THE 110TH CONGRESSIONAL DISTRICT ATLAS

THE 110TH CONGRESSIONAL DISTRICT ATLAS

Edited by Deirdre A. Gaquin and Katherine A. DeBrandt

Published in the United States of America
by Bernan Press, a wholly owned subsidiary of
The Rowman & Littlefield Publishing Group, Inc.
4501 Forbes Boulevard, Suite 200
Lanham, Maryland 20706

Bernan Press
800-865-3457
info@bernan.com
www.bernan.com

ISBN 10: 1-59888-240-6
ISBN 13: 978-1-59888-240-7

∞™ The paper used in this publication meets the minimum requirements of
American National Standard for Information Sciences—Permanence of
Paper for Printed Library Materials, ANSI/NISO Z39.48-1992.
Manufactured in the United States of America.

Contents

Preface

The 110th Congressional District Atlas reflects the congressional district boundaries that will be in effect until the 113th Congress unless a state initiative or court-ordered redistricting requires additional changes.

The 110th Congressional District Atlas was edited by Deirdre A. Gaquin and Katherine A. DeBrandt. Ms. Gaquin has been a data use consultant to private organizations, government agencies, and universities for over 20 years. Prior to that, she was Director of Data Access Services at Data Use & Access Laboratories, a pioneer in private sector distribution of federal statistical data. A former president of the Association of Public Data Users, Ms. Gaquin has served on numerous boards, panels, and task forces concerned with federal statistical data and has worked on four decennial censuses. She holds a Master of Urban Planning degree from Hunter College. Ms. Gaquin is also an editor of Bernan Press' *The Who, What, and Where of America: Understanding the Census Results*; *County and City Extra: Annual Metro, City*, and *County Data Book*; and *Places, Towns and Townships*.

Ms. DeBrandt is the managing editor at Bernan Press. She received her B.A. in political science from Colgate University. She is also a co-editor of *The Almanac of American Education*; *State Profiles: The Population and Economy of Each U.S. State*; and *Social Change in America: The Historical Handbook,* all published by Bernan Press.

Responsibility of the editors and publisher of this publication is limited to reasonable care in the reproduction and presentation of data obtained from sources believed to be reliable.

As always, we are especially grateful to the many federal agency personnel who assisted us in obtaining the data, provided excellent resources on their Web sites, and patiently answered our questions.

Introduction

The Atlas is organized into two sections—Part I: Maps and Part II: Tables. The maps are presented on the national and state level and detail the districts of the 110th Congress, as well as the nonvoting delegate districts. After the 2000 census, the 435 seats in the U.S. House of Representatives were reapportioned among the states based on the new population data. These populations included states' resident populations along with their overseas populations of military and federal civilian employees, along with their dependents. The apportionment population is not adjusted to reflect overcounting or undercounting in the decennial census.

As required by Article 1, Section 2 of the Constitution, a census is conducted every 10 years for the purpose of reapportioning the seats of the House of Representatives among the 50 states (neither the District of Columbia nor the territories have voting representation). The number of representatives has been set at 435 since the 1910 census, except for a brief period with 437 representatives to account for the new states of Alaska and Hawaii in the 1950s.

As a result of the new population counts, many state legislatures and, in some states, bipartisan commissions redrew districts to reflect reapportionment and changes in population. Redistricting can be a contentious issue, as in some states the political party with the majority can design districts to suit its own interests. The total population in the 50 states exceeded 280,000,000 in 2000, giving the average congressional district a population of about 645,000 people. The population counts from the 2000 census are used by states to create new boundaries for congressional districts that must be equal in population.

Number of Representatives by State, 1890–2000

State	2000 Apportionment population [1]	Number of apportioned Representatives	Change from 1990 Census apportionment	Number of apportioned Representatives 1990	1980	1970	1960	1950	1940	1930	1920	1910	1900	1890
United States	281 424 177	435	X	435	435	435	435	437	435	435	435	435	391	357
Alabama	4 461 130	7	0	7	7	7	8	9	9	9	10	10	9	9
Alaska	628 933	1	0	1	1	1	1	1	X	X	X	X	X	X
Arizona	5 140 683	8	2	6	5	4	3	2	2	1	1	1	X	X
Arkansas	2 679 733	4	0	4	4	4	4	6	7	7	7	7	7	6
California	33 930 798	53	1	52	45	43	38	30	23	20	11	11	8	7
Colorado	4 311 882	7	1	6	6	5	4	4	4	4	4	4	3	2
Connecticut	3 409 535	5	-1	6	6	6	6	6	6	6	5	5	5	4
Delaware	785 068	1	0	1	1	1	1	1	1	1	1	1	1	1
Florida	16 028 890	25	2	23	19	15	12	8	6	5	4	4	3	2
Georgia	8 206 975	13	2	11	10	10	10	10	10	10	12	12	11	11
Hawaii	1 216 642	2	0	2	2	2	2	1	X	X	X	X	X	X
Idaho	1 297 274	2	0	2	2	2	2	2	2	2	2	2	1	1
Illinois	12 439 042	19	-1	20	22	24	24	25	26	27	27	27	25	22
Indiana	6 090 782	9	-1	10	10	11	11	11	11	12	13	13	13	13
Iowa	2 931 923	5	0	5	6	6	7	8	8	9	11	11	11	11
Kansas	2 693 824	4	0	4	5	5	5	6	6	7	8	8	8	8
Kentucky	4 049 431	6	0	6	7	7	7	8	9	9	11	11	11	11
Louisiana	4 480 271	7	0	7	8	8	8	8	8	8	8	8	7	6
Maine	1 277 731	2	0	2	2	2	2	3	3	3	4	4	4	4
Maryland	5 307 886	8	0	8	8	8	8	7	6	6	6	6	6	6
Massachusetts	6 355 568	10	0	10	11	12	12	14	14	15	16	16	14	13
Michigan	9 955 829	15	-1	16	18	19	19	18	17	17	13	13	12	12
Minnesota	4 925 670	8	0	8	8	8	8	9	9	9	10	10	9	7
Mississippi	2 852 927	4	-1	5	5	5	5	6	7	7	8	8	8	7
Missouri	5 606 260	9	0	9	9	10	10	11	13	13	16	16	16	15
Montana	905 316	1	0	1	2	2	2	2	2	2	2	2	1	1
Nebraska	1 715 369	3	0	3	3	3	3	4	4	5	6	6	6	6
Nevada	2 002 032	3	1	2	2	1	1	1	1	1	1	1	1	1
New Hampshire	1 238 415	2	0	2	2	2	2	2	2	2	2	2	2	2
New Jersey	8 424 354	13	0	13	14	15	15	14	14	14	12	12	10	8
New Mexico	1 823 821	3	0	3	3	2	2	2	2	1	1	1	X	X
New York	19 004 973	29	-2	31	34	39	41	43	45	45	43	43	37	34
North Carolina	8 067 673	13	1	12	11	11	11	12	12	11	10	10	10	9
North Dakota	643 756	1	0	1	1	1	2	2	2	2	3	3	2	1
Ohio	11 374 540	18	-1	19	21	23	24	23	23	24	22	22	21	21
Oklahoma	3 458 819	5	-1	6	6	6	6	6	8	9	8	8	5	X
Oregon	3 428 543	5	0	5	5	4	4	4	4	3	3	3	2	2
Pennsylvania	12 300 670	19	-2	21	23	25	27	30	33	34	36	36	32	30
Rhode Island	1 049 662	2	0	2	2	2	2	2	2	2	3	3	2	2
South Carolina	4 025 061	6	0	6	6	6	6	6	6	6	7	7	7	7
South Dakota	756 874	1	0	1	1	2	2	2	2	2	3	3	2	2
Tennessee	5 700 037	9	0	9	9	8	9	9	10	9	10	10	10	10
Texas	20 903 994	32	2	30	27	24	23	22	21	21	18	18	16	13
Utah	2 236 714	3	0	3	3	2	2	2	2	2	2	2	1	1
Vermont	609 890	1	0	1	1	1	1	1	1	1	2	2	2	2
Virginia	7 100 702	11	0	11	10	10	10	10	9	9	10	10	10	10
Washington	5 908 684	9	0	9	8	7	7	7	6	6	5	5	3	2
West Virginia	1 813 077	3	0	3	4	4	5	6	6	6	6	6	5	4
Wisconsin	5 371 210	8	-1	9	9	9	10	10	10	10	11	11	11	10
Wyoming	495 304	1	0	1	1	1	1	1	1	1	1	1	1	1

[1] Includes the resident population for the 50 states and counts of overseas U.S. military and federal civilian employees (and their dependents living with them) allocated to their home state, as reported by the employing federal agencies. The total United States apportionment population excludes the population of the District of Columbia.
X = Not applicable.

The 108th Congress was the first to reflect the new district boundaries based on the 2000 census. From the 108th to 109th Congress, three states—Maine, Pennsylvania, and Texas—made additional changes to their district boundaries. Georgia and Texas redistricted for the 110th Congress. The United States Congressional Districts map reflecting the 109th district boundaries is included in the introduction.

California has the most seats in the House of Representatives with 53, followed by Texas (32) and New York (29). Arizona, Florida, Georgia, and Texas all gained two seats from 1990 to 2000. New York and Pennsylvania each lost two seats as a result of the census count. Another 12 states lost or gained one seat, primarily reflecting the higher population growth in southern and western states. Utah lost a court challenge as North Carolina's population growth edged Utah out of a new seat. (North Carolina's overseas military residents helped the state gain an edge over Utah.) There are six states—Alaska, Delaware, Montana, North Dakota, South Dakota, and Wyoming—with just one "At Large" representative. Montana has the largest population among the six states with about 900,000, which is too small to earn a second representative.

The state-based tables show the relationship between the congressional districts and counties or county equivalents. Data from the 2006 American Community Survey have been collected for the 109th districts and data from the 2000 decennial census have been retabulated for the 109th districts. Data from the 2002 Census of Agriculture were tabulated for the 108th Congress, so they do not reflect the boundary changes in Georgia, Maine, Pennsylvania, and Texas. Complete source notes for each item are included in the notes and definitions on page 463.

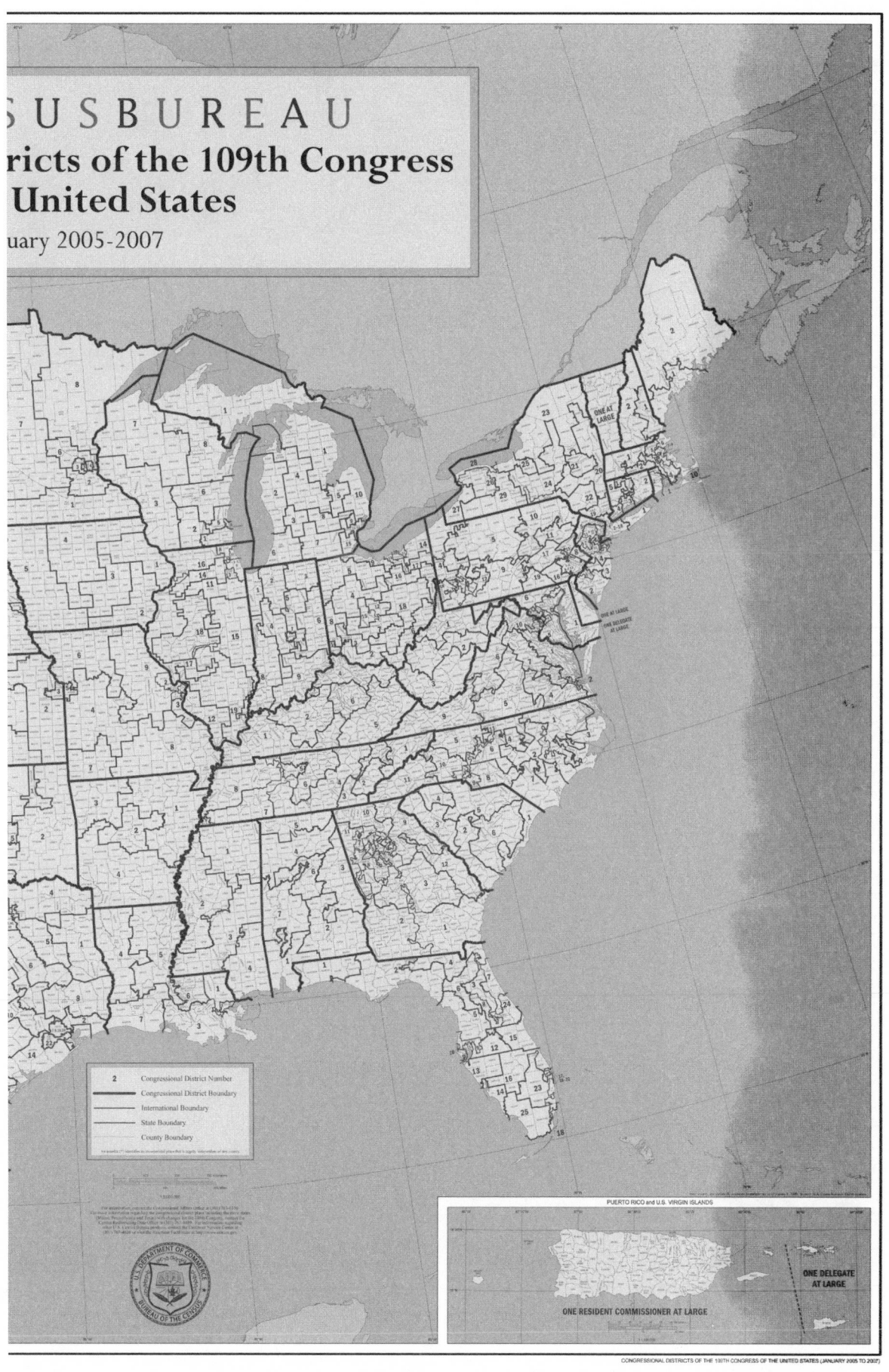

SUSBUREAU
ricts of the 109th Congress
United States
uary 2005-2007

PART I: MAPS

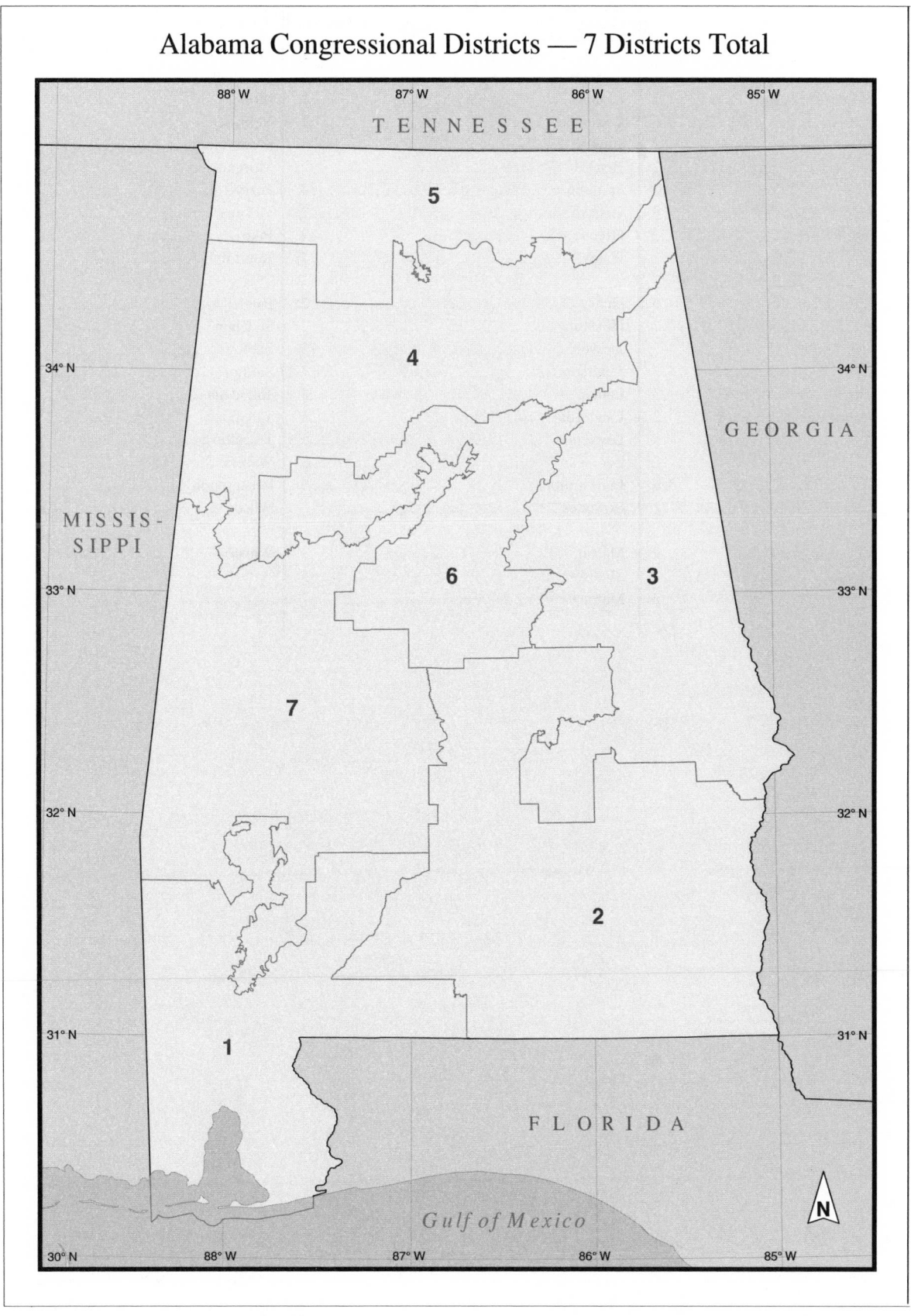

Alabama Congressional Districts — 7 Districts Total

ALABAMA—110th CONGRESSIONAL DISTRICTS BY COUNTIES

County	Congressional District
Autauga	2
Baldwin	1
Barbour	2
Bibb	6
Blount	4
Bullock	2
Butler	2
Calhoun	3
Chambers	3
Cherokee	3
Chilton	6
Choctaw	7
Clarke	1, 7
Clay	3
Cleburne	3
Coffee	2
Colbert	5
Conecuh	2
Coosa	3, 6
Covington	2
Crenshaw	2
Cullman	4
Dale	2

County	Congressional District
Dallas	7
DeKalb	4
Elmore	2
Escambia	1
Etowah	4
Fayette	4
Franklin	4
Geneva	2
Greene	7
Hale	7
Henry	2
Houston	2
Jackson	5
Jefferson	6, 7
Lamar	4
Lauderdale	5
Lawrence	5
Lee	3
Limestone	5
Lowndes	2
Macon	3
Madison	5
Marengo	7

County	Congressional District
Marion	4
Marshall	4
Mobile	1
Monroe	1
Montgomery	2, 3
Morgan	4, 5
Perry	7
Pickens	4, 7
Pike	2
Randolph	3
Russell	3
St. Clair	4, 6
Shelby	6
Sumter	7
Talladega	3
Tallapoosa	3
Tuscaloosa	6, 7
Walker	4
Washington	1
Wilcox	7
Winston	4

Congressional District 1

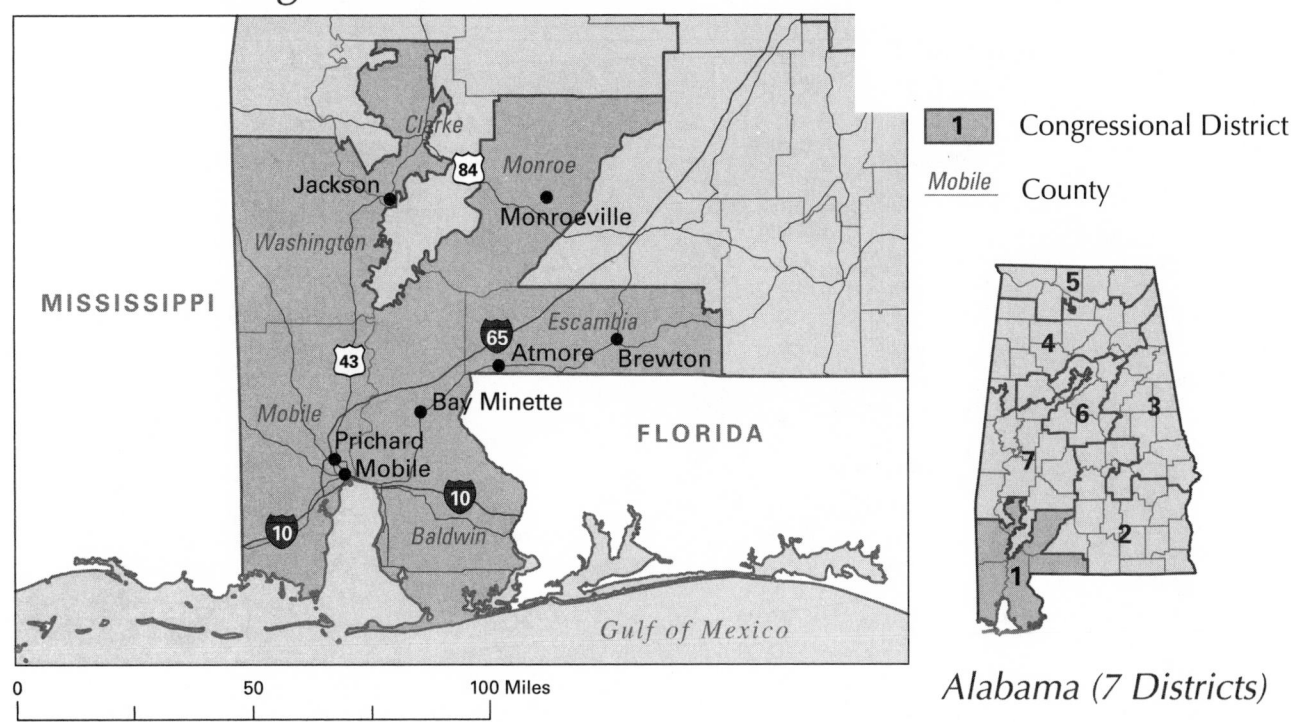

Alabama (7 Districts)

Congressional District 2

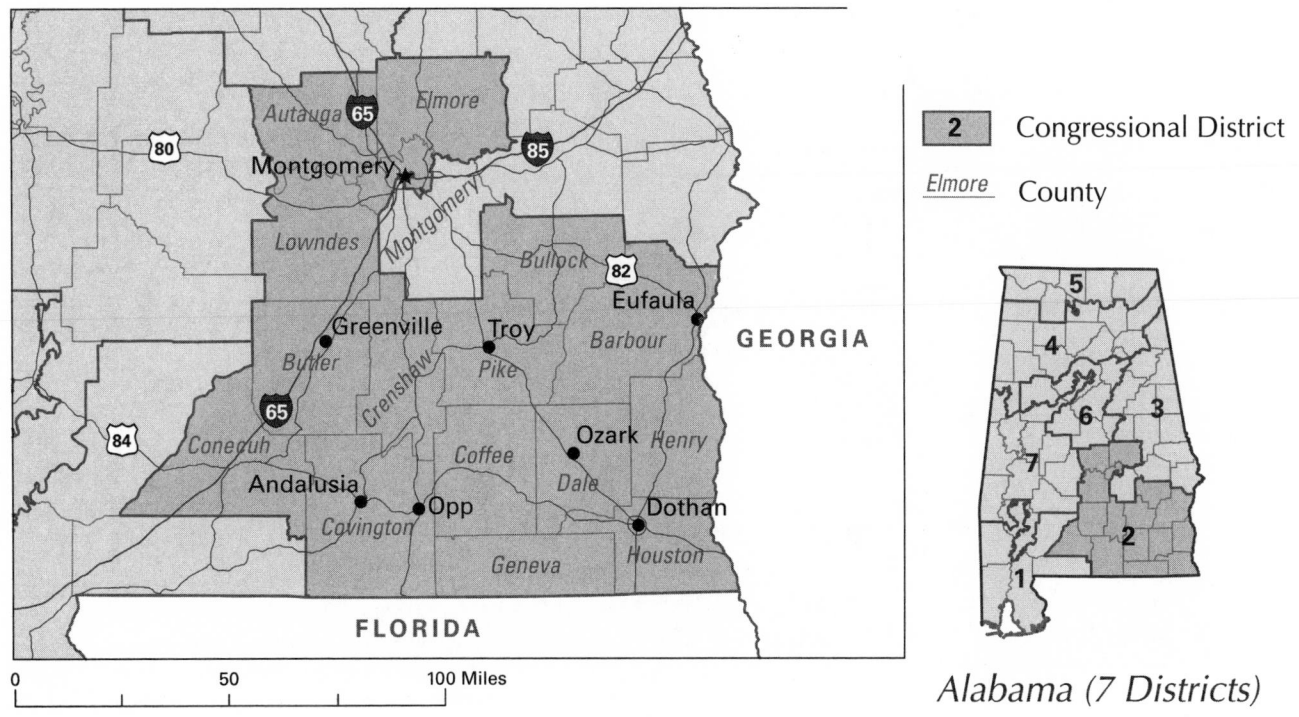

Alabama (7 Districts)

Congressional District 3

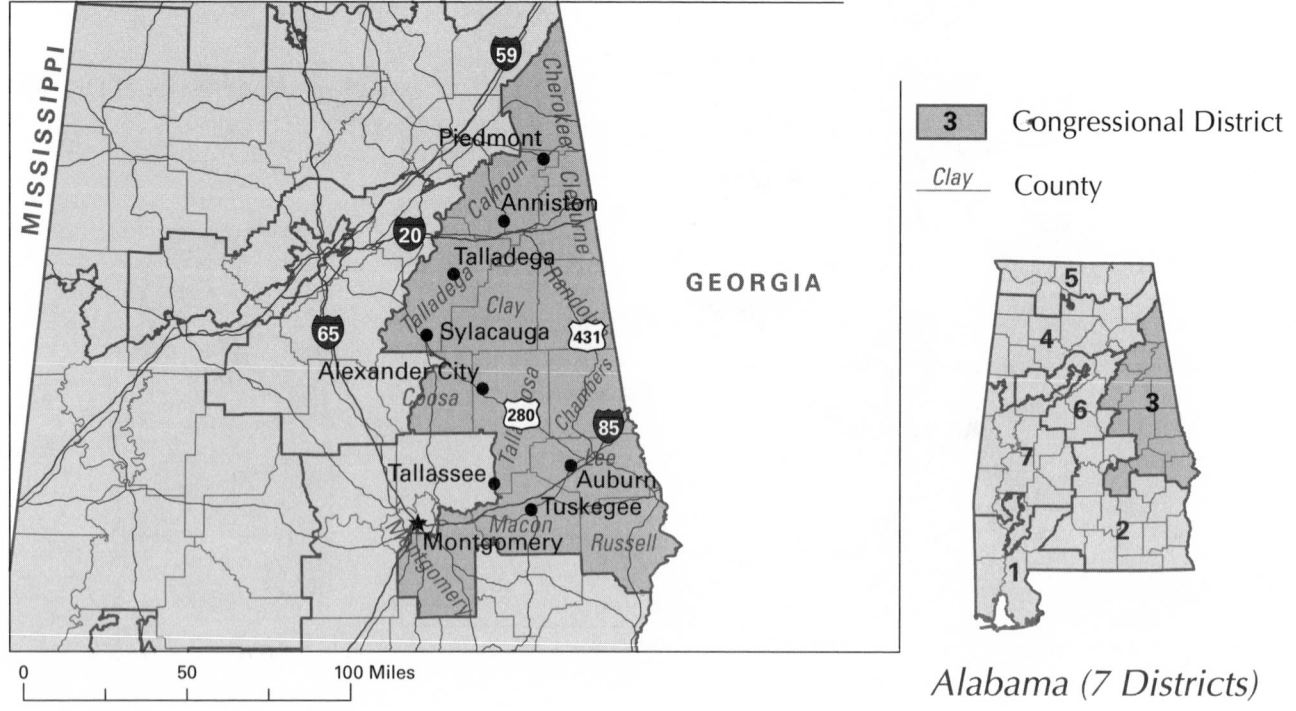

Alabama (7 Districts)

Congressional District 4

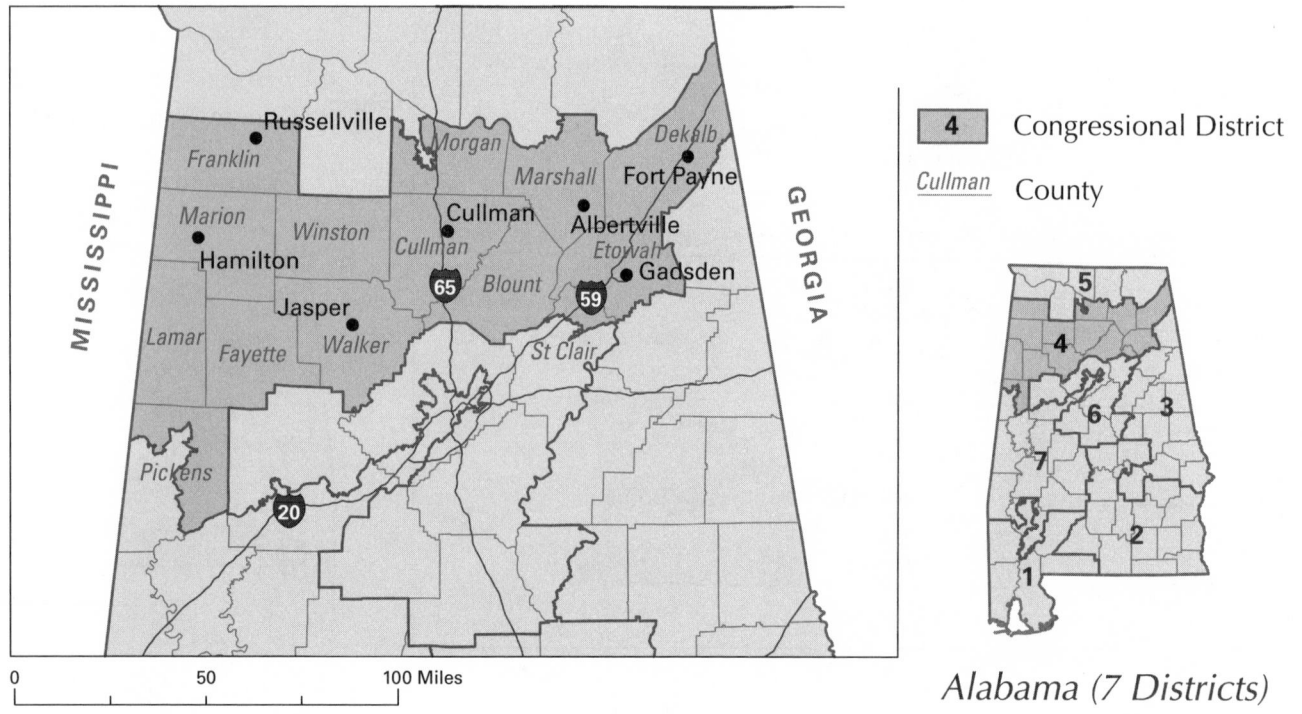

Alabama (7 Districts)

Congressional District 5

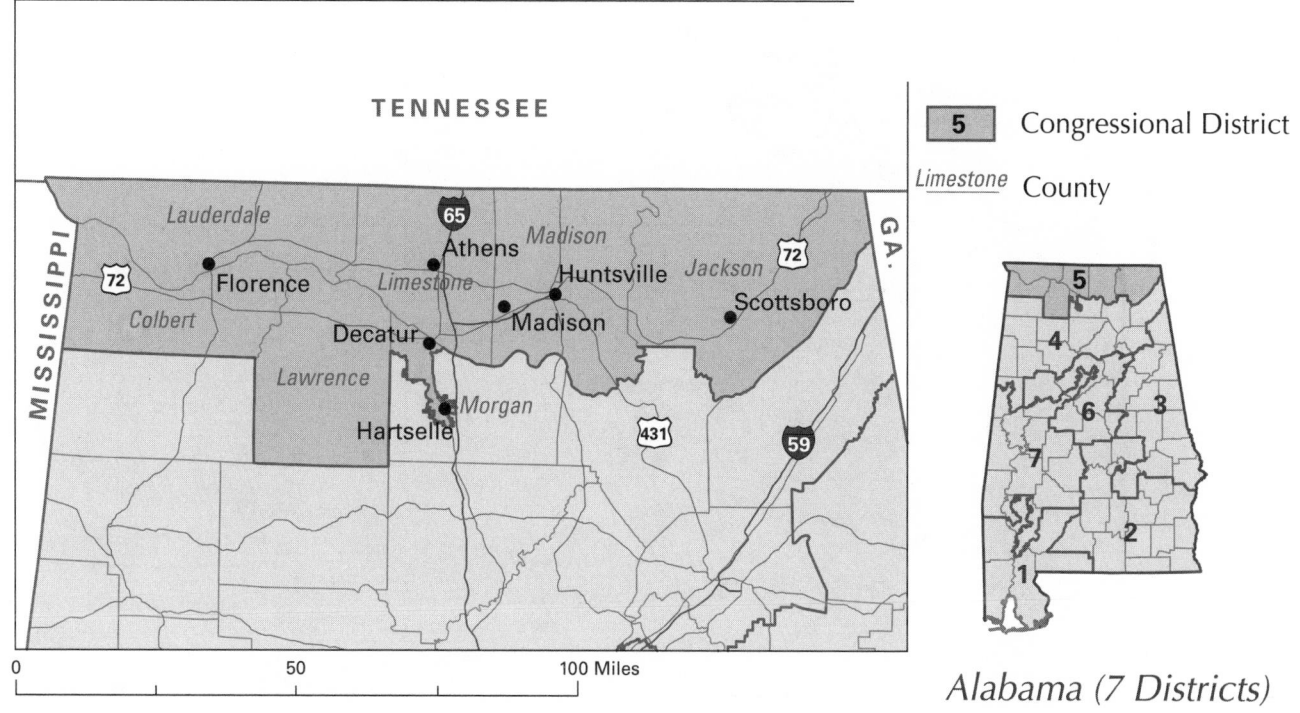

Alabama (7 Districts)

Congressional District 6

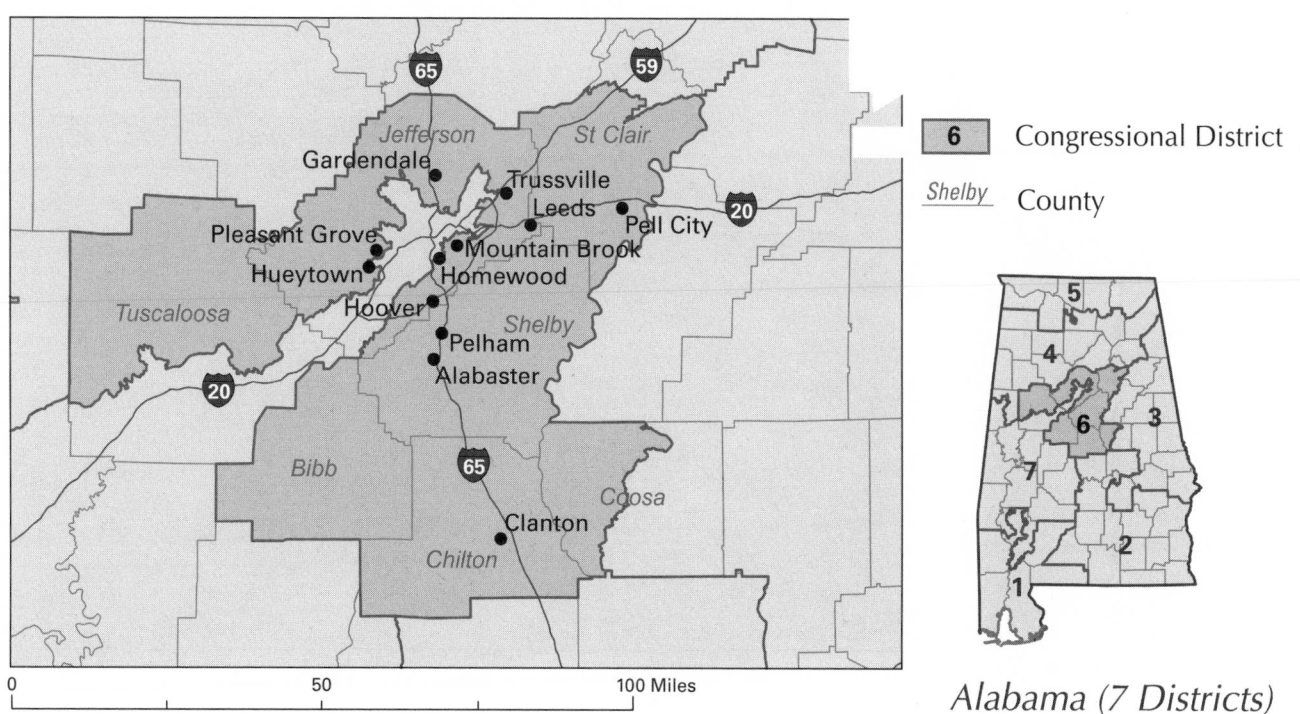

Alabama (7 Districts)

Congressional District 7

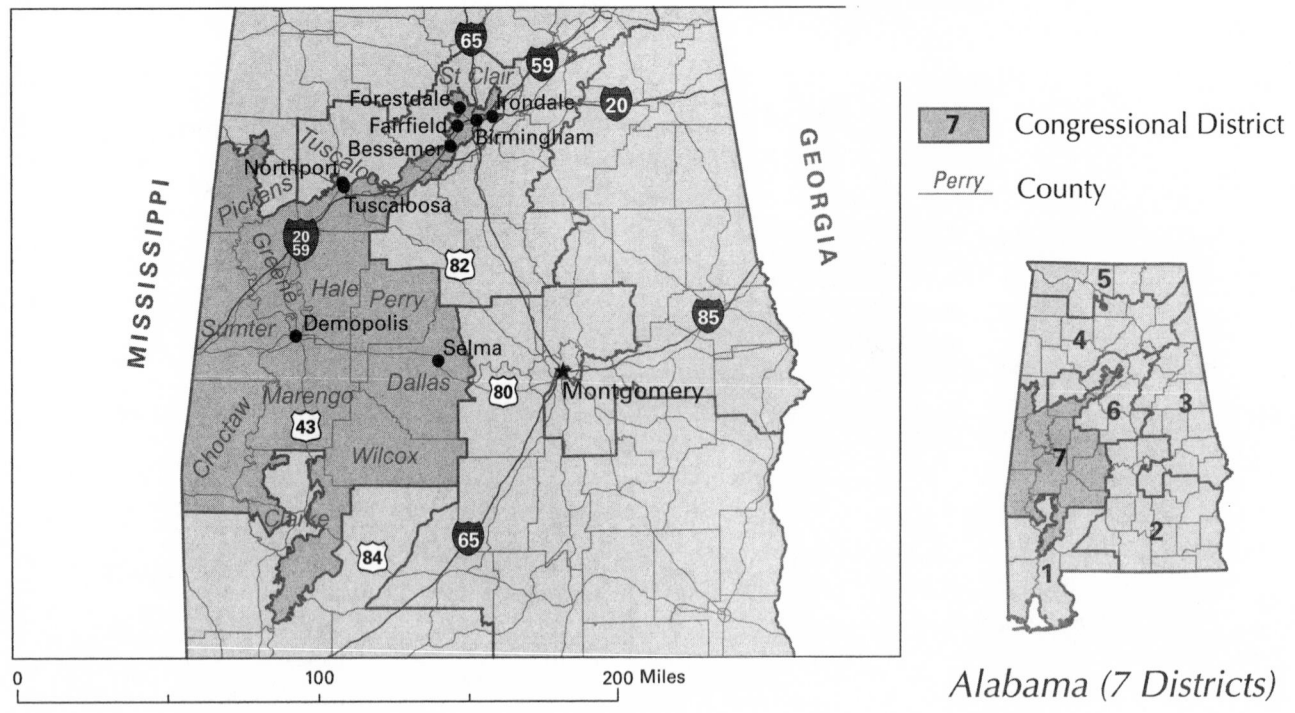

0   100   200 Miles

Legend:

7   Congressional District

Perry   County

Alabama (7 Districts)

Alaska–
Congressional District: At large

Alaska (1 district)

ALASKA—110th CONGRESSIONAL DISTRICTS BY COUNTIES

County	Congressional District
Aleutians East Borough	1
Aleutians West Census Area	1
Anchorage	1
Bethel	1
Bristol Bay	1
Denali Borough	1
Dillingham	1
Fairbanks North Star	1
Haines	1
Juneau	1

County	Congressional District
Kenai Peninsula	1
Ketchikan Gateway	1
Kodiak Island	1
Lake and Peninsula Borough	1
Matanuska-Susitna	1
Nome	1
North Slope	1
Northwest Arctic Borough	1
Prince of Wales-Outer Ketchikan	1
Sitka	1

County	Congressional District
Skagway-Hoonah-Angoon	1
Southeast Fairbanks	1
Valdez-Cordova	1
Wade Hampton	1
Wrangell-Petersburg	1
Yakutat Borough	1
Yukon-Koyukuk	1

Arizona Congressional Districts — 8 Districts Total

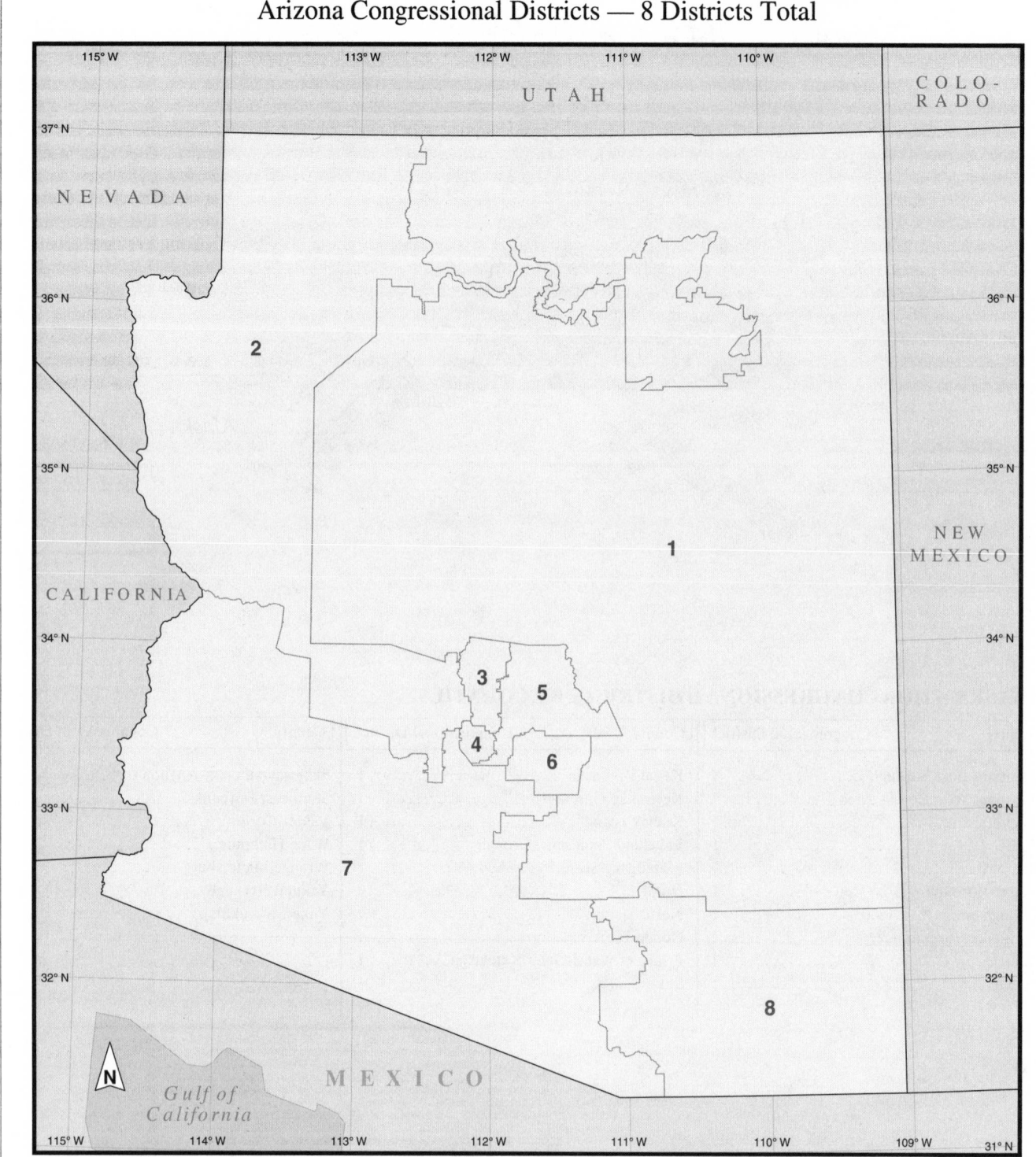

ARIZONA—110th CONGRESSIONAL DISTRICTS BY COUNTIES

County	Congressional District	County	Congressional District	County	Congressional District
Apache	1	Greenlee	1	Pima	7,8
Cochise	8	La Paz	2,7	Pinal	1, 6–8
Coconino	1,2	Maricopa	2–7	Santa Cruz	7,8
Gila	1	Mohave	2	Yavapai	1,2
Graham	1	Navajo	1,2	Yuma	7

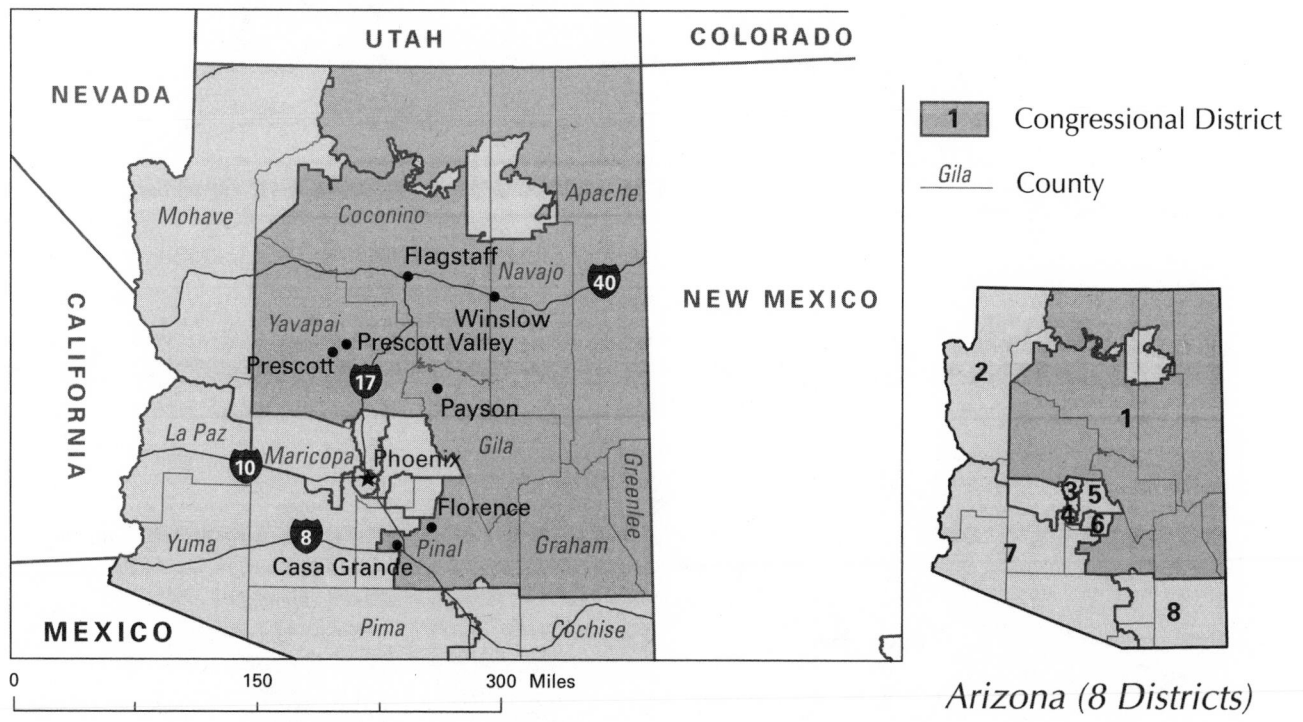

Congressional District 1

1   Congressional District

Gila   County

Arizona (8 Districts)

0   150   300   Miles

Congressional District 2

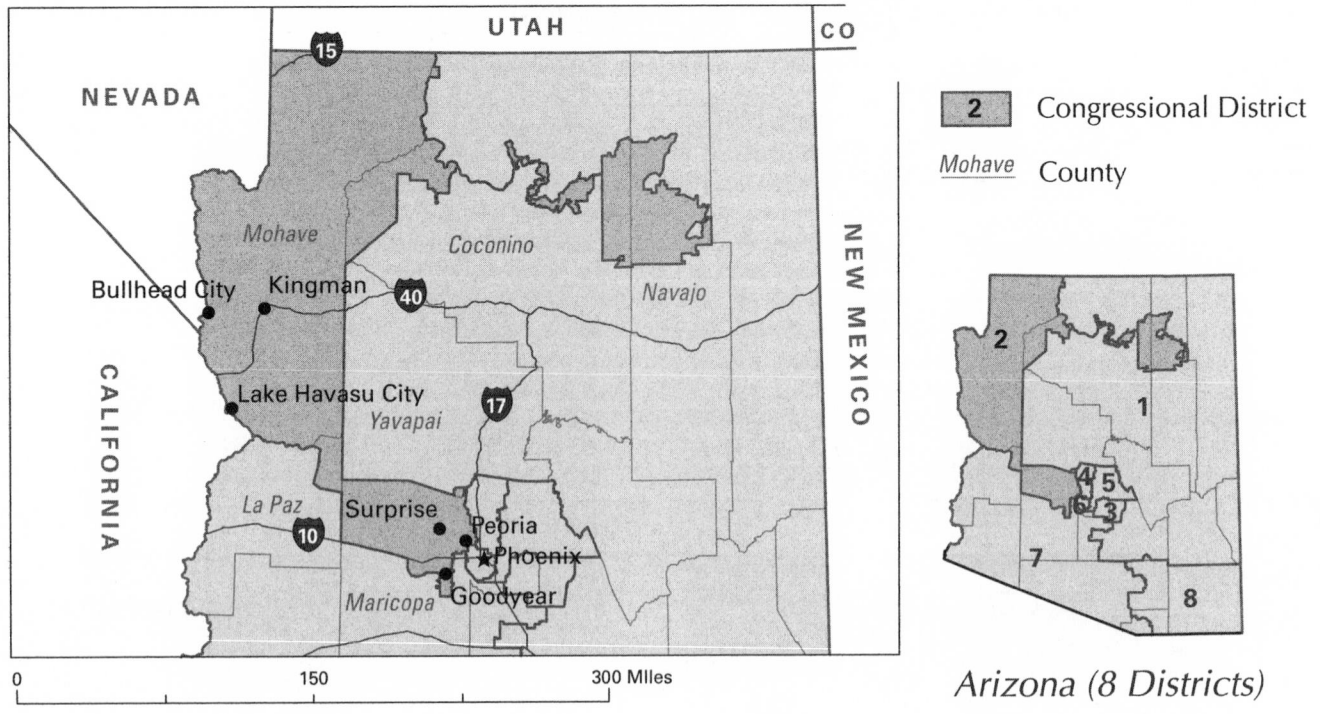

Arizona (8 Districts)

Congressional District 3

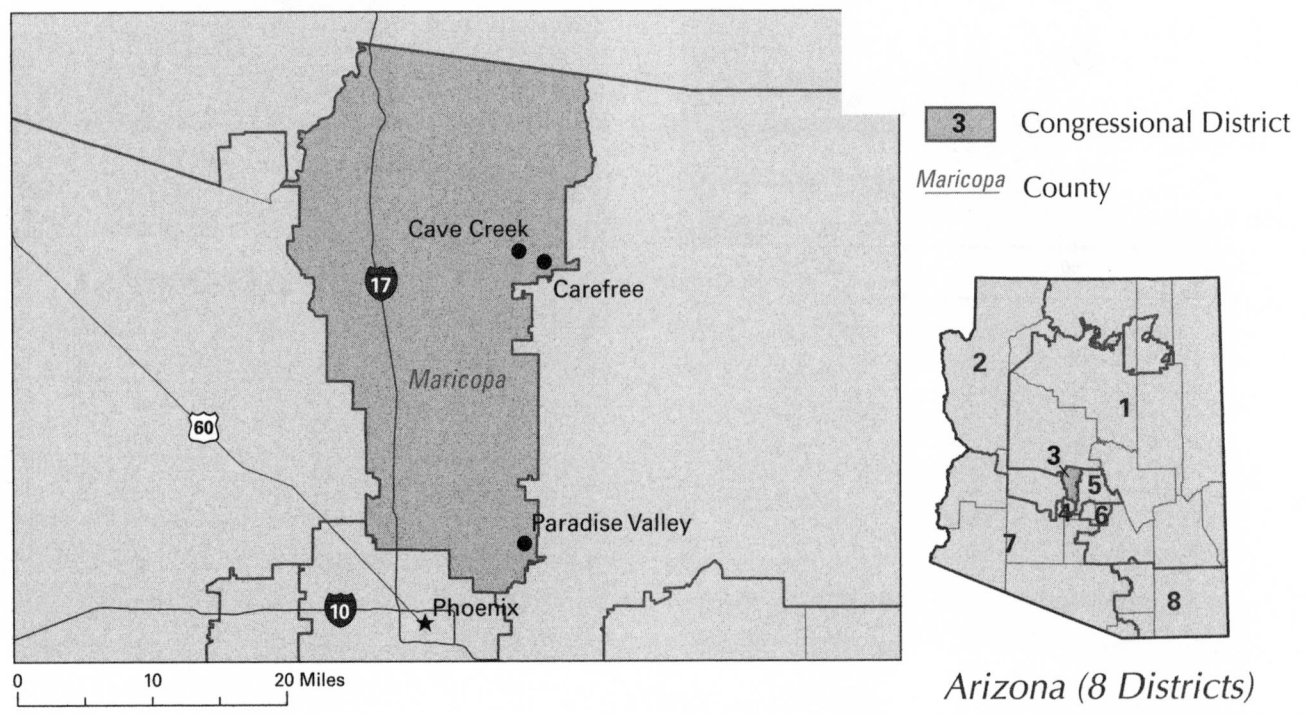

Arizona (8 Districts)

Congressional District 4

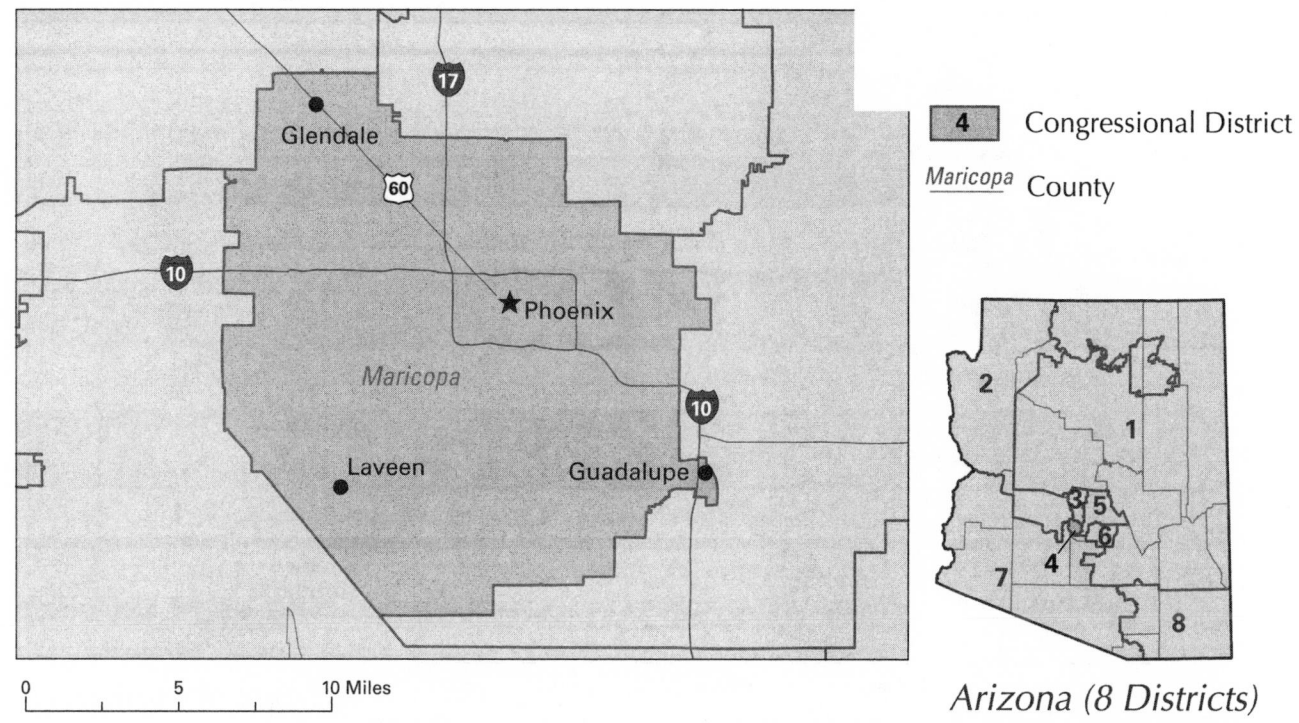

Arizona (8 Districts)

Congressional District 5

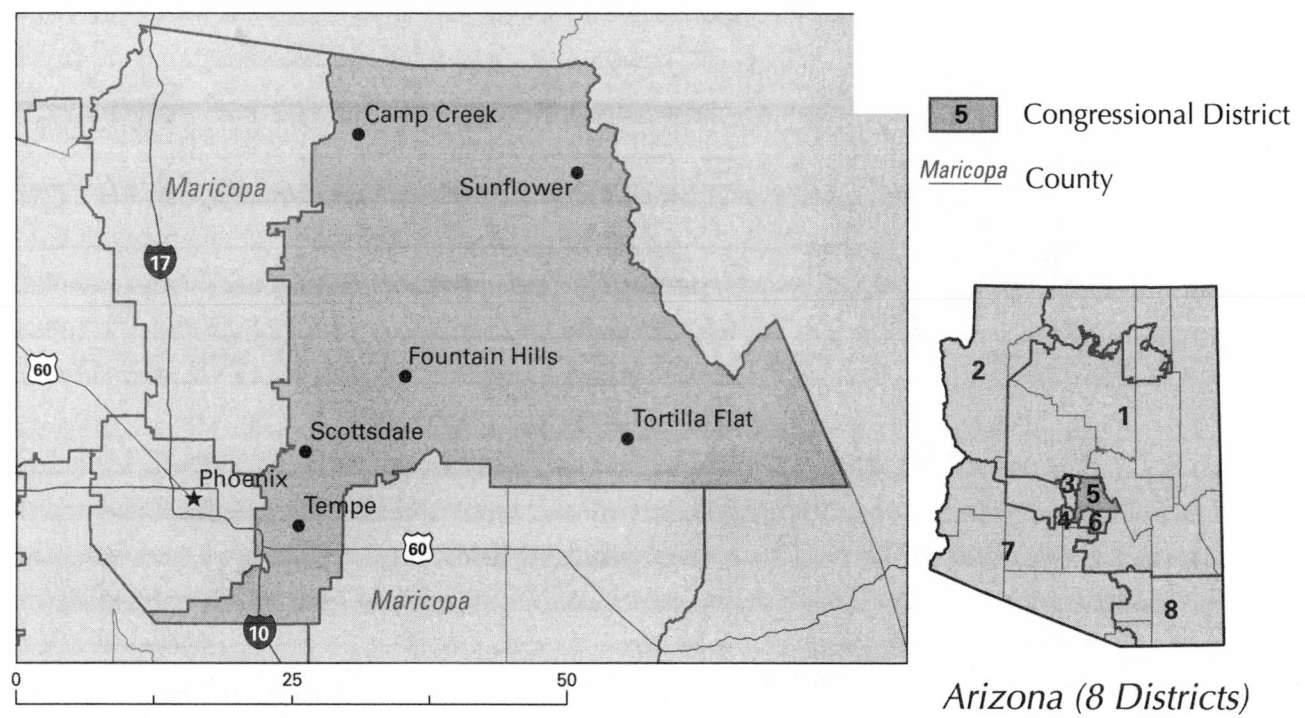

Arizona (8 Districts)

Congressional District 6

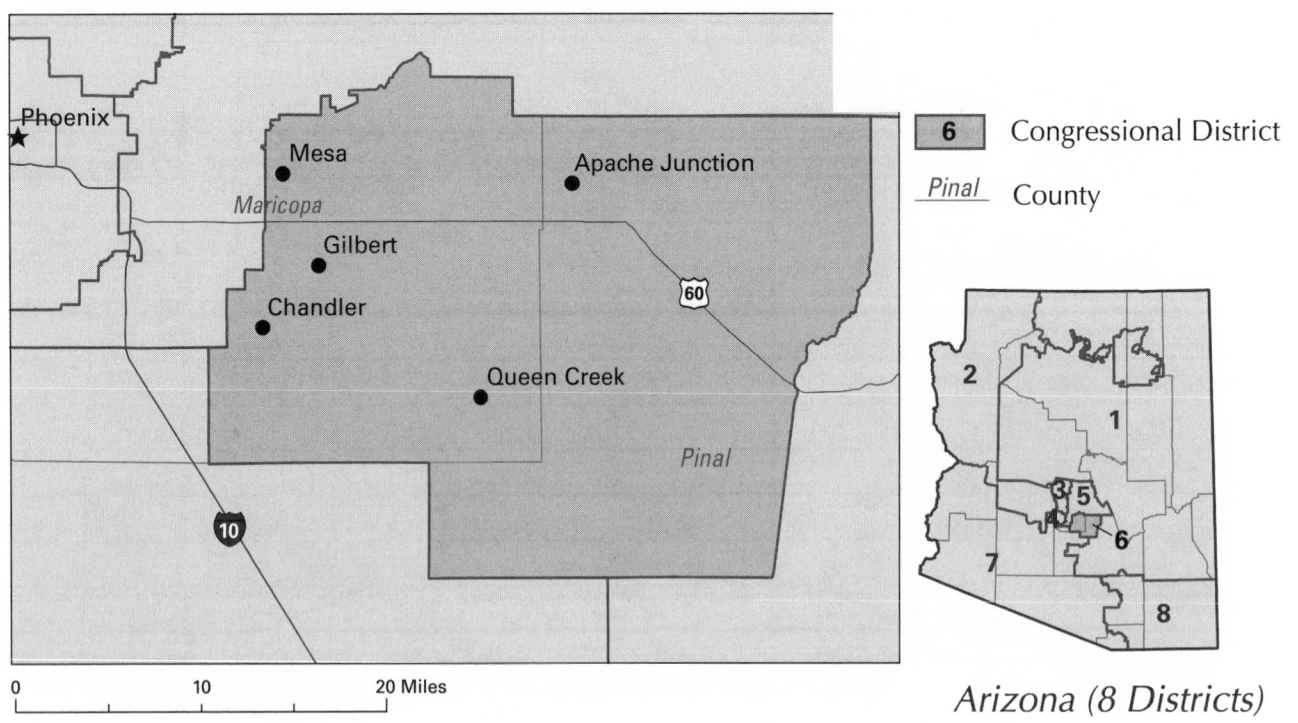

Arizona (8 Districts)

Congressional District 7

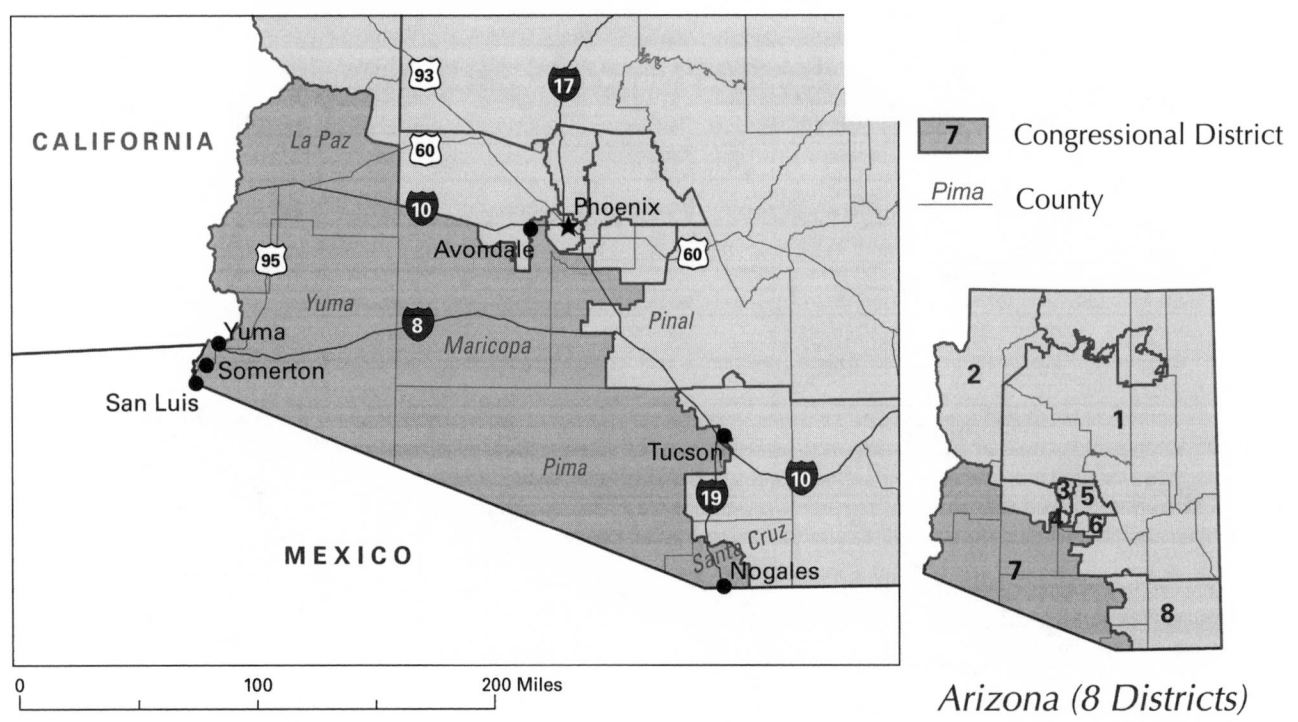

Arizona (8 Districts)

Congressional District 8

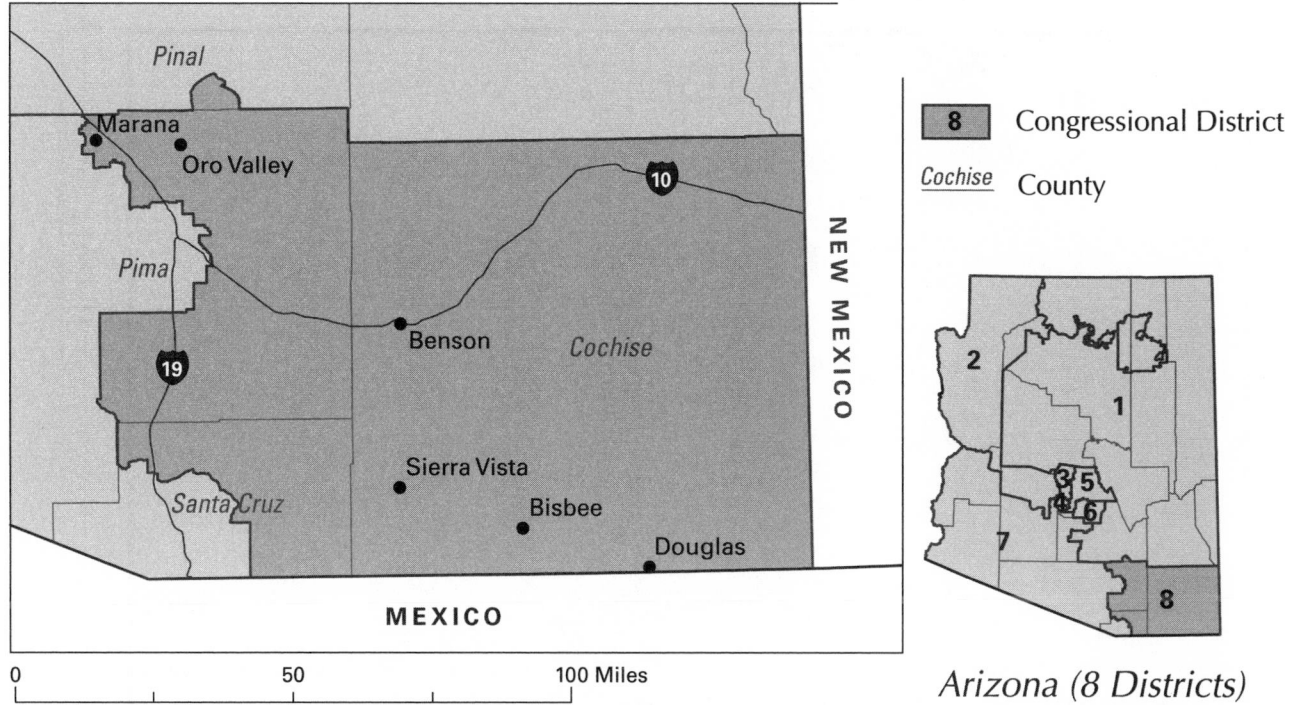

Arizona (8 Districts)

Arkansas Congressional Districts — 4 Districts Total

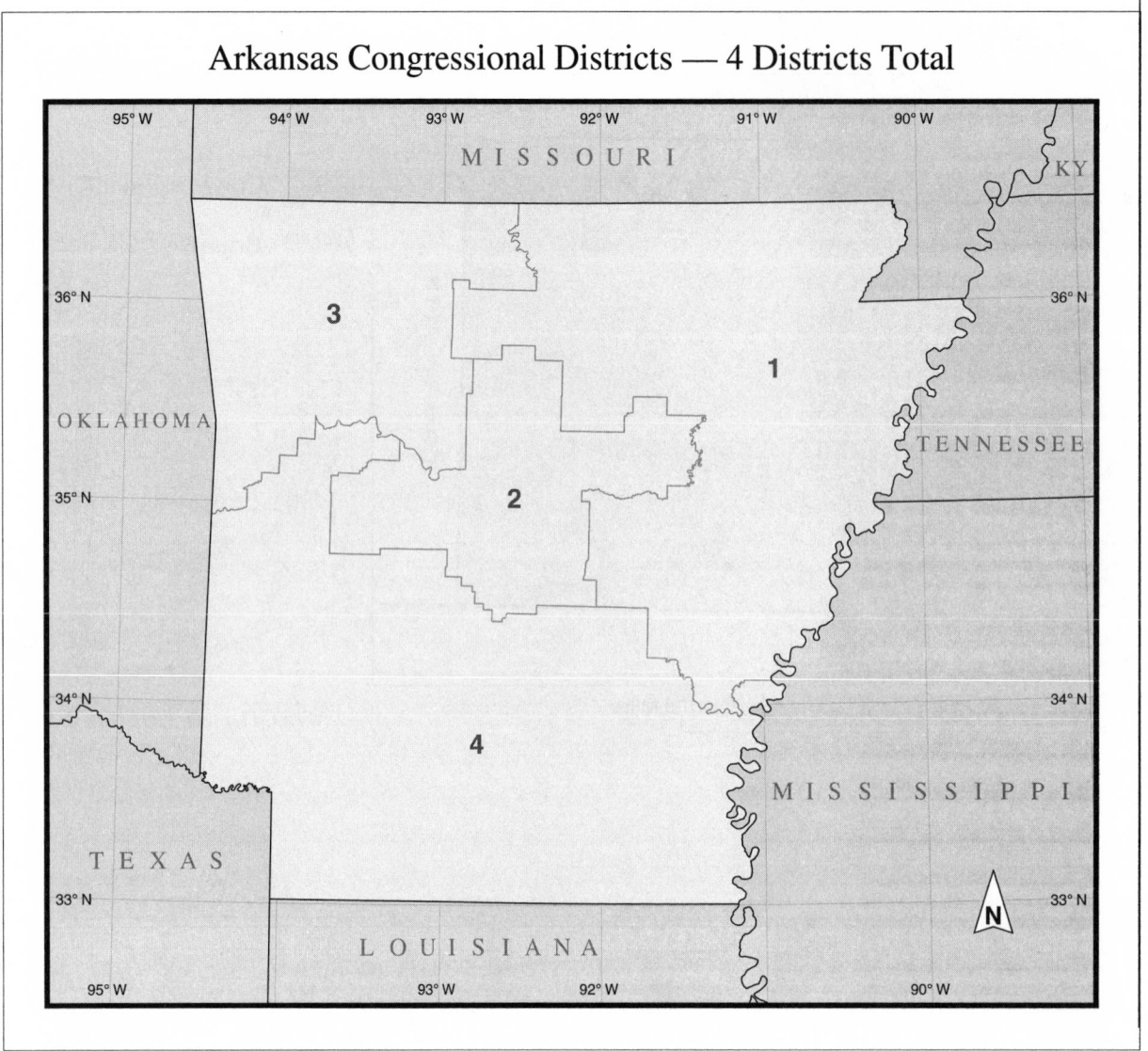

ARKANSAS—110th CONGRESSIONAL DISTRICTS BY COUNTIES

County	Congressional District	County	Congressional District	County	Congressional District
Arkansas	1	Garland	4	Newton	3
Ashley	4	Grant	4	Ouachita	4
Baxter	1	Greene	1	Perry	2
Benton	3	Hempstead	4	Phillips	1
Boone	3	Hot Spring	4	Pike	4
Bradley	4	Howard	4	Poinsett	1
Calhoun	4	Independence	1	Polk	4
Carroll	3	Izard	1	Pope	3
Chicot	4	Jackson	1	Prairie	1
Clark	4	Jefferson	4	Pulaski	2
Clay	1	Johnson	3	Randolph	1
Cleburne	1	Lafayette	4	St. Francis	1
Cleveland	4	Lawrence	1	Saline	2
Columbia	4	Lee	1	Scott	4
Conway	2	Lincoln	4	Searcy	1
Craighead	1	Little River	4	Sebastian	3
Crawford	3	Logan	4	Sevier	4
Crittenden	1	Lonoke	1	Sharp	1
Cross	1	Madison	3	Stone	1
Dallas	4	Marion	3	Union	4
Desha	4	Miller	4	Van Buren	2
Drew	4	Mississippi	1	Washington	3
Faulkner	2	Monroe	1	White	2
Franklin	3	Montgomery	4	Woodruff	1
Fulton	1	Nevada	4	Yell	2

Congressional District 1

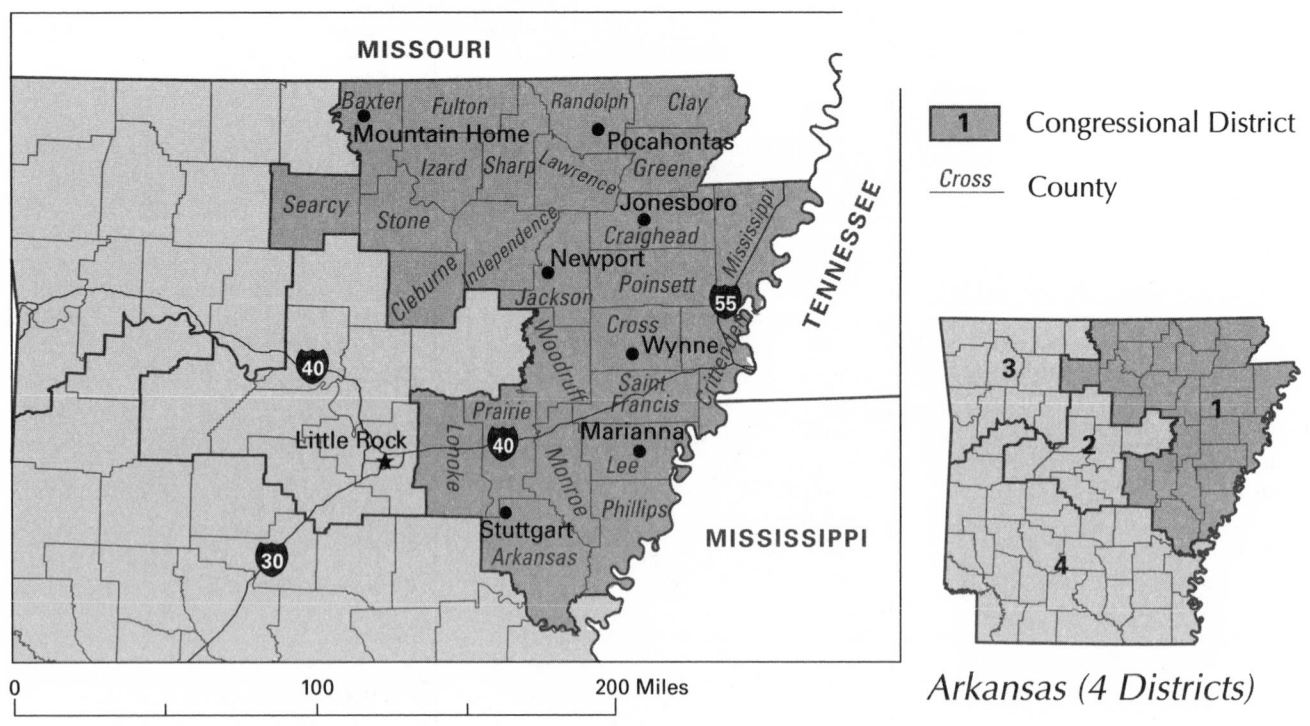

Arkansas (4 Districts)

Congressional District 2

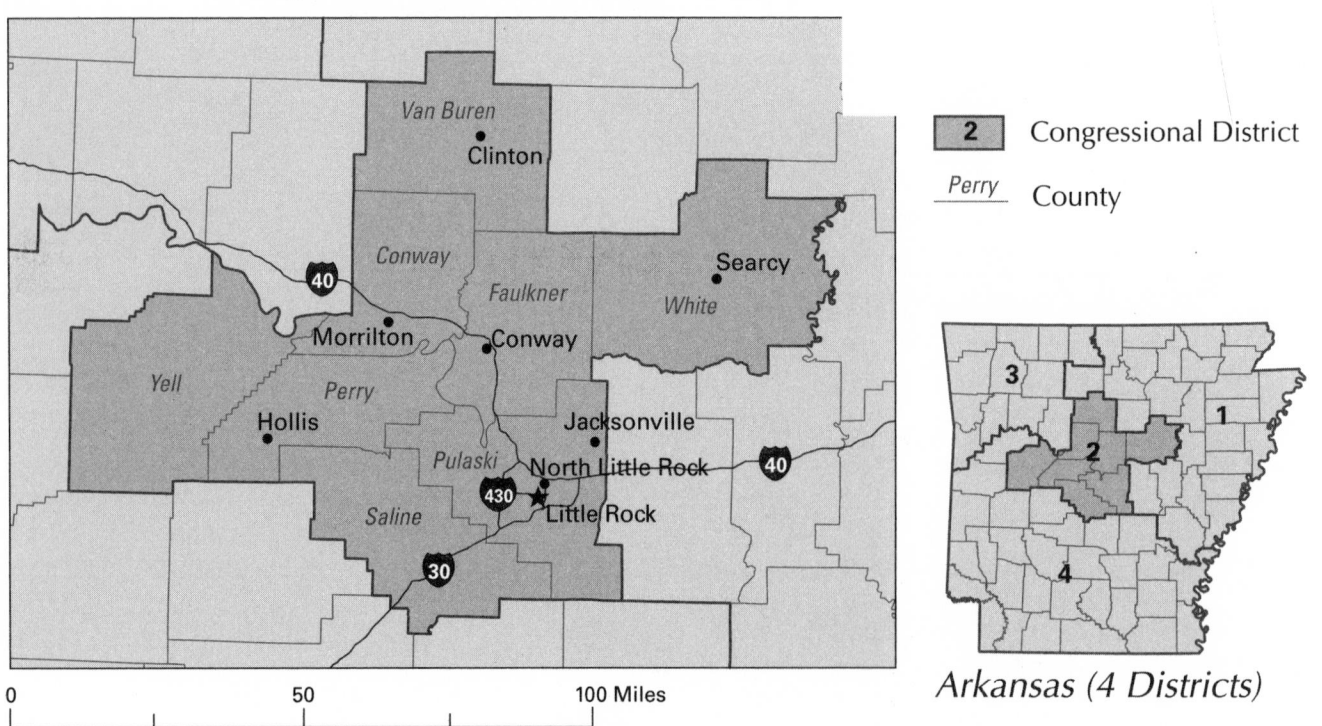

Arkansas (4 Districts)

Congressional District 3

3 Congressional District

Franklin County

Arkansas (4 Districts)

Congressional District 4

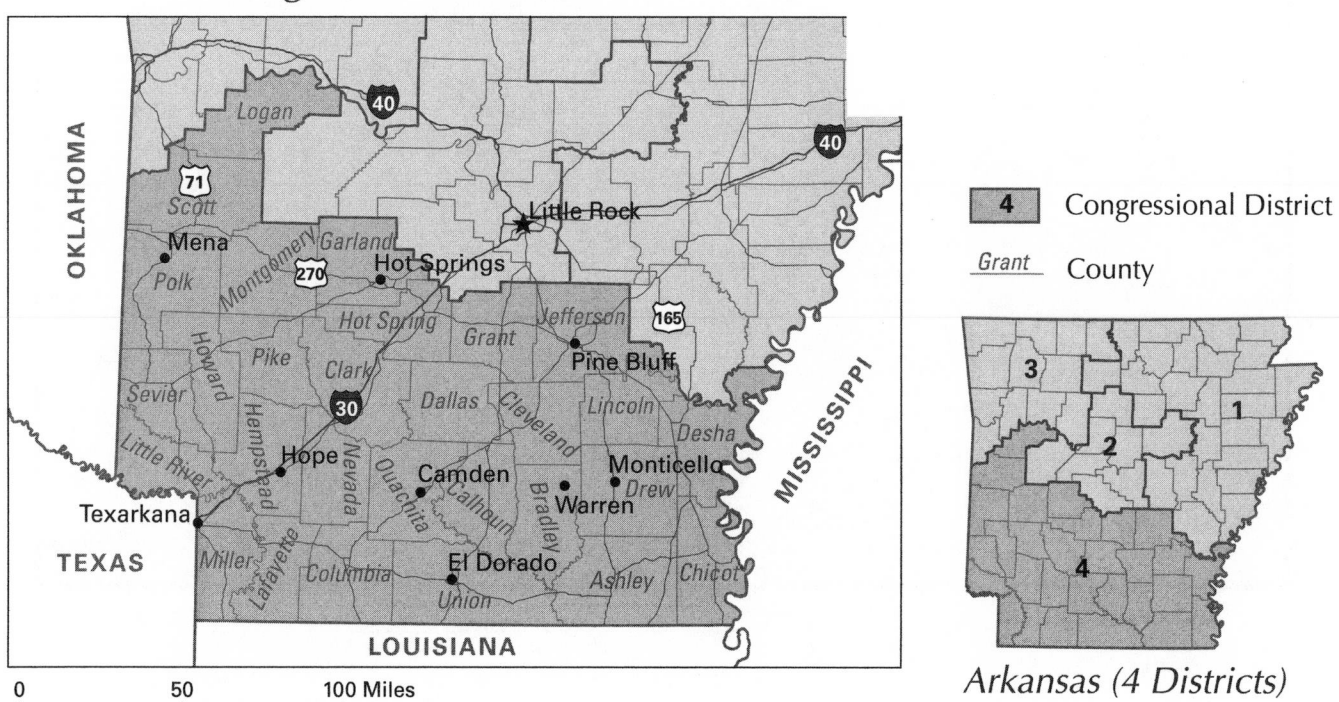

4 Congressional District

Grant County

Arkansas (4 Districts)

California Congressional Districts — 53 Districts Total

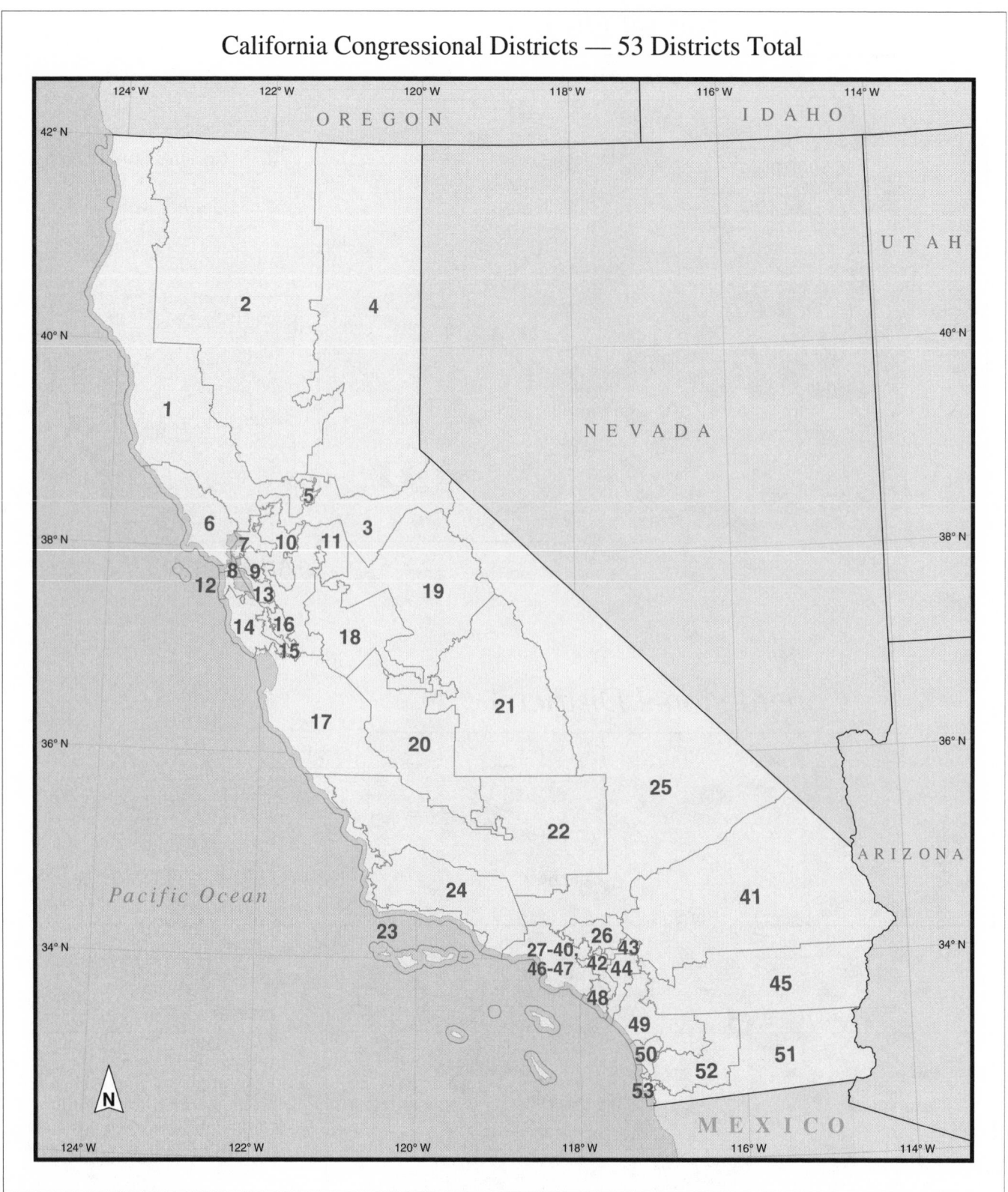

CALIFORNIA—110th CONGRESSIONAL DISTRICTS BY COUNTIES

County	Congressional District
Alameda	9–11, 13
Alpine	3
Amador	3
Butte	2, 4
Calaveras	3
Colusa	2
Contra Costa	7, 10, 11
Del Norte	1
El Dorado	4
Fresno	18–21
Glenn	2
Humboldt	1
Imperial	51
Inyo	25
Kern	20, 22
Kings	20
Lake	1
Lassen	4
Los Angeles	22, 25–39, 42, 46
Madera	18, 19

County	Congressional District
Marin	6
Mariposa	19
Mendocino	1
Merced	18
Modoc	4
Mono	25
Monterey	17
Napa	1
Nevada	4
Orange	40, 42, 44, 46–48
Placer	4
Plumas	4
Riverside	41, 44, 45, 49
Sacramento	3–5, 10
San Benito	17
San Bernardino	25, 26, 41–43
San Diego	49–53
San Francisco	8, 12
San Joaquin	11, 18
San Luis Obispo	22, 23

County	Congressional District
San Mateo	12, 14
Santa Barbara	23, 24
Santa Clara	11, 14–16
Santa Cruz	14, 17
Shasta	2
Sierra	4
Siskiyou	2
Solano	3, 7, 10
Sonoma	1, 6
Stanislaus	18, 19
Sutter	2
Tehama	2
Trinity	2
Tulare	21
Tuolumne	19
Ventura	23, 24
Yolo	1, 2
Yuba	2

Congressional District 1

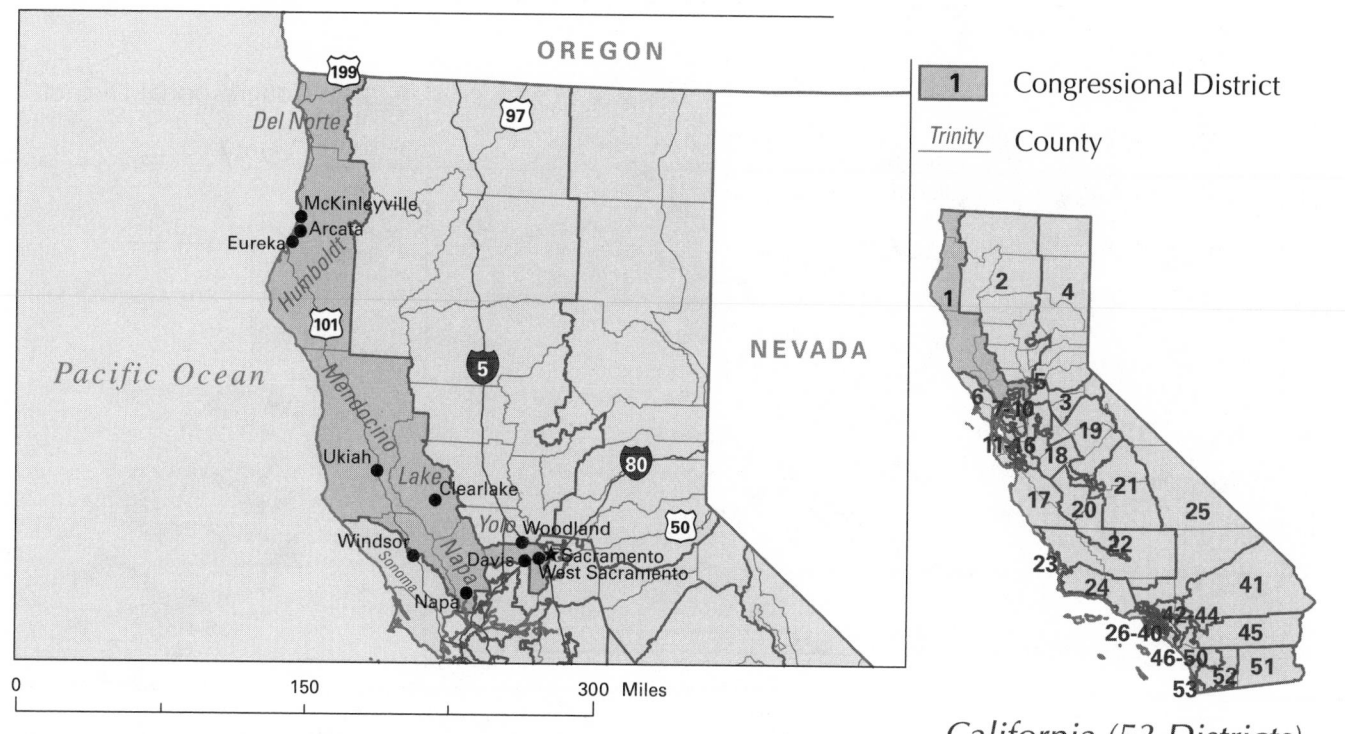

California (53 Districts)

Congressional District 2

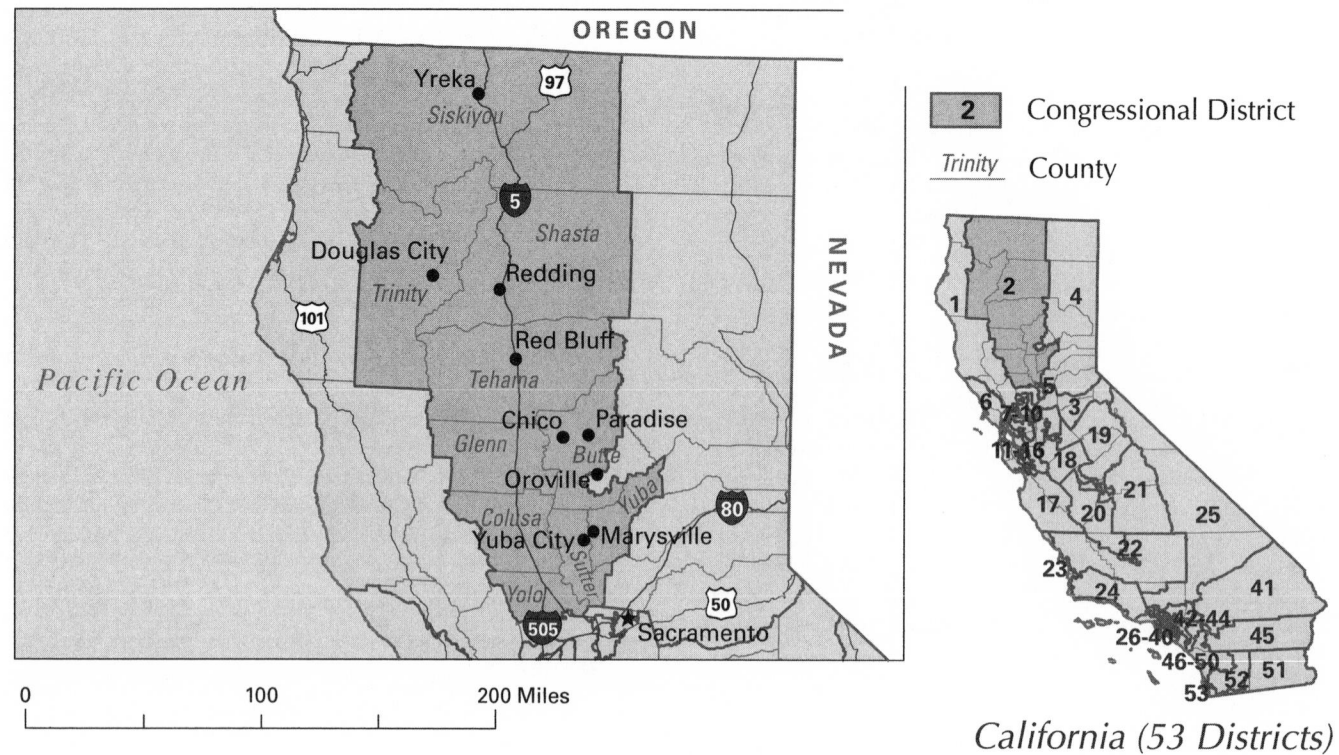

California (53 Districts)

Congressional District 3

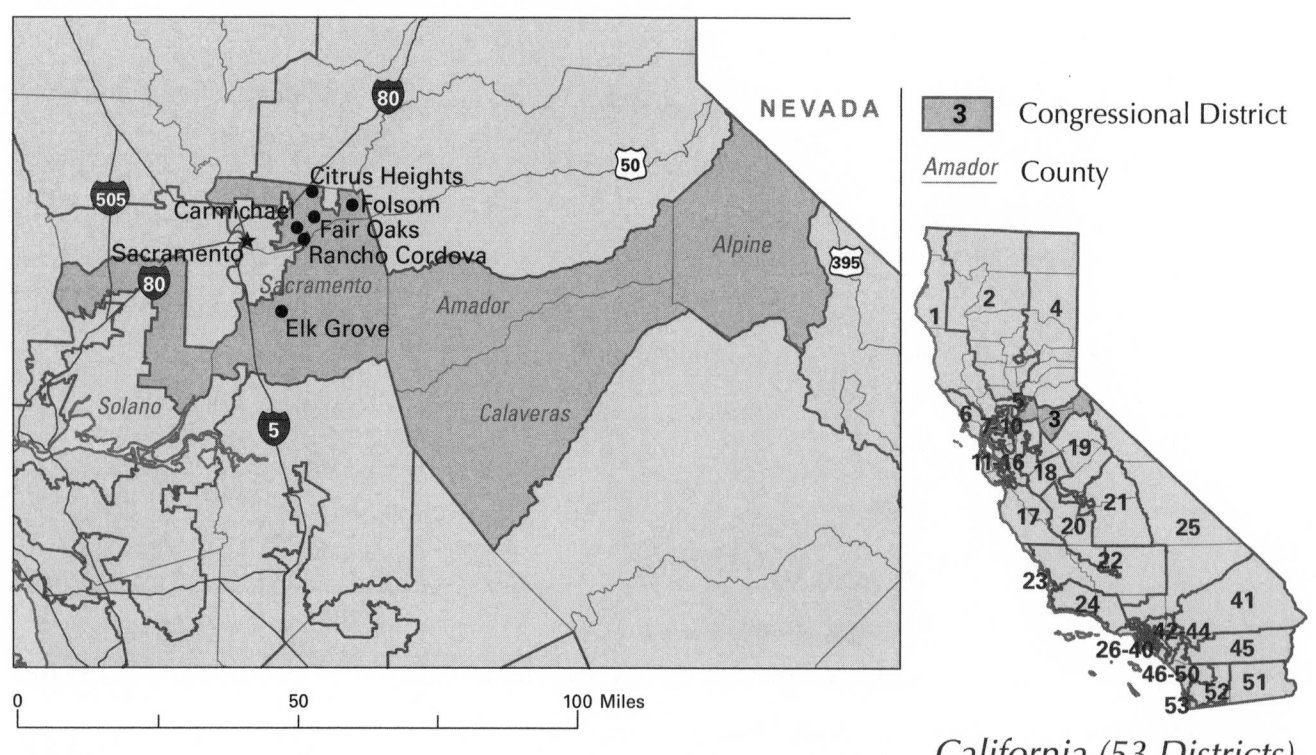

California (53 Districts)

Congressional District 4

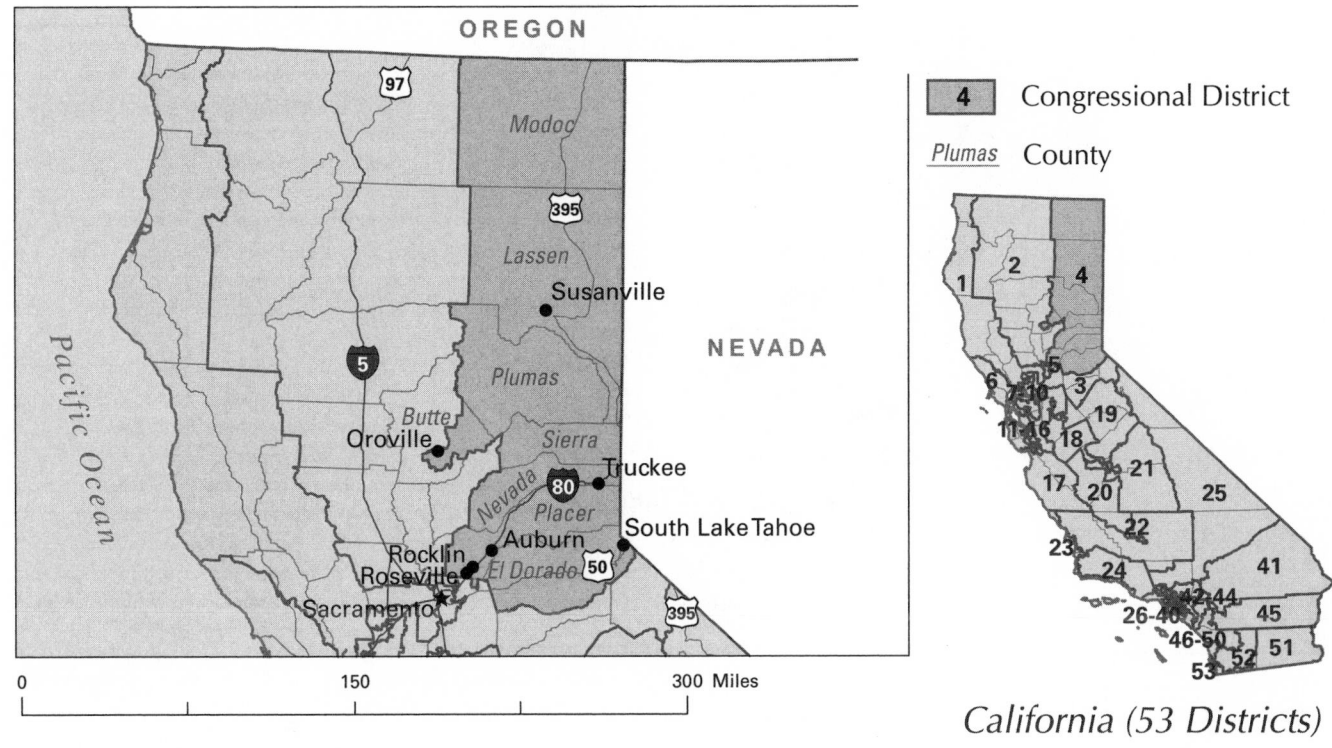

4 Congressional District

Plumas County

California (53 Districts)

Congressional District 5

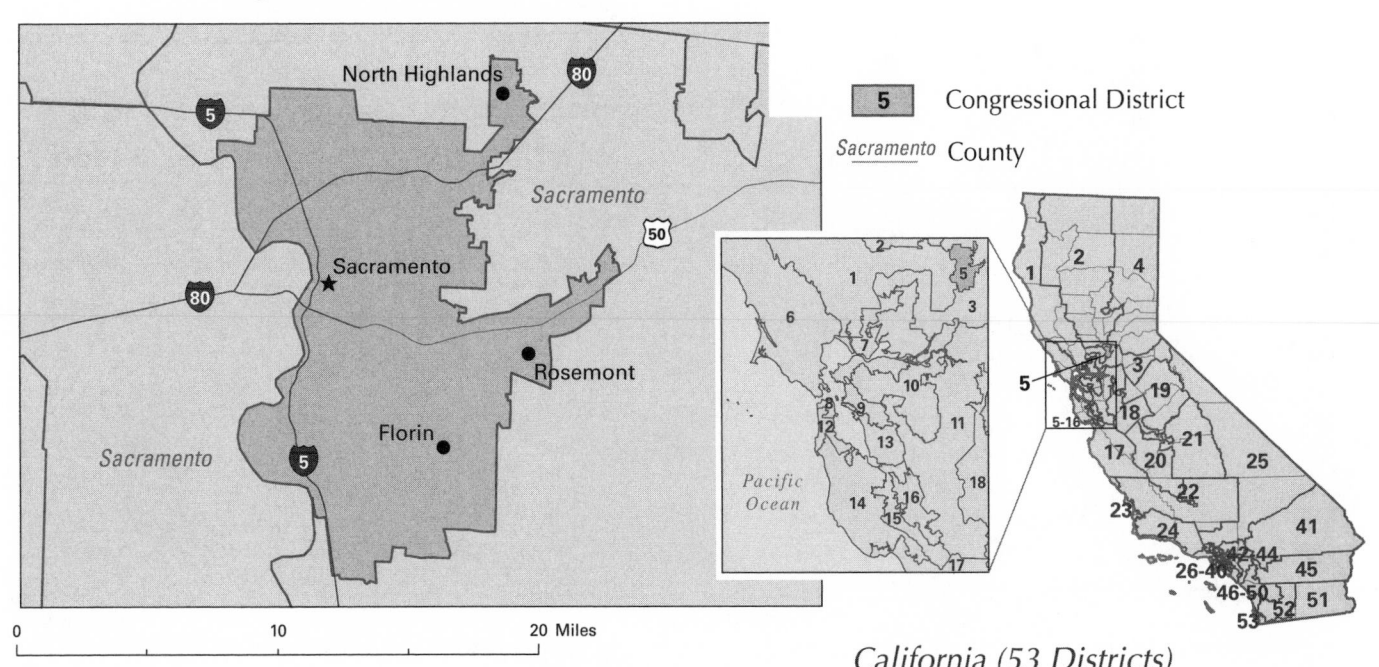

5 Congressional District

Sacramento County

California (53 Districts)

Congressional District 6

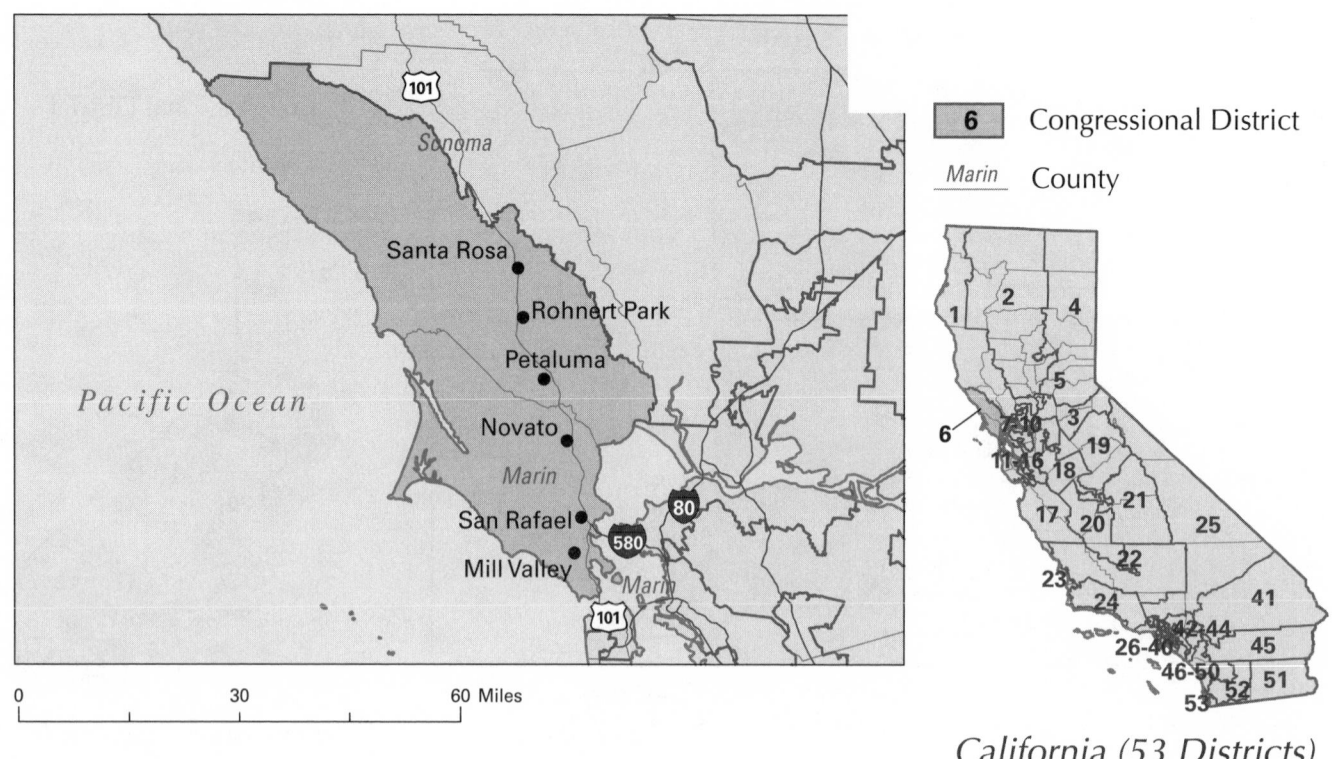

California (53 Districts)

Congressional District 7

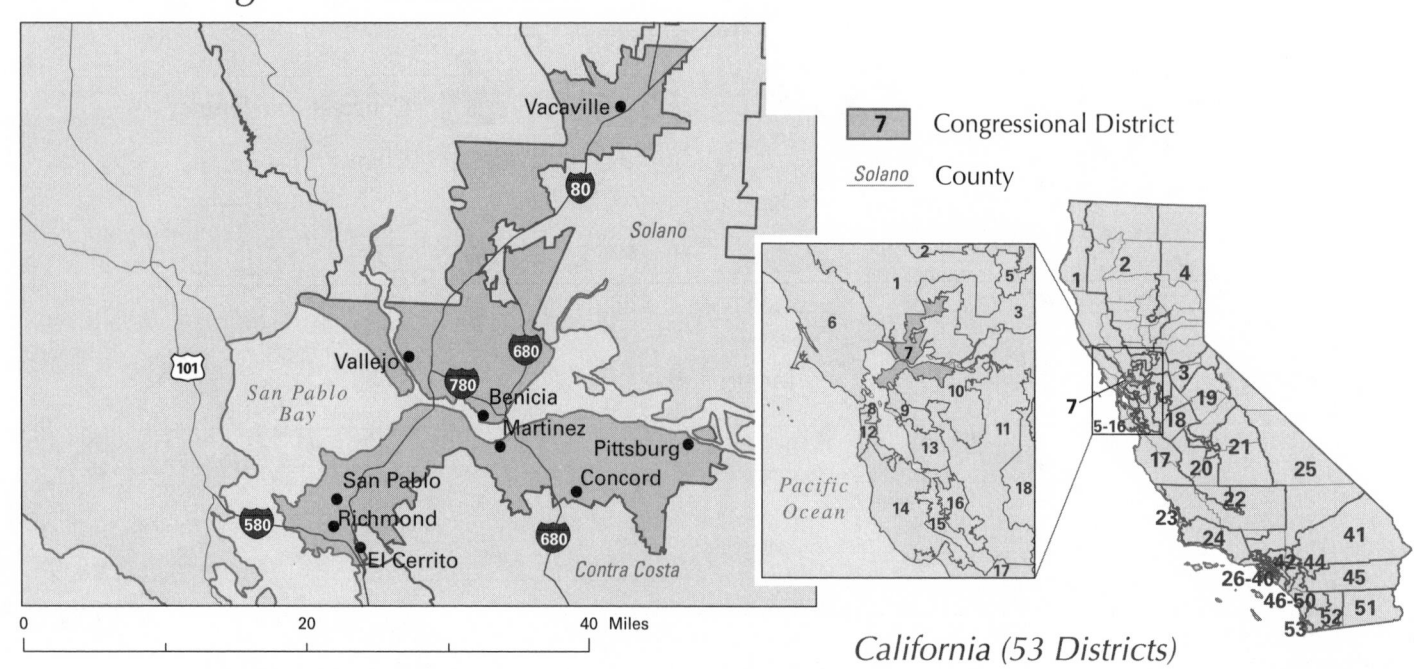

California (53 Districts)

Congressional District 8

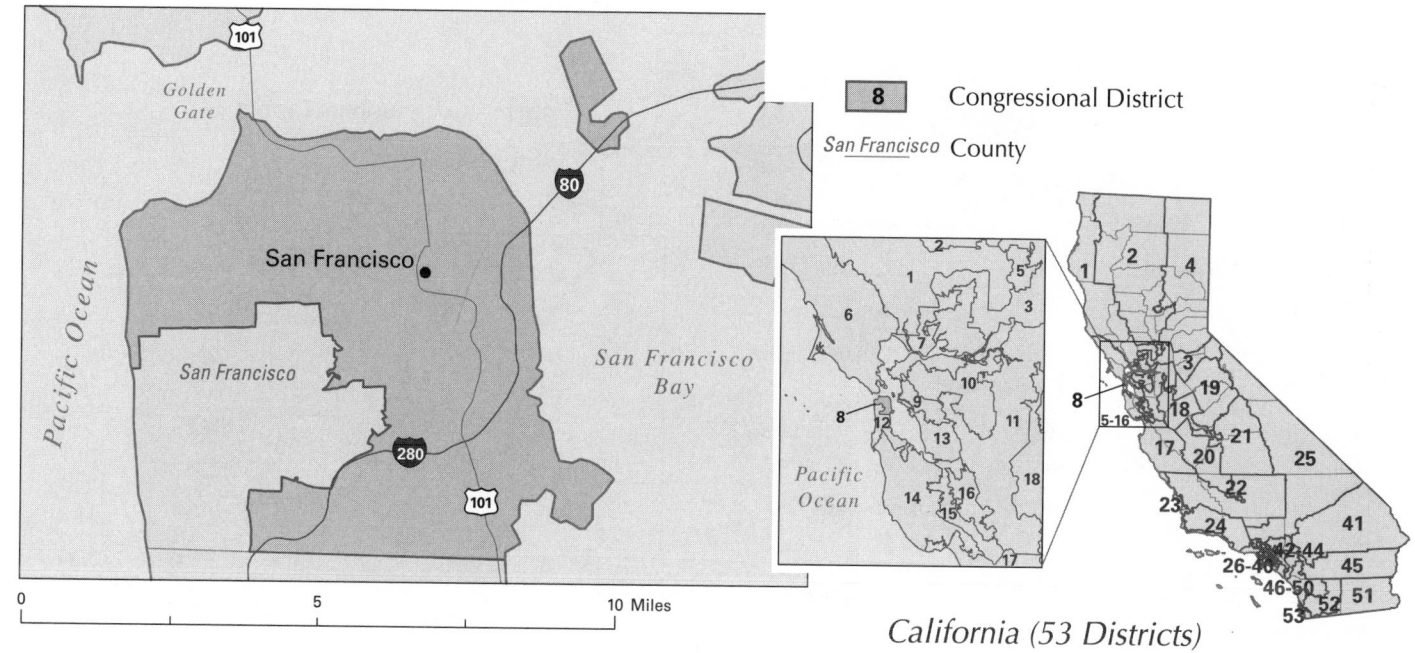

California (53 Districts)

Congressional District 9

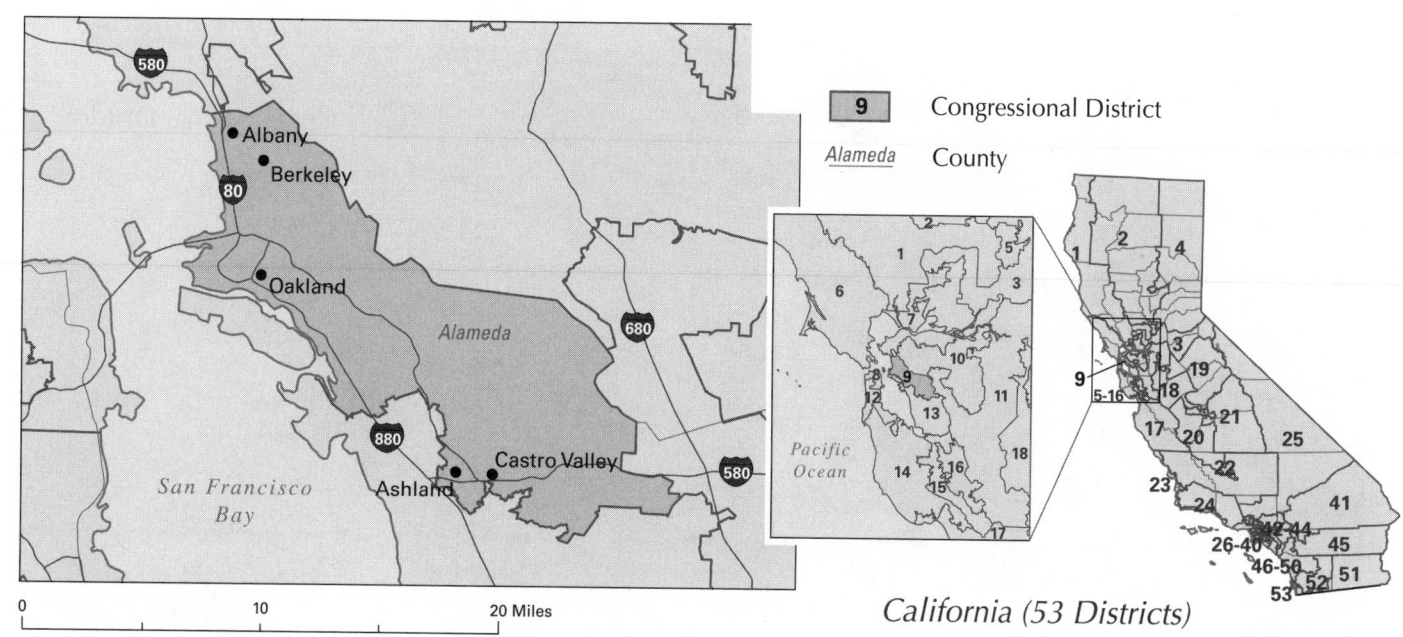

California (53 Districts)

Congressional District 10

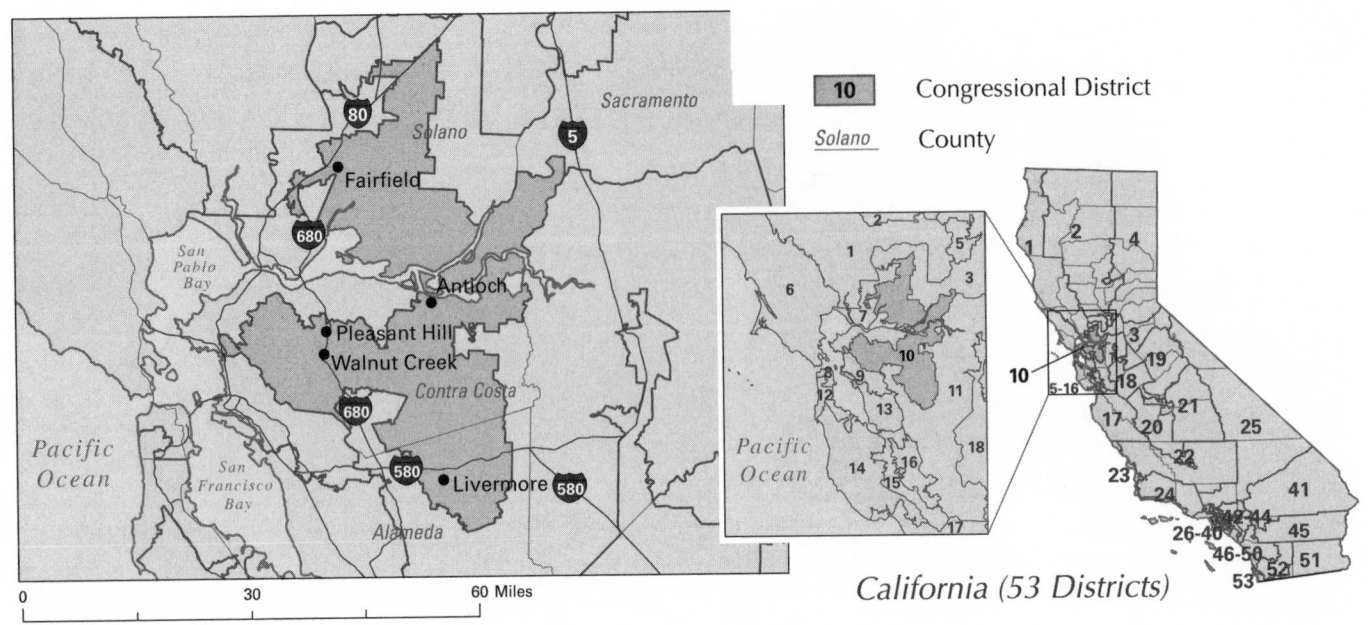

California (53 Districts)

Congressional District 11

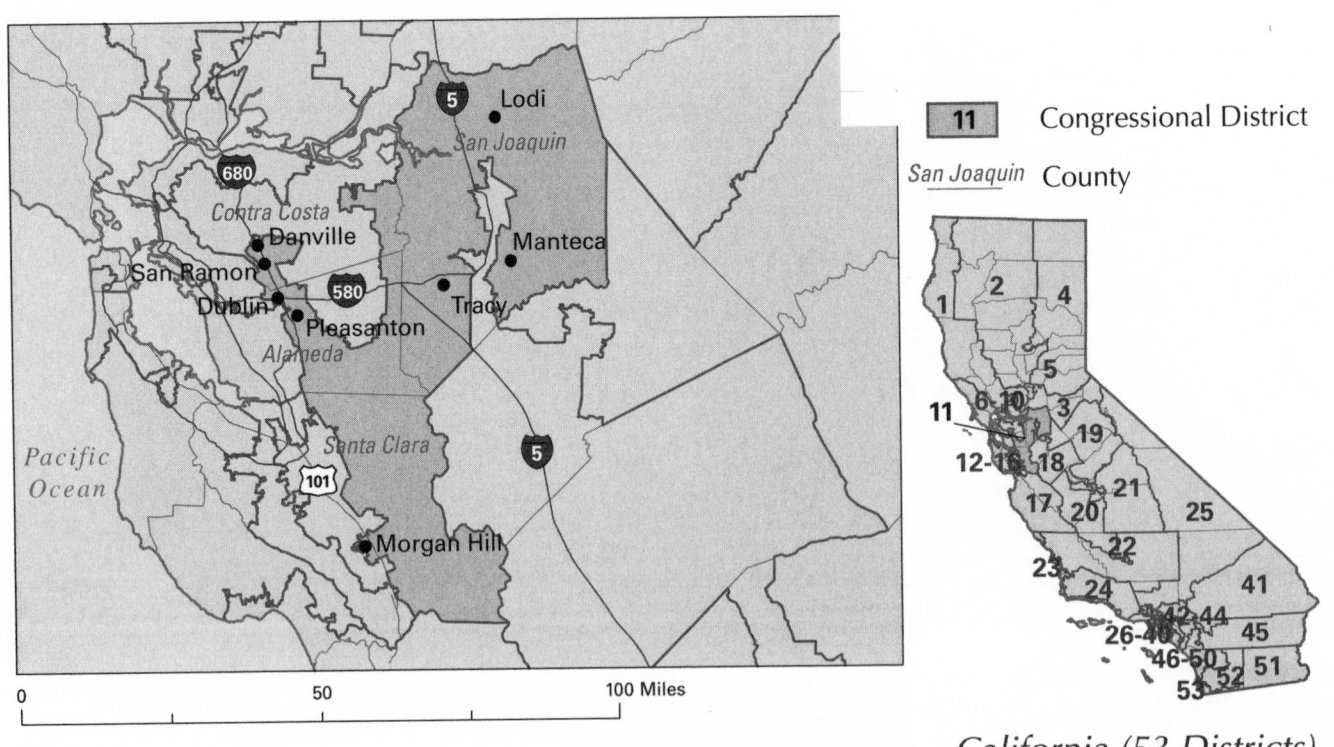

California (53 Districts)

Congressional District 12

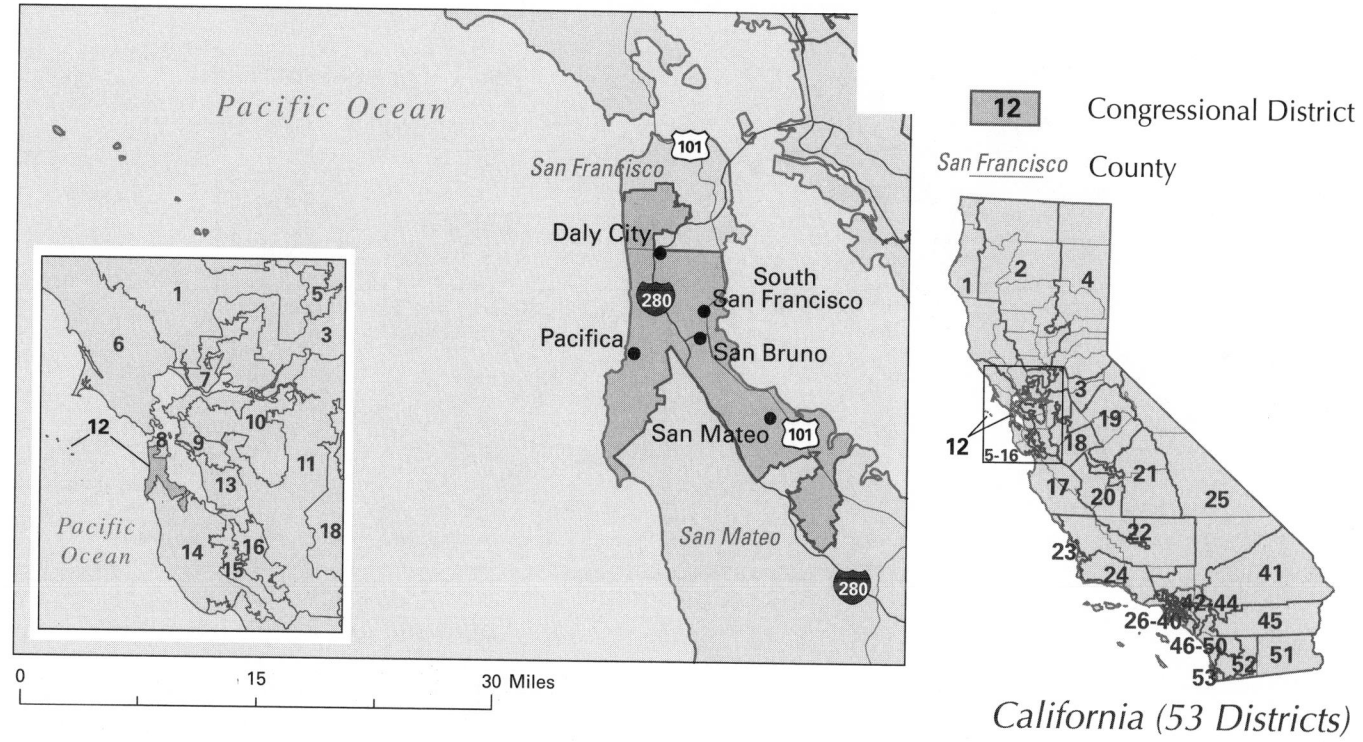

California (53 Districts)

Congressional District 13

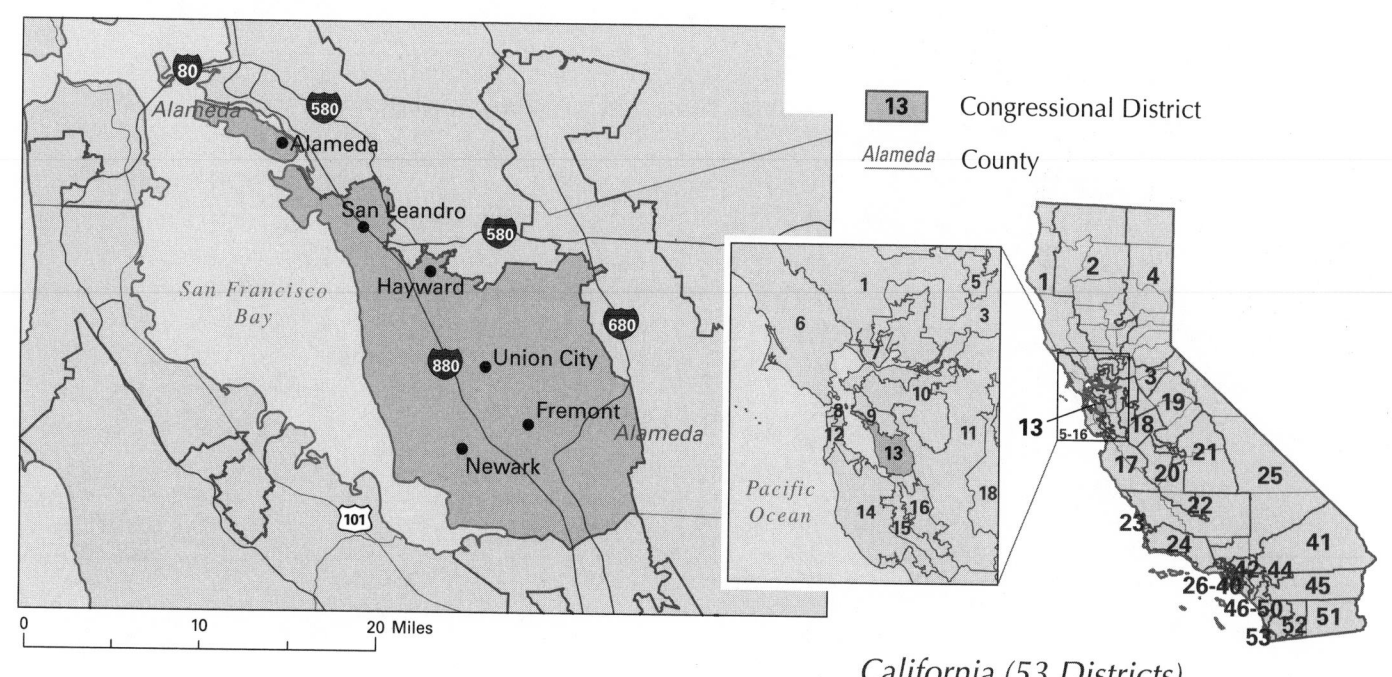

California (53 Districts)

Congressional District 14

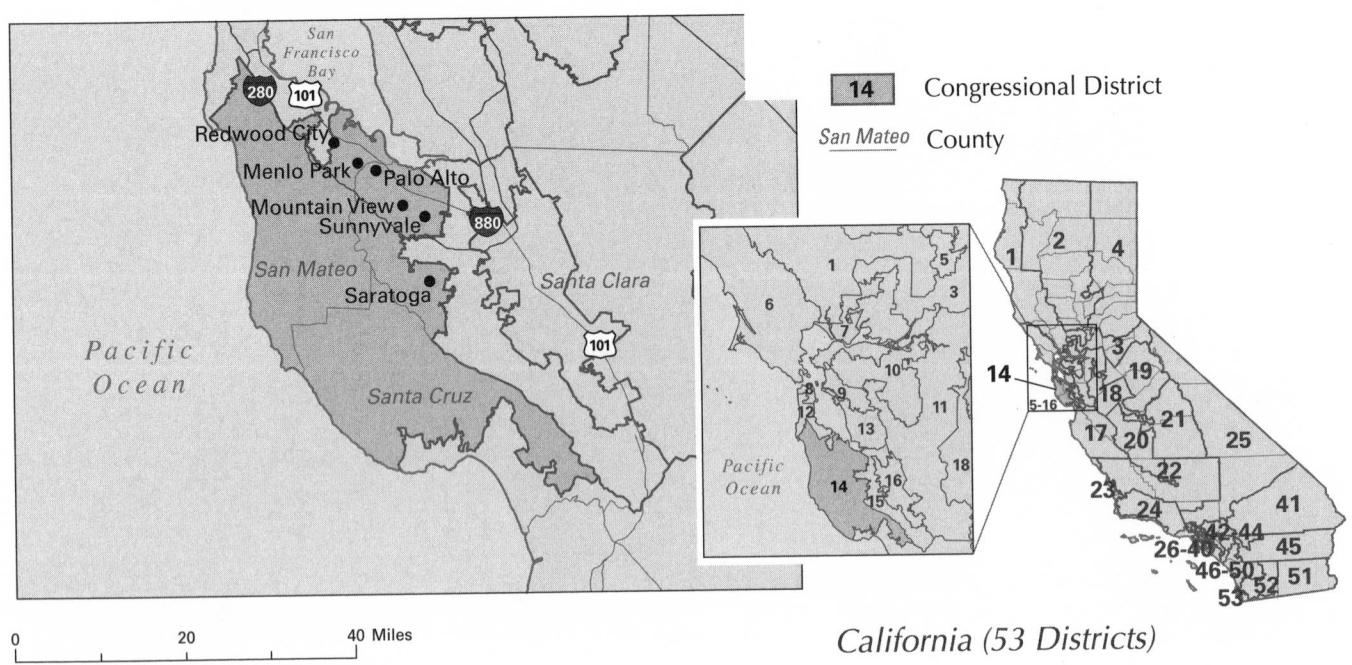

14 Congressional District
San Mateo County

California (53 Districts)

Congressional District 15

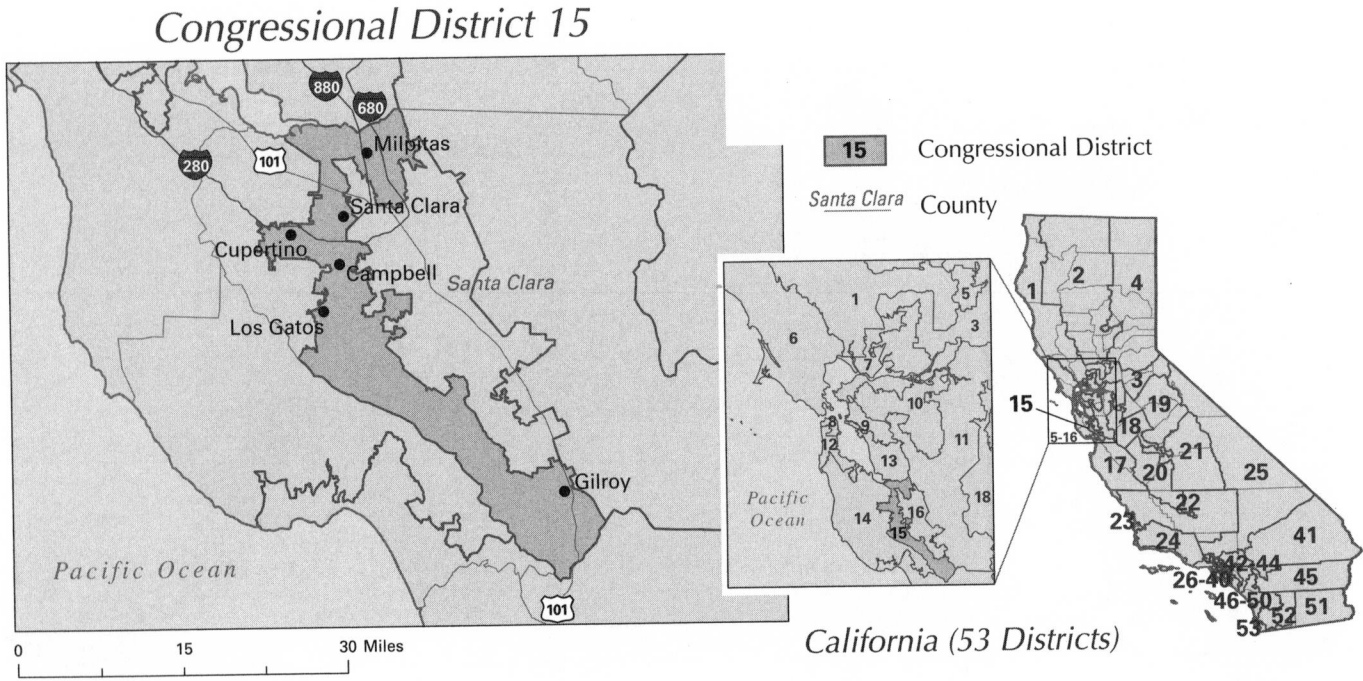

15 Congressional District
Santa Clara County

California (53 Districts)

Congressional District 16

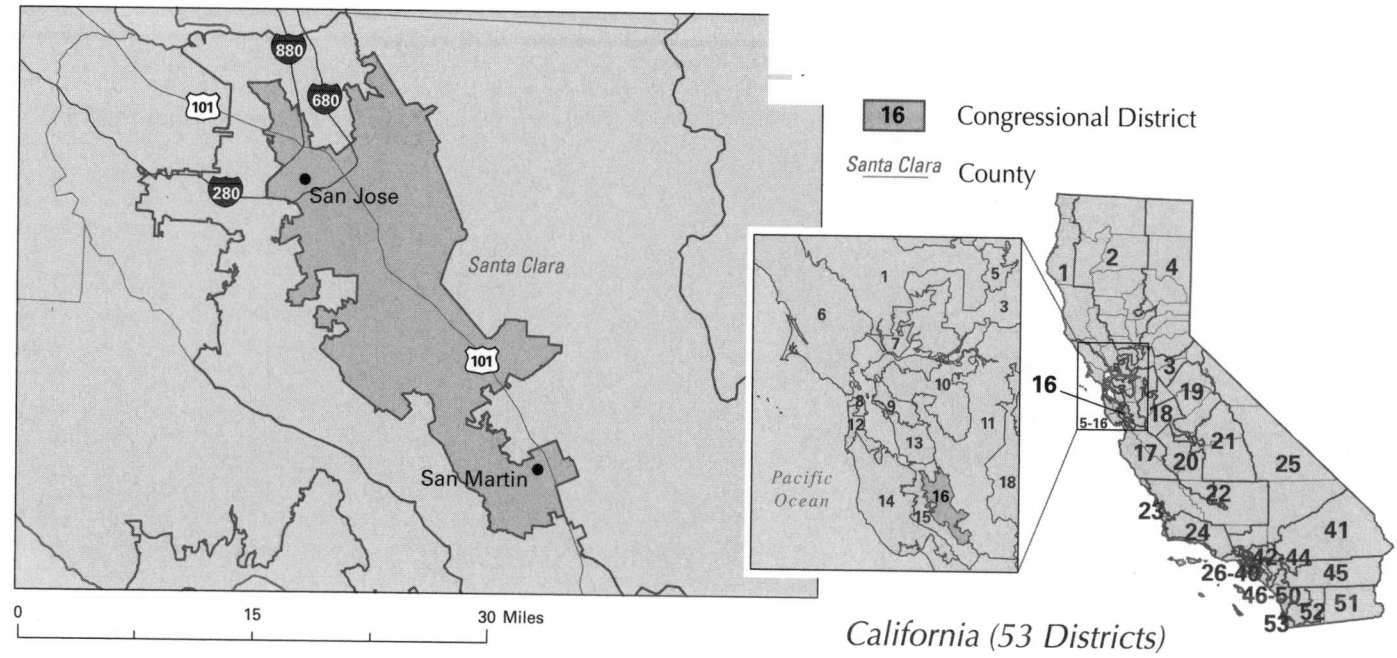

California (53 Districts)

Congressional District 17

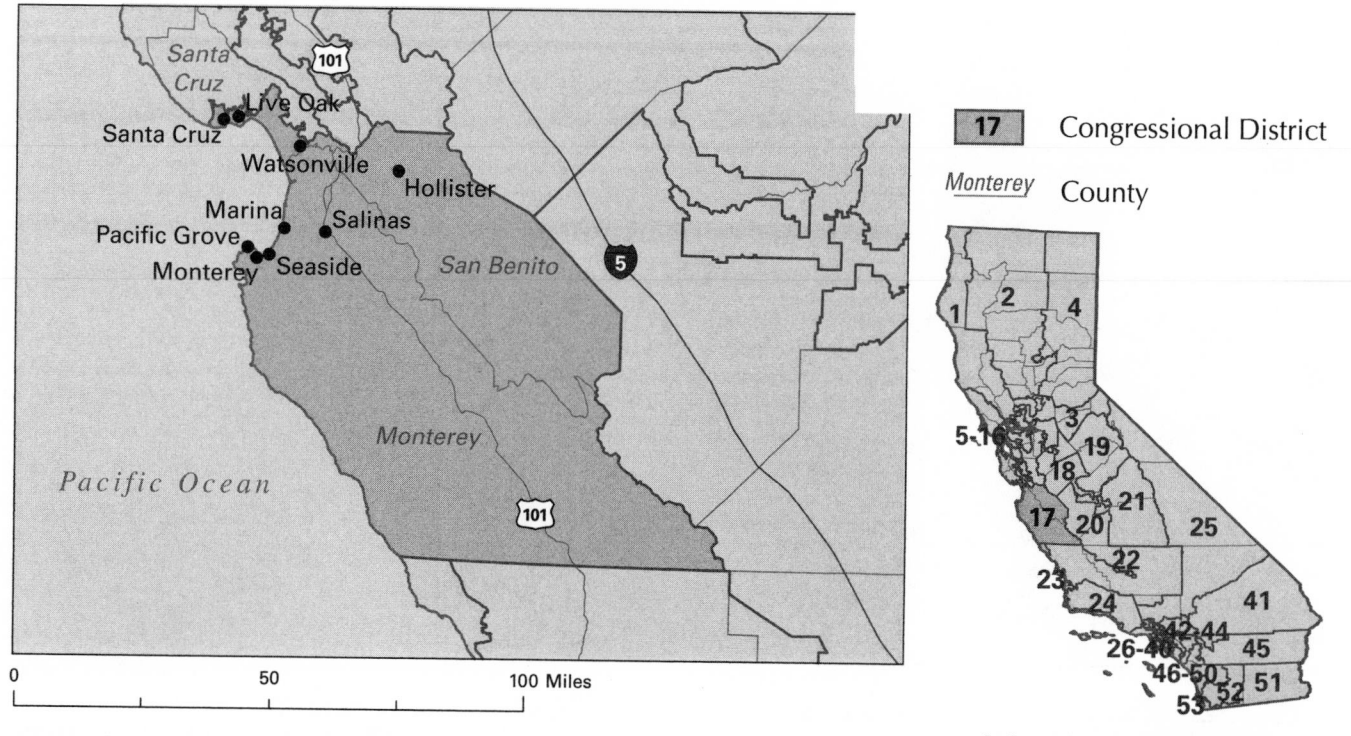

California (53 Districts)

Congressional District 18

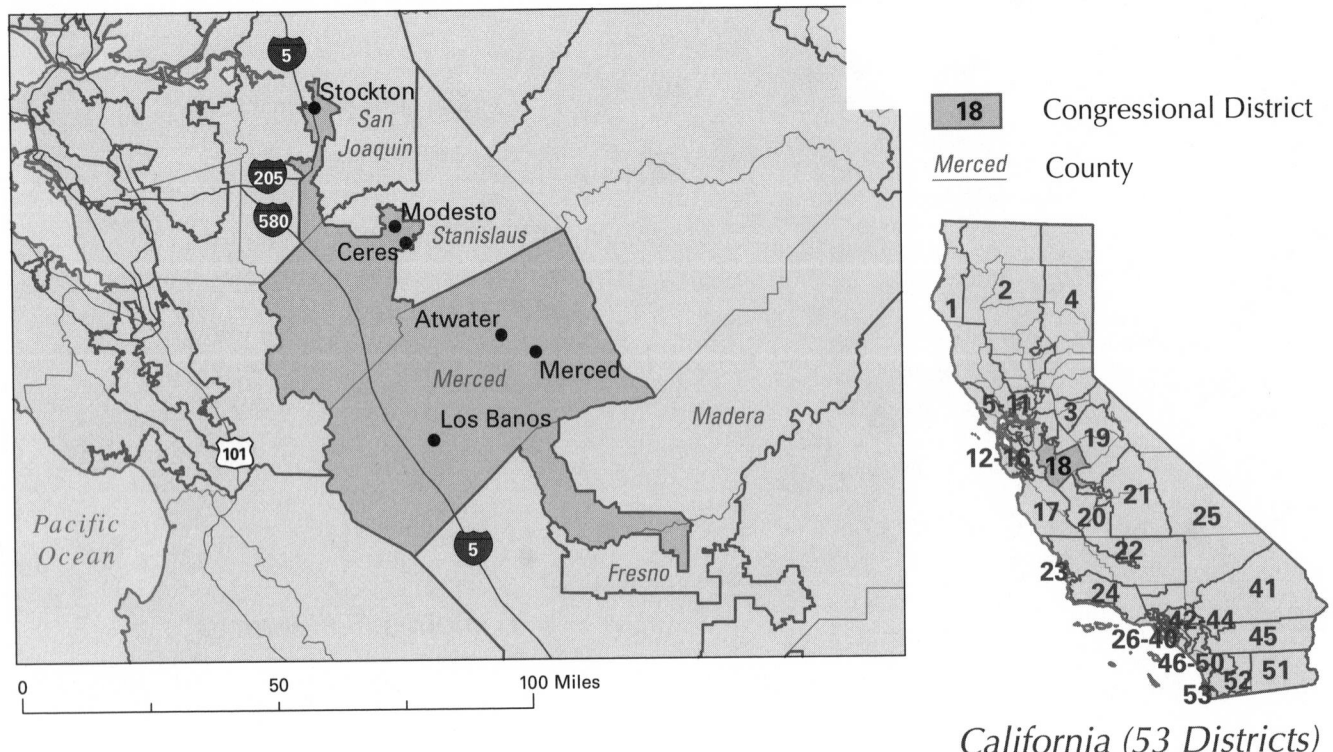

California (53 Districts)

Congressional District 19

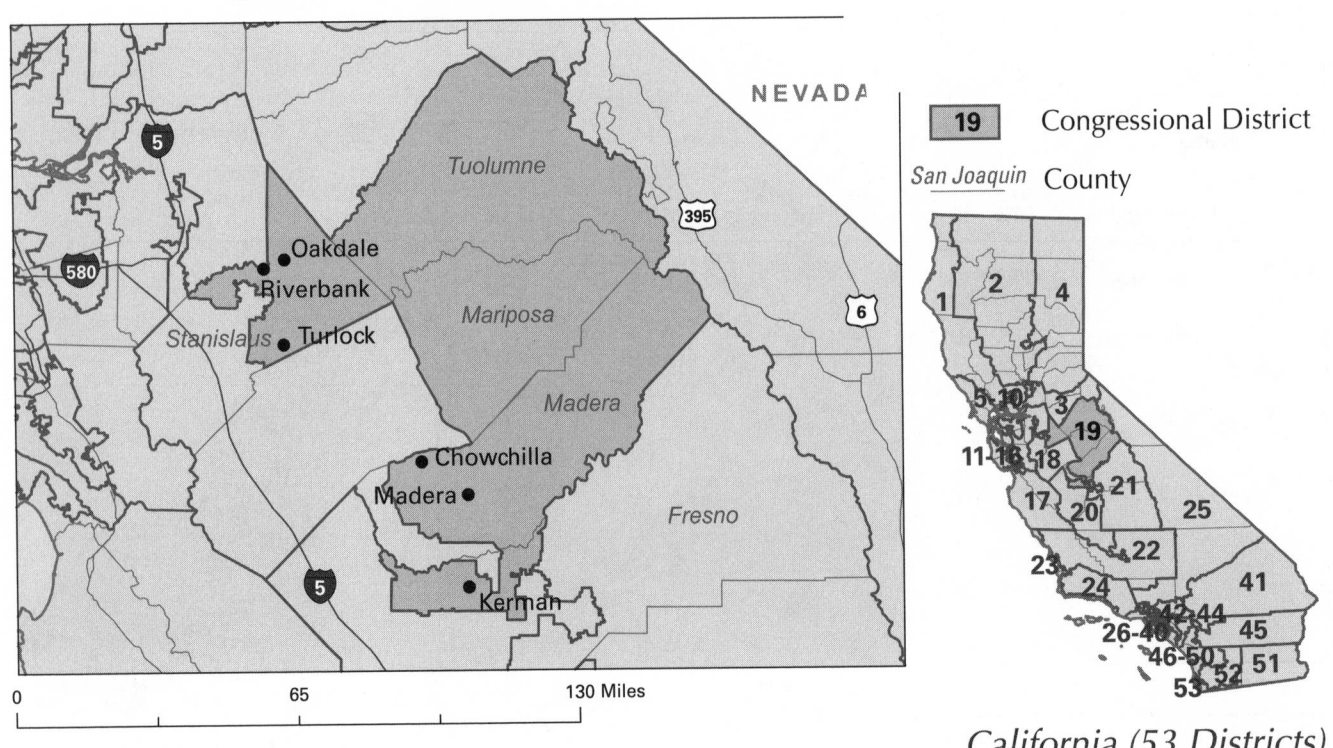

California (53 Districts)

Congressional District 20

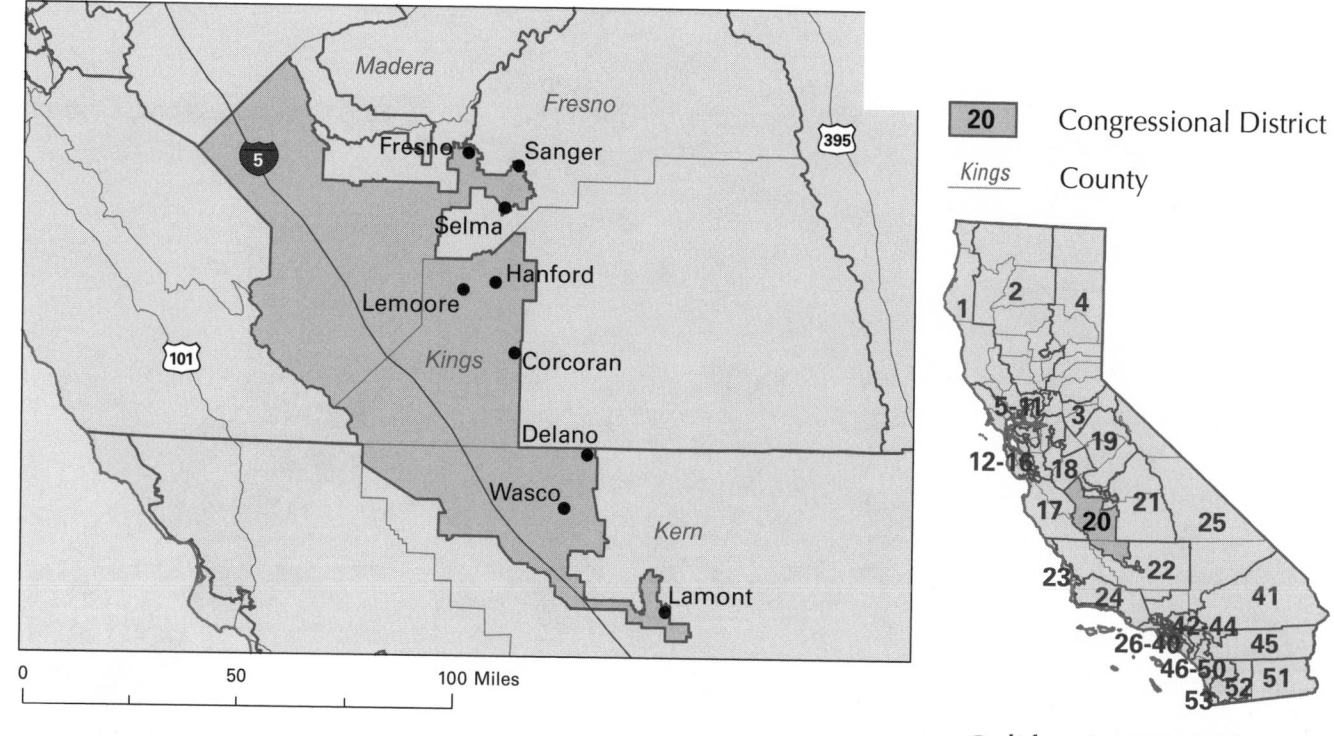

California (53 Districts)

Congressional District 21

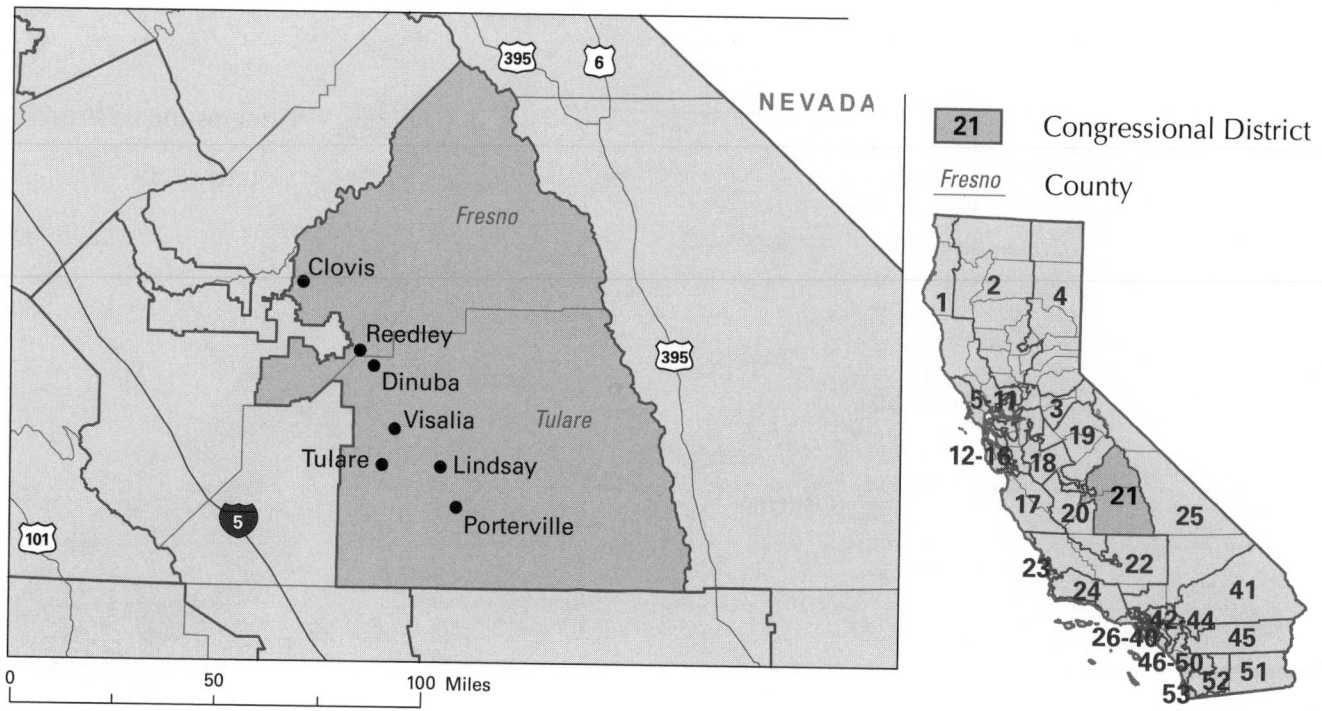

California (53 Districts)

Congressional District 22

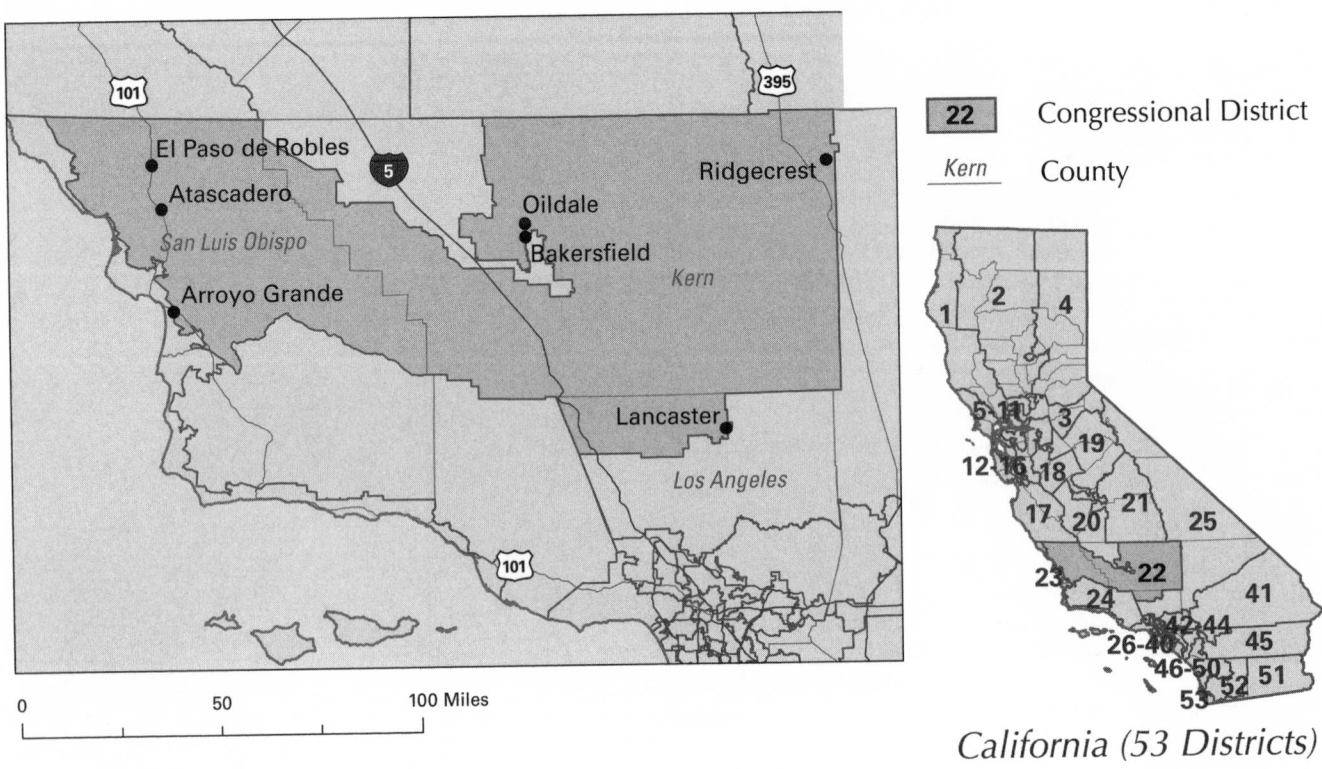

California (53 Districts)

Congressional District 23

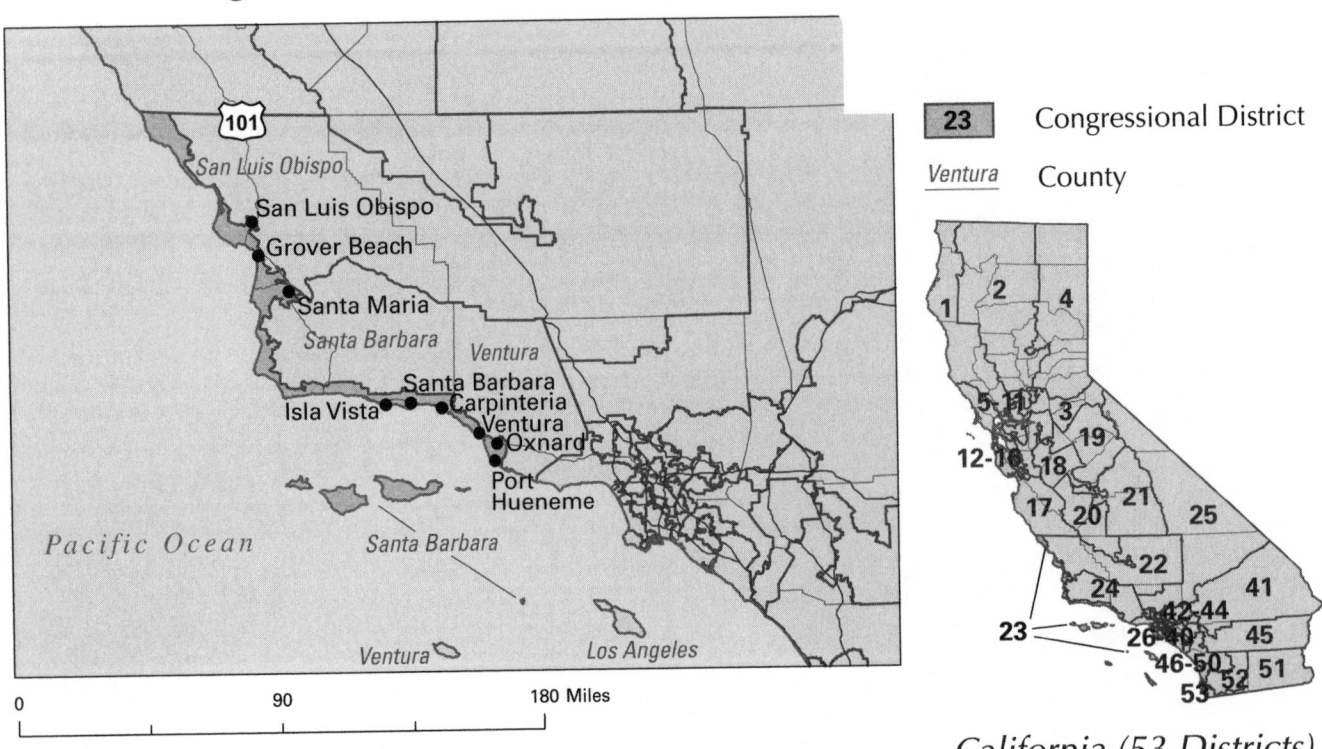

California (53 Districts)

Congressional District 24

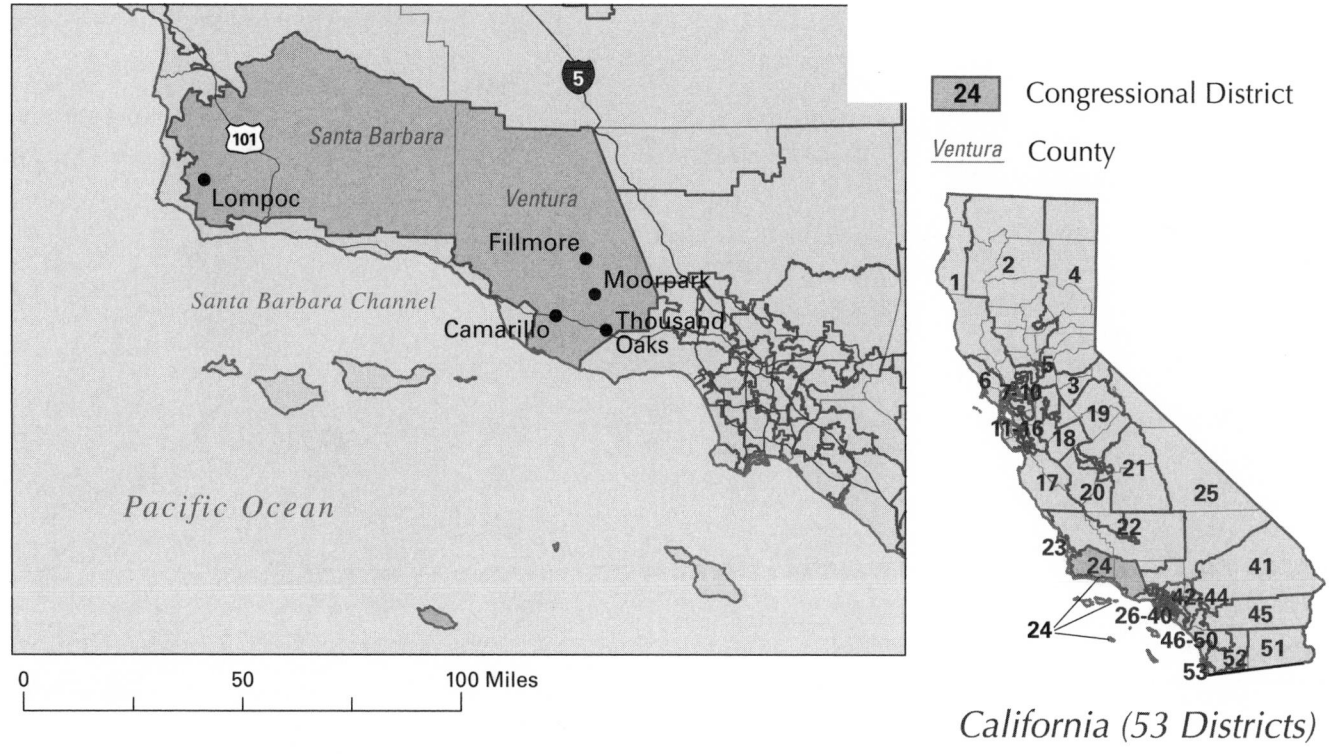

24   Congressional District

Ventura   County

California (53 Districts)

Congressional District 25

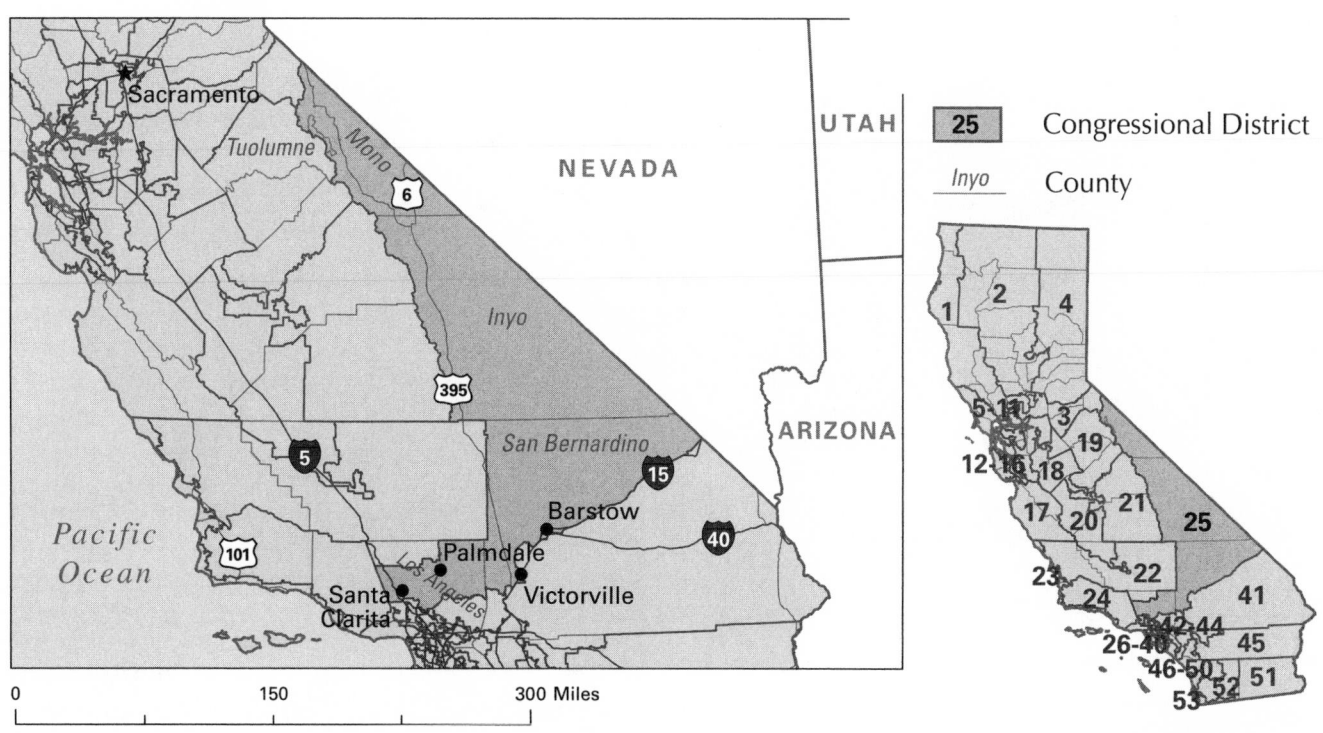

25   Congressional District

Inyo   County

California (53 Districts)

Congressional District 26

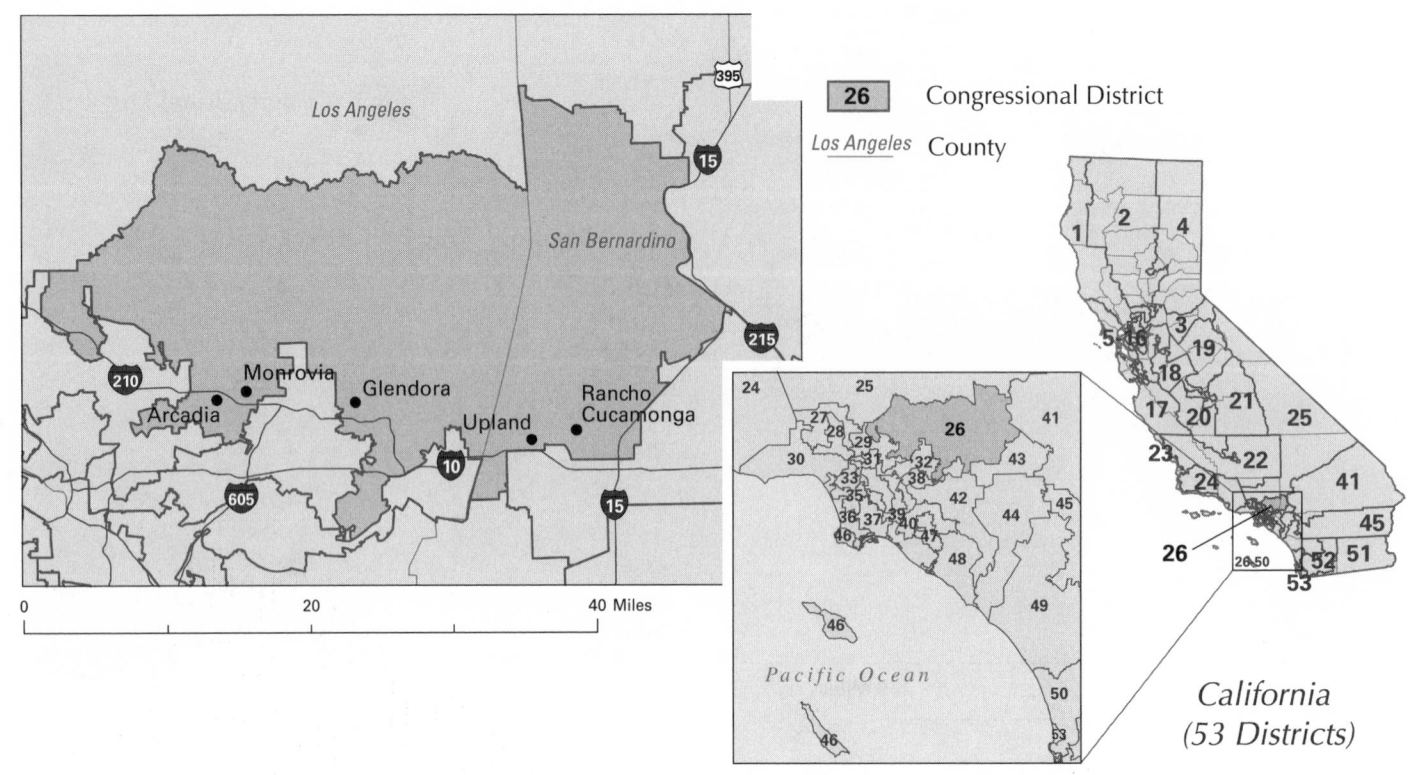

Congressional District 27

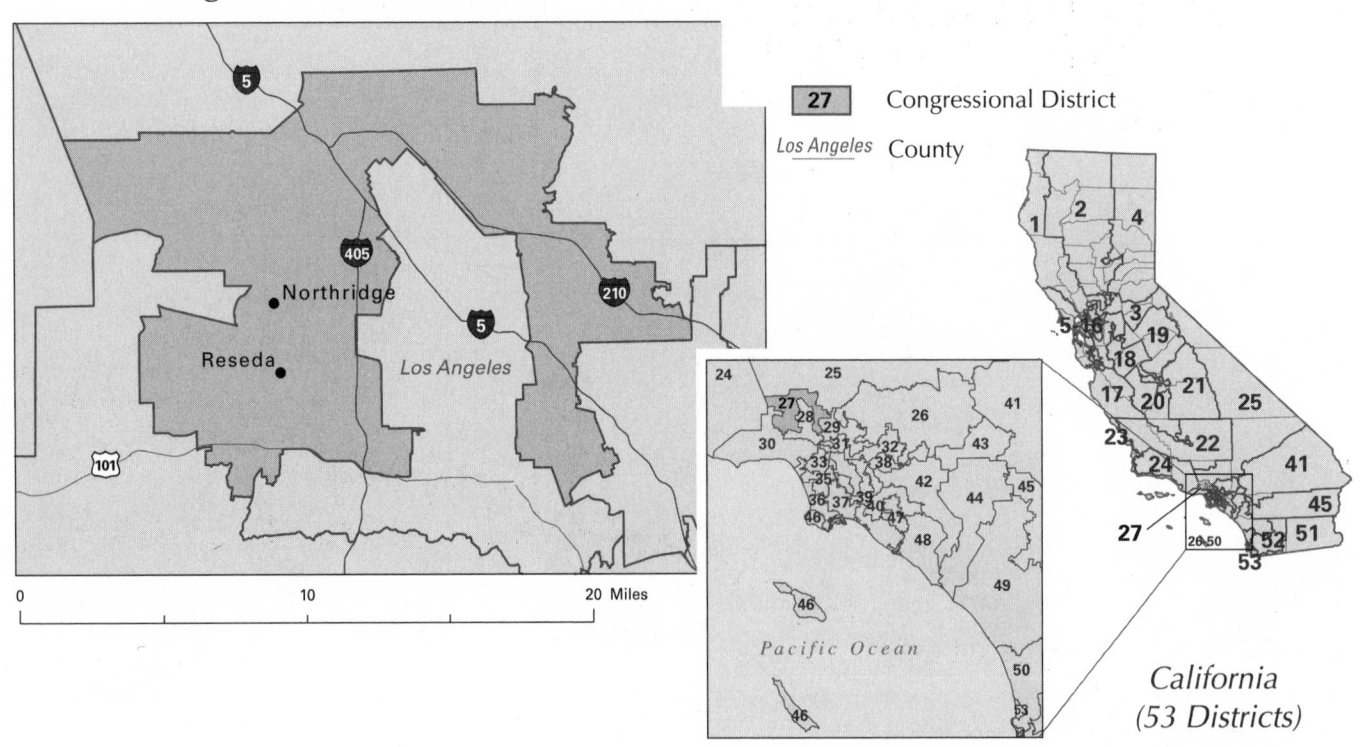

Congressional District 28

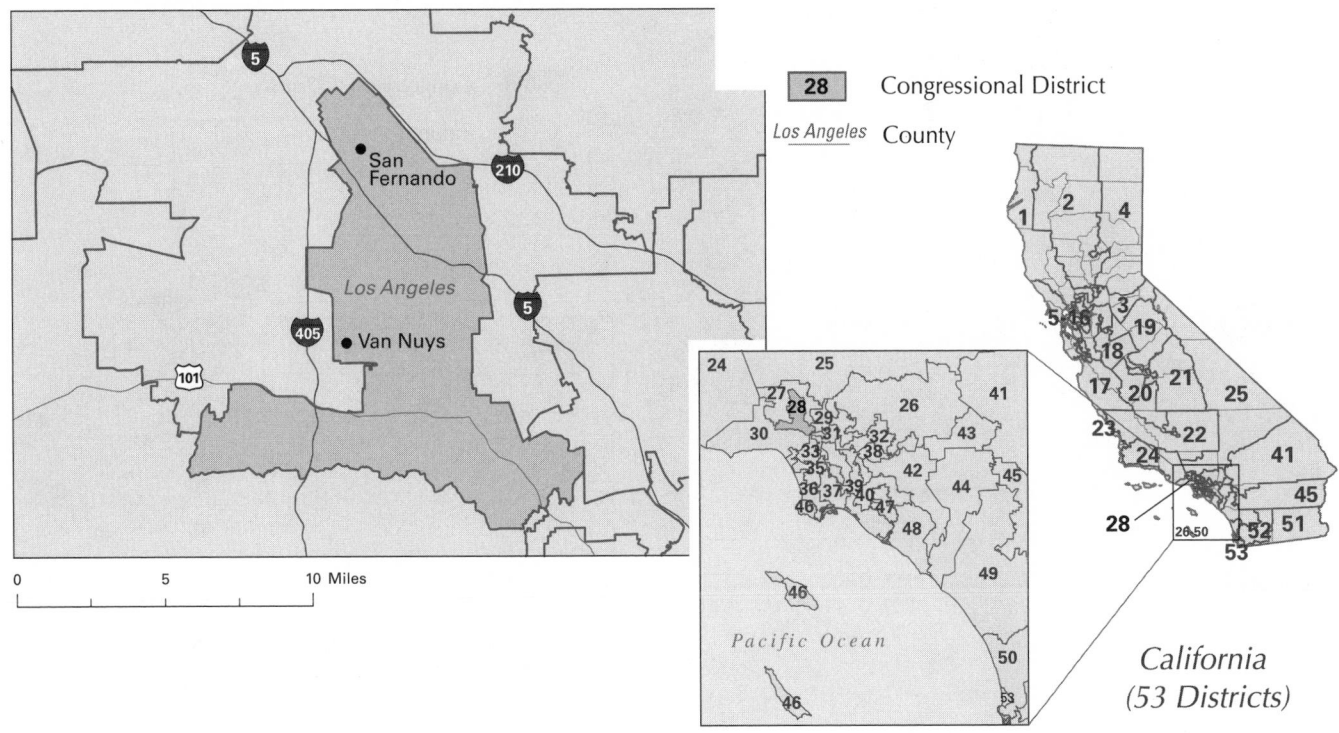

Congressional District 29

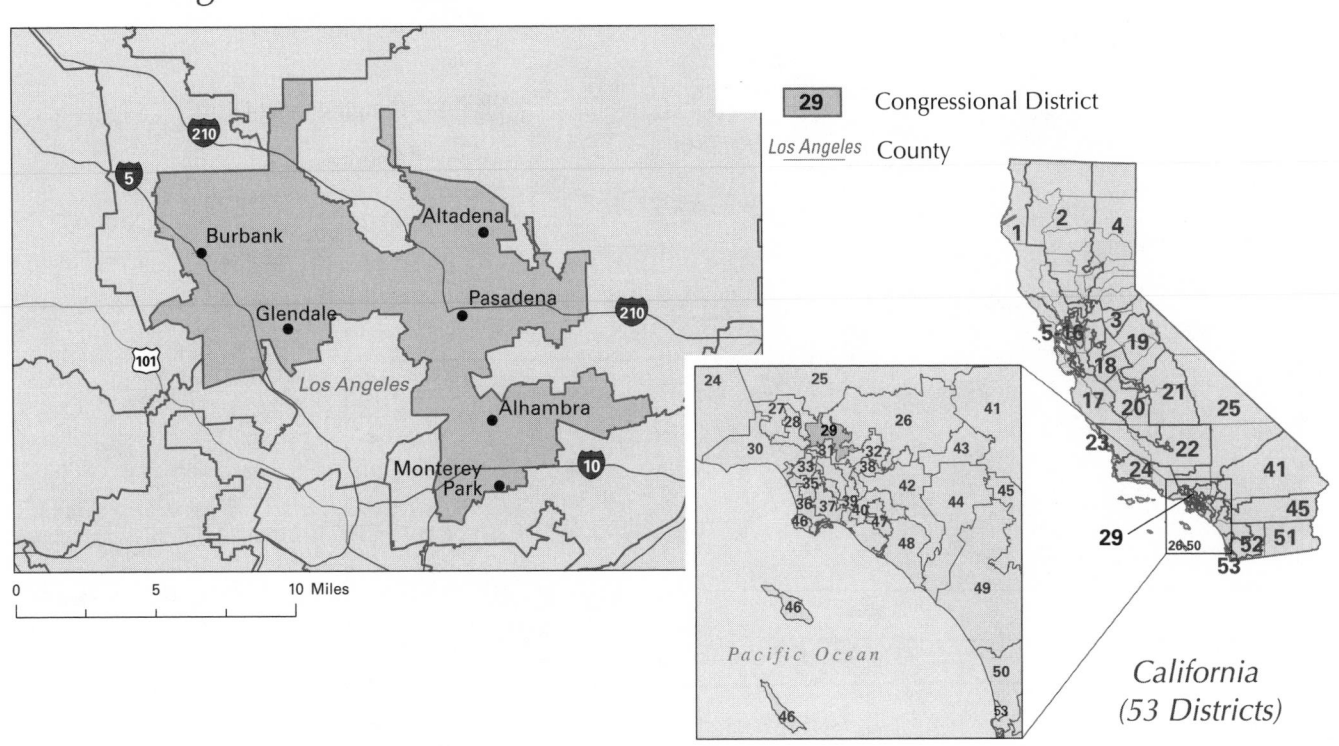

Congressional District 30

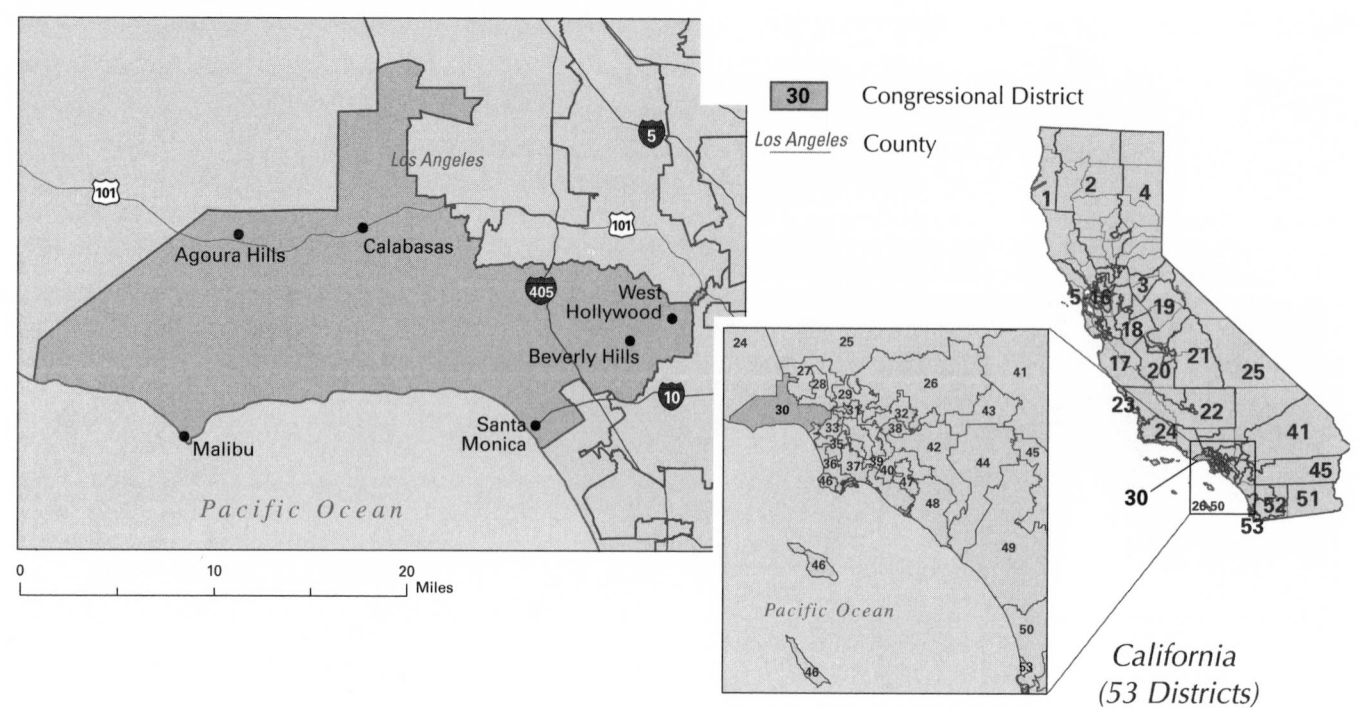

Congressional District 31

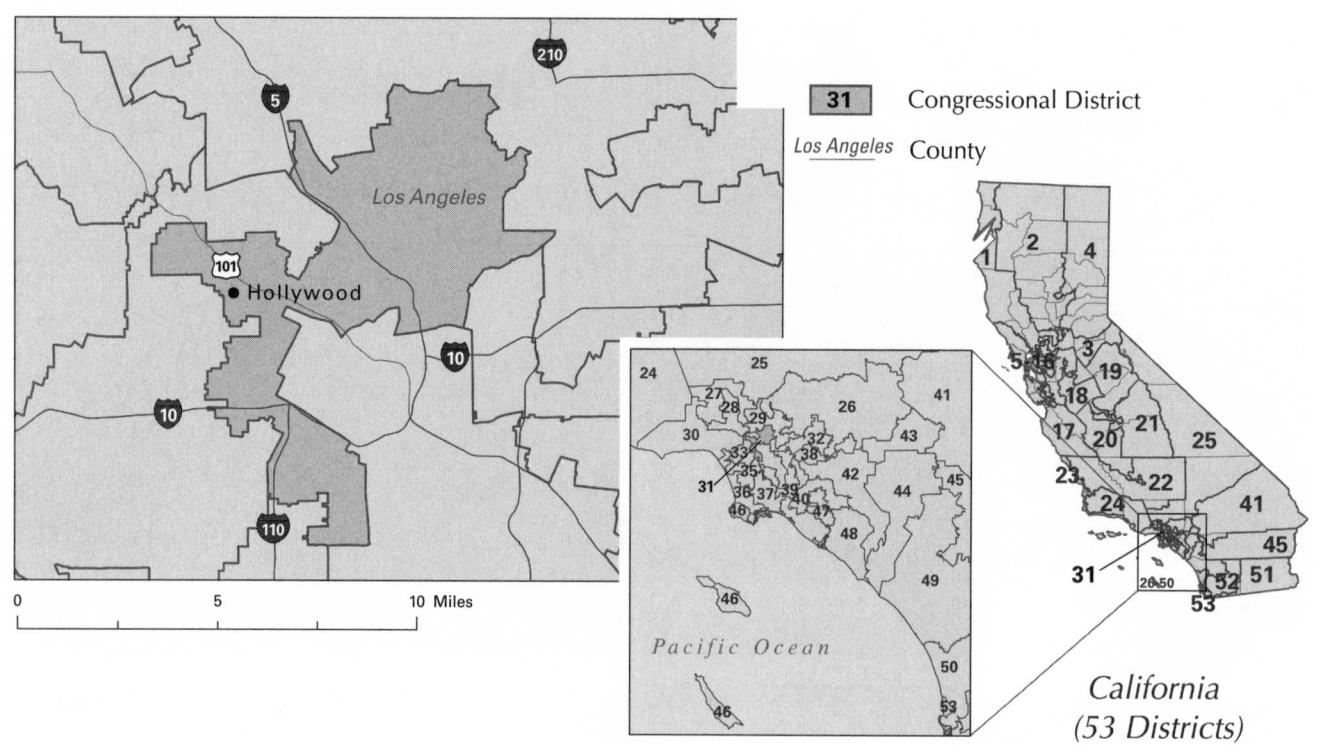

Congressional District 32

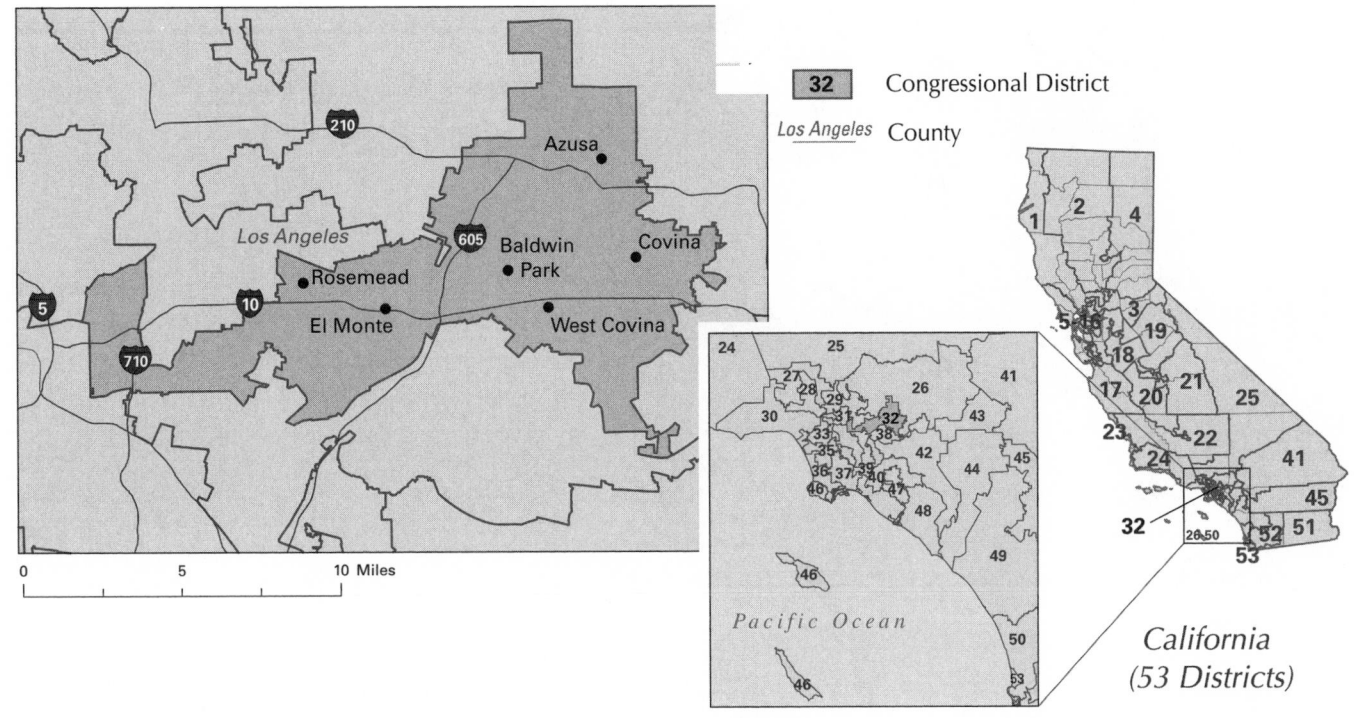

Congressional District 33

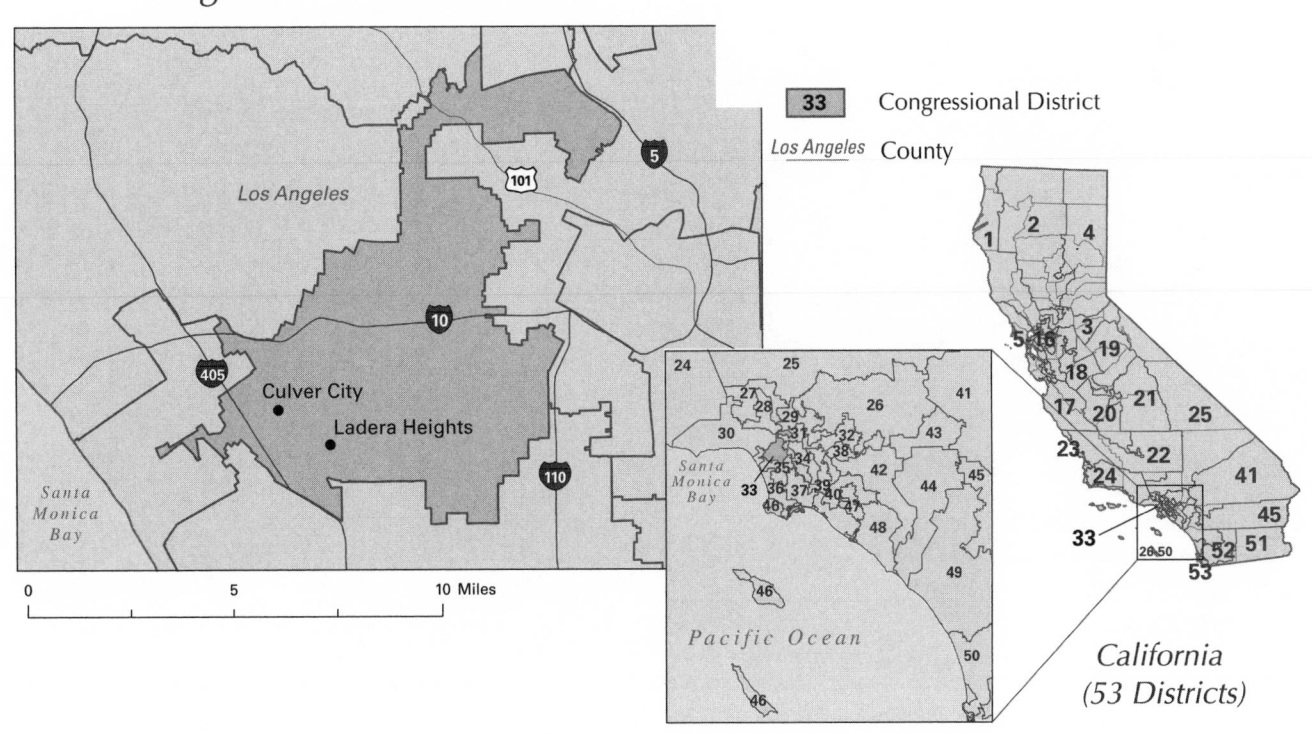

Congressional District 34

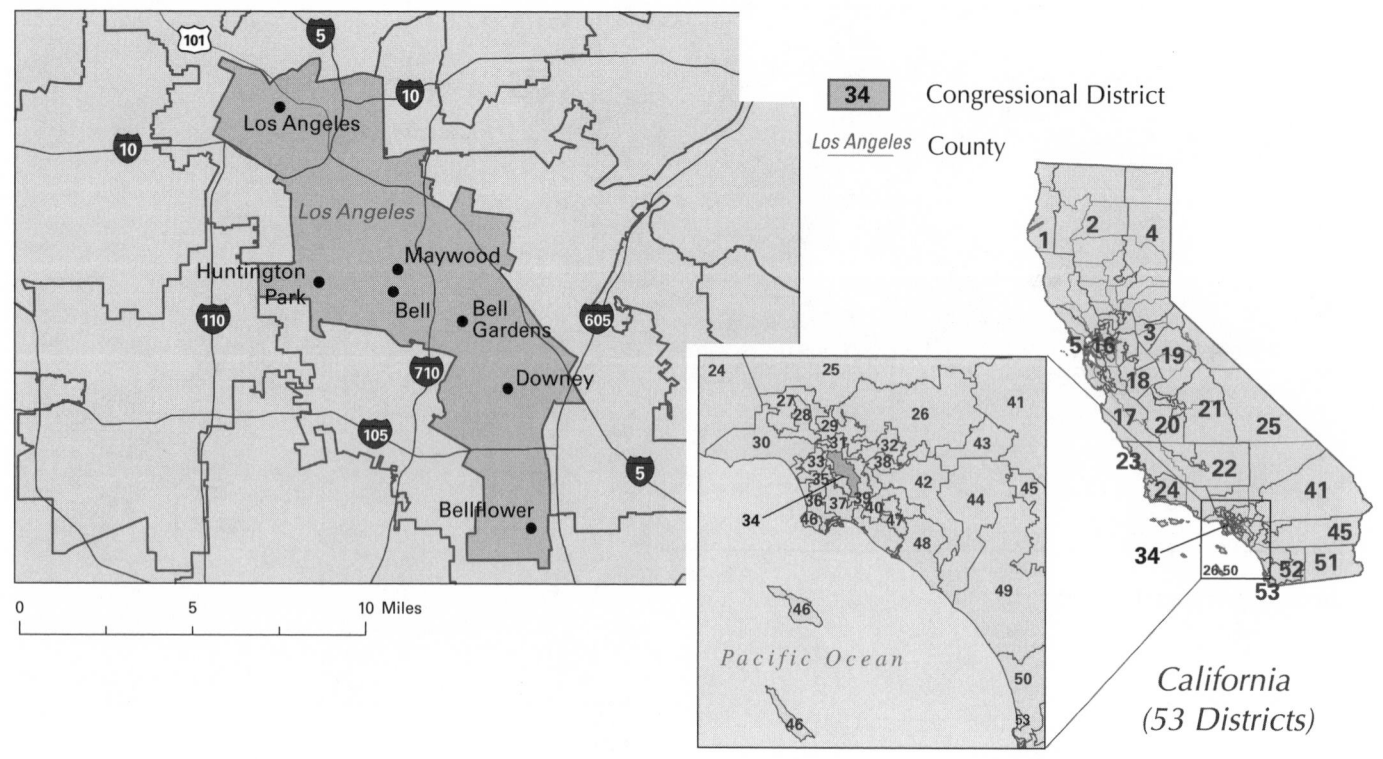

Congressional District 35

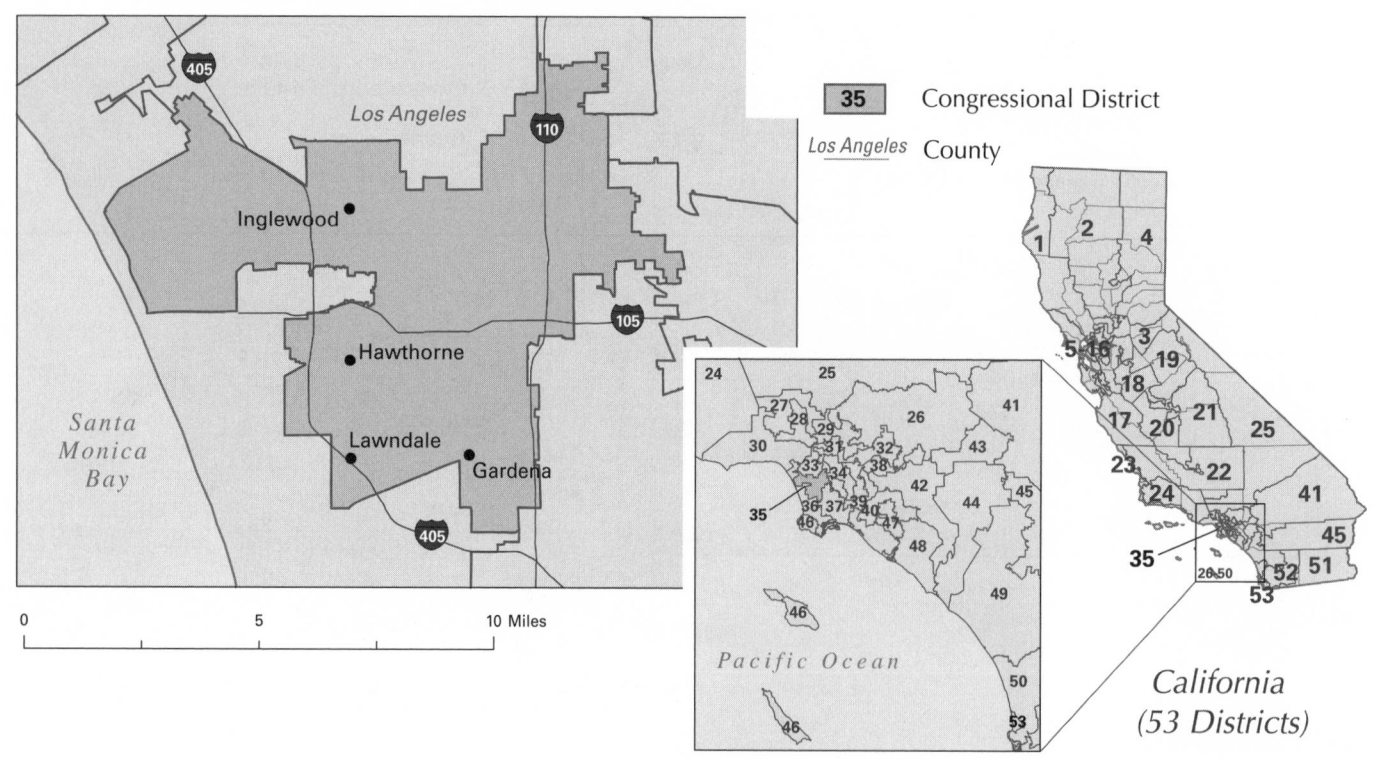

Congressional District 36

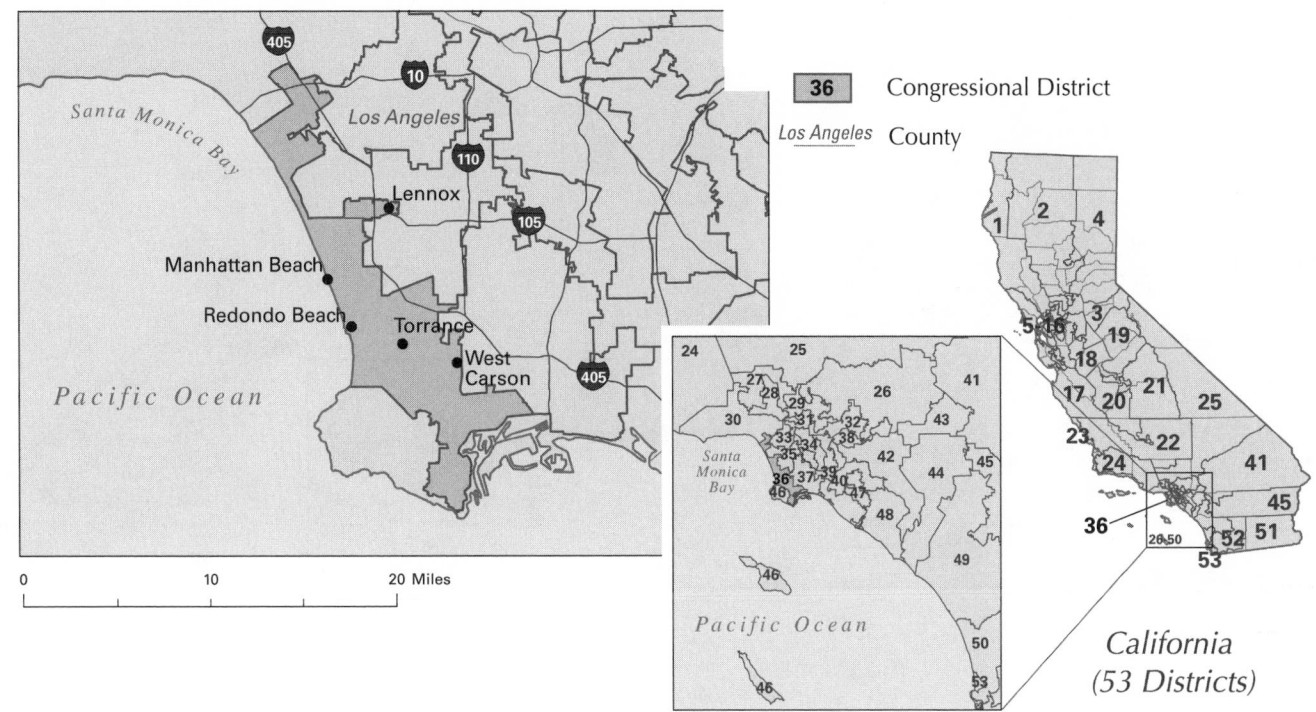

Congressional District 37

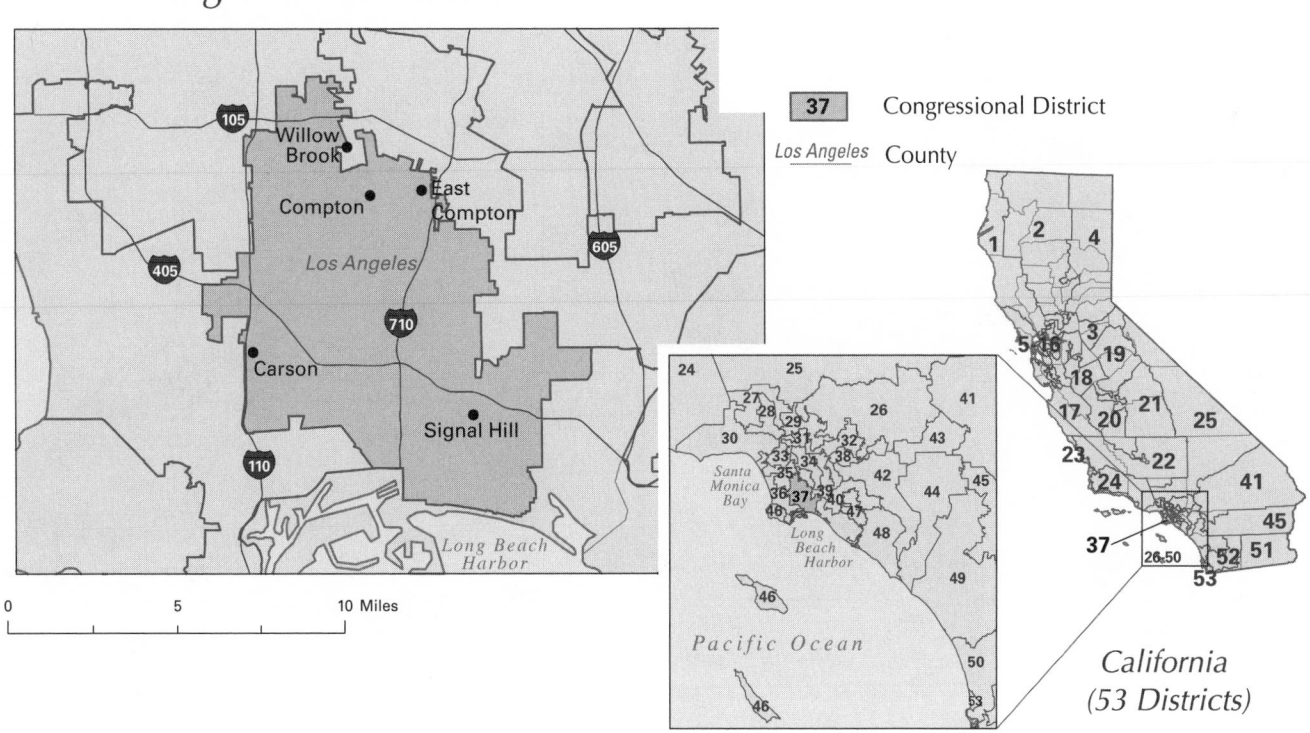

Congressional District 38

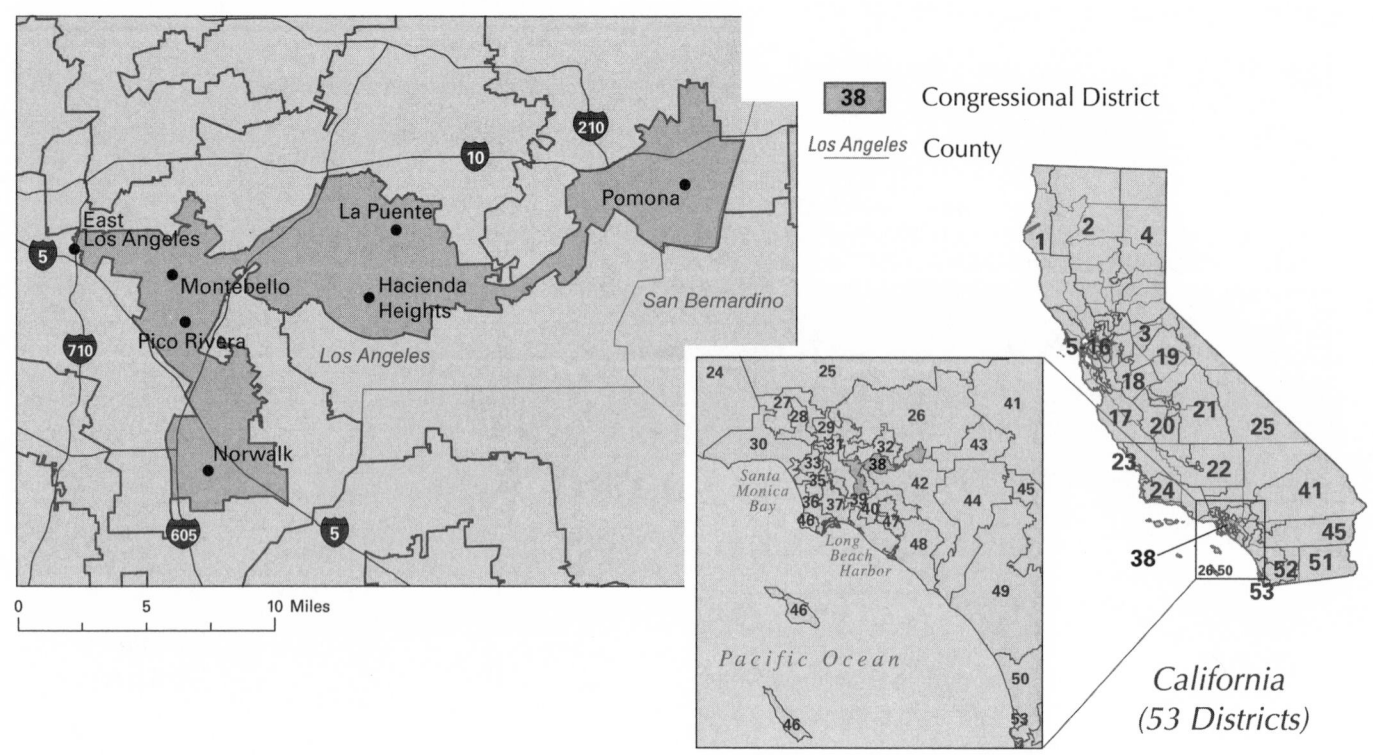

Congressional District 39

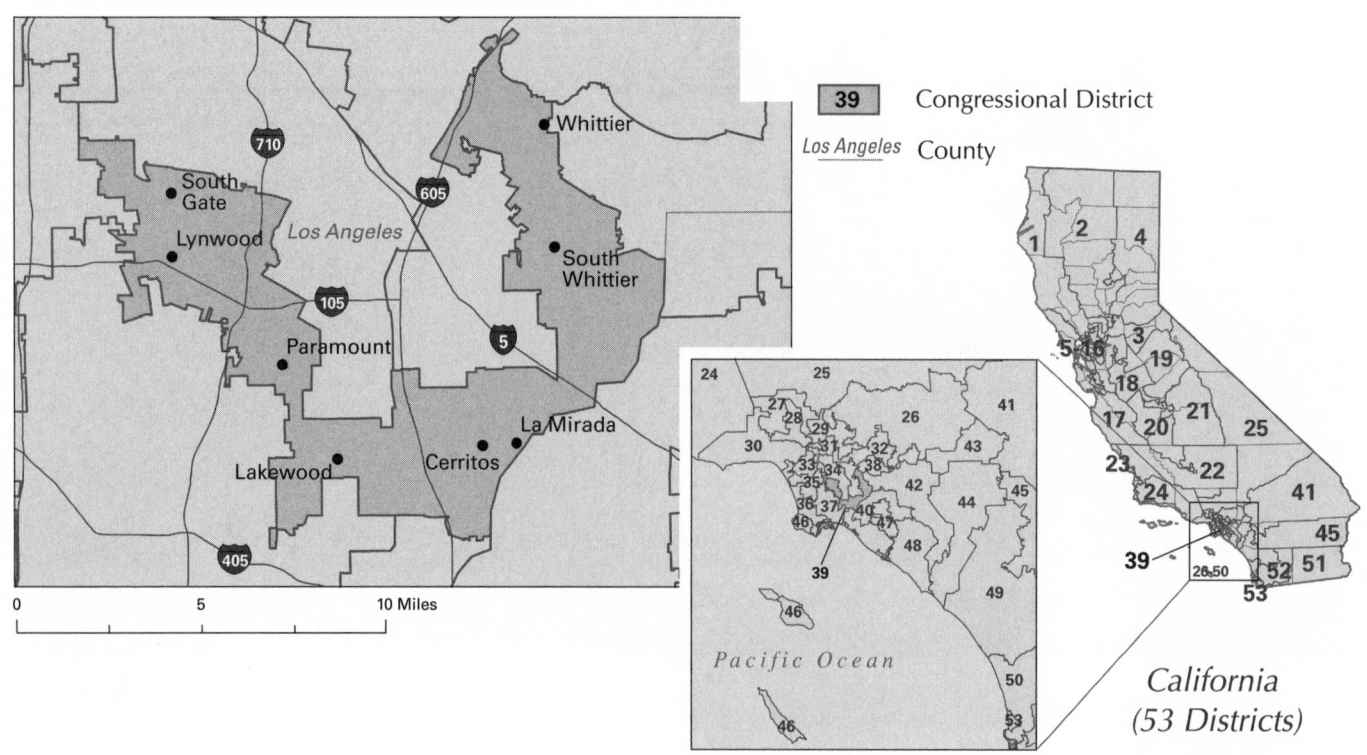

Congressional District 40

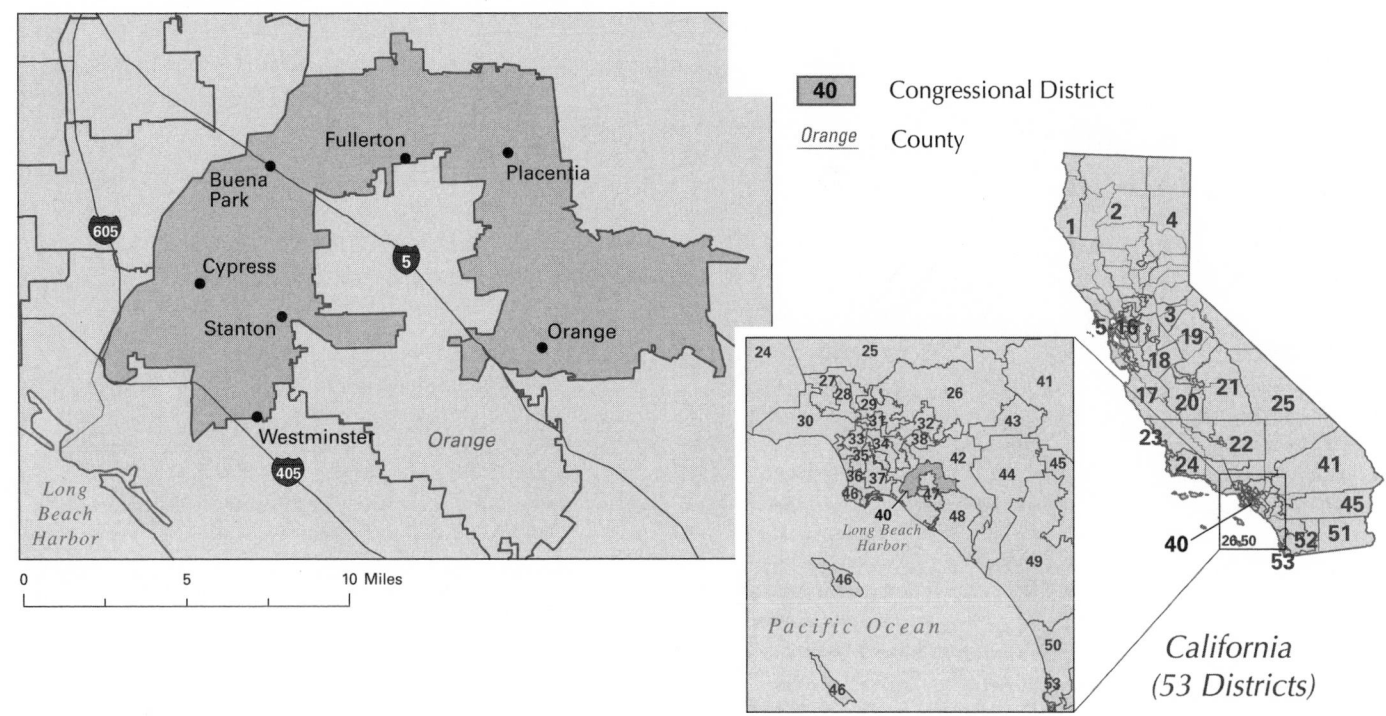

40 Congressional District

Orange County

California
(53 Districts)

Congressional District 41

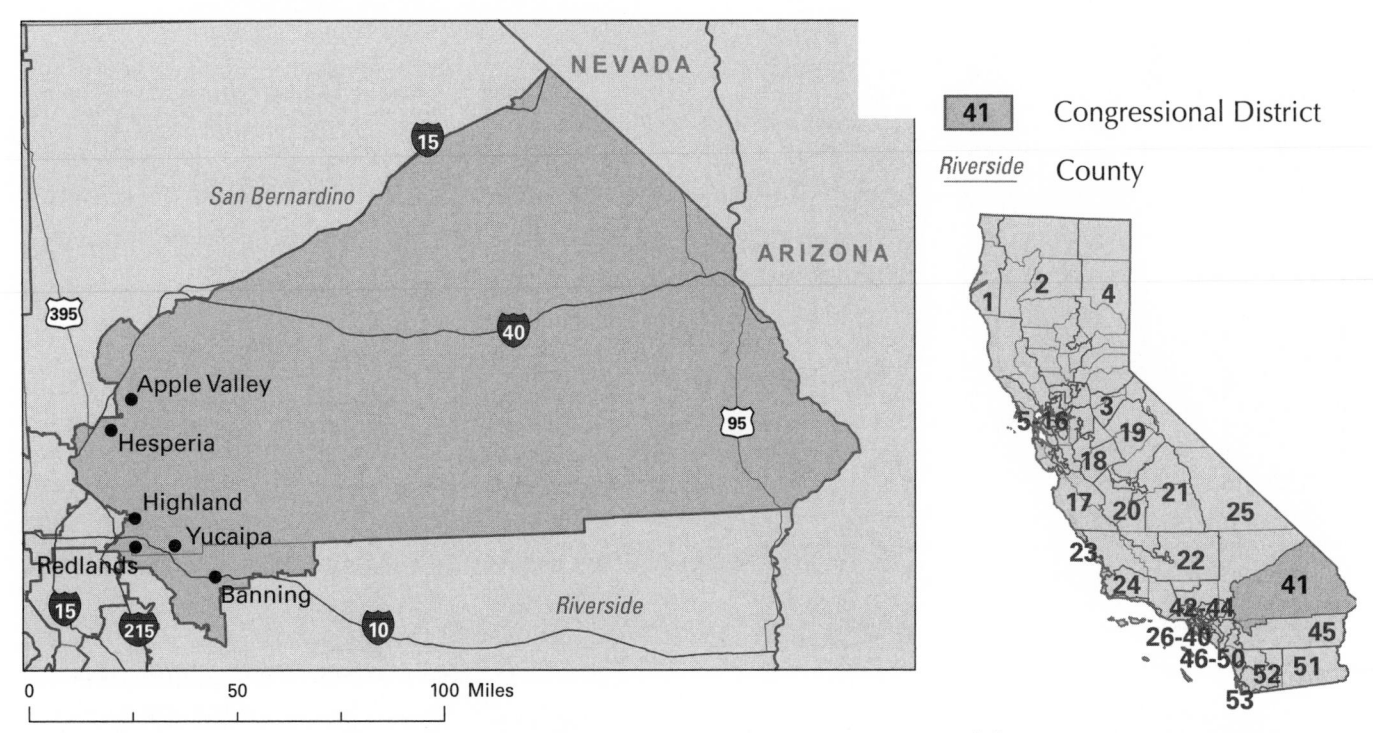

41 Congressional District

Riverside County

California (53 Districts)

Congressional District 42

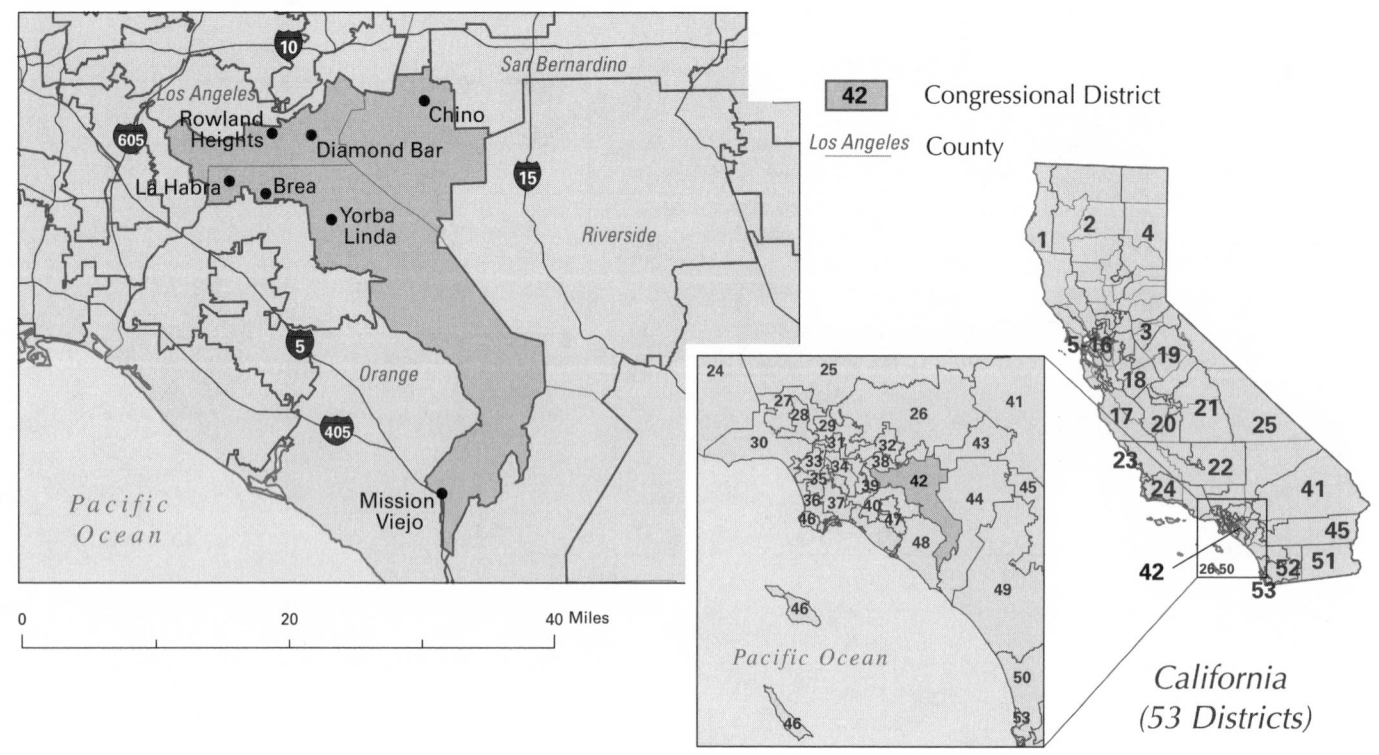

Congressional District 43

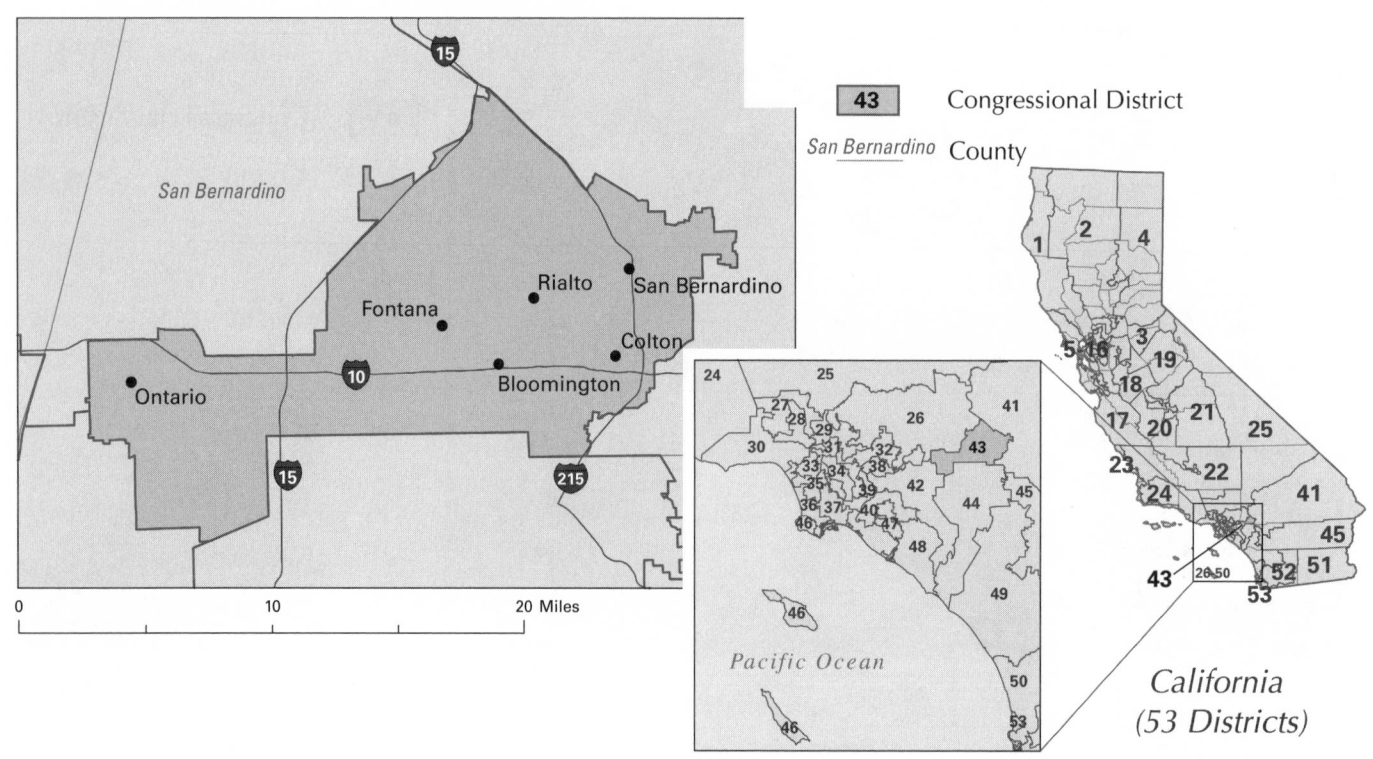

Congressional District 44

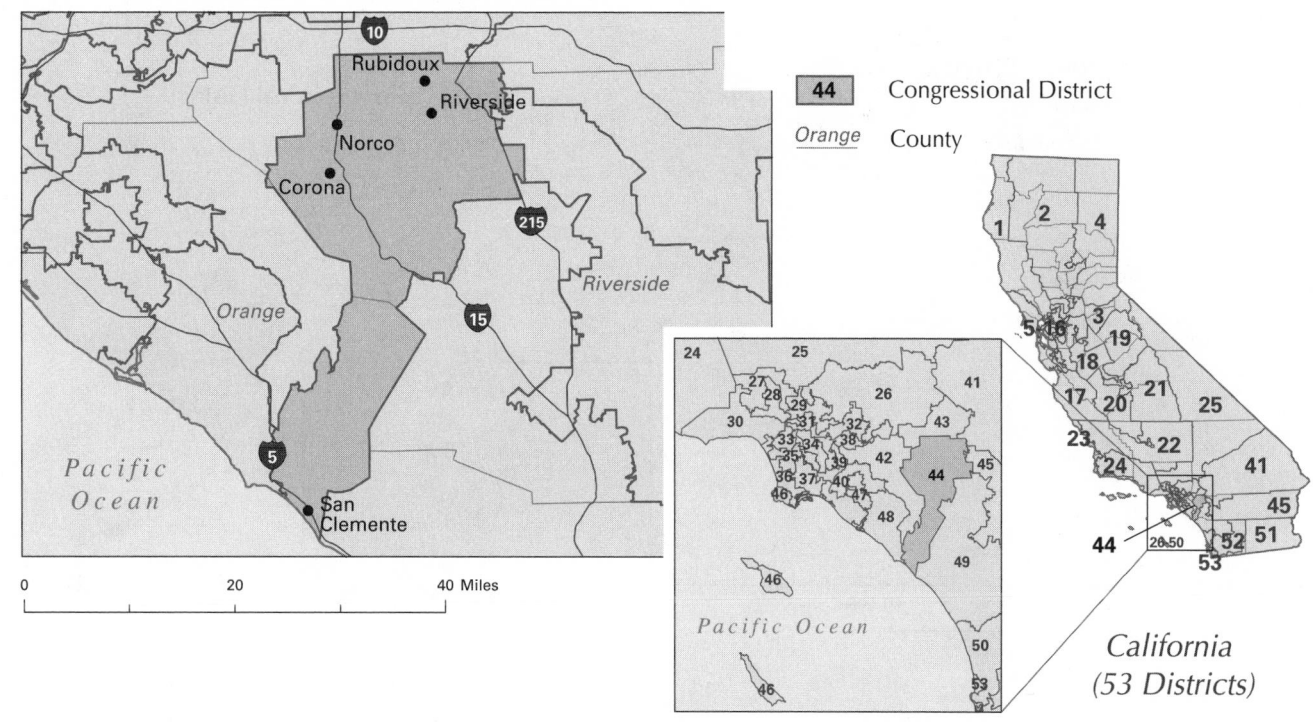

Congressional District 45

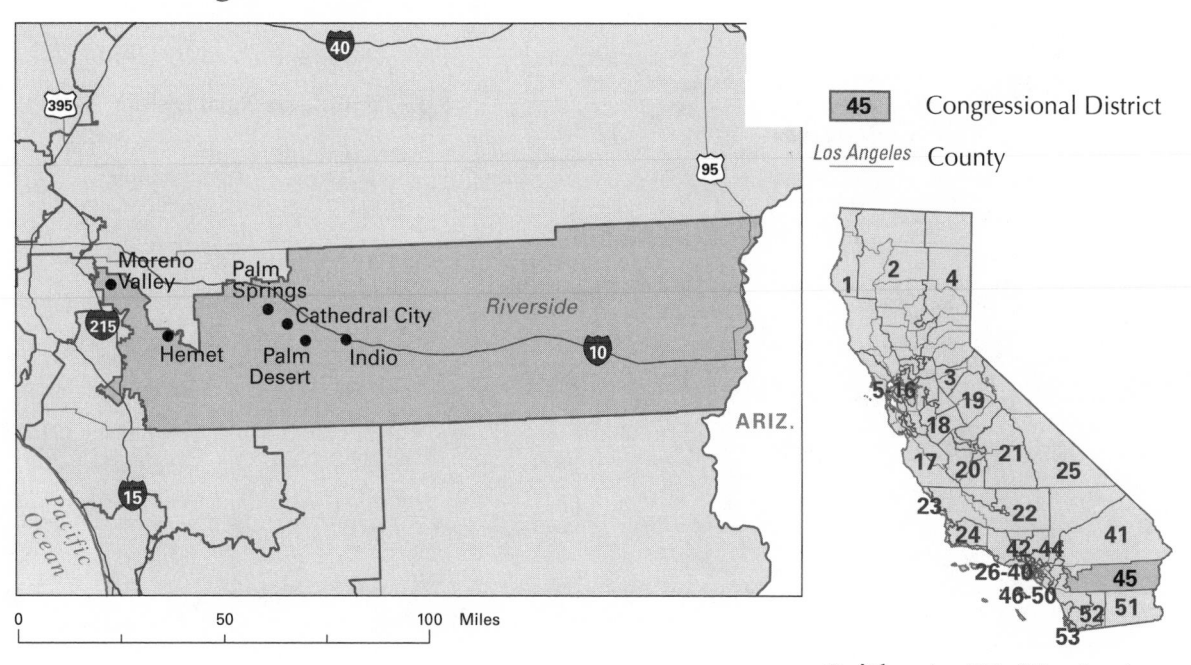

Congressional District 46

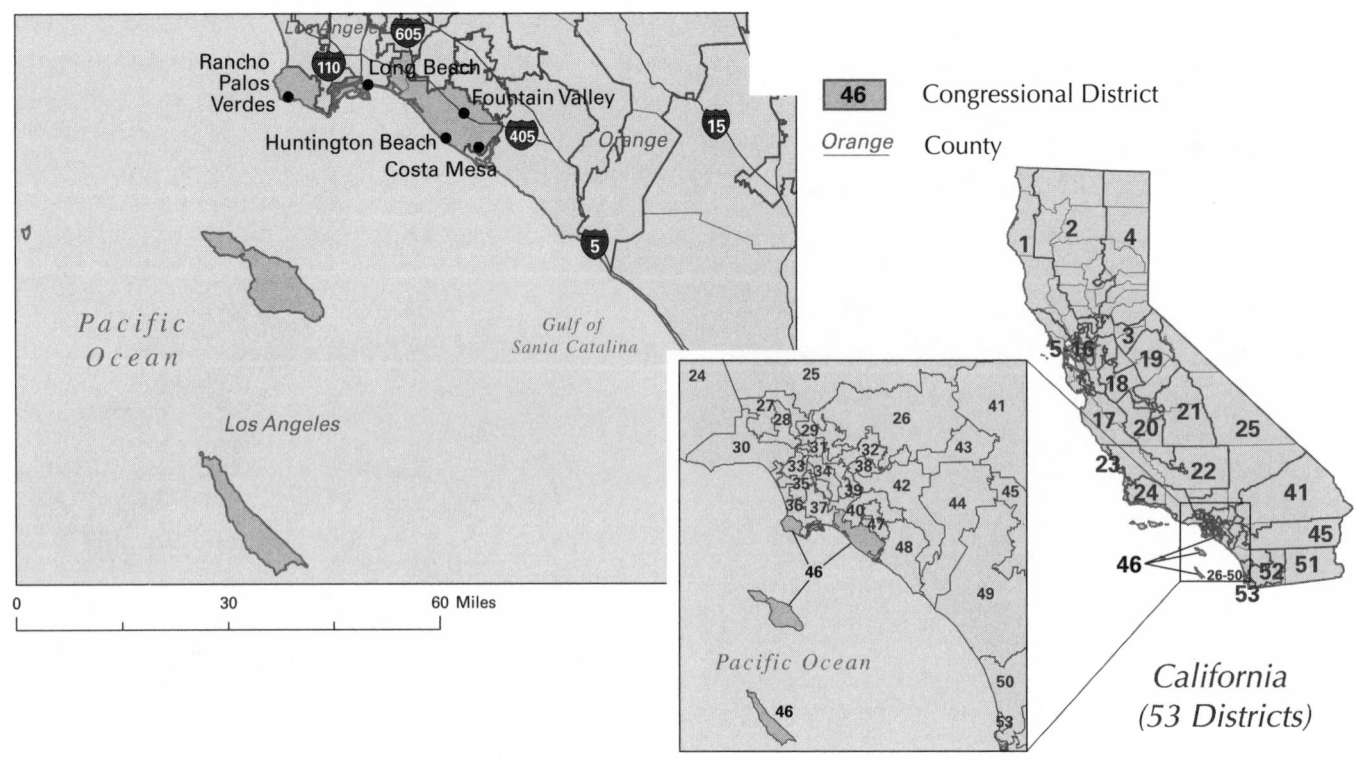

Congressional District 47

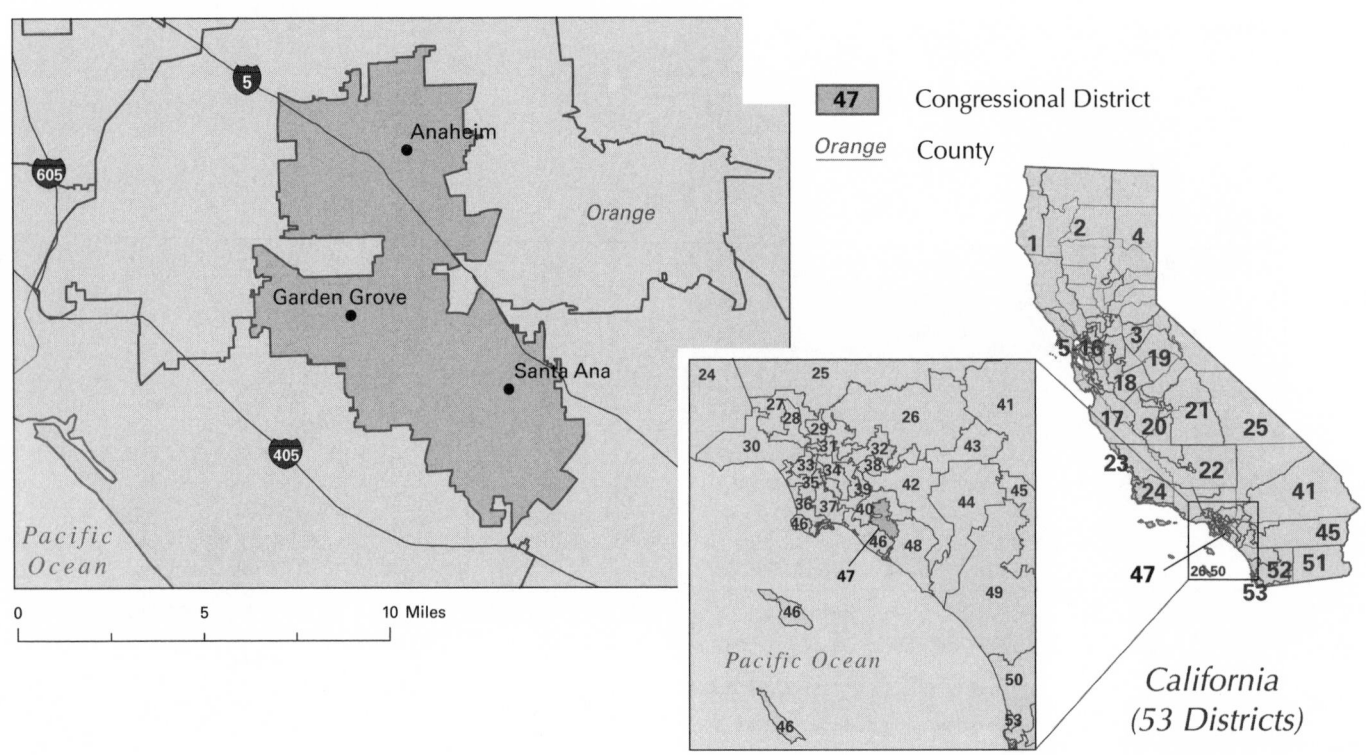

Congressional District 48

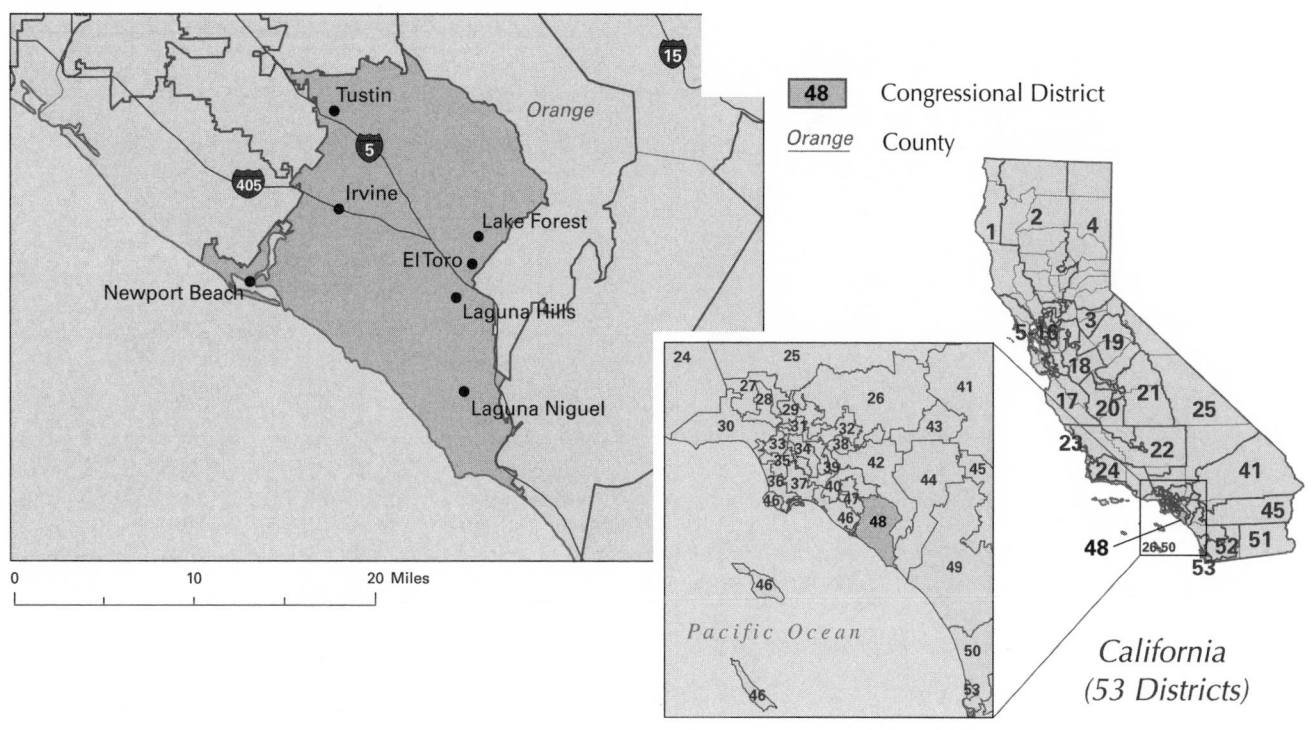

Congressional District 49

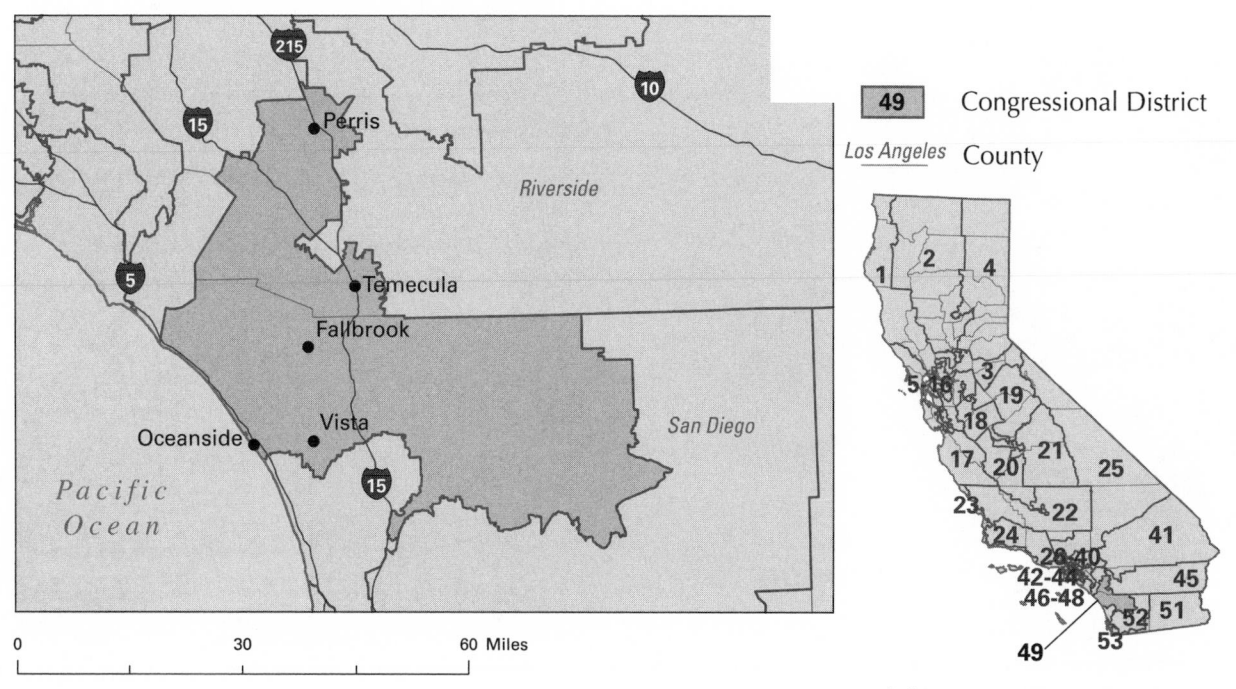

California (53 Districts)

Congressional District 50

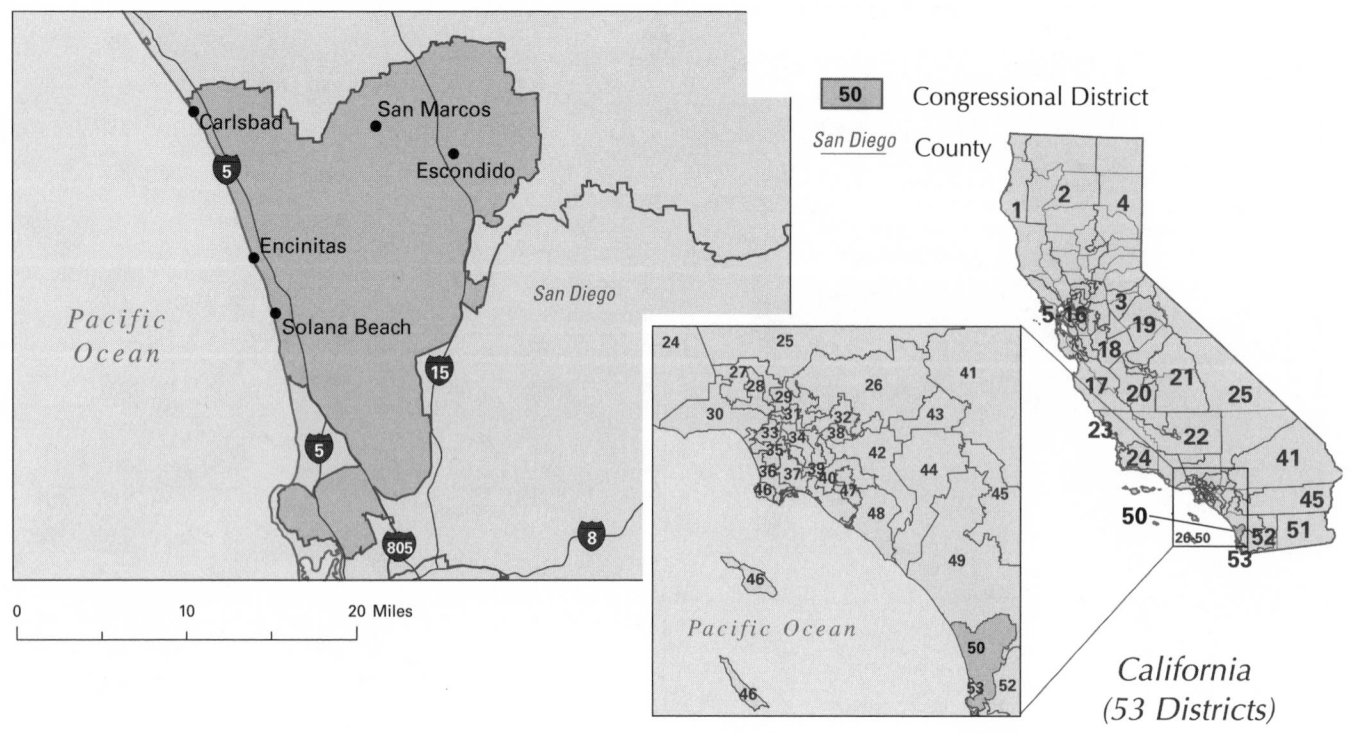

Congressional District 51

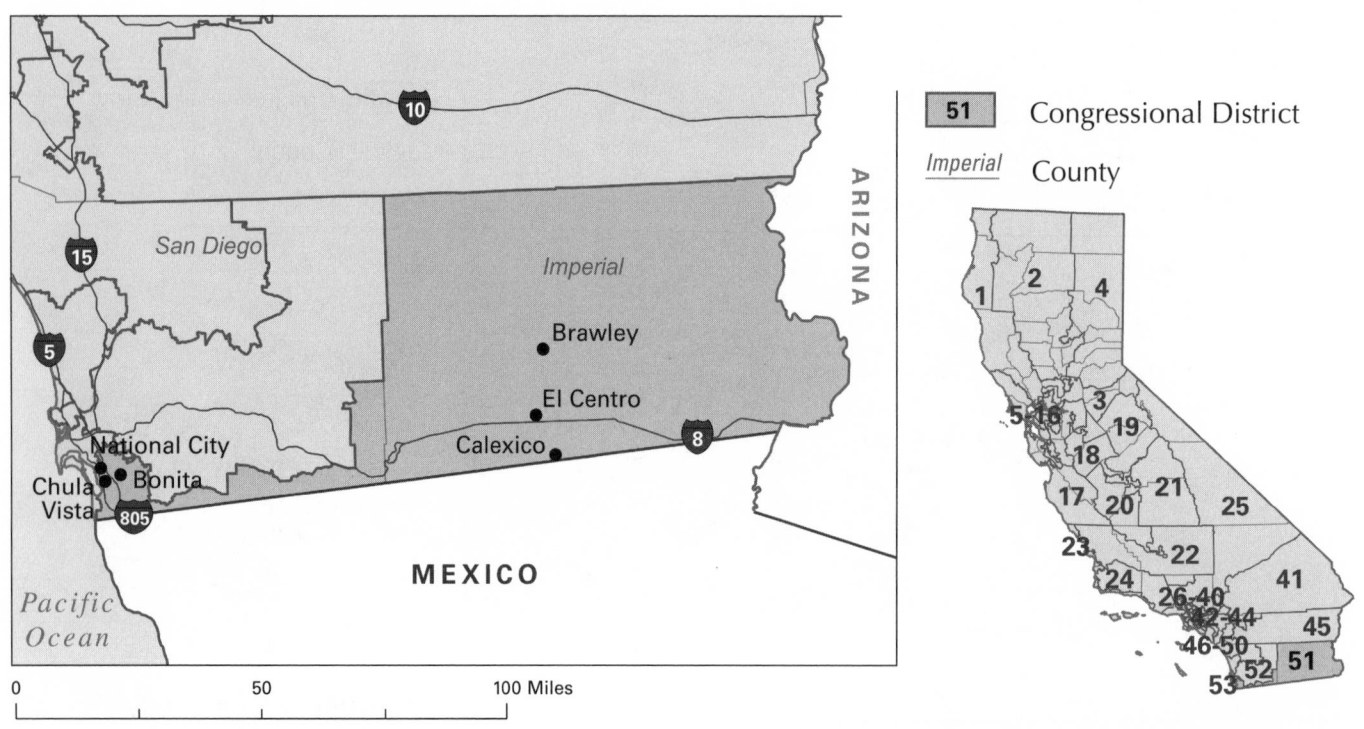

California (53 Districts)

Congressional District 52

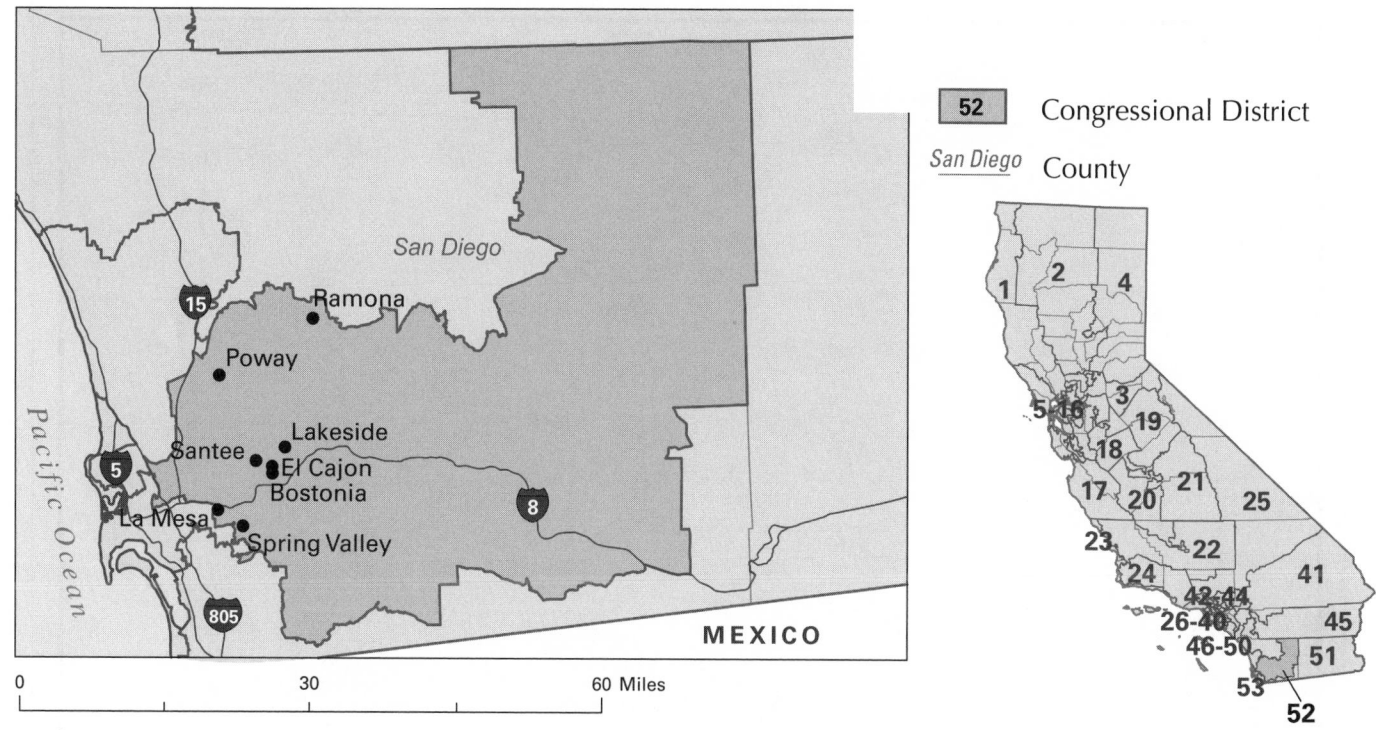

52   Congressional District
San Diego   County

California (53 Districts)

Congressional District 53

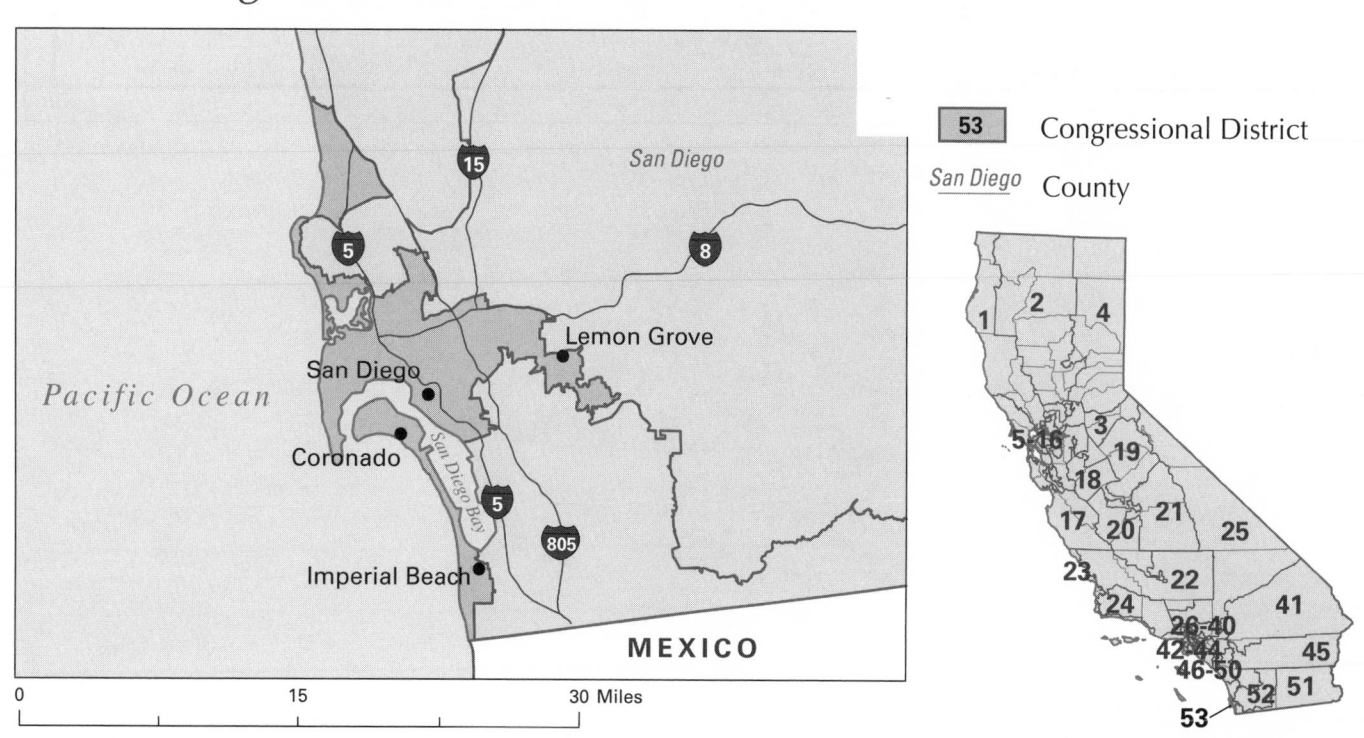

53   Congressional District
San Diego   County

California (53 Districts)

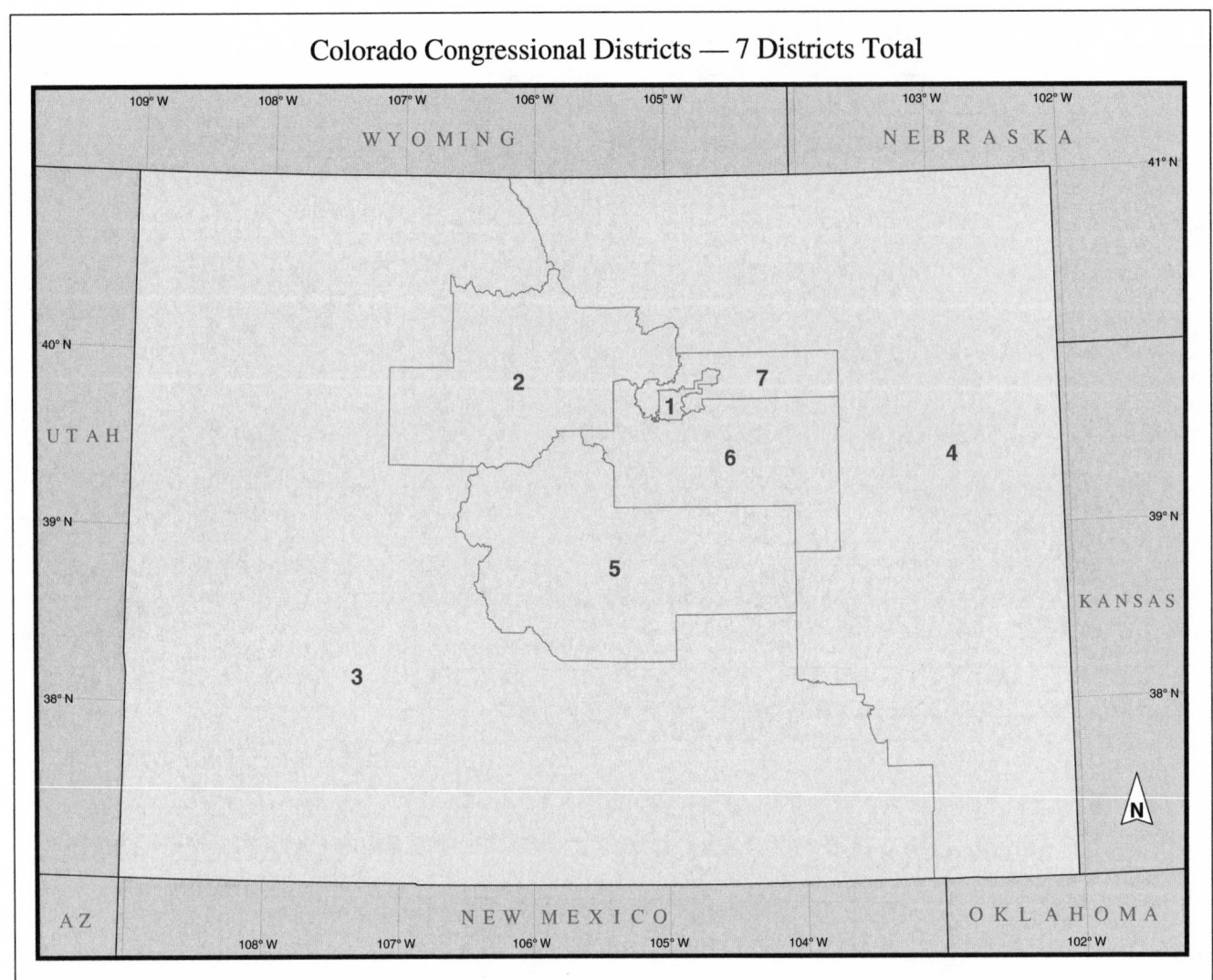

Colorado Congressional Districts — 7 Districts Total

COLORADO—110th CONGRESSIONAL DISTRICTS BY COUNTIES

County	Congressional District
Adams	1, 2, 7
Alamosa	3
Arapahoe	1, 6, 7
Archuleta	3
Baca	4
Bent	4
Boulder	2, 4
Chaffee	5
Cheyenne	4
Clear Creek	2
Conejos	3
Costilla	3
Crowley	4
Custer	3
Delta	3
Denver	1
Dolores	3
Douglas	6
Eagle	2
Elbert	6
El Paso	5
Fremont	5

County	Congressional District
Garfield	3
Gilpin	2
Grand	2
Gunnison	3
Hinsdale	3
Huerfano	3
Jackson	3
Jefferson	1, 2, 6, 7
Kiowa	4
Kit Carson	4
Lake	5
La Plata	3
Larimer	4
Las Animas	3
Lincoln	4
Logan	4
Mesa	3
Mineral	3
Moffat	3
Montezuma	3
Montrose	3
Morgan	4

County	Congressional District
Otero	3, 4
Ouray	3
Park	5, 6
Phillips	4
Pitkin	3
Prowers	4
Pueblo	3
Rio Blanco	3
Rio Grande	3
Routt	3
Saguache	3
San Juan	3
San Miguel	3
Sedgwick	4
Summit	2
Teller	5
Washington	4
Weld	2, 4
Yuma	4

Congressional District 1

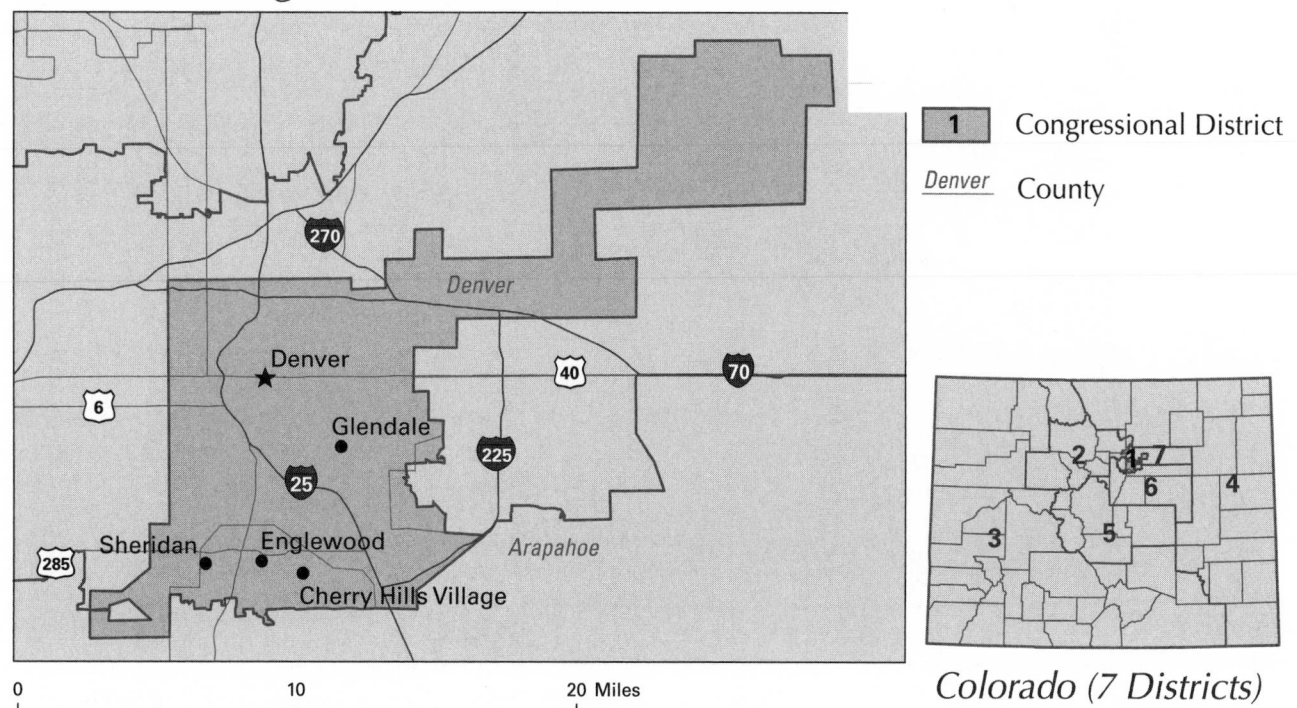

1	Congressional District
Denver	County

Colorado (7 Districts)

Congressional District 2

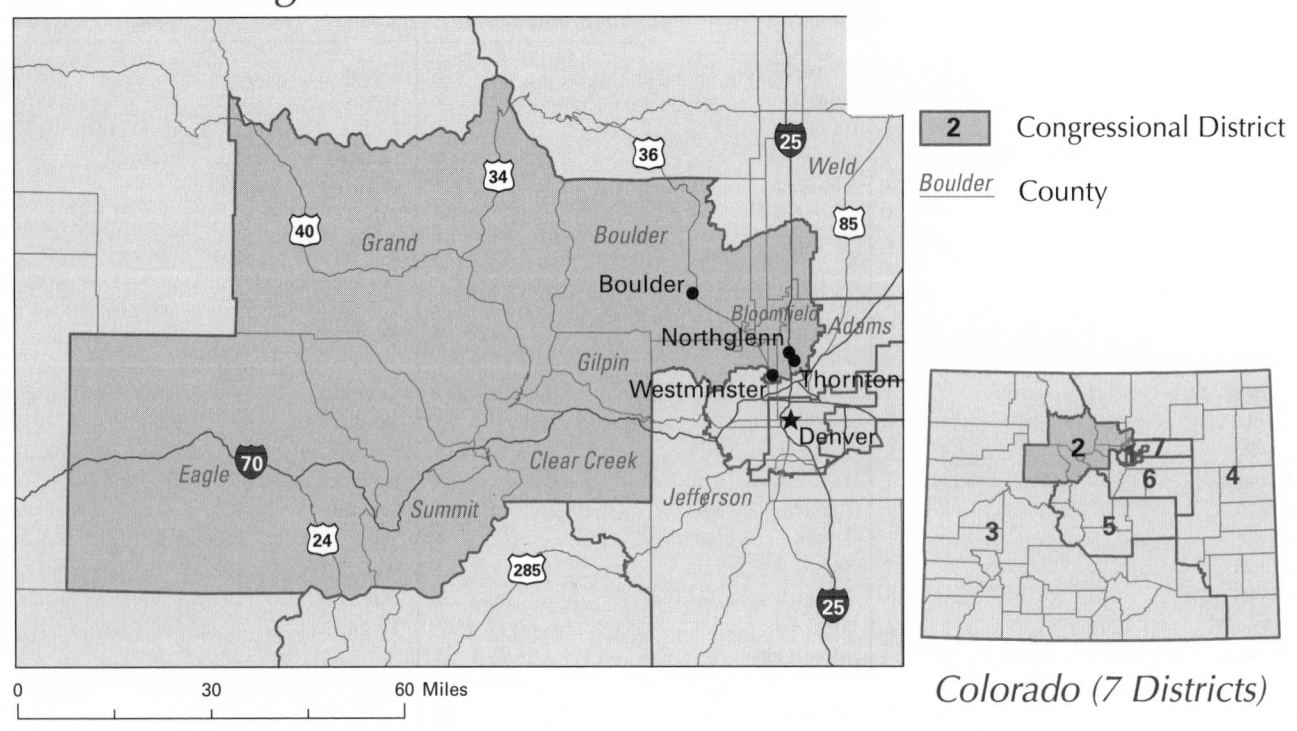

2 Congressional District

Boulder County

Colorado (7 Districts)

Congressional District 3

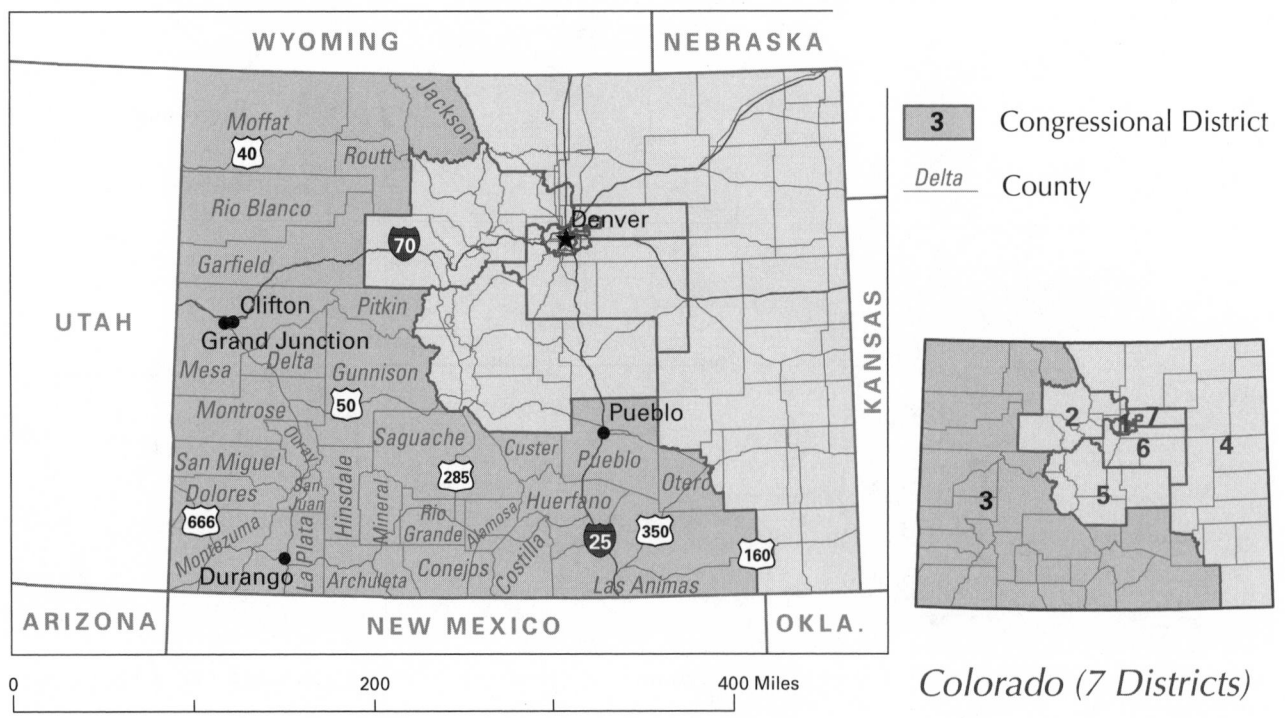

3 Congressional District

Delta County

Colorado (7 Districts)

Congressional District 4

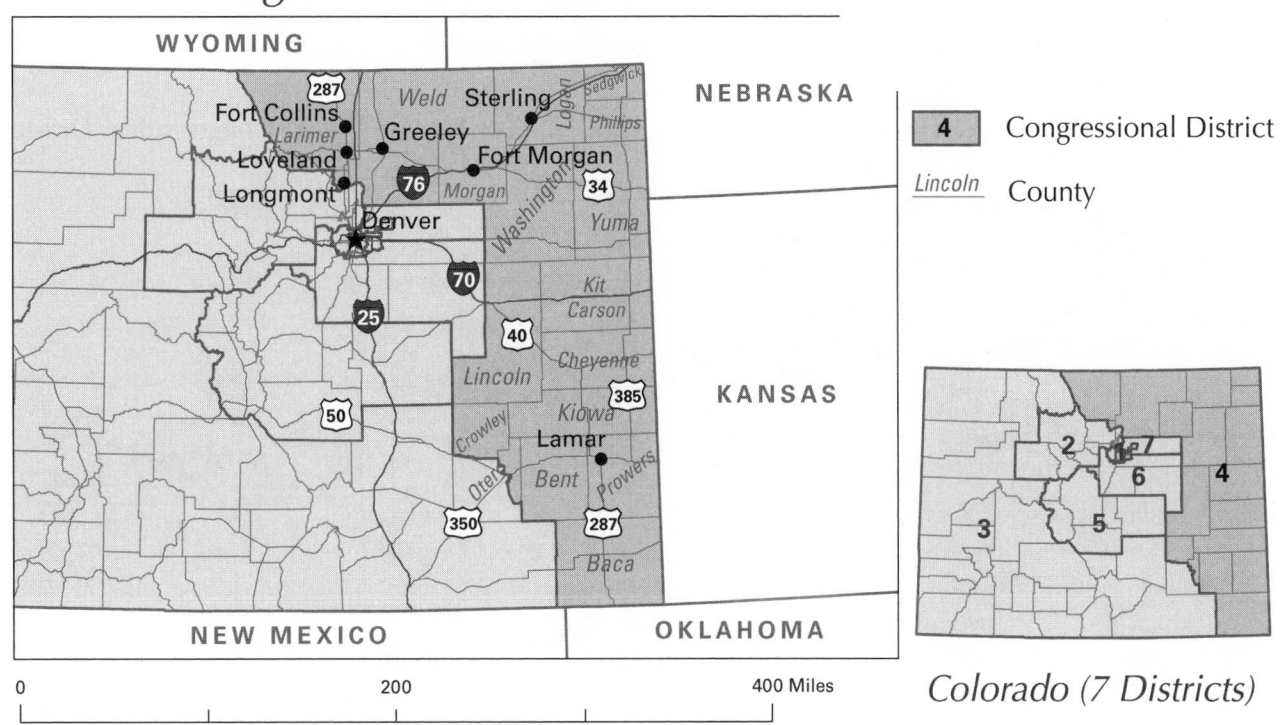

Colorado (7 Districts)

Congressional District 5

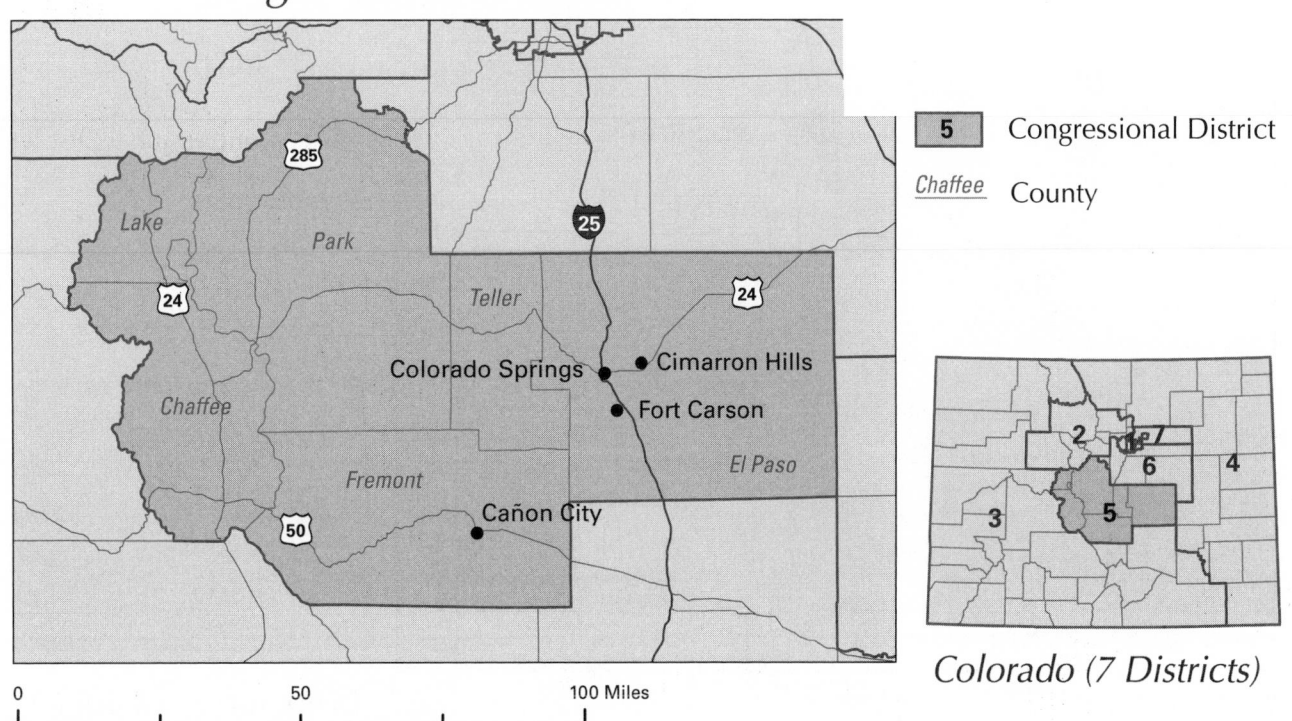

Colorado (7 Districts)

Congressional District 6

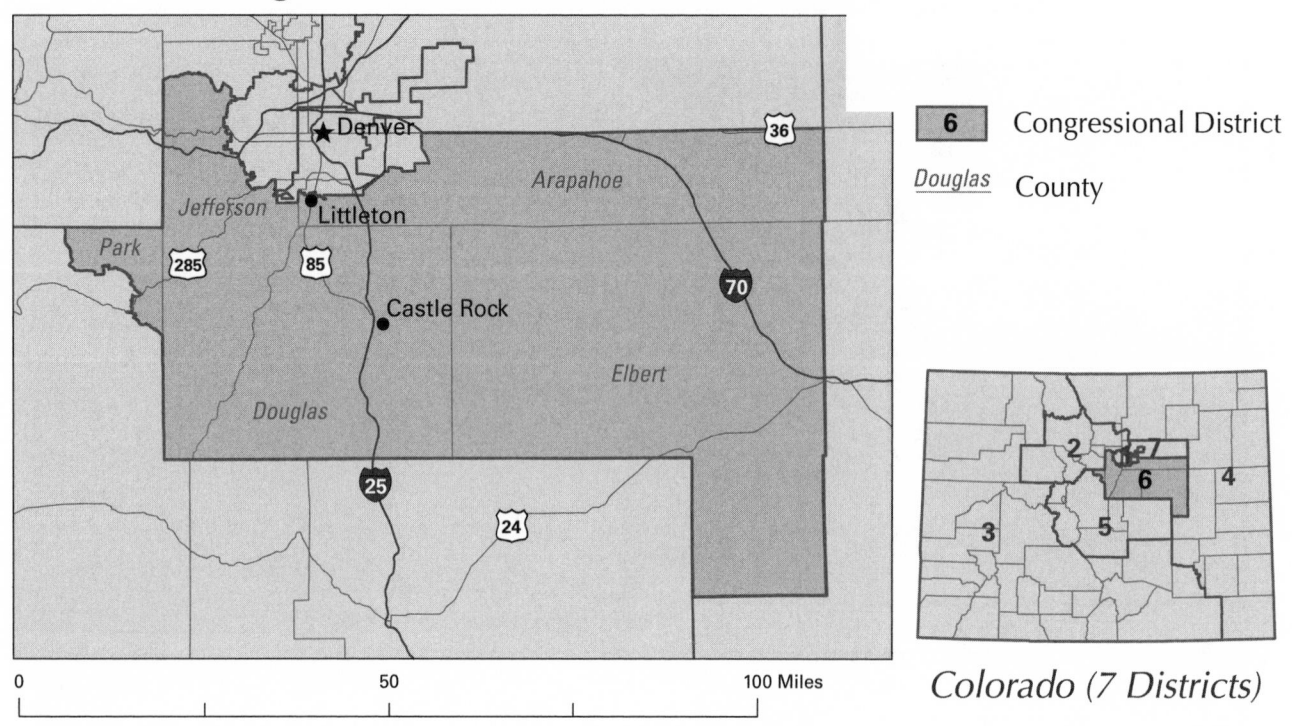

0   50   100 Miles

6 Congressional District

Douglas County

Colorado (7 Districts)

Congressional District 7

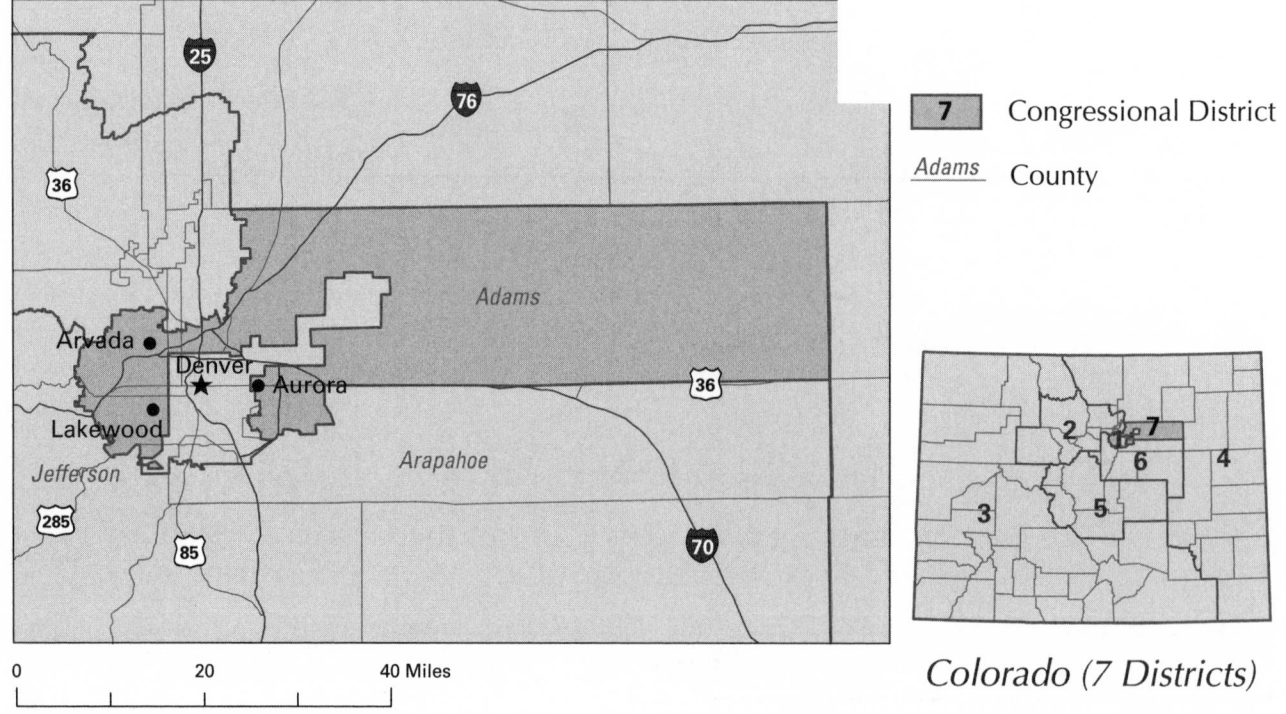

0   20   40 Miles

7 Congressional District

Adams County

Colorado (7 Districts)

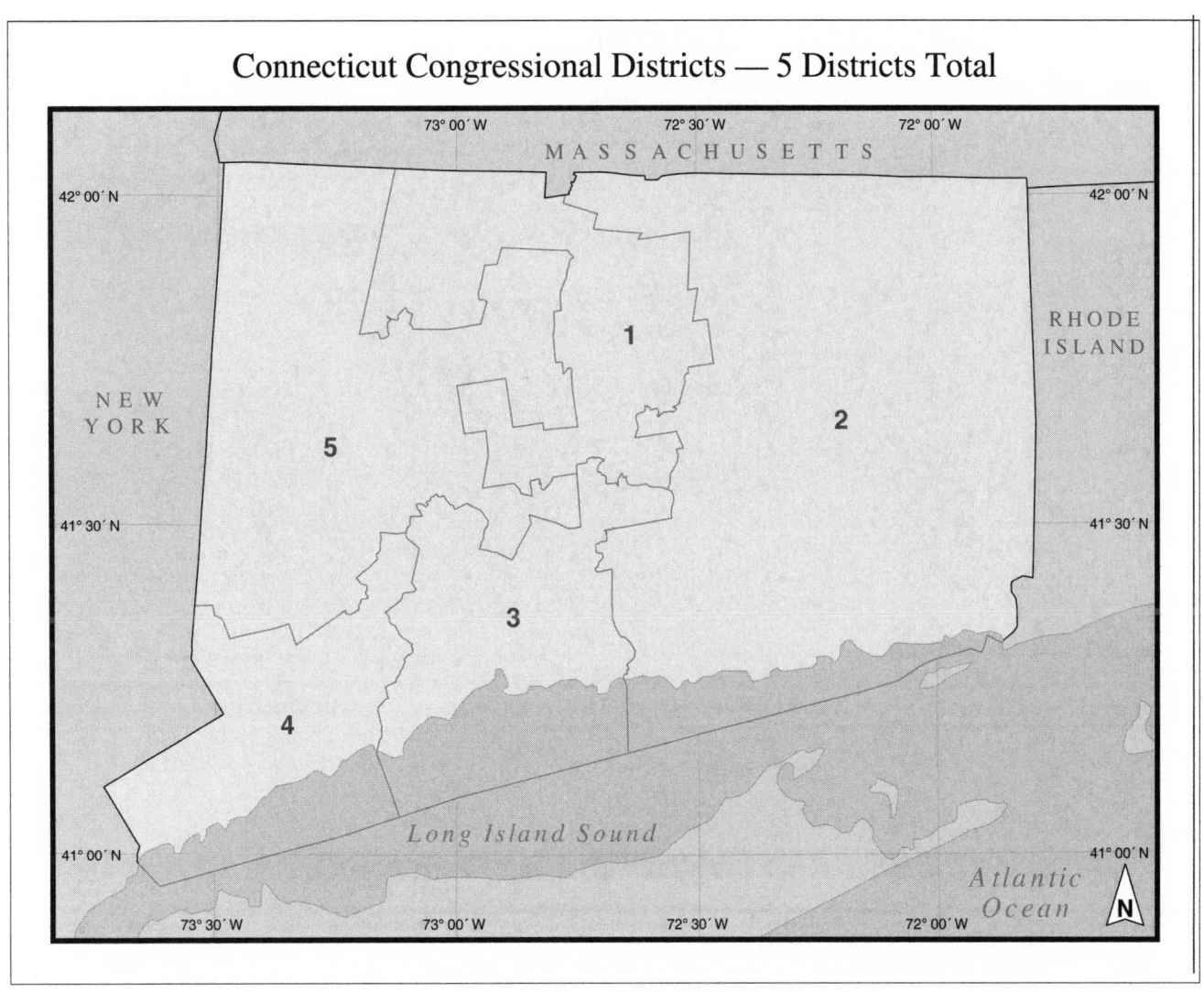

Connecticut Congressional Districts — 5 Districts Total

CONNECTICUT—110th CONGRESSIONAL DISTRICTS BY COUNTIES

County	Congressional District
Fairfield	3–5
Hartford	1, 2, 5
Litchfield	1, 5
Middlesex	1–3
New Haven	2–5
New London	2
Tolland	2
Windham	2

Congressional District 1

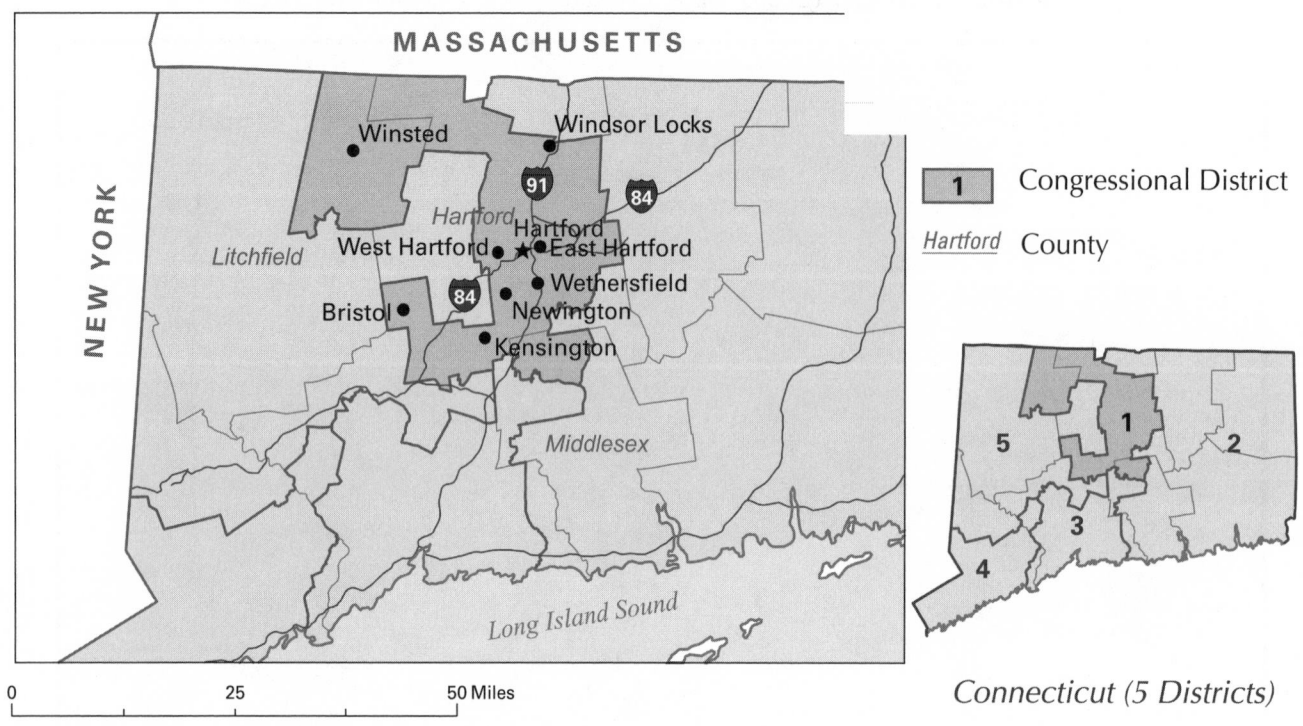

Connecticut (5 Districts)

Congressional District 2

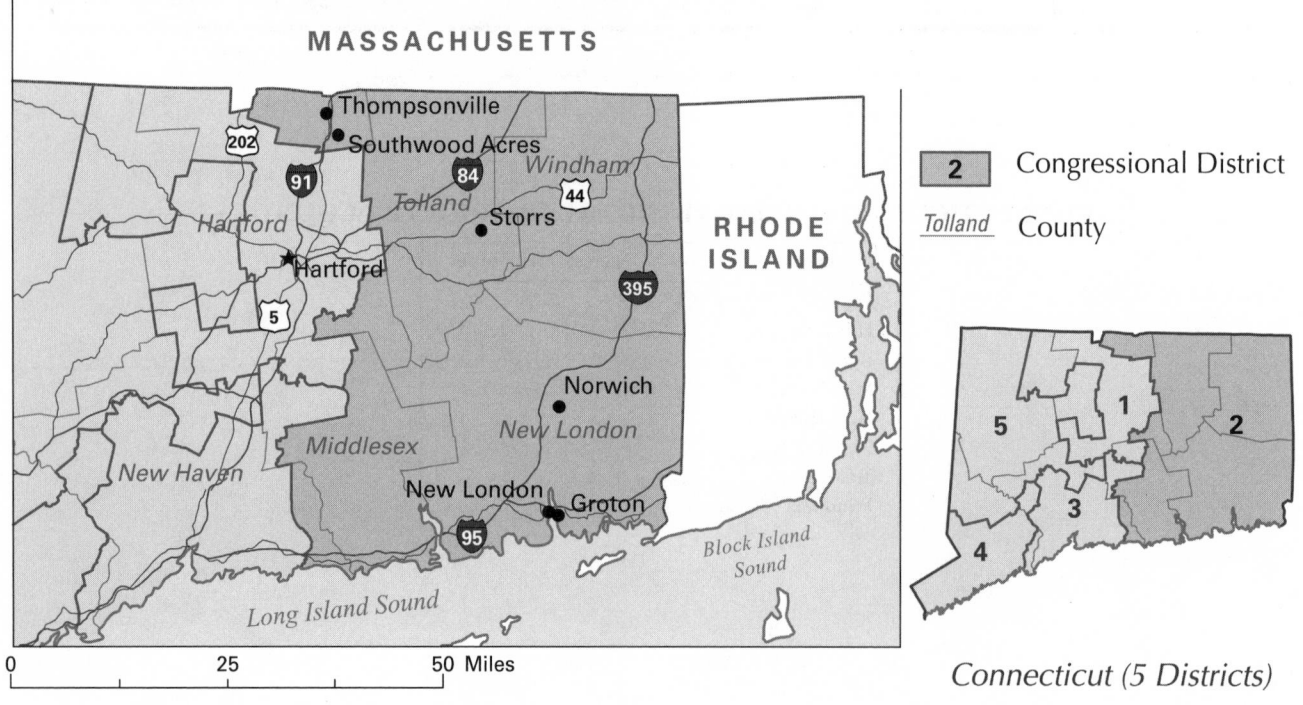

Connecticut (5 Districts)

Congressional District 3

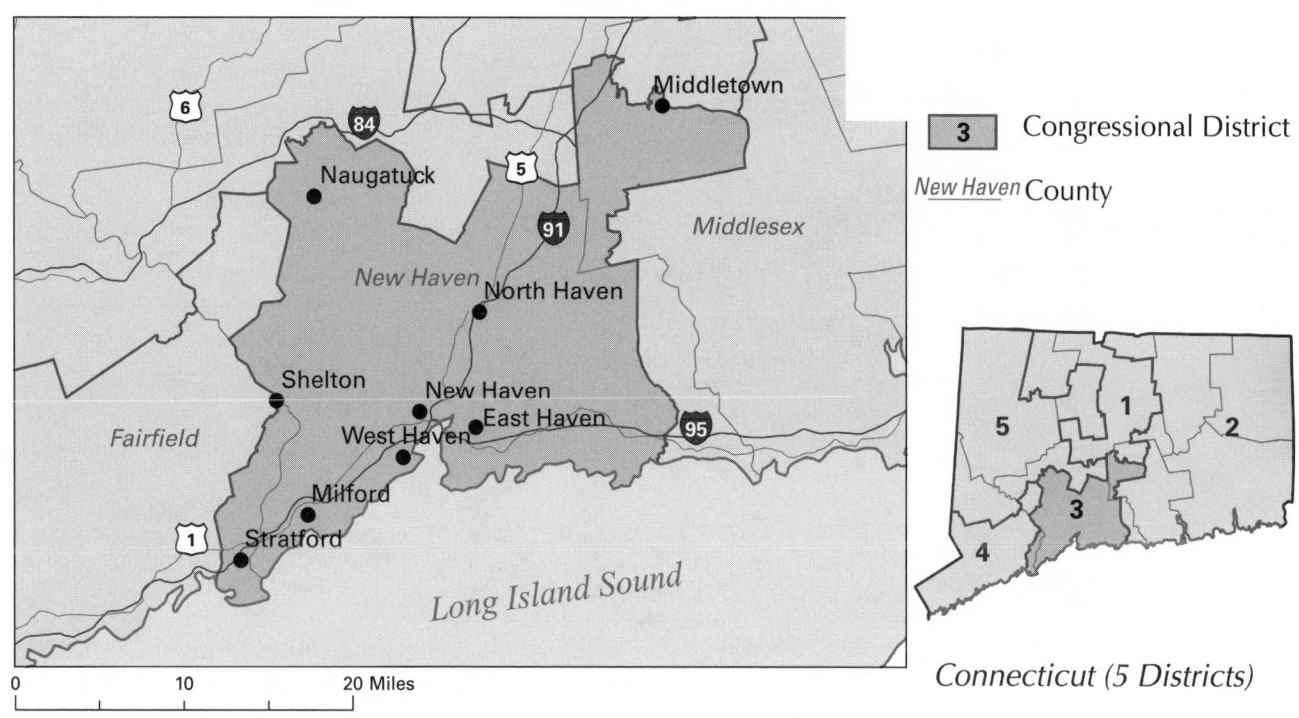

Connecticut (5 Districts)

Congressional District 4

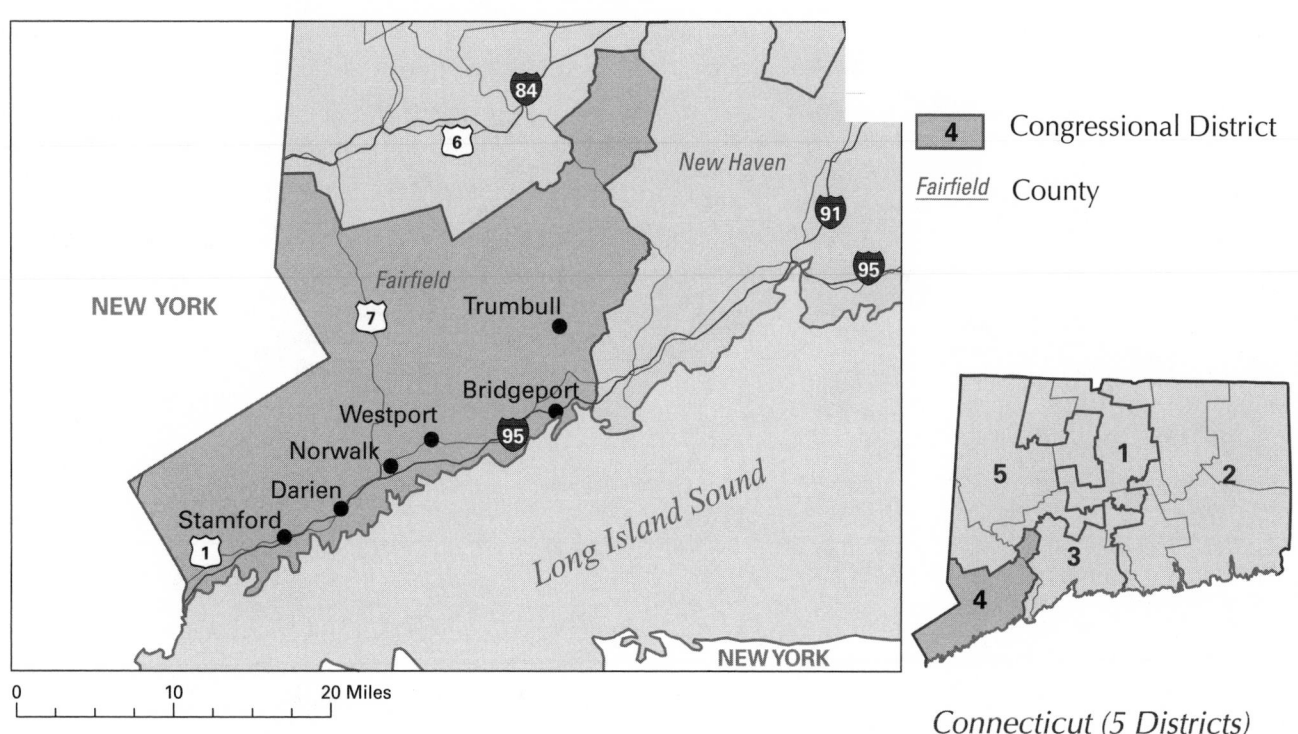

Connecticut (5 Districts)

Congressional District 5

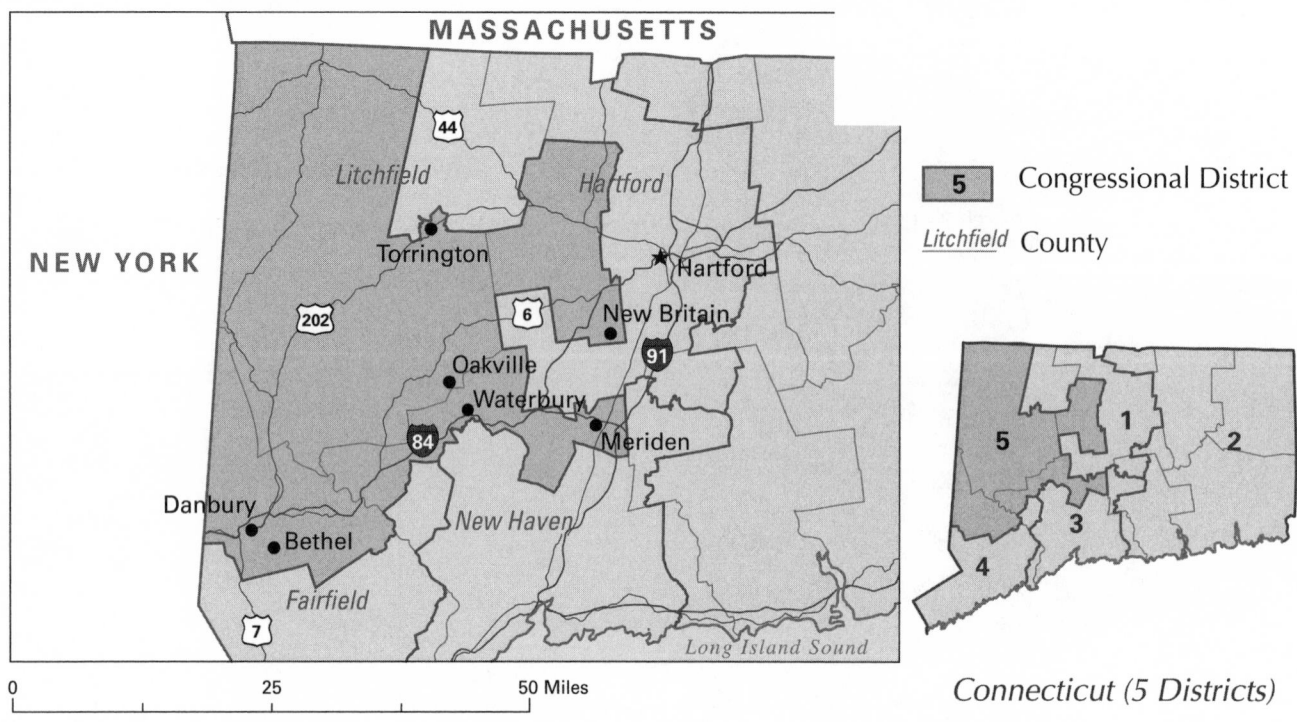

Connecticut (5 Districts)

Delaware—
Congressional District: At large

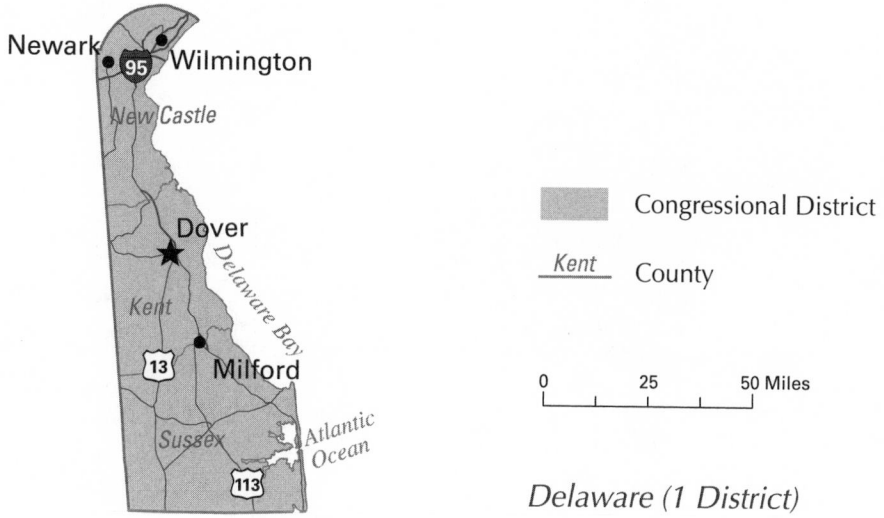

Congressional District

Kent   County

0   25   50 Miles

Delaware (1 District)

DELAWARE—110th CONGRESSIONAL DISTRICTS BY COUNTIES

County	Congressional District
Kent	1
New Castle	1
Sussex	1

District of Columbia—Delegate District

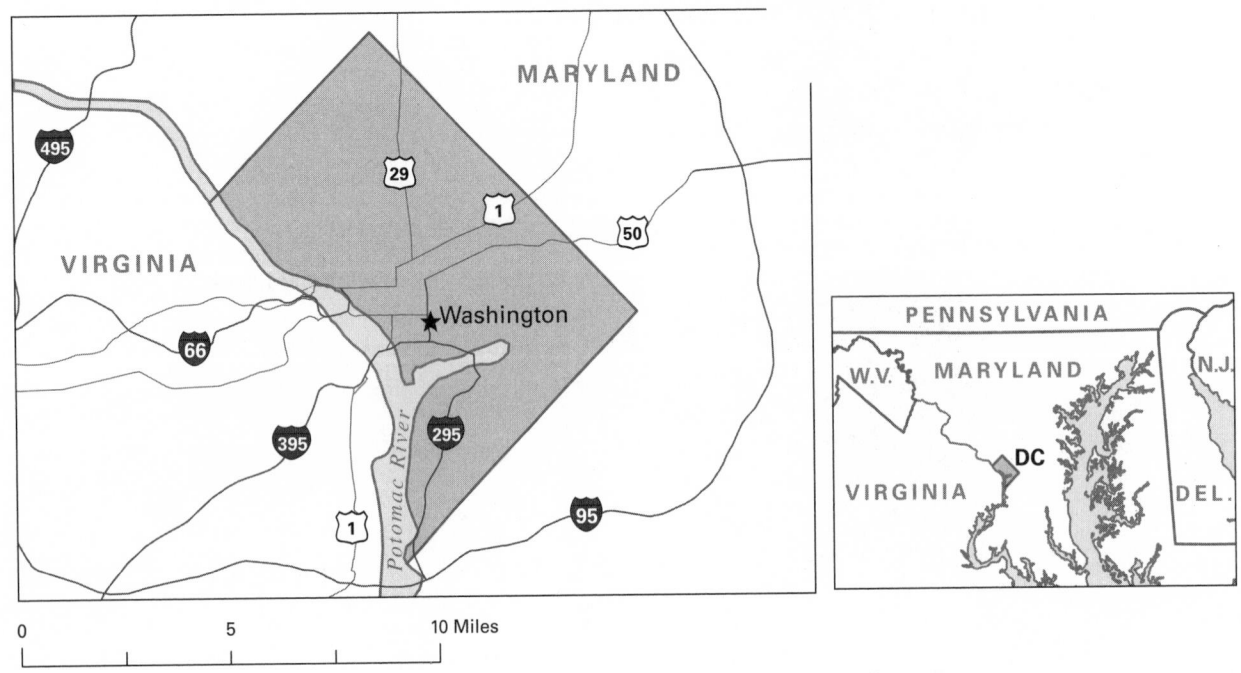

0   5   10 Miles

Florida Congressional Districts — 25 Districts Total

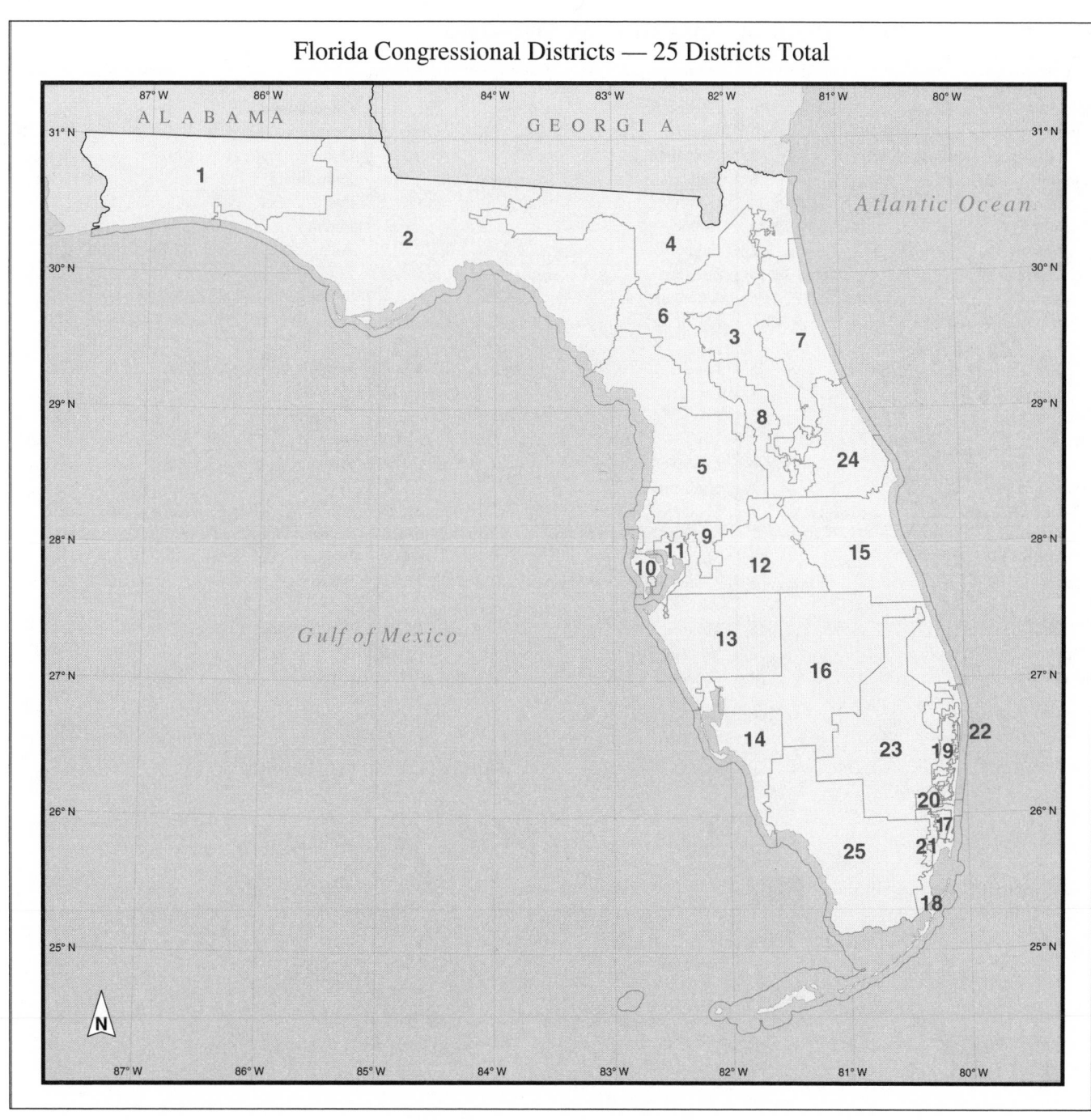

FLORIDA—110th CONGRESSIONAL DISTRICTS BY COUNTIES

County	Congressional District
Alachua	3, 6
Baker	4
Bay	2
Bradford	6
Brevard	15, 24
Broward	17, 19–23
Calhoun	2
Charlotte	13, 14, 16
Citrus	5
Clay	3, 6
Collier	14, 25
Columbia	4
DeSoto	13
Dixie	2
Duval	3, 4, 6
Escambia	1
Flagler	7
Franklin	2
Gadsden	2
Gilchrist	6
Glades	16
Gulf	2
Hamilton	4

County	Congressional District
Hardee	13
Hendry	16, 23
Hernando	5
Highlands	16
Hillsborough	9, 11, 12
Holmes	1
Indian River	15
Jackson	2
Jefferson	2, 4
Lafayette	2
Lake	3, 5, 6, 8
Lee	14
Leon	2, 4
Levy	5, 6
Liberty	2
Madison	4
Manatee	11, 13
Marion	3, 5, 6, 8
Martin	16, 23
Miami-Dade	17, 18, 20, 21, 25
Monroe	18, 25
Nassau	4
Okaloosa	1, 2

County	Congressional District
Okeechobee	16
Orange	3, 7, 8, 24
Osceola	8, 12, 15
Palm Beach	16, 19, 22, 23
Pasco	5, 9
Pinellas	9–11
Polk	5, 12, 15
Putnam	3, 7
St. Johns	7
St. Lucie	16, 23
Santa Rosa	1
Sarasota	13
Seminole	3, 7, 24
Sumter	5
Suwannee	2
Taylor	2
Union	4
Volusia	3, 7, 24
Wakulla	2
Walton	1, 2
Washington	1

Congressional District 1

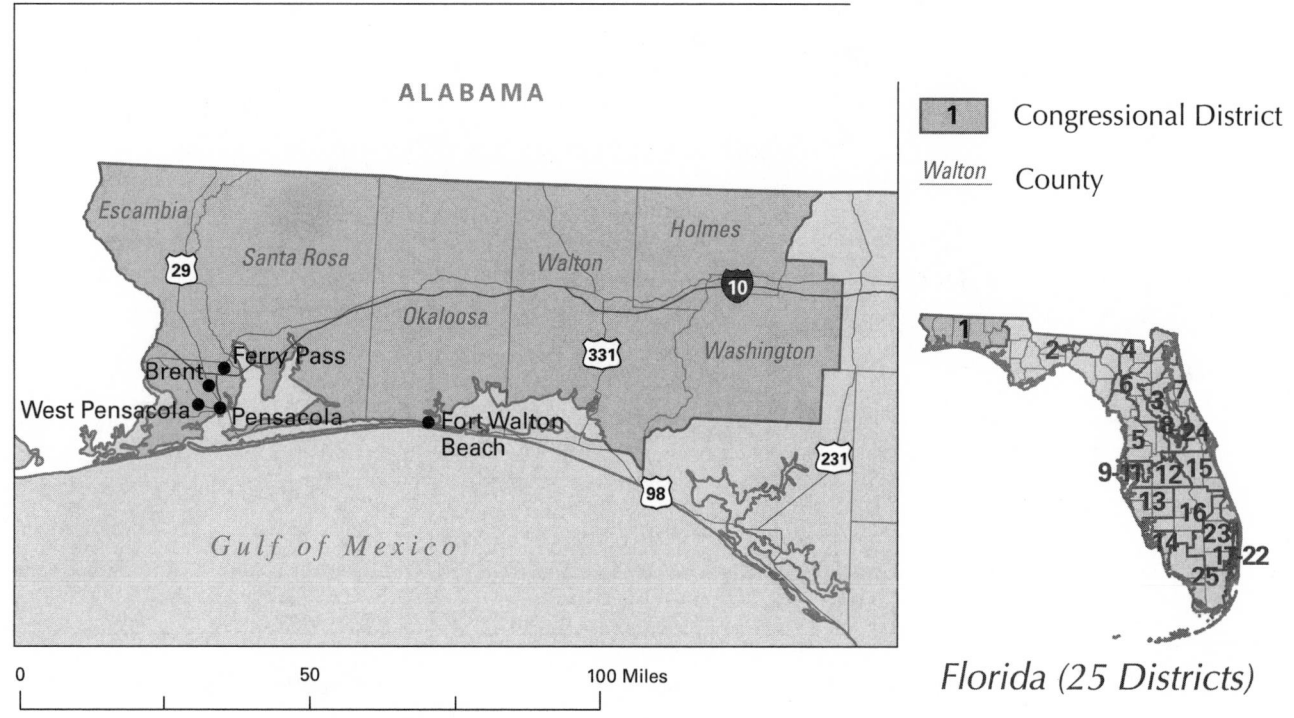

Florida (25 Districts)

Congressional District 2

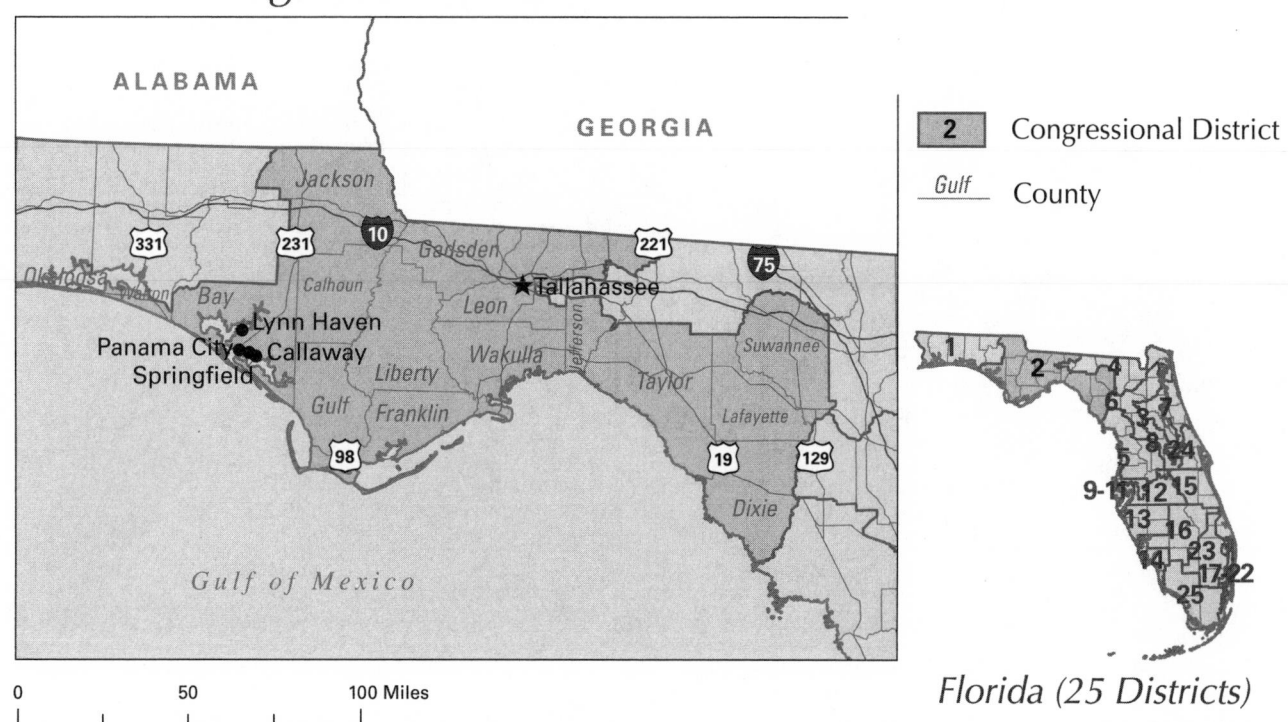

Florida (25 Districts)

Congressional District 3

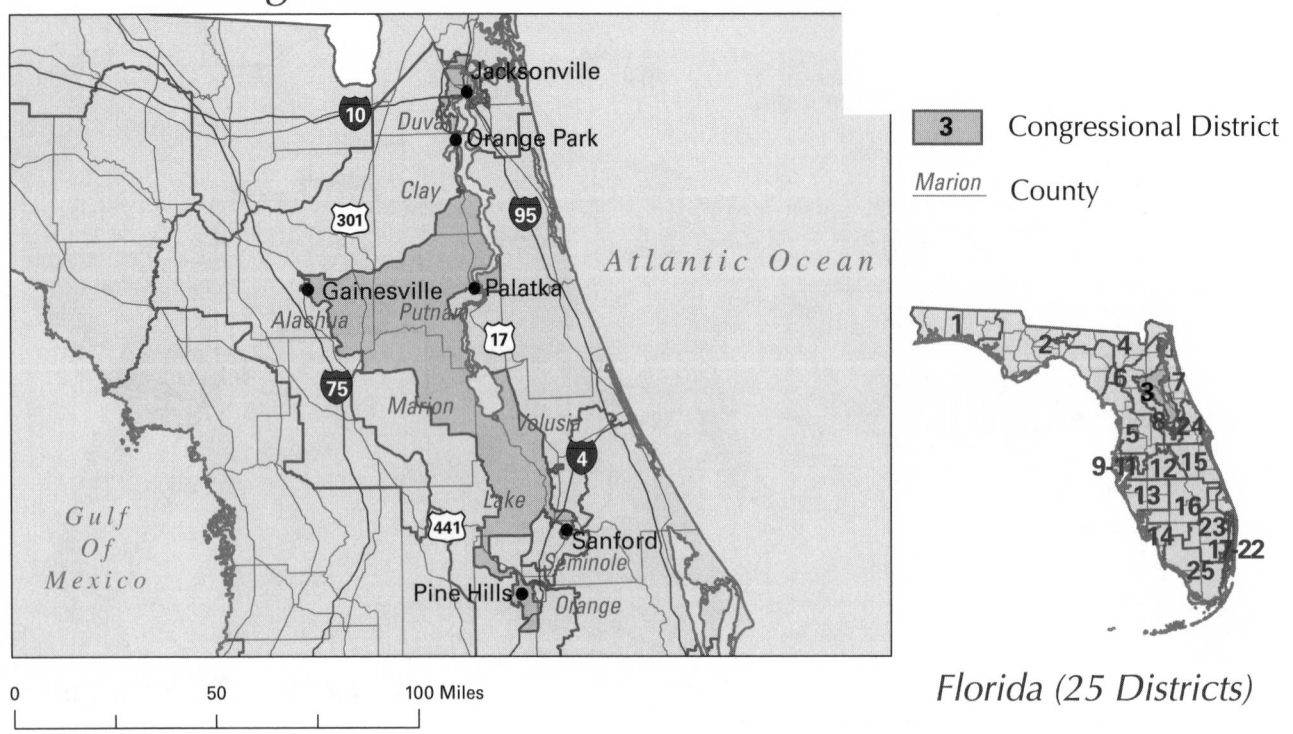

Florida (25 Districts)

Congressional District 4

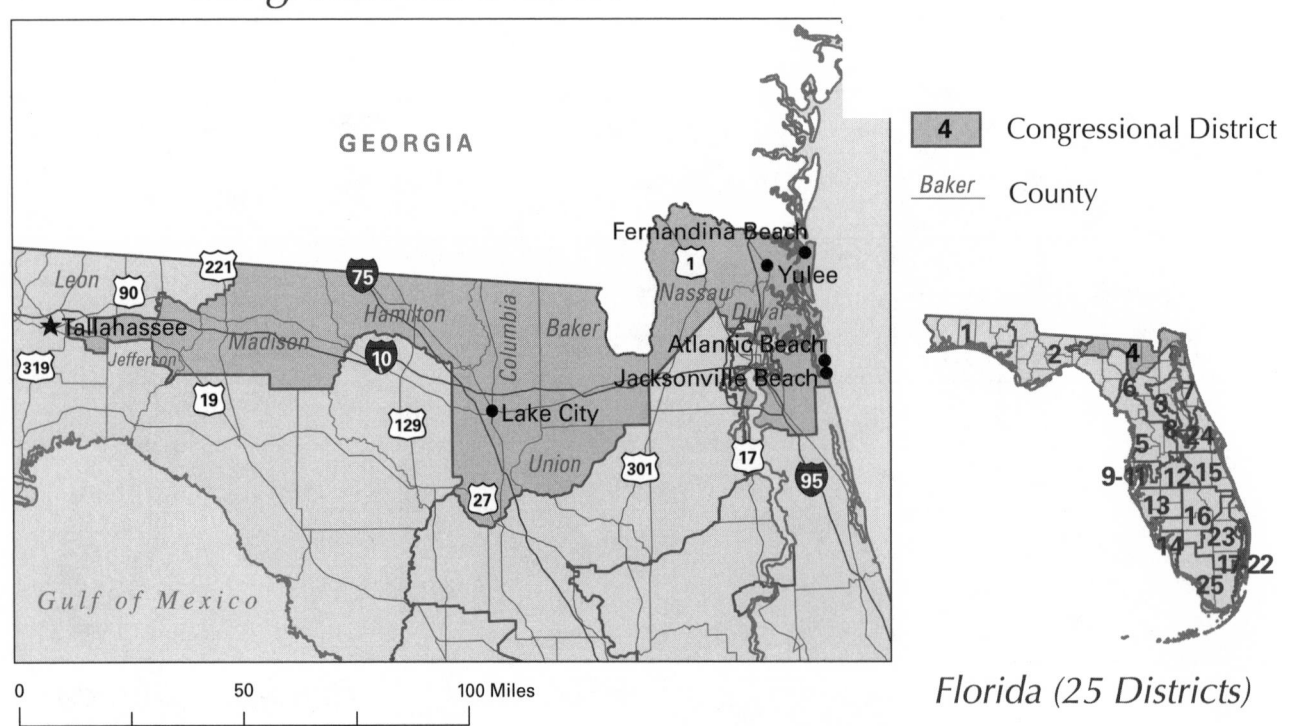

Florida (25 Districts)

Congressional District 5

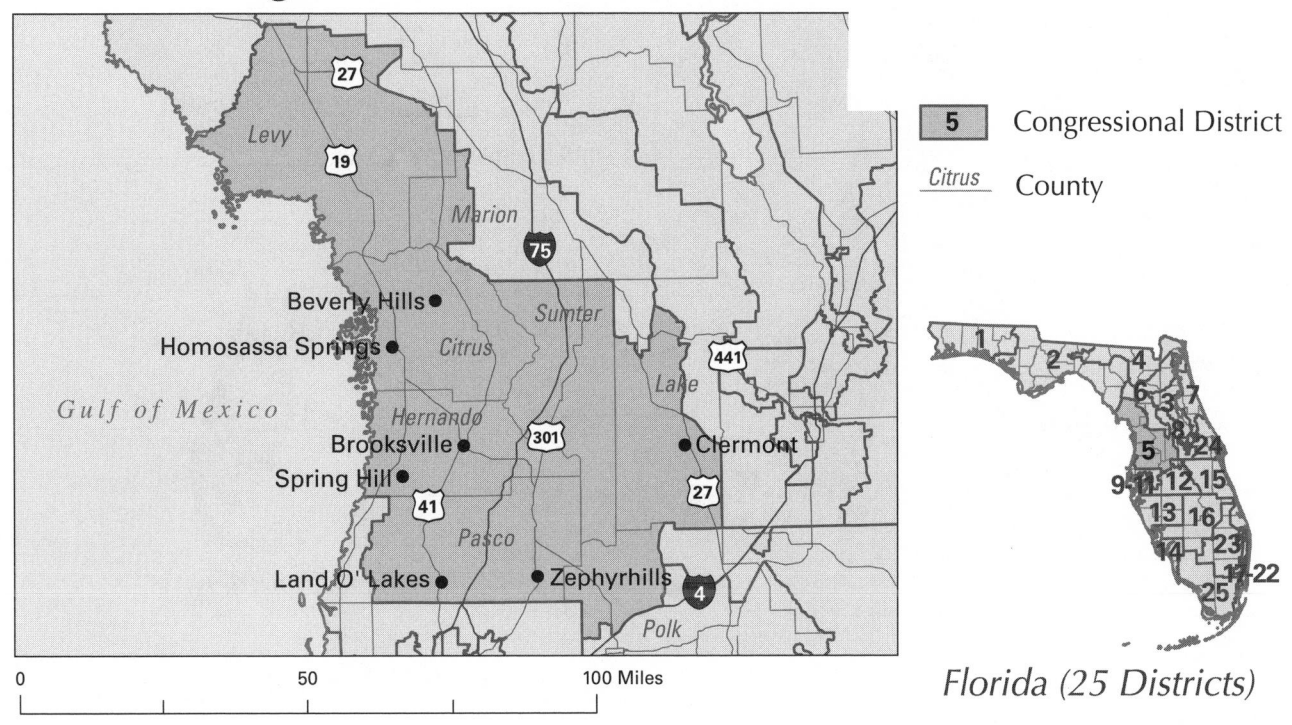

5 Congressional District

Citrus County

Florida (25 Districts)

Congressional District 6

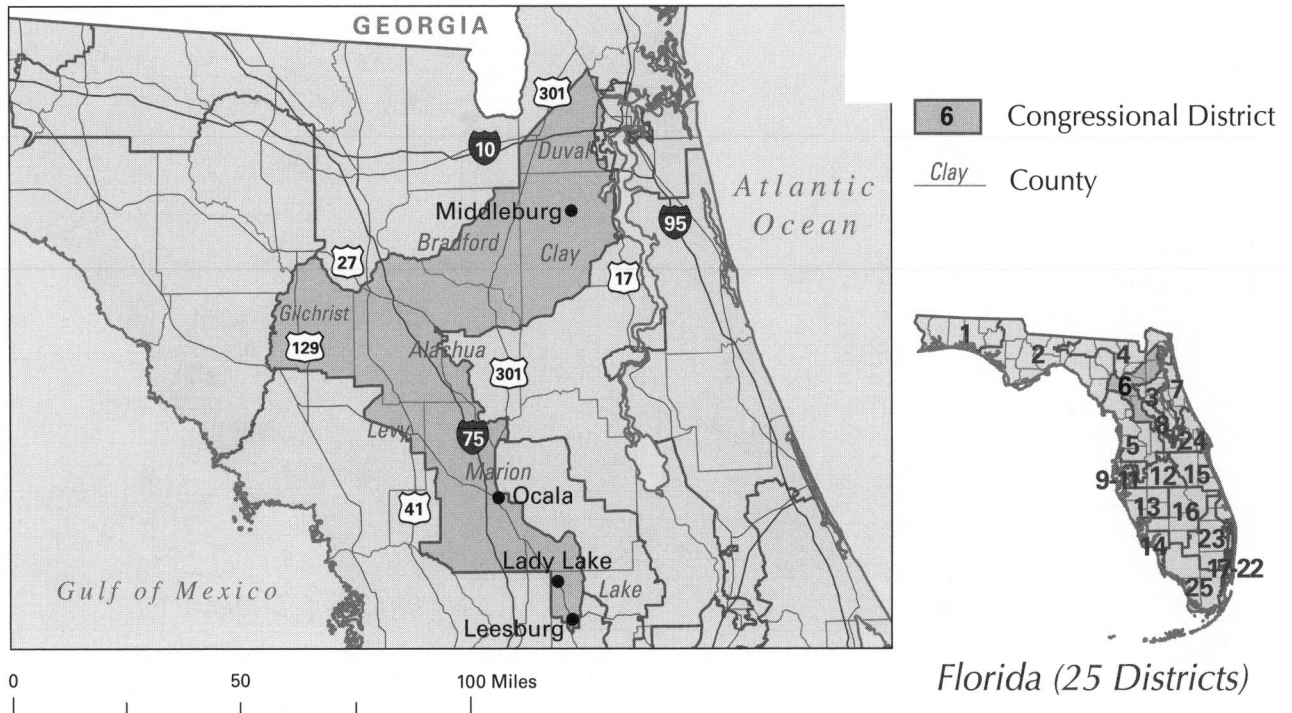

6 Congressional District

Clay County

Florida (25 Districts)

Congressional District 7

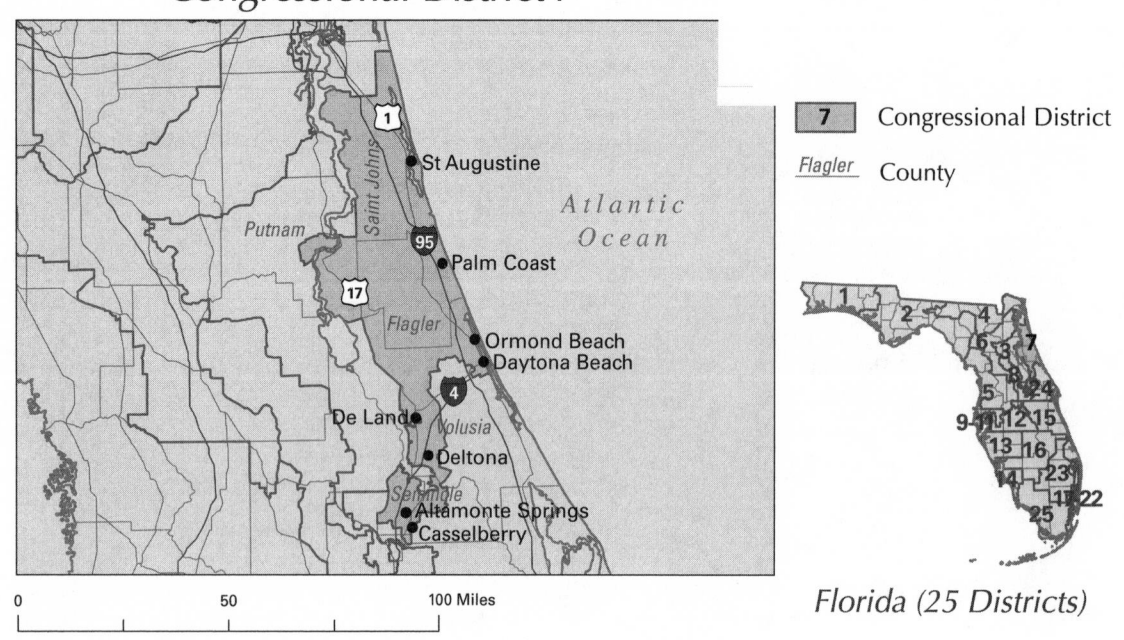

7	Congressional District
Flagler	County

Florida (25 Districts)

Congressional District 8

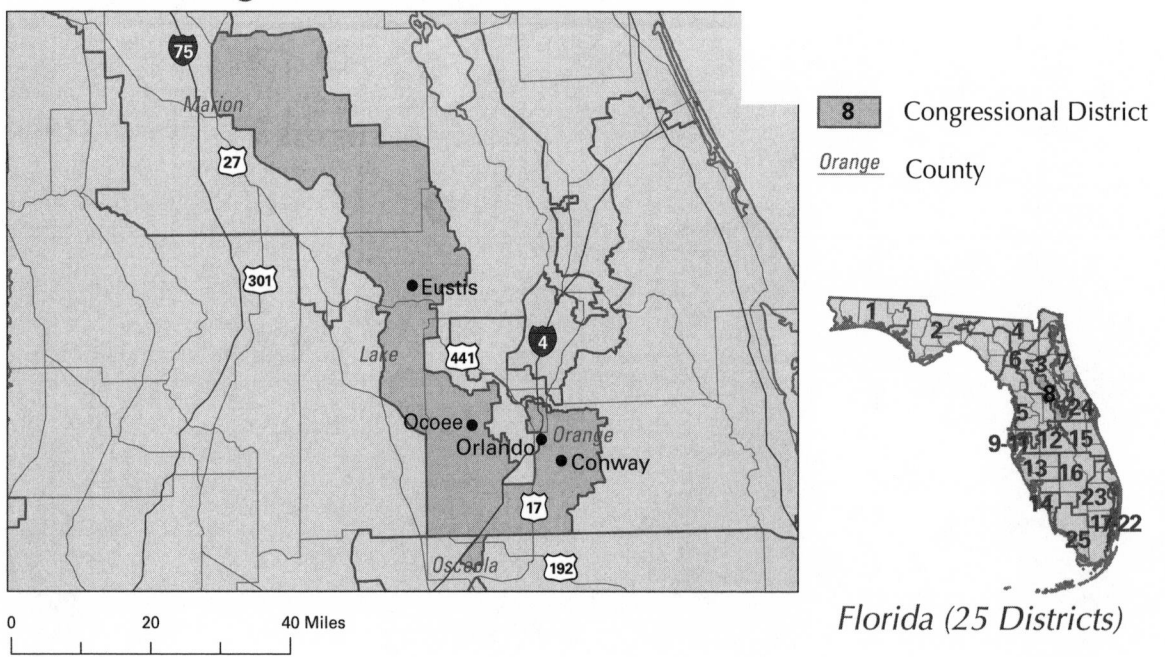

8	Congressional District
Orange	County

Florida (25 Districts)

Congressional District 9

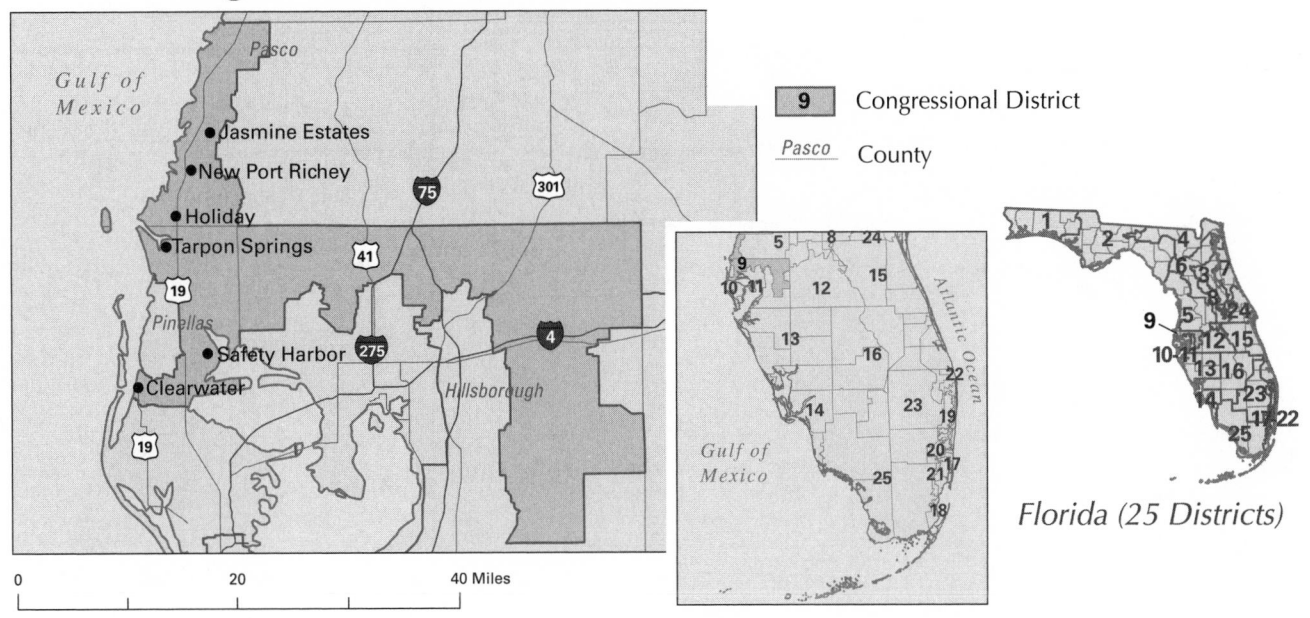

Congressional District 10

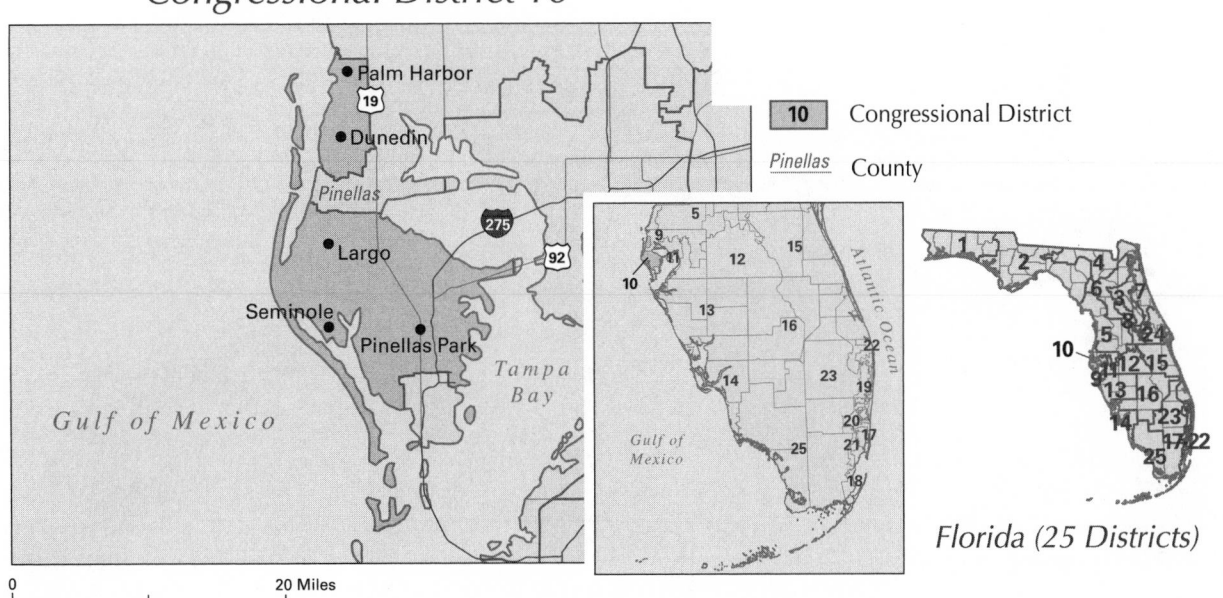

Congressional District 11

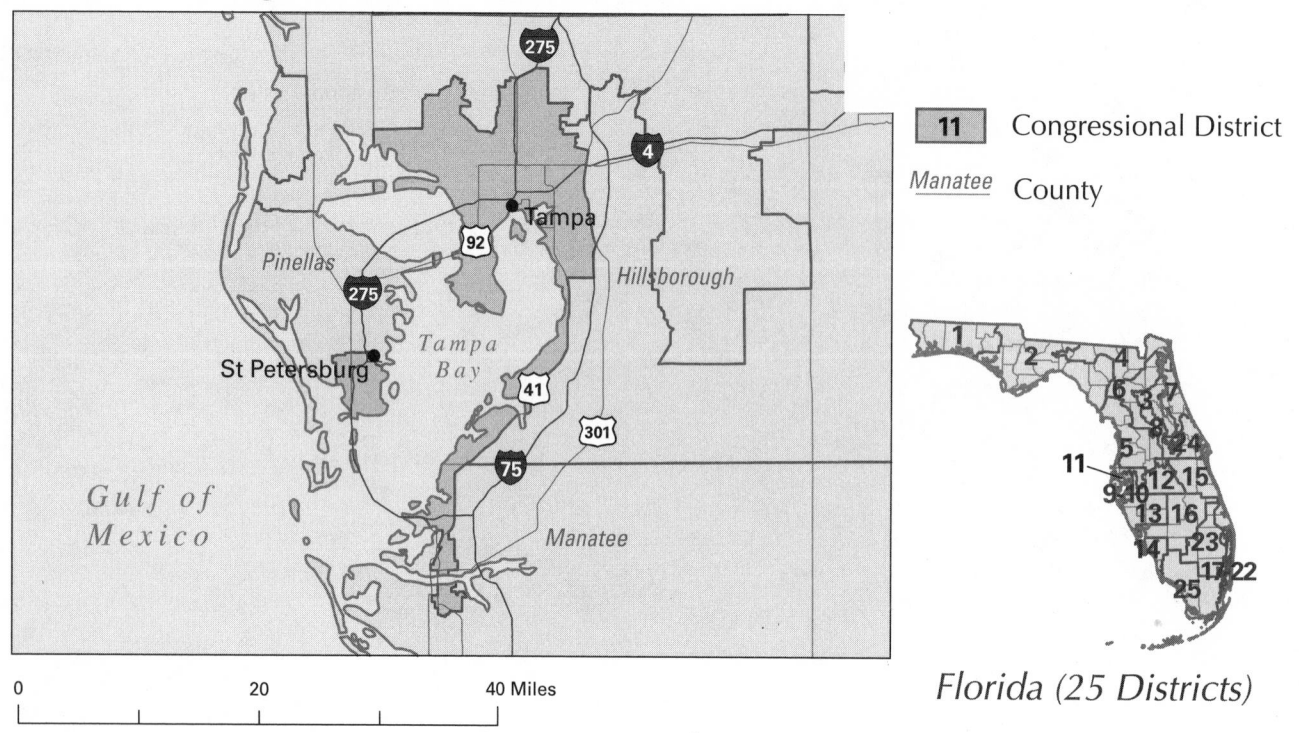

Congressional District 12

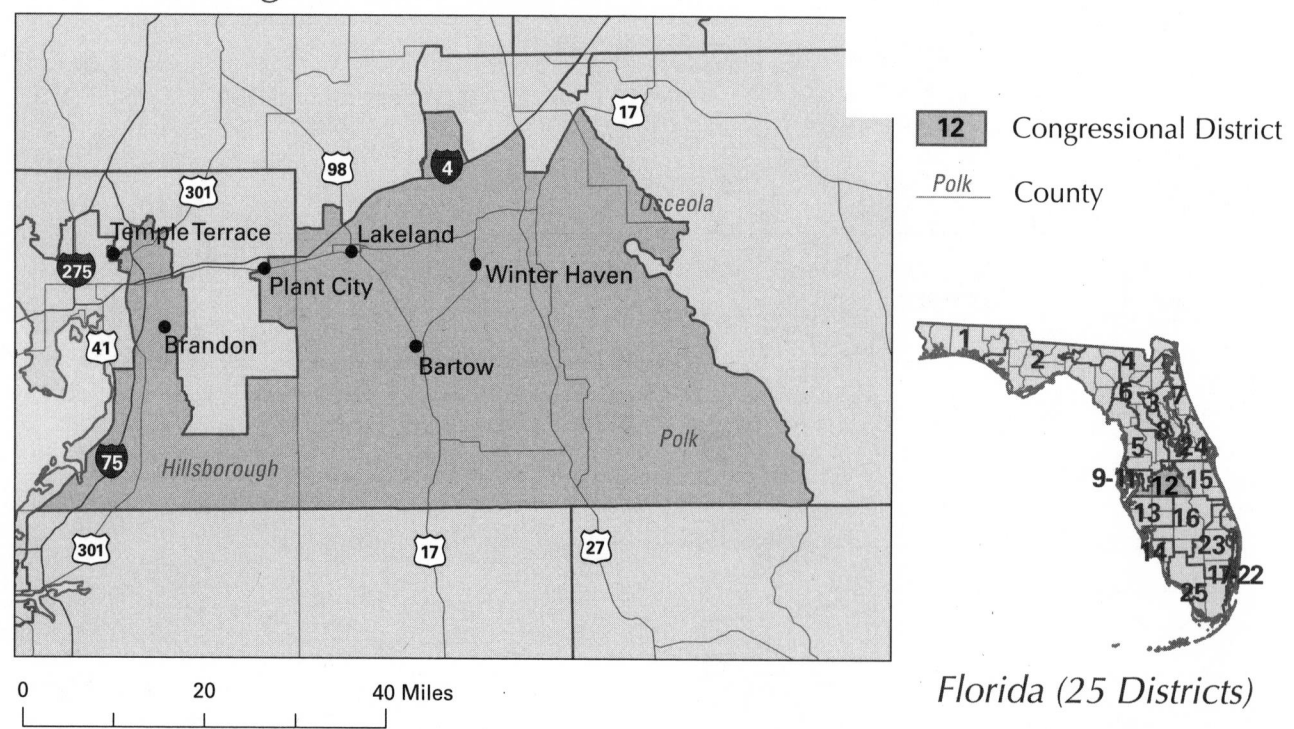

Congressional District 13

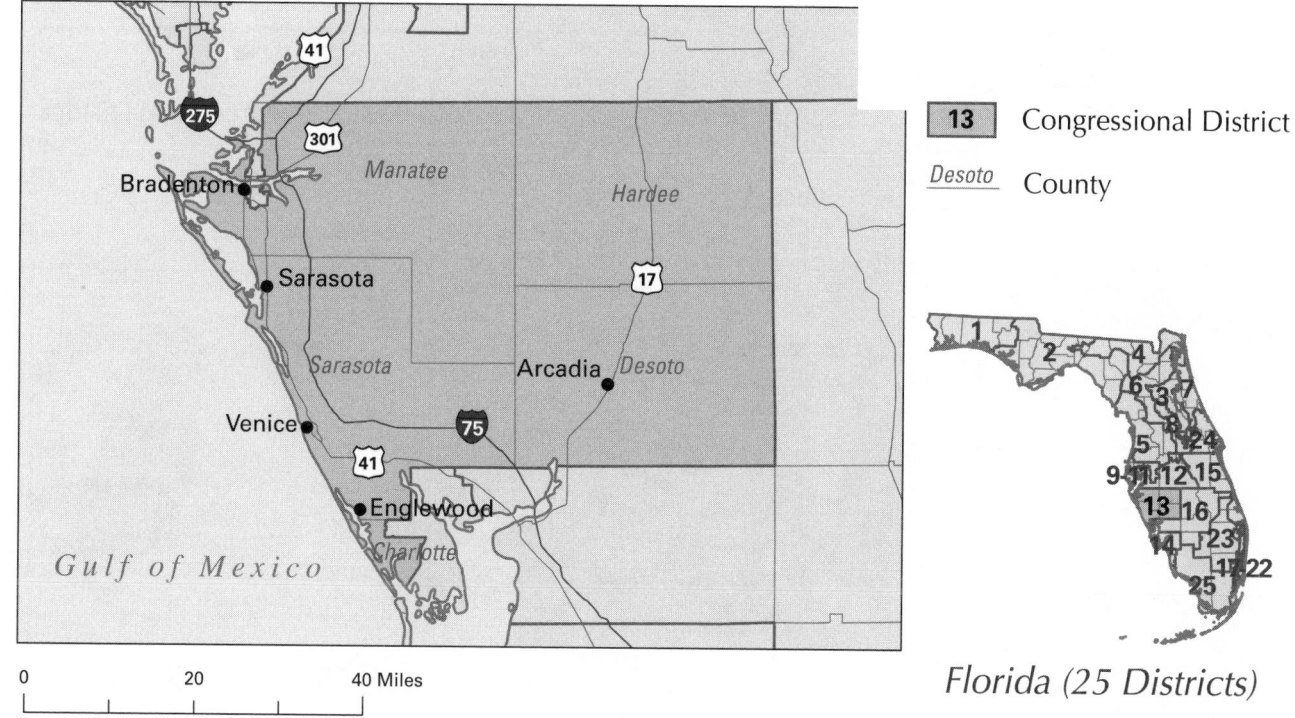

13   Congressional District

Desoto   County

Florida (25 Districts)

Congressional District 14

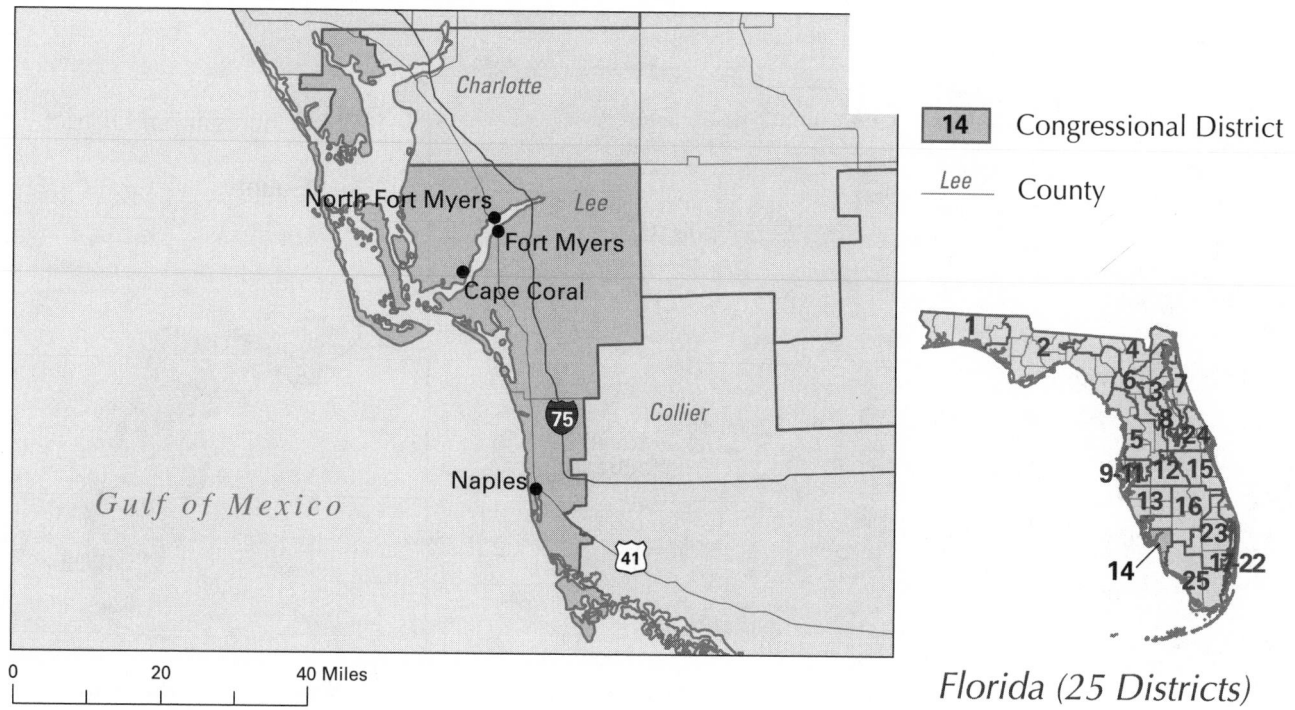

14   Congressional District

Lee   County

Florida (25 Districts)

Congressional District 15

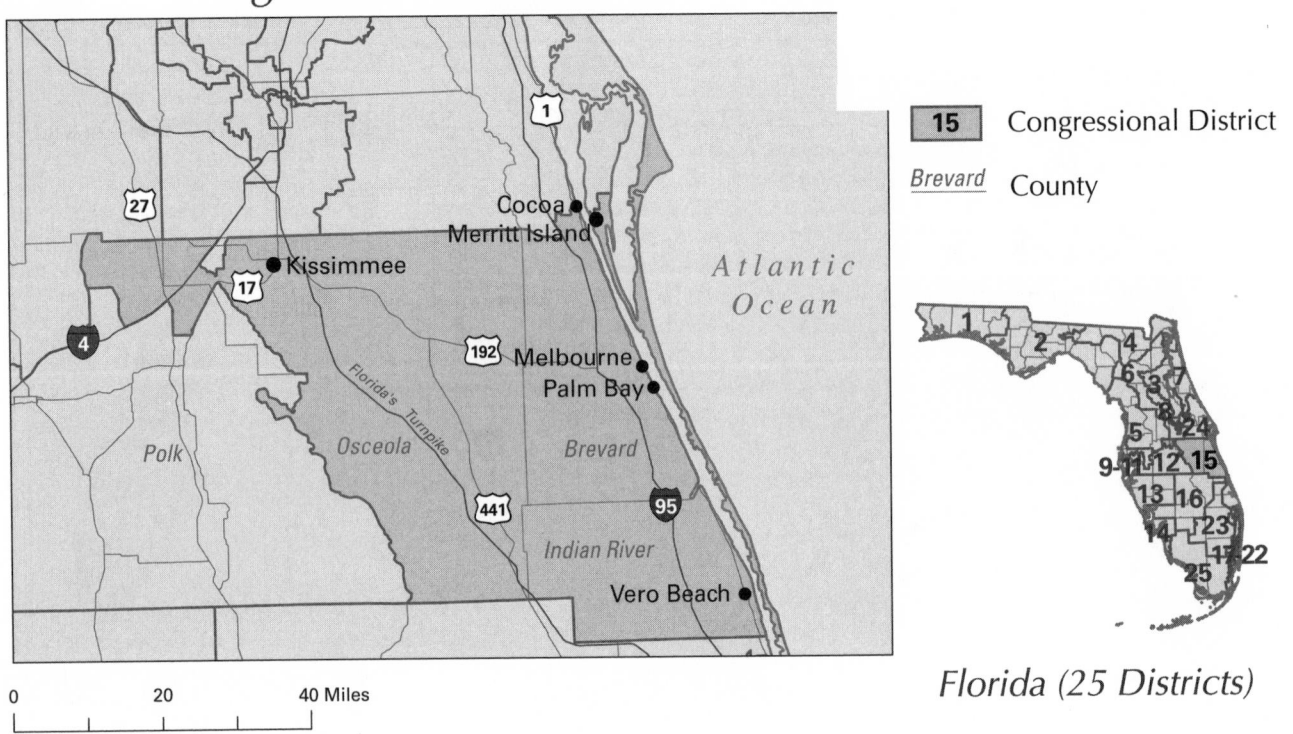

| 15 | Congressional District |
| *Brevard* | County |

Florida (25 Districts)

Congressional District 16

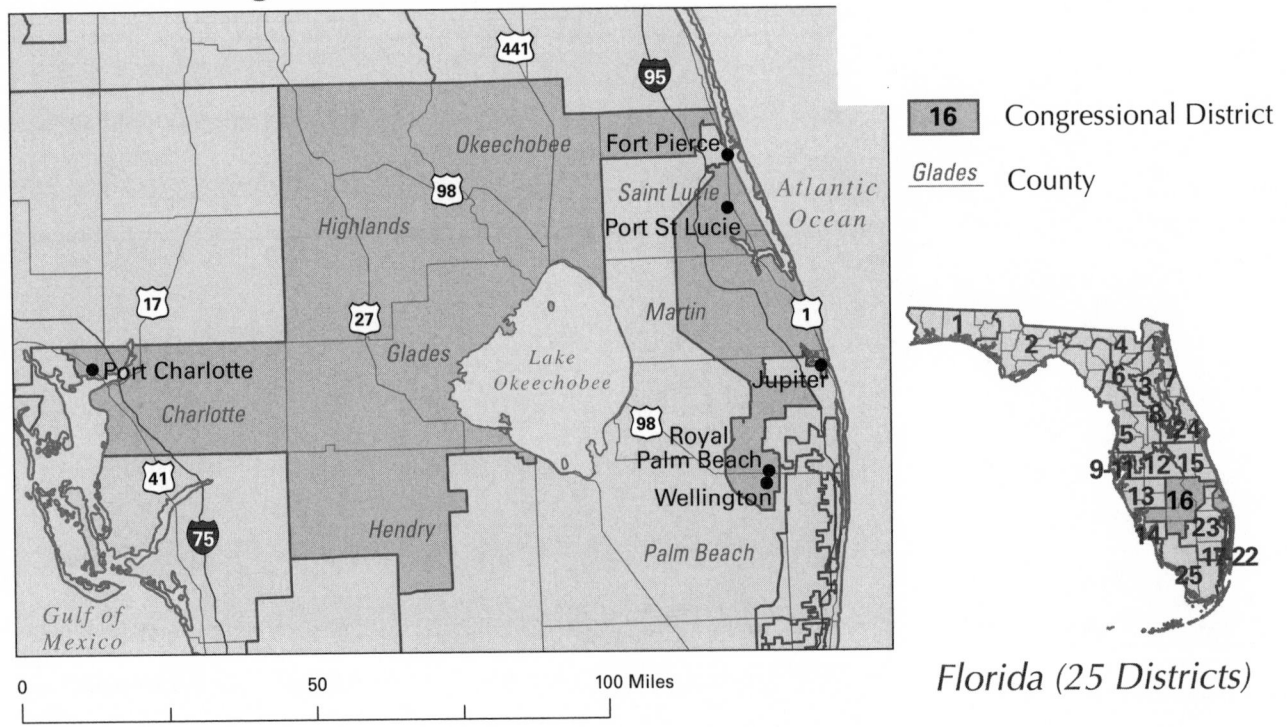

| 16 | Congressional District |
| *Glades* | County |

Florida (25 Districts)

Congressional District 17

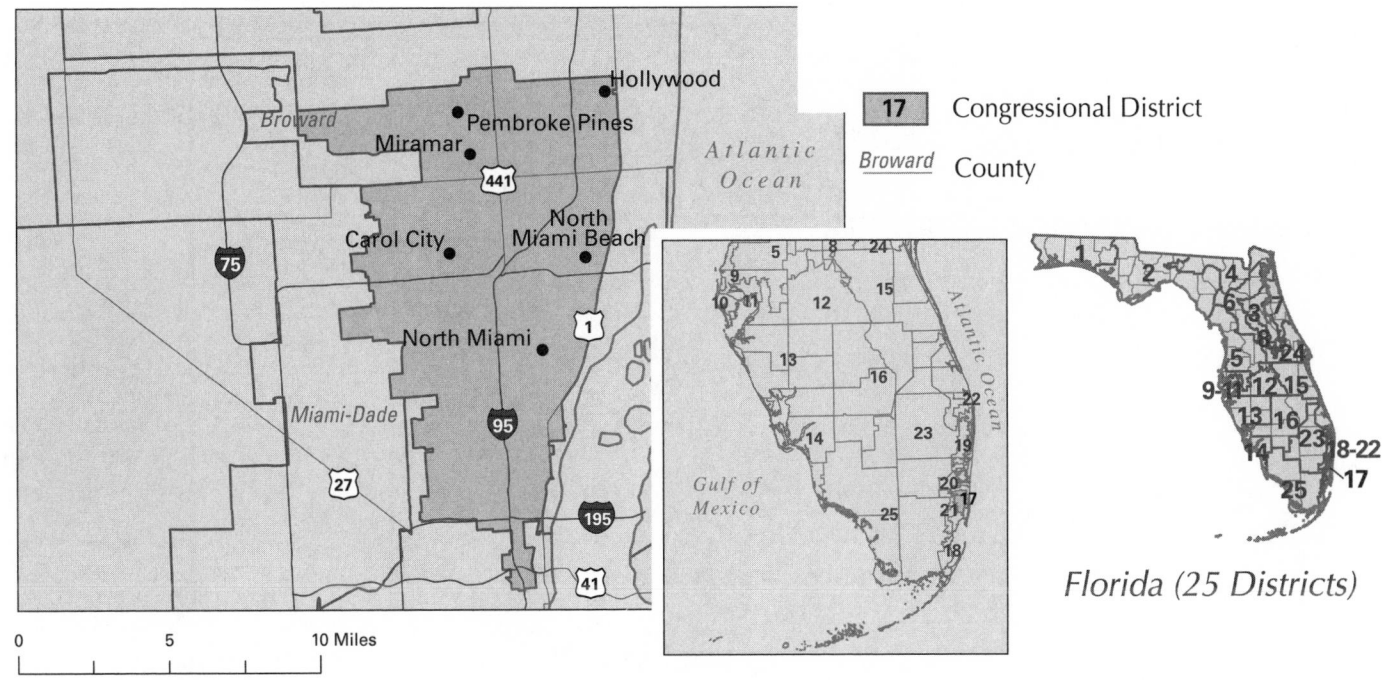

Congressional District 18

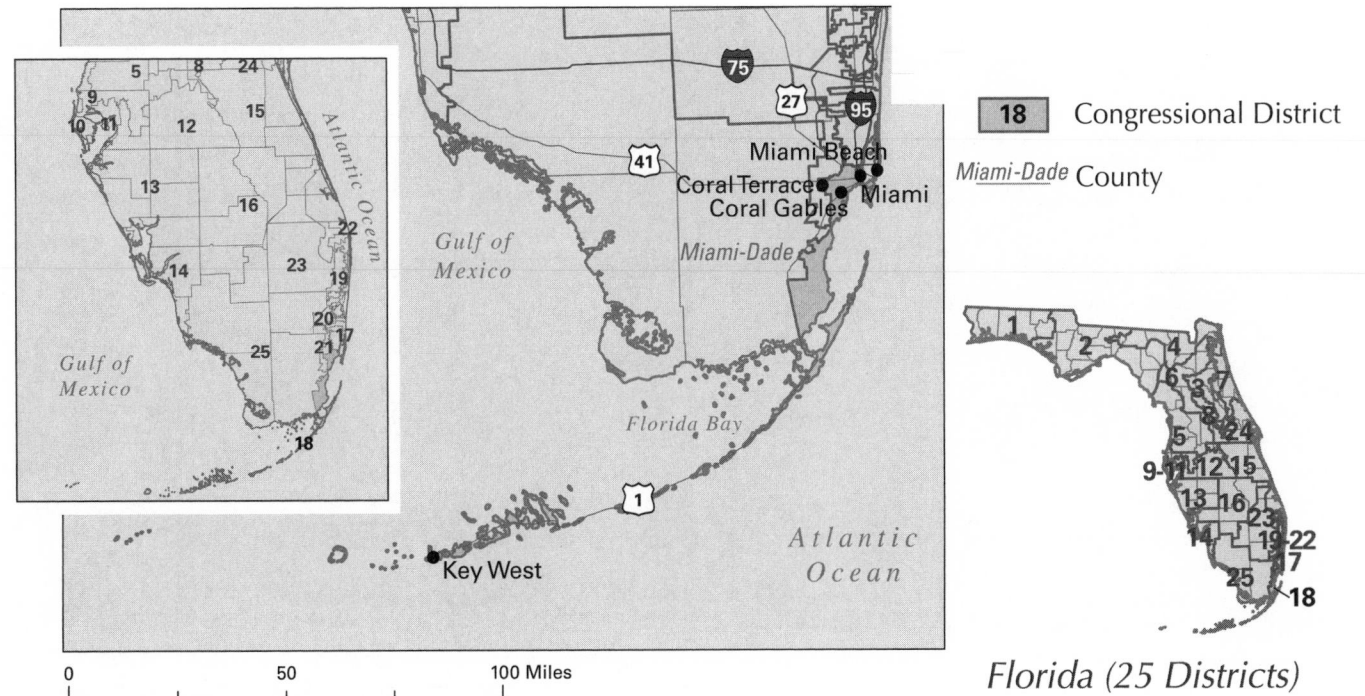

Congressional District 19

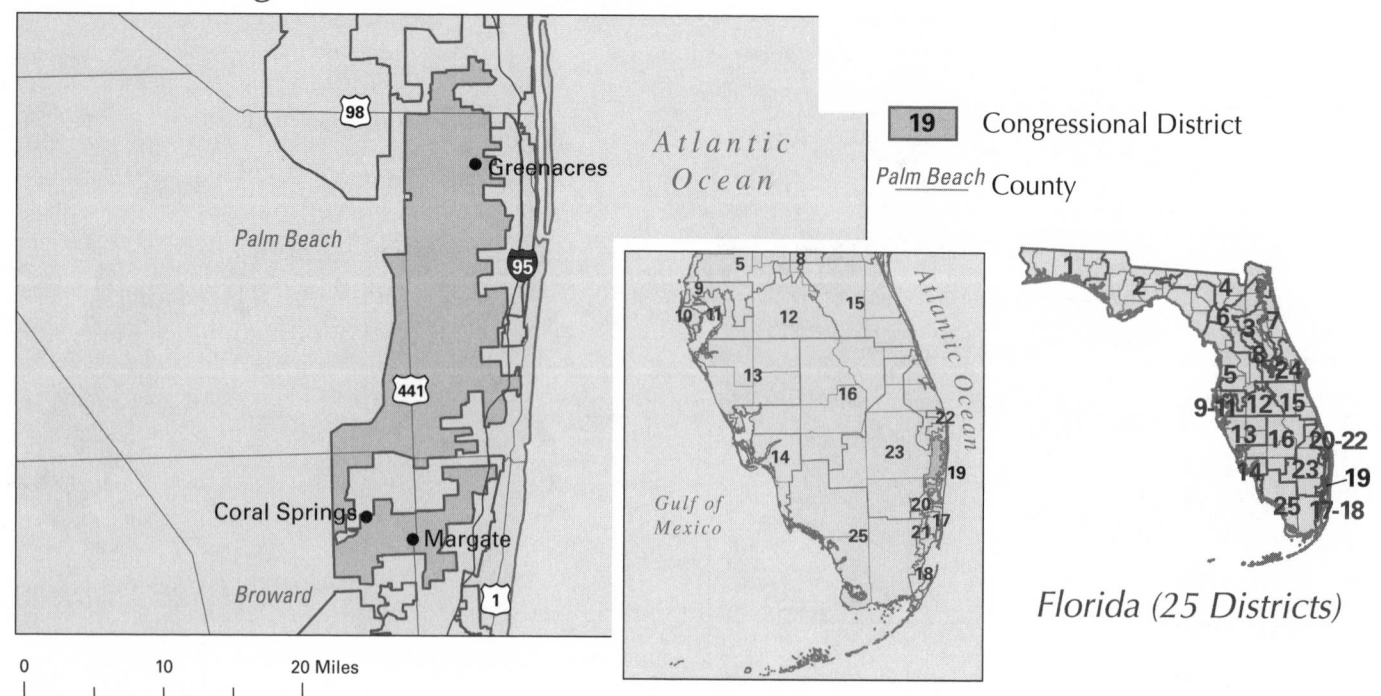

Congressional District 20

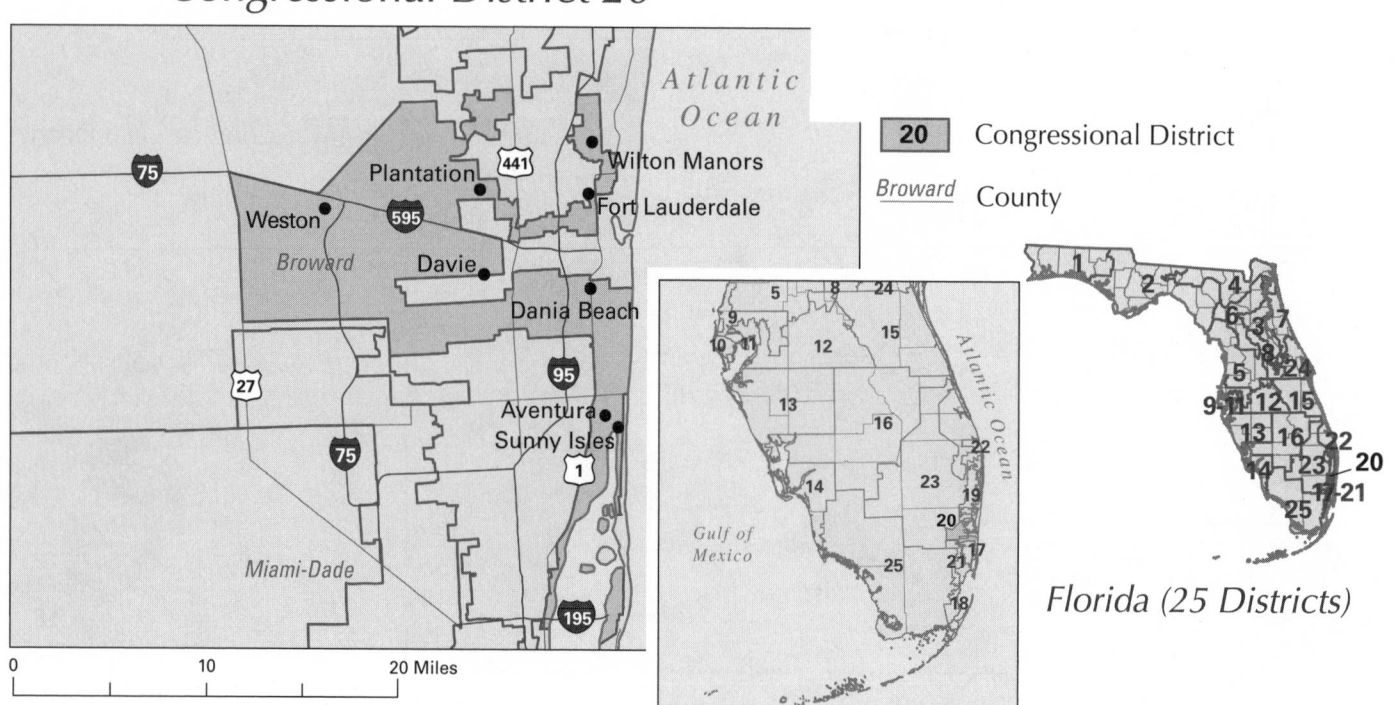

Congressional District 21

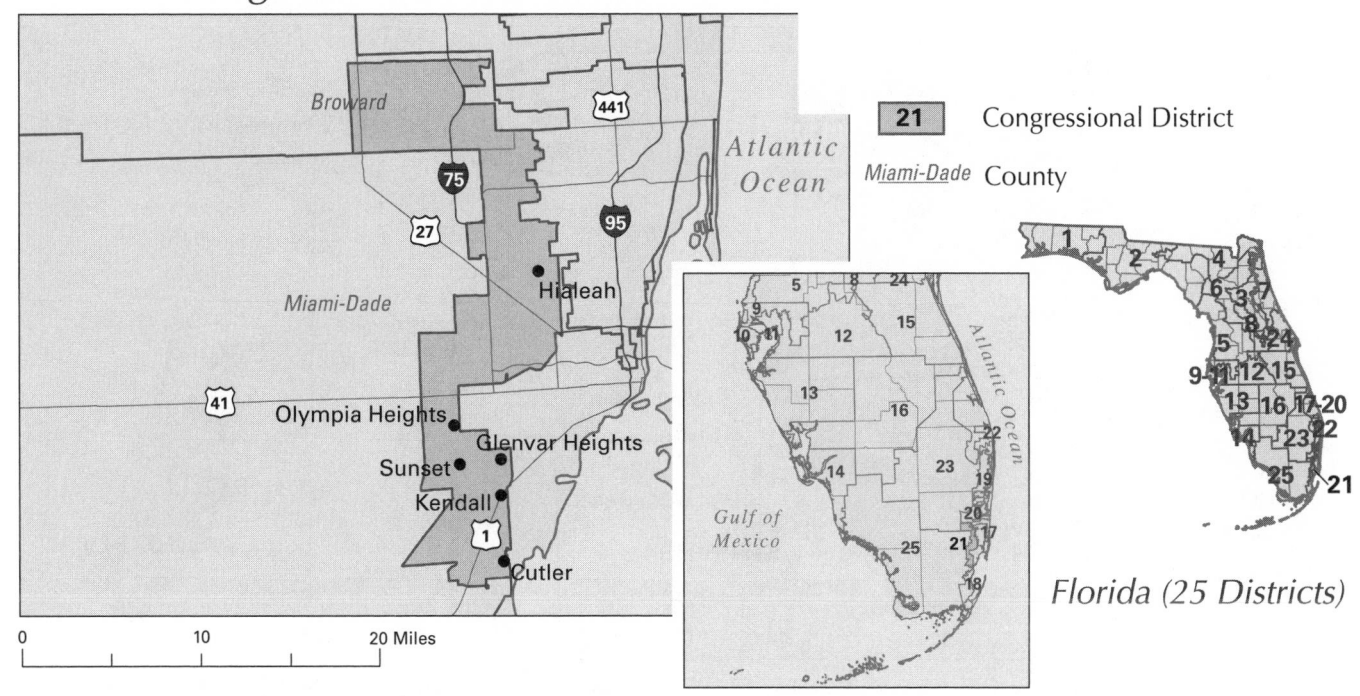

21 Congressional District

Miami-Dade County

Florida (25 Districts)

Congressional District 22

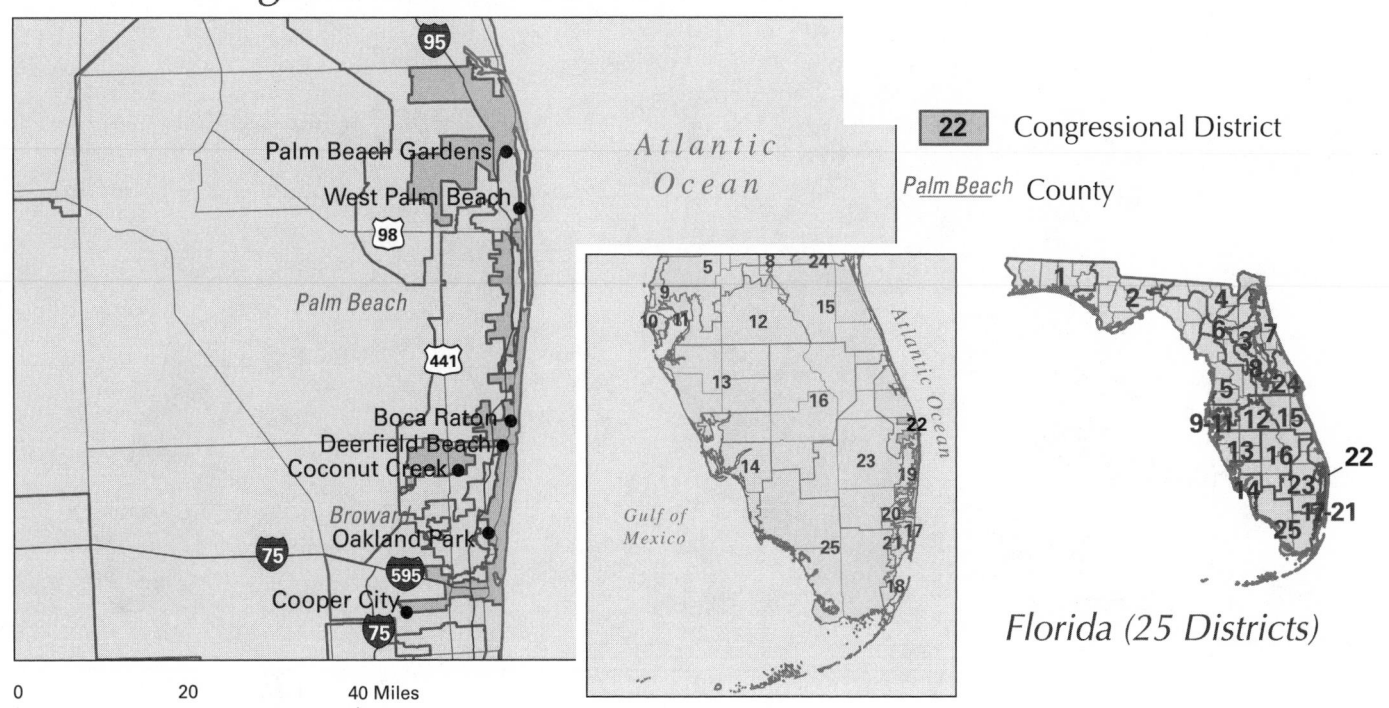

22 Congressional District

Palm Beach County

Florida (25 Districts)

Congressional District 23

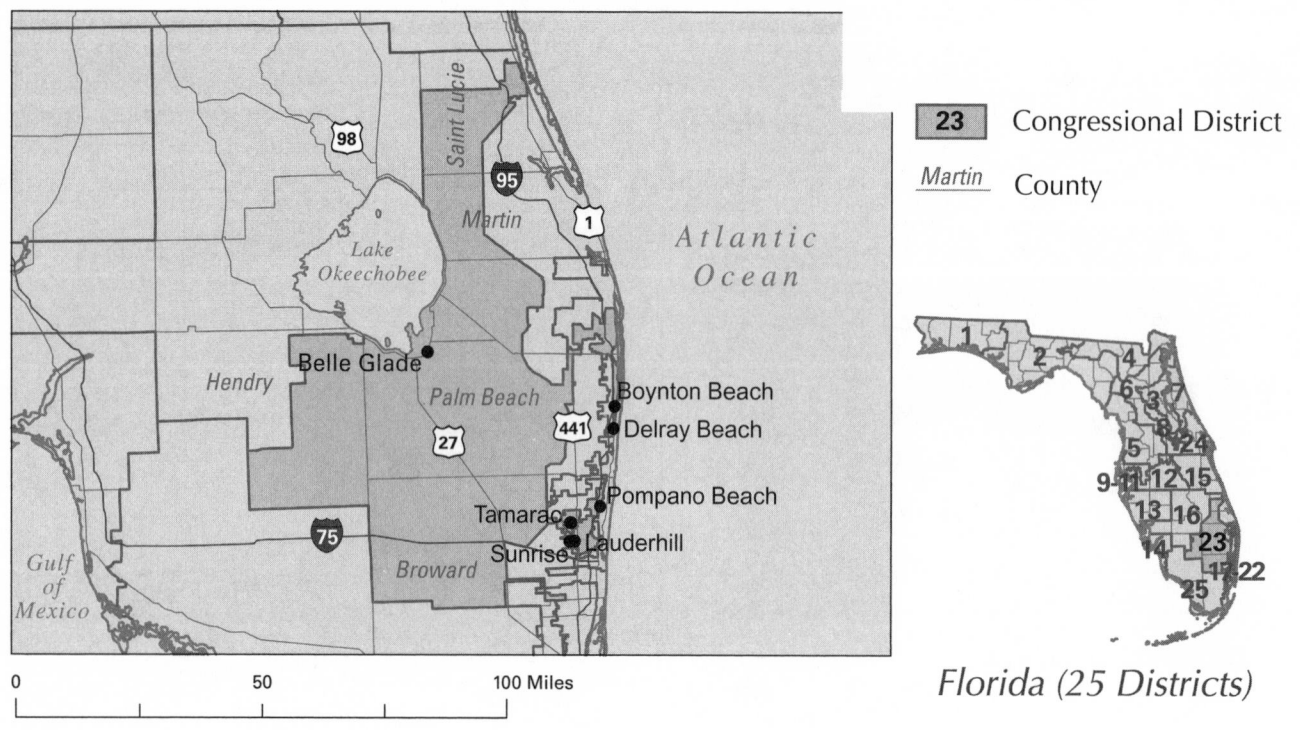

Florida (25 Districts)

Congressional District 24

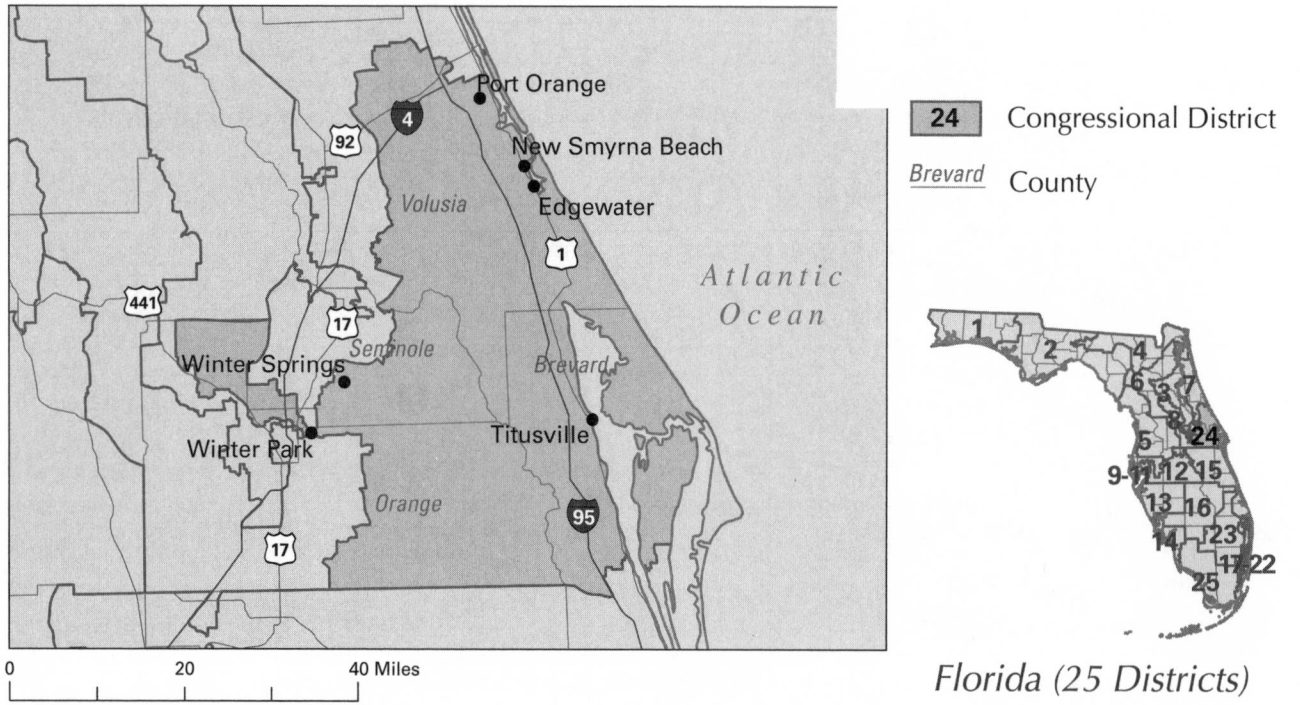

Florida (25 Districts)

Congressional District 25

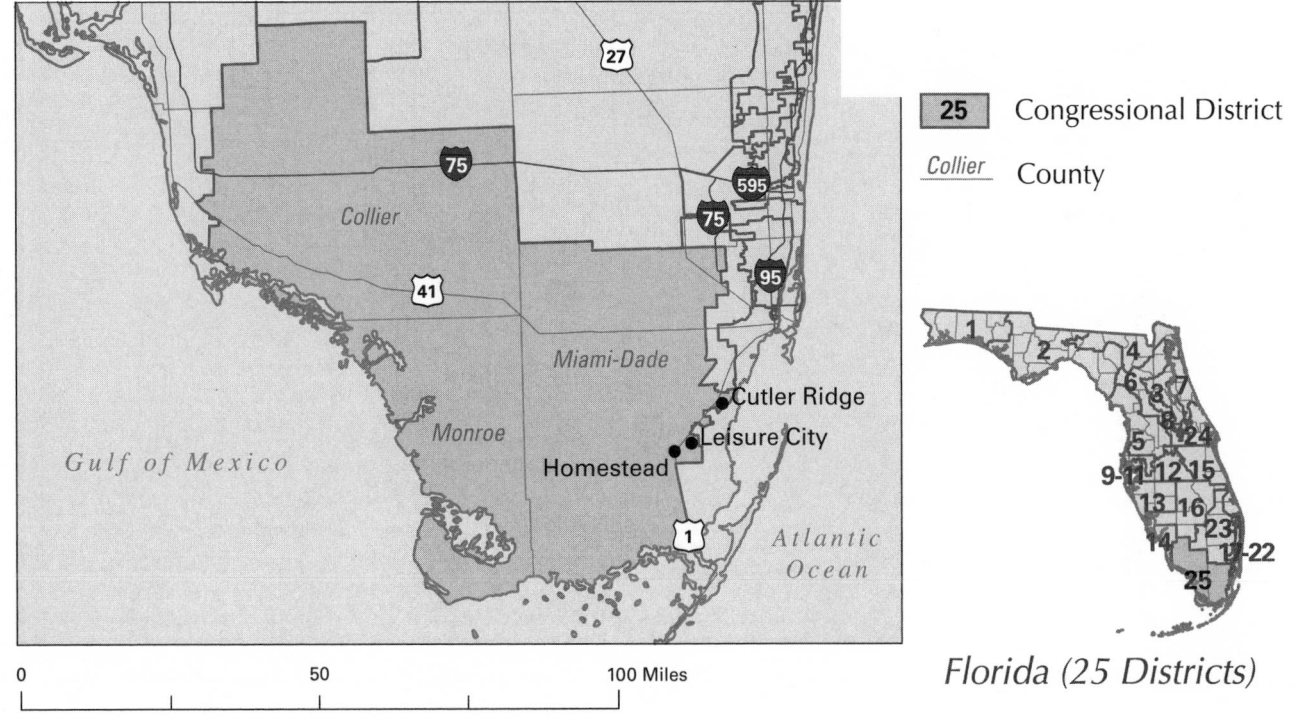

Florida (25 Districts)

Georgia — Counties

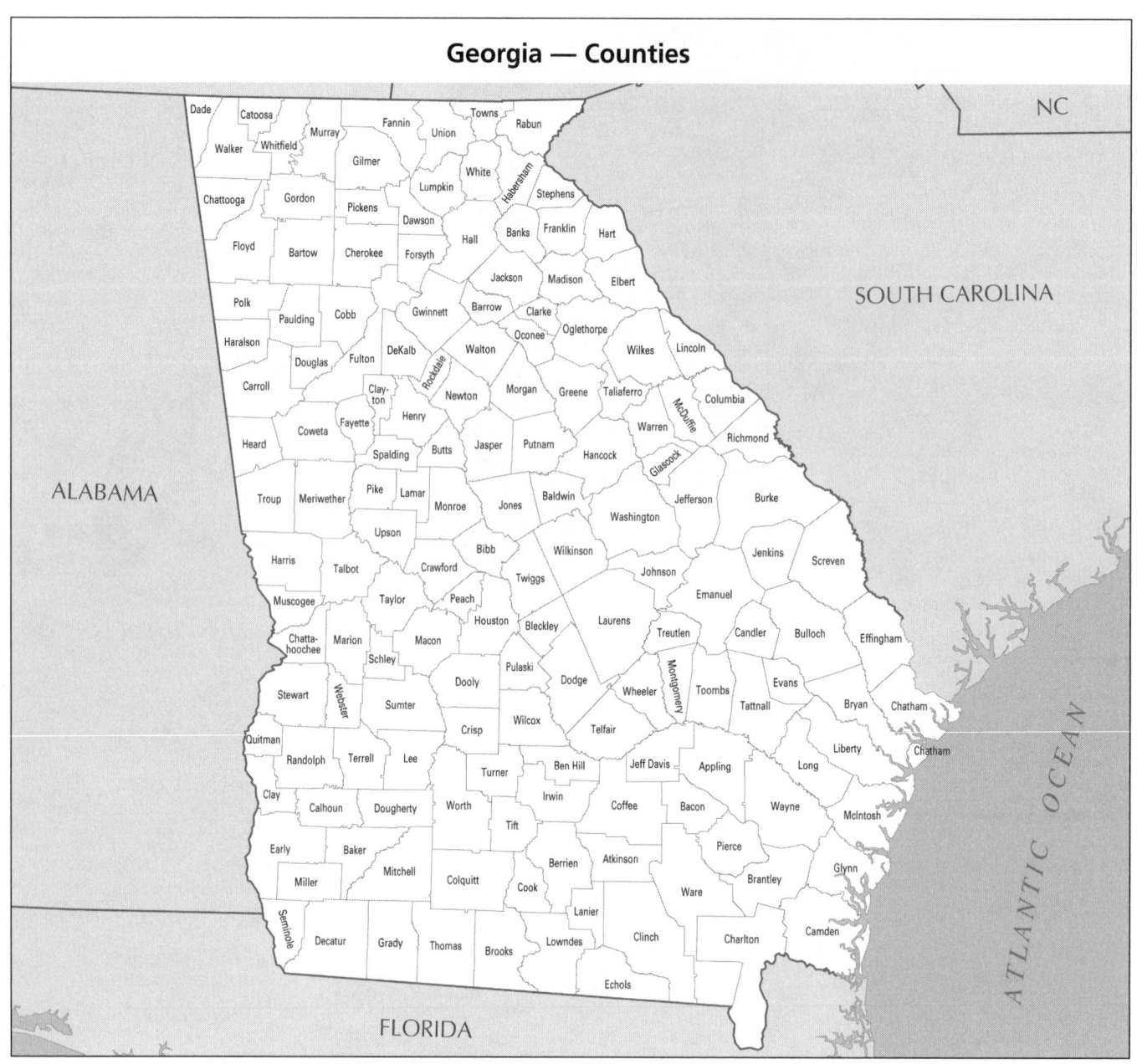

GEORGIA—110th CONGRESSIONAL DISTRICTS BY COUNTIES

County	Congressional District	County	Congressional District	County	Congressional District
Appling	1	Dade	9	Jefferson	12
Atkinson	1	Dawson	9	Jenkins	12
Bacon	1	Decatur	2	Johnson	12
Baker	2	DeKalb	4–6, 13	Jones	8
Baldwin	8, 12	Dodge	8	Lamar	3
Banks	10	Dooly	2	Lanier	1
Barrow	7	Dougherty	2	Laurens	8
Bartow	11	Douglas	3, 13	Lee	2
Ben Hill	8	Early	2	Liberty	1
Berrien	1	Echols	1	Lincoln	10
Bibb	8	Effingham	12	Long	1
Bleckley	8	Elbert	10	Lowndes	1, 2
Brantley	1	Emanuel	12	Lumpkin	9
Brooks	2	Evans	12	McDuffie	10
Bryan	1	Fannin	9	McIntosh	1
Bulloch	12	Fayette	3	Macon	2
Burke	12	Floyd	11	Madison	10
Butts	8	Forsyth	7, 9	Marion	2
Calhoun	2	Franklin	10	Meriwether	3
Camden	1	Fulton	5, 6, 13	Miller	2
Candler	12	Gilmer	9	Mitchell	2
Carroll	3, 11	Glascock	12	Monroe	8
Catoosa	9	Glynn	1	Montgomery	12
Charlton	1	Gordon	9, 11	Morgan	10
Chatham	1, 12	Grady	2	Murray	9
Chattahoochee	2	Greene	10	Muscogee	2, 3
Chattooga	11	Gwinnett	4, 7	Newton	7, 8
Cherokee	6	Habersham	10	Oconee	10
Clarke	10	Hall	9	Oglethorpe	10
Clay	2	Hancock	12	Paulding	11
Clayton	5, 13	Haralson	11	Peach	2
Clinch	1	Harris	3	Pickens	9
Cobb	6, 11, 13	Hart	10	Pierce	1
Coffee	1	Heard	3	Pike	3
Colquitt	8	Henry	3, 13	Polk	11
Columbia	10	Houston	8	Pulaski	8
Cook	1	Irwin	8	Putnam	10
Coweta	3	Jackson	10	Quitman	2
Crawford	2	Jasper	8	Rabun	10
Crisp	2	Jeff Davis	1	Randolph	2

GEORGIA — 110th CONGRESSIONAL DISTRICTS BY COUNTIES

County	Congressional District
Richmond	10, 12
Rockdale	3, 4
Schley	2
Screven	12
Seminole	2
Spalding	3
Stephens	10
Stewart	2
Sumter	2
Talbot	2
Taliaferro	12
Tattnall	12
Taylor	2

County	Congressional District
Telfair	1
Terrell	2
Thomas	2
Tift	8
Toombs	12
Towns	10
Treutlen	12
Troup	3
Turner	8
Twiggs	8
Union	9
Upson	3
Walker	9

County	Congressional District
Walton	7
Ware	1
Warren	12
Washington	12
Wayne	1
Webster	2
Wheeler	1
White	9
Whitfield	9
Wilcox	8
Wilkes	10
Wilkinson	8
Worth	2, 8

Congressional District 1

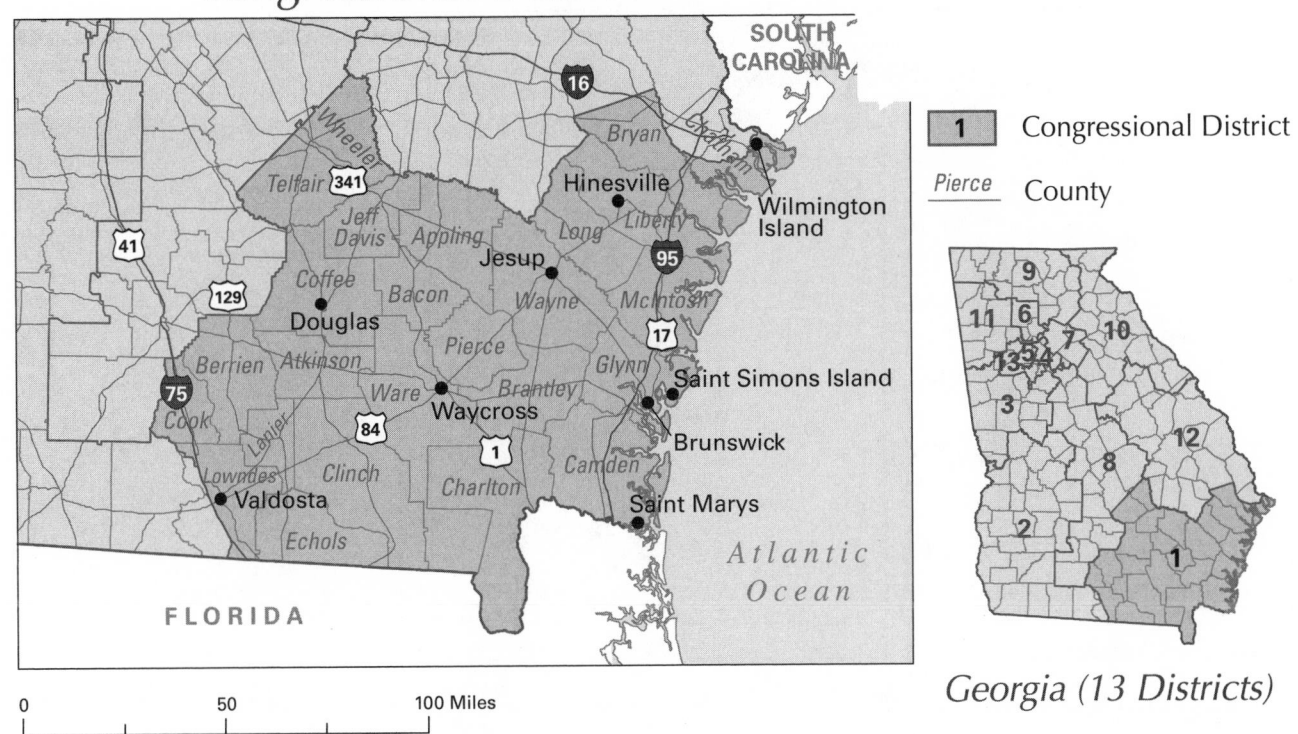

Georgia (13 Districts)

0   50   100 Miles

Congressional District 2

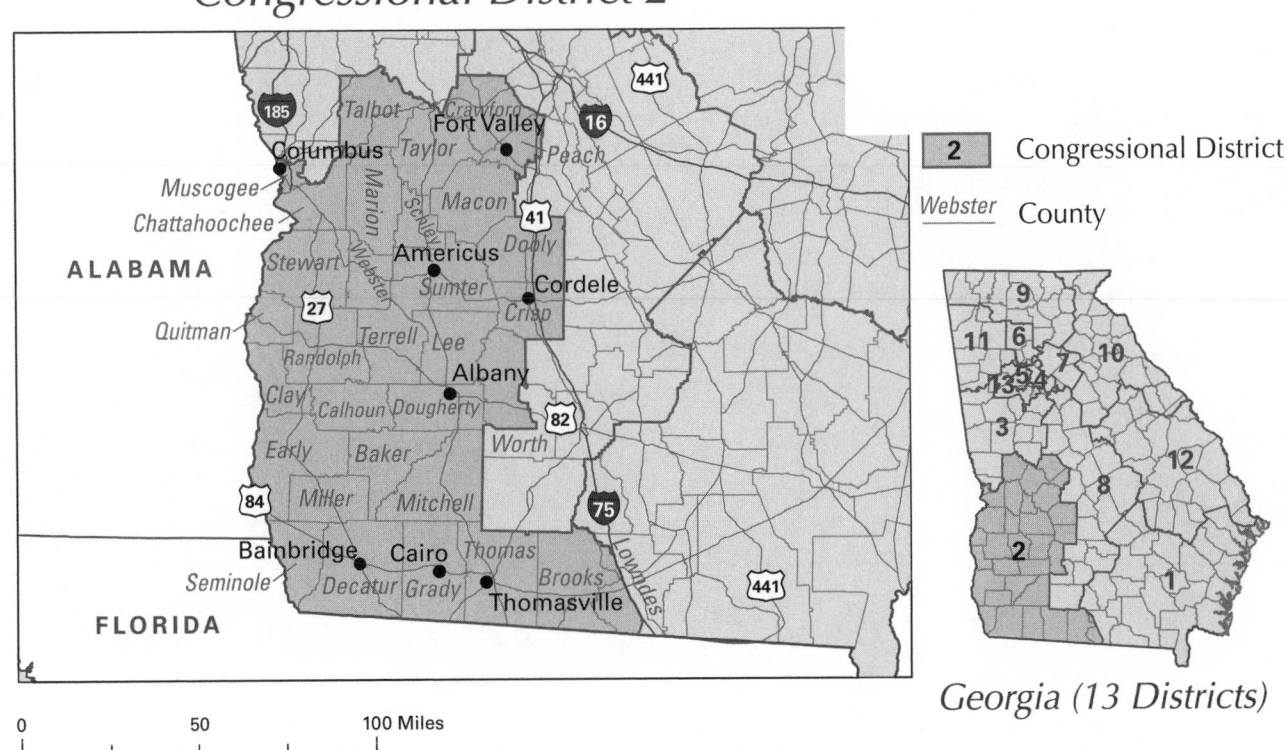

Georgia (13 Districts)

0   50   100 Miles

Congressional District 3

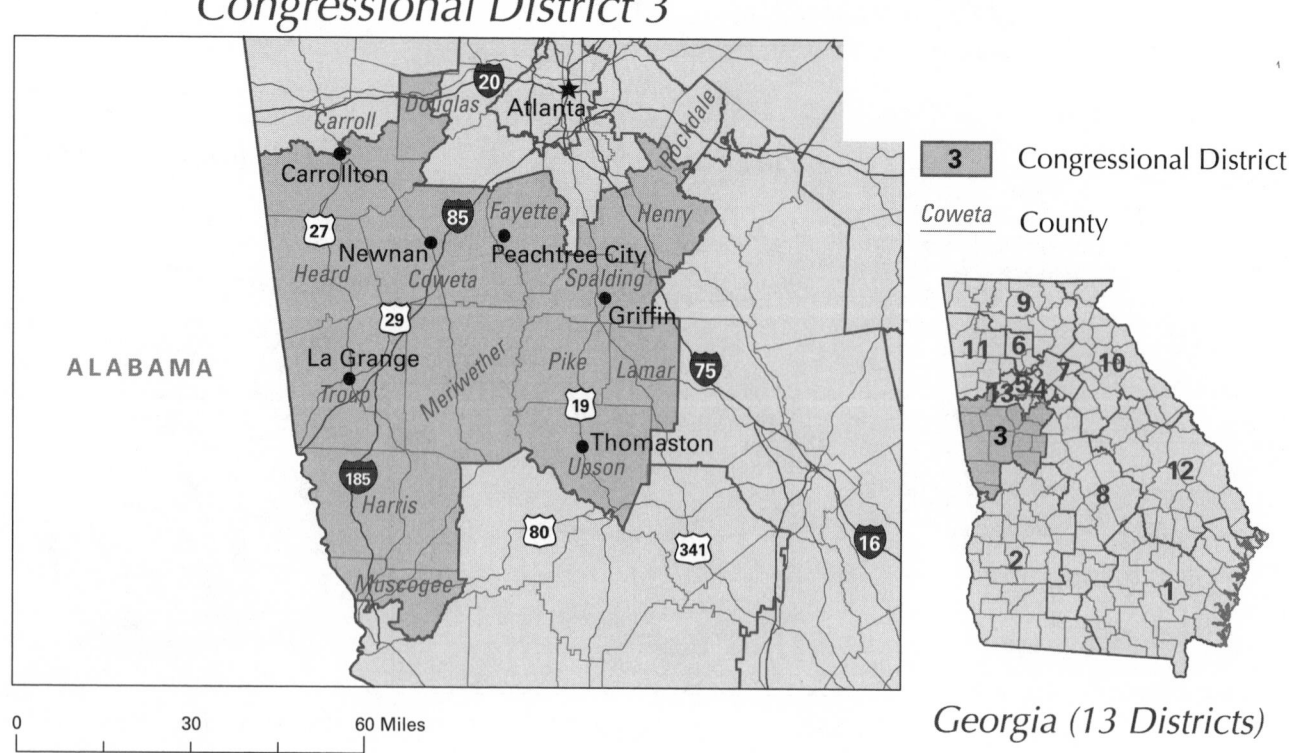

3	Congressional District
Coweta	County

Georgia (13 Districts)

Congressional District 4

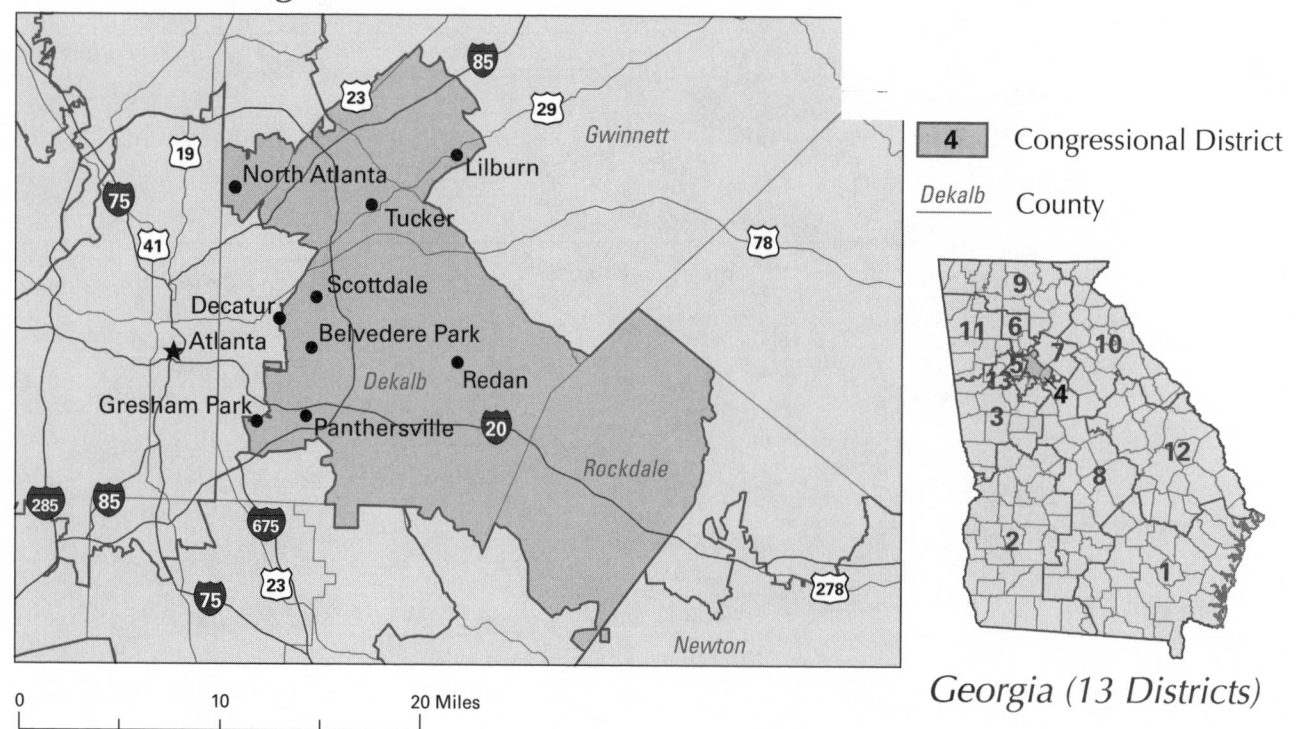

4	Congressional District
Dekalb	County

Georgia (13 Districts)

Congressional District 5

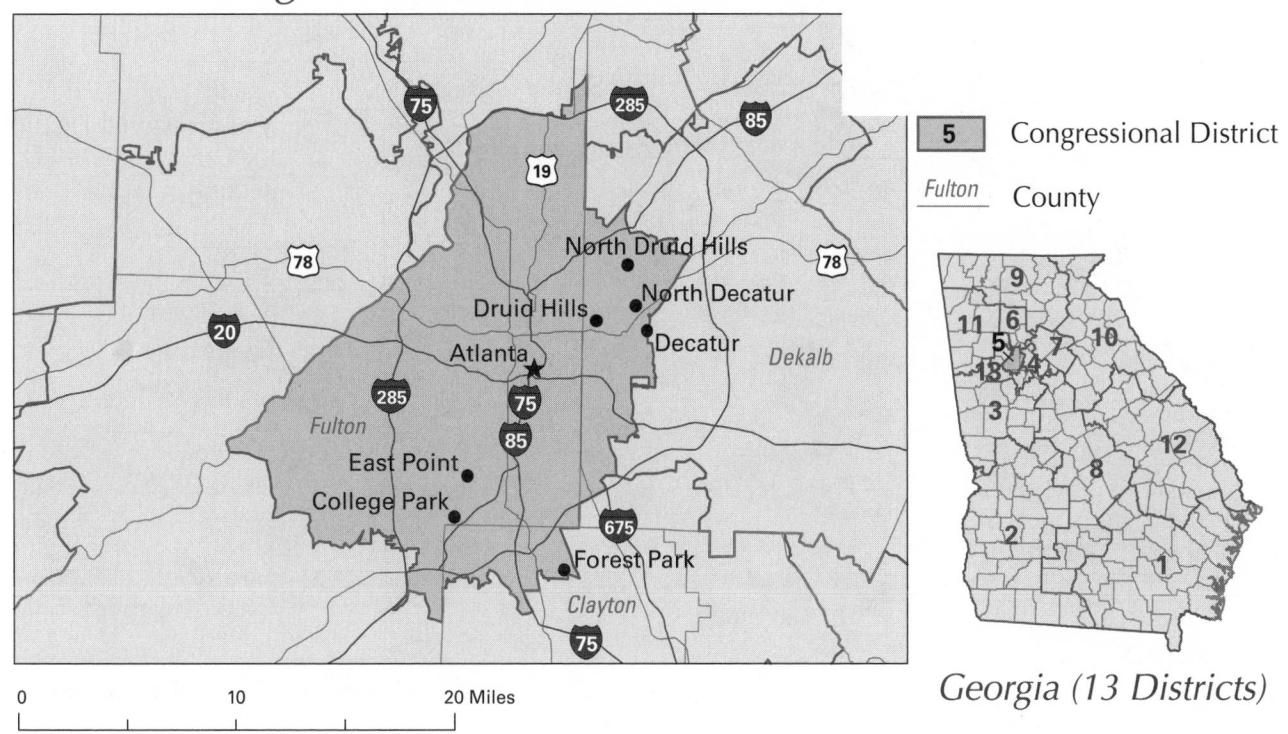

5 | Congressional District

Fulton | County

Georgia (13 Districts)

Congressional District 6

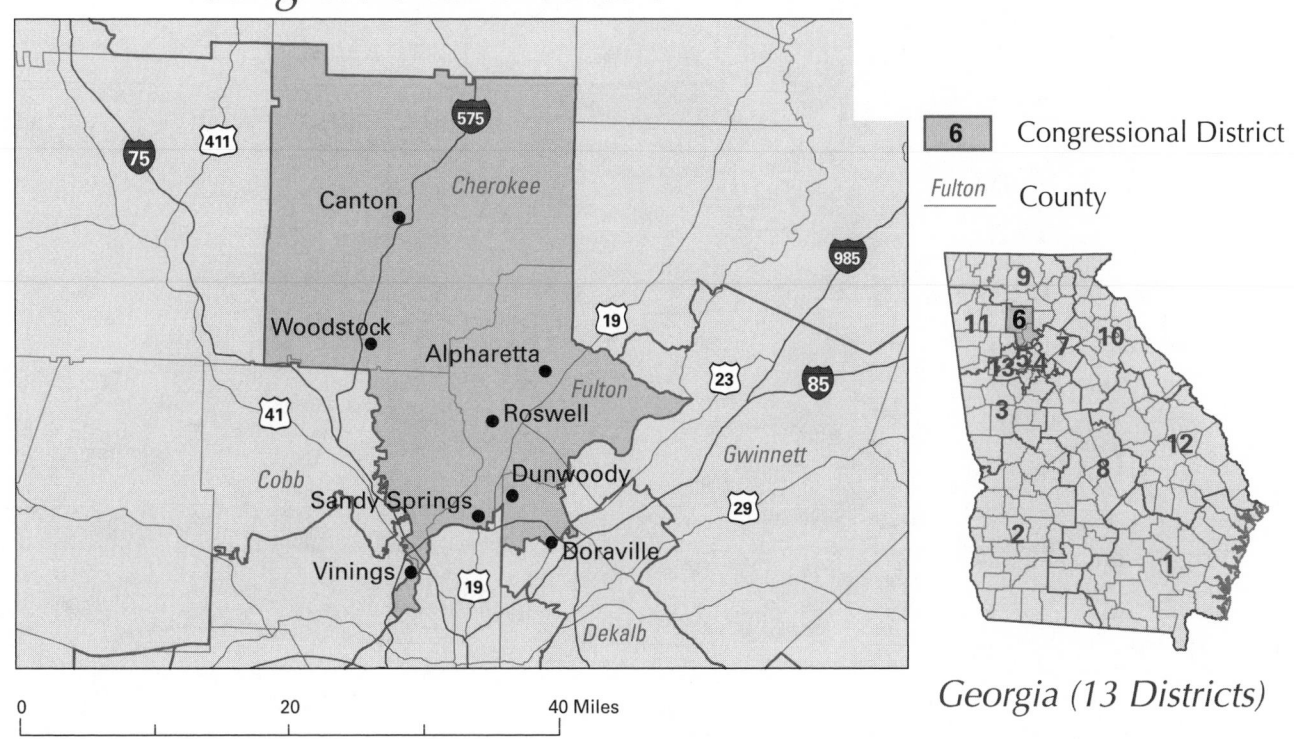

6 | Congressional District

Fulton | County

Georgia (13 Districts)

Congressional District 7

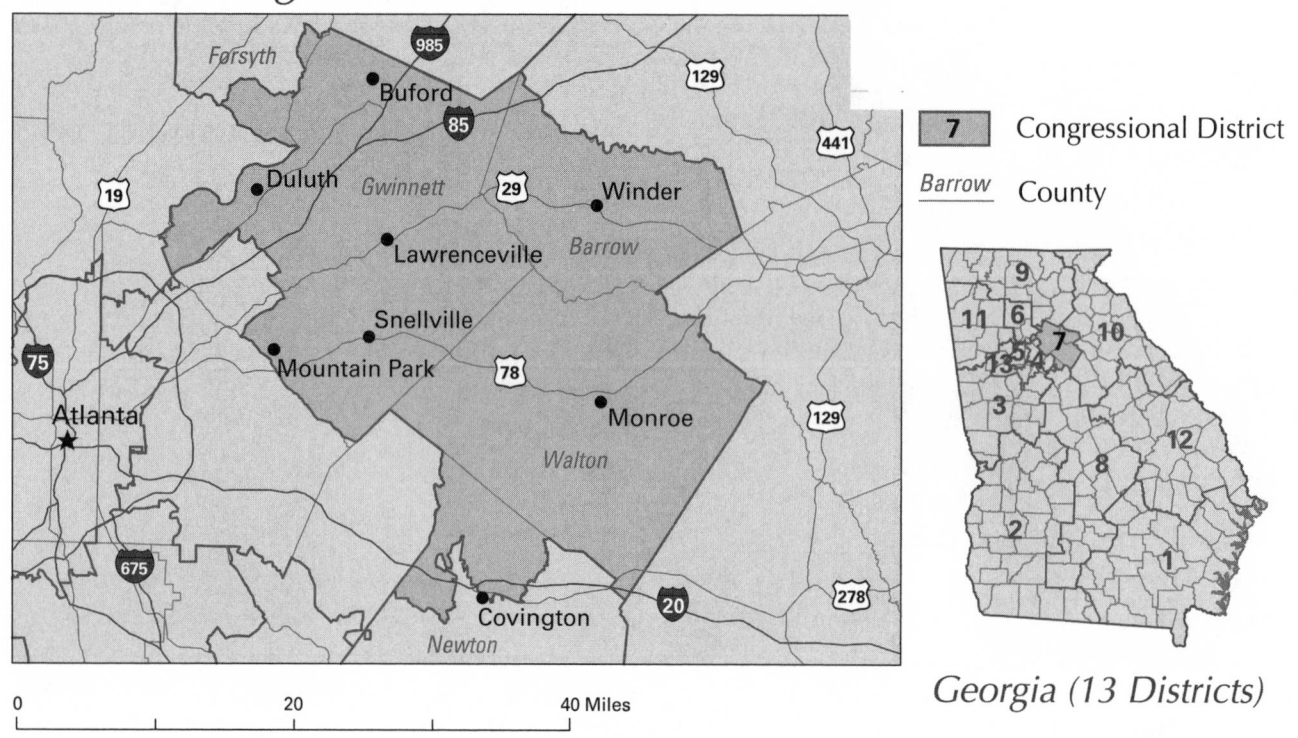

7 — Congressional District
Barrow — County

Georgia (13 Districts)

Congressional District 8

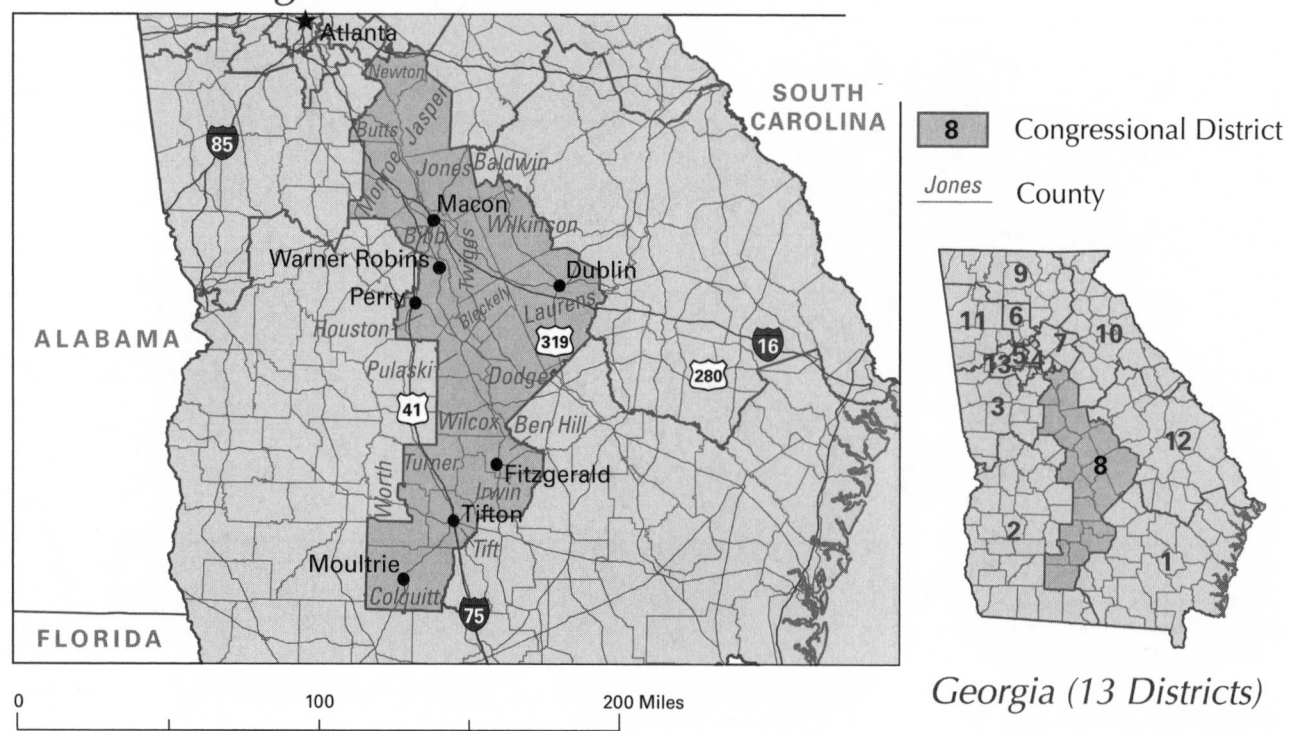

8 — Congressional District
Jones — County

Georgia (13 Districts)

Congressional District 9

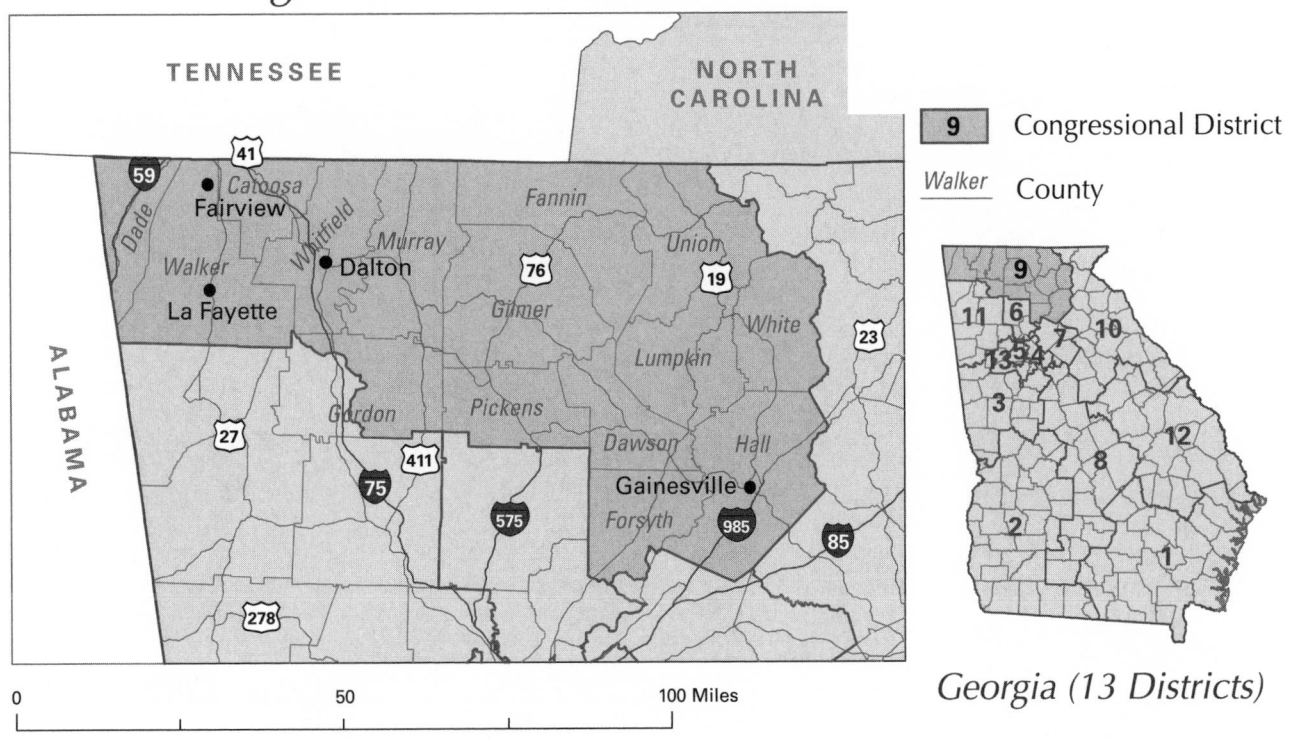

Georgia (13 Districts)

Congressional District 10

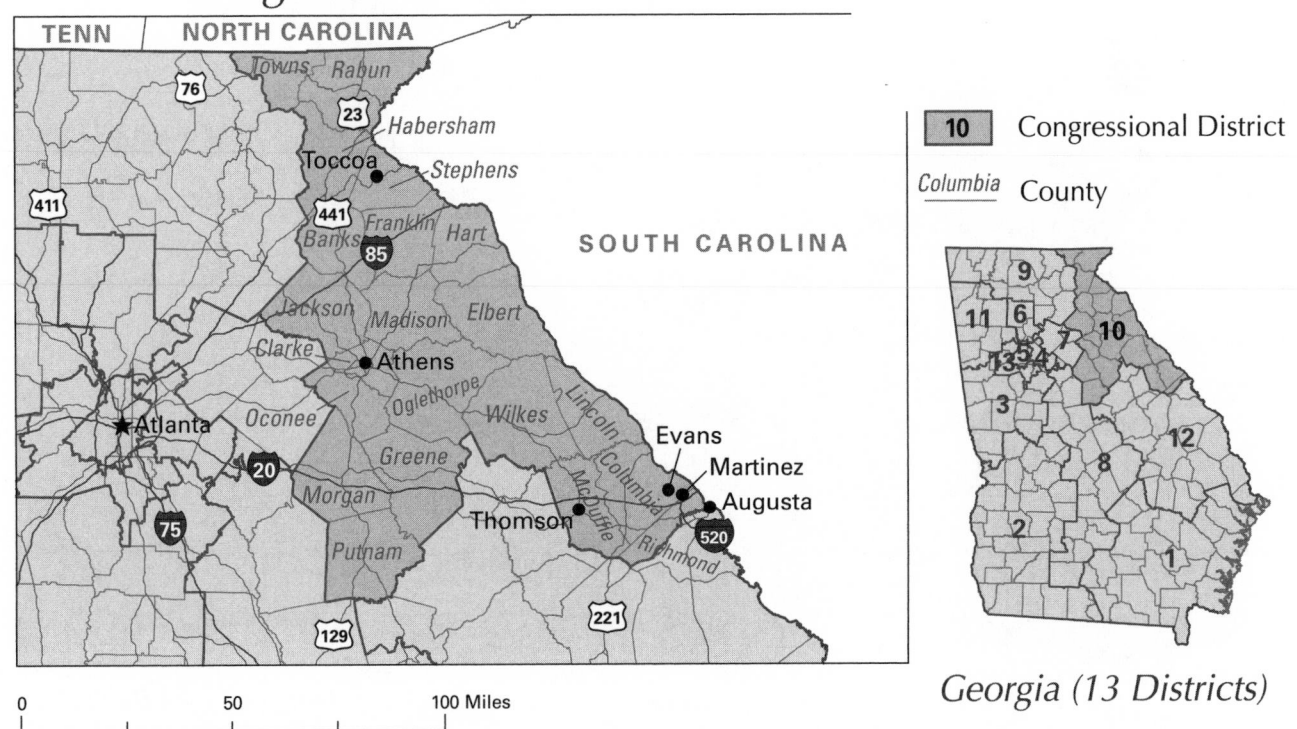

Georgia (13 Districts)

Congressional District 11

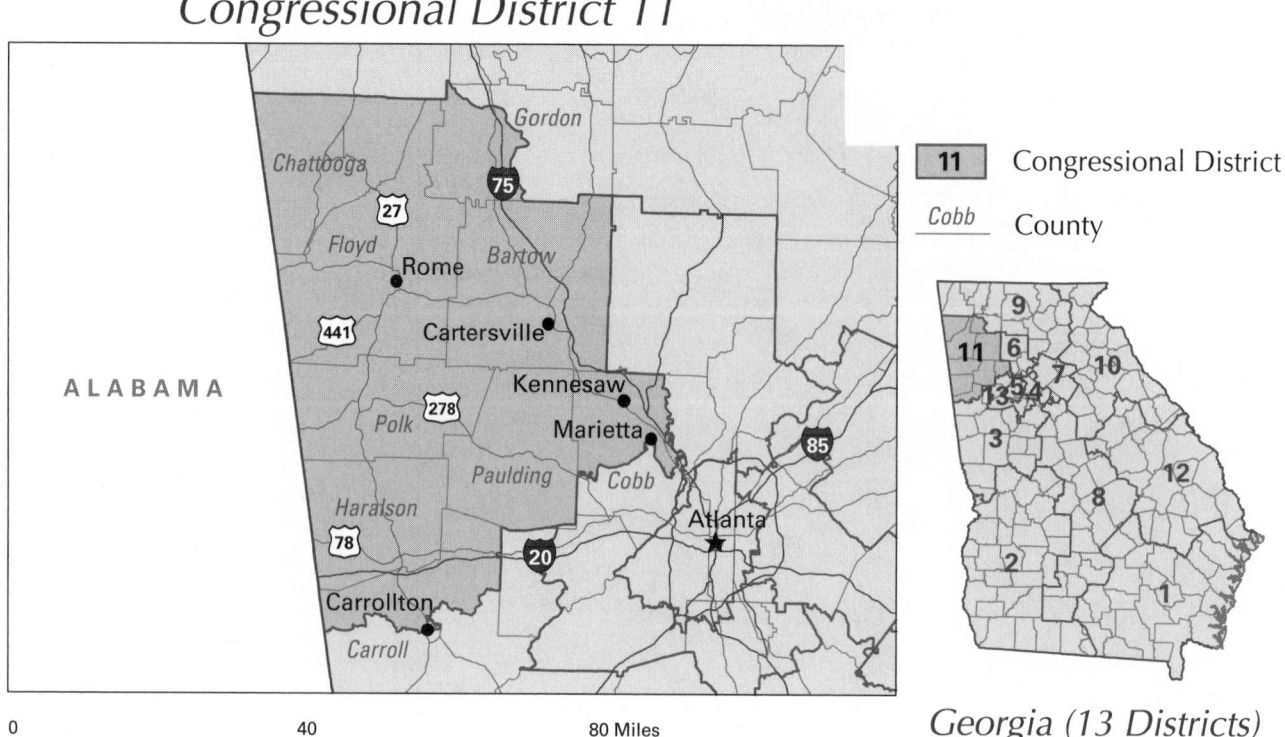

11 Congressional District
Cobb County

Georgia (13 Districts)

Congressional District 12

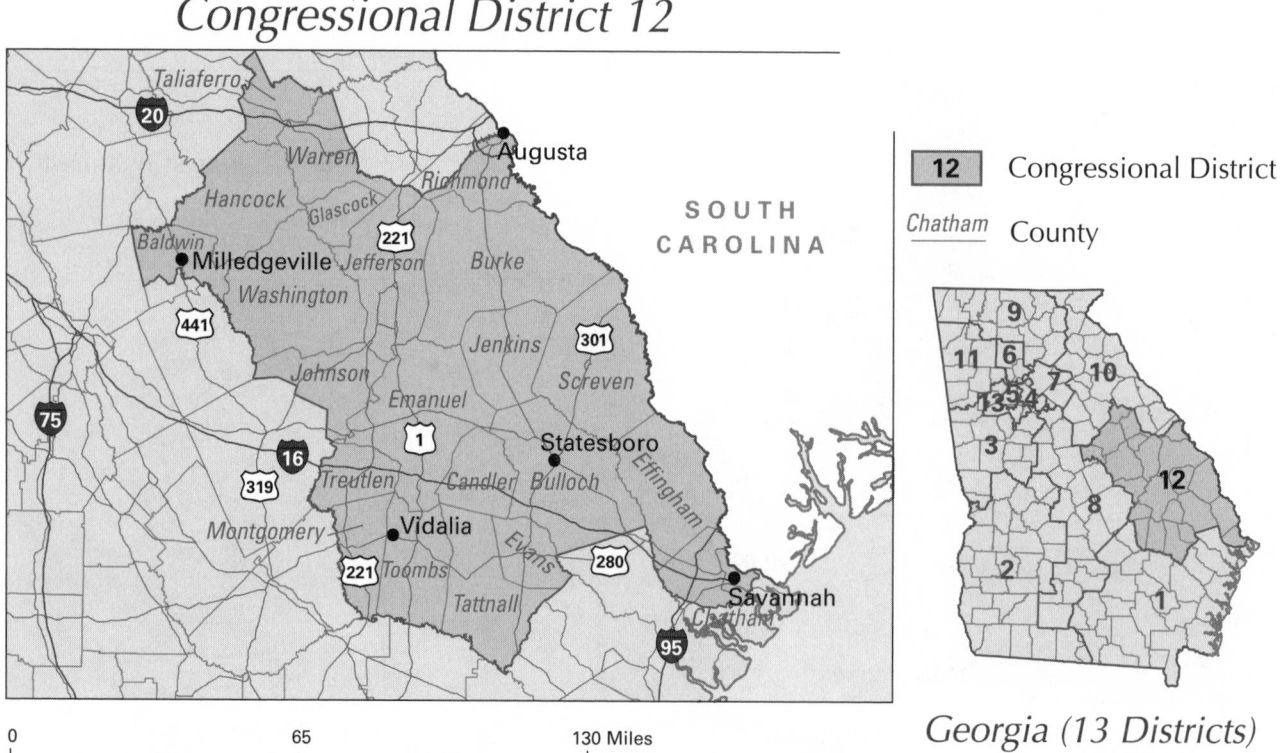

12 Congressional District
Chatham County

Georgia (13 Districts)

Congressional District 13

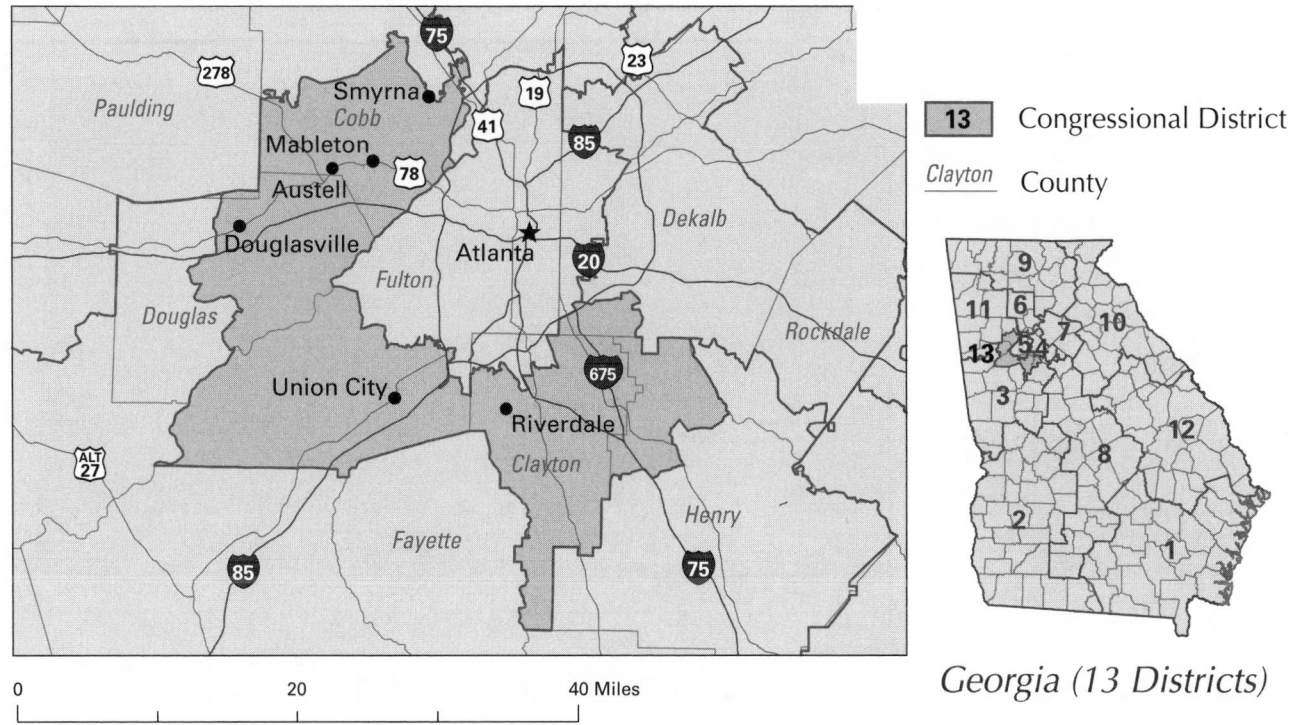

13 Congressional District

Clayton County

Georgia (13 Districts)

Hawaii Congressional Districts — 2 Districts Total

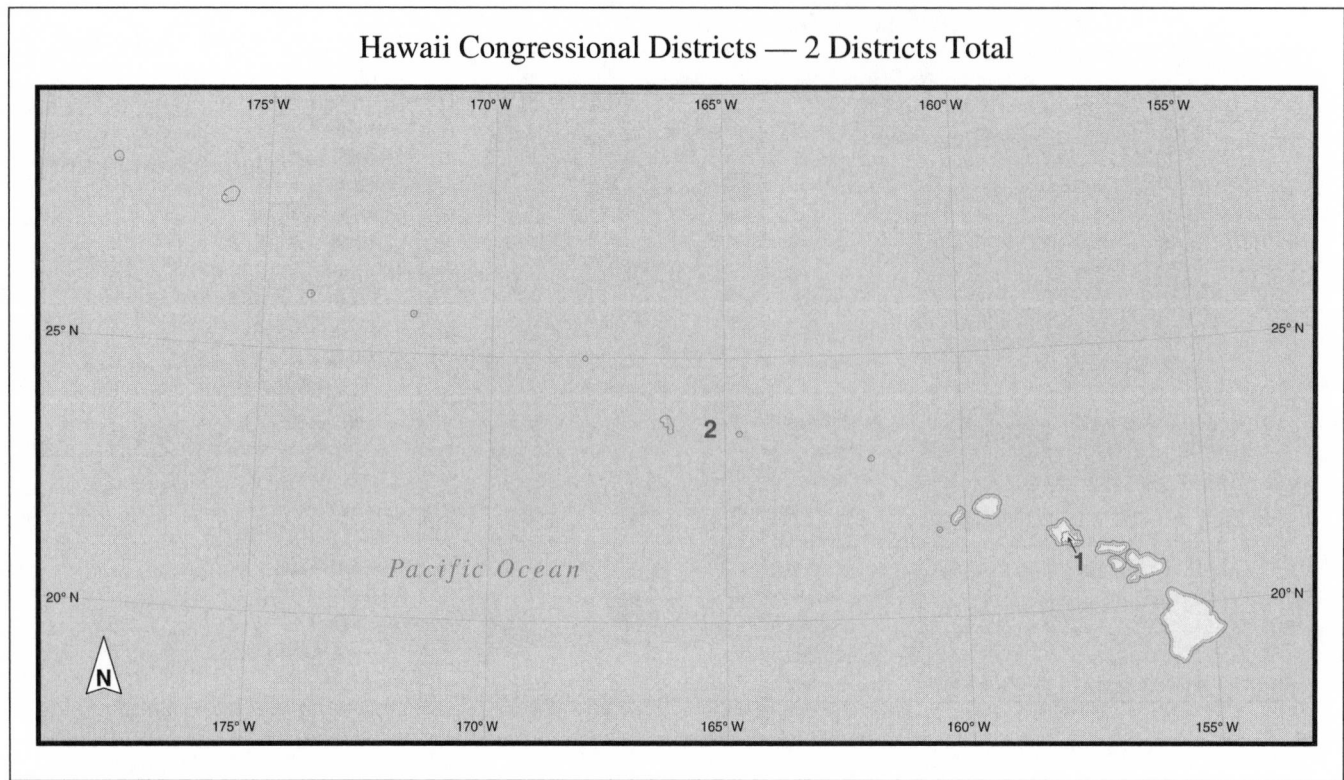

HAWAII—110th CONGRESSIONAL DISTRICTS BY COUNTIES

County	Congressional District
Hawaii	2
Honolulu	1, 2
Kalawao	2
Kauai	2
Maui	2

Congressional District 1

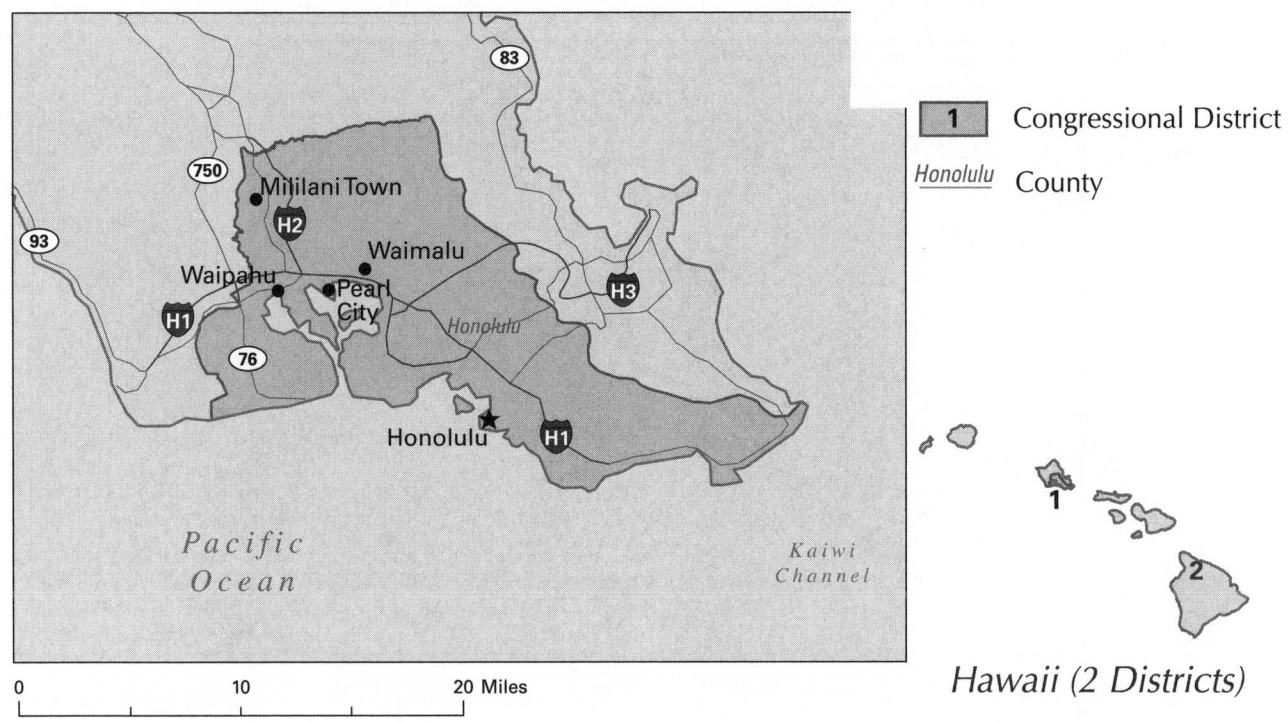

Mililani Town
Waimalu
Waipahu
Pearl City
Honolulu

Honolulu

Pacific Ocean

Kaiwi Channel

0   10   20 Miles

1 Congressional District
Honolulu County

Hawaii (2 Districts)

Congressional District 2

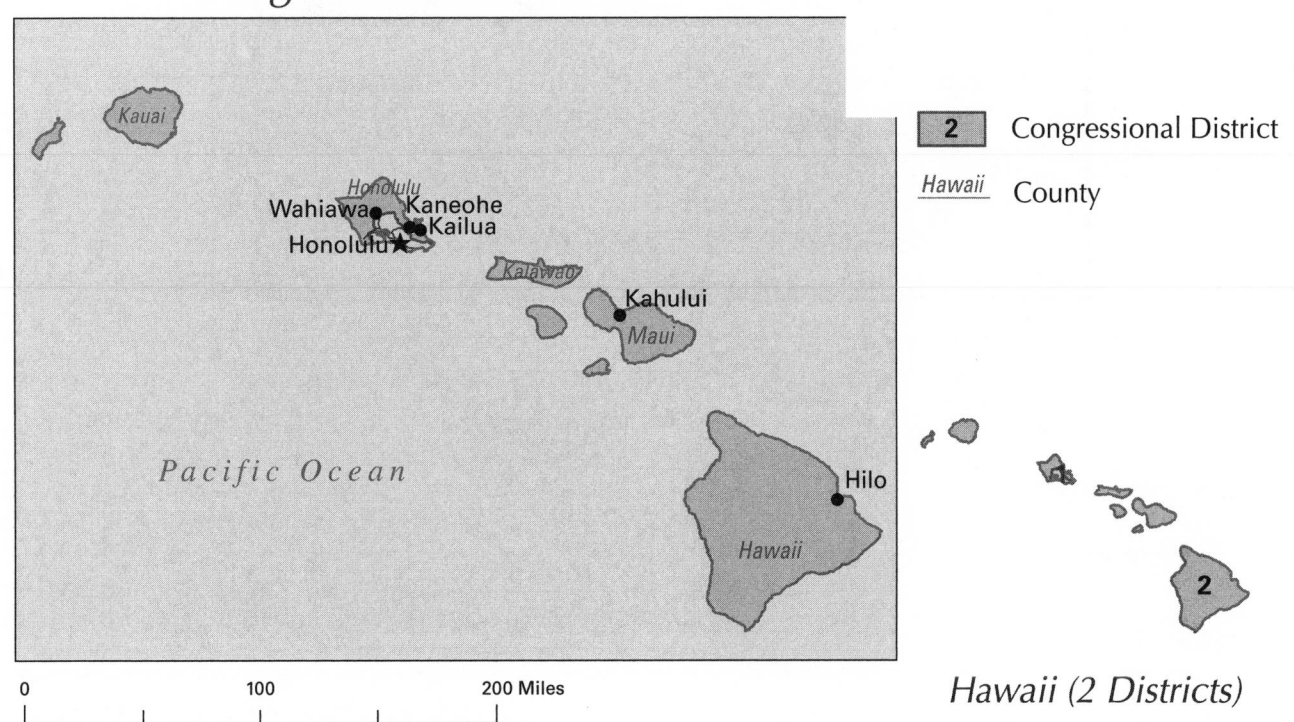

Kauai

Honolulu
Wahiawa Kaneohe
Honolulu Kailua

Kalawao

Kahului
Maui

Pacific Ocean

Hilo

Hawaii

0   100   200 Miles

2 Congressional District
Hawaii County

Hawaii (2 Districts)

Idaho Congressional Districts — 2 Districts Total

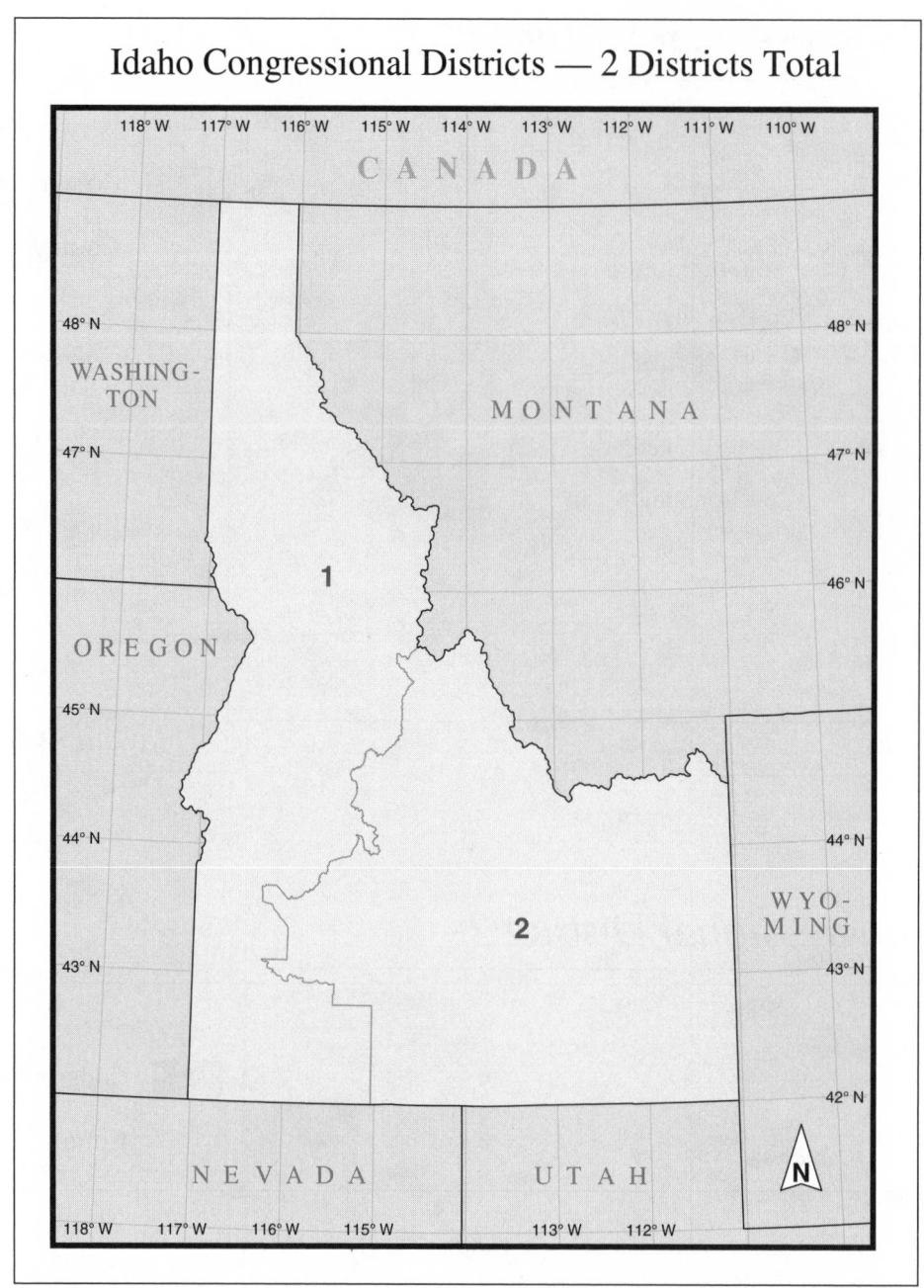

IDAHO—110th CONGRESSIONAL DISTRICTS BY COUNTIES

County	Congressional District	County	Congressional District	County	Congressional District
Ada	1, 2	Cassia	2	Lewis	1
Adams	1	Clark	2	Lincoln	2
Bannock	2	Clearwater	1	Madison	2
Bear Lake	2	Custer	2	Minidoka	2
Benewah	1	Elmore	2	Nez Perce	1
Bingham	2	Franklin	2	Oneida	2
Blaine	2	Fremont	2	Owyhee	1
Boise	1	Gem	1	Payette	1
Bonner	1	Gooding	2	Power	2
Bonneville	2	Idaho	1	Shoshone	1
Boundary	1	Jefferson	2	Teton	2
Butte	2	Jerome	2	Twin Falls	2
Camas	2	Kootenai	1	Valley	1
Canyon	1	Latah	1	Washington	1
Caribou	2	Lemhi	2		

Congressional District 1

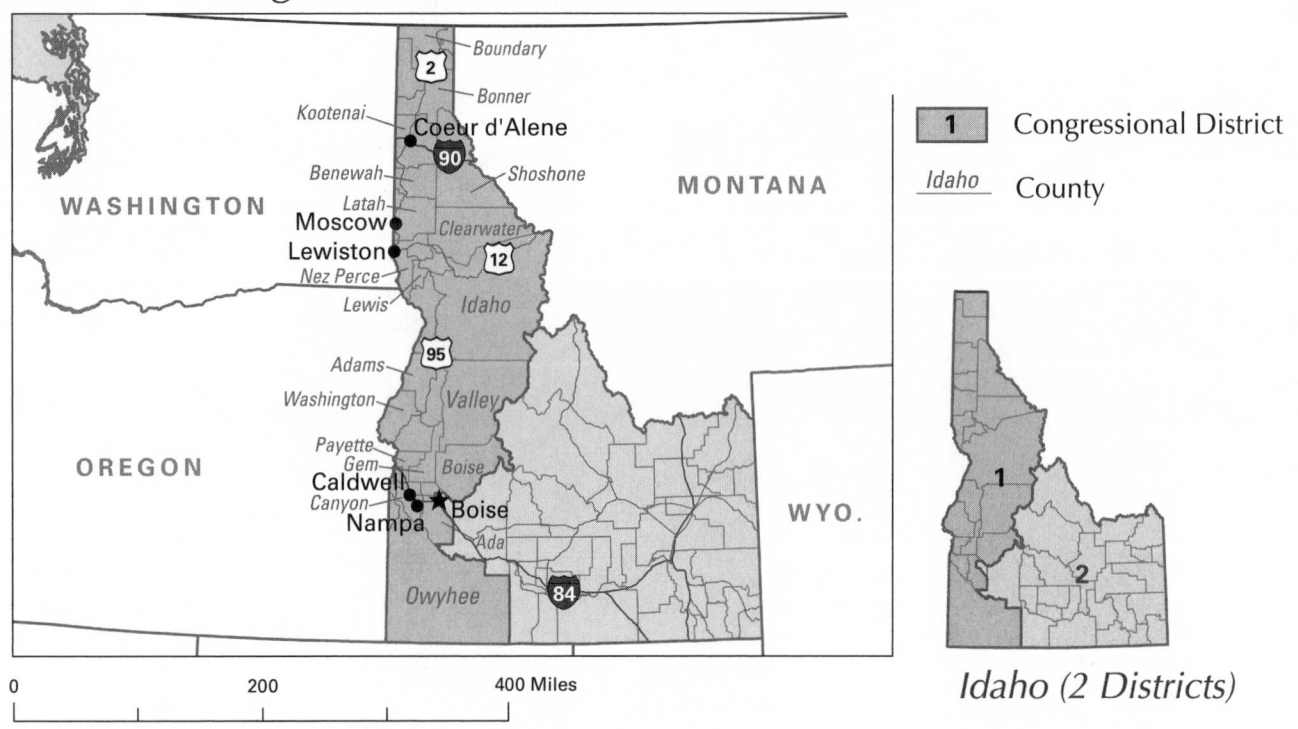

Congressional District 2

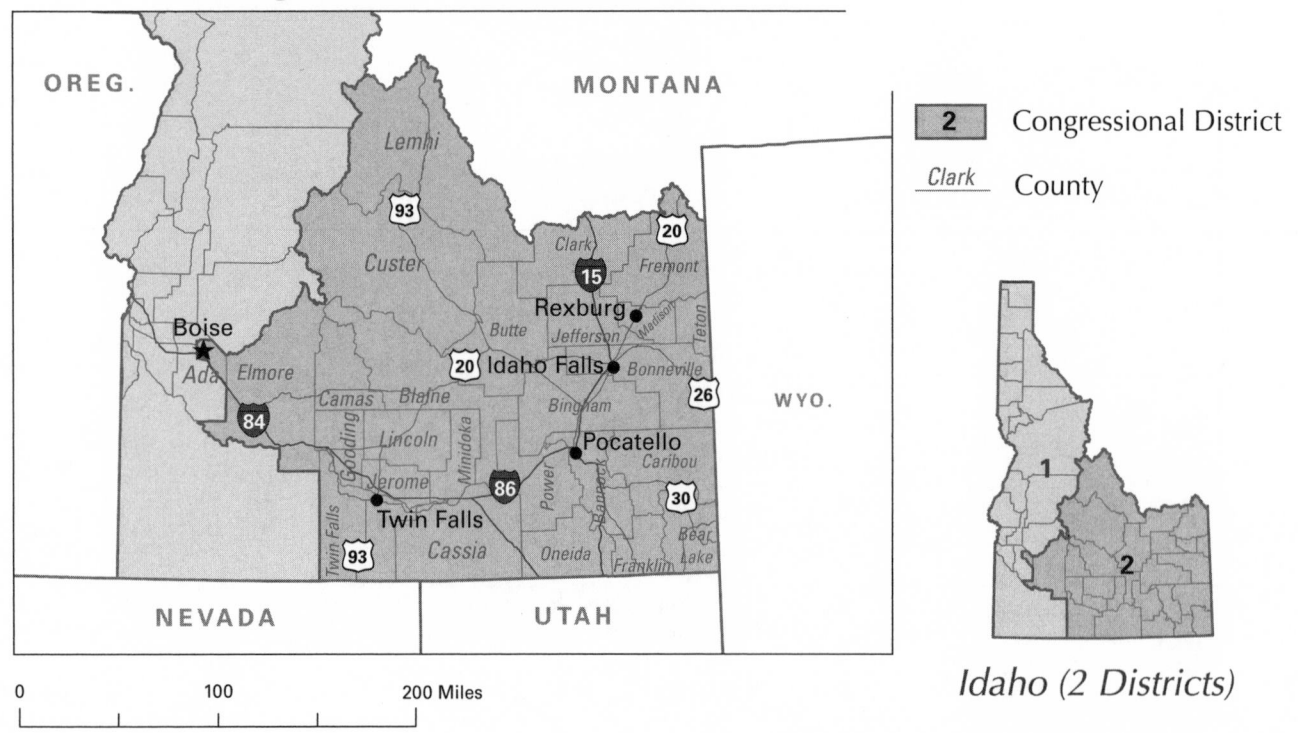

Illinois Congressional Districts — 19 Districts Total

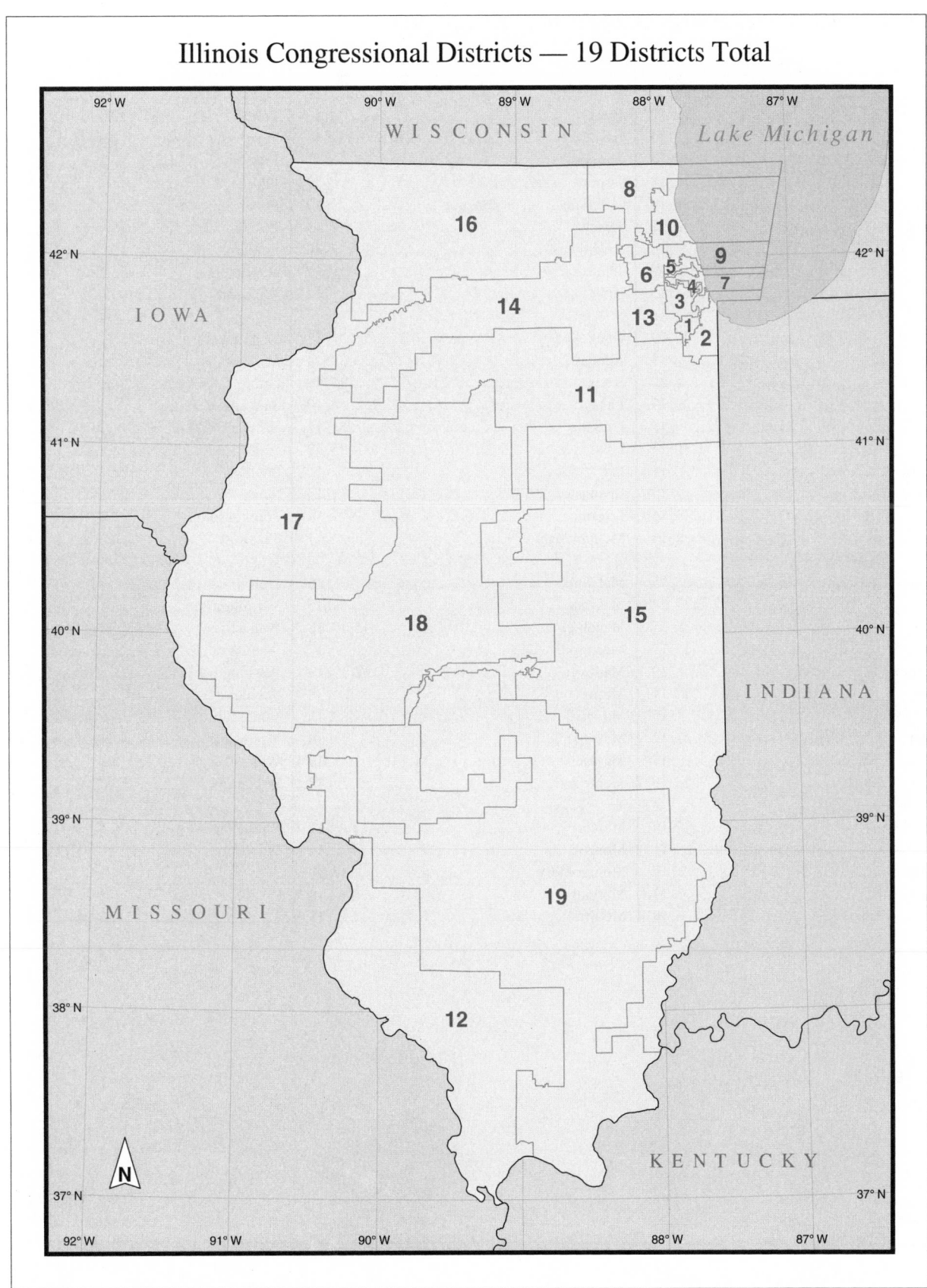

ILLINOIS — 110th CONGRESSIONAL DISTRICTS BY COUNTIES

County	Congressional District	County	Congressional District	County	Congressional District
Adams	17, 18	Henderson	17	Ogle	16
Alexander	12	Henry	14, 17	Peoria	18
Bond	19	Iroquois	15	Perry	12
Boone	16	Jackson	12	Piatt	15
Brown	18	Jasper	19	Pike	17, 18
Bureau	11, 14, 18	Jefferson	19	Pope	19
Calhoun	17	Jersey	17, 19	Pulaski	12
Carroll	16	Jo Daviess	16	Putnam	18
Cass	18	Johnson	19	Randolph	12
Champaign	15	Kane	14	Richland	19
Christian	17, 19	Kankakee	11	Rock Island	17
Clark	15	Kendall	14	St. Clair	12
Clay	19	Knox	17, 18	Saline	15, 19
Clinton	19	Lake	8, 10	Sangamon	17–19
Coles	15	La Salle	11	Schuyler	18
Cook	1–10, 13	Lawrence	15, 19	Scott	18
Crawford	15	Lee	14	Shelby	17, 19
Cumberland	15	Livingston	11, 15	Stark	18
DeKalb	14, 16	Logan	18	Stephenson	16
De Witt	15	McDonough	17	Tazewell	18
Douglas	15	McHenry	8, 16	Union	12
DuPage	6, 13, 14	McLean	11, 15	Vermilion	15
Edgar	15	Macon	15, 17, 18	Wabash	15, 19
Edwards	15, 19	Macoupin	17	Warren	17
Effingham	19	Madison	12, 17, 19	Washington	19
Fayette	17, 19	Marion	19	Wayne	19
Ford	15	Marshall	18	White	15, 19
Franklin	12	Mason	18	Whiteside	14, 16, 17
Fulton	17	Massac	19	Will	2, 11, 13
Gallatin	15, 19	Menard	18	Williamson	12, 19
Greene	17, 19	Mercer	17	Winnebago	16
Grundy	11	Monroe	12	Woodford	11, 18
Hamilton	19	Montgomery	17, 19		
Hancock	17	Morgan	18		
Hardin	19	Moultrie	15		

Congressional District 1

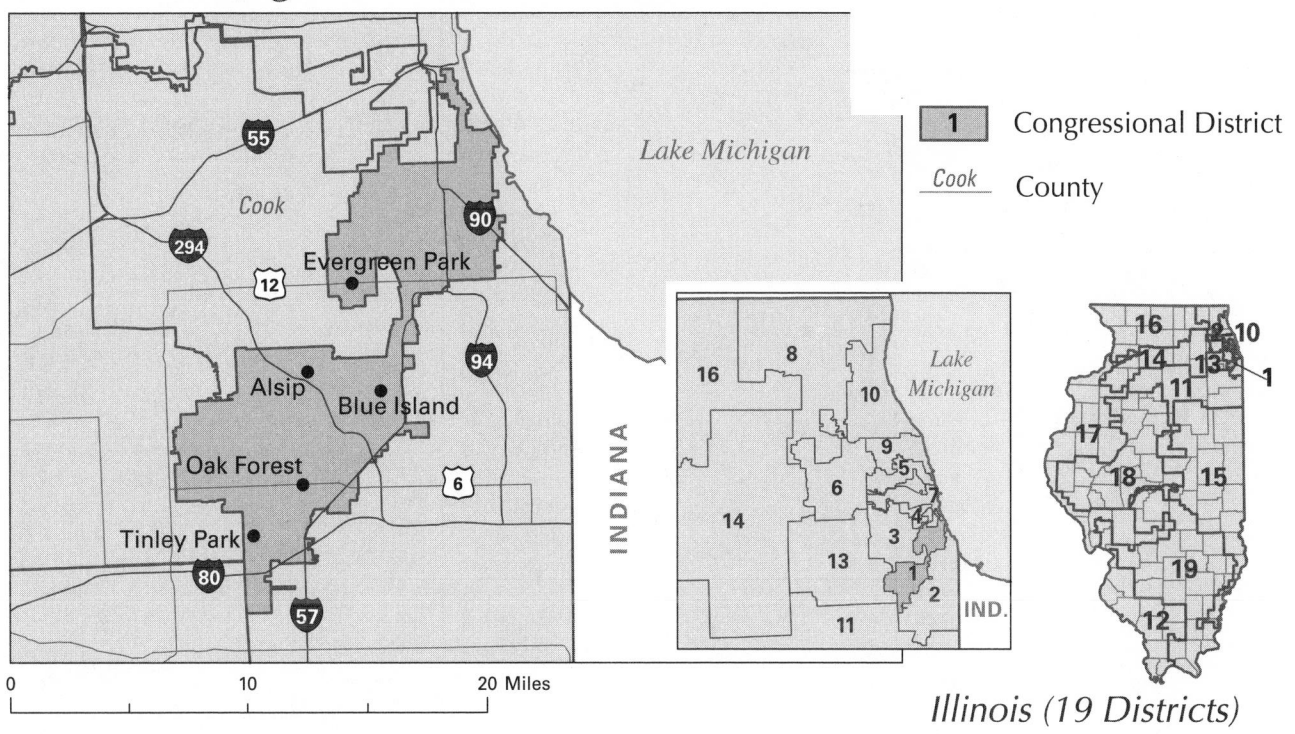

Illinois (19 Districts)

Congressional District 2

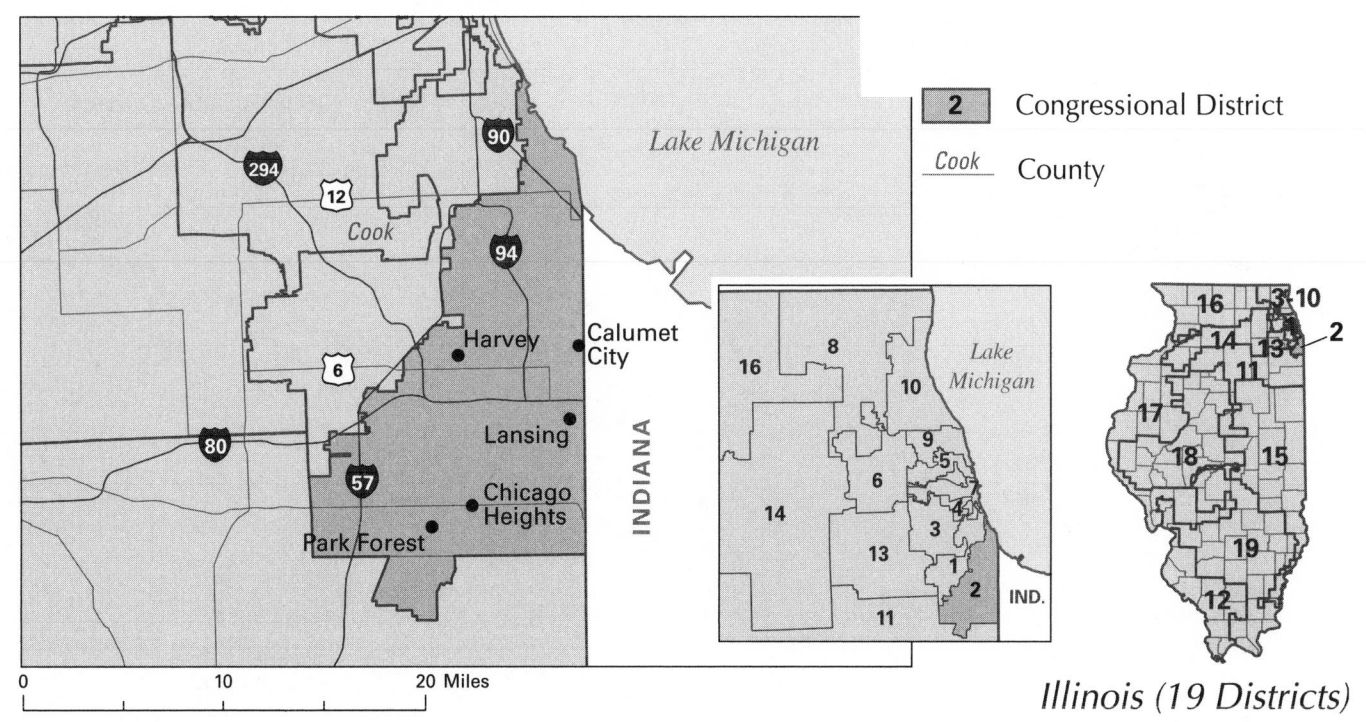

Illinois (19 Districts)

Congressional District 3

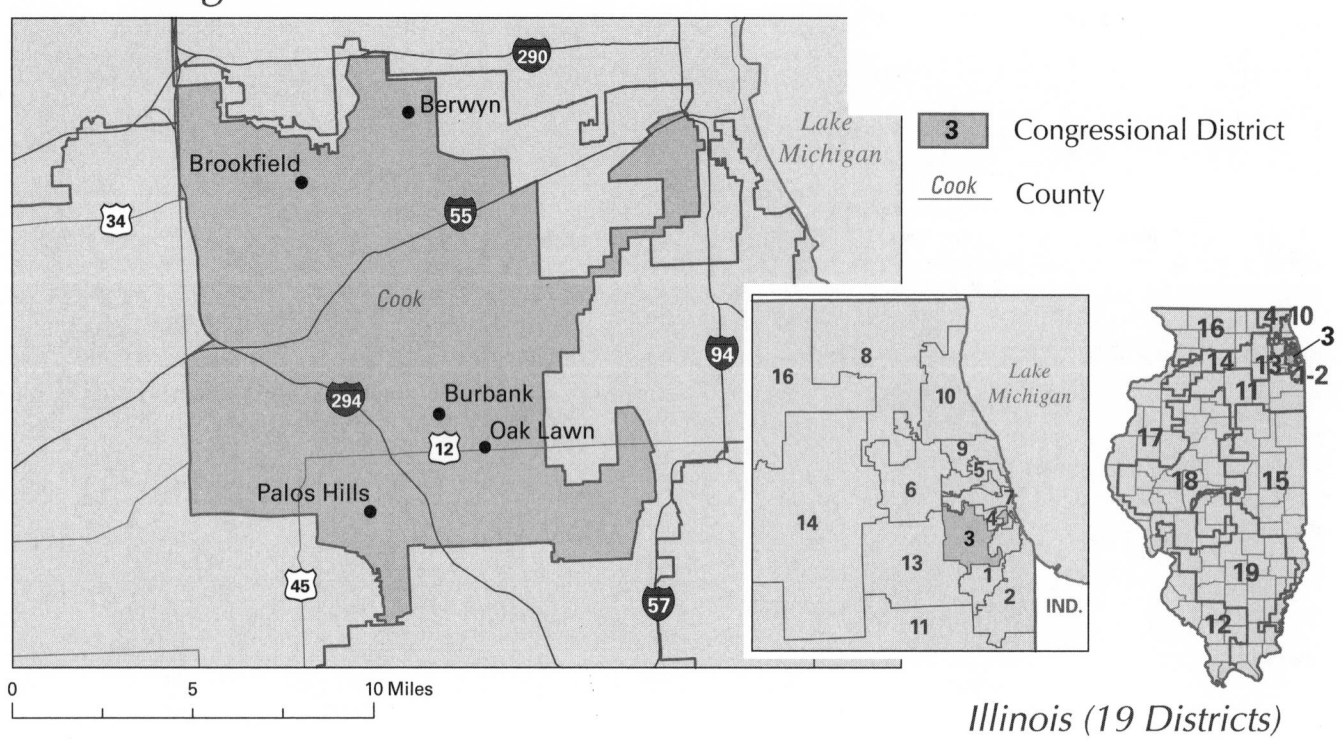

Illinois (19 Districts)

Congressional District 4

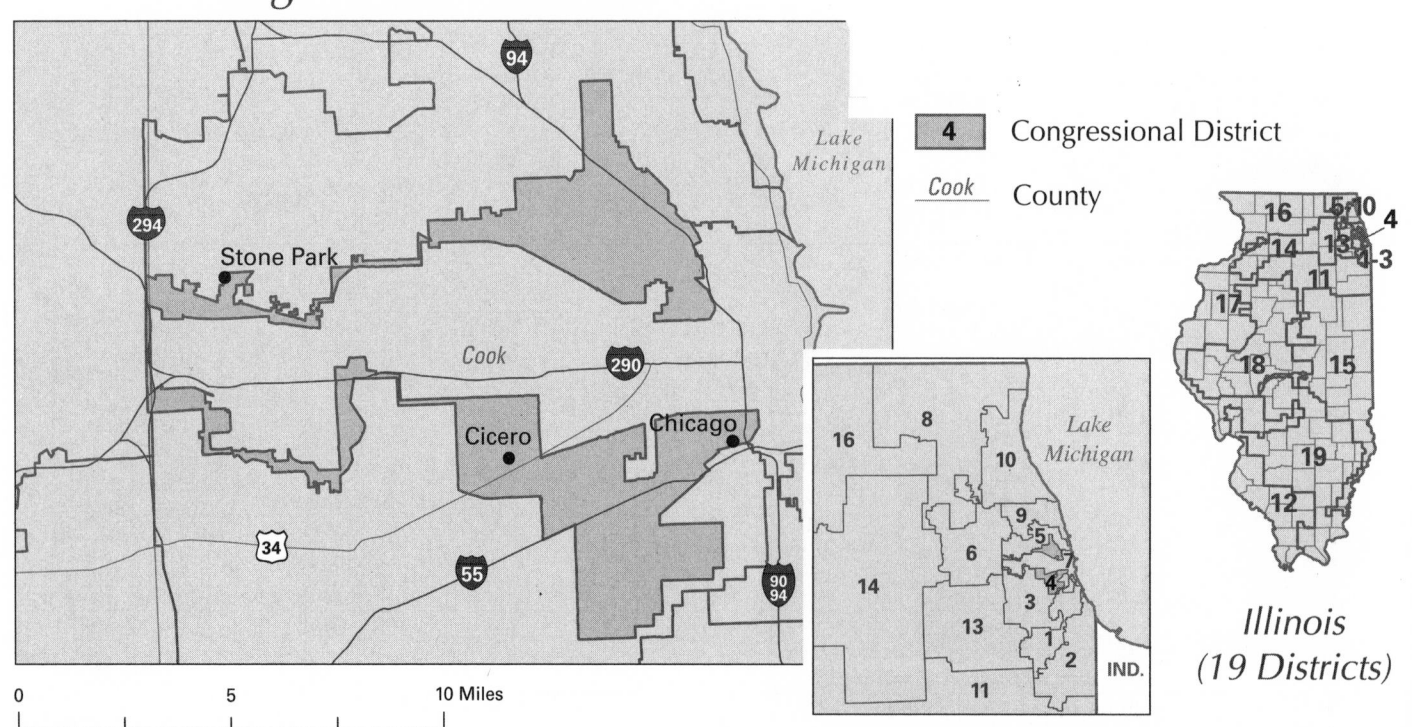

Illinois (19 Districts)

Congressional District 5

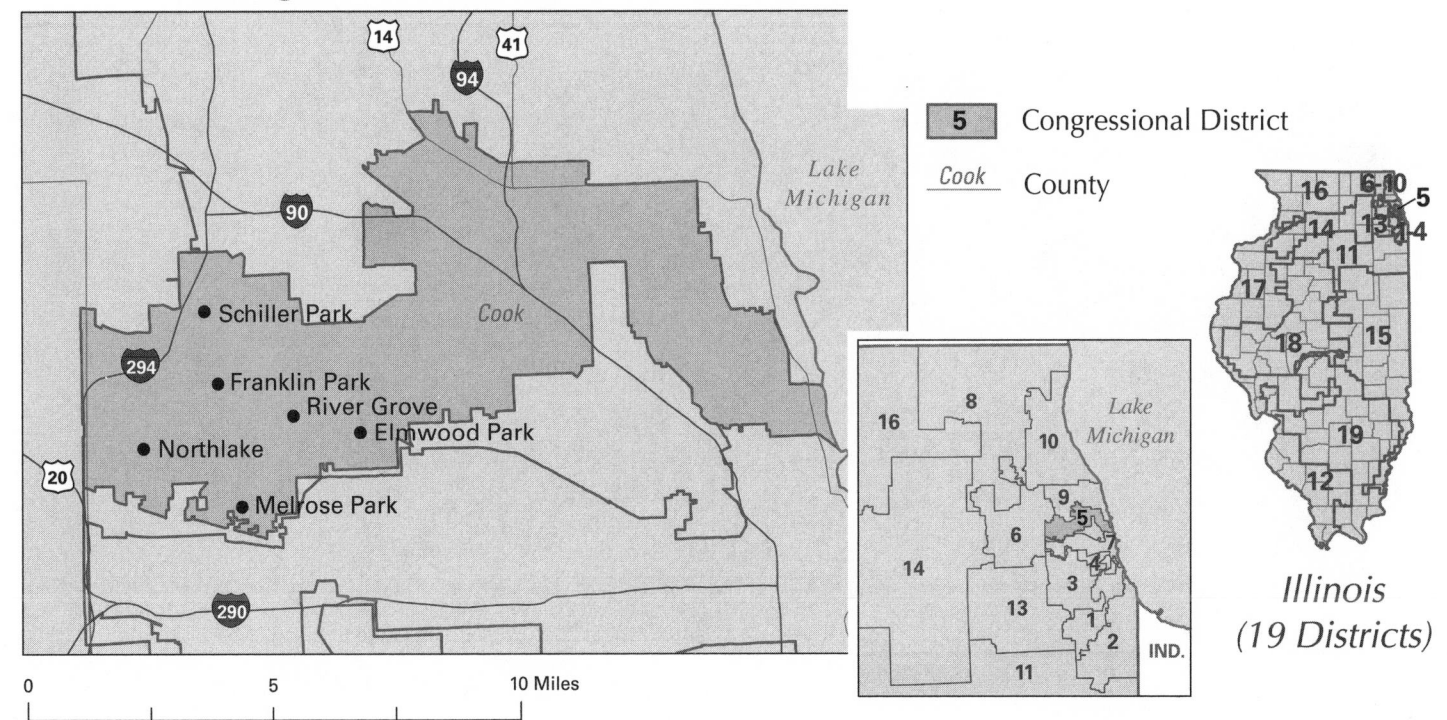

Congressional District 6

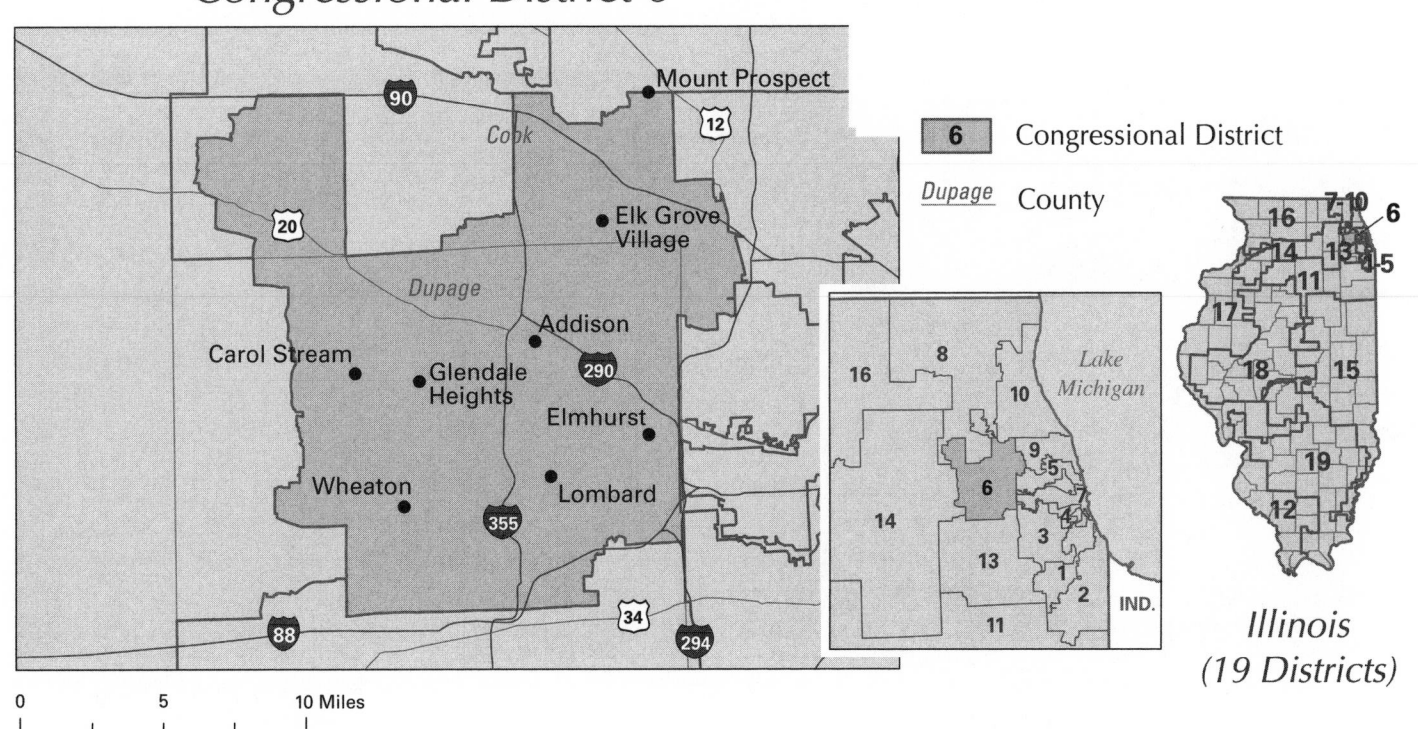

Congressional District 7

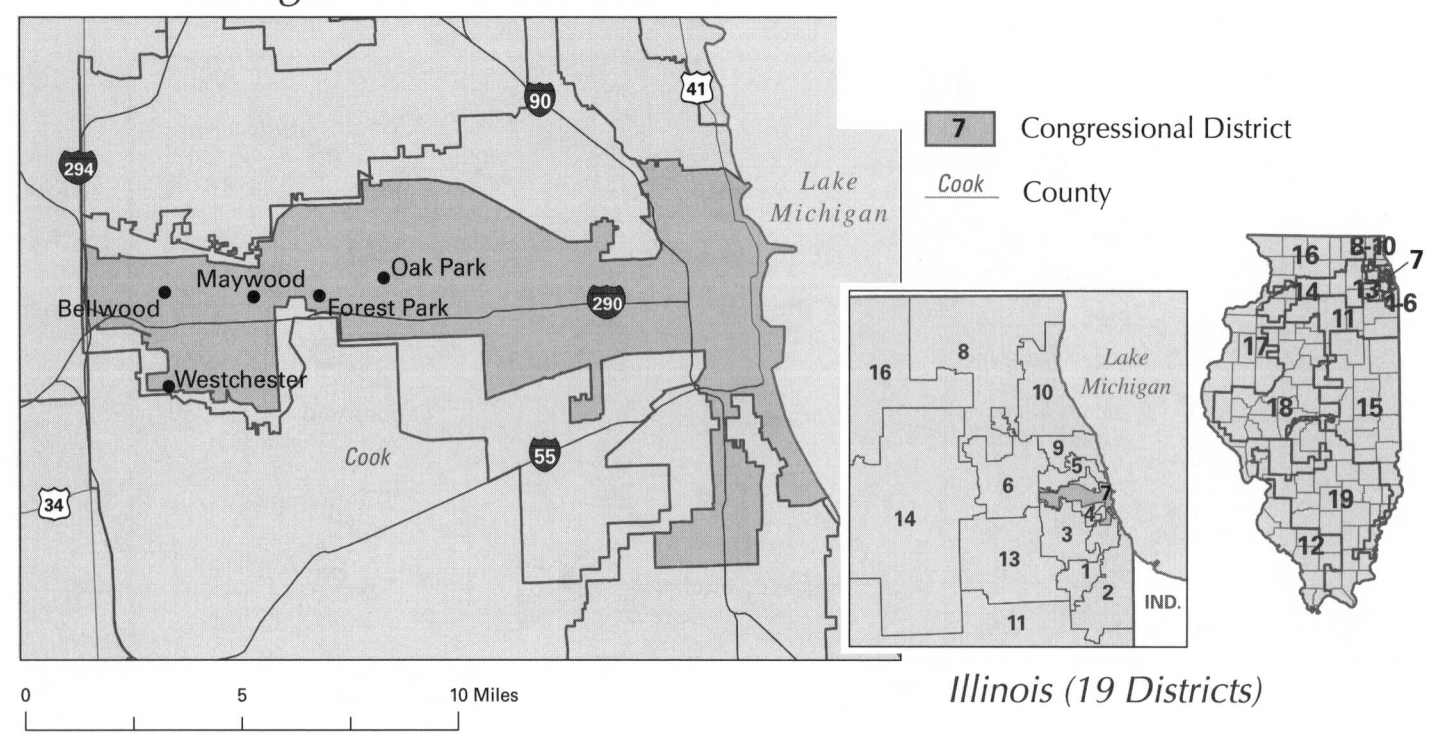

Illinois (19 Districts)

Congressional District 8

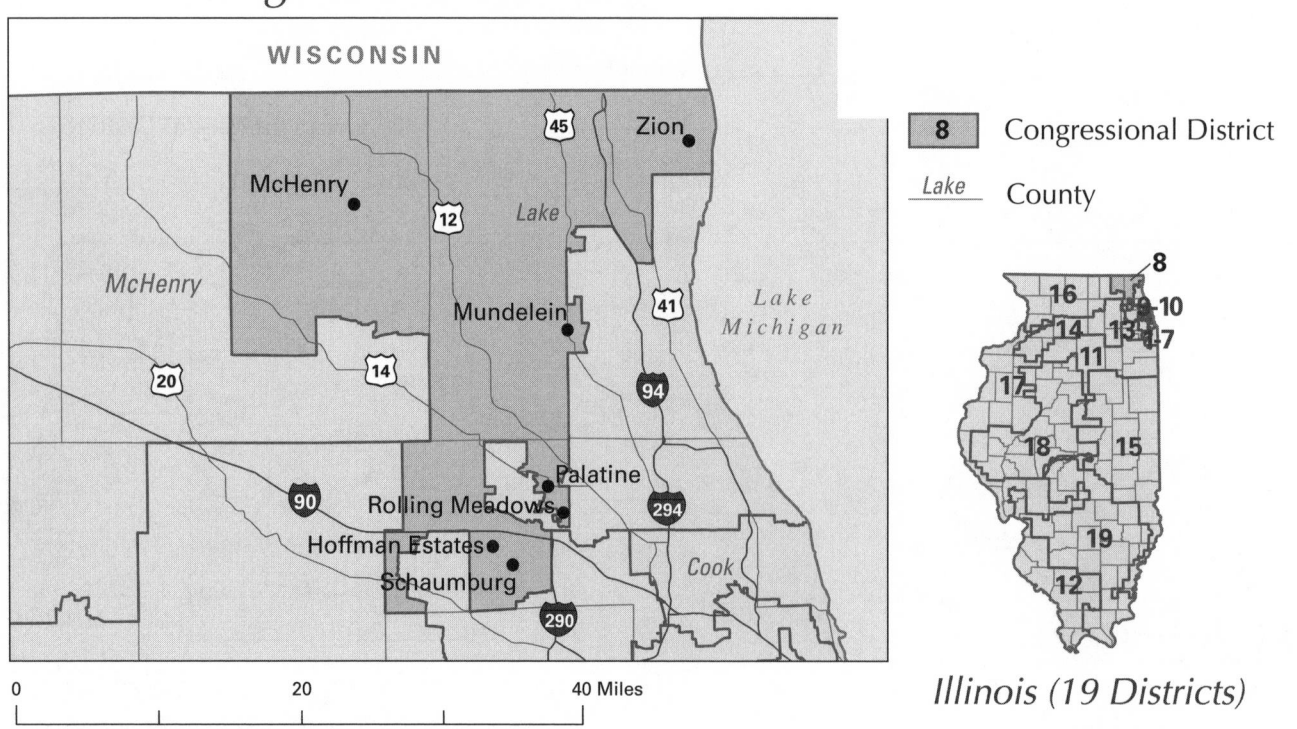

Illinois (19 Districts)

Congressional District 9

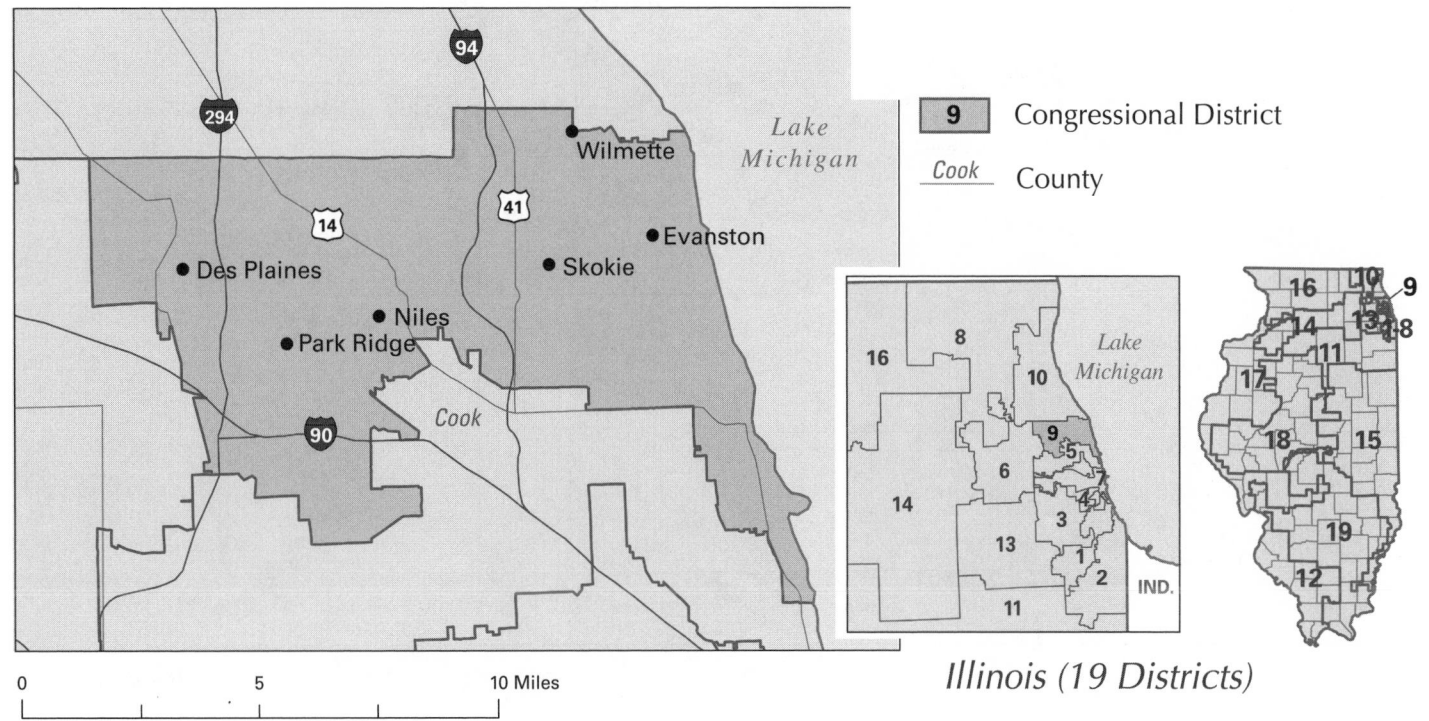

Illinois (19 Districts)

Congressional District 10

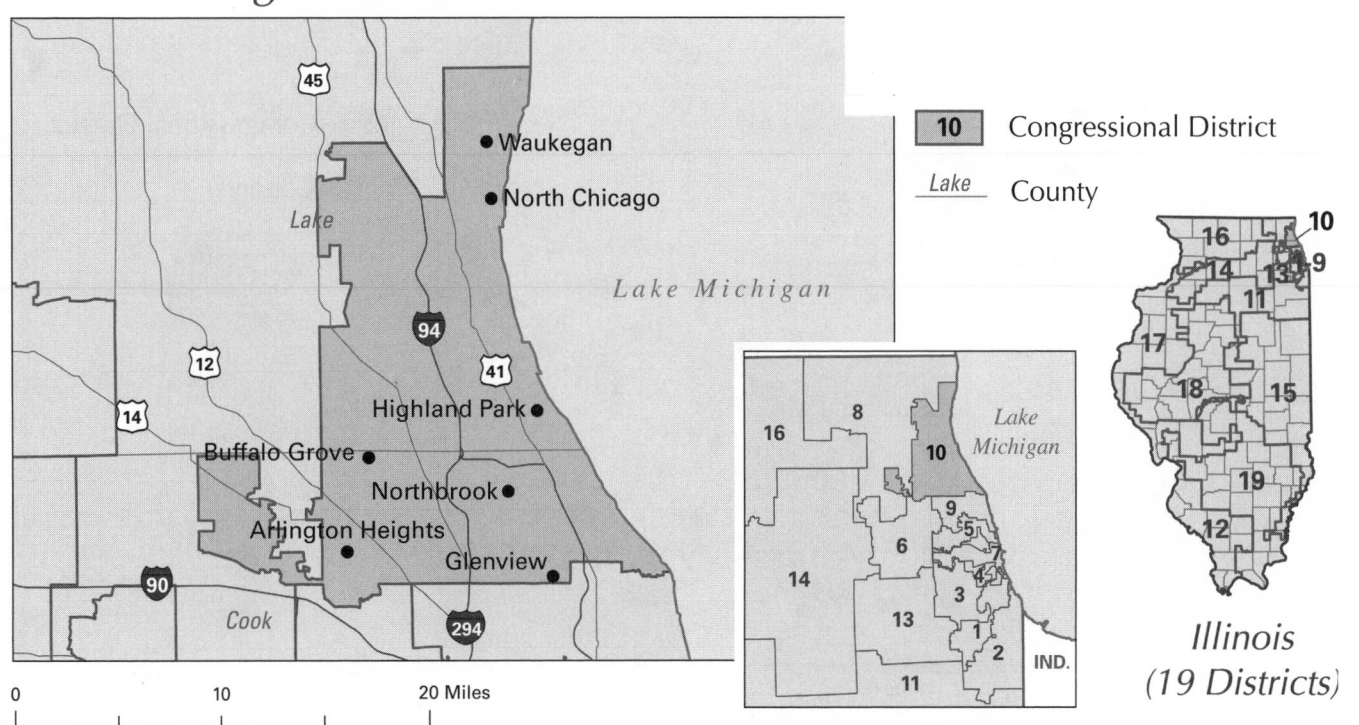

Illinois
(19 Districts)

Congressional District 11

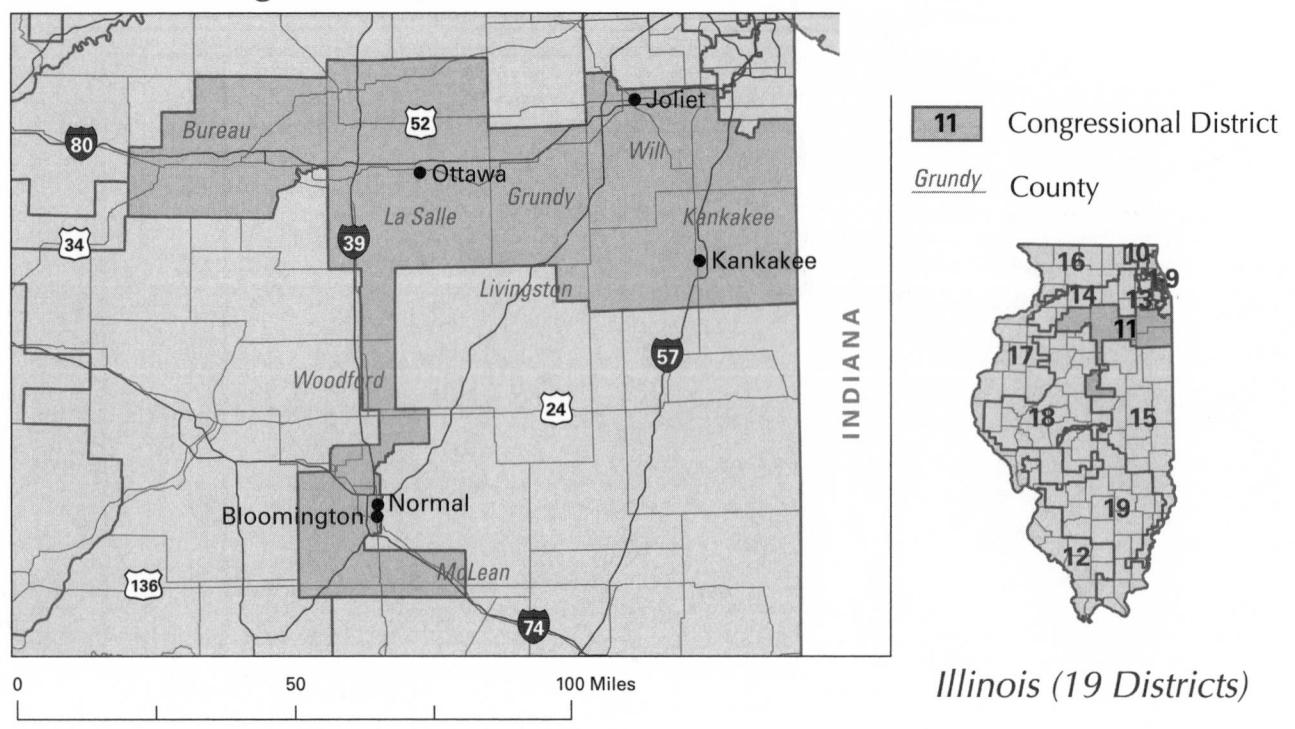

Illinois (19 Districts)

Congressional District 12

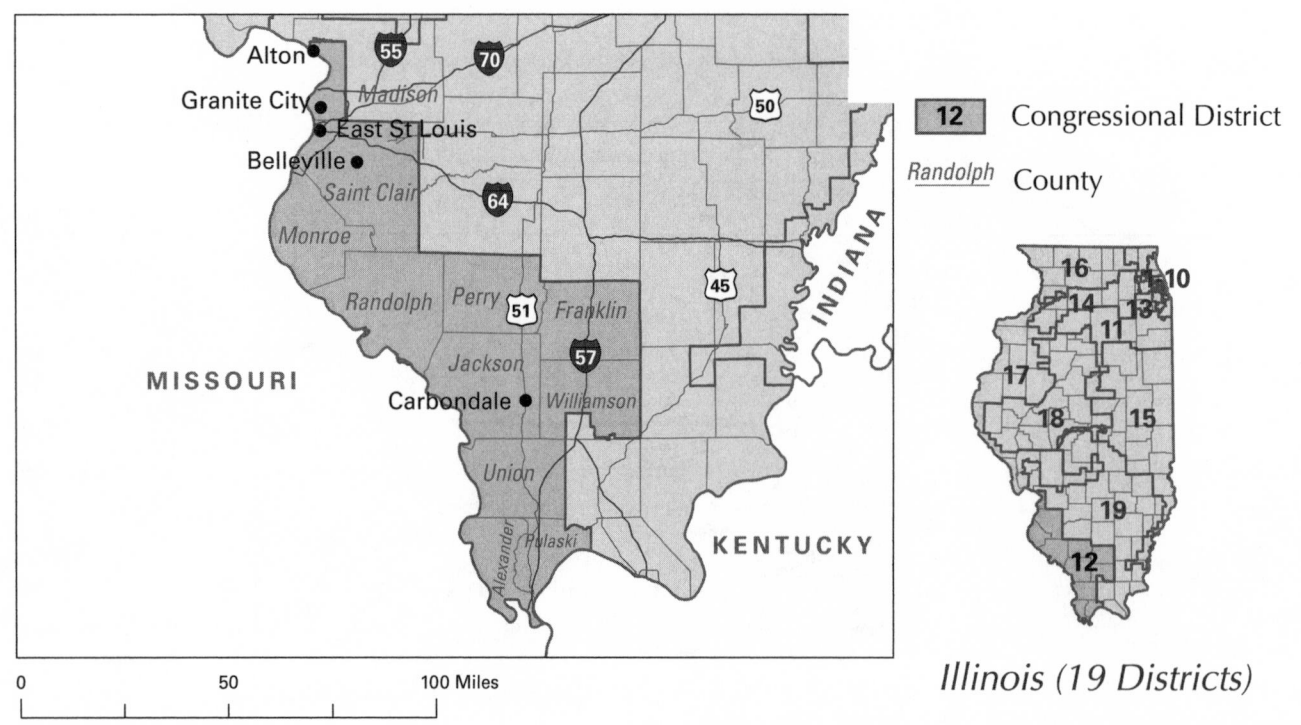

Illinois (19 Districts)

Congressional District 13

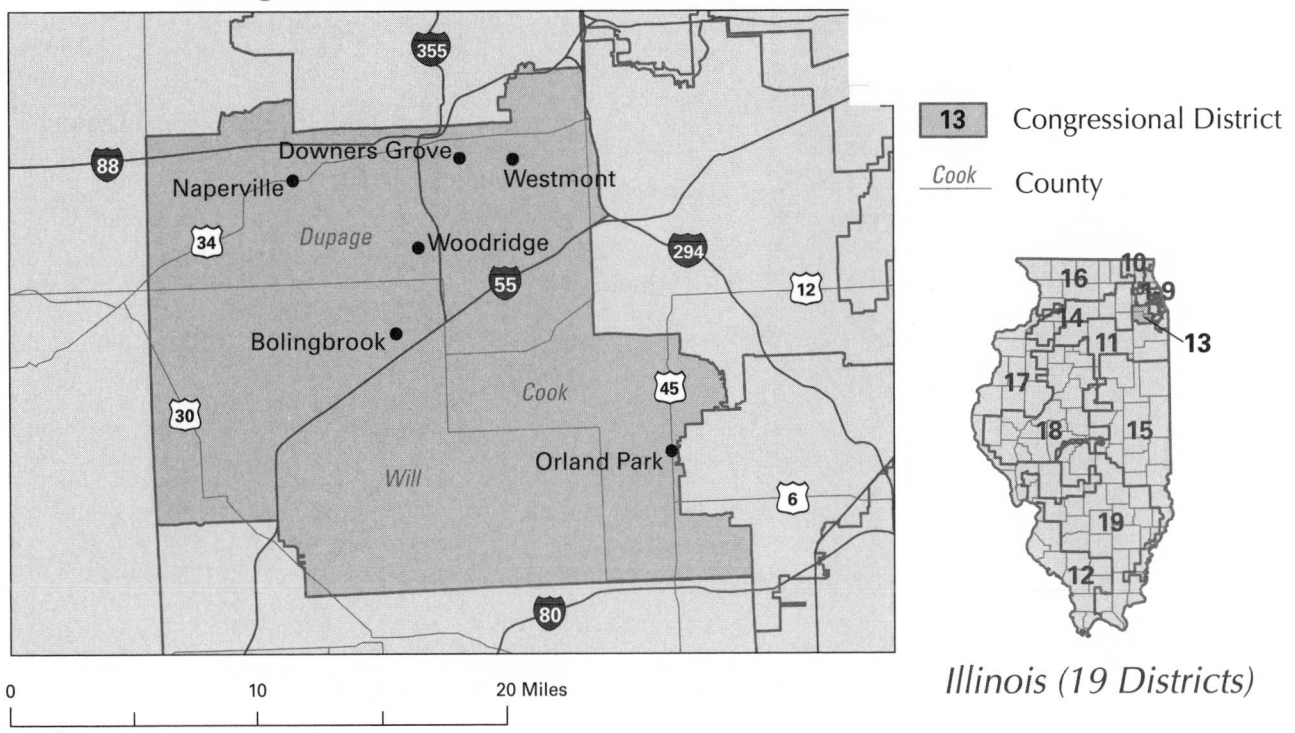

13 Congressional District

Cook County

Illinois (19 Districts)

0   10   20 Miles

Congressional District 14

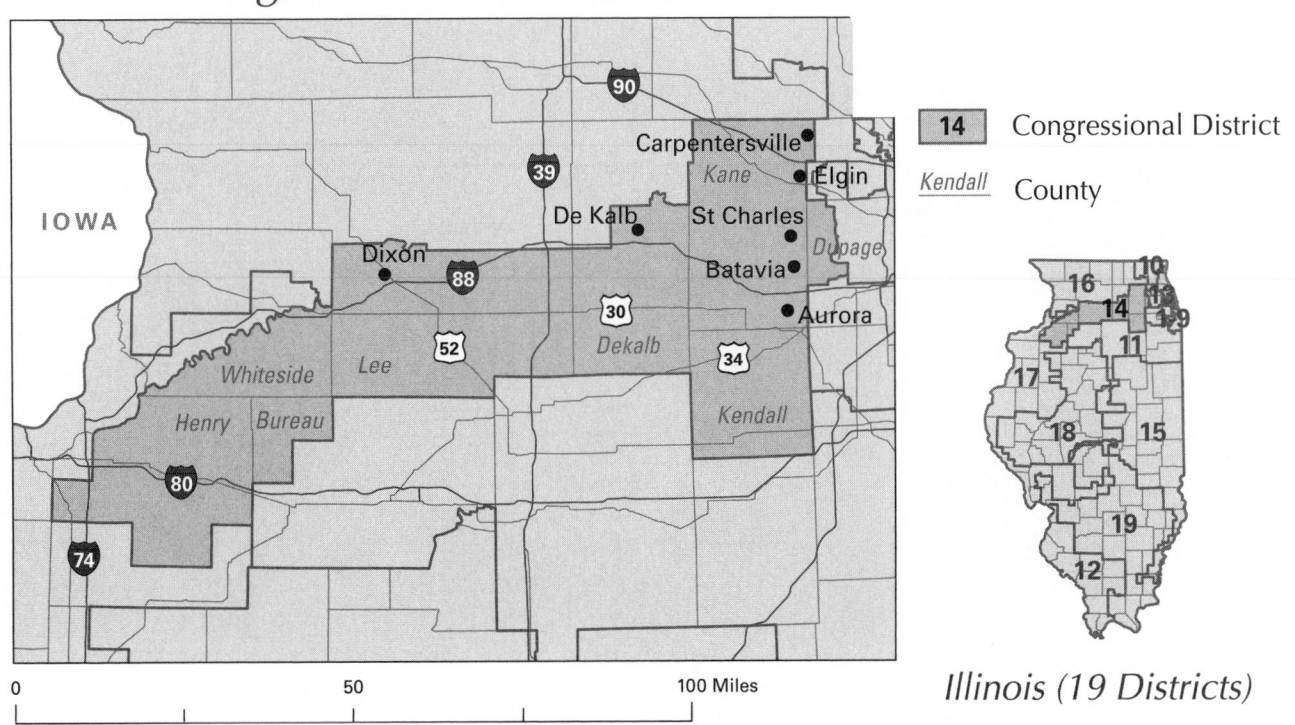

14 Congressional District

Kendall County

Illinois (19 Districts)

0   50   100 Miles

Congressional District 15

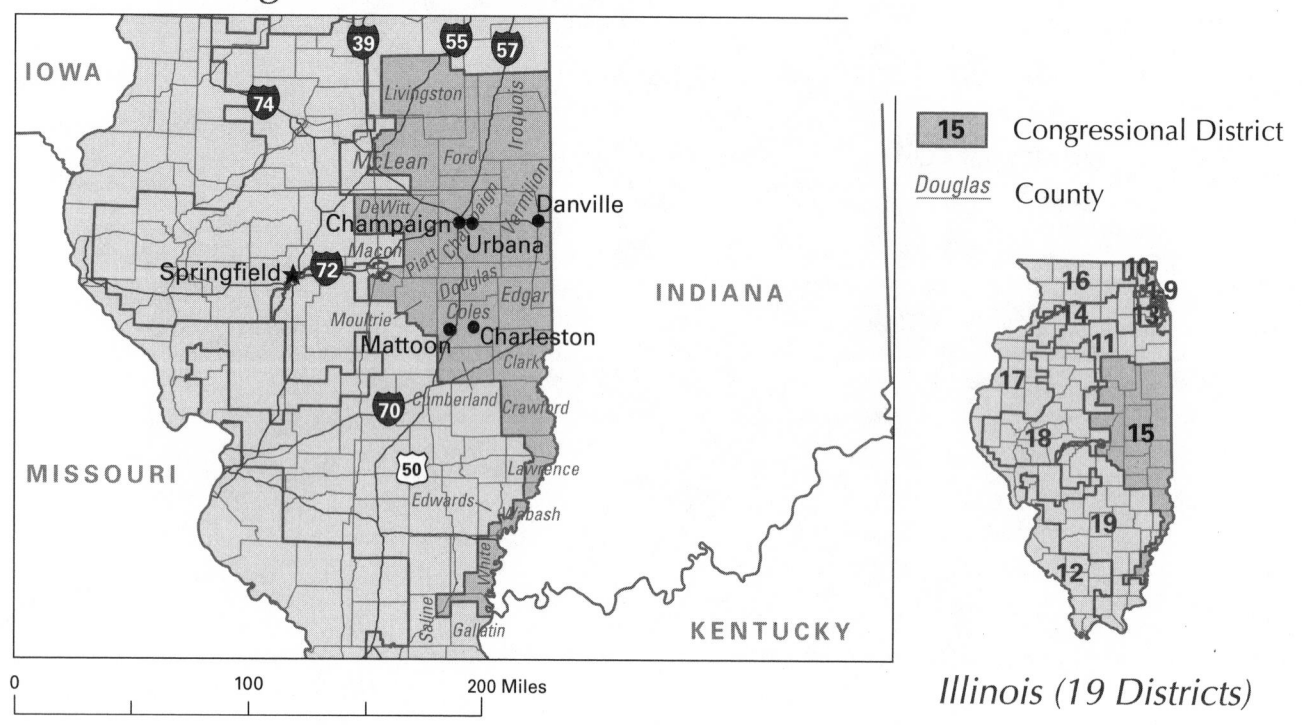

Illinois (19 Districts)

Congressional District 16

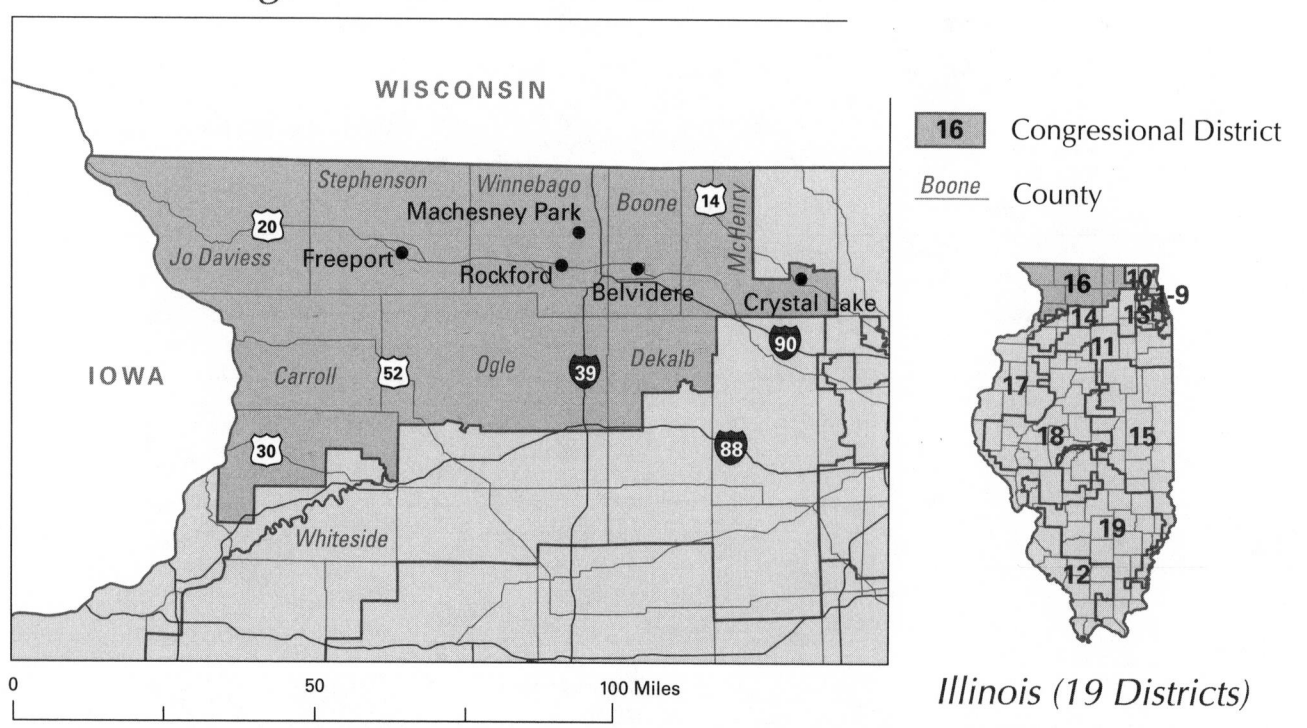

Illinois (19 Districts)

Congressional District 17

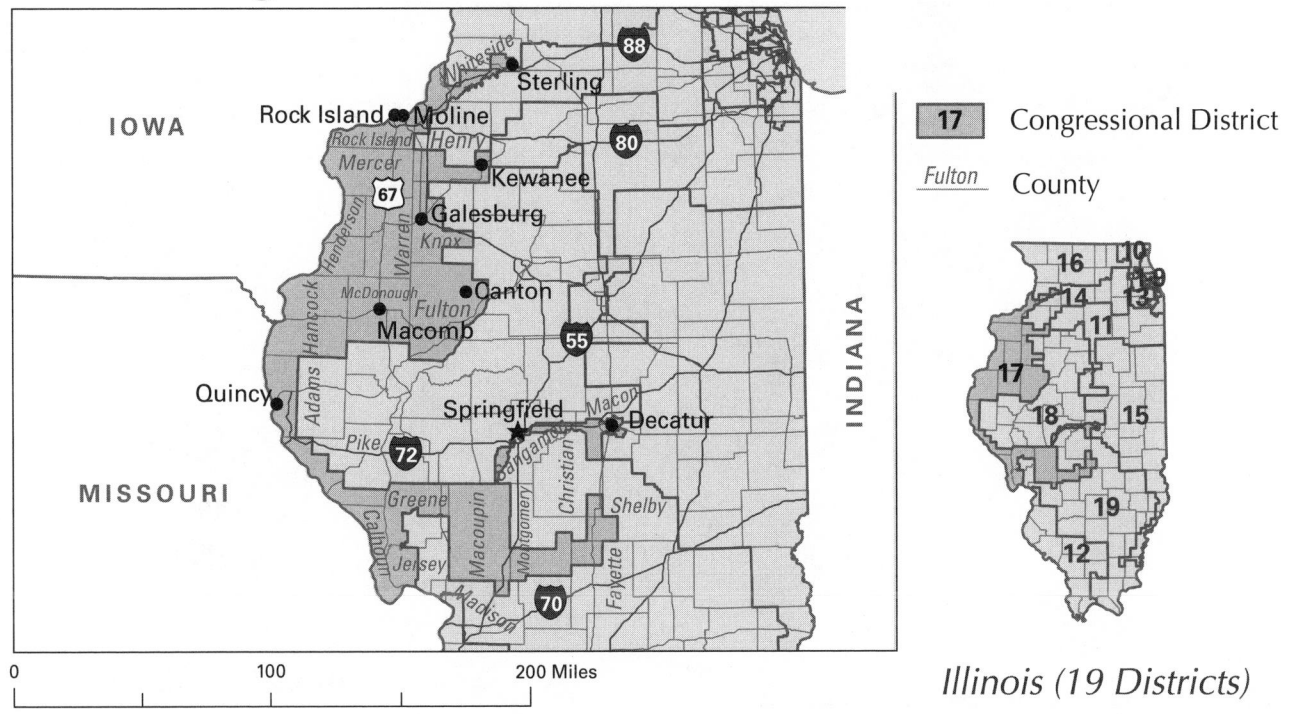

Illinois (19 Districts)

Congressional District 18

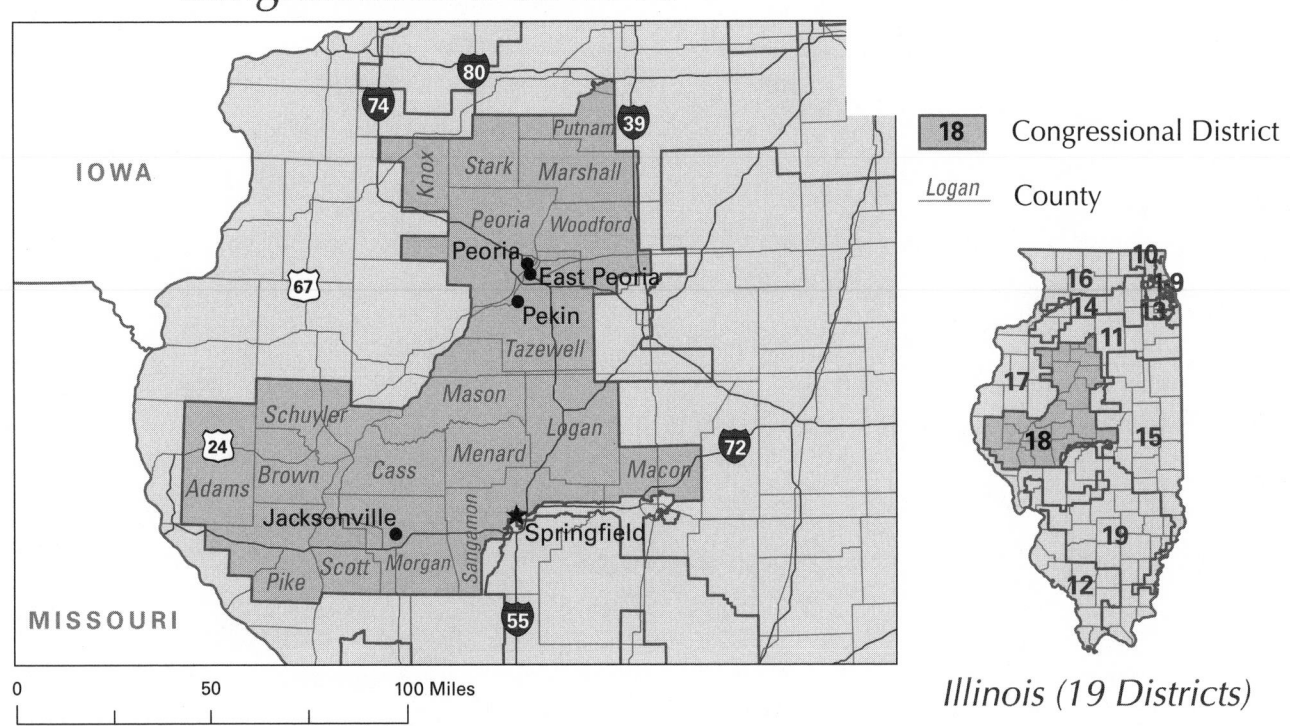

Illinois (19 Districts)

Congressional District 19

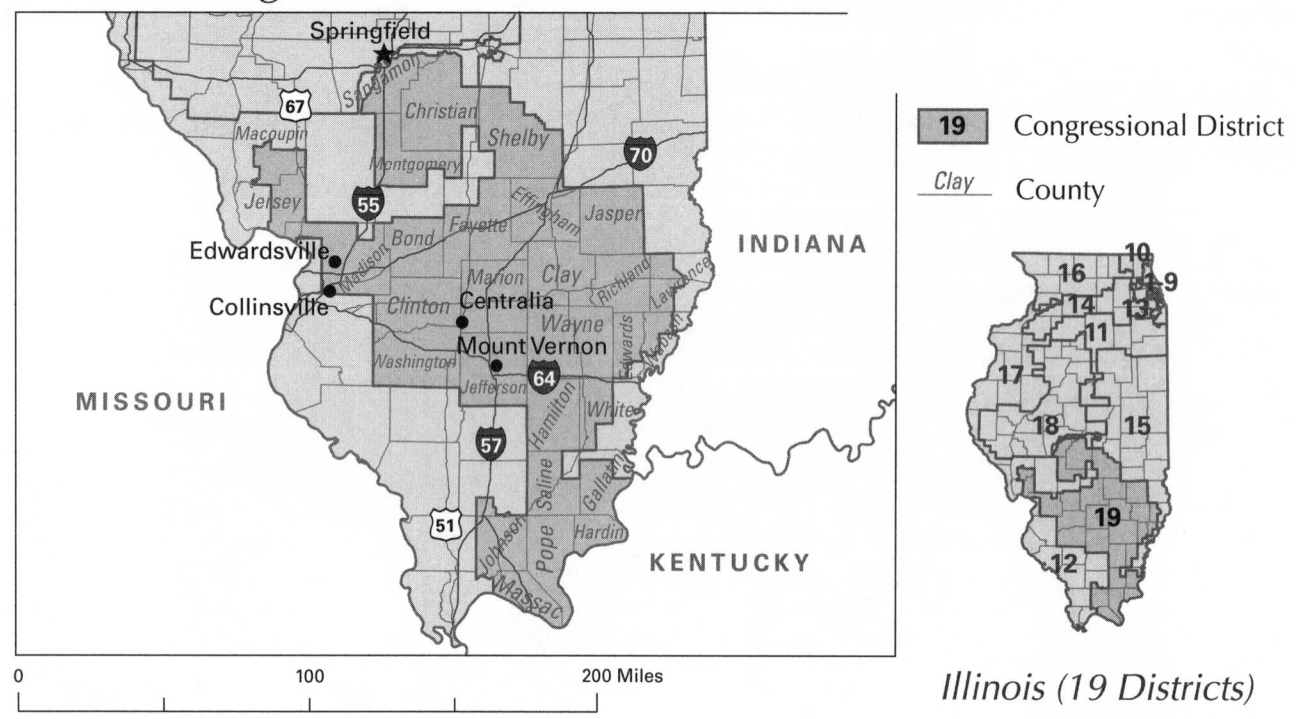

Illinois (19 Districts)

Indiana Congressional Districts — 9 Districts Total

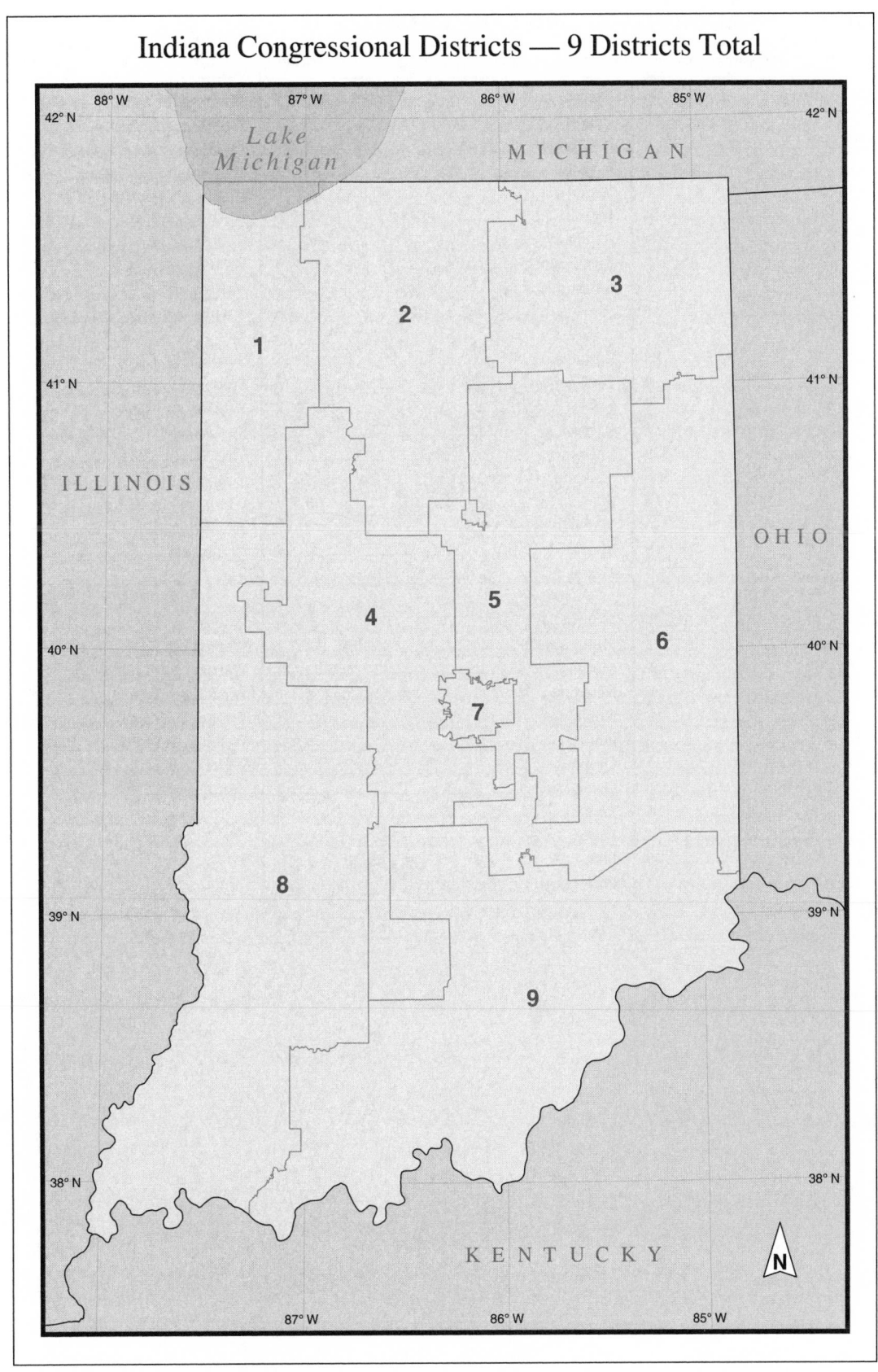

INDIANA—110th CONGRESSIONAL DISTRICTS BY COUNTIES

County	Congressional District	County	Congressional District	County	Congressional District
Adams	6	Henry	6	Posey	8
Allen	3, 6	Howard	2, 5	Pulaski	2
Bartholomew	6, 9	Huntington	5	Putnam	8
Benton	1	Jackson	9	Randolph	6
Blackford	6	Jasper	1	Ripley	9
Boone	4	Jay	6	Rush	6
Brown	9	Jefferson	9	St. Joseph	2
Carroll	2	Jennings	9	Scott	9
Cass	2	Johnson	4–6	Shelby	5, 6
Clark	9	Knox	8	Spencer	9
Clay	8	Kosciusko	3	Starke	2
Clinton	4	LaGrange	3	Steuben	3
Crawford	9	Lake	1	Sullivan	8
Daviess	8	LaPorte	2	Switzerland	9
Dearborn	6, 9	Lawrence	4	Tippecanoe	4
Decatur	6	Madison	6	Tipton	5
DeKalb	3	Marion	4, 5, 7	Union	6
Delaware	6	Marshall	2	Vanderburgh	8
Dubois	9	Martin	8	Vermillion	8
Elkhart	2, 3	Miami	5	Vigo	8
Fayette	6	Monroe	4, 9	Wabash	5
Floyd	9	Montgomery	4	Warren	8
Fountain	4, 8	Morgan	4	Warrick	8
Franklin	6	Newton	1	Washington	9
Fulton	2	Noble	3	Wayne	6
Gibson	8	Ohio	9	Wells	6
Grant	5	Orange	9	White	2, 4
Greene	8	Owen	8	Whitley	3
Hamilton	5	Parke	8		
Hancock	5	Perry	9		
Harrison	9	Pike	8		
Hendricks	4	Porter	1, 2		

Congressional District 1

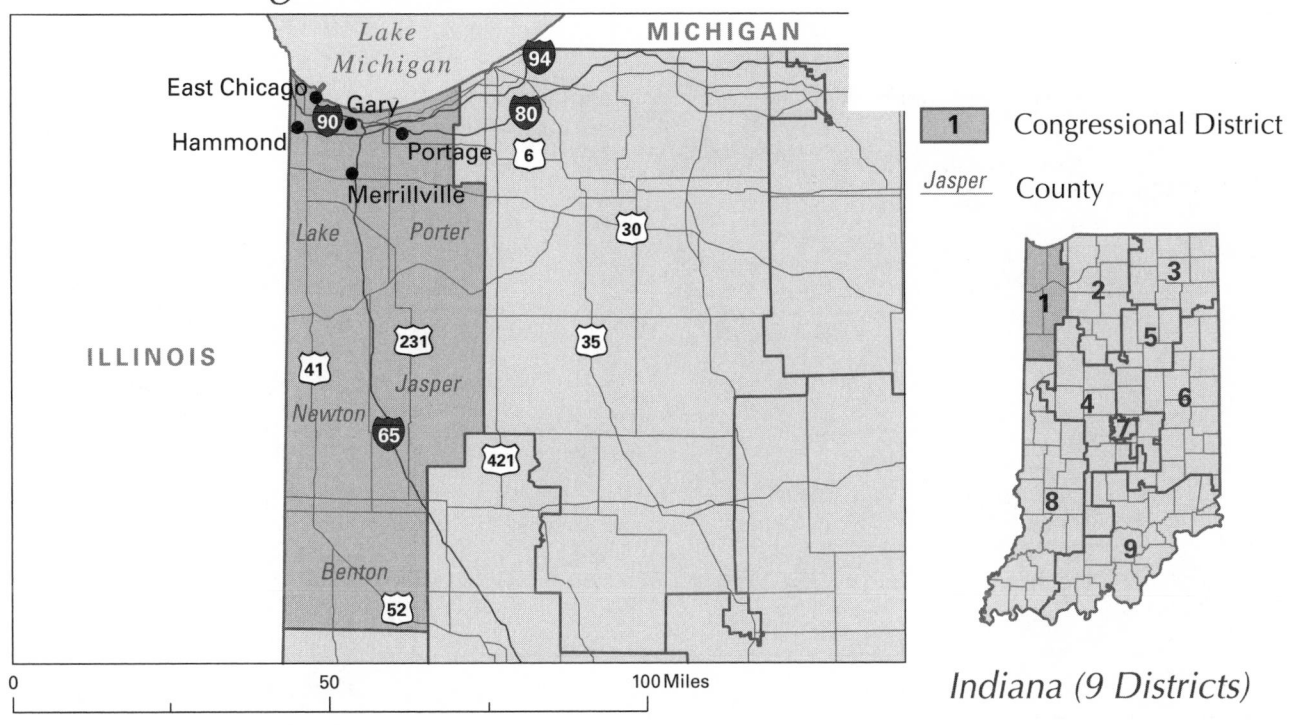

Indiana (9 Districts)

Congressional District 2

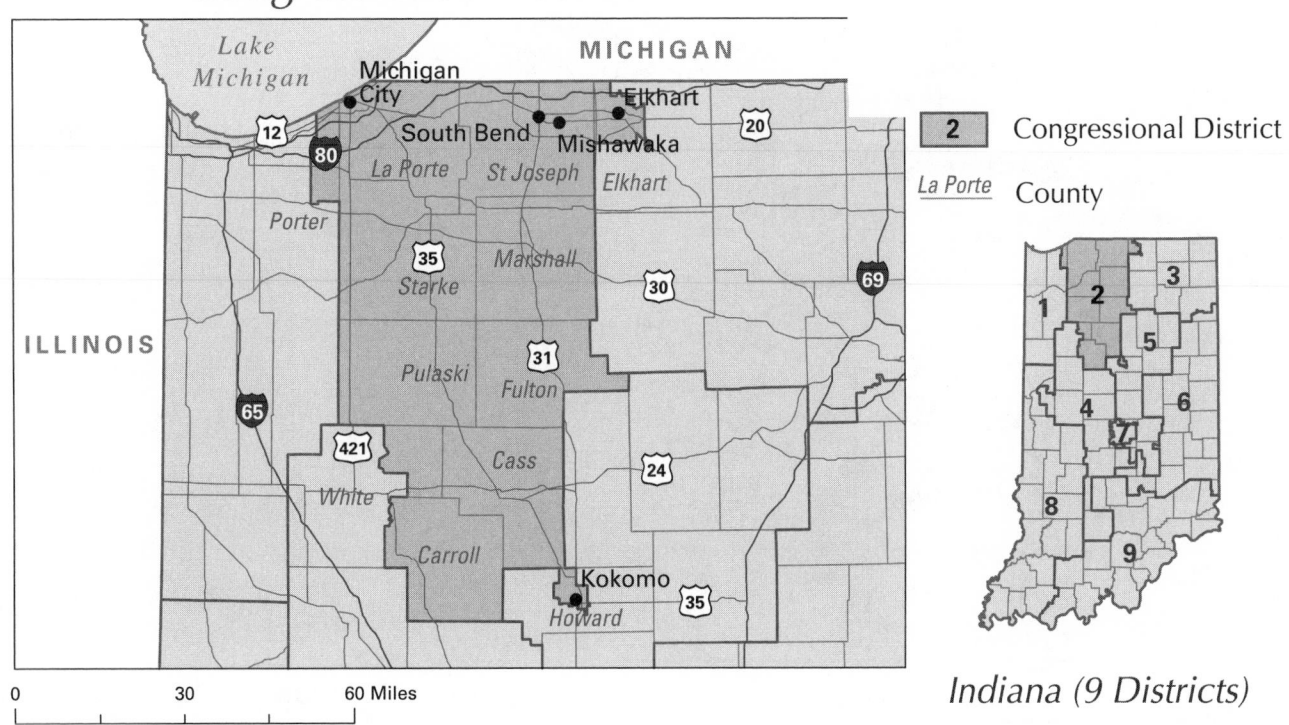

Indiana (9 Districts)

Congressional District 3

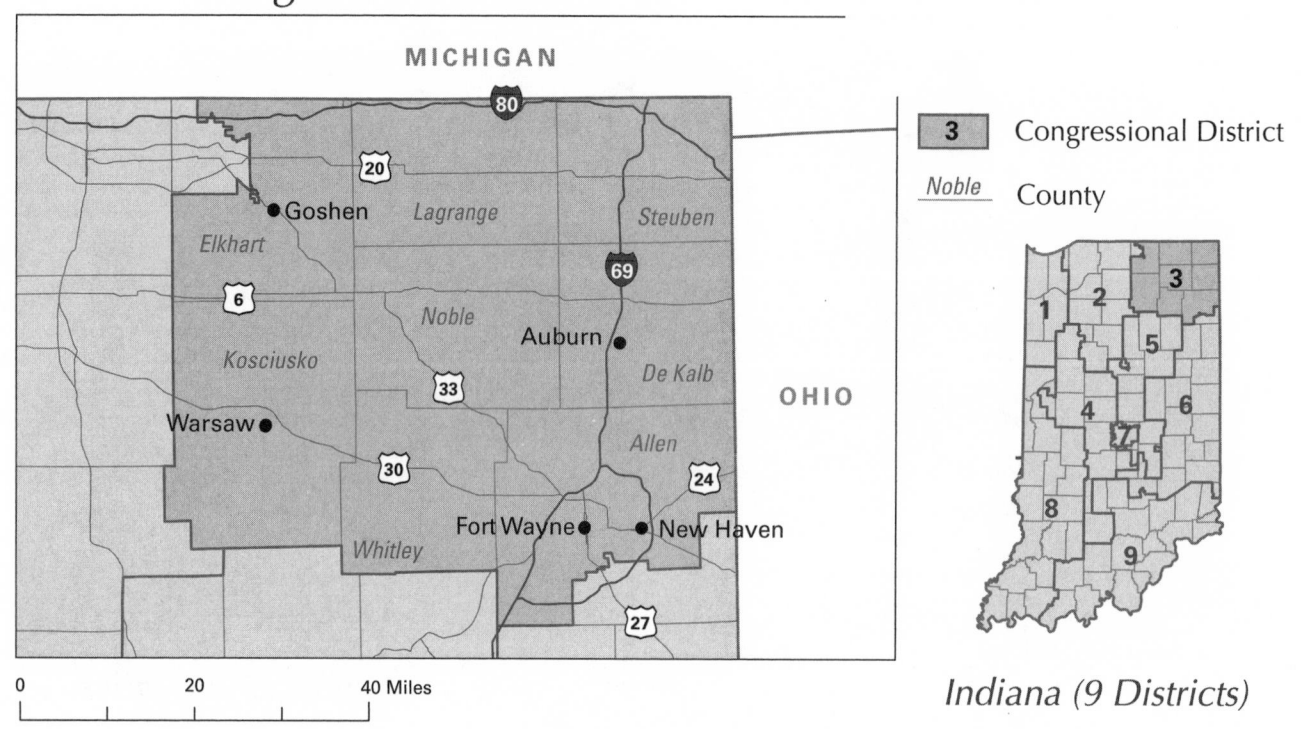

Indiana (9 Districts)

Congressional District 4

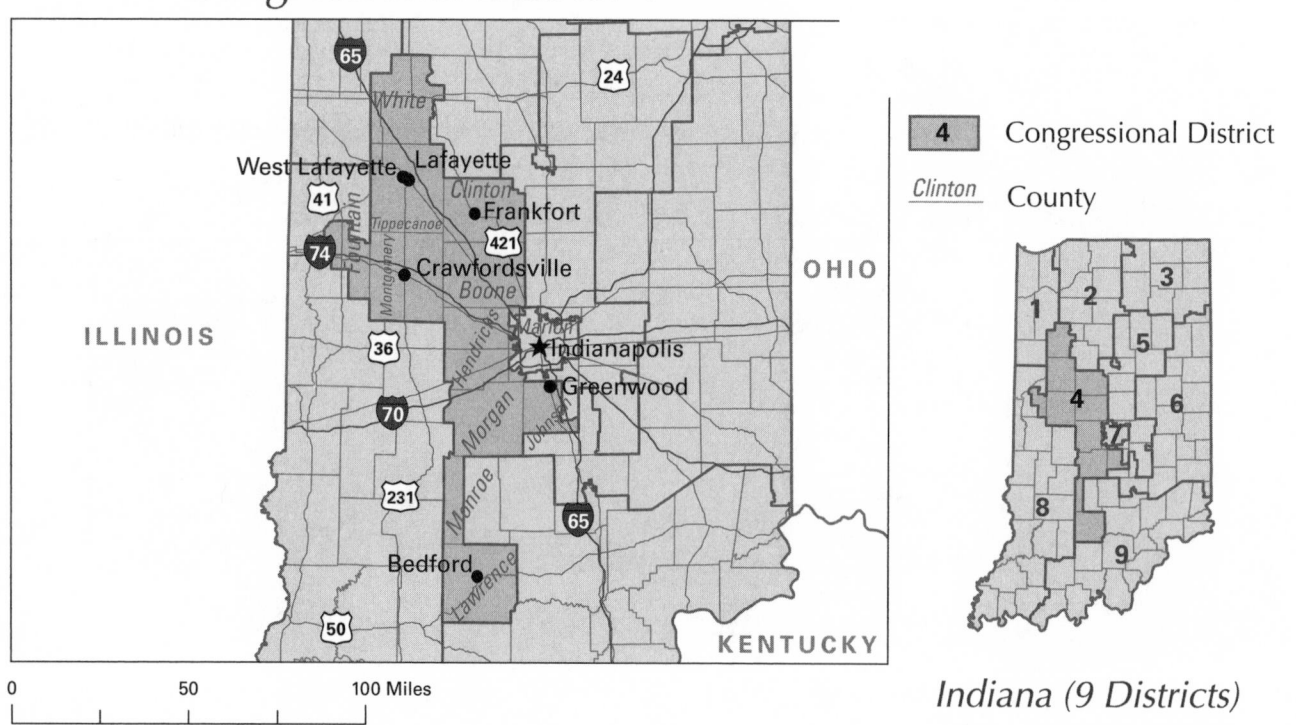

Indiana (9 Districts)

Congressional District 5

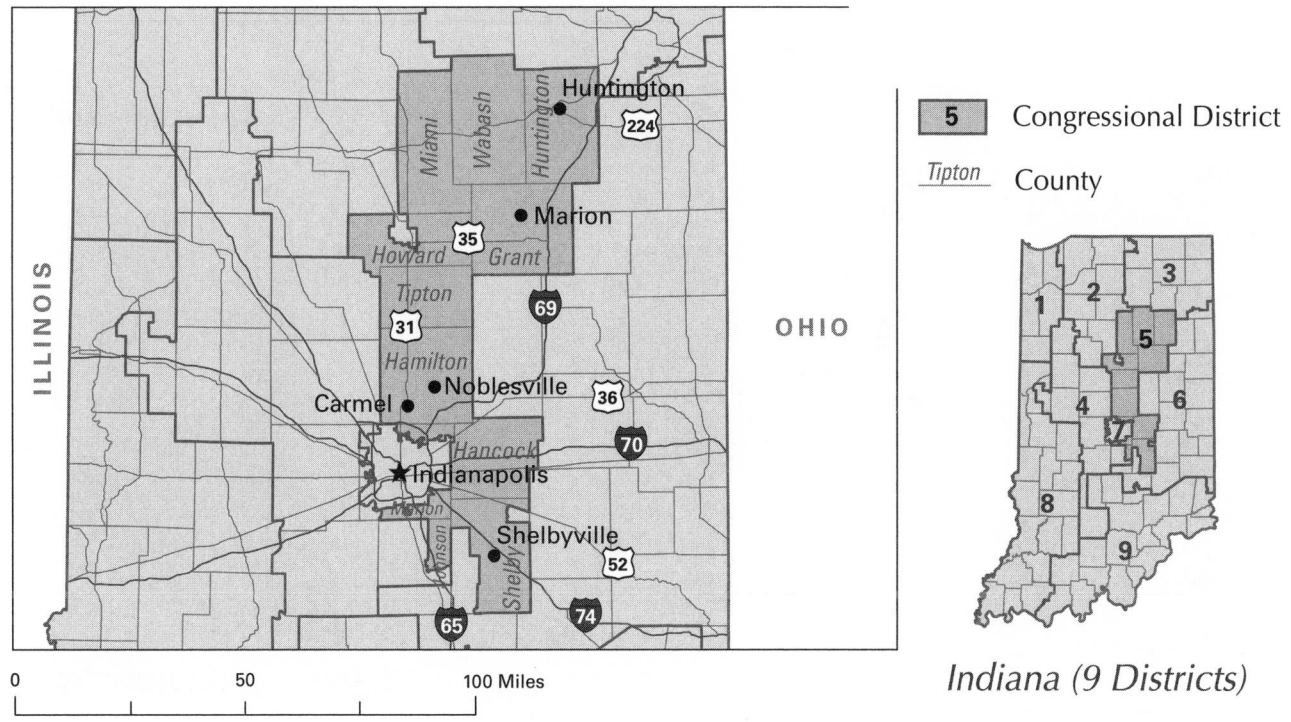

Indiana (9 Districts)

Congressional District 6

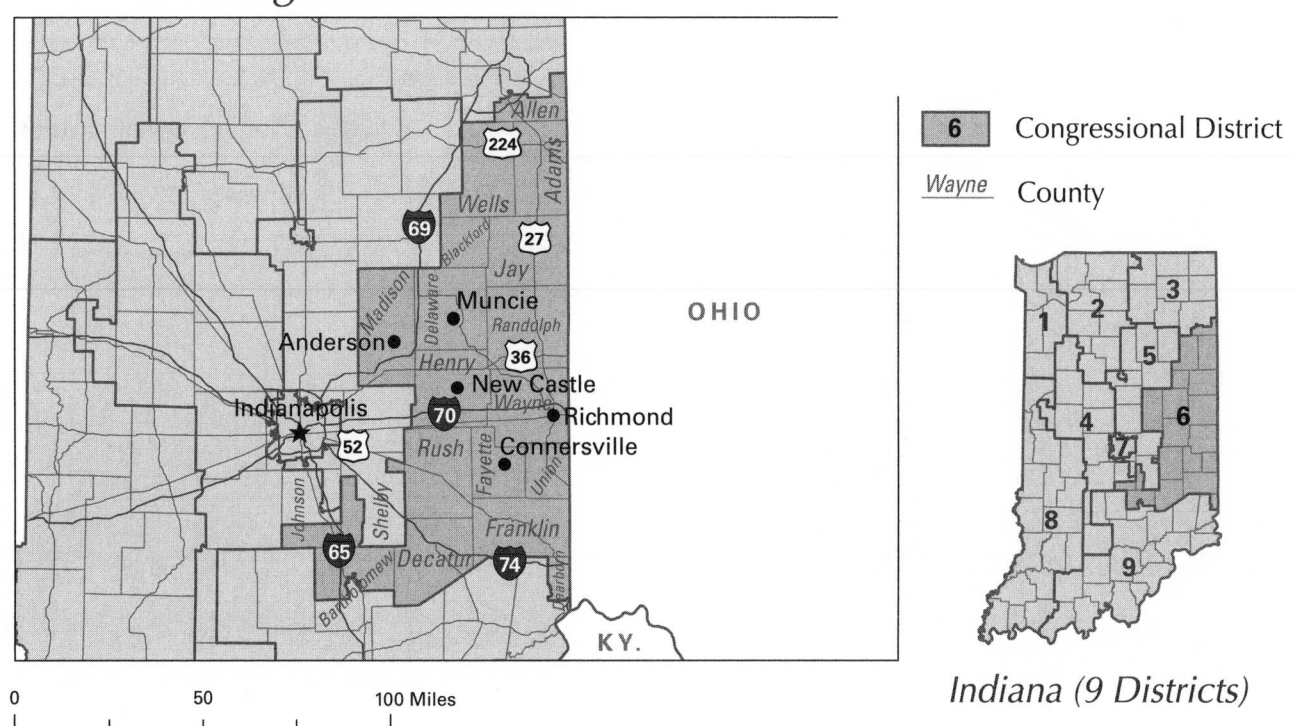

Indiana (9 Districts)

Congressional District 7

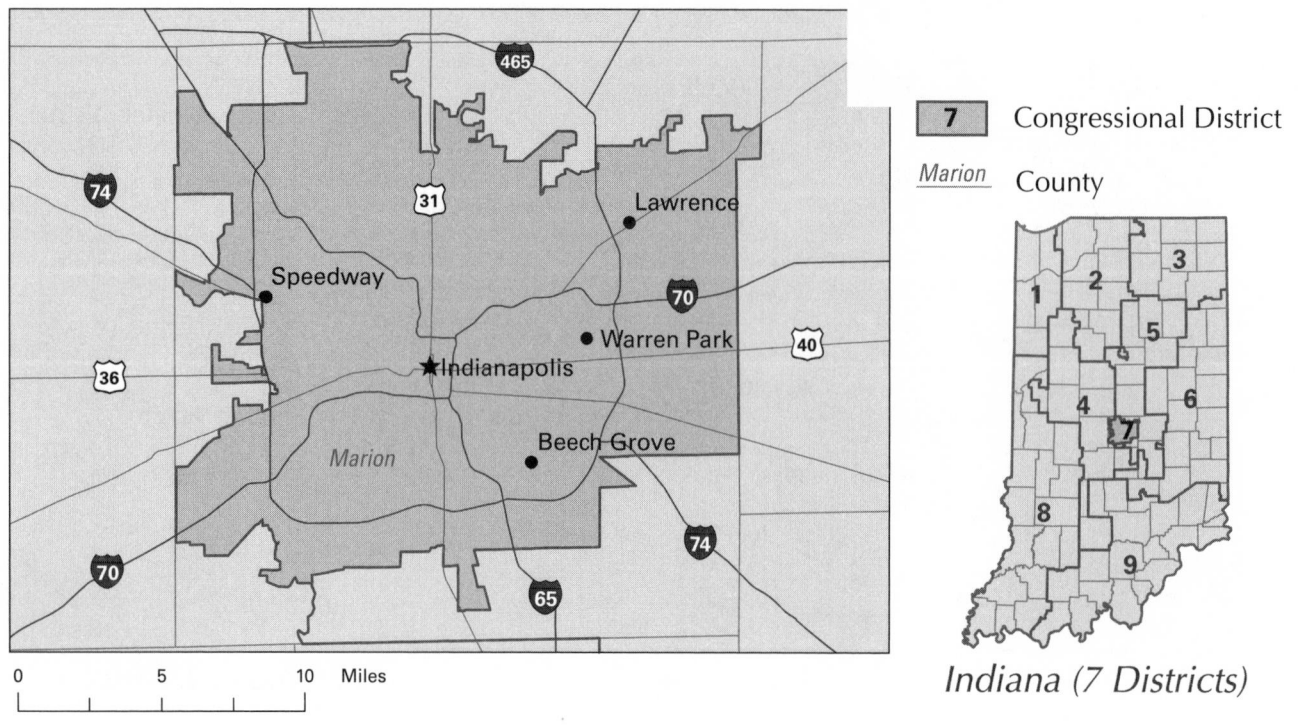

Indiana (7 Districts)

Congressional District 8

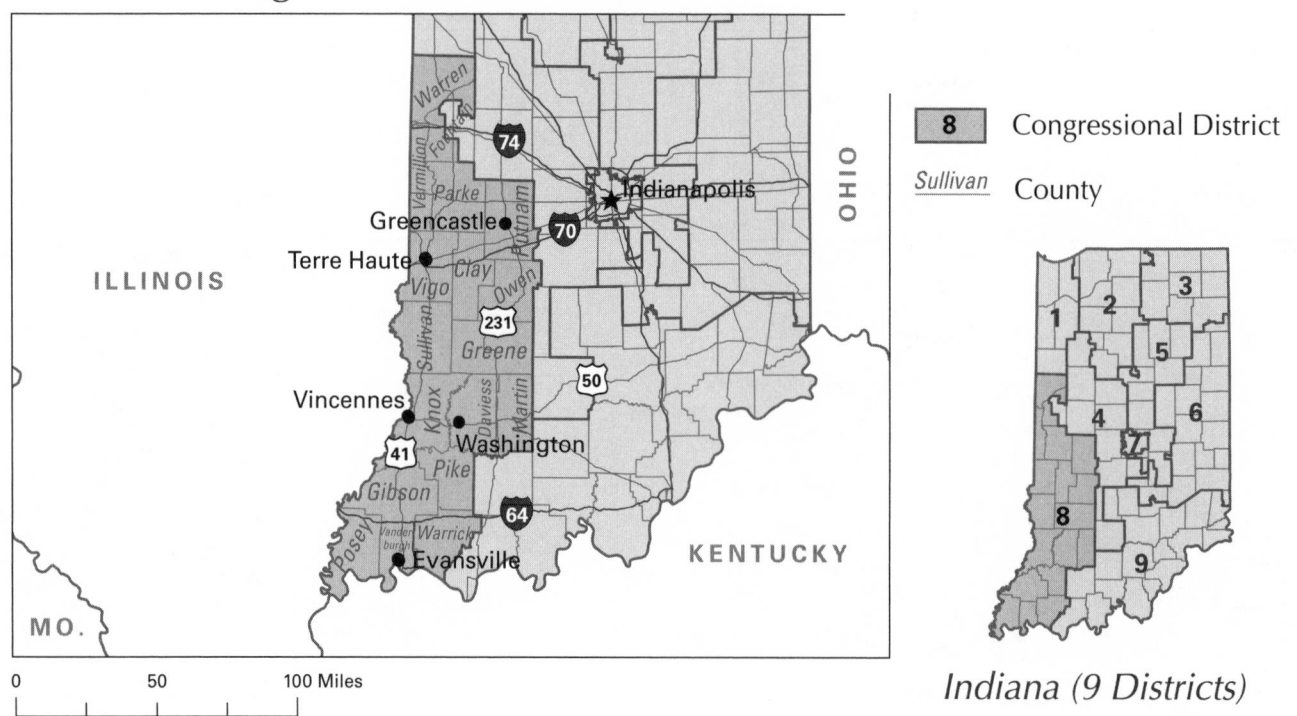

Indiana (9 Districts)

Congressional District 9

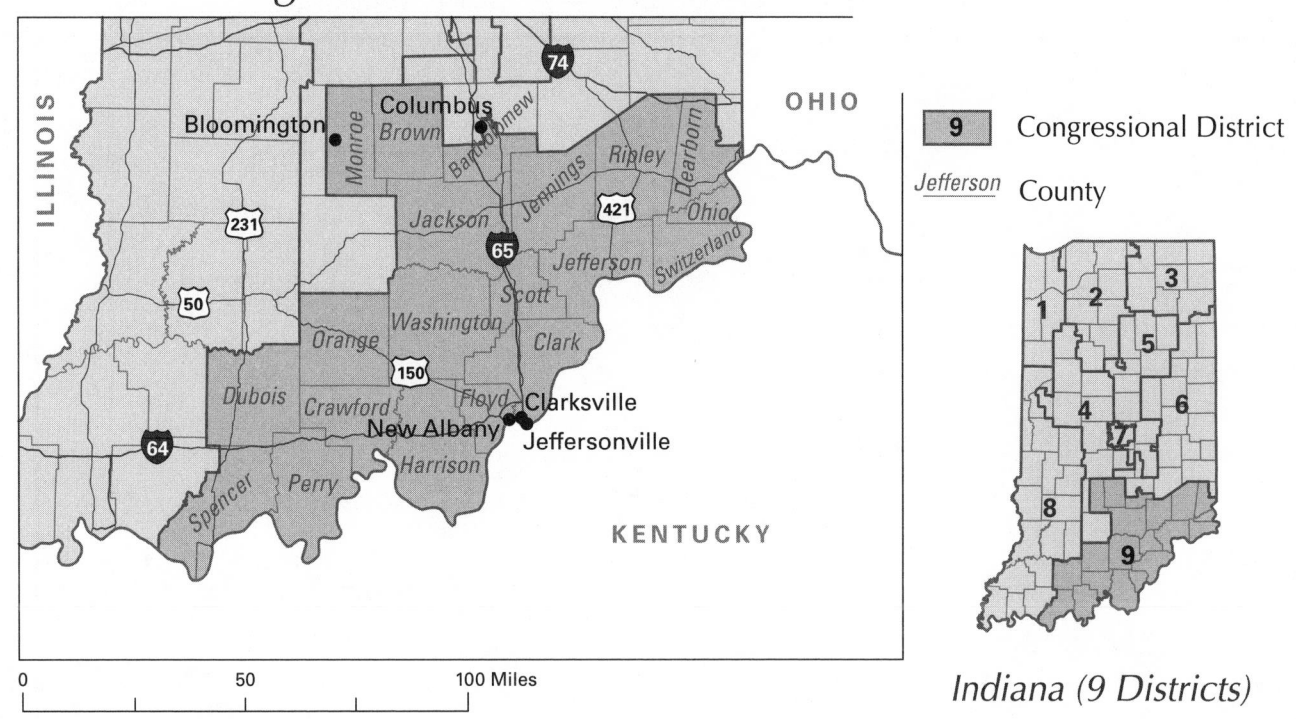

Indiana (9 Districts)

Iowa Congressional Districts — 5 Districts Total

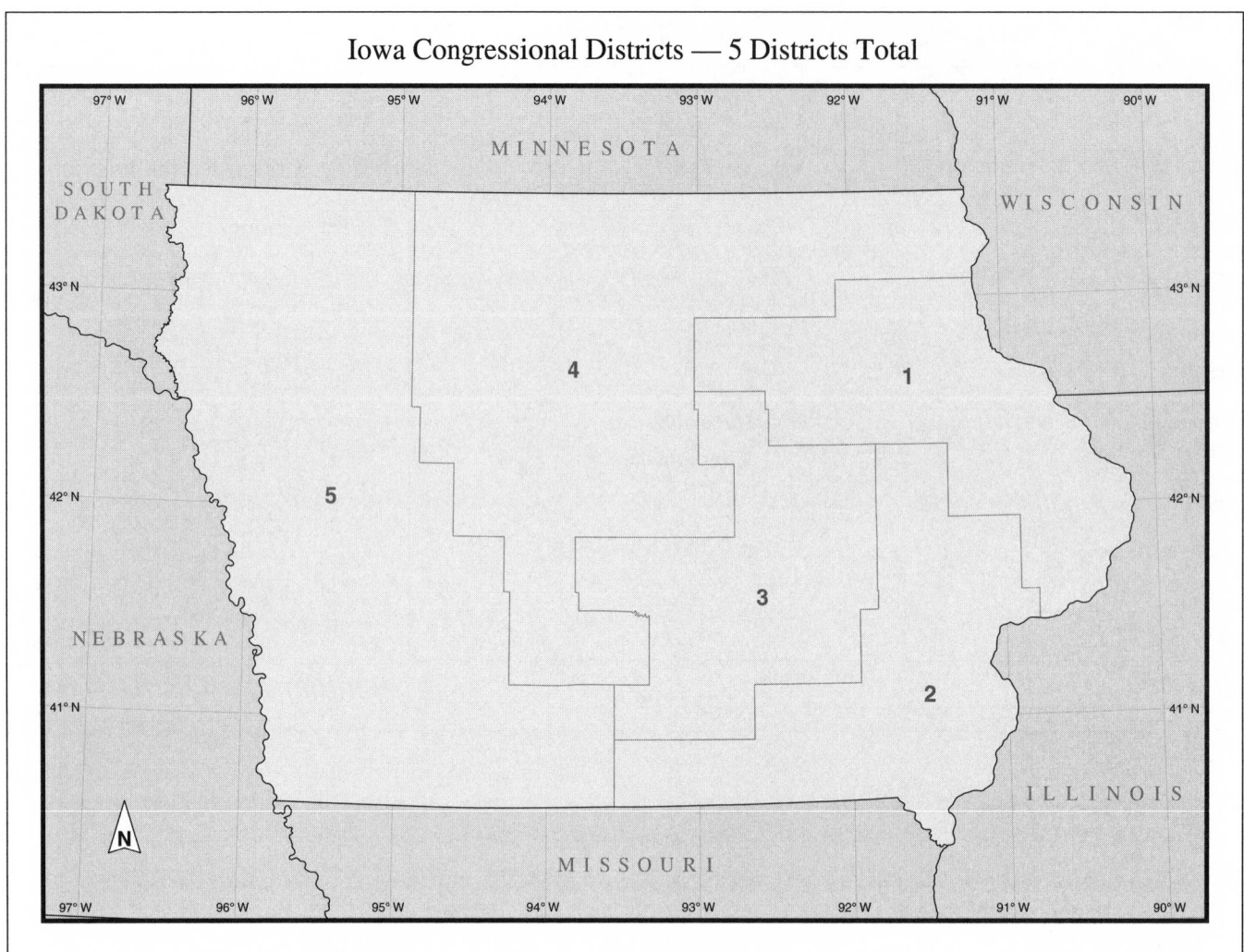

IOWA—110th CONGRESSIONAL DISTRICTS BY COUNTIES

County	Congressional District
Adair	5
Adams	5
Allamakee	4
Appanoose	2
Audubon	5
Benton	3
Black Hawk	1
Boone	4
Bremer	1
Buchanan	1
Buena Vista	5
Butler	1
Calhoun	4
Carroll	5
Cass	5
Cedar	2
Cerro Gordo	4
Cherokee	5
Chickasaw	4
Clarke	5
Clay	5
Clayton	1
Clinton	1
Crawford	5
Dallas	4
Davis	2
Decatur	5
Delaware	1
Des Moines	2
Dickinson	5
Dubuque	1
Emmet	4
Fayette	1

County	Congressional District
Floyd	4
Franklin	4
Fremont	5
Greene	4
Grundy	3
Guthrie	5
Hamilton	4
Hancock	4
Hardin	4
Harrison	5
Henry	2
Howard	4
Humboldt	4
Ida	5
Iowa	3
Jackson	1
Jasper	3
Jefferson	2
Johnson	2
Jones	1
Keokuk	3
Kossuth	4
Lee	2
Linn	2
Louisa	2
Lucas	3
Lyon	5
Madison	4
Mahaska	3
Marion	3
Marshall	4
Mills	5
Mitchell	4

County	Congressional District
Monona	5
Monroe	3
Montgomery	5
Muscatine	2
O'Brien	5
Osceola	5
Page	5
Palo Alto	4
Plymouth	5
Pocahontas	4
Polk	3
Pottawattamie	5
Poweshiek	3
Ringgold	5
Sac	5
Scott	1
Shelby	5
Sioux	5
Story	4
Tama	3
Taylor	5
Union	5
Van Buren	2
Wapello	2
Warren	4
Washington	2
Wayne	2
Webster	4
Winnebago	4
Winneshiek	4
Woodbury	5
Worth	4
Wright	4

Congressional District 1

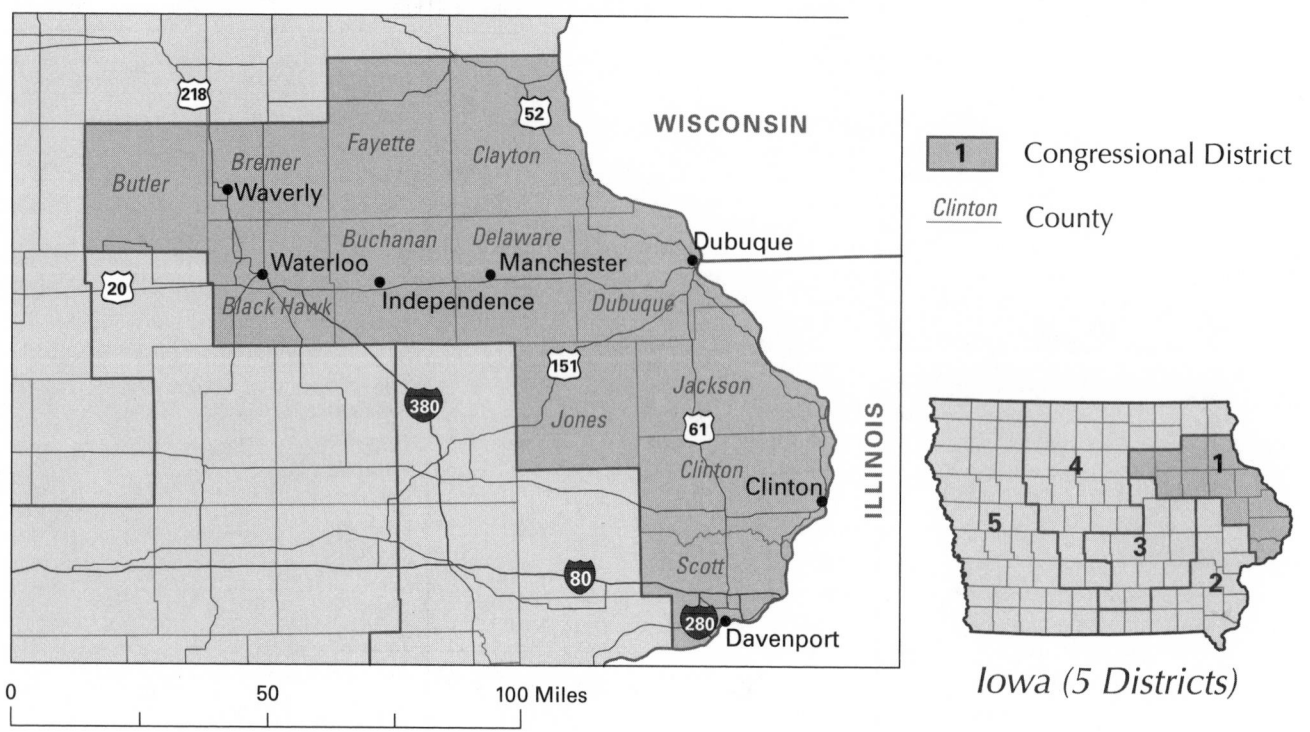

Iowa (5 Districts)

Congressional District 2

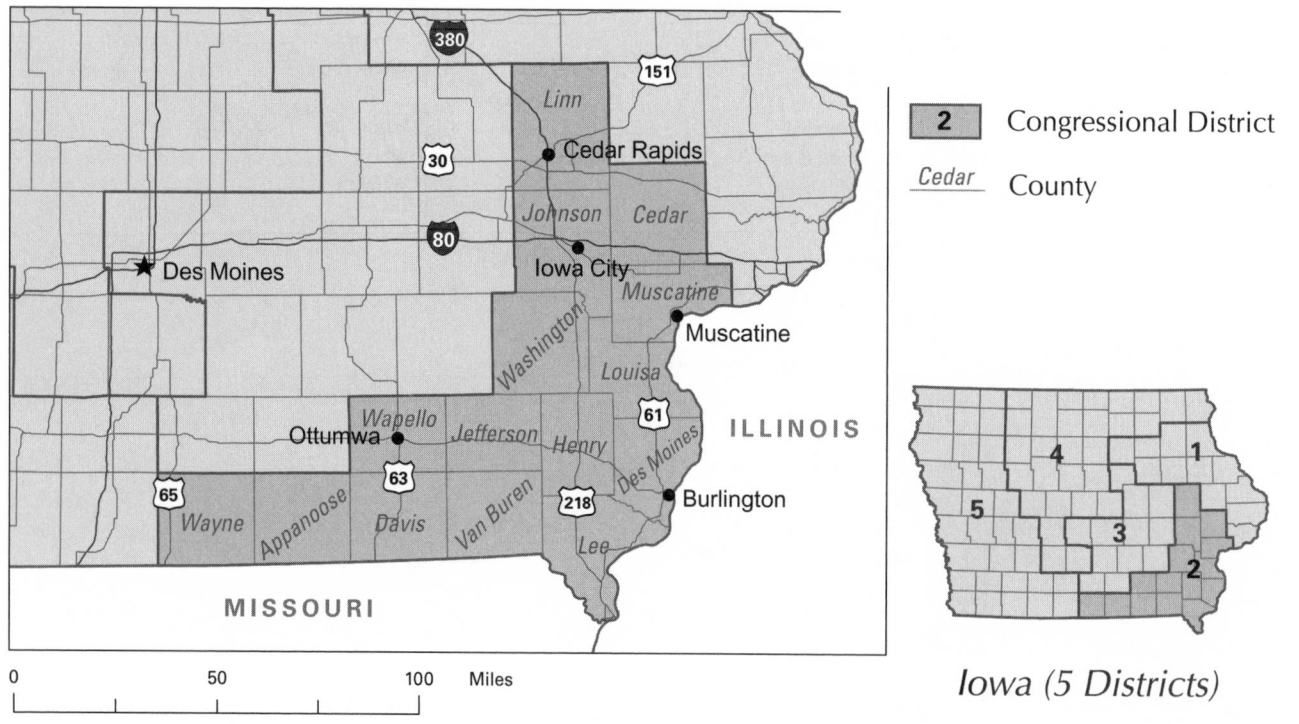

Iowa (5 Districts)

Congressional District 3

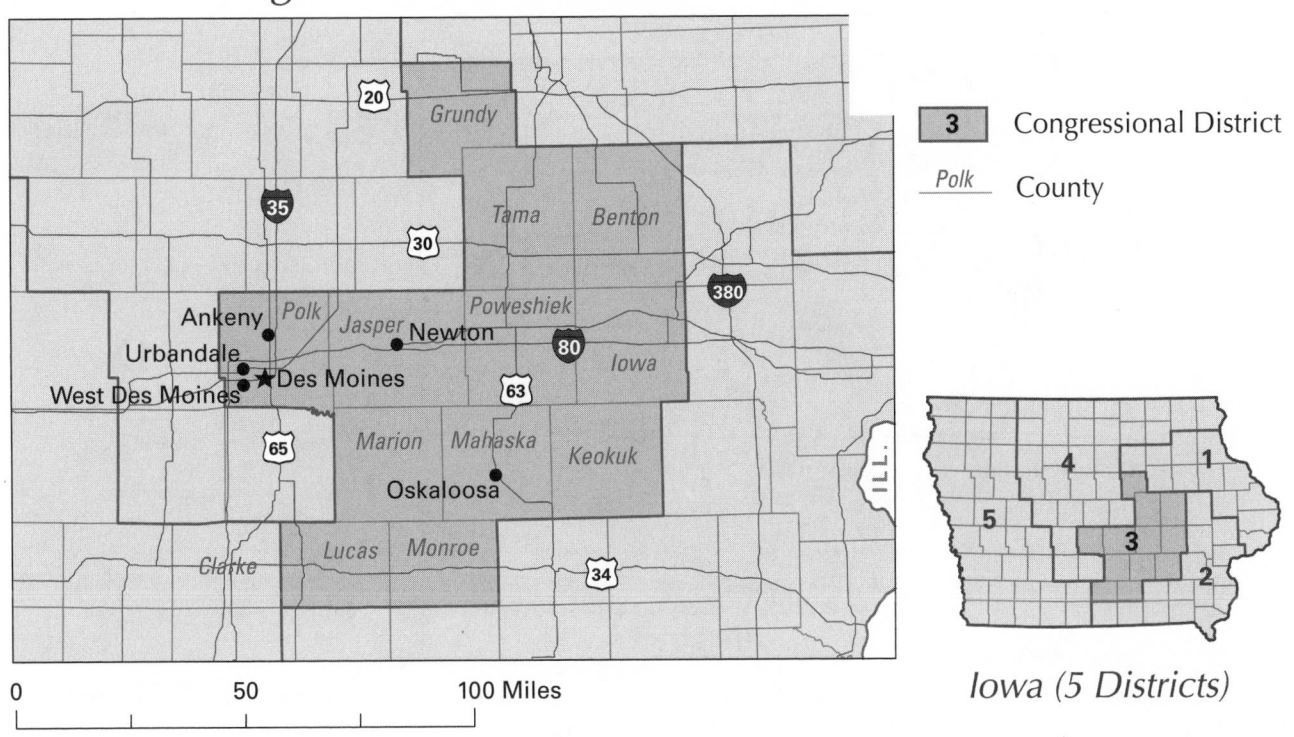

3 Congressional District
Polk County

Iowa (5 Districts)

0   50   100 Miles

Congressional District 4

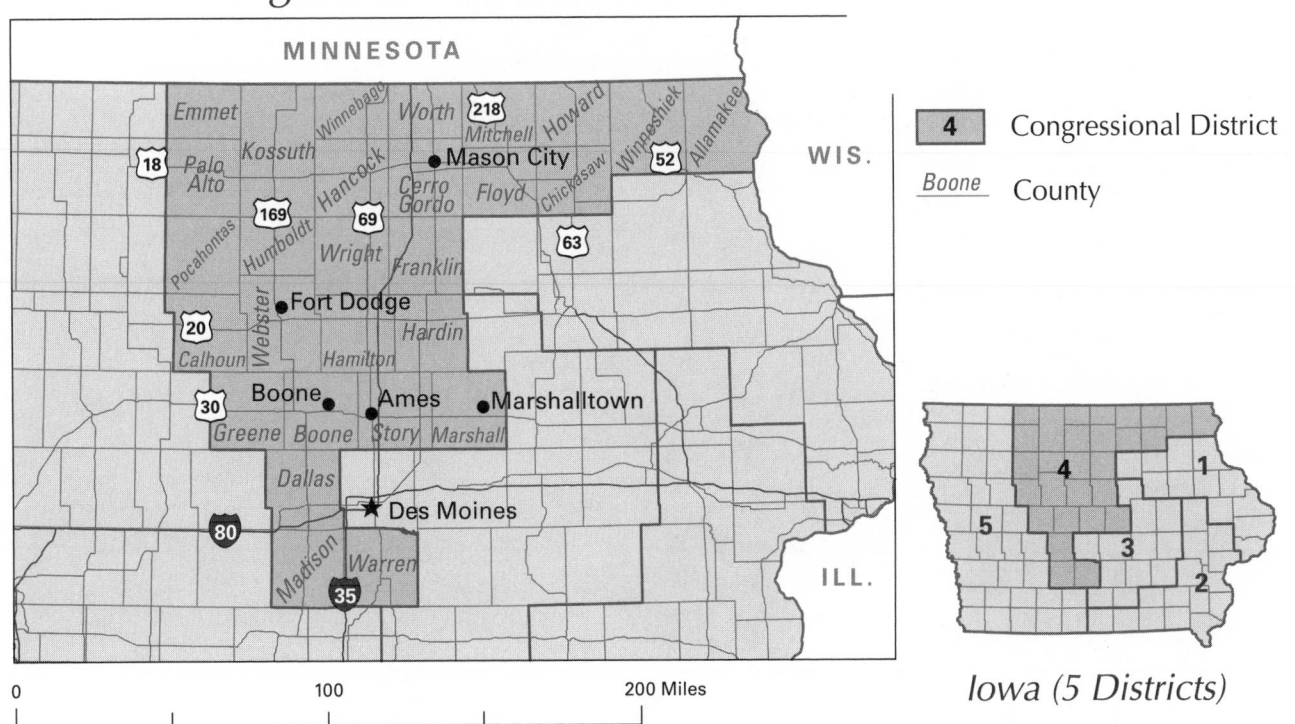

4 Congressional District
Boone County

Iowa (5 Districts)

0   100   200 Miles

Congressional District 5

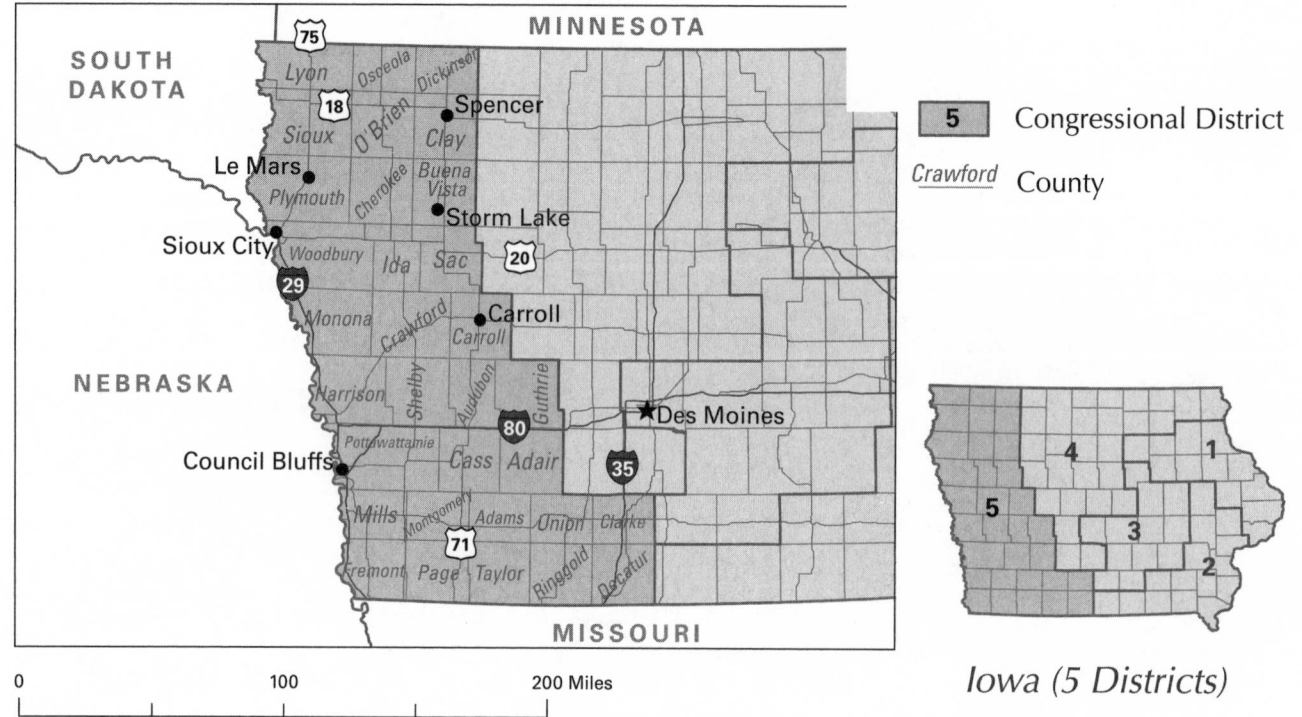

Iowa (5 Districts)

Kansas Congressional Districts — 4 Districts Total

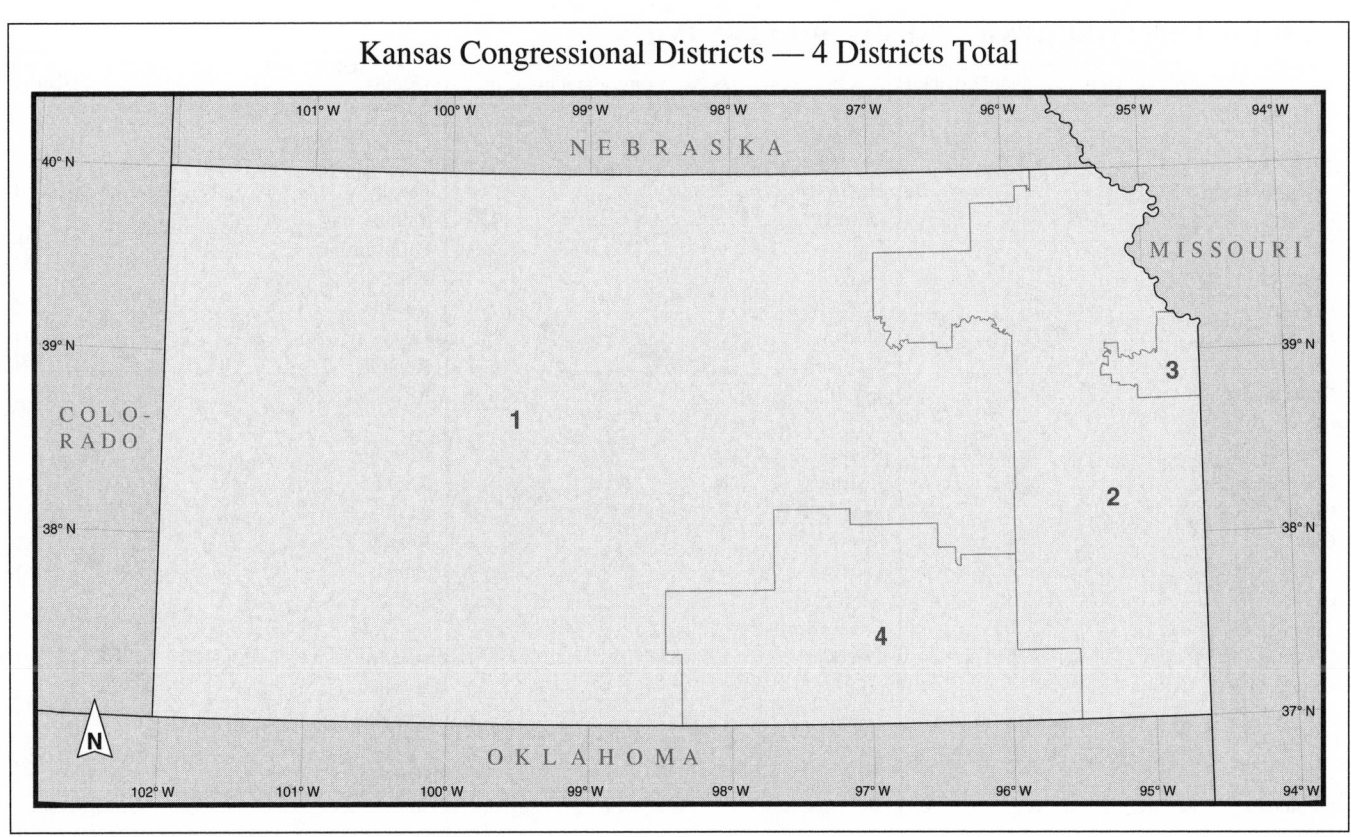

KANSAS—110th CONGRESSIONAL DISTRICTS BY COUNTIES

County	Congressional District	County	Congressional District	County	Congressional District
Allen	2	Greeley	1	Osborne	1
Anderson	2	Greenwood	1, 4	Ottawa	1
Atchison	2	Hamilton	1	Pawnee	1
Barber	1	Harper	4	Phillips	1
Barton	1	Harvey	4	Pottawatomie	2
Bourbon	2	Haskell	1	Pratt	1
Brown	2	Hodgeman	1	Rawlins	1
Butler	4	Jackson	2	Reno	1
Chase	1	Jefferson	2	Republic	1
Chautauqua	4	Jewell	1	Rice	1
Cherokee	2	Johnson	3	Riley	2
Cheyenne	1	Kearny	1	Rooks	1
Clark	1	Kingman	4	Rush	1
Clay	1	Kiowa	1	Russell	1
Cloud	1	Labette	2	Saline	1
Coffey	2	Lane	1	Scott	1
Comanche	1	Leavenworth	2	Sedgwick	4
Cowley	4	Lincoln	1	Seward	1
Crawford	2	Linn	2	Shawnee	2
Decatur	1	Logan	1	Sheridan	1
Dickinson	1	Lyon	1	Sherman	1
Doniphan	2	McPherson	1	Smith	1
Douglas	2, 3	Marion	1	Stafford	1
Edwards	1	Marshall	1	Stanton	1
Elk	4	Meade	1	Stevens	1
Ellis	1	Miami	2	Sumner	4
Ellsworth	1	Mitchell	1	Thomas	1
Finney	1	Montgomery	4	Trego	1
Ford	1	Morris	1	Wabaunsee	1
Franklin	2	Morton	1	Wallace	1
Geary	1, 2	Nemaha	1, 2	Washington	1
Gove	1	Neosho	2	Wichita	1
Graham	1	Ness	1	Wilson	2
Grant	1	Norton	1	Woodson	2
Gray	1	Osage	2	Wyandotte	3

Congressional District 1

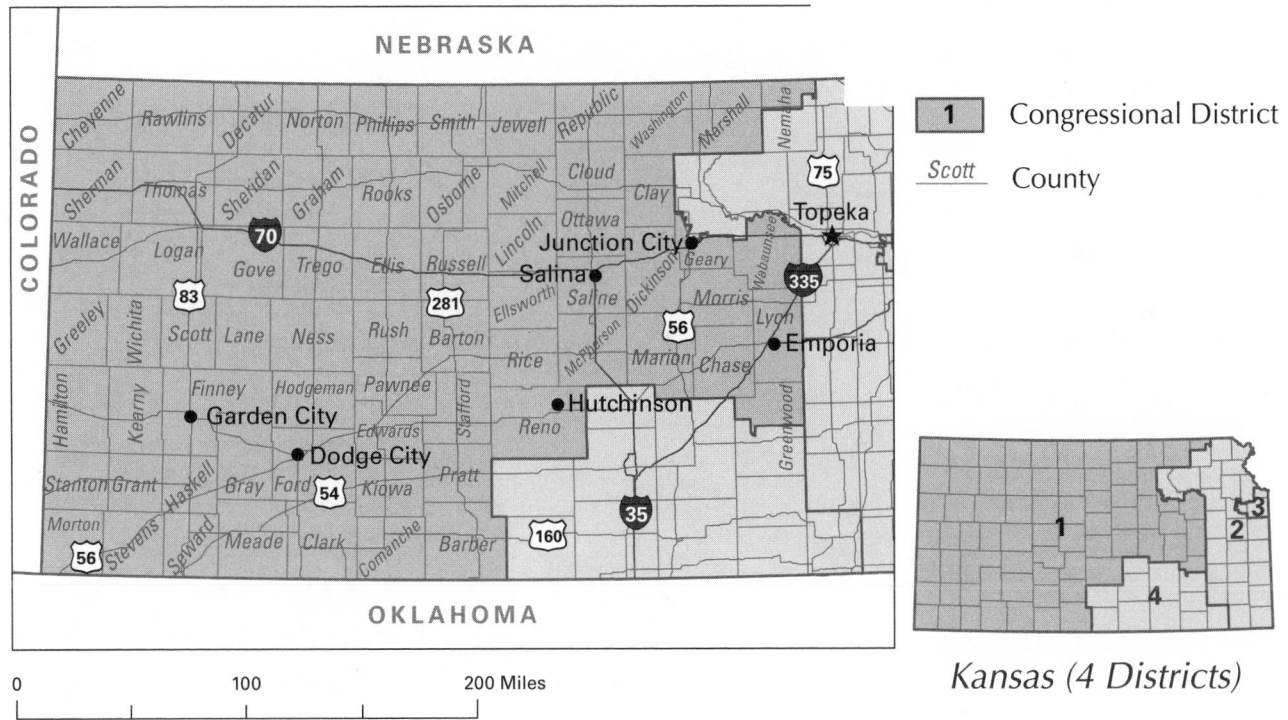

Kansas (4 Districts)

Congressional District 2

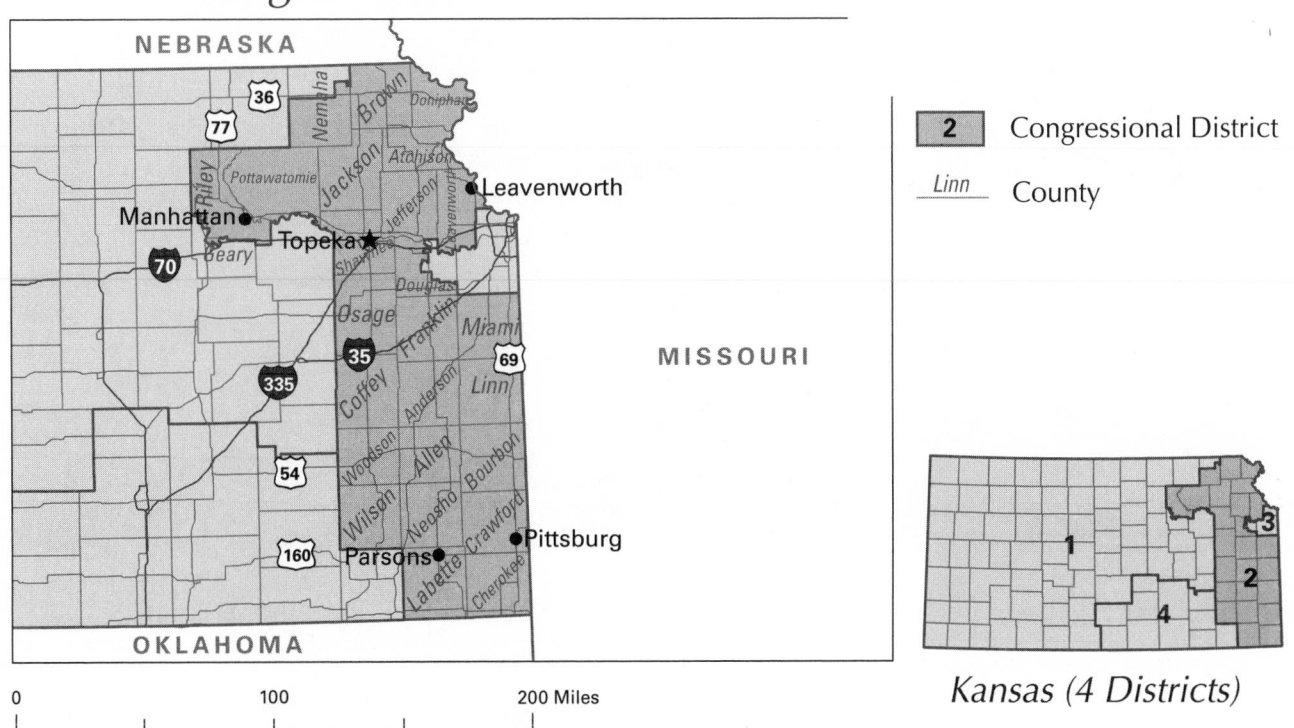

Kansas (4 Districts)

Congressional District 3

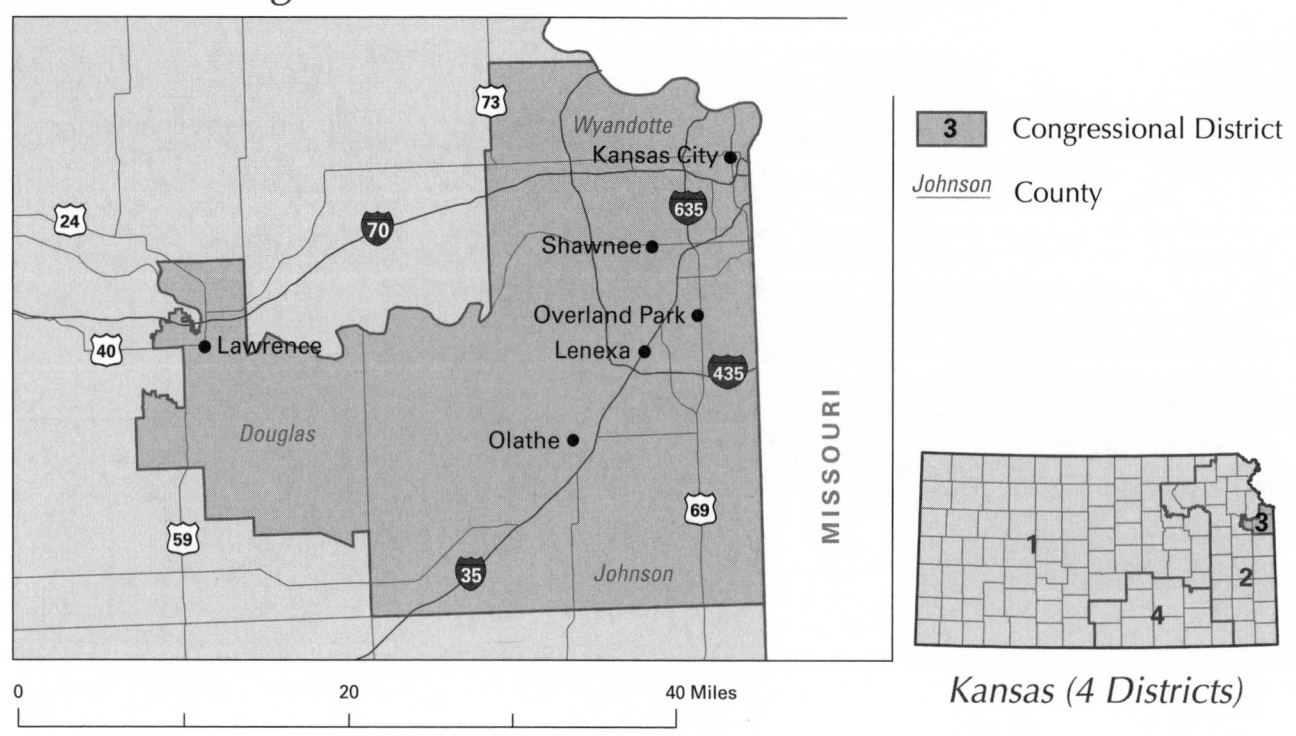

3 Congressional District
Johnson County

Kansas (4 Districts)

Congressional District 4

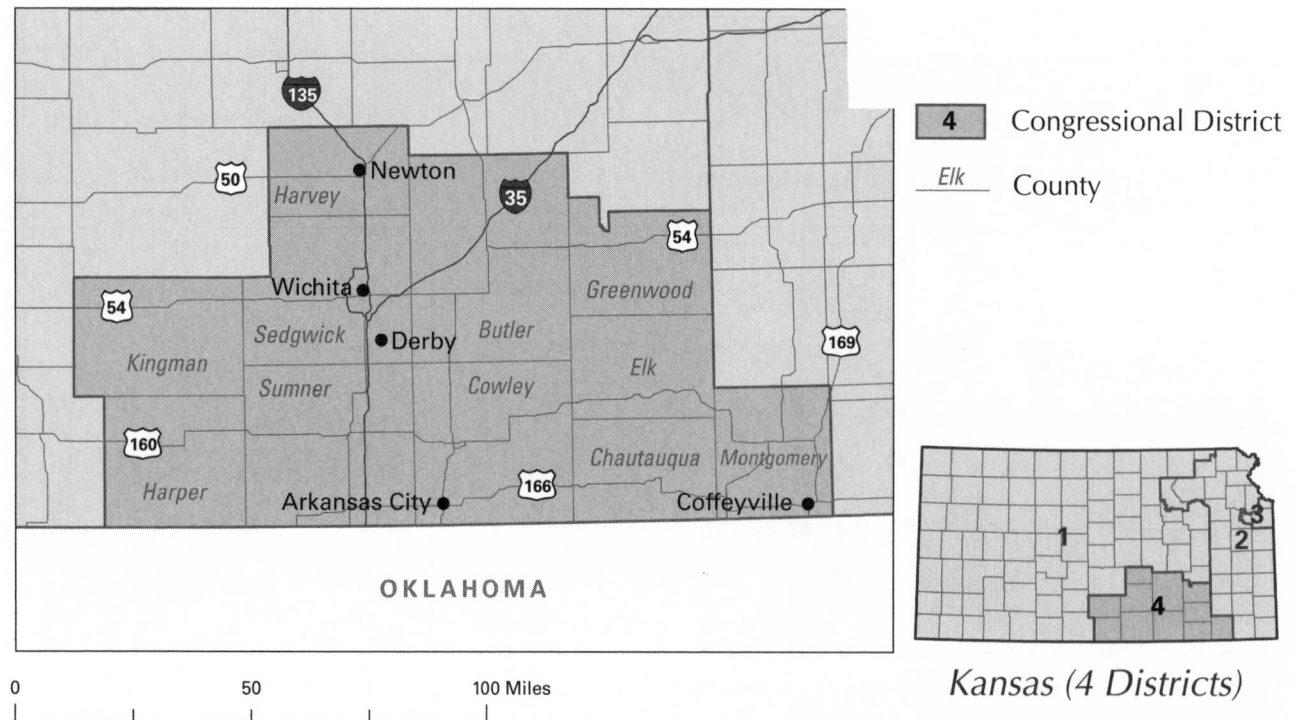

4 Congressional District
Elk County

Kansas (4 Districts)

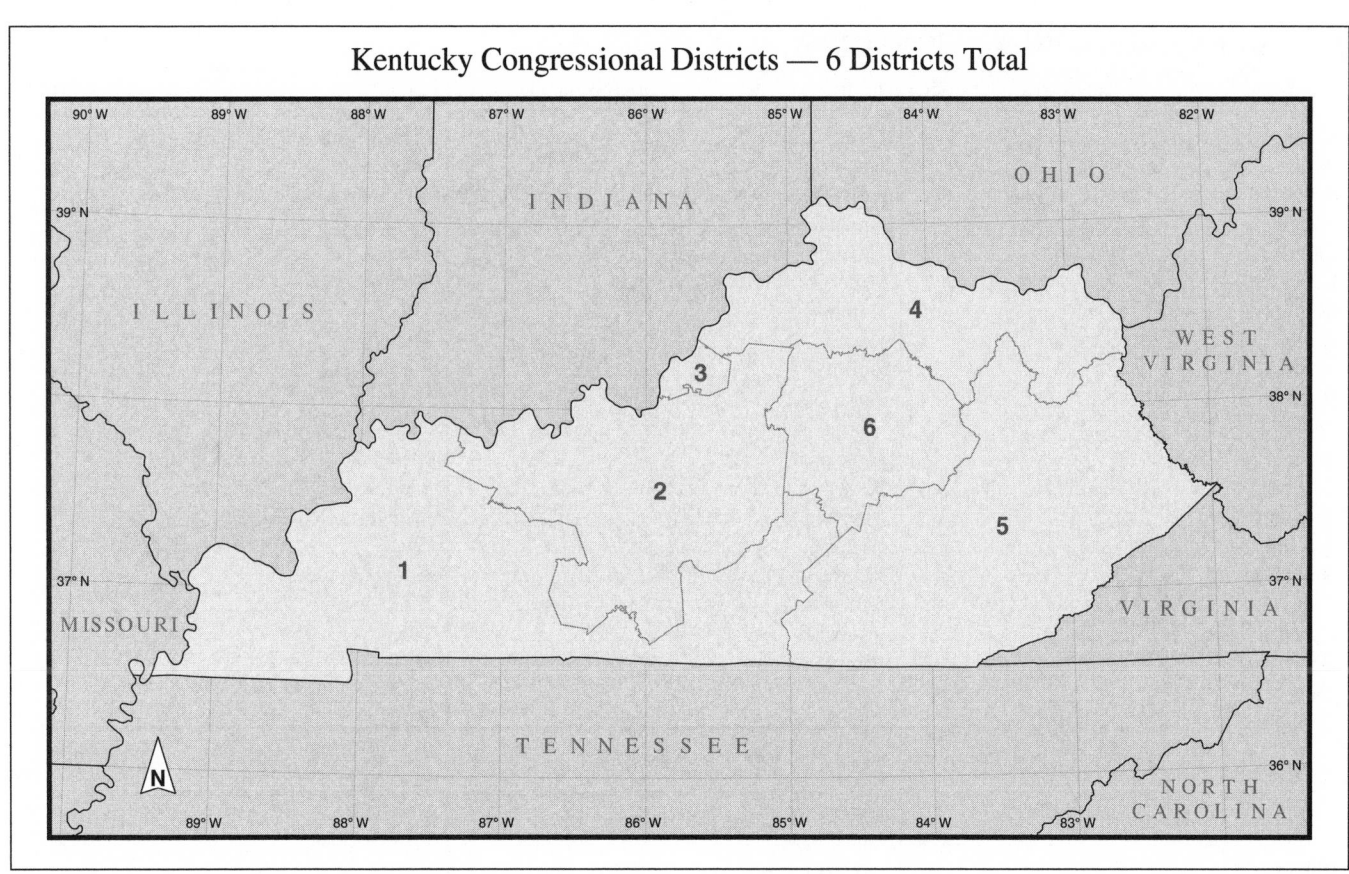

Kentucky Congressional Districts — 6 Districts Total

KENTUCKY—110th CONGRESSIONAL DISTRICTS BY COUNTIES

County	Congressional District	County	Congressional District	County	Congressional District
Adair	1	Grant	4	Mason	4
Allen	1	Graves	1	Meade	2
Anderson	6	Grayson	2	Menifee	5
Ballard	1	Green	2	Mercer	6
Barren	2	Greenup	4	Metcalfe	1
Bath	4, 5	Hancock	2	Monroe	1
Bell	5	Hardin	2	Montgomery	6
Boone	4	Harlan	5	Morgan	5
Bourbon	6	Harrison	4	Muhlenberg	1
Boyd	4	Hart	2	Nelson	2
Boyle	6	Henderson	1	Nicholas	4
Bracken	4	Henry	4	Ohio	1, 2
Breathitt	5	Hickman	1	Oldham	4
Breckinridge	2	Hopkins	1	Owen	4
Bullitt	2	Jackson	5	Owsley	5
Butler	1	Jefferson	2, 3	Pendleton	4
Caldwell	1	Jessamine	6	Perry	5
Calloway	1	Johnson	5	Pike	5
Campbell	4	Kenton	4	Powell	6
Carlisle	1	Knott	5	Pulaski	5
Carroll	4	Knox	5	Robertson	4
Carter	4	Larue	2	Rockcastle	5
Casey	1	Laurel	5	Rowan	5
Christian	1	Lawrence	5	Russell	1
Clark	6	Lee	5	Scott	4, 6
Clay	5	Leslie	5	Shelby	2
Clinton	1	Letcher	5	Simpson	1
Crittenden	1	Lewis	4	Spencer	2
Cumberland	1	Lincoln	1, 6	Taylor	2
Daviess	2	Livingston	1	Todd	1
Edmonson	2	Logan	1	Trigg	1
Elliott	4	Lyon	1	Trimble	4
Estill	6	McCracken	1	Union	1
Fayette	6	McCreary	5	Warren	2
Fleming	4	McLean	1	Washington	2
Floyd	5	Madison	6	Wayne	5
Franklin	6	Magoffin	5	Webster	1
Fulton	1	Marion	2	Whitley	5
Gallatin	4	Marshall	1	Wolfe	5
Garrard	6	Martin	5	Woodford	6

Congressional District 1

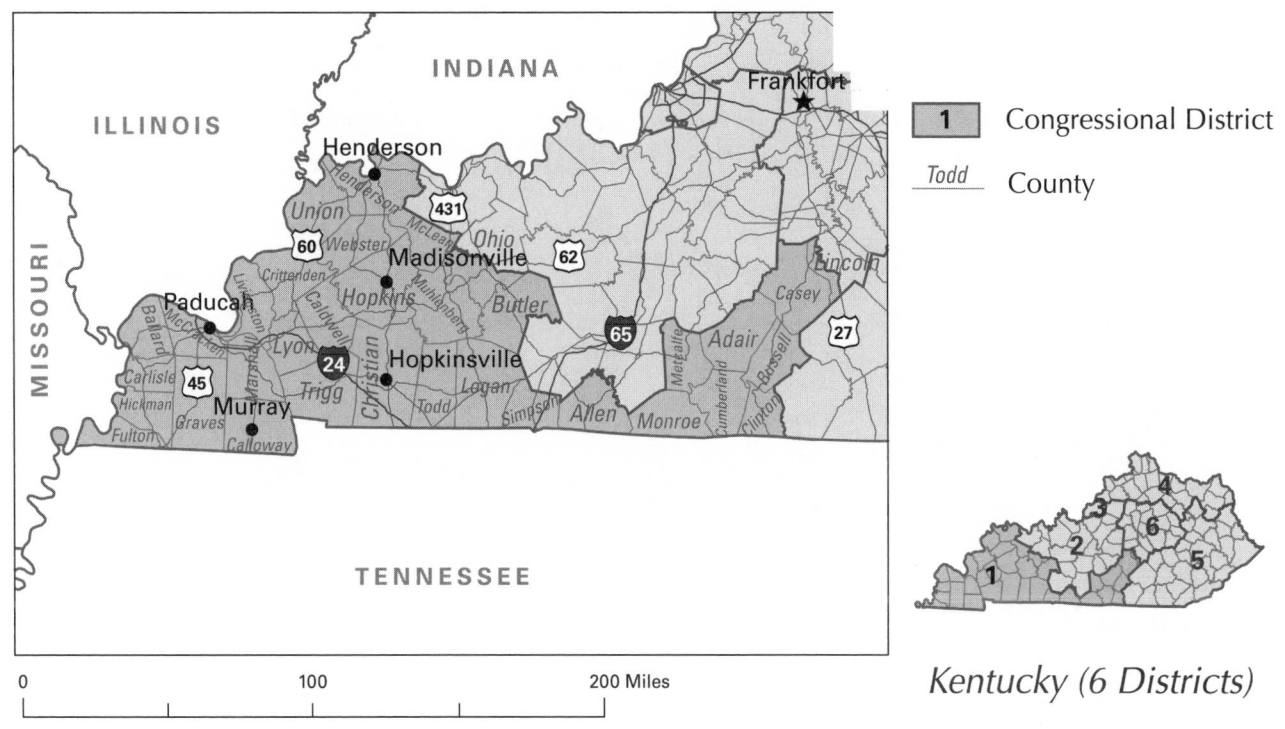

1 Congressional District
Todd County

Kentucky (6 Districts)

Congressional District 2

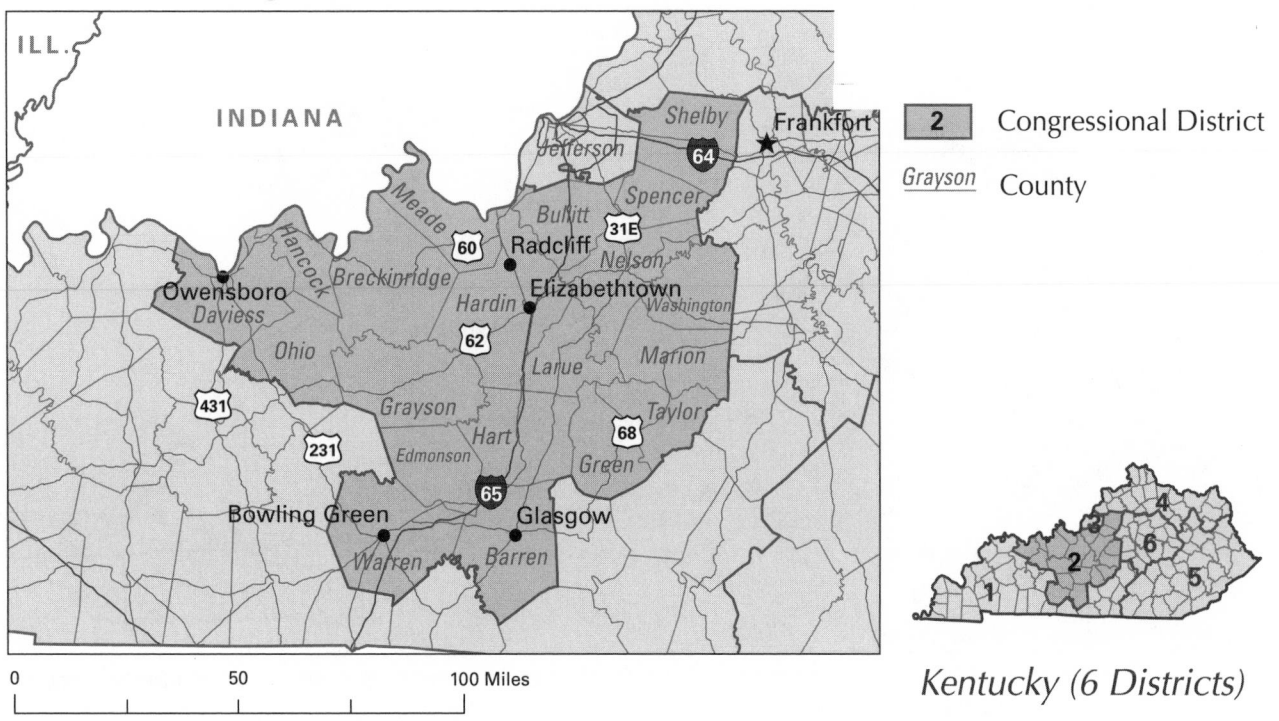

2 Congressional District
Grayson County

Kentucky (6 Districts)

Congressional District 3

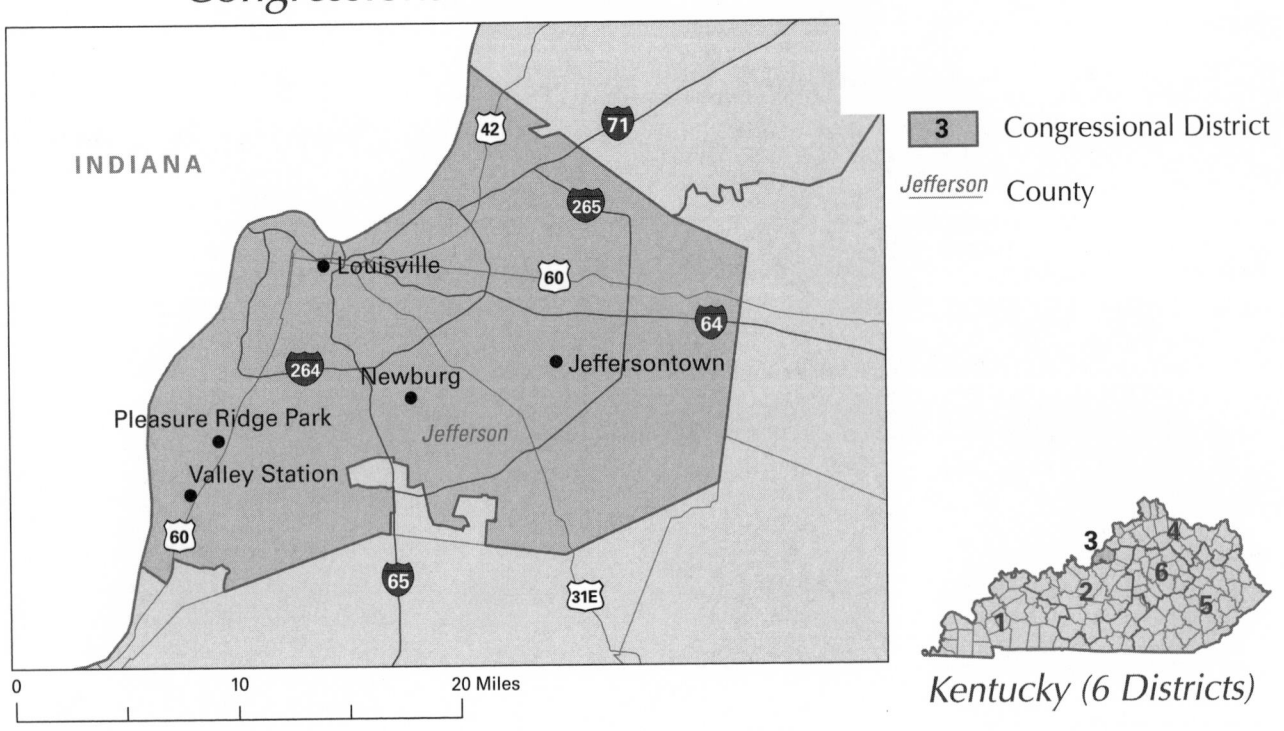

Congressional District 4

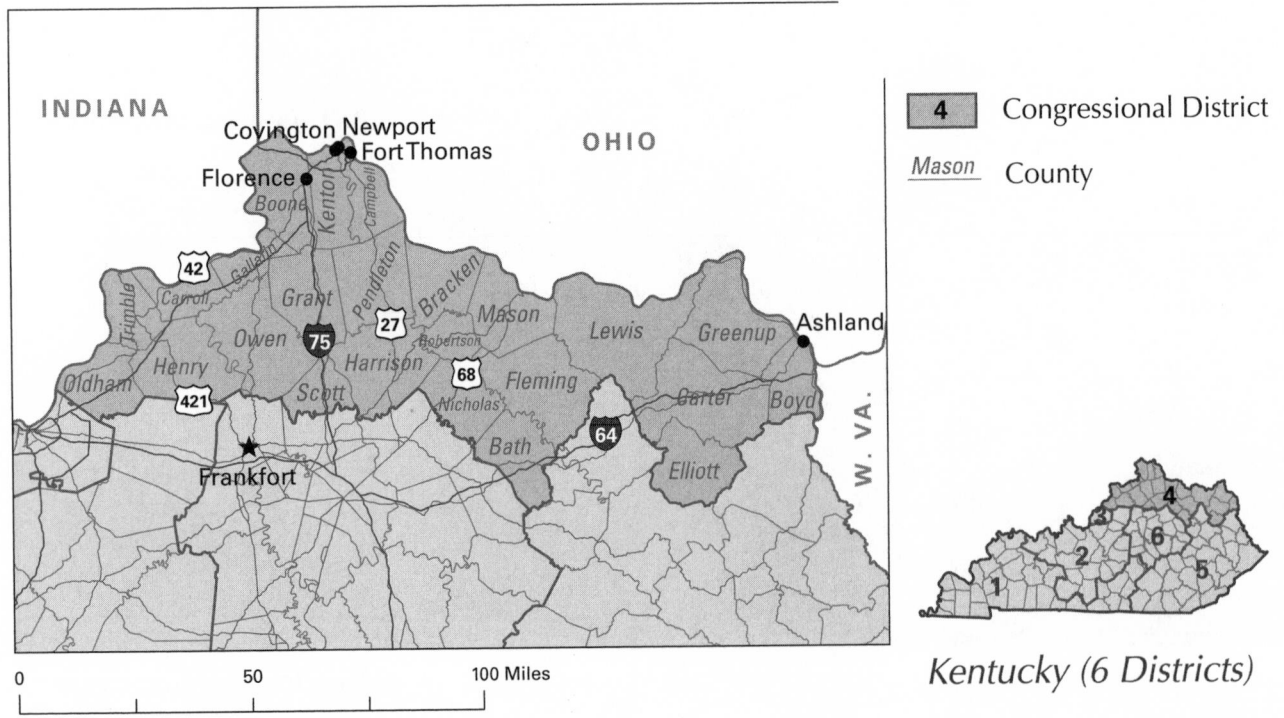

Congressional District 5

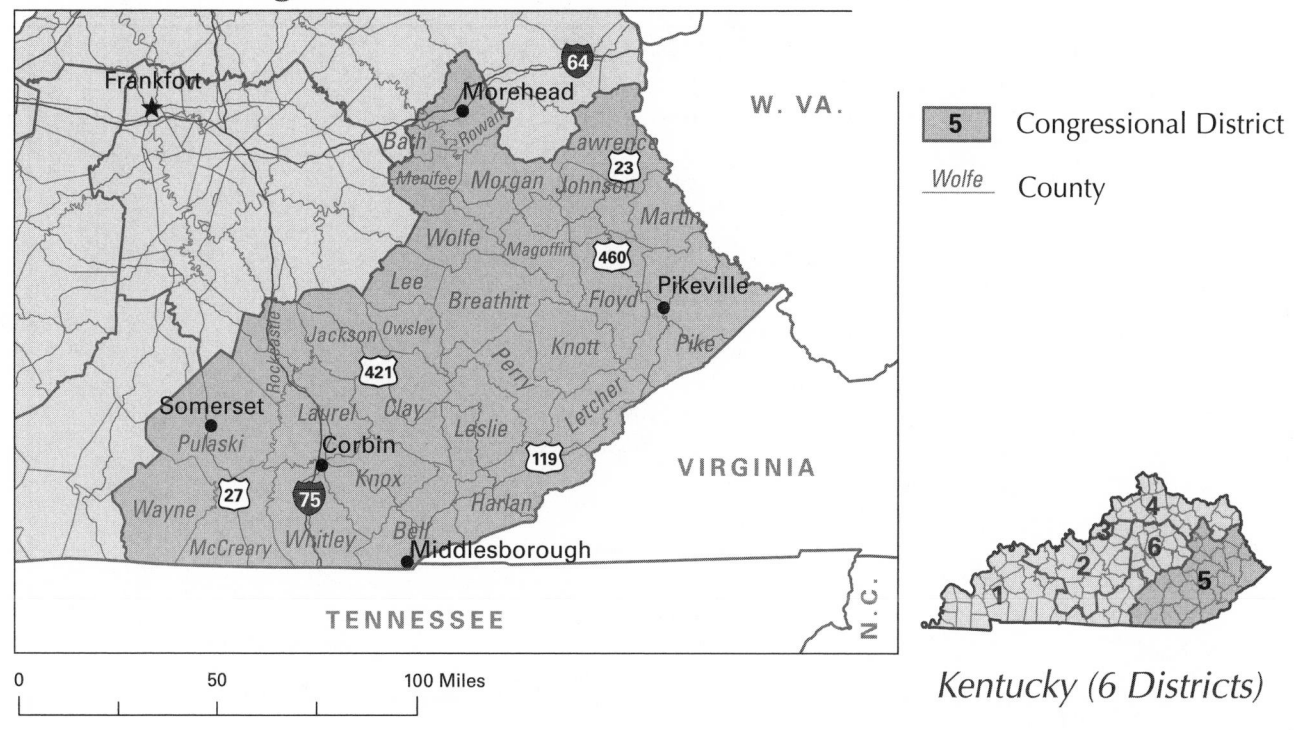

Kentucky (6 Districts)

Congressional District 6

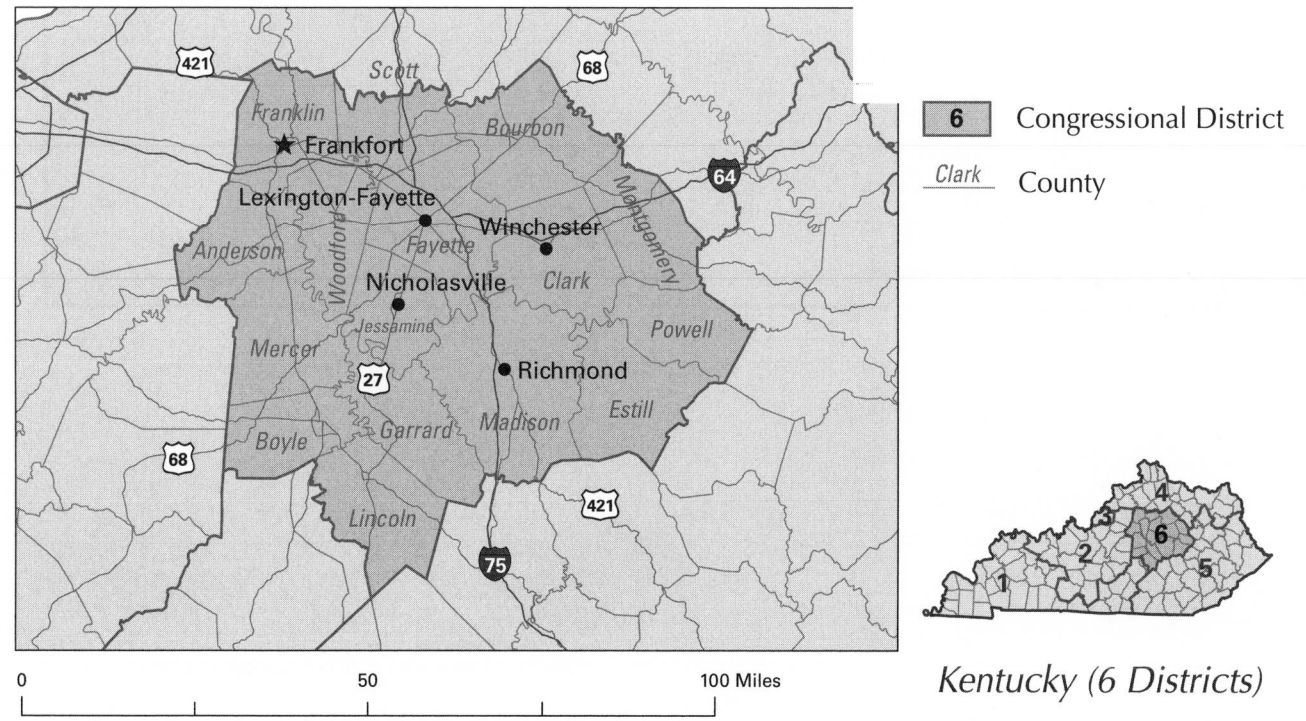

Kentucky (6 Districts)

Louisiana Congressional Districts — 7 Districts Total

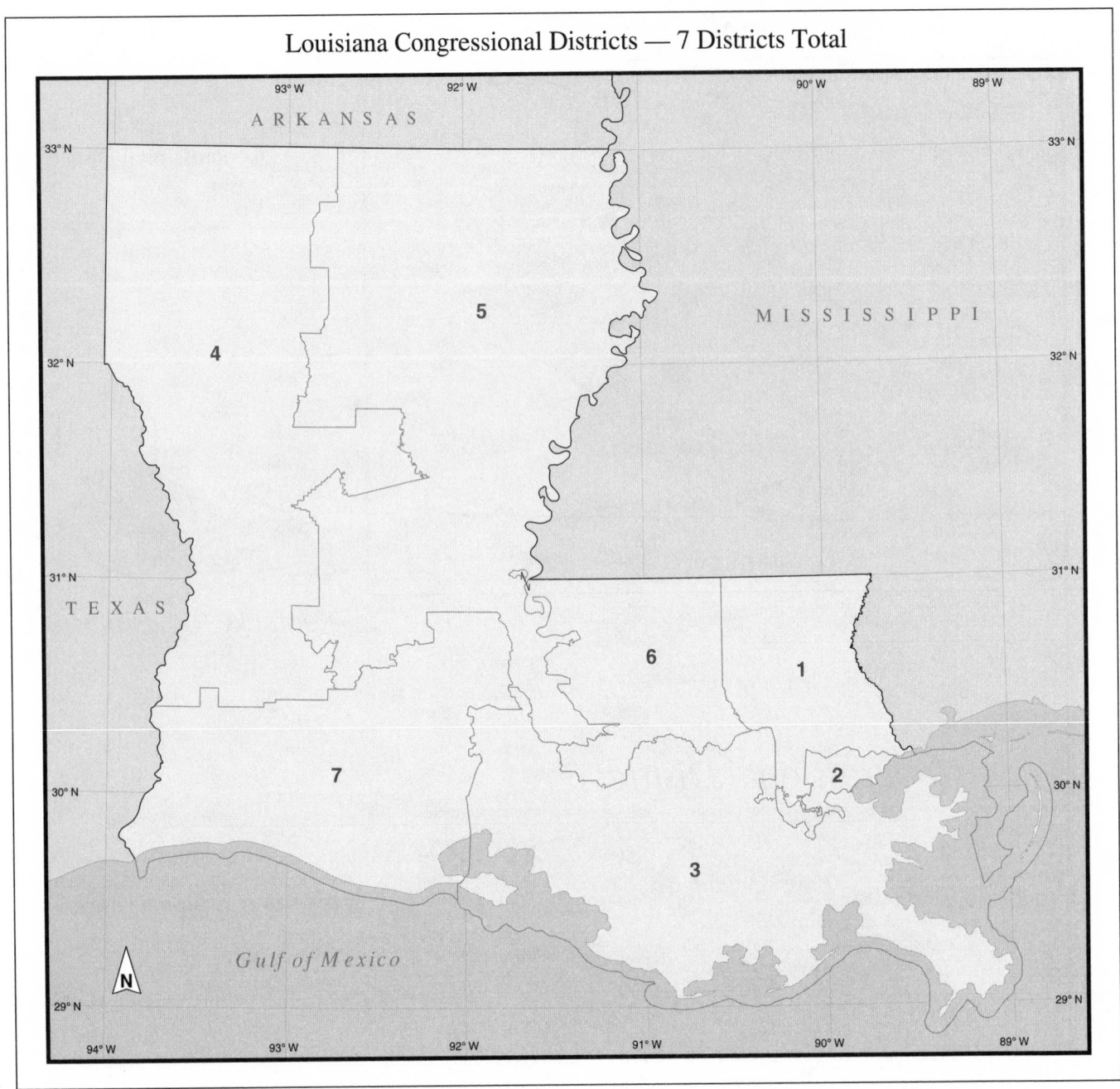

LOUISIANA—110th CONGRESSIONAL DISTRICTS BY COUNTIES

County	Congressional District
Acadia	7
Allen	4, 5
Ascension	3, 6
Assumption	3
Avoyelles	5
Beauregard	4
Bienville	4
Bossier	4
Caddo	4
Calcasieu	7
Caldwell	5
Cameron	7
Catahoula	5
Claiborne	4
Concordia	5
De Soto	4
East Baton Rouge	6
East Carroll	5
East Feliciana	6
Evangeline	5, 7
Franklin	5
Grant	4

County	Congressional District
Iberia	3
Iberville	5, 6
Jackson	5
Jefferson	1–3
Jefferson Davis	7
Lafayette	7
Lafourche	3
La Salle	5
Lincoln	5
Livingston	6
Madison	5
Morehouse	5
Natchitoches	4
Orleans	1, 2
Ouachita	5
Plaquemines	3
Pointe Coupee	5, 6
Rapides	5
Red River	4
Richland	5
Sabine	4
St. Bernard	3

County	Congressional District
St. Charles	1, 3
St. Helena	6
St. James	3
St. John the Baptist	3
St. Landry	7
St. Martin	3
St. Mary	3
St. Tammany	1
Tangipahoa	1
Tensas	5
Terrebonne	3
Union	5
Vermilion	7
Vernon	4
Washington	1
Webster	4
West Baton Rouge	6
West Carroll	5
West Feliciana	6
Winn	5

Congressional District 1

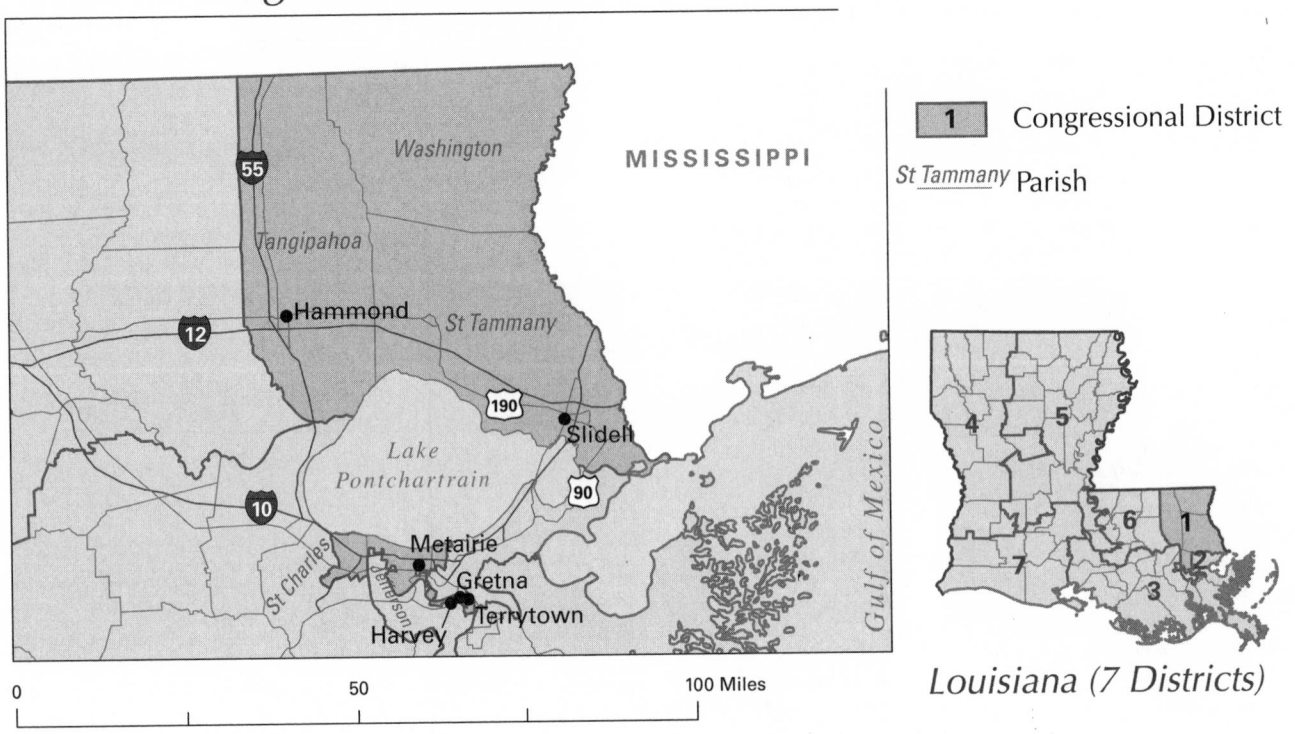

Louisiana (7 Districts)

Congressional District 2

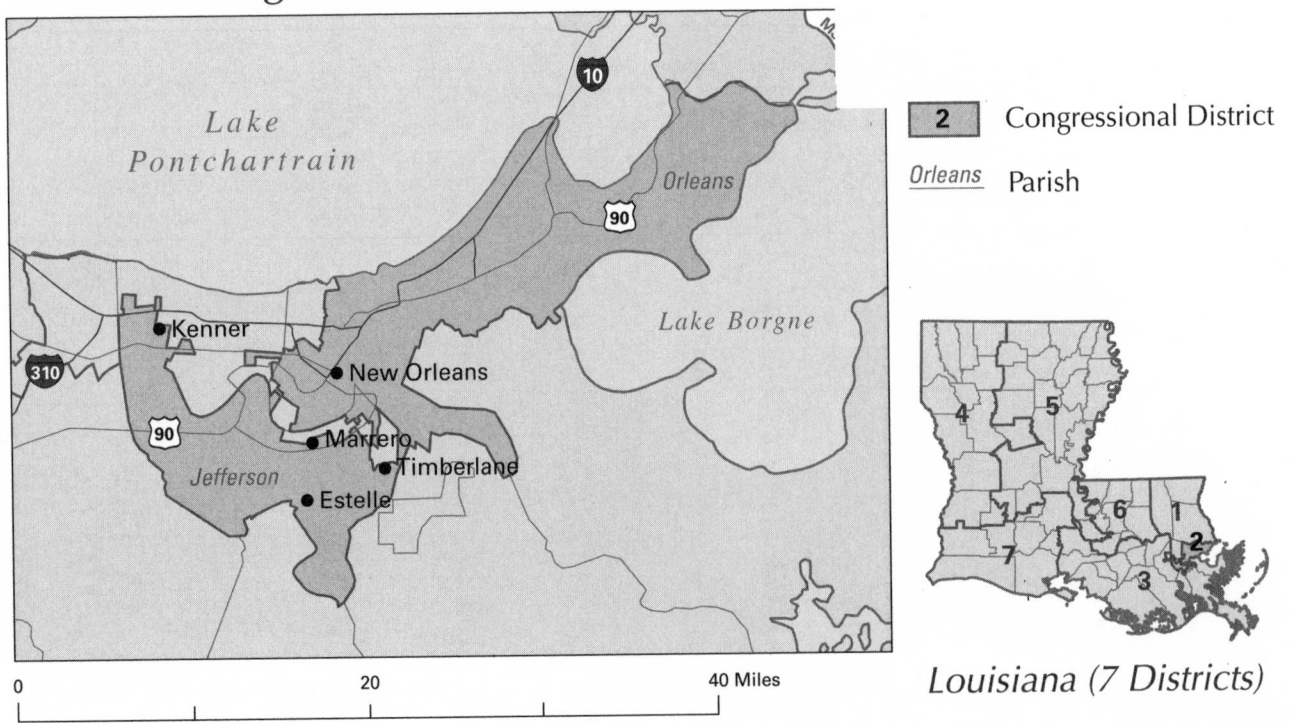

Louisiana (7 Districts)

Congressional District 3

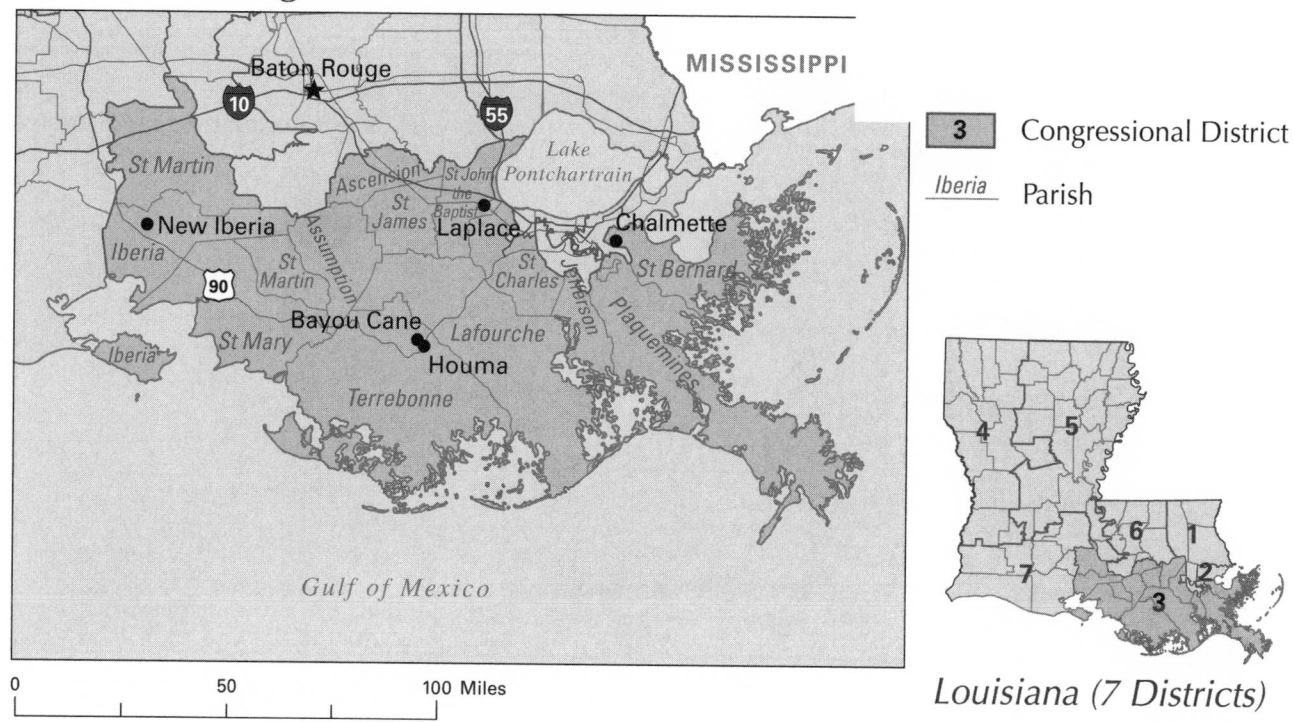

3 Congressional District

Iberia Parish

Louisiana (7 Districts)

Congressional District 4

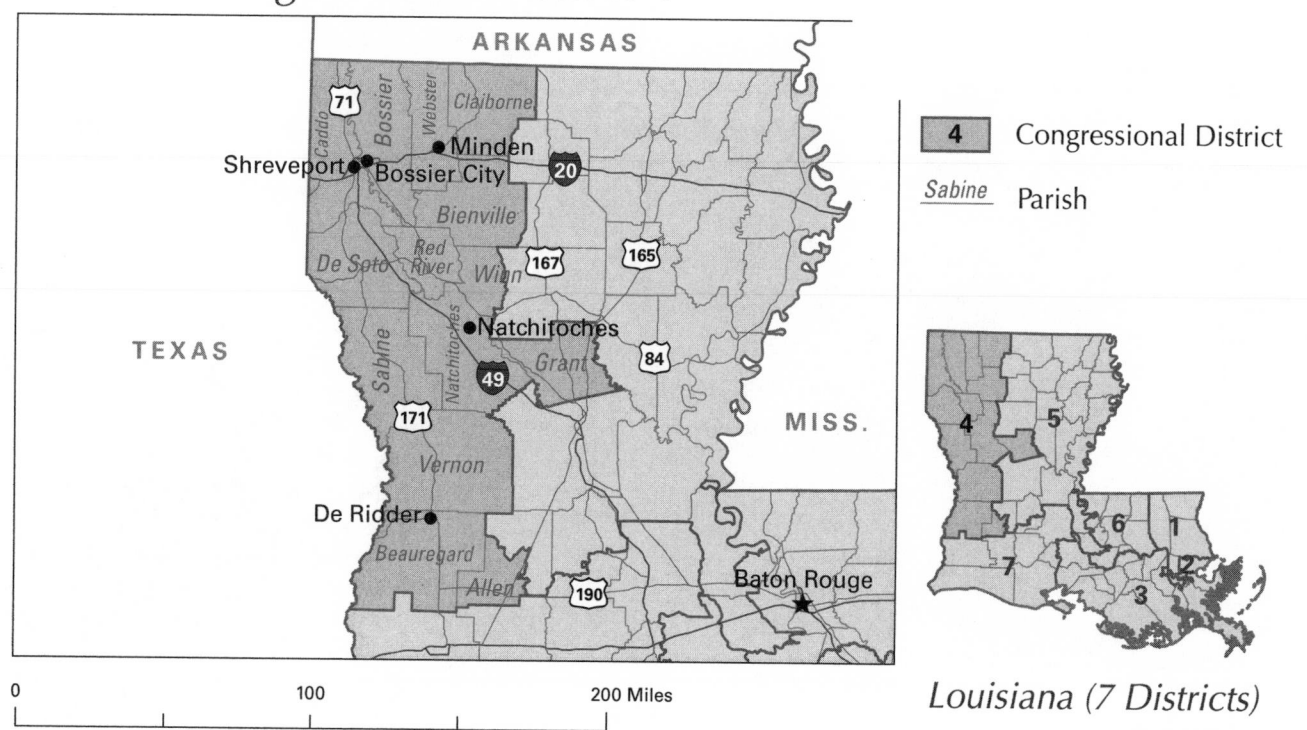

4 Congressional District

Sabine Parish

Louisiana (7 Districts)

Congressional District 5

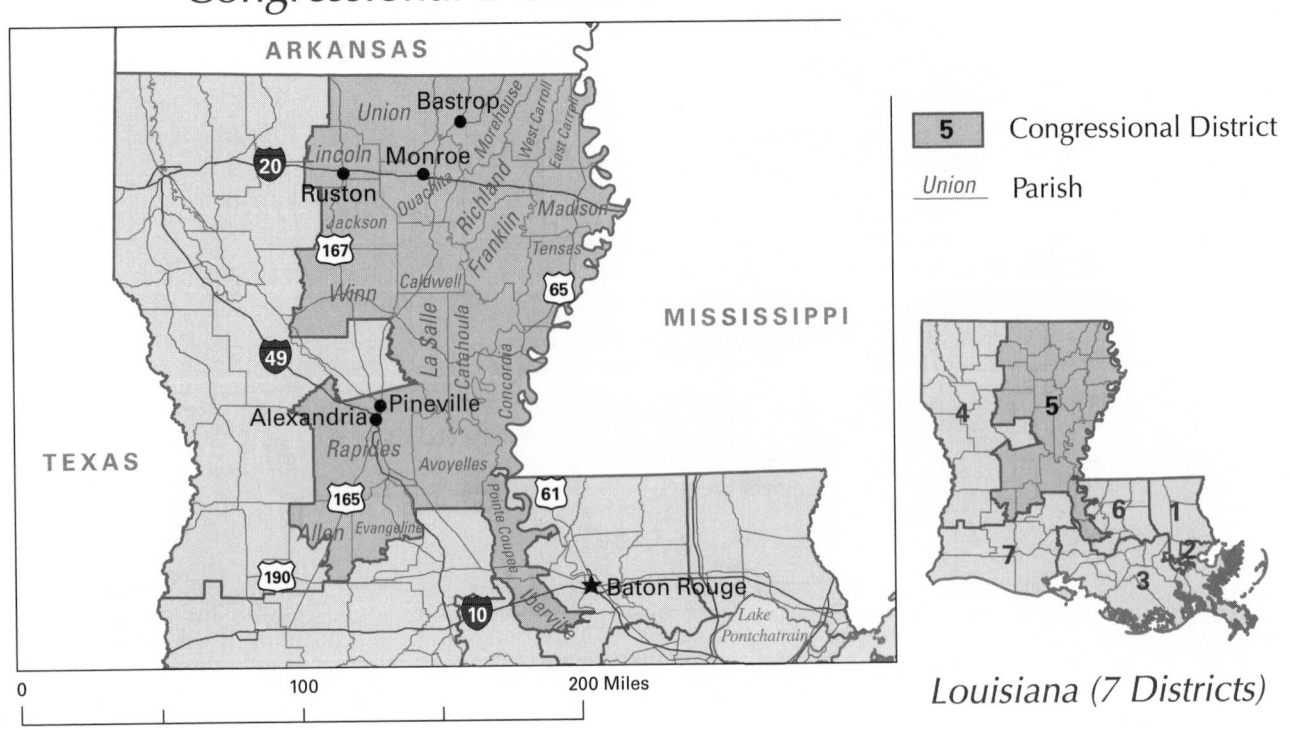

Louisiana (7 Districts)

Congressional District 6

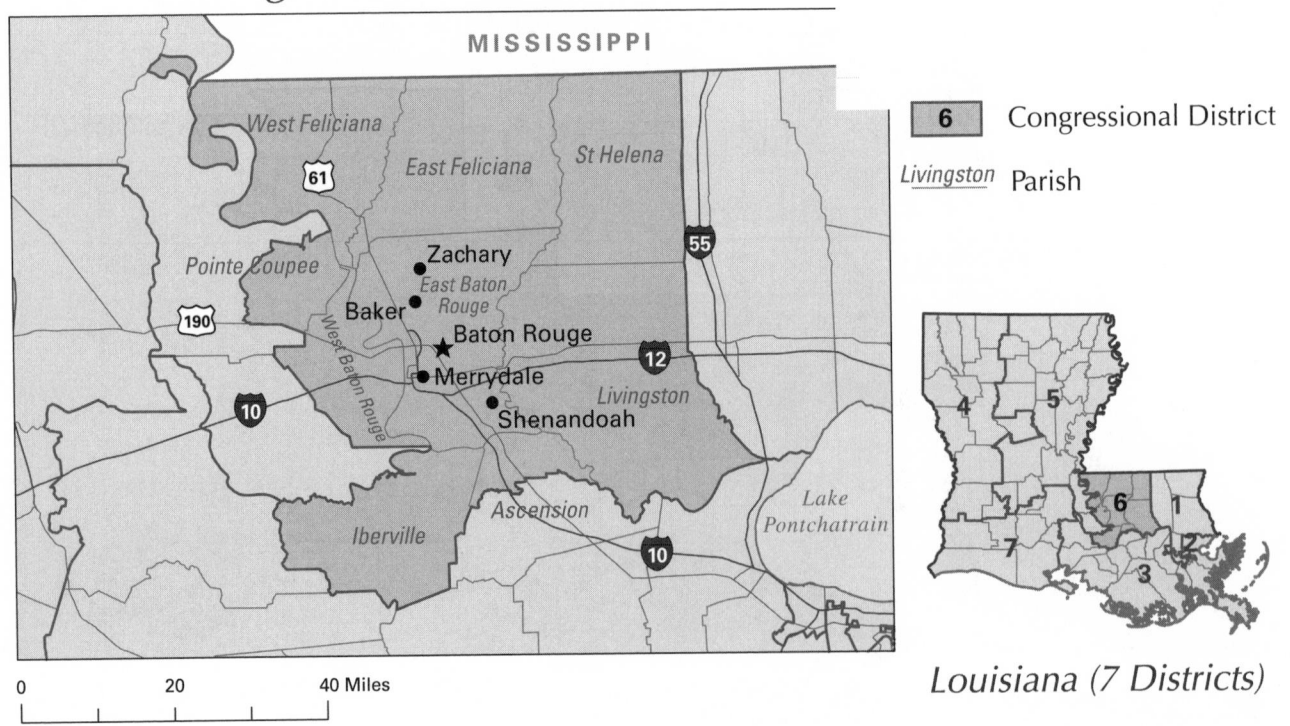

Louisiana (7 Districts)

Congressional District 7

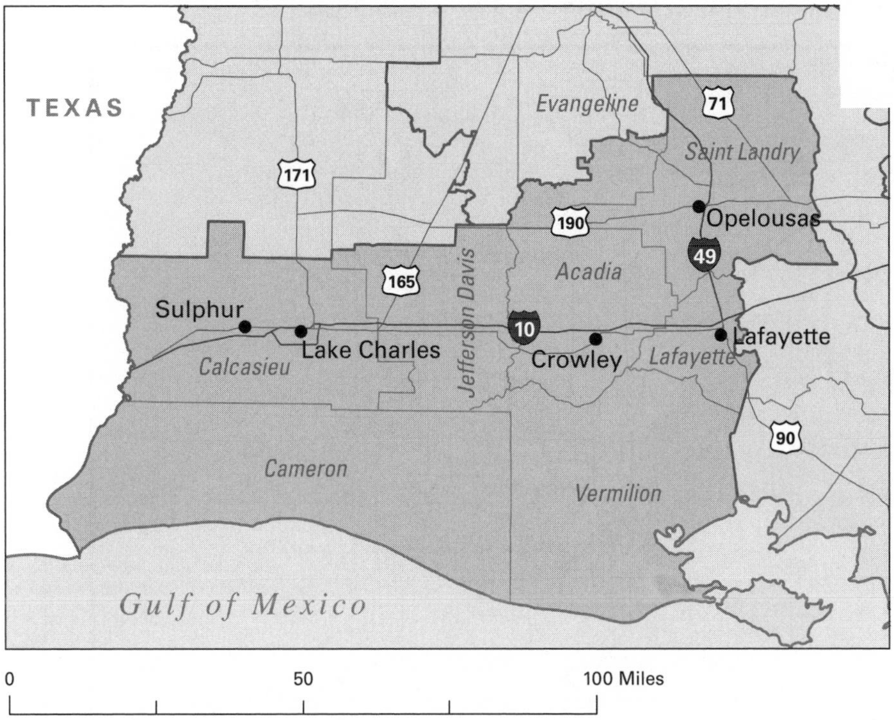

7	Congressional District
Cameron	Parish

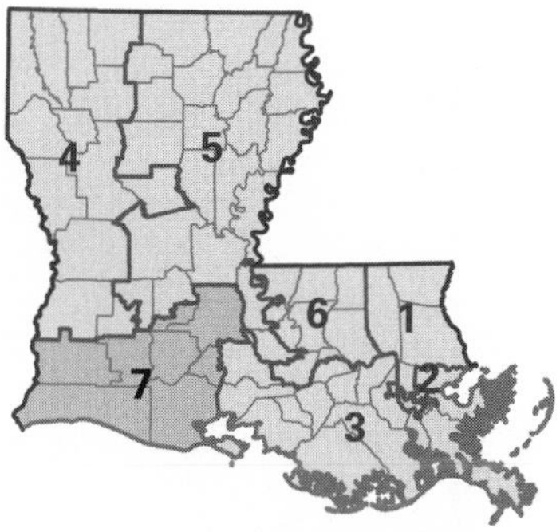

TEXAS

Evangeline

Saint Landry

171

190

Opelousas

165

49

Acadia

Sulphur

Lake Charles

10

Crowley

Lafayette

Calcasieu

Jefferson Davis

Lafayette

90

Cameron

Vermilion

Gulf of Mexico

0   50   100 Miles

Louisiana (7 Districts)

Maine Congressional Districts - 2 Districts Total

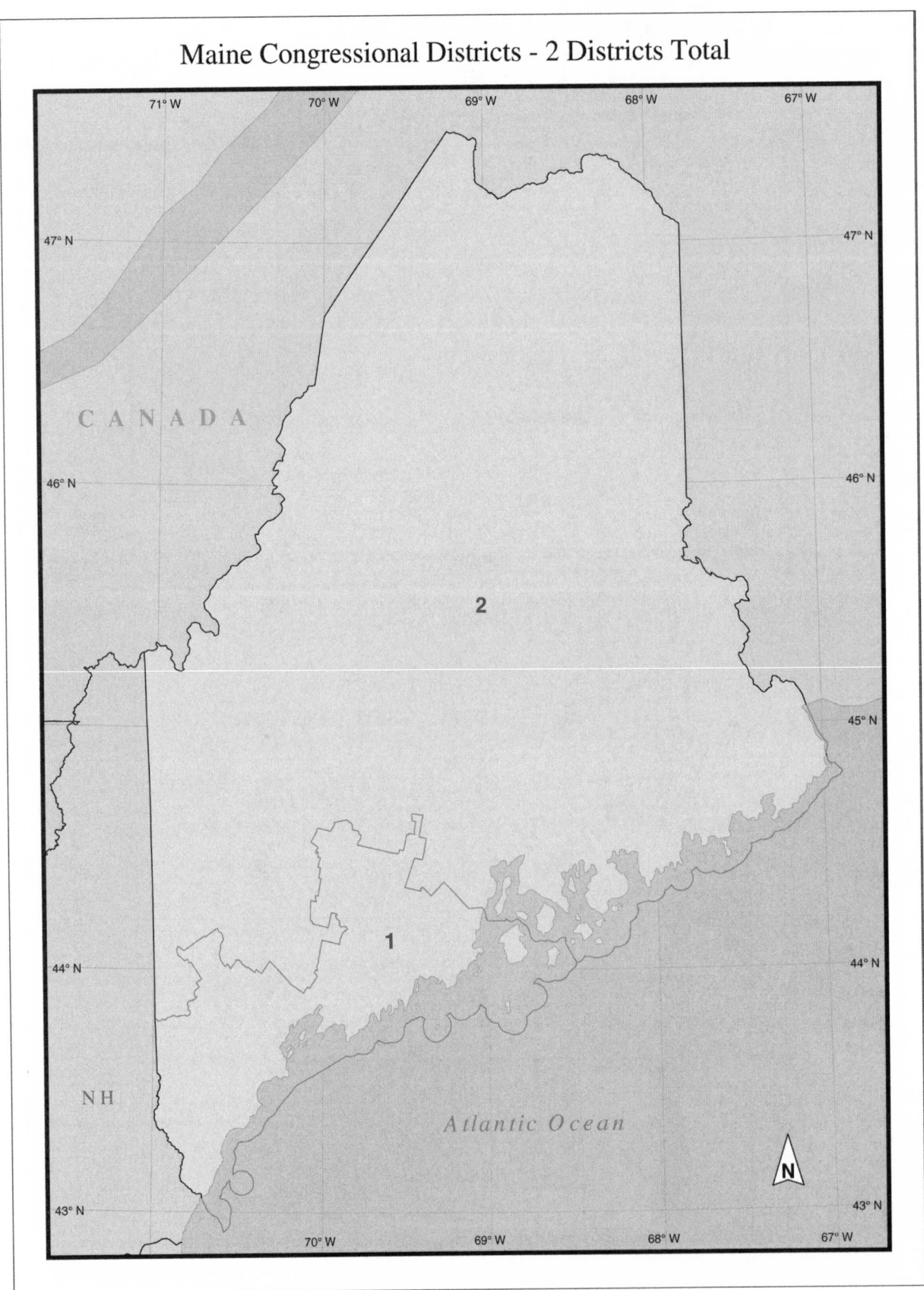

MAINE—110th CONGRESSIONAL DISTRICTS BY COUNTIES

County	Congressional District	County	Congressional District
Androscoggin	2	Penobscot	2
Aroostook	2	Piscataquis	2
Cumberland	1	Sagadahoc	1
Franklin	2	Somerset	2
Hancock	2	Waldo	2
Kennebec	1, 2	Washington	2
Knox	1	York	1
Lincoln	1		
Oxford	2		

Congressional District 1

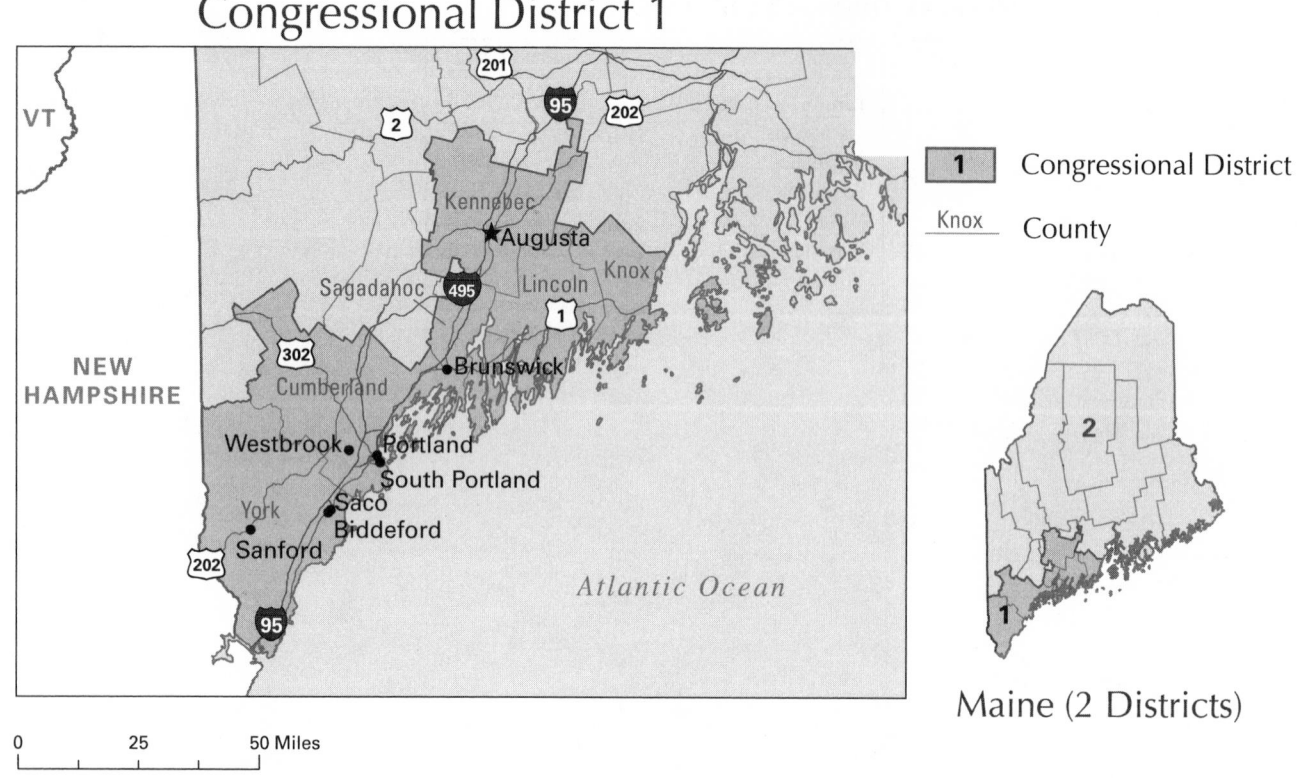

0   25   50 Miles

1 Congressional District

Knox County

Maine (2 Districts)

Congressional District 2

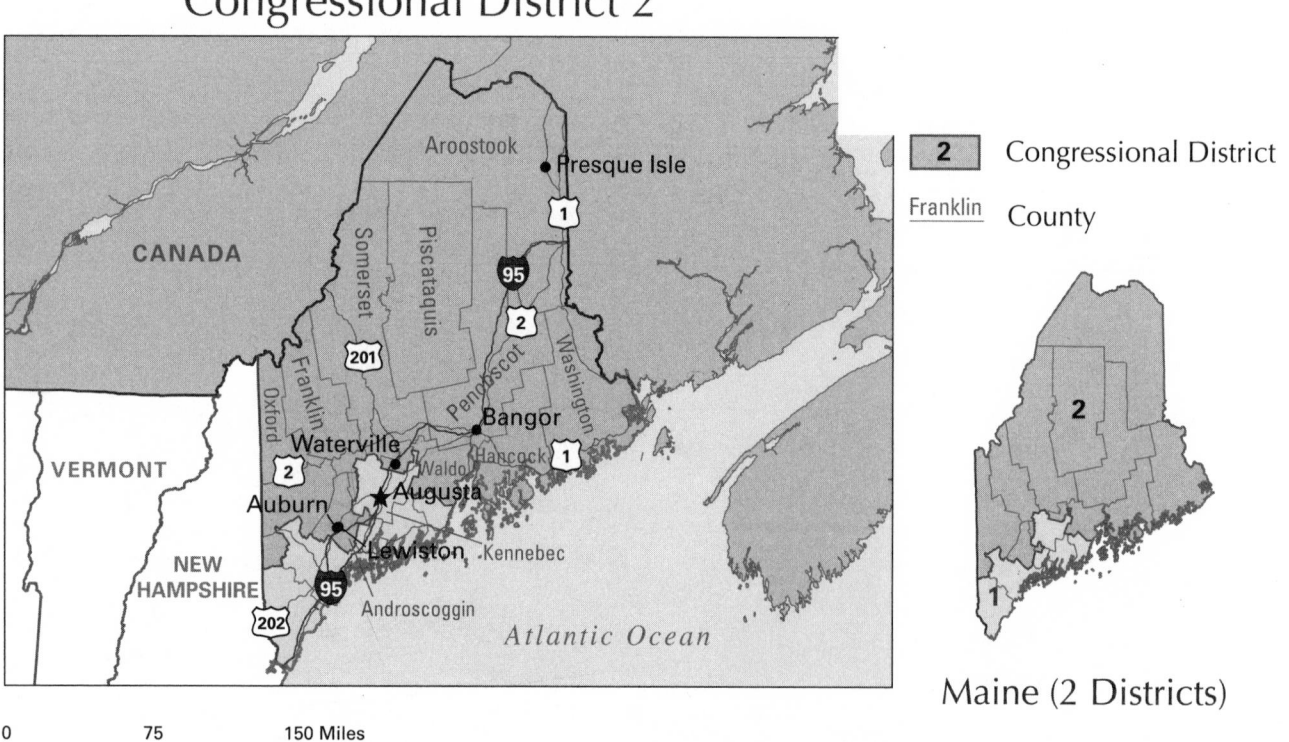

0   75   150 Miles

2 Congressional District

Franklin County

Maine (2 Districts)

Maryland Congressional Districts — 8 Districts Total

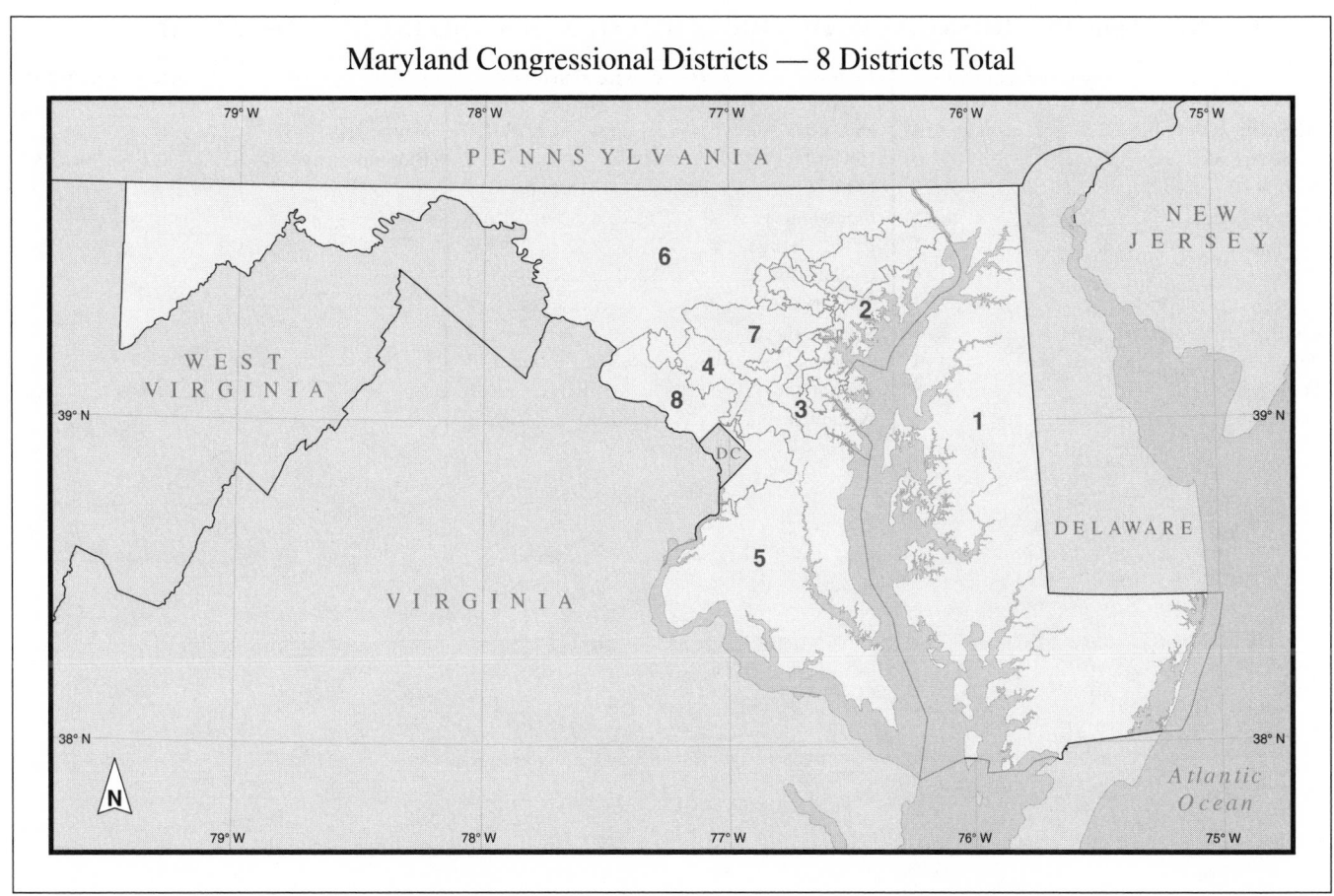

MARYLAND—110th CONGRESSIONAL DISTRICTS BY COUNTIES AND INDEPENDENT CITIES

County	Congressional District
Allegany	6
Anne Arundel	1–3, 5
Baltimore	1–3, 6, 7
Calvert	5
Caroline	1
Carroll	6
Cecil	1
Charles	5
Dorchester	1
Frederick	6
Garrett	6

County	Congressional District
Harford	1, 2, 6
Howard	3, 7
Kent	1
Montgomery	4, 6, 8
Prince George's	4, 5, 8
Queen Anne's	1
St. Mary's	5
Somerset	1
Talbot	1
Washington	6
Wicomico	1

County	Congressional District
Worcester	1
Baltimore city	2, 3, 7

Congressional District 1

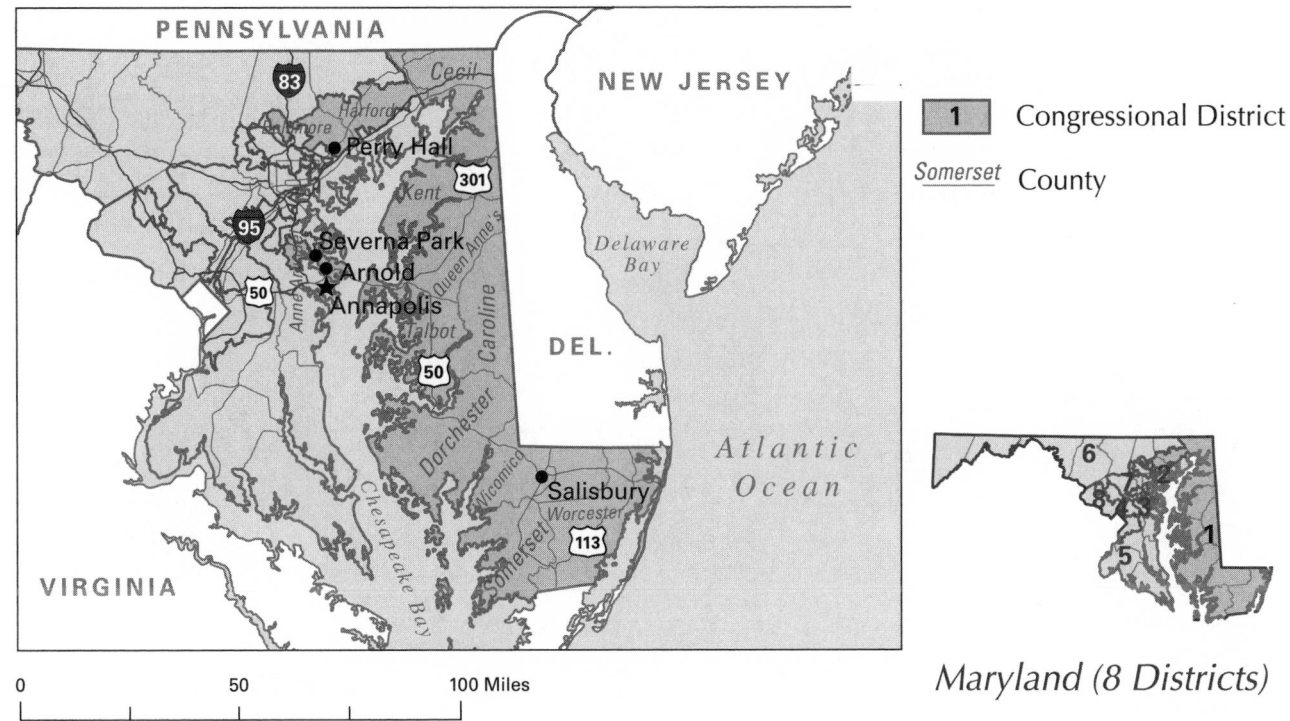

1	Congressional District
Somerset	County

Maryland (8 Districts)

Congressional District 2

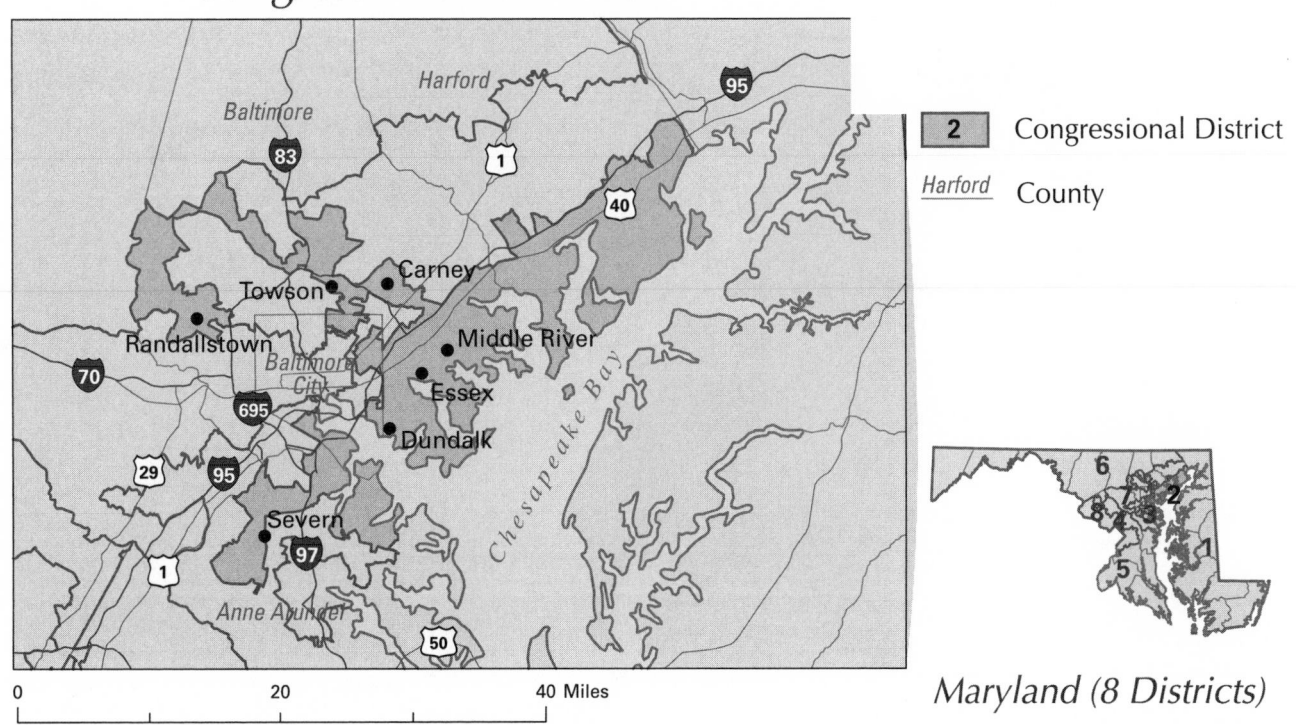

2	Congressional District
Harford	County

Maryland (8 Districts)

Congressional District 3

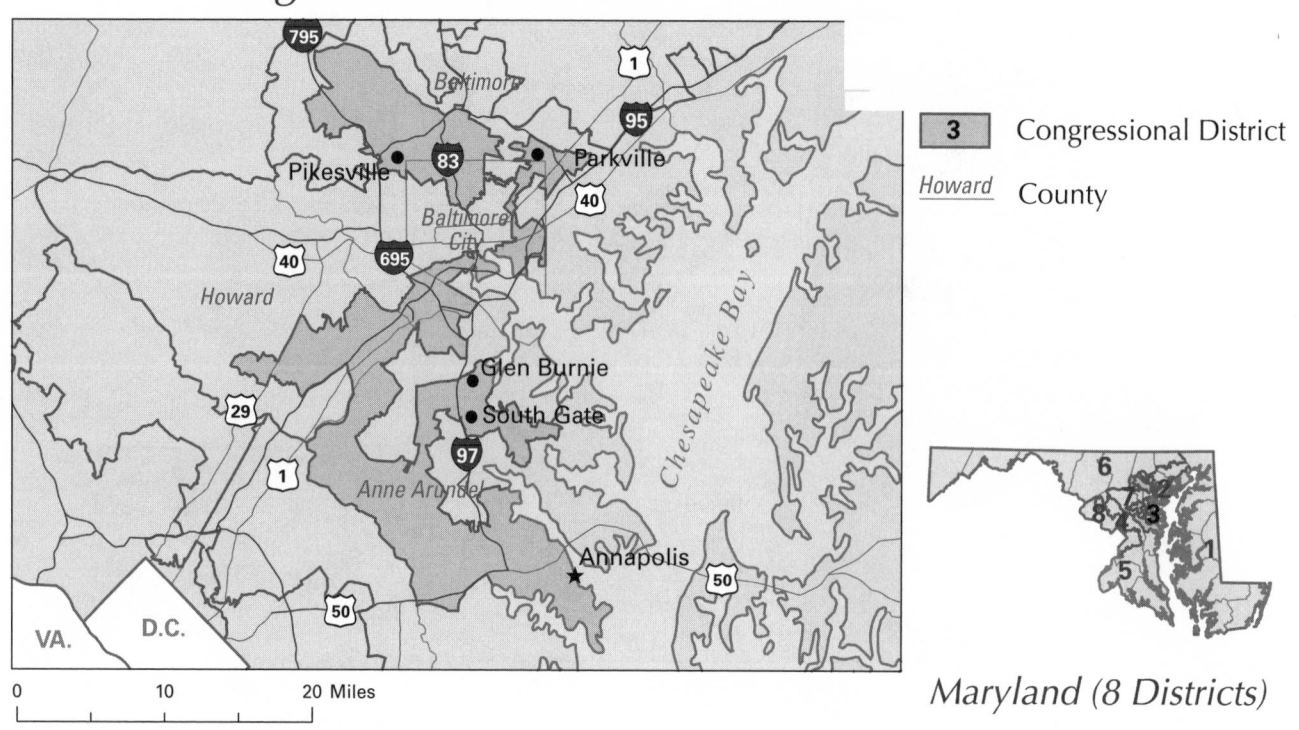

3 Congressional District

Howard County

Maryland (8 Districts)

Congressional District 4

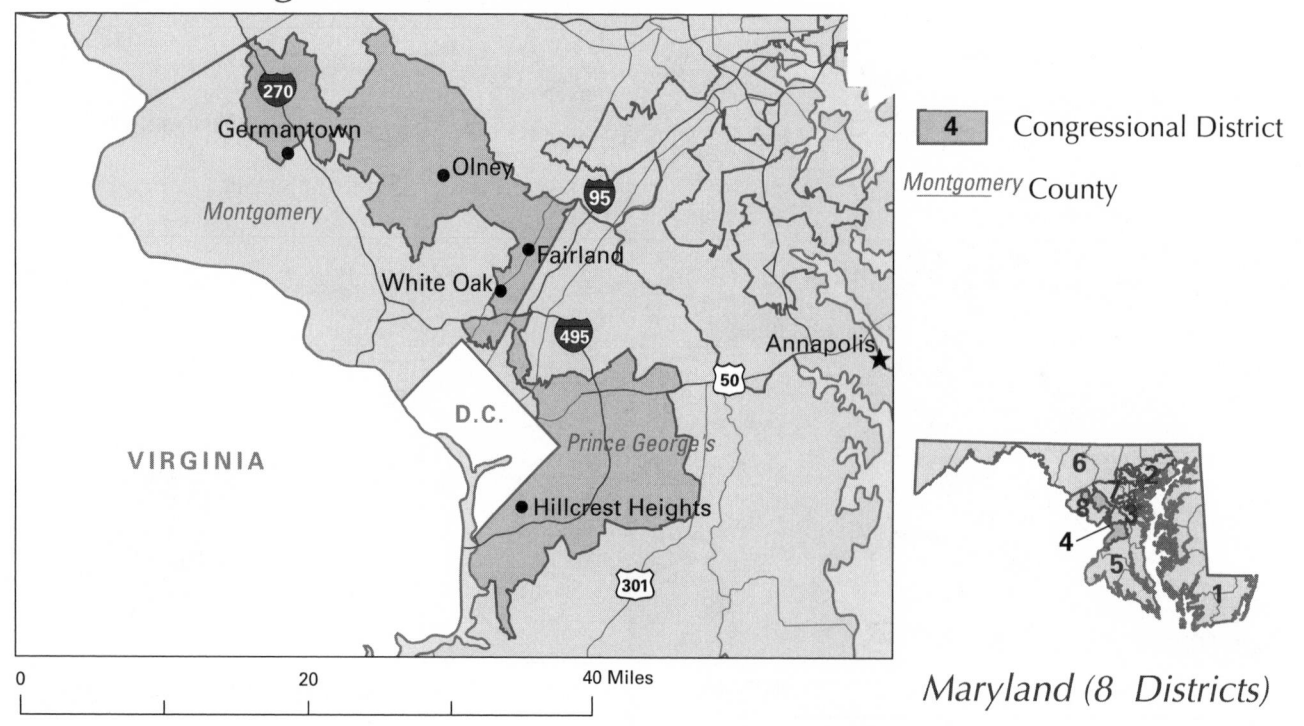

4 Congressional District

Montgomery County

Maryland (8 Districts)

Congressional District 5

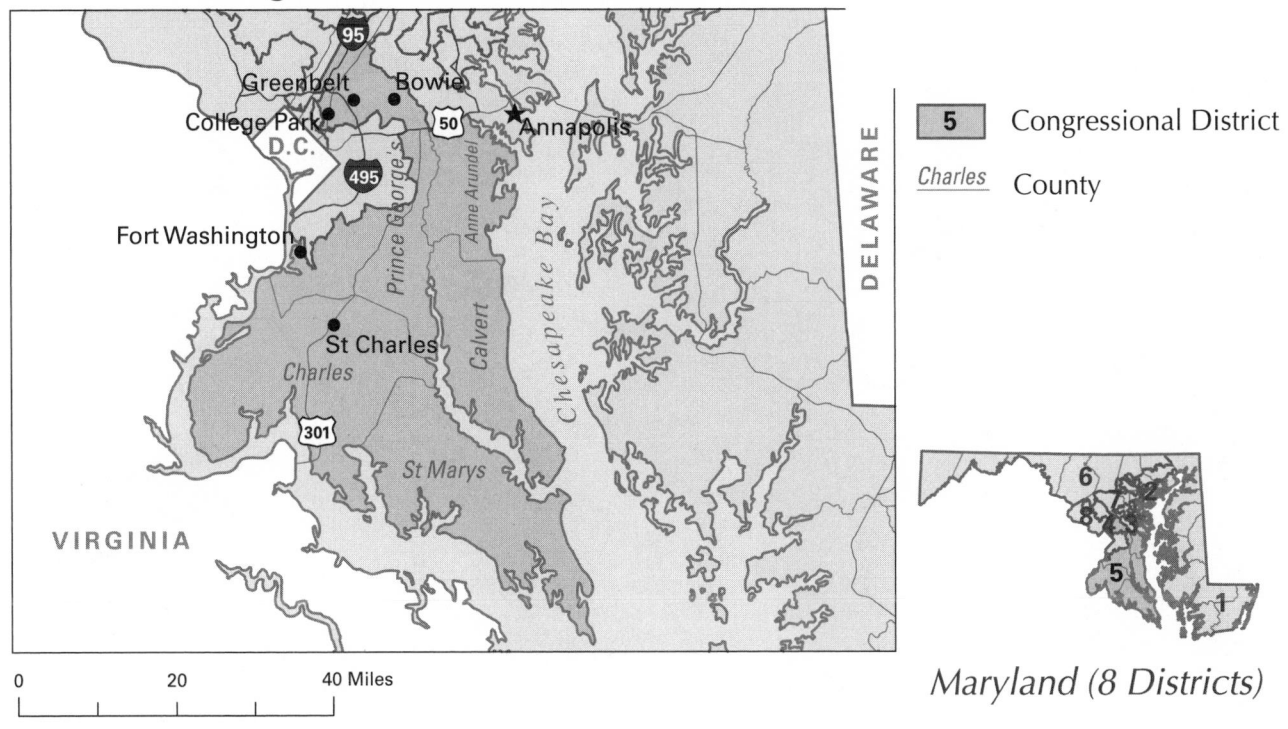

5	Congressional District
Charles	County

Maryland (8 Districts)

0   20   40 Miles

Congressional District 6

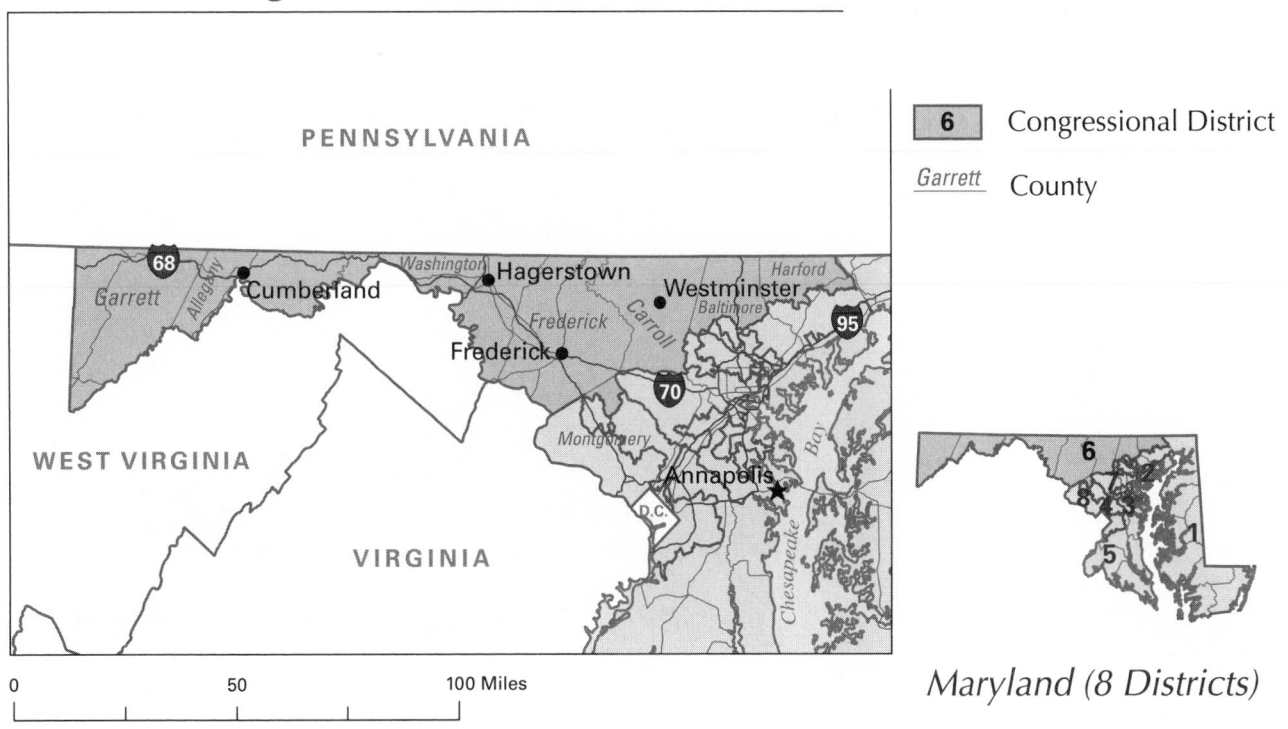

6	Congressional District
Garrett	County

Maryland (8 Districts)

0   50   100 Miles

Congressional District 7

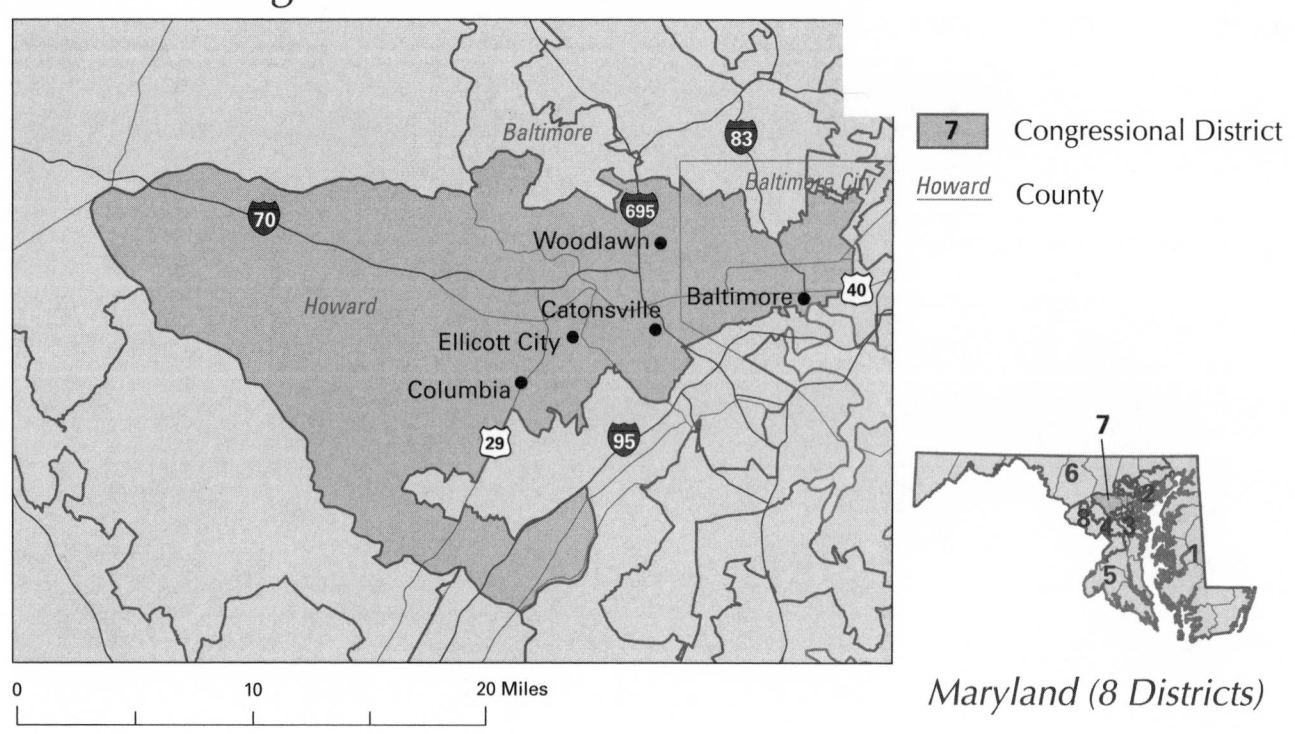

7	Congressional District
Howard	County

Maryland (8 Districts)

Congressional District 8

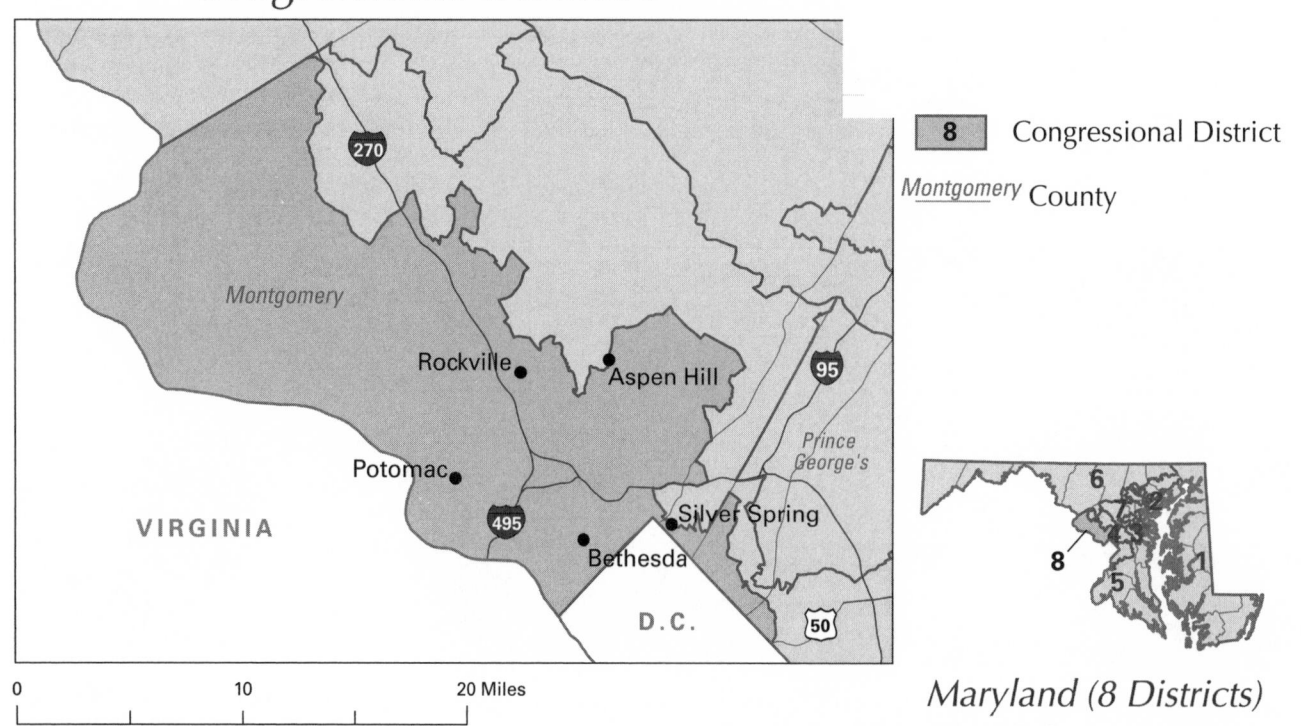

8	Congressional District
Montgomery	County

Maryland (8 Districts)

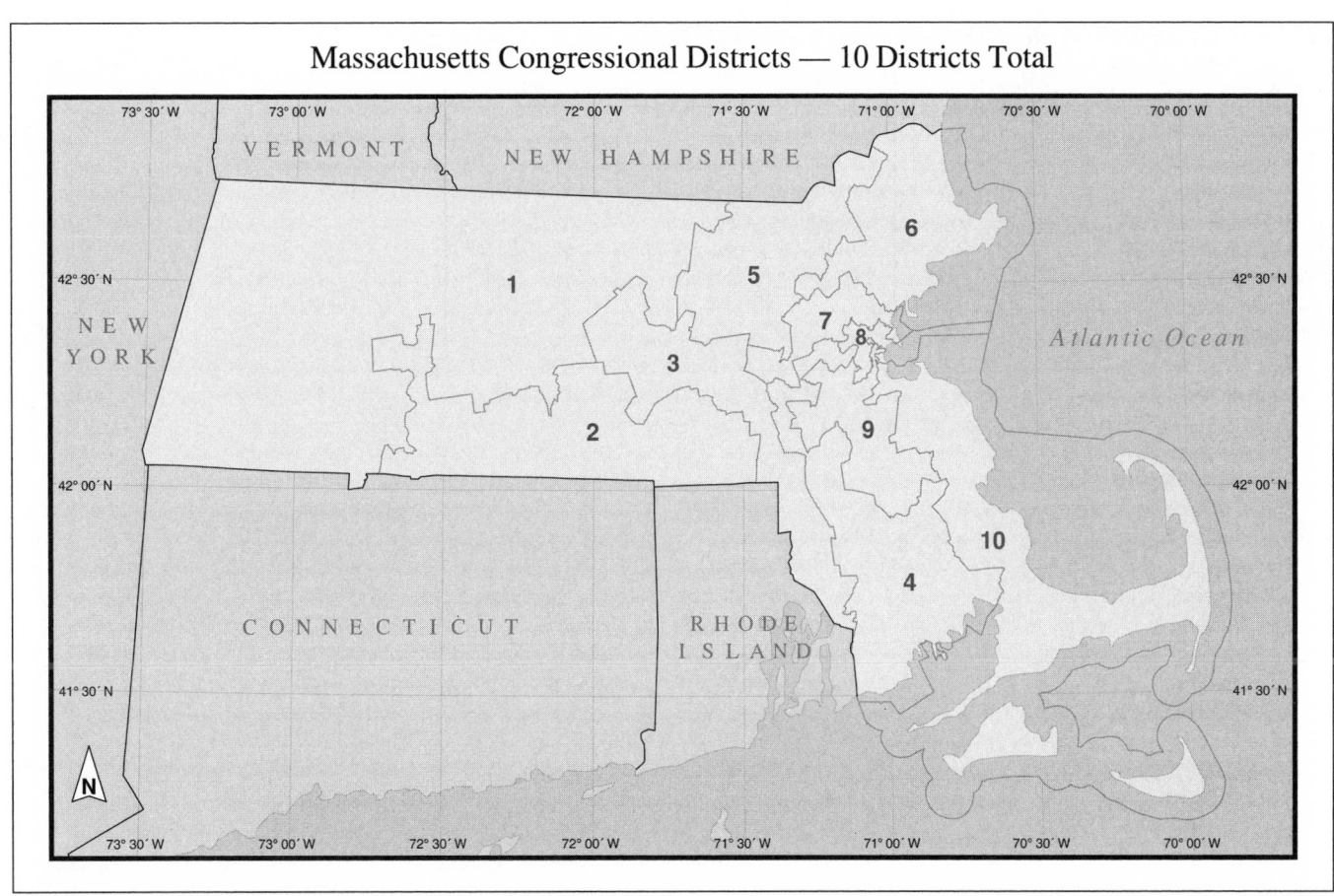

Massachusetts Congressional Districts — 10 Districts Total

MASSACHUSETTS—110th CONGRESSIONAL DISTRICTS BY COUNTIES

County	Congressional District	County	Congressional District
Barnstable	10	Middlesex	1, 3–8
Berkshire	1	Nantucket	10
Bristol	3, 4, 9, 10	Norfolk	2–4, 9, 10
Dukes	10	Plymouth	4, 9, 10
Essex	5, 6	Suffolk	7–9
Franklin	1	Worcester	1–3, 5
Hampden	1, 2		
Hampshire	1, 2		

Congressional District 1

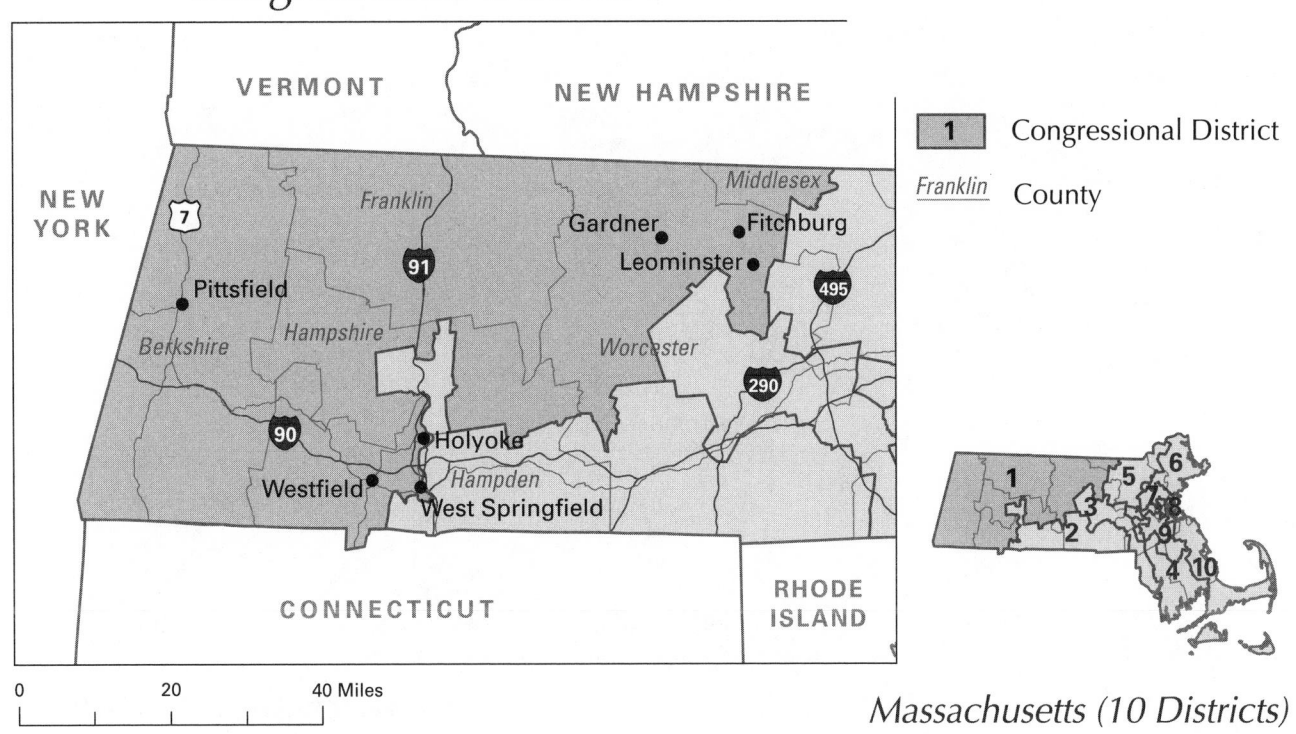

1 Congressional District
Franklin County

Massachusetts (10 Districts)

Congressional District 2

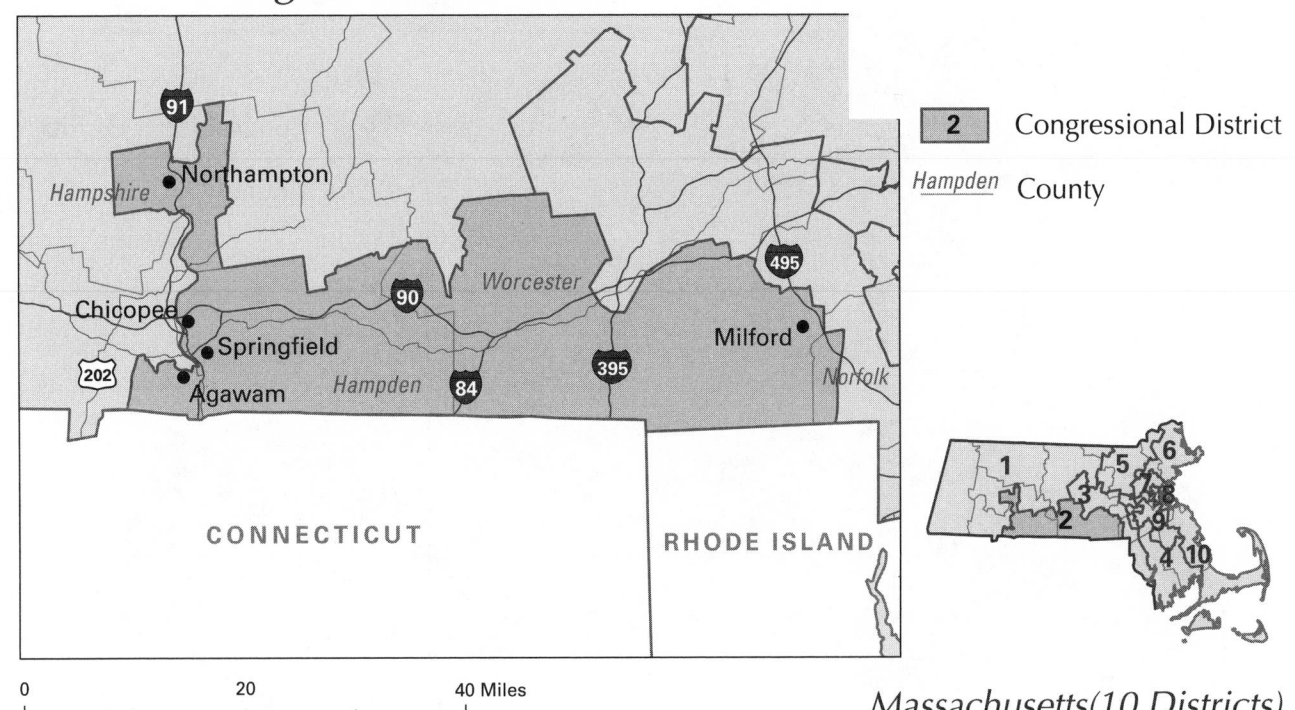

2 Congressional District
Hampden County

Massachusetts(10 Districts)

Congressional District 3

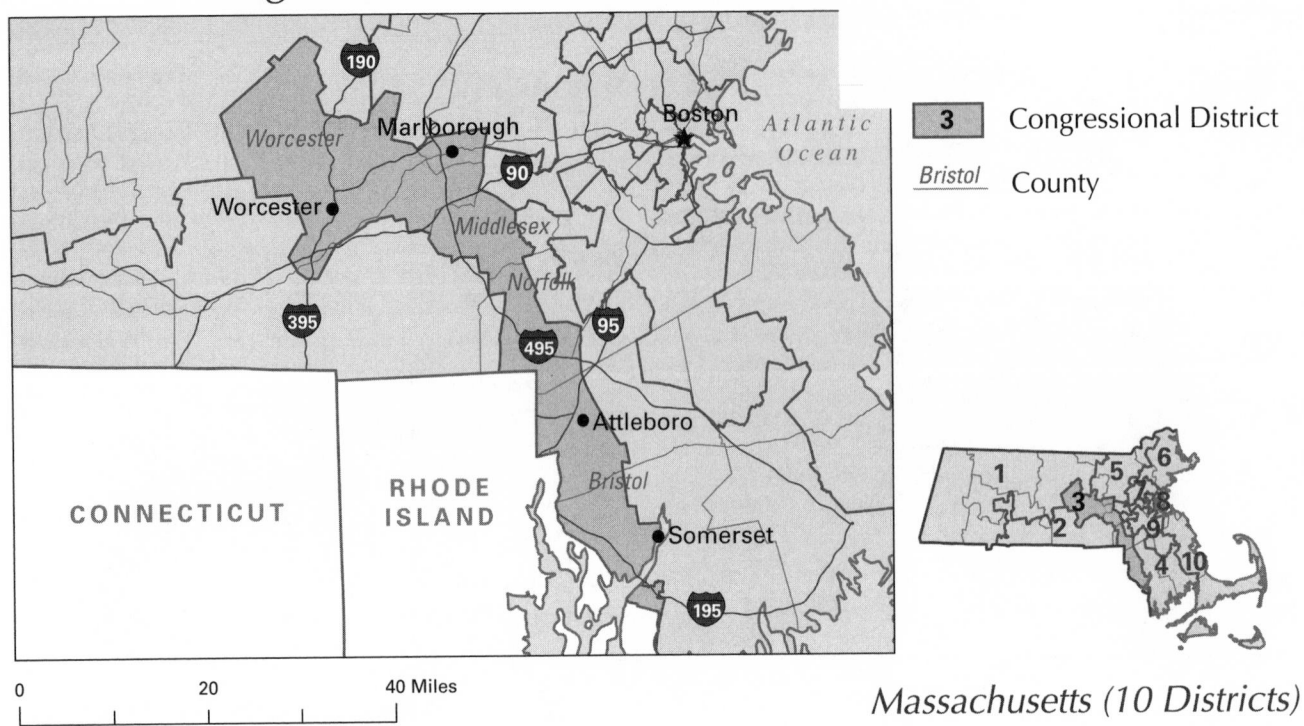

Massachusetts (10 Districts)

Congressional District 4

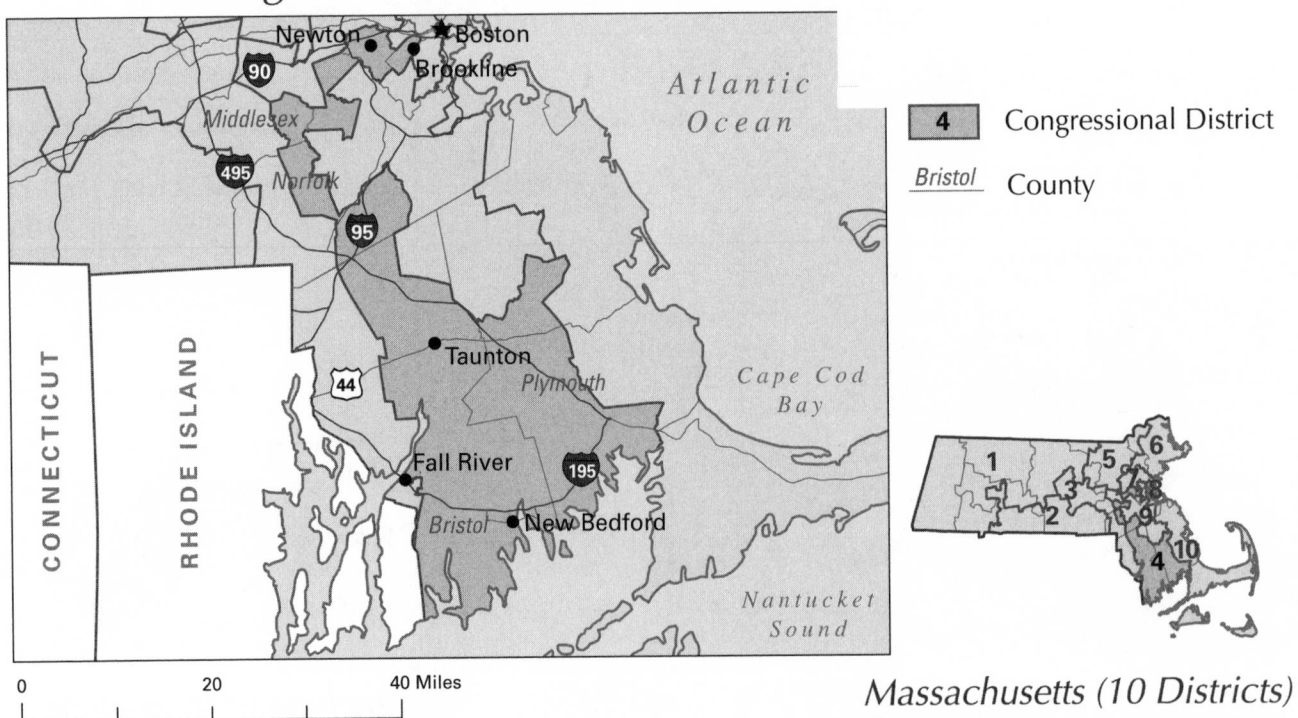

Massachusetts (10 Districts)

Congressional District 5

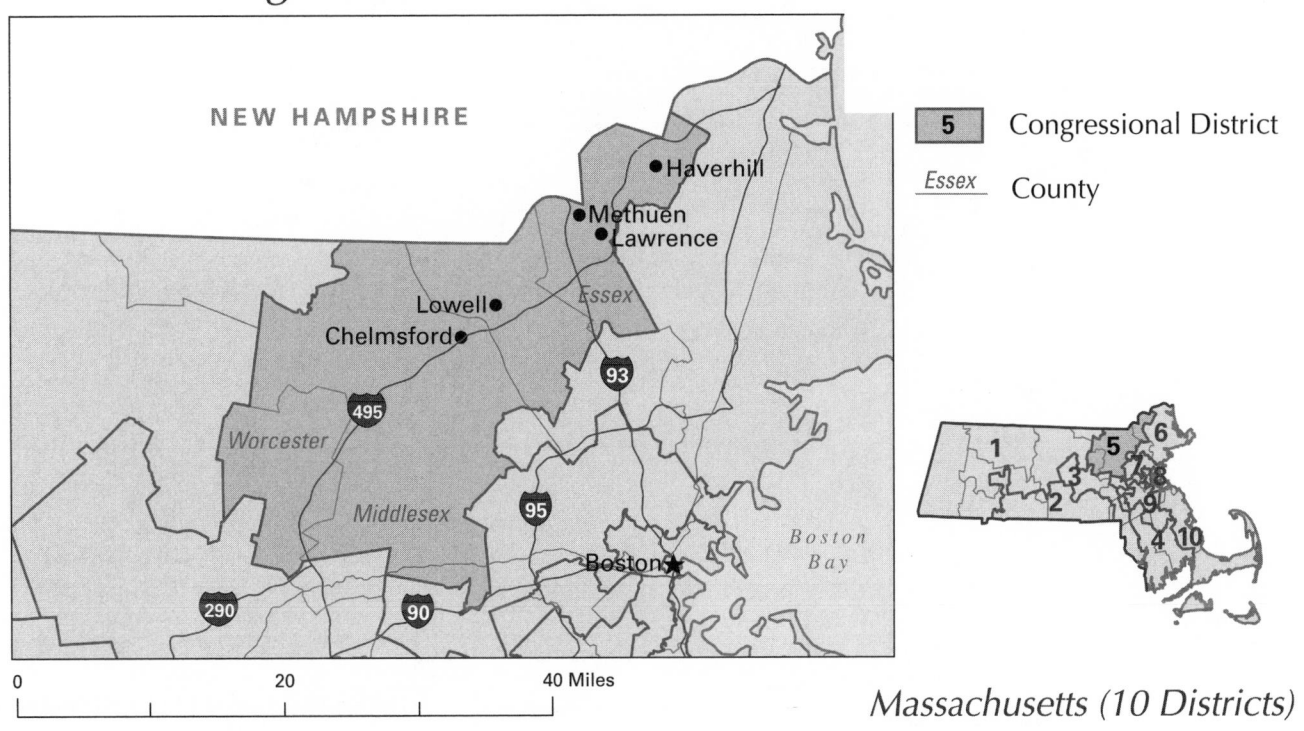

Massachusetts (10 Districts)

Congressional District 6

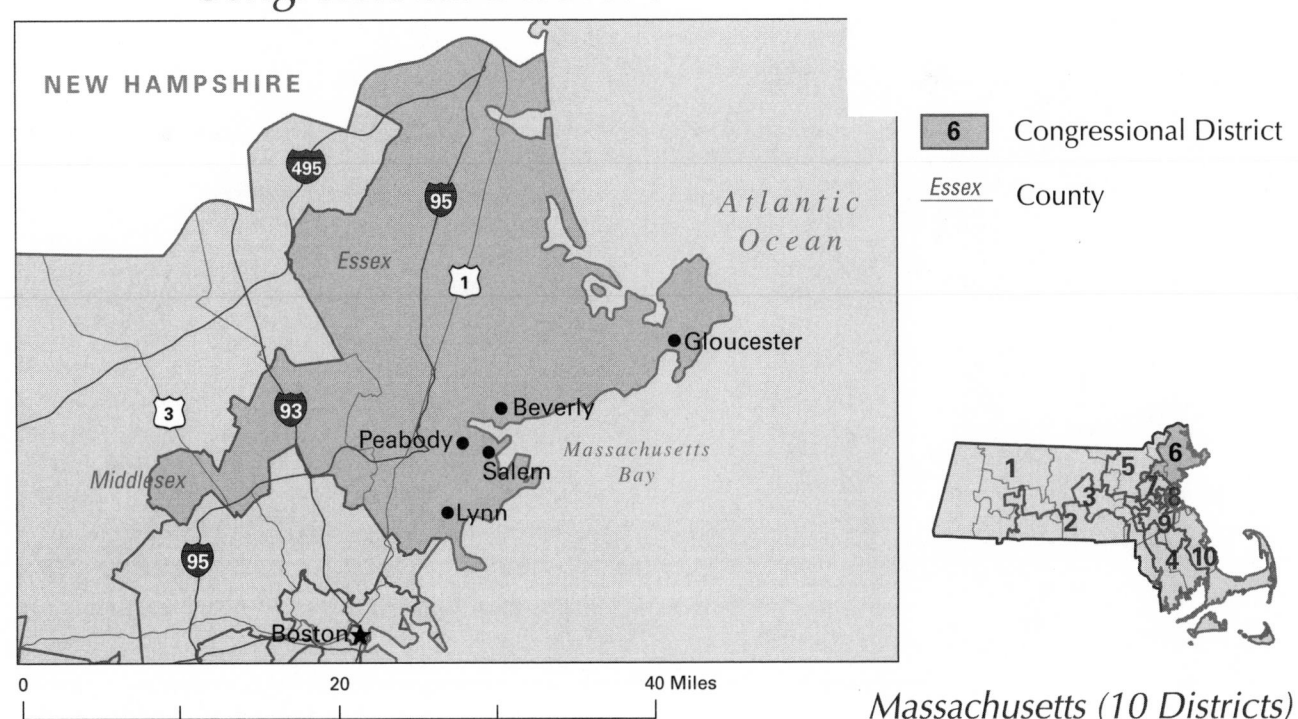

Massachusetts (10 Districts)

Congressional District 7

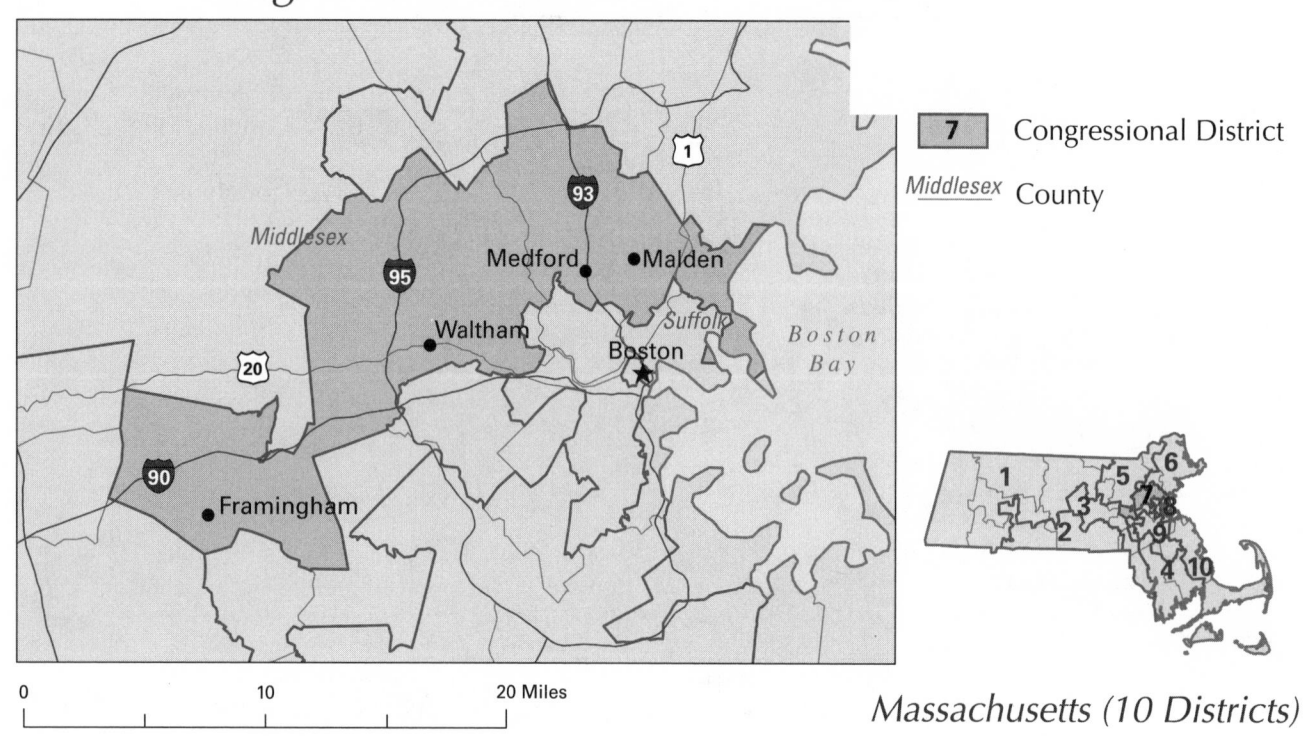

Massachusetts (10 Districts)

Congressional District 8

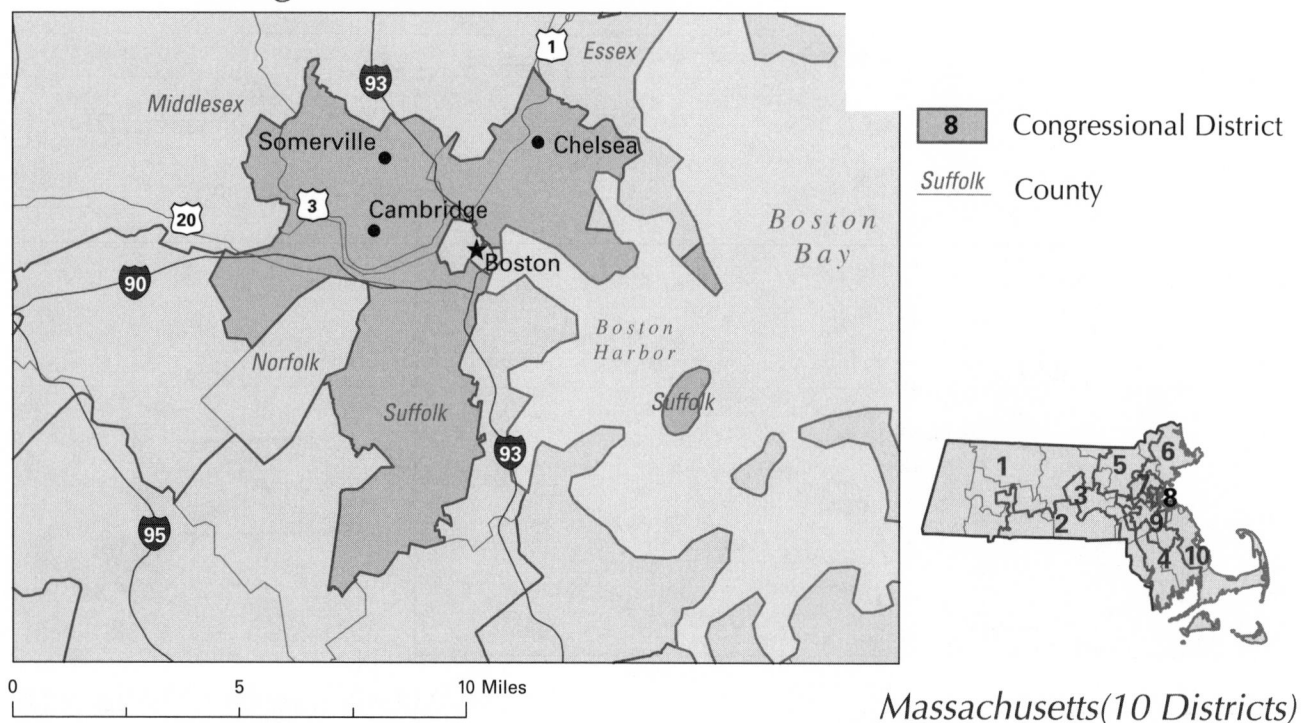

Massachusetts(10 Districts)

Congressional District 9

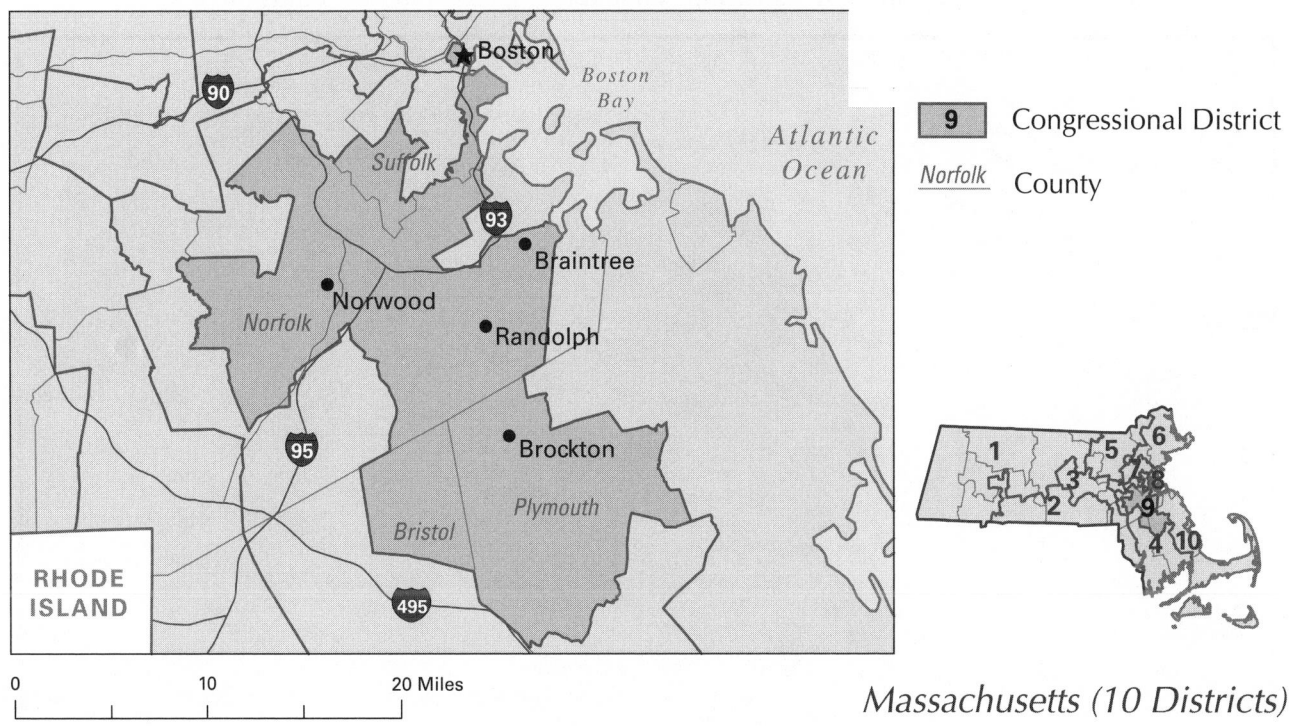

9 Congressional District
Norfolk County

Massachusetts (10 Districts)

Congressional District 10

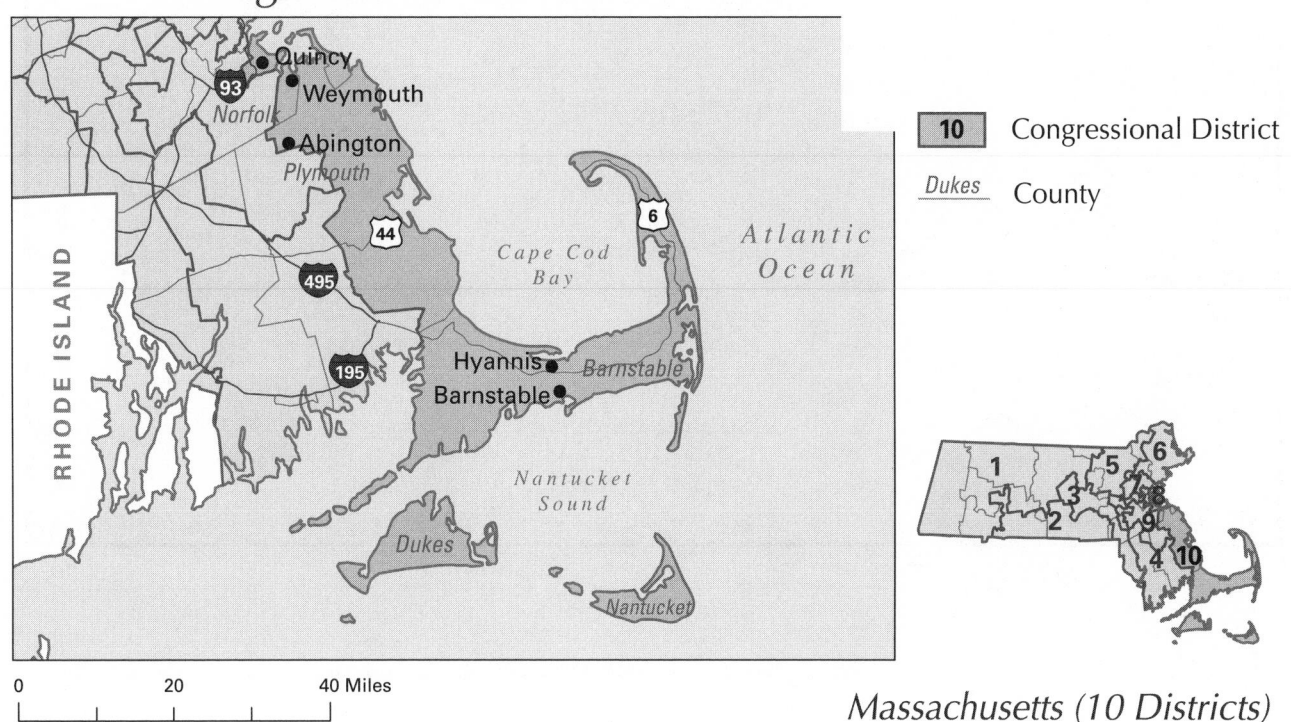

10 Congressional District
Dukes County

Massachusetts (10 Districts)

Michigan Congressional Districts — 15 Districts Total

MICHIGAN—110th CONGRESSIONAL DISTRICTS BY COUNTIES

County	Congressional District
Alcona	1
Alger	1
Allegan	2, 6
Alpena	1
Antrim	1
Arenac	1
Baraga	1
Barry	3
Bay	1, 5
Benzie	2
Berrien	6
Branch	7
Calhoun	6, 7
Cass	6
Charlevoix	1
Cheboygan	1
Chippewa	1
Clare	4
Clinton	8
Crawford	1
Delta	1
Dickinson	1
Eaton	7
Emmet	1
Genesee	5
Gladwin	1
Gogebic	1
Grand Traverse	4

County	Congressional District
Gratiot	4
Hillsdale	7
Houghton	1
Huron	10
Ingham	8
Ionia	3
Iosco	1
Iron	1
Isabella	4
Jackson	7
Kalamazoo	6
Kalkaska	4
Kent	2, 3
Keweenaw	1
Lake	2
Lapeer	10
Leelanau	4
Lenawee	7
Livingston	8
Luce	1
Mackinac	1
Macomb	10, 12
Manistee	2
Marquette	1
Mason	2
Mecosta	4
Menominee	1
Midland	4

County	Congressional District
Missaukee	4
Monroe	15
Montcalm	4
Montmorency	1
Muskegon	2
Newaygo	2
Oakland	8, 9, 11, 12
Oceana	2
Ogemaw	1
Ontonagon	1
Osceola	4
Oscoda	1
Otsego	1
Ottawa	2
Presque Isle	1
Roscommon	4
Saginaw	4, 5
St. Clair	10
St. Joseph	6
Sanilac	10
Schoolcraft	1
Shiawassee	4, 8
Tuscola	5
Van Buren	6
Washtenaw	7, 15
Wayne	11, 13–15
Wexford	2

Congressional District 1

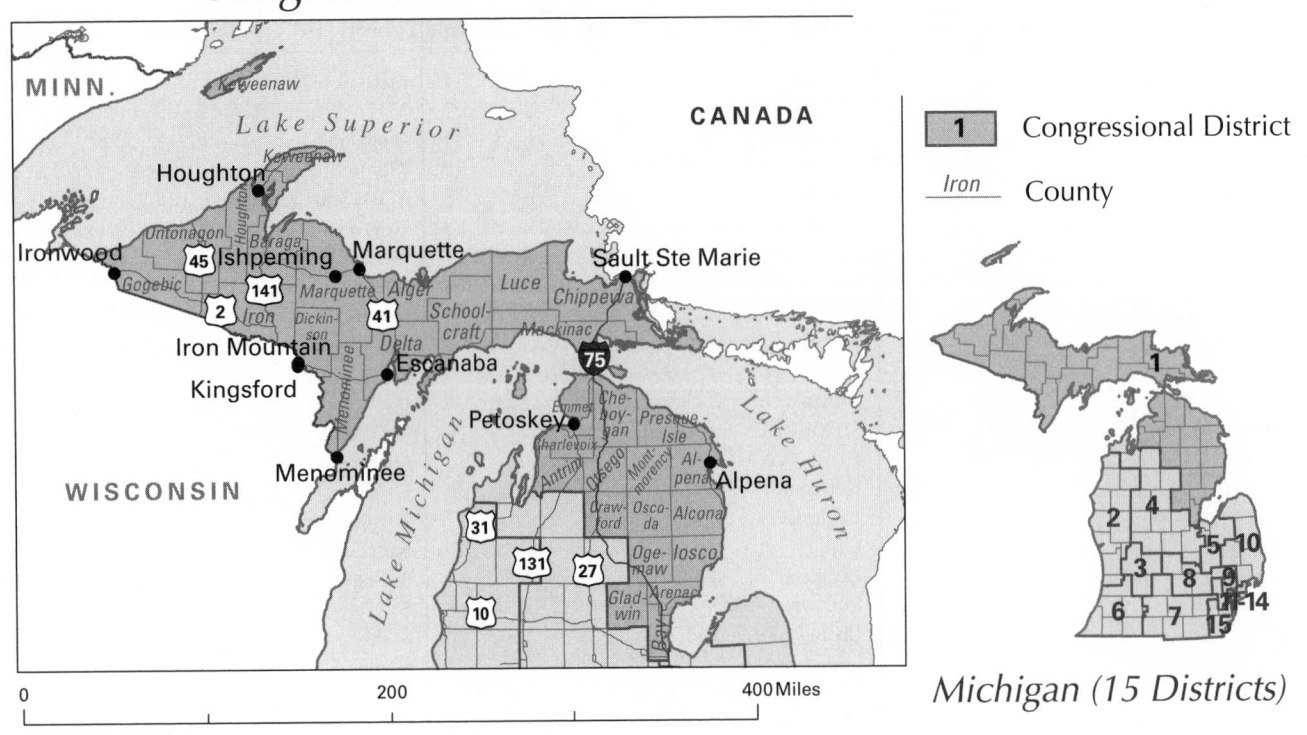

Michigan (15 Districts)

Congressional District 2

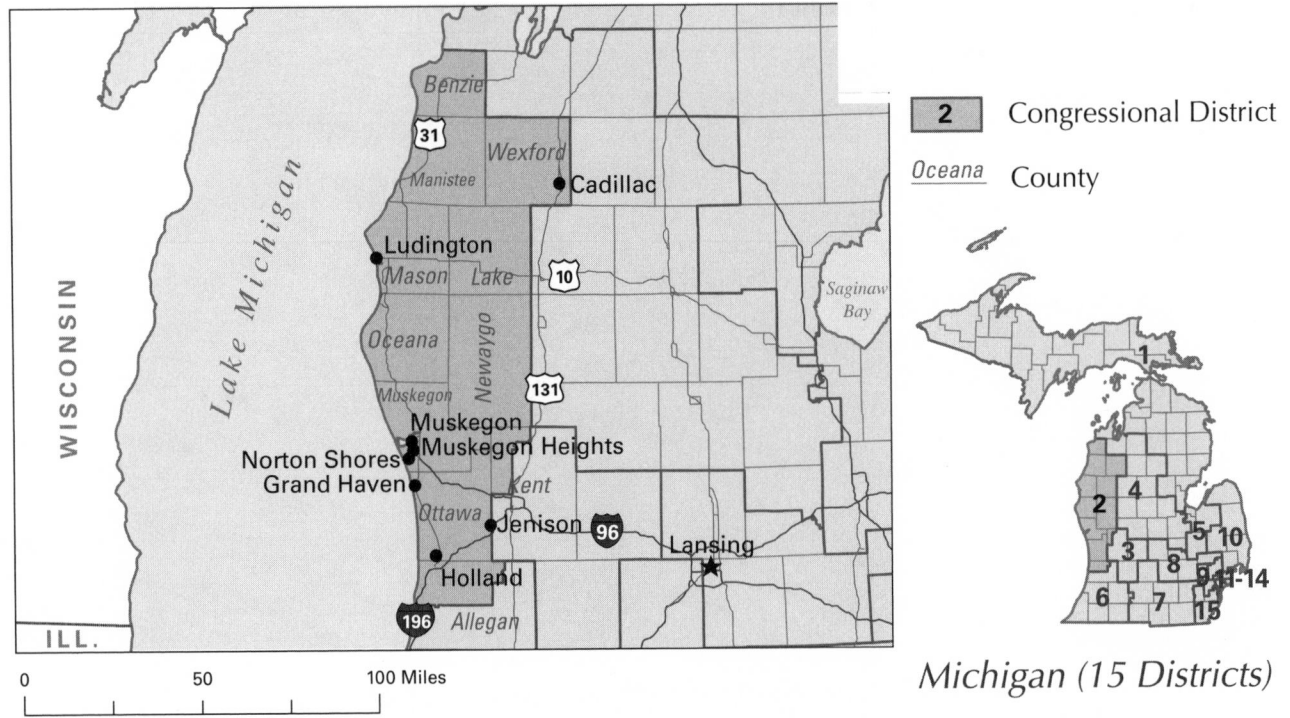

Michigan (15 Districts)

Congressional District 3

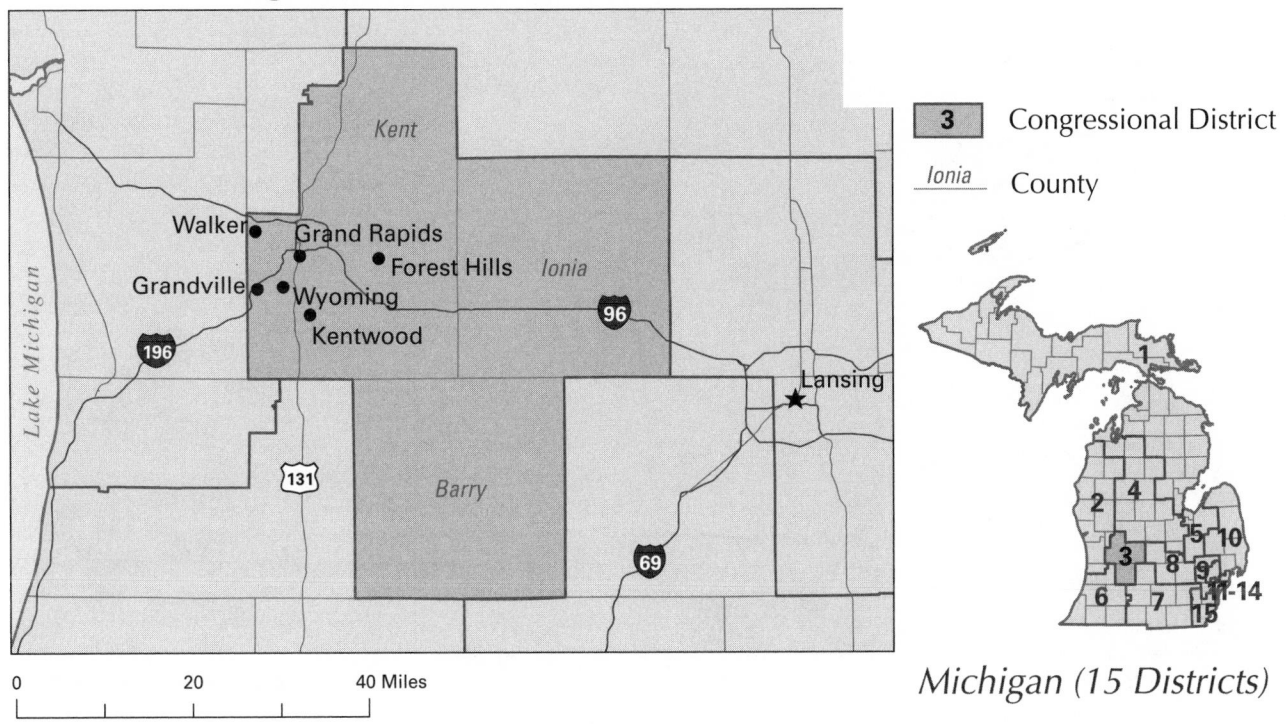

3   Congressional District

Ionia   County

Michigan (15 Districts)

Congressional District 4

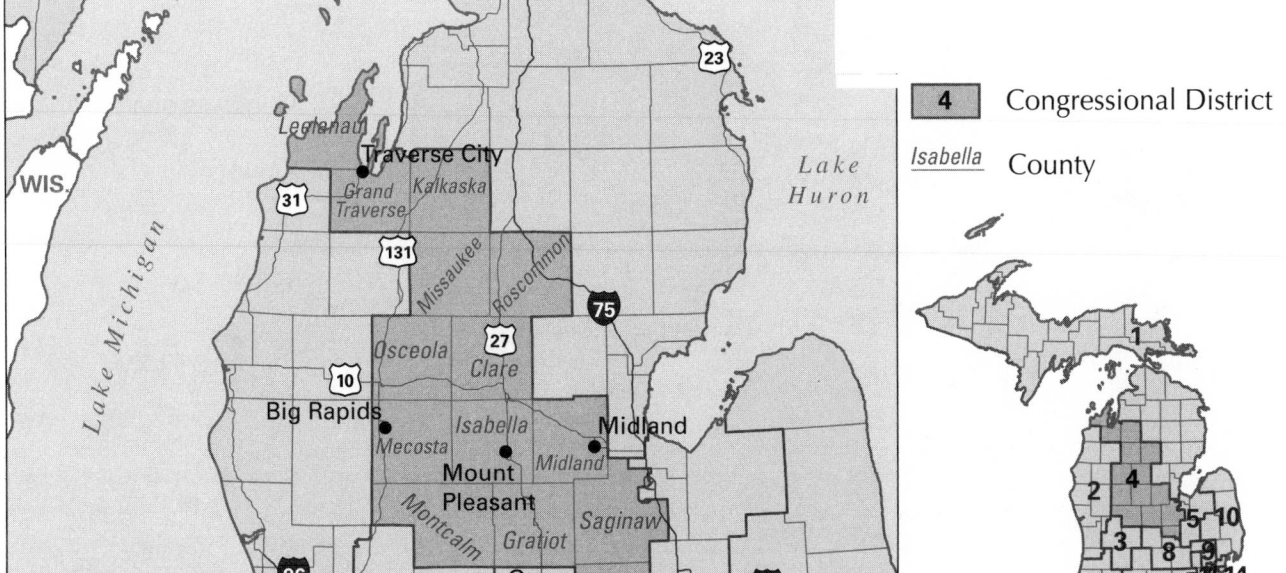

4   Congressional District

Isabella   County

Michigan (15 Districts)

Congressional District 5

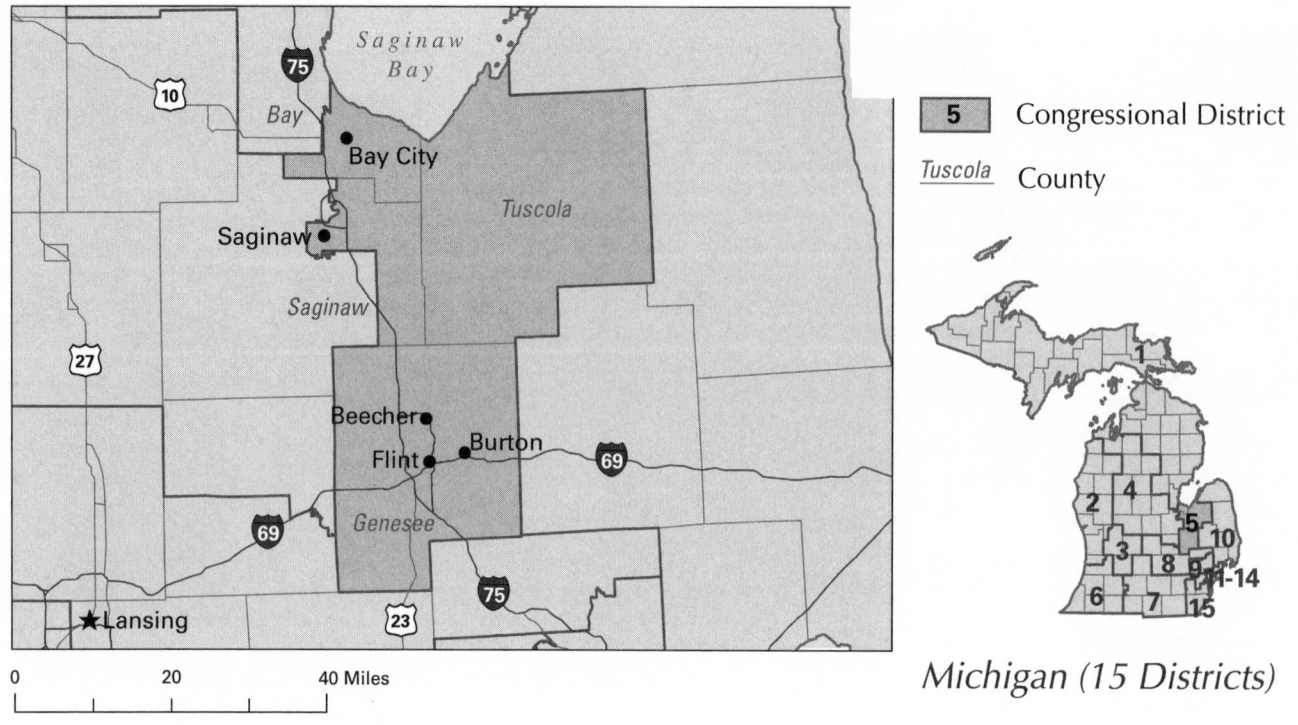

Michigan (15 Districts)

Congressional District 6

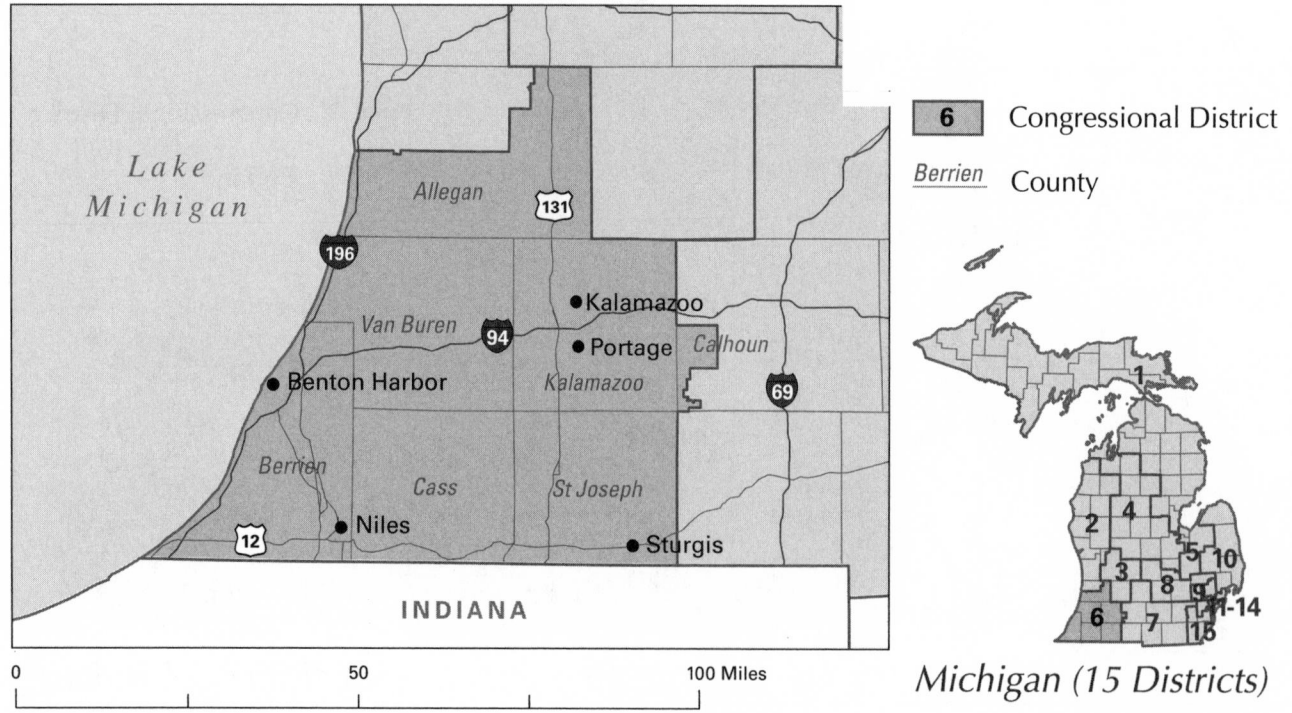

Michigan (15 Districts)

Congressional District 7

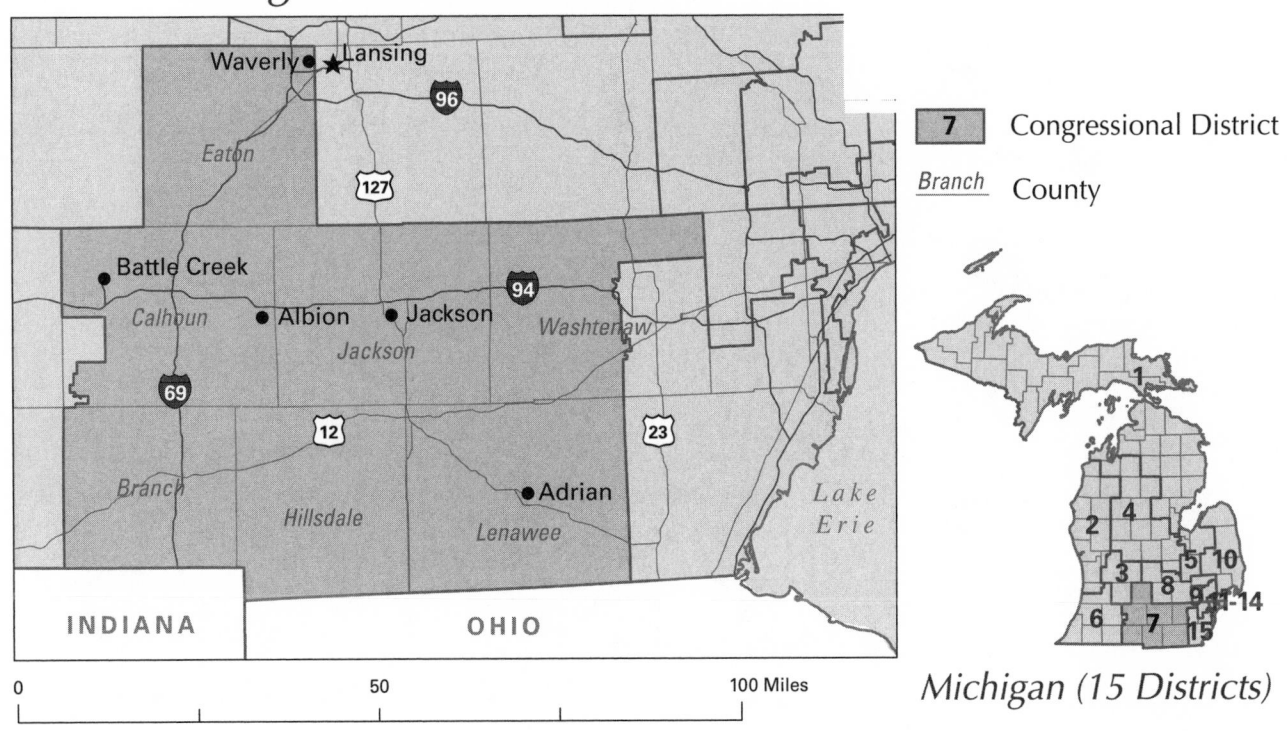

7 Congressional District

Branch County

Michigan (15 Districts)

Congressional District 8

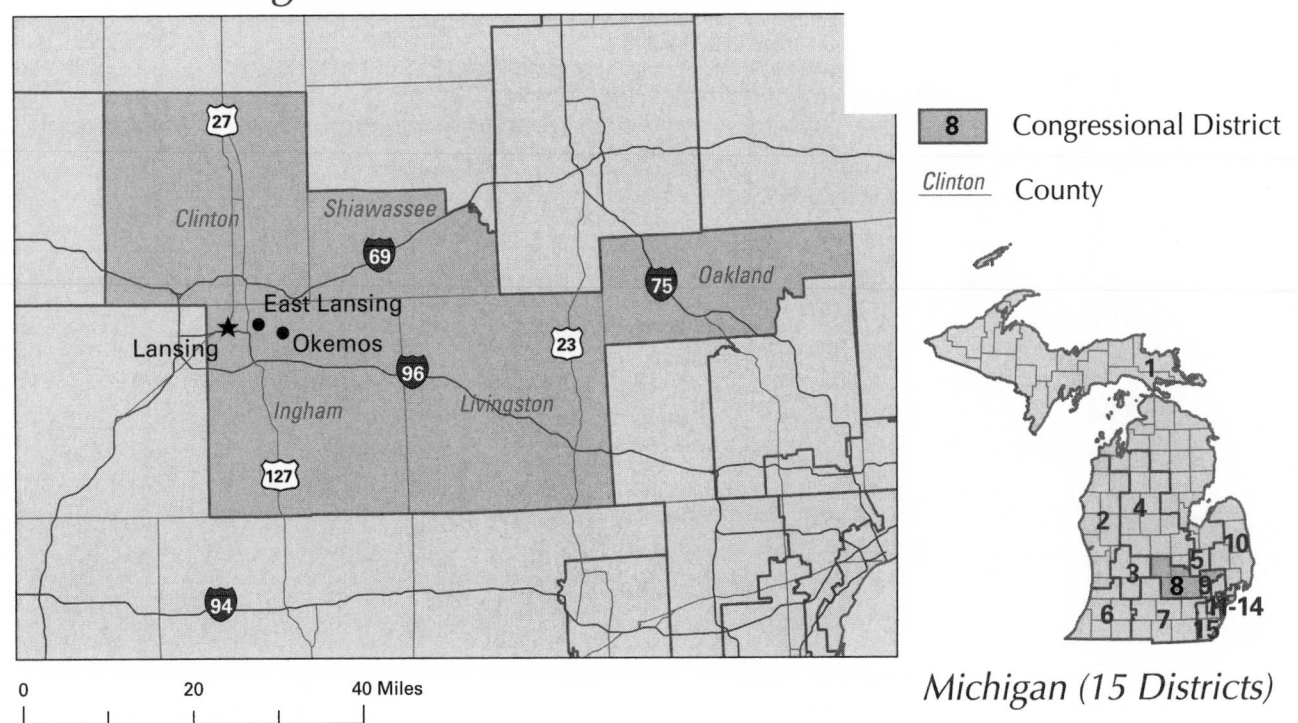

8 Congressional District

Clinton County

Michigan (15 Districts)

Congressional District 9

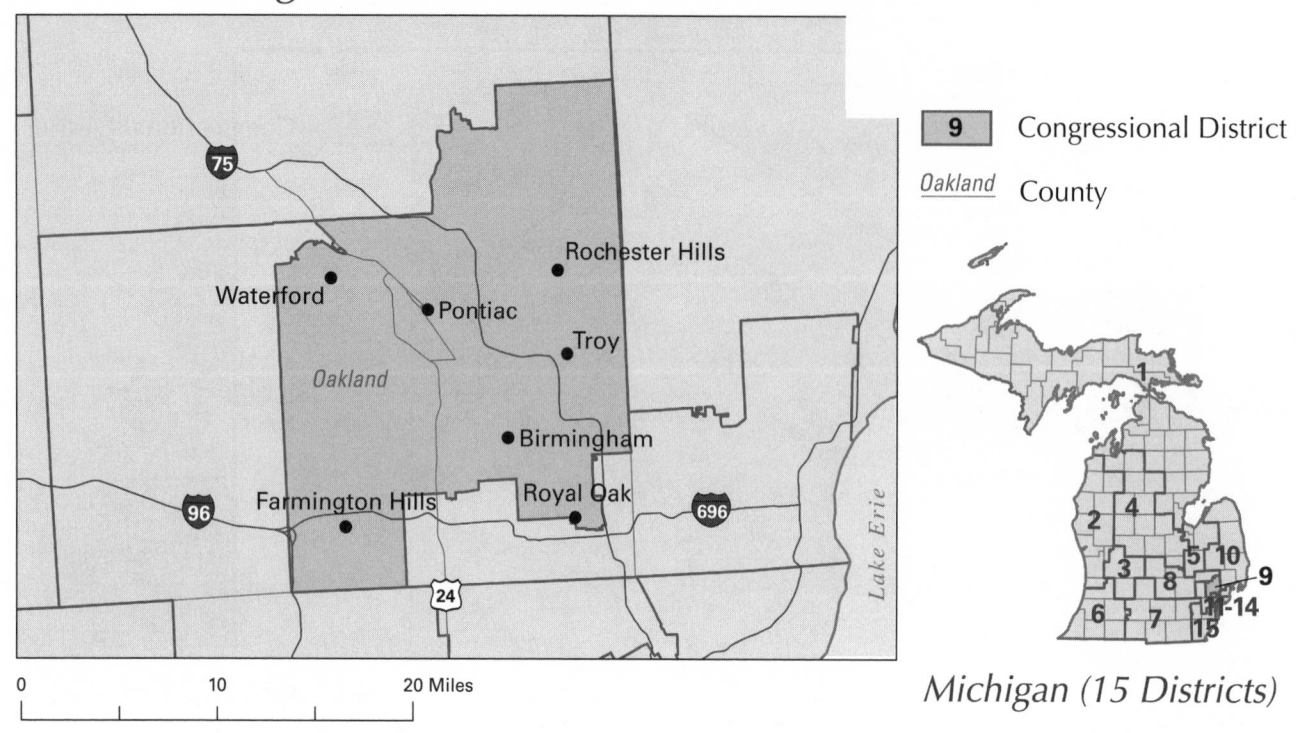

0   10   20 Miles

9 Congressional District
Oakland County

Michigan (15 Districts)

Congressional District 10

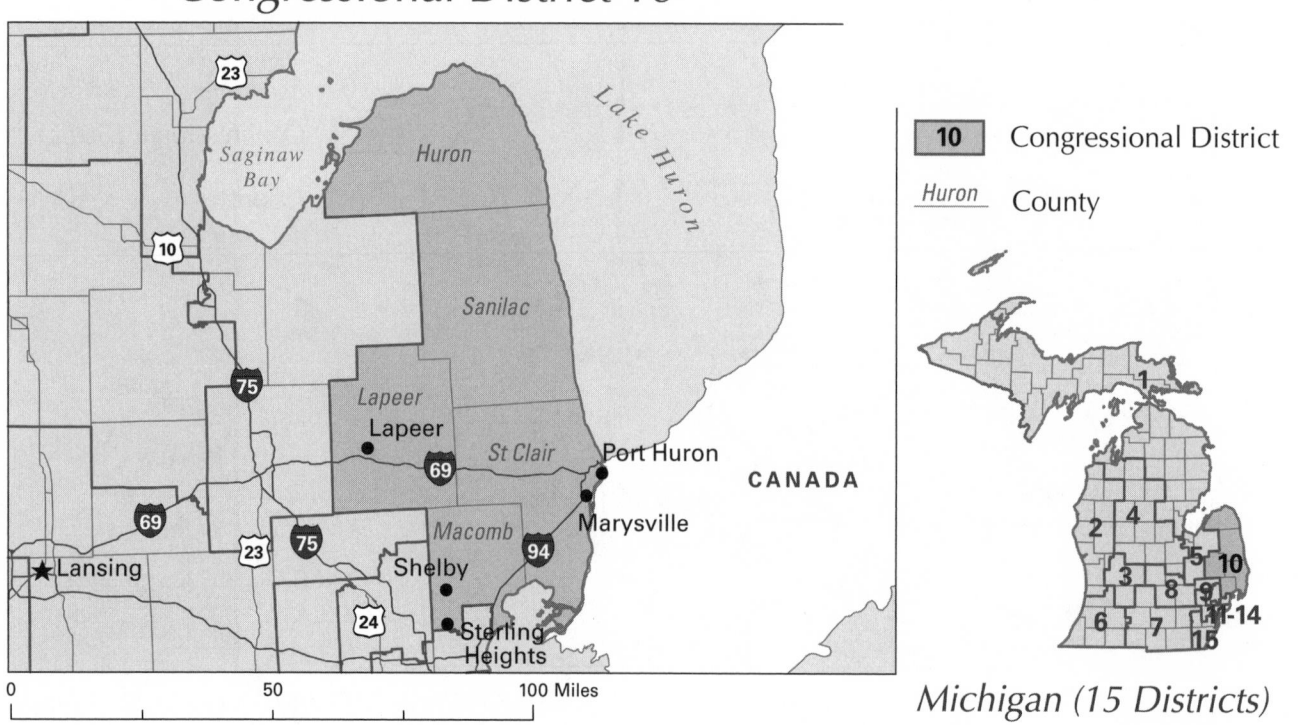

0   50   100 Miles

10 Congressional District
Huron County

Michigan (15 Districts)

Congressional District 11

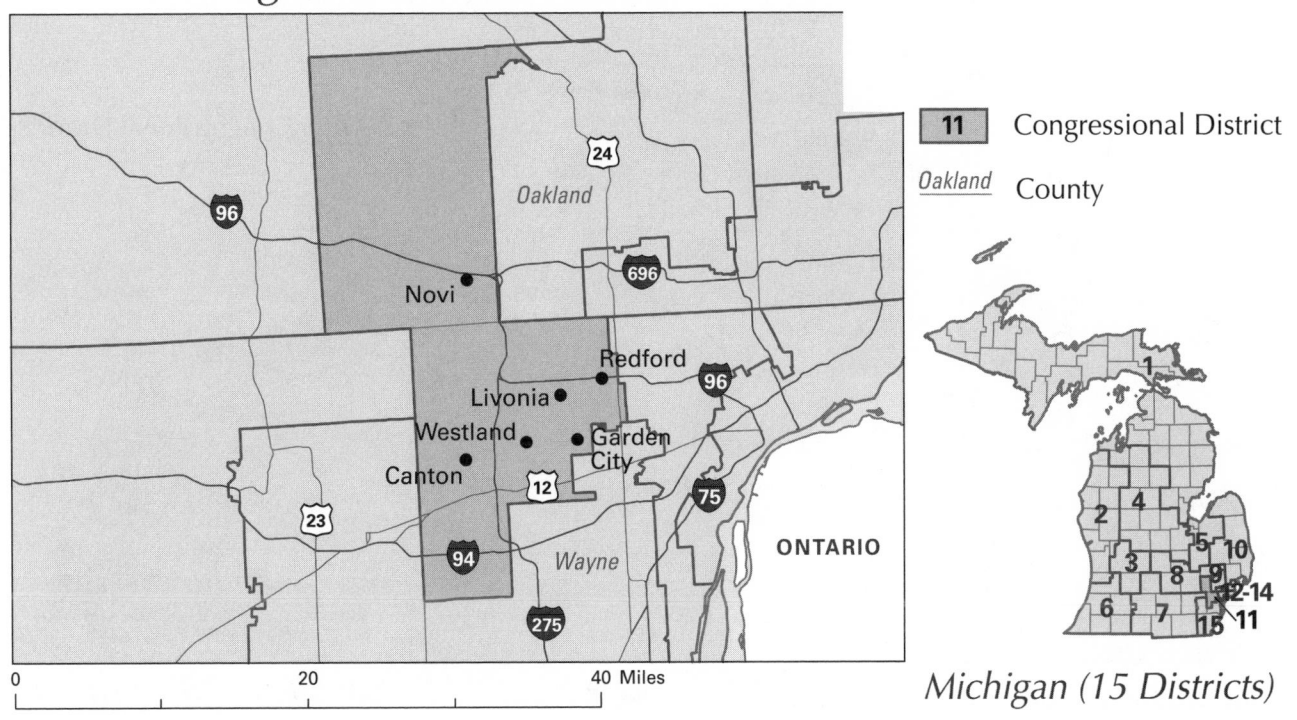

Congressional District 12

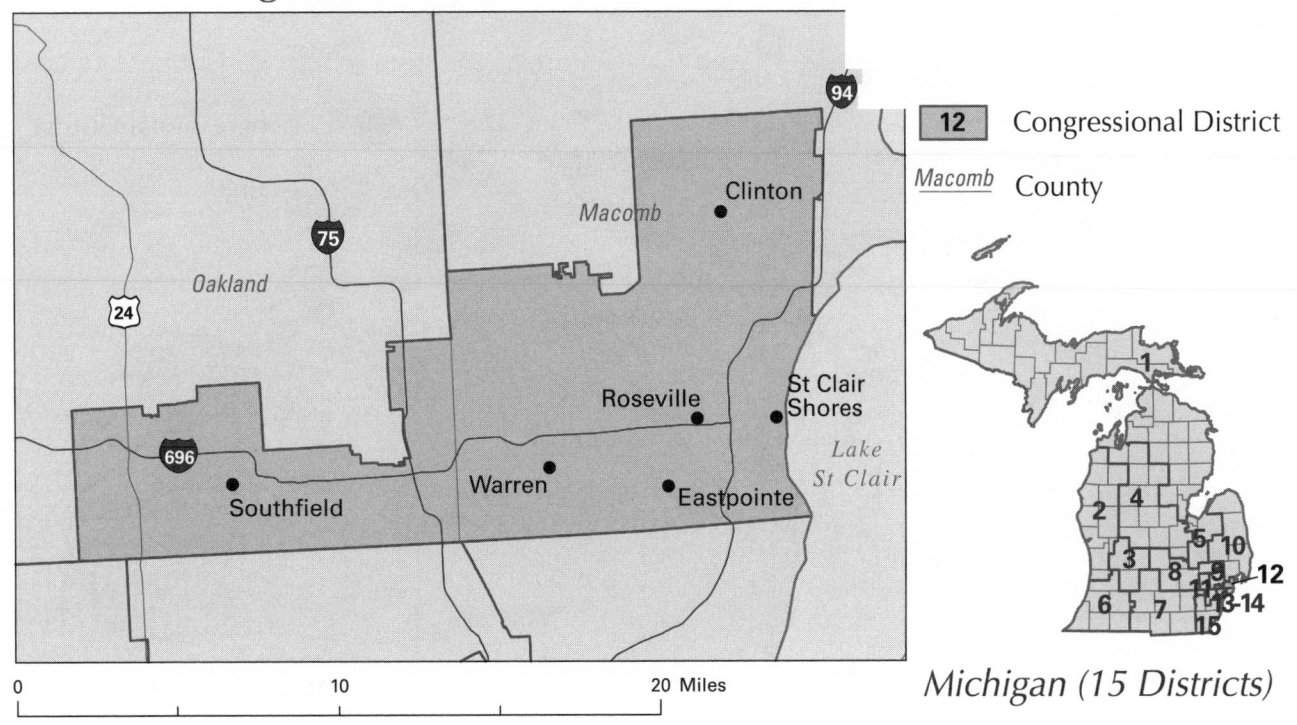

Congressional District 13

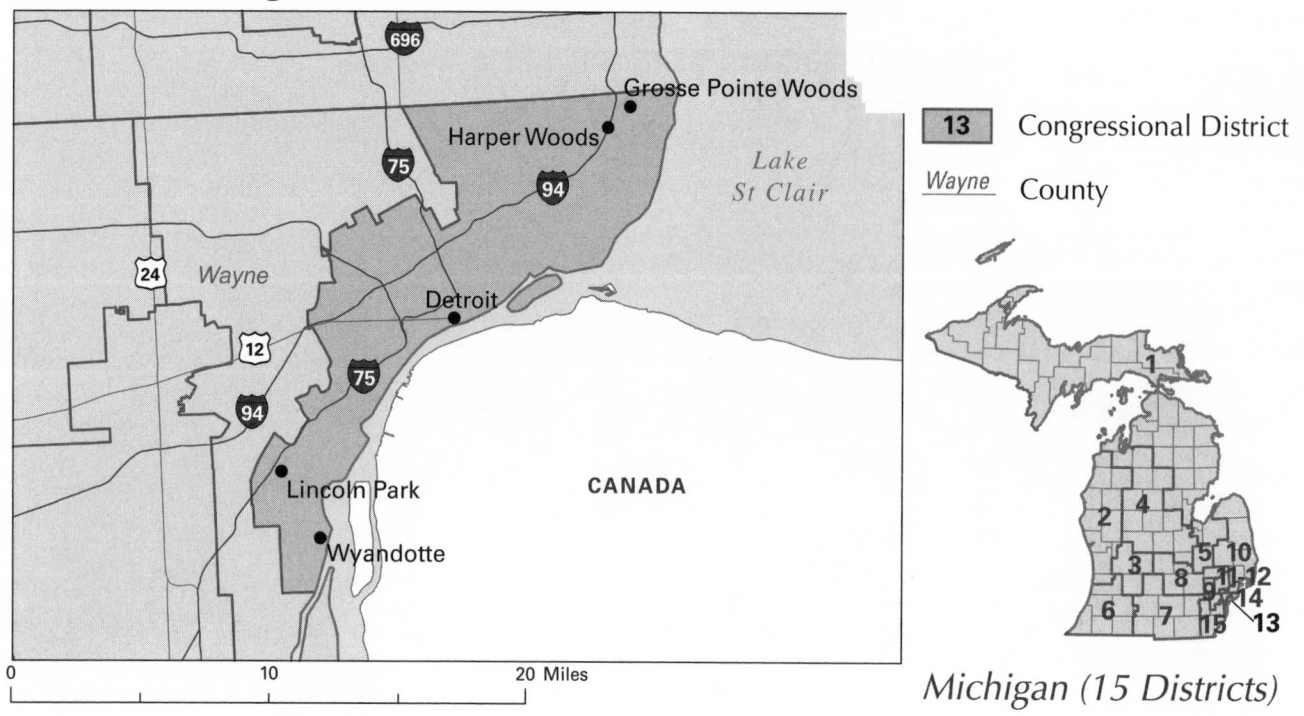

Congressional District 14

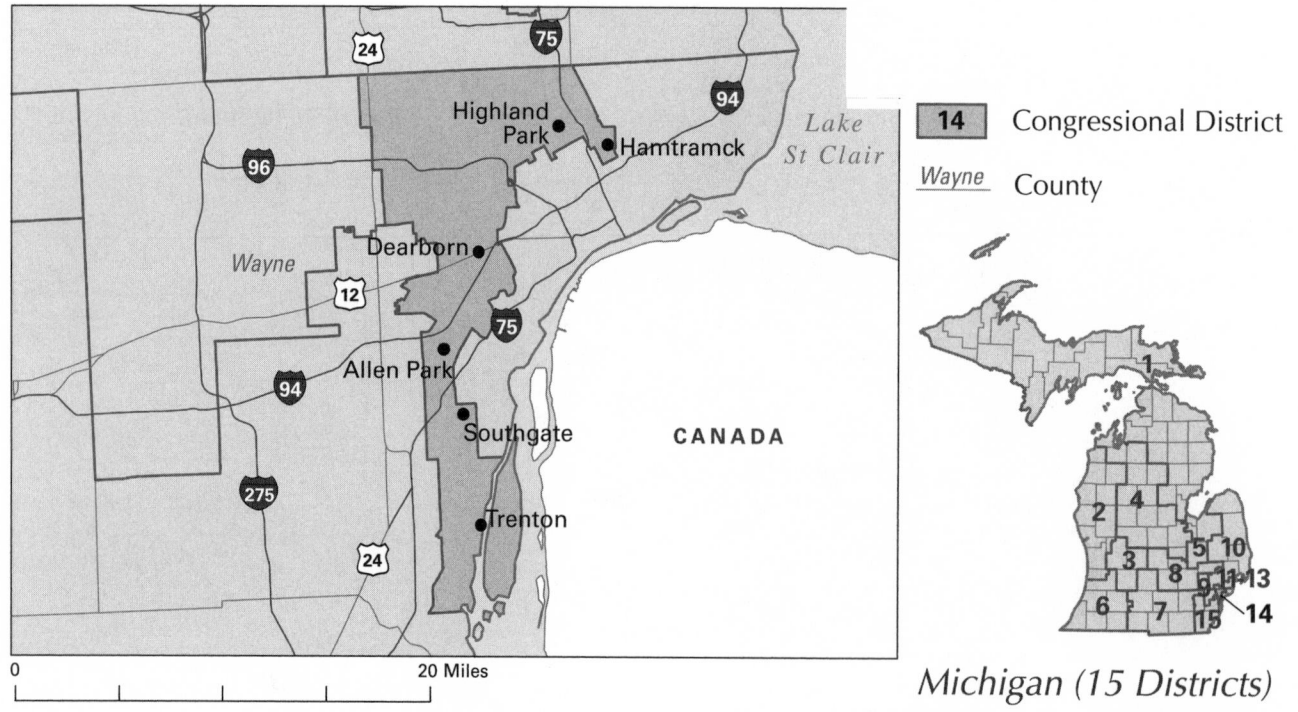

Congressional District 15

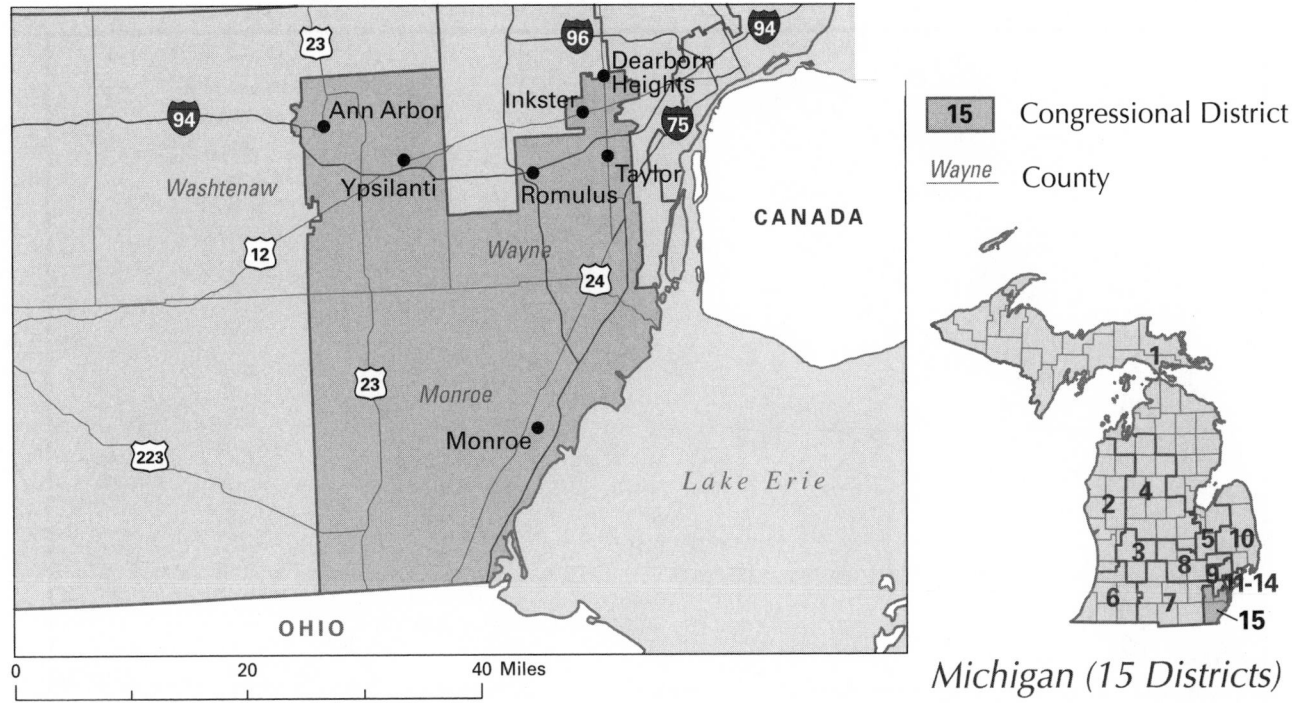

Michigan (15 Districts)

Minnesota Congressional Districts — 8 Districts Total

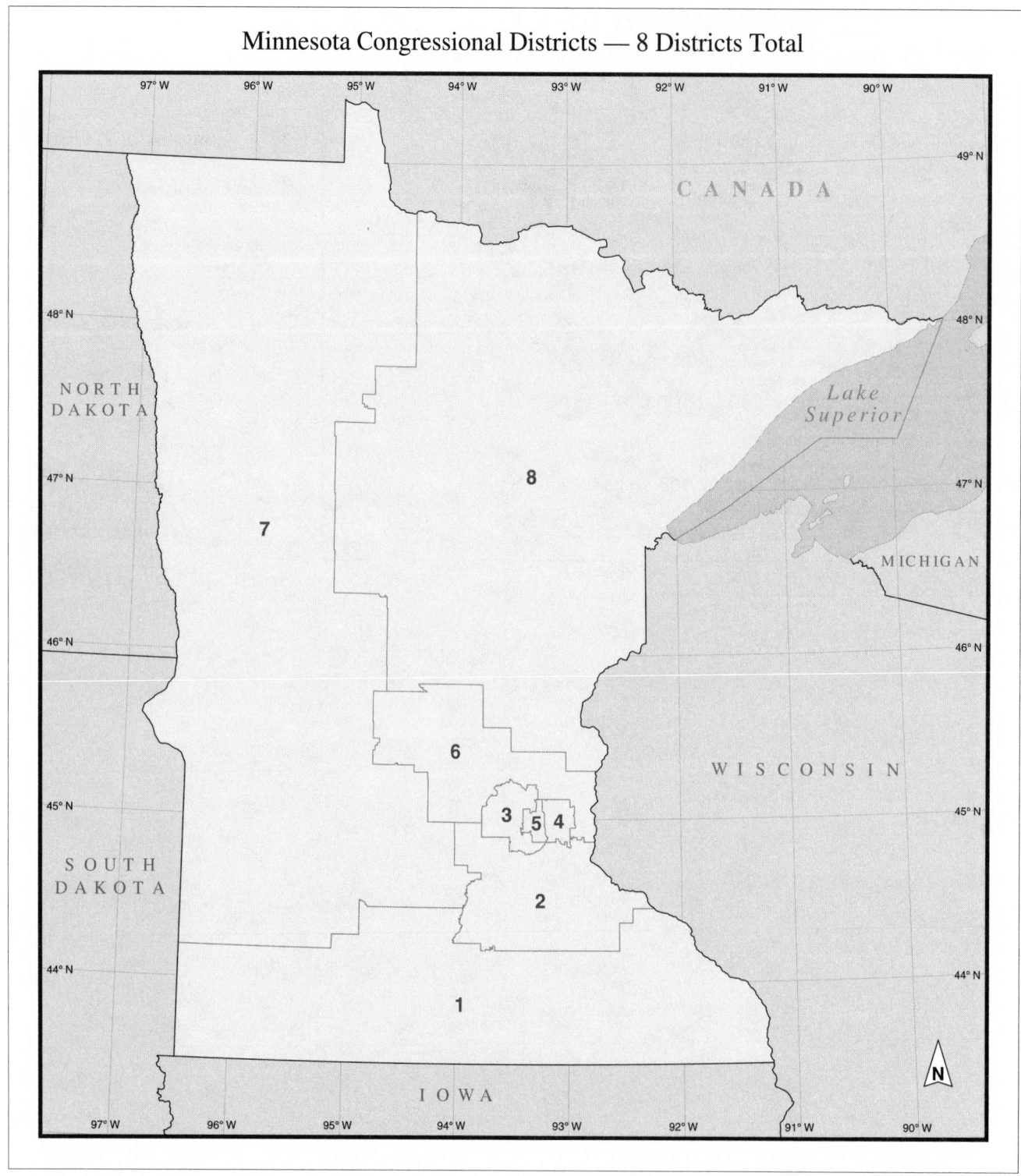

MINNESOTA — 110th CONGRESSIONAL DISTRICTS BY COUNTIES

County	Congressional District	County	Congressional District	County	Congressional District
Aitkin	8	Isanti	8	Pipestone	1
Anoka	3, 5, 6	Itasca	8	Polk	7
Becker	7	Jackson	1	Pope	7
Beltrami	7, 8	Kanabec	8	Ramsey	4–6
Benton	6	Kandiyohi	7	Red Lake	7
Big Stone	7	Kittson	7	Redwood	7
Blue Earth	1	Koochiching	8	Renville	7
Brown	1	Lac qui Parle	7	Rice	2
Carlton	8	Lake	8	Rock	1
Carver	2	Lake of the Woods	7	Roseau	7
Cass	8	Le Sueur	1, 2	St. Louis	8
Chippewa	7	Lincoln	7	Scott	2
Chisago	8	Lyon	7	Sherburne	6
Clay	7	McLeod	7	Sibley	7
Clearwater	7	Mahnomen	7	Stearns	6, 7
Cook	8	Marshall	7	Steele	1
Cottonwood	1	Martin	1	Stevens	7
Crow Wing	8	Meeker	7	Swift	7
Dakota	2, 4	Mille Lacs	8	Todd	7
Dodge	1	Morrison	8	Traverse	7
Douglas	7	Mower	1	Wabasha	1
Faribault	1	Murray	1	Wadena	8
Fillmore	1	Nicollet	1	Waseca	1
Freeborn	1	Nobles	1	Washington	2, 4, 6
Goodhue	2	Norman	7	Watonwan	1
Grant	7	Olmsted	1	Wilkin	7
Hennepin	2, 3, 5, 6	Otter Tail	7	Winona	1
Houston	1	Pennington	7	Wright	6
Hubbard	8	Pine	8	Yellow Medicine	7

Congressional District 1

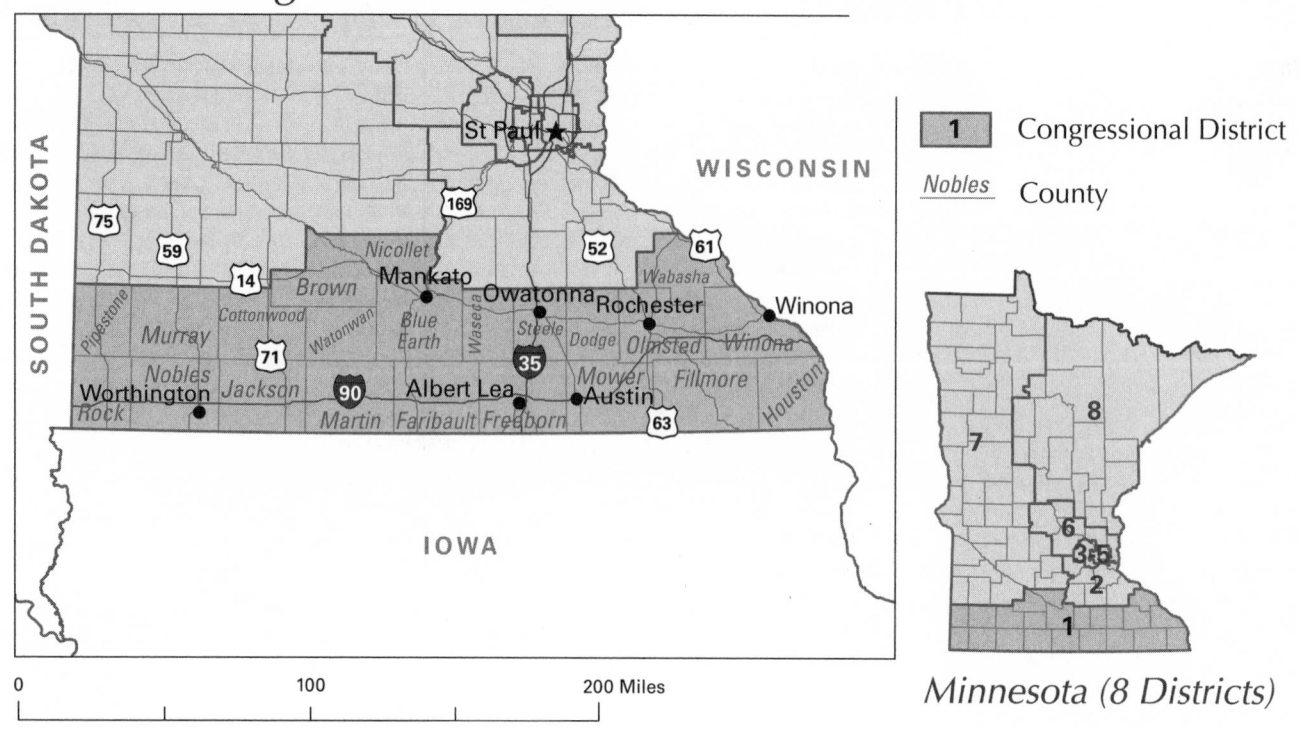

1 Congressional District

Nobles County

Minnesota (8 Districts)

Congressional District 2

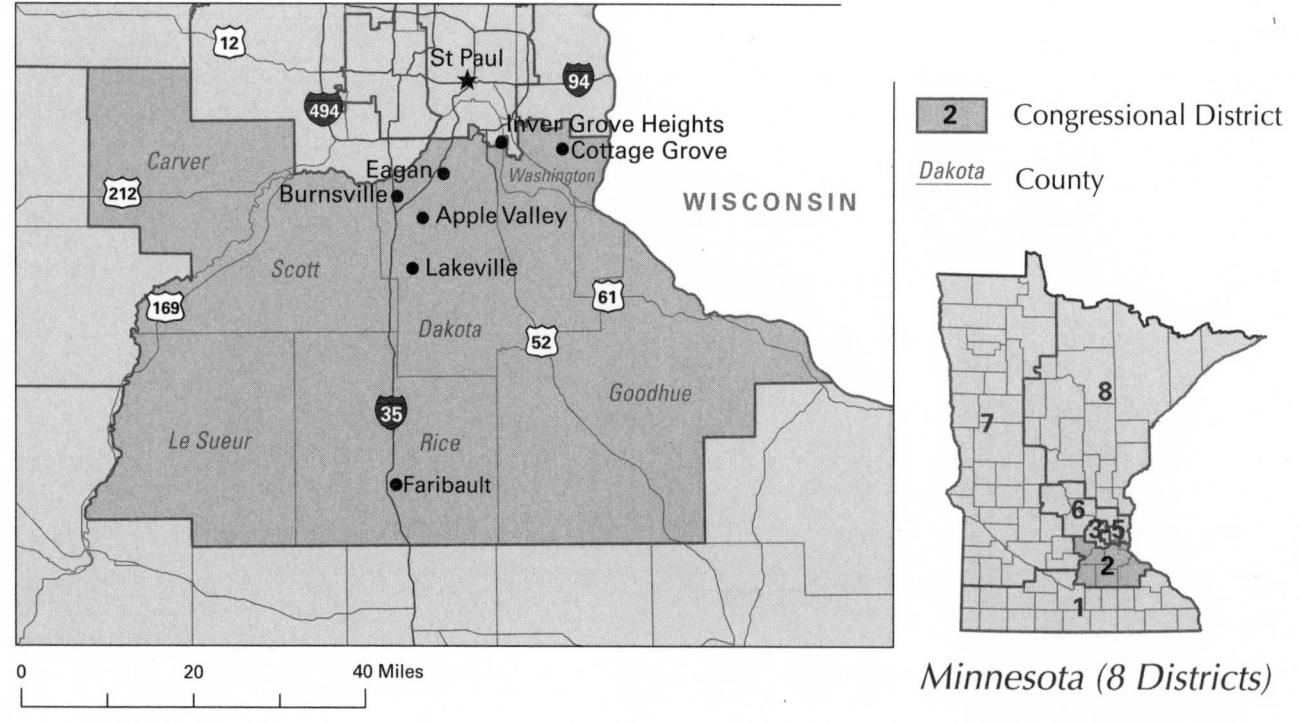

2 Congressional District

Dakota County

Minnesota (8 Districts)

Congressional District 3

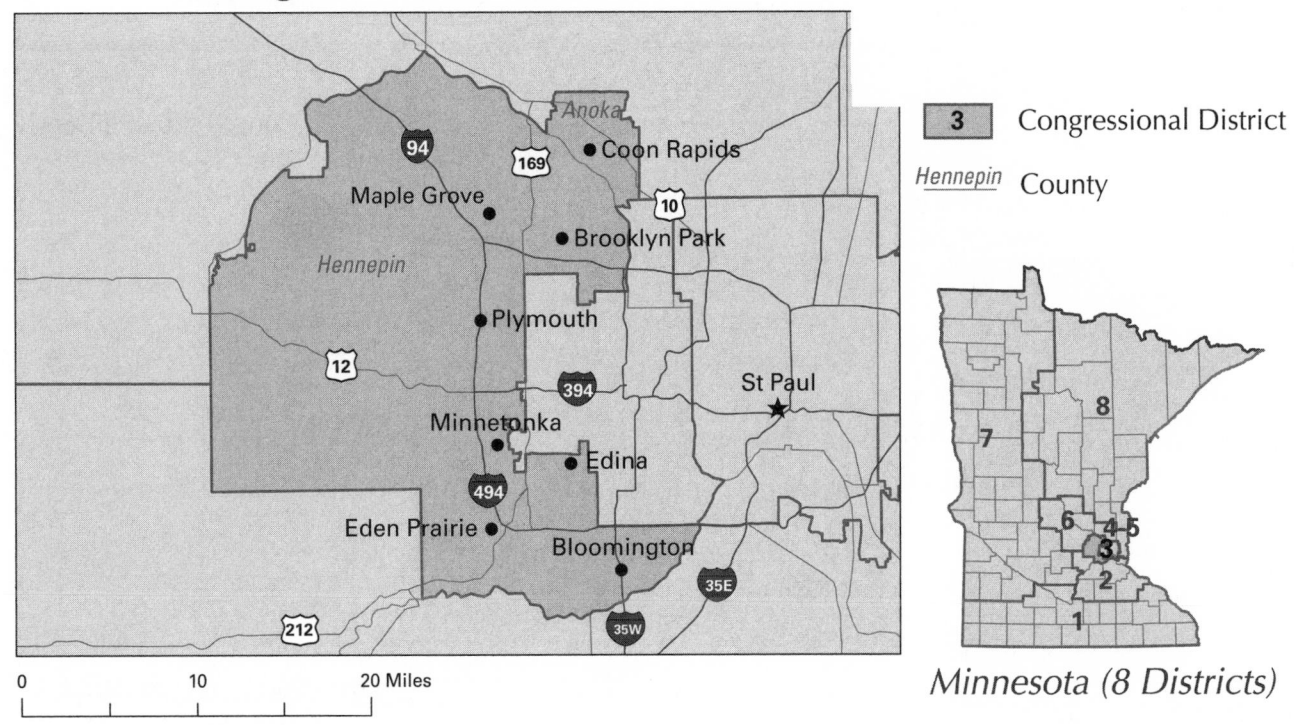

3 Congressional District

Hennepin County

Minnesota (8 Districts)

Congressional District 4

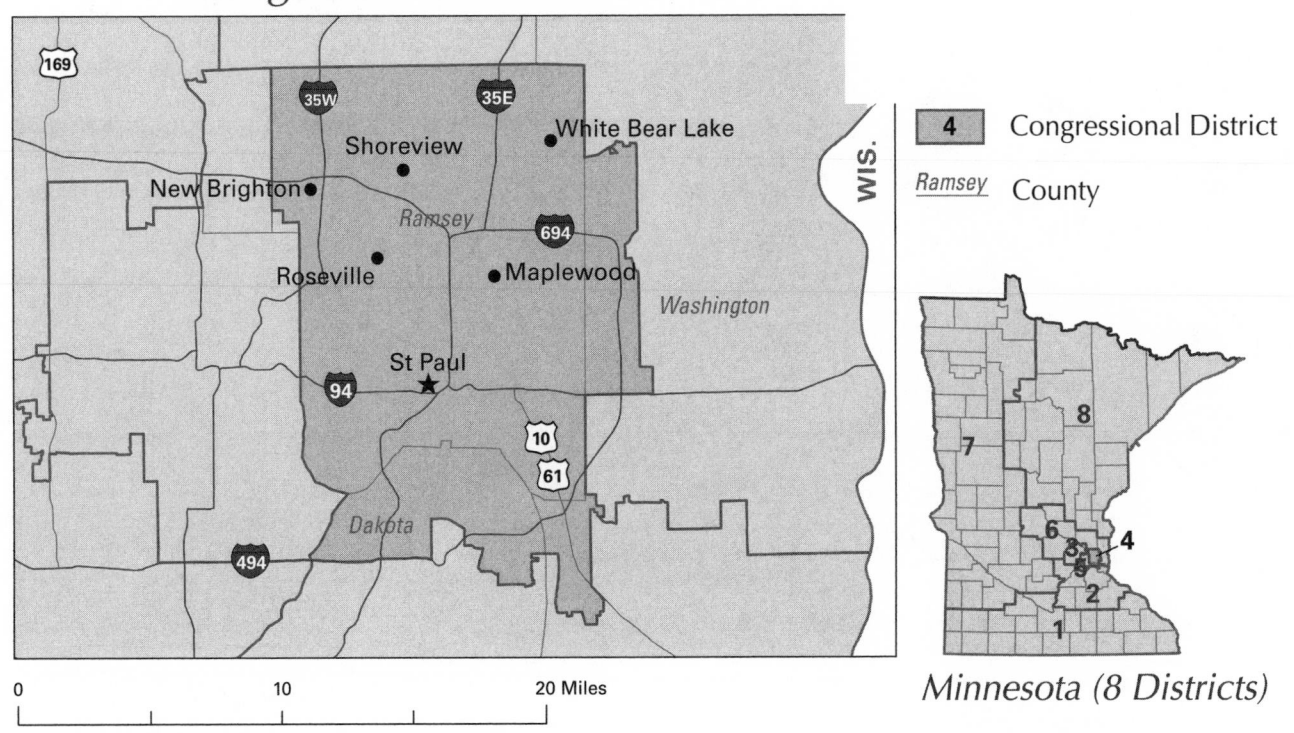

4 Congressional District

Ramsey County

Minnesota (8 Districts)

Congressional District 5

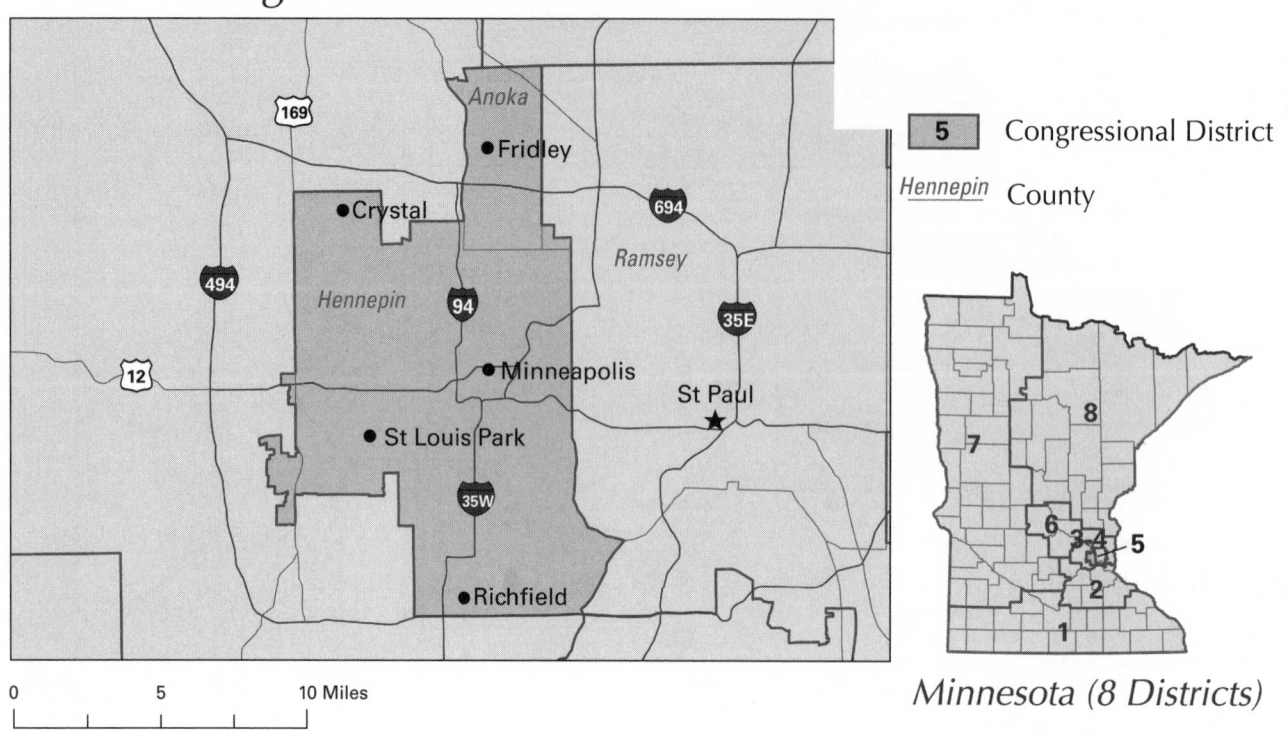

5 | Congressional District
Hennepin | County

Minnesota (8 Districts)

Congressional District 6

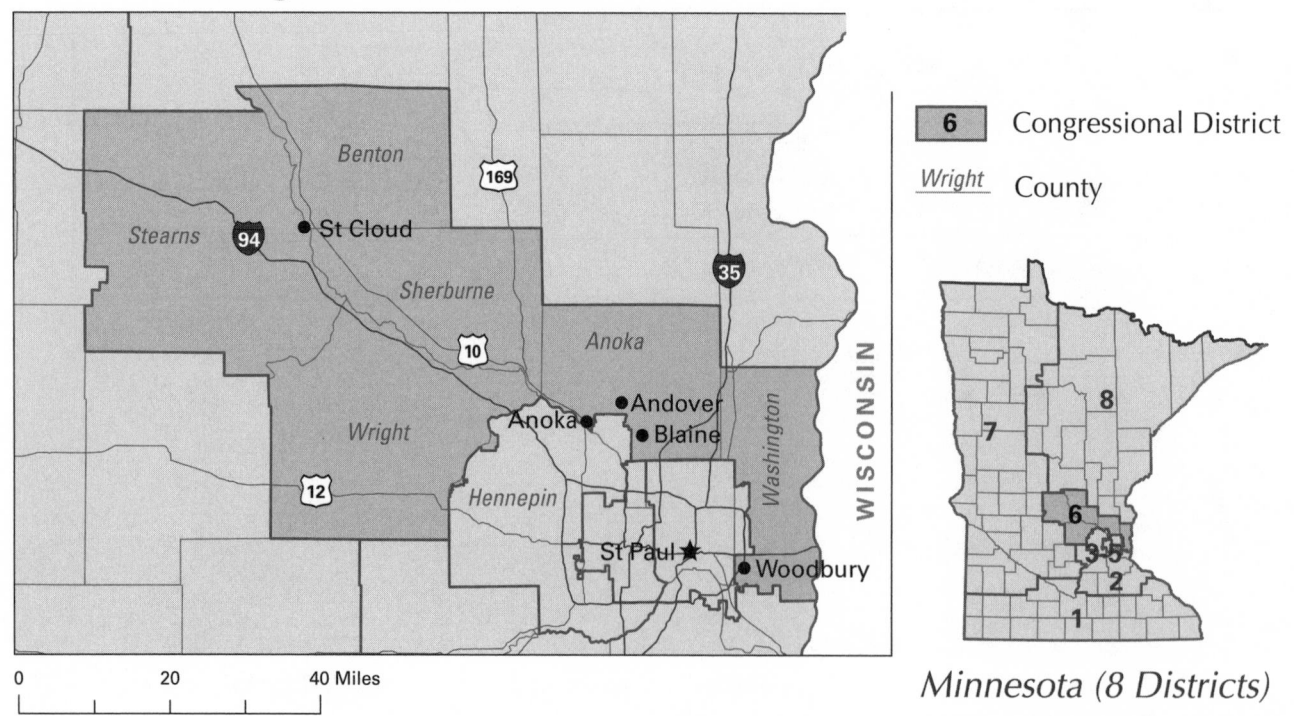

6 | Congressional District
Wright | County

Minnesota (8 Districts)

Congressional District 7

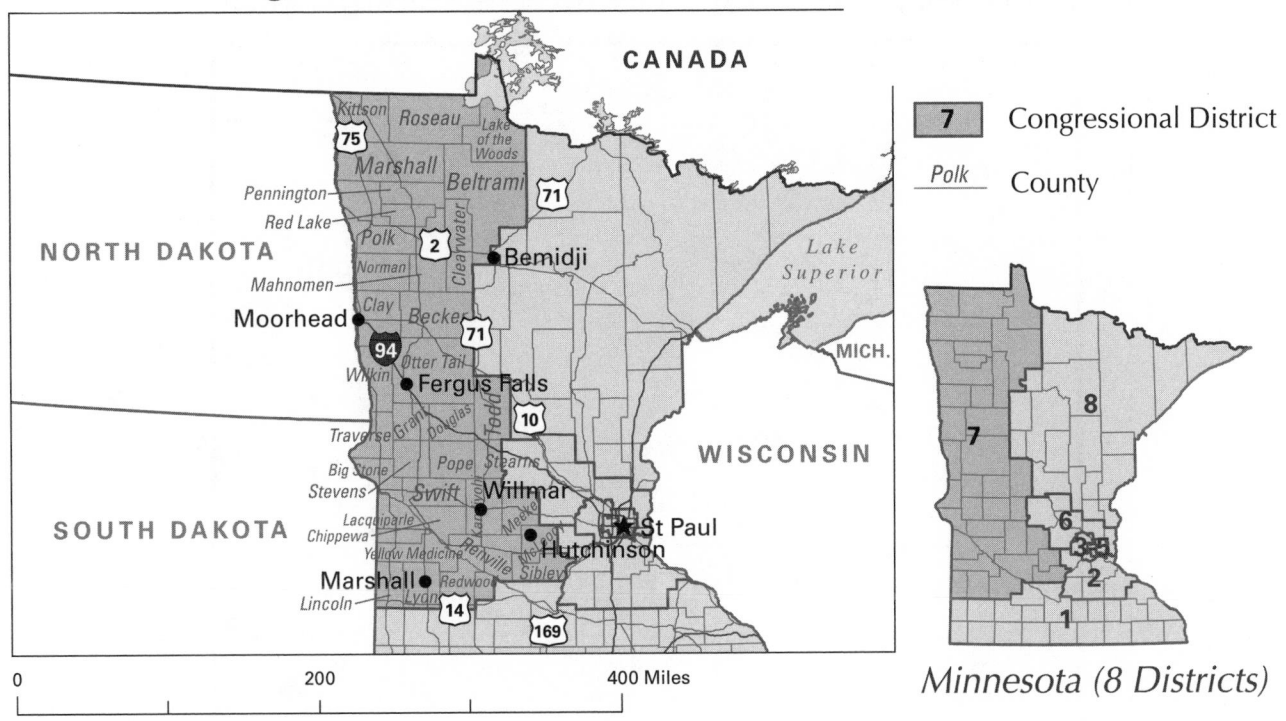

Minnesota (8 Districts)

Congressional District 8

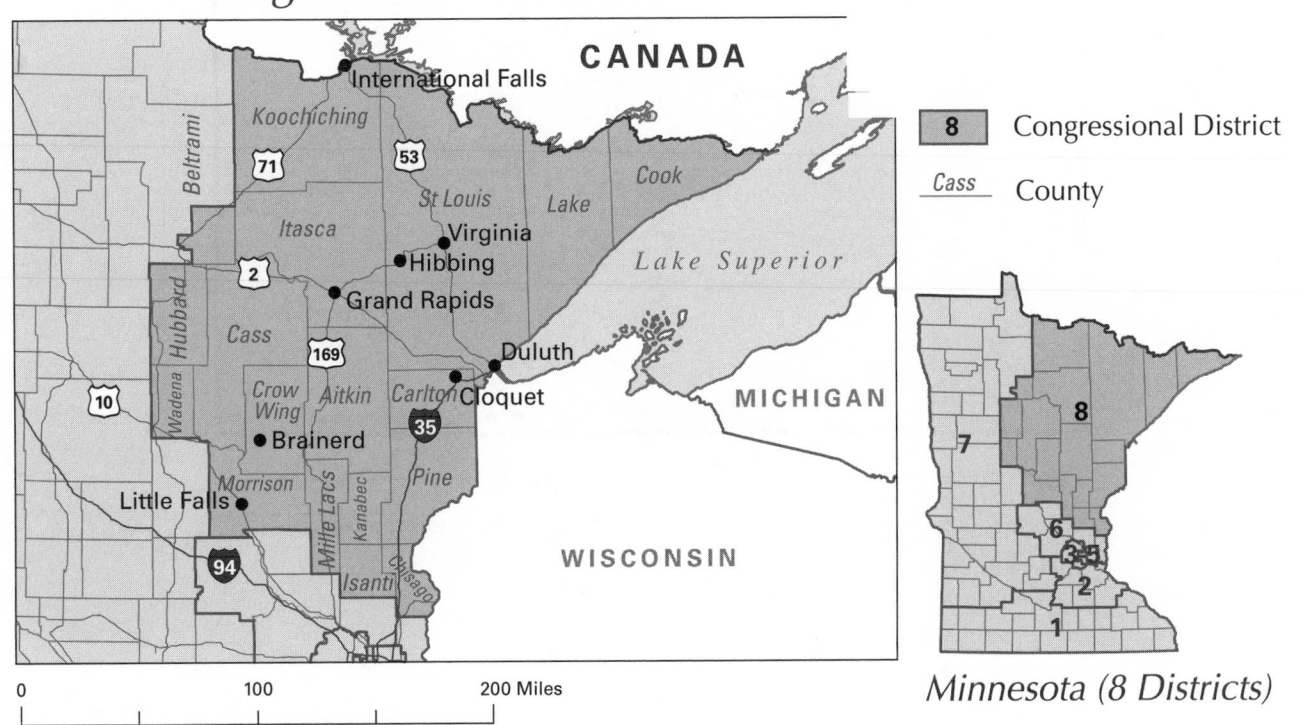

Minnesota (8 Districts)

Mississippi Congressional Districts — 4 Districts Total

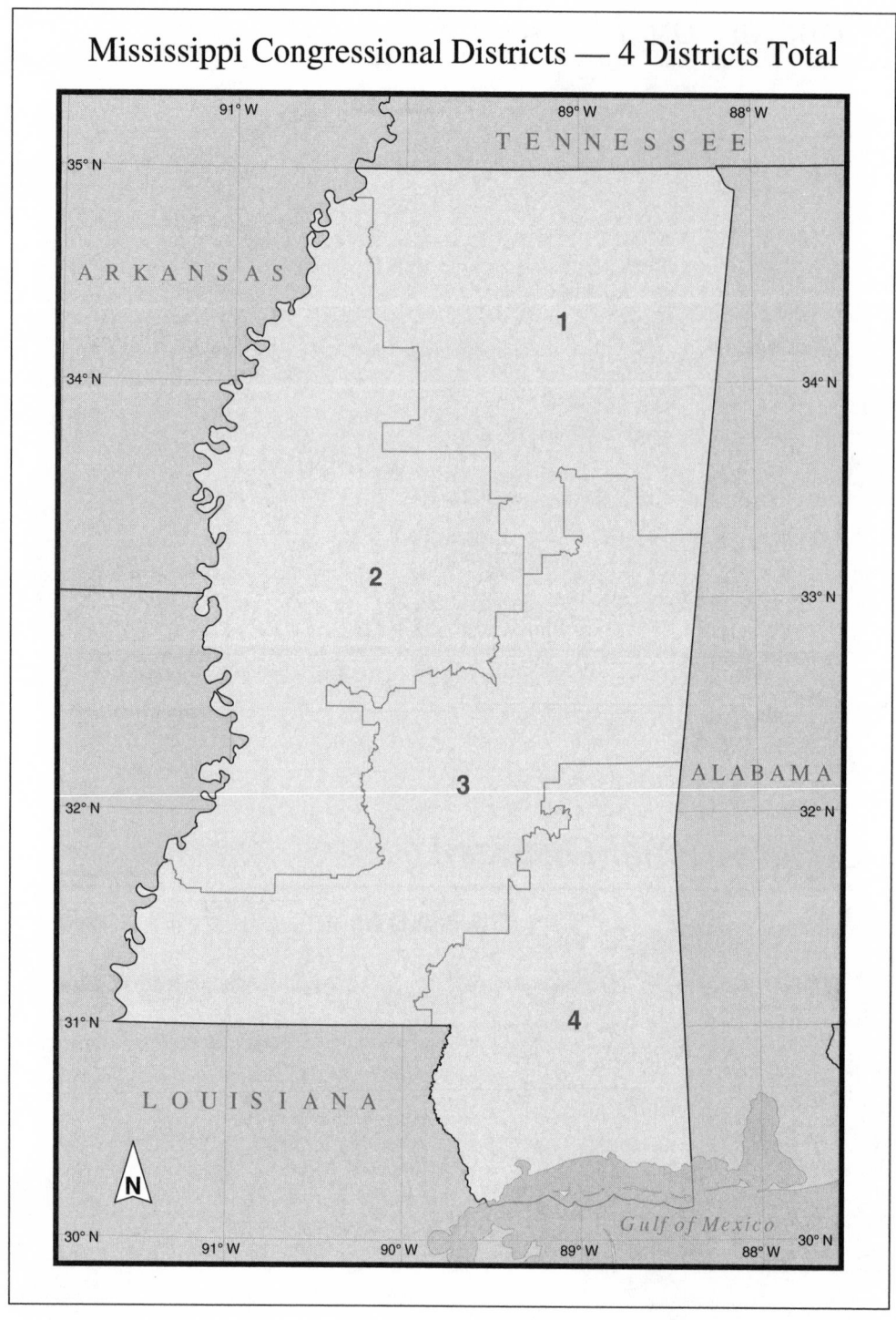

MISSISSIPPI—110th CONGRESSIONAL DISTRICTS BY COUNTIES

County	Congressional District
Adams	3
Alcorn	1
Amite	3
Attala	2
Benton	1
Bolivar	2
Calhoun	1
Carroll	2
Chickasaw	1
Choctaw	1
Claiborne	2
Clarke	4
Clay	1
Coahoma	2
Copiah	2
Covington	3
DeSoto	1
Forrest	4
Franklin	3
George	4
Greene	4
Grenada	1
Hancock	4
Harrison	4
Hinds	2, 3
Holmes	2
Humphreys	2
Issaquena	2

County	Congressional District
Itawamba	1
Jackson	4
Jasper	3, 4
Jefferson	2
Jefferson Davis	3
Jones	3, 4
Kemper	3
Lafayette	1
Lamar	4
Lauderdale	3
Lawrence	3
Leake	2, 3
Lee	1
Leflore	2
Lincoln	3
Lowndes	1
Madison	2, 3
Marion	3, 4
Marshall	1
Monroe	1
Montgomery	2
Neshoba	3
Newton	3
Noxubee	3
Oktibbeha	3
Panola	1
Pearl River	4
Perry	4

County	Congressional District
Pike	3
Pontotoc	1
Prentiss	1
Quitman	2
Rankin	3
Scott	3
Sharkey	2
Simpson	3
Smith	3
Stone	4
Sunflower	2
Tallahatchie	2
Tate	1
Tippah	1
Tishomingo	1
Tunica	2
Union	1
Walthall	3
Warren	2
Washington	2
Wayne	4
Webster	1, 3
Wilkinson	3
Winston	1, 3
Yalobusha	1
Yazoo	2

Congressional District 1

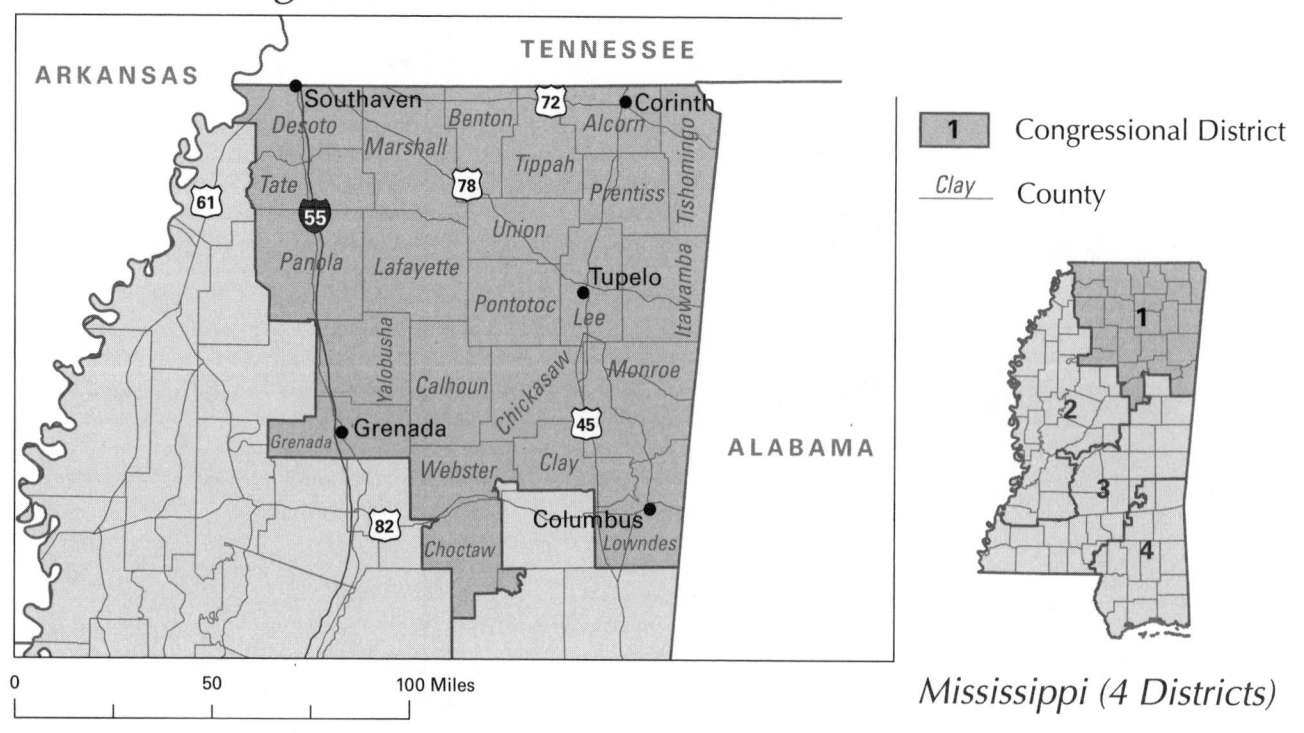

Mississippi (4 Districts)

Congressional District 2

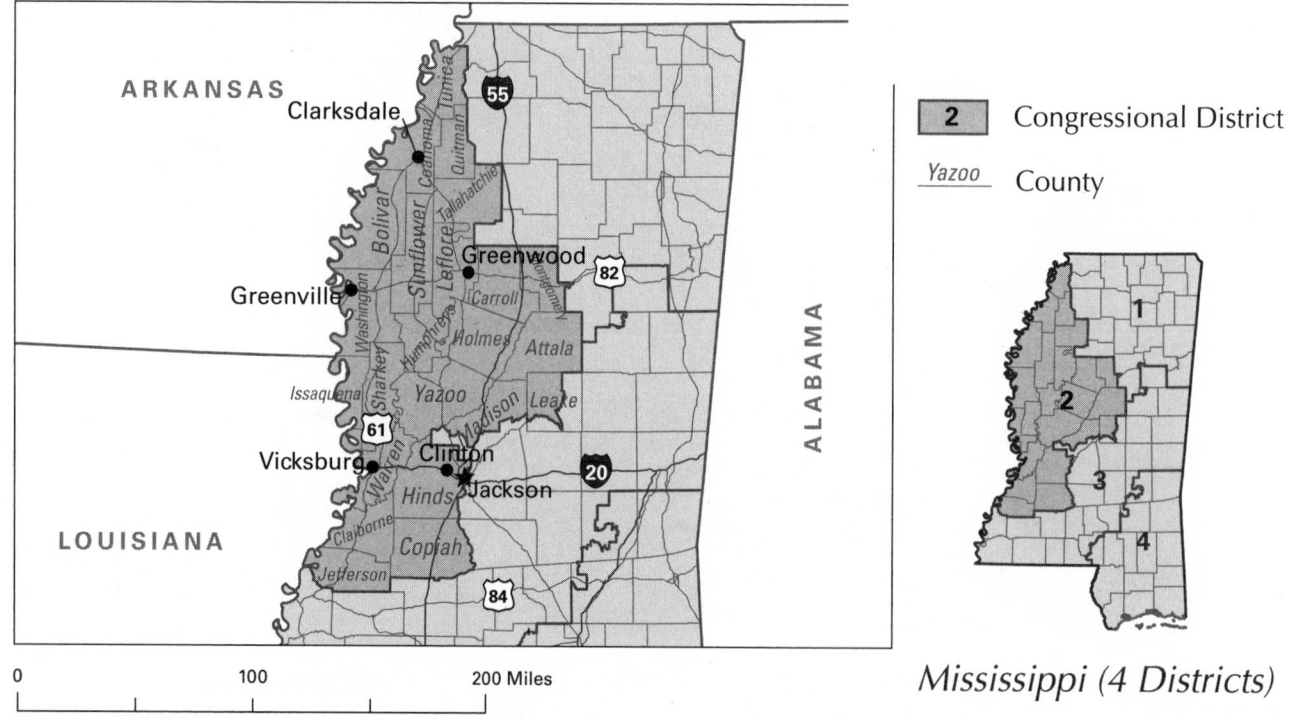

Mississippi (4 Districts)

Congressional District 3

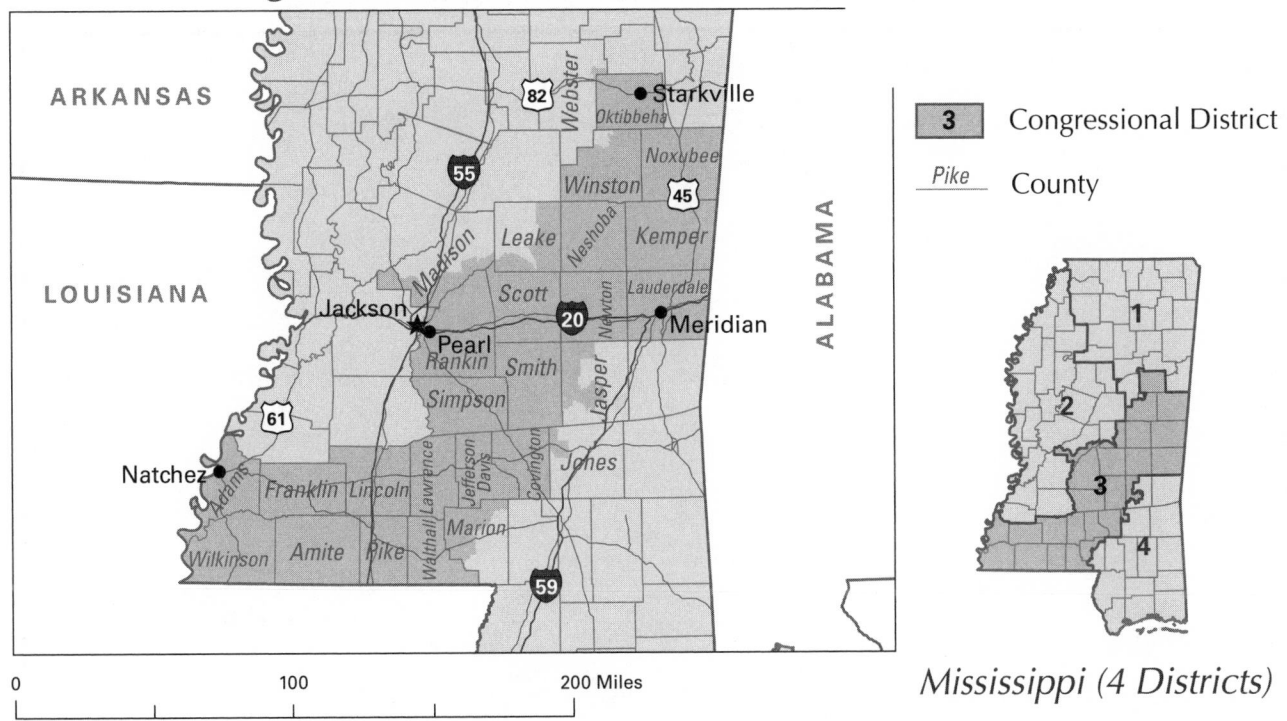

Mississippi (4 Districts)

Congressional District 4

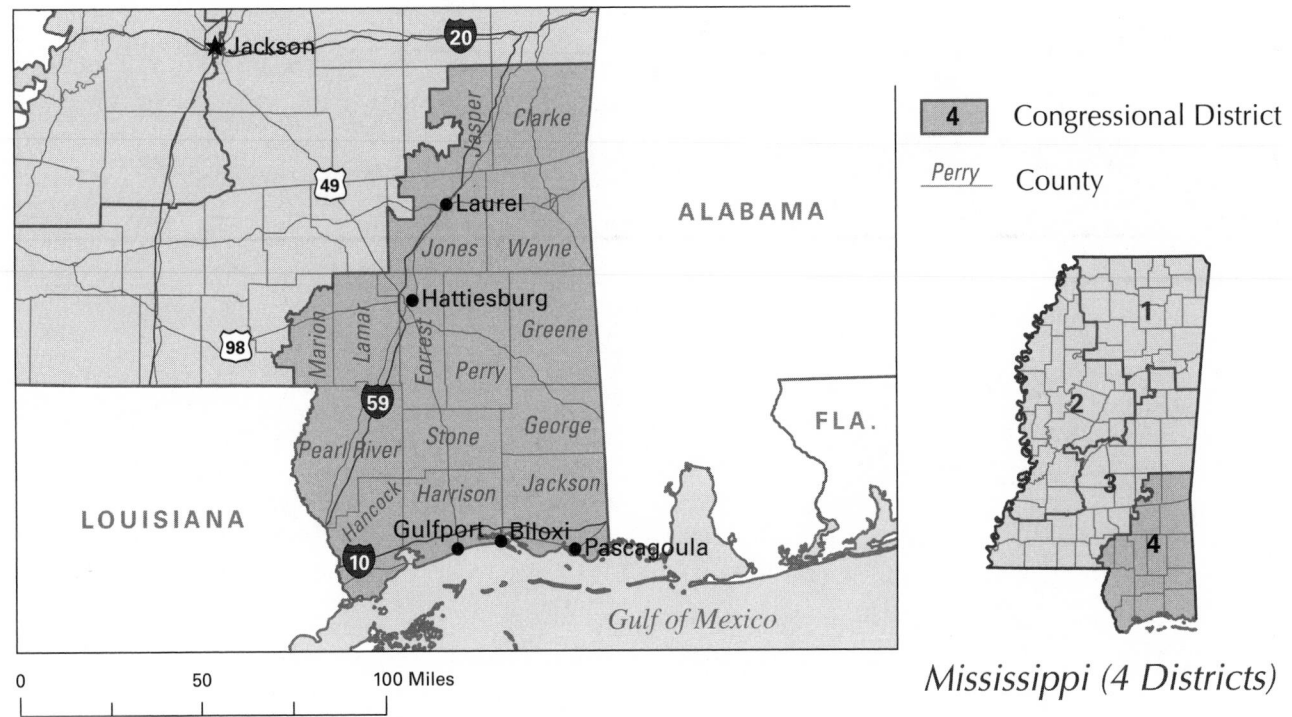

Mississippi (4 Districts)

Missouri Congressional Districts — 9 Districts Total

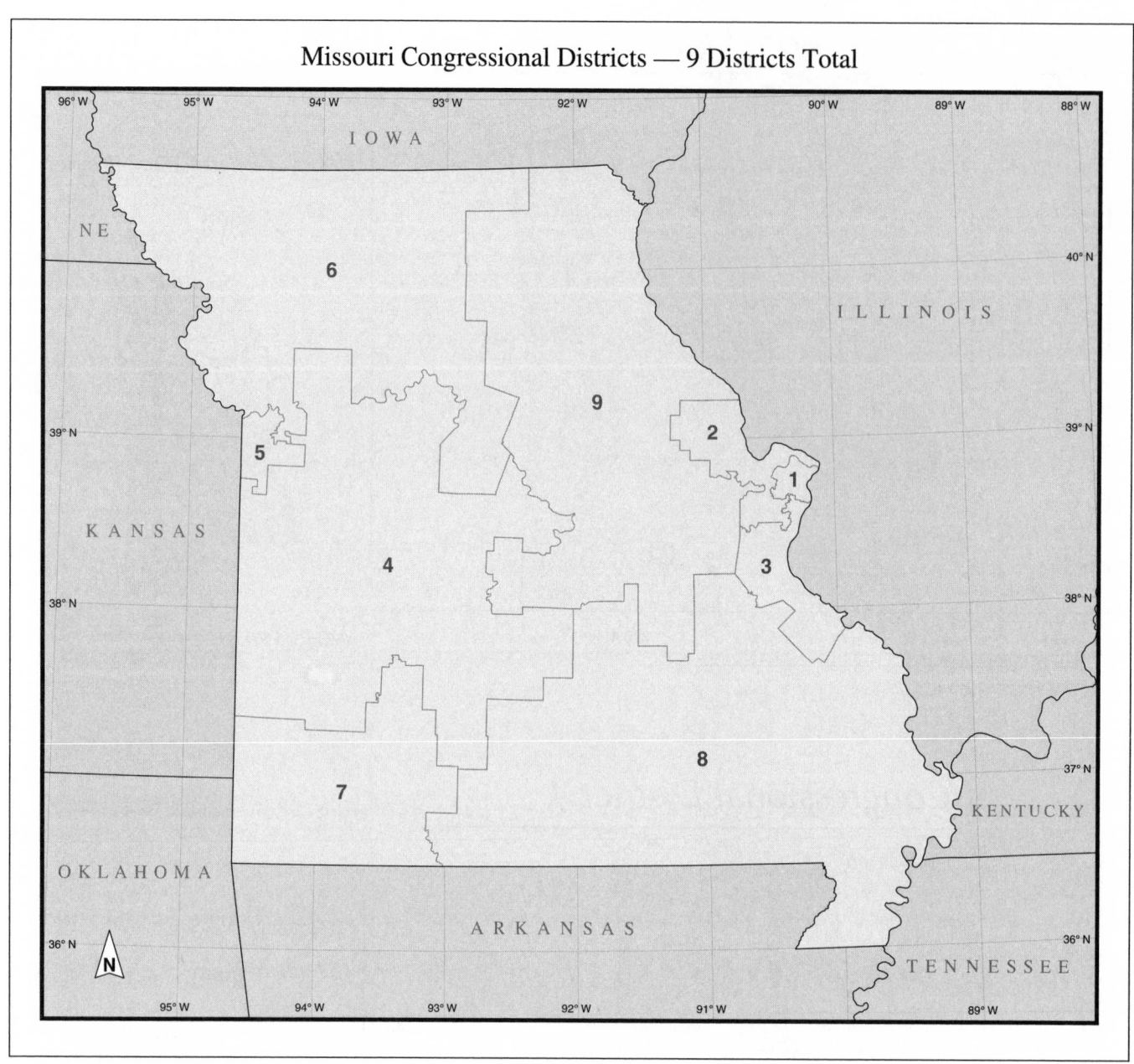

MISSOURI—110th CONGRESSIONAL DISTRICTS BY COUNTIES AND INDEPENDENT CITIES

County	Congressional District	County	Congressional District	County	Congressional District
Adair	9	Grundy	6	Perry	8
Andrew	6	Harrison	6	Pettis	4
Atchison	6	Henry	4	Phelps	8
Audrain	9	Hickory	4	Pike	9
Barry	7	Holt	6	Platte	6
Barton	4	Howard	6	Polk	4, 7
Bates	4	Howell	8	Pulaski	4
Benton	4	Iron	8	Putnam	6
Bollinger	8	Jackson	4–6	Ralls	9
Boone	9	Jasper	7	Randolph	9
Buchanan	6	Jefferson	3	Ray	4
Butler	8	Johnson	4	Reynolds	8
Caldwell	6	Knox	9	Ripley	8
Callaway	9	Laclede	4	St. Charles	2, 9
Camden	4, 9	Lafayette	4	St. Clair	4
Cape Girardeau	8	Lawrence	7	Ste. Genevieve	3
Carroll	6	Lewis	9	St. Francois	8
Carter	8	Lincoln	2	St. Louis	1–3
Cass	4, 5	Linn	6	Saline	4
Cedar	4	Livingston	6	Schuyler	6
Chariton	6	McDonald	7	Scotland	9
Christian	7	Macon	9	Scott	8
Clark	9	Madison	8	Shannon	8
Clay	6	Maries	9	Shelby	9
Clinton	6	Marion	9	Stoddard	8
Cole	4	Mercer	6	Stone	7
Cooper	6	Miller	9	Sullivan	6
Crawford	9	Mississippi	8	Taney	7, 8
Dade	4	Moniteau	4	Texas	8
Dallas	4	Monroe	9	Vernon	4
Daviess	6	Montgomery	9	Warren	9
DeKalb	6	Morgan	4	Washington	8
Dent	8	New Madrid	8	Wayne	8
Douglas	8	Newton	7	Webster	4
Dunklin	8	Nodaway	6	Worth	6
Franklin	9	Oregon	8	Wright	8
Gasconade	9	Osage	9	St. Louis city	1, 3
Gentry	6	Ozark	8		
Greene	7	Pemiscot	8		

Congressional District 1

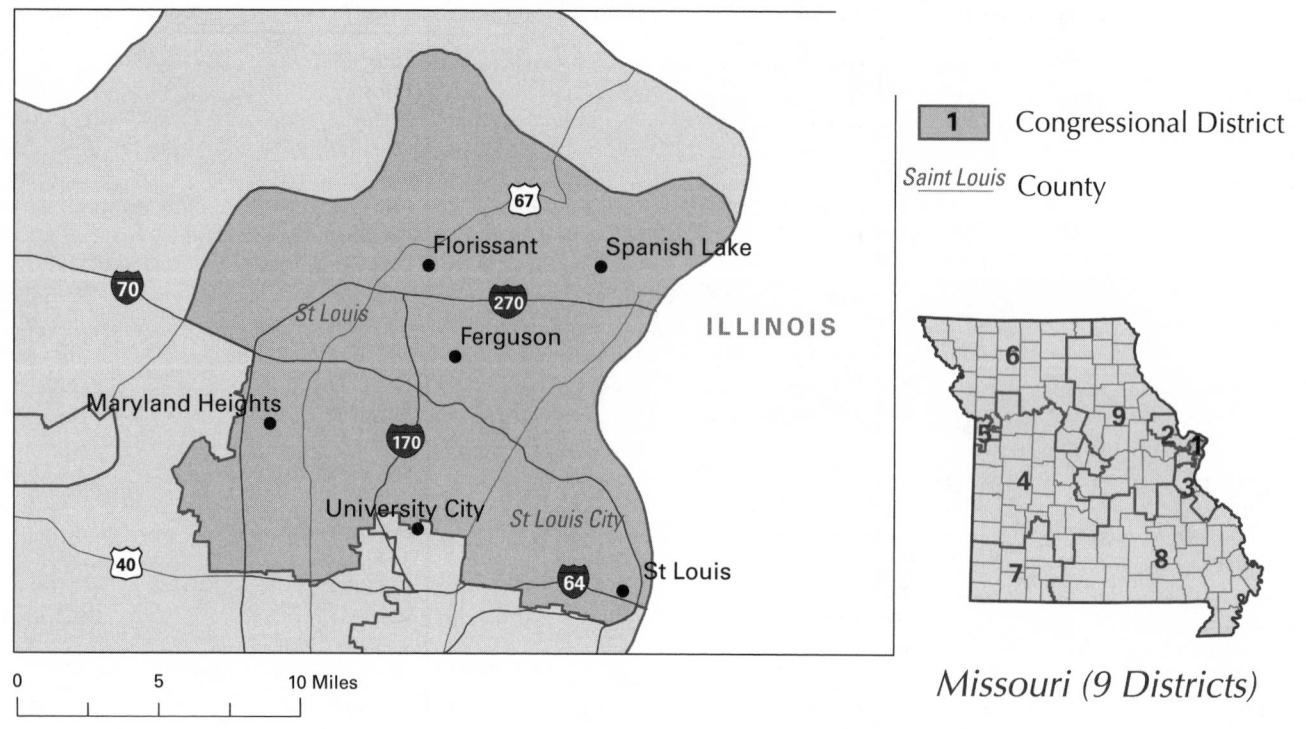

1 Congressional District

Saint Louis County

Missouri (9 Districts)

Congressional District 2

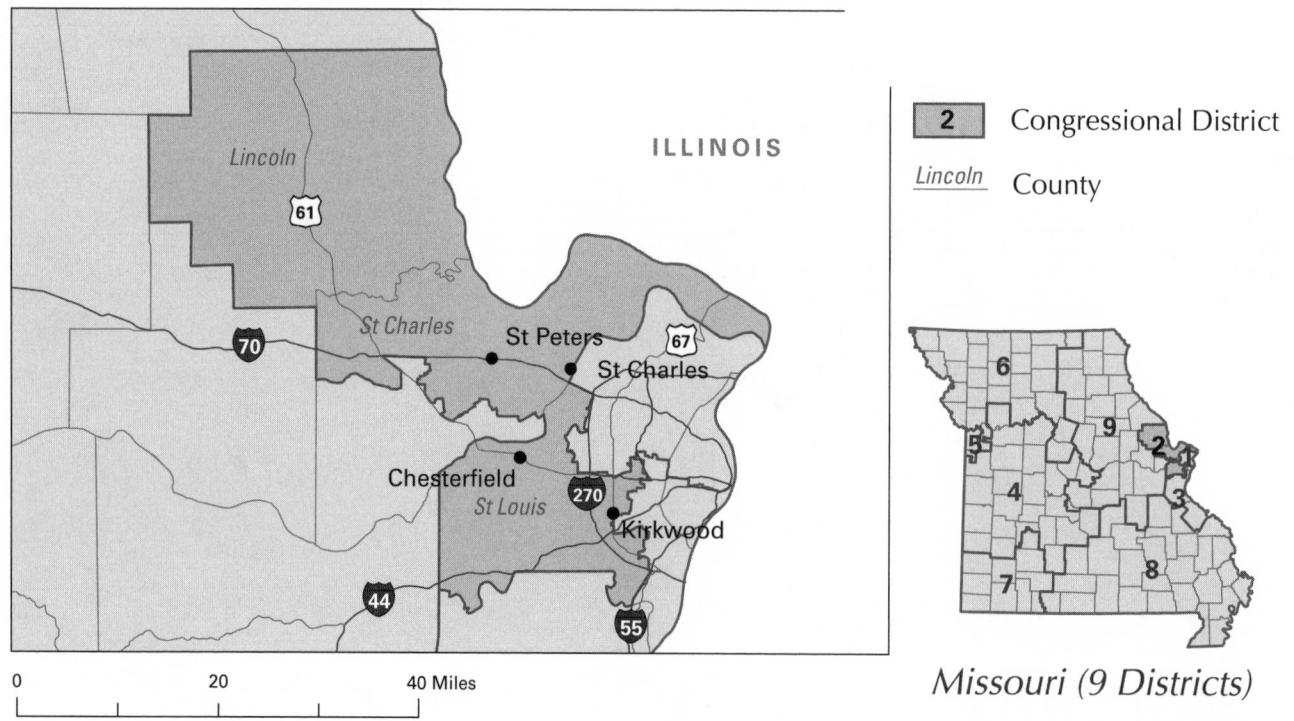

2 Congressional District

Lincoln County

Missouri (9 Districts)

Congressional District 3

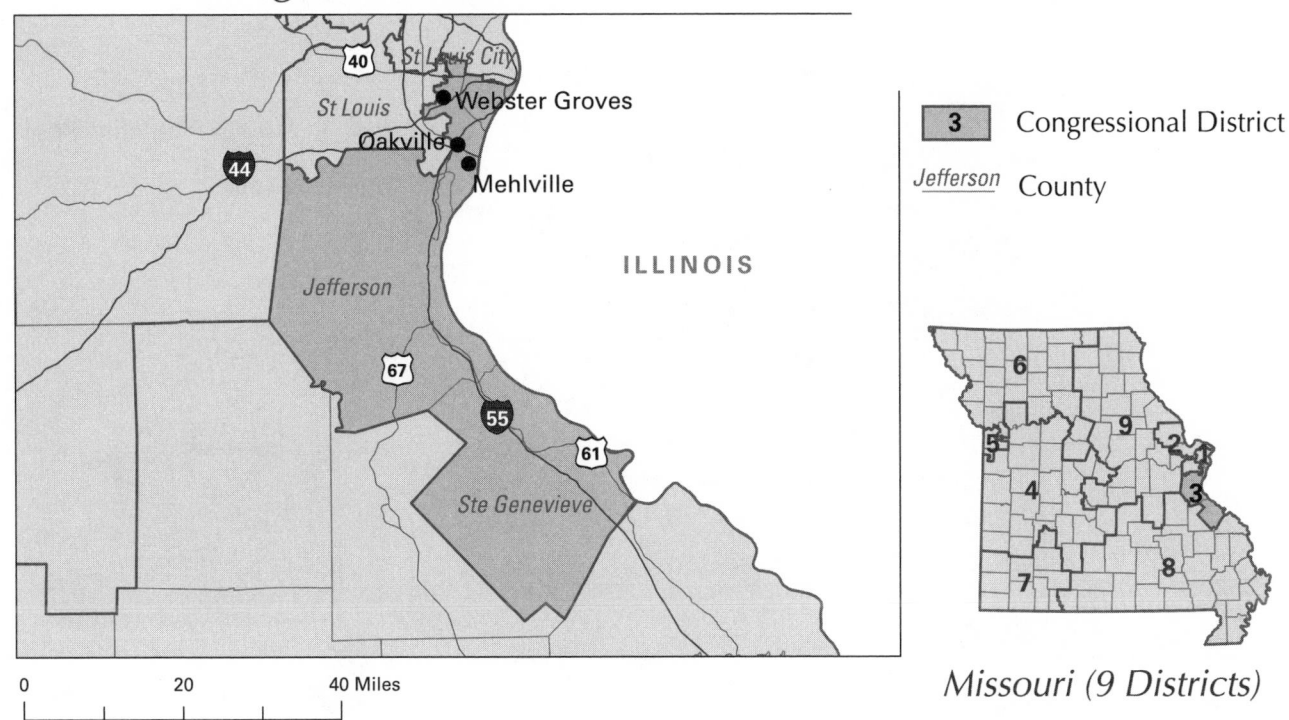

3 — Congressional District
Jefferson — County

Missouri (9 Districts)

0   20   40 Miles

Congressional District 4

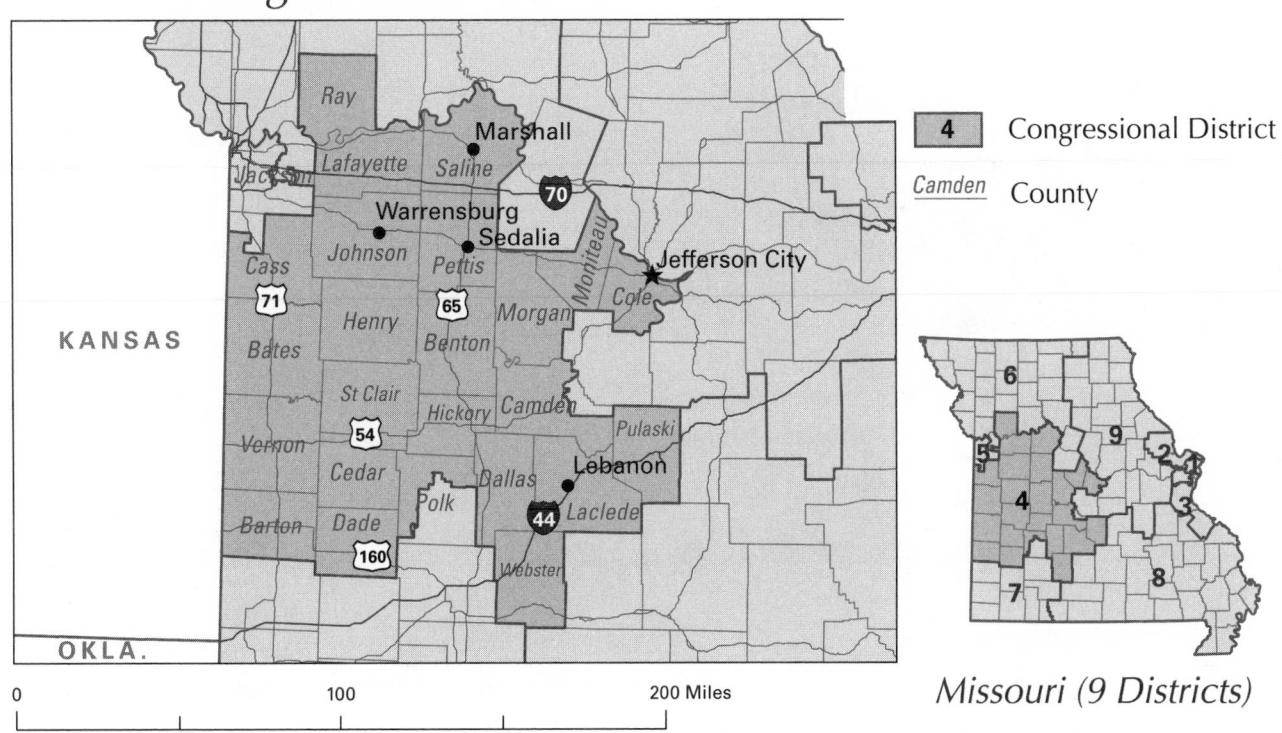

4 — Congressional District
Camden — County

Missouri (9 Districts)

0   100   200 Miles

Congressional District 5

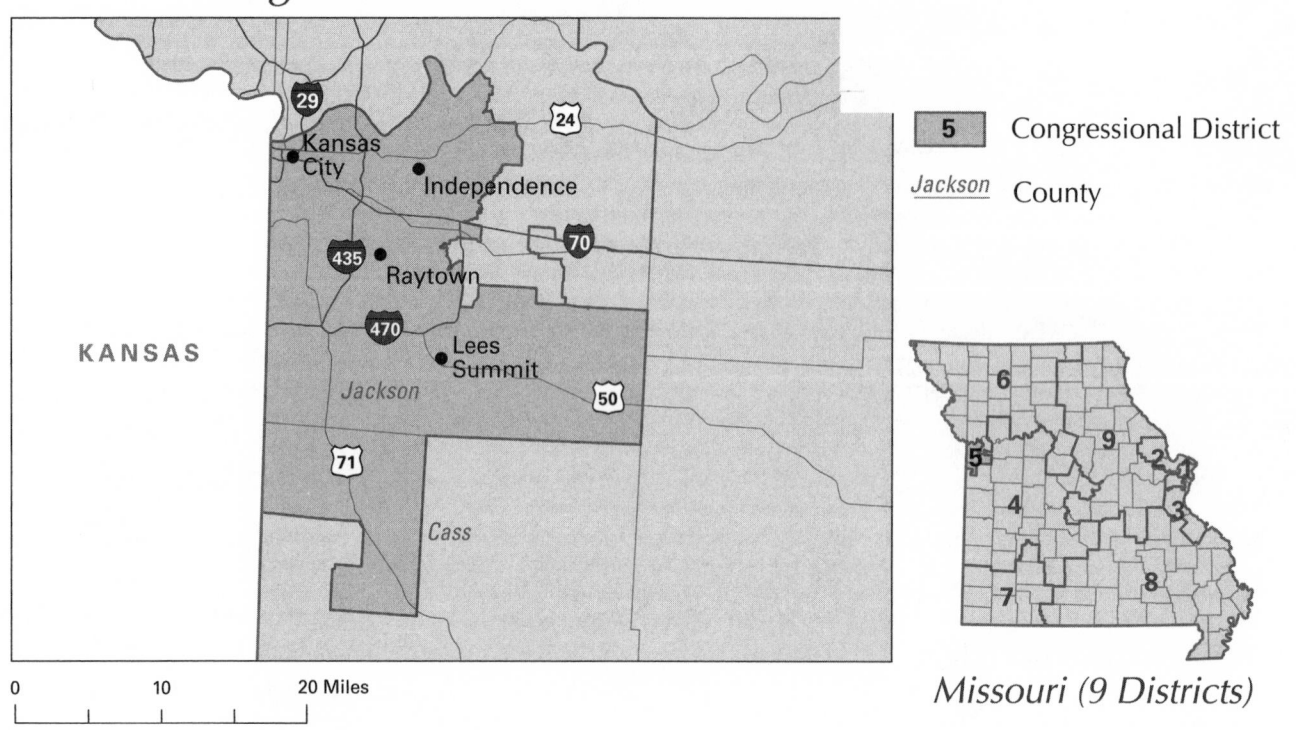

0   10   20 Miles

Missouri (9 Districts)

Congressional District 6

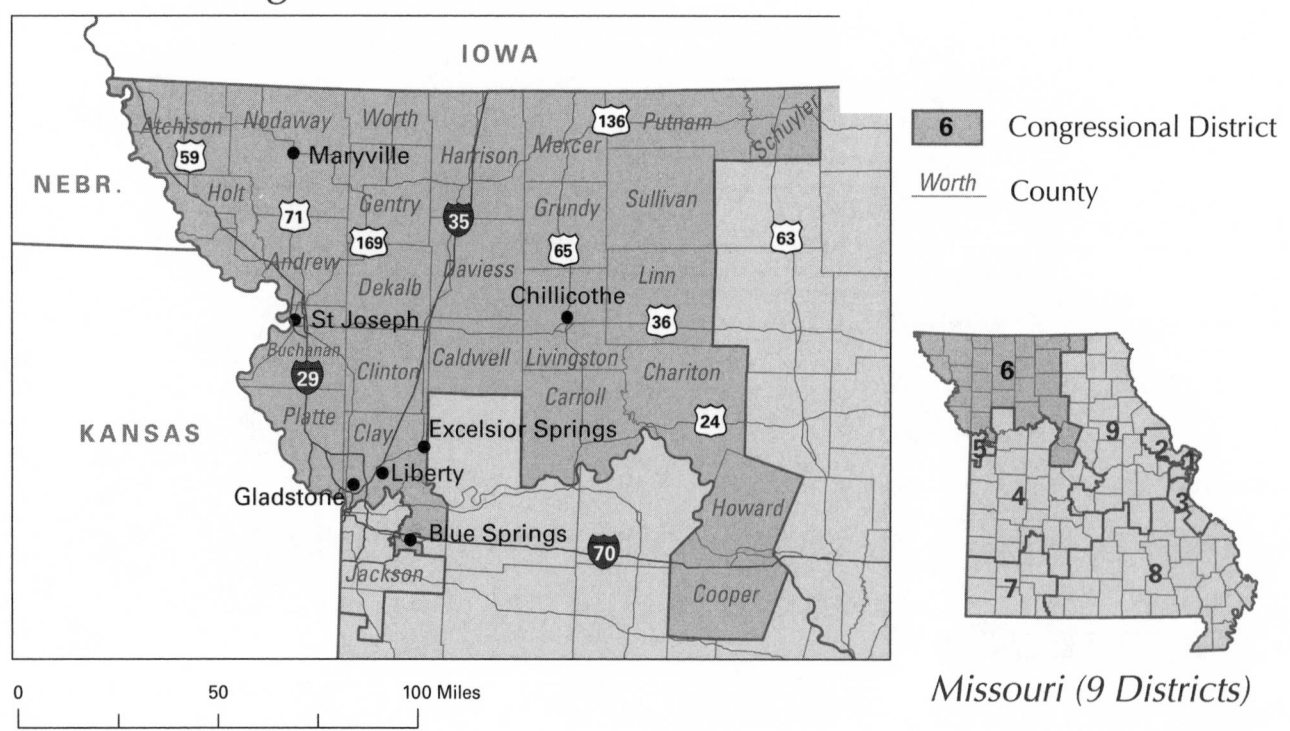

0   50   100 Miles

Missouri (9 Districts)

Congressional District 7

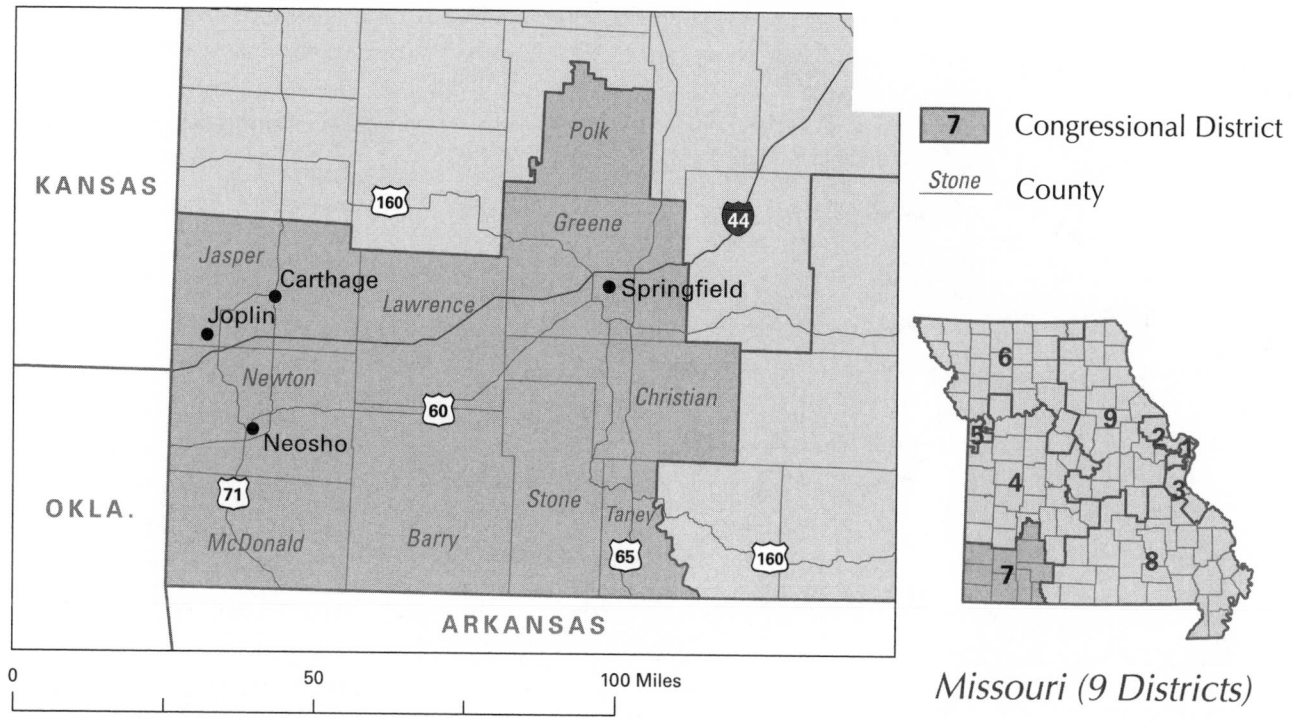

Congressional District 8

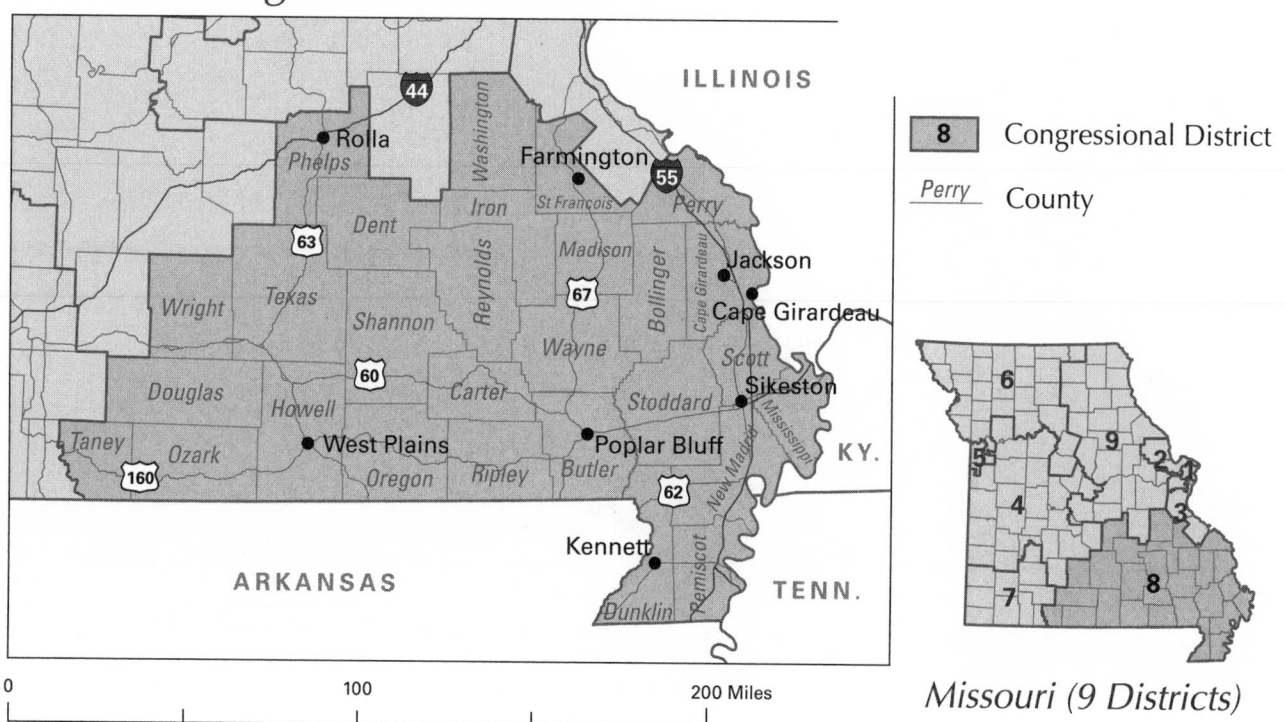

Congressional District 9

Missouri (9 Districts)

Montana—
Congressional District: At large

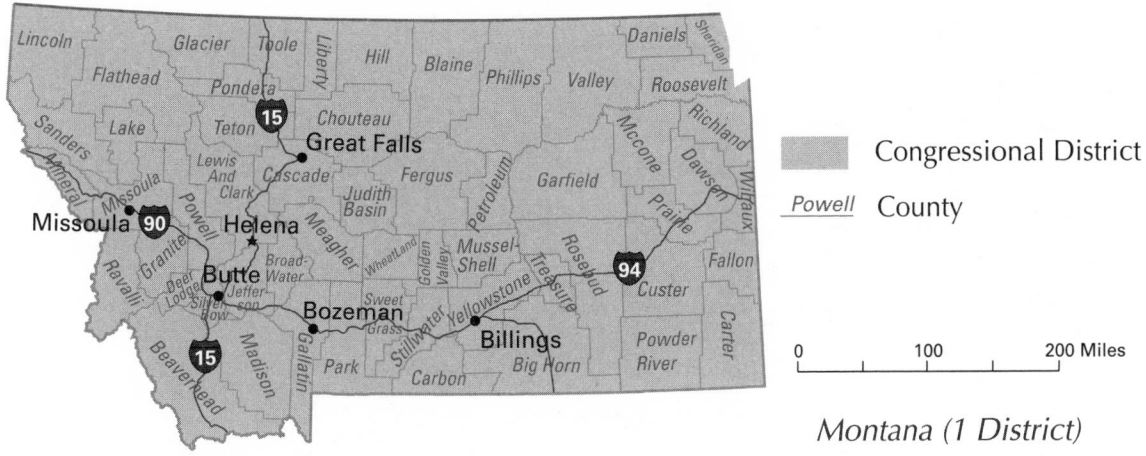

Congressional District

Powell County

0   100   200 Miles

Montana (1 District)

MONTANA—110th CONGRESSIONAL DISTRICTS BY COUNTIES

County	Congressional District	County	Congressional District	County	Congressional District
Beaverhead	1	Granite	1	Powell	1
Big Horn	1	Hill	1	Prairie	1
Blaine	1	Jefferson	1	Ravalli	1
Broadwater	1	Judith Basin	1	Richland	1
Carbon	1	Lake	1	Roosevelt	1
Carter	1	Lewis and Clark	1	Rosebud	1
Cascade	1	Liberty	1	Sanders	1
Chouteau	1	Lincoln	1	Sheridan	1
Custer	1	McCone	1	Silver Bow	1
Daniels	1	Madison	1	Stillwater	1
Dawson	1	Meagher	1	Sweet Grass	1
Deer Lodge	1	Mineral	1	Teton	1
Fallon	1	Missoula	1	Toole	1
Fergus	1	Musselshell	1	Treasure	1
Flathead	1	Park	1	Valley	1
Gallatin	1	Petroleum	1	Wheatland	1
Garfield	1	Phillips	1	Wibaux	1
Glacier	1	Pondera	1	Yellowstone	1
Golden Valley	1	Powder River	1		

Nebraska Congressional Districts — 3 Districts Total

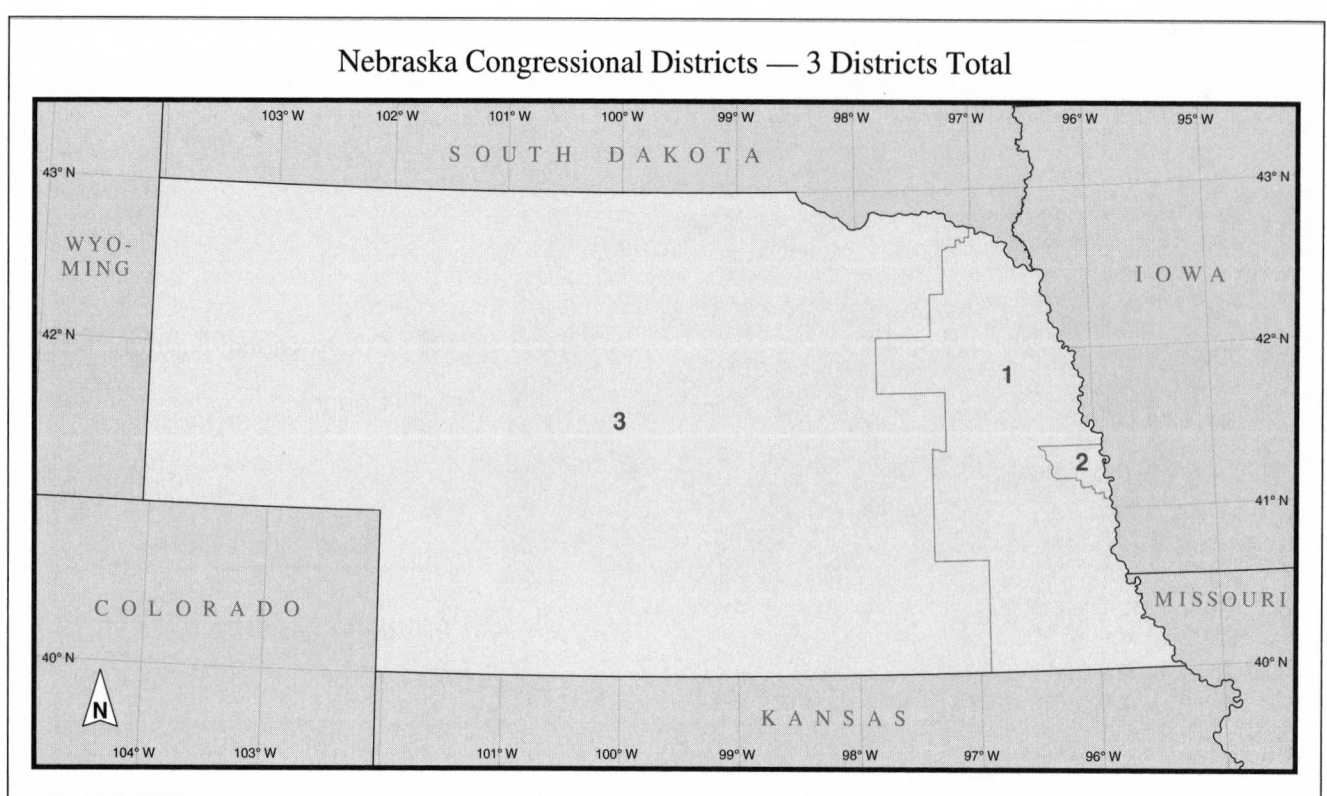

NEBRASKA—110th CONGRESSIONAL DISTRICTS BY COUNTIES

County	Congressional District
Adams	3
Antelope	3
Arthur	3
Banner	3
Blaine	3
Boone	3
Box Butte	3
Boyd	3
Brown	3
Buffalo	3
Burt	1
Butler	1
Cass	1
Cedar	1, 3
Chase	3
Cherry	3
Cheyenne	3
Clay	3
Colfax	1
Cuming	1
Custer	3
Dakota	1
Dawes	3
Dawson	3
Deuel	3
Dixon	1
Dodge	1
Douglas	2
Dundy	3
Fillmore	3
Franklin	3

County	Congressional District
Frontier	3
Furnas	3
Gage	1
Garden	3
Garfield	3
Gosper	3
Grant	3
Greeley	3
Hall	3
Hamilton	3
Harlan	3
Hayes	3
Hitchcock	3
Holt	3
Hooker	3
Howard	3
Jefferson	3
Johnson	1
Kearney	3
Keith	3
Keya Paha	3
Kimball	3
Knox	3
Lancaster	1
Lincoln	3
Logan	3
Loup	3
McPherson	3
Madison	1
Merrick	3
Morrill	3

County	Congressional District
Nance	3
Nemaha	1
Nuckolls	3
Otoe	1
Pawnee	1
Perkins	3
Phelps	3
Pierce	3
Platte	3
Polk	3
Red Willow	3
Richardson	1
Rock	3
Saline	3
Sarpy	1, 2
Saunders	1
Scotts Bluff	3
Seward	1
Sheridan	3
Sherman	3
Sioux	3
Stanton	1
Thayer	3
Thomas	3
Thurston	1
Valley	3
Washington	1
Wayne	1
Webster	3
Wheeler	3
York	3

Congressional District 1

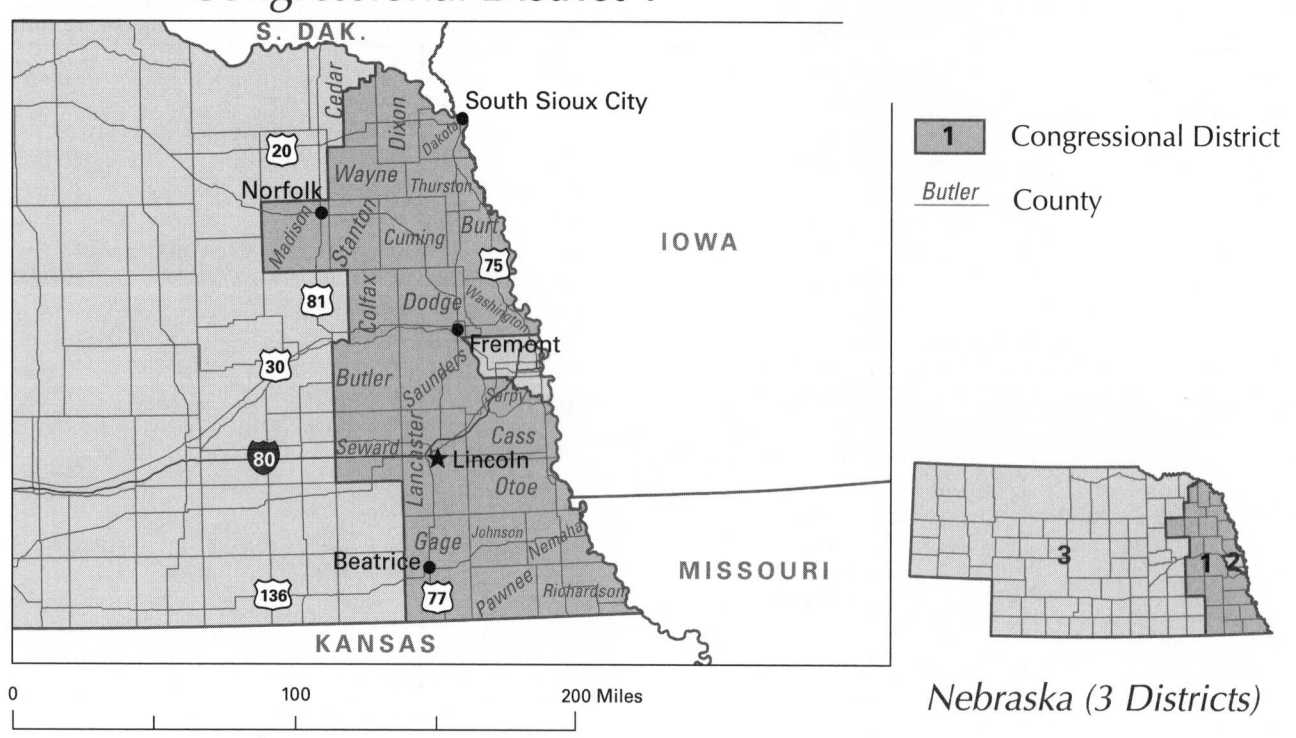

Nebraska (3 Districts)

Congressional District 2

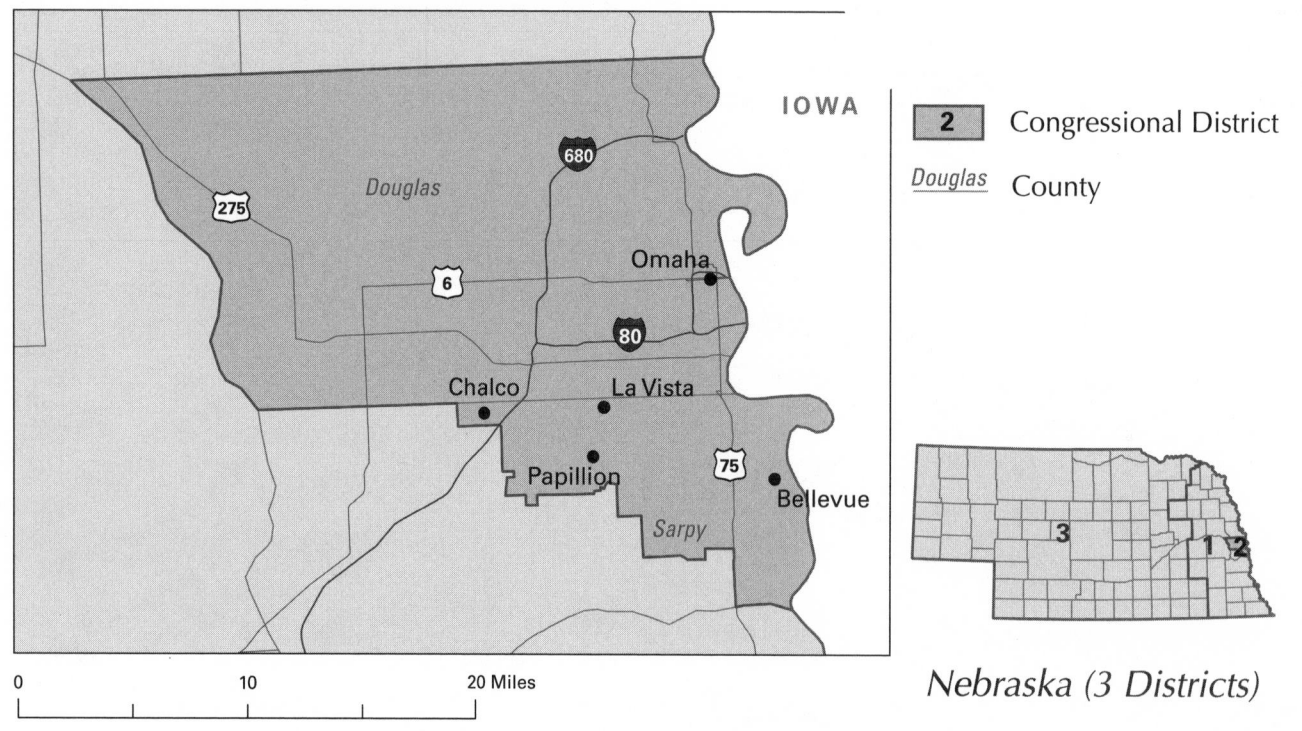

Nebraska (3 Districts)

Congressional District 3

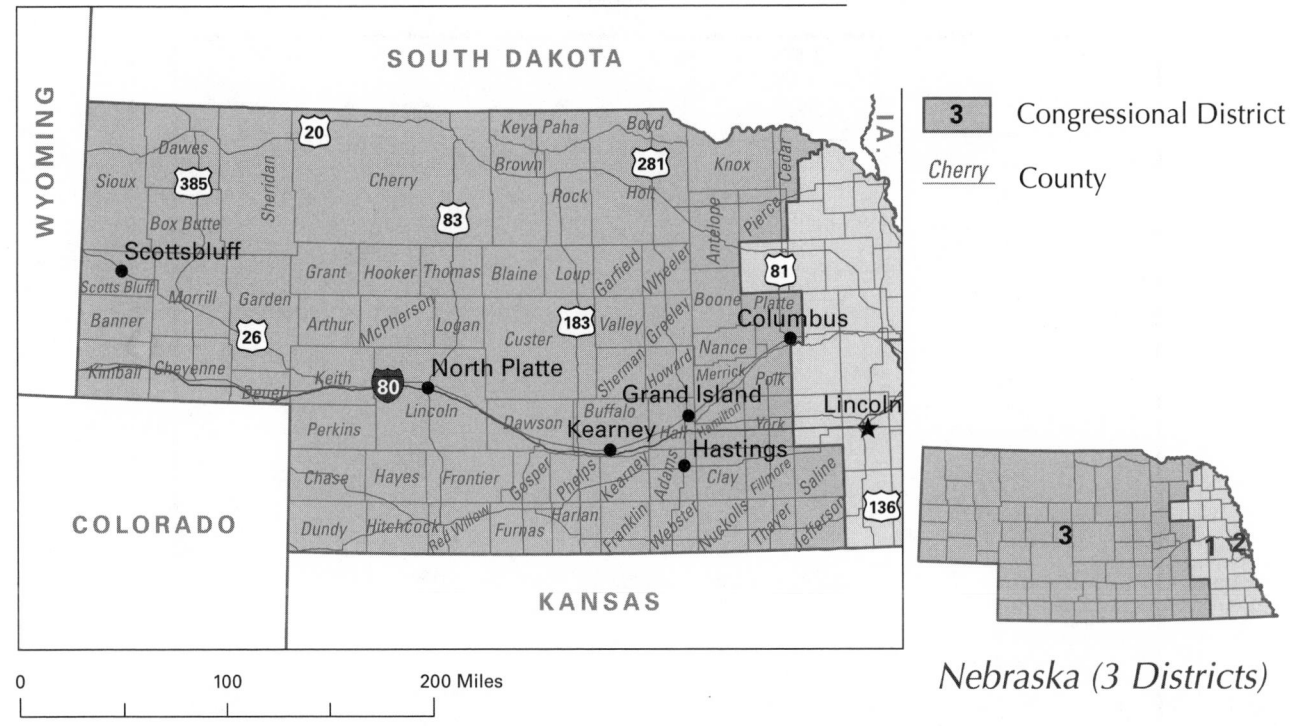

Nebraska (3 Districts)

Nevada Congressional Districts — 3 Districts Total

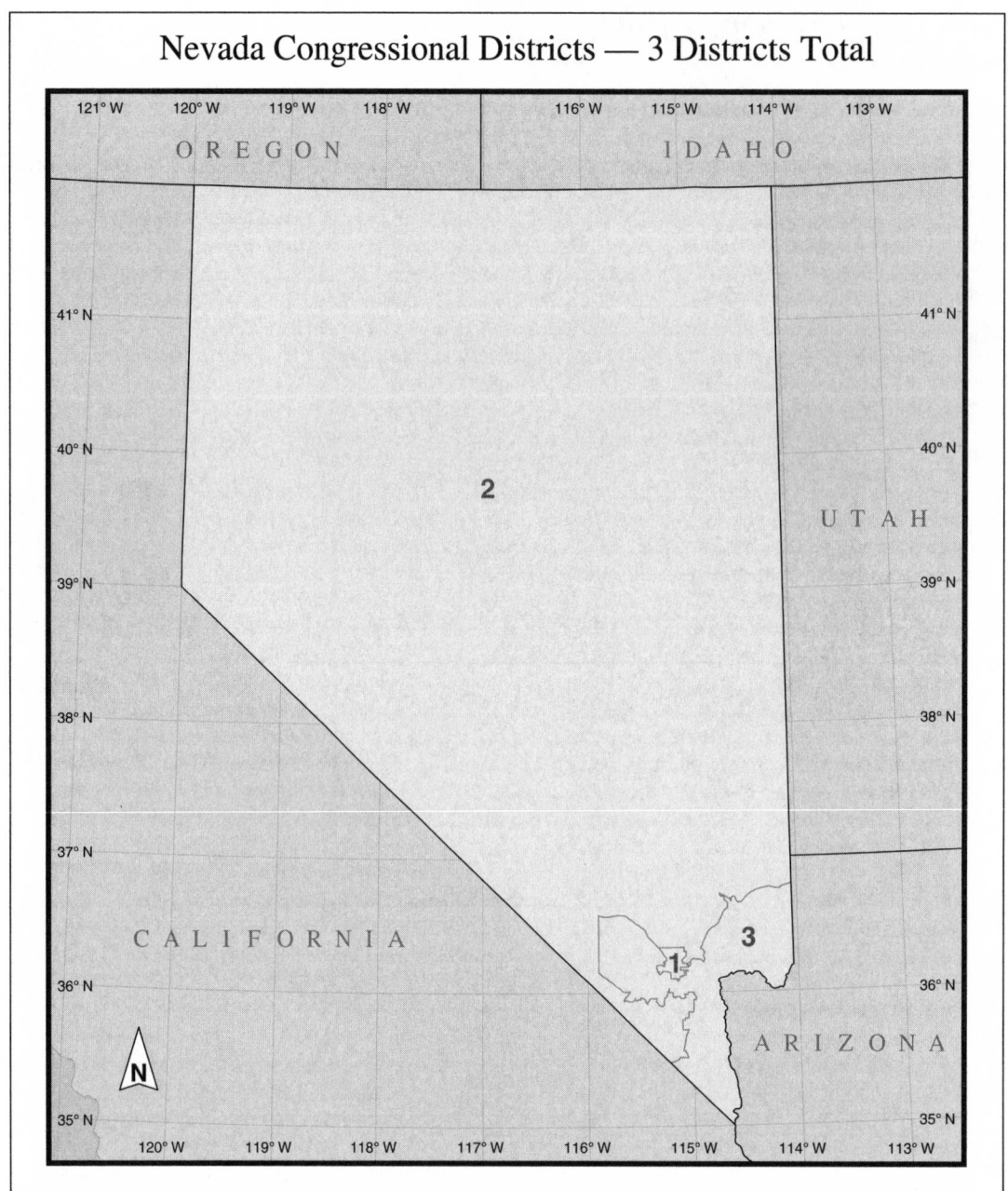

NEVADA—110th CONGRESSIONAL DISTRICTS BY COUNTIES AND INDEPENDENT CITIES

County	Congressional District
Churchill	2
Clark	1–3
Douglas	2
Elko	2
Esmeralda	2
Eureka	2
Humboldt	2
Lander	2
Lincoln	2
Lyon	2

County	Congressional District
Mineral	2
Nye	2
Pershing	2
Storey	2
Washoe	2
White Pine	2
Carson City	2

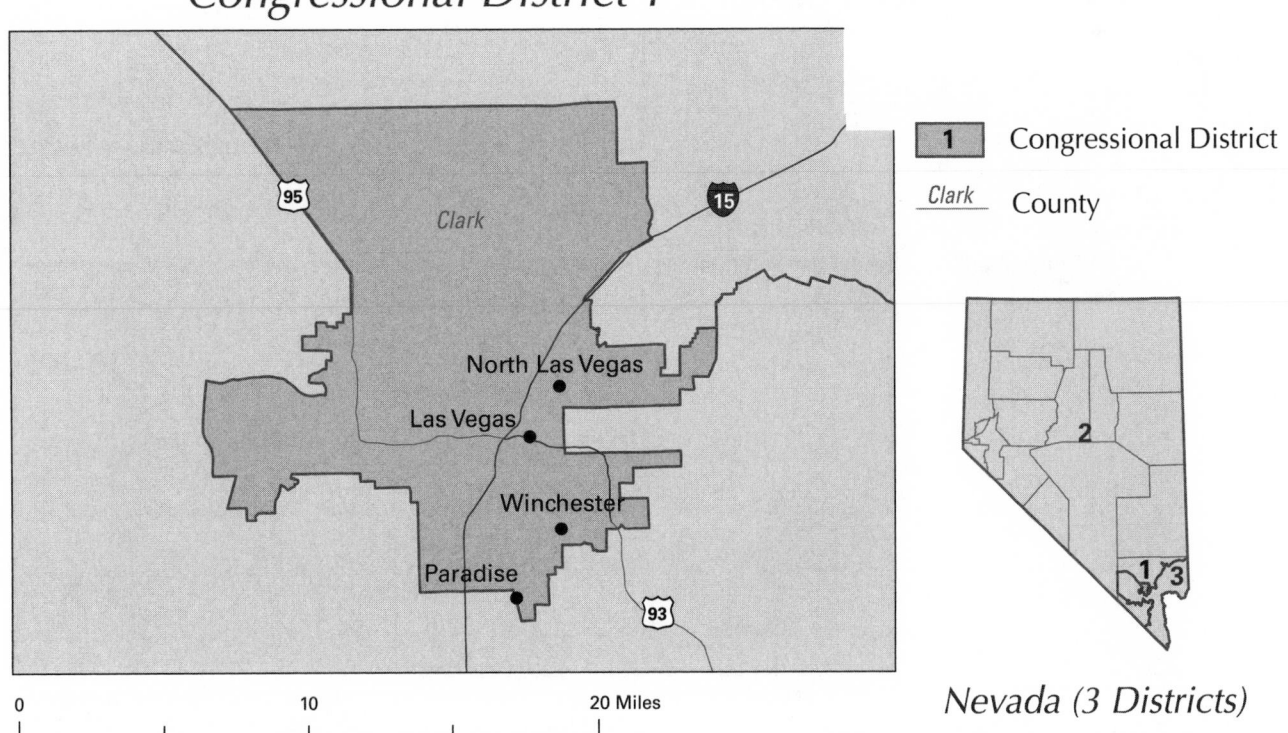

Congressional District 1

1 Congressional District

Clark County

Nevada (3 Districts)

Congressional District 2

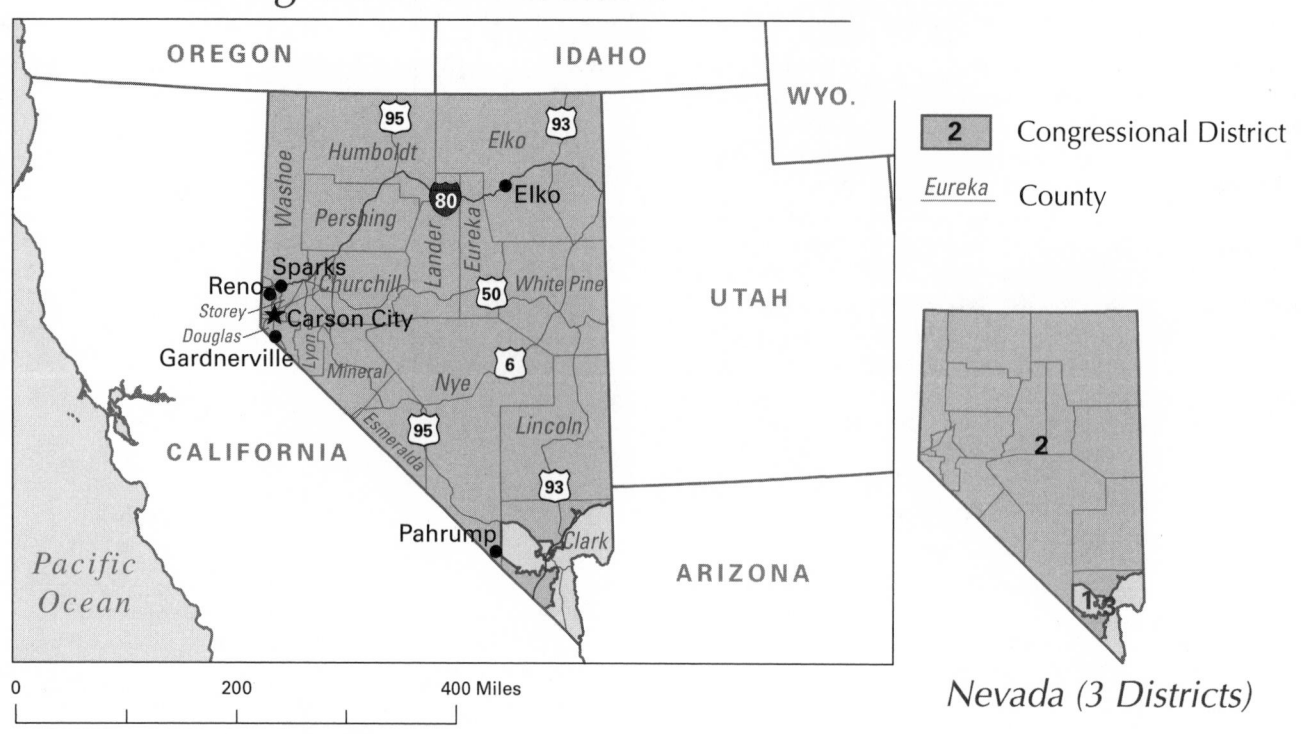

Nevada (3 Districts)

Congressional District 3

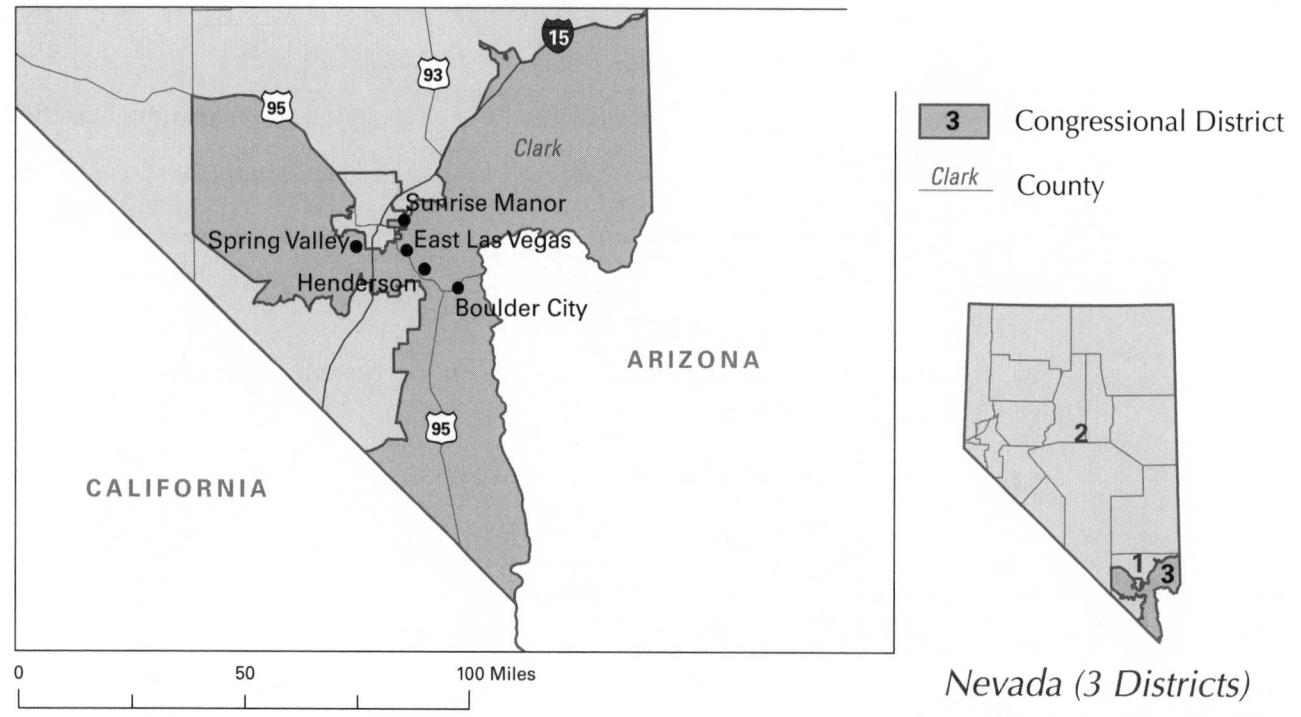

Nevada (3 Districts)

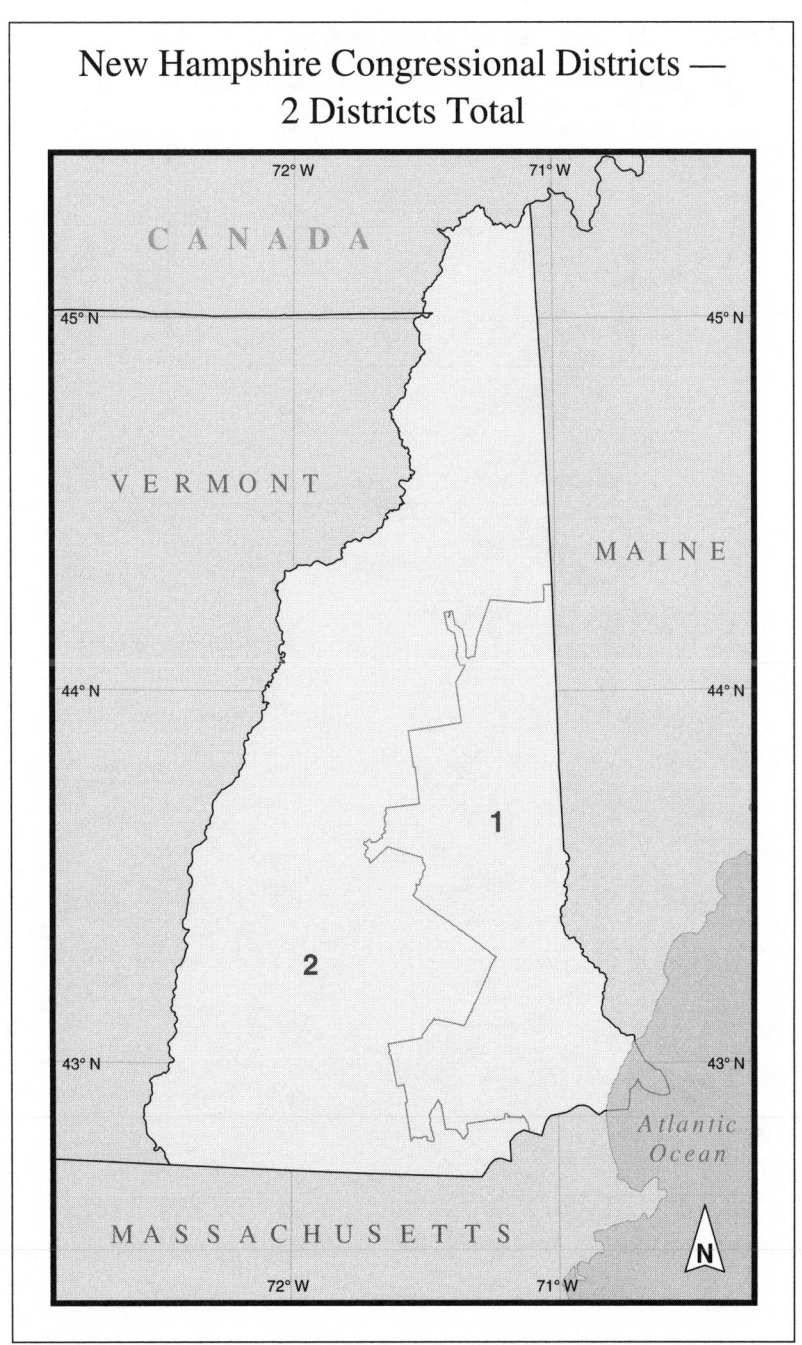

New Hampshire Congressional Districts —
2 Districts Total

NEW HAMPSHIRE—110th CONGRESSIONAL DISTRICTS BY COUNTIES

County	Congressional District	County	Congressional District
Belknap	1, 2	Strafford	1
Carroll	1, 2	Sullivan	2
Cheshire	2		
Coos	2		
Grafton	2		
Hillsborough	1, 2		
Merrimack	1, 2		
Rockingham	1, 2		

Congressional District 1

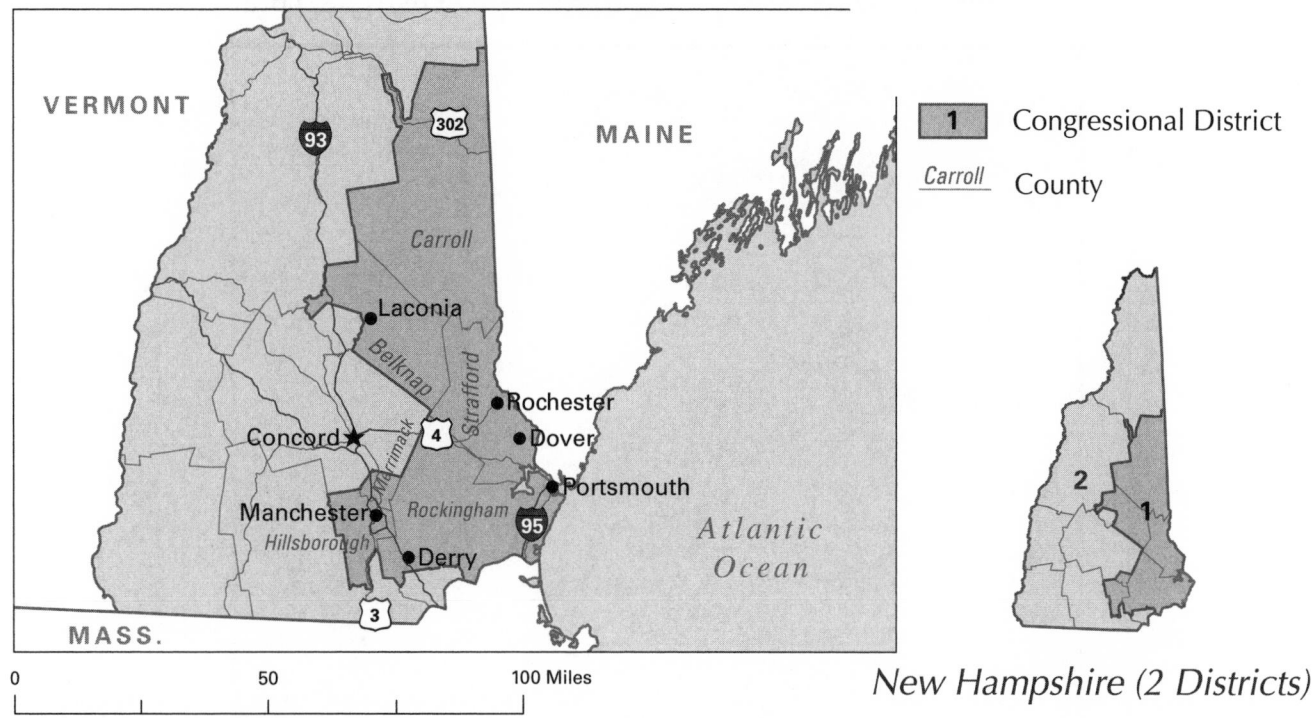

New Hampshire (2 Districts)

Congressional District 2

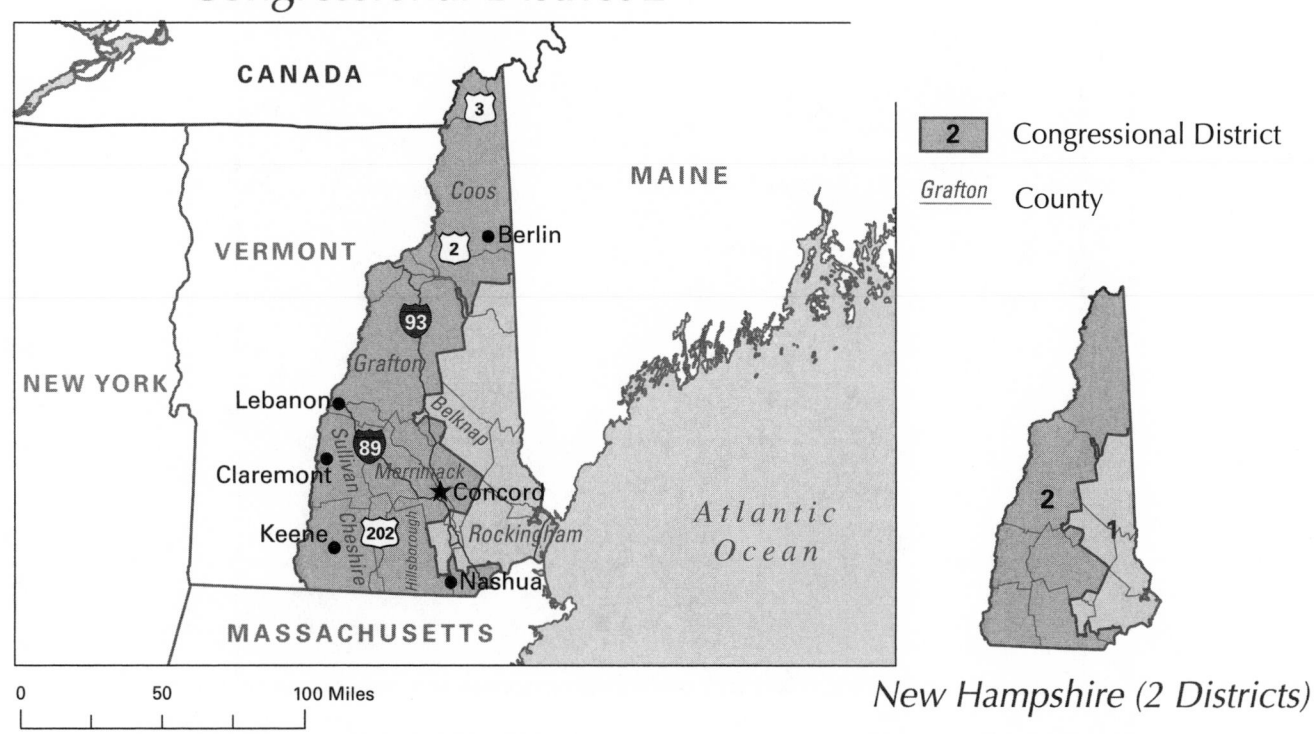

New Hampshire (2 Districts)

New Jersey Congressional Districts — 13 Districts Total

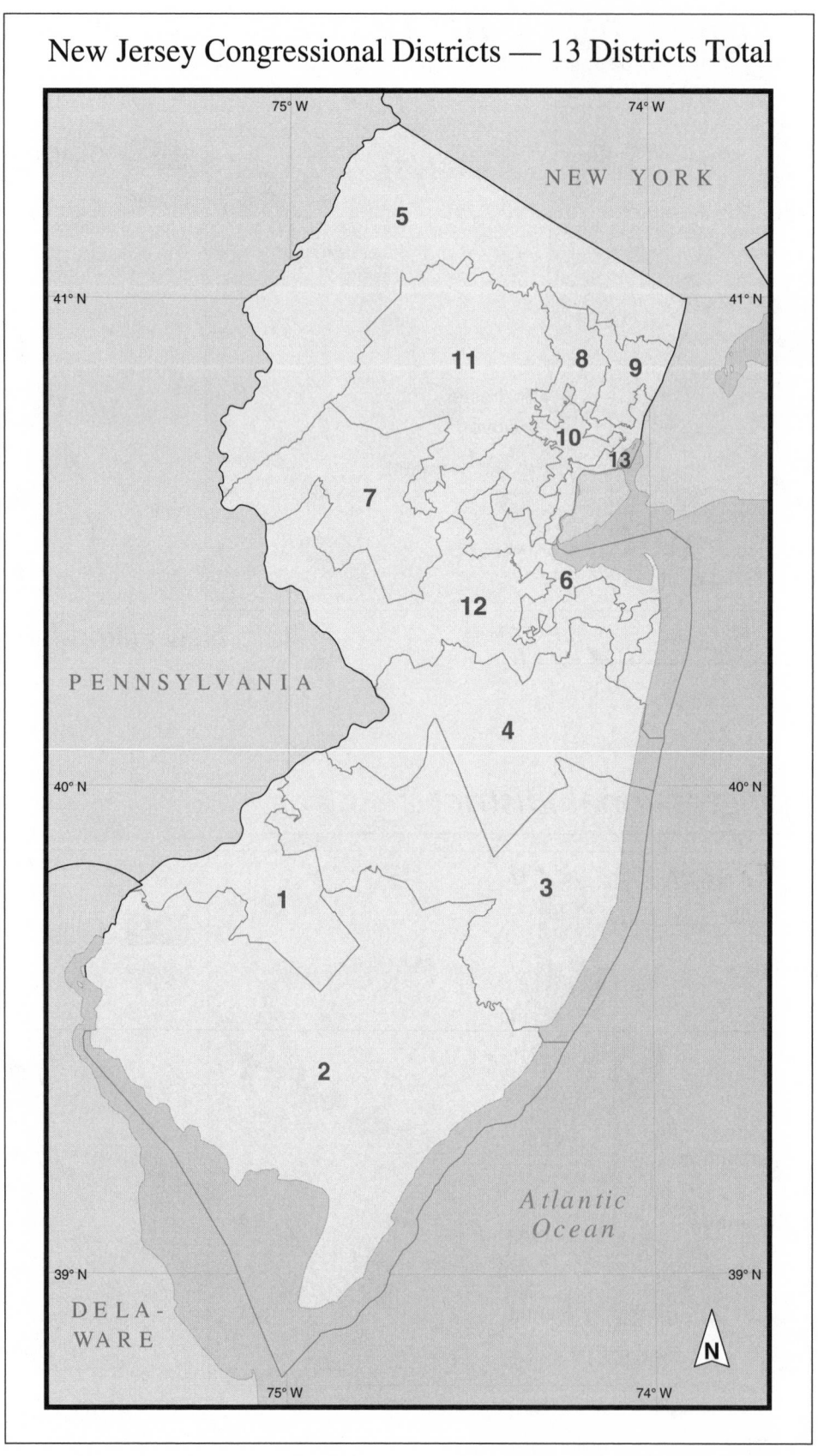

NEW JERSEY—110th CONGRESSIONAL DISTRICTS BY COUNTIES

County	Congressional District	County	Congressional District
Atlantic	2	Middlesex	6, 7, 12, 13
Bergen	5, 9	Monmouth	4, 6, 12
Burlington	1–4	Morris	11
Camden	1–3	Ocean	3, 4
Cape May	2	Passaic	5, 8, 9, 11
Cumberland	2	Salem	2
Essex	8, 10, 11, 13	Somerset	6, 7, 11, 12
Gloucester	1, 2	Sussex	5, 11
Hudson	9, 10, 13	Union	6, 7, 10, 13
Hunterdon	7, 12	Warren	5
Mercer	4, 12		

Congressional District 1

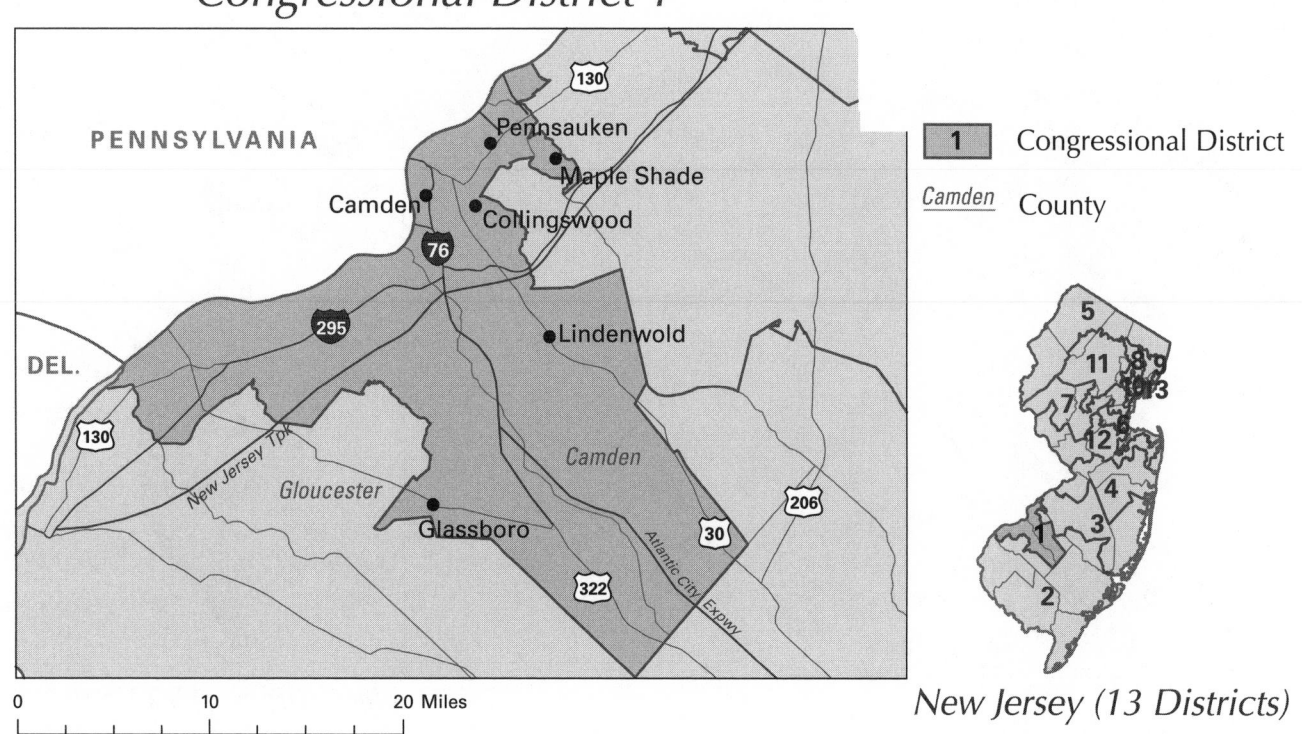

1 Congressional District

Camden County

New Jersey (13 Districts)

Congressional District 2

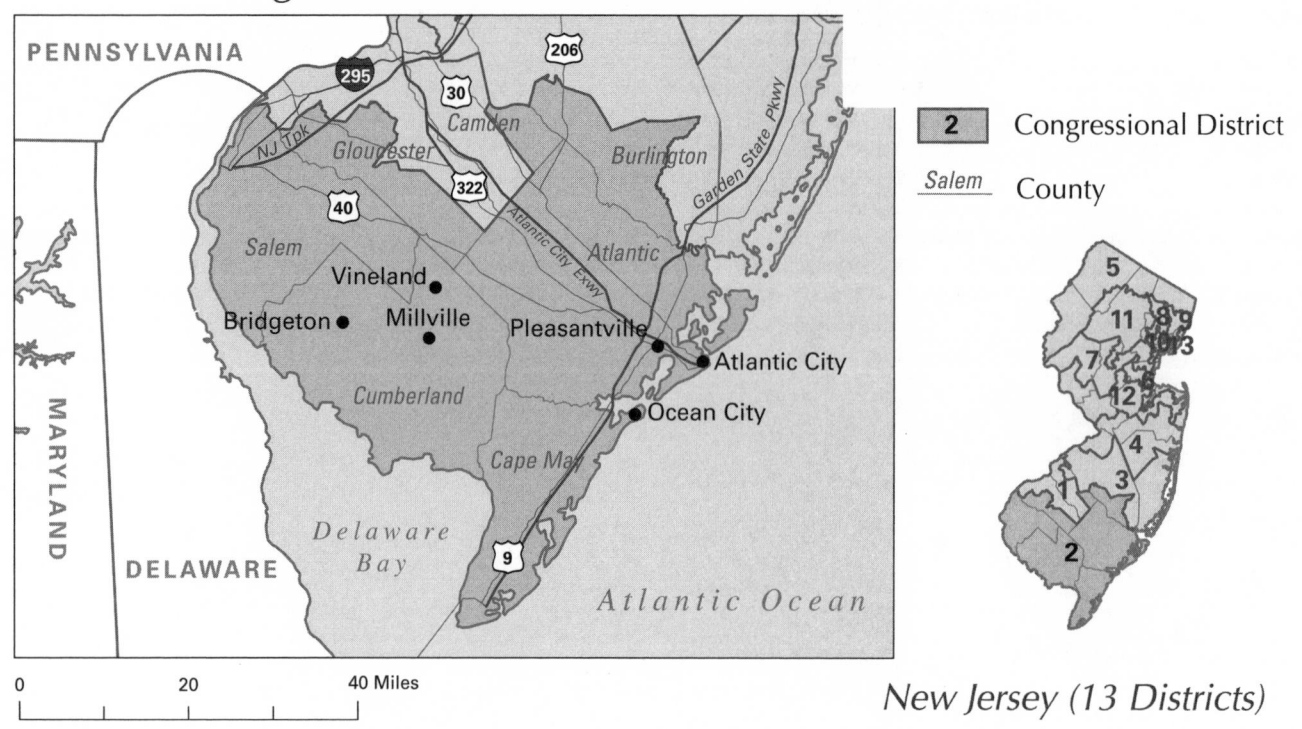

New Jersey (13 Districts)

Congressional District 3

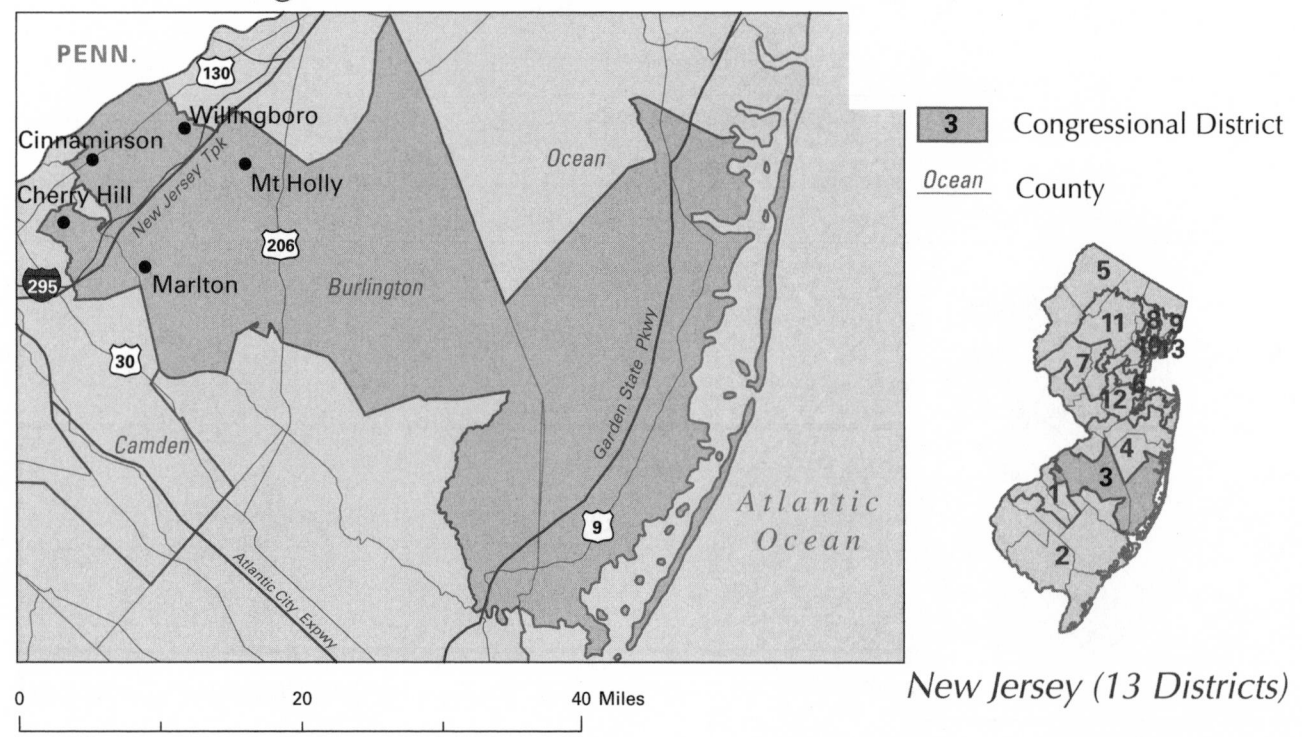

New Jersey (13 Districts)

Congressional District 4

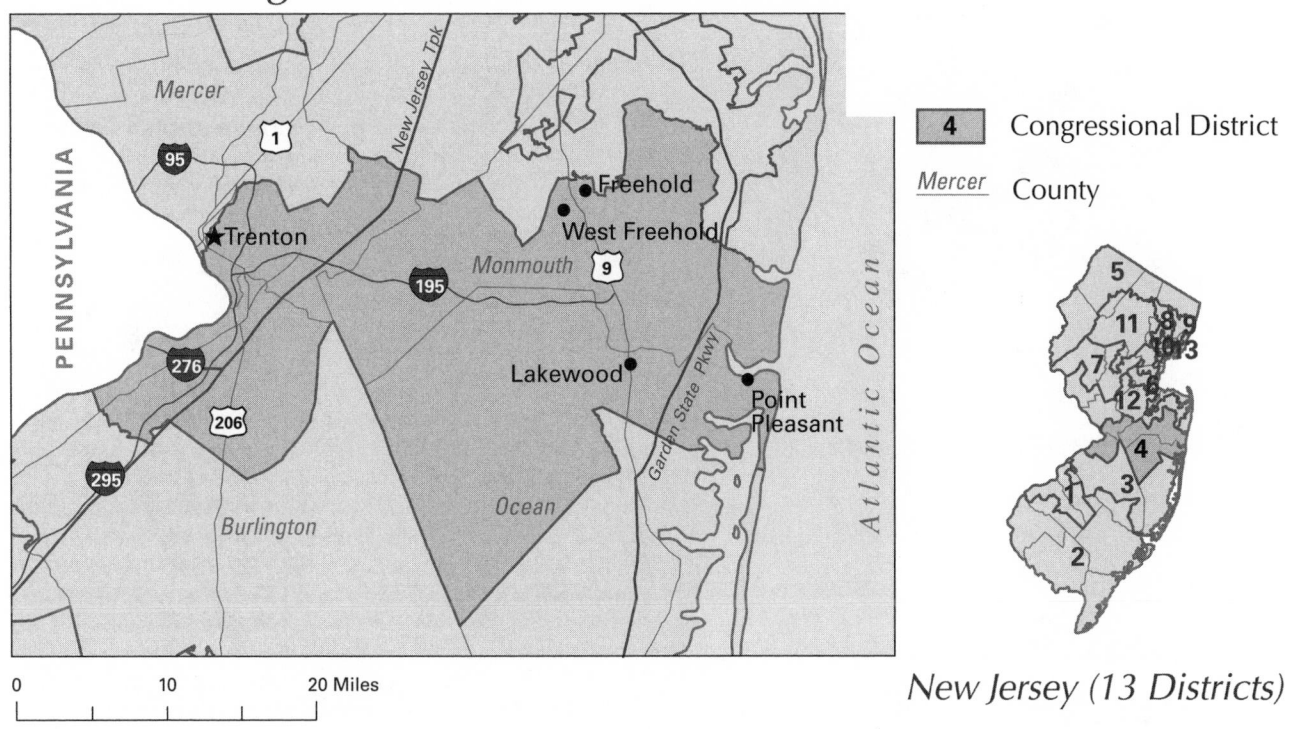

New Jersey (13 Districts)

Congressional District 5

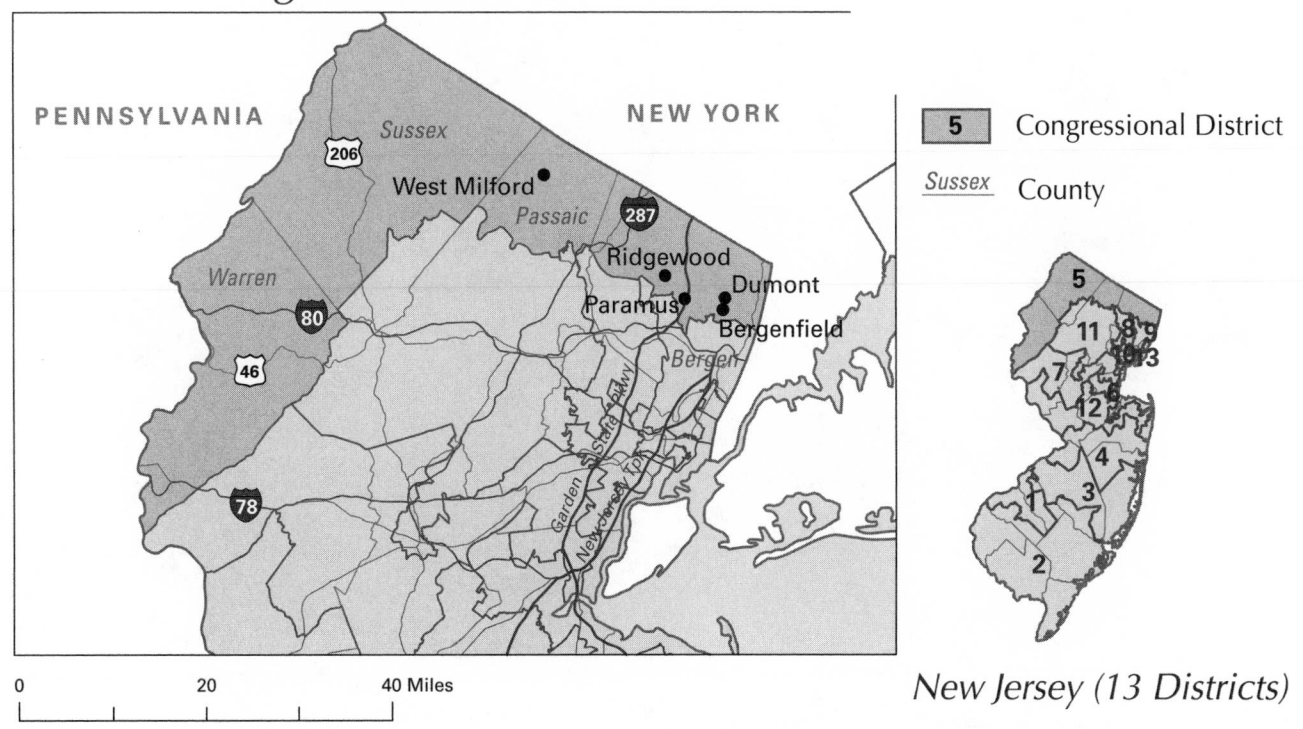

New Jersey (13 Districts)

Congressional District 6

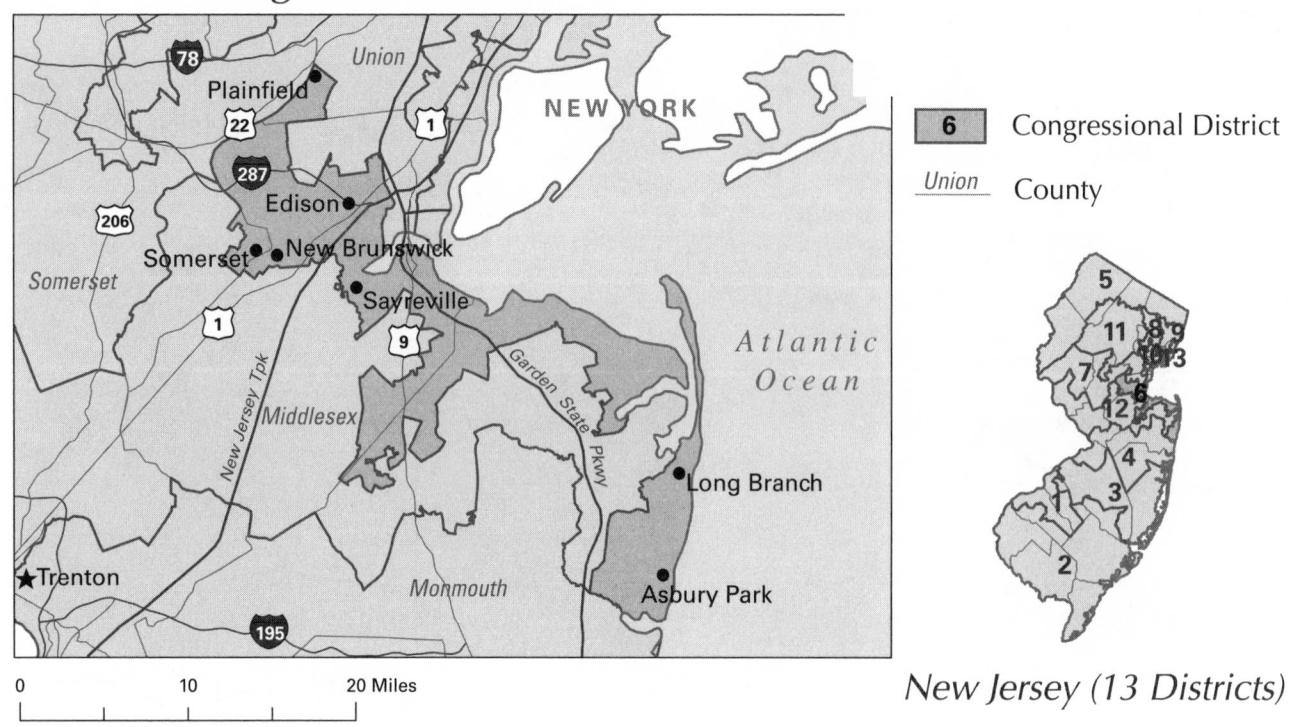

0   10   20 Miles

6   Congressional District

Union   County

New Jersey (13 Districts)

Congressional District 7

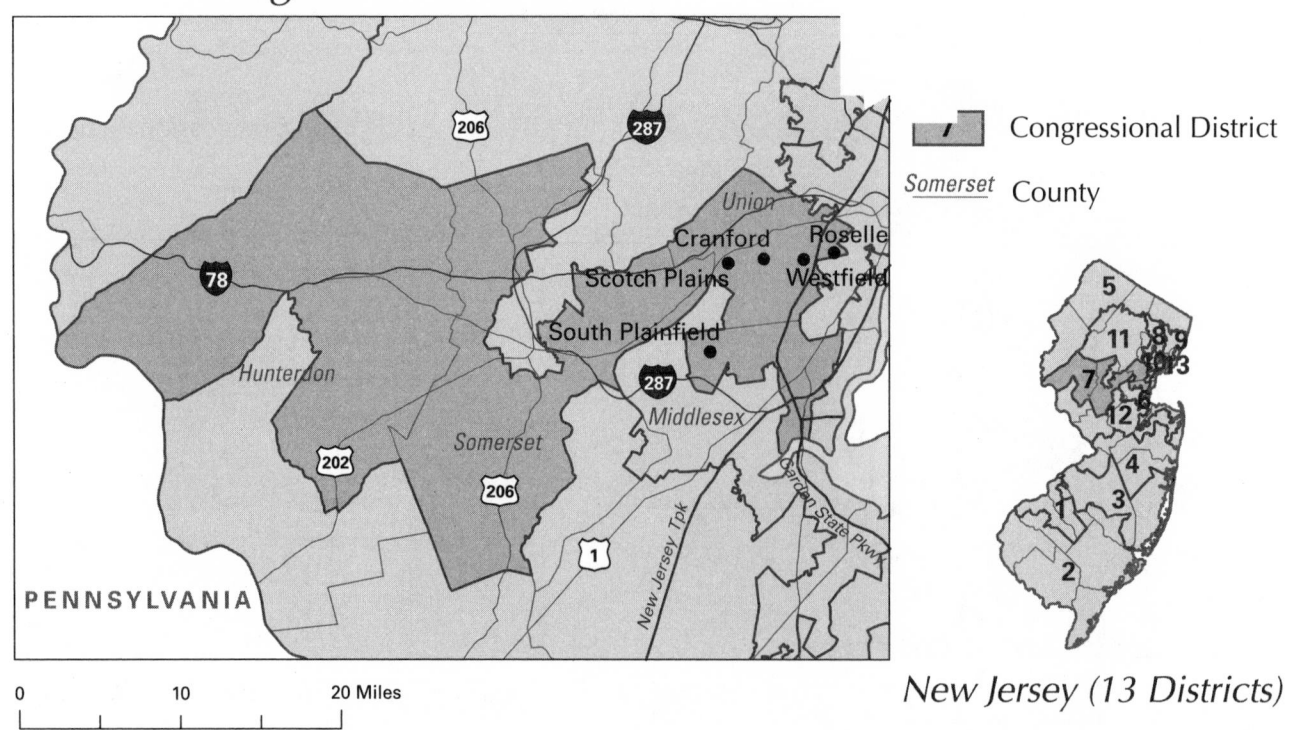

0   10   20 Miles

7   Congressional District

Somerset   County

New Jersey (13 Districts)

Congressional District 8

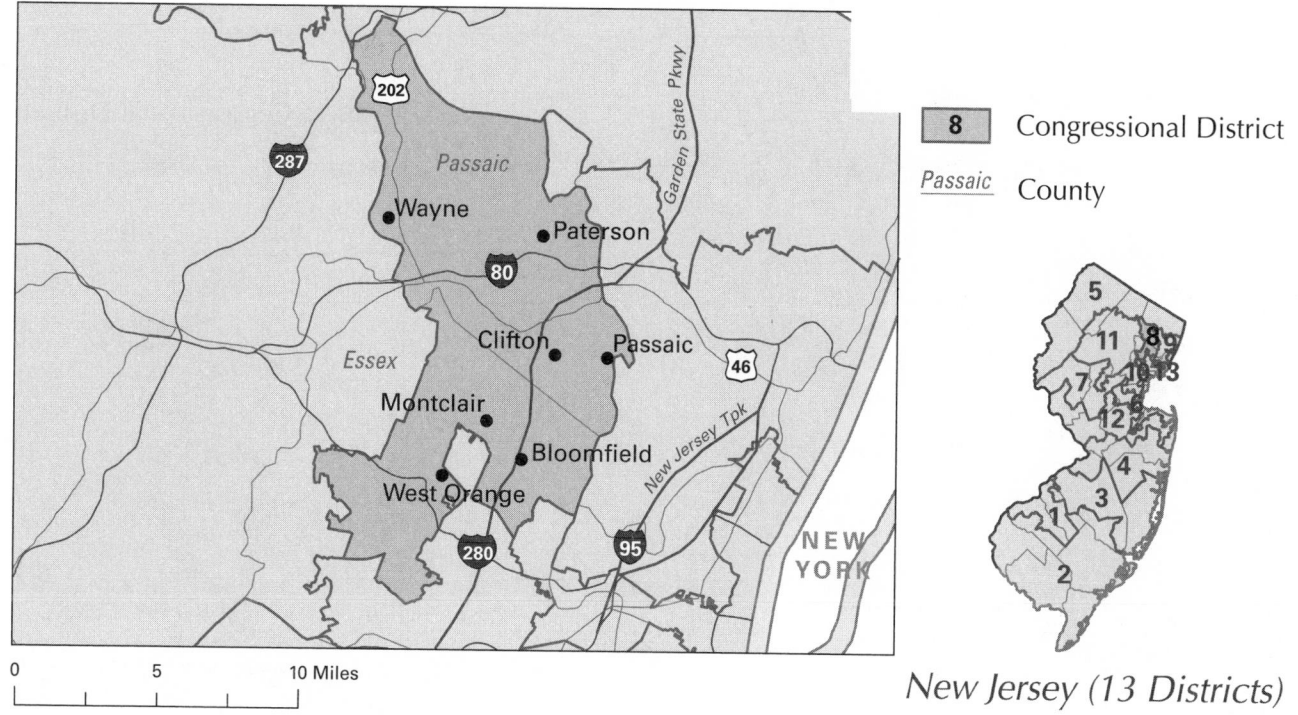

New Jersey (13 Districts)

Congressional District 9

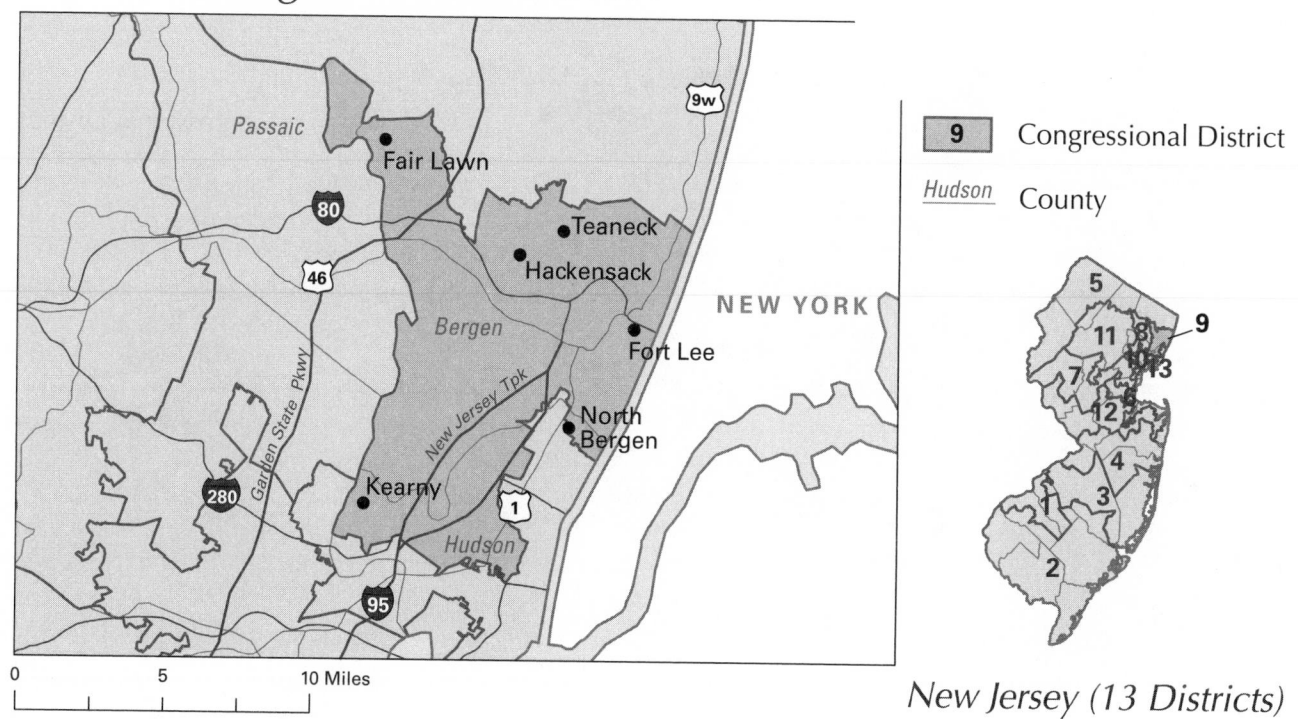

New Jersey (13 Districts)

Congressional District 10

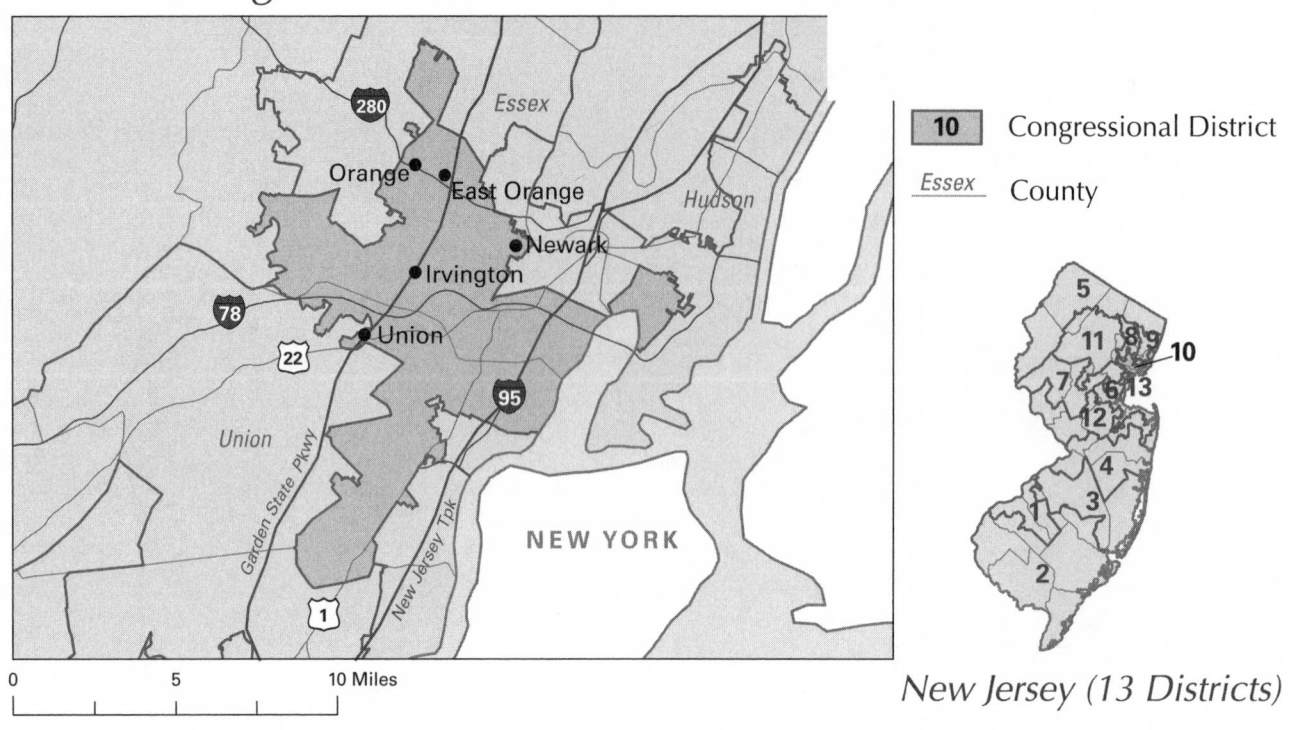

New Jersey (13 Districts)

Congressional District 11

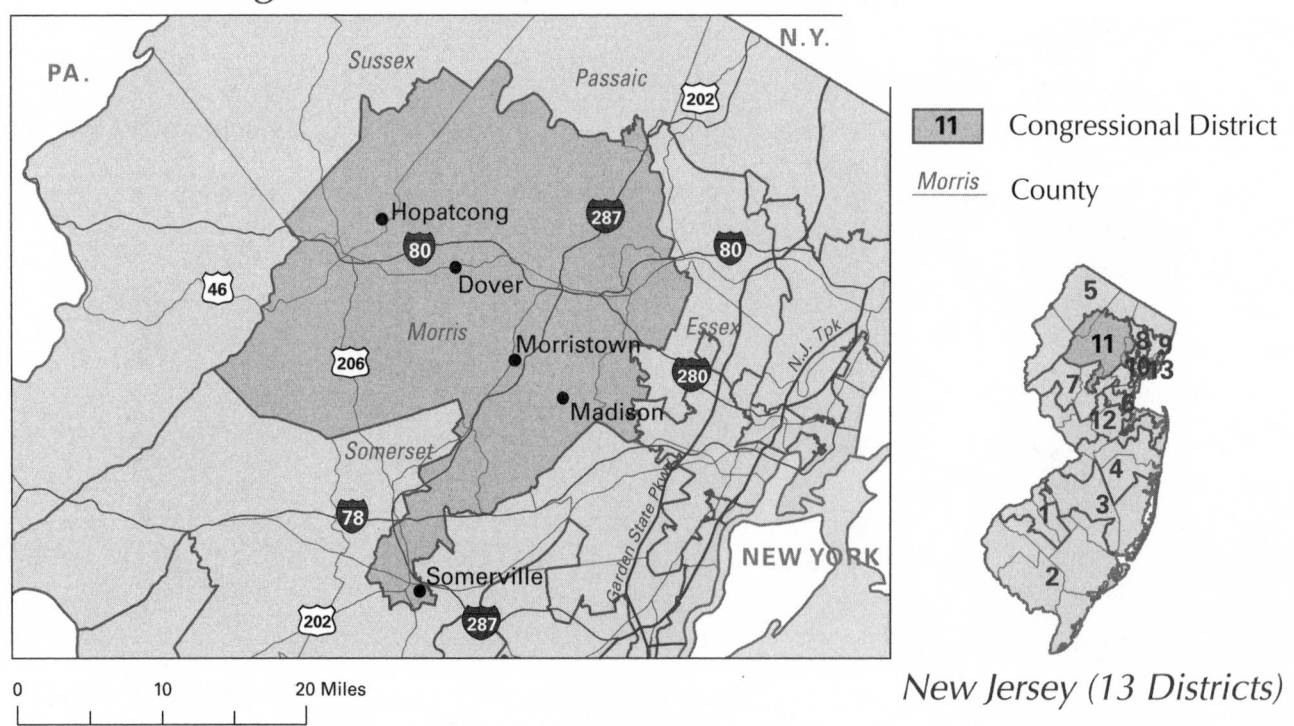

New Jersey (13 Districts)

Congressional District 12

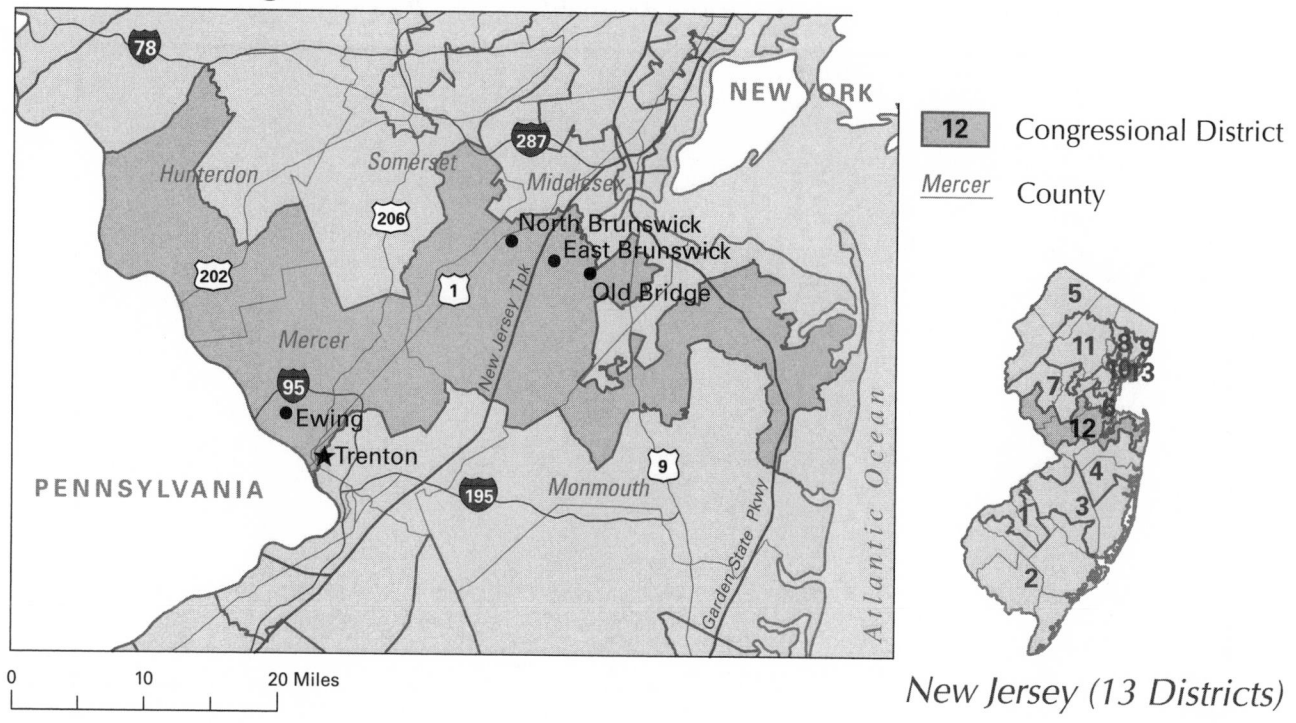

Congressional District 13

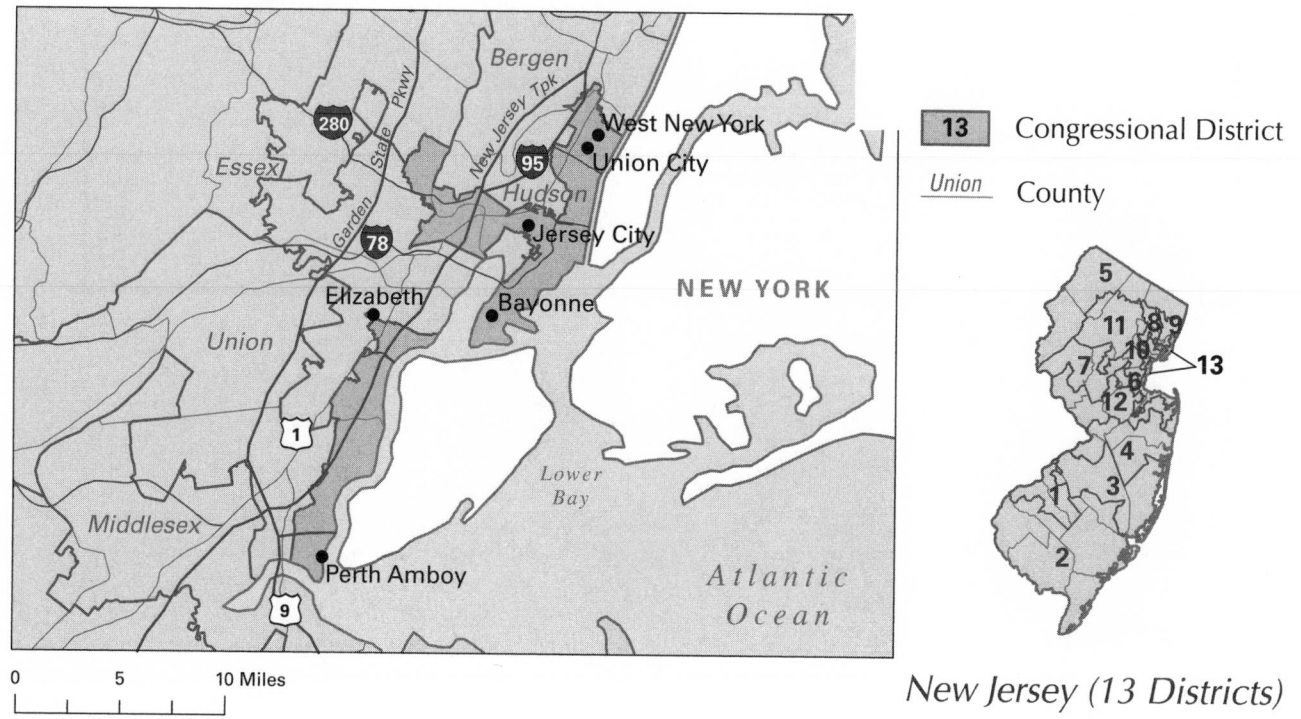

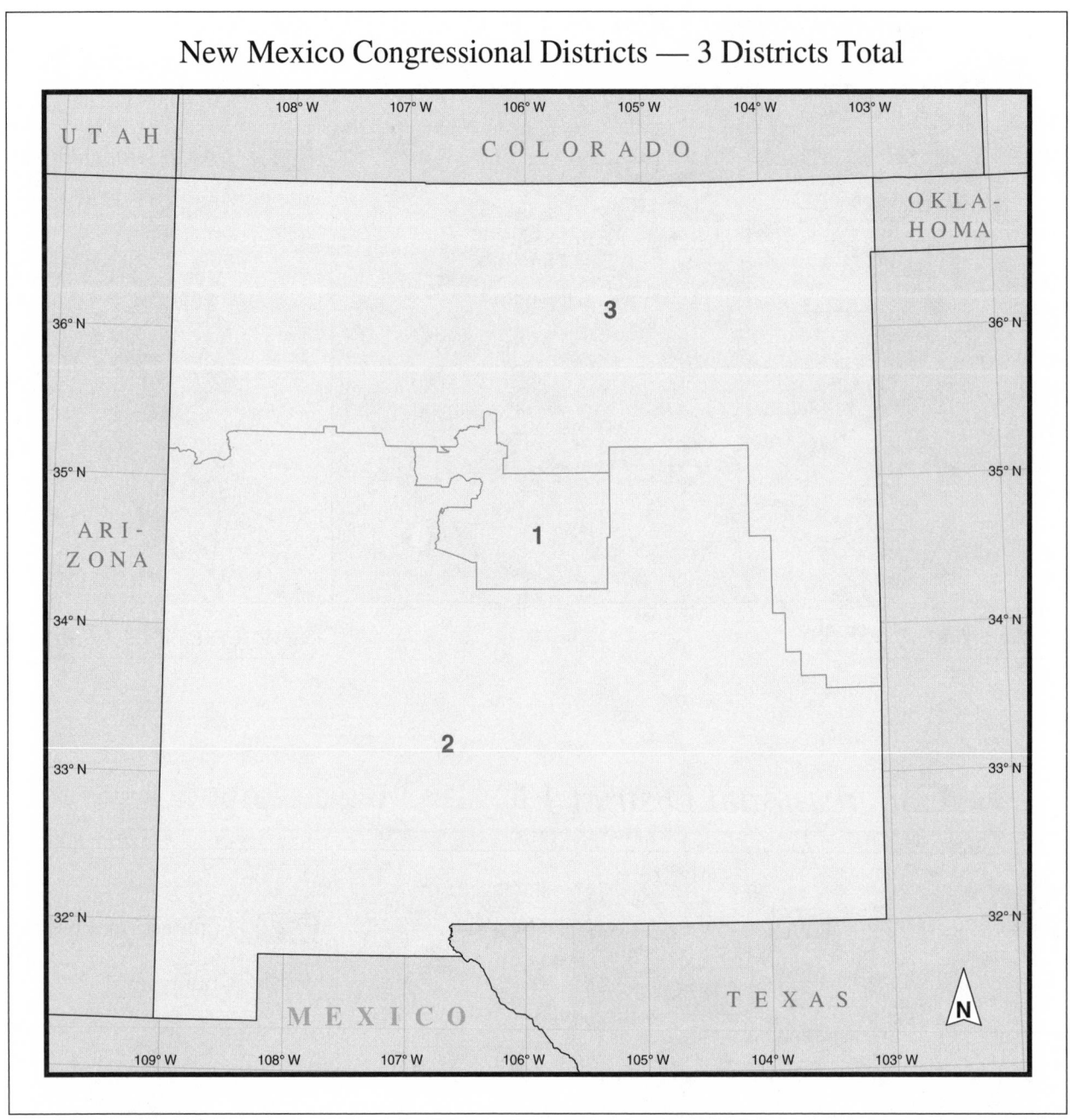

New Mexico Congressional Districts — 3 Districts Total

NEW MEXICO—110th CONGRESSIONAL DISTRICTS BY COUNTIES

County	Congressional District	County	Congressional District	County	Congressional District
Bernalillo	1–3	Harding	3	Roosevelt	3
Catron	2	Hidalgo	2	Sandoval	1, 3
Chaves	2	Lea	2	San Juan	3
Cibola	2	Lincoln	2	San Miguel	3
Colfax	3	Los Alamos	3	Santa Fe	1, 3
Curry	3	Luna	2	Sierra	2
De Baca	2	McKinley	2, 3	Socorro	2
Dona Ana	2	Mora	3	Taos	3
Eddy	2	Otero	2	Torrance	1
Grant	2	Quay	3	Union	3
Guadalupe	2	Rio Arriba	3	Valencia	1, 2

Congressional District 1

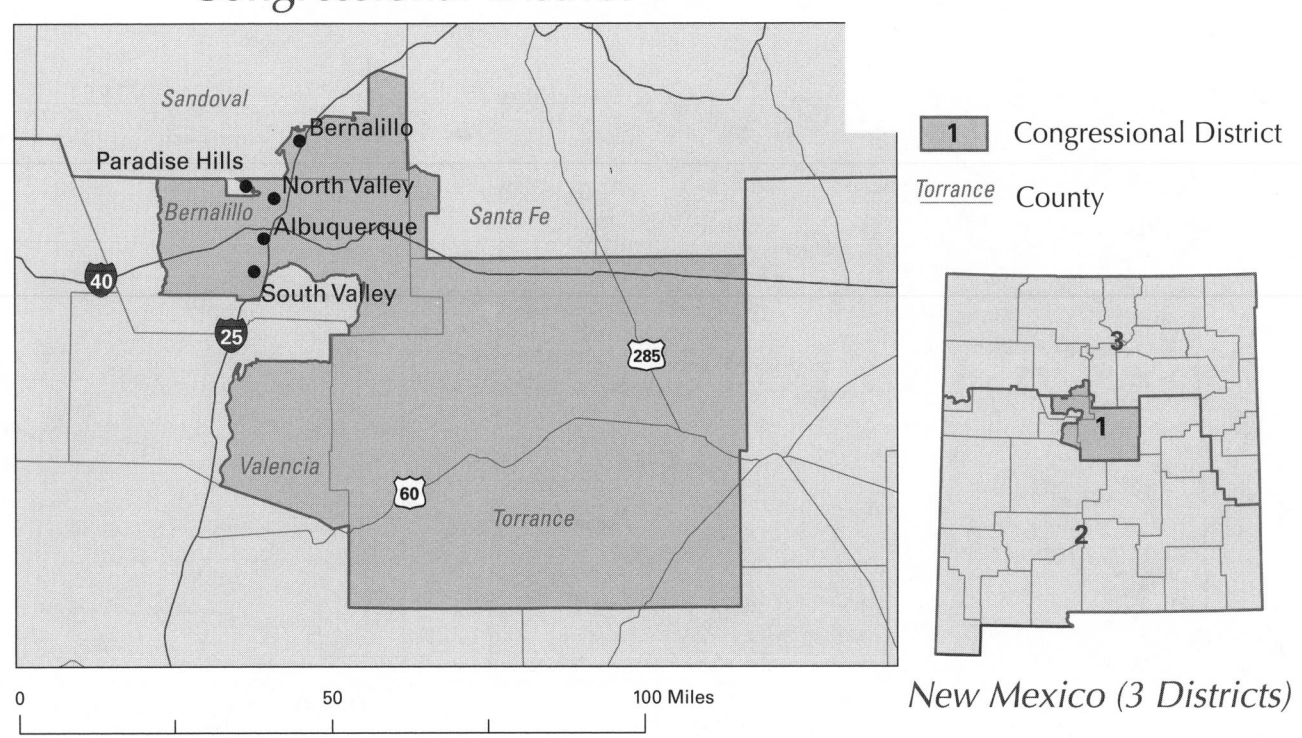

1 Congressional District

Torrance County

New Mexico (3 Districts)

Congressional District 2

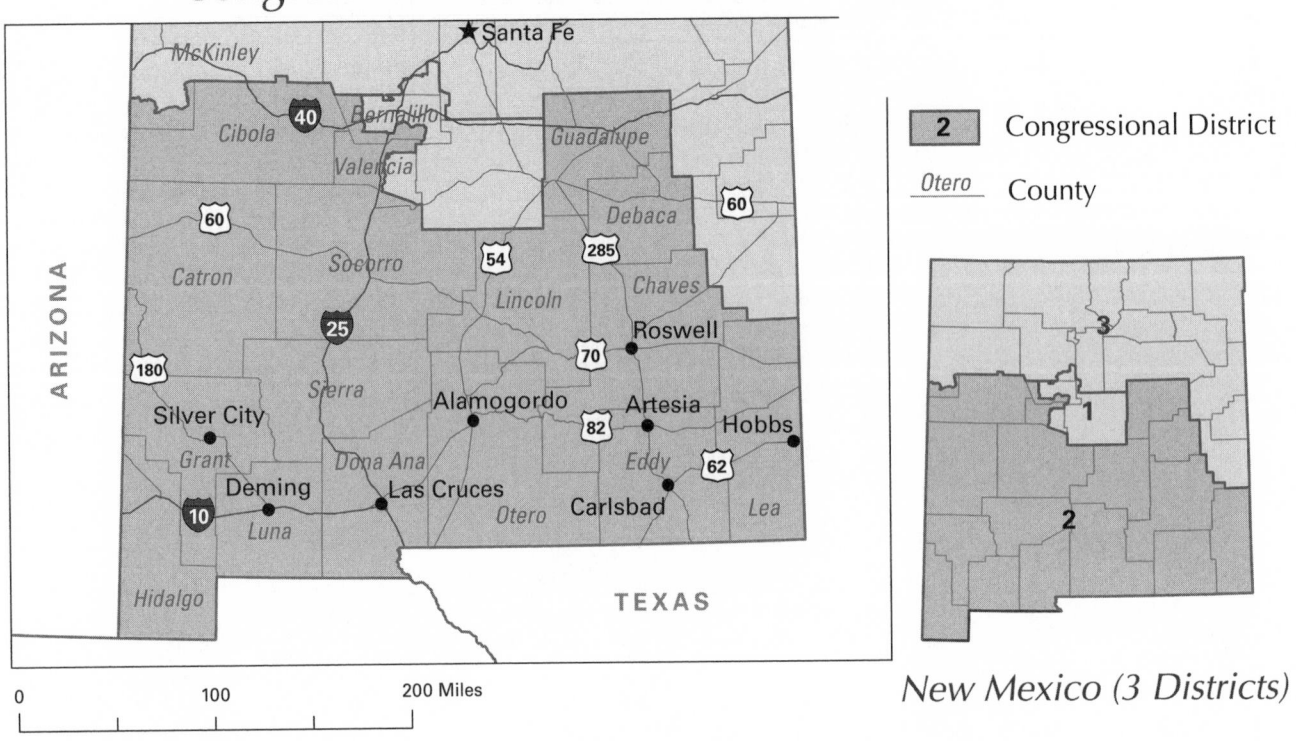

New Mexico (3 Districts)

Congressional District 3

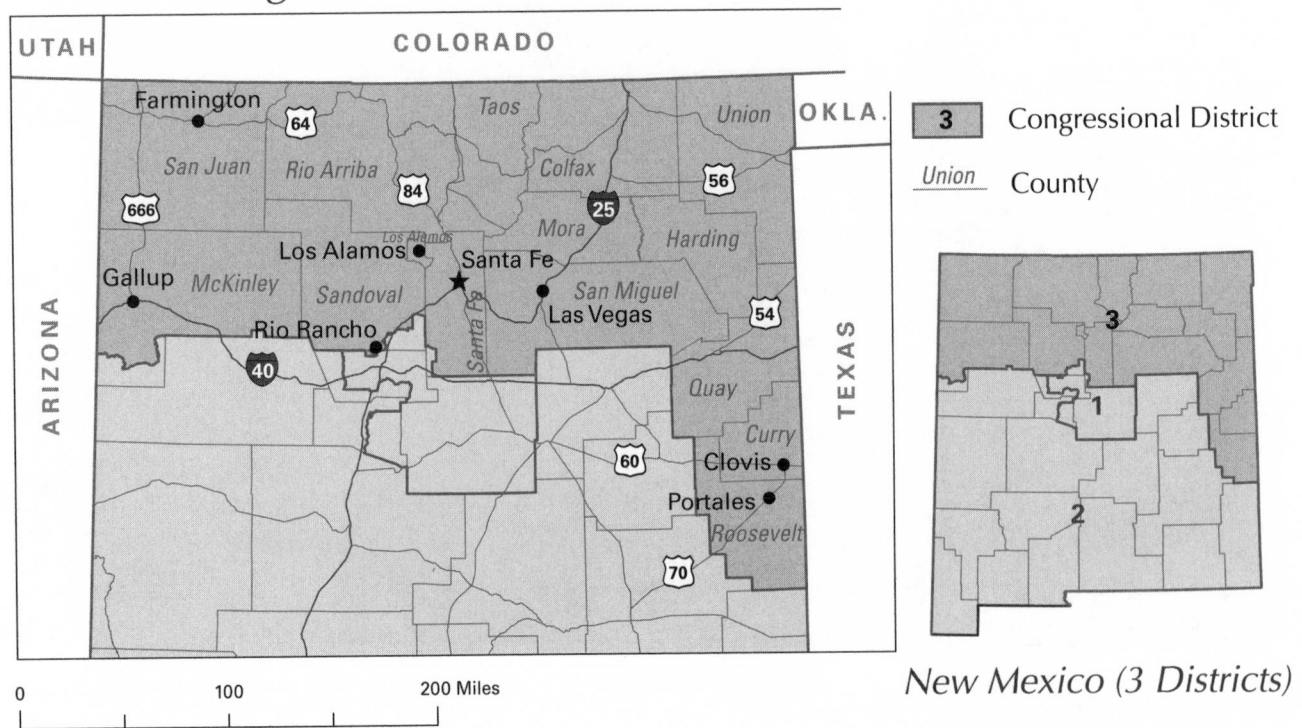

New Mexico (3 Districts)

New York Congressional Districts — 29 Districts Total

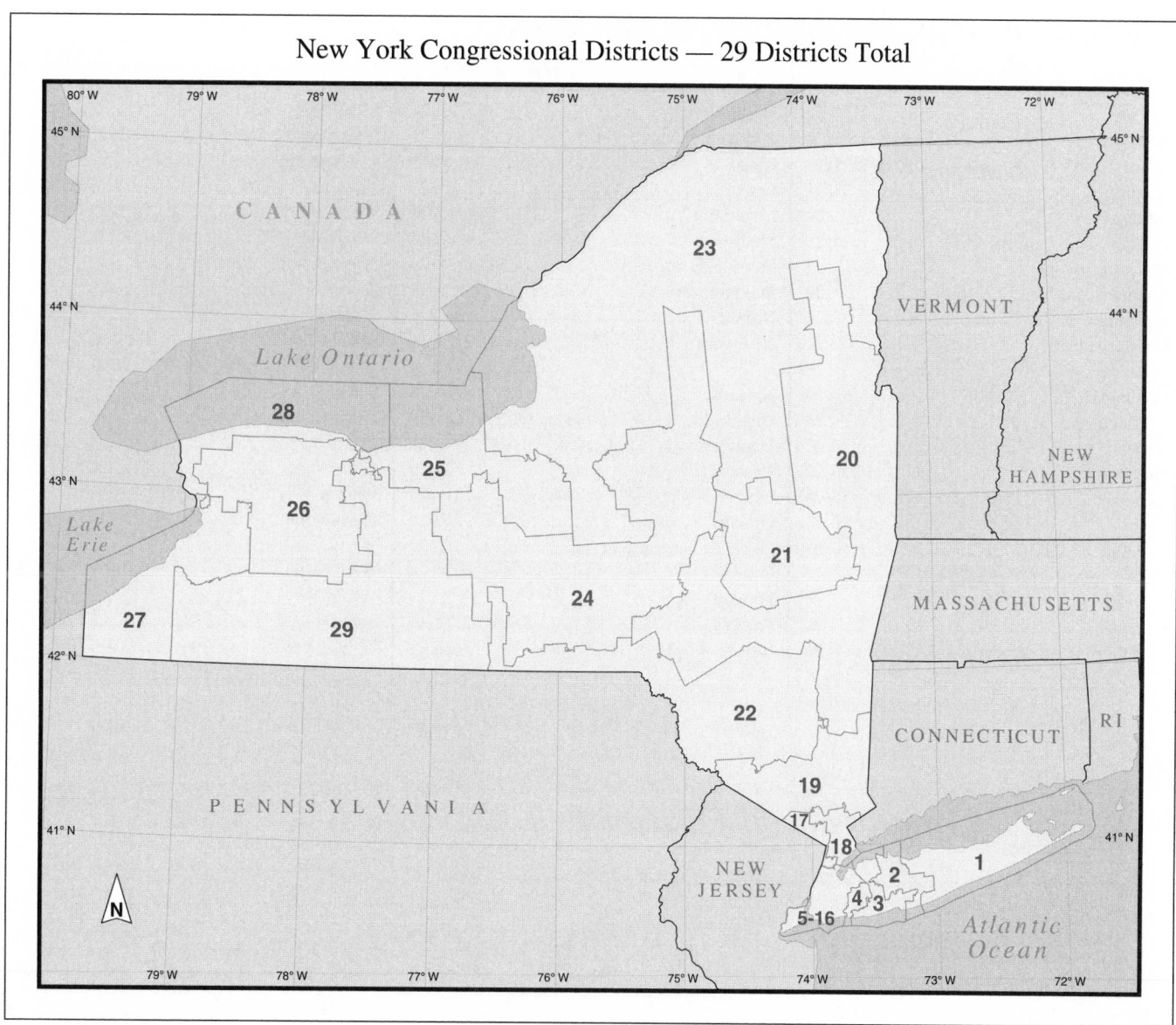

NEW YORK—110th CONGRESSIONAL DISTRICTS BY COUNTIES

County	Congressional District
Albany	21
Allegany	29
Bronx	7, 15–17
Broome	22, 24
Cattaraugus	29
Cayuga	24, 25
Chautauqua	27
Chemung	29
Chenango	24
Clinton	23
Columbia	20
Cortland	24
Delaware	20, 22
Dutchess	19, 20, 22
Erie	26–28
Essex	20, 23
Franklin	23
Fulton	21, 23
Genesee	26
Greene	20
Hamilton	23

County	Congressional District
Herkimer	24
Jefferson	23
Kings	8–13
Lewis	23
Livingston	26
Madison	23
Monroe	25, 26, 28, 29
Montgomery	21
Nassau	2–5
New York	8, 12, 14, 15
Niagara	26, 28
Oneida	23, 24
Onondaga	25
Ontario	24, 29
Orange	19, 22
Orleans	26, 28
Oswego	23
Otsego	20, 24
Putnam	19
Queens	5–7, 9, 12, 14, 15
Rensselaer	20, 21

County	Congressional District
Richmond	13
Rockland	17–19
St. Lawrence	23
Saratoga	20, 21
Schenectady	21
Schoharie	21
Schuyler	29
Seneca	24
Steuben	29
Suffolk	1–3
Sullivan	22
Tioga	22, 24
Tompkins	22, 24
Ulster	22
Warren	20
Washington	20
Wayne	25
Westchester	17–19
Wyoming	26
Yates	29

Congressional District 1

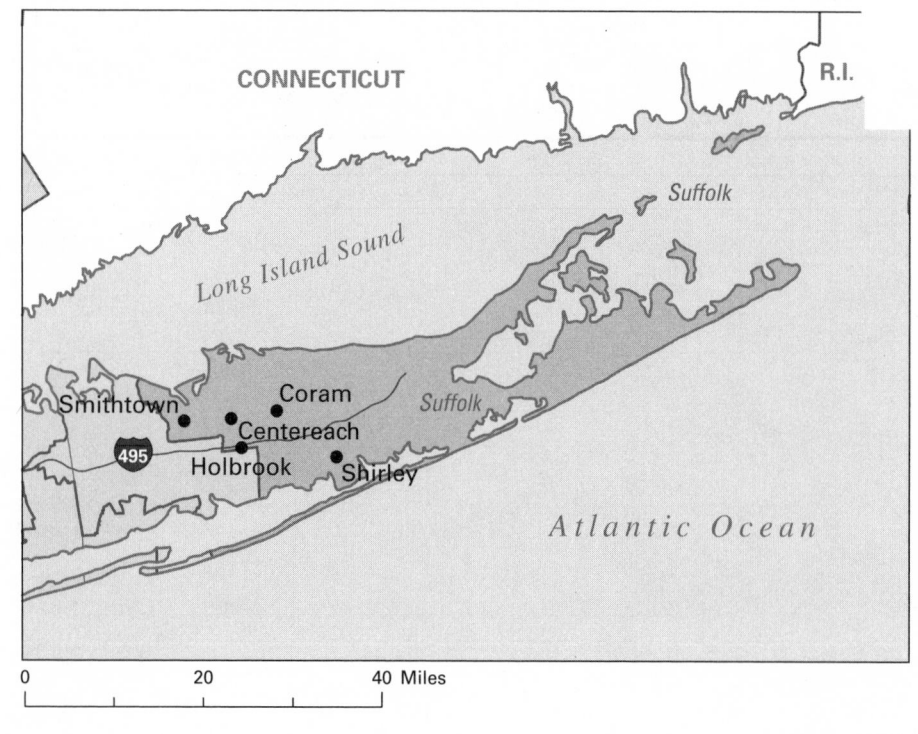

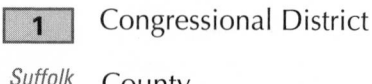

Congressional District

Suffolk County

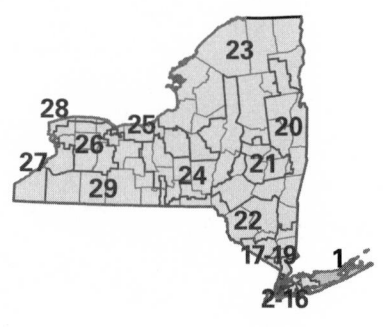

New York (29 Districts)

Congressional District 2

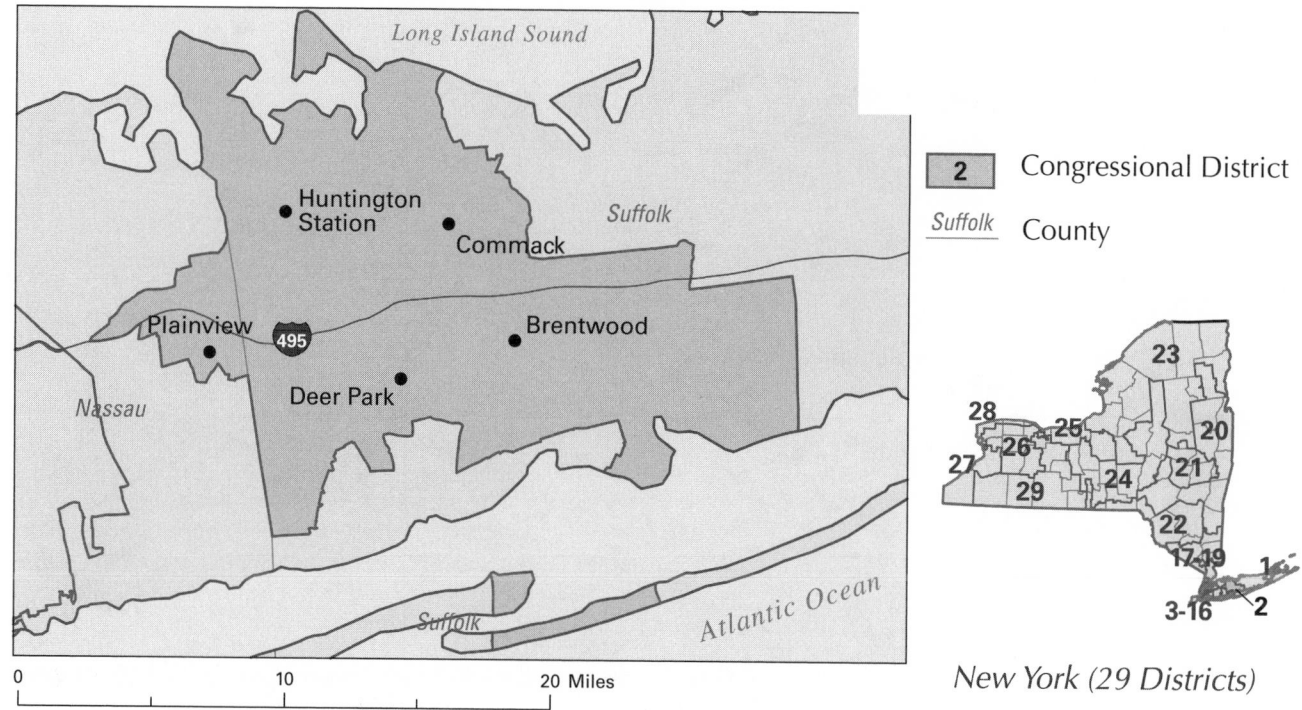

New York (29 Districts)

Congressional District 3

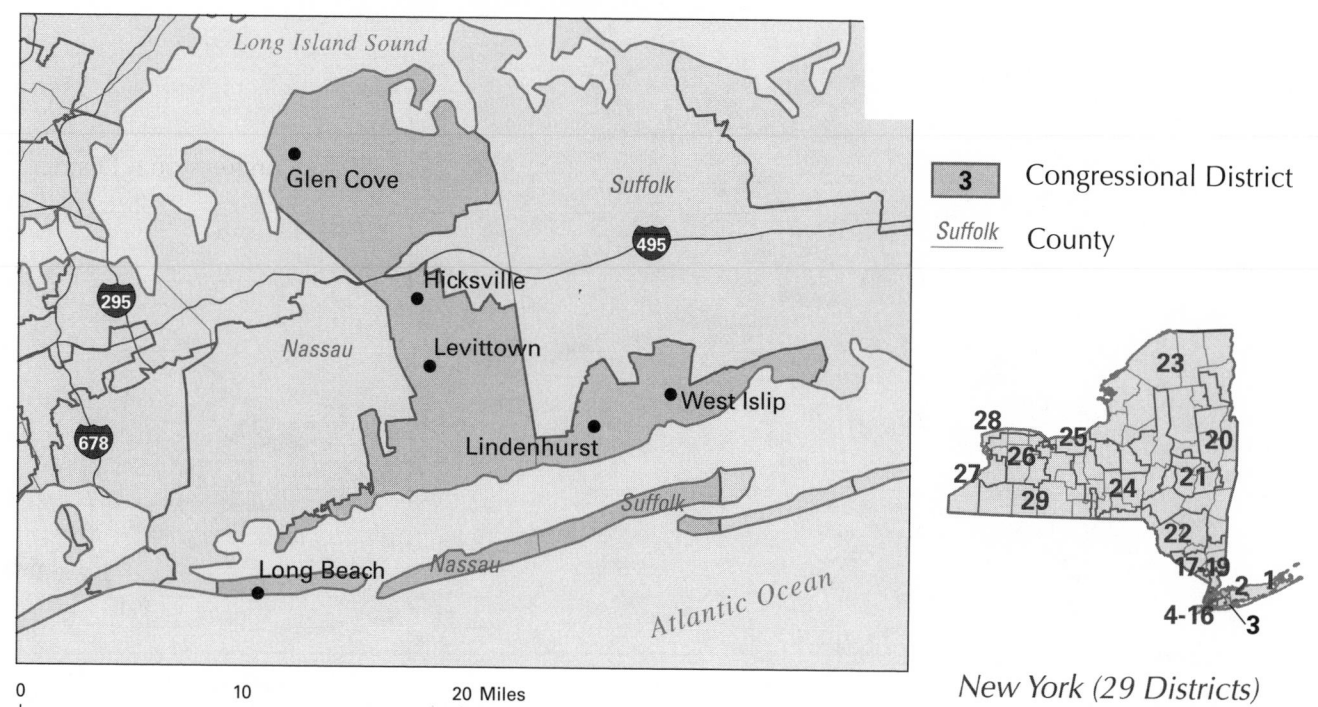

New York (29 Districts)

Congressional District 4

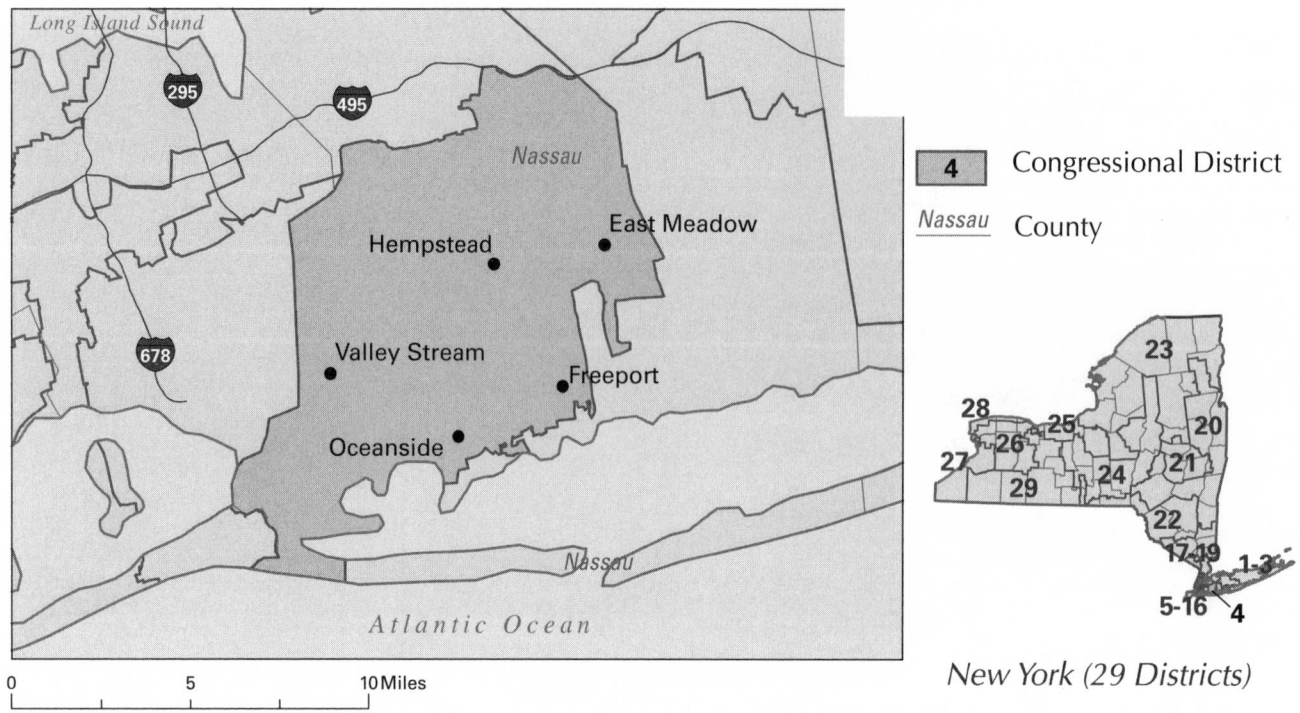

New York (29 Districts)

Congressional District 5

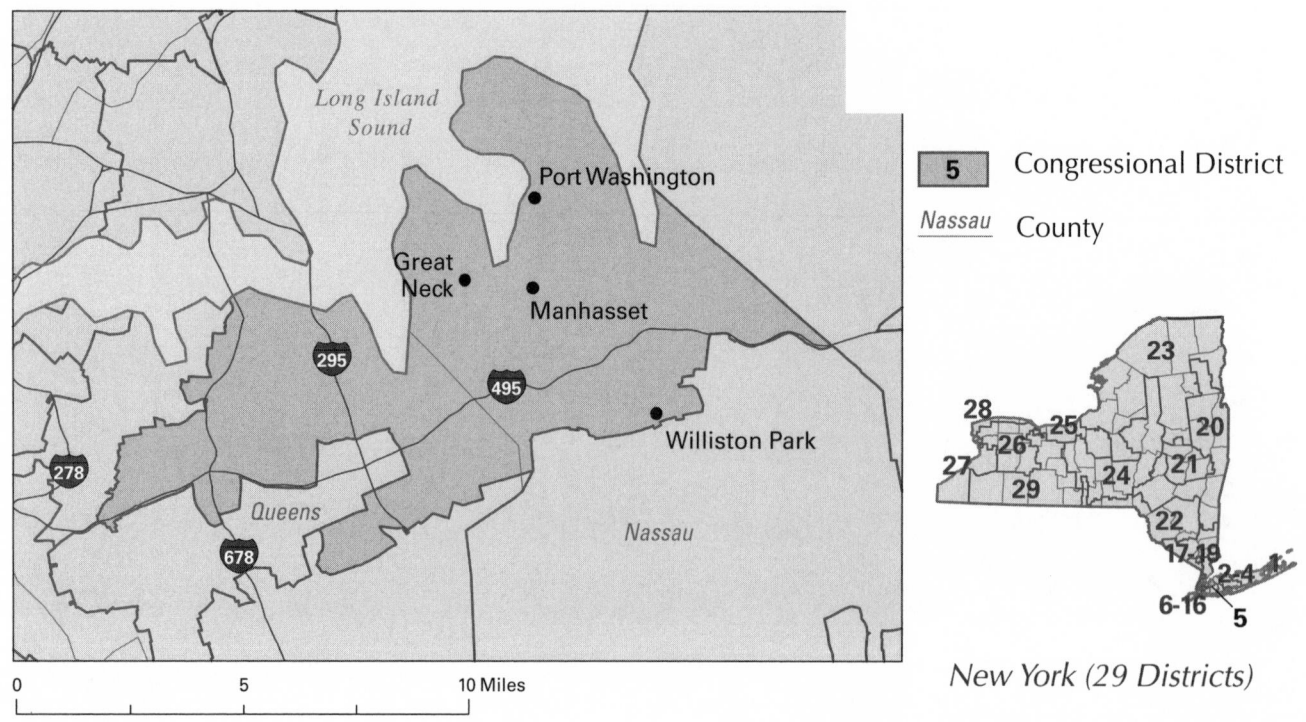

New York (29 Districts)

Congressional District 6

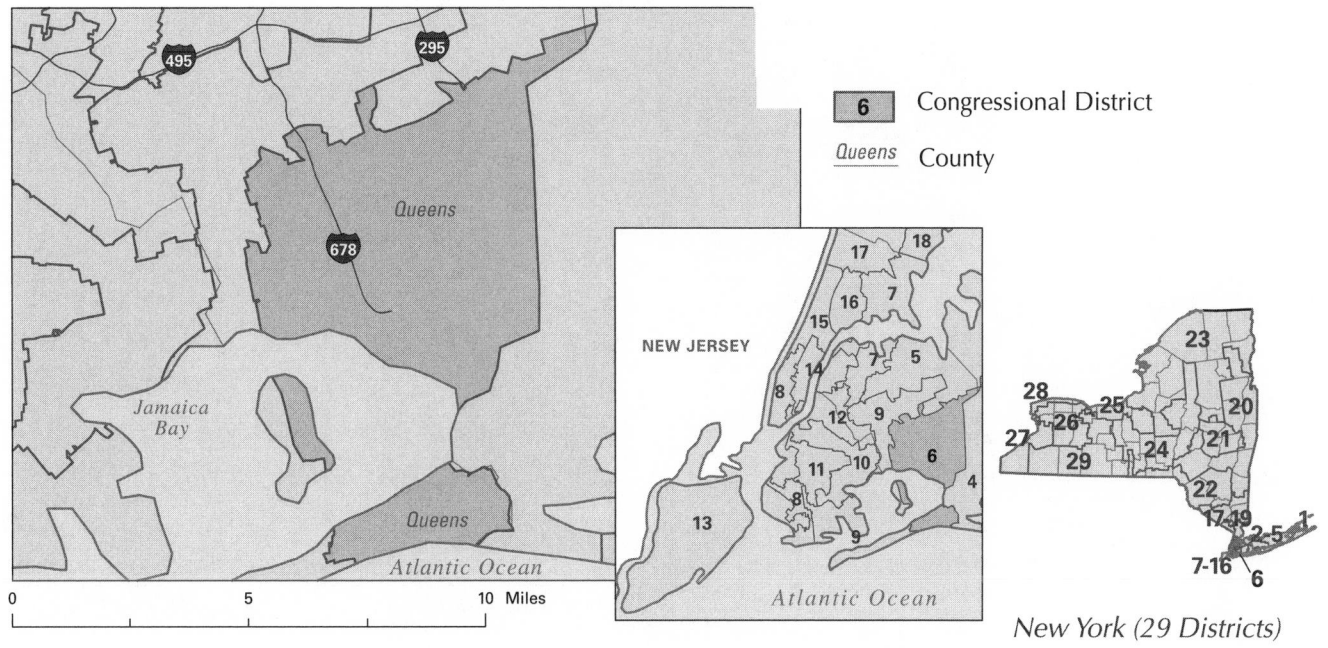

6 Congressional District
Queens County

New York (29 Districts)

Congressional District 7

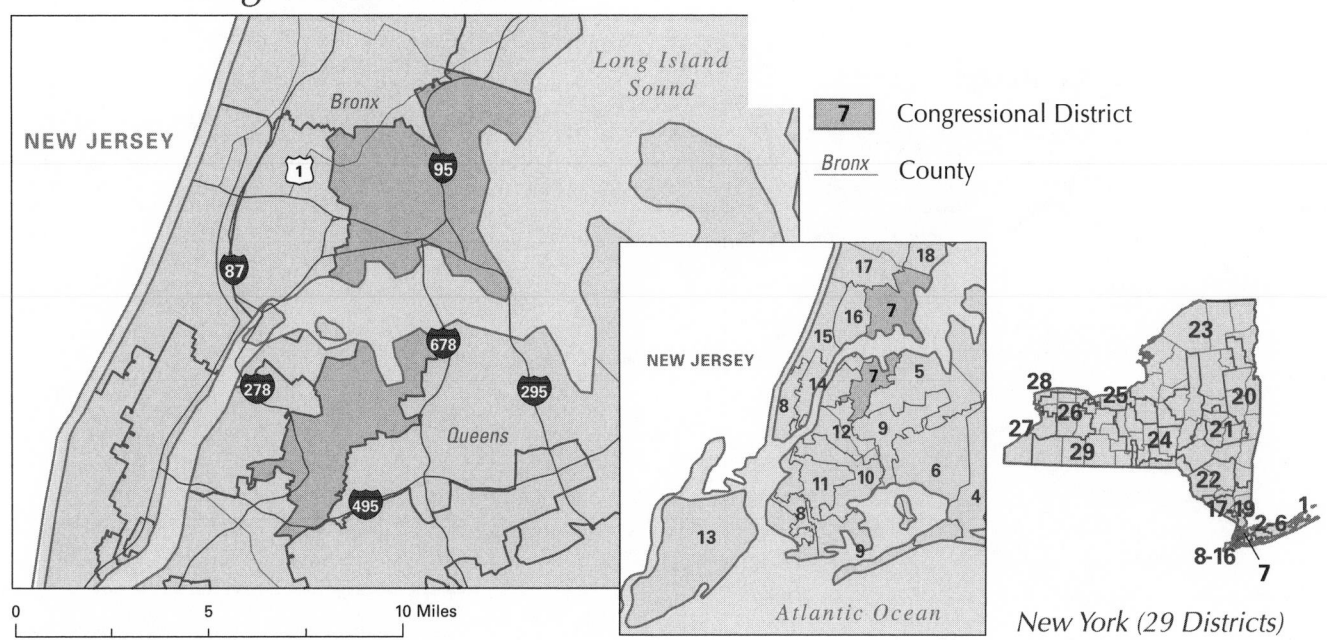

7 Congressional District
Bronx County

New York (29 Districts)

Congressional District 8

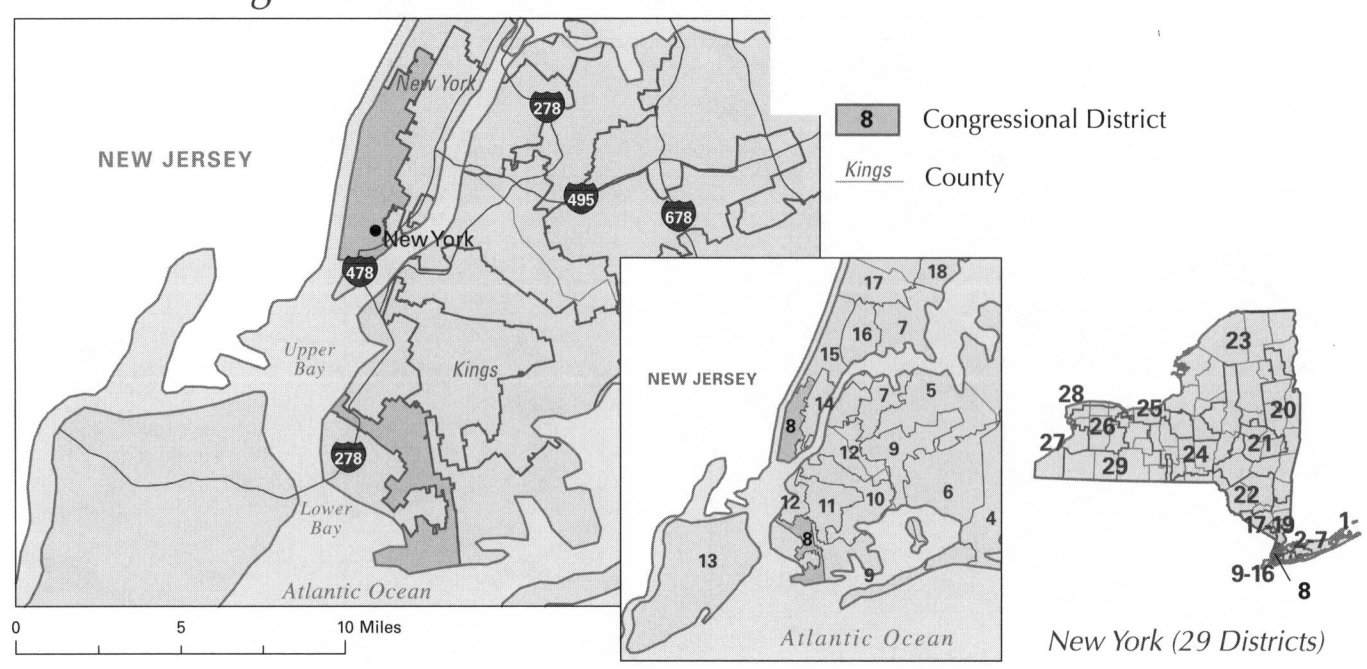

Congressional District 9

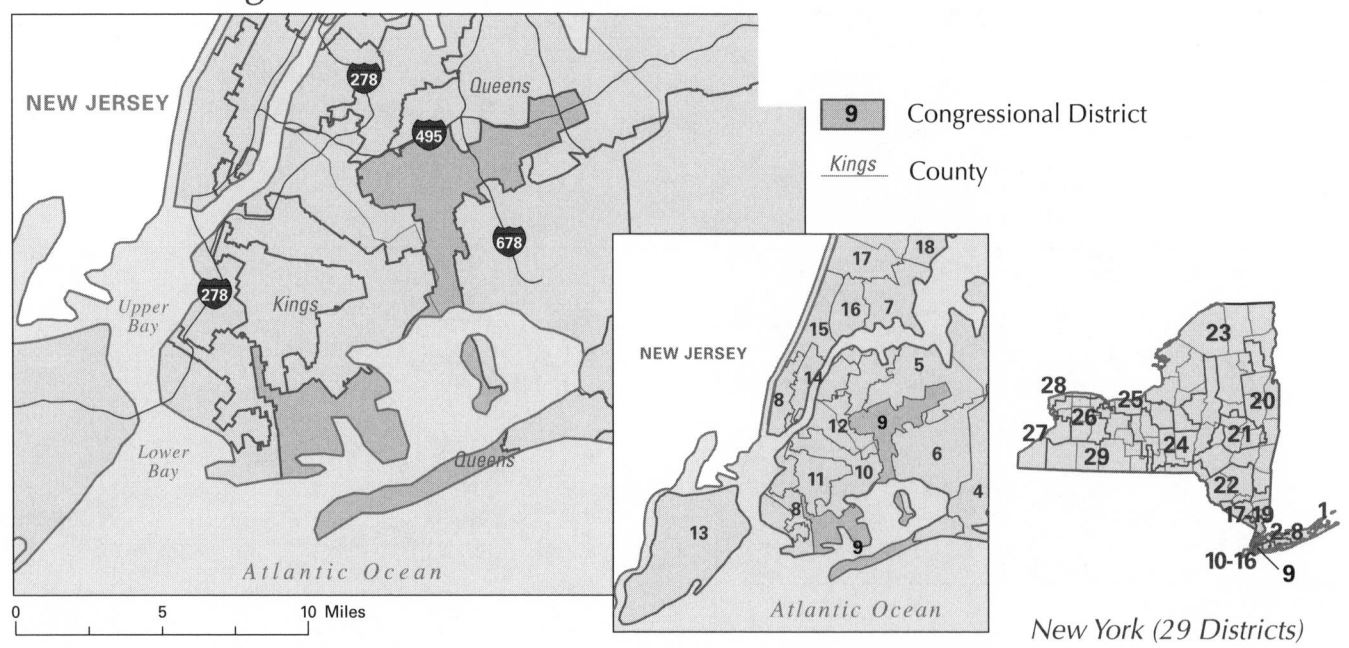

Congressional District 10

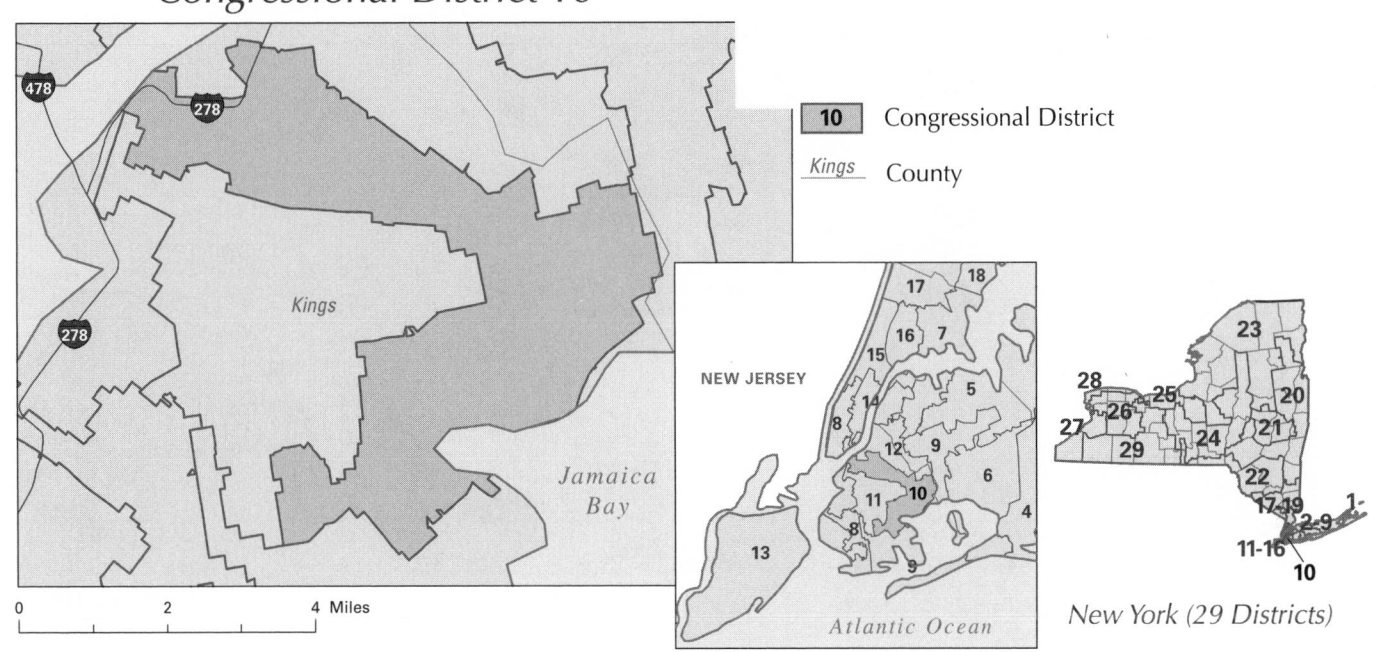

Congressional District 11

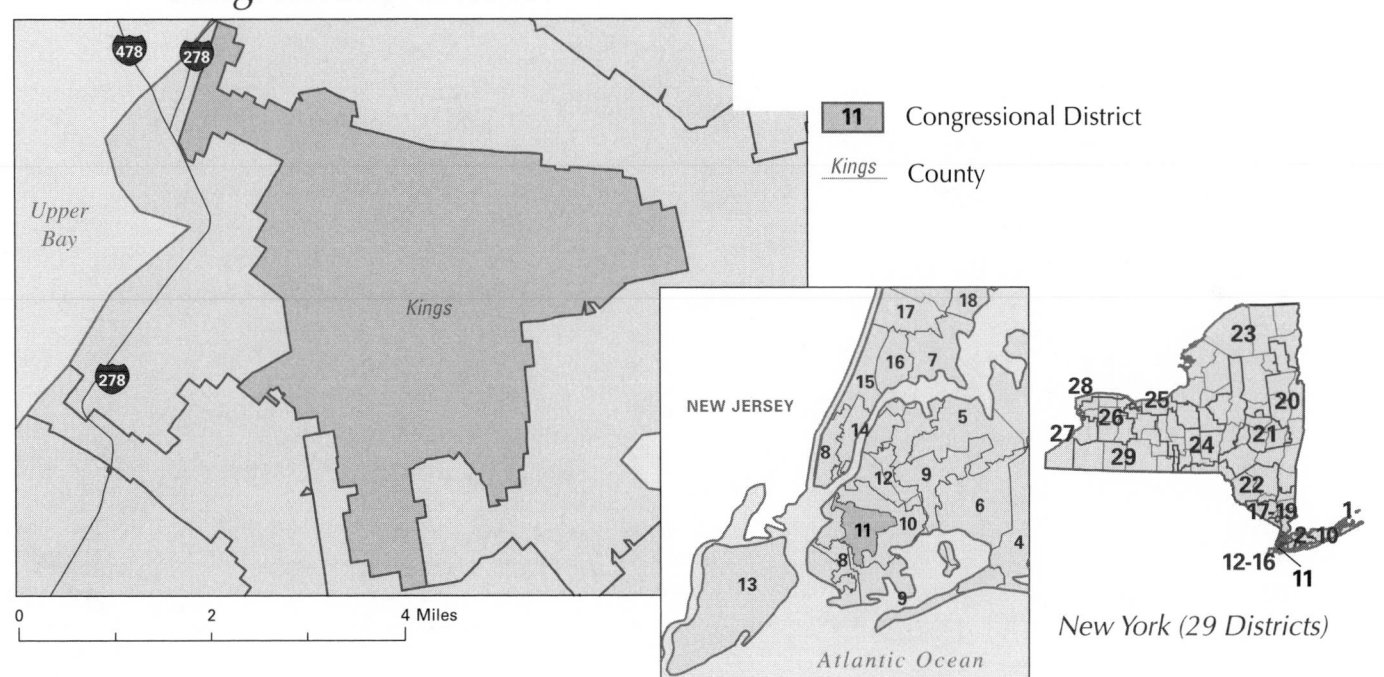

Congressional District 12

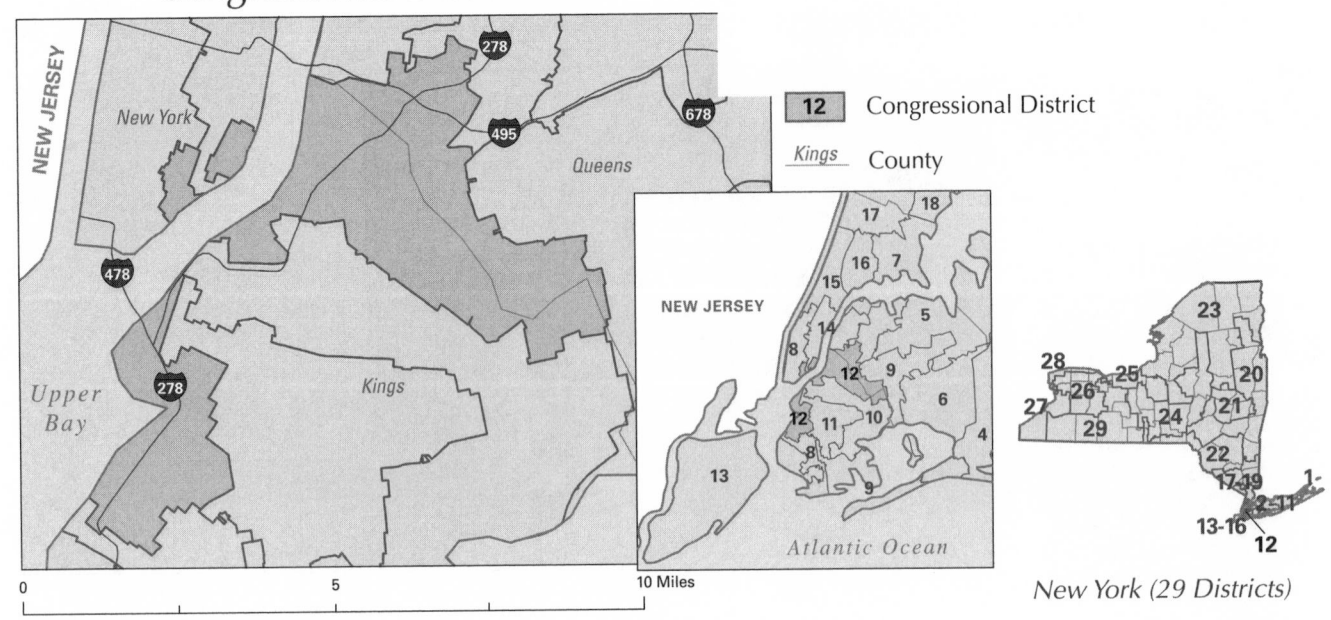

12   Congressional District
Kings   County

New York (29 Districts)

Congressional District 13

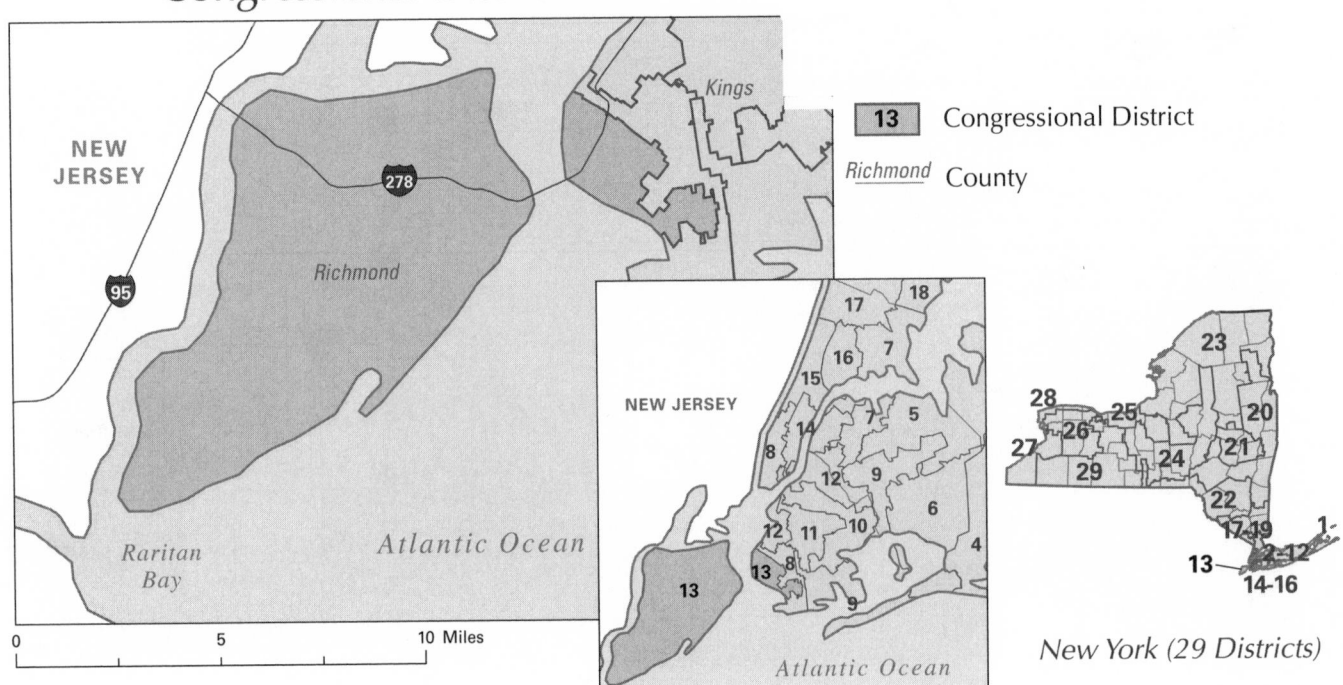

13   Congressional District
Richmond   County

New York (29 Districts)

Congressional District 14

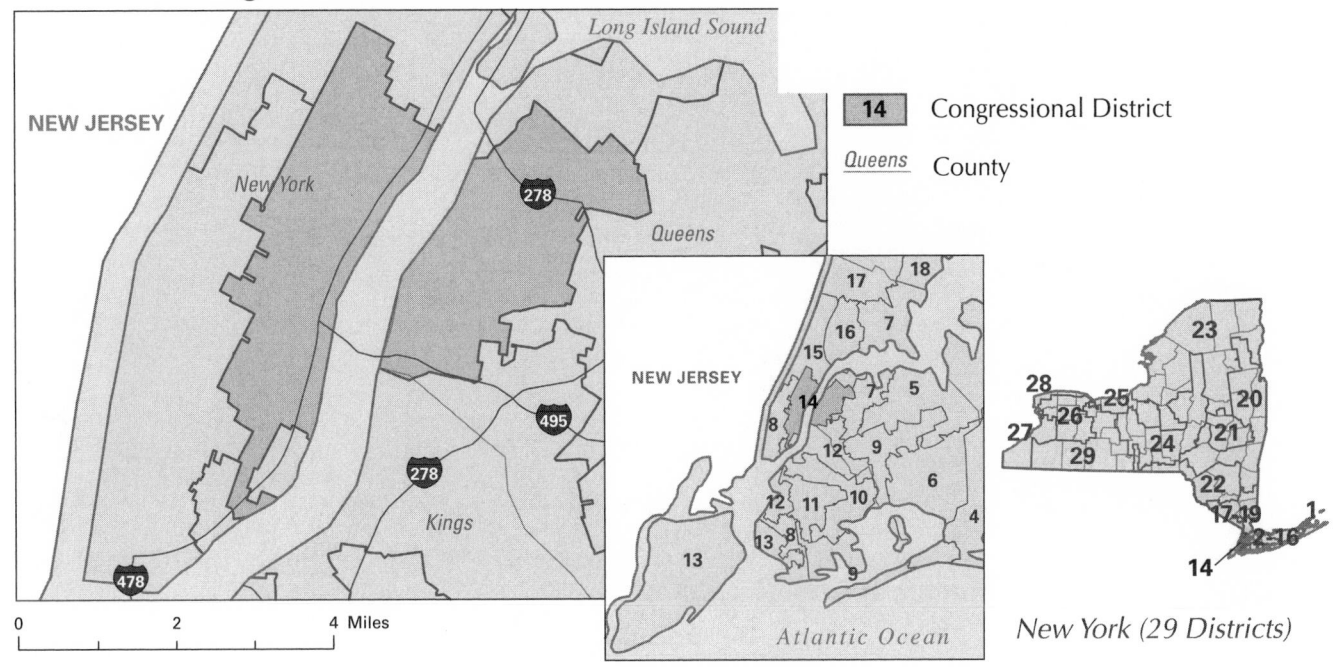

Congressional District 15

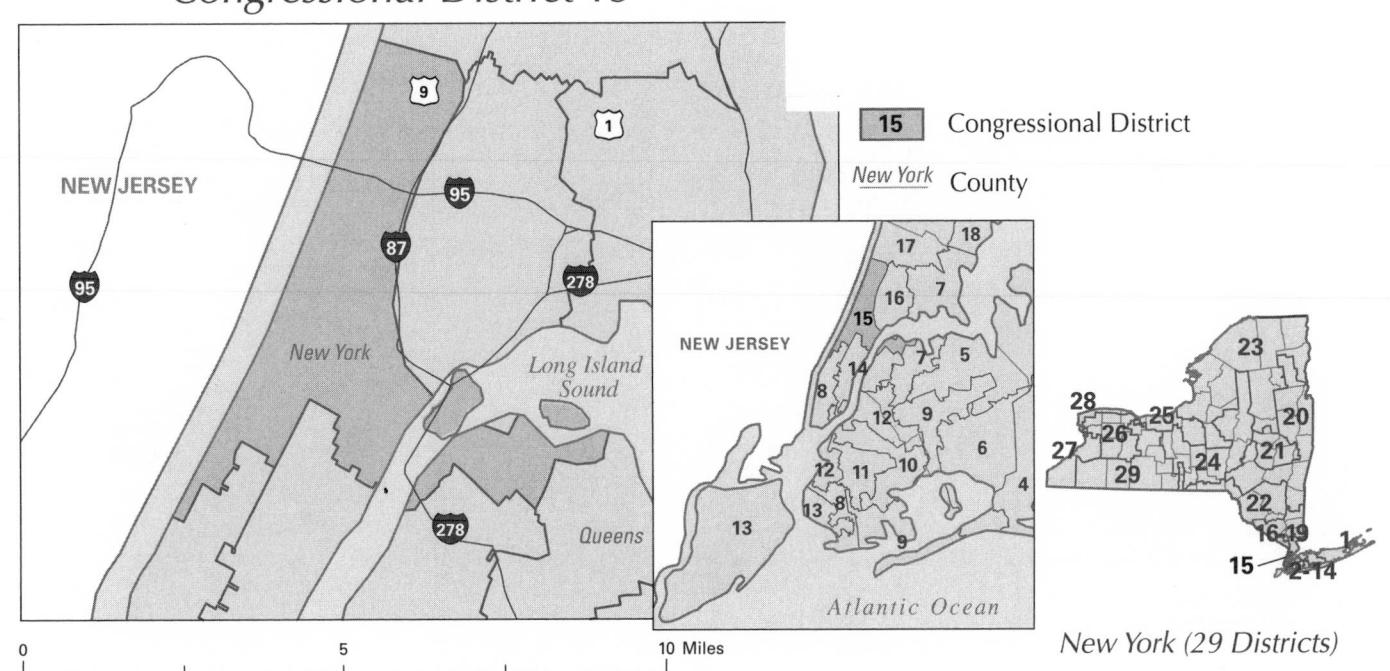

Congressional District 16

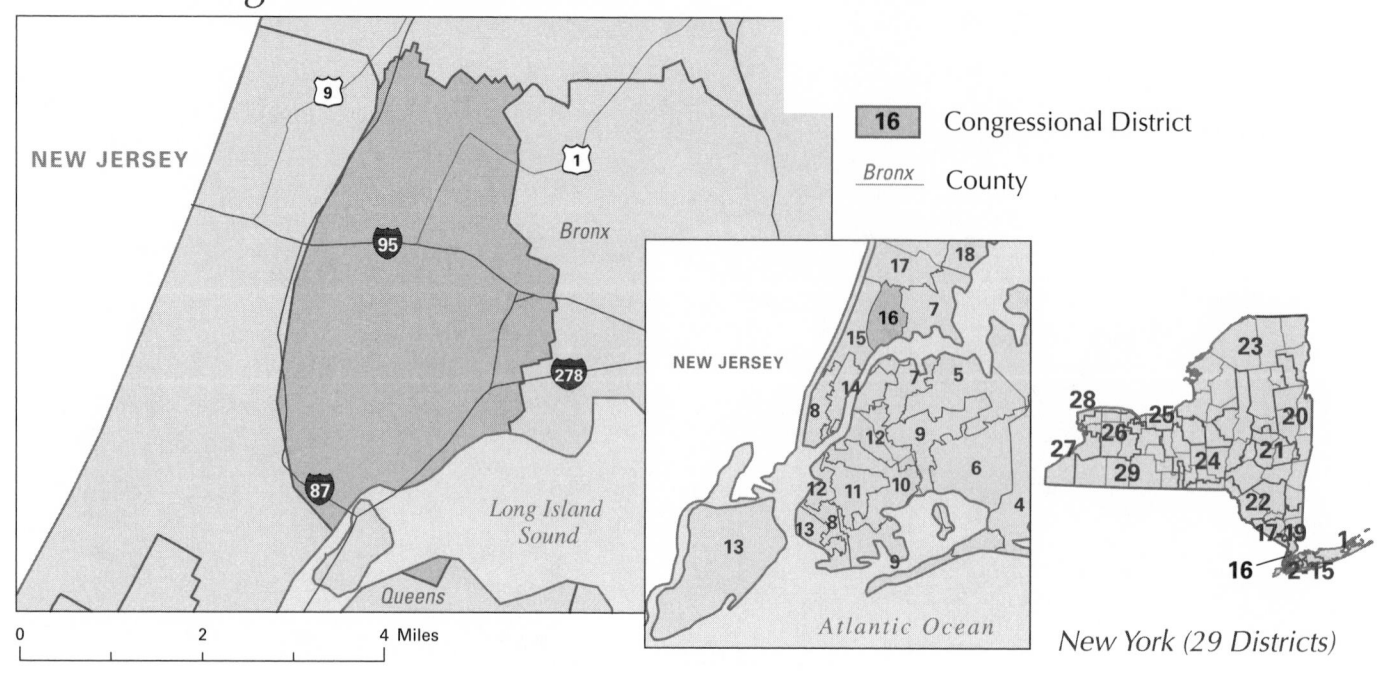

16 Congressional District

Bronx County

New York (29 Districts)

Congressional District 17

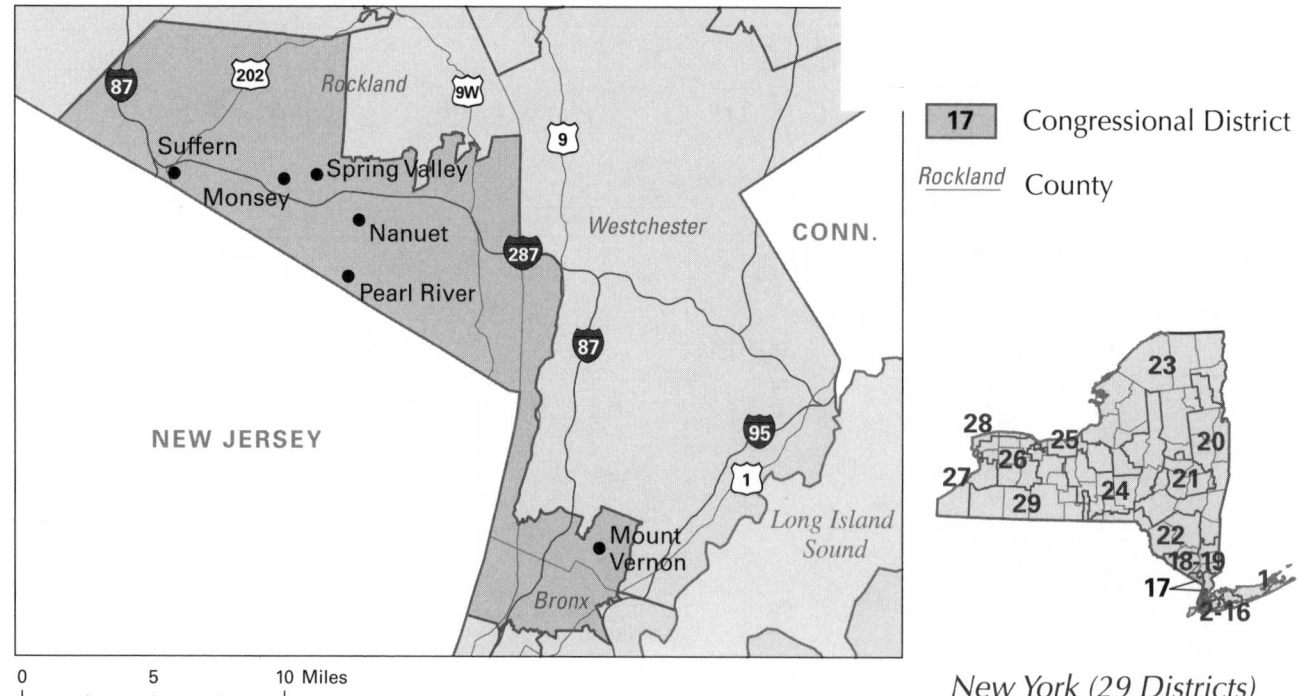

17 Congressional District

Rockland County

New York (29 Districts)

Congressional District 18

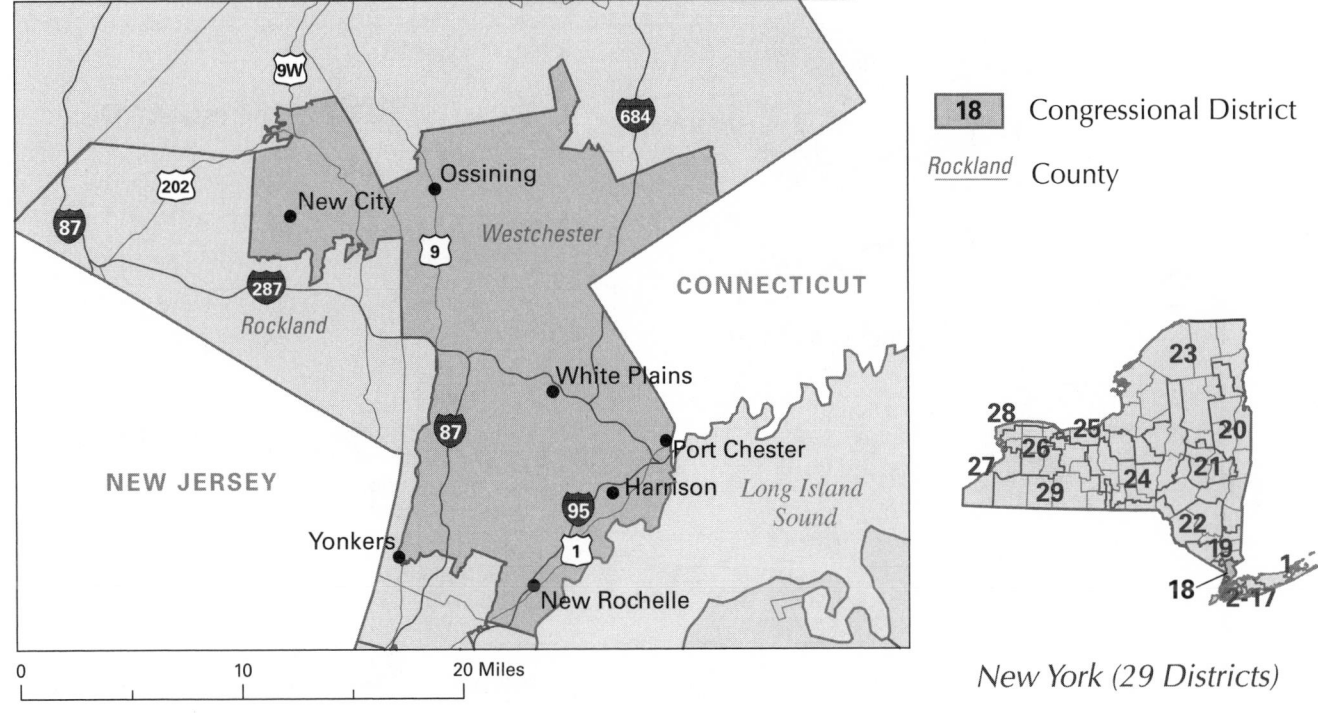

Congressional District 19

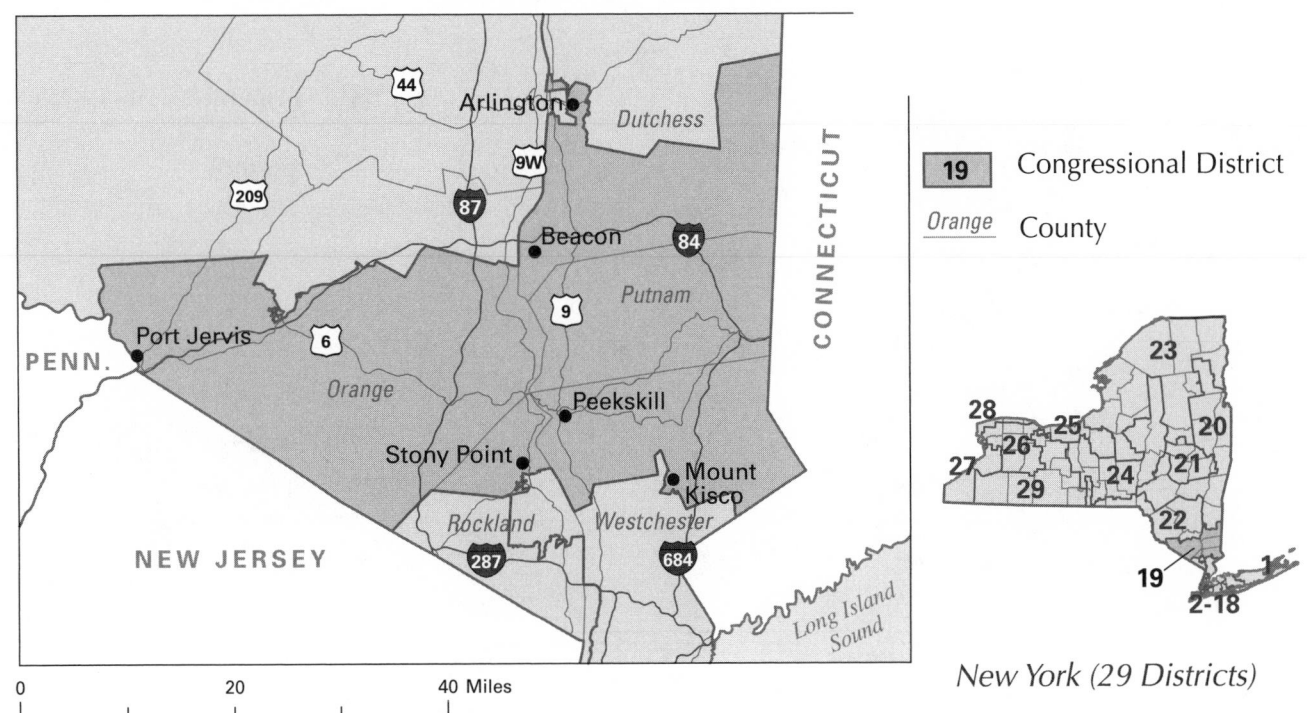

Congressional District 20

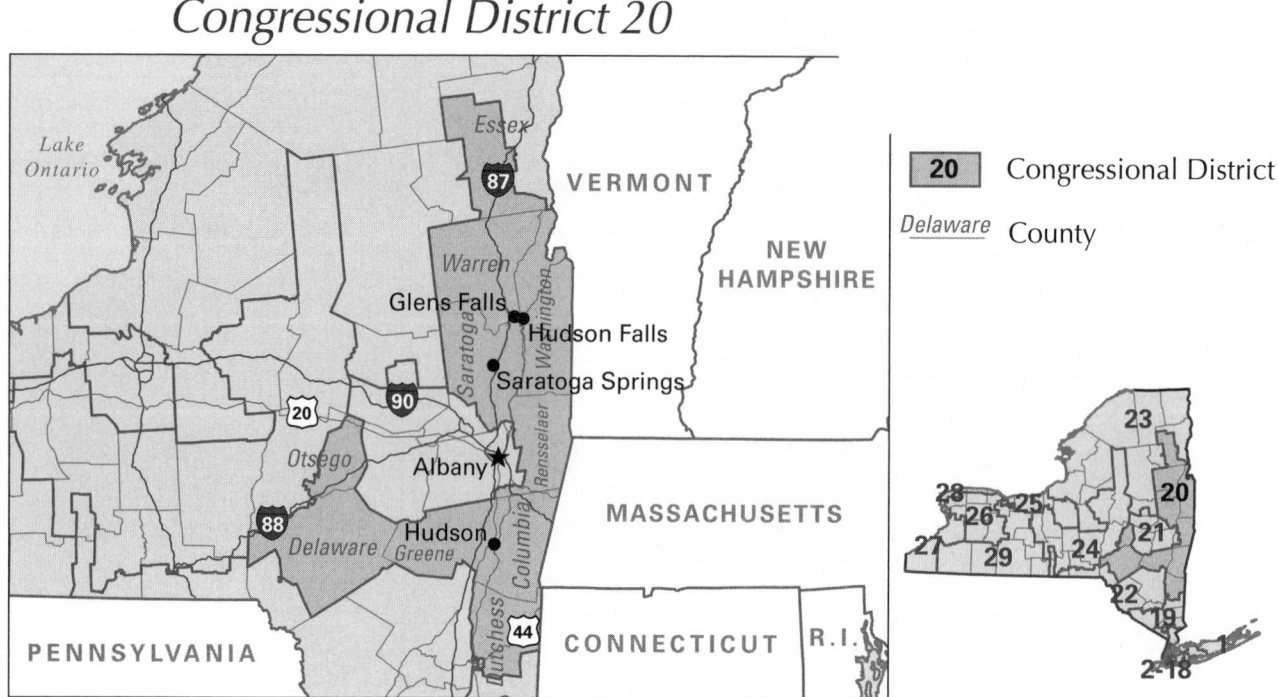

New York (29 Districts)

Congressional District 21

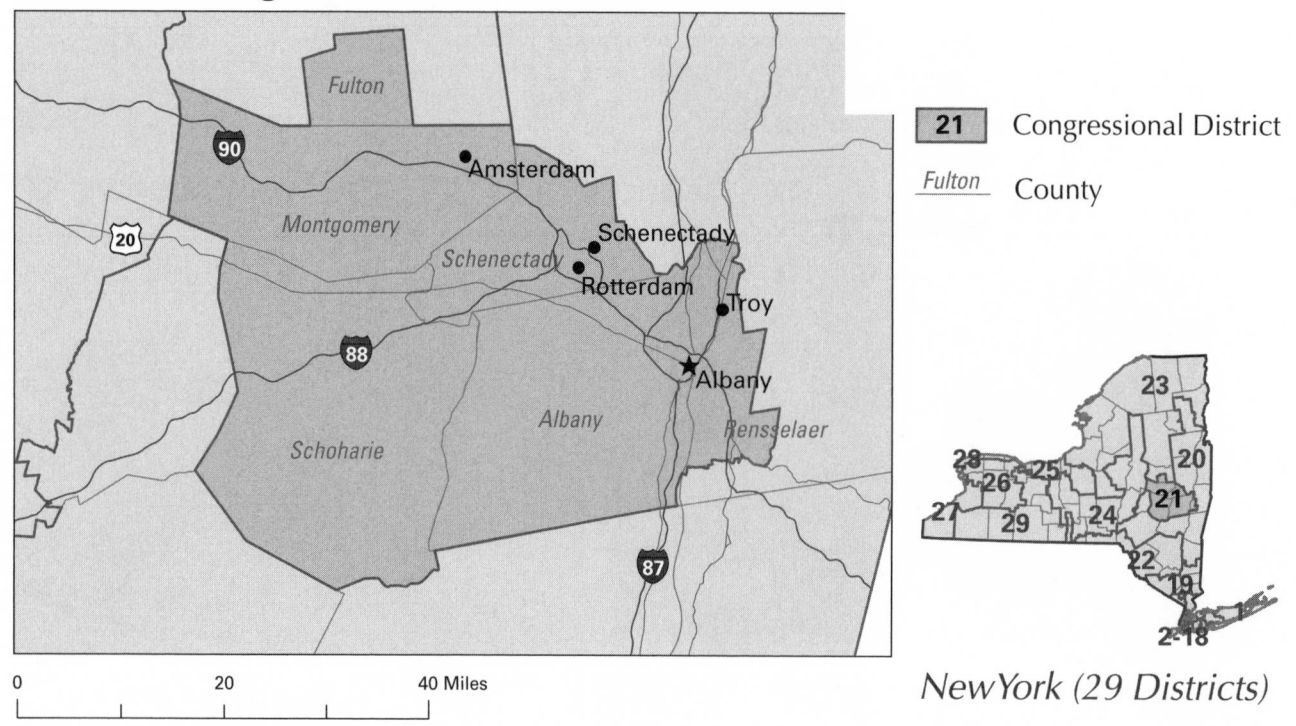

NewYork (29 Districts)

Congressional District 22

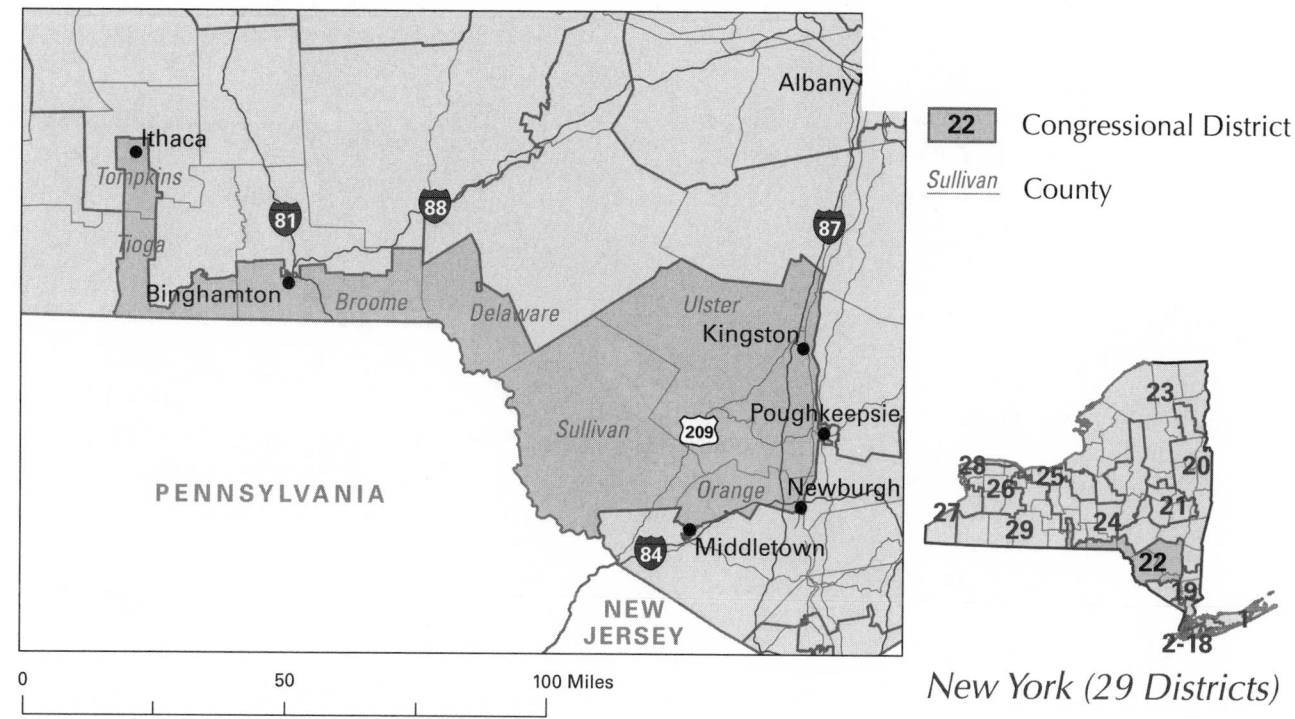

Congressional District 23

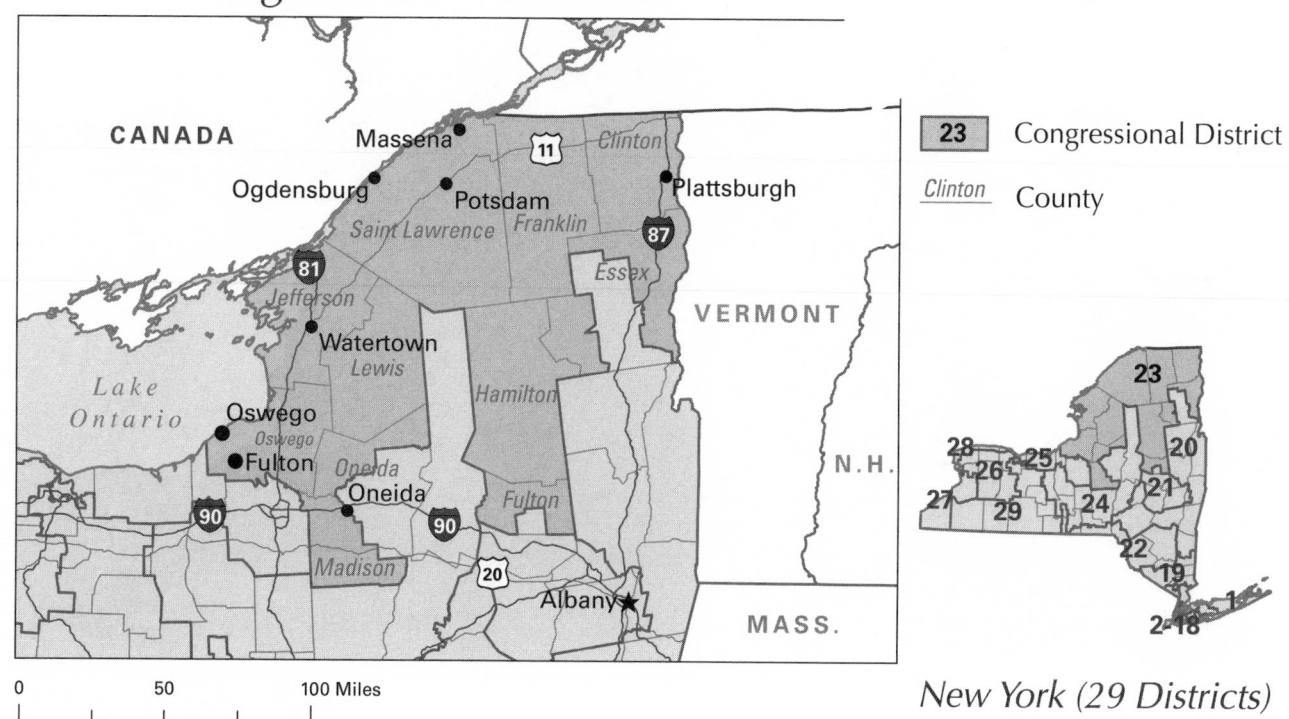

Congressional District 24

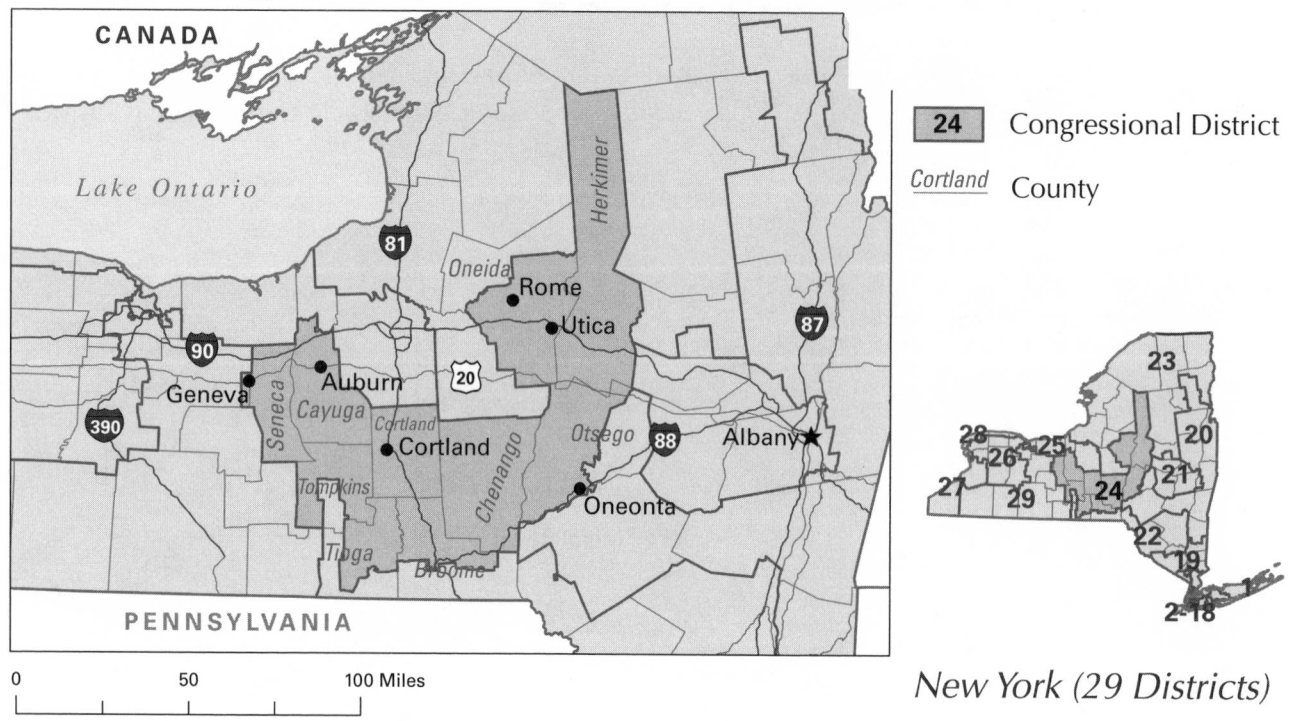

24 Congressional District

Cortland County

New York (29 Districts)

Congressional District 25

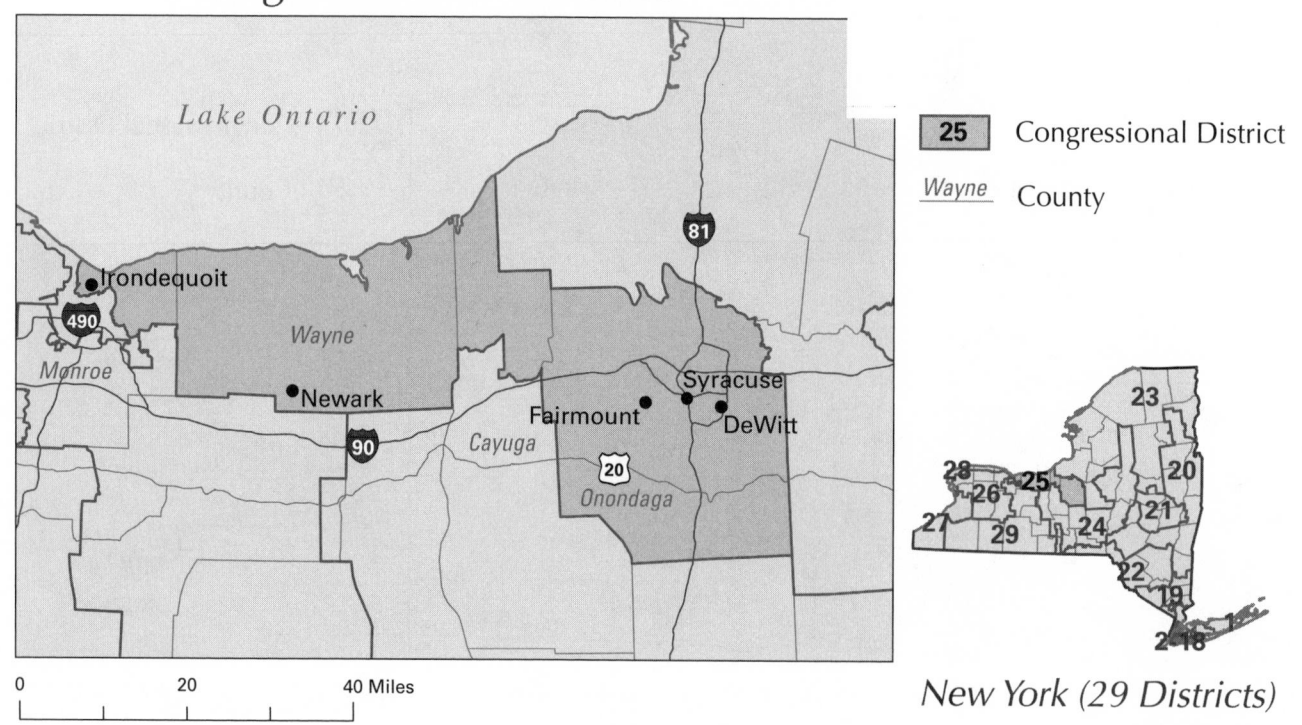

25 Congressional District

Wayne County

New York (29 Districts)

Congressional District 26

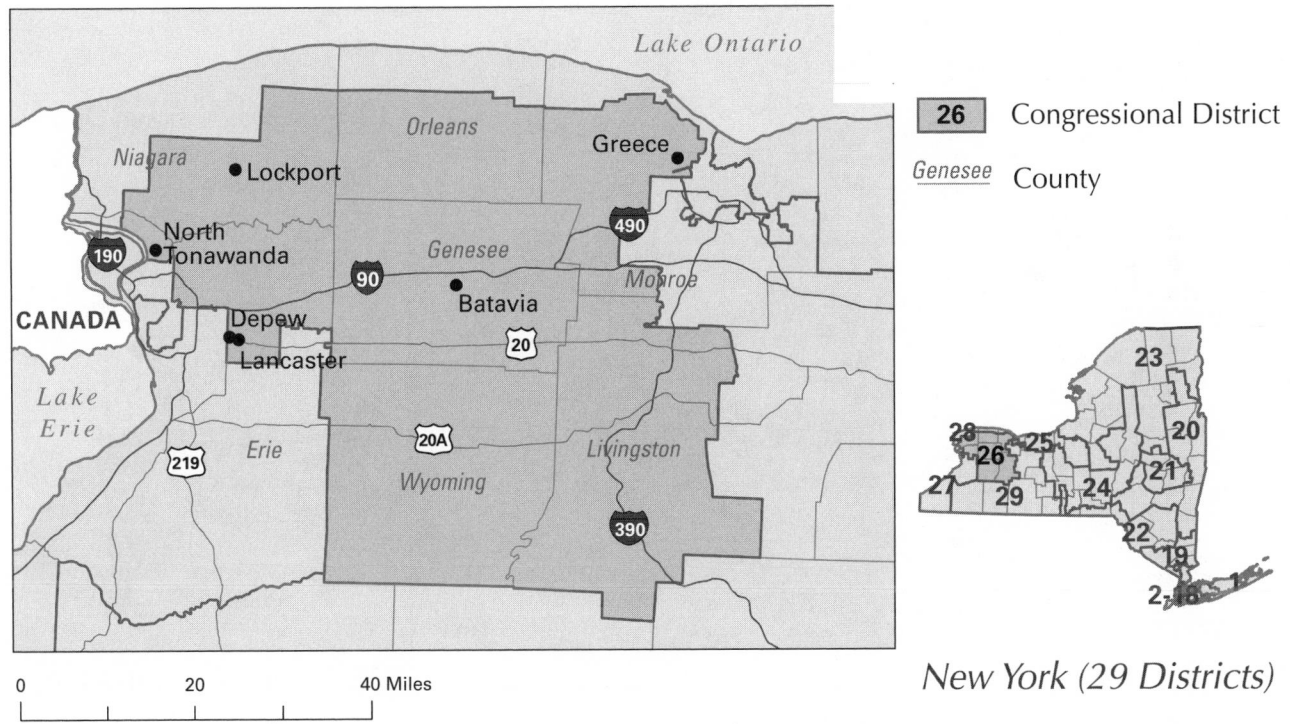

| 26 | Congressional District |
| *Genesee* | County |

New York (29 Districts)

Congressional District 27

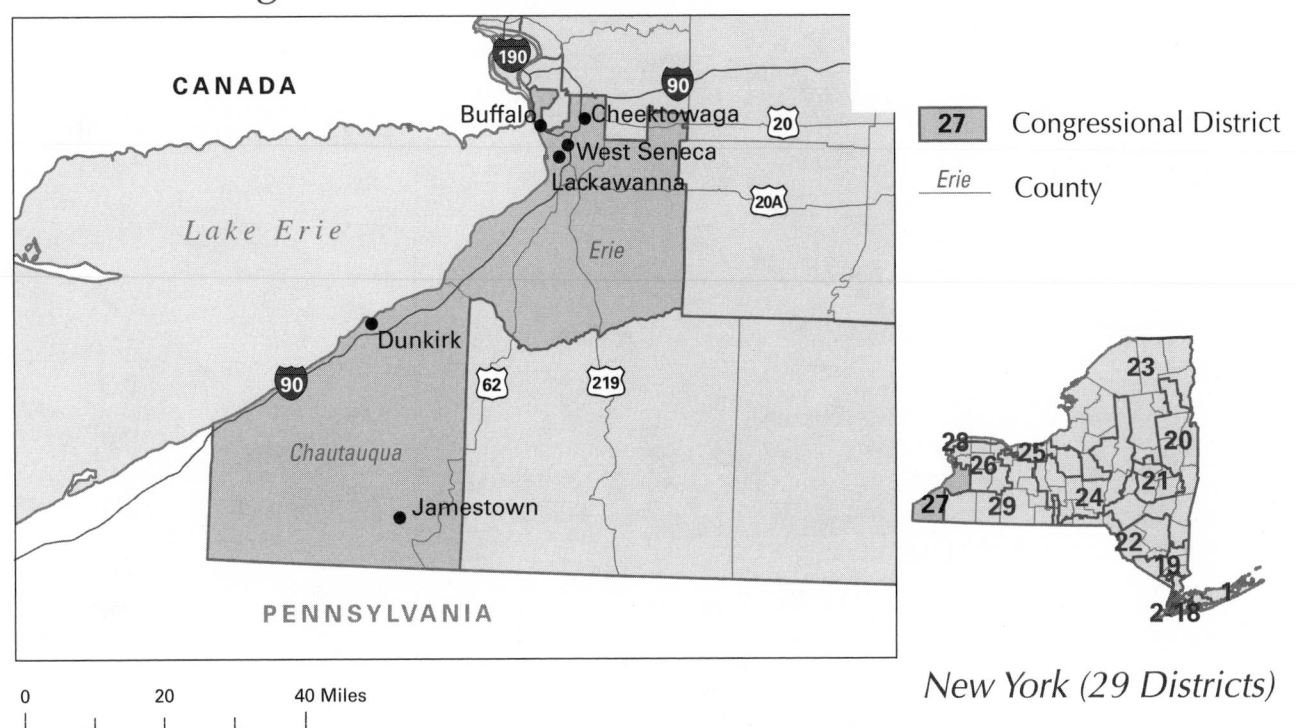

| 27 | Congressional District |
| *Erie* | County |

New York (29 Districts)

Congressional District 28

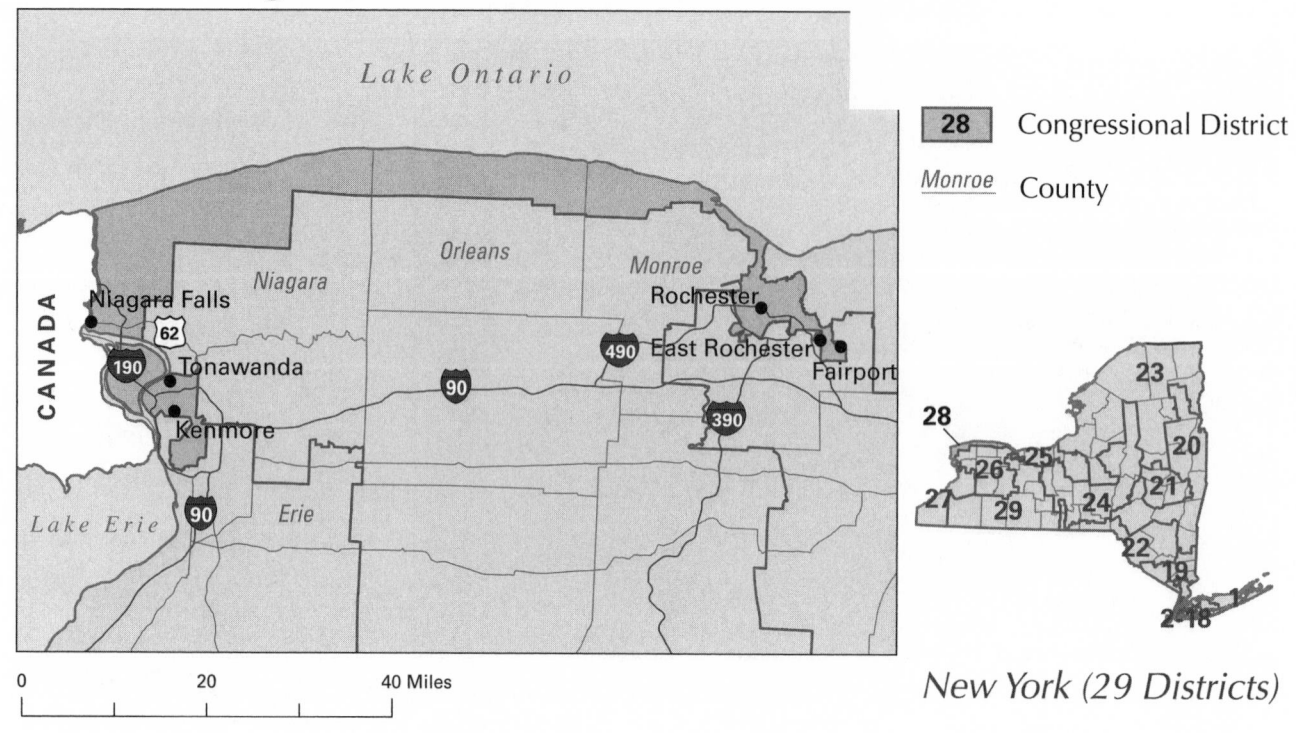

28   Congressional District
Monroe   County

New York (29 Districts)

Congressional District 29

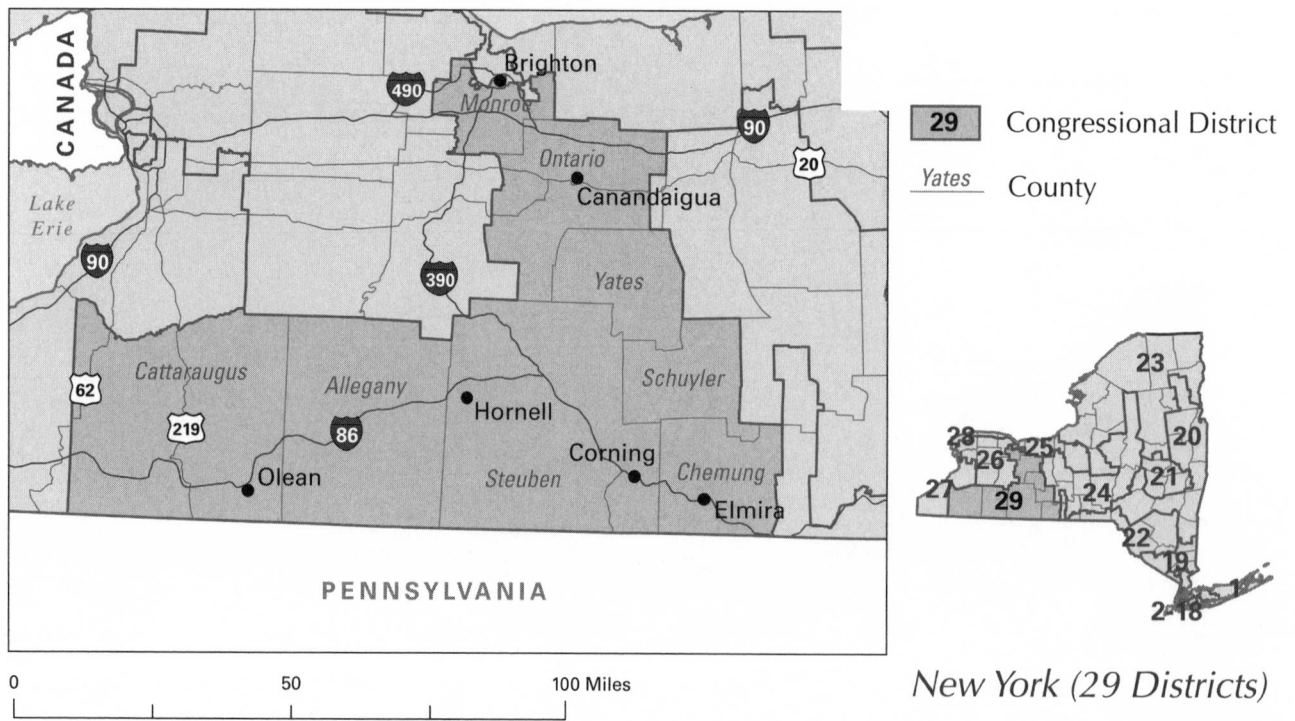

29   Congressional District
Yates   County

New York (29 Districts)

North Carolina Congressional Districts — 13 Districts Total

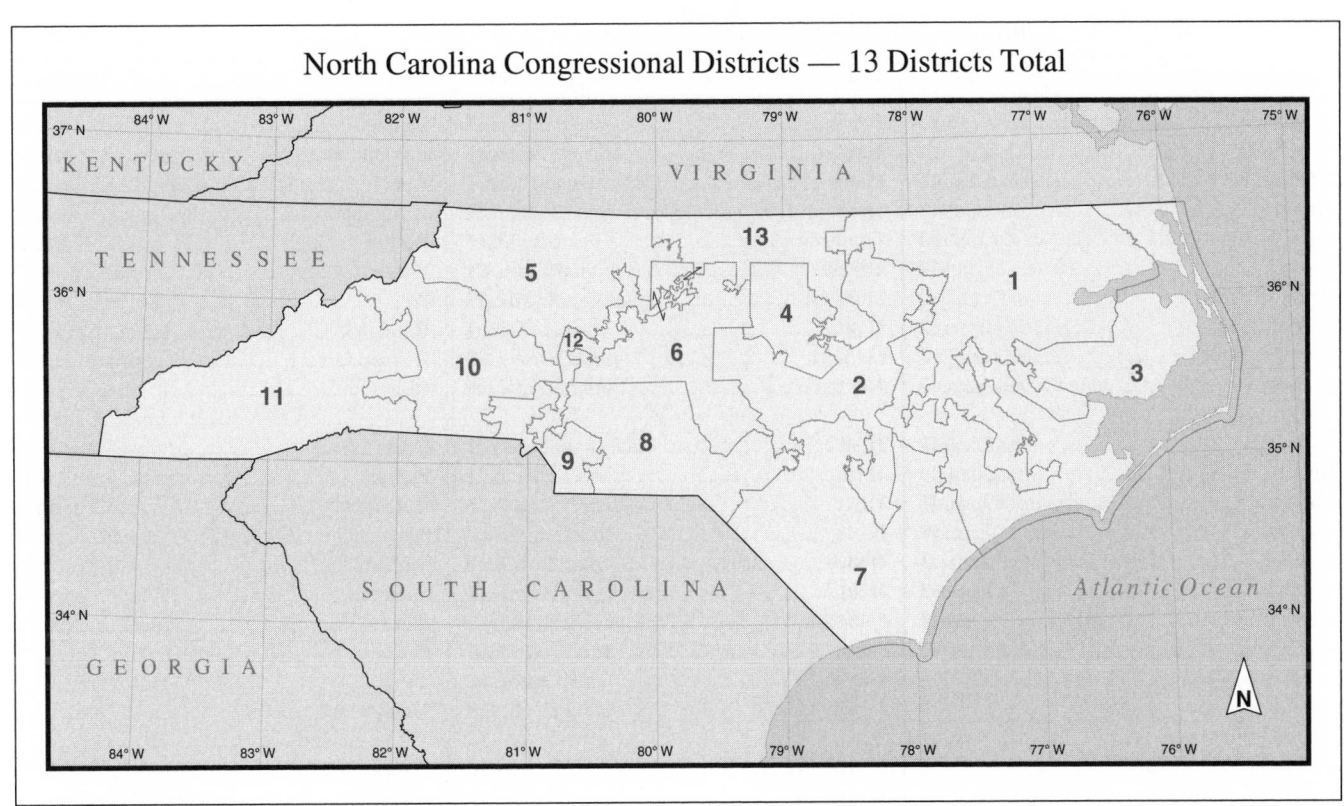

NORTH CAROLINA — 110th CONGRESSIONAL DISTRICTS BY COUNTIES

County	Congressional District	County	Congressional District	County	Congressional District
Alamance	6, 13	Franklin	2	Pamlico	3
Alexander	5	Gaston	9, 10	Pasquotank	1
Alleghany	5	Gates	1	Pender	7
Anson	8	Graham	11	Perquimans	1
Ashe	5	Granville	1, 13	Person	13
Avery	10	Greene	1	Pitt	1, 3
Beaufort	1, 3	Guilford	6, 12, 13	Polk	11
Bertie	1	Halifax	1	Randolph	6
Bladen	7	Harnett	2	Richmond	8
Brunswick	7	Haywood	11	Robeson	7
Buncombe	11	Henderson	11	Rockingham	5, 13
Burke	10	Hertford	1	Rowan	6, 12
Cabarrus	8, 12	Hoke	8	Rutherford	10, 11
Caldwell	10	Hyde	3	Sampson	2, 7
Camden	3	Iredell	5, 10	Scotland	7, 8
Carteret	3	Jackson	11	Stanly	8
Caswell	13	Johnston	2	Stokes	5
Catawba	10	Jones	1, 3	Surry	5
Chatham	2, 4	Lee	2	Swain	11
Cherokee	11	Lenoir	1, 3	Transylvania	11
Chowan	1	Lincoln	10	Tyrrell	3
Clay	11	McDowell	11	Union	8, 9
Cleveland	10	Macon	11	Vance	1, 2
Columbus	7	Madison	11	Wake	2, 4, 13
Craven	1, 3	Martin	1	Warren	1
Cumberland	2, 7, 8	Mecklenburg	8, 9, 12	Washington	1
Currituck	3	Mitchell	10	Watauga	5
Dare	3	Montgomery	8	Wayne	1, 3
Davidson	6, 12	Moore	6	Wilkes	5
Davie	5	Nash	1–3	Wilson	1, 3
Duplin	3, 7	New Hanover	7	Yadkin	5
Durham	4	Northampton	1	Yancey	11
Edgecombe	1	Onslow	3		
Forsyth	5, 12	Orange	4		

Congressional District 1

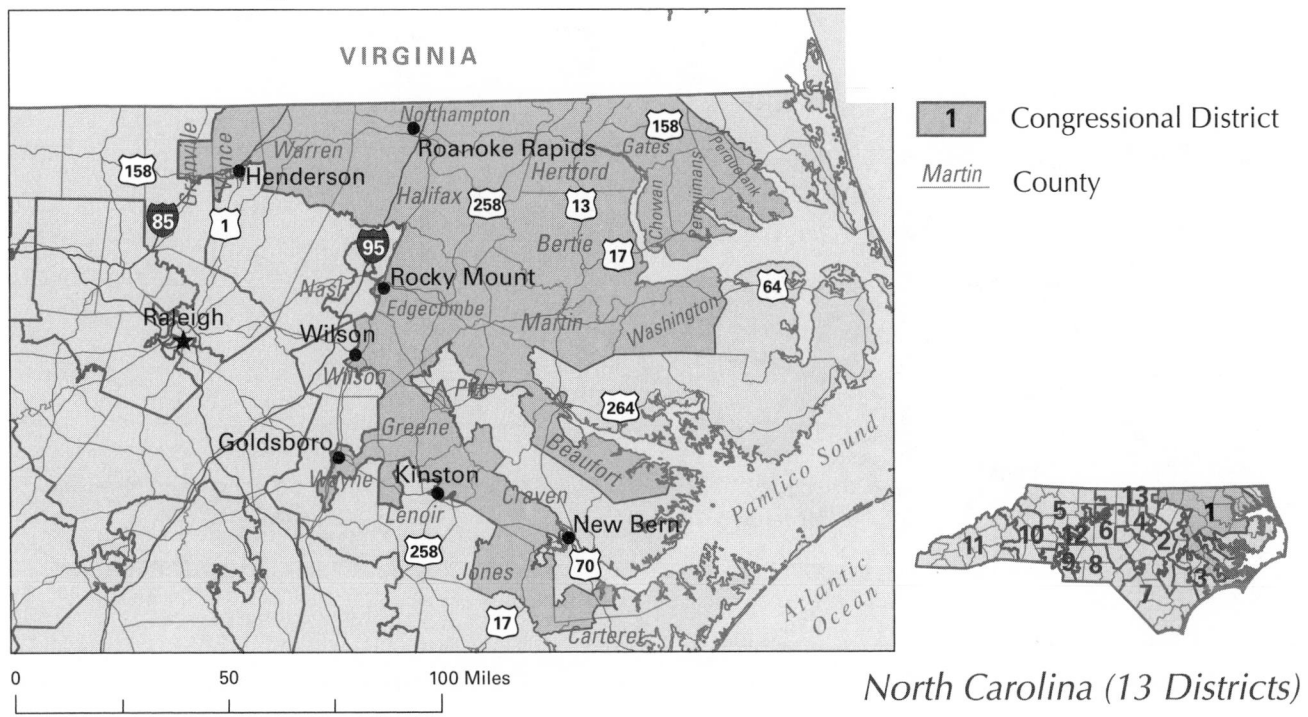

North Carolina (13 Districts)

Congressional District 2

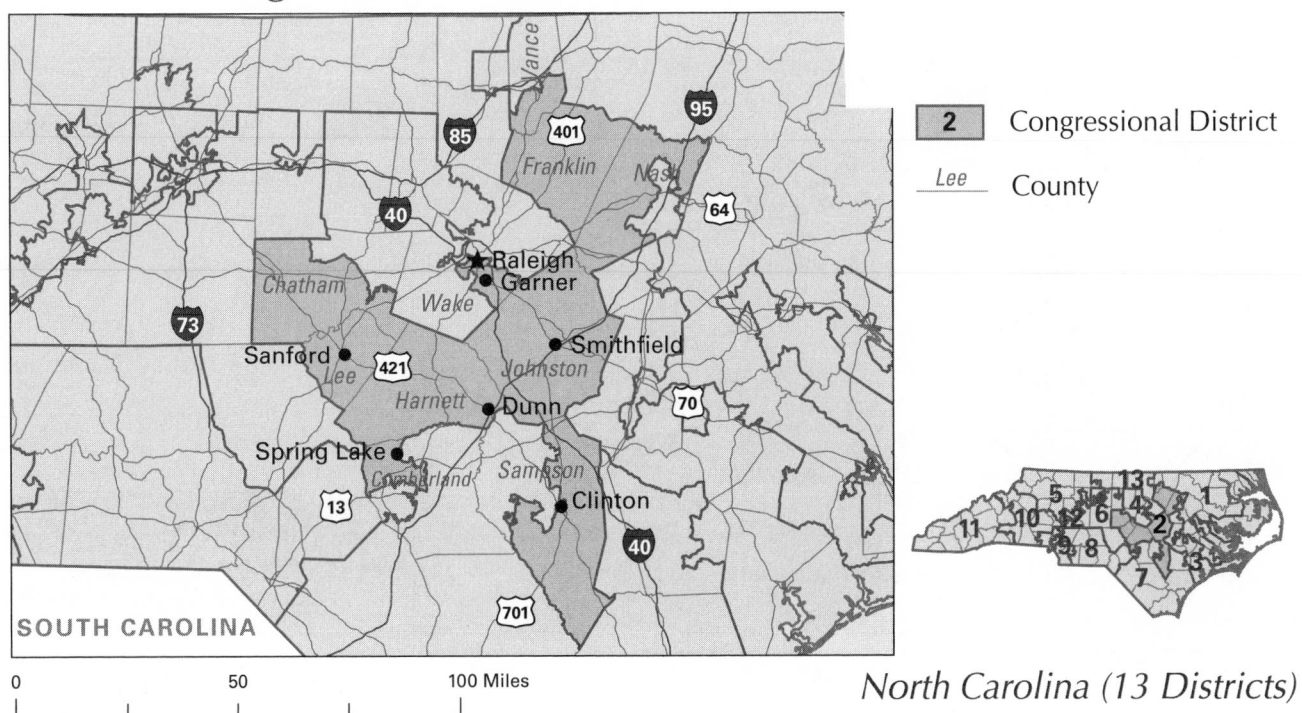

North Carolina (13 Districts)

Congressional District 3

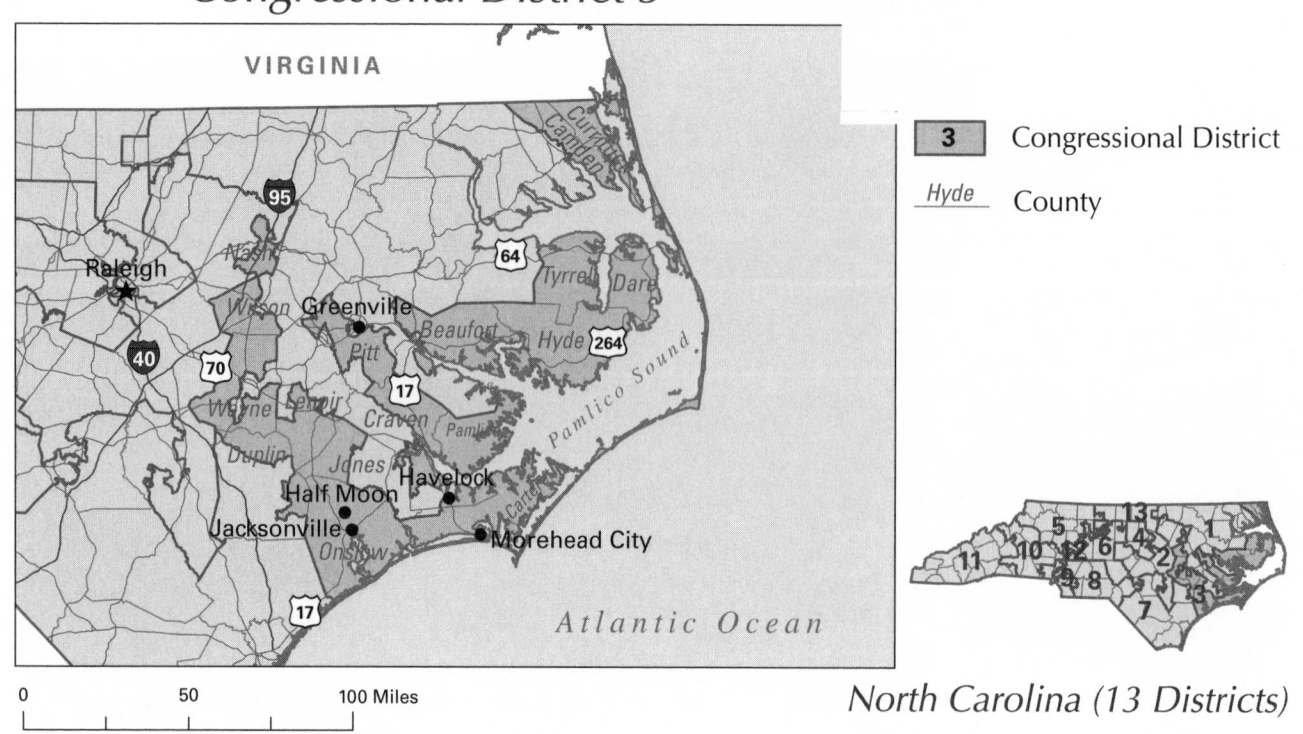

North Carolina (13 Districts)

Congressional District 4

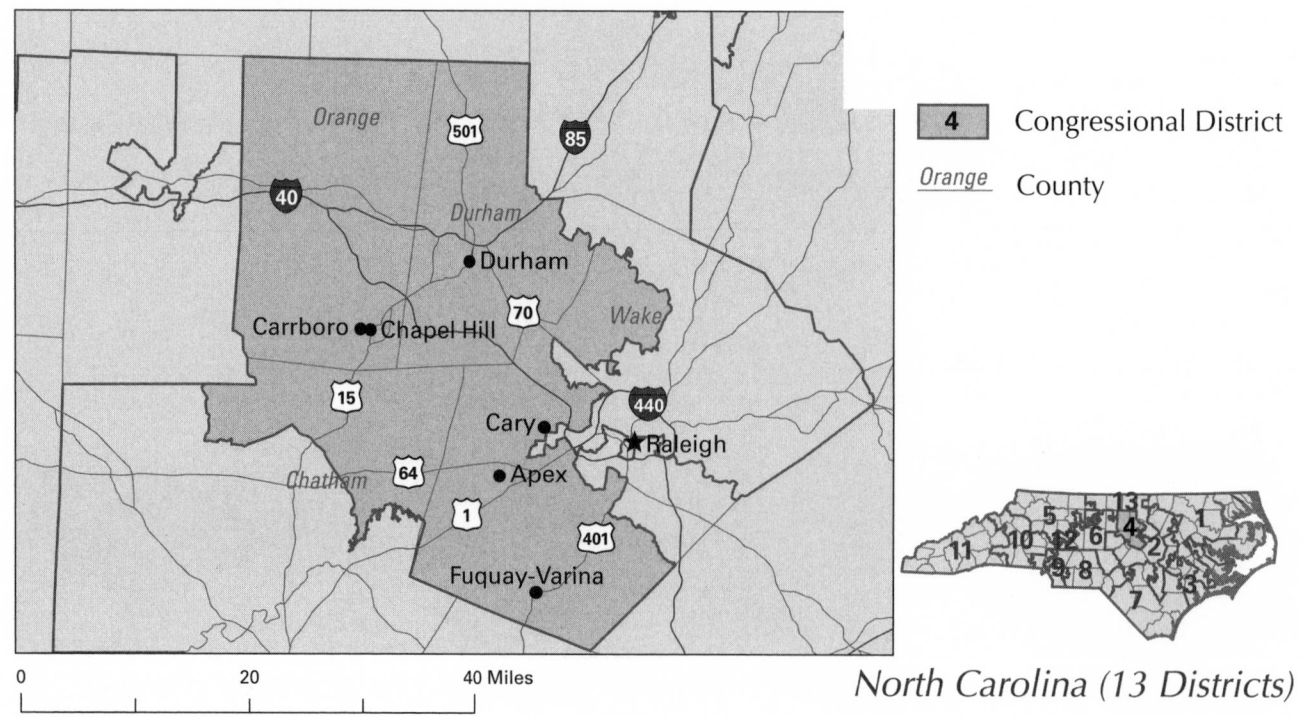

North Carolina (13 Districts)

Congressional District 5

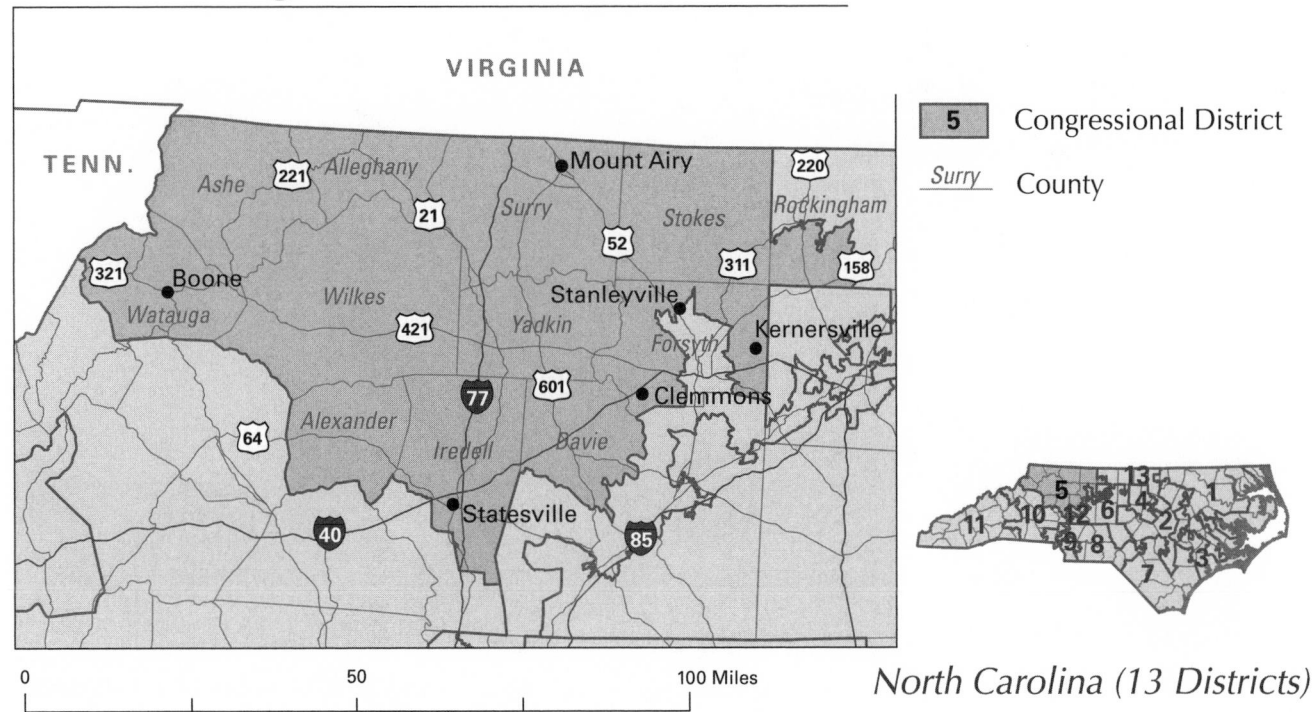

North Carolina (13 Districts)

Congressional District 6

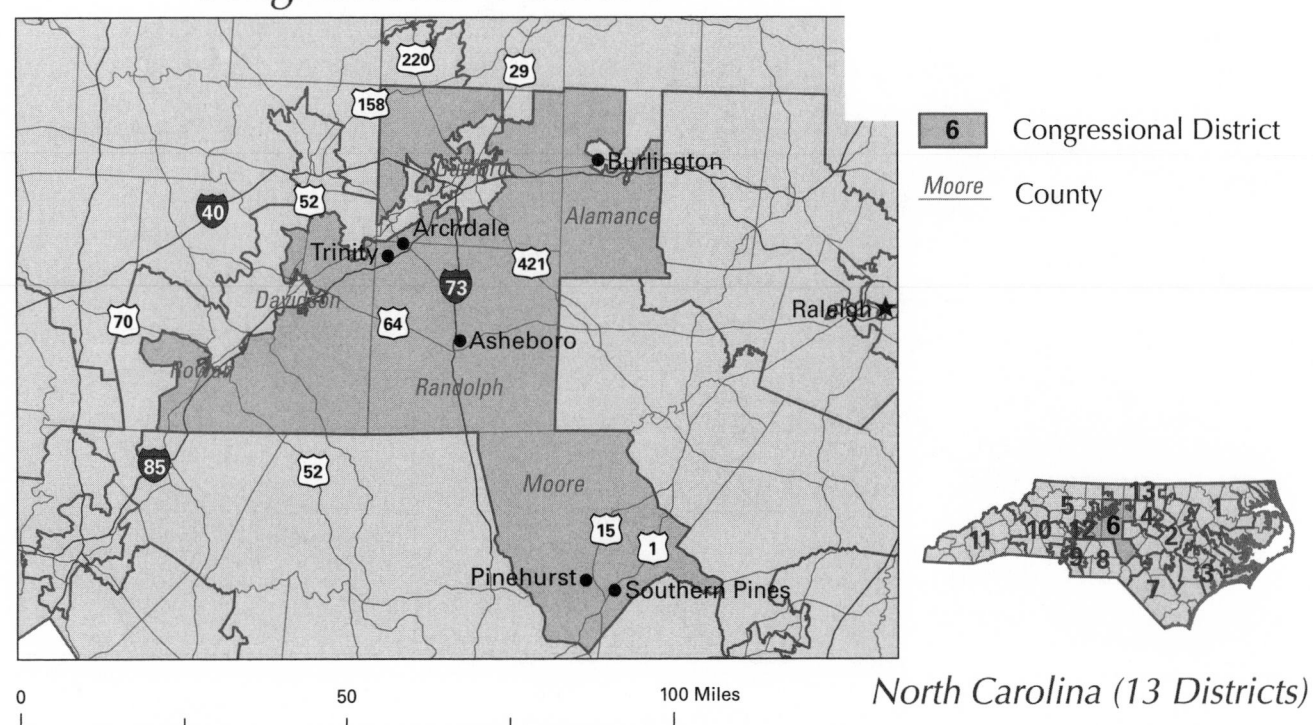

North Carolina (13 Districts)

Congressional District 7

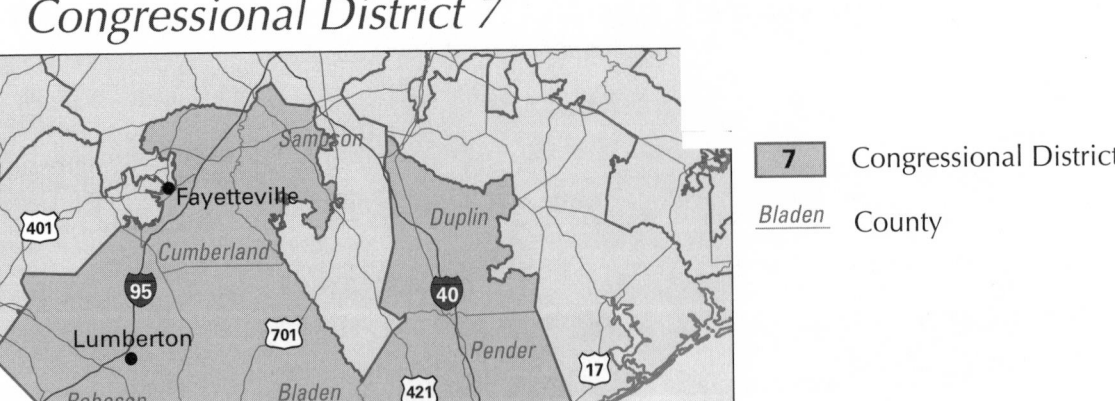

North Carolina (13 Districts)

Congressional District 8

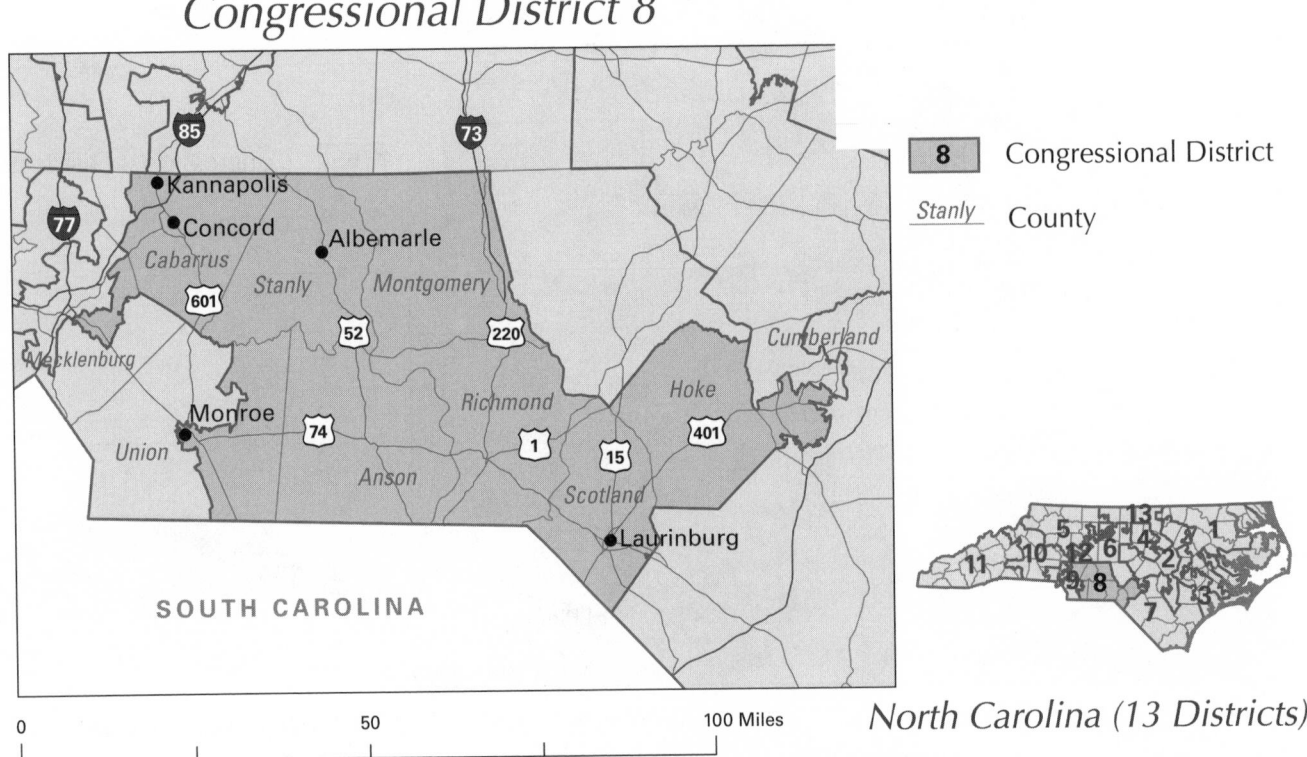

North Carolina (13 Districts)

Congressional District 9

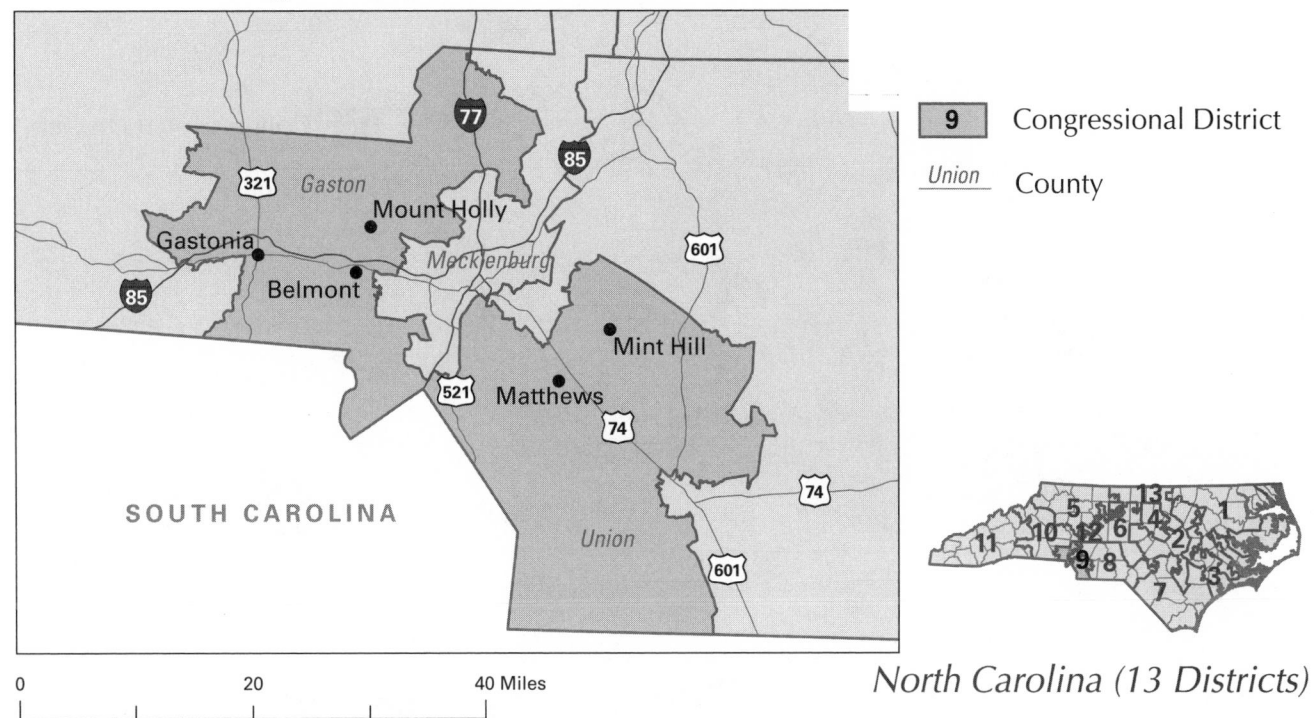

North Carolina (13 Districts)

Congressional District 10

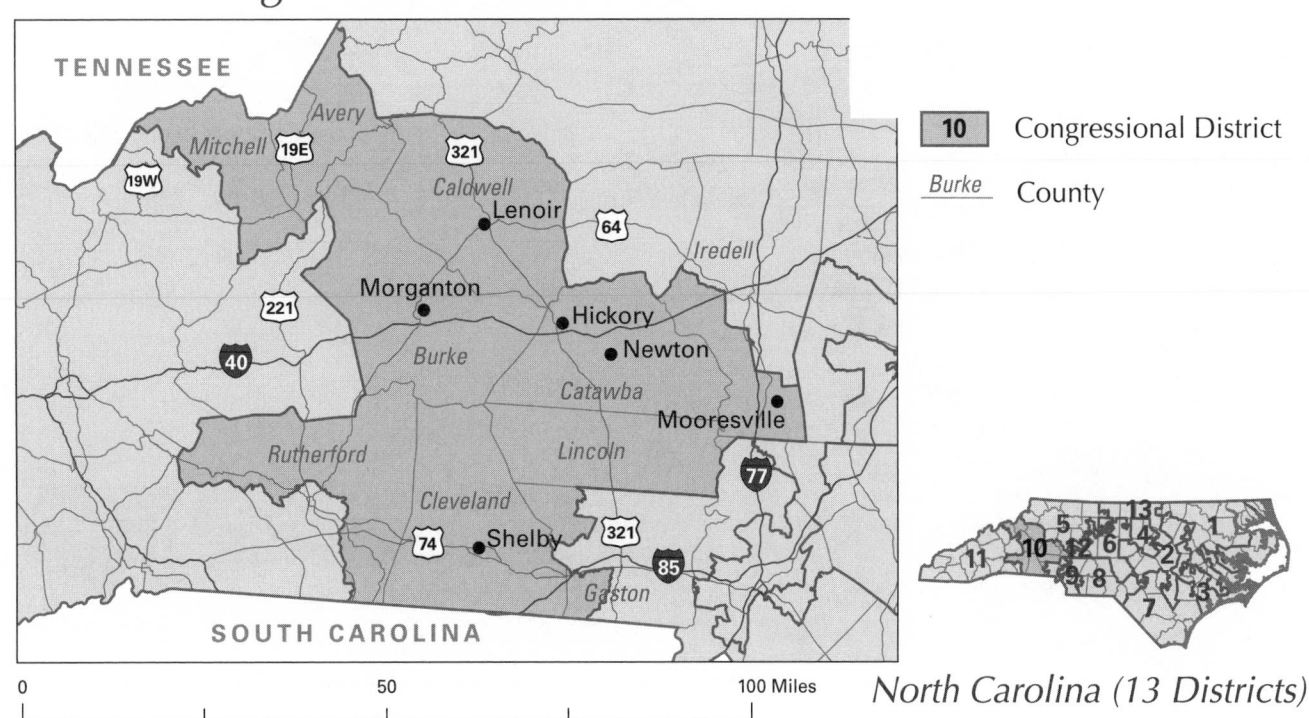

North Carolina (13 Districts)

Congressional District 11

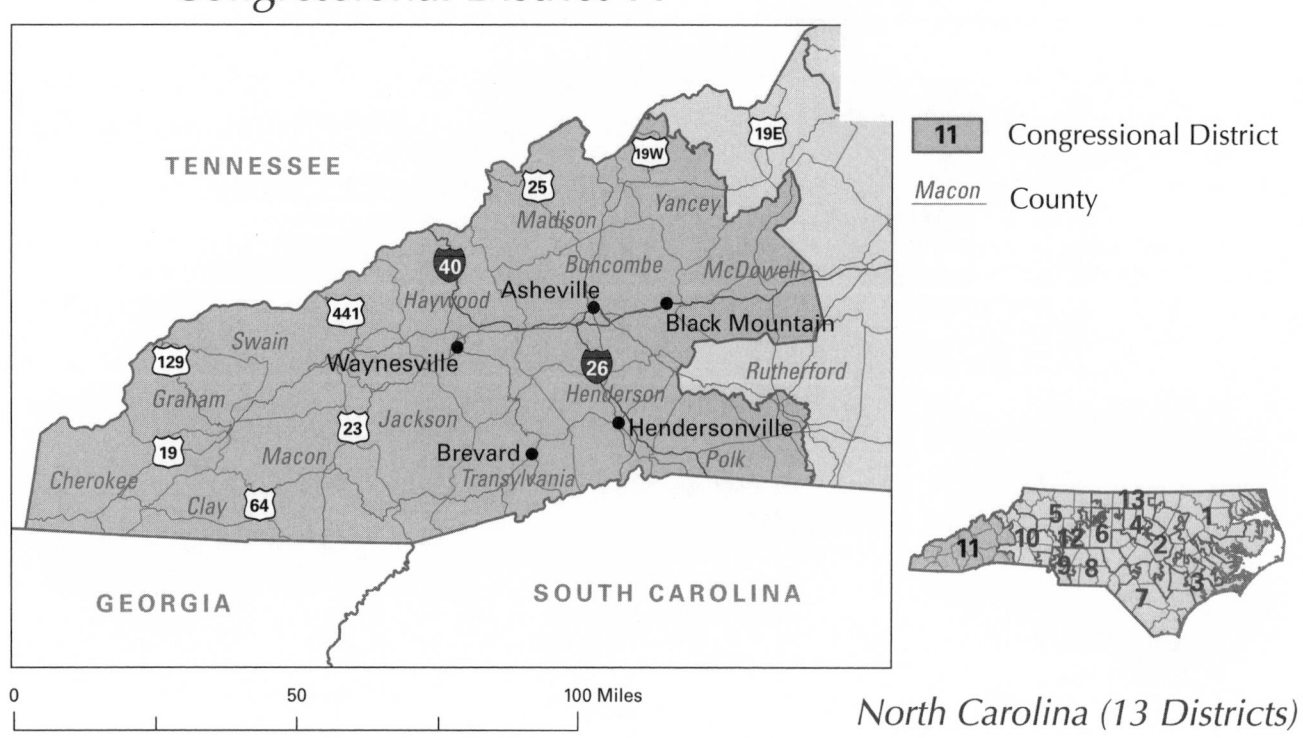

North Carolina (13 Districts)

Congressional District 12

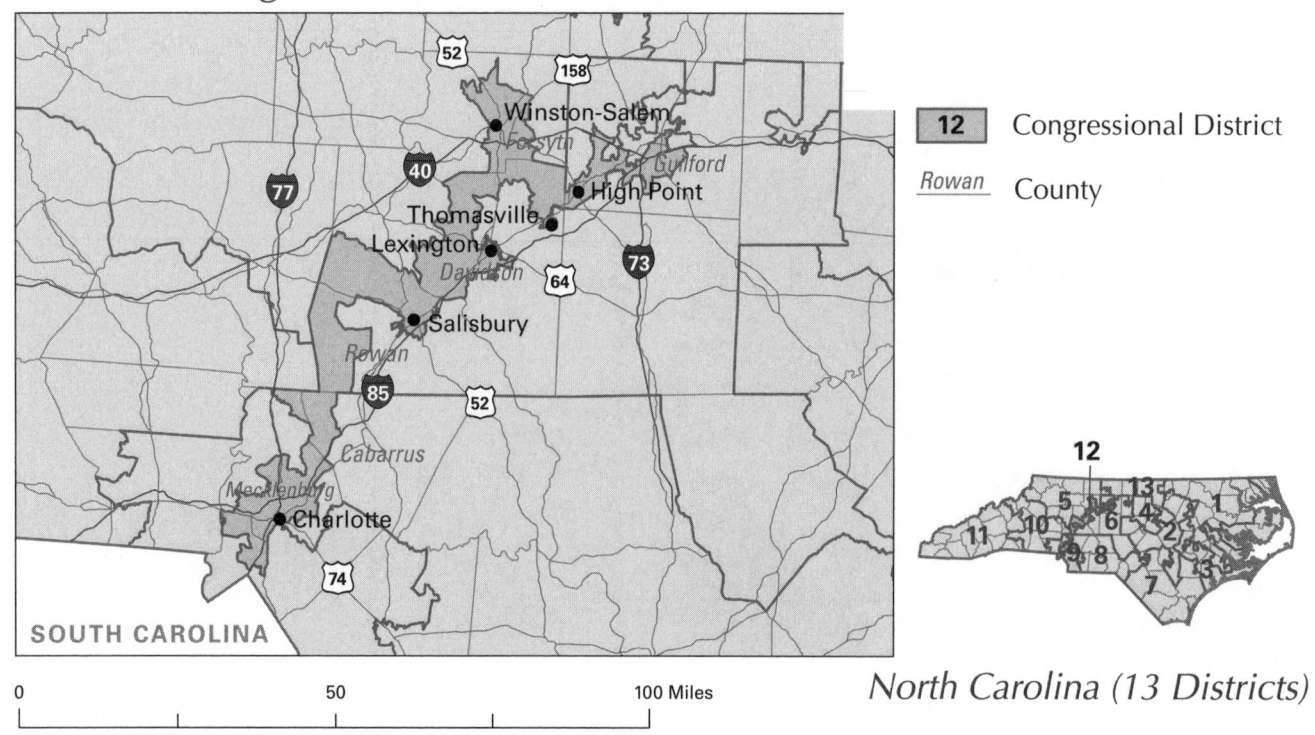

North Carolina (13 Districts)

Congressional District 13

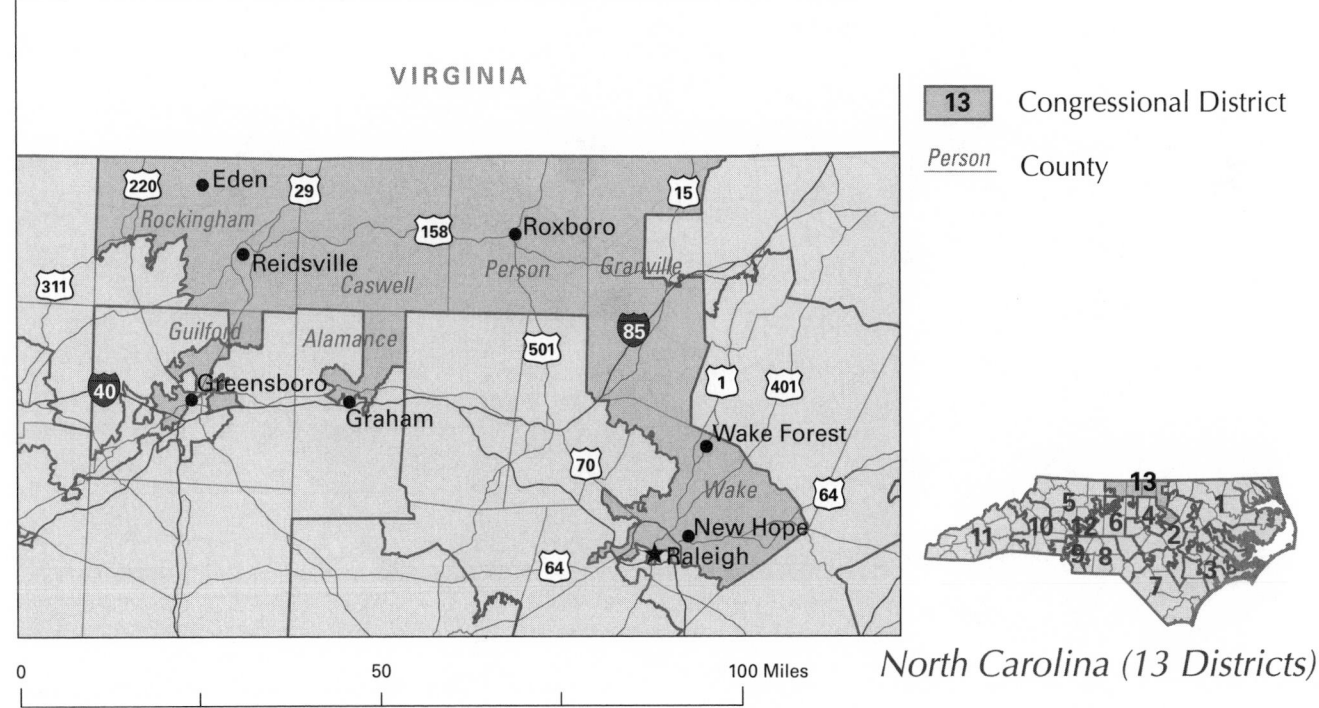

North Carolina (13 Districts)

North Dakota—
Congressional District: At large

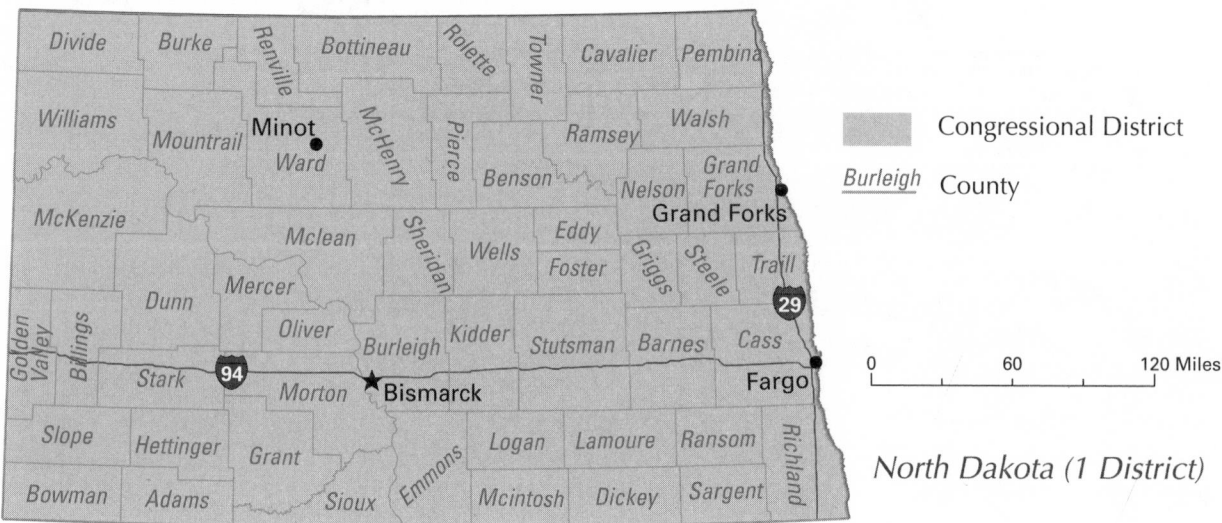

Congressional District

Burleigh County

North Dakota (1 District)

NORTH DAKOTA—110th CONGRESSIONAL DISTRICTS BY COUNTIES

County	Congressional District	County	Congressional District	County	Congressional District
Adams	1	Grant	1	Ransom	1
Barnes	1	Griggs	1	Renville	1
Benson	1	Hettinger	1	Richland	1
Billings	1	Kidder	1	Rolette	1
Bottineau	1	La Moure	1	Sargent	1
Bowman	1	Logan	1	Sheridan	1
Burke	1	McHenry	1	Sioux	1
Burleigh	1	McIntosh	1	Slope	1
Cass	1	McKenzie	1	Stark	1
Cavalier	1	McLean	1	Steele	1
Dickey	1	Mercer	1	Stutsman	1
Divide	1	Morton	1	Towner	1
Dunn	1	Mountrail	1	Traill	1
Eddy	1	Nelson	1	Walsh	1
Emmons	1	Oliver	1	Ward	1
Foster	1	Pembina	1	Wells	1
Golden Valley	1	Pierce	1	Williams	1
Grand Forks	1	Ramsey	1		

Ohio Congressional Districts — 18 Districts Total

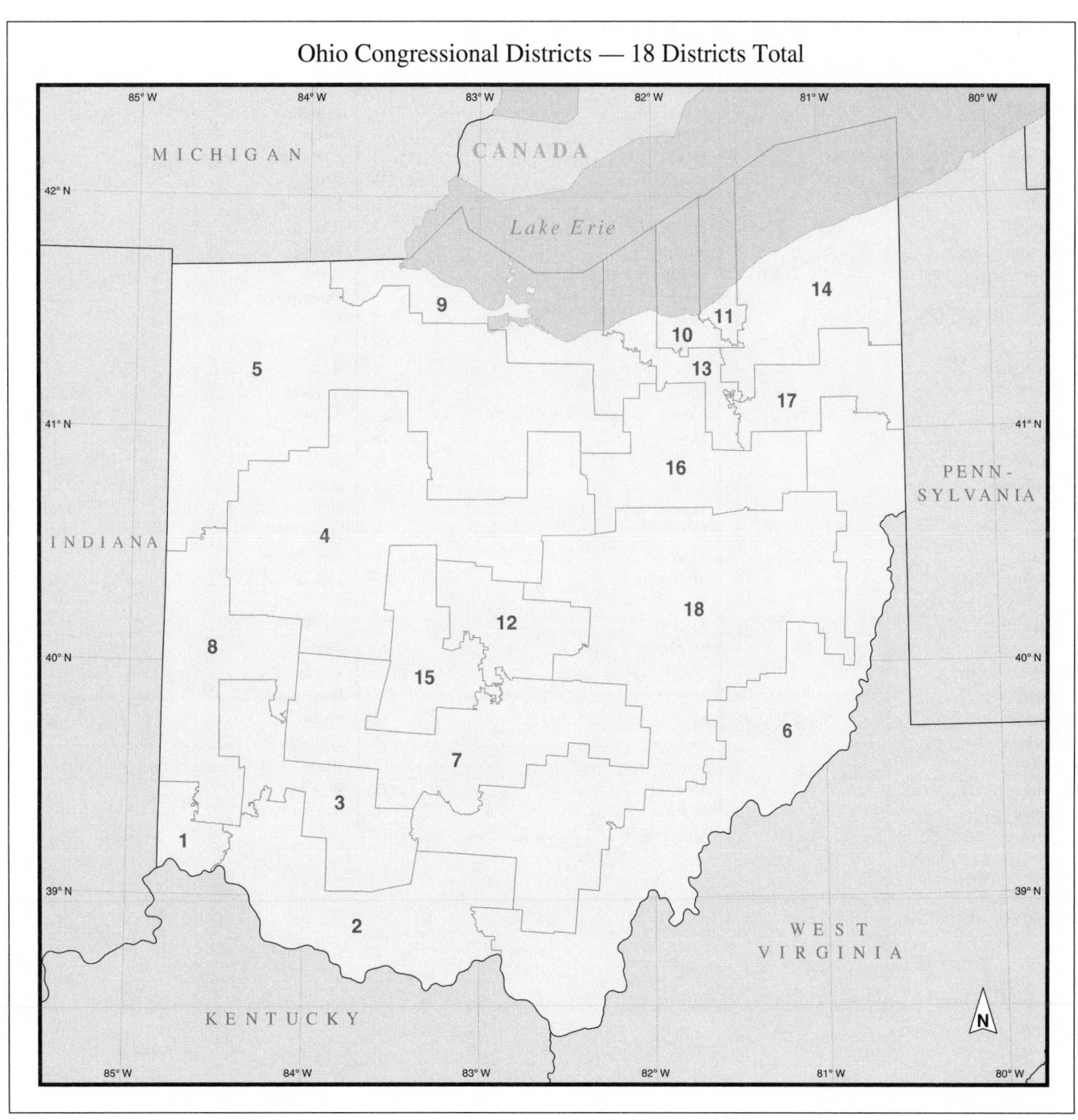

OHIO—110th CONGRESSIONAL DISTRICTS BY COUNTIES

County	Congressional District	County	Congressional District	County	Congressional District
Adams	2	Hamilton	1, 2	Noble	6
Allen	4	Hancock	4	Ottawa	9
Ashland	5, 16	Hardin	4	Paulding	5
Ashtabula	14	Harrison	18	Perry	7
Athens	6, 18	Henry	5	Pickaway	7
Auglaize	4	Highland	3	Pike	2
Belmont	6, 18	Hocking	18	Portage	14, 17
Brown	2	Holmes	18	Preble	8
Butler	1, 8	Huron	5	Putnam	5
Carroll	18	Jackson	18	Richland	4
Champaign	4	Jefferson	6	Ross	7, 18
Clark	7	Knox	12, 18	Sandusky	5
Clermont	2	Lake	14	Scioto	2, 6
Clinton	3	Lawrence	6	Seneca	5
Columbiana	6	Licking	12, 18	Shelby	4
Coshocton	18	Logan	4	Stark	16
Crawford	5	Lorain	9, 13	Summit	13, 14, 17
Cuyahoga	10, 11, 13, 14	Lucas	5, 9	Trumbull	14, 17
Darke	8	Madison	15	Tuscarawas	18
Defiance	5	Mahoning	6, 17	Union	15
Delaware	12	Marion	4	Van Wert	5
Erie	9	Medina	13, 16	Vinton	18
Fairfield	7	Meigs	6	Warren	2, 3
Fayette	7	Mercer	5, 8	Washington	6
Franklin	7, 12, 15	Miami	8	Wayne	16
Fulton	5	Monroe	6	Williams	5
Gallia	6	Montgomery	3, 8	Wood	5
Geauga	14	Morgan	18	Wyandot	4, 5
Greene	7	Morrow	4		
Guernsey	18	Muskingum	18		

Congressional District 1

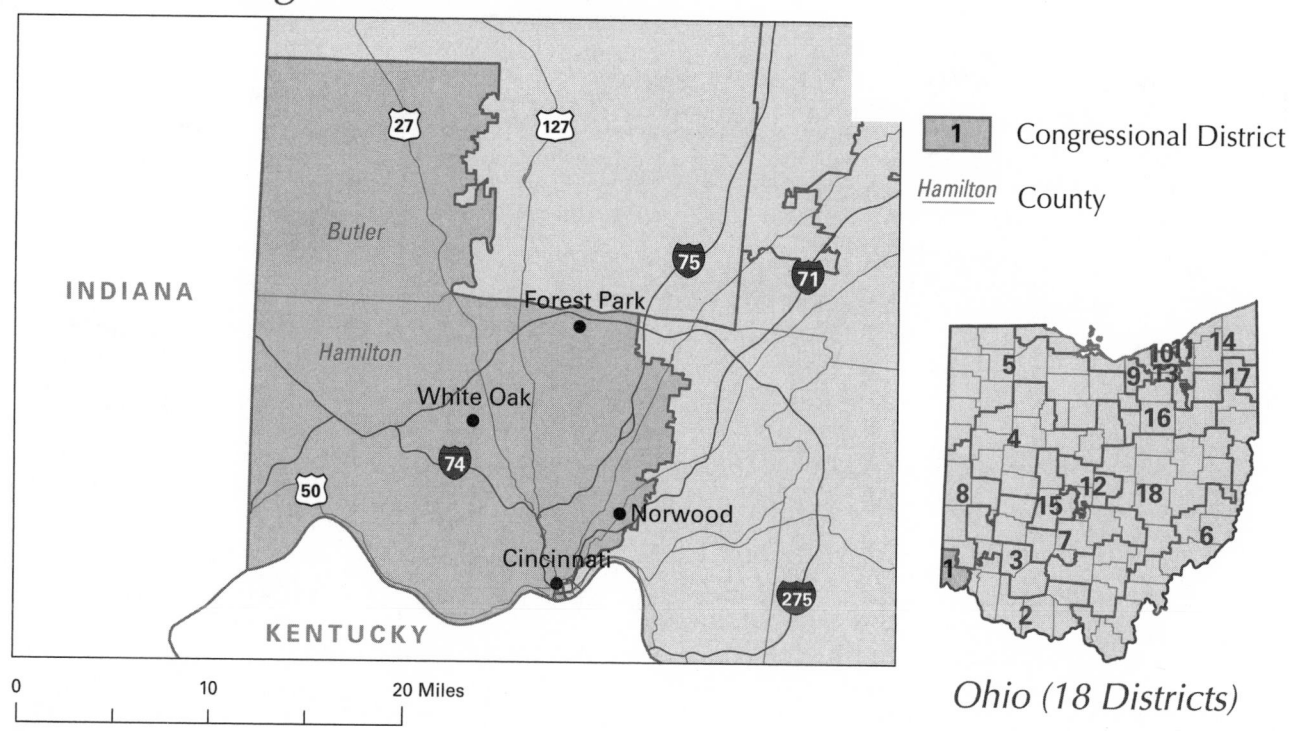

Ohio (18 Districts)

Congressional District 2

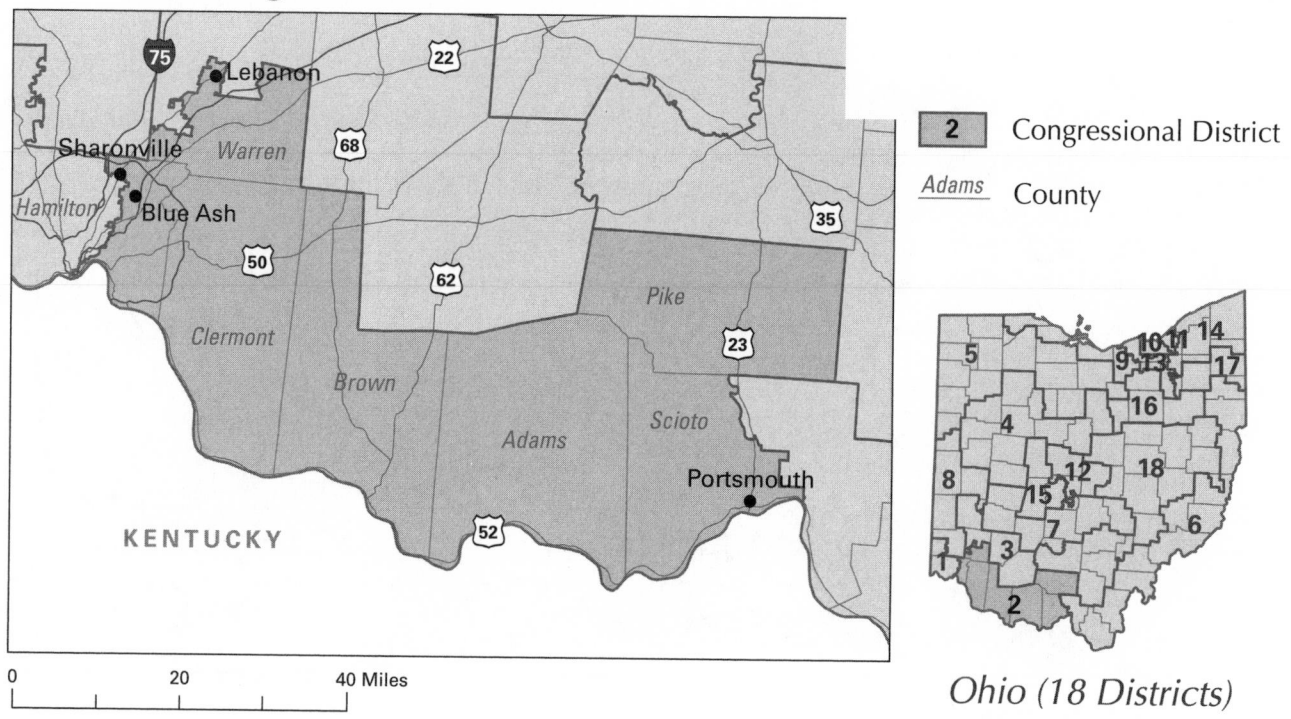

Ohio (18 Districts)

Congressional District 3

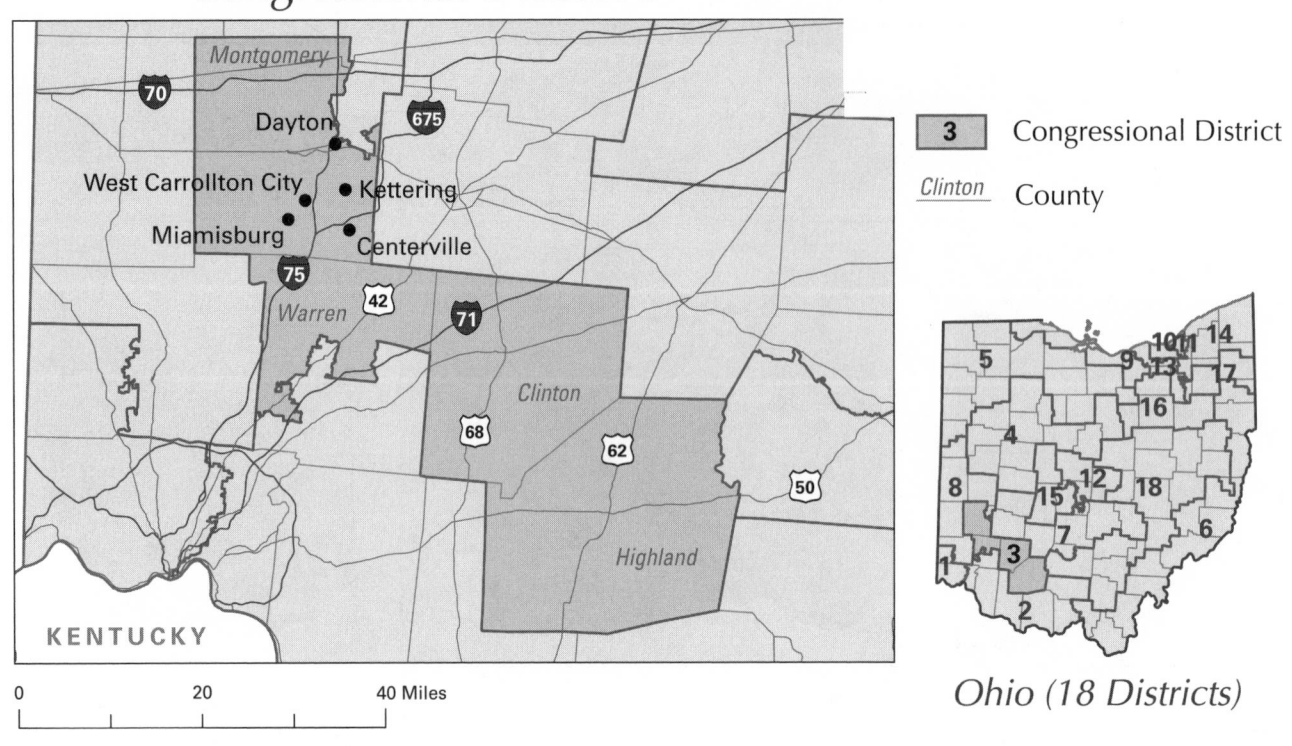

| 3 | Congressional District |
| *Clinton* | County |

Ohio (18 Districts)

Congressional District 4

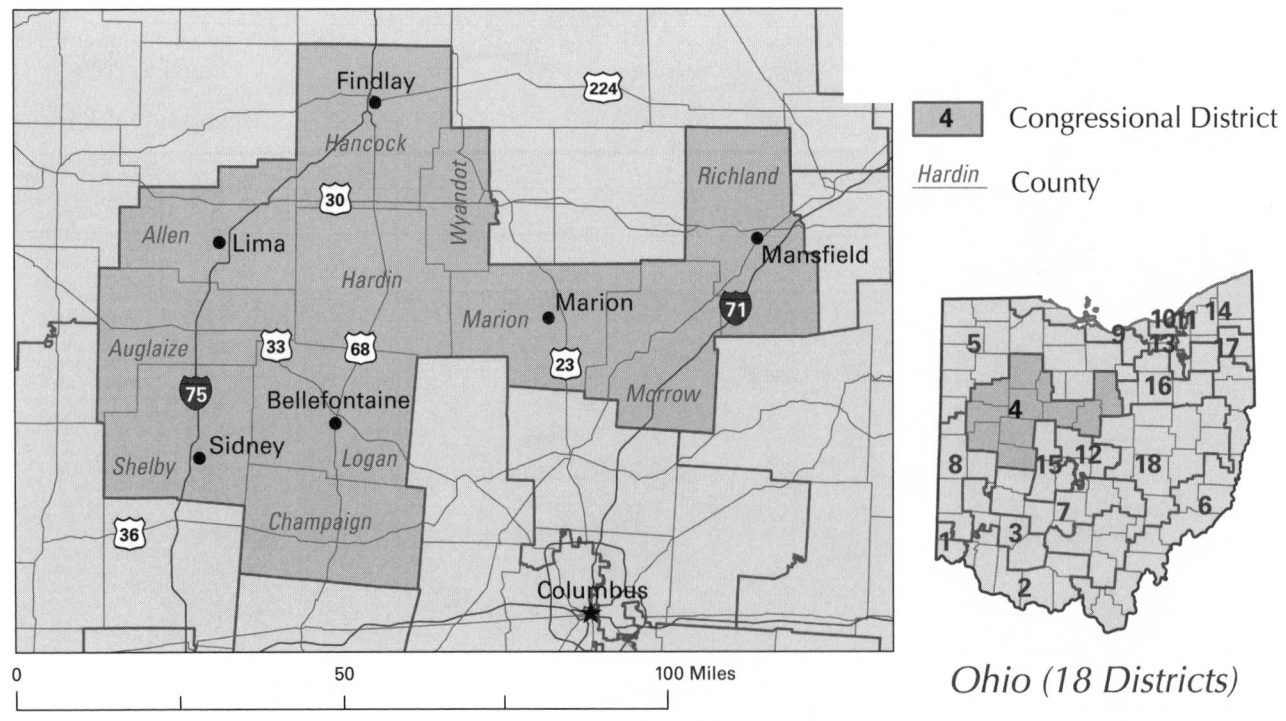

| 4 | Congressional District |
| *Hardin* | County |

Ohio (18 Districts)

Congressional District 5

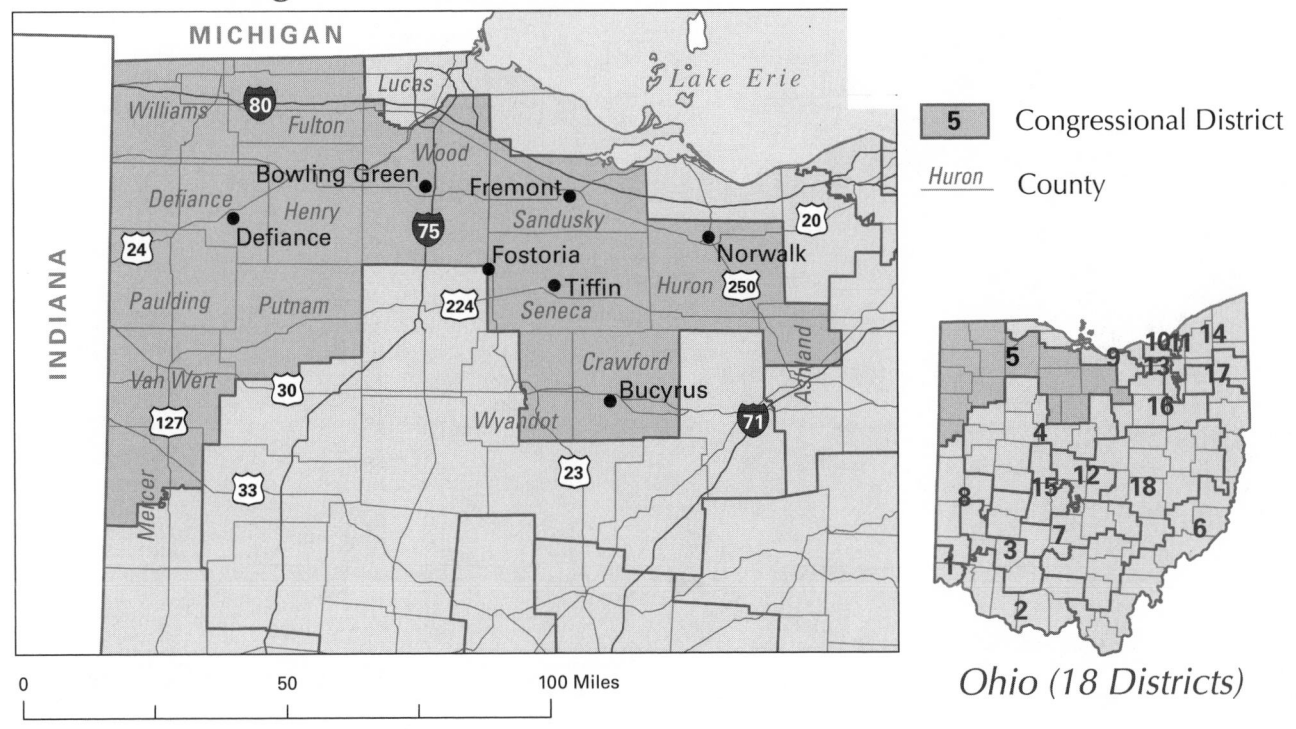

Congressional District 6

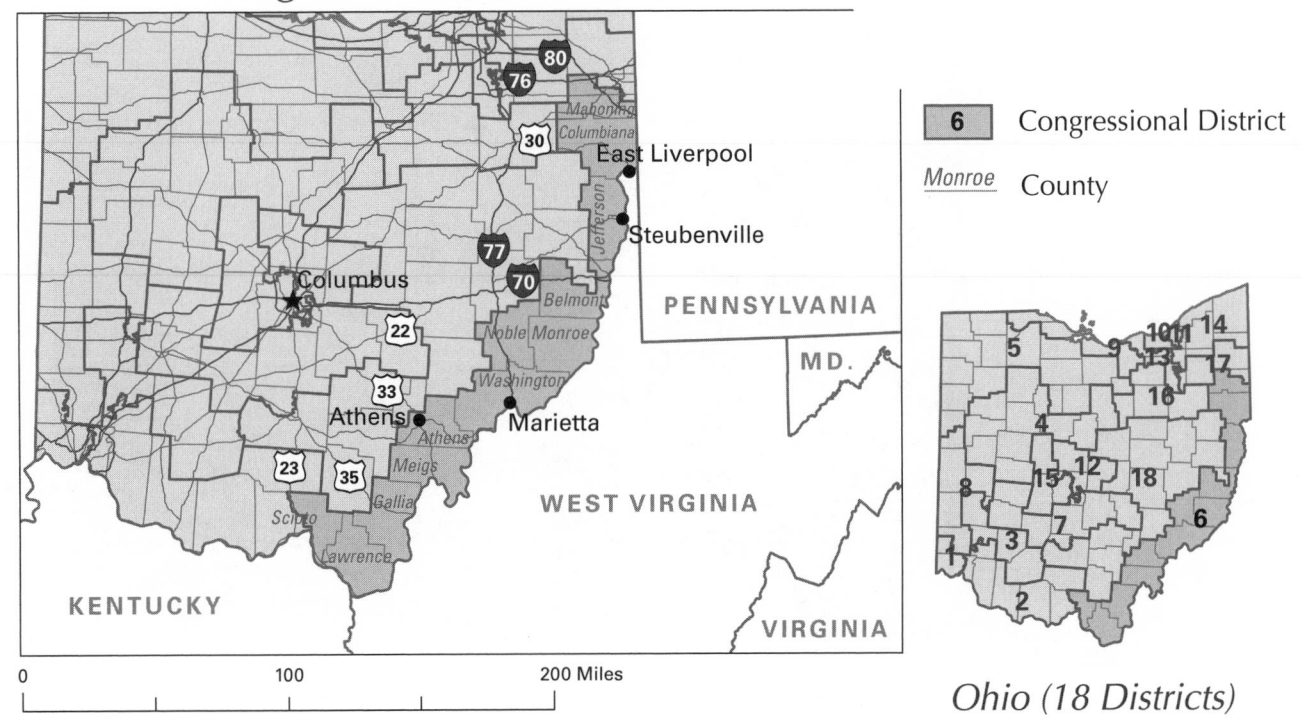

Congressional District 7

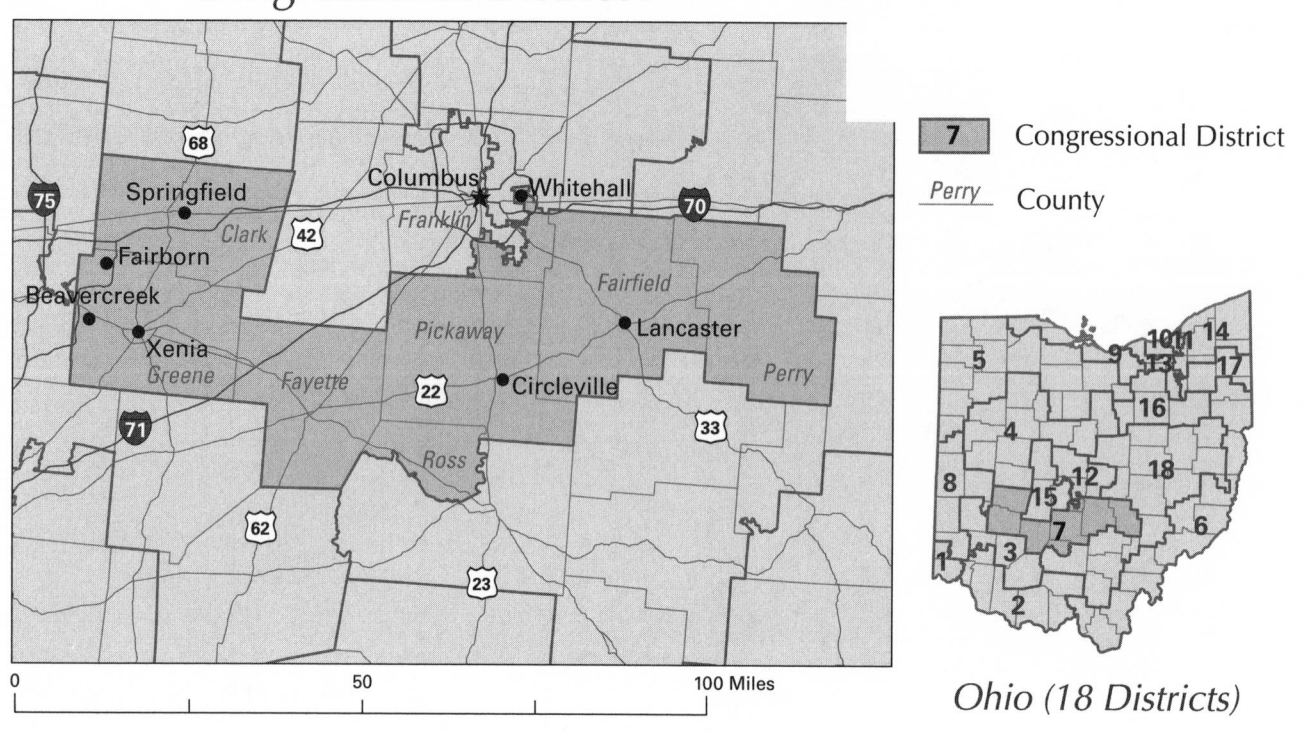

7 Congressional District
Perry County

Ohio (18 Districts)

Congressional District 8

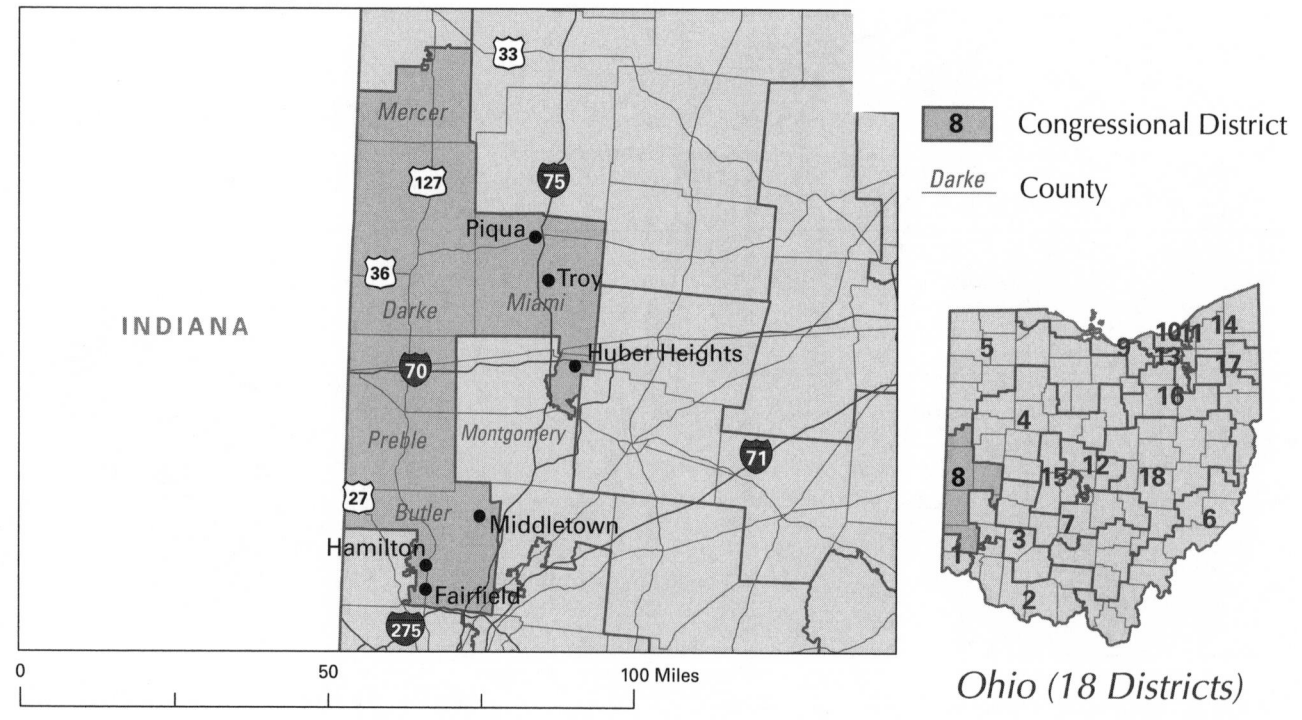

8 Congressional District
Darke County

Ohio (18 Districts)

Congressional District 9

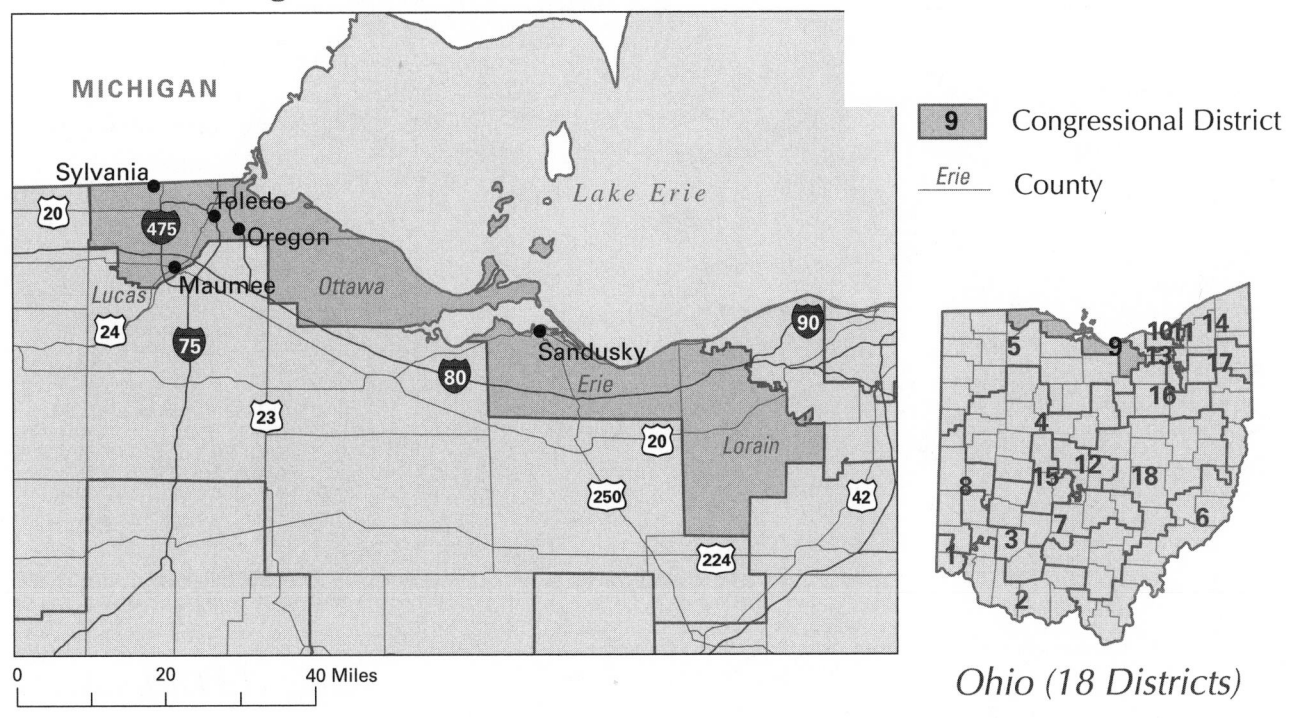

Ohio (18 Districts)

Congressional District 10

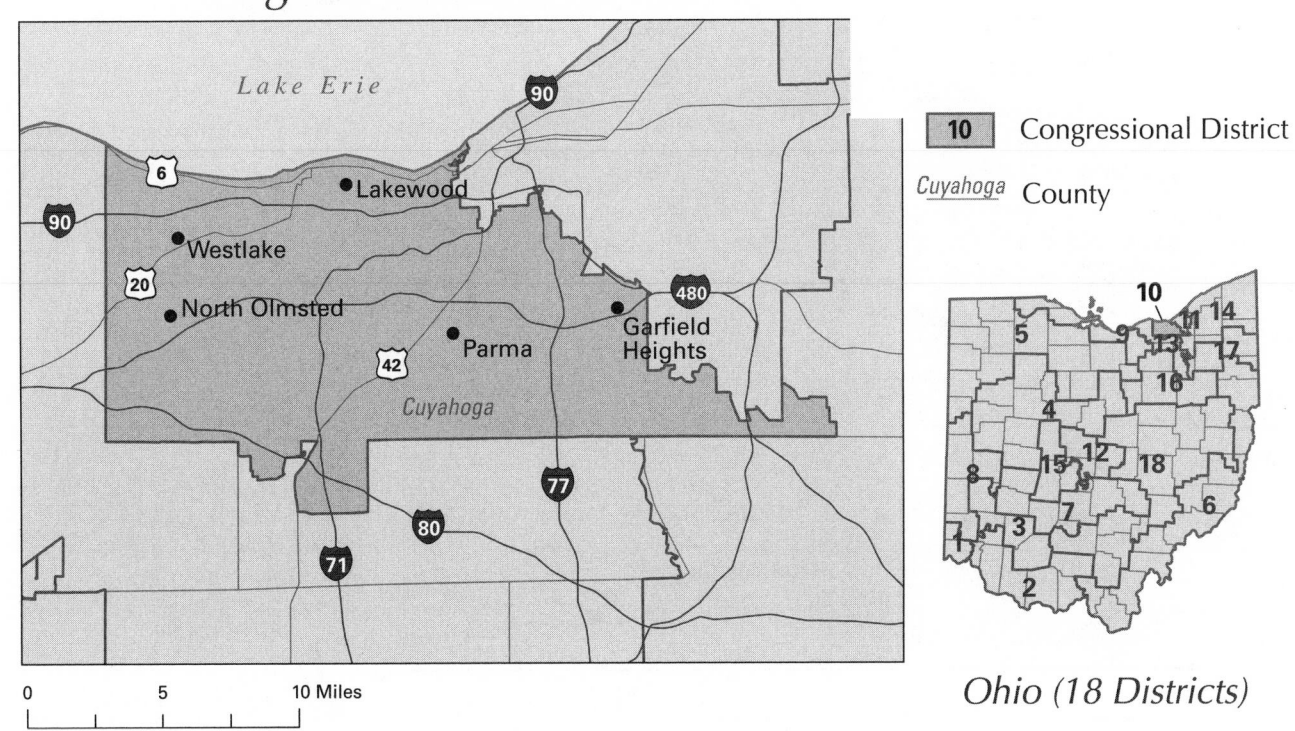

Ohio (18 Districts)

Congressional District 11

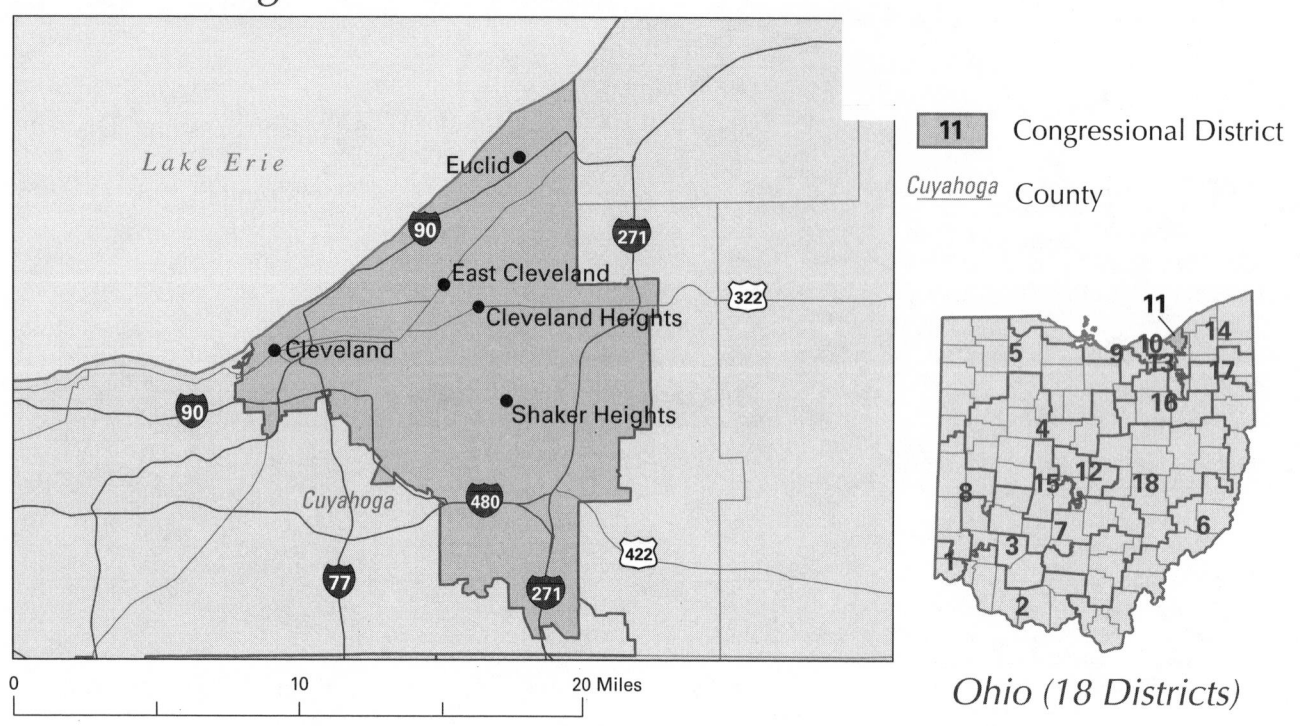

11 Congressional District

Cuyahoga County

Ohio (18 Districts)

Congressional District 12

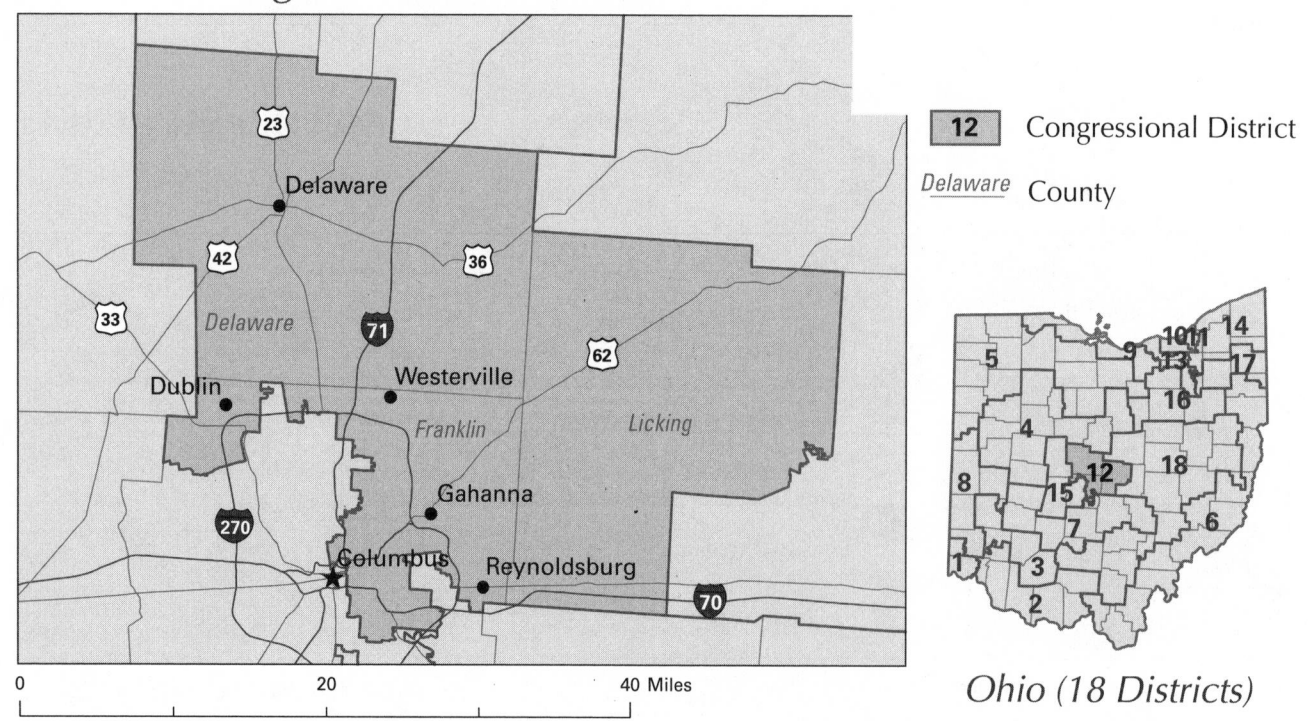

12 Congressional District

Delaware County

Ohio (18 Districts)

Congressional District 13

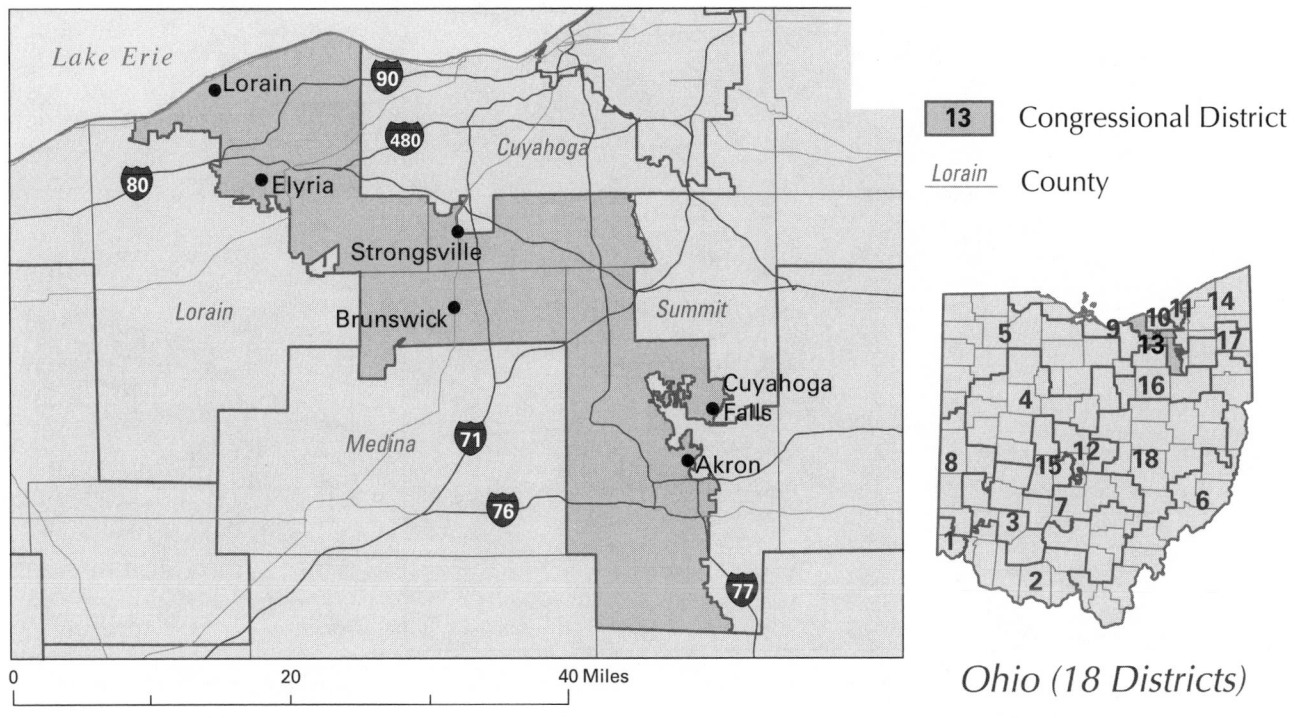

13   Congressional District

Lorain   County

Ohio (18 Districts)

Congressional District 14

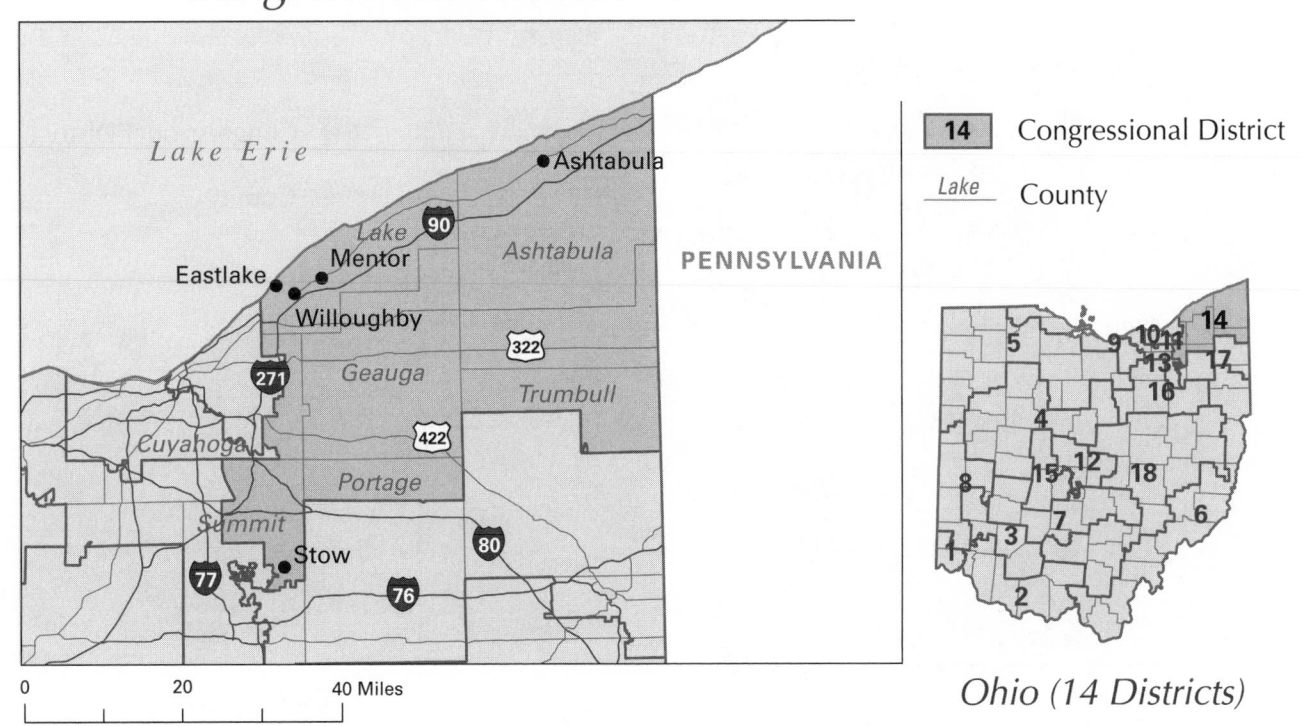

14   Congressional District

Lake   County

Ohio (14 Districts)

Congressional District 15

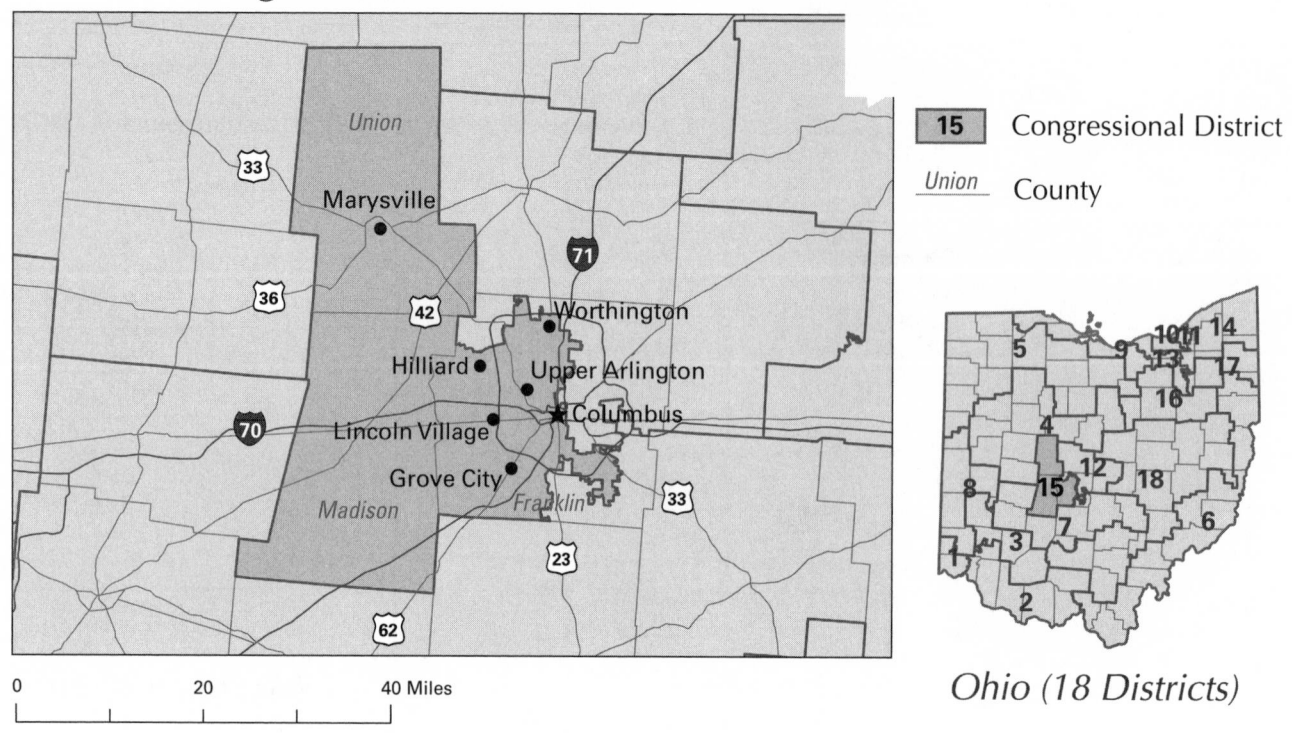

Ohio (18 Districts)

Congressional District 16

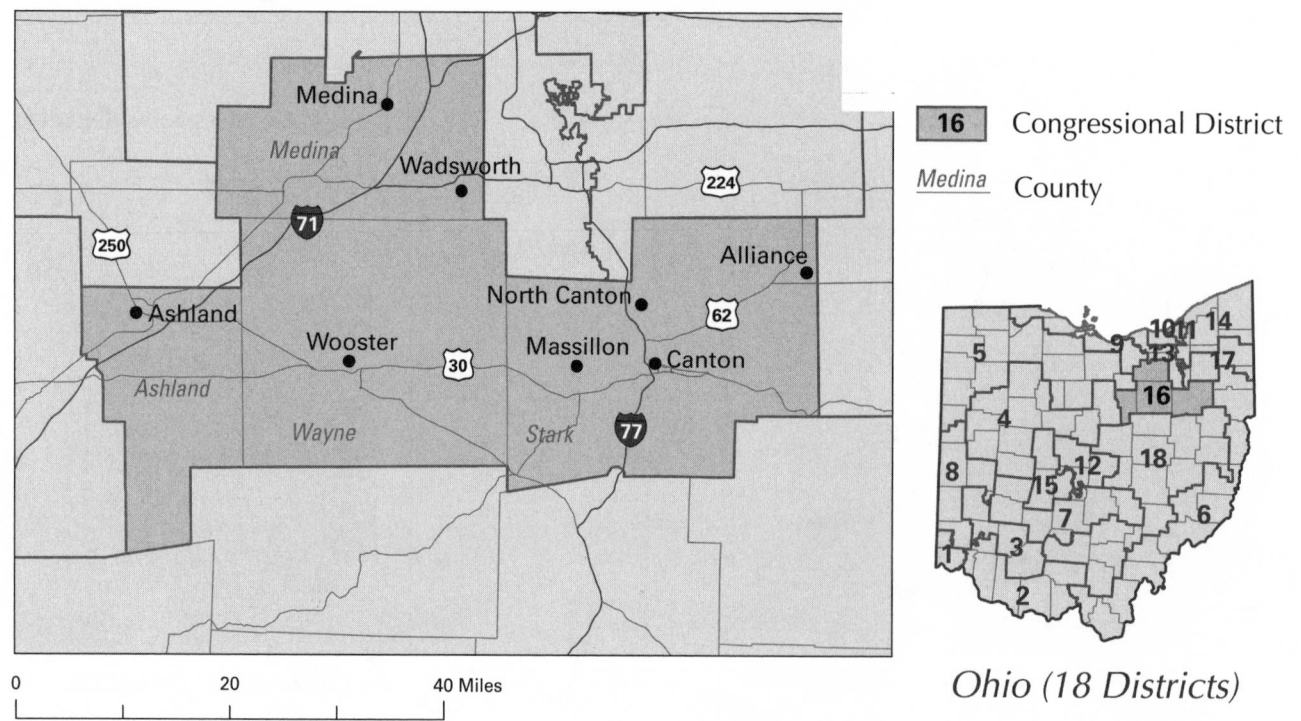

Ohio (18 Districts)

Congressional District 17

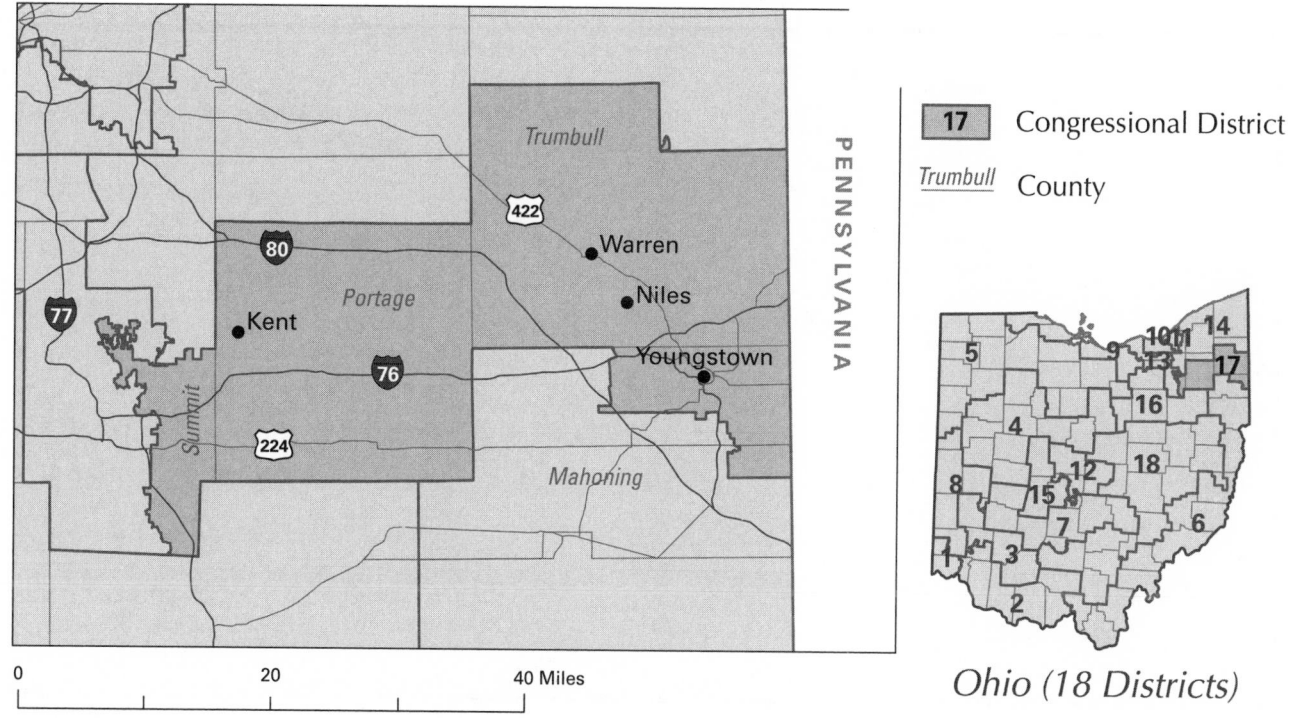

Ohio (18 Districts)

Congressional District 18

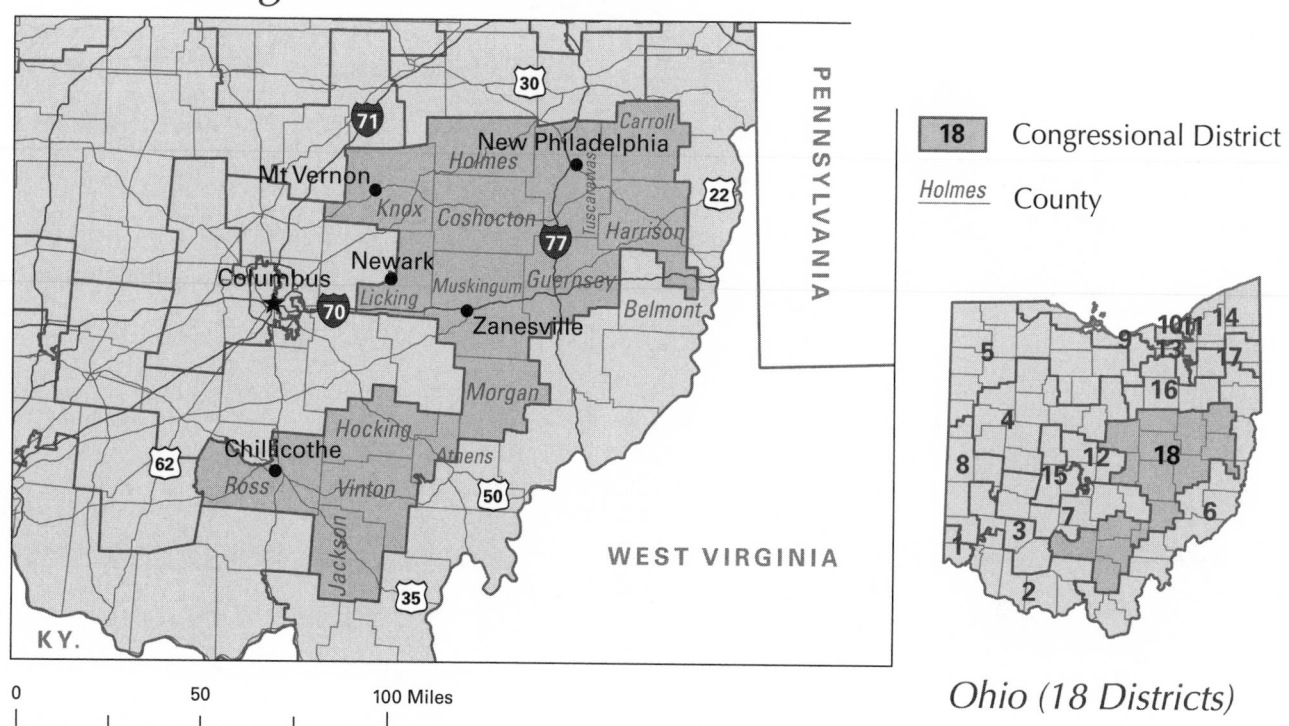

Ohio (18 Districts)

Oklahoma Congressional Districts — 5 Districts Total

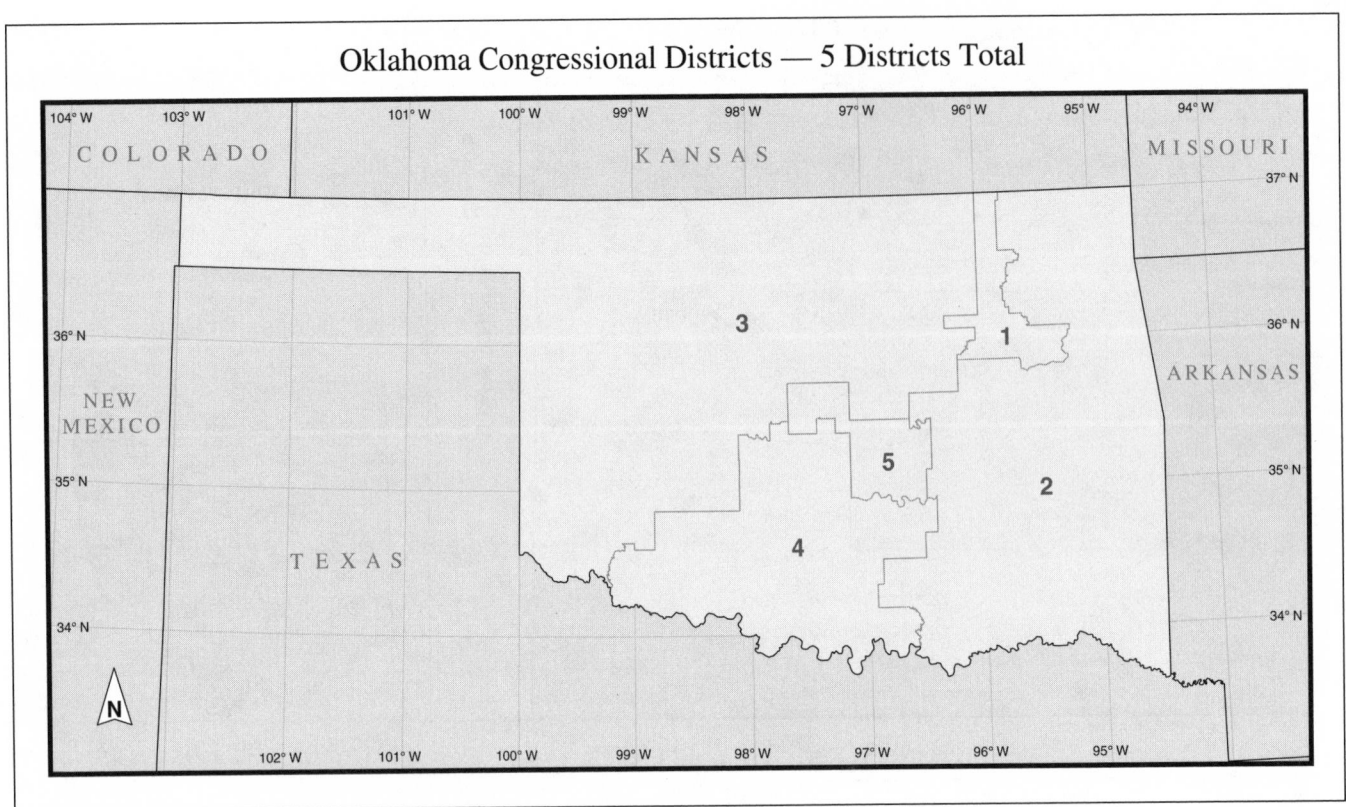

OKLAHOMA—110th CONGRESSIONAL DISTRICTS BY COUNTIES

County	Congressional District
Adair	2
Alfalfa	3
Atoka	2
Beaver	3
Beckham	3
Blaine	3
Bryan	2
Caddo	3
Canadian	3, 4
Carter	4
Cherokee	2
Choctaw	2
Cimarron	3
Cleveland	4
Coal	2
Comanche	4
Cotton	4
Craig	2
Creek	1, 3
Custer	3
Delaware	2
Dewey	3
Ellis	3
Garfield	3
Garvin	4
Grady	4

County	Congressional District
Grant	3
Greer	3
Harmon	3
Harper	3
Haskell	2
Hughes	2
Jackson	3
Jefferson	4
Johnston	2
Kay	3
Kingfisher	3
Kiowa	3
Latimer	2
Le Flore	2
Lincoln	3
Logan	3
Love	4
McClain	4
McCurtain	2
McIntosh	2
Major	3
Marshall	4
Mayes	2
Murray	4
Muskogee	2
Noble	3

County	Congressional District
Nowata	2
Okfuskee	2
Oklahoma	4, 5
Okmulgee	2
Osage	3
Ottawa	2
Pawnee	3
Payne	3
Pittsburg	2
Pontotoc	4
Pottawatomie	5
Pushmataha	2
Roger Mills	3
Rogers	1, 2
Seminole	5
Sequoyah	2
Stephens	4
Texas	3
Tillman	4
Tulsa	1
Wagoner	1
Washington	1
Washita	3
Woods	3
Woodward	3

Congressional District 1

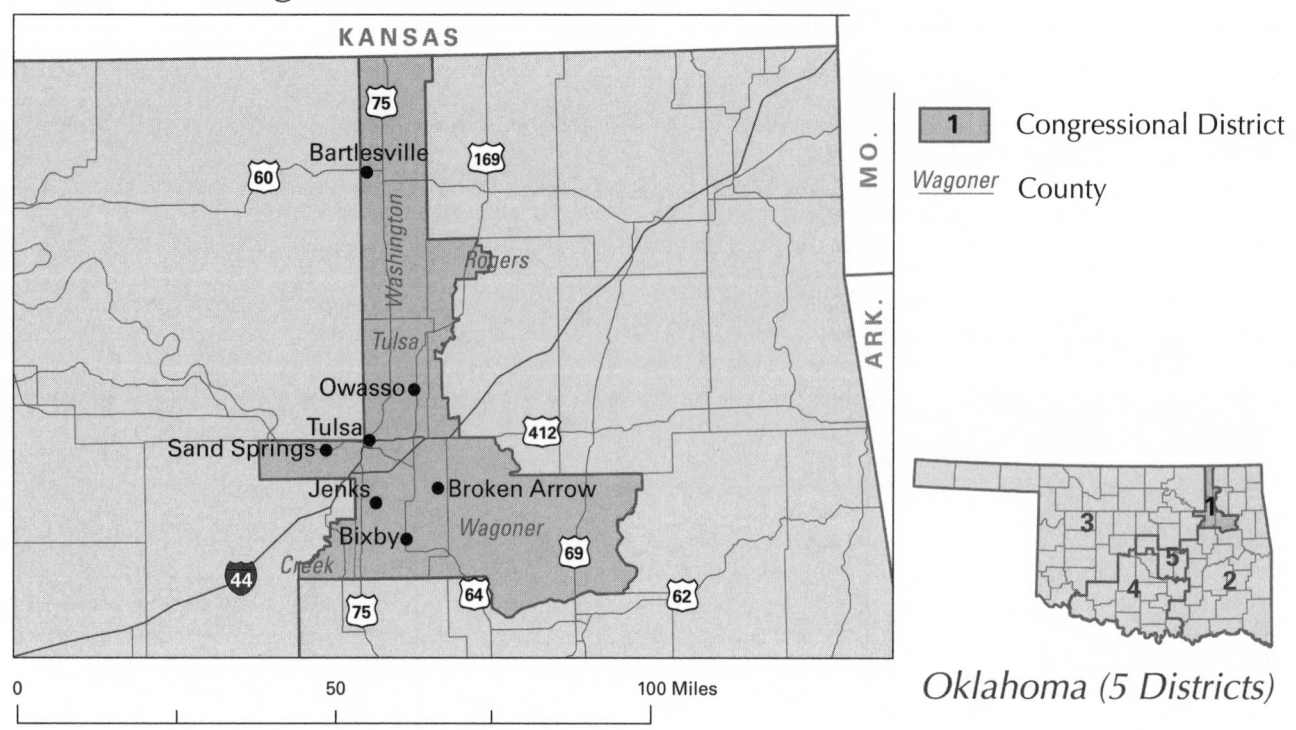

Oklahoma (5 Districts)

Congressional District 2

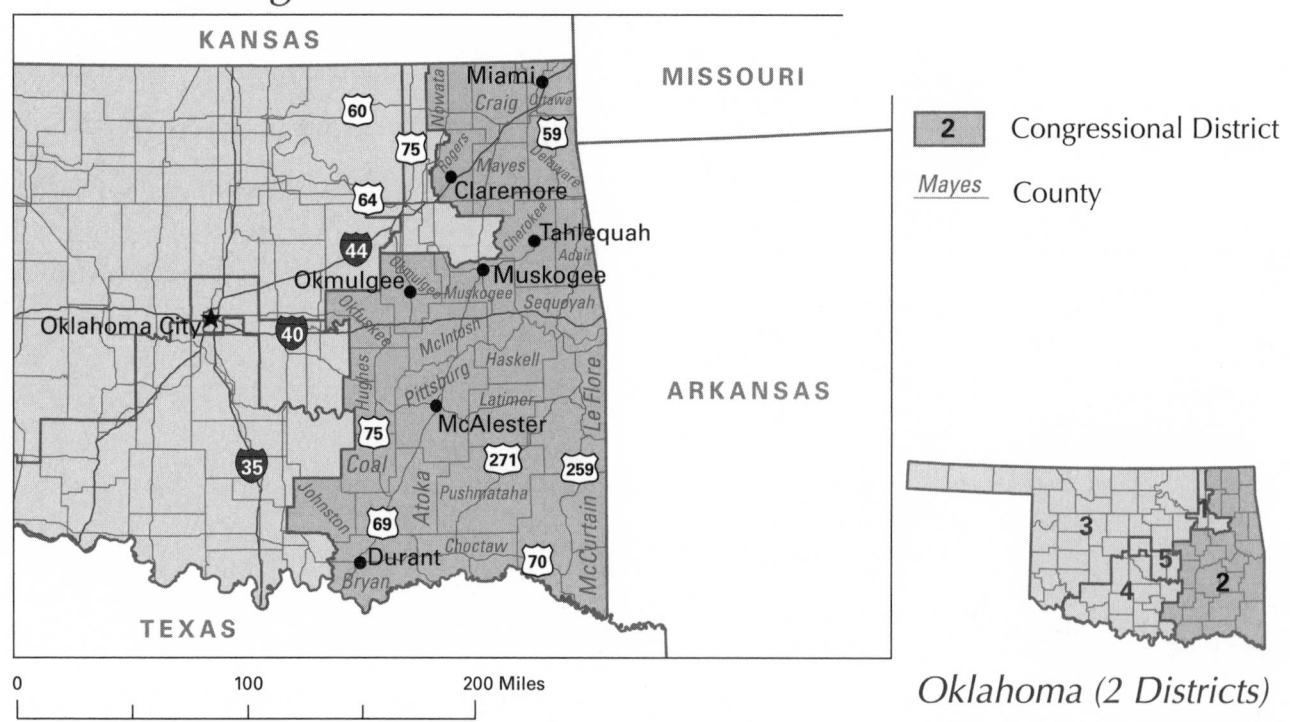

Oklahoma (2 Districts)

Congressional District 3

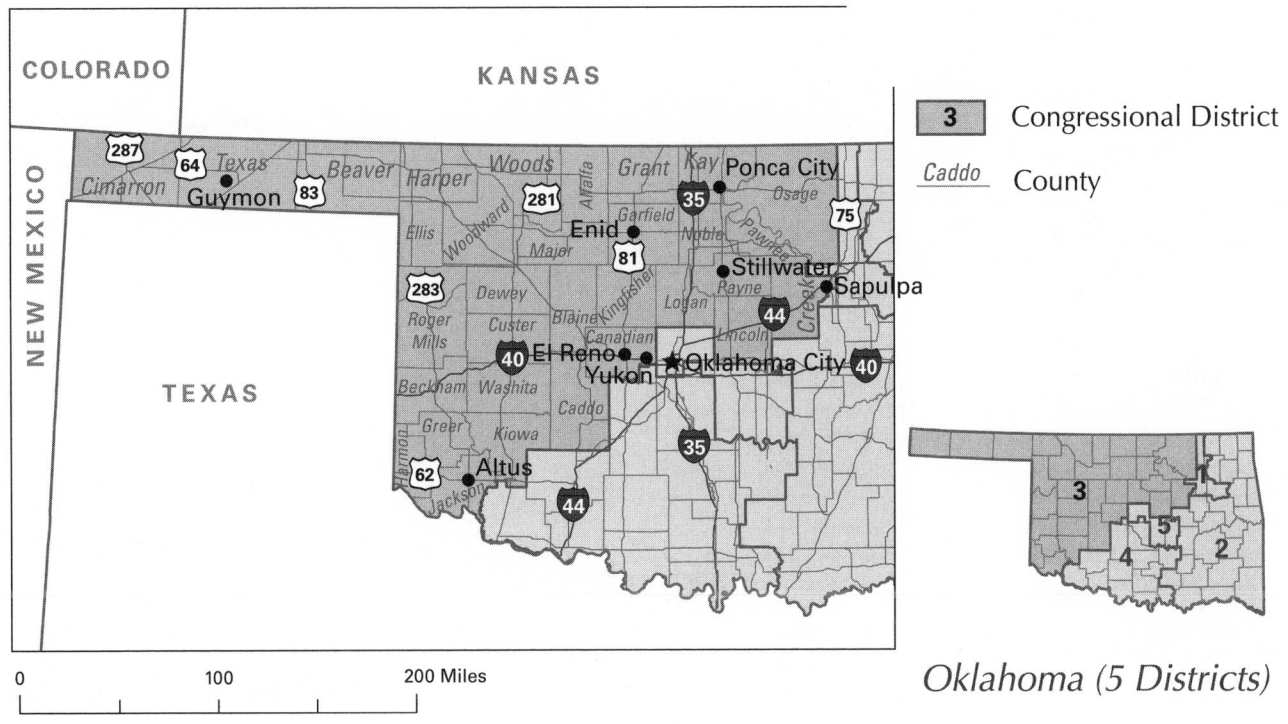

Oklahoma (5 Districts)

Congressional District 4

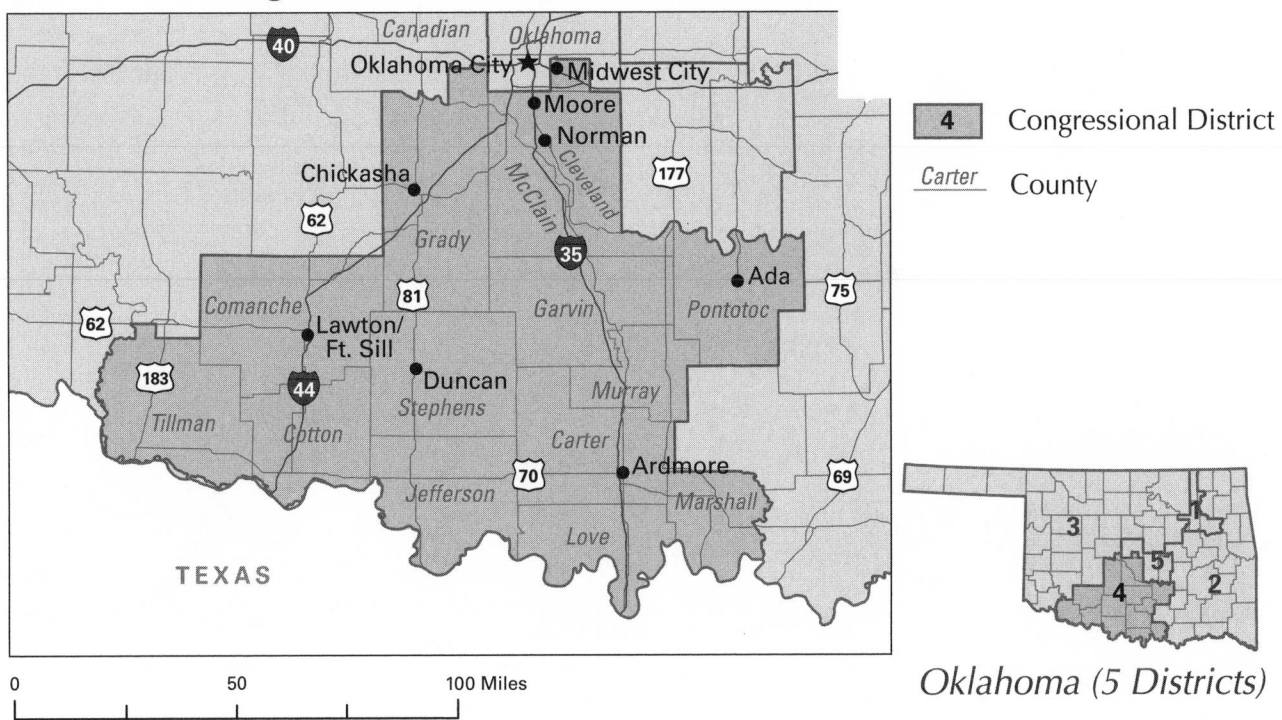

Oklahoma (5 Districts)

Congressional District 5

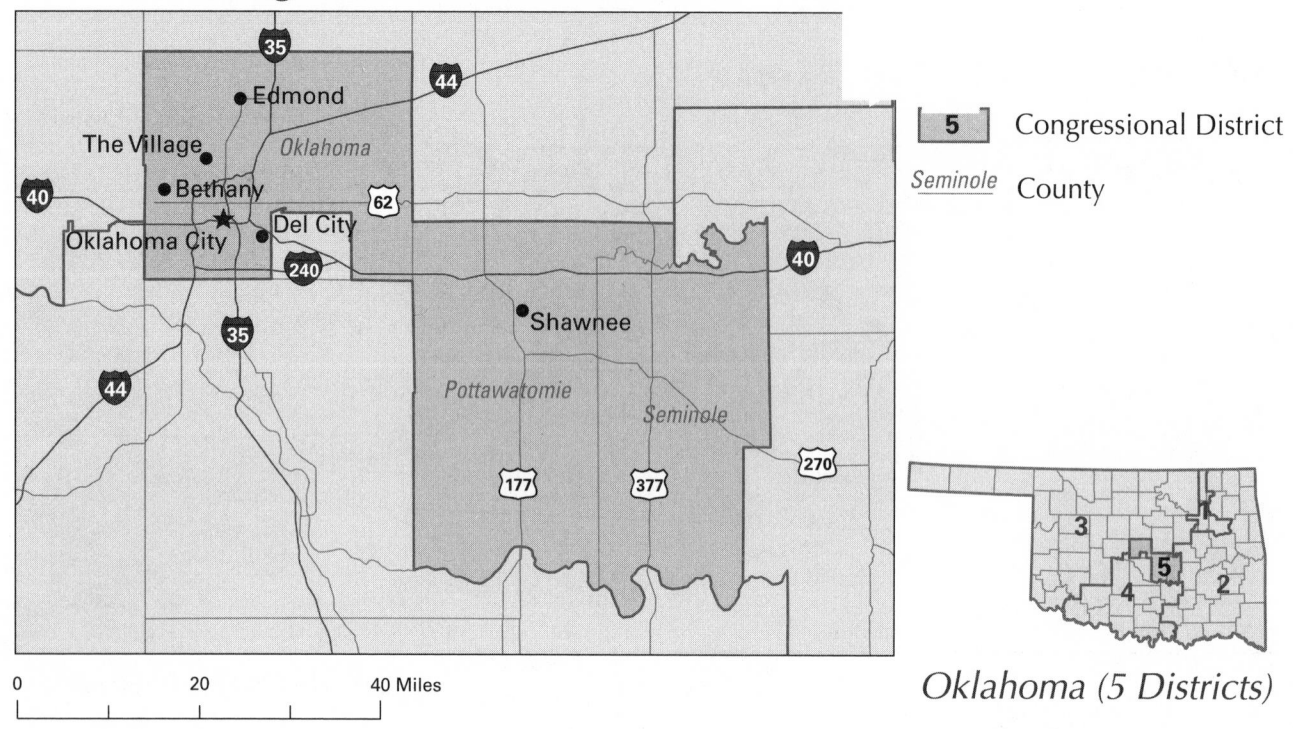

5	Congressional District
Seminole	County

Oklahoma (5 Districts)

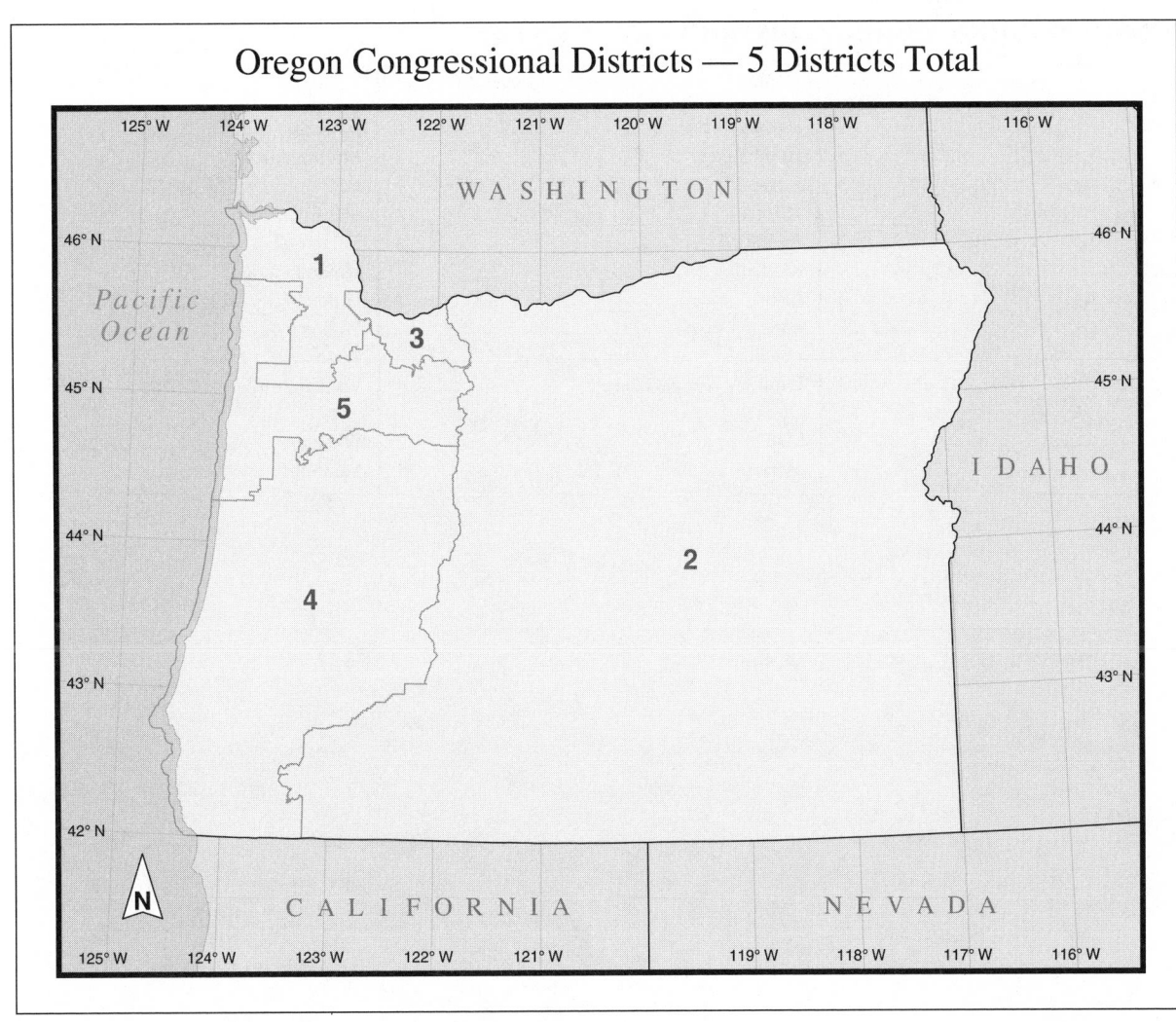

Oregon Congressional Districts — 5 Districts Total

OREGON—110th CONGRESSIONAL DISTRICTS BY COUNTIES

County	Congressional District
Baker	2
Benton	4, 5
Clackamas	3, 5
Clatsop	1
Columbia	1
Coos	4
Crook	2
Curry	4
Deschutes	2
Douglas	4
Gilliam	2
Grant	2

County	Congressional District
Harney	2
Hood River	2
Jackson	2
Jefferson	2
Josephine	2, 4
Klamath	2
Lake	2
Lane	4
Lincoln	5
Linn	4
Malheur	2
Marion	5

County	Congressional District
Morrow	2
Multnomah	1, 3, 5
Polk	5
Sherman	2
Tillamook	5
Umatilla	2
Union	2
Wallowa	2
Wasco	2
Washington	1
Wheeler	2
Yamhill	1

Congressional District 1

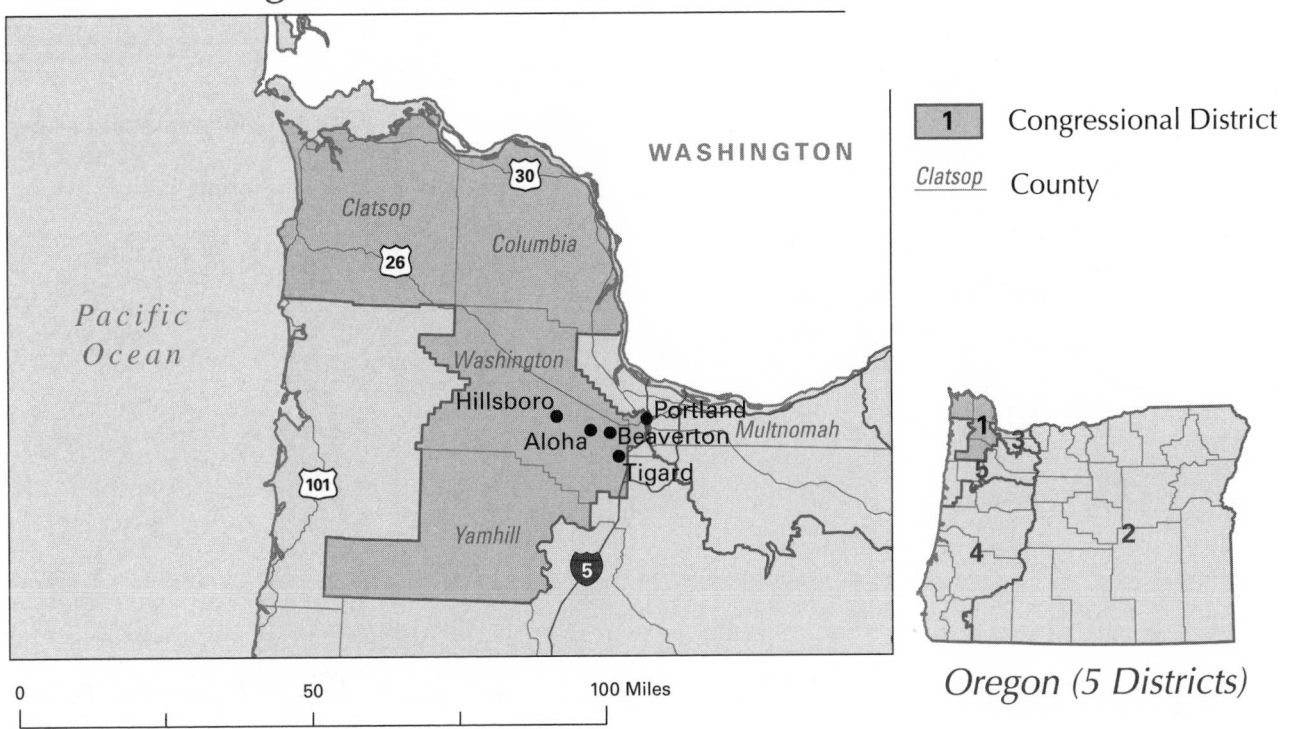

Oregon (5 Districts)

Congressional District 2

Oregon (5 Districts)

Congressional District 3

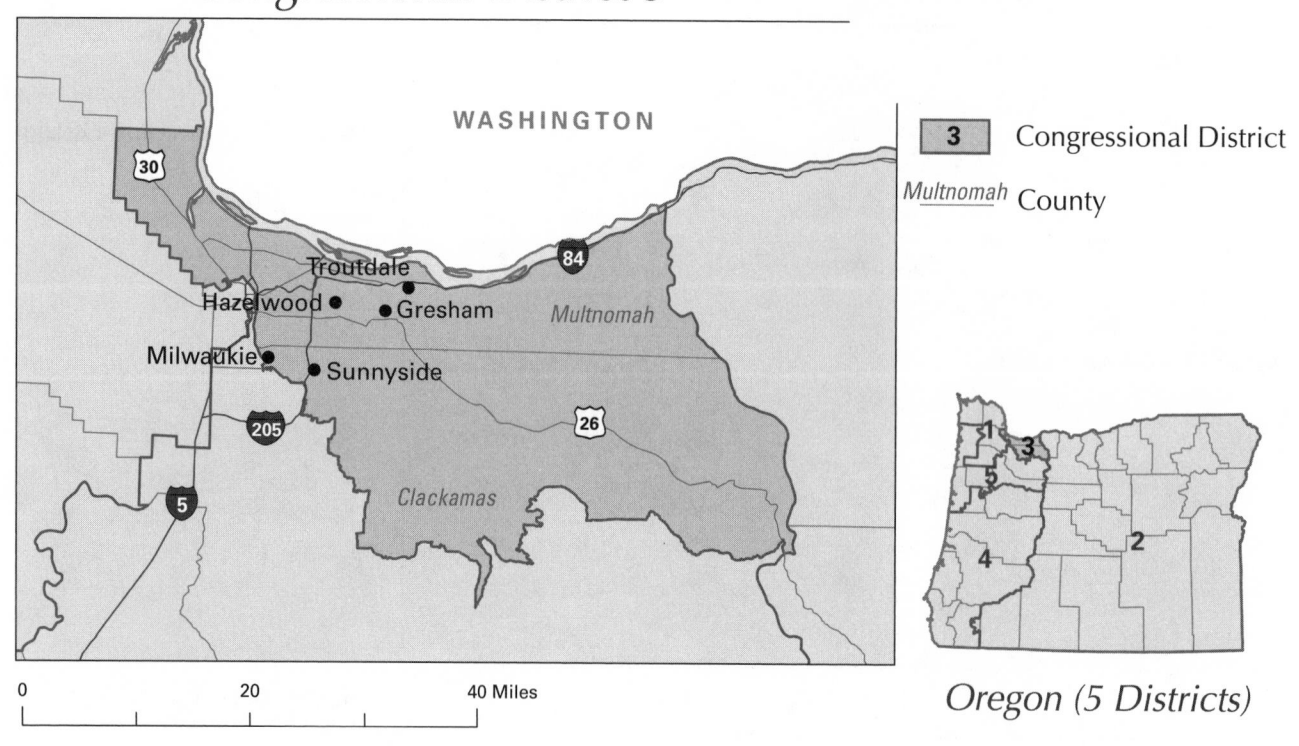

Oregon (5 Districts)

Congressional District 4

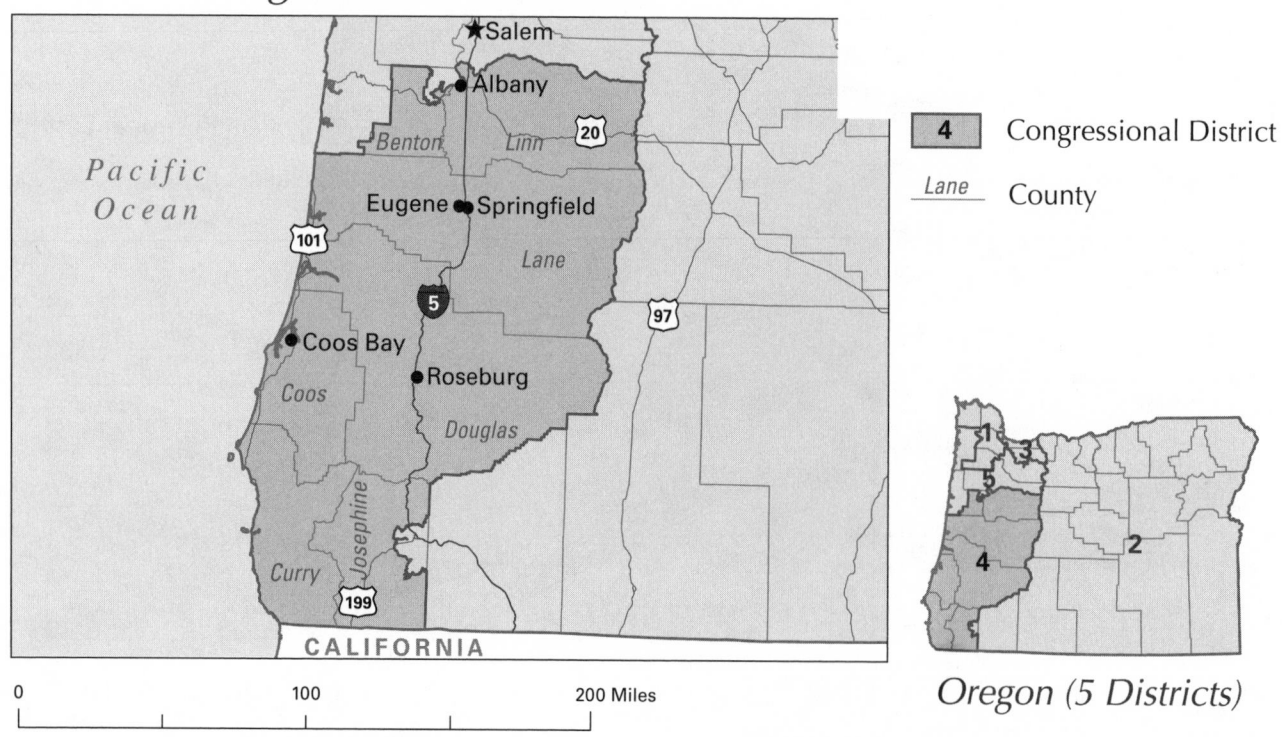

Oregon (5 Districts)

Congressional District 5

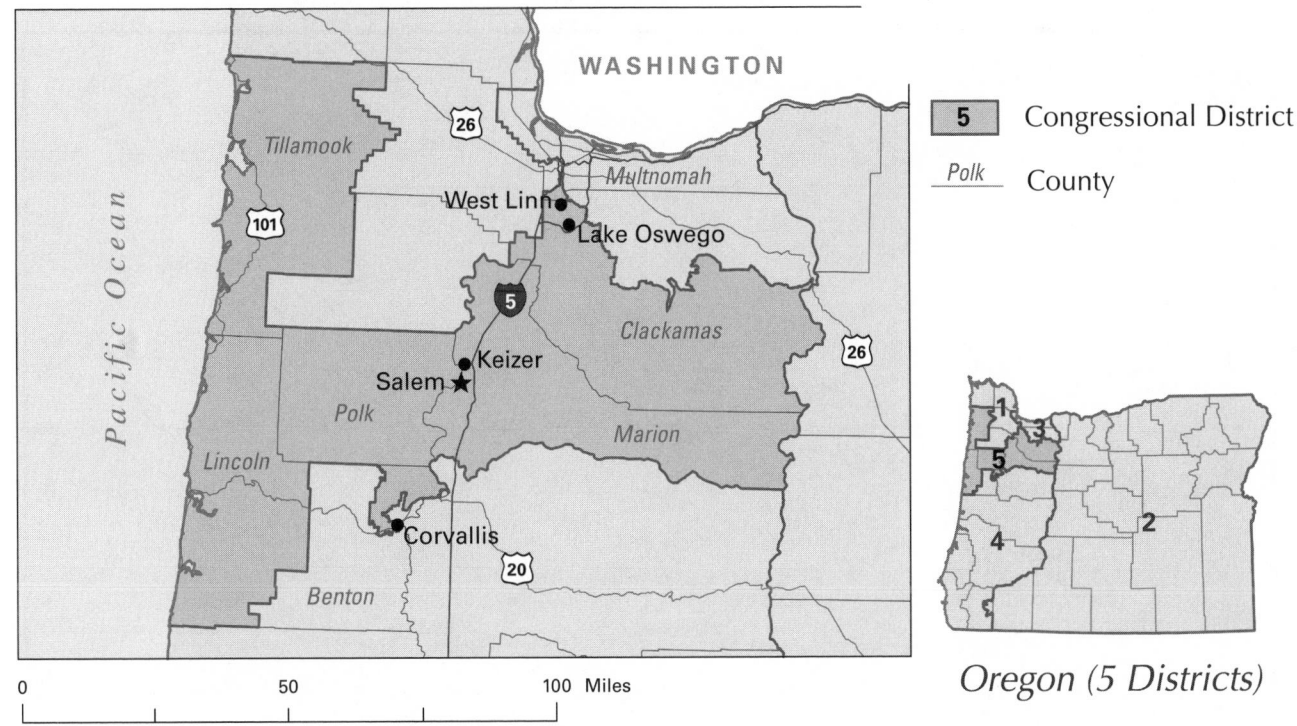

Oregon (5 Districts)

Pennsylvania Congressional Districts - 19 Districts Total

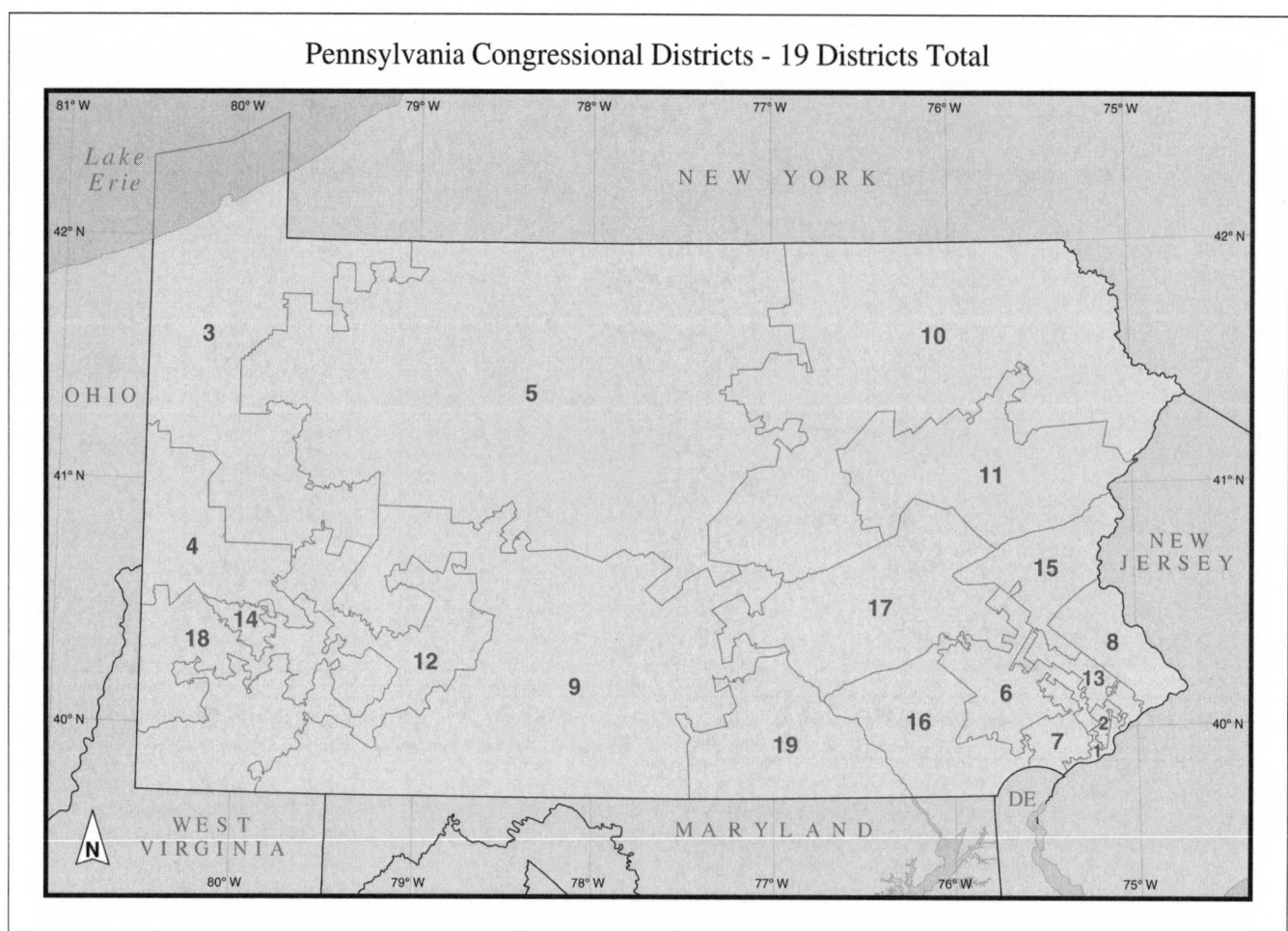

PENNSYLVANIA—110th CONGRESSIONAL DISTRICTS BY COUNTIES

County	Congressional District
Adams County	19
Allegheny County	4, 12, 14, 18
Armstrong County	3, 12
Beaver County	4, 18
Bedford County	9
Berks County	6, 15, 16, 17
Blair County	9
Bradford County	10
Bucks County	8
Butler County	3, 4
Cambria County	9, 12
Cameron County	5
Carbon County	11
Centre County	5, 10
Chester County	6, 7, 16
Clarion County	5
Clearfield County	5, 9
Clinton County	5
Columbia County	11
Crawford County	3, 5
Cumberland County	9, 19
Dauphin County	17
Delaware County	1, 7
Elk County	5

County	Congressional District
Erie County	3
Fayette County	9, 12
Forest County	5
Franklin County	9, 19
Fulton County	9
Greene County	12
Huntingdon County	9
Indiana County	9, 12
Jefferson County	5
Juniata County	5, 9
Lackawanna County	10, 11
Lancaster County	16
Lawrence County	4
Lebanon County	17
Lehigh County	6, 8, 15
Luzerne County	10, 11
Lycoming County	5, 10, 11
McKean County	5
Mercer County	3, 4
Mifflin County	5, 9
Monroe County	11
Montgomery County	2, 6, 7, 8, 13, 15
Montour County	10
Northampton County	15

County	Congressional District
Northumberland County	10
Perry County	9, 17
Philadelphia County	1, 2, 8, 13
Pike County	10
Potter County	5
Schuylkill County	17
Snyder County	10
Somerset County	9, 12
Sullivan County	10
Susquehanna County	10
Tioga County	5, 10
Union County	10
Venango County	3, 5
Warren County	3, 5
Washington County	12, 18
Wayne County	10
Westmoreland County	4, 9, 12, 18
Wyoming County	10
York County	19

Congressional District 1

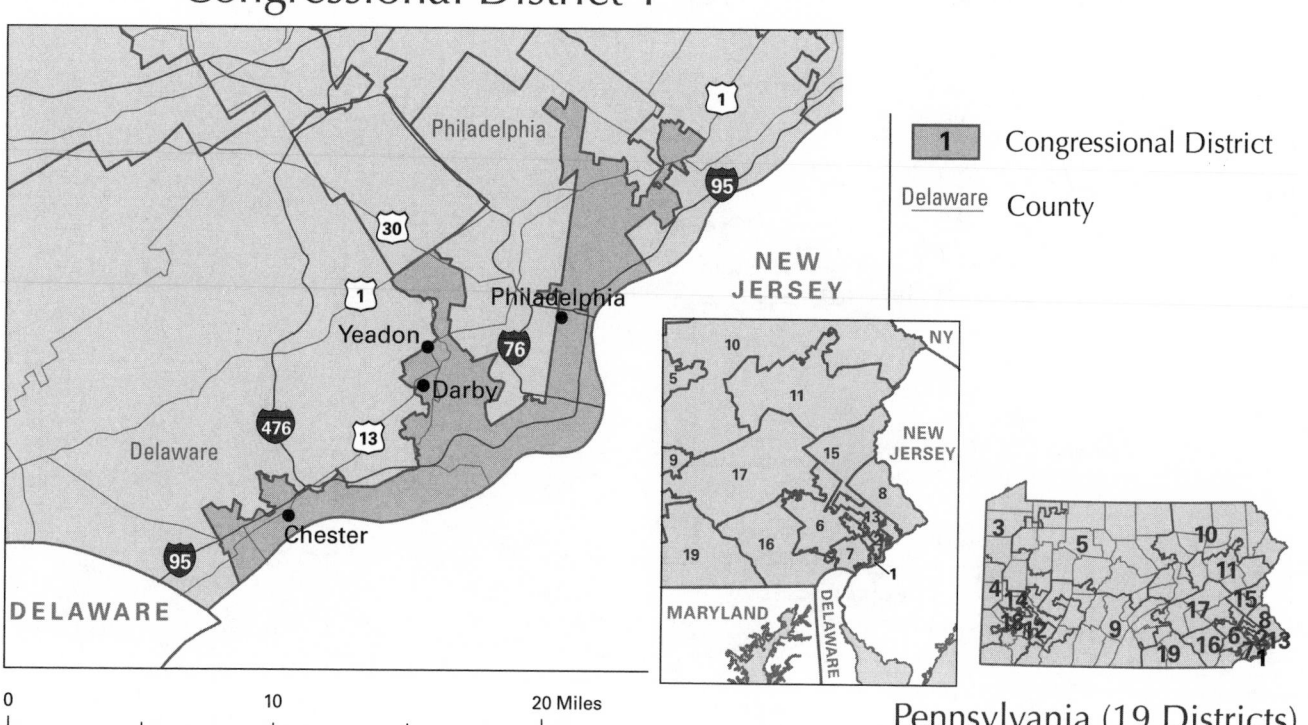

Pennsylvania (19 Districts)

Congressional District 2

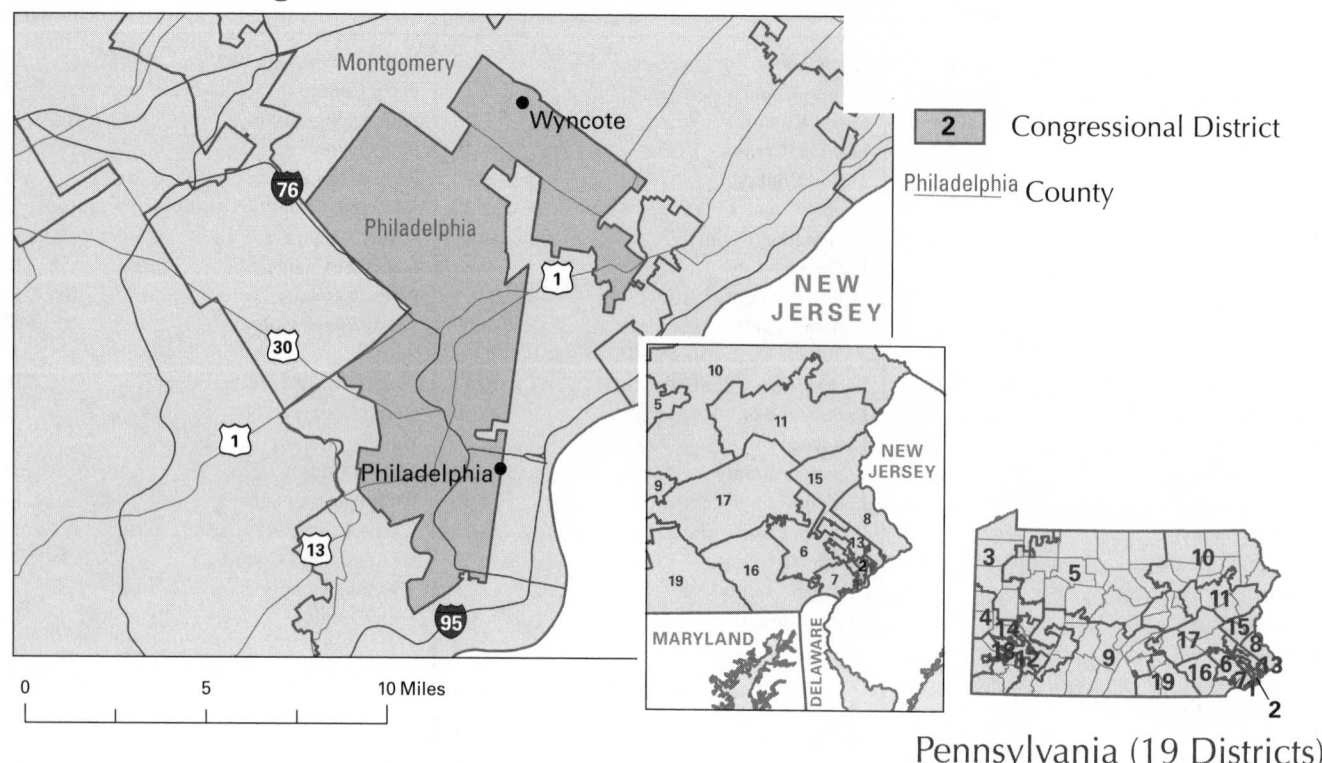

Pennsylvania (19 Districts)

Congressional District 3

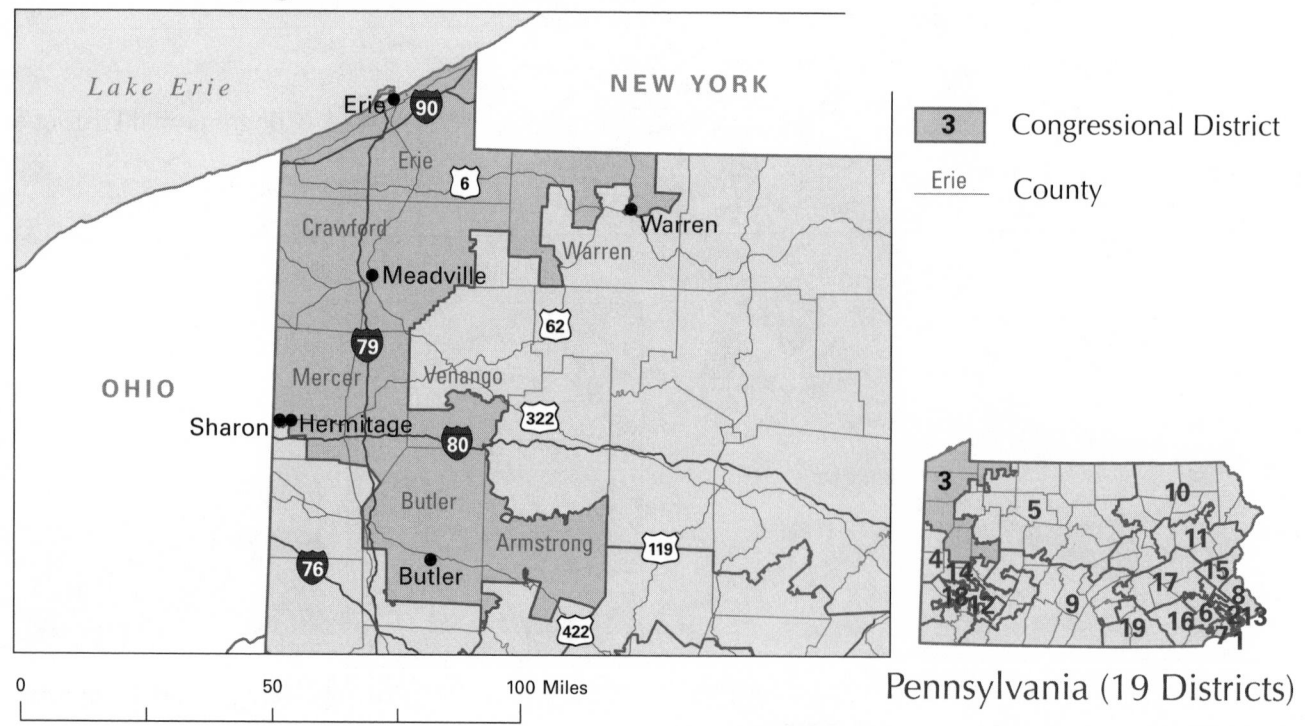

Pennsylvania (19 Districts)

Congressional District 4

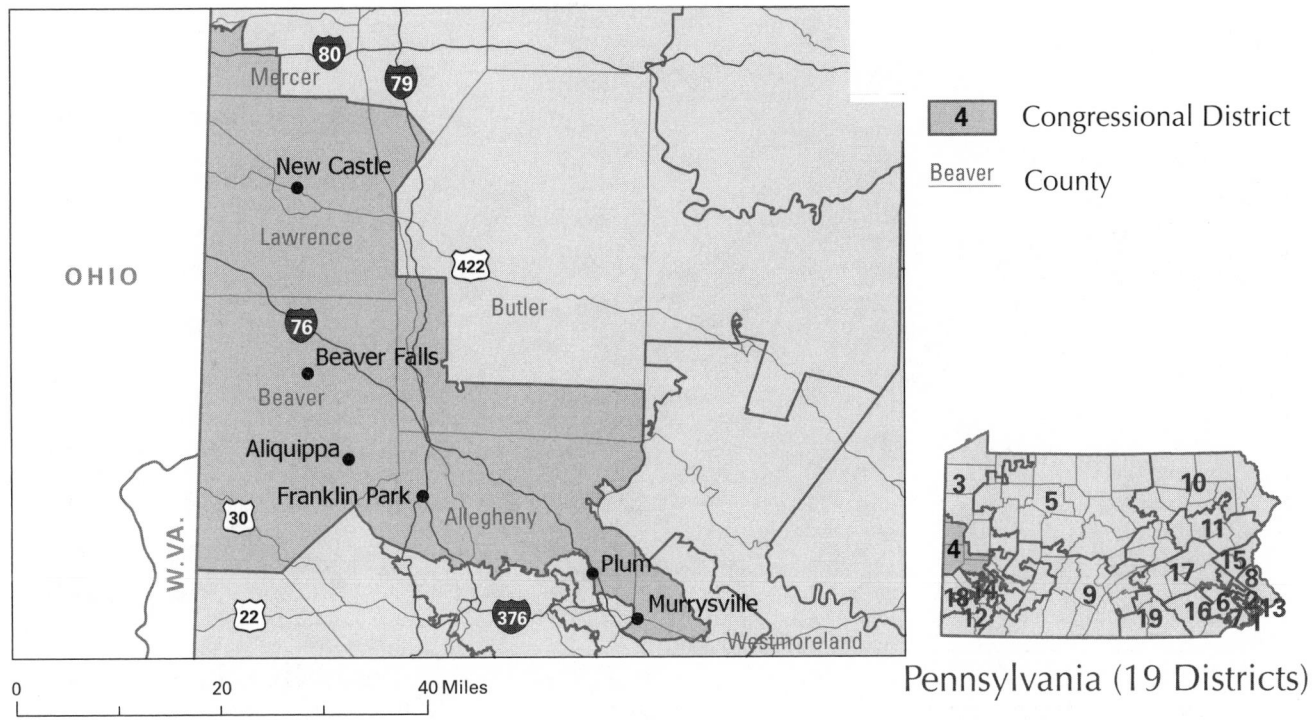

4 Congressional District
Beaver County

Pennsylvania (19 Districts)

Congressional District 5

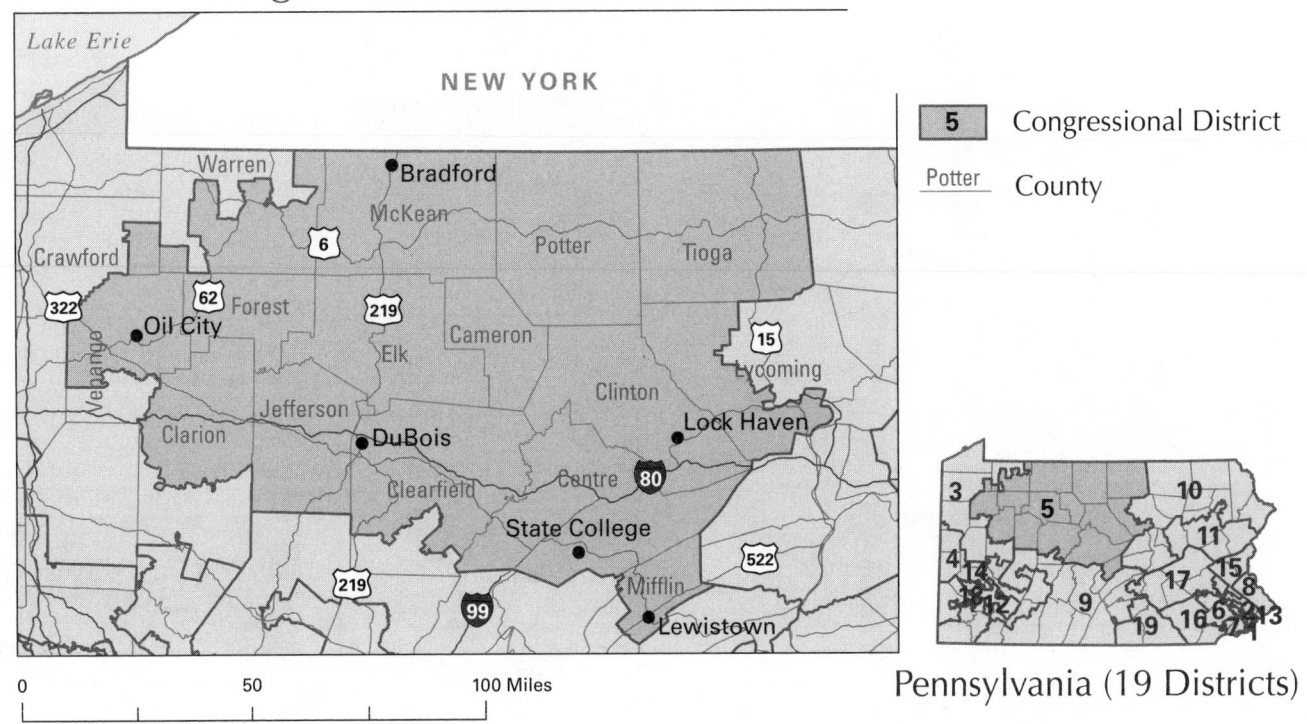

5 Congressional District
Potter County

Pennsylvania (19 Districts)

Congressional District 6

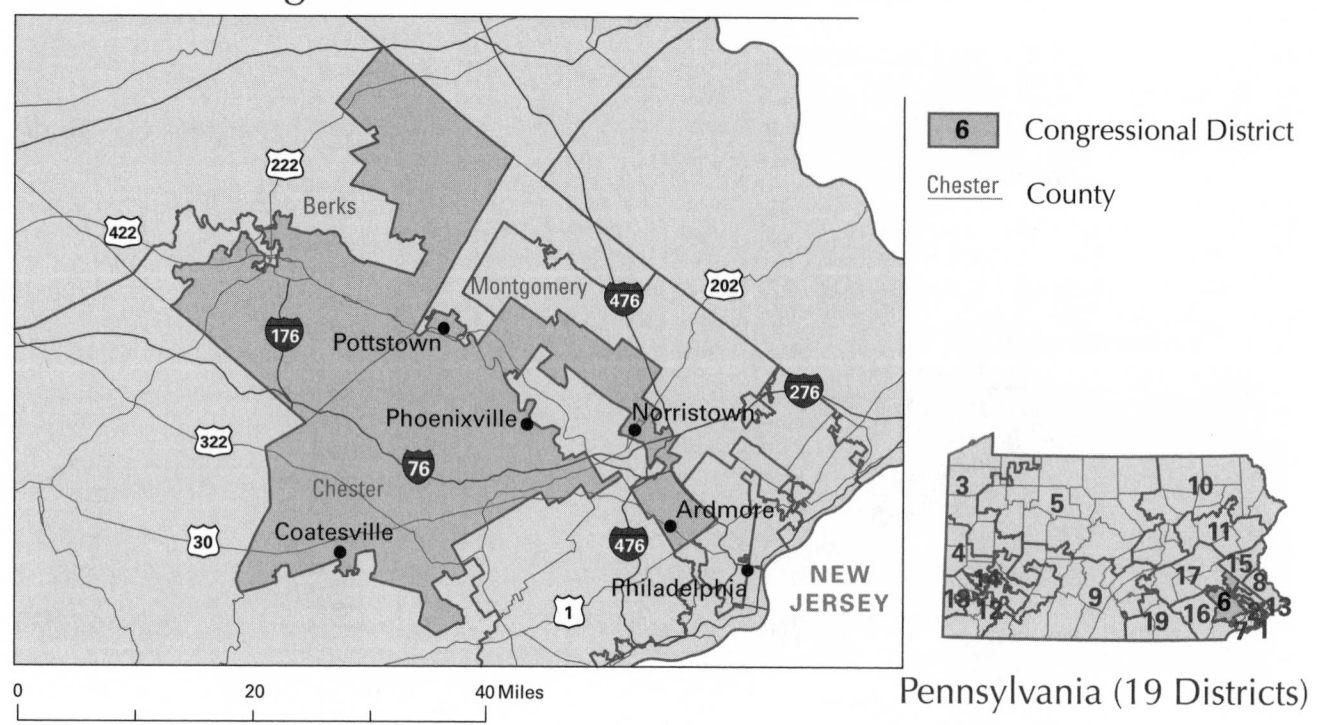

6 Congressional District

Chester County

Pennsylvania (19 Districts)

Congressional District 7

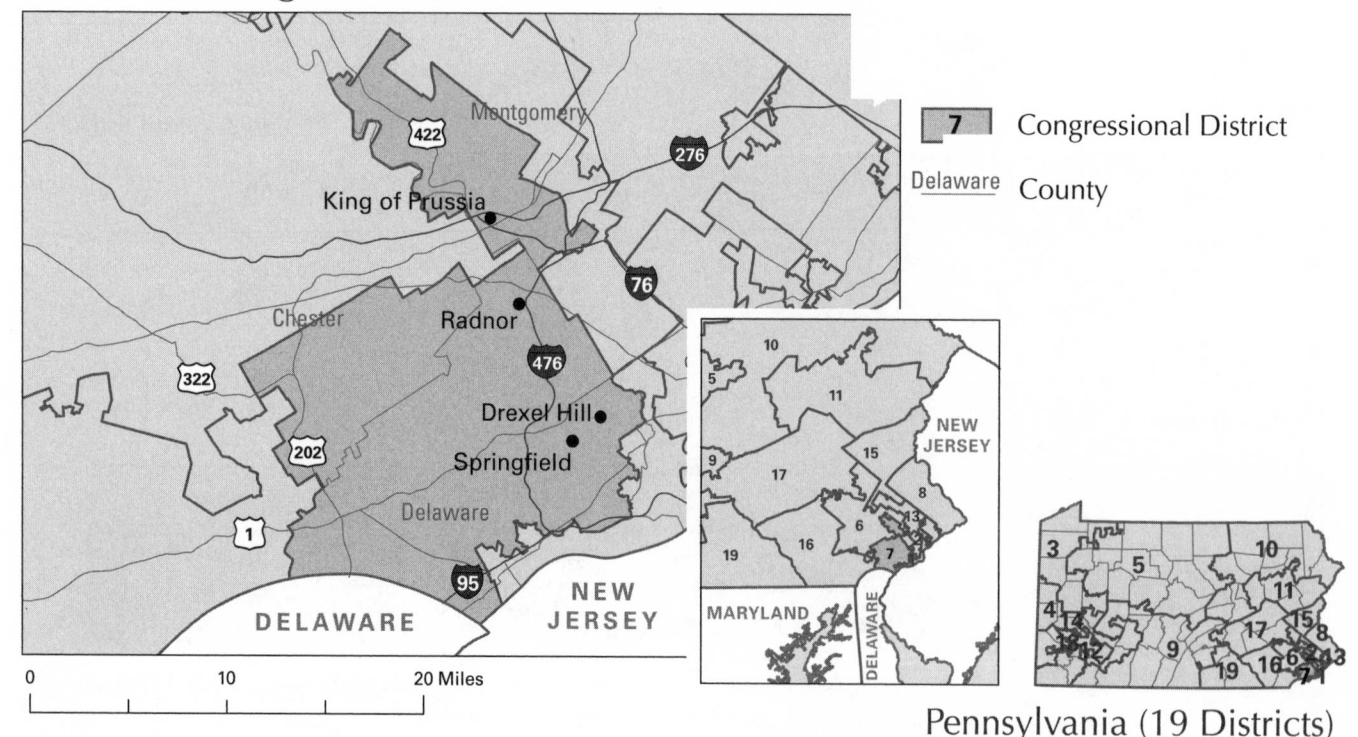

7 Congressional District

Delaware County

Pennsylvania (19 Districts)

Congressional District 8

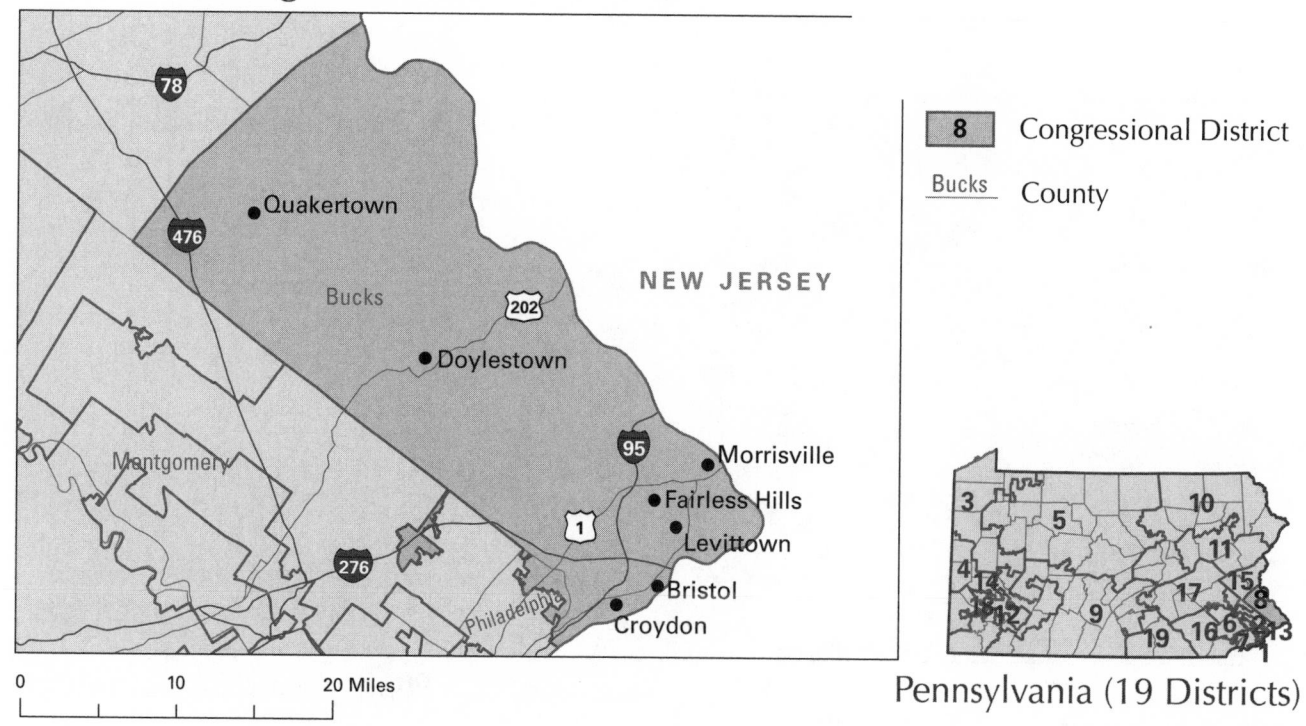

8   Congressional District

Bucks   County

Pennsylvania (19 Districts)

Congressional District 9

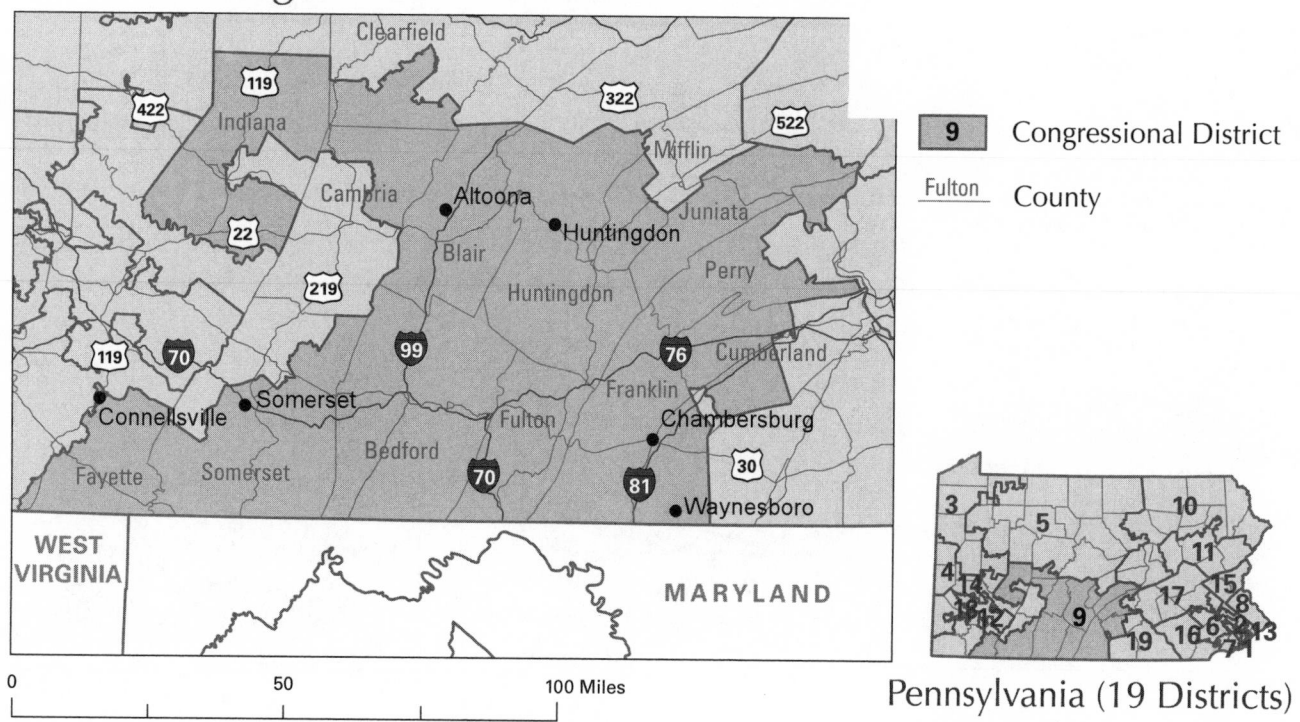

9   Congressional District

Fulton   County

Pennsylvania (19 Districts)

Congressional District 10

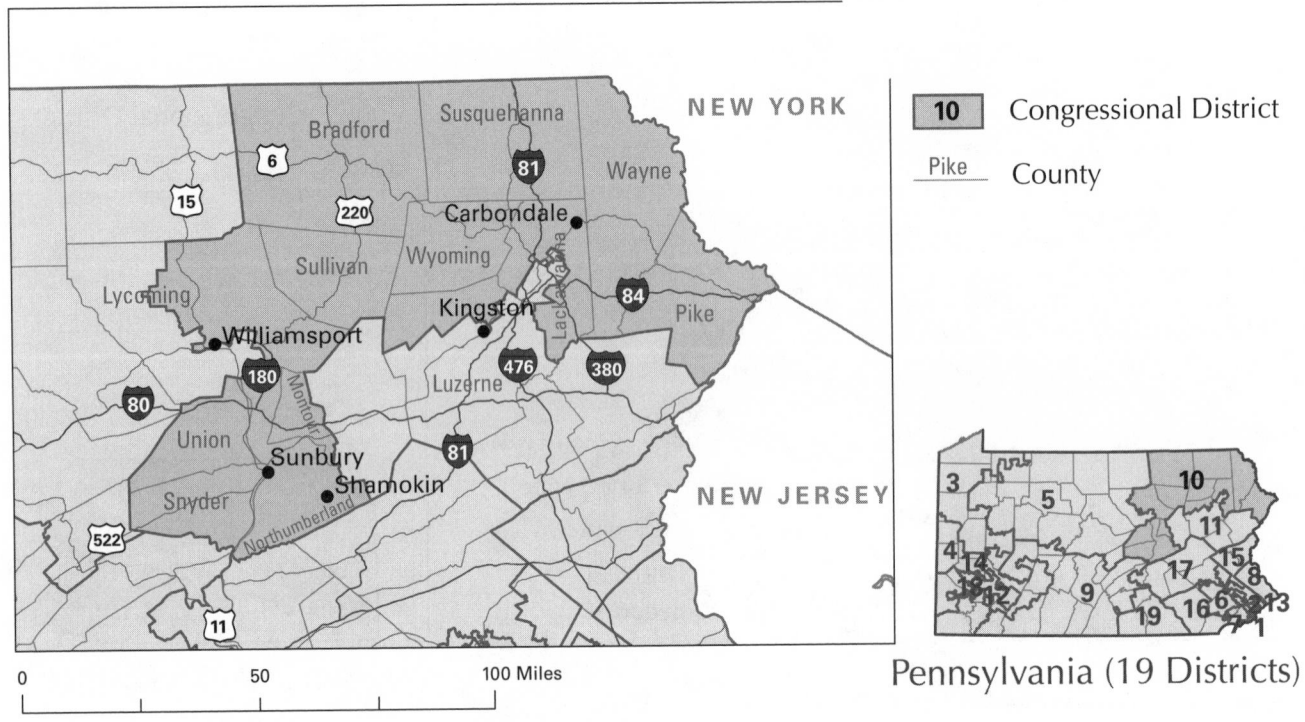

Pennsylvania (19 Districts)

Congressional District 11

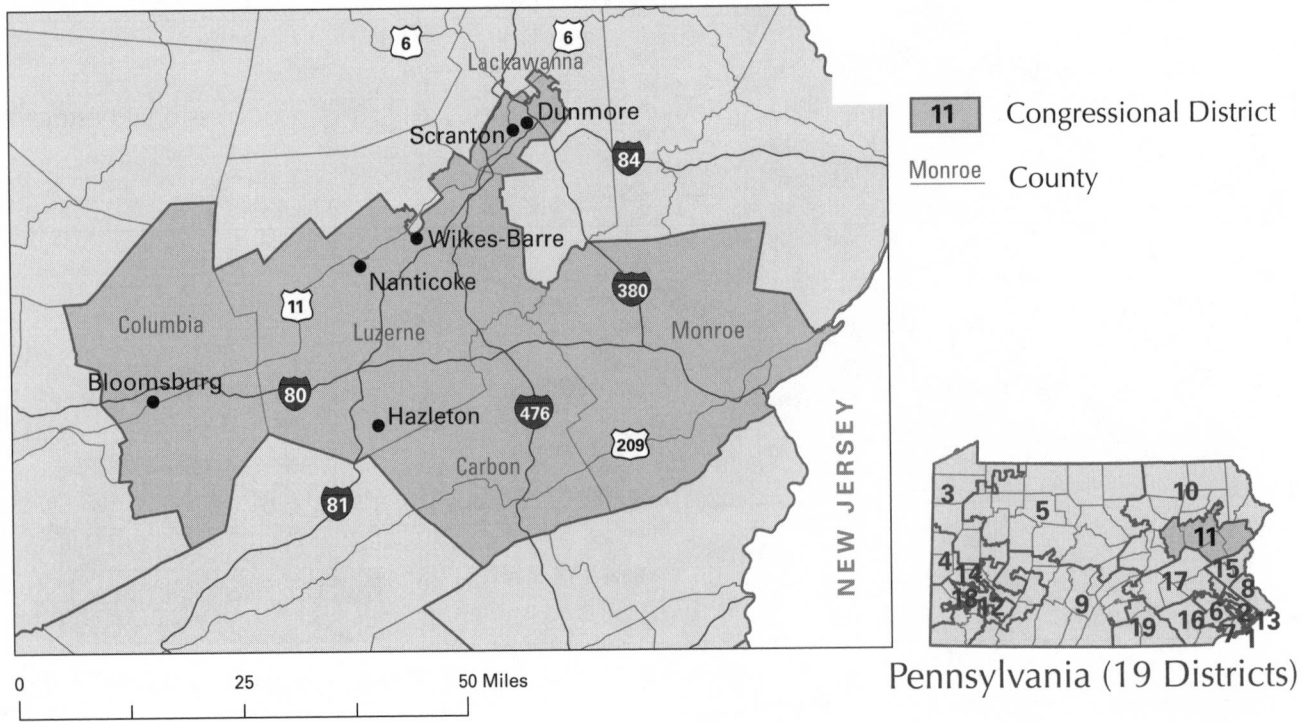

Pennsylvania (19 Districts)

Congressional District 12

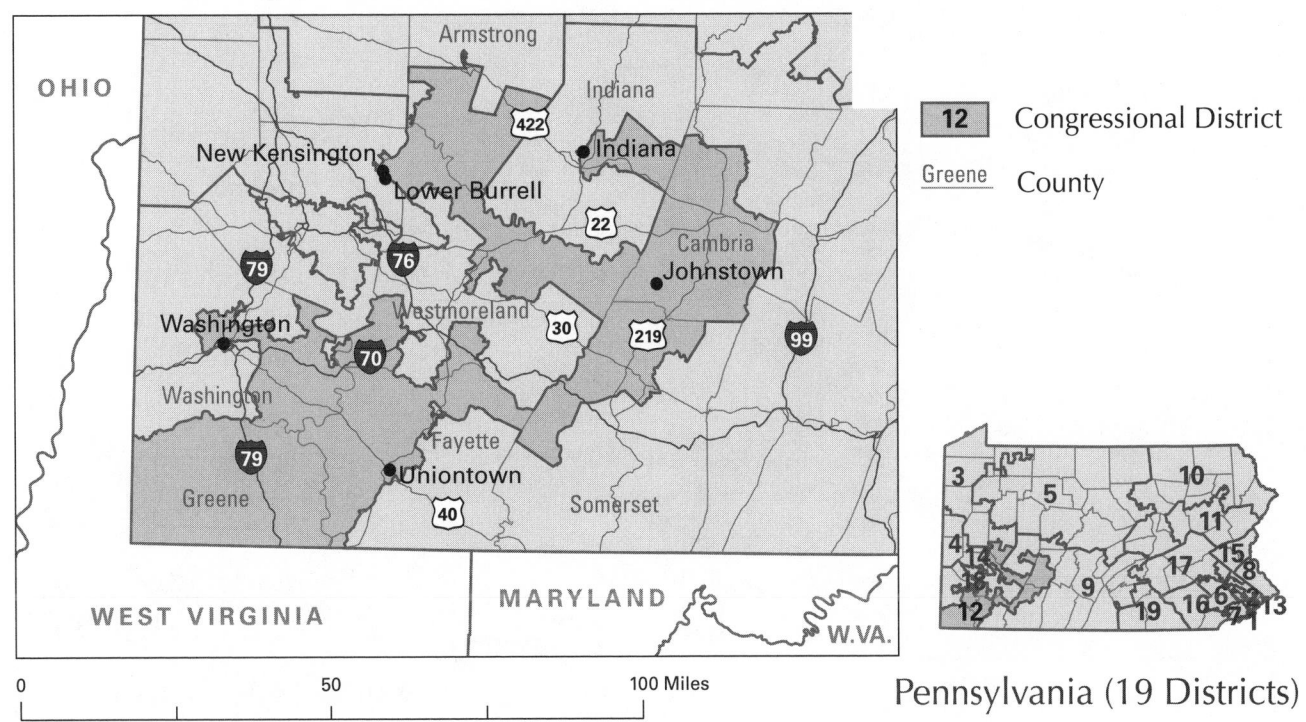

12 Congressional District

Greene County

Pennsylvania (19 Districts)

Congressional District 13

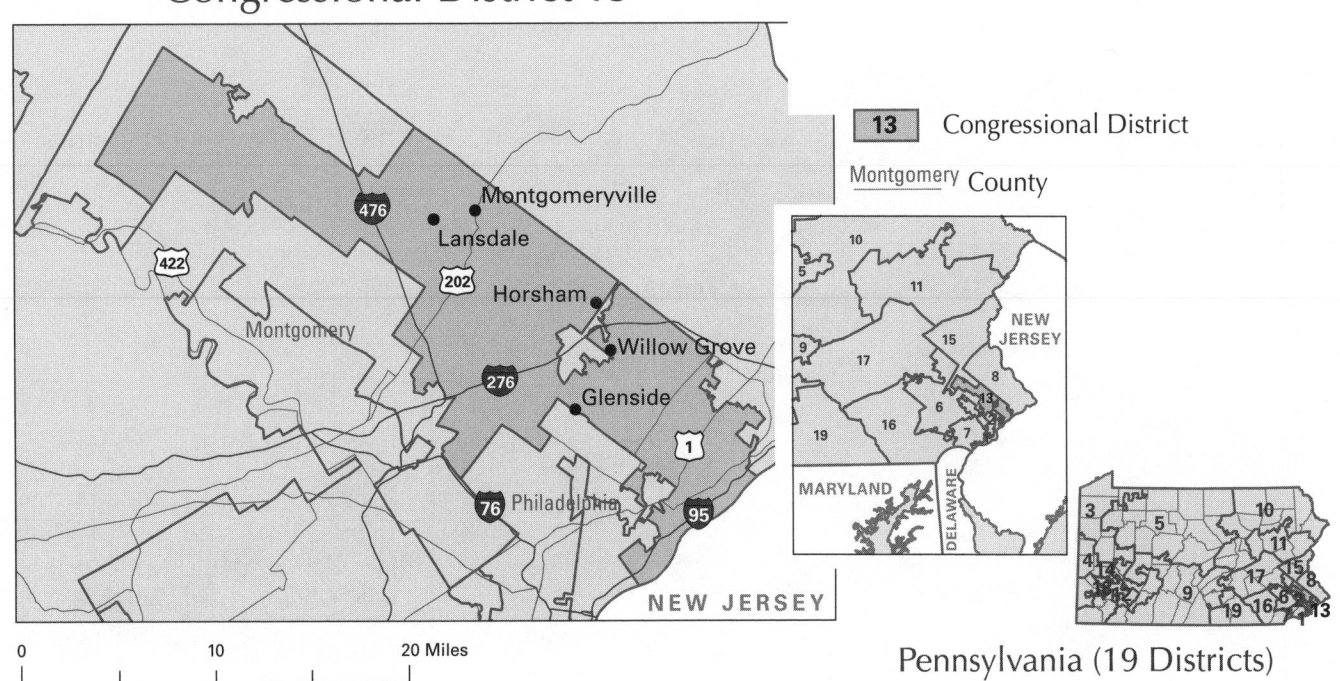

13 Congressional District

Montgomery County

Pennsylvania (19 Districts)

Congressional District 14

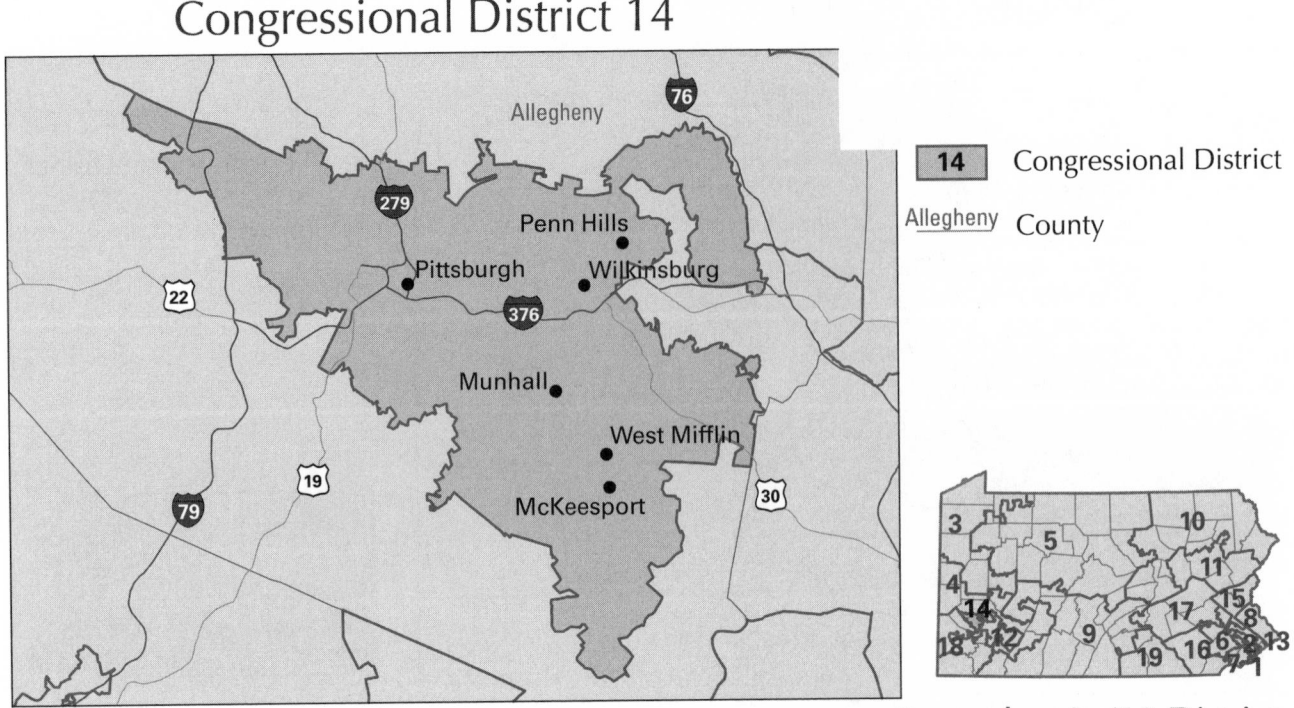

Pennsylvania (19 Districts)

Congressional District 15

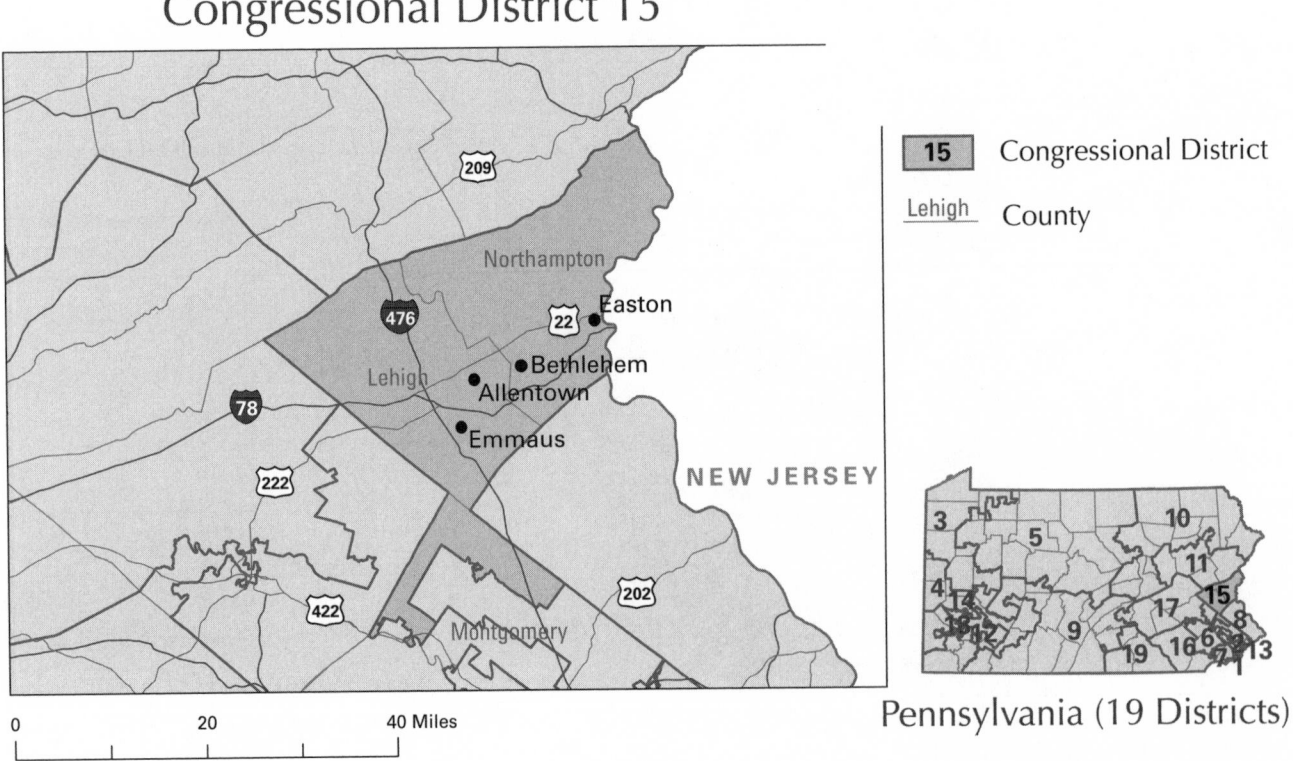

Pennsylvania (19 Districts)

Congressional District 16

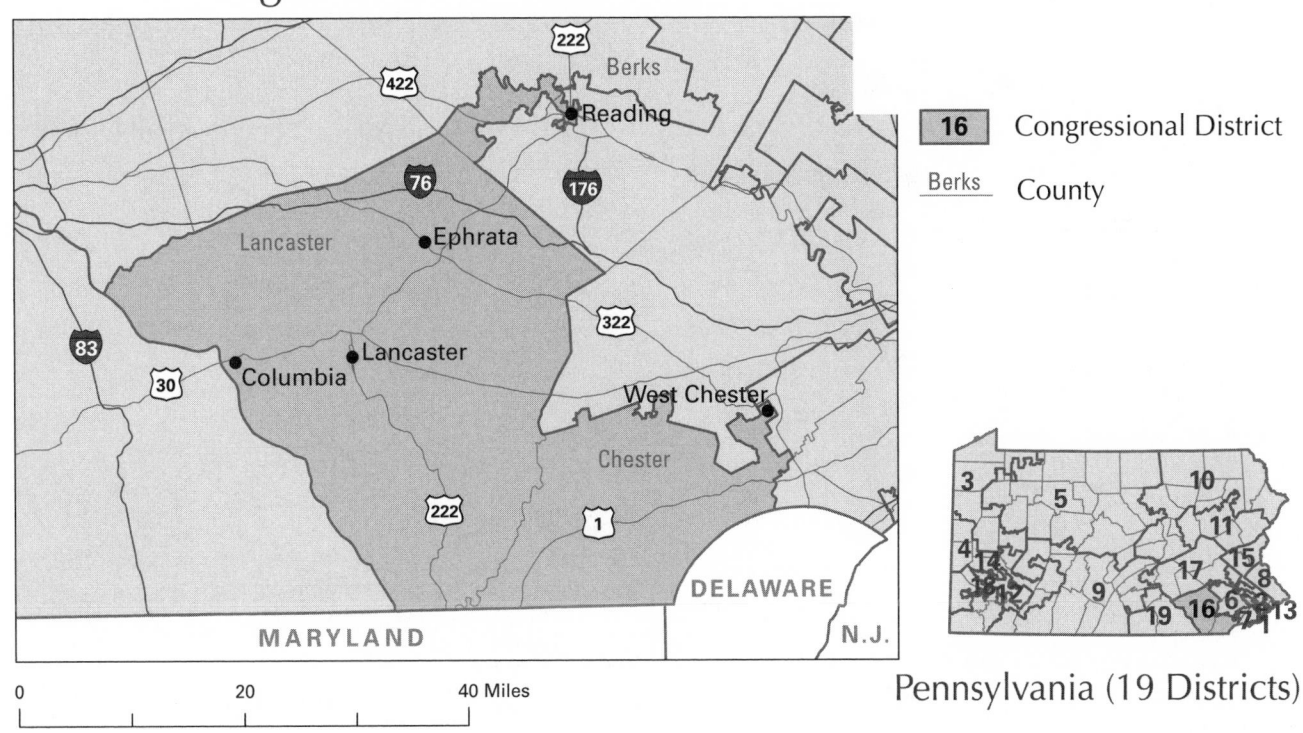

16 Congressional District

Berks County

Pennsylvania (19 Districts)

Congressional District 17

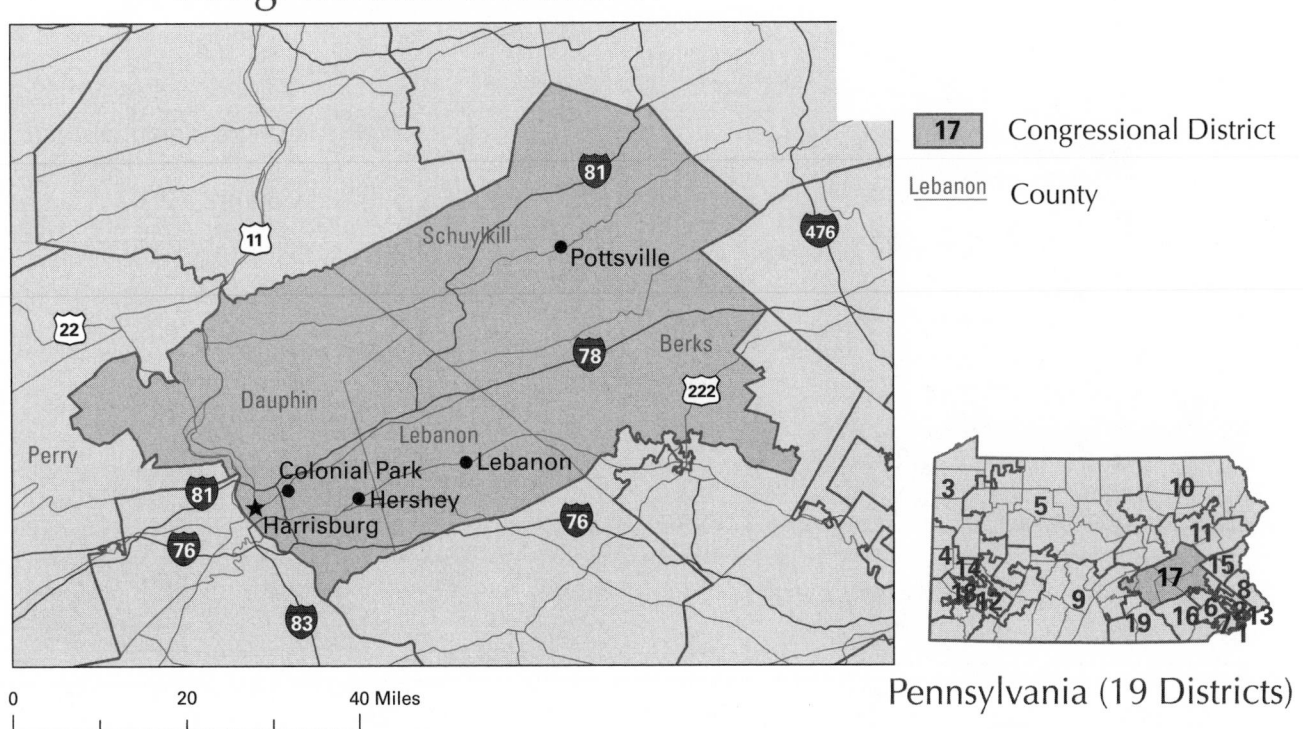

17 Congressional District

Lebanon County

Pennsylvania (19 Districts)

Congressional District 18

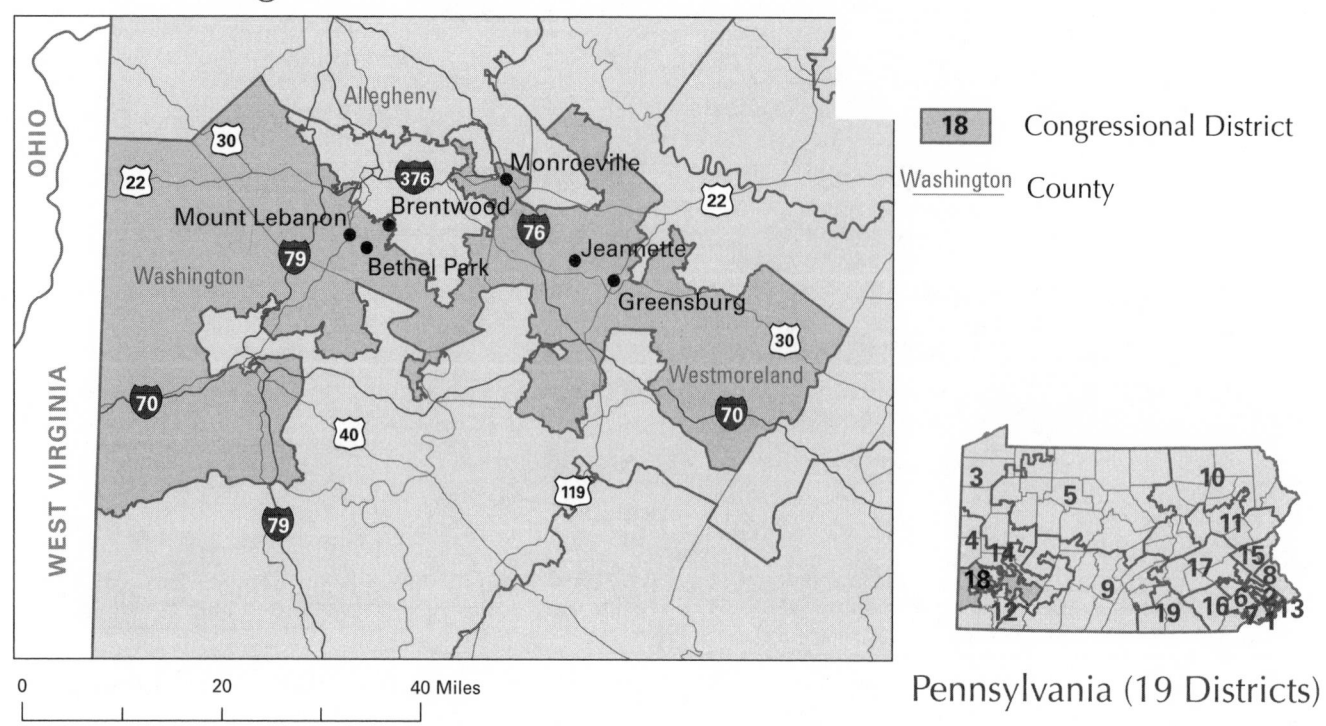

Pennsylvania (19 Districts)

Congressional District 19

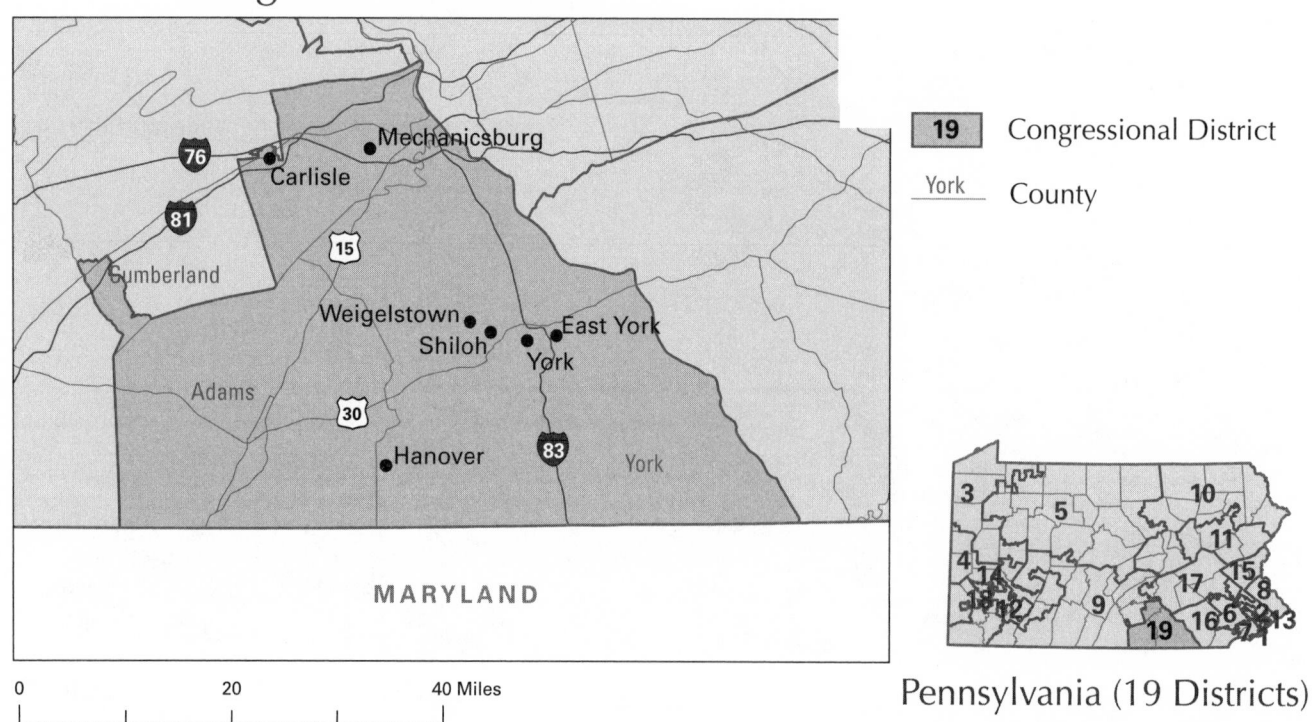

Pennsylvania (19 Districts)

Rhode Island Congressional Districts — 2 Districts Total

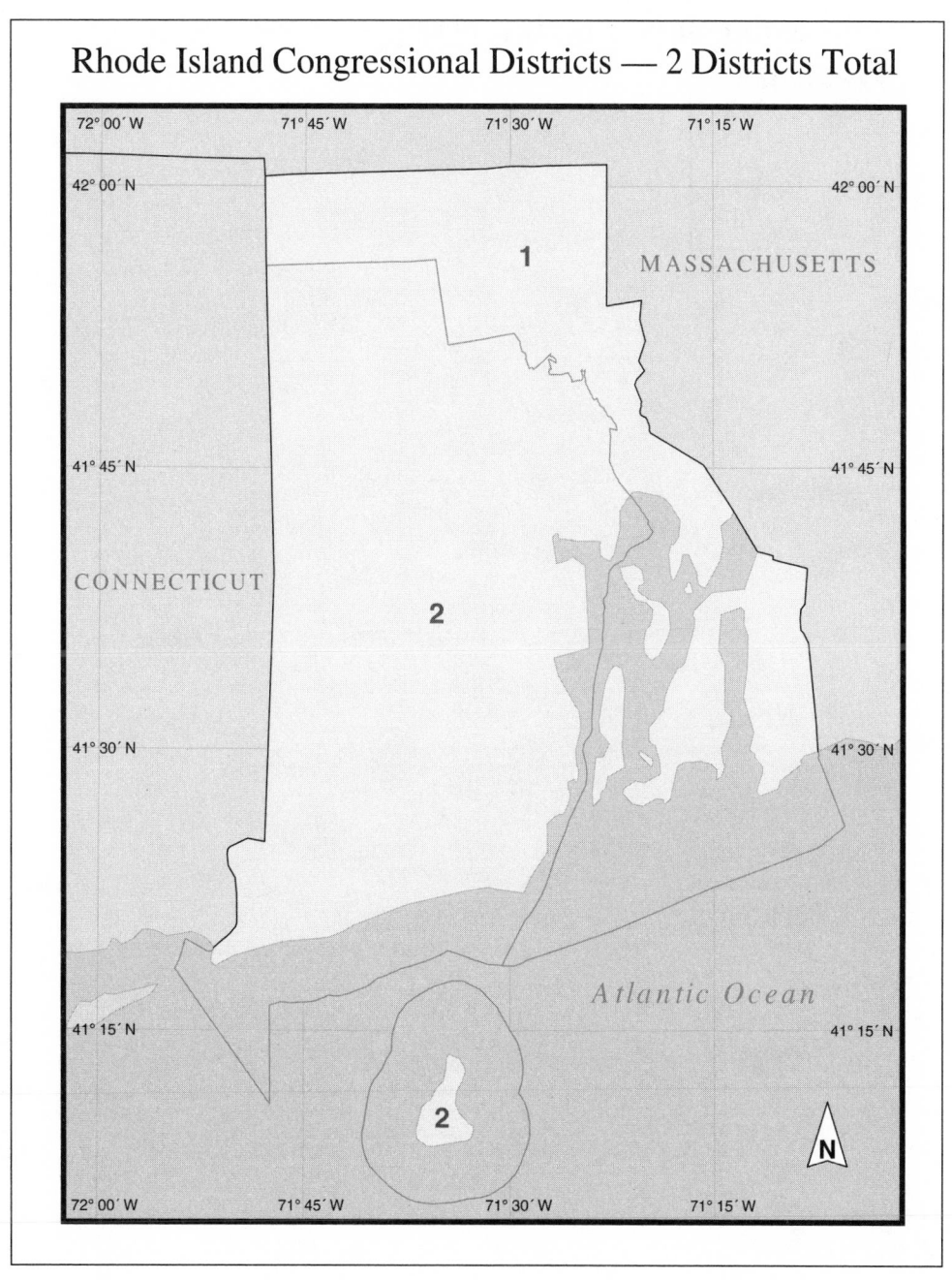

RHODE ISLAND—110th CONGRESSIONAL DISTRICTS BY COUNTIES

County	Congressional District
Bristol	1
Kent	2
Newport	1
Providence	1, 2
Washington	2

Congressional District 1

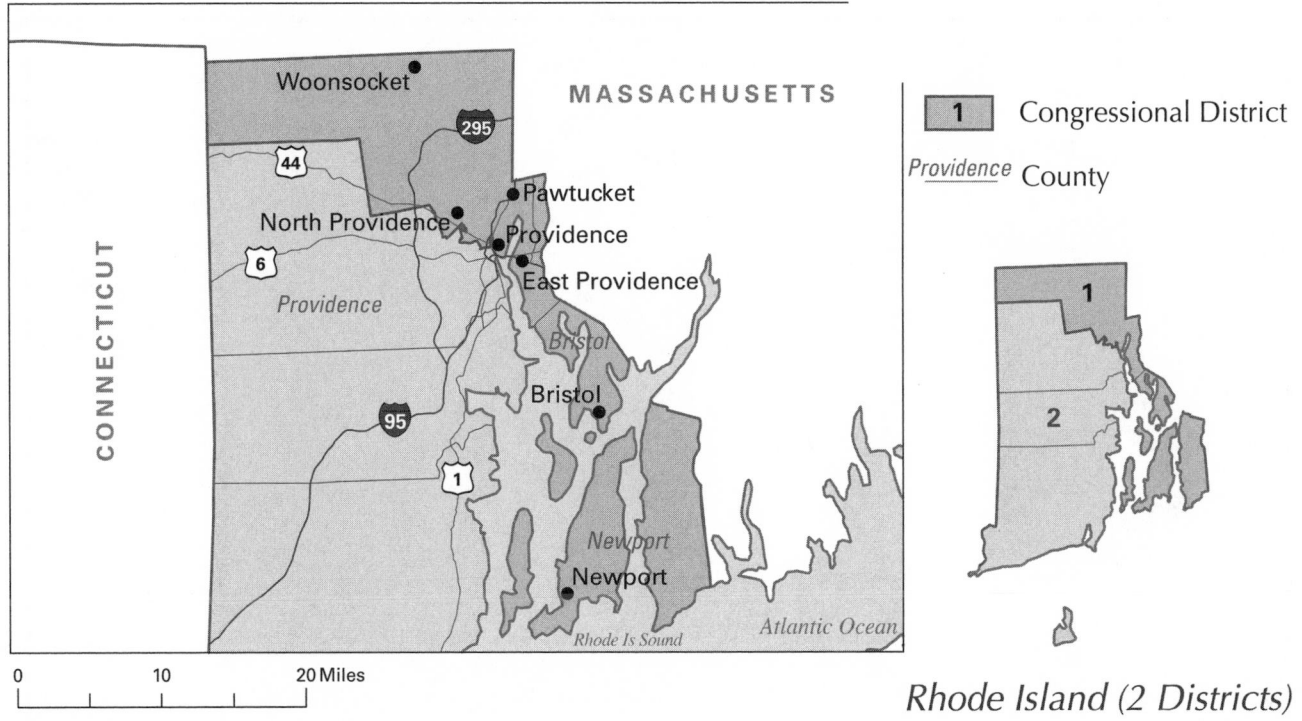

Rhode Island (2 Districts)

Congressional District 2

Rhode Island (2 Districts)

South Carolina Congressional Districts — 6 Districts Total

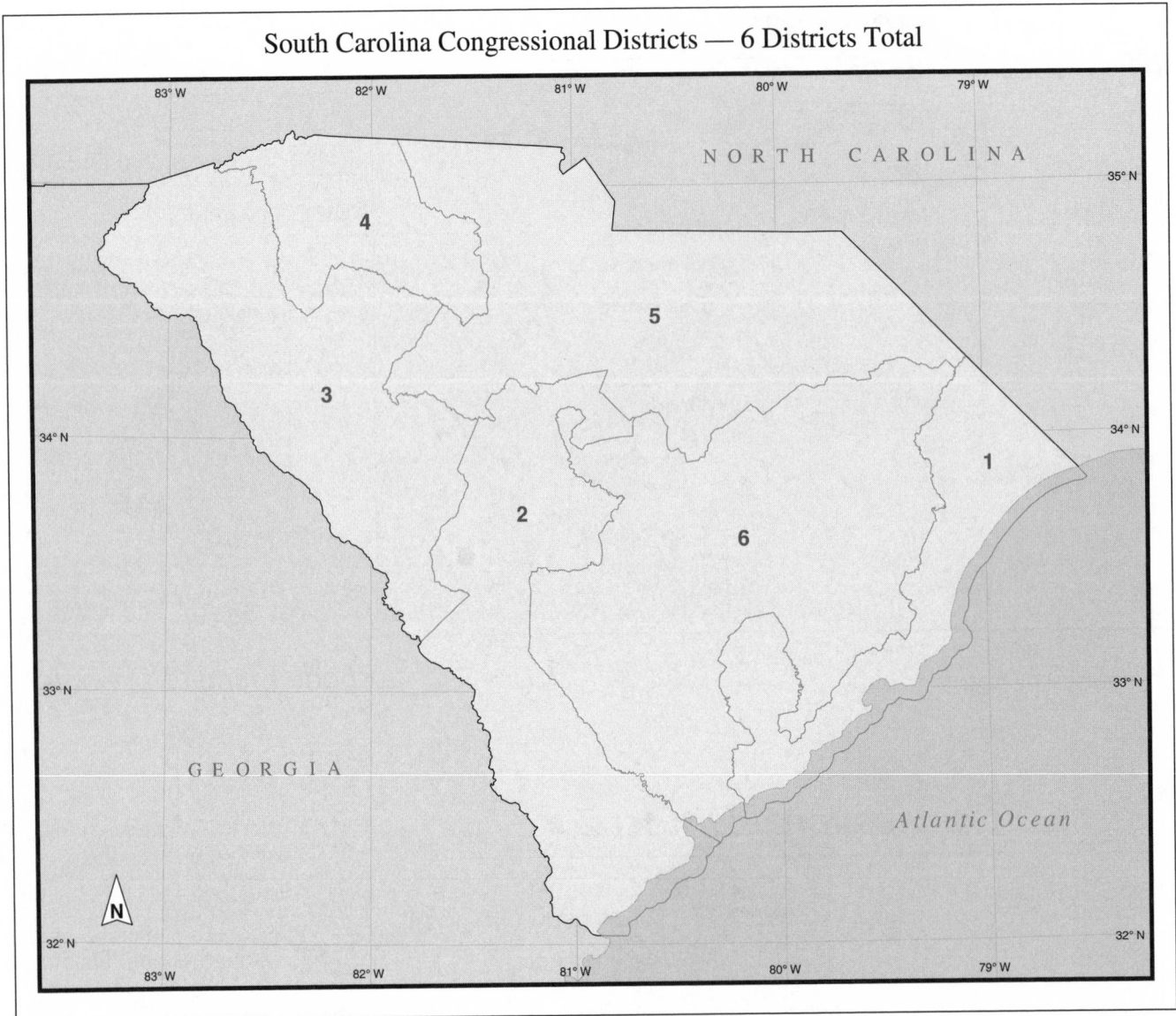

SOUTH CAROLINA—110th CONGRESSIONAL DISTRICTS BY COUNTIES

County	Congressional District
Abbeville	3
Aiken	2, 3
Allendale	2
Anderson	3
Bamberg	6
Barnwell	2
Beaufort	2
Berkeley	1, 6
Calhoun	2, 6
Charleston	1, 6
Cherokee	5
Chester	5
Chesterfield	5
Clarendon	6
Colleton	6
Darlington	5

County	Congressional District
Dillon	5
Dorchester	1, 6
Edgefield	3
Fairfield	5
Florence	5, 6
Georgetown	1, 6
Greenville	4
Greenwood	3
Hampton	2
Horry	1
Jasper	2
Kershaw	5
Lancaster	5
Laurens	3, 4
Lee	5, 6
Lexington	2

County	Congressional District
McCormick	3
Marion	6
Marlboro	5
Newberry	5
Oconee	3
Orangeburg	2, 6
Pickens	3
Richland	2, 6
Saluda	3
Spartanburg	4
Sumter	5, 6
Union	4
Williamsburg	6
York	5

Congressional District 1

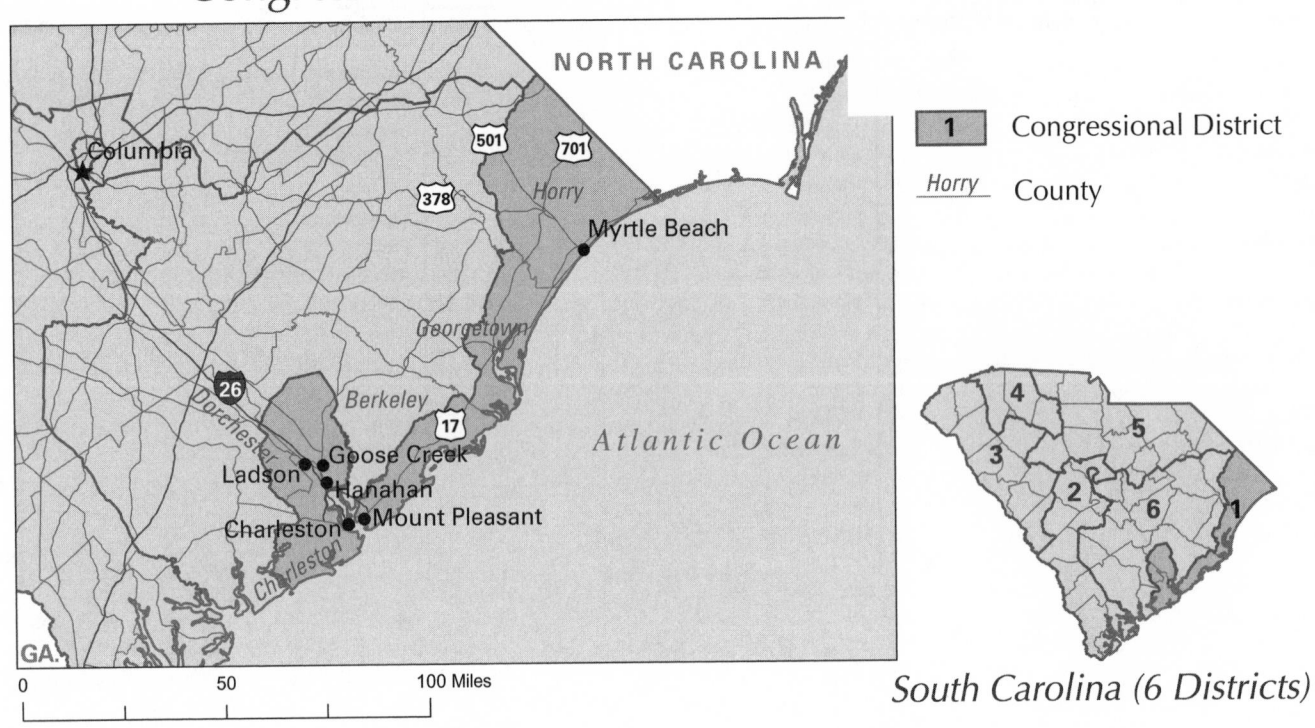

Legend:
1 Congressional District
Horry County

South Carolina (6 Districts)

Congressional District 2

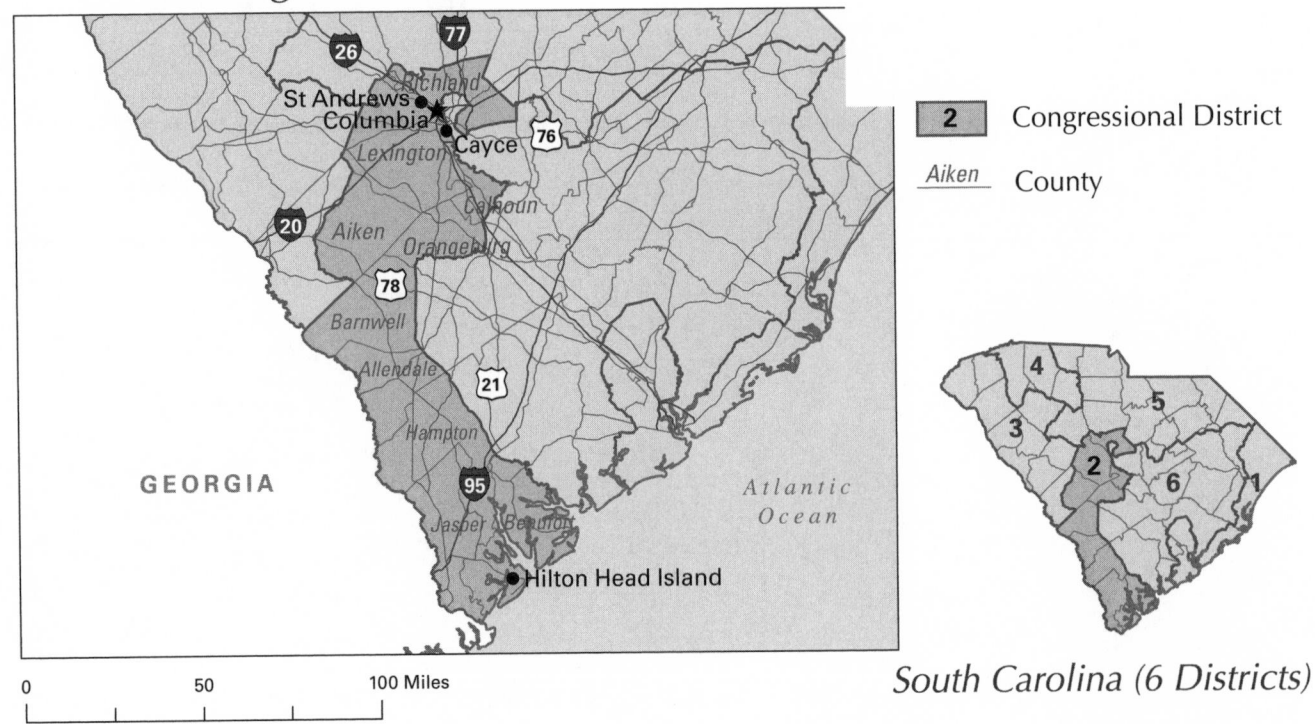

Legend:
2 Congressional District
Aiken County

South Carolina (6 Districts)

Congressional District 3

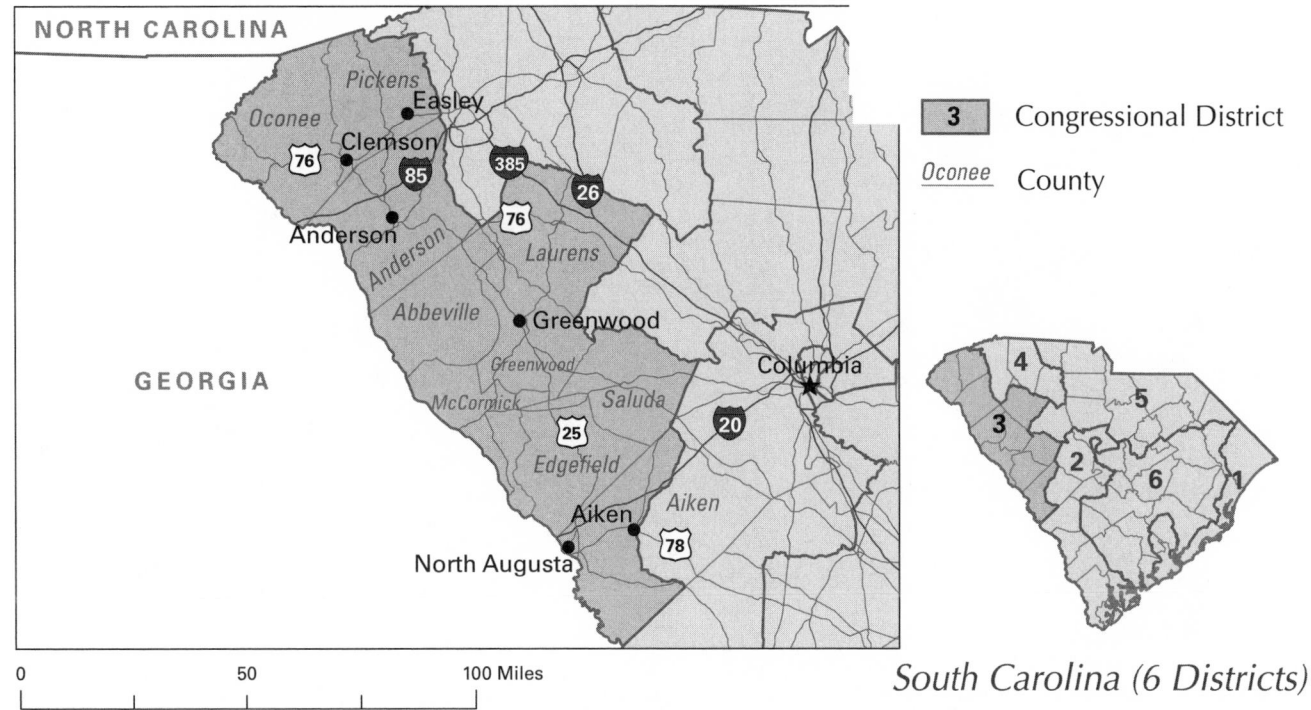

South Carolina (6 Districts)

Congressional District 4

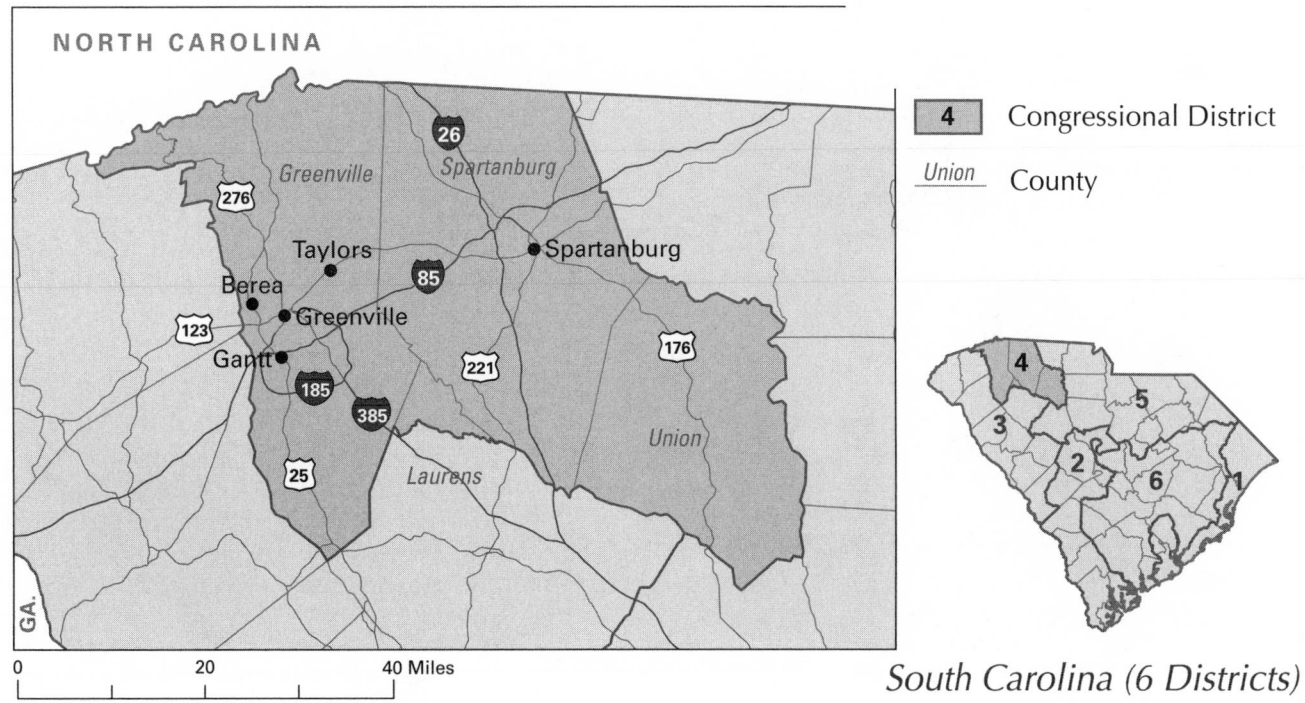

South Carolina (6 Districts)

Congressional District 5

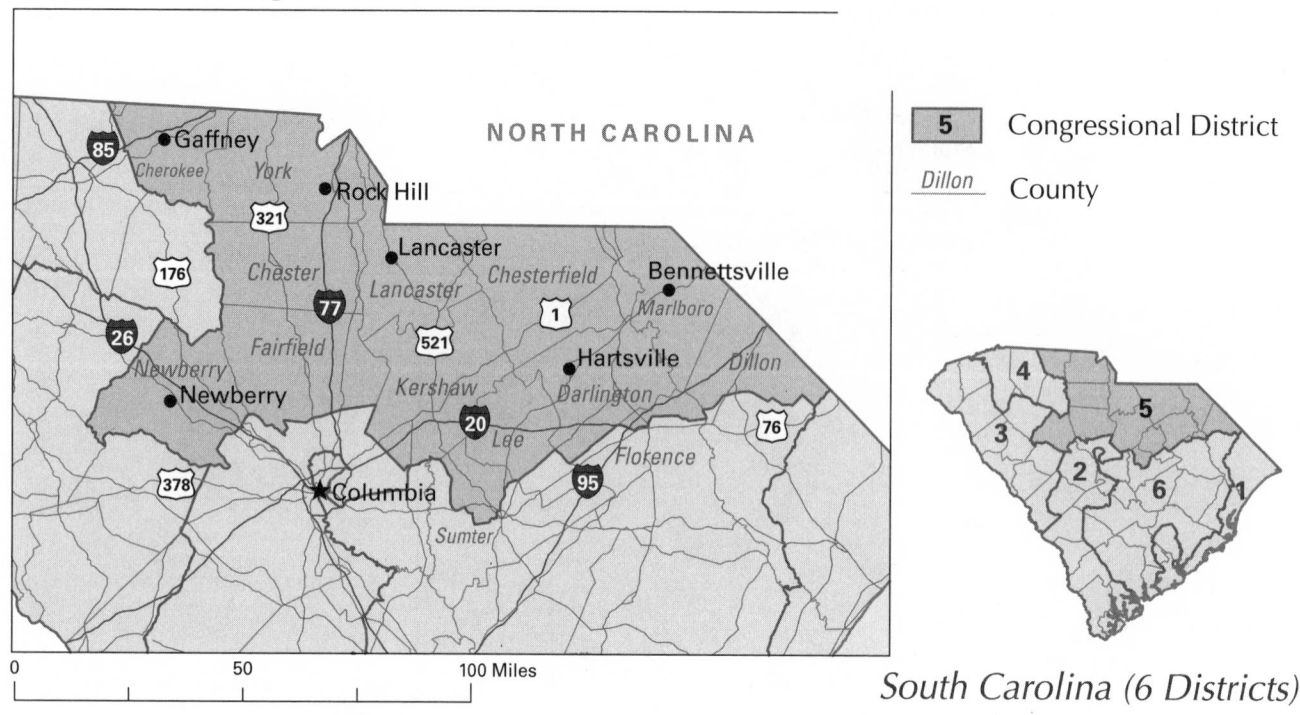

South Carolina (6 Districts)

Congressional District 6

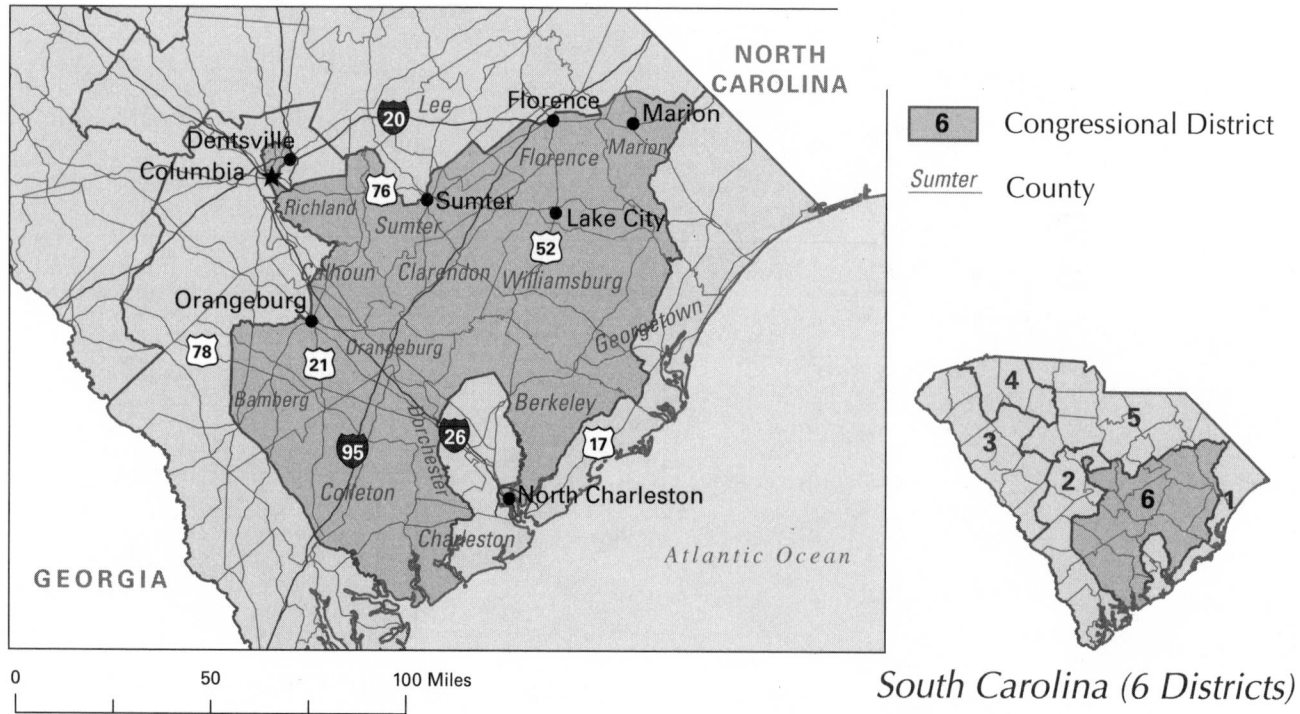

South Carolina (6 Districts)

South Dakota—
Congressional District: At large

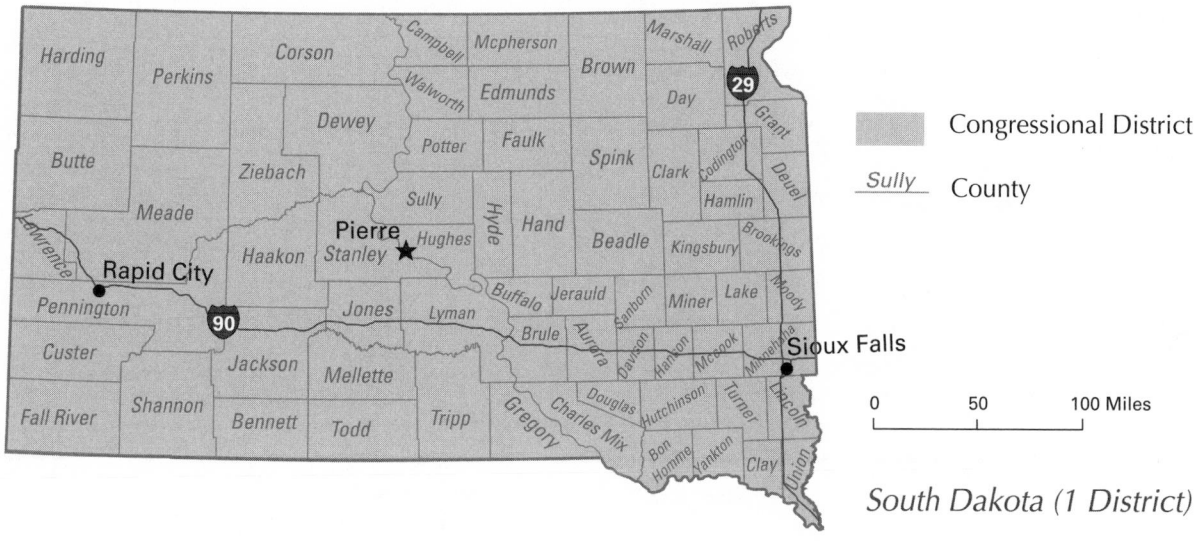

Congressional District

Sully   County

South Dakota (1 District)

SOUTH DAKOTA—110th CONGRESSIONAL DISTRICTS BY COUNTIES

County	Congressional District	County	Congressional District	County	Congressional District
Adams	1	Grant	1	Ransom	1
Barnes	1	Griggs	1	Renville	1
Benson	1	Hettinger	1	Richland	1
Billings	1	Kidder	1	Rolette	1
Bottineau	1	La Moure	1	Sargent	1
Bowman	1	Logan	1	Sheridan	1
Burke	1	McHenry	1	Sioux	1
Burleigh	1	McIntosh	1	Slope	1
Cass	1	McKenzie	1	Stark	1
Cavalier	1	McLean	1	Steele	1
Dickey	1	Mercer	1	Stutsman	1
Divide	1	Morton	1	Towner	1
Dunn	1	Mountrail	1	Traill	1
Eddy	1	Nelson	1	Walsh	1
Emmons	1	Oliver	1	Ward	1
Foster	1	Pembina	1	Wells	1
Golden Valley	1	Pierce	1	Williams	1
Grand Forks	1	Ramsey	1		

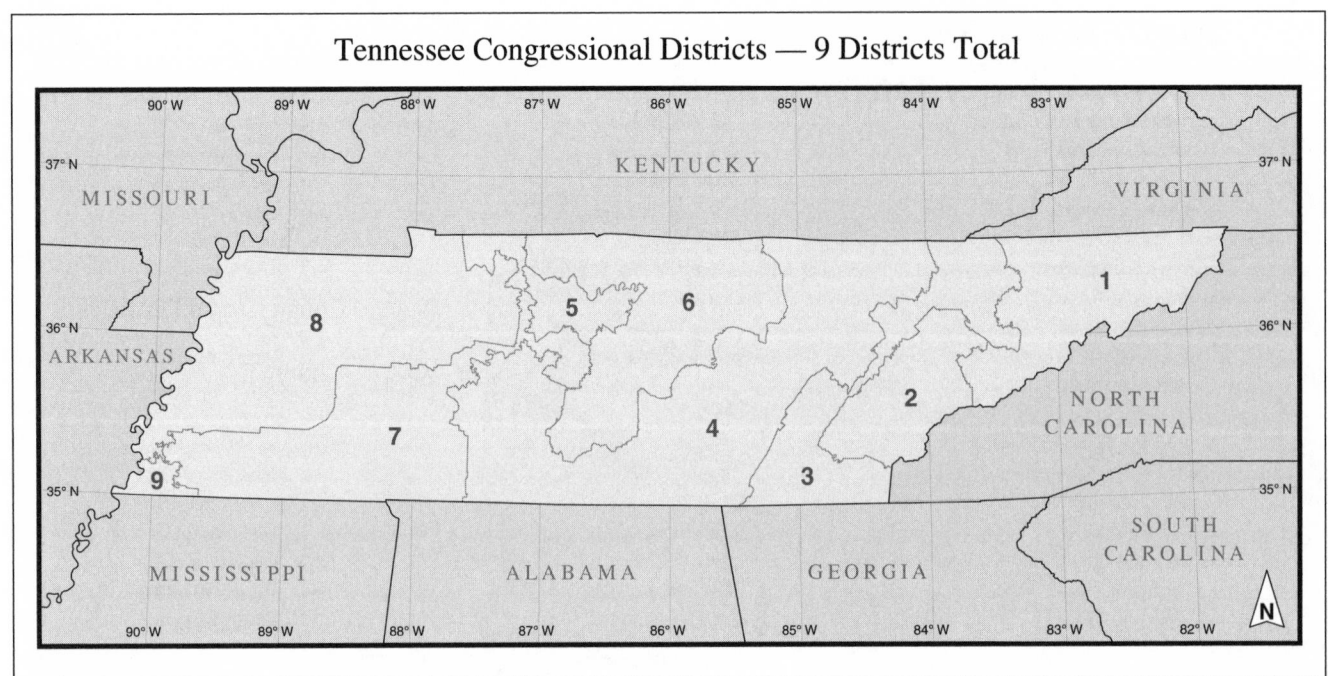

Tennessee Congressional Districts — 9 Districts Total

TENNESSEE—110th CONGRESSIONAL DISTRICTS BY COUNTIES

County	Congressional District	County	Congressional District	County	Congressional District
Anderson	3	Hamilton	3	Morgan	4
Bedford	6	Hancock	1	Obion	8
Benton	8	Hardeman	7	Overton	6
Bledsoe	4	Hardin	7	Perry	7
Blount	2	Hawkins	1	Pickett	4
Bradley	3	Haywood	8	Polk	3
Campbell	4	Henderson	7	Putnam	6
Cannon	6	Henry	8	Rhea	3
Carroll	8	Hickman	4, 7	Roane	3, 4
Carter	1	Houston	8	Robertson	6
Cheatham	5, 7	Humphreys	8	Rutherford	6
Chester	7	Jackson	6	Scott	4
Claiborne	3	Jefferson	1, 3	Sequatchie	4
Clay	6	Johnson	1	Sevier	1, 2
Cocke	1	Knox	2	Shelby	7–9
Coffee	4	Lake	8	Smith	6
Crockett	8	Lauderdale	8	Stewart	8
Cumberland	4	Lawrence	4	Sullivan	1
Davidson	5, 7	Lewis	4	Sumner	6
Decatur	7	Lincoln	4	Tipton	8
DeKalb	6	Loudon	2	Trousdale	6
Dickson	7, 8	McMinn	2	Unicoi	1
Dyer	8	McNairy	7	Union	3
Fayette	7	Macon	6	Van Buren	4
Fentress	4	Madison	8	Warren	4
Franklin	4	Marion	4	Washington	1
Gibson	8	Marshall	6	Wayne	7
Giles	4	Maury	4	Weakley	8
Grainger	3	Meigs	3	White	4
Greene	1	Monroe	2	Williamson	4, 7
Grundy	4	Montgomery	7, 8	Wilson	5, 6
Hamblen	1	Moore	4		

Congressional District 1

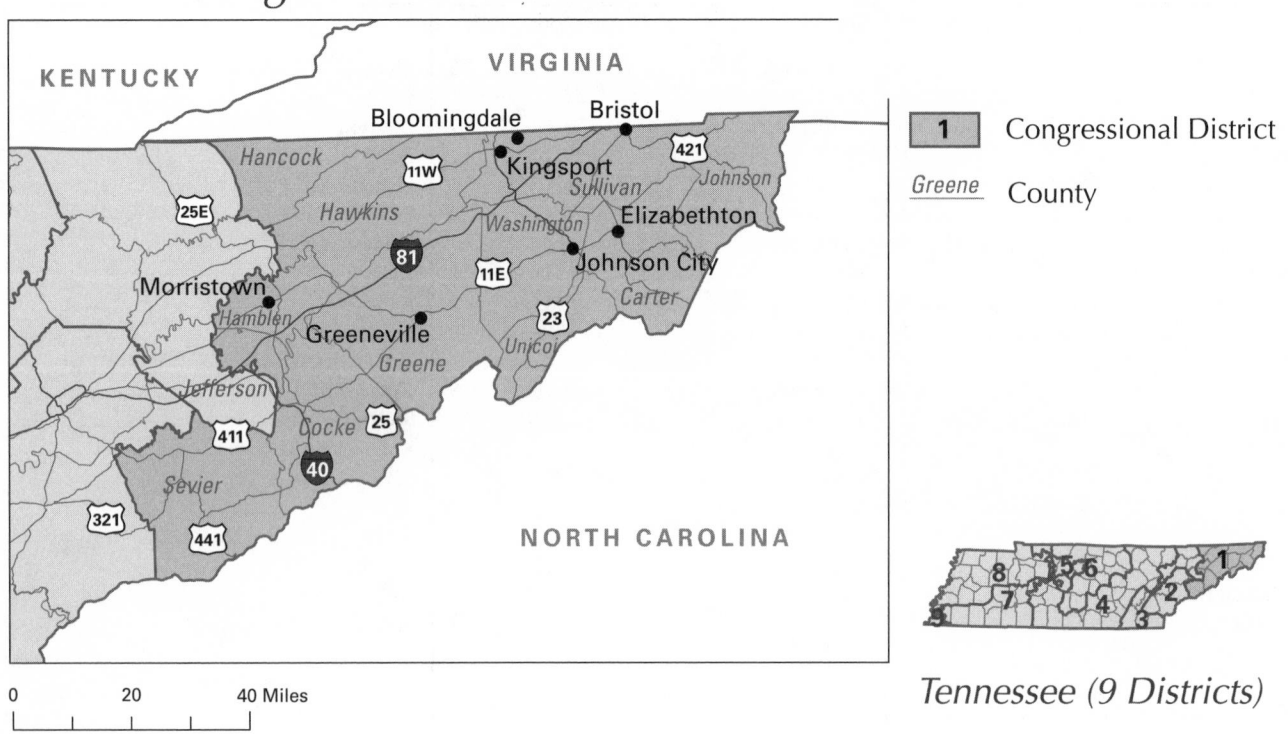

Tennessee (9 Districts)

Congressional District 2

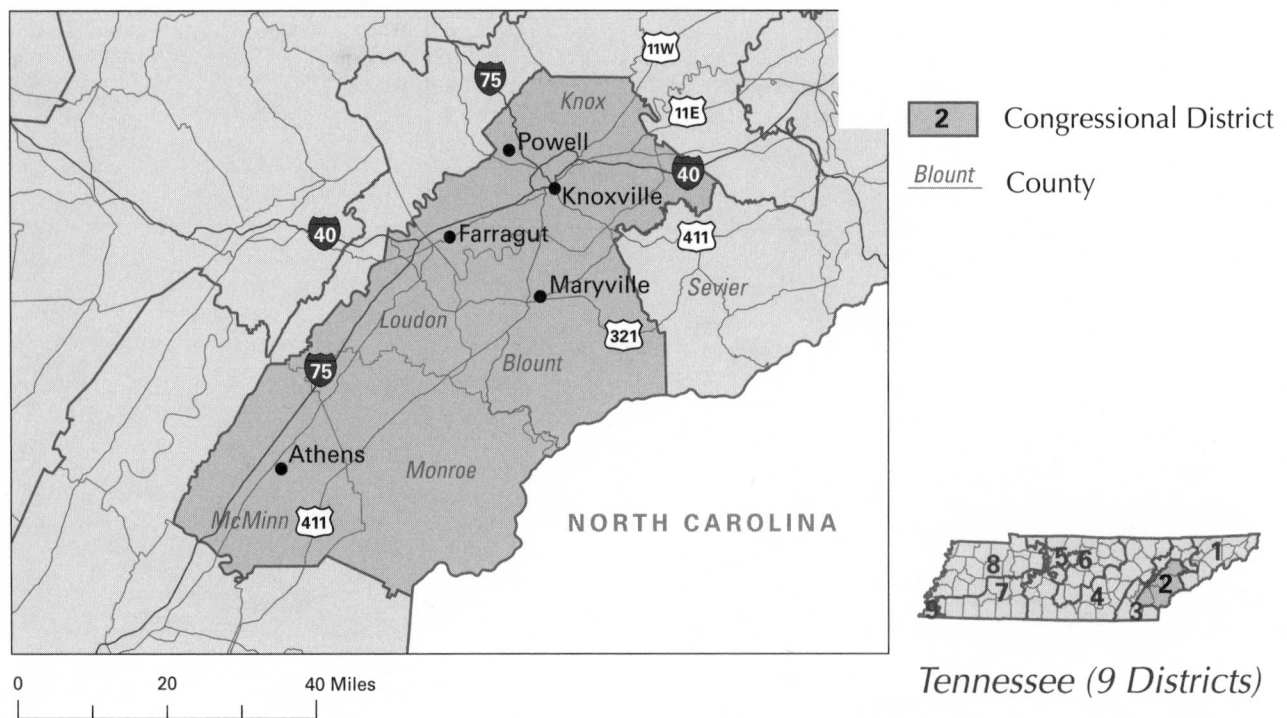

Tennessee (9 Districts)

Congressional District 3

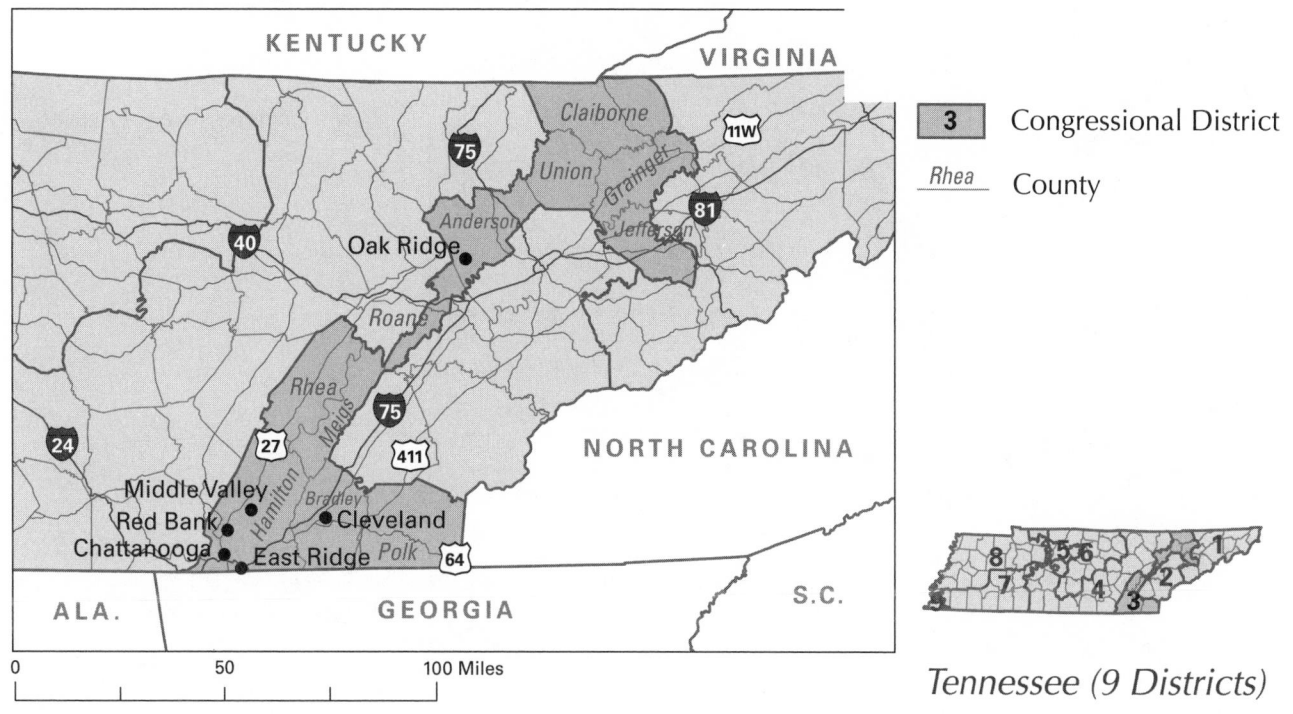

Tennessee (9 Districts)

Congressional District 4

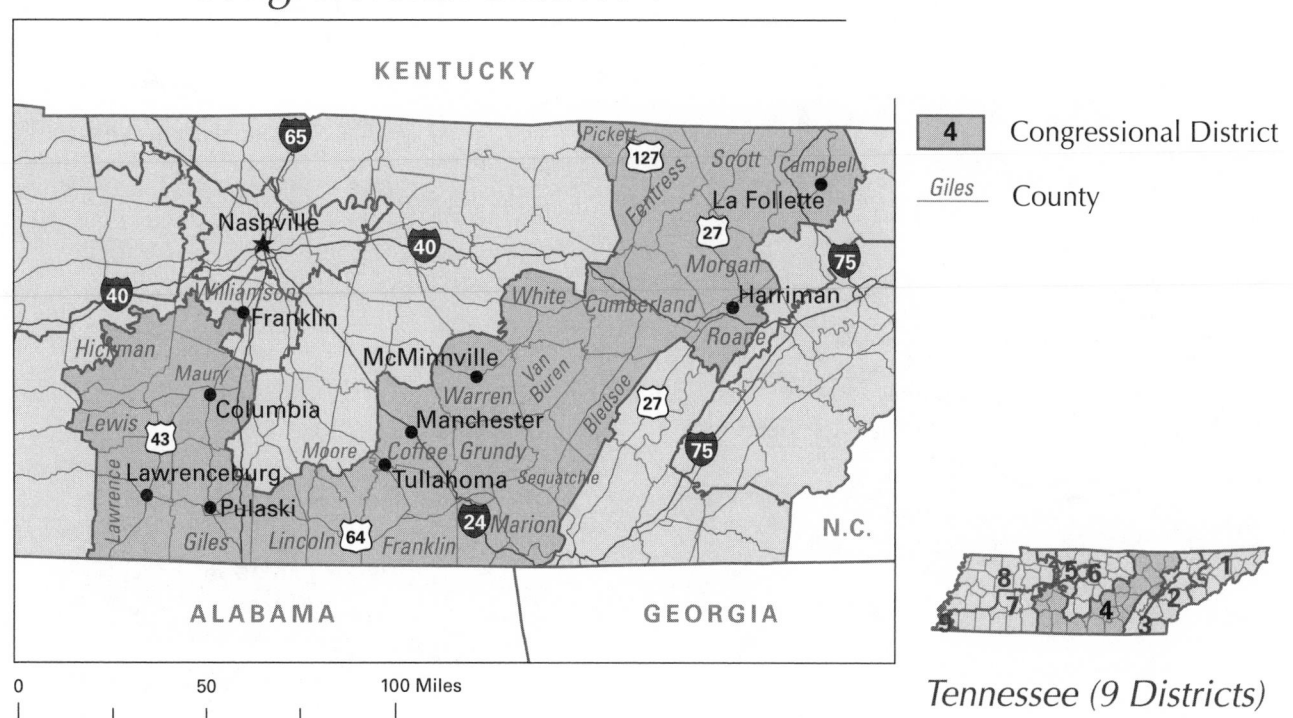

Tennessee (9 Districts)

Congressional District 5

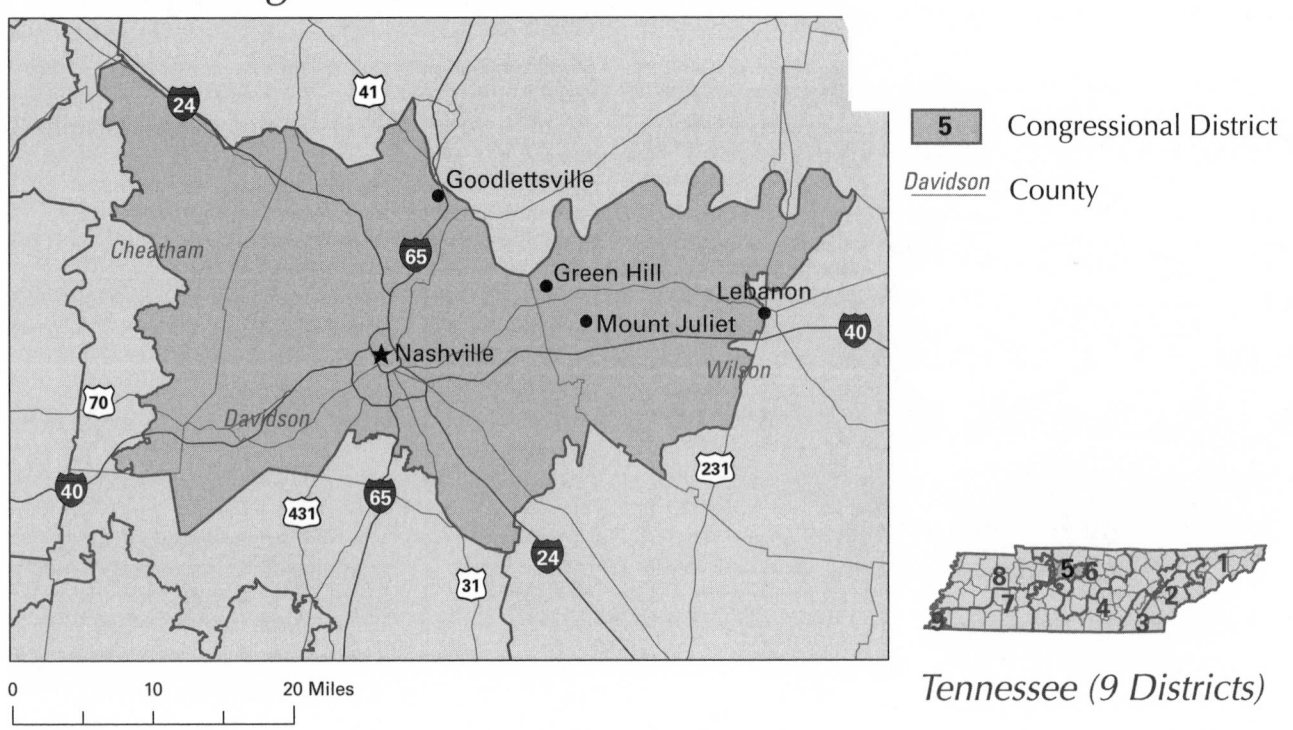

Congressional District 6

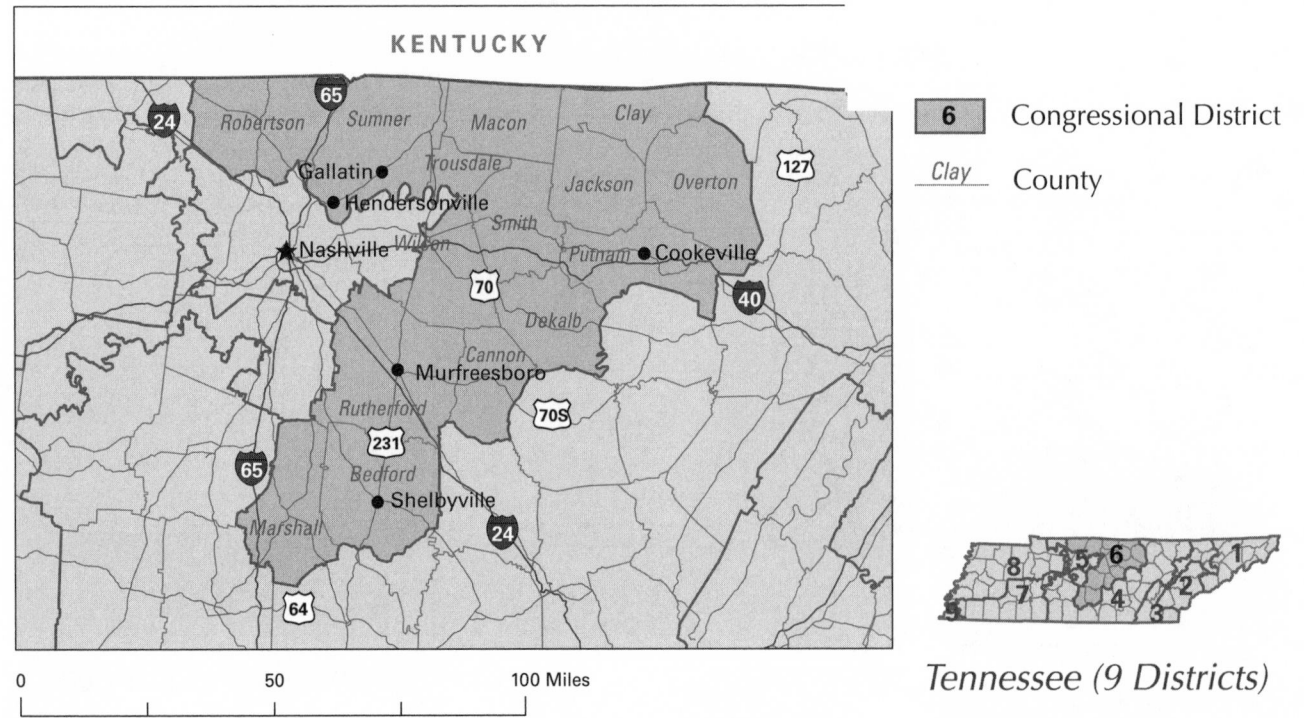

Congressional District 7

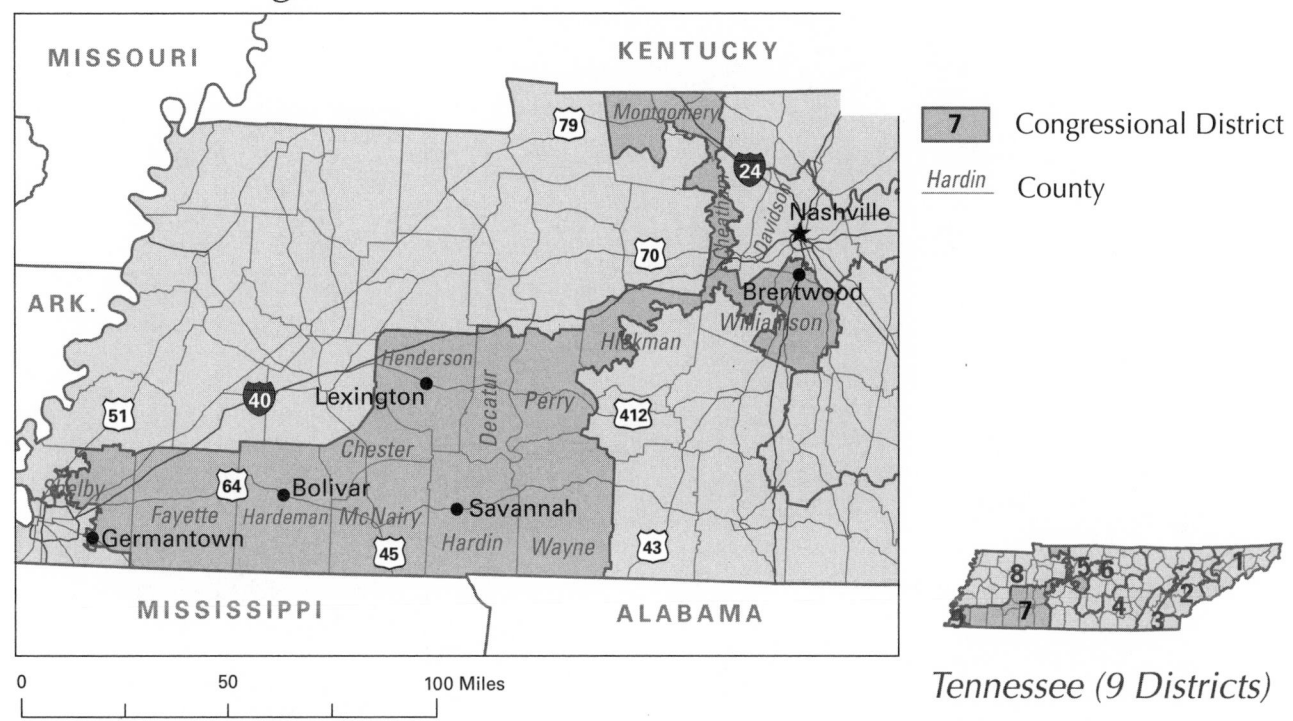

Congressional District 8

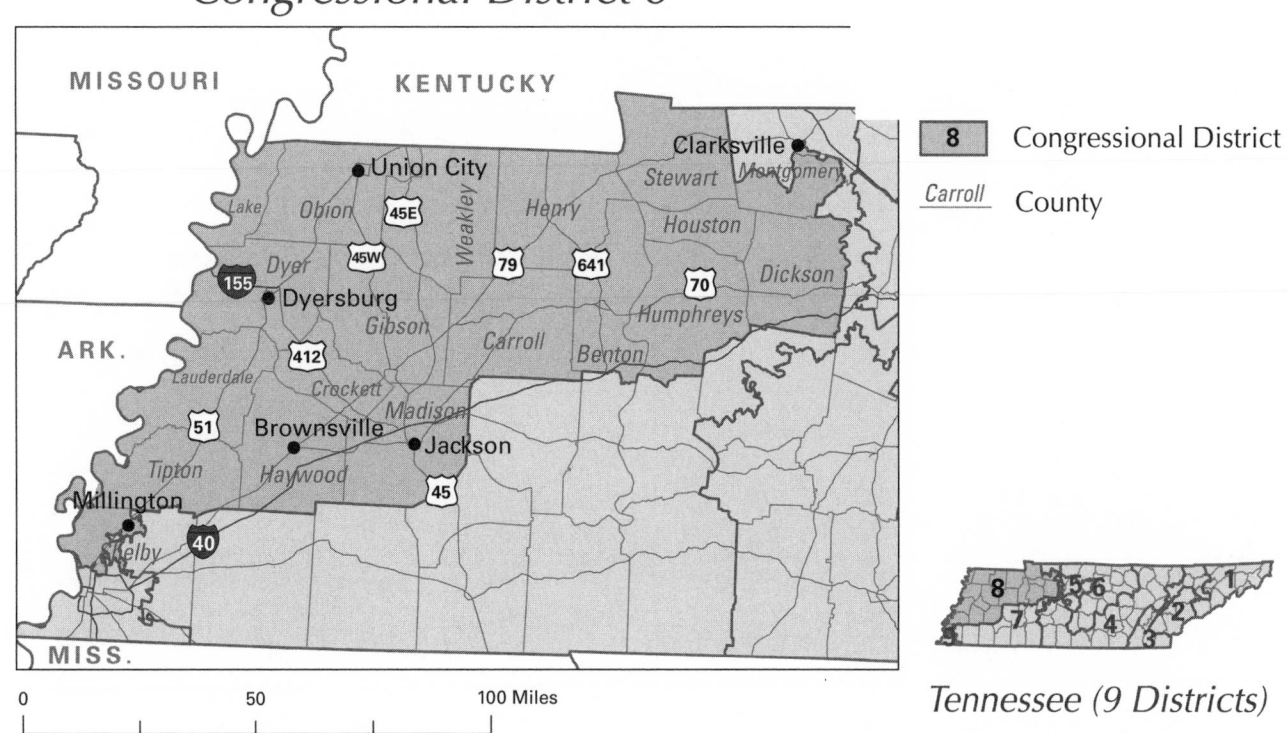

Congressional District 9

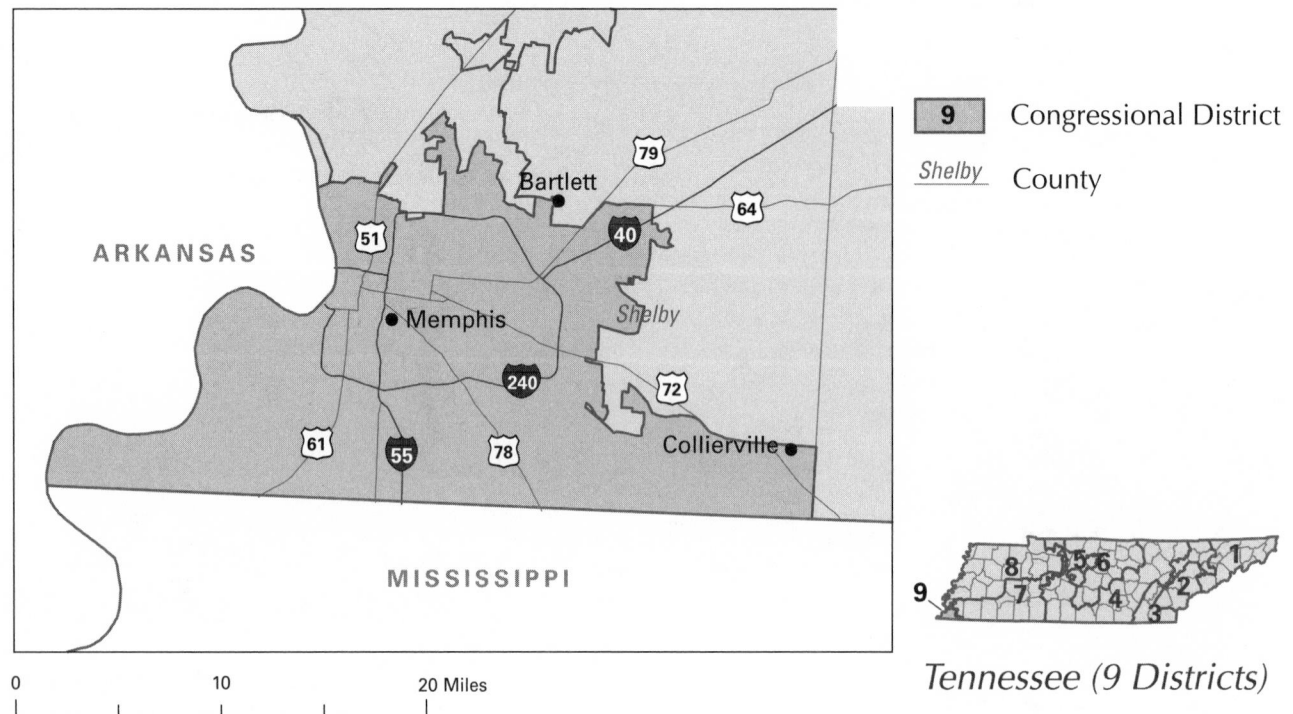

ARKANSAS

Bartlett

Shelby

Memphis

Collierville

MISSISSIPPI

| 9 | Congressional District |
| *Shelby* | County |

0   10   20 Miles

Tennessee (9 Districts)

Texas — Counties

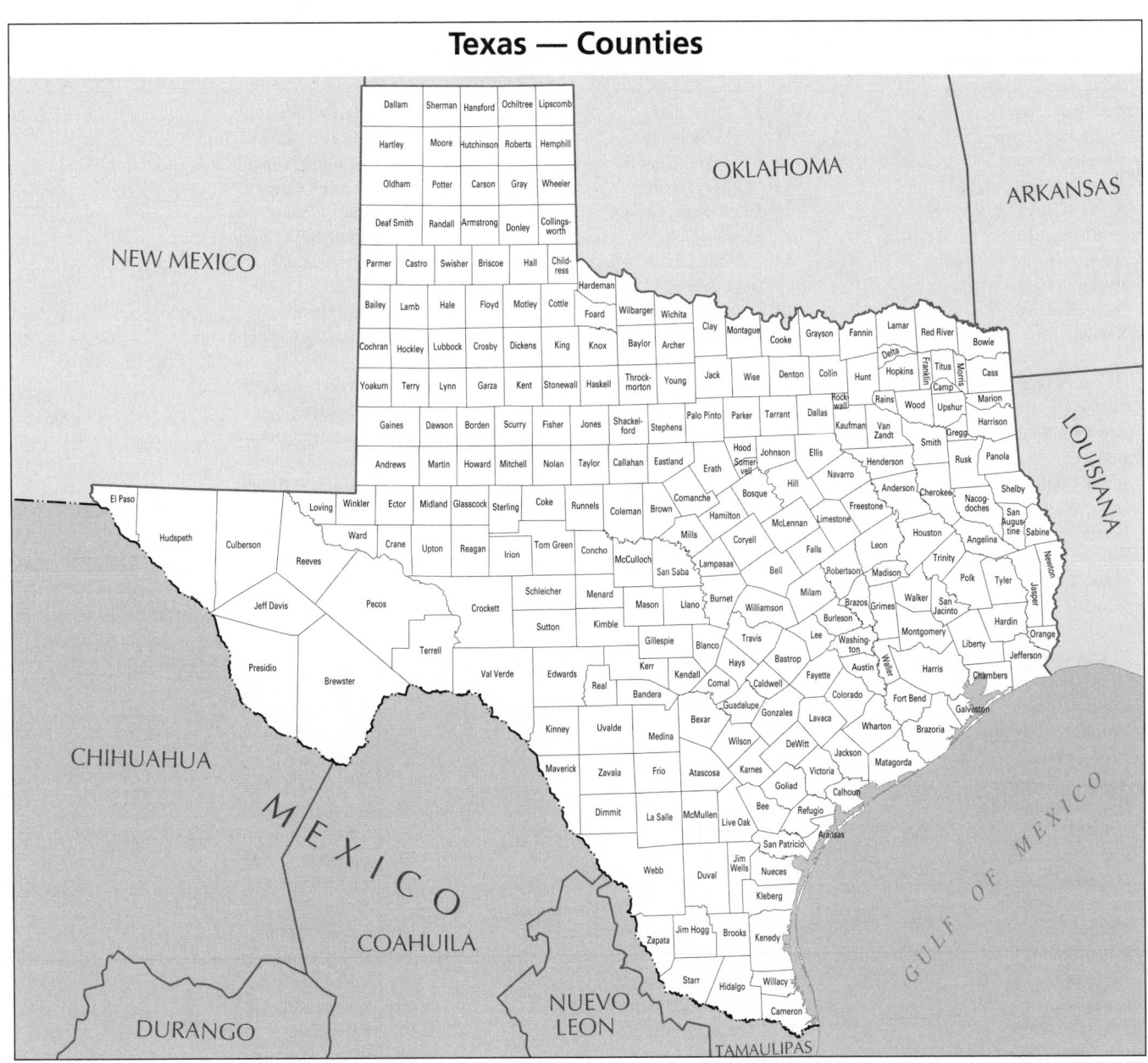

TEXAS—110th CONGRESSIONAL DISTRICTS BY COUNTIES

County	Congressional District
Anderson County	5
Andrews County	11
Angelina County	1
Aransas County	14
Archer County	13, 19
Armstrong County	13
Atascosa County	28
Austin County	10
Bailey County	19
Bandera County	21
Bastrop County	10, 25
Baylor County	13
Bee County	15
Bell County	31
Bexar County	20, 21, 23, 28
Blanco County	21
Borden County	19
Bosque County	17
Bowie County	4
Brazoria County	14, 22
Brazos County	17
Brewster County	23
Briscoe County	13
Brooks County	15
Brown County	11
Burleson County	10, 17
Burnet County	11
Caldwell County	25
Calhoun County	14
Callahan County	19
Cameron County	15, 27
Camp County	4
Carson County	13
Cass County	1, 4
Castro County	19
Chambers County	14
Cherokee County	5
Childress County	13
Clay County	13
Cochran County	19
Coke County	11
Coleman County	11
Collin County	3, 4
Collingsworth County	13
Colorado County	25
Comal County	21
Comanche County	11
Concho County	11
Cooke County	13, 26
Coryell County	31

County	Congressional District
Cottle County	13
Crane County	11
Crockett County	23
Crosby County	13
Culberson County	23
Dallam County	13
Dallas County	3, 5, 24, 26, 30, 32
Dawson County	11
Deaf Smith County	19
Delta County	4
Denton County	24, 26
DeWitt County	15
Dickens County	13
Dimmit County	23
Donley County	13
Duval County	15
Eastland County	19
Ector County	11
Edwards County	23
Ellis County	6
El Paso County	16, 23
Erath County	31
Falls County	31
Fannin County	4
Fayette County	25
Fisher County	19
Floyd County	19
Foard County	13
Fort Bend County	9, 14, 22
Franklin County	4
Freestone County	6
Frio County	28
Gaines County	19
Galveston County	14, 22
Garza County	19
Gillespie County	11
Glasscock County	11
Goliad County	15
Gonzales County	25
Gray County	13
Grayson County	4
Gregg County	1
Grimes County	17
Guadalupe County	28
Hale County	19
Hall County	13
Hamilton County	31
Hansford County	13
Hardeman County	13
Hardin County	8

County	Congressional District
Harris County	2, 7, 9, 10, 18, 22, 29
Harrison County	1
Hartley County	13
Haskell County	13
Hays County	25
Hemphill County	13
Henderson County	5
Hidalgo County	15, 28
Hill County	17
Hockley County	19
Hood County	17
Hopkins County	4
Houston County	6
Howard County	19
Hudspeth County	23
Hunt County	4
Hutchinson County	13
Irion County	11
Jack County	13
Jackson County	14
Jasper County	8
Jeff Davis County	23
Jefferson County	2
Jim Hogg County	28
Jim Wells County	15
Johnson County	17
Jones County	13
Karnes County	15
Kaufman County	5
Kendall County	21
Kenedy County	27
Kent County	19
Kerr County	21
Kimble County	11
King County	13
Kinney County	23
Kleberg County	27
Knox County	13
Lamar County	4
Lamb County	19
Lampasas County	11
La Salle County	28
Lavaca County	25
Lee County	10
Leon County	6
Liberty County	2, 8
Limestone County	6, 17
Lipscomb County	13
Live Oak County	15
Llano County	11

TEXAS—110th CONGRESSIONAL DISTRICTS BY COUNTIES

County	Congressional District
Loving County	11
Lubbock County	19
Lynn County	19
Madison County	17
Marion County	1
Martin County	11
Mason County	11
Matagorda County	14
Maverick County	23
McCulloch County	11
McLennan County	17
McMullen County	28
Medina County	23
Menard County	11
Midland County	11
Milam County	31
Mills County	11
Mitchell County	11
Montague County	13
Montgomery County	8
Moore County	13
Morris County	4
Motley County	13
Nacogdoches County	1
Navarro County	6
Newton County	8
Nolan County	11, 19
Nueces County	27
Ochiltree County	13
Oldham County	13
Orange County	8
Palo Pinto County	13
Panola County	1
Parker County	12
Parmer County	19

County	Congressional District
Pecos County	23
Polk County	8
Potter County	13
Presidio County	23
Rains County	4
Randall County	13
Reagan County	11
Real County	21
Red River County	4
Reeves County	23
Refugio County	15
Roberts County	13
Robertson County	17, 31
Rockwall County	4
Runnels County	11
Rusk County	1
Sabine County	1
San Augustine County	1
San Jacinto County	8
San Patricio County	15, 27
San Saba County	11
Schleicher County	11
Scurry County	11
Shackelford County	19
Shelby County	1
Sherman County	13
Smith County	1
Somervell County	17
Starr County	28
Stephens County	19
Sterling County	11
Stonewall County	13
Sutton County	11, 23
Swisher County	13
Tarrant County	6, 12, 24, 26

County	Congressional District
Taylor County	19
Terrell County	23
Terry County	19
Throckmorton County	13
Titus County	4
Tom Green County	11
Travis County	10, 21, 25
Trinity County	6, 8
Tyler County	8
Upshur County	1
Upton County	11
Uvalde County	23
Val Verde County	23
Van Zandt County	5
Victoria County	14
Walker County	8
Waller County	10
Ward County	11
Washington County	10
Webb County	28
Wharton County	14
Wheeler County	13
Wichita County	13
Wilbarger County	13
Willacy County	27
Williamson County	31
Wilson County	28
Winkler County	11
Wise County	12
Wood County	5
Yoakum County	19
Young County	19
Zapata County	28
Zavala County	23

Congressional District 1

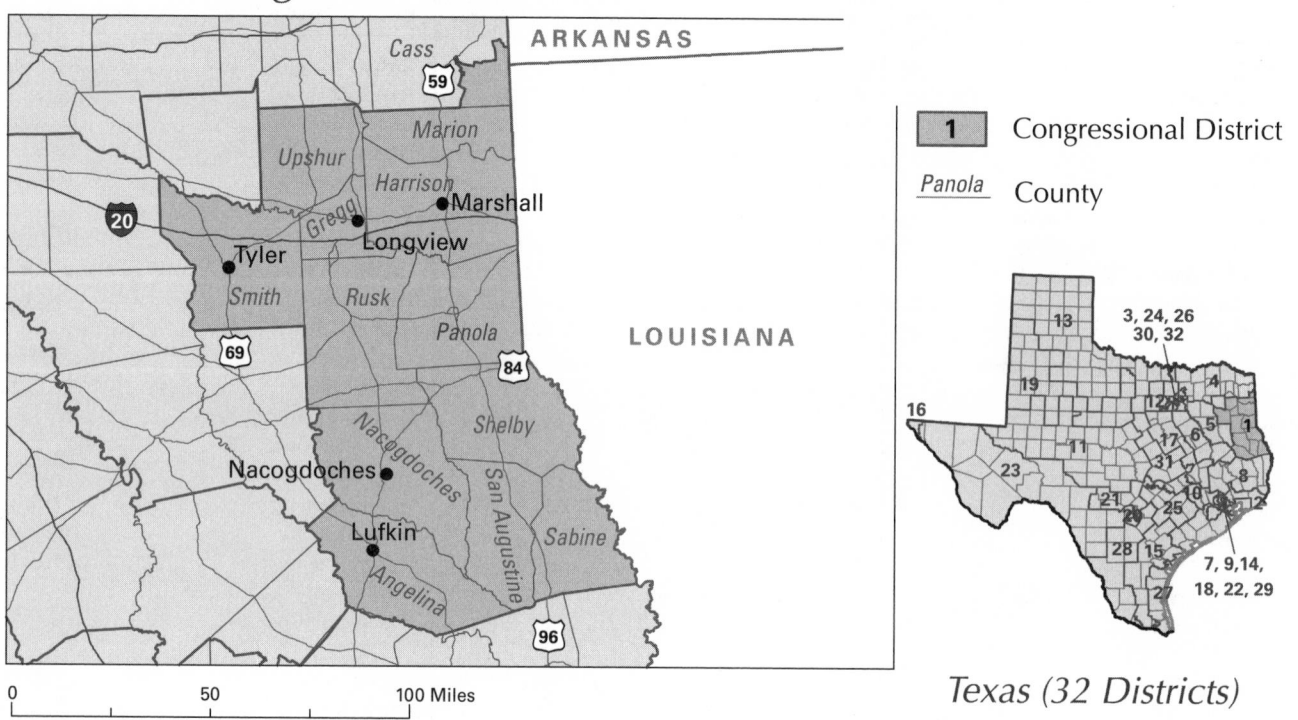

Texas (32 Districts)

Congressional District 2

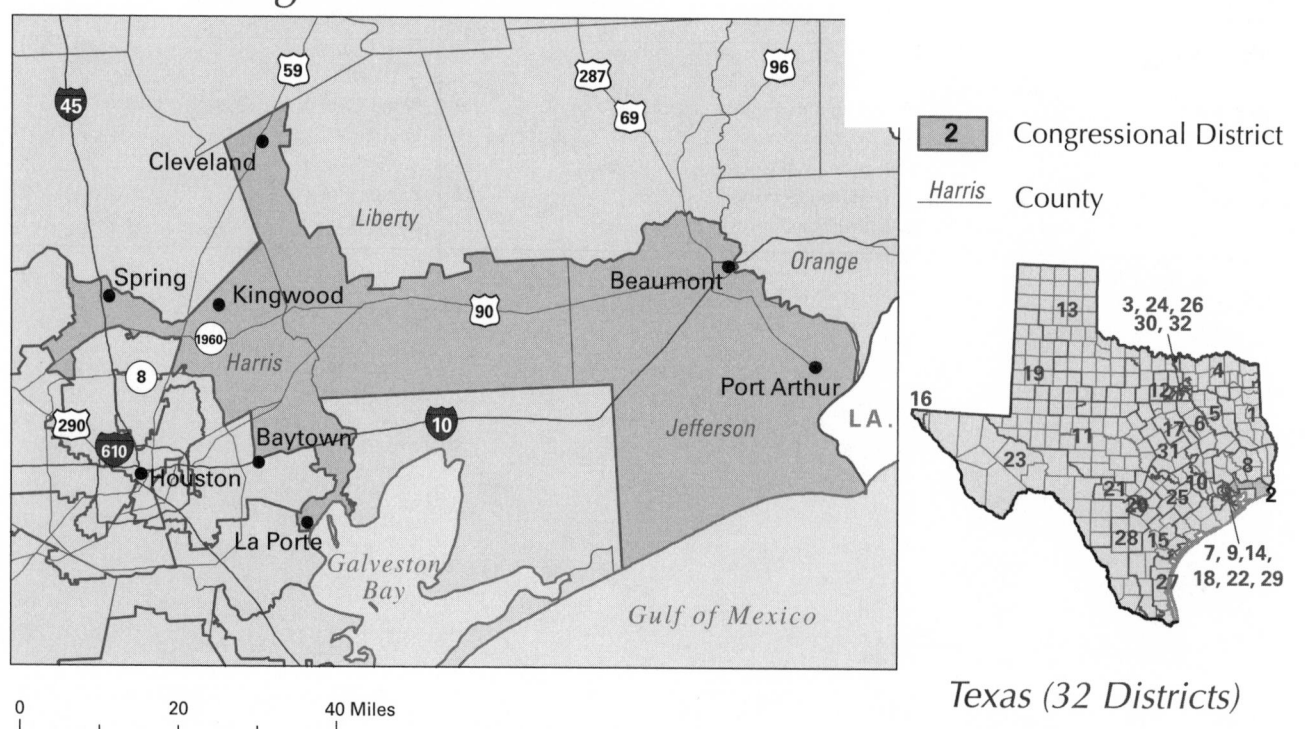

Texas (32 Districts)

Congressional District 3

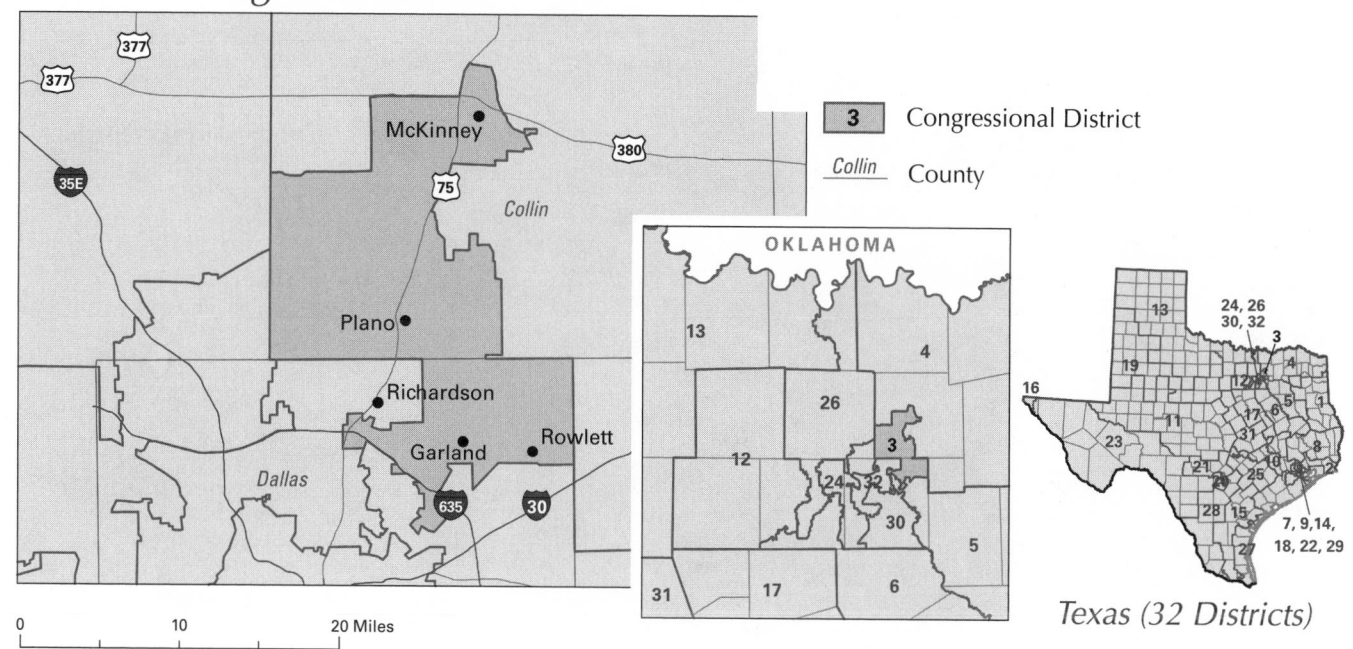

Texas (32 Districts)

Congressional District 4

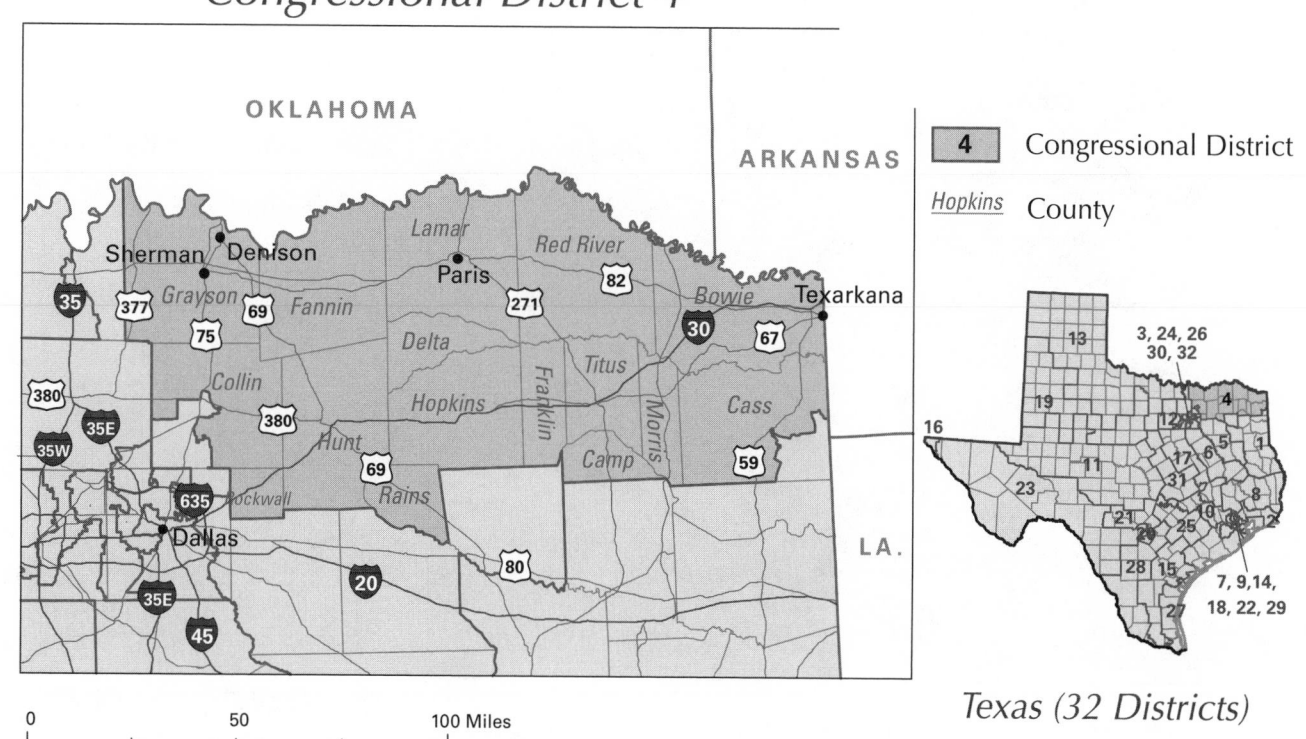

Texas (32 Districts)

Congressional District 5

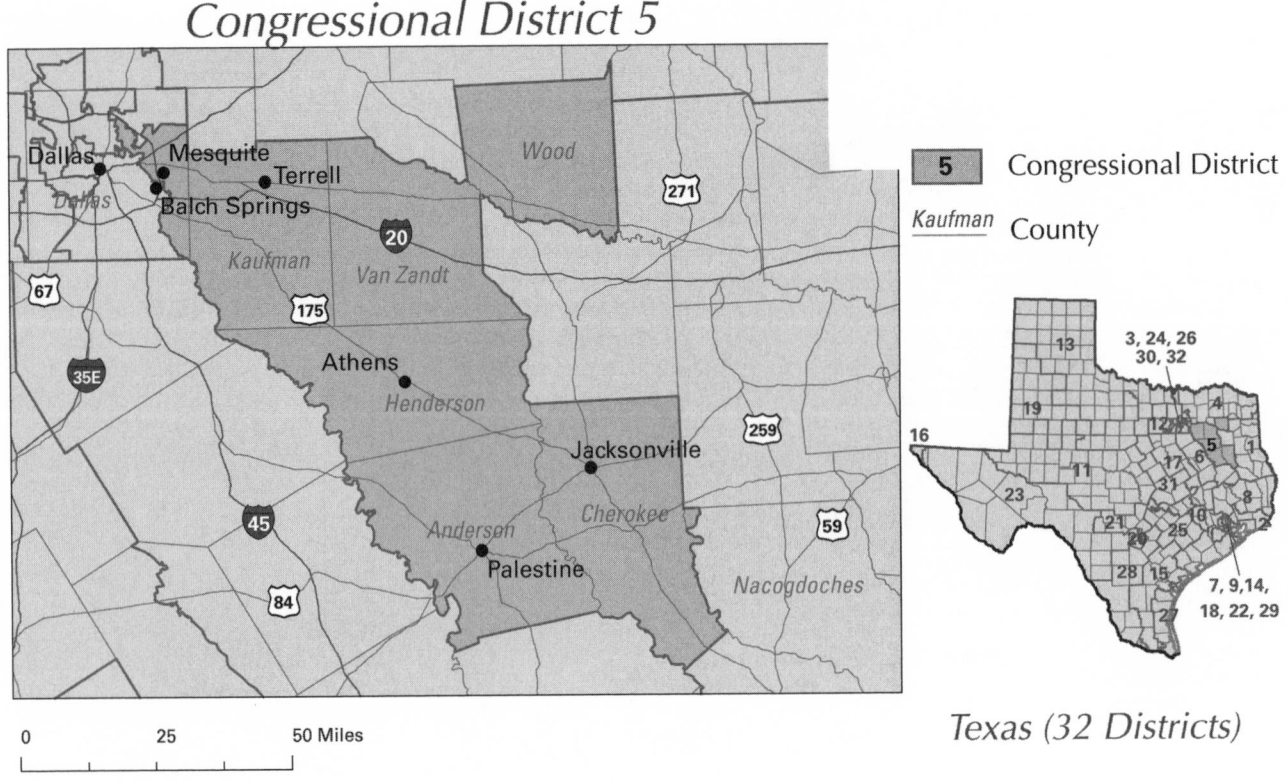

0   25   50 Miles

5 Congressional District

Kaufman County

Texas (32 Districts)

Congressional District 6

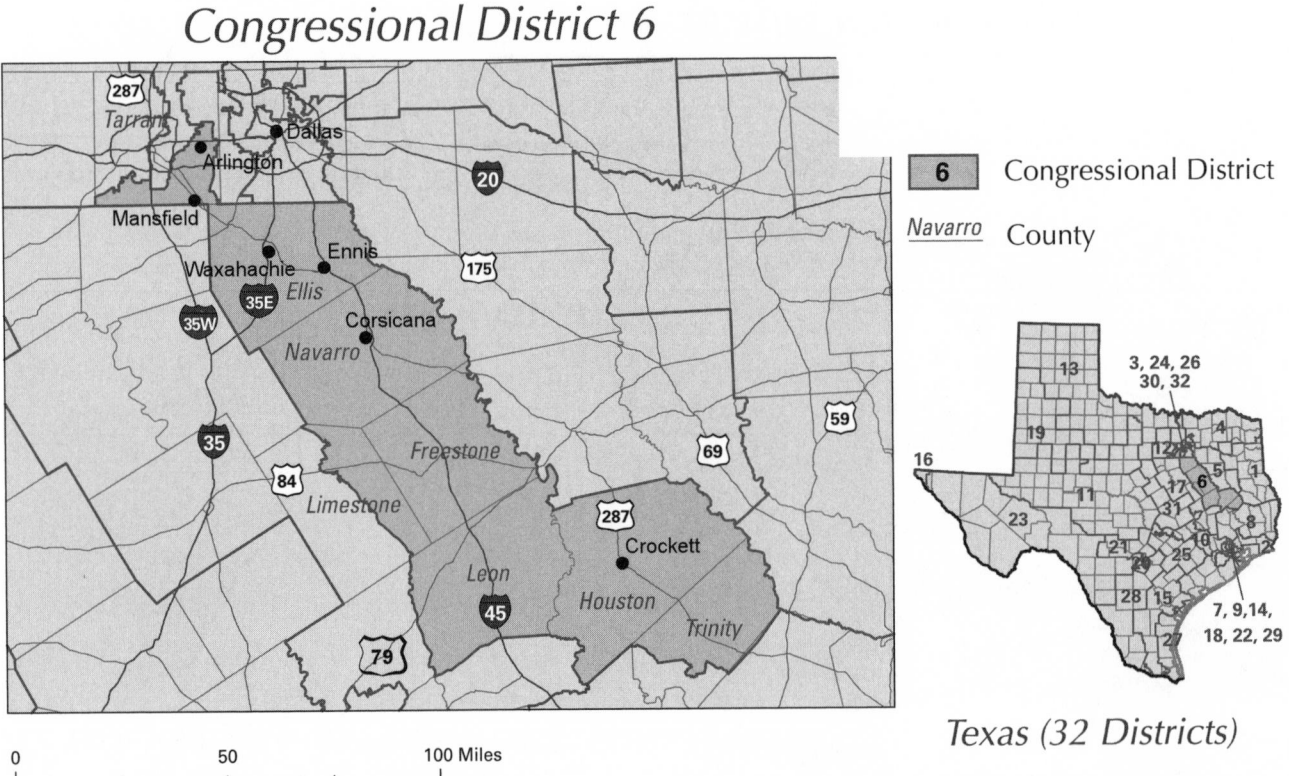

0   50   100 Miles

6 Congressional District

Navarro County

Texas (32 Districts)

Congressional District 7

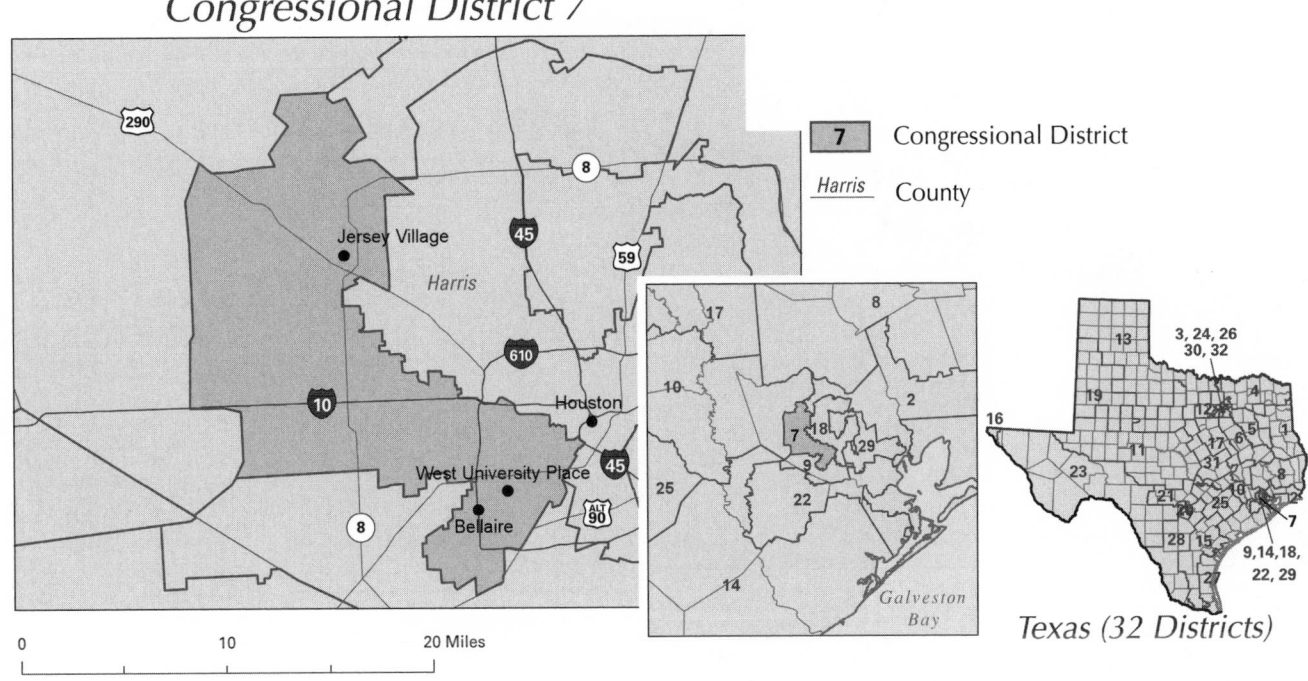

Texas (32 Districts)

Congressional District 8

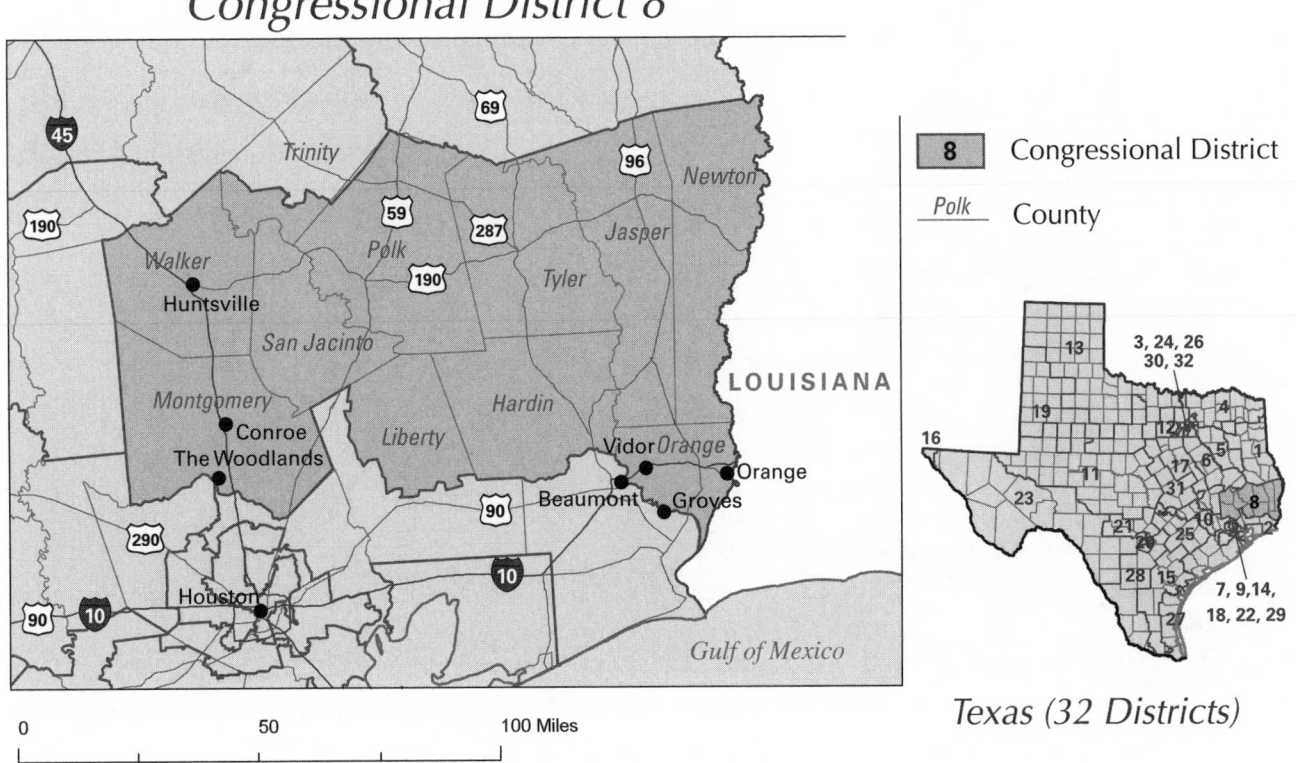

Texas (32 Districts)

Congressional District 9

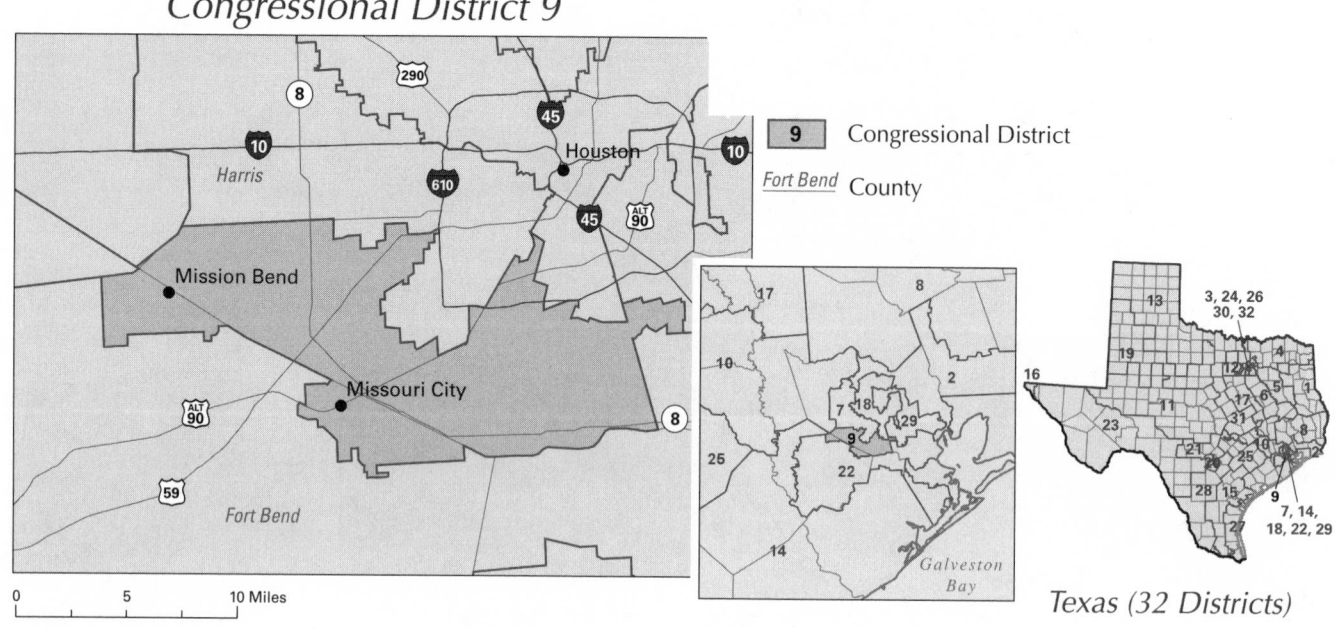

Congressional District 10

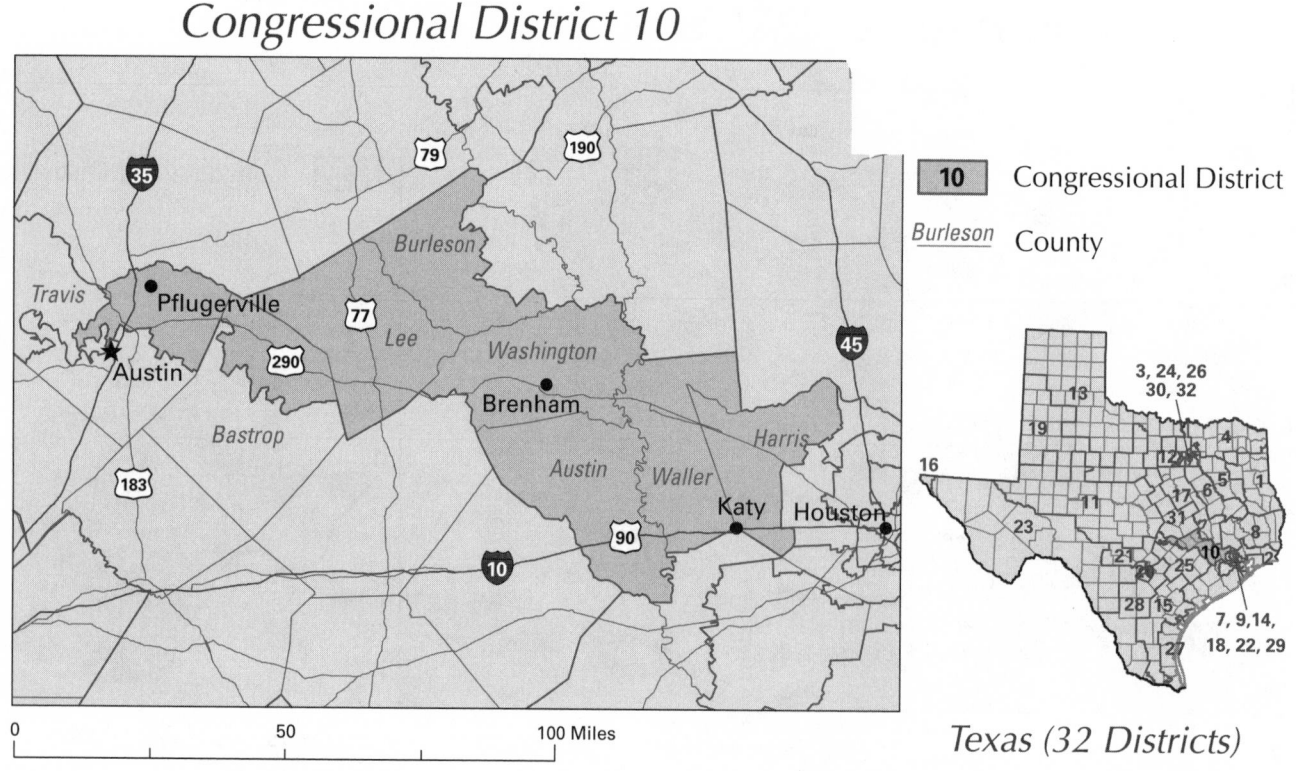

Congressional District 11

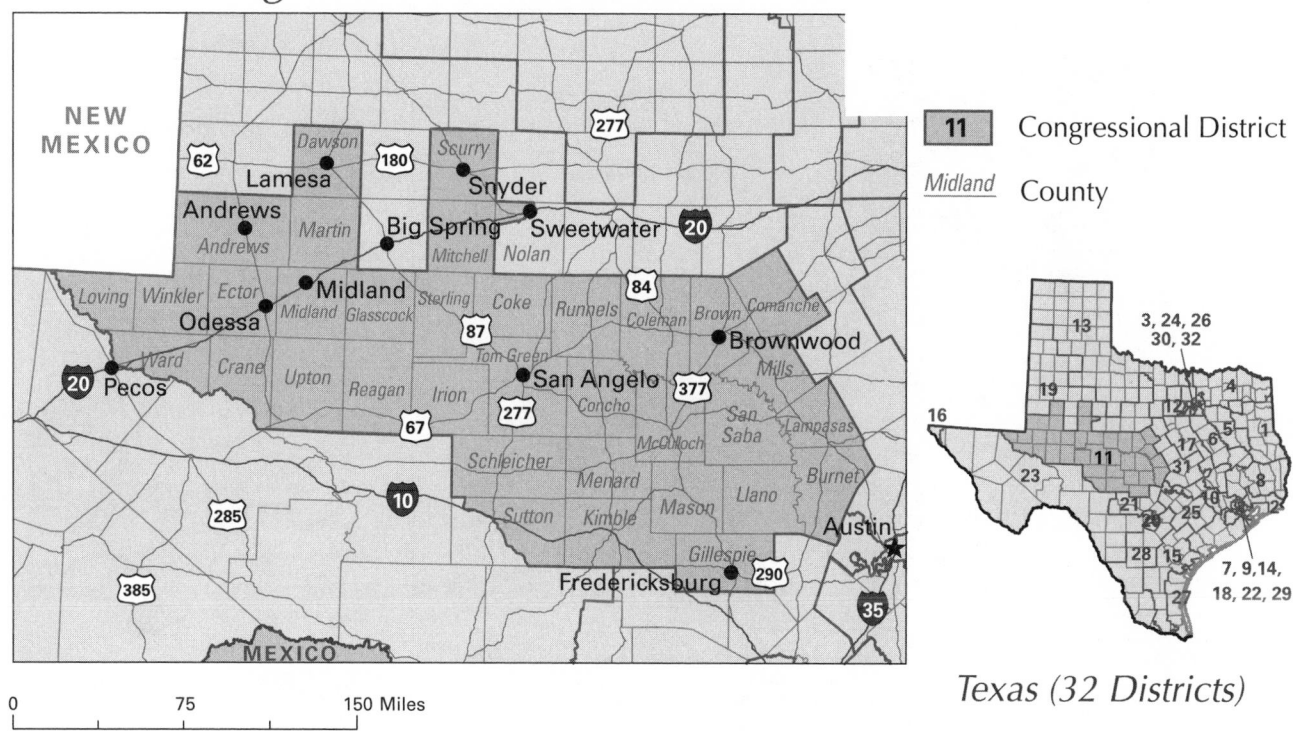

11   Congressional District
Midland   County

Texas (32 Districts)

Congressional District 12

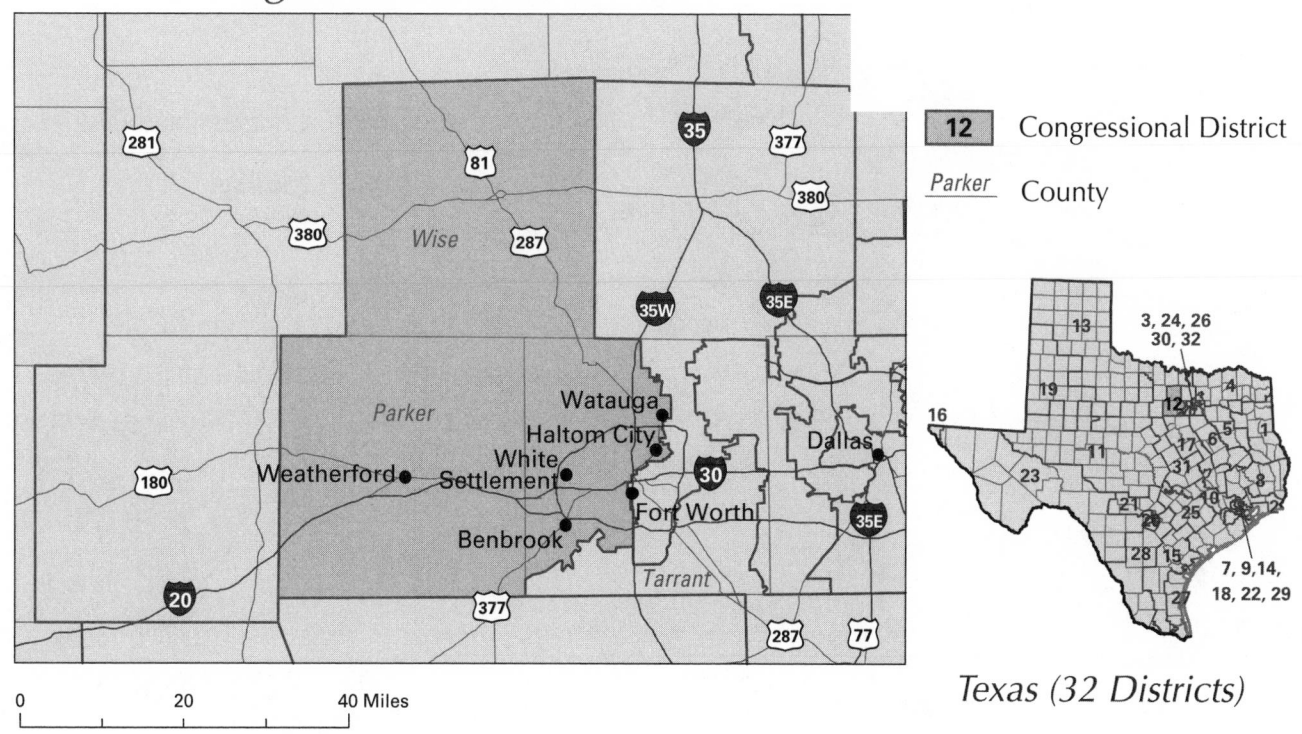

12   Congressional District
Parker   County

Texas (32 Districts)

Congressional District 13

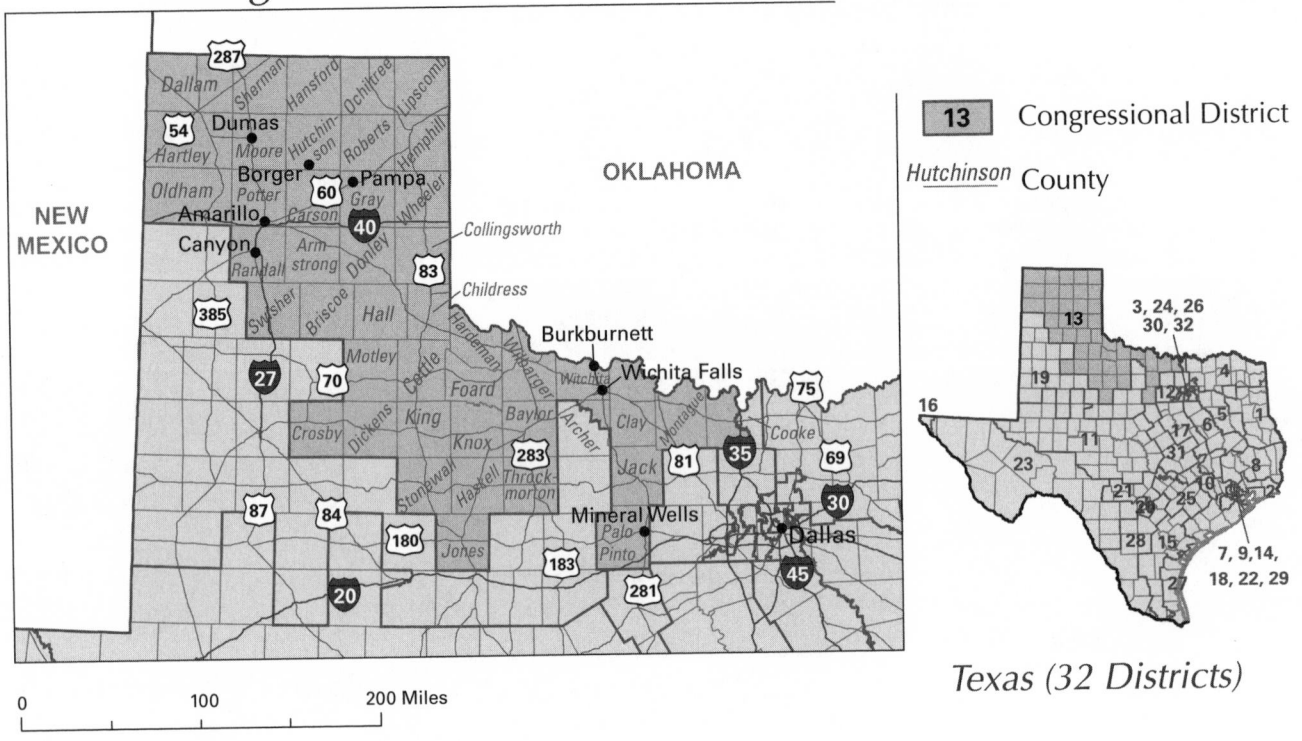

Texas (32 Districts)

Congressional District 14

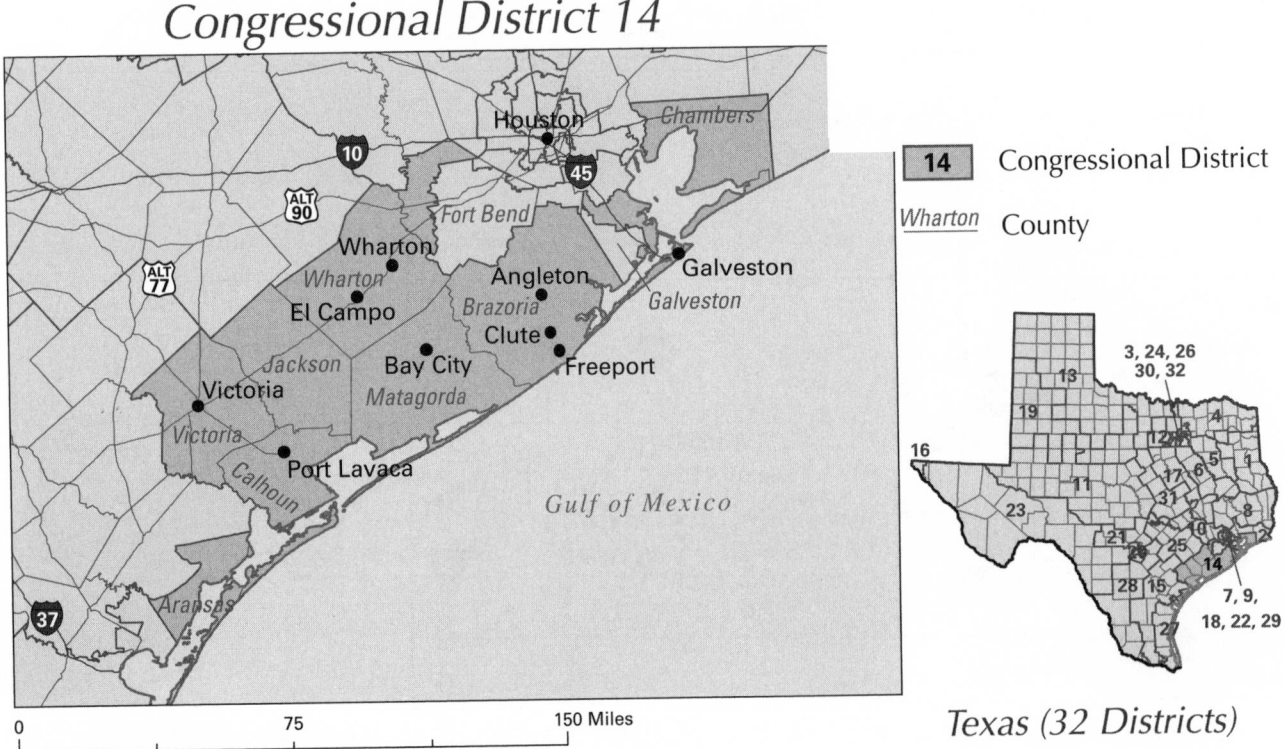

Texas (32 Districts)

Congressional District 15

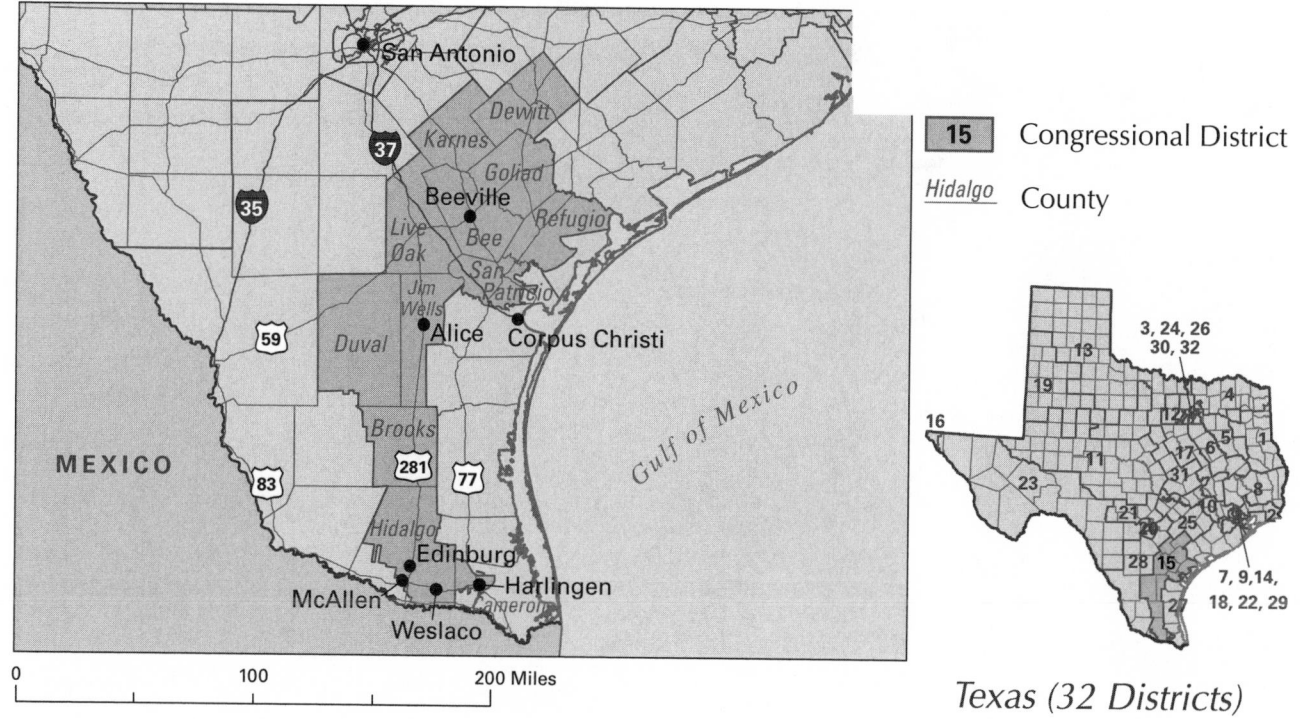

Texas (32 Districts)

Congressional District 16

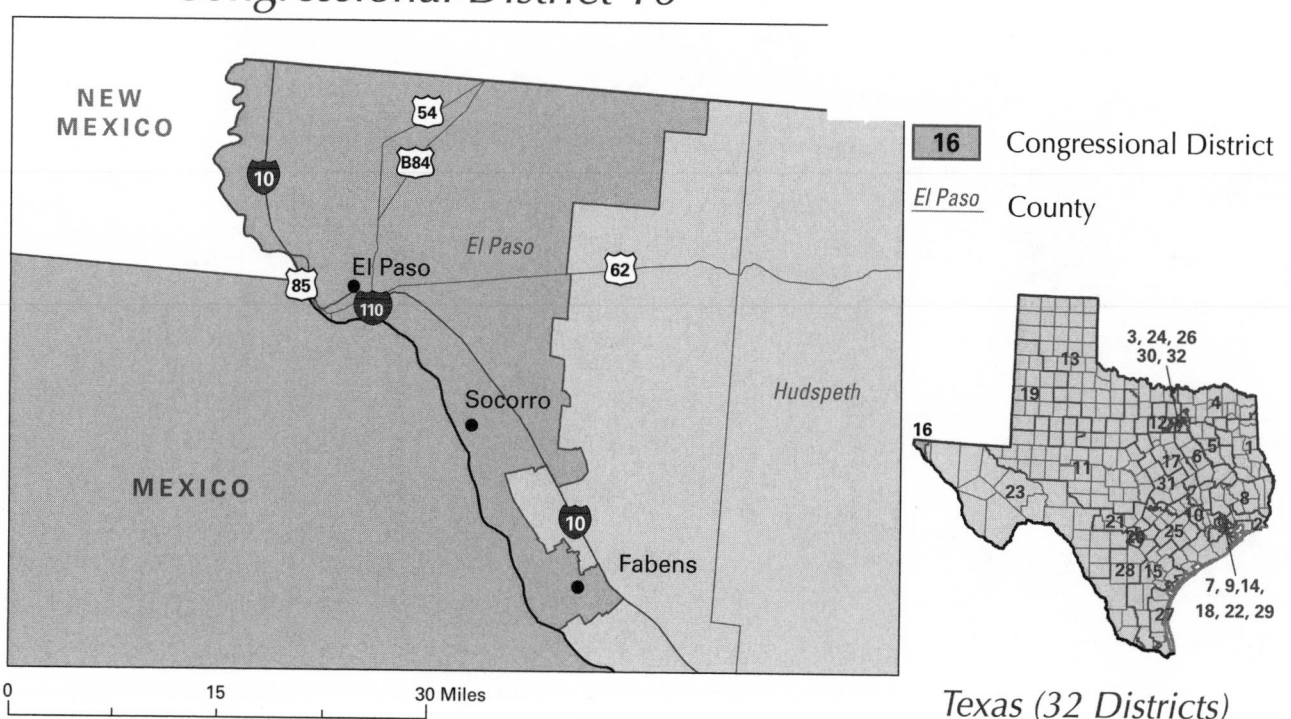

Texas (32 Districts)

Congressional District 17

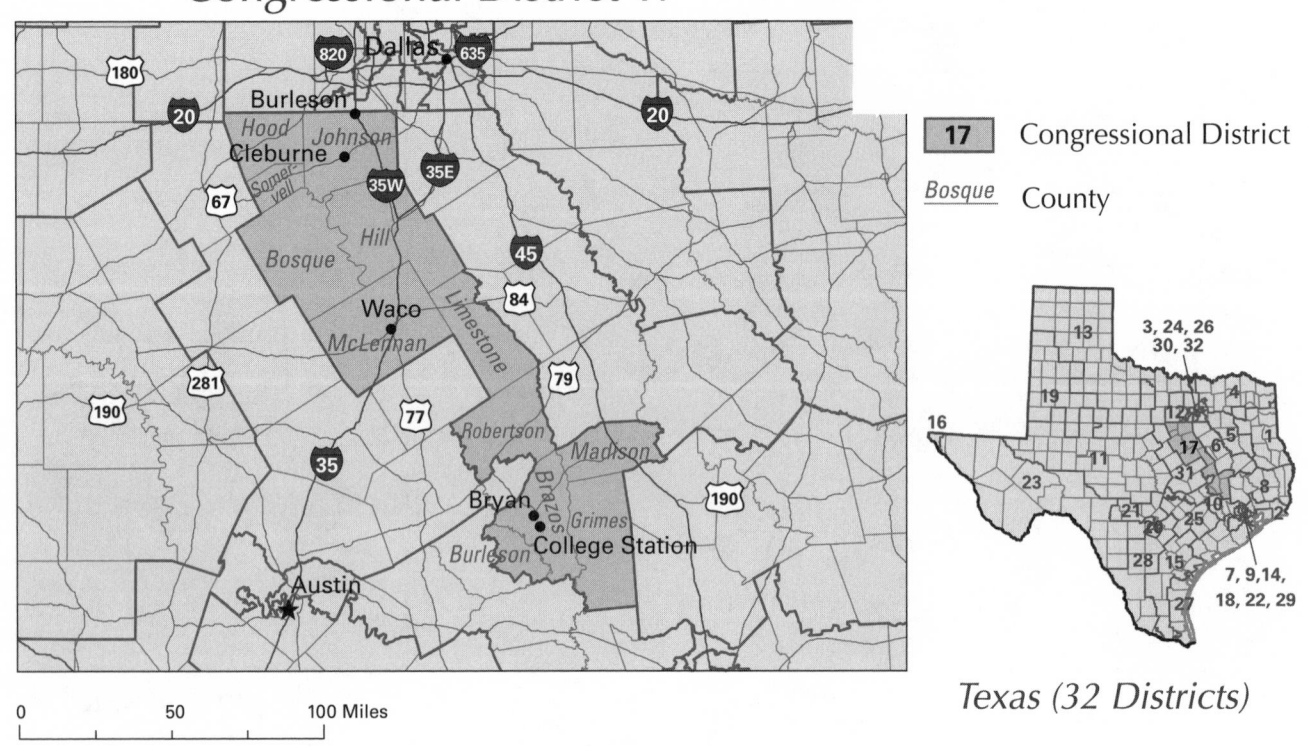

17	Congressional District
Bosque	County

Texas (32 Districts)

Congressional District 18

18	Congressional District
Harris	County

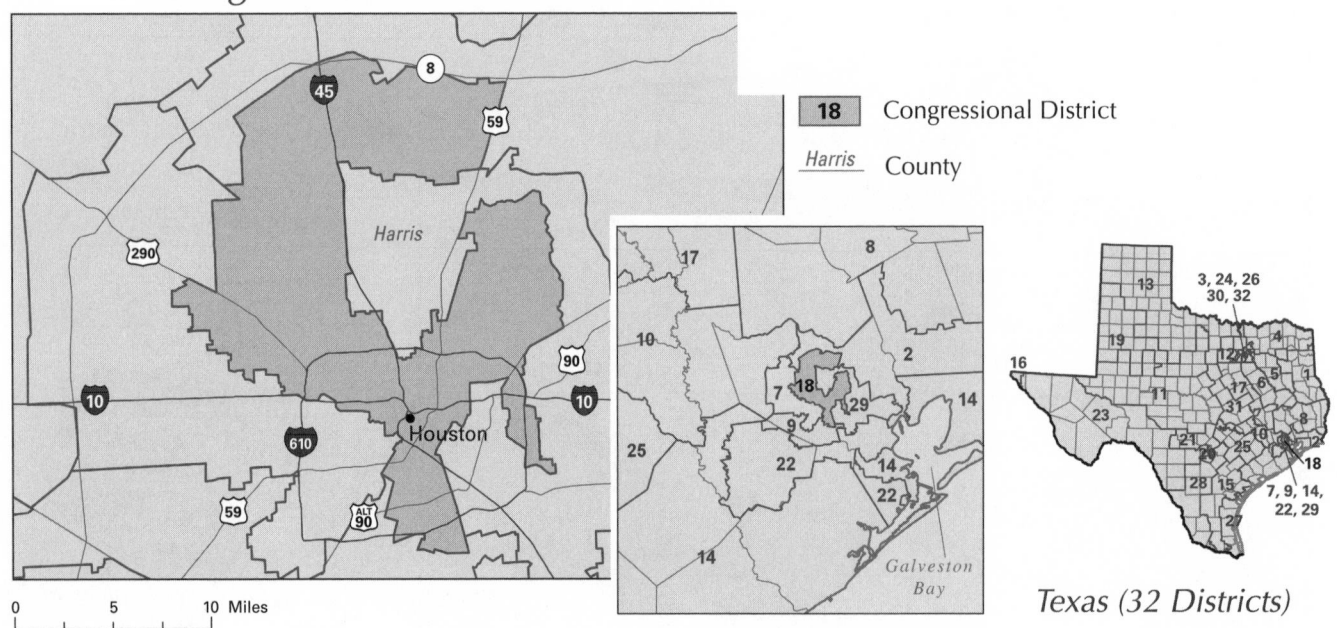

Texas (32 Districts)

Congressional District 19

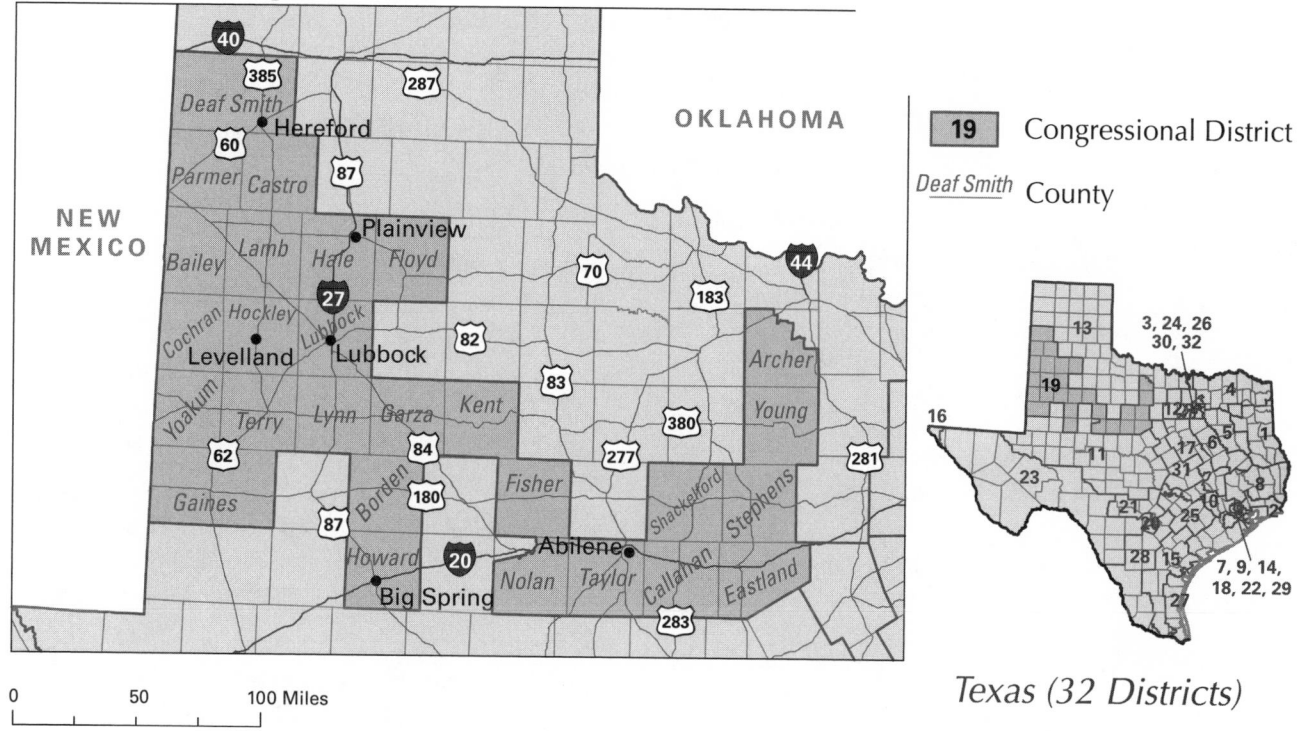

Congressional District 20

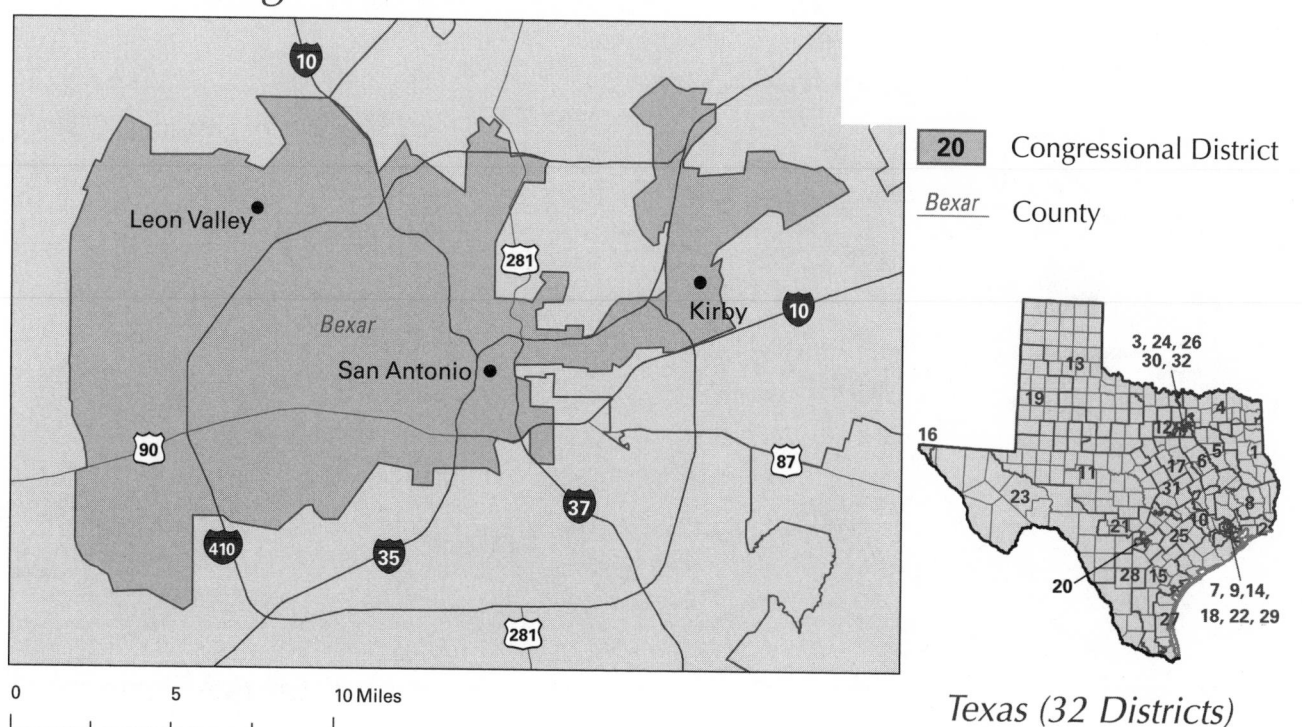

Congressional District 21

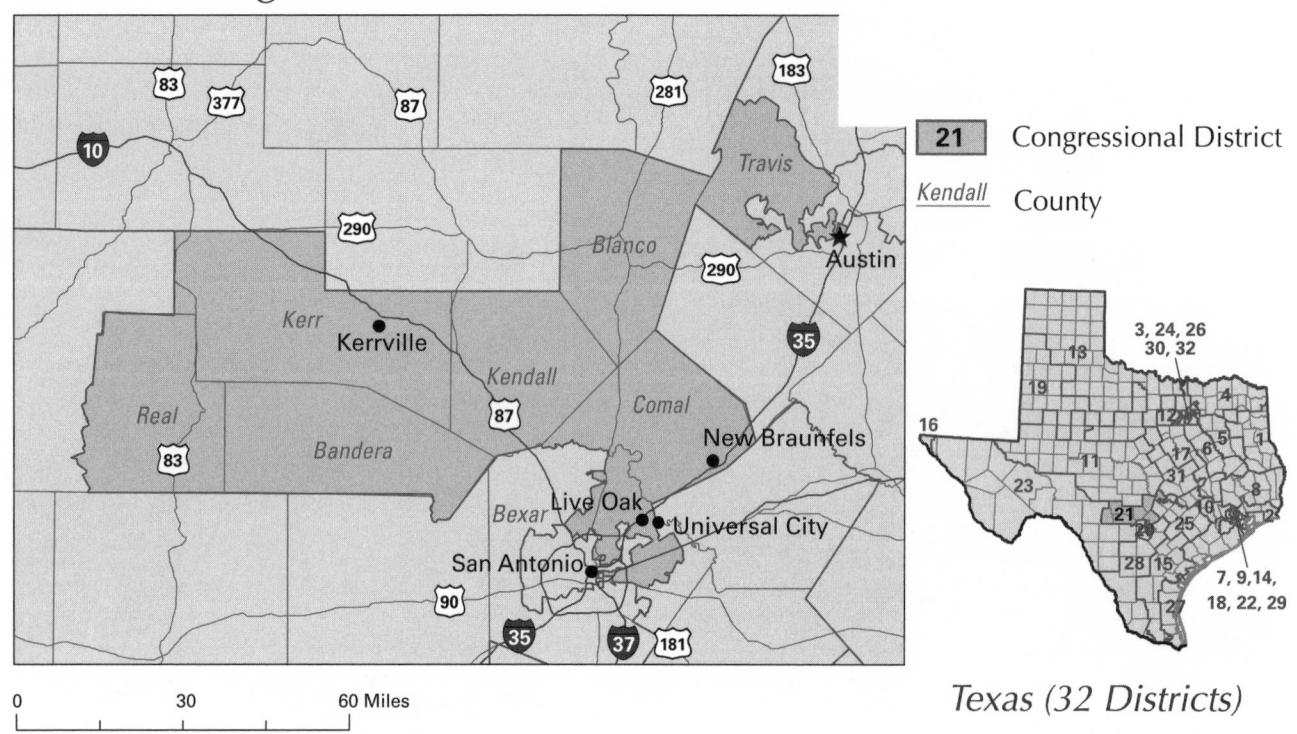

Texas (32 Districts)

Congressional District 22

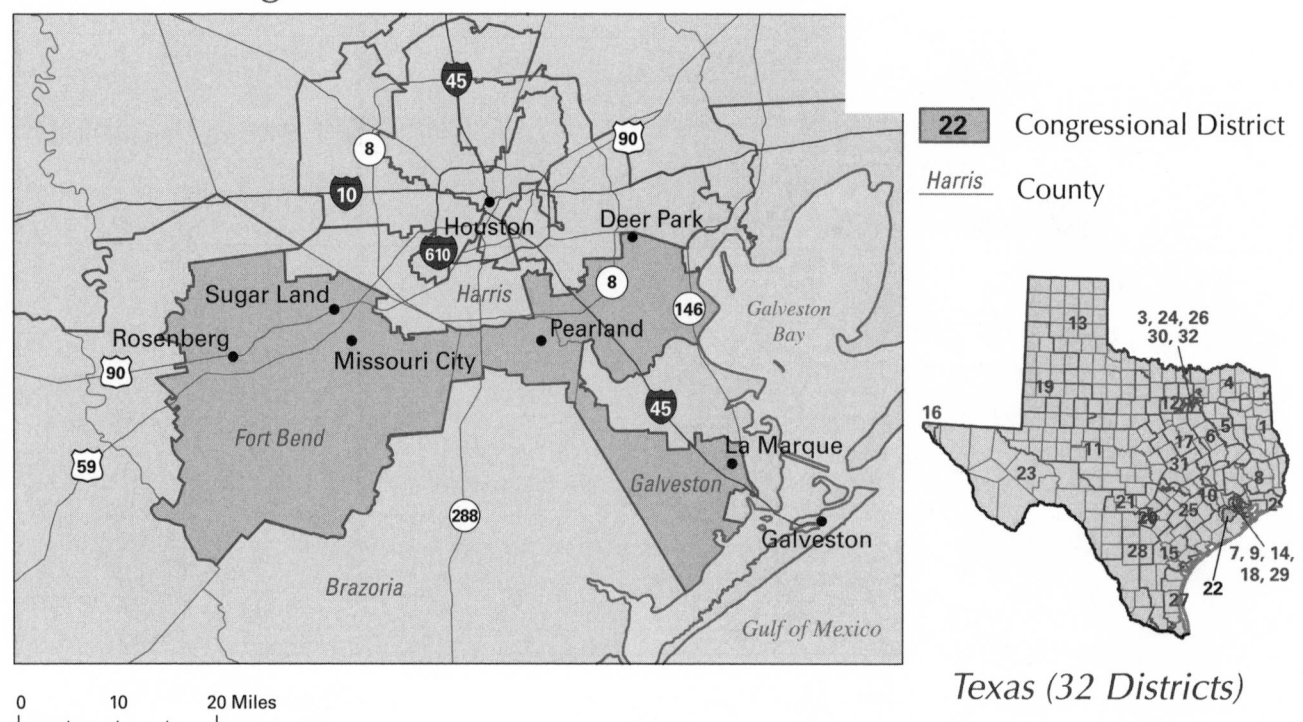

Texas (32 Districts)

Congressional District 23

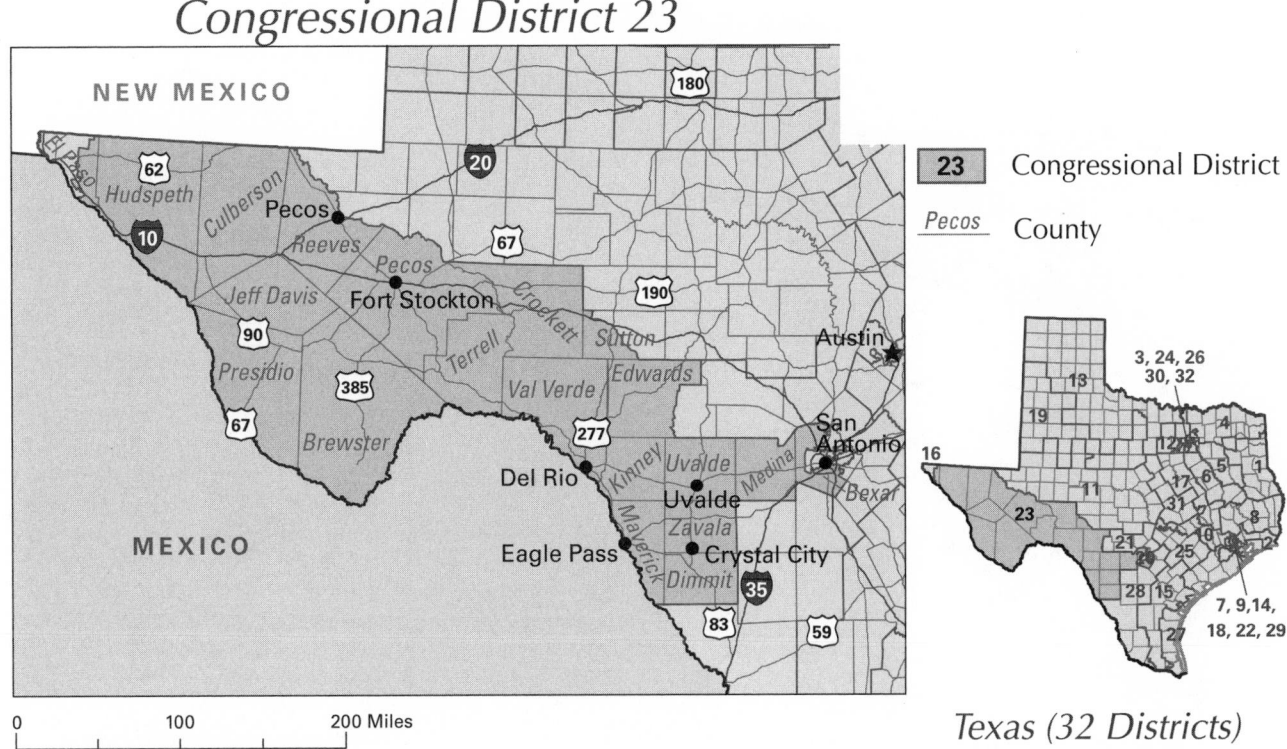

Texas (32 Districts)

Congressional District 24

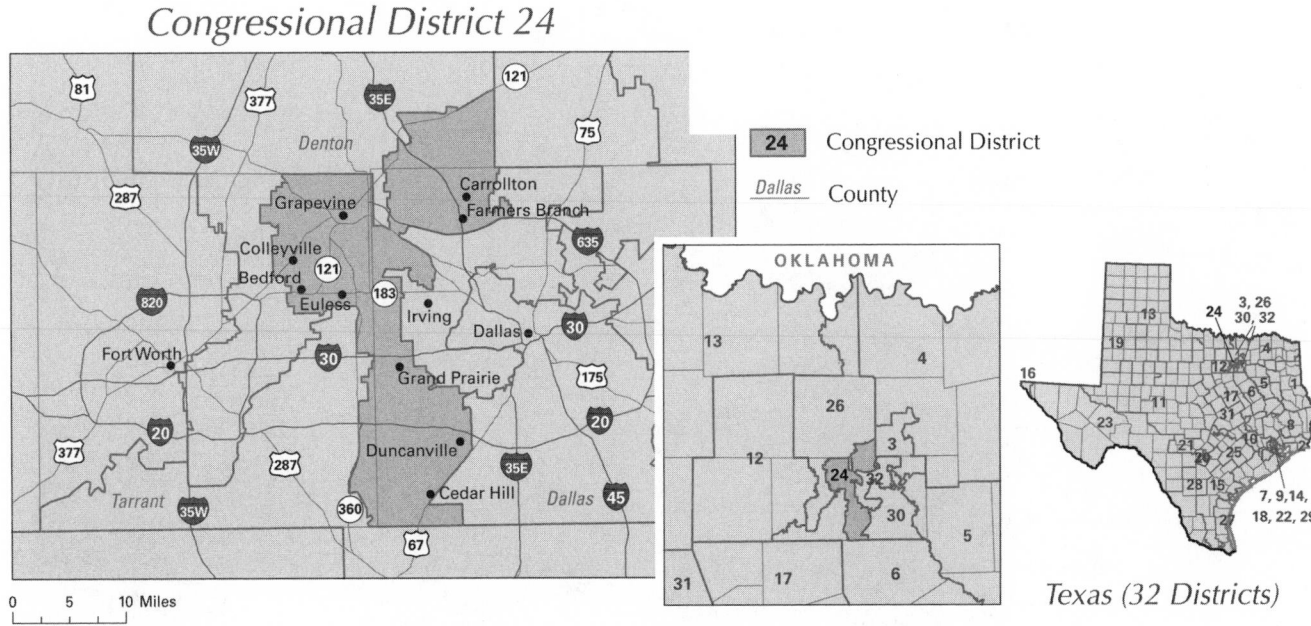

Texas (32 Districts)

Congressional District 25

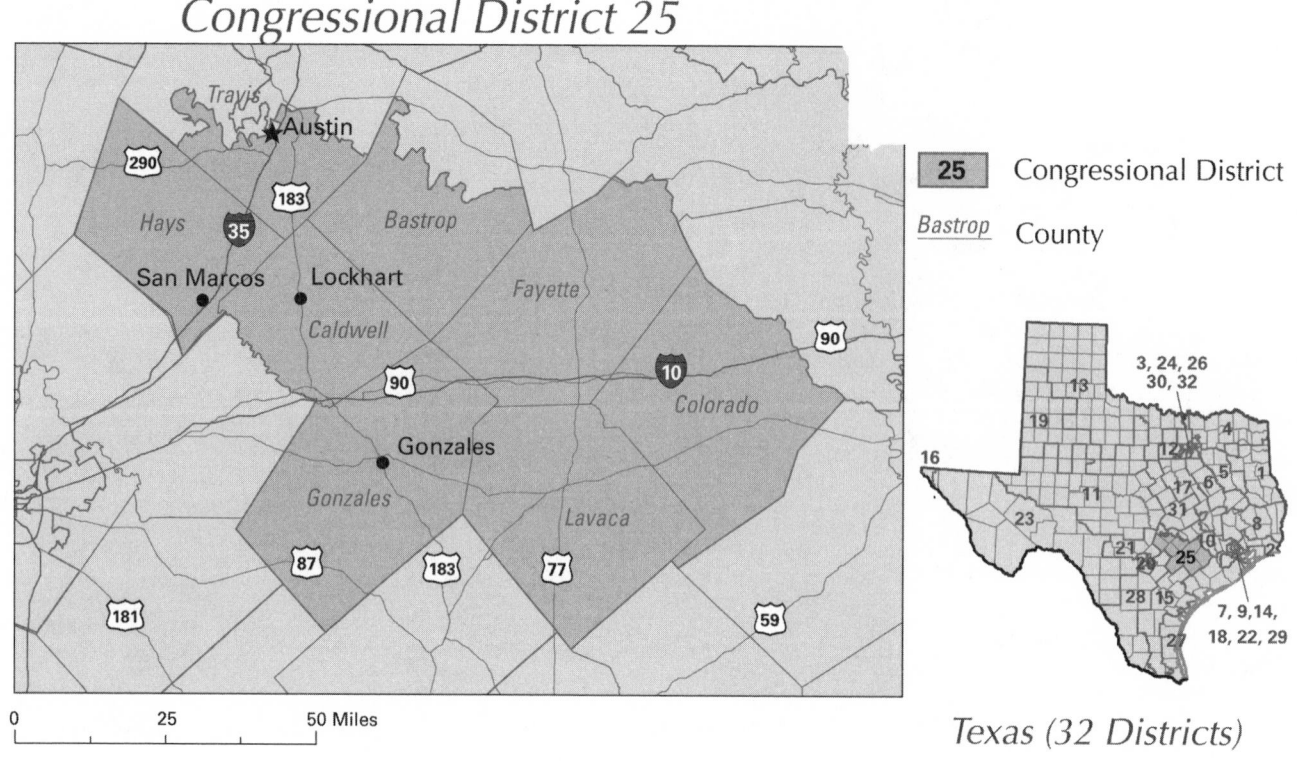

Texas (32 Districts)

Congressional District 26

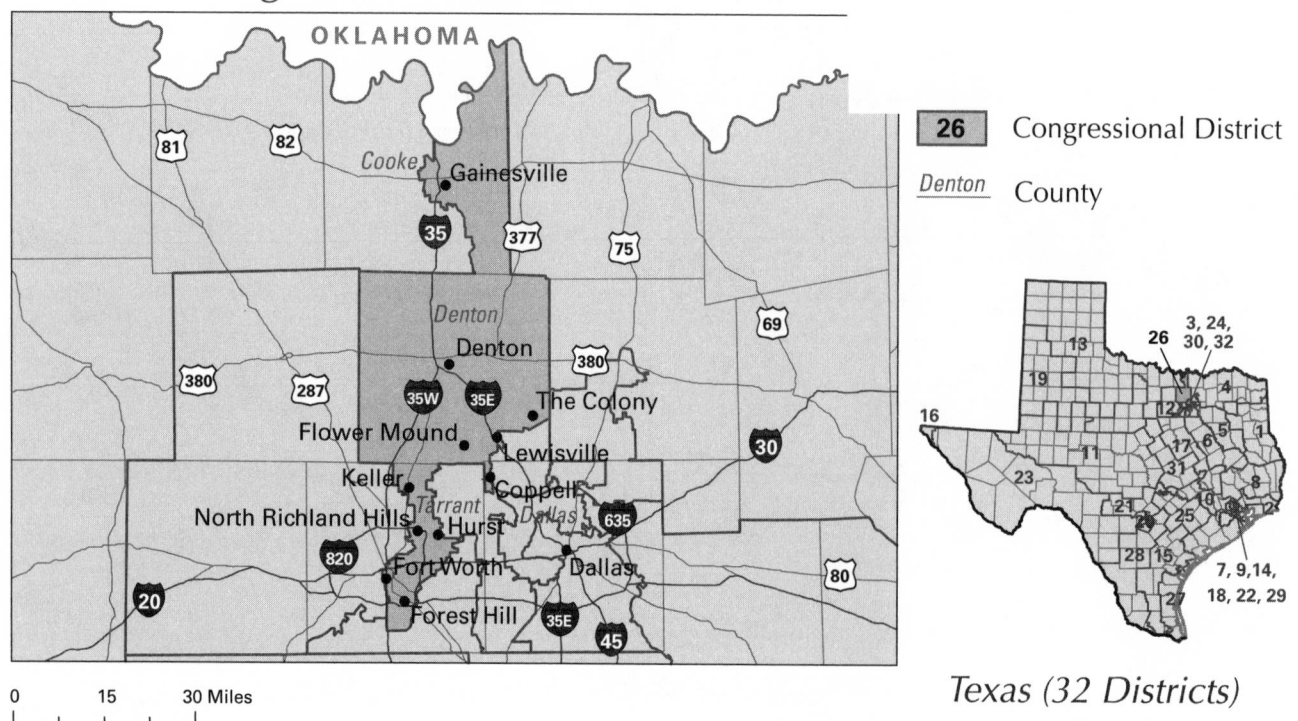

Texas (32 Districts)

Congressional District 27

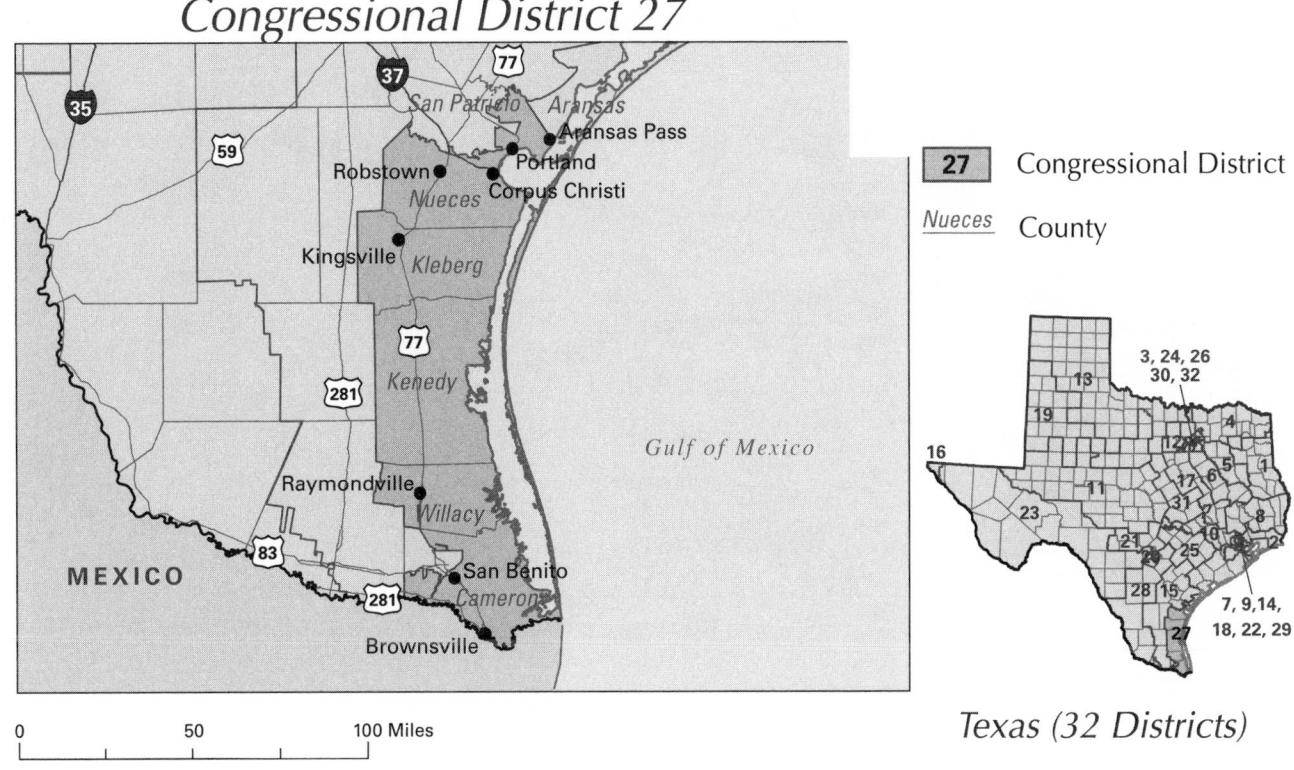

27 Congressional District

Nueces County

Texas (32 Districts)

Congressional District 28

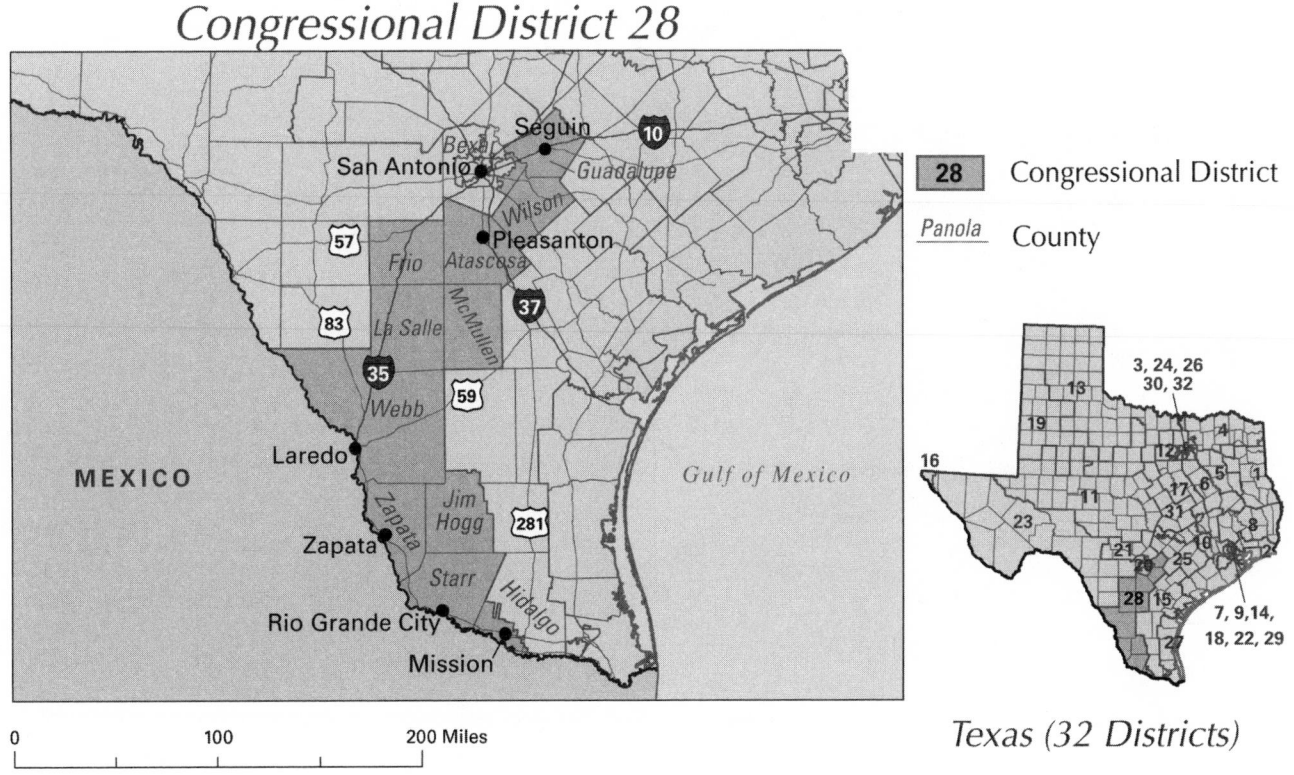

28 Congressional District

Panola County

Texas (32 Districts)

Congressional District 29

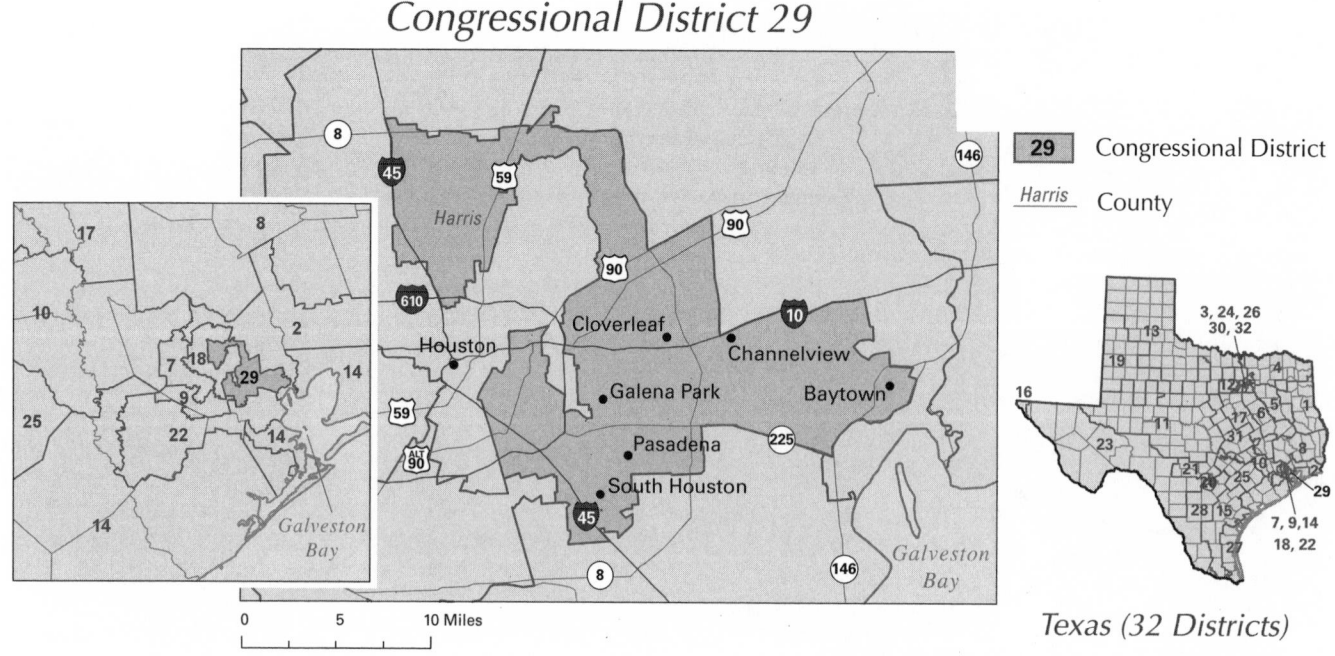

Congressional District 30

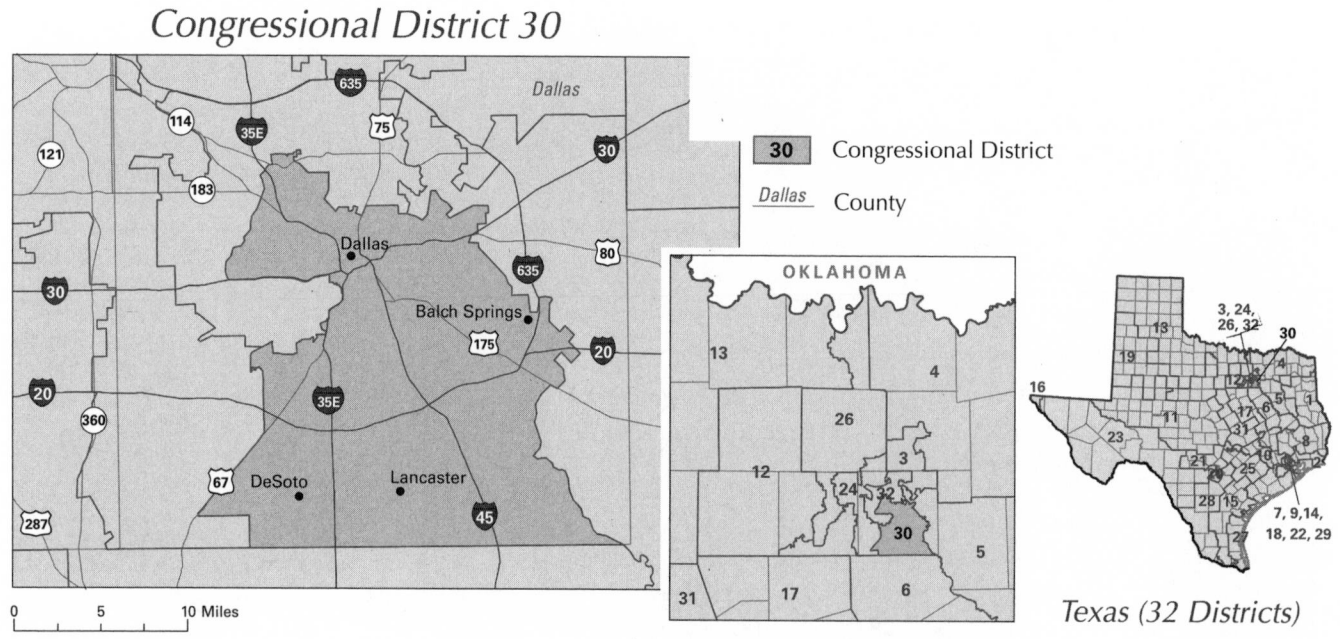

Congressional District 31

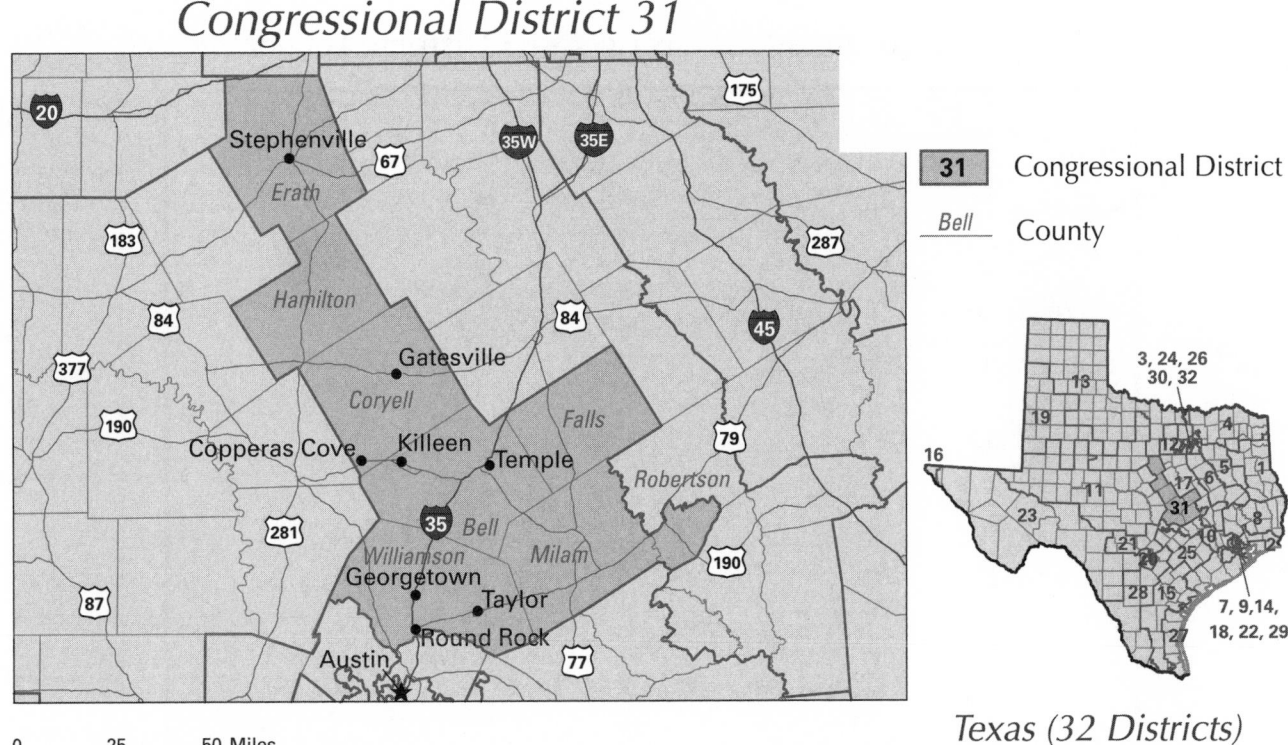

31 Congressional District

Bell County

Texas (32 Districts)

Congressional District 32

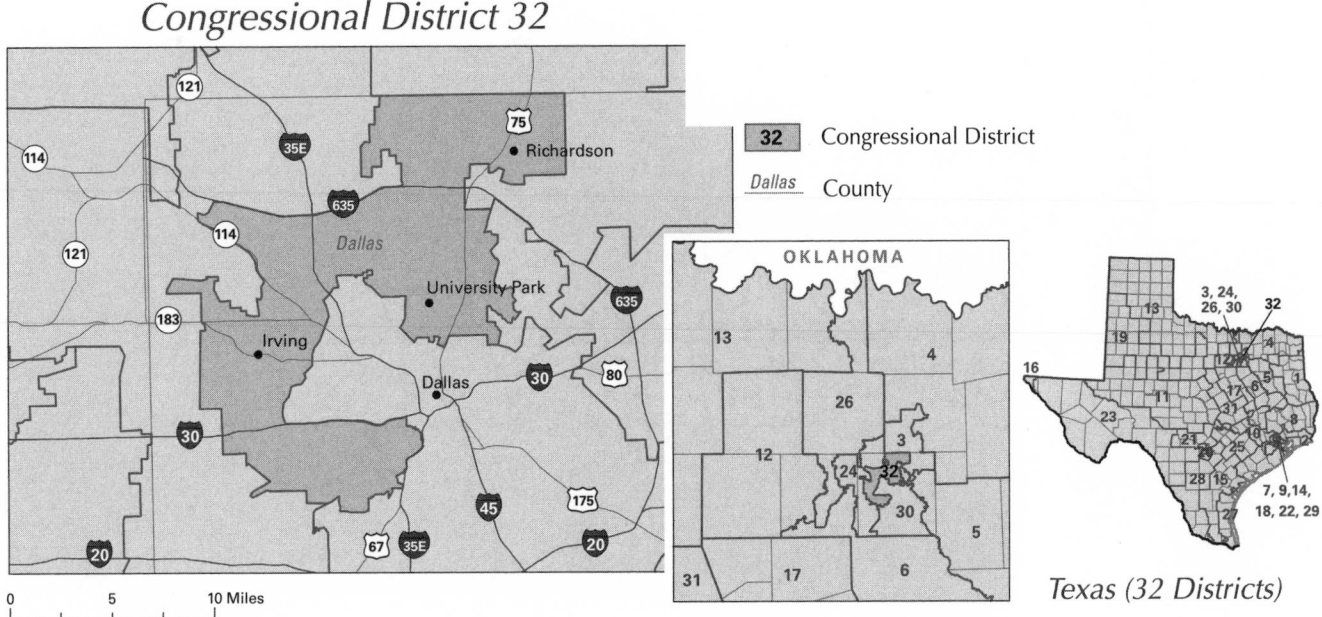

32 Congressional District

Dallas County

Texas (32 Districts)

Utah Congressional Districts — 3 Districts Total

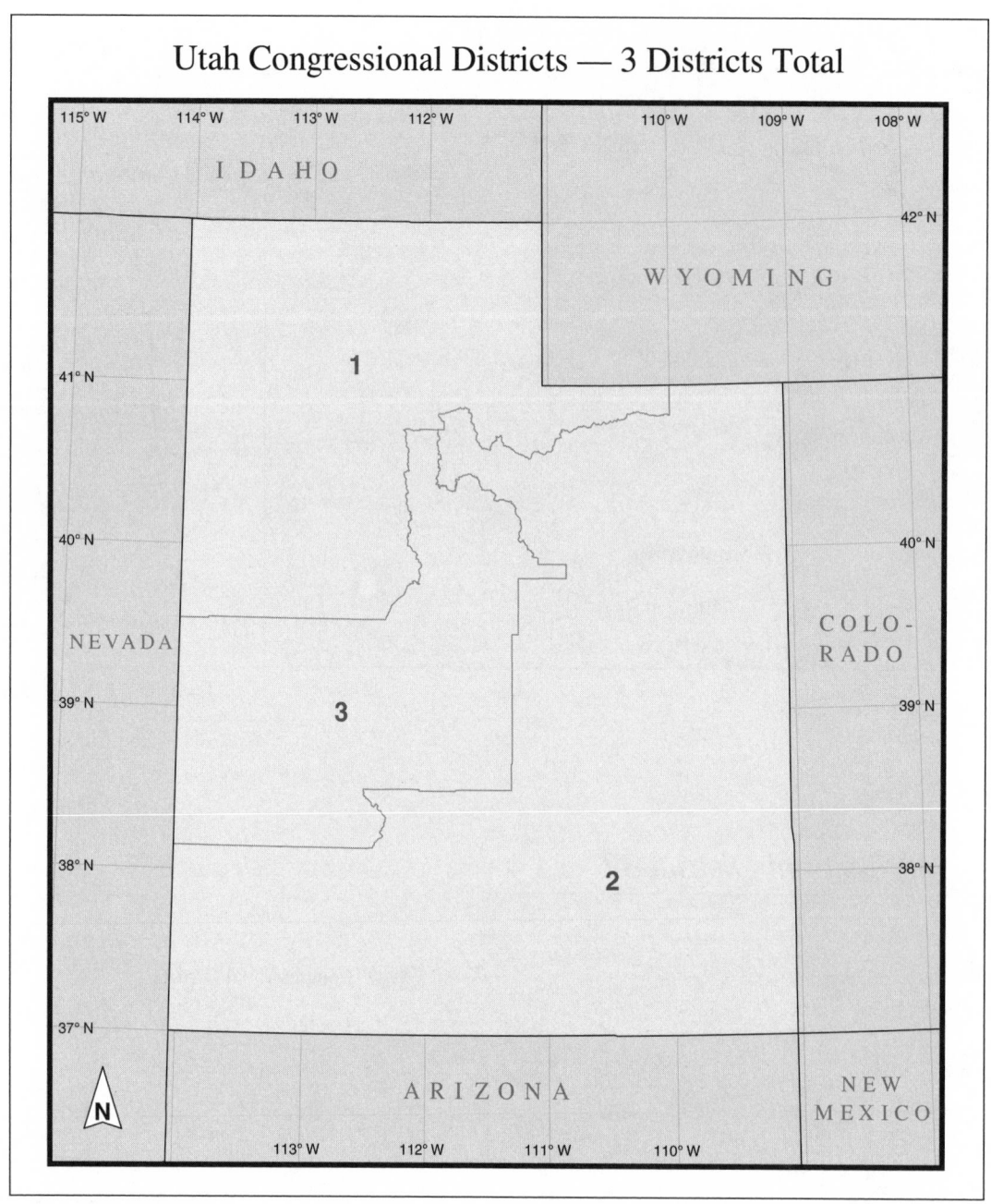

UTAH—110th CONGRESSIONAL DISTRICTS BY COUNTIES

County	Congressional District	County	Congressional District	County	Congressional District
Beaver	3	Iron	2	Sevier	3
Box Elder	1	Juab	1,3	Summit	1
Cache	1	Kane	2	Tooele	1
Carbon	2	Millard	3	Uintah	2
Daggett	2	Morgan	1	Utah	2,3
Davis	1	Piute	2	Wasatch	2
Duchesne	2	Rich	1	Washington	2
Emery	2	Salt Lake	1–3	Wayne	2
Garfield	2	San Juan	2	Weber	1
Grand	2	Sanpete	3		

Congressional District 1

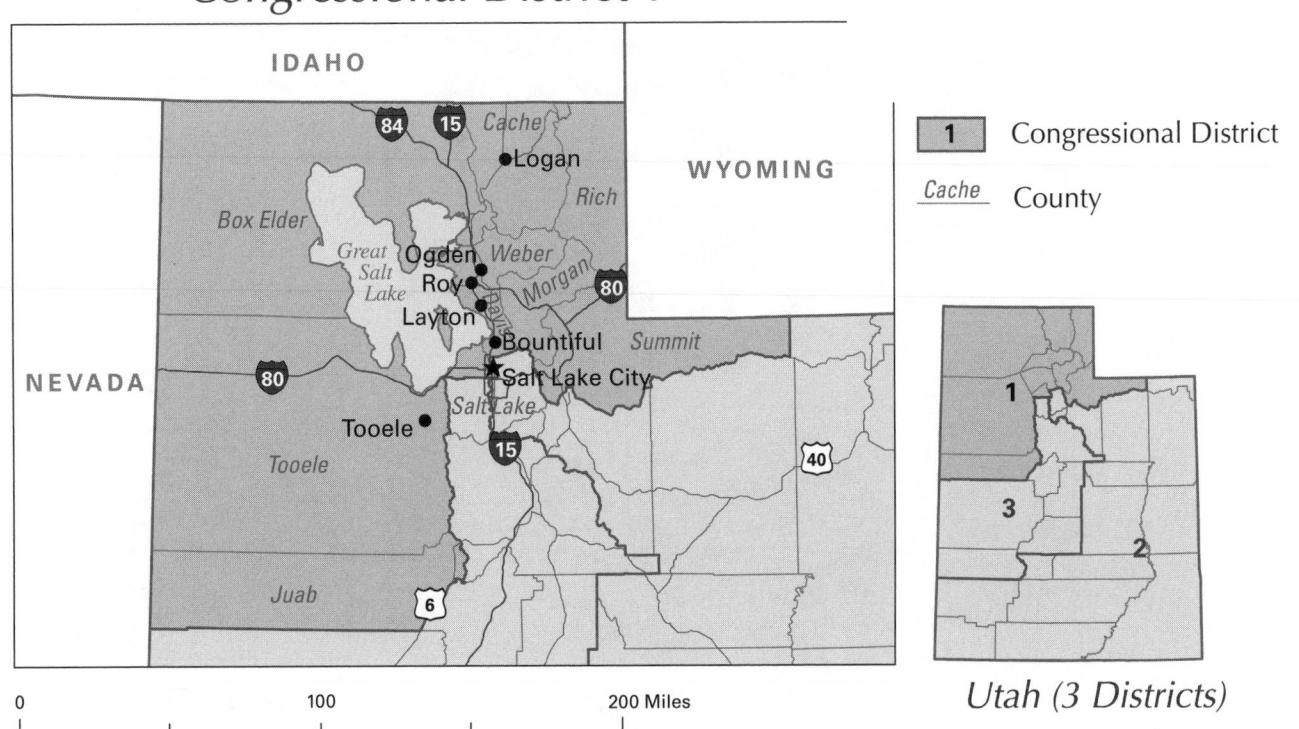

Utah (3 Districts)

Congressional District 2

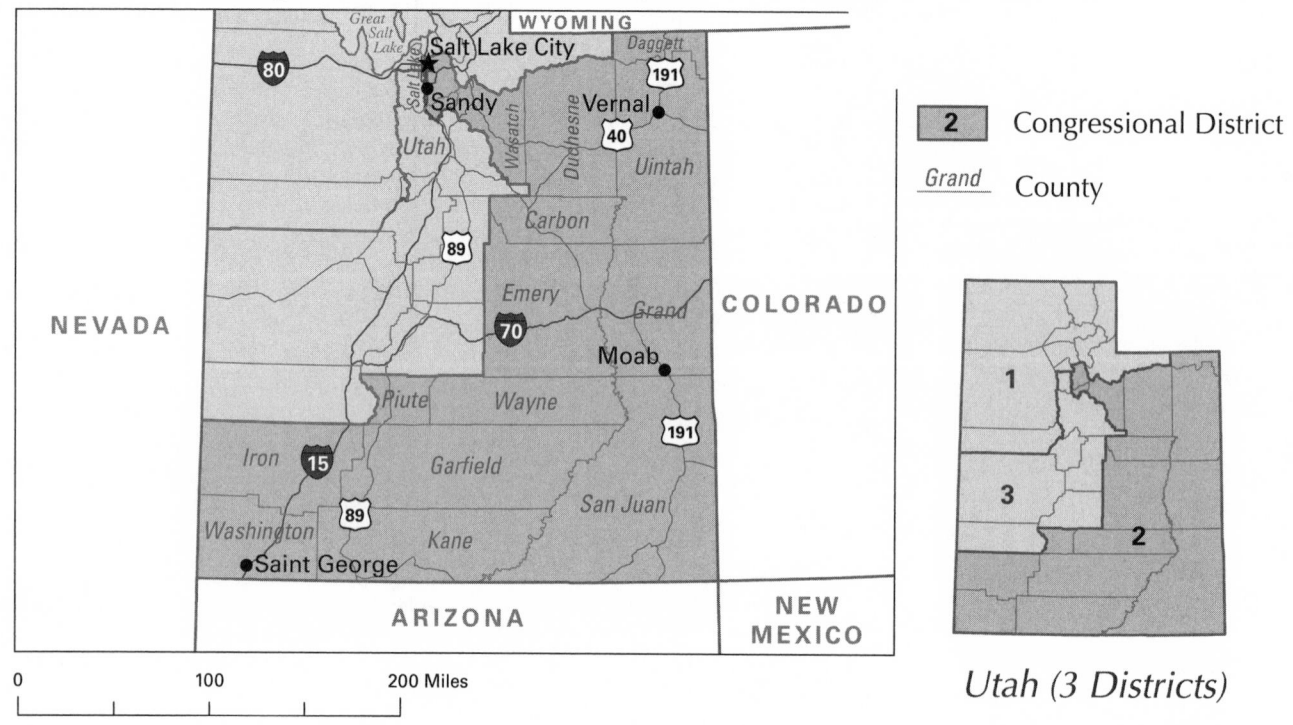

Utah (3 Districts)

Congressional District 3

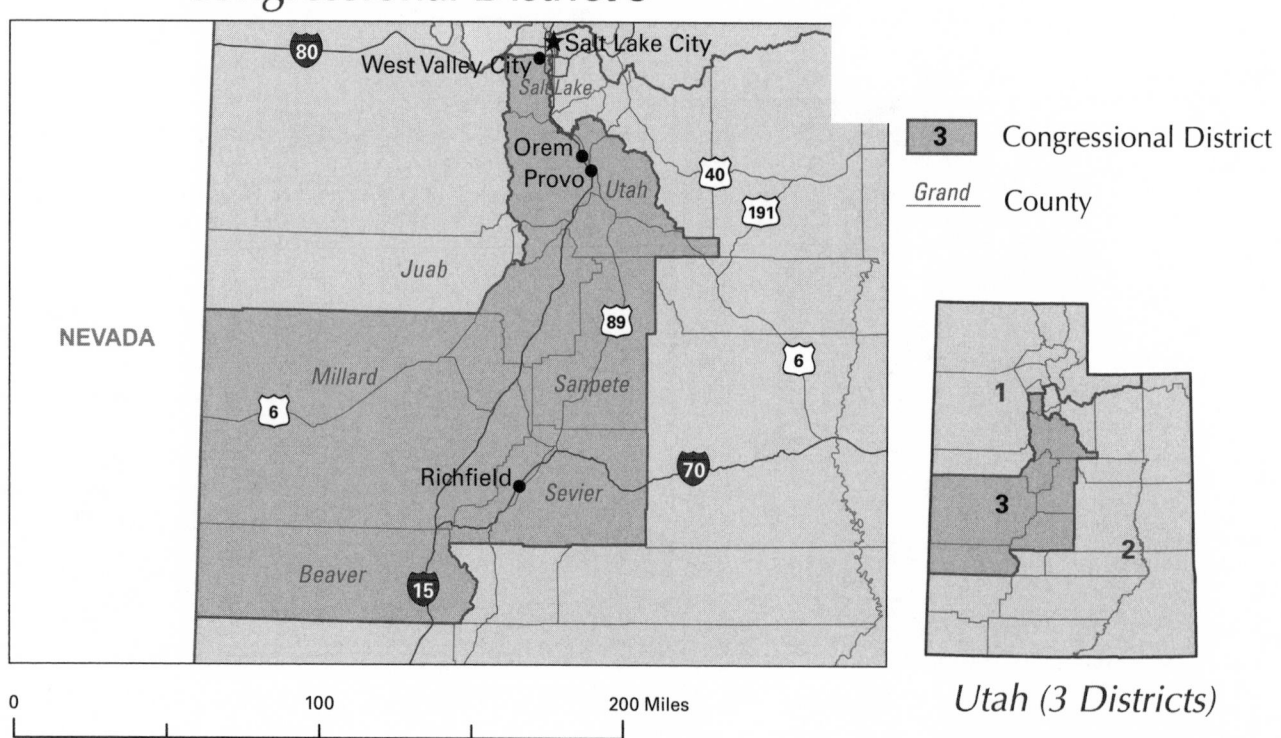

Utah (3 Districts)

Vermont—

Congressional District: At large

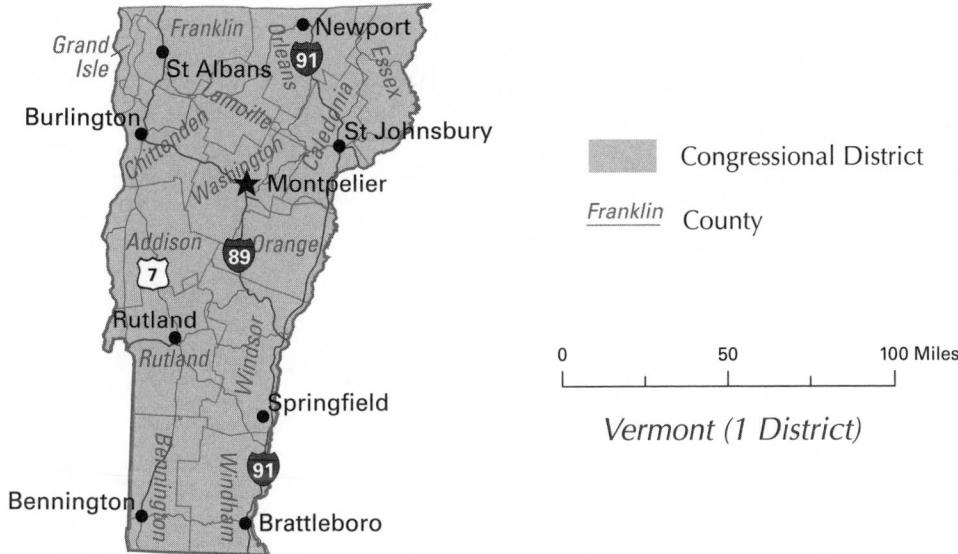

Congressional District

Franklin County

0   50   100 Miles

Vermont (1 District)

VERMONT—110th CONGRESSIONAL DISTRICTS BY COUNTIES

County	Congressional District	County	Congressional District
Addison	1	Lamoille	1
Bennington	1	Orange	1
Caledonia	1	Orleans	1
Chittenden	1	Rutland	1
Essex	1	Washington	1
Franklin	1	Windham	1
Grand Isle	1	Windsor	1

Virginia Congressional Districts — 11 Districts Total

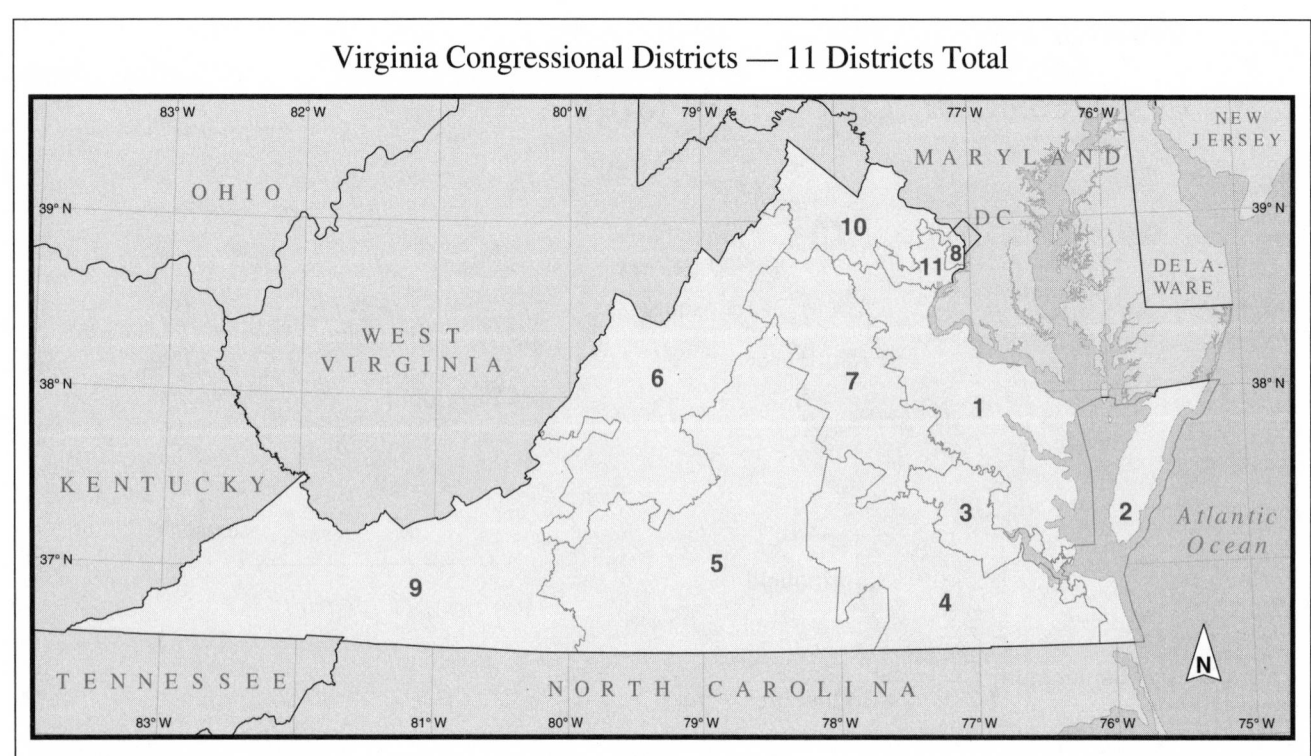

VIRGINIA—110th CONGRESSIONAL DISTRICTS BY COUNTIES AND INDEPENDENT CITIES

County	Congressional District
Accomack	2
Albemarle	5
Alleghany	6, 9
Amelia	4
Amherst	6
Appomattox	5
Arlington	8
Augusta	6
Bath	6
Bedford	5, 6
Bland	9
Botetourt	6
Brunswick	4, 5
Buchanan	9
Buckingham	5
Campbell	5
Caroline	1, 7
Carroll	9
Charles City	3
Charlotte	5
Chesterfield	4, 7
Clarke	10
Craig	9
Culpeper	7
Cumberland	5
Dickenson	9
Dinwiddie	4
Essex	1
Fairfax	8, 10, 11
Fauquier	1, 10
Floyd	9
Fluvanna	5
Franklin	5
Frederick	10
Giles	9
Gloucester	1
Goochland	7
Grayson	9
Greene	5
Greensville	4
Halifax	5
Hanover	7
Henrico	3, 7
Henry	5, 9
Highland	6
Isle of Wight	3, 4

County	Congressional District
James City	1, 3
King and Queen	1
King George	1
King William	1
Lancaster	1
Lee	9
Loudoun	10
Louisa	7
Lunenburg	5
Madison	7
Mathews	1
Mecklenburg	5
Middlesex	1
Montgomery	9
Nelson	5
New Kent	3
Northampton	2
Northumberland	1
Nottoway	4
Orange	7
Page	7
Patrick	9
Pittsylvania	5
Powhatan	4
Prince Edward	5
Prince George	3, 4
Prince William	1, 10, 11
Pulaski	9
Rappahannock	7
Richmond	1
Roanoke	6, 9
Rockbridge	6
Rockingham	6
Russell	9
Scott	9
Shenandoah	6
Smyth	9
Southampton	4
Spotsylvania	1, 7
Stafford	1
Surry	3
Sussex	4
Tazewell	9
Warren	10
Washington	9
Westmoreland	1

County	Congressional District
Wise	9
Wythe	9
York	1
Alexandria city	8
Bedford city	5
Bristol city	9
Buena Vista city	6
Charlottesville city	5
Chesapeake city	4
Clifton Forge city	9
Colonial Heights city	4
Covington city	6, 9
Danville city	5
Emporia city	4
Fairfax city	11
Falls Church city	8
Franklin city	4
Fredericksburg city	1
Galax city	9
Hampton city	1–3
Harrisonburg city	6
Hopewell city	4
Lexington city	6
Lynchburg city	6
Manassas city	10
Manassas Park city	10
Martinsville city	5
Newport News city	1, 3
Norfolk city	2, 3
Norton city	9
Petersburg city	4
Poquoson city	1
Portsmouth city	3
Radford city	9
Richmond city	3, 7
Roanoke city	6
Salem city	6
Staunton city	6
Suffolk city	4
Virginia Beach city	2
Waynesboro city	6
Williamsburg city	1
Winchester city	10

Congressional District 1

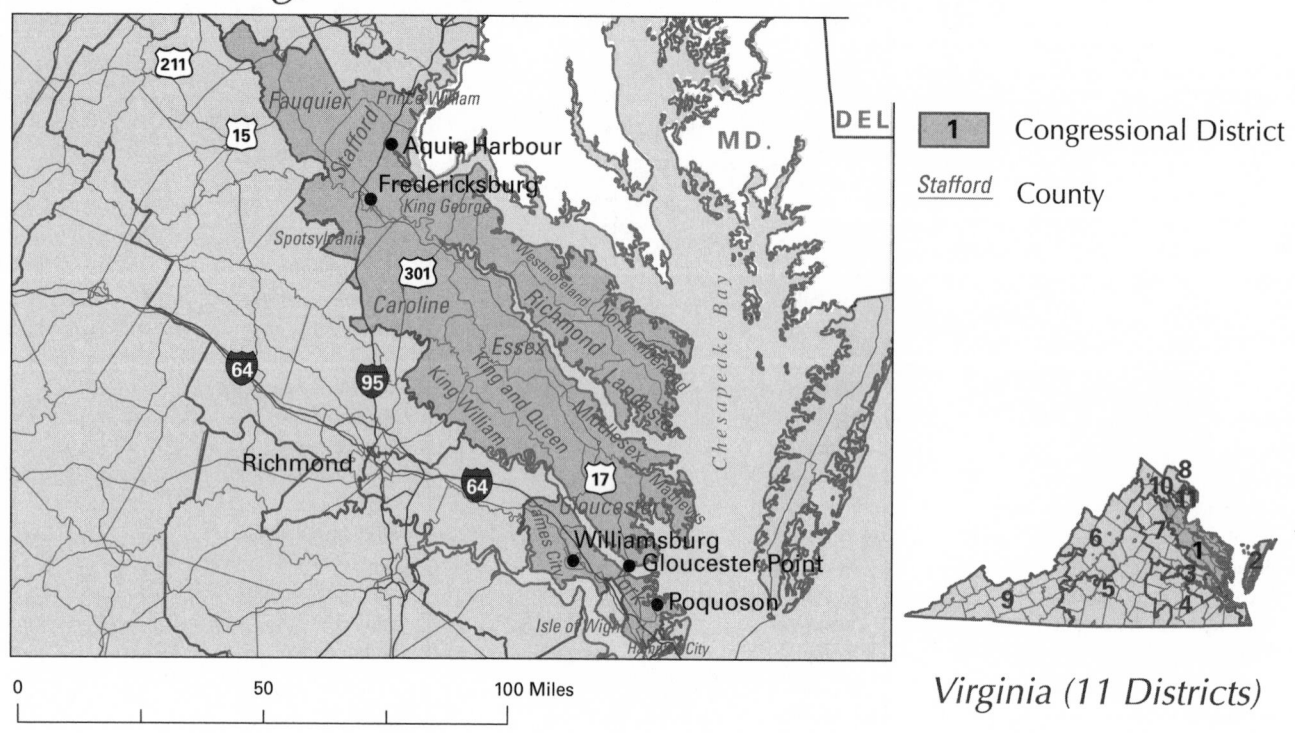

Virginia (11 Districts)

Congressional District 2

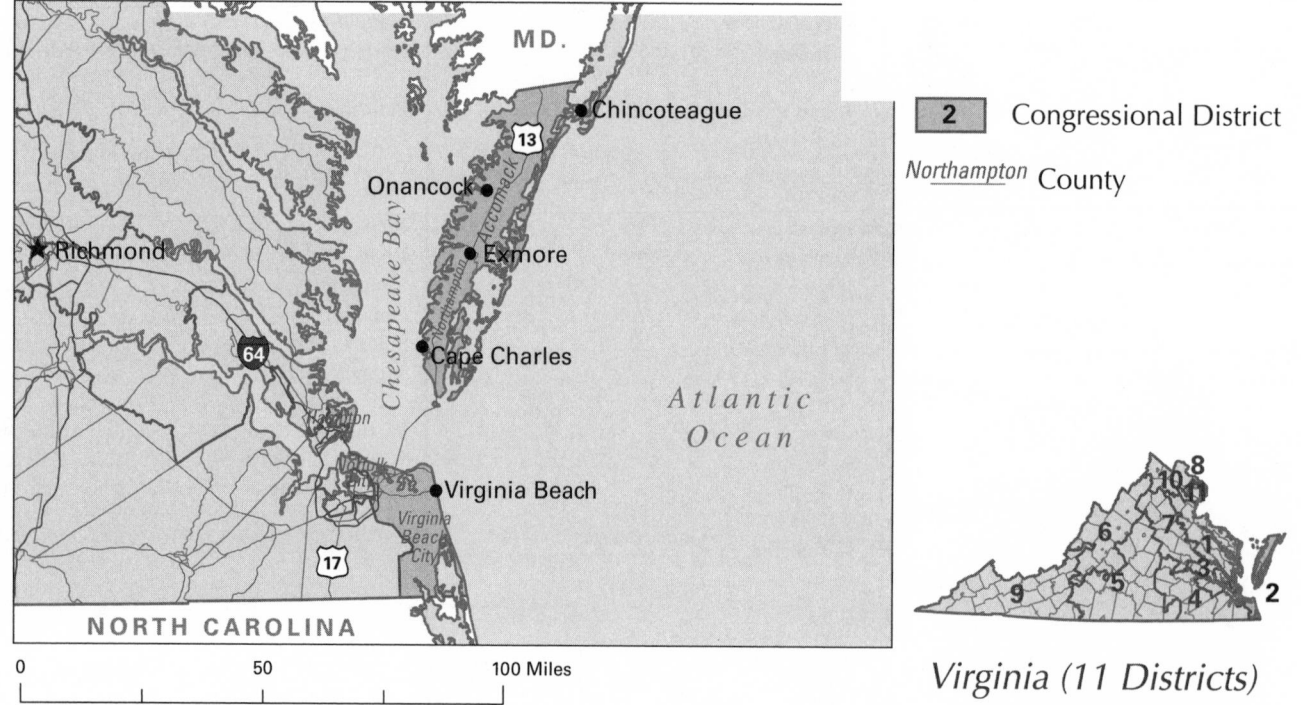

Virginia (11 Districts)

Congressional District 3

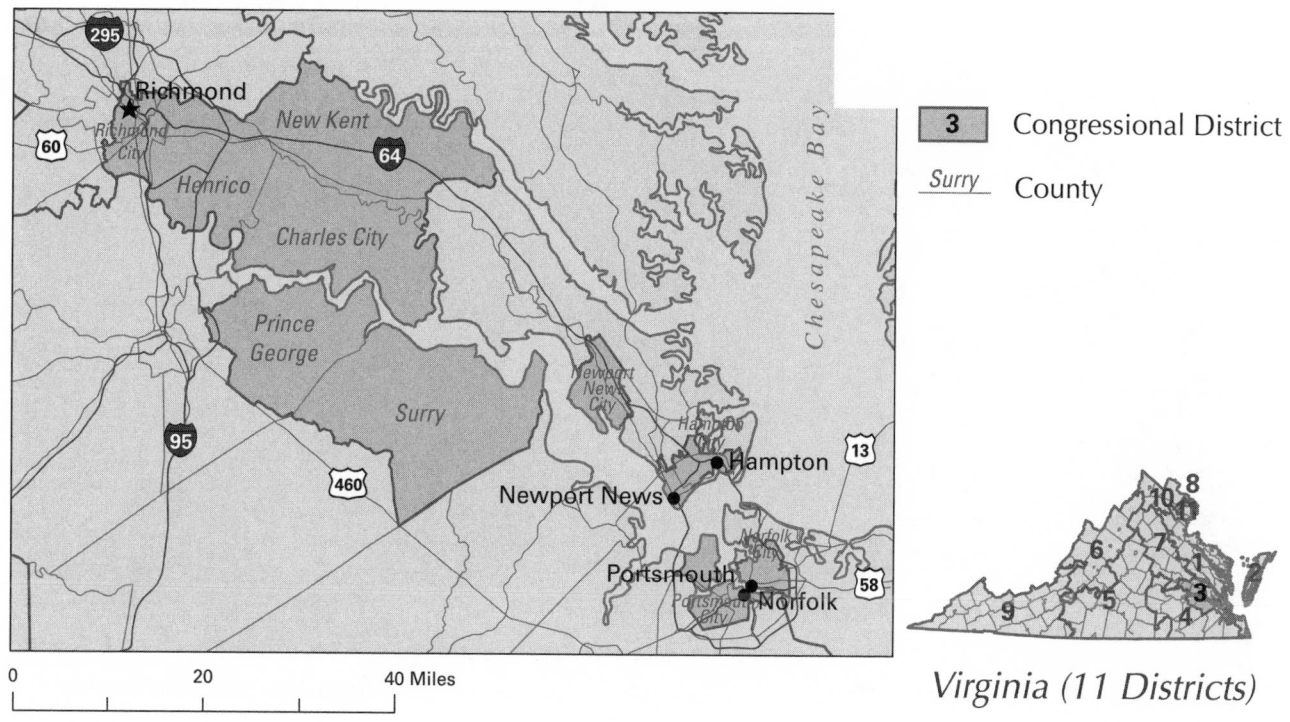

| 3 | Congressional District |
| *Surry* | County |

Virginia (11 Districts)

Congressional District 4

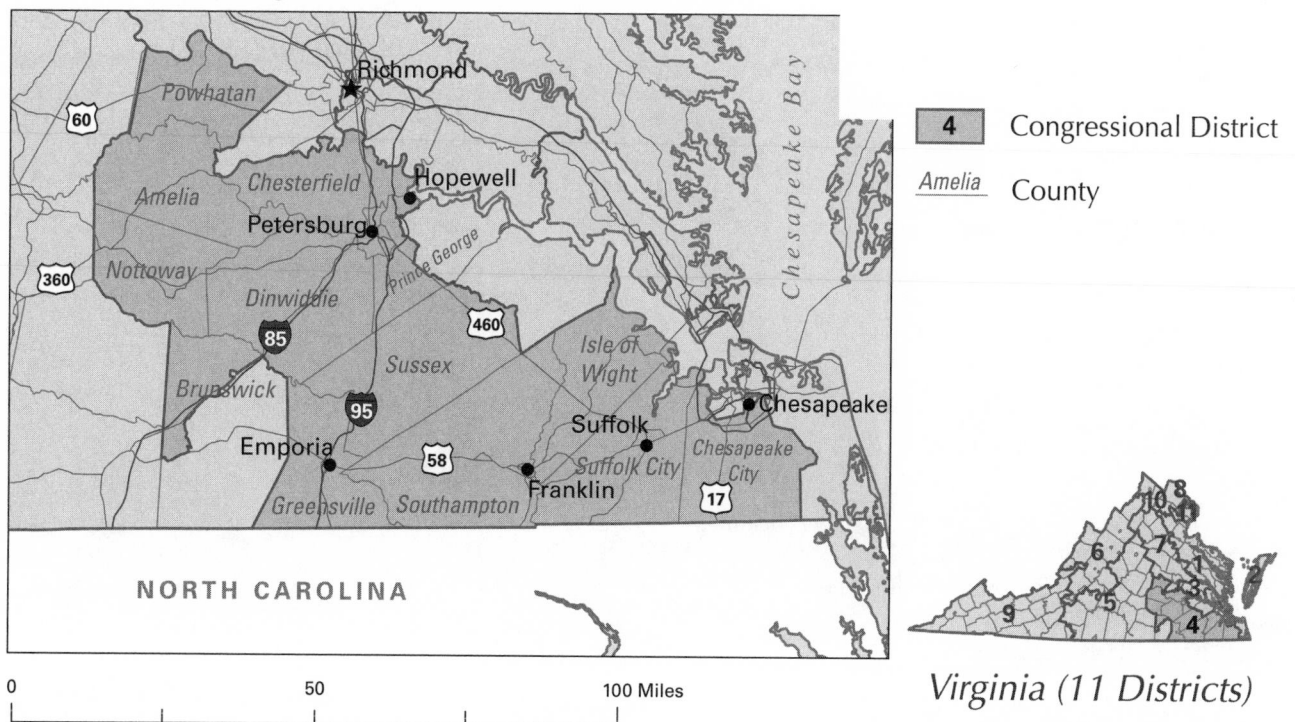

| 4 | Congressional District |
| *Amelia* | County |

Virginia (11 Districts)

Congressional District 5

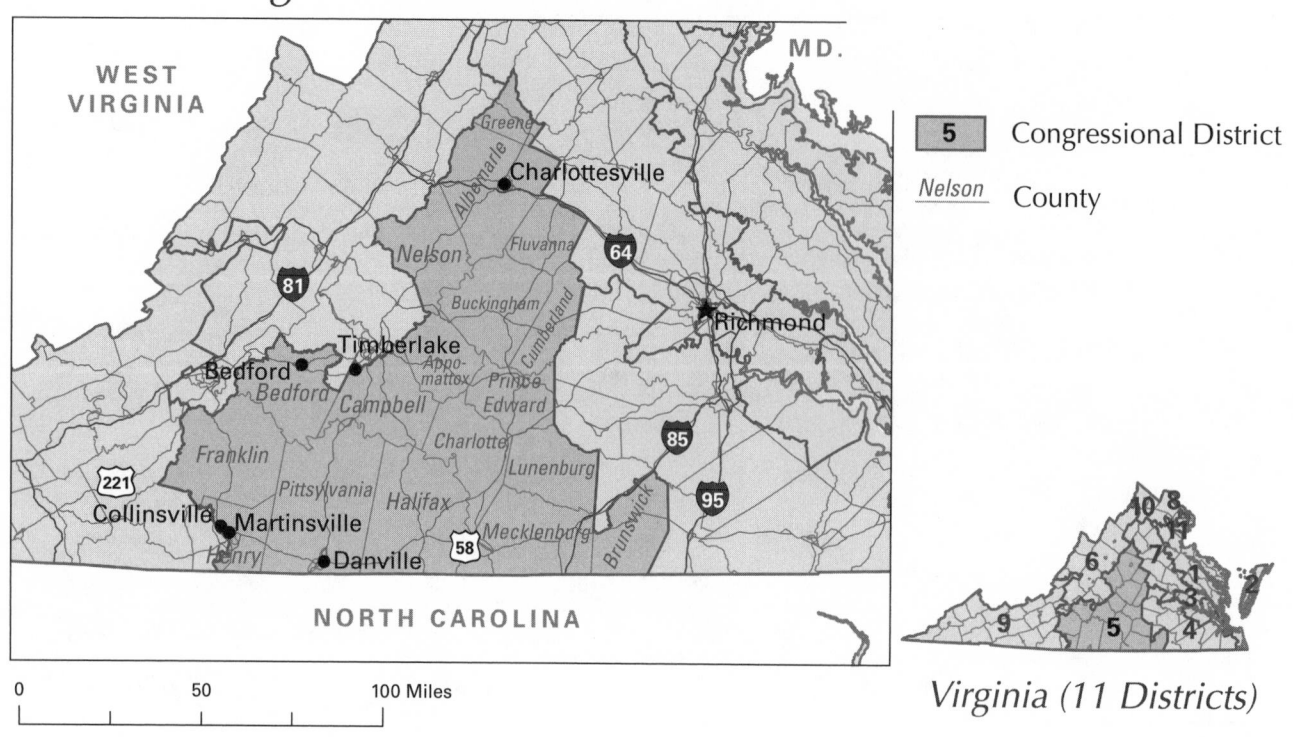

Virginia (11 Districts)

Congressional District 6

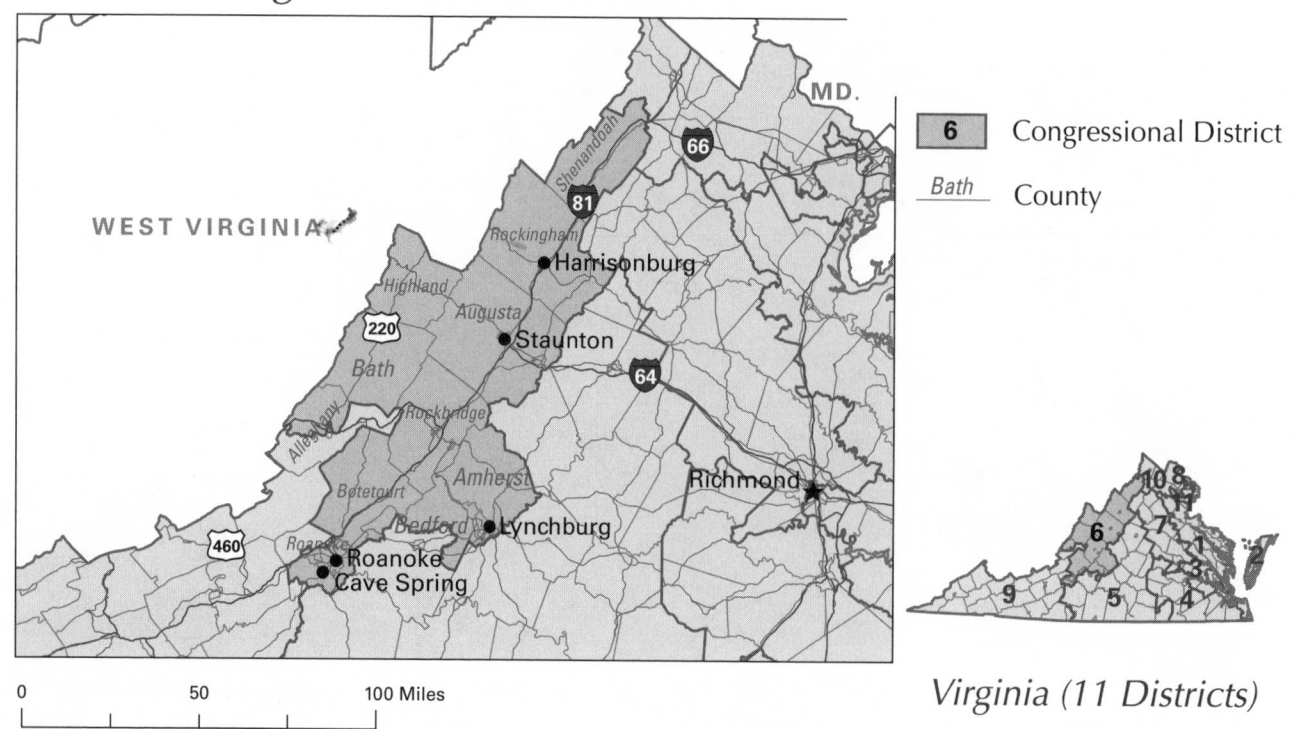

Virginia (11 Districts)

Congressional District 7

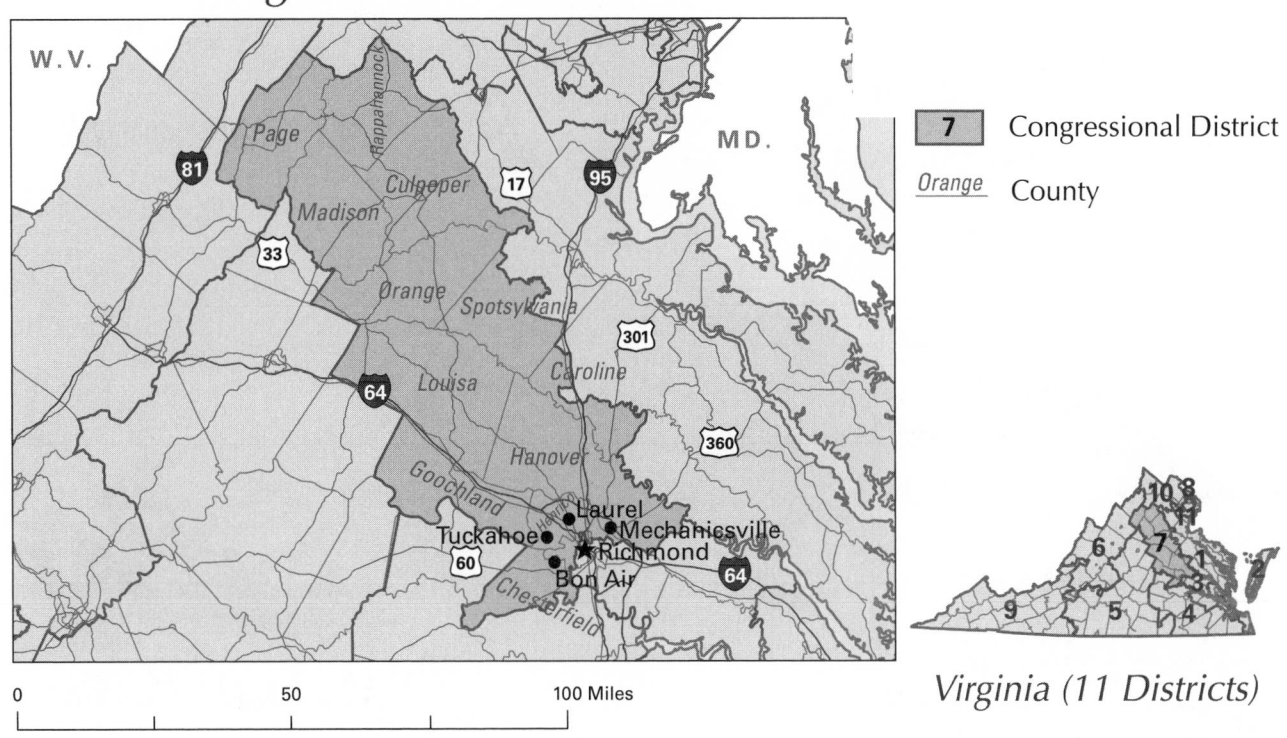

| 7 | Congressional District |
| *Orange* | County |

0   50   100 Miles

Virginia (11 Districts)

Congressional District 8

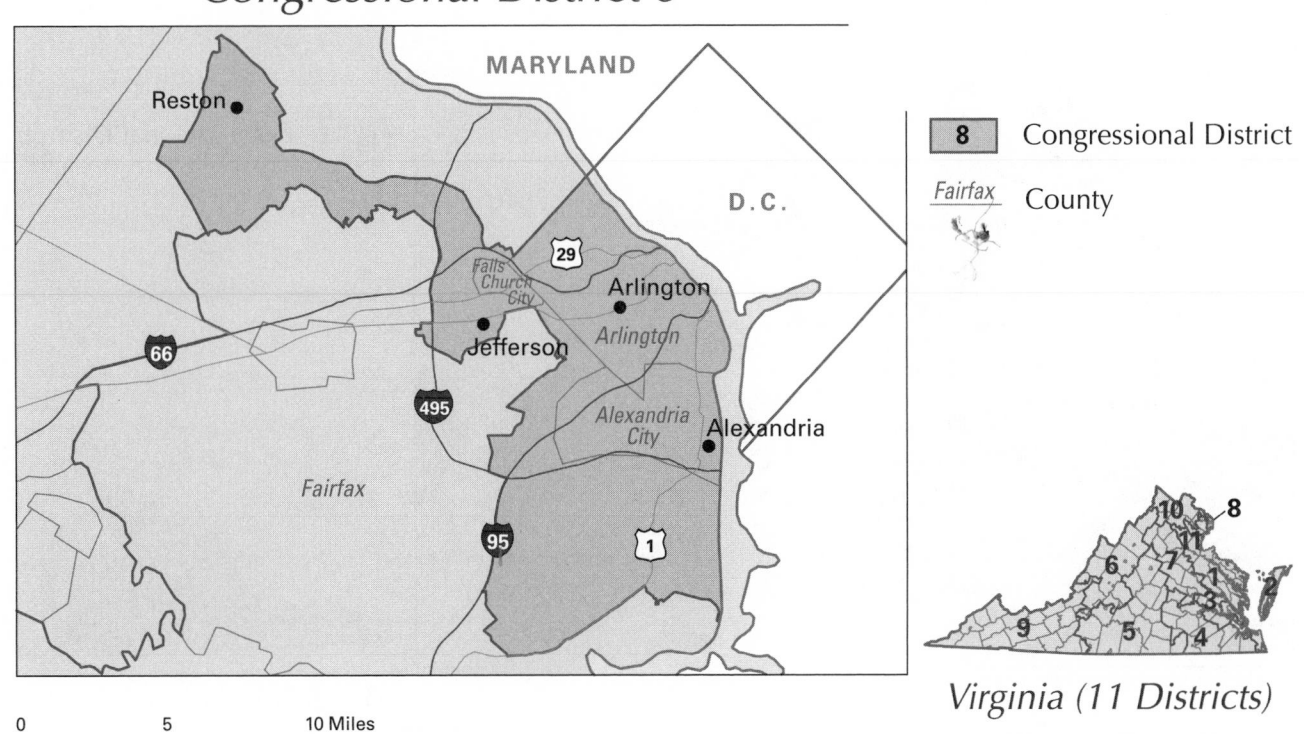

| 8 | Congressional District |
| *Fairfax* | County |

0   5   10 Miles

Virginia (11 Districts)

Congressional District 9

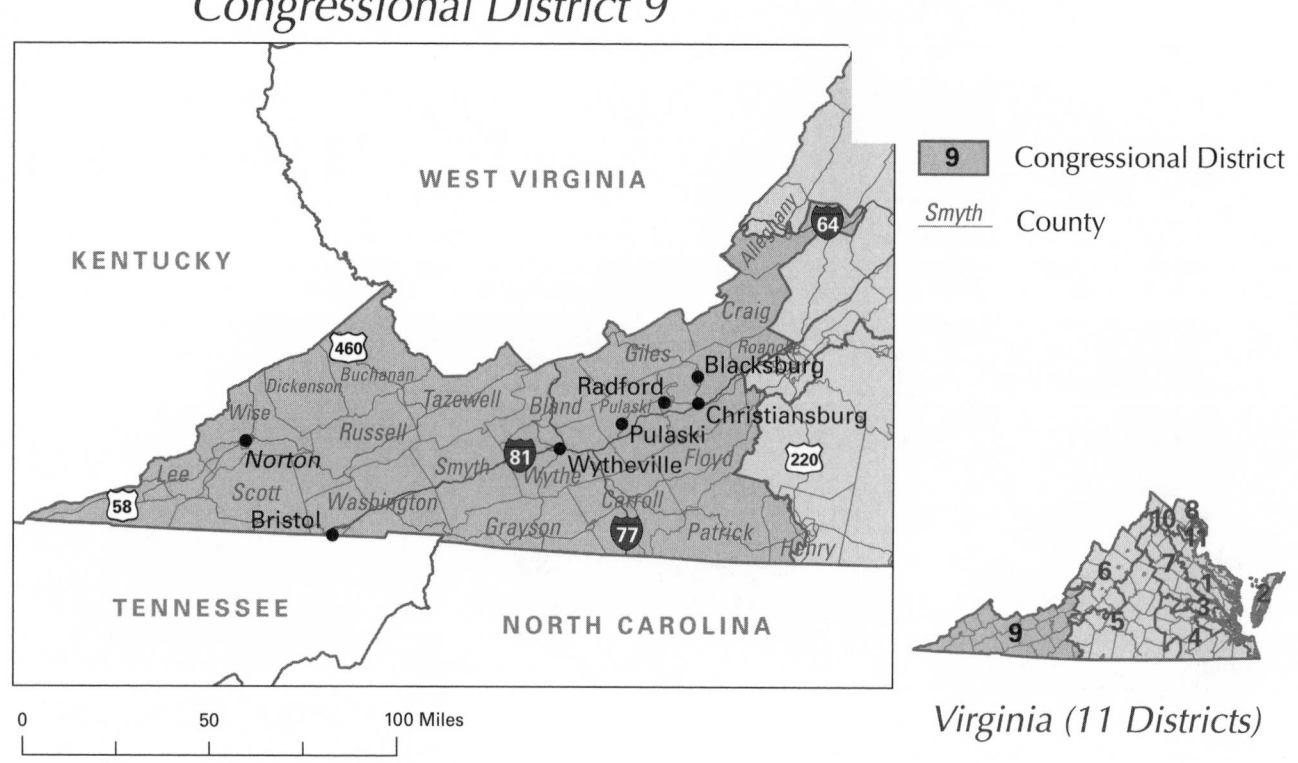

0   50   100 Miles

Congressional District 10

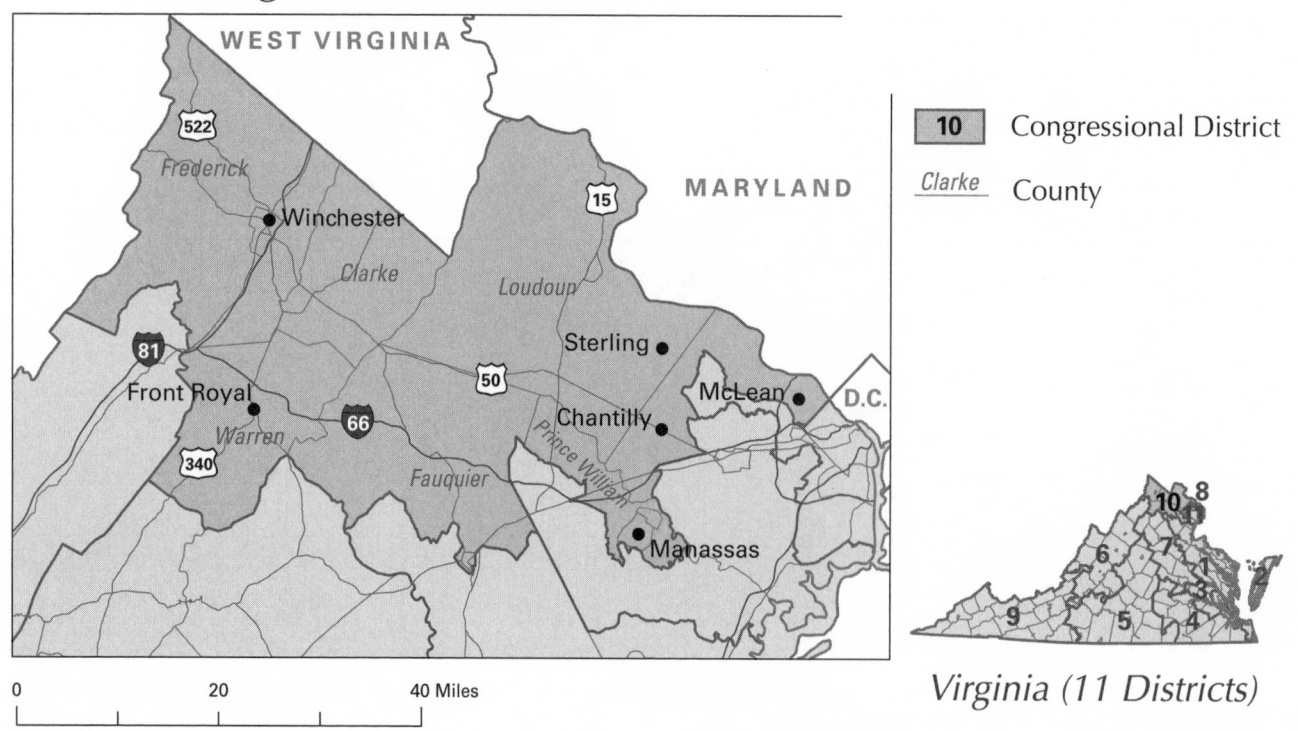

0   20   40 Miles

Congressional District 11

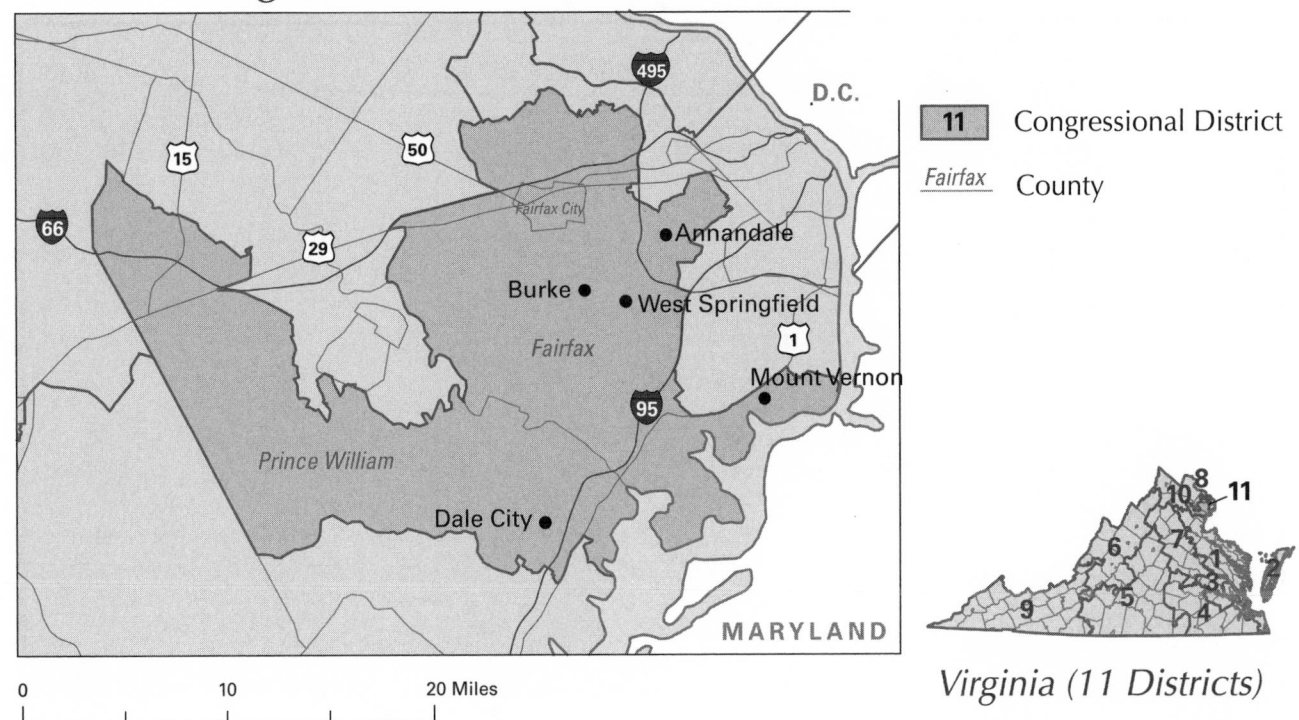

Virginia (11 Districts)

Washington Congressional Districts — 9 Districts Total

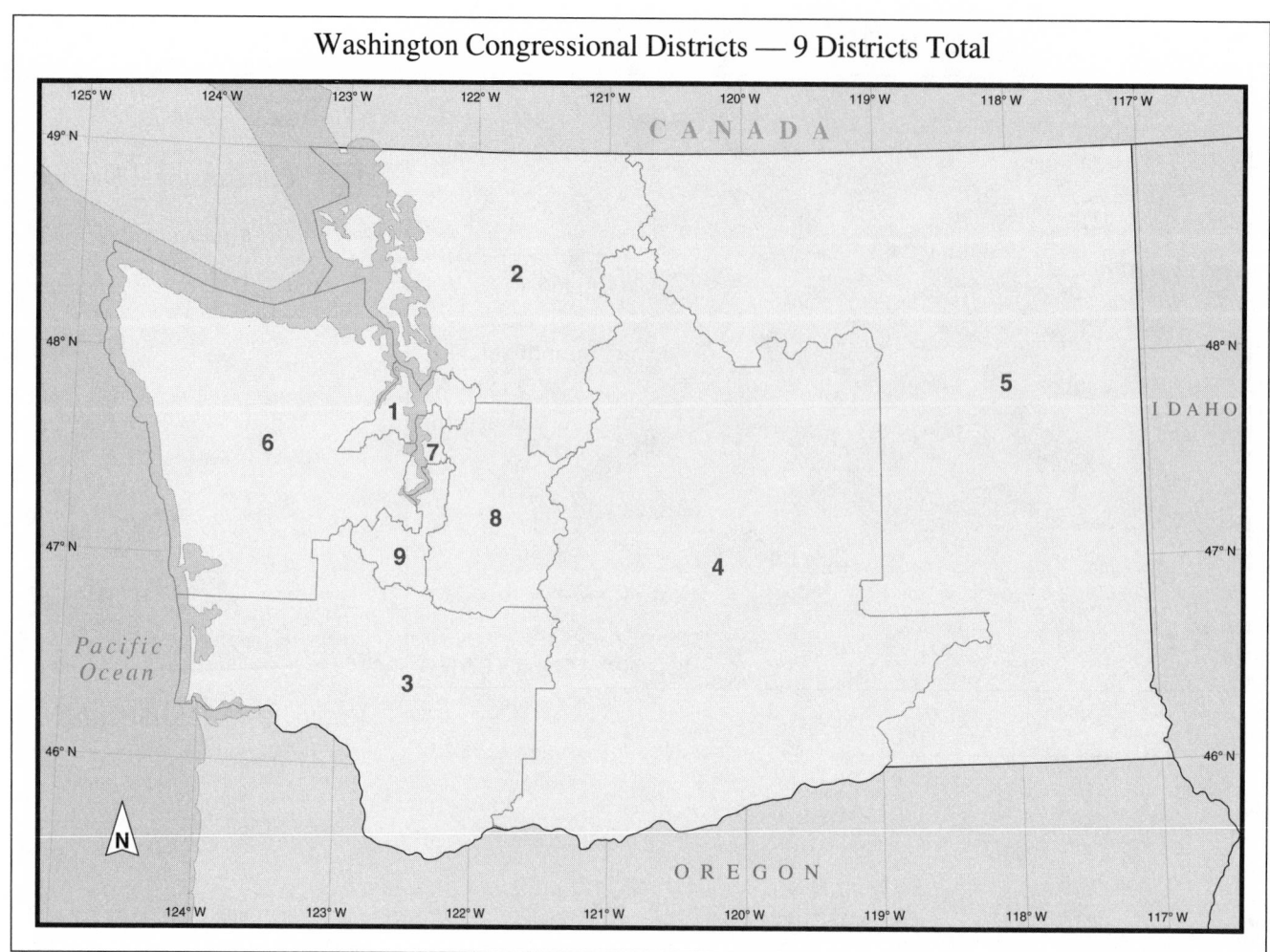

WASHINGTON—110th CONGRESSIONAL DISTRICTS BY COUNTIES

County	Congressional District
Adams	4, 5
Asotin	5
Benton	4
Chelan	4
Clallam	6
Clark	3
Columbia	5
Cowlitz	3
Douglas	4
Ferry	5
Franklin	4
Garfield	5
Grant	4

County	Congressional District
Grays Harbor	6
Island	2
Jefferson	6
King	1, 2, 7–9
Kitsap	1, 6
Kittitas	4
Klickitat	4
Lewis	3
Lincoln	5
Mason	6
Okanogan	5
Pacific	3
Pend Oreille	5

County	Congressional District
Pierce	6, 8, 9
San Juan	2
Skagit	2
Skamania	3, 4
Snohomish	1, 2
Spokane	5
Stevens	5
Thurston	3, 9
Wahkiakum	3
Walla Walla	5
Whatcom	2
Whitman	5
Yakima	4

Congressional District 1

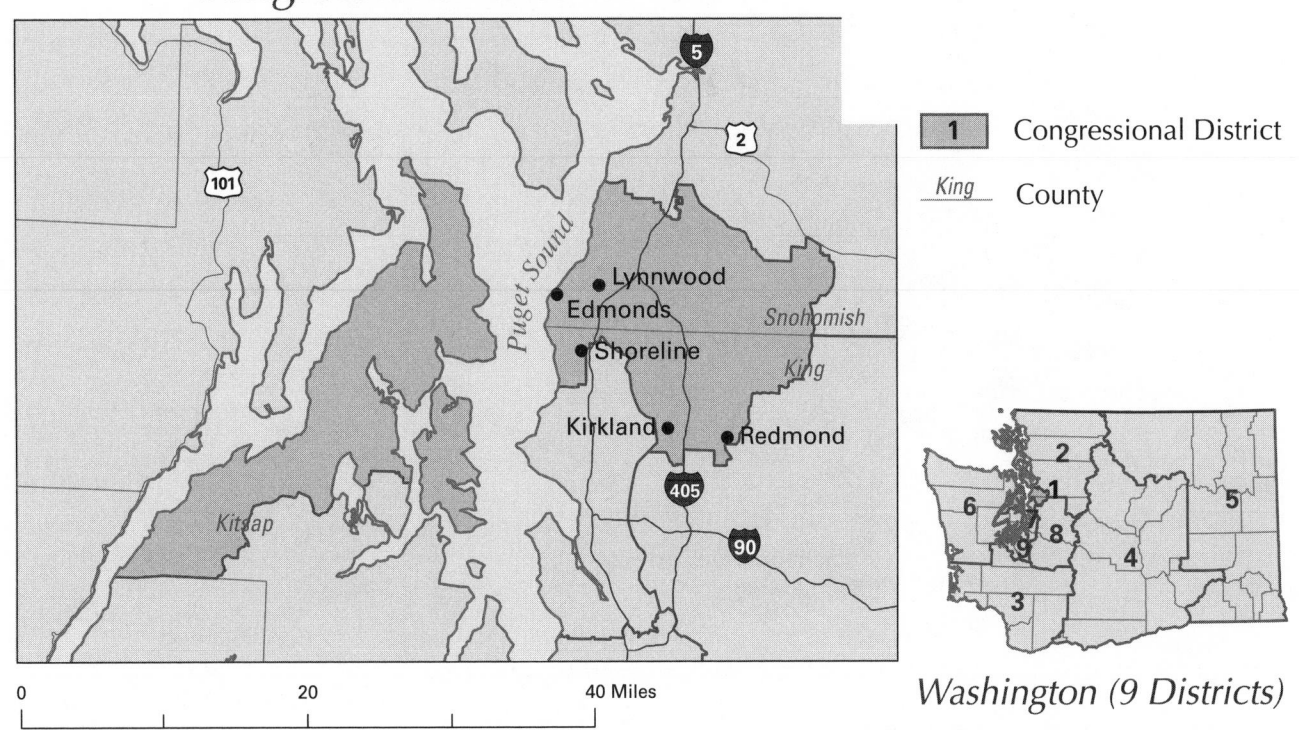

Washington (9 Districts)

Congressional District 2

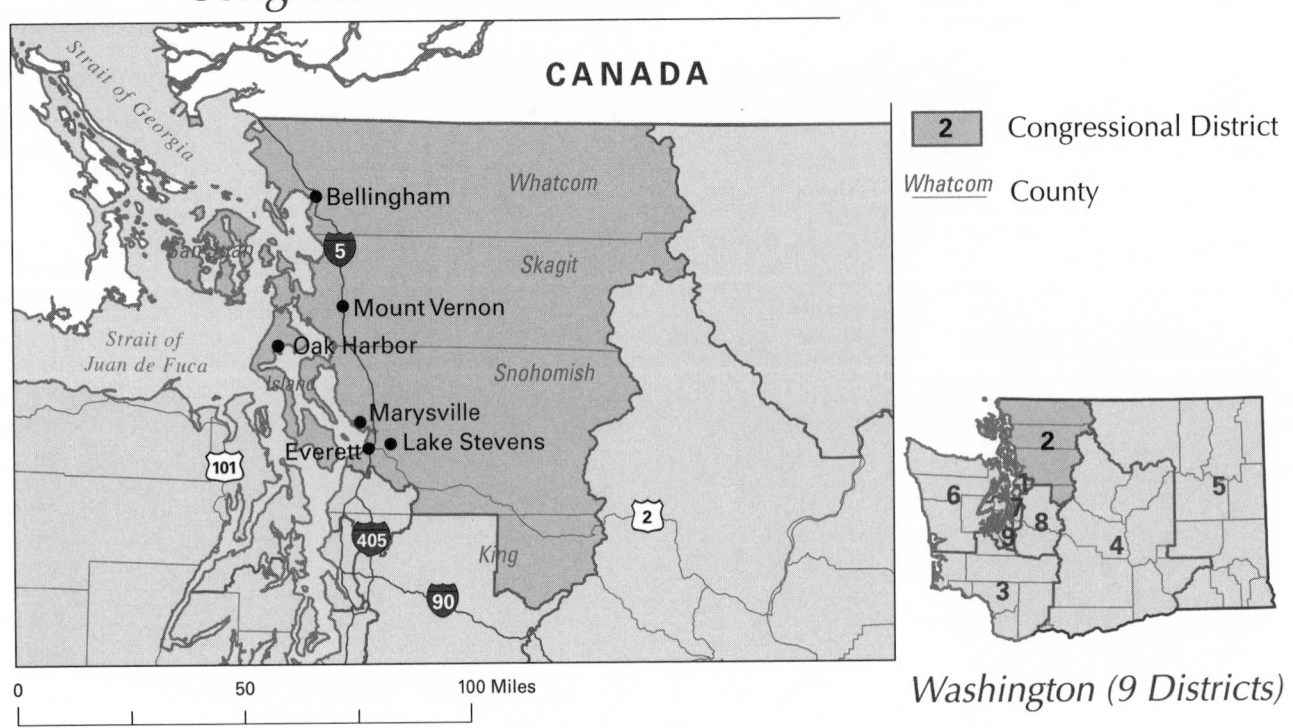

Washington (9 Districts)

Congressional District 3

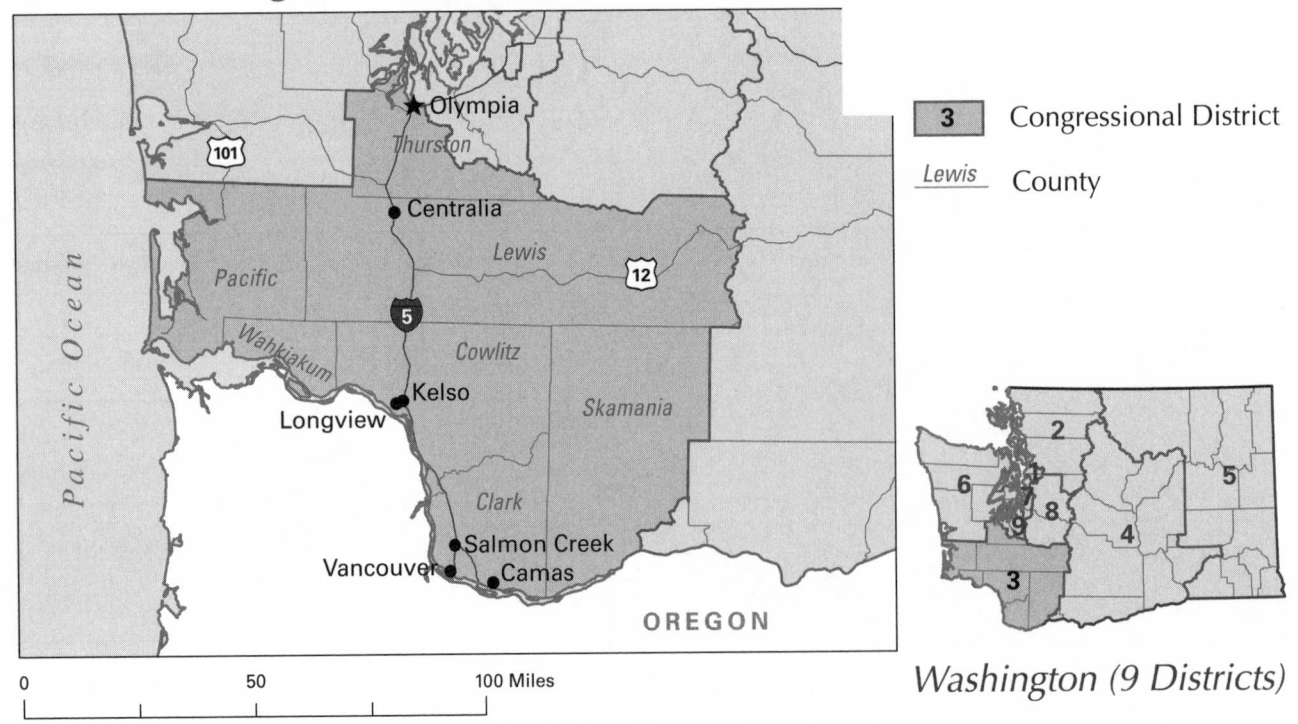

Washington (9 Districts)

Congressional District 4

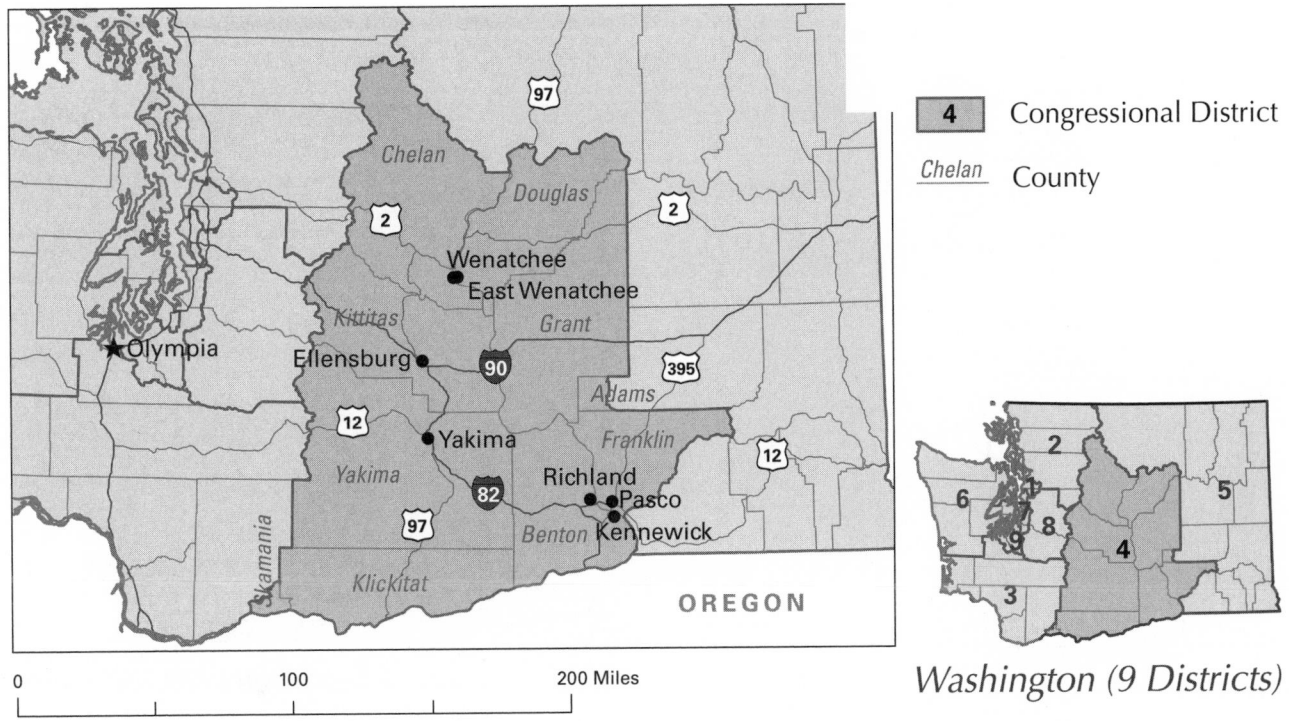

4 Congressional District
Chelan County

Washington (9 Districts)

Congressional District 5

5 Congressional District
Ferry County

Washington (5 Districts)

Congressional District 6

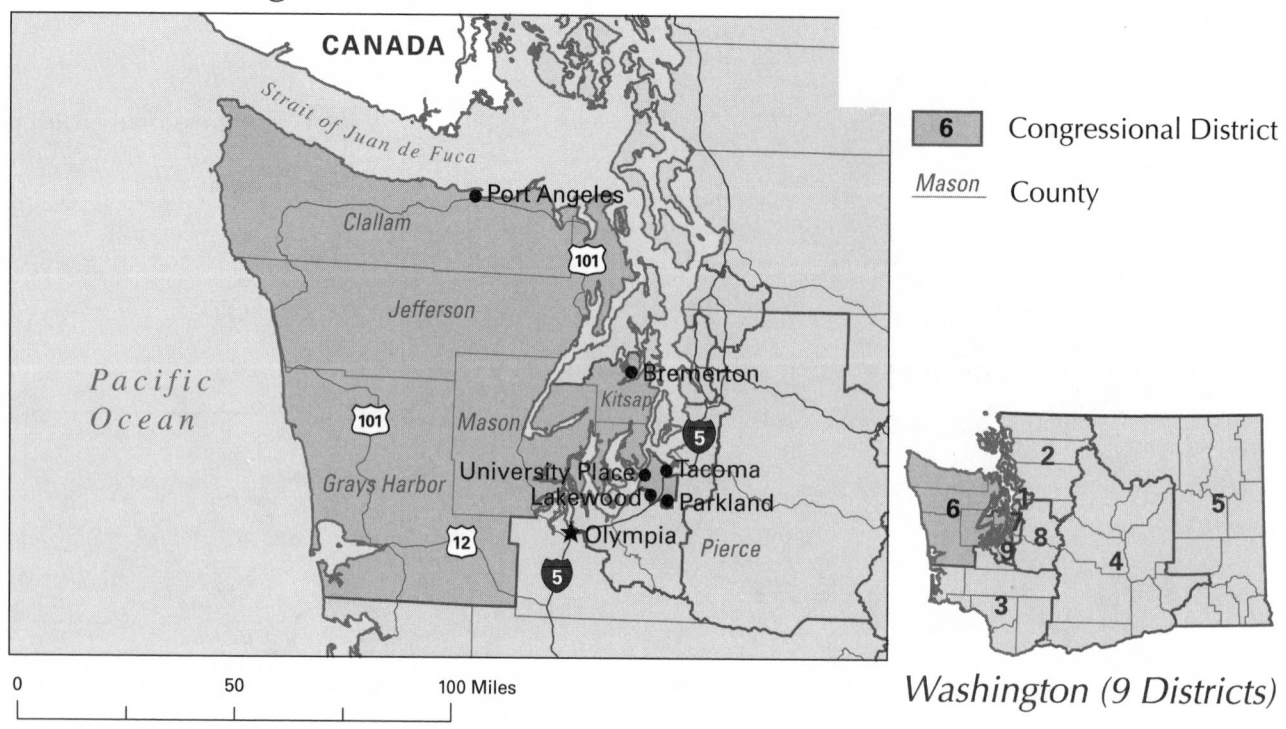

Washington (9 Districts)

Congressional District 7

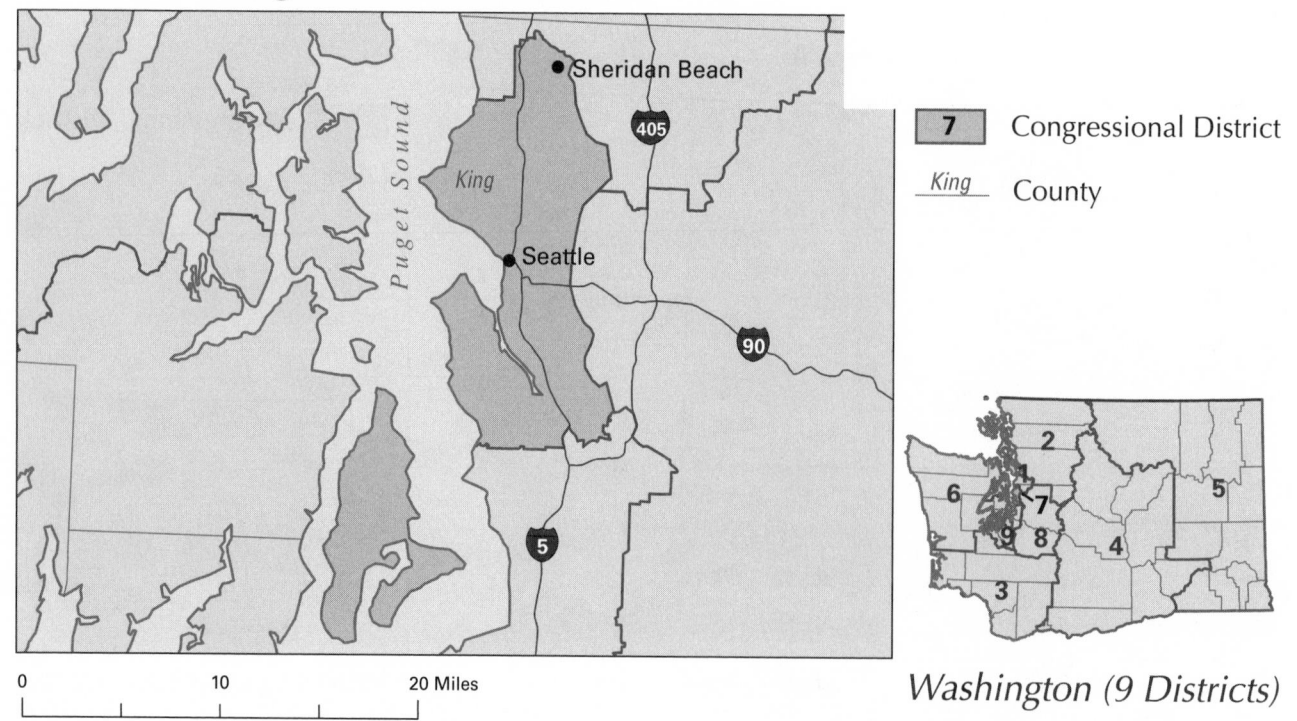

Washington (9 Districts)

Congressional District 8

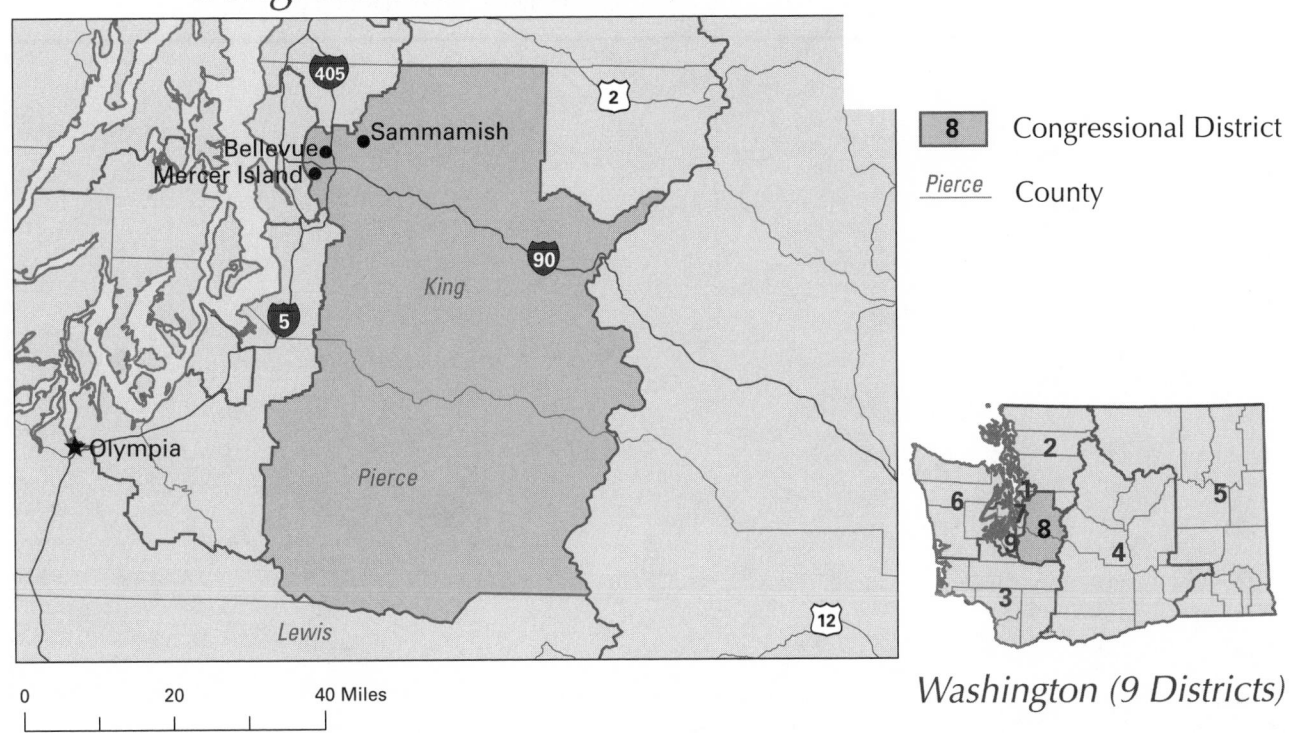

8 Congressional District

Pierce County

Washington (9 Districts)

Congressional District 9

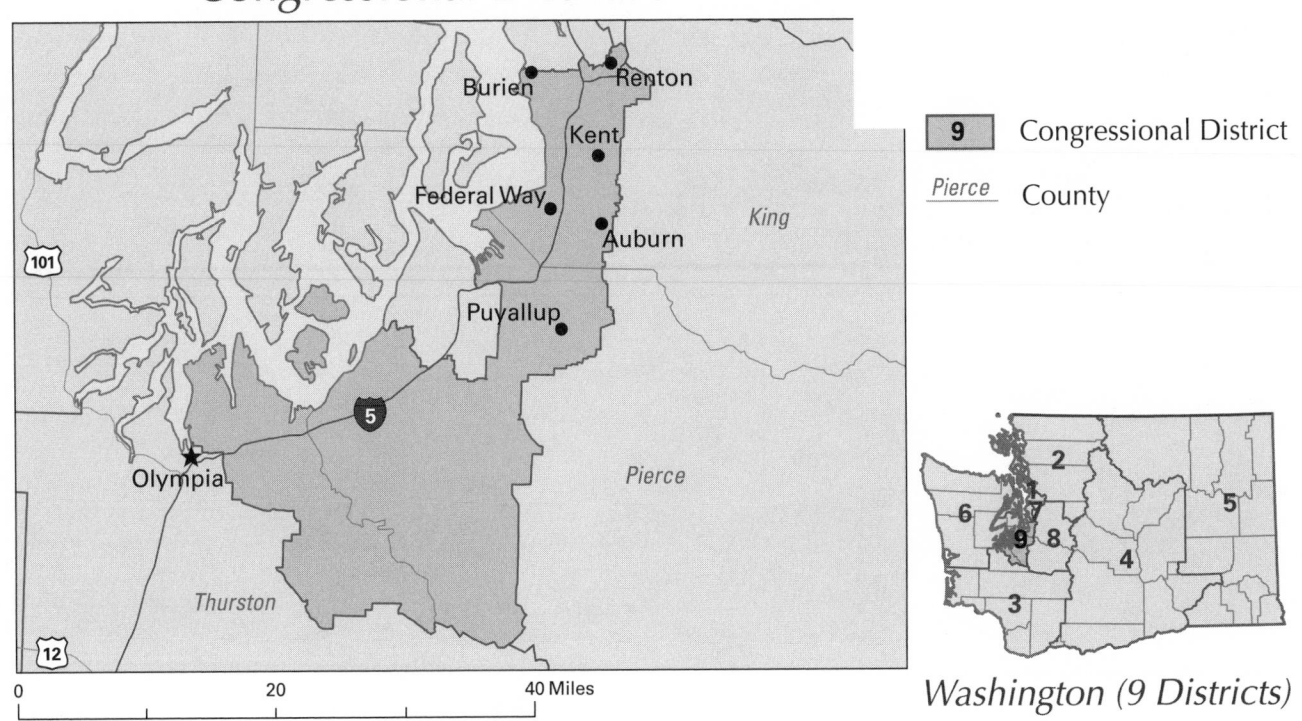

9 Congressional District

Pierce County

Washington (9 Districts)

West Virginia Congressional Districts — 3 Districts Total

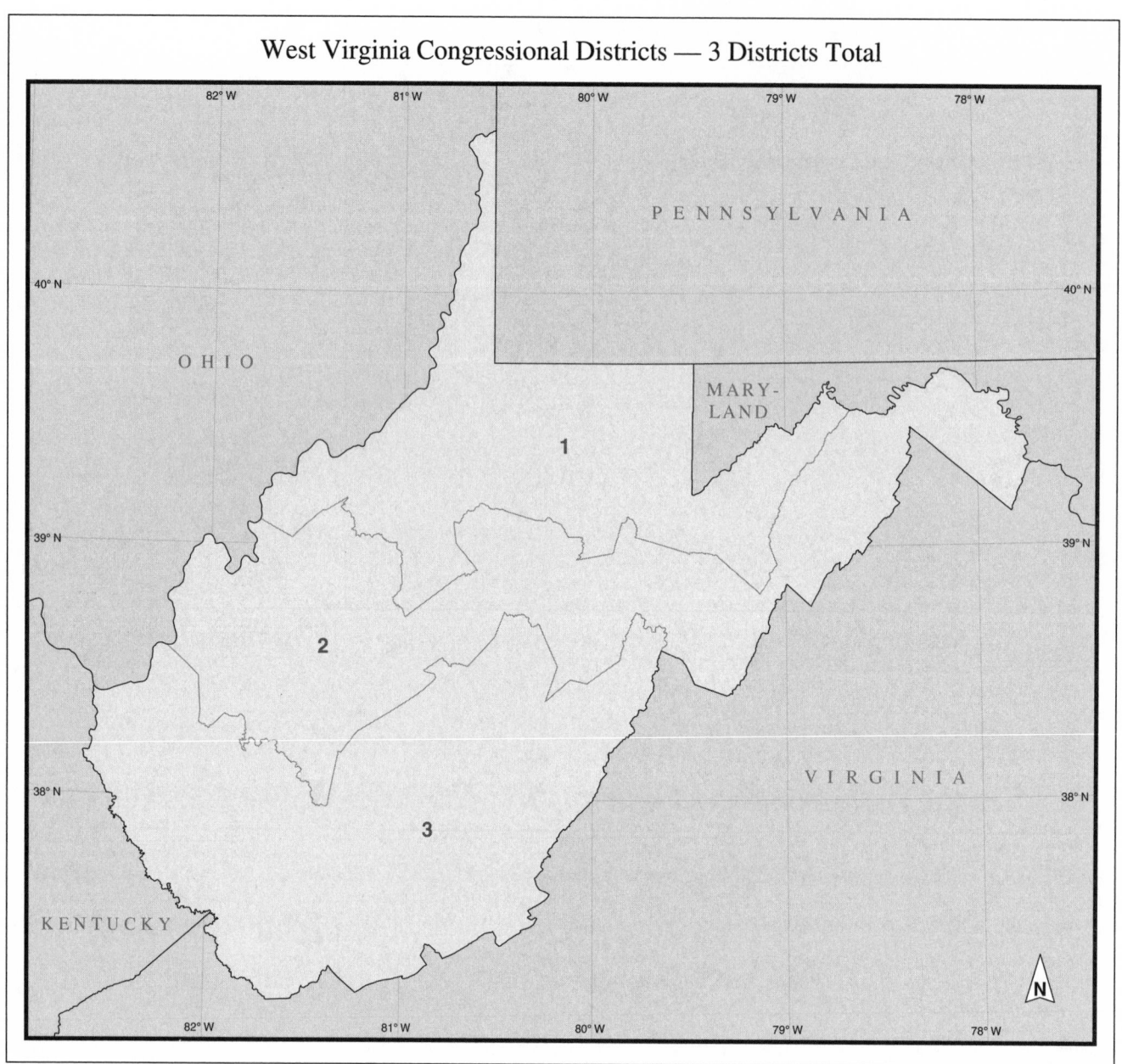

WEST VIRGINIA—110th CONGRESSIONAL DISTRICTS BY COUNTIES

County	Congressional District	County	Congressional District	County	Congressional District
Barbour	1	Kanawha	2	Preston	1
Berkeley	2	Lewis	2	Putnam	2
Boone	3	Lincoln	3	Raleigh	3
Braxton	2	Logan	3	Randolph	2
Brooke	1	McDowell	3	Ritchie	1
Cabell	3	Marion	1	Roane	2
Calhoun	2	Marshall	1	Summers	3
Clay	2	Mason	2	Taylor	1
Doddridge	1	Mercer	3	Tucker	1
Fayette	3	Mineral	1	Tyler	1
Gilmer	1	Mingo	3	Upshur	2
Grant	1	Monongalia	1	Wayne	3
Greenbrier	3	Monroe	3	Webster	3
Hampshire	2	Morgan	2	Wetzel	1
Hancock	1	Morgan	2	Wirt	2
Hardy	2	Nicholas	3	Wood	1
Harrison	1	Ohio	1	Wyoming	3
Jackson	2	Pendleton	2		
Jefferson	2	Pleasants	1		
		Pocahontas	3		

Congressional District 1

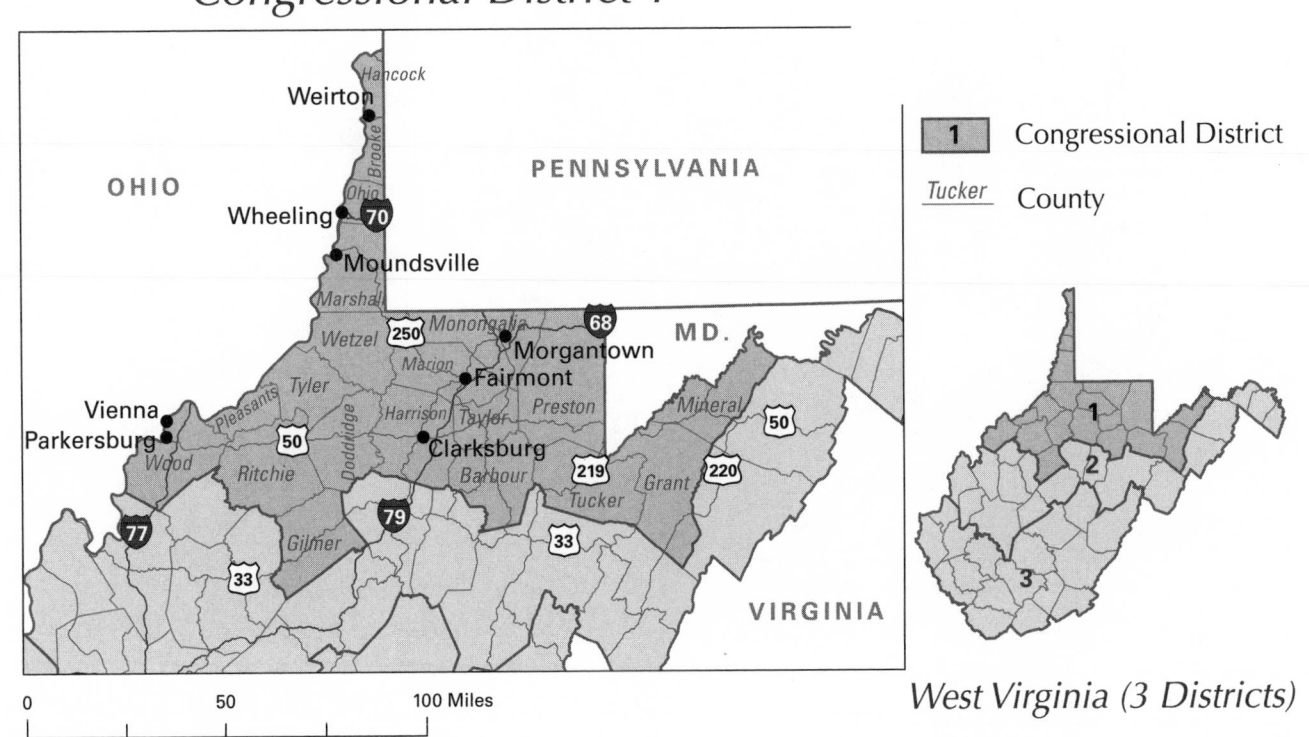

West Virginia (3 Districts)

Congressional District 2

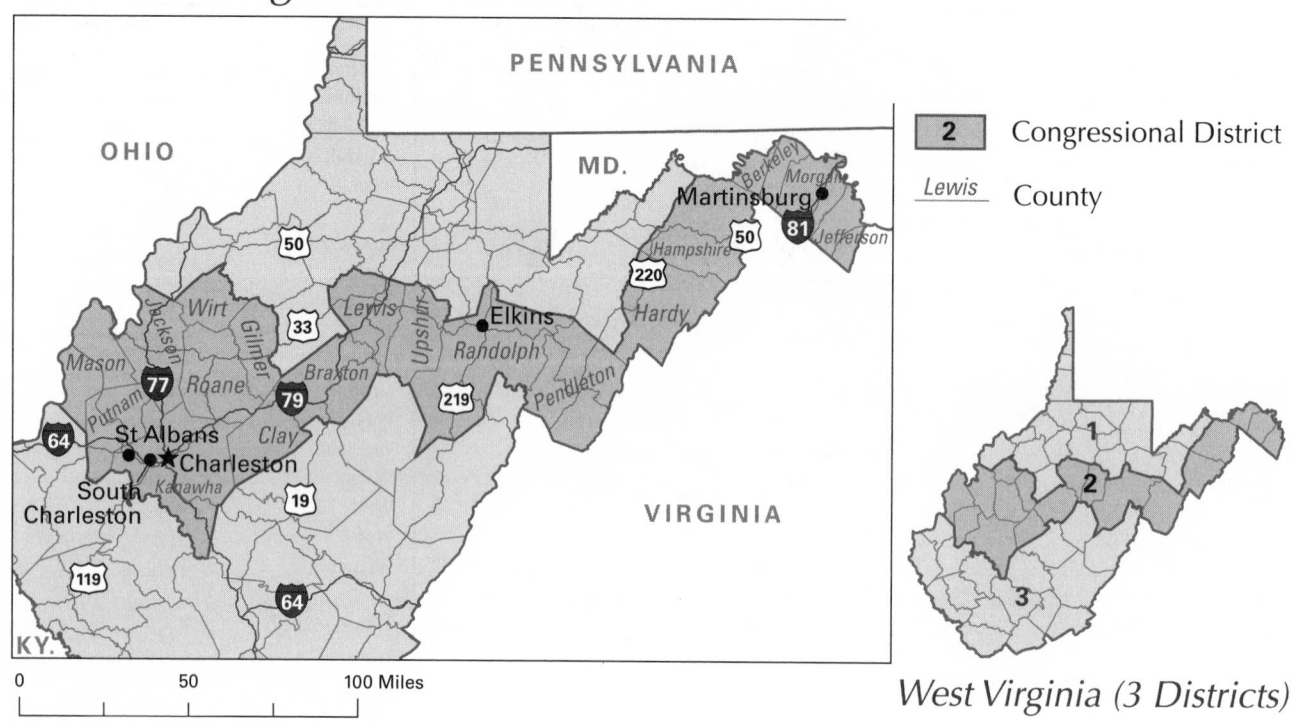

West Virginia (3 Districts)

Congressional District 3

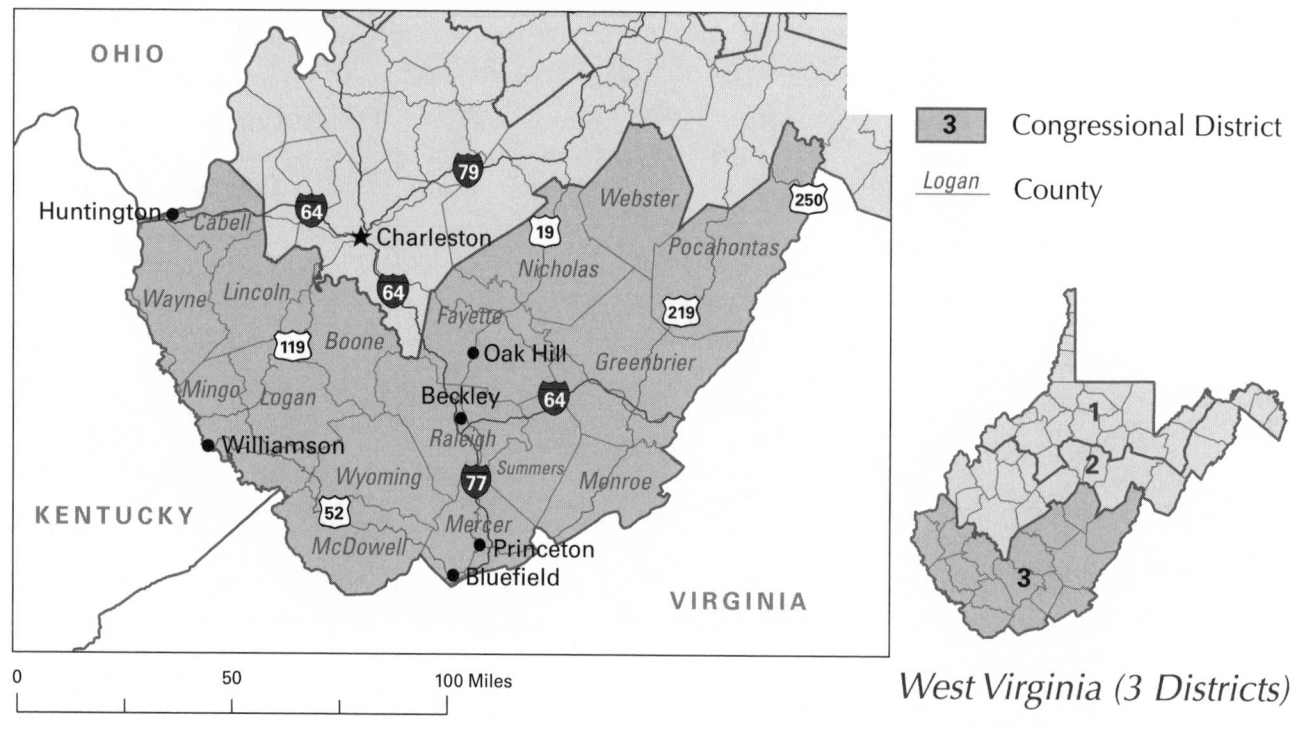

West Virginia (3 Districts)

Wisconsin Congressional Districts — 8 Districts Total

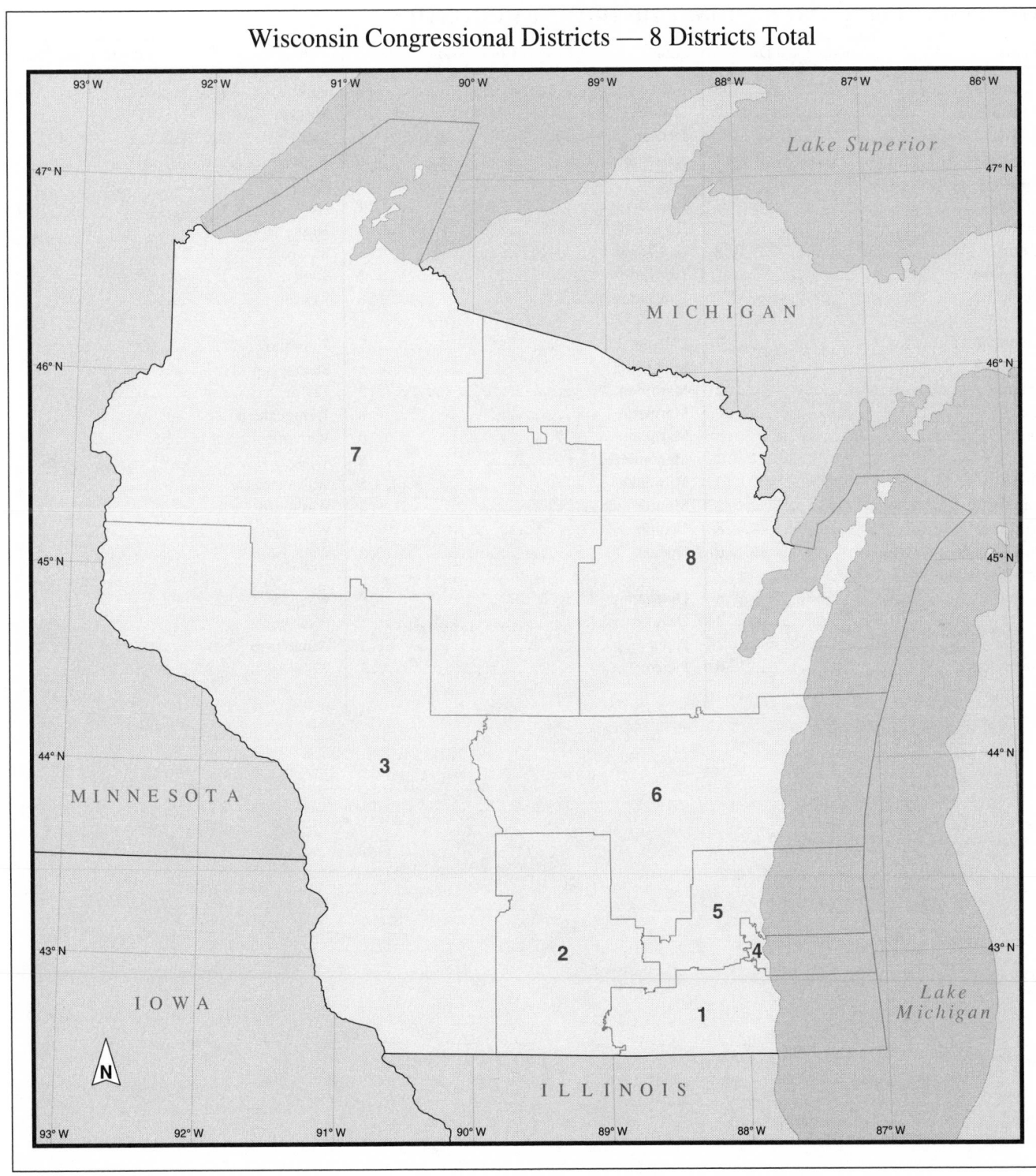

WISCONSIN—110th CONGRESSIONAL DISTRICTS BY COUNTIES

County	Congressional District	County	Congressional District	County	Congressional District
Adams	6	Iowa	3	Polk	7
Ashland	7	Iron	7	Portage	7
Barron	7	Jackson	3	Price	7
Bayfield	7	Jefferson	2, 5, 6	Racine	1
Brown	8	Juneau	3	Richland	3
Buffalo	3	Kenosha	1	Rock	1, 2
Burnett	7	Kewaunee	8	Rusk	7
Calumet	6, 8	La Crosse	3	St. Croix	3
Chippewa	7	Lafayette	3	Sauk	2, 3
Clark	3, 7	Langlade	7, 8	Sawyer	7
Columbia	2	Lincoln	7	Shawano	8
Crawford	3	Manitowoc	6	Sheboygan	6
Dane	2	Marathon	7	Taylor	7
Dodge	6	Marinette	8	Trempealeau	3
Door	8	Marquette	6	Vernon	3
Douglas	7	Menominee	8	Vilas	8
Dunn	3	Milwaukee	1, 4, 5	Walworth	1, 2
Eau Claire	3	Monroe	3	Washburn	7
Florence	8	Oconto	8	Washington	5
Fond du Lac	6	Oneida	7, 8	Waukesha	1, 5
Forest	8	Outagamie	6, 8	Waupaca	8
Grant	3	Ozaukee	5	Waushara	6
Green	2	Pepin	3	Winnebago	6
Green Lake	6	Pierce	3	Wood	7

Congressional District 1

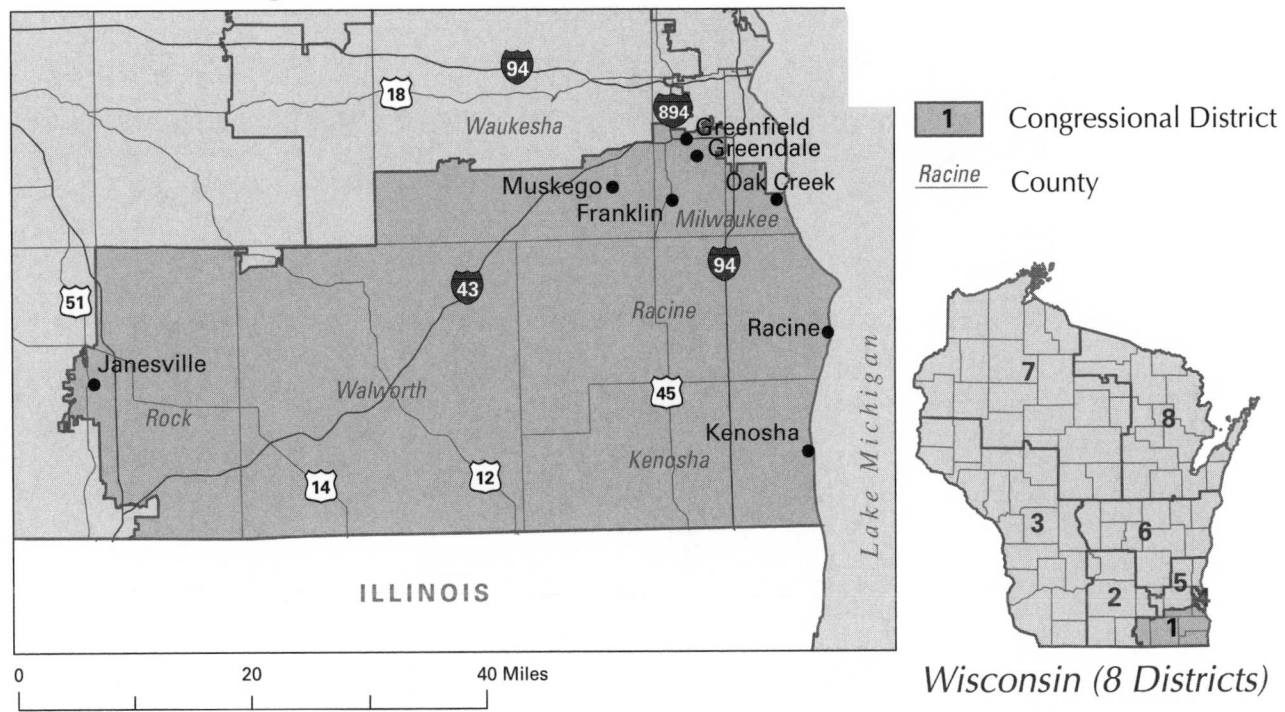

1 Congressional District
Racine County

Wisconsin (8 Districts)

Congressional District 2

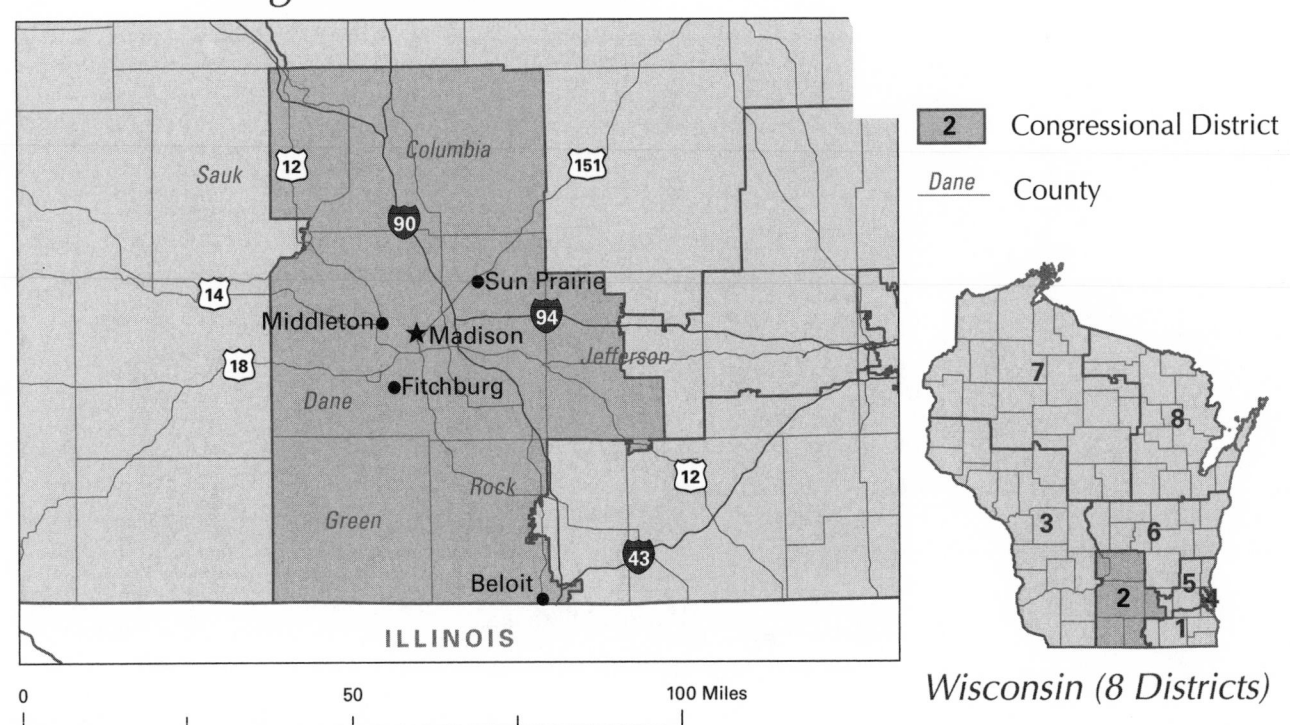

2 Congressional District
Dane County

Wisconsin (8 Districts)

Congressional District 3

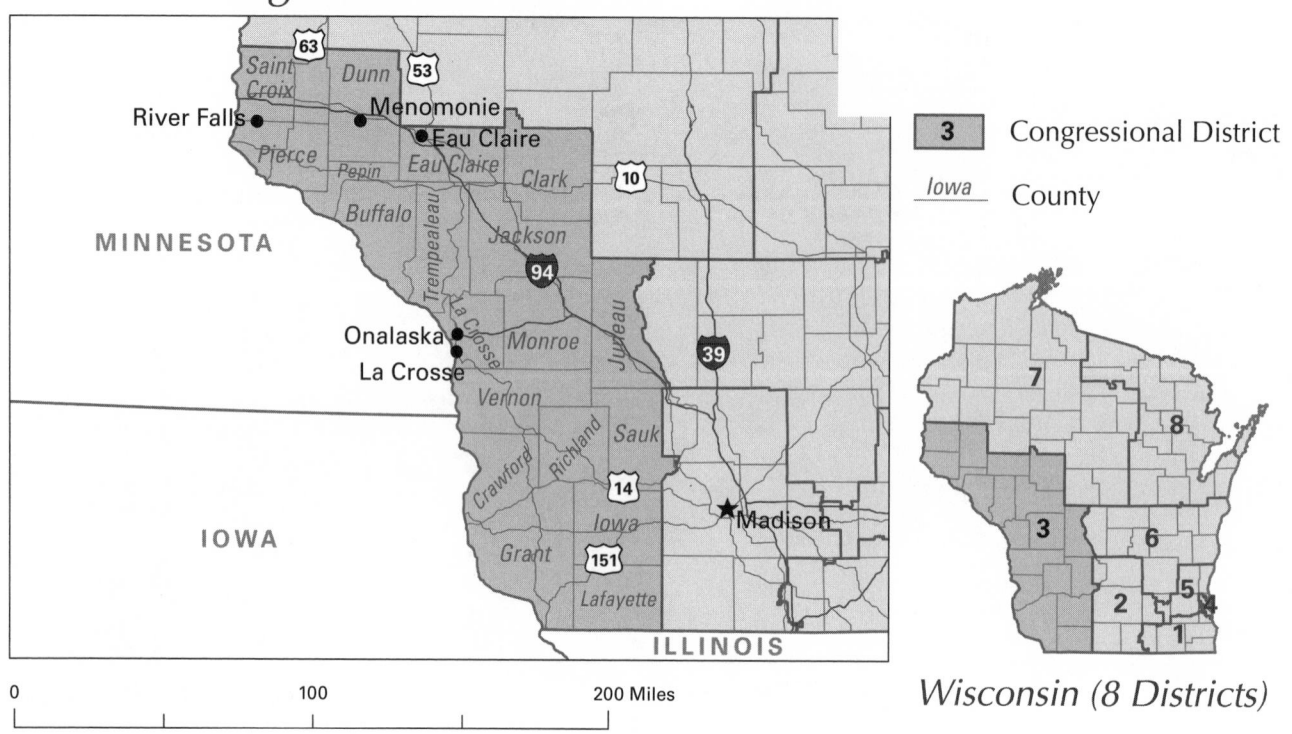

3 ▢ Congressional District
Iowa County

Wisconsin (8 Districts)

0   100   200 Miles

Congressional District 4

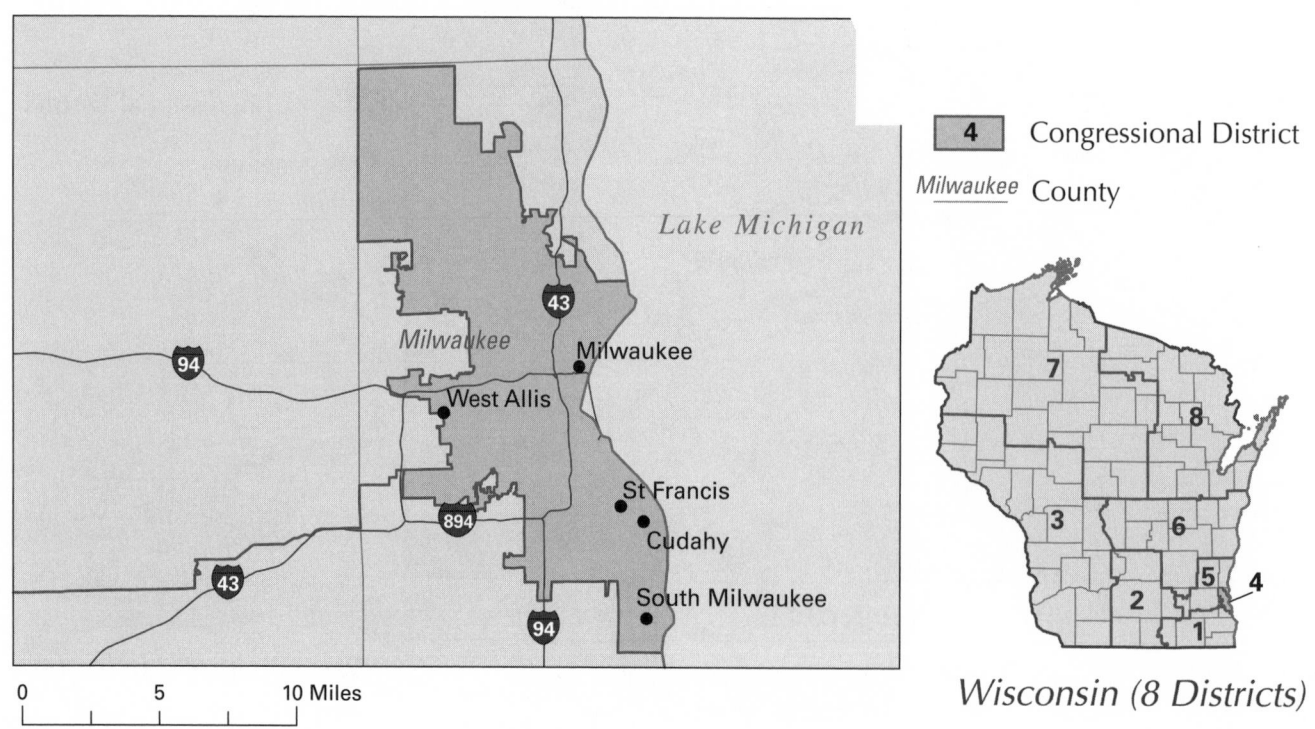

4 ▢ Congressional District
Milwaukee County

Wisconsin (8 Districts)

0   5   10 Miles

Congressional District 5

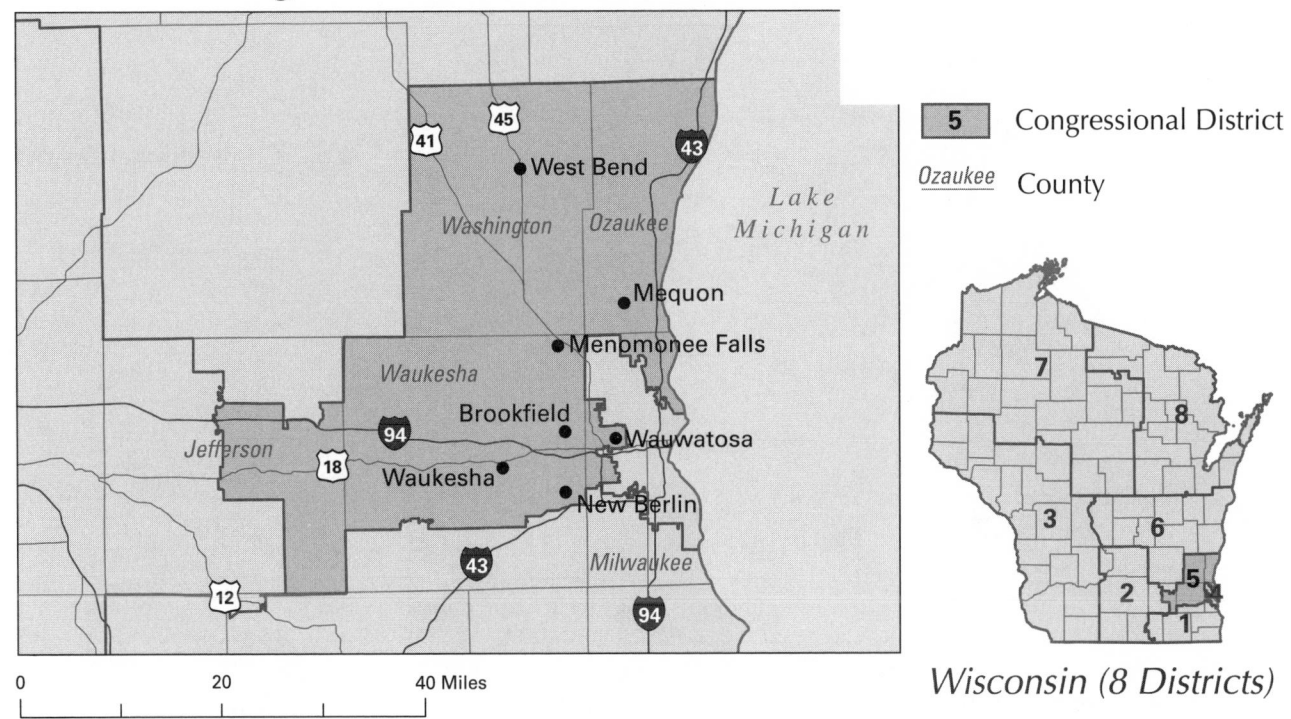

5 Congressional District
Ozaukee County

Wisconsin (8 Districts)

Congressional District 6

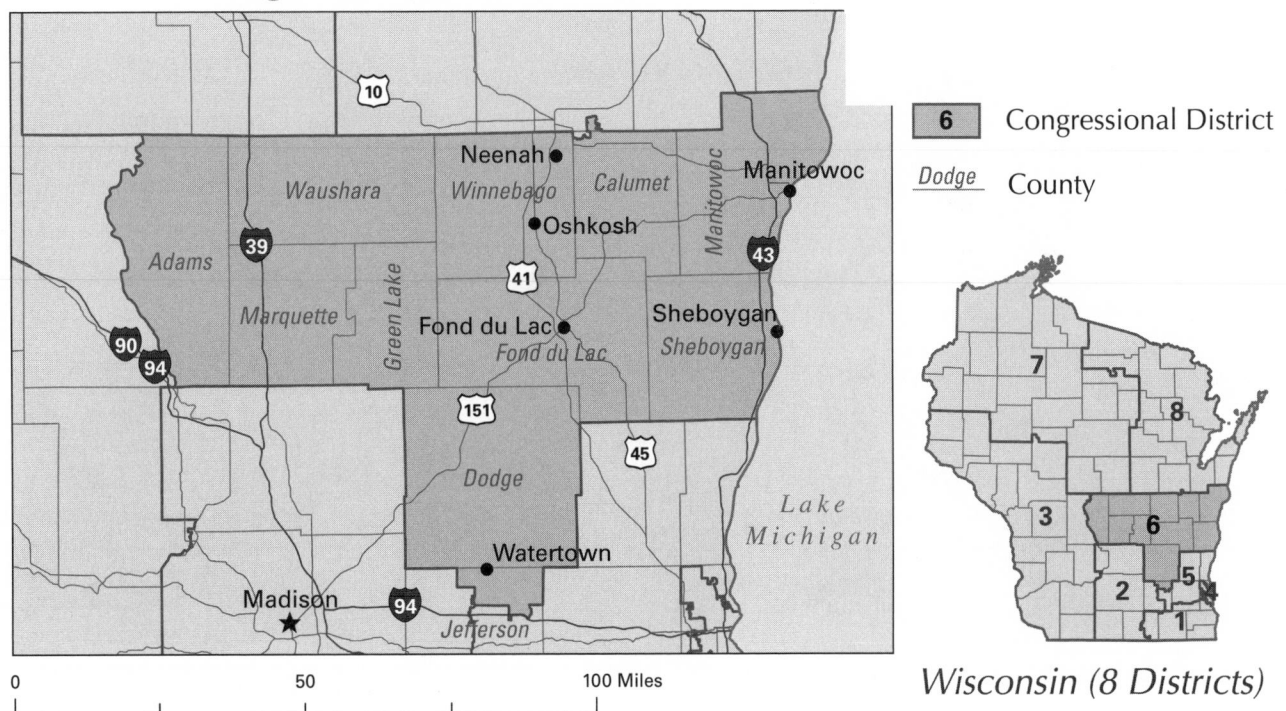

6 Congressional District
Dodge County

Wisconsin (8 Districts)

Congressional District 7

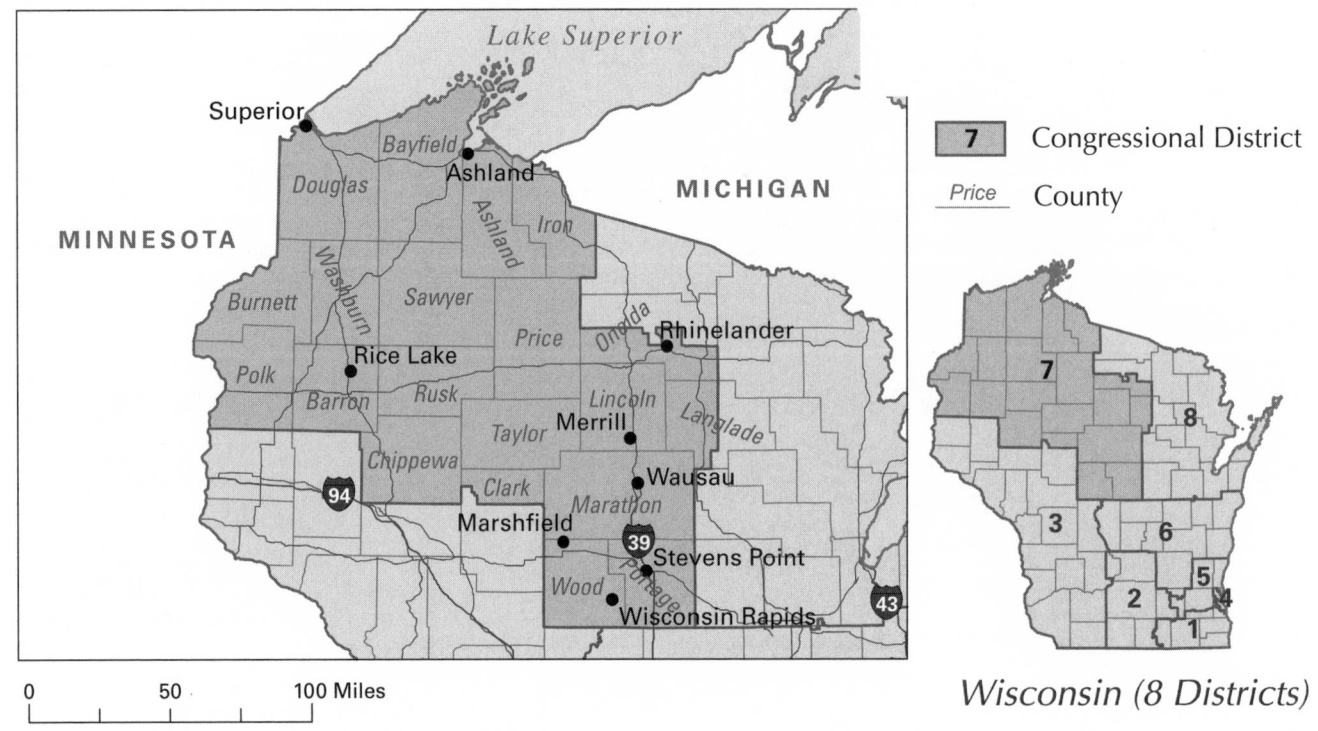

Wisconsin (8 Districts)

Congressional District 8

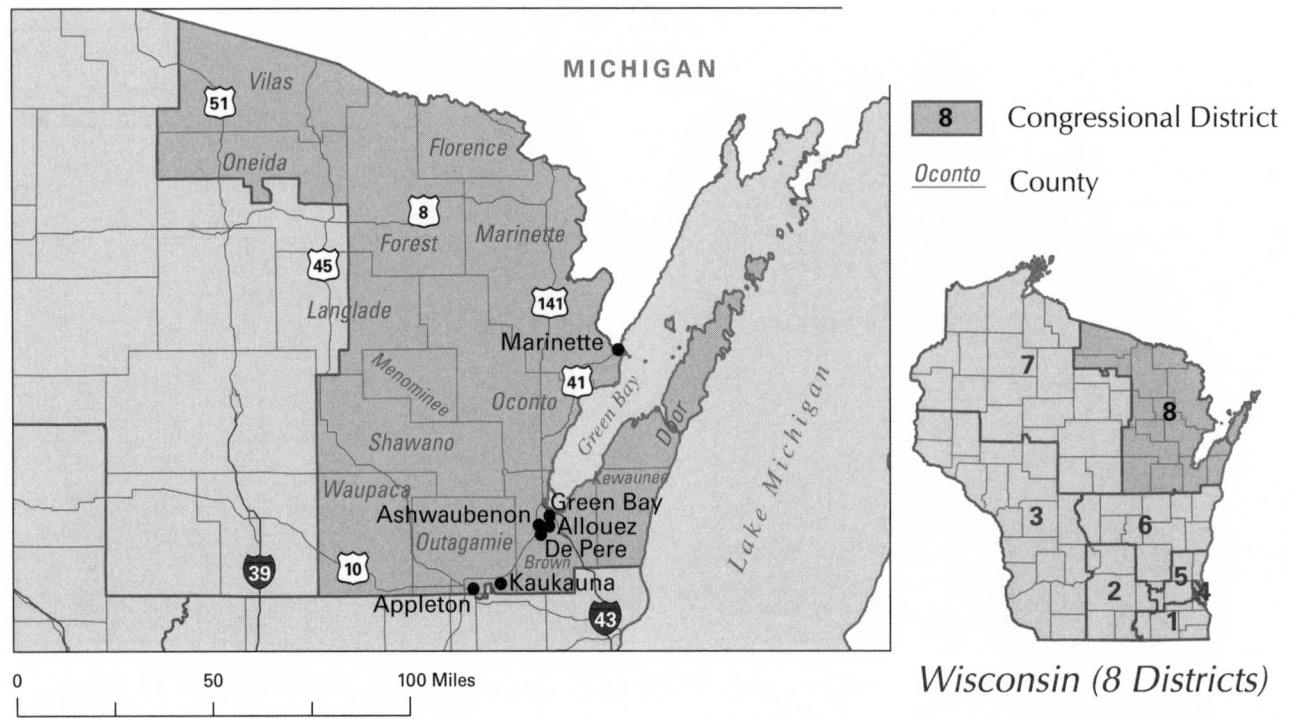

Wisconsin (8 Districts)

Wyoming—
Congressional District: At large

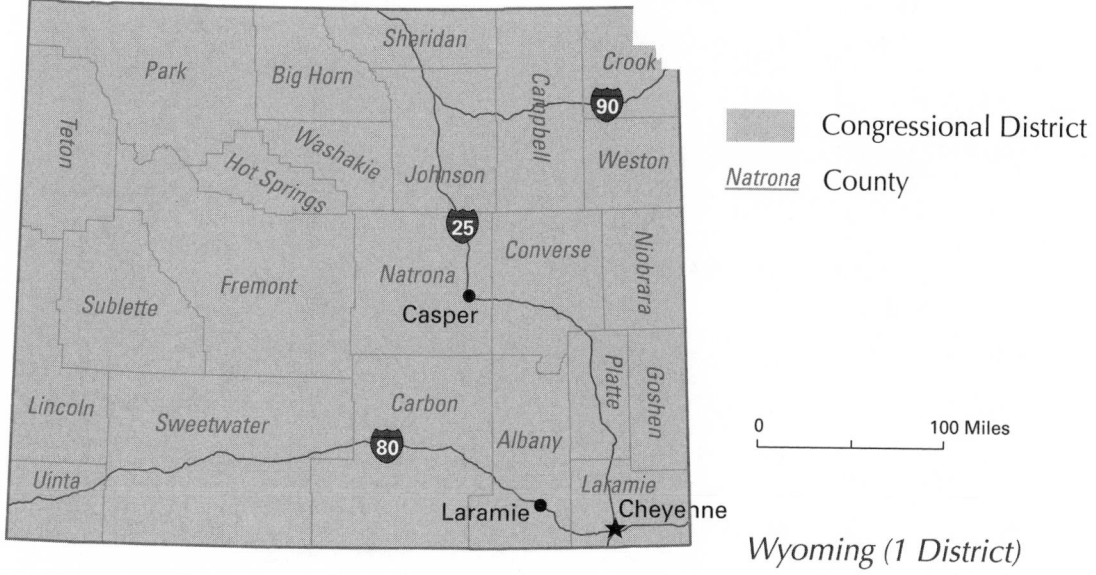

Congressional District

Natrona   County

Wyoming (1 District)

WYOMING—110th CONGRESSIONAL DISTRICTS BY COUNTIES

County	Congressional District
Albany	1
Big Horn	1
Campbell	1
Carbon	1
Converse	1
Crook	1
Fremont	1
Goshen	1
Hot Springs	1
Johnson	1
Laramie	1
Lincoln	1

County	Congressional District
Natrona	1
Niobrara	1
Park	1
Platte	1
Sheridan	1
Sublette	1
Sweetwater	1
Teton	1
Uinta	1
Washakie	1
Weston	1

American Samoa—Delegate District

Congressional District: At large

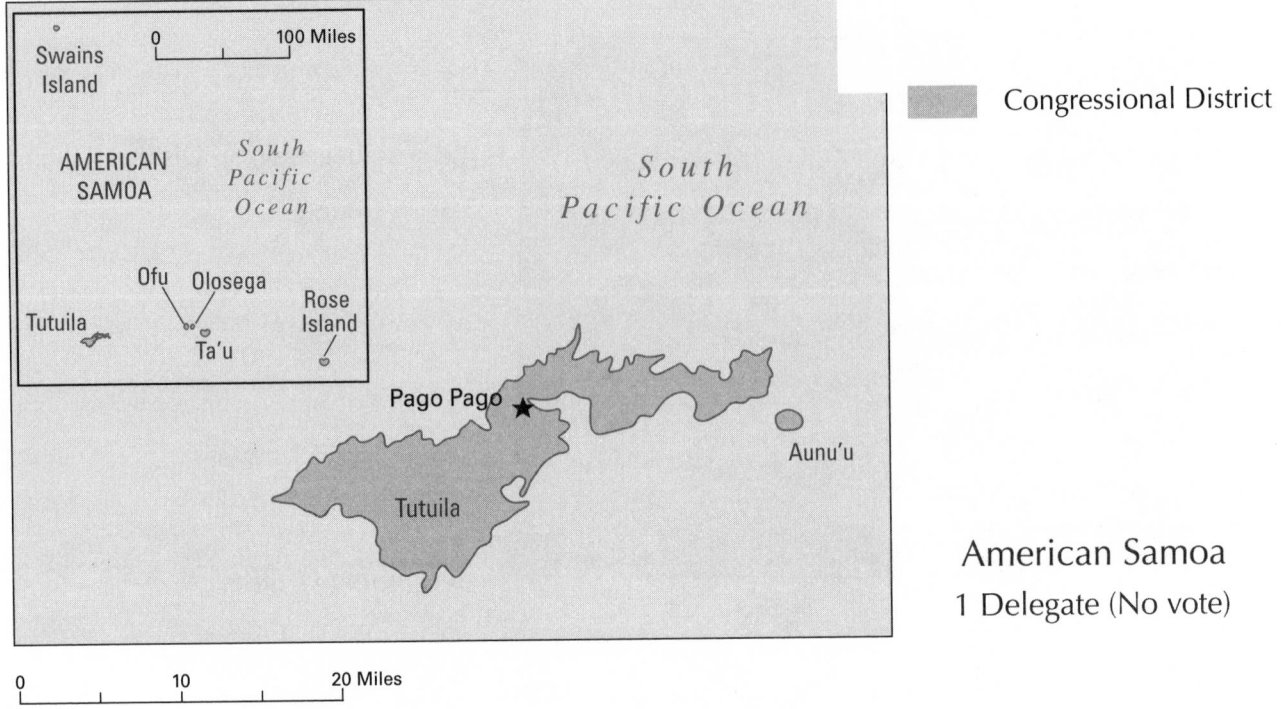

American Samoa
1 Delegate (No vote)

AMERICAN SAMOA—110th DELEGATE DISTRICTS BY COUNTIES

County	Delegate District
Eastern District	1
Manu'a District	1
Rose Island	1
Swains Island	1
Western District	1

Guam—Delegate District
Congressional District: At large

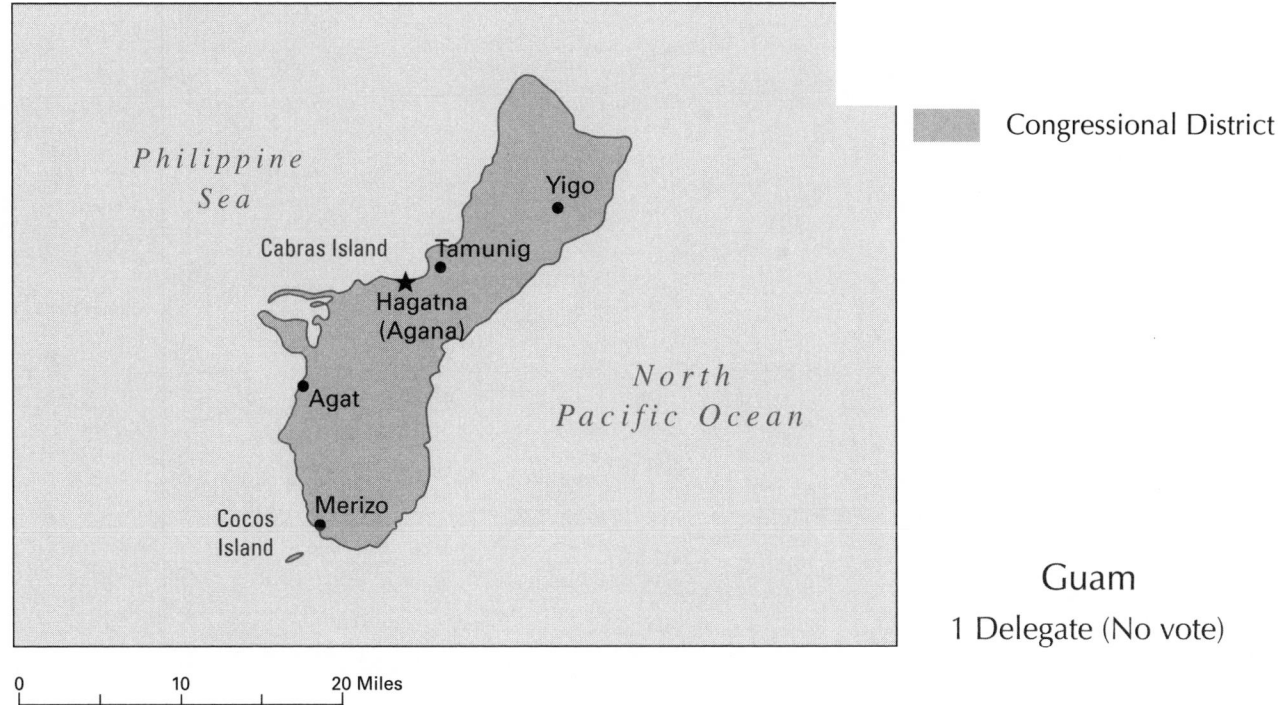

Congressional District

Guam
1 Delegate (No vote)

Northern Mariana Islands—Resident Representative District

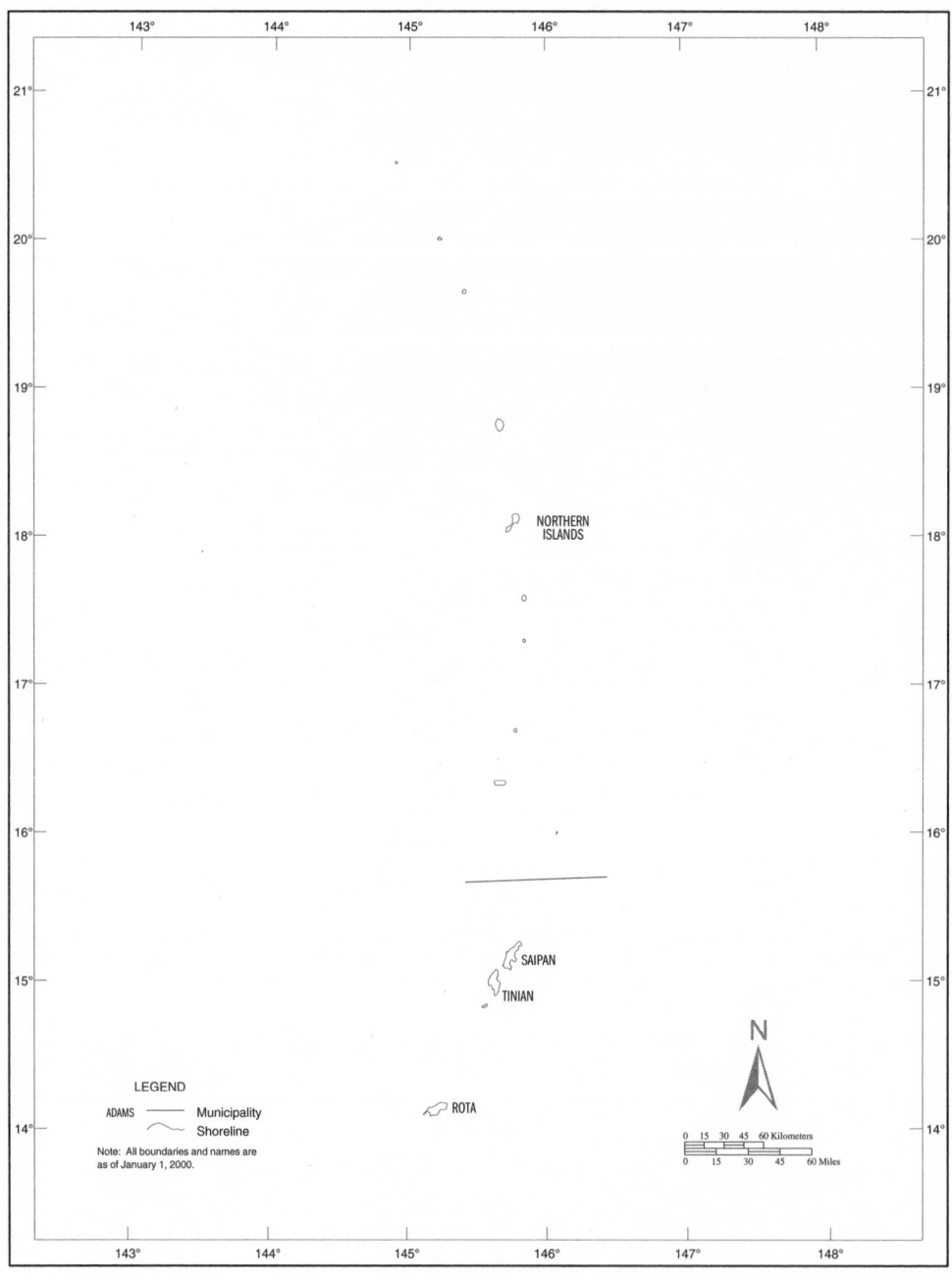

NORTHERN MARIANA ISLANDS—110th REPRESENTATIVE DISTRICT BY COUNTIES

County	Representative District
Northern Islands Municipality	1
Rota Municipality	1
Saipan Municipality	1
Tinian Municipality	1

Commonwealth of Puerto Rico—Delegate District

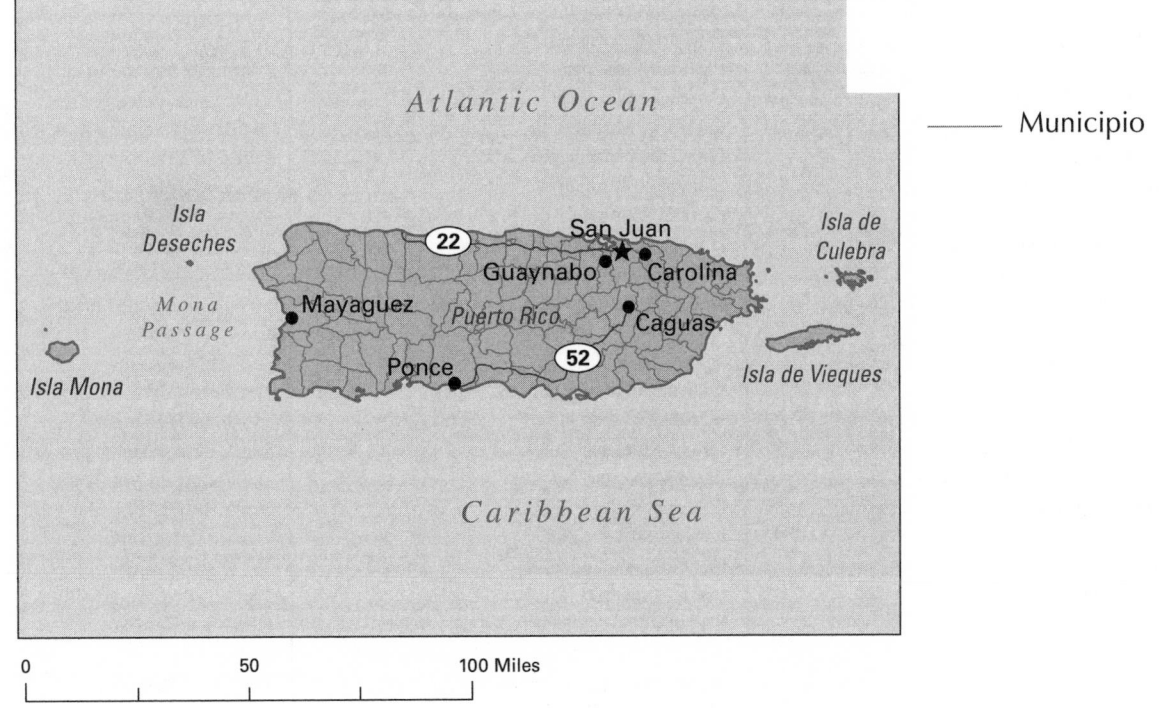

Municipio

PUERTO RICO—110th DELEGATE DISTRICTS BY COUNTIES

County	Delegate District	County	Delegate District	County	Delegate District
Adjuntas Municipio	1	Fajardo Municipio	1	Naguabo Municipio	1
Aguada Municipio	1	Florida Municipio	1	Naranjito Municipio	1
Aguadilla Municipio	1	Guánica Municipio	1	Orocovis Municipio	1
Aguas Buenas Municipio	1	Guayama Municipio	1	Patillas Municipio	1
Aibonito Municipio	1	Guayanilla Municipio	1	Peñuelas Municipio	1
Añasco Municipio	1	Guaynabo Municipio	1	Ponce Municipio	1
Arecibo Municipio	1	Gurabo Municipio	1	Quebradillas Municipio	1
Arroyo Municipio	1	Hatillo Municipio	1	Rincón Municipio	1
Barceloneta Municipio	1	Hormigueros Municipio	1	Río Grande Municipio	1
Barranquitas Municipio	1	Humacao Municipio	1	Sabana Grande Municipio	1
Bayamón Municipio	1	Isabela Municipio	1	Salinas Municipio	1
Cabo Rojo Municipio	1	Jayuya Municipio	1	San Germán Municipio	1
Caguas Municipio	1	Juana Díaz Municipio	1	San Juan Municipio	1
Camuy Municipio	1	Juncos Municipio	1	San Lorenzo Municipio	1
Canóvanas Municipio	1	Lajas Municipio	1	San Sebastián Municipio	1
Carolina Municipio	1	Lares Municipio	1	Santa Isabel Municipio	1
Cataño Municipio	1	Las Marías Municipio	1	Toa Alta Municipio	1
Cayey Municipio	1	Las Piedras Municipio	1	Toa Baja Municipio	1
Ceiba Municipio	1	Loíza Municipio	1	Trujillo Alto Municipio	1
Ciales Municipio	1	Luquillo Municipio	1	Utuado Municipio	1
Cidra Municipio	1	Manatí Municipio	1	Vega Alta Municipio	1
Coamo Municipio	1	Maricao Municipio	1	Vega Baja Municipio	1
Comerío Municipio	1	Maunabo Municipio	1	Vieques Municipio	1
Corozal Municipio	1	Mayagüez Municipio	1	Villalba Municipio	1
Culebra Municipio	1	Moca Municipio	1	Yabucoa Municipio	1
Dorado Municipio	1	Morovis Municipio	1	Yauco Municipio	1

United States Virgin Islands—Delegate District

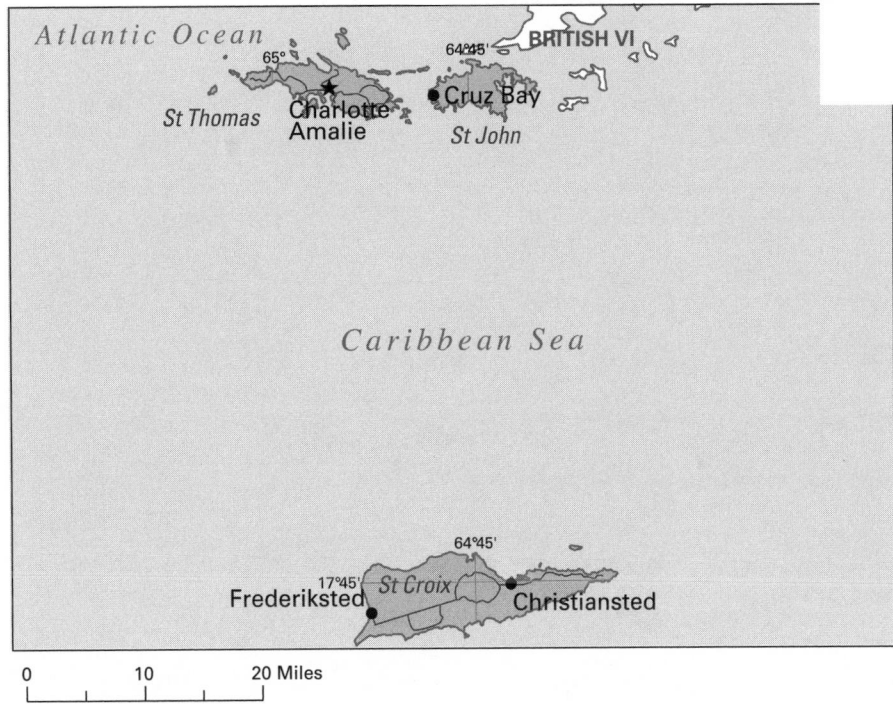

VIRGIN ISLANDS—110th DELEGATE DISTRICTS BY COUNTIES

County	Delegate District
Northern Islands Municipality	1
St. Croix Island	1
St. John Island	1
St. Thomas Island	1

PART II: TABLES

110th Congressional District Rankings[1]

(Top 30 and lowest 30 districts by rank.)

Largest Land Area,[2] 2006			Smallest Land Area,[2] 2006		
Rank	Congressional district	Land area (square kilometers)	Rank	Congressional district	Land area (square kilometers)
1	Alaska, Congressional District (At Large)	1 481 347	1	New York, Congressional District 15	27
2	Montana, Congressional District (At Large)	376 979	2	New York, Congressional District 11	31
3	Nevada, Congressional District 2	272 153	2	New York, Congressional District 16	31
4	Wyoming, Congressional District (At Large)	251 489	4	New York, Congressional District 14	33
5	South Dakota, Congressional District (At Large)	196 540	5	New York, Congressional District 8	39
6	New Mexico, Congressional District 2	179 986	6	New York, Congressional District 10	46
7	Oregon, Congressional District 2	179 982	7	New York, Congressional District 12	49
8	North Carolina, Congressional District 1	178 647	8	New York, Congressional District 7	68
9	Nebraska, Congressional District 3	167 083	9	California, Congressional District 8	92
10	Arizona, Congressional District 1	151 795	10	New York, Congressional District 9	96
11	Kansas, Congressional District 1	148 596	11	Illinois, Congressional District 4	101
12	Colorado, Congressional District 3	139 765	12	California, Congressional District 31	102
13	Texas, Congressional District 23	125 501	12	New York, Congressional District 6	102
14	New Mexico, Congressional District 3	122 108	14	Massachusetts, Congressional District 8	105
15	Utah, Congressional District 2	118 166	15	California, Congressional District 33	125
16	Idaho, Congressional District 2	111 946	16	California, Congressional District 47	142
17	Texas, Congressional District 13	104 111	17	California, Congressional District 35	144
18	Idaho, Congressional District 1	102 369	18	Illinois, Congressional District 7	146
19	Texas, Congressional District 11	90 636	19	New Jersey, Congressional District 13	147
20	Oklahoma, Congressional District 3	88 289	20	Illinois, Congressional District 5	148
21	Minnesota, Congressional District 7	82 353	21	California, Congressional District 34	151
22	Colorado, Congressional District 4	80 025	22	Pennsylvania, Congressional District 1	152
23	Minnesota, Congressional District 8	71 439	22	Pennsylvania, Congressional District 2	152
24	Maine, Congressional District 2	70 775	24	District of Columbia, Delegate District (At Large)	159
25	Texas, Congressional District 19	65 445	25	California, Congressional District 39	168
26	Michigan, Congressional District 1	64 458	25	New York, Congressional District 13	168
27	Arizona, Congressional District 7	59 240	27	New Jersey, Congressional District 10	171
28	Washington, Congressional District 5	59 217	28	New York, Congressional District 5	172
29	California, Congressional District 2	56 353	29	California, Congressional District 37	193
30	California, Congressional District 25	55 644	30	California, Congressional District 36	194

Most Densely Populated, 2006			Least Densely Populated, 2006		
Rank	Congressional district	Population density (persons per square kilometer)	Rank	Congressional district	Population density (persons per square kilometer)
1	New York, Congressional District 15	24 873.5	1	Alaska, Congressional District (At Large)	0.5
2	New York, Congressional District 16	21 610.0	2	Wyoming, Congressional District (At Large)	2.0
3	New York, Congressional District 11	21 172.4	3	Montana, Congressional District (At Large)	2.5
4	New York, Congressional District 14	19 475.0	4	Nevada, Congressional District 2	2.9
5	New York, Congressional District 8	17 764.7	5	Nebraska, Congressional District 3	3.4
6	New York, Congressional District 10	14 882.8	6	New Mexico, Congressional District 2	3.5
7	New York, Congressional District 12	13 832.4	7	North Carolina, Congressional District 1	3.6
8	New York, Congressional District 7	9 776.5	8	South Dakota, Congressional District (At Large)	4.0
9	New York, Congressional District 9	7 029.6	9	Oregon, Congressional District 2	4.2
10	New York, Congressional District 6	6 587.8	10	Kansas, Congressional District 1	4.4
11	California, Congressional District 8	6 544.6	11	Arizona, Congressional District 1	4.8
12	California, Congressional District 31	6 320.7	11	Colorado, Congressional District 3	4.8
13	Illinois, Congressional District 4	5 977.2	13	New Mexico, Congressional District 3	5.3
14	Massachusetts, Congressional District 8	5 663.3	14	Idaho, Congressional District 2	6.1
15	California, Congressional District 33	5 188.3	15	Texas, Congressional District 23	6.2
16	California, Congressional District 35	4 762.5	16	Texas, Congressional District 13	6.3
17	California, Congressional District 47	4 570.7	17	Utah, Congressional District 2	7.2
18	Illinois, Congressional District 5	4 489.4	18	Minnesota, Congressional District 7	7.5
19	California, Congressional District 34	4 418.1	18	Texas, Congressional District 11	7.5
20	New Jersey, Congressional District 13	4 387.0	20	Idaho, Congressional District 1	7.6
21	Illinois, Congressional District 7	4 292.0	21	Oklahoma, Congressional District 3	7.9
22	California, Congressional District 39	4 206.7	22	Colorado, Congressional District 4	8.6
23	Pennsylvania, Congressional District 1	4 200.3	23	Minnesota, Congressional District 8	9.1
24	New York, Congressional District 13	4 099.1	24	Maine, Congressional District 2	9.2
25	New York, Congressional District 5	3 802.5	25	Texas, Congressional District 19	10.0
26	New Jersey, Congressional District 10	3 754.5	26	Michigan, Congressional District 1	10.3
27	Pennsylvania, Congressional District 2	3 672.7	27	Washington, Congressional District 5	11.7
28	District of Columbia, Delegate District (At Large)	3 657.4	28	Iowa, Congressional District 5	12.2
29	California, Congressional District 36	3 422.7	29	California, Congressional District 2	12.4
30	California, Congressional District 37	3 397.1	30	Arkansas, Congressional District 4	12.5

[1]Includes 435 state congressional districts and the District of Columbia. Georgia and Texas data are for 109th congressional districts and the boundaries for the 110th Congress have changed.
[2]Dry land or land partially or temporarily covered by water.

110th Congressional District Rankings[1]—*Continued*

(Top 30 and lowest 30 districts by rank.)

	Highest Proportion of Non-Hispanic White Population, 2006			Lowest Proportion of Non-Hispanic White Population, 2006	
Rank	Congressional district	Percent non-Hispanic White	Rank	Congressional district	Percent non-Hispanic White
1	Pennsylvania, Congressional District 9	95.7	1	New York, Congressional District 16	2.2
2	Ohio, Congressional District 18	95.6	2	California, Congressional District 34	8.3
2	Vermont, Congressional District (At Large)	95.6	3	California, Congressional District 35	8.5
4	Maine, Congressional District 1	95.5	4	California, Congressional District 31	10.5
5	West Virginia, Congressional District 1	95.3	5	California, Congressional District 38	11.4
6	Wisconsin, Congressional District 3	95.2	6	New York, Congressional District 6	11.5
7	Pennsylvania, Congressional District 5	95.1	7	California, Congressional District 32	12.7
8	Maine, Congressional District 2	95.0	8	Texas, Congressional District 9	13.2
9	Ohio, Congressional District 6	94.8	9	California, Congressional District 47	13.4
10	Wisconsin, Congressional District 7	94.4	10	Texas, Congressional District 16	14.2
11	Pennsylvania, Congressional District 12	94.2	11	Florida, Congressional District 17	14.6
11	West Virginia, Congressional District 3	94.2	12	California, Congressional District 37	14.7
13	Kentucky, Congressional District 4	93.9	13	Texas, Congressional District 18	15.4
13	Minnesota, Congressional District 8	93.9	14	Texas, Congressional District 29	15.7
13	New Hampshire, Congressional District 1	93.9	15	Florida, Congressional District 21	16.2
13	Pennsylvania, Congressional District 10	93.9	16	California, Congressional District 39	16.7
17	Tennessee, Congressional District 1	93.8	17	California, Congressional District 43	17.0
18	Illinois, Congressional District 19	93.5	18	New Jersey, Congressional District 10	17.3
18	Iowa, Congressional District 4	93.5	19	Texas, Congressional District 30	17.4
20	New Hampshire, Congressional District 2	93.3	20	Illinois, Congressional District 4	17.9
21	Indiana, Congressional District 8	93.2	21	New York, Congressional District 10	18.0
21	Indiana, Congressional District 9	93.2	22	California, Congressional District 51	18.1
23	Michigan, Congressional District 1	93.1	23	Texas, Congressional District 25	18.7
23	Pennsylvania, Congressional District 3	93.1	24	Illinois, Congressional District 2	18.8
25	Ohio, Congressional District 5	93.0	25	California, Congressional District 20	19.0
25	West Virginia, Congressional District 2	93.0	26	Hawaii, Congressional District 1	19.1
27	Pennsylvania, Congressional District 4	92.8	27	New York, Congressional District 15	19.9
28	New York, Congressional District 23	92.5	28	Florida, Congressional District 25	20.0
28	Virginia, Congressional District 9	92.5	29	Texas, Congressional District 20	20.8
28	Wisconsin, Congressional District 6	92.5	30	California, Congressional District 33	21.9

	Highest Proportion of Black Alone Population, 2006			Lowest Proportion of Black Alone Population, 2006	
Rank	Congressional district	Percent Black alone	Rank	Congressional district	Percent Black alone
1	Illinois, Congressional District 2	68.3	1	Nebraska, Congressional District 3	0.2
2	Mississippi, Congressional District 2	66.4	2	Idaho, Congressional District 1	0.4
3	Illinois, Congressional District 1	64.4	2	Oregon, Congressional District 2	0.4
4	Alabama, Congressional District 7	63.7	2	Wisconsin, Congressional District 7	0.4
5	Tennessee, Congressional District 9	63.4	5	Idaho, Congressional District 2	0.5
6	Michigan, Congressional District 14	61.7	5	Minnesota, Congressional District 7	0.5
7	New York, Congressional District 10	61.6	5	Montana, Congressional District (At Large)	0.5
8	Pennsylvania, Congressional District 2	60.9	8	Iowa, Congressional District 5	0.6
9	Michigan, Congressional District 13	59.9	8	Utah, Congressional District 3	0.6
10	Ohio, Congressional District 11	59.1	10	Colorado, Congressional District 4	0.7
11	New Jersey, Congressional District 10	58.3	10	Iowa, Congressional District 4	0.7
12	Maryland, Congressional District 7	57.8	10	South Dakota, Congressional District (At Large)	0.7
13	New York, Congressional District 11	57.6	10	Utah, Congressional District 2	0.7
14	Florida, Congressional District 17	57.4	10	Wisconsin, Congressional District 3	0.7
15	Lousiana, Congressional District 2	56.4	10	Wyoming, Congressional District (At Large)	0.7
16	Virginia, Congressional District 3	56.1	16	Colorado, Congressional District 3	0.8
17	Florida, Congressional District 23	56.0	16	Oregon, Congressional District 4	0.8
18	Illinois, Congressional District 7	55.8	16	Vermont, Congressional District (At Large)	0.8
19	Maryland, Congressional District 4	55.7	19	Colorado, Congressional District 2	0.9
20	South Carolina, Congressional District 6	55.6	19	Minnesota, Congressional District 8	0.9
21	District of Columbia, Delegate District (At Large)	55.4	19	North Carolina, Congressional District 1	0.9
22	Georgia, Congressional District 4	54.1	19	Washington, Congressional District 4	0.9
23	Missouri, Congressional District 1	53.8	19	Wisconsin, Congressional District 8	0.9
24	Georgia, Congressional District 5	53.6	24	Maine, Congressional District 2	1.0
25	New York, Congressional District 6	52.4	24	New Hampshire, Congressional District 2	1.0
26	Florida, Congressional District 3	51.8	24	Oregon, Congressional District 5	1.0
27	North Carolina, Congressional District 2	50.8	27	California, Congressional District 2	1.1
28	Georgia, Congressional District 13	50.7	27	Maine, Congressional District 1	1.1
29	Pennsylvania, Congressional District 1	49.9	27	New Hampshire, Congressional District 1	1.1
30	North Carolina, Congressional District 13	44.0	30	Arizona, Congressional District 1	1.2
			30	California, Congressional District 4	1.2
			30	California, Congressional District 47	1.2
			30	Kentucky, Congressional District 5	1.2
			30	Missouri, Congressional District 7	1.2
			30	Ohio, Congressional District 5	1.2

[1]Includes 435 state congressional districts and the District of Columbia. Georgia and Texas data are for 109th congressional districts and the boundaries for the 110th Congress have changed.

110th Congressional District Rankings[1]—*Continued*

(Top 30 and lowest 30 districts by rank.)

Highest Proportion of Foreign-Born Population, 2006			Lowest Proportion of Foreign-Born Population, 2006		
Rank	Congressional district	Percent foreign born	Rank	Congressional district	Percent foreign born
1	Florida, Congressional District 21	54.3	1	Kentucky, Congressional District 5	0.7
2	Florida, Congressional District 18	53.3	1	Ohio, Congressional District 18	0.7
3	California, Congressional District 31	51.4	1	West Virginia, Congressional District 3	0.7
4	California, Congressional District 47	49.3	4	Pennsylvania, Congressional District 12	1.0
5	New York, Congressional District 5	49.1	5	Mississippi, Congressional District 2	1.1
6	Florida, Congressional District 25	46.6	6	Arkansas, Congressional District 1	1.2
7	California, Congressional District 34	43.9	6	Illinois, Congressional District 19	1.2
7	New York, Congressional District 6	43.9	6	Lousiana, Congressional District 5	1.2
9	California, Congressional District 28	43.5	6	Missouri, Congressional District 8	1.2
10	California, Congressional District 29	42.1	10	Pennsylvania, Congressional District 9	1.3
10	New Jersey, Congressional District 13	42.1	10	West Virginia, Congressional District 2	1.3
12	New York, Congressional District 12	41.9	12	Minnesota, Congressional District 8	1.4
12	New York, Congressional District 9	41.9	13	Mississippi, Congressional District 3	1.5
14	California, Congressional District 32	41.2	14	Indiana, Congressional District 6	1.6
15	New York, Congressional District 7	39.2	14	Indiana, Congressional District 8	1.6
16	New York, Congressional District 11	39.1	14	Ohio, Congressional District 4	1.6
17	California, Congressional District 16	38.9	14	West Virginia, Congressional District 1	1.6
18	California, Congressional District 38	38.1	18	Kentucky, Congressional District 1	1.7
19	California, Congressional District 13	38.0	18	Ohio, Congressional District 6	1.7
20	Illinois, Congressional District 4	37.8	20	Alabama, Congressional District 2	1.9
21	California, Congressional District 27	37.6	20	Kentucky, Congressional District 4	1.9
22	Florida, Congressional District 17	37.2	20	Lousiana, Congressional District 7	1.9
23	California, Congressional District 15	36.1	20	Michigan, Congressional District 1	1.9
24	California, Congressional District 8	35.7	20	Montana, Congressional District (At Large)	1.9
24	Texas, Congressional District 9	35.7	20	Oklahoma, Congressional District 2	1.9
26	New Jersey, Congressional District 9	35.5	20	Tennessee, Congressional District 4	1.9
26	New York, Congressional District 16	35.5	20	Tennessee, Congressional District 8	1.9
28	California, Congressional District 33	35.3	28	Michigan, Congressional District 4	2.0
29	California, Congressional District 12	35.1	28	Michigan, Congressional District 5	2.0
30	Texas, Congressional District 29	34.3	28	Mississippi, Congressional District 1	2.0
			28	Missouri, Congressional District 9	2.0
			28	Ohio, Congressional District 5	2.0
			28	Virginia, Congressional District 9	2.0
			28	Wisconsin, Congressional District 3	2.0
			28	Wisconsin, Congressional District 7	2.0

Highest Proportion of Population Born in State of Residence, 2006			Lowest Proportion of Population Born in State of Residence, 2006		
Rank	Congressional district	Percent born in state of residence	Rank	Congressional district	Percent born in state of residence
1	Lousiana, Congressional District 3	87.5	1	Maryland, Congressional District 8	19.2
2	Pennsylvania, Congressional District 12	87.1	2	Nevada, Congressional District 3	20.1
3	Lousiana, Congressional District 7	85.2	3	Florida, Congressional District 19	20.4
4	Ohio, Congressional District 18	84.6	4	Virginia, Congressional District 8	21.1
5	Mississippi, Congressional District 2	84.4	5	Florida, Congressional District 14	21.3
6	Michigan, Congressional District 10	83.6	6	Maryland, Congressional District 4	22.6
7	Michigan, Congressional District 4	83.4	7	Nevada, Congressional District 1	22.7
7	New York, Congressional District 26	83.4	8	Florida, Congressional District 18	24.2
7	Pennsylvania, Congressional District 18	83.4	9	Florida, Congressional District 13	24.5
10	Pennsylvania, Congressional District 3	82.7	10	Florida, Congressional District 22	25.2
11	Ohio, Congressional District 4	82.6	11	Florida, Congressional District 15	26.2
12	Pennsylvania, Congressional District 5	82.2	12	Nevada, Congressional District 2	26.8
13	Michigan, Congressional District 5	82.1	13	Arizona, Congressional District 5	27.5
14	New York, Congressional District 27	81.9	13	Florida, Congressional District 20	27.5
15	Pennsylvania, Congressional District 9	81.7	15	Florida, Congressional District 10	27.8
16	Pennsylvania, Congressional District 4	81.5	16	Virginia, Congressional District 11	28.1
16	Pennsylvania, Congressional District 14	81.5	17	Arizona, Congressional District 2	28.2
18	Alabama, Congressional District 7	81.4	17	Florida, Congressional District 21	28.2
19	New York, Congressional District 3	81.2	19	Florida, Congressional District 16	29.3
20	Wisconsin, Congressional District 6	81.1	20	Florida, Congressional District 9	29.5
21	Ohio, Congressional District 5	81.0	21	Florida, Congressional District 8	31.0
22	Ohio, Congressional District 16	80.6	22	Arizona, Congressional District 8	31.3
23	Illinois, Congressional District 18	80.5	23	Florida, Congressional District 5	31.5
23	New York, Congressional District 24	80.5	24	Florida, Congressional District 24	31.6
25	Pennsylvania, Congressional District 17	80.4	25	Colorado, Congressional District 5	32.0
26	Kentucky, Congressional District 5	80.2	26	Florida, Congressional District 7	32.8
27	New York, Congressional District 23	80.1	27	Arizona, Congressional District 3	33.1
28	Lousiana, Congressional District 5	80.0	28	Arizona, Congressional District 6	33.2
28	Michigan, Congressional District 2	80.0	28	Georgia, Congressional District 6	33.2
28	West Virginia, Congressional District 3	80.0	30	Florida, Congressional District 25	34.1

[1] Includes 435 state congressional districts and the District of Columbia. Georgia and Texas data are for 109th congressional districts and the boundaries for the 110th Congress have changed.

110th Congressional District Rankings[1]—Continued

(Top 30 districts and lowest 30 districts by rank.)

	Highest Proportion with a Bachelor's Degree or More,[3] 2006			Lowest Proportion with a Bachelor's Degree or More,[3] 2006	
Rank	Congressional district	Percent with bachelor's degree or more	Rank	Congressional district	Percent with bachelor's degree or more
1	New York, Congressional District 14	62.1	1	Texas, Congressional District 29	7.1
2	Virginia, Congressional District 8	60.4	2	California, Congressional District 20	7.2
3	California, Congressional District 30	58.5	3	California, Congressional District 18	9.6
4	Maryland, Congressional District 8	56.3	4	California, Congressional District 34	10.2
5	New York, Congressional District 8	55.9	4	New York, Congressional District 16	10.2
6	California, Congressional District 14	55.5	6	California, Congressional District 43	11.0
7	Georgia, Congressional District 6	53.3	7	Texas, Congressional District 28	12.1
8	California, Congressional District 48	52.4	8	Lousiana, Congressional District 3	12.3
9	Virginia, Congressional District 11	51.7	8	Ohio, Congressional District 18	12.3
10	Illinois, Congressional District 10	50.8	10	North Carolina, Congressional District 1	12.5
11	Washington, Congressional District 7	50.5	11	Alabama, Congressional District 4	12.6
12	North Carolina, Congressional District 4	49.8	11	California, Congressional District 47	12.6
13	California, Congressional District 8	48.8	11	Kentucky, Congressional District 5	12.6
14	New York, Congressional District 18	48.3	14	West Virginia, Congressional District 3	12.9
15	New Jersey, Congressional District 12	47.8	15	Arkansas, Congressional District 1	13.3
16	New Jersey, Congressional District 11	47.7	15	Tennessee, Congressional District 4	13.3
17	Michigan, Congressional District 9	47.3	17	Kentucky, Congressional District 1	13.7
17	Texas, Congressional District 7	47.3	17	Missouri, Congressional District 8	13.7
19	Colorado, Congressional District 6	47.2	19	Arizona, Congressional District 4	13.8
19	Texas, Congressional District 21	47.2	20	California, Congressional District 38	13.9
21	California, Congressional District 12	46.6	21	Georgia, Congressional District 3	14.0
22	Virginia, Congressional District 10	46.5	22	Tennessee, Congressional District 8	14.3
23	District of Columbia, Delegate District (At Large)	45.9	22	Virginia, Congressional District 9	14.3
24	Illinois, Congressional District 13	45.5	24	Oklahoma, Congressional District 2	14.4
25	California, Congressional District 15	45.3	25	Arizona, Congressional District 7	14.7
26	Massachusetts, Congressional District 8	44.9	25	Arkansas, Congressional District 4	14.7
27	California, Congressional District 50	44.5	25	Michigan, Congressional District 13	14.7
28	New Jersey, Congressional District 7	44.3	28	Pennsylvania, Congressional District 9	14.9
29	Connecticut, Congressional District 4	43.9	28	Texas, Congressional District 15	14.9
30	Kansas, Congressional District 3	42.8	30	Florida, Congressional District 3	15.0

	Highest Median Household Income, 2006			Lowest Median Household Income, 2006	
Rank	Congressional district	Median household income (dollars)	Rank	Congressional district	Median household income (dollars)
1	Virginia, Congressional District 11	97 753	1	New York, Congressional District 16	21 088
2	New Jersey, Congressional District 11	92 765	2	Kentucky, Congressional District 5	26 967
3	Virginia, Congressional District 10	87 512	3	Mississippi, Congressional District 2	27 955
4	California, Congressional District 14	87 055	4	Alabama, Congressional District 7	28 298
5	New Jersey, Congressional District 7	87 020	5	Pennsylvania, Congressional District 1	29 448
6	California, Congressional District 42	86 983	6	North Carolina, Congressional District 1	30 872
7	New York, Congressional District 3	86 932	7	Michigan, Congressional District 13	31 169
8	New Jersey, Congressional District 5	84 443	8	West Virginia, Congressional District 3	31 282
9	Virginia, Congressional District 8	84 260	9	Georgia, Congressional District 2	31 296
10	New Jersey, Congressional District 12	84 020	10	Texas, Congressional District 15	31 502
11	California, Congressional District 48	83 652	11	Lousiana, Congressional District 5	31 713
12	Maryland, Congressional District 8	82 987	12	Pennsylvania, Congressional District 2	31 730
13	New York, Congressional District 2	82 196	13	South Carolina, Congressional District 6	31 833
14	California, Congressional District 15	82 085	14	Texas, Congressional District 27	31 990
15	New York, Congressional District 18	81 538	15	Texas, Congressional District 25	32 113
16	Colorado, Congressional District 6	80 873	16	California, Congressional District 20	32 212
17	Illinois, Congressional District 13	80 703	17	Arkansas, Congressional District 4	32 284
18	Georgia, Congressional District 6	80 175	18	Texas, Congressional District 16	32 290
19	Maryland, Congressional District 5	79 916	19	Florida, Congressional District 3	32 373
20	California, Congressional District 12	79 035	20	Pennsylvania, Congressional District 14	32 466
21	Illinois, Congressional District 10	78 269	21	Missouri, Congressional District 8	32 604
22	New York, Congressional District 4	78 147	22	Arkansas, Congressional District 1	32 702
23	Connecticut, Congressional District 4	78 014	23	Oklahoma, Congressional District 2	32 848
24	New York, Congressional District 19	77 721	24	New York, Congressional District 15	32 890
25	Washington, Congressional District 8	76 115	25	Georgia, Congressional District 3	32 916
26	California, Congressional District 11	75 008	26	Virginia, Congressional District 9	33 069
27	California, Congressional District 50	74 613	27	Ohio, Congressional District 11	33 661
28	California, Congressional District 24	74 529	28	Texas, Congressional District 29	33 725
29	California, Congressional District 10	74 338	29	Georgia, Congressional District 12	34 136
30	California, Congressional District 30	74 235	30	West Virginia, Congressional District 1	34 198

[1]Includes 435 state congressional districts and the District of Columbia. Georgia and Texas data are for 109th congressional districts and the boundaries for the 110th Congress have changed.
[3]Persons 25 years old and over.

110th Congressional District Rankings[1]—*Continued*

(Top 30 districts and lowest 30 districts by rank.)

Rank	Highest Unemployment Rate,[4] 2006 Congressional district	Unemployment rate	Rank	Lowest Unemployment Rate,[4] 2006 Congressional district	Unemployment rate
1	Michigan, Congressional District 13	18.8	1	Virginia, Congressional District 8	2.8
2	Michigan, Congressional District 14	17.5	2	Virginia, Congressional District 10	2.9
3	Illinois, Congressional District 2	14.7	3	North Carolina, Congressional District 1	3.3
4	Pennsylvania, Congressional District 1	14.2	4	Wyoming, Congressional District (At Large)	3.5
5	New York, Congressional District 16	14.2	5	Arizona, Congressional District 6	3.6
6	Illinois, Congressional District 1	13.0	5	Wisconsin, Congressional District 5	3.6
7	California, Congressional District 20	12.9	7	California, Congressional District 48	3.7
8	Ohio, Congressional District 11	12.5	8	Arizona, Congressional District 5	3.8
9	Mississippi, Congressional District 2	12.1	8	Florida, Congressional District 14	3.8
10	California, Congressional District 18	11.8	8	Maryland, Congressional District 6	3.8
11	Pennsylvania, Congressional District 2	11.8	11	Missouri, Congressional District 2	3.9
12	South Carolina, Congressional District 6	11.6	11	Nebraska, Congressional District 3	3.9
13	Lousiana, Congressional District 2	11.6	11	Virginia, Congressional District 11	3.9
14	Illinois, Congressional District 7	11.5	14	Alabama, Congressional District 6	4.0
15	Tennessee, Congressional District 9	11.2	14	Florida, Congressional District 18	4.0
16	New Jersey, Congressional District 10	11.0	14	Kansas, Congressional District 1	4.0
17	Michigan, Congressional District 5	10.9	14	New Hampshire, Congressional District 2	4.0
18	Alabama, Congressional District 7	10.4	14	Pennsylvania, Congressional District 16	4.0
19	Michigan, Congressional District 12	10.4	19	Arizona, Congressional District 3	4.1
20	New York, Congressional District 15	10.3	19	Florida, Congressional District 22	4.1
21	Texas, Congressional District 30	10.2	19	Florida, Congressional District 7	4.1
22	Michigan, Congressional District 4	10.2	19	Maryland, Congressional District 8	4.1
23	Missouri, Congressional District 1	10.1	19	New York, Congressional District 3	4.1
24	Texas, Congressional District 29	10.1	19	Utah, Congressional District 2	4.1
25	Indiana, Congressional District 7	10.0	25	Colorado, Congressional District 6	4.2
26	Georgia, Congressional District 13	9.8	25	Florida, Congressional District 13	4.2
27	Wisconsin, Congressional District 4	9.8	25	Iowa, Congressional District 4	4.2
28	California, Congressional District 17	9.8	25	Massachusetts, Congressional District 6	4.2
29	North Carolina, Congressional District 13	9.7	25	Minnesota, Congressional District 1	4.2
30	Lousiana, Congressional District 5	9.5	25	New Jersey, Congressional District 11	4.2
30	Washington, Congressional District 4	9.5	25	Pennsylvania, Congressional District 18	4.2
			25	Virginia, Congressional District 6	4.2
			25	Wisconsin, Congressional District 2	4.2

Rank	Highest Poverty Rate, 2006 Congressional district	Poverty rate	Rank	Lowest Poverty Rate, 2006 Congressional district	Poverty rate
1	New York, Congressional District 16	40.8	1	New Jersey, Congressional District 7	3.5
2	Pennsylvania, Congressional District 1	30.7	2	New Jersey, Congressional District 5	3.7
3	Texas, Congressional District 25	30.6	3	New Jersey, Congressional District 11	3.8
4	Michigan, Congressional District 13	30.3	4	Illinois, Congressional District 13	4.1
4	Texas, Congressional District 15	30.3	5	Colorado, Congressional District 6	4.2
6	California, Congressional District 20	30.2	5	Virginia, Congressional District 11	4.2
7	Mississippi, Congressional District 2	28.9	7	Missouri, Congressional District 2	4.4
8	Texas, Congressional District 27	28.4	8	Minnesota, Congressional District 2	4.6
9	New York, Congressional District 15	27.8	8	Pennsylvania, Congressional District 8	4.6
10	New York, Congressional District 10	27.5	10	Wisconsin, Congressional District 5	5.1
11	Texas, Congressional District 16	27.1	11	Georgia, Congressional District 6	5.2
12	Kentucky, Congressional District 5	26.3	11	New York, Congressional District 3	5.2
13	Pennsylvania, Congressional District 2	26.0	13	Virginia, Congressional District 10	5.3
14	Alabama, Congressional District 7	25.5	14	Illinois, Congressional District 10	5.4
15	Georgia, Congressional District 2	25.0	15	California, Congressional District 42	5.5
15	New York, Congressional District 12	25.0	15	New York, Congressional District 2	5.5
15	Texas, Congressional District 30	25.0	17	Massachusetts, Congressional District 10	5.6
18	Arizona, Congressional District 4	24.9	17	Minnesota, Congressional District 3	5.6
18	Texas, Congressional District 18	24.9	17	Pennsylvania, Congressional District 7	5.6
20	South Carolina, Congressional District 6	24.6	20	Maryland, Congressional District 8	5.7
21	Wisconsin, Congressional District 4	24.3	21	Maryland, Congressional District 6	5.8
22	California, Congressional District 31	24.2	21	New York, Congressional District 4	5.8
23	Lousiana, Congressional District 5	24.1	23	Connecticut, Congressional District 2	5.9
24	California, Congressional District 35	23.6	23	Maryland, Congressional District 3	5.9
25	Illinois, Congressional District 4	23.3	25	Illinois, Congressional District 8	6.0
26	Illinois, Congressional District 7	23.2	25	New Jersey, Congressional District 12	6.0
27	Michigan, Congressional District 14	23.0	25	Washington, Congressional District 1	6.0
27	Texas, Congressional District 9	23.0	28	New Jersey, Congressional District 3	6.1
29	North Carolina, Congressional District 2	22.9	29	Washington, Congressional District 8	6.2
30	Florida, Congressional District 3	22.8	30	Michigan, Congressional District 11	6.3
30	Georgia, Congressional District 3	22.8			

[1] Includes 435 state congressional districts and the District of Columbia. Georgia and Texas data are for 109th congressional districts and the boundaries for the 110th Congress have changed.
[4] Percent of civilian labor force.

110th Congressional District Rankings[1]—*Continued*

(Top 30 districts and lowest 30 districts by rank.)

	Highest Proportion of One-Person Households, 2006			Lowest Proportion of One-Person Households, 2006	
Rank	Congressional district	Percent one-person household	Rank	Congressional district	Percent one-person household
1	New York, Congressional District 14	50.1	1	Texas, Congressional District 27	20.3
2	New York, Congressional District 8	47.5	1	Texas, Congressional District 28	20.3
3	District of Columbia, Delegate District (At Large)	47.2	1	California, Congressional District 40	20.3
4	Georgia, Congressional District 5	45.5	4	California, Congressional District 49	20.2
5	Pennsylvania, Congressional District 2	45.0	4	Minnesota, Congressional District 6	20.2
6	California, Congressional District 8	43.5	6	California, Congressional District 34	20.1
7	Pennsylvania, Congressional District 14	42.6	6	Utah, Congressional District 1	20.1
8	Virginia, Congressional District 8	41.8	6	Texas, Congressional District 22	20.1
9	Washington, Congressional District 7	41.6	9	Florida, Congressional District 21	20.0
10	New York, Congressional District 15	41.5	9	California, Congressional District 18	20.0
11	California, Congressional District 30	41.4	11	Texas, Congressional District 29	19.8
12	Colorado, Congressional District 1	41.2	11	New York, Congressional District 3	19.8
13	Illinois, Congressional District 7	40.0	13	New Jersey, Congressional District 5	19.7
14	Ohio, Congressional District 11	39.8	13	Colorado, Congressional District 6	19.7
15	Massachusetts, Congressional District 8	39.7	15	California, Congressional District 11	19.6
16	Minnesota, Congressional District 5	39.3	16	Georgia, Congressional District 8	19.5
17	California, Congressional District 53	38.4	17	California, Congressional District 21	18.9
17	Florida, Congressional District 10	38.4	18	Texas, Congressional District 15	18.8
19	Illinois, Congressional District 9	37.9	19	California, Congressional District 44	18.7
20	California, Congressional District 33	37.6	20	California, Congressional District 20	17.9
21	New York, Congressional District 28	37.5	21	California, Congressional District 25	17.3
22	Pennsylvania, Congressional District 1	37.1	22	New York, Congressional District 2	17.2
23	Wisconsin, Congressional District 4	36.7	23	Georgia, Congressional District 7	17.0
24	California, Congressional District 9	36.2	24	Florida, Congressional District 25	16.5
25	Ohio, Congressional District 1	35.6	25	California, Congressional District 42	16.3
25	Texas, Congressional District 7	35.6	26	California, Congressional District 38	15.8
27	Michigan, Congressional District 12	35.4	27	California, Congressional District 51	15.7
28	Indiana, Congressional District 7	35.2	28	Utah, Congressional District 3	15.2
28	Missouri, Congressional District 1	35.2	29	California, Congressional District 32	15.1
28	Tennessee, Congressional District 9	35.2	29	California, Congressional District 43	15.1
			30	California, Congressional District 39	14.1
			30	California, Congressional District 47	13.7

	Highest Median Owner-Occupied Housing Value, 2006			Lowest Median Owner-Occupied Housing Value, 2006	
Rank	Congressional district	Median housing value (dollars)	Rank	Congressional district	Median housing value (dollars)
1	California, Congressional District 30	920 200	1	Kentucky, Congressional District 5	65 000
2	California, Congressional District 14	875 600	2	Texas, Congressional District 15	69 400
3	California, Congressional District 12	809 400	3	Mississippi, Congressional District 2	72 900
4	California, Congressional District 8	779 800	4	Texas, Congressional District 11	73 800
5	California, Congressional District 48	762 800	5	Arkansas, Congressional District 4	74 000
6	California, Congressional District 15	740 700	6	Texas, Congressional District 19	74 700
7	California, Congressional District 46	734 600	7	West Virginia, Congressional District 3	74 800
8	New York, Congressional District 8	726 100	8	Pennsylvania, Congressional District 14	76 900
9	New York, Congressional District 14	723 300	8	Texas, Congressional District 13	76 900
10	California, Congressional District 36	711 400	10	Texas, Congressional District 28	77 100
11	California, Congressional District 6	701 000	11	Oklahoma, Congressional District 2	78 100
12	California, Congressional District 17	695 300	12	Arkansas, Congressional District 1	79 000
13	California, Congressional District 16	680 700	13	Kentucky, Congressional District 1	79 200
14	California, Congressional District 42	670 900	14	Texas, Congressional District 25	79 400
15	California, Congressional District 23	655 300	15	Kansas, Congressional District 1	79 800
16	California, Congressional District 50	652 100	16	Texas, Congressional District 27	80 600
17	California, Congressional District 24	646 900	17	Lousiana, Congressional District 5	80 700
18	California, Congressional District 9	639 800	18	Texas, Congressional District 20	81 600
19	California, Congressional District 10	634 900	19	Oklahoma, Congressional District 3	82 400
20	California, Congressional District 29	633 200	20	Alabama, Congressional District 7	82 900
21	California, Congressional District 40	631 500	21	Illinois, Congressional District 17	83 200
22	California, Congressional District 13	628 100	22	Georgia, Congressional District 3	83 900
23	New York, Congressional District 5	614 400	23	Texas, Congressional District 29	84 200
24	California, Congressional District 28	610 600	24	Nebraska, Congressional District 3	85 200
25	California, Congressional District 11	607 900	25	New York, Congressional District 28	85 800
26	New York, Congressional District 18	607 600	26	Lousiana, Congressional District 4	86 000
27	California, Congressional District 26	604 300	27	North Carolina, Congressional District 2	86 300
28	California, Congressional District 33	602 900	28	Texas, Congressional District 1	86 400
29	California, Congressional District 27	598 200	29	Pennsylvania, Congressional District 12	86 500
30	Connecticut, Congressional District 4	596 700	30	Alabama, Congressional District 4	87 100

[1]Includes 435 state congressional districts and the District of Columbia. Georgia and Texas data are for 109th congressional districts and the boundaries for the 110th Congress have changed.

110th Congressional District Rankings[1]—Continued

(Top 75 districts by rank.)

	Highest Number of Farms, 2002			Highest Value of Agricultural Products Sold, 2002	
Rank	Congressional district	Number of farms	Rank	Congressional district	Market value of agricultural products sold ($1,000)
1	Kansas, Congressional District 1	34 746	1	Kansas, Congressional District 1	7 176 335
2	Minnesota, Congressional District 7	32 629	2	Nebraska, Congressional District 3	7 174 525
3	Nebraska, Congressional District 3	31 774	3	Texas, Congressional District 13	5 656 446
4	South Dakota, Congressional District (At Large)	31 736	4	Iowa, Congressional District 5	4 480 496
5	North Dakota, Congressional District (At Large)	30 619	5	South Dakota, Congressional District (At Large)	3 834 625
6	Oklahoma, Congressional District 3	30 462	6	Iowa, Congressional District 4	3 813 075
7	Oklahoma, Congressional District 2	30 416	7	Minnesota, Congressional District 7	3 792 754
8	Montana, Congressional District (At Large)	27 870	8	Colorado, Congressional District 4	3 456 724
9	Wisconsin, Congressional District 3	27 124	9	California, Congressional District 21	3 282 057
10	Iowa, Congressional District 5	26 562	10	North Dakota, Congressional District (At Large)	3 233 366
11	Missouri, Congressional District 4	26 556	11	Minnesota, Congressional District 1	3 186 486
12	Texas, Congressional District 14	26 242	12	California, Congressional District 20	3 022 243
13	Texas, Congressional District 17	25 433	13	Idaho, Congressional District 2	3 011 342
14	Iowa, Congressional District 4	24 501	14	Washington, Congressional District 4	2 924 142
15	Kentucky, Congressional District 1	24 157	15	California, Congressional District 17	2 627 098
16	Kentucky, Congressional District 2	23 291	16	Oklahoma, Congressional District 3	2 528 847
17	Missouri, Congressional District 9	22 595	17	Nebraska, Congressional District 1	2 489 414
18	Minnesota, Congressional District 1	21 384	18	California, Congressional District 18	2 011 986
19	Texas, Congressional District 1	21 053	19	Montana, Congressional District (At Large)	1 882 114
20	Missouri, Congressional District 6	20 879	20	California, Congressional District 19	1 867 389
21	Missouri, Congressional District 8	19 816	21	Wisconsin, Congressional District 3	1 649 004
22	Kansas, Congressional District 2	19 459	22	Iowa, Congressional District 1	1 642 021
23	Tennessee, Congressional District 4	19 059	23	North Carolina, Congressional District 7	1 641 469
24	Illinois, Congressional District 19	18 783	24	Arkansas, Congressional District 1	1 574 413
25	Tennessee, Congressional District 6	17 959	25	Arkansas, Congressional District 4	1 566 116
26	Texas, Congressional District 13	17 197	26	California, Congressional District 22	1 556 281
27	Nebraska, Congressional District 1	17 159	27	Illinois, Congressional District 15	1 533 084
28	Wisconsin, Congressional District 7	16 407	28	Arkansas, Congressional District 3	1 454 448
29	Texas, Congressional District 4	16 085	29	California, Congressional District 2	1 450 753
30	Kentucky, Congressional District 4	15 394	30	Texas, Congressional District 19	1 427 265
31	Oklahoma, Congressional District 4	14 907	31	Alabama, Congressional District 4	1 384 212
32	Oregon, Congressional District 2	14 768	32	Illinois, Congressional District 19	1 374 345
33	Arkansas, Congressional District 1	14 524	33	Georgia, Congressional District 9	1 330 465
34	Arkansas, Congressional District 3	14 277	34	Mississippi, Congressional District 3	1 308 446
35	Virginia, Congressional District 9	14 103	35	Oregon, Congressional District 2	1 302 248
36	Texas, Congressional District 2	14 099	36	Kentucky, Congressional District 1	1 289 939
37	Iowa, Congressional District 1	14 046	37	Oklahoma, Congressional District 2	1 289 267
38	Iowa, Congressional District 2	13 904	38	Iowa, Congressional District 3	1 245 663
39	Idaho, Congressional District 2	13 757	39	Illinois, Congressional District 18	1 222 379
40	Alabama, Congressional District 4	13 754	40	California, Congressional District 11	1 206 548
41	Texas, Congressional District 31	13 511	41	Arizona, Congressional District 7	1 195 488
42	Texas, Congressional District 11	13 461	42	Missouri, Congressional District 4	1 169 374
43	Tennessee, Congressional District 1	13 428	43	Texas, Congressional District 1	1 136 605
44	Mississippi, Congressional District 3	13 241	44	Illinois, Congressional District 17	1 133 509
45	Missouri, Congressional District 7	13 028	45	Pennsylvania, Congressional District 16	1 121 589
46	Mississippi, Congressional District 1	12 947	46	Florida, Congressional District 16	1 093 314
47	Texas, Congressional District 5	12 764	47	Iowa, Congressional District 2	1 092 379
48	Tennessee, Congressional District 8	12 620	48	North Carolina, Congressional District 1	1 083 751
49	Minnesota, Congressional District 8	12 619	49	California, Congressional District 1	1 081 764
50	Kentucky, Congressional District 6	12 448	50	Washington, Congressional District 5	1 081 288
51	Ohio, Congressional District 5	12 354	51	California, Congressional District 23	1 078 883
52	Colorado, Congressional District 4	12 156	52	Mississippi, Congressional District 2	1 066 712
53	Colorado, Congressional District 3	12 015	53	California, Congressional District 51	1 066 057
54	Arkansas, Congressional District 4	11 944	54	Missouri, Congressional District 6	1 061 393
55	Washington, Congressional District 4	11 752	55	Wisconsin, Congressional District 7	1 048 406
56	Ohio, Congressional District 18	11 737	56	Texas, Congressional District 17	1 036 036
57	Iowa, Congressional District 3	11 642	57	Texas, Congressional District 14	995 563
58	Illinois, Congressional District 15	11 576	58	Wisconsin, Congressional District 6	981 682
59	Indiana, Congressional District 9	11 428	59	North Carolina, Congressional District 3	981 552
60	Idaho, Congressional District 1	11 260	60	Georgia, Congressional District 2	944 223
61	Texas, Congressional District 21	11 022	61	Missouri, Congressional District 8	943 180
62	Indiana, Congressional District 6	10 845	62	Missouri, Congressional District 9	924 717
63	Kentucky, Congressional District 5	10 761	63	New Mexico, Congressional District 2	914 991
64	Wisconsin, Congressional District 6	10 625	64	Idaho, Congressional District 1	896 919
65	Illinois, Congressional District 17	10 613	65	North Carolina, Congressional District 2	892 784
66	California, Congressional District 2	10 253	66	Kansas, Congressional District 2	887 080
67	North Carolina, Congressional District 5	10 156	67	Maryland, Congressional District 1	875 979
68	Illinois, Congressional District 18	10 105	68	Wyoming, Congressional District (At Large)	863 887
69	Virginia, Congressional District 5	10 059	69	Ohio, Congressional District 5	859 731
70	Georgia, Congressional District 9	10 034	70	Indiana, Congressional District 6	859 457
71	Wisconsin, Congressional District 8	9 853	71	Wisconsin, Congressional District 8	830 563
72	Ohio, Congressional District 4	9 610	72	Alabama, Congressional District 2	802 683
73	Wyoming, Congressional District (At Large)	9 422	73	Oregon, Congressional District 5	796 286
74	Washington, Congressional District 5	9 367	74	Colorado, Congressional District 3	781 245
75	Kansas, Congressional District 4	9 168	75	California, Congressional District 24	777 345

[1]Includes 435 state congressional districts and the District of Columbia. Georgia and Texas data are for 108th congressional districts and the boundaries for the 110th Congress have changed.

Table A. 110th Congressional Districts

(Number, percent.)

STATE Congressional district	Representative	Land area,[1] (sq km)	Total population	Persons per square kilometer	Race alone (percent)				Some other race (percent)	Two or more races (percent)	Hispanic or Latino[2] (percent)	Non-Hispanic White (percent)
					White	Black	American Indian/ Alaska Native	Asian and Pacific Islander				
	1	2	3	4	5	6	7	8	9	10	11	12
UNITED STATES[3]		9 161 924	299 398 485	32.7	73.9	12.4	0.8	4.5	6.3	2.0	14.8	66.2
ALABAMA		131 426	4 599 030	35.0	70.4	26.3	0.4	1.1	0.8	1.0	2.4	69.0
District 1	Rep. Jo Bonner (R)	16 361	666 932	40.8	68.3	28.0	0.8	1.3	0.7	1.0	1.6	67.5
District 2	Rep. Terry Everett (R)	27 199	649 951	23.9	66.2	31.0	0.3	0.8	0.7	1.0	1.9	65.2
District 3	Rep. Mike Rogers (R)	20 290	657 814	32.4	65.2	32.0	0.3	1.1	0.5	1.0	1.5	64.4
District 4	Rep. Robert B. Aderholt (R)	21 684	652 585	30.1	91.5	5.2	0.6	0.7	1.0	1.0	4.6	88.5
District 5	Rep. Robert E. "Bud" Cramer Jr. (D)	11 618	670 041	57.7	78.2	17.3	0.7	1.3	0.9	1.7	2.8	76.4
District 6	Rep. Spencer Bachus (R)	11 821	697 031	59.0	85.7	11.0	0.2	1.7	0.6	0.8	2.2	84.2
District 7	Rep. Artur Davis (D)	22 453	604 676	26.9	34.0	63.7	0.2	0.5	1.0	0.7	2.5	32.7
ALASKA		1 481 347	670 053	0.5	68.7	3.2	13.1	5.1	1.8	8.1	5.6	66.3
At Large	Rep. Don Young (R)	1 481 347	670 053	0.5	68.7	3.2	13.1	5.1	1.8	8.1	5.6	66.3
ARIZONA		294 312	6 166 318	21.0	76.9	3.4	4.5	2.5	10.3	2.4	29.2	59.5
District 1	Rep. Rick Renzi (R)	151 795	730 163	4.8	65.8	1.2	21.2	0.8	8.5	2.5	18.7	57.1
District 2	Rep. Trent Franks (R)	52 369	897 525	17.1	82.3	3.2	2.1	2.3	7.6	2.5	19.3	72.0
District 3	Rep. John B. Shadegg (R)	1 550	699 585	451.3	86.1	3.0	1.2	2.7	5.3	1.7	20.2	71.9
District 4	Rep. Ed Pastor (D)	516	707 088	1 370.3	67.9	7.8	2.7	1.7	18.0	2.0	65.0	22.6
District 5	Rep. Harry E. Mitchell (D)	3 641	671 465	184.4	84.0	3.0	2.5	5.1	3.4	2.0	16.9	71.3
District 6	Rep. Jeff Flake (R)	1 874	948 360	506.1	84.7	2.3	0.9	3.3	6.5	2.4	21.5	70.7
District 7	Rep. Raúl M. Grijalva (D)	59 240	787 055	13.3	60.6	3.6	5.7	1.8	24.7	3.5	54.8	34.6
District 8	Rep. Gabrielle Giffords (D)	23 327	725 077	31.1	82.2	3.2	0.9	2.5	8.4	2.7	19.9	71.8
ARKANSAS		134 856	2 810 872	20.8	78.6	15.6	0.8	1.1	2.4	1.6	4.9	76.3
District 1	Rep. Marion Berry (D)	44 422	675 114	15.2	80.4	16.9	0.5	0.4	0.5	1.2	1.8	79.5
District 2	Rep. Vic Snyder (D)	15 338	704 974	46.0	75.0	20.8	0.6	1.2	1.1	1.3	3.5	72.9
District 3	Rep. John Boozman (R)	21 989	765 390	34.8	86.6	2.4	1.4	1.9	5.6	2.0	9.9	82.7
District 4	Rep. Mike Ross (D)	53 107	665 394	12.5	71.1	23.9	0.7	0.6	2.1	1.7	3.9	69.6
CALIFORNIA		403 933	36 457 549	90.3	59.8	6.2	0.7	12.7	17.3	3.3	35.9	42.8
District 1	Rep. Mike Thompson (D)	28 505	686 677	24.1	78.2	1.8	2.5	6.1	8.3	3.2	21.4	66.3
District 2	Rep. Wally Herger (R)	56 353	701 123	12.4	80.7	1.1	1.9	4.1	7.3	4.9	16.7	73.1
District 3	Rep. Daniel E. Lungren (R)	8 739	785 650	89.9	71.3	6.0	0.9	11.3	6.8	3.5	13.6	65.7
District 4	Rep. John T. Doolittle (R)	42 614	748 169	17.6	85.5	1.2	1.3	4.7	4.6	2.7	9.8	80.9
District 5	Rep. Doris O. Matsui (D)	381	658 493	1 728.3	51.1	14.1	1.3	16.7	11.7	5.1	25.7	39.3
District 6	Rep. Lynn C. Woolsey (D)	4 208	641 428	152.4	80.1	2.3	0.5	5.1	9.1	2.8	17.9	72.1
District 7	Rep. George Miller (D)	904	654 534	724.0	47.7	15.7	0.7	16.3	15.5	4.1	26.4	38.3
District 8	Rep. Nancy Pelosi (D)	92	602 099	6 544.6	53.4	7.9	0.5	29.5	5.6	3.1	16.0	43.6
District 9	Rep. Barbara Lee (D)	343	623 539	1 817.9	44.6	21.8	0.7	17.9	11.6	3.5	21.7	35.2
District 10	Rep. Ellen O. Tauscher (D)	2 624	683 572	260.5	64.8	7.2	0.5	11.4	12.0	4.1	19.3	58.3
District 11	Rep. Jerry McNerney (D)	5 897	792 039	134.3	67.3	4.7	0.6	14.5	8.4	4.4	23.6	53.7
District 12	Vacant	303	642 844	2 121.6	54.0	2.3	0.4	34.2	5.7	3.5	15.9	44.7
District 13	Rep. Fortney "Pete" Stark (D)	573	643 902	1 123.7	40.4	7.1	0.5	35.4	13.1	3.6	23.4	31.7
District 14	Rep. Anna G. Eshoo (D)	2 138	651 056	304.5	68.4	3.0	0.4	18.9	6.3	3.1	19.4	55.9
District 15	Rep. Michael M. Honda (D)	741	664 233	896.4	48.9	2.4	0.6	35.1	9.6	3.5	18.9	40.7
District 16	Rep. Zoe Lofgren (D)	595	647 847	1 088.8	47.1	3.1	0.5	27.5	18.1	3.6	39.9	27.3
District 17	Rep. Sam Farr (D)	12 484	641 114	51.4	68.7	2.3	0.7	6.2	17.8	4.3	47.0	42.1
District 18	Rep. Dennis A. Cardoza (D)	7 906	700 850	88.6	63.0	5.6	1.1	10.0	16.4	3.9	49.6	32.7
District 19	Rep. George Radanovich (R)	17 333	748 104	43.2	75.5	3.3	0.9	5.0	11.6	3.7	33.8	55.0
District 20	Rep. Jim Costa (D)	12 904	702 391	54.4	55.2	6.4	1.0	5.4	28.7	3.3	67.7	19.0
District 21	Rep. Devin Nunes (R)	20 787	749 852	36.1	70.1	2.4	1.2	7.2	16.5	2.6	47.4	40.8
District 22	Rep. Kevin McCarthy (R)	26 980	738 104	27.4	68.9	5.9	1.0	4.0	15.8	4.4	27.6	59.5
District 23	Rep. Lois Capps (D)	2 698	637 864	236.4	72.6	2.2	0.8	6.1	14.9	3.4	44.1	46.0
District 24	Rep. Elton Gallegly (R)	10 057	687 724	68.4	72.4	1.6	0.7	5.9	15.9	3.5	26.8	63.2
District 25	Rep. Howard P. "Buck" McKeon (R)	55 644	786 155	14.1	58.8	9.8	1.0	5.7	20.7	3.9	35.7	45.8
District 26	Rep. David Dreier (R)	1 947	687 990	353.4	56.6	4.7	0.4	18.7	15.1	4.5	28.0	46.4
District 27	Rep. Brad Sherman (D)	390	668 799	1 714.9	52.9	4.2	0.6	12.9	25.5	4.0	40.3	41.0
District 28	Rep. Howard L. Berman (D)	200	654 761	3 273.8	54.6	3.0	0.4	6.8	30.7	4.6	57.1	31.7
District 29	Rep. Adam B. Schiff (D)	263	651 759	2 478.2	52.3	5.8	0.3	25.7	13.6	2.3	24.8	42.2
District 30	Rep. Henry A. Waxman (D)	740	650 728	879.4	78.8	3.1	0.2	11.2	4.0	2.5	8.6	74.9
District 31	Rep. Xavier Becerra (D)	102	644 707	6 320.7	32.8	4.1	0.6	14.2	46.5	1.7	70.0	10.5
District 32	Rep. Hilda L. Solis (D)	238	656 579	2 758.7	35.6	2.2	0.6	20.9	38.5	2.1	63.2	12.7
District 33	Rep. Diane E. Watson (D)	125	648 535	5 188.3	35.4	27.0	0.6	11.6	22.9	2.4	36.7	21.9
District 34	Rep. Lucille Roybal-Allard (D)	151	667 136	4 418.1	44.4	4.8	0.8	5.9	42.6	1.5	80.0	8.3
District 35	Rep. Maxine Waters (D)	144	685 806	4 762.5	31.9	29.3	0.2	5.3	31.1	2.2	56.0	8.5
District 36	Rep. Jane Harman (D)	194	664 004	3 422.7	59.7	4.1	0.6	14.6	16.4	4.7	33.4	44.9
District 37	Rep. Laura Richardson (D)	193	655 632	3 397.1	27.2	24.3	0.4	13.3	32.0	2.7	46.2	14.7
District 38	Rep. Grace F. Napolitano (D)	269	660 653	2 456.0	43.4	3.0	0.6	11.4	39.7	2.0	73.9	11.4
District 39	Rep. Linda T. Sánchez (D)	168	706 730	4 206.7	39.4	6.0	0.8	10.8	39.8	3.3	64.9	16.7
District 40	Rep. Edward R. Royce (R)	259	672 377	2 596.1	57.5	2.3	0.5	19.5	16.9	3.2	32.8	43.0

[1]Dry land or land partially or temporarily covered by water.
[2]May be of any race.
[3]United States totals do not include Puerto Rico.

Table A. 110th Congressional Districts—*Continued*

(Number, percent.)

STATE Congressional district	Percent female	Percent foreign born	Percent born in state of residence	Under 5 years	5 to 18 years	18 to 24 years	25 to 34 years	35 to 44 years	45 to 54 years	55 to 64 years	65 to 74 years	75 years and over
	13	14	15	16	17	18	19	20	21	22	23	24
UNITED STATES[3]	50.8	12.5	58.9	6.8	17.8	9.9	13.3	14.7	14.5	10.6	6.3	6.1
ALABAMA	51.5	2.8	70.9	6.4	17.9	10.0	12.7	14.1	14.4	11.3	7.1	6.2
District 1	51.5	2.5	68.5	6.4	18.9	9.1	12.9	13.6	14.4	11.4	7.1	6.2
District 2	50.9	1.9	70.4	6.5	18.0	9.9	12.4	14.6	14.0	10.9	7.2	6.5
District 3	51.9	2.1	67.3	6.3	17.7	12.7	12.2	13.2	13.9	11.1	6.9	5.9
District 4	51.0	3.4	75.7	6.4	16.7	8.8	13.1	13.8	13.9	12.2	8.1	7.0
District 5	51.3	3.9	62.0	6.1	17.6	9.4	12.5	14.9	15.0	11.3	7.5	5.8
District 6	51.0	3.5	72.1	6.4	17.6	8.1	12.9	15.6	15.3	11.8	6.5	5.8
District 7	53.2	2.4	81.4	6.7	18.6	12.4	12.5	12.9	14.3	10.1	6.2	6.3
ALASKA	48.5	7.0	38.9	7.1	19.7	11.2	14.0	15.0	16.3	10.1	3.9	2.7
At Large	48.5	7.0	38.9	7.1	19.7	11.2	14.0	15.0	16.3	10.1	3.9	2.7
ARIZONA	50.0	15.1	35.7	7.8	18.6	9.5	14.6	13.9	12.8	10.0	6.6	6.2
District 1	49.5	5.8	50.8	6.8	18.5	11.0	12.7	12.4	13.2	10.9	7.6	6.8
District 2	51.0	10.1	28.2	7.4	17.6	7.2	13.1	12.8	11.9	11.7	8.9	9.4
District 3	50.5	14.9	33.1	7.0	18.1	8.0	15.1	15.5	15.1	10.7	5.5	4.9
District 4	47.2	33.3	40.1	10.8	22.1	10.3	19.0	14.5	10.5	6.6	3.4	2.7
District 5	49.8	14.2	27.5	5.8	14.5	12.6	15.3	14.6	14.9	11.0	6.1	5.3
District 6	50.0	12.5	33.2	8.9	20.7	7.9	15.0	15.5	11.7	8.5	6.1	5.7
District 7	49.6	21.7	42.6	8.7	20.6	11.2	15.2	13.0	11.4	8.7	5.7	5.4
District 8	51.7	9.8	31.3	6.2	15.9	8.8	11.7	13.1	14.3	12.3	8.8	8.8
ARKANSAS	51.0	3.8	61.3	6.9	17.7	9.6	13.0	13.7	13.9	11.3	7.2	6.6
District 1	51.0	1.2	65.8	6.6	18.0	8.6	12.8	13.3	13.7	11.7	7.9	7.3
District 2	51.6	3.5	66.7	7.1	17.5	9.9	13.3	14.2	14.4	11.2	6.6	5.8
District 3	50.3	7.1	49.4	7.4	18.0	10.0	14.2	13.8	13.6	10.5	6.5	6.0
District 4	51.2	3.0	64.8	6.5	17.3	9.9	11.6	13.4	14.0	11.8	8.0	7.4
CALIFORNIA	50.0	27.2	52.4	7.3	18.8	10.4	14.4	15.2	13.8	9.4	5.5	5.3
District 1	50.4	15.7	61.1	6.0	16.4	13.2	13.2	13.7	14.2	10.6	6.2	6.5
District 2	50.4	10.0	64.8	6.2	17.2	12.3	13.2	12.6	13.8	10.9	6.9	7.1
District 3	50.5	15.6	59.8	6.7	19.7	8.2	12.8	15.6	14.8	10.3	6.2	5.7
District 4	50.0	7.9	62.7	5.1	16.4	10.0	13.6	13.9	15.6	11.5	7.2	6.8
District 5	51.1	23.5	57.1	7.8	17.9	11.1	17.5	13.8	12.7	8.7	5.4	5.2
District 6	50.1	18.2	54.7	5.9	15.7	9.2	11.1	14.4	16.4	13.7	6.7	6.7
District 7	50.6	25.3	53.2	6.6	18.2	9.5	13.9	14.2	15.9	10.9	5.3	5.4
District 8	48.6	35.7	36.3	5.3	8.9	7.4	18.6	20.6	14.6	10.1	6.9	7.5
District 9	50.7	27.0	48.4	7.1	15.3	11.3	14.0	15.7	14.3	11.2	5.6	5.4
District 10	50.6	19.8	55.7	6.6	18.7	9.5	12.1	15.4	15.0	10.5	6.3	5.9
District 11	49.8	20.6	59.5	7.4	20.7	9.0	12.7	16.0	14.6	9.9	5.2	4.4
District 12	51.1	35.1	47.2	6.5	14.1	7.7	12.0	16.7	16.2	12.5	7.1	7.3
District 13	50.9	38.0	46.8	7.1	18.0	7.8	14.3	16.3	15.3	10.4	5.5	5.3
District 14	48.8	29.5	45.9	7.3	17.7	7.6	12.5	16.2	15.5	11.2	6.0	5.9
District 15	49.4	36.1	45.7	7.9	16.4	8.2	14.0	18.0	14.8	10.0	5.7	5.1
District 16	48.3	38.9	47.3	7.7	18.2	10.3	14.7	16.8	14.1	9.2	5.2	3.8
District 17	48.7	25.7	54.3	7.9	18.1	12.6	14.5	13.8	13.5	9.5	4.8	5.2
District 18	49.7	26.0	60.1	8.7	22.5	10.9	15.7	13.9	11.3	7.6	4.8	4.5
District 19	50.4	15.2	66.7	7.5	18.5	11.4	14.9	13.8	13.0	9.7	5.8	5.5
District 20	46.5	30.7	56.9	9.1	23.4	12.3	16.7	14.0	11.4	6.2	3.8	3.1
District 21	50.0	21.2	64.0	8.7	21.9	11.7	14.7	13.1	12.1	8.2	5.0	4.7
District 22	49.1	12.2	64.6	7.3	19.7	10.7	14.0	14.4	13.9	9.1	5.5	5.3
District 23	49.1	25.1	53.6	7.2	16.0	15.4	14.1	13.2	12.2	9.3	6.1	6.5
District 24	50.2	17.9	55.4	6.8	19.8	9.1	11.7	14.6	15.9	10.8	5.9	5.4
District 25	49.5	19.3	59.6	8.5	24.0	9.5	12.3	15.7	14.3	8.0	4.6	3.1
District 26	51.3	23.2	56.8	5.9	19.8	9.7	11.3	14.9	16.1	10.5	6.0	5.9
District 27	50.8	37.6	45.4	7.2	18.1	9.4	13.7	16.5	14.4	9.7	5.5	5.5
District 28	50.1	43.5	41.8	8.1	19.4	9.9	16.3	16.4	12.5	7.6	5.1	4.7
District 29	52.2	42.1	39.7	5.7	15.0	8.9	13.7	15.6	15.7	11.3	7.1	7.2
District 30	51.4	26.6	39.4	4.5	13.2	9.5	13.6	16.3	15.9	11.8	6.9	8.2
District 31	49.5	51.4	39.7	8.5	19.4	11.4	17.4	15.7	11.9	7.6	4.1	4.1
District 32	49.3	41.2	50.0	7.5	20.4	11.3	13.9	14.9	12.9	8.7	5.6	4.8
District 33	50.9	35.3	41.8	6.3	15.7	12.2	17.0	16.2	13.5	9.7	5.3	4.1
District 34	49.1	43.9	48.3	9.4	22.1	11.2	16.7	14.8	10.9	7.3	3.8	4.0
District 35	50.3	33.6	50.2	9.7	22.1	10.7	15.3	14.3	11.7	8.0	4.6	3.6
District 36	50.8	28.0	48.4	6.8	17.3	7.3	16.0	17.9	14.0	10.0	5.7	5.1
District 37	50.8	29.3	54.6	8.0	22.8	11.4	14.1	15.9	12.4	7.4	4.5	3.4
District 38	50.8	38.1	52.9	8.6	20.8	10.9	14.2	14.6	13.0	8.1	5.2	4.5
District 39	50.4	33.2	56.3	8.3	23.5	11.6	13.5	14.4	12.4	8.3	4.2	3.9
District 40	50.0	30.1	51.5	7.8	18.9	10.5	12.3	15.5	14.1	9.6	5.9	5.4

[3]United States totals do not include Puerto Rico.

Table A. 110th Congressional Districts—*Continued*

(Number, percent.)

STATE Congressional district	Households, 2006						Group quarters, 2006		Group quarters, 2000			
	Number	Average household size	Family households (percent)	Married-couple family (percent)	Female family house-holder[4] (percent)	One-person households (percent)	Total in group quarters	Percent 65 years and over	Persons in correctional institutions	Persons in nursing homes	Persons in college dormitories	Persons in military quarters
	25	26	27	28	29	30	31	32	33	34	35	36
UNITED STATES[3]	111 617 402	2.61	66.8	49.7	12.5	27.3	8 065 644	23.4	1 976 019	1 720 500	2 064 128	355 155
ALABAMA	1 796 058	2.50	68.1	49.5	14.4	27.7	115 155	23.7	33 542	26 697	31 086	5 370
District 1	255 369	2.57	71.3	51.5	15.8	24.3	11 793	21.4	3 825	3 113	3 083	61
District 2	251 129	2.50	67.6	48.3	15.0	28.7	21 141	26.3	11 533	3 833	1 765	4 715
District 3	256 372	2.48	65.9	46.0	16.0	29.1	21 834	21.4	4 965	4 446	9 213	4
District 4	252 430	2.53	70.8	53.8	11.8	25.5	13 125	43.6	2 019	4 856	409	0
District 5	264 761	2.47	69.6	54.0	11.5	26.3	15 077	25.3	4 268	2 892	4 792	587
District 6	275 821	2.48	69.3	57.2	8.9	26.8	11 954	11.2	4 223	3 220	2 749	0
District 7	240 176	2.43	61.6	33.9	23.3	33.4	20 231	18.2	2 709	4 337	9 075	3
ALASKA	229 878	2.81	68.7	51.0	12.2	24.9	23 100	6.9	3 331	803	1 748	3 970
At Large	229 878	2.81	68.7	51.0	12.2	24.9	23 100	6.9	3 331	803	1 748	3 970
ARIZONA	2 224 992	2.72	66.3	49.7	11.5	26.8	109 501	14.0	45 783	13 607	17 340	5 256
District 1	256 336	2.70	67.4	50.8	12.1	26.6	36 793	7.5	19 019	2 410	4 248	0
District 2	333 983	2.66	69.0	53.8	10.0	25.5	9 485	33.1	4 316	3 160	573	681
District 3	262 492	2.64	64.6	48.3	11.3	28.5	5 338	59.6	1 229	408	137	0
District 4	206 071	3.35	65.8	40.7	16.9	26.3	15 797	11.1	8 656	1 421	491	0
District 5	269 535	2.47	58.2	44.0	8.9	31.4	6 925	9.1	60	1 169	4 600	0
District 6	331 639	2.85	70.6	56.4	9.7	23.2	4 245	11.1	0	2 073	69	0
District 7	263 288	2.93	71.4	49.2	15.9	22.2	16 501	4.1	4 758	875	7 094	1 677
District 8	301 648	2.36	62.8	49.3	9.9	31.3	14 417	18.6	7 745	2 091	128	2 898
ARKANSAS	1 103 428	2.48	68.7	51.4	12.9	26.8	78 322	25.2	20 565	21 379	18 280	1 290
District 1	264 334	2.49	70.1	52.1	14.3	26.3	16 427	29.5	7 787	6 049	2 150	0
District 2	284 752	2.39	67.9	50.5	13.4	26.7	23 906	18.8	2 763	4 460	5 950	1 246
District 3	292 545	2.57	68.5	54.0	9.6	26.5	12 160	26.6	1 416	4 407	5 863	27
District 4	261 797	2.44	68.5	48.8	14.5	28.0	25 829	27.7	8 599	6 463	4 317	17
CALIFORNIA	12 151 227	2.93	68.3	49.8	12.8	24.6	863 207	20.2	248 516	120 724	126 715	58 810
District 1	255 033	2.61	61.0	45.4	11.4	28.4	21 594	17.2	5 410	2 903	7 287	1
District 2	263 364	2.62	65.2	49.9	11.2	26.0	11 036	22.3	2 366	2 760	3 270	512
District 3	279 831	2.74	71.8	56.3	10.9	22.8	18 796	29.0	8 143	2 934	6	235
District 4	280 364	2.61	70.3	56.3	9.7	22.4	17 689	21.4	10 152	2 551	224	0
District 5	248 870	2.61	59.7	37.4	15.2	31.4	9 601	20.5	2 104	2 649	907	104
District 6	251 176	2.47	61.8	47.2	9.9	29.4	20 365	12.5	7 730	2 994	1 892	331
District 7	221 503	2.87	70.2	48.8	15.2	23.7	18 544	15.1	10 352	2 143	0	25
District 8	268 969	2.17	42.2	30.1	8.2	43.5	18 355	19.3	1 369	1 582	2 428	36
District 9	238 290	2.54	54.0	37.1	12.4	36.2	18 838	8.9	979	2 595	5 116	0
District 10	241 866	2.79	69.8	54.4	10.8	23.7	9 395	38.2	1 109	2 967	1 473	2 019
District 11	259 294	3.00	75.7	58.8	11.4	19.6	15 044	31.2	7 216	2 622	1 854	15
District 12	234 319	2.72	65.1	51.9	9.7	27.3	5 721	66.4	20	2 670	1 498	0
District 13	213 399	2.99	72.0	54.0	11.9	21.9	5 641	54.5	40	2 327	636	224
District 14	241 935	2.63	64.5	51.6	8.4	29.2	14 828	20.6	2 019	2 684	8 309	281
District 15	230 349	2.82	70.7	55.5	10.2	23.5	13 551	35.8	3 112	2 810	2 075	0
District 16	197 859	3.23	72.3	53.8	11.8	21.1	7 892	15.5	1 255	1 102	2 294	0
District 17	205 174	2.99	67.9	51.1	11.2	24.9	27 842	8.6	12 888	2 009	4 644	2 478
District 18	209 643	3.26	74.6	49.9	17.1	20.0	17 217	29.9	6 821	2 373	26	3
District 19	246 821	2.94	71.6	53.0	12.8	22.5	21 651	6.4	11 476	1 649	630	0
District 20	184 986	3.54	78.2	49.2	20.4	17.9	47 328	6.2	39 151	2 157	118	1 085
District 21	225 254	3.27	76.2	55.3	13.5	18.9	12 752	29.2	1 222	3 039	1 420	0
District 22	247 943	2.83	72.2	53.1	13.2	22.1	36 927	7.3	22 515	2 213	3 032	742
District 23	222 110	2.74	62.6	47.1	10.6	25.5	28 516	22.7	959	2 098	7 604	892
District 24	233 065	2.91	73.7	58.4	10.1	21.0	10 231	30.3	5 466	1 896	1 266	1 029
District 25	230 672	3.32	77.6	57.8	13.8	17.3	20 864	6.2	9 342	1 288	925	1 632
District 26	224 318	3.00	74.3	57.1	12.5	20.9	14 624	26.5	1 971	2 861	5 279	0
District 27	220 363	2.99	68.2	46.6	14.5	23.9	9 172	49.9	24	4 155	2 352	0
District 28	208 471	3.10	65.1	45.4	13.6	27.1	9 279	71.2	144	1 088	16	0
District 29	233 677	2.72	65.7	47.2	13.0	28.2	15 524	59.7	42	5 296	1 395	0
District 30	286 650	2.19	47.9	38.5	6.5	41.4	23 977	35.0	107	3 205	12 709	0
District 31	195 228	3.23	65.6	38.6	17.8	24.5	13 275	39.0	367	2 359	1 397	0
District 32	173 757	3.73	80.7	55.3	17.4	15.1	8 757	52.5	102	2 023	1 738	0
District 33	244 264	2.57	53.0	31.4	15.5	37.6	21 615	10.6	190	1 919	5 356	0
District 34	175 801	3.63	75.1	47.5	19.2	20.1	28 184	14.3	11 903	1 817	0	0
District 35	202 563	3.34	70.6	39.3	23.1	24.8	8 835	42.5	185	1 279	2 251	0
District 36	256 894	2.57	59.1	43.1	11.6	32.3	4 417	54.1	8	1 894	361	44
District 37	196 428	3.30	68.9	39.9	21.4	24.0	6 940	23.8	52	2 604	930	0
District 38	170 154	3.83	79.9	53.6	17.9	15.8	8 856	23.5	45	2 300	2 349	0
District 39	181 564	3.83	81.8	55.7	17.9	14.1	10 952	16.6	1 205	1 955	1 417	0
District 40	208 355	3.18	74.2	55.2	13.3	20.3	10 575	19.9	2 446	2 872	1 775	0

[3]United States totals do not include Puerto Rico.
[4]No spouse present.

Table A. 110th Congressional Districts—*Continued*

(Number, percent.)

STATE Congressional district	Education, 2006				Income, 2006			Poverty, 2006		
	School enrollment[5]		Attainment level[6] (percent)		Per capita income (dollars)	Median household income (dollars)	Percent of households with income over $100,000	Persons below poverty level (percent)	Families below poverty level (percent)	Percent of households receiving food stamps in past 12 months
	Total	Private (percent)	High school graduate or more	Bachelor's degree or more						
	37	38	39	40	41	42	43	44	45	46
UNITED STATES[3]	79 121 944	16.8	84.1	27.0	25 267	48 451	17.9	13.3	9.8	8.1
ALABAMA	1 179 725	15.2	80.1	21.1	21 270	38 783	11.9	16.6	12.6	10.1
District 1	173 181	19.7	82.0	20.0	20 568	39 550	11.3	17.3	14.7	15.7
District 2	161 467	14.9	78.7	18.1	20 168	37 031	10.1	17.8	13.5	12.3
District 3	182 353	13.1	77.0	19.5	19 252	34 998	9.4	18.7	14.2	10.9
District 4	145 852	8.8	74.3	12.6	18 246	34 723	8.2	16.1	12.6	8.2
District 5	173 945	14.8	82.4	25.9	23 344	44 200	15.5	13.7	9.5	7.0
District 6	174 226	19.2	87.3	33.0	30 105	54 382	21.2	8.1	5.5	3.2
District 7	168 701	14.6	78.0	16.8	16 205	28 298	6.6	25.5	20.1	14.7
ALASKA	189 863	10.4	89.7	26.9	26 919	59 393	22.6	10.9	8.2	8.3
At Large	189 863	10.4	89.7	26.9	26 919	59 393	22.6	10.9	8.2	8.3
ARIZONA	1 625 354	10.9	83.8	25.5	24 110	47 265	16.9	14.2	10.1	6.8
District 1	193 628	9.1	82.6	18.5	18 454	38 317	10.0	19.0	13.3	9.9
District 2	212 584	11.5	85.8	20.6	24 690	49 553	16.1	11.0	7.8	5.9
District 3	174 782	18.7	88.3	31.8	31 439	55 367	24.3	11.1	7.6	5.1
District 4	191 721	6.8	63.4	13.8	15 351	36 439	9.1	24.9	21.3	11.7
District 5	184 714	14.2	91.5	41.6	34 819	57 383	25.9	10.4	5.8	2.8
District 6	264 064	9.7	88.1	27.7	25 333	56 392	20.6	7.8	5.3	3.6
District 7	227 659	6.4	74.8	14.7	16 792	37 783	8.9	20.8	16.0	12.2
District 8	176 202	13.4	90.9	34.2	26 987	47 695	17.4	10.6	7.4	5.7
ARKANSAS	701 027	10.9	80.5	18.2	19 758	36 599	9.2	17.3	13.1	11.9
District 1	168 156	7.7	76.9	13.3	17 335	32 702	6.9	20.3	15.8	15.6
District 2	180 131	16.1	85.4	25.2	23 341	41 904	12.8	13.9	10.2	9.9
District 3	191 965	10.4	79.8	19.3	20 134	39 237	9.6	14.9	10.9	7.8
District 4	160 775	9.0	79.8	14.7	17 987	32 284	7.3	20.5	15.7	15.2
CALIFORNIA	10 385 391	14.1	80.1	29.0	26 974	56 645	24.6	13.1	9.7	4.3
District 1	188 707	9.0	84.2	28.3	24 660	46 363	18.1	15.9	9.2	5.5
District 2	193 494	8.3	83.9	19.1	21 718	42 037	13.2	16.6	12.1	7.2
District 3	220 492	14.1	89.3	29.2	28 554	63 291	25.9	8.4	5.7	4.0
District 4	190 250	13.4	90.1	28.4	31 090	61 588	26.6	7.5	4.6	2.2
District 5	181 551	9.9	79.4	24.8	21 905	43 961	14.0	16.2	12.9	9.5
District 6	162 687	16.1	88.4	39.3	37 287	67 321	31.0	9.4	5.6	2.3
District 7	173 407	14.9	82.9	24.8	26 084	60 881	24.1	10.3	7.6	4.3
District 8	114 720	29.5	84.1	48.8	41 887	61 745	30.9	13.3	7.8	2.9
District 9	176 893	17.7	81.9	39.9	29 246	51 171	23.8	16.7	12.3	4.2
District 10	186 269	15.5	90.2	36.8	36 088	74 338	35.2	8.2	5.9	2.2
District 11	232 567	16.3	86.4	31.7	32 463	75 008	35.6	8.7	5.7	3.6
District 12	160 510	26.0	90.0	46.6	38 962	79 035	38.4	6.8	4.6	1.0
District 13	173 193	14.0	86.3	36.2	29 467	70 945	32.4	7.8	5.5	2.4
District 14	179 466	26.3	90.2	55.5	48 400	87 055	44.4	7.7	5.0	1.5
District 15	179 507	21.5	88.8	45.3	36 045	82 085	40.4	7.4	5.3	2.4
District 16	177 557	14.4	79.7	31.8	29 238	70 287	34.0	11.7	8.9	3.5
District 17	188 073	12.1	74.3	26.1	25 350	56 290	22.5	11.2	7.3	4.4
District 18	205 120	6.4	65.6	9.6	16 558	40 364	10.6	19.3	15.5	10.0
District 19	208 371	10.4	80.3	20.5	23 334	50 655	17.8	14.2	11.1	6.5
District 20	212 608	5.5	55.0	7.2	12 338	32 212	6.3	30.2	25.9	16.5
District 21	234 028	7.6	72.7	16.9	18 959	45 303	16.0	18.9	15.2	10.3
District 22	209 569	13.1	82.6	20.5	23 482	50 637	19.5	15.0	11.4	6.4
District 23	190 588	11.8	76.5	28.0	26 113	52 268	20.9	17.0	10.6	4.3
District 24	201 637	16.6	87.1	32.5	32 468	74 529	34.5	7.2	4.8	1.9
District 25	256 800	11.8	79.7	20.1	22 438	58 803	23.5	15.1	11.3	6.1
District 26	211 834	20.0	89.6	35.8	32 297	72 701	32.6	6.6	4.9	2.0
District 27	189 775	17.5	80.3	28.6	24 655	55 600	23.0	10.9	8.6	2.2
District 28	179 570	16.5	71.4	26.0	24 296	46 486	19.4	17.1	14.1	5.1
District 29	160 595	20.2	82.4	37.3	29 078	54 712	24.9	11.6	9.6	2.7
District 30	166 418	33.5	94.3	58.5	54 003	74 235	38.2	8.6	3.8	0.6
District 31	186 086	11.6	59.7	18.5	15 495	34 517	9.2	24.2	22.3	7.7
District 32	200 314	11.4	66.9	16.3	17 657	49 392	16.5	13.3	11.0	6.0
District 33	186 455	26.8	77.9	32.5	23 801	40 588	15.0	20.2	16.5	4.5
District 34	204 897	6.9	54.3	10.2	14 042	36 597	9.3	22.0	18.4	8.9
District 35	210 039	9.9	66.0	15.5	16 238	38 944	10.6	23.6	20.9	8.4
District 36	172 901	16.3	85.7	40.7	33 857	62 338	29.6	11.8	9.0	2.6
District 37	215 254	7.7	70.6	18.7	17 664	41 927	14.5	21.0	18.3	9.7
District 38	201 896	9.4	65.2	13.9	17 290	51 283	15.4	13.8	11.4	5.4
District 39	233 797	10.3	67.7	16.3	18 311	53 205	19.2	12.8	11.1	6.0
District 40	204 183	17.2	82.3	29.9	25 862	64 443	26.6	9.8	6.9	2.4

[3]United States totals do not include Puerto Rico.
[5]All persons 3 years old and over enrolled in nursery school through college.
[6]Persons 25 years old and over.

Table A. 110th Congressional Districts—*Continued*

(Number, percent.)

STATE Congressional district	Total	Total occupied units	Owner-occupied units						Median cost as percent of income	
			Percent owner-occupied units	Median value (dollars)	Percent valued at $500,000 or more	Median real estate taxes (dollars)	Median monthly costs (dollars)	Percent with second mort-gage or home equity loan	With a mortgage	Without a mortgage
	47	48	49	50	51	52	53	54	55	56
UNITED STATES[3]	126 311 823	111 617 402	67.3	185 200	13.7	1 742	1 040	18.1	24.9	13.0
ALABAMA	2 110 139	1 796 058	71.8	107 000	2.9	328	685	13.1	21.7	11.7
District 1	315 517	255 369	72.5	114 700	3.8	371	718	12.2	22.8	11.3
District 2	296 638	251 129	68.9	92 000	1.2	228	612	11.8	20.4	10.9
District 3	306 776	256 372	69.4	94 900	2.8	285	658	10.6	22.1	12.1
District 4	294 101	252 430	76.0	87 100	1.2	194	525	8.7	21.0	12.0
District 5	299 265	264 761	74.1	116 600	2.1	371	739	15.3	19.8	10.2
District 6	307 293	275 821	78.6	163 700	6.8	661	950	20.5	21.9	11.1
District 7	290 549	240 176	61.8	82 900	1.0	321	653	10.4	25.3	14.8
ALASKA	276 590	229 878	64.5	213 200	5.5	2 216	1 233	14.3	24.3	10.7
At Large	276 590	229 878	64.5	213 200	5.5	2 216	1 233	14.3	24.3	10.7
ARIZONA	2 605 095	2 224 992	68.5	236 500	13.6	1 216	1 062	19.4	25.3	10.7
District 1	344 644	256 336	69.6	167 100	9.1	763	649	12.2	25.6	10.8
District 2	387 085	333 983	75.8	243 400	9.1	1 166	1 033	20.3	26.2	10.4
District 3	296 251	262 492	67.1	322 900	26.4	1 449	1 328	25.3	24.8	10.4
District 4	234 326	206 071	51.9	189 100	4.3	1 031	1 086	14.9	28.5	12.4
District 5	310 042	269 535	63.3	354 300	30.9	1 477	1 299	24.4	23.2	10.6
District 6	378 090	331 639	76.3	271 100	14.4	1 231	1 264	23.5	25.6	11.1
District 7	313 729	263 288	67.0	154 500	2.7	965	825	13.4	26.9	10.6
District 8	340 928	301 648	68.9	226 200	10.6	1 506	985	17.7	23.7	10.1
ARKANSAS	1 273 433	1 103 428	68.3	93 900	2.1	469	611	7.5	20.7	11.7
District 1	315 006	264 334	68.9	79 000	0.9	376	539	5.8	20.8	11.4
District 2	316 948	284 752	66.9	109 100	2.6	611	764	10.2	20.5	11.6
District 3	327 794	292 545	67.2	120 400	3.5	606	694	8.9	21.2	11.3
District 4	313 685	261 797	70.3	74 000	1.2	360	501	4.9	19.9	12.3
CALIFORNIA	13 174 781	12 151 227	58.4	535 700	54.3	2 510	1 737	24.8	31.0	11.7
District 1	286 653	255 033	59.0	461 100	45.0	1 926	1 294	20.0	31.4	12.3
District 2	293 175	263 364	63.3	289 200	13.0	1 329	1 007	19.9	28.2	12.5
District 3	307 601	279 831	71.1	432 400	33.7	2 327	1 690	29.9	29.1	11.2
District 4	338 189	280 364	73.1	470 600	44.1	2 457	1 585	26.9	28.9	12.5
District 5	274 201	248 870	51.9	346 500	14.2	1 523	1 423	23.4	31.1	11.0
District 6	274 891	251 176	64.2	701 000	77.5	3 397	1 978	26.6	31.7	12.5
District 7	242 412	221 503	65.9	519 800	53.2	2 562	1 910	28.5	32.5	11.3
District 8	299 861	268 969	34.5	779 800	88.2	3 762	2 149	19.8	30.8	11.6
District 9	264 221	238 290	48.6	639 800	71.7	3 707	1 959	26.6	33.0	12.3
District 10	258 273	241 866	71.4	634 900	70.3	3 372	2 186	30.1	31.9	11.0
District 11	275 235	259 294	70.3	607 900	63.2	3 472	2 207	30.1	31.1	12.3
District 12	246 536	234 319	64.1	809 400	88.3	3 665	2 205	25.4	31.2	10.5
District 13	227 823	213 399	63.4	628 100	75.9	3 084	2 013	28.2	29.6	10.1
District 14	256 007	241 935	60.3	875 600	86.0	4 205	2 412	27.4	28.8	9.6
District 15	239 668	230 349	58.4	740 700	84.8	4 126	2 331	27.3	29.2	8.9
District 16	205 809	197 859	64.2	680 700	82.2	4 046	2 363	26.6	33.3	13.1
District 17	228 985	205 174	55.8	695 300	77.4	2 937	1 843	27.5	33.2	11.0
District 18	229 283	209 643	57.5	343 800	13.0	1 381	1 335	19.2	33.7	12.2
District 19	272 732	246 821	63.3	362 700	21.9	1 698	1 367	20.3	28.8	12.7
District 20	198 276	184 986	48.9	209 800	3.7	1 069	960	18.7	29.0	11.2
District 21	244 905	225 254	59.6	274 700	15.0	1 313	1 102	18.3	26.6	10.6
District 22	273 999	247 943	66.2	325 600	20.7	1 812	1 329	22.0	28.0	12.9
District 23	242 152	222 110	52.2	655 300	69.0	2 592	1 691	22.2	32.5	11.1
District 24	243 009	233 065	70.9	646 900	74.7	3 102	2 036	29.1	29.9	11.5
District 25	258 326	230 672	70.8	389 400	32.4	2 292	1 665	25.7	30.0	13.7
District 26	236 726	224 318	69.0	604 300	65.5	2 735	1 906	25.8	29.2	11.2
District 27	233 534	220 363	56.9	598 200	69.6	2 720	1 938	27.9	33.9	14.4
District 28	217 057	208 471	45.3	610 600	65.2	3 016	2 072	27.8	36.9	12.6
District 29	245 348	233 677	45.3	633 200	70.5	2 919	1 909	25.5	30.4	11.5
District 30	307 369	286 650	50.2	920 200	86.7	4 266	2 530	28.3	32.6	12.7
District 31	208 136	195 228	23.7	525 200	54.0	2 147	1 635	18.7	33.3	12.6
District 32	181 275	173 757	56.8	469 400	40.6	2 240	1 528	20.8	31.8	10.3
District 33	261 421	244 264	32.0	602 900	61.6	2 454	1 847	22.6	35.0	13.3
District 34	187 028	175 801	30.8	513 100	52.1	2 238	1 585	16.5	33.2	10.8
District 35	215 778	202 563	40.9	476 200	43.6	2 199	1 554	19.5	34.1	12.2
District 36	274 267	256 894	46.9	711 400	79.0	3 278	1 932	26.8	29.7	10.4
District 37	210 668	196 428	47.6	454 900	39.6	2 004	1 517	20.7	32.5	12.2
District 38	176 743	170 154	60.8	460 500	36.8	2 047	1 468	18.9	31.8	10.9
District 39	186 137	181 564	59.8	516 400	52.9	2 214	1 613	23.1	30.4	9.2
District 40	217 059	208 355	59.8	631 500	76.5	2 420	1 770	25.1	29.4	9.1

[3]United States totals do not include Puerto Rico.

Table A. 110th Congressional Districts—*Continued*

(Number, percent.)

STATE Congressional district	Housing units, 2006—Continued			Civilian labor force, 2006			Civilian employment and occupation, 2006			
	Renter-occupied units		Sub-standard housing units (percent)[7]	Total	Unemployment		Total civilian employment	Management, professional, and related (percent)	Service, sales, and office (percent)	Construction and production (percent)
	Median gross rent (dollars)	Median gross rent as a percent of income			Total	Rate[8]				
	57	58	59	60	61	62	63	64	65	66
UNITED STATES[3]	763	29.9	3.4	151 203 992	9 702 558	6.4	141 501 434	34.0	42.4	22.9
ALABAMA	573	29.1	2.1	2 163 696	149 223	6.9	2 014 473	30.8	40.2	28.3
District 1	654	29.6	2.6	302 952	19 061	6.3	283 891	30.1	42.2	26.9
District 2	566	27.4	2.1	297 650	21 076	7.1	276 574	27.9	41.6	29.7
District 3	537	31.3	1.9	306 532	28 209	9.2	278 323	29.5	39.1	30.7
District 4	480	25.2	2.2	301 370	19 213	6.4	282 157	23.9	38.0	36.8
District 5	542	28.6	1.7	328 936	19 123	5.8	309 813	34.4	38.8	26.4
District 6	722	26.6	1.2	353 666	14 092	4.0	339 574	40.1	38.9	20.7
District 7	569	34.0	2.8	272 590	28 449	10.4	244 141	26.9	44.0	28.5
ALASKA	883	27.6	10.3	356 243	33 625	9.4	322 618	35.0	41.1	22.5
At Large	883	27.6	10.3	356 243	33 625	9.4	322 618	35.0	41.1	22.5
ARIZONA	762	29.4	5.1	2 936 092	143 286	4.9	2 792 806	32.6	44.7	22.2
District 1	684	28.6	8.1	306 872	15 423	5.0	291 449	25.9	44.8	28.3
District 2	877	30.1	2.9	403 435	19 448	4.8	383 987	30.2	47.1	22.5
District 3	797	29.2	3.0	387 775	16 001	4.1	371 774	37.7	45.2	17.0
District 4	696	31.0	13.0	313 243	16 912	5.4	296 331	20.1	43.0	36.3
District 5	876	28.1	2.9	383 966	14 430	3.8	369 536	41.5	44.5	14.0
District 6	877	28.5	3.7	457 664	16 373	3.6	441 291	35.3	43.0	21.4
District 7	622	29.8	8.8	349 654	29 303	8.4	320 351	25.6	45.8	26.8
District 8	691	29.8	2.1	333 483	15 396	4.6	318 087	40.2	44.0	15.6
ARKANSAS	566	29.5	2.8	1 344 722	93 646	7.0	1 251 076	28.6	41.3	28.7
District 1	510	30.9	2.7	307 023	26 364	8.6	280 659	24.9	42.1	30.6
District 2	640	28.8	2.4	354 557	19 422	5.5	335 135	34.7	42.2	22.7
District 3	598	28.5	3.0	380 709	20 494	5.4	360 215	27.7	40.7	30.6
District 4	517	30.7	2.9	302 433	27 366	9.0	275 067	26.1	40.0	31.6
CALIFORNIA	1 029	32.4	8.2	17 926 638	1 185 700	6.6	16 740 938	34.7	42.7	21.2
District 1	872	32.9	5.4	338 248	23 937	7.1	314 311	33.3	44.5	18.5
District 2	726	33.0	3.9	328 554	30 625	9.3	297 929	29.0	45.8	22.3
District 3	979	32.0	2.9	390 054	22 802	5.8	367 252	38.0	44.6	17.1
District 4	977	31.2	2.7	384 658	22 397	5.8	362 261	35.2	44.3	19.8
District 5	870	34.7	5.7	321 725	29 032	9.0	292 693	32.4	45.7	21.7
District 6	1 232	35.7	3.2	344 010	17 453	5.1	326 557	38.5	43.8	16.8
District 7	1 089	34.7	5.1	328 792	21 883	6.7	306 909	31.9	46.3	21.7
District 8	1 144	27.0	7.7	353 814	21 694	6.1	332 120	50.8	38.5	10.6
District 9	996	33.5	5.6	320 613	28 050	8.7	292 563	46.2	36.0	17.7
District 10	1 179	32.7	3.2	353 596	21 590	6.1	332 006	40.5	40.4	18.7
District 11	1 086	30.7	4.9	389 180	25 101	6.4	364 079	40.4	39.3	18.7
District 12	1 364	28.2	4.8	349 804	16 382	4.7	333 422	45.6	40.5	13.9
District 13	1 177	30.4	5.7	338 438	20 886	6.2	317 552	37.5	41.6	20.9
District 14	1 261	26.3	6.0	331 243	15 907	4.8	315 336	56.5	31.4	11.3
District 15	1 227	27.4	5.8	345 921	19 733	5.7	326 188	48.5	35.4	15.6
District 16	1 176	31.9	9.0	331 400	23 408	7.1	307 992	36.8	40.4	22.5
District 17	1 066	33.0	8.2	317 989	31 117	9.8	286 872	30.9	41.3	18.8
District 18	789	34.2	9.8	304 382	36 028	11.8	268 354	19.7	41.0	33.7
District 19	836	32.6	5.8	354 466	29 588	8.3	324 878	29.7	44.2	22.5
District 20	610	32.5	18.1	287 177	37 156	12.9	250 021	14.1	40.3	28.3
District 21	711	29.2	10.2	338 758	30 232	8.9	308 526	26.4	42.3	22.1
District 22	824	31.4	5.4	334 855	23 643	7.1	311 212	31.6	42.1	24.6
District 23	1 141	36.2	7.9	321 957	18 112	5.6	303 845	31.4	44.5	19.3
District 24	1 315	31.0	4.4	353 878	17 760	5.0	336 118	39.8	42.5	16.4
District 25	1 039	35.0	6.2	348 486	26 051	7.5	322 435	31.5	45.2	23.1
District 26	1 167	31.0	4.5	349 007	21 013	6.0	327 994	42.6	41.7	15.5
District 27	1 042	34.0	9.4	348 234	16 262	4.7	331 972	33.5	46.4	20.0
District 28	968	35.2	14.6	330 053	19 479	5.9	310 574	30.3	43.0	26.6
District 29	1 089	32.1	8.0	336 338	18 498	5.5	317 840	42.2	42.3	15.4
District 30	1 362	30.5	2.2	360 059	20 781	5.8	339 278	58.1	36.9	4.9
District 31	822	33.7	28.9	321 099	23 383	7.3	297 716	22.0	48.7	29.2
District 32	984	34.3	15.5	309 797	21 224	6.9	288 573	23.8	45.3	30.2
District 33	922	33.6	12.3	344 490	30 094	8.7	314 396	36.0	44.4	19.5
District 34	822	32.9	24.2	288 842	21 536	7.5	267 306	18.1	44.2	37.4
District 35	889	35.8	16.3	313 102	20 514	6.6	292 588	21.2	47.4	31.1
District 36	1 147	29.0	6.9	362 229	19 627	5.4	342 602	41.9	42.2	15.9
District 37	891	35.0	16.2	296 608	26 856	9.1	269 752	26.0	46.8	27.0
District 38	994	34.2	17.0	313 124	20 939	6.7	292 185	21.8	45.6	32.2
District 39	963	34.0	16.3	321 929	21 126	6.6	300 803	25.1	45.0	29.7
District 40	1 197	34.3	8.9	337 487	16 805	5.0	320 682	34.1	44.3	21.4

[3]United States totals do not include Puerto Rico.
[7]Overcrowded or lacking complete plumbing facilities.
[8]Percent of civilian labor force.

Table A. 110th Congressional Districts—*Continued*

(Number, percent.)

STATE Congressional district	Social Security Beneficiaries (OASDI), December 2006							Supplemental Security Income, December 2006			
	Total	Rate per 1,000 population	Retired workers[9]	Disabled workers	Widow(er)s[10]	Spouses[11]	Children[12]	Total	Aged	Blind	Disabled
	67	68	69	70	71	72	73	74	75	76	77
UNITED STATES[3]	47 894 380	160.0	30 330 882	6 650 045	4 502 395	2 495 068	3 915 990	7 200 238	1 206 025	73 024	5 921 188
ALABAMA	920 843	200.2	502 502	178 375	95 762	45 299	98 905	164 782	16 652	927	147 203
District 1	134 557	201.8	74 348	23 472	14 133	7 388	15 216	20 758	2 084	120	18 554
District 2	131 600	202.5	73 202	25 505	12 745	5 639	14 509	26 539	2 909	135	23 495
District 3	131 844	200.4	71 783	28 620	12 146	4 913	14 382	25 654	2 456	208	22 990
District 4	147 105	225.4	78 883	29 774	16 145	8 054	14 249	23 202	2 688	123	20 391
District 5	128 105	191.2	73 895	21 853	13 485	7 566	11 306	17 801	1 922	107	107
District 6	123 135	176.7	71 571	19 837	13 373	7 128	11 226	12 443	994	65	11 384
District 7	124 497	205.9	58 820	29 314	13 735	4 611	18 017	38 385	3 599	169	34 617
ALASKA	66 906	99.9	40 237	10 211	5 103	2 904	8 451	11 343	2 112	102	9 129
At Large	66 906	99.9	40 237	10 211	5 103	2 904	8 451	11 343	2 112	102	9 129
ARIZONA	940 213	152.5	617 724	125 727	76 392	48 045	72 325	99 418	13 466	880	85 072
District 1	138 561	189.8	87 470	19 703	11 373	7 742	12 273	20 174	2 578	204	17 392
District 2	188 011	209.5	133 586	21 022	13 939	8 572	10 892	11 165	1 414	107	9 644
District 3	95 228	136.1	61 117	14 089	7 819	4 197	8 006	9 425	1 101	78	8 246
District 4	59 061	83.5	29 973	13 638	4 955	2 552	7 943	18 323	1 985	125	16 213
District 5	86 823	129.3	60 653	9 047	7 214	4 626	5 283	4 712	658	49	4 005
District 6	124 441	131.2	84 653	14 865	10 138	5 866	8 919	7 344	925	60	6 359
District 7	98 061	124.6	57 155	16 012	8 674	5 717	10 503	17 995	3 393	151	14 451
District 8	150 027	206.9	103 117	17 351	12 280	8 773	8 506	10 280	1 412	106	8 762
ARKANSAS	576 997	205.3	327 697	109 118	55 616	27 067	57 499	92 810	9 147	771	82 892
District 1	156 060	231.2	86 872	30 273	16 037	7 325	15 553	30 570	3 431	221	26 918
District 2	129 821	184.2	74 927	24 309	11 421	5 493	13 671	19 815	1 457	206	18 152
District 3	141 549	184.9	81 861	27 279	12 284	6 673	13 452	16 824	1 524	131	15 169
District 4	149 567	224.8	84 037	27 257	15 874	7 576	14 823	25 601	2 735	213	22 653
CALIFORNIA	4 504 672	123.6	2 912 853	570 084	394 166	272 968	354 601	1 224 864	359 971	21 245	843 648
District 1	115 233	167.8	71 078	18 618	10 428	6 041	9 068	25 106	3 335	387	21 384
District 2	136 917	195.3	82 308	23 457	12 297	7 767	11 088	32 214	4 089	513	27 612
District 3	108 613	138.2	69 473	14 999	9 371	5 853	8 917	19 811	3 776	380	15 655
District 4	134 083	179.2	90 550	16 966	10 689	7 445	8 433	16 108	2 022	280	13 806
District 5	84 365	128.1	48 323	16 081	7 566	3 808	8 587	39 599	6 034	669	32 896
District 6	101 508	158.3	69 706	11 304	8 975	5 502	6 021	12 398	2 098	217	10 083
District 7	82 651	126.3	50 414	13 243	7 116	4 202	7 676	21 443	4 643	403	16 397
District 8	83 421	138.6	56 063	13 338	5 951	3 820	4 249	41 517	18 069	623	22 825
District 9	75 397	120.9	47 564	11 658	6 317	3 506	6 352	29 765	7 236	494	22 035
District 10	95 614	139.9	63 529	10 396	8 909	6 283	6 497	12 994	3 210	243	9 541
District 11	96 529	121.9	61 806	12 609	8 264	5 415	8 435	17 386	3 790	337	13 259
District 12	91 948	143.0	66 963	7 740	7 551	5 393	4 301	14 708	7 699	221	6 788
District 13	73 897	114.8	47 713	9 780	6 371	4 422	5 611	19 602	7 851	312	11 439
District 14	79 372	121.9	57 279	6 362	6 488	5 719	3 524	9 411	4 103	146	5 162
District 15	68 044	102.4	46 997	6 920	5 614	4 322	4 191	15 927	7 611	255	8 061
District 16	64 448	99.5	40 949	8 809	4 989	4 097	5 604	23 692	9 107	348	14 237
District 17	80 030	124.8	51 269	10 320	7 350	4 928	6 163	14 972	3 885	274	10 813
District 18	84 861	121.1	47 257	15 500	7 967	4 697	9 440	36 720	6 640	639	29 441
District 19	110 473	147.7	69 555	15 124	9 879	6 265	9 650	24 578	5 111	436	19 031
District 20	71 385	101.6	37 710	12 890	6 696	4 129	9 960	39 011	8 552	643	29 816
District 21	94 971	126.7	57 839	13 500	8 582	5 619	9 431	31 321	7 097	579	23 645
District 22	106 982	144.9	64 742	16 766	9 563	5 981	9 930	23 660	3 227	436	19 997
District 23	92 854	145.6	60 186	11 866	7 936	6 001	6 865	17 861	4 637	267	12 957
District 24	99 307	144.4	67 522	10 271	8 763	6 142	6 609	11 161	3 063	176	7 922
District 25	80 847	102.8	47 108	12 759	6 891	4 219	9 870	23 201	4 399	421	18 381
District 26	86 240	125.4	58 846	8 184	7 736	5 549	5 925	15 662	6 290	343	9 029
District 27	75 605	113.0	49 838	9 048	6 186	4 578	5 955	24 004	9 314	370	14 320
District 28	58 684	89.6	38 267	7 247	4 831	4 034	4 305	24 435	8 788	420	15 227
District 29	75 691	116.1	52 602	7 366	6 100	4 902	4 721	38 986	17 370	643	20 973
District 30	96 915	148.9	69 805	8 017	8 374	6 729	3 990	21 000	8 336	328	12 336
District 31	45 187	70.1	29 029	6 076	3 324	2 963	3 795	32 713	13 681	524	18 508
District 32	67 954	103.5	42 672	7 575	6 195	5 181	6 331	30 492	13 348	557	16 587
District 33	67 945	104.8	44 722	9 215	5 342	2 949	5 717	35 362	10 266	600	24 496
District 34	54 355	81.5	32 543	7 516	4 893	4 230	5 173	32 307	12 783	502	19 022
District 35	63 617	92.8	38 925	9 739	5 313	2 893	6 747	31 412	6 100	556	24 756
District 36	79 429	119.6	55 210	7 654	6 990	4 734	4 841	15 088	5 238	245	9 605
District 37	63 231	96.4	36 763	10 628	5 641	3 319	6 880	34 282	7 161	642	26 479
District 38	71 543	108.3	44 272	8 300	6 649	5 760	6 562	26 736	10 443	487	15 806
District 39	65 581	92.8	41 038	7 923	6 080	4 752	5 788	21 901	7 660	412	13 829
District 40	79 047	117.6	54 299	7 328	7 023	5 386	5 011	15 619	6 186	295	9 138

[3]United States totals do not include Puerto Rico.
[9]Includes special age-72 beneficiaries.
[10]Includes nondisabled widow(er)s, disabled widow(er)s, widowed mothers and fathers, and parents receiving payment on the record of a worker who is deceased.
[11]These beneficiaries receive payment on the record of a worker who is retired or disabled.
[12]These beneficiaries receive payment on the record of a worker who is retired, deceased, or disabled.

Table A. 110th Congressional Districts—*Continued*

(Number, percent.)

STATE Congressional district	Total farms	Farms by size (percent) 1 to 49 acres	50 to 999 acres	1,000 acres or more	Land in farms Total acreage	Average size of farms (acres)	Percent of farms where principal operator's primary occupation is farming	Value of all agricultural products sold Total ($1,000)	Percent of farms with value of: Less than $50,000	$50,000 to $249,999	$250,000 or more	Payments from federal farm programs Total ($1,000)	Number of farms that receive payments	Percent of farms that receive payments
	78	79	80	81	82	83	84	85	86	87	88	89	90	91
UNITED STATES[3]	2 128 982	34.9	56.8	8.3	938 279 056	441	57.5	200 646 355	78.8	14.1	7.2	6 545 679	707 596	33.2
ALABAMA	45 126	37.1	59.6	3.3	8 904 387	197	53.1	3 264 949	86.9	5.6	7.5	77 930	12 863	28.5
District 1	3 275	44.0	52.9	3.1	605 168	185	54.1	203 142	87.8	8.0	4.2	7 550	840	25.6
District 2	8 885	26.7	68.0	5.3	2 434 064	274	52.3	802 683	84.2	7.3	8.5	31 990	3 855	43.4
District 3	5 370	31.2	65.0	3.8	1 178 279	219	53.7	301 216	90.1	5.0	4.9	6 376	1 267	23.6
District 4	13 754	43.3	55.8	1.0	1 656 852	120	54.2	1 384 212	83.0	4.7	12.2	6 457	2 967	21.6
District 5	7 592	43.8	53.6	2.7	1 241 928	164	50.8	321 987	91.2	4.3	4.5	16 061	2 360	31.1
District 6	2 518	42.2	56.2	1.6	364 603	145	52.0	80 085	93.6	4.1	2.3	1 317	326	12.9
District 7	3 732	24.8	66.0	9.3	1 423 493	381	54.3	171 623	88.7	7.0	4.3	8 179	1 248	33.4
ALASKA	609	42.0	48.6	9.4	900 715	1 479	60.8	46 143	82.8	11.0	6.2	1 765	72	11.8
At Large	609	42.0	48.6	9.4	900 715	1 479	60.8	46 143	82.8	11.0	6.2	1 765	72	11.8
ARIZONA	7 294	58.0	30.5	11.5	26 586 577	3 645	58.9	2 395 447	79.4	8.6	12.0	31 760	833	11.4
District 1	2 441	51.7	35.2	13.1	19 310 231	7 911	58.9	493 023	82.3	8.8	8.9	8 156	298	12.2
District 2	769	61.0	26.3	12.7	2 040 011	2 653	62.7	243 542	77.9	7.8	14.3	5 103	106	13.8
District 3	364	89.8	8.0	2.2	100 362	276	49.2	36 952	91.2	4.4	4.4	572	6	1.6
District 4	183	76.5	19.7	3.8	27 243	149	62.3	99 751	66.1	7.7	26.2	318	12	6.6
District 5	182	74.2	22.0	3.8	180 266	990	55.5	17 186	87.9	7.7	4.4	483	8	4.4
District 6	778	82.6	15.6	1.8	64 320	83	53.3	191 311	85.6	5.4	9.0	1 725	40	5.1
District 7	1 201	55.7	30.6	13.7	1 223 087	1 018	59.2	1 195 488	64.5	10.4	25.1	11 937	166	13.8
District 8	1 376	42.5	41.5	16.0	3 641 057	2 646	62.3	118 194	82.3	10.2	7.4	3 465	197	14.3
ARKANSAS	47 483	27.3	65.7	7.0	14 502 793	305	57.7	4 950 397	78.1	9.5	12.3	238 577	7 811	16.5
District 1	14 524	20.0	65.3	14.7	7 268 862	500	61.8	1 574 413	72.4	14.2	13.4	181 865	4 706	32.4
District 2	6 738	32.0	65.1	2.9	1 347 815	200	53.7	355 420	87.3	6.2	6.4	7 958	745	11.1
District 3	14 277	32.3	65.4	2.3	2 537 053	178	54.6	1 454 448	82.7	6.4	10.9	3 884	970	6.8
District 4	11 944	27.5	66.8	5.7	3 349 063	280	58.7	1 566 116	74.5	9.4	16.1	44 870	1 390	11.6
CALIFORNIA	79 631	61.7	32.3	6.0	27 589 027	346	61.7	25 737 173	66.9	17.7	15.5	168 698	7 228	9.1
District 1	6 057	58.9	34.0	7.0	2 248 591	371	58.1	1 081 764	70.3	18.6	11.0	6 745	414	6.8
District 2	10 253	48.8	44.1	7.1	4 125 002	402	63.1	1 450 753	66.5	21.2	12.3	50 553	1 896	18.5
District 3	2 676	60.7	32.1	7.1	866 501	324	58.3	284 961	81.7	11.0	7.3	3 320	210	7.8
District 4	4 579	67.1	27.0	5.9	1 674 734	366	56.6	159 450	89.4	7.6	3.0	3 718	338	7.4
District 5	114	63.2	30.7	6.1	20 613	181	63.2	14 352	74.6	14.9	10.5	419	19	16.7
District 6	2 836	69.6	26.4	4.0	560 354	198	55.3	428 735	74.8	14.8	10.4	2 247	172	6.1
District 7	416	69.7	27.6	2.6	61 199	147	53.6	89 897	85.3	9.9	4.8	328	22	5.3
District 8	8	100.0	0.0	0.0	. . .	. . .	37.5	1 012	62.5	12.5	25.0	. . .	. . .	. . .
District 9	72	66.7	33.3	0.0	7 300	101	52.8	2 436	87.5	8.3	4.2	. . .	1	1.4
District 10	784	52.2	36.4	11.5	434 222	554	58.4	159 248	69.3	13.5	17.2	2 066	109	13.9
District 11	4 438	64.5	31.2	4.3	953 808	215	66.1	1 206 548	62.7	19.3	18.1	6 548	325	7.3
District 12	64	87.5	12.5	0.0	1 915	30	54.7	10 702	71.9	17.2	10.9	. . .	. . .	. . .
District 13	94	52.1	42.6	5.3	31 270	333	40.4	21 234	75.5	10.6	13.8	51	7	7.4
District 14	799	69.6	27.9	2.5	92 324	116	63.0	295 179	68.3	16.3	15.4	174	24	3.0
District 15	204	65.7	29.9	4.4	26 740	131	55.4	63 826	84.8	3.9	11.3	24	7	3.4
District 16	372	79.8	15.1	5.1	123 660	332	55.1	64 604	81.2	14.0	4.8	31	4	1.1
District 17	2 199	49.5	37.7	12.8	1 863 180	847	65.0	2 627 098	58.3	12.9	28.8	1 511	157	7.1
District 18	4 566	51.8	41.9	6.3	1 429 594	313	71.3	2 011 986	52.9	23.5	23.7	15 117	597	13.1
District 19	6 521	59.0	36.3	4.6	1 718 145	263	65.9	1 867 389	63.6	20.0	16.4	13 170	485	7.4
District 20	3 719	46.4	42.0	11.6	2 046 714	550	73.1	3 022 243	44.7	23.3	32.0	26 257	690	18.6
District 21	8 787	62.1	33.8	4.1	2 170 193	247	66.0	3 282 057	56.4	24.9	18.7	17 745	692	7.9
District 22	3 621	49.1	39.2	11.7	3 426 156	946	61.9	1 556 281	69.6	13.9	16.5	9 323	435	12.0
District 23	1 368	63.7	29.9	6.4	481 690	352	65.0	1 078 883	56.1	16.7	27.2	546	77	5.6
District 24	2 815	69.3	25.6	5.0	770 148	274	57.3	777 345	65.0	19.7	15.3	1 549	129	4.6
District 25	858	77.4	17.9	4.7	373 393	435	58.4	178 809	85.2	6.5	8.3	168	14	1.6
District 26	277	87.7	10.5	1.8	21 992	79	53.4	31 824	81.2	9.0	9.7	85	8	2.9
District 27	117	90.6	6.8	2.6	9 244	79	48.7	18 358	81.2	10.3	8.5	. . .	2	3.8
District 28	52	78.8	21.2	0.0	3 702	71	59.6	3 617	84.6	7.7	7.7	. . .	1	2.6
District 29	39	92.3	7.7	0.0	565	14	43.6	2 417	87.2	2.6	10.3	. . .	1	2.6
District 30	148	84.5	14.9	0.7	8 367	57	51.4	10 649	85.8	8.1	6.1	. . .	2	1.4
District 31	4	75.0	25.0	0.0	. . .	. . .	25.0	8	100.0	0.0	0.0	. . .	1	25.0
District 32	50	82.0	18.0	0.0	1 896	38	78.0	83 532	48.0	8.0	44.0	. . .	. . .	. . .
District 33	12	91.7	8.3	0.0	127	11	50.0	733	58.3	41.7	0.0	. . .	. . .	. . .
District 34	14	85.7	14.3	0.0	387	28	57.1	6 831	50.0	35.7	14.3	. . .	1	7.1
District 35	40	100.0	0.0	0.0	311	8	77.5	13 719	27.5	52.5	20.0	. . .	. . .	. . .
District 36	54	74.1	25.9	0.0	2 806	52	48.1	24 909	61.1	11.1	27.8	3	4	7.4
District 37	24	87.5	12.5	0.0	344	14	75.0	22 312	54.2	12.5	33.3	. . .	1	4.2
District 38	56	87.5	8.9	3.6	3 862	69	58.9	7 319	58.9	21.4	19.6	. . .	. . .	. . .
District 39	34	91.2	8.8	0.0	715	21	47.1	2 975	55.9	20.6	23.5	. . .	2	5.9
District 40	62	83.9	16.1	0.0	3 117	50	53.2	31 072	58.1	14.5	27.4	1	3	4.8

[3]United States totals do not include Puerto Rico.
. . . = Not available.

Table A. 110th Congressional Districts—*Continued*

(Number, percent.)

STATE Congressional district	Representative	Land area,[1] (sq km)	Population and population characteristics, 2006									
			Total population	Persons per square kilometer	Race alone (percent)				Some other race (percent)	Two or more races (percent)	Hispanic or Latino[2] (percent)	Non-Hispanic White (percent)
					White	Black	American Indian/ Alaska Native	Asian and Pacific Islander				
	1	2	3	4	5	6	7	8	9	10	11	12
CALIFORNIA—*Continued*												
District 41	Rep. Jerry Lewis (R)	34 484	770 206	22.3	71.6	5.8	1.1	4.3	14.4	2.7	33.3	54.2
District 42	Rep. Gary G. Miller (R)	813	687 751	845.9	58.6	3.3	0.5	20.5	14.2	3.1	26.2	48.1
District 43	Rep. Joe Baca (D)	494	729 476	1 476.7	58.2	11.6	0.7	4.5	22.0	3.0	65.2	17.0
District 44	Rep. Ken Calvert (R)	1 352	827 843	612.3	61.4	4.9	0.8	6.6	22.6	3.7	41.7	44.5
District 45	Rep. Mary Bono Mack (R)	15 488	826 129	53.3	62.7	6.7	0.6	5.0	21.4	3.5	39.9	43.4
District 46	Rep. Dana Rohrabacher (R)	683	644 395	943.5	69.2	1.7	0.3	17.4	8.9	2.5	19.0	59.9
District 47	Rep. Loretta Sanchez (D)	142	649 040	4 570.7	57.2	1.2	0.3	15.0	24.9	1.4	69.4	13.4
District 48	Rep. John Campbell (R)	550	689 639	1 253.9	70.7	1.8	0.4	16.9	7.6	2.5	16.6	61.8
District 49	Rep. Darrell E. Issa (R)	4 378	749 162	171.1	67.7	4.7	1.1	4.8	18.1	3.6	35.4	52.1
District 50	Rep. Brian P. Bilbray (R)	778	710 358	913.1	75.3	1.6	0.3	13.8	5.8	3.2	20.9	61.2
District 51	Rep. Bob Filner (D)	11 868	683 959	57.6	60.6	7.4	0.7	12.2	15.4	3.7	59.7	18.1
District 52	Rep. Duncan Hunter (R)	5 473	650 592	118.9	79.1	3.8	0.7	8.9	3.7	3.8	16.7	67.8
District 53	Rep. Susan A. Davis (D)	246	643 440	2 615.6	68.6	7.6	0.9	9.3	10.5	3.1	31.6	49.3
COLORADO		268 627	4 753 377	17.7	82.8	3.7	0.9	2.9	7.1	2.6	19.7	71.5
District 1	Rep. Diana DeGette (D)	444	624 028	1 405.5	69.2	10.0	0.9	3.2	14.0	2.8	33.2	51.3
District 2	Rep. Mark Udall (D)	14 542	681 241	46.8	85.6	0.9	0.8	4.3	6.1	2.3	18.0	75.0
District 3	Rep. John T. Salazar (D)	139 765	676 395	4.8	88.1	0.8	1.8	0.6	6.3	2.5	22.4	73.3
District 4	Rep. Marilyn N. Musgrave (R)	80 025	688 513	8.6	87.8	0.7	0.4	1.9	7.1	2.1	19.2	76.6
District 5	Rep. Doug Lamborn (R)	19 963	679 861	34.1	81.7	5.4	1.0	2.9	5.0	4.0	12.7	75.9
District 6	Rep. Thomas G. Tancredo (R)	10 629	744 831	70.1	88.7	2.6	0.4	3.8	2.5	2.0	7.2	84.5
District 7	Rep. Ed Perlmutter (D)	3 259	658 508	202.1	76.6	6.5	0.8	3.4	9.9	2.8	27.5	60.8
CONNECTICUT		12 548	3 504 809	279.3	79.9	9.5	0.2	3.4	5.2	1.8	11.2	74.5
District 1	Rep. John B. Larson (D)	1 691	696 667	412.0	72.9	13.8	0.2	3.6	7.5	1.9	12.7	68.2
District 2	Rep. Joe Courtney (D)	5 253	706 619	134.5	87.9	3.9	0.4	2.6	3.3	1.9	5.5	86.4
District 3	Rep. Rosa L. DeLauro (D)	1 189	709 165	596.4	77.4	12.9	0.2	3.6	4.2	1.7	10.0	72.1
District 4	Rep. Christopher Shays (R)	1 183	694 419	587.0	76.7	11.2	0.1	4.2	6.5	1.4	15.0	68.4
District 5	Rep. Christopher S. Murphy (D)	3 231	697 939	216.0	84.5	5.7	0.2	2.8	4.6	2.1	12.9	77.2
DELAWARE		5 060	853 476	168.7	72.1	20.7	0.3	2.9	2.5	1.4	6.3	68.8
At Large	Rep. Michael N. Castle (R)	5 060	853 476	168.7	72.1	20.7	0.3	2.9	2.5	1.4	6.3	68.8
DISTRICT OF COLUMBIA		159	581 530	3 657.4	34.5	55.4	0.3	3.4	4.8	1.5	8.2	31.6
Delegate District (At Large)	Del. Eleanor Holmes Norton (D)	159	581 530	3 657.4	34.5	55.4	0.3	3.4	4.8	1.5	8.2	31.6
FLORIDA		139 670	18 089 889	129.5	76.1	15.4	0.3	2.2	4.3	1.8	20.1	61.0
District 1	Rep. Jeff Miller (R)	12 022	681 180	56.7	78.9	14.4	0.5	2.4	1.1	2.8	3.7	76.5
District 2	Rep. Allen Boyd (D)	24 410	686 565	28.1	73.8	21.6	0.3	1.5	1.2	1.7	3.6	71.7
District 3	Rep. Corrine Brown (D)	4 652	679 832	146.1	39.4	51.8	0.4	1.7	5.2	1.5	10.7	34.6
District 4	Rep. Ander Crenshaw (R)	10 665	705 650	66.2	78.1	14.4	0.3	3.3	1.9	2.0	6.0	74.1
District 5	Rep. Ginny Brown-Waite (R)	10 474	852 578	81.4	88.2	5.2	0.5	1.5	3.1	1.5	8.8	82.5
District 6	Rep. Cliff Stearns (R)	7 541	751 577	99.7	79.6	13.7	0.3	3.1	1.6	1.7	6.6	75.3
District 7	Rep. John L. Mica (R)	4 654	777 881	167.1	83.9	9.0	0.4	2.4	2.7	1.5	9.8	77.3
District 8	Rep. Ric Keller (R)	2 556	746 635	292.1	76.4	9.4	0.2	3.5	8.3	2.3	22.3	63.2
District 9	Rep. Gus M. Bilirakis (R)	1 642	772 245	470.3	87.5	5.5	0.2	2.9	2.4	1.4	11.0	79.0
District 10	Rep. C.W. Bill Young (R)	452	621 223	1 374.4	88.2	5.2	0.3	3.1	1.3	1.8	6.1	83.6
District 11	Rep. Kathy Castor (D)	632	661 212	1 046.2	62.4	28.4	0.3	2.6	4.6	1.7	25.3	42.9
District 12	Rep. Adam H. Putnam (R)	5 066	771 683	152.3	74.6	14.4	0.3	1.6	6.8	2.3	18.7	63.8
District 13	Rep. Vern Buchanan (R)	6 732	736 109	109.3	89.4	4.9	0.2	1.3	3.2	0.8	10.3	82.5
District 14	Rep. Connie Mack (R)	2 736	813 476	297.3	86.8	5.8	0.2	1.3	4.9	1.0	15.4	76.5
District 15	Rep. Dave Weldon, (R)	6 591	764 771	116.0	81.5	9.1	0.4	2.5	4.3	2.3	16.1	70.8
District 16	Rep. Tim Mahoney (D)	11 755	763 215	64.9	85.0	8.3	0.3	1.2	3.7	1.5	14.5	74.8
District 17	Rep. Kendrick B. Meek (D)	250	676 629	2 706.5	32.7	57.4	0.4	2.1	5.6	1.8	25.7	14.6
District 18	Rep. Ileana Ros-Lehtinen (R)	919	638 719	695.0	86.3	6.4	0.2	1.5	4.2	1.5	65.1	28.0
District 19	Rep. Robert Wexler (D)	598	727 647	1 216.8	79.3	9.5	0.1	2.4	7.4	1.2	18.5	68.1
District 20	Rep. Debbie Wasserman Schultz (D)	416	672 781	1 617.3	79.5	10.6	0.2	2.8	4.2	2.6	25.8	59.4
District 21	Rep. Lincoln Diaz-Balart (R)	349	665 532	1 907.0	82.2	8.2	0.2	2.5	5.7	1.3	73.8	16.2
District 22	Rep. Ron Klein (D)	694	692 476	997.8	87.0	5.9	0.2	2.4	3.0	1.4	14.8	75.5
District 23	Rep. Alcee L. Hastings (D)	8 708	692 406	79.5	33.5	56.0	0.4	1.6	6.4	2.0	17.2	23.7
District 24	Rep. Tom Feeney (R)	4 101	740 876	180.7	82.6	7.3	0.4	3.1	4.5	2.1	13.5	74.5
District 25	Rep. Mario Diaz-Balart (R)	11 054	796 991	72.1	75.8	11.7	0.2	1.7	8.4	2.2	66.6	20.0
GEORGIA[13]		149 976	9 363 941	62.4	62.1	29.8	0.2	2.8	3.8	1.3	7.4	58.7
District 1	Rep. Jack Kingston (R)	29 542	681 860	23.1	72.1	22.7	0.3	1.3	2.0	1.5	4.4	70.0
District 2	Rep. Sanford D. Bishop Jr. (D)	28 079	646 921	23.0	53.0	43.2	0.3	0.5	1.7	1.3	4.0	50.9
District 3	Rep. Lynn A. Westmoreland (R)	10 650	640 378	60.1	55.7	40.9	0.1	0.6	1.7	0.9	3.4	54.4
District 4	Rep. Henry C. "Hank" Johnson Jr. (D)	854	683 079	799.9	34.3	54.1	0.2	4.4	6.0	1.1	10.6	30.3
District 5	Rep. John Lewis (D)	636	674 043	1 059.8	37.6	53.6	0.3	2.7	4.7	1.1	7.3	35.1

[1]Dry land or land partially or temporarily covered by water.
[2]May be of any race.
[13]Data are for 109th congressional districts. The boundaries for districts for the 110th Congress have changed.

Table A. 110th Congressional Districts—*Continued*

(Number, percent.)

STATE Congressional district	Percent female	Percent foreign born	Percent born in state of residence	Under 5 years	5 to 18 years	18 to 24 years	25 to 34 years	35 to 44 years	45 to 54 years	55 to 64 years	65 to 74 years	75 years and over
	13	14	15	16	17	18	19	20	21	22	23	24
CALIFORNIA—*Continued*												
District 41	51.2	15.6	59.8	7.7	19.8	10.5	14.0	13.7	12.9	9.4	6.4	5.7
District 42	49.8	25.2	54.4	6.3	20.3	8.8	11.9	16.5	16.7	10.2	5.1	4.2
District 43	49.8	29.8	58.7	8.6	23.4	12.4	17.7	13.8	11.5	6.5	3.2	2.9
District 44	49.2	24.0	57.2	7.4	20.6	11.5	16.4	15.8	12.9	7.7	3.9	3.8
District 45	50.2	22.6	51.6	7.0	19.5	9.8	15.4	13.4	12.0	8.2	7.0	7.7
District 46	50.9	23.6	49.9	5.5	15.9	8.5	12.2	16.2	15.5	12.0	7.2	7.0
District 47	47.7	49.3	43.0	9.6	22.1	11.2	17.5	14.7	10.7	6.9	3.9	3.4
District 48	51.3	25.1	47.0	6.4	16.7	9.5	13.0	16.7	14.4	11.0	6.3	6.0
District 49	48.8	20.5	50.9	8.0	19.5	11.9	15.7	14.1	12.4	7.4	5.2	5.9
District 50	50.0	23.5	43.1	7.8	18.2	8.6	12.4	16.4	14.7	9.7	5.8	6.5
District 51	50.3	34.0	49.5	8.5	22.0	11.1	13.6	14.7	12.4	7.6	5.3	4.9
District 52	51.0	15.2	50.8	7.2	18.2	8.4	12.9	15.0	16.2	11.0	5.5	5.7
District 53	48.4	23.5	43.2	6.7	13.3	17.3	20.8	13.9	11.3	7.4	4.0	5.1
COLORADO	49.6	10.3	42.1	7.1	17.5	9.8	15.0	15.1	15.2	10.3	5.4	4.6
District 1	49.3	17.3	42.8	8.8	15.6	8.1	17.7	16.3	13.2	9.7	4.9	5.8
District 2	48.6	11.1	40.8	7.1	17.1	10.8	16.1	16.3	15.5	9.9	4.3	2.9
District 3	50.0	5.2	51.7	6.2	16.8	10.3	13.7	13.1	15.1	11.3	6.9	6.7
District 4	49.9	8.6	45.9	6.9	17.4	12.3	15.0	13.9	14.4	9.6	5.3	5.2
District 5	49.5	7.1	32.0	6.8	18.1	9.8	15.1	15.1	15.2	10.1	5.7	4.3
District 6	50.1	7.4	37.9	6.9	20.0	7.4	12.2	16.4	17.5	11.4	4.8	3.3
District 7	50.0	16.5	43.8	7.5	16.9	9.8	15.5	15.0	14.9	9.9	6.0	4.4
CONNECTICUT	51.3	12.9	55.7	5.8	17.6	9.1	11.6	15.6	15.7	11.2	6.4	7.0
District 1	52.2	14.6	58.8	5.8	16.9	9.1	12.5	14.8	15.3	11.7	6.5	7.5
District 2	49.9	6.3	56.4	5.2	17.1	10.0	11.8	15.9	16.3	11.0	6.5	6.1
District 3	52.2	11.3	64.1	5.7	17.2	9.9	12.4	15.2	14.9	10.9	6.3	7.5
District 4	51.6	19.6	42.6	6.6	19.1	8.3	10.2	15.8	16.0	11.1	6.4	6.5
District 5	50.8	12.9	56.5	5.5	17.6	8.3	11.2	16.0	16.1	11.3	6.5	7.3
DELAWARE	51.5	8.1	47.0	6.7	17.2	9.8	12.9	14.7	14.3	11.1	7.1	6.3
At Large	51.5	8.1	47.0	6.7	17.2	9.8	12.9	14.7	14.3	11.1	7.1	6.3
DISTRICT OF COLUMBIA	53.1	12.7	40.1	6.0	13.7	12.2	18.0	14.6	12.9	10.3	6.2	6.0
Delegate District (At Large)	53.1	12.7	40.1	6.0	13.7	12.2	18.0	14.6	12.9	10.3	6.2	6.0
FLORIDA	50.9	18.9	33.6	6.2	16.0	8.9	12.4	14.4	14.0	11.3	8.0	8.7
District 1	50.1	4.2	41.1	6.5	16.6	10.6	12.4	14.0	14.7	11.9	7.5	5.8
District 2	50.1	4.2	53.4	6.0	15.5	12.6	13.3	13.5	14.3	11.9	7.0	5.9
District 3	51.6	12.1	52.0	7.7	18.9	10.9	14.5	13.2	14.0	9.7	5.8	5.4
District 4	49.3	8.1	45.8	7.1	16.8	9.5	13.4	15.6	14.7	11.4	6.4	5.1
District 5	50.9	7.1	31.5	5.1	14.6	7.3	11.9	14.3	12.6	11.7	11.2	11.4
District 6	50.9	6.9	41.7	6.0	15.0	12.0	12.9	13.8	13.2	11.3	7.8	8.1
District 7	51.1	8.6	32.8	5.4	15.6	9.2	11.8	13.5	15.1	12.7	8.2	8.6
District 8	51.2	15.0	31.0	6.6	17.1	8.5	14.3	16.1	14.3	10.2	6.3	6.6
District 9	51.8	11.7	29.5	5.5	16.9	7.2	11.6	14.4	14.7	12.0	7.7	10.0
District 10	51.8	12.1	27.8	5.4	13.5	7.0	10.3	13.7	15.6	13.3	8.9	12.3
District 11	50.8	17.4	42.4	7.2	17.0	10.4	15.2	14.4	14.2	10.3	5.9	5.4
District 12	50.9	12.1	39.2	7.1	17.3	8.9	13.9	13.9	12.7	10.6	7.8	7.9
District 13	51.5	12.4	24.5	4.8	13.0	6.8	11.1	12.2	13.2	12.8	11.4	14.9
District 14	50.6	16.0	21.3	5.2	13.5	7.0	12.0	12.6	12.6	12.5	11.7	13.0
District 15	50.9	12.5	26.2	5.6	15.3	8.4	12.0	14.0	13.9	11.7	9.4	9.7
District 16	50.4	14.2	29.3	5.1	15.9	7.8	11.1	13.0	13.3	11.0	10.0	12.8
District 17	51.9	37.2	43.1	7.9	19.8	11.5	13.0	14.0	13.7	9.7	5.5	4.9
District 18	50.7	53.3	24.2	5.2	13.1	8.5	11.8	16.5	14.5	12.4	8.8	9.3
District 19	52.6	24.2	20.4	4.8	14.2	6.8	10.4	12.7	12.9	12.5	9.4	16.4
District 20	51.5	30.5	27.5	5.7	16.2	7.1	12.0	16.1	15.8	11.0	7.1	9.0
District 21	52.0	54.3	28.2	6.5	17.4	8.7	11.7	16.7	14.2	10.0	8.1	6.7
District 22	50.8	19.6	25.2	5.6	14.3	6.7	9.6	15.6	16.3	12.6	8.7	10.6
District 23	50.2	31.1	40.4	8.9	18.7	10.6	14.6	15.1	12.9	8.7	5.0	5.5
District 24	49.2	10.6	31.6	5.7	16.0	9.7	13.0	15.4	14.5	11.1	7.8	6.8
District 25	50.3	46.6	34.1	8.4	19.2	9.7	12.8	16.2	13.7	9.3	5.7	4.9
GEORGIA[13]	50.7	9.2	55.5	7.5	18.7	10.1	14.3	15.7	14.1	10.0	5.4	4.3
District 1	49.6	4.1	60.7	7.6	19.4	10.3	13.2	14.5	14.0	10.0	6.2	4.8
District 2	51.1	2.9	71.3	7.3	19.3	12.3	13.3	13.2	12.7	9.9	6.3	5.8
District 3	50.1	2.9	78.0	6.7	18.4	11.7	12.7	14.0	13.7	10.4	6.8	5.5
District 4	51.2	17.0	44.3	8.0	17.5	9.3	14.8	17.5	14.6	9.9	4.6	3.6
District 5	49.7	10.2	51.1	7.3	15.2	10.9	18.5	16.7	13.5	9.8	4.4	3.7

[13]Data are for 109th congressional districts. The boundaries for districts for the 110th Congress have changed.

Table A. 110th Congressional Districts—*Continued*

(Number, percent.)

STATE Congressional district	Households, 2006						Group quarters, 2006		Group quarters, 2000			
	Number	Average household size	Family households (percent)	Married-couple family (percent)	Female family house-holder[4] (percent)	One-person households (percent)	Total in group quarters	Percent 65 years and over	Persons in correctional institutions	Persons in nursing homes	Persons in college dormitories	Persons in military quarters
	25	26	27	28	29	30	31	32	33	34	35	36
CALIFORNIA—*Continued*												
District 41	258 892	2.91	71.8	52.9	13.6	22.2	16 787	22.6	2 019	2 290	1 590	5 583
District 42	217 053	3.11	80.0	64.3	10.4	16.3	12 954	9.3	9 726	569	714	0
District 43	192 897	3.75	81.0	53.0	18.2	15.1	6 747	29.8	2 257	1 703	0	0
District 44	247 888	3.28	75.3	57.1	11.5	18.7	13 559	12.4	5 968	2 049	2 814	1
District 45	278 391	2.92	70.3	52.5	11.9	23.0	14 419	14.1	9 748	1 971	0	0
District 46	241 656	2.63	62.9	48.8	8.6	30.1	9 428	18.3	1 375	1 618	2 617	154
District 47	152 064	4.21	80.9	54.4	16.9	13.7	8 807	28.4	2 473	1 653	28	0
District 48	263 019	2.59	63.6	50.7	9.2	28.2	8 784	30.1	944	1 850	7 122	0
District 49	242 837	2.99	73.8	58.9	10.0	20.2	22 799	7.6	1 141	1 026	497	15 770
District 50	254 837	2.75	68.7	54.6	9.5	23.7	10 407	31.8	148	2 512	36	4 114
District 51	200 120	3.30	81.0	55.2	19.5	15.7	24 334	7.3	17 028	942	0	2 700
District 52	239 044	2.68	70.6	54.5	10.9	22.6	9 707	24.4	1 280	3 288	400	0
District 53	251 953	2.32	46.8	32.2	10.3	38.4	59 275	6.4	2 402	2 611	12 638	18 800
COLORADO	1 846 988	2.52	64.8	50.6	9.8	28.2	102 994	17.8	30 136	18 495	23 631	8 512
District 1	272 044	2.25	50.6	35.3	10.9	41.2	11 078	17.0	3 059	3 257	2 027	0
District 2	257 853	2.59	64.3	50.7	8.7	26.2	13 512	11.6	782	1 579	6 125	0
District 3	265 023	2.49	66.5	53.1	9.7	27.7	16 374	23.2	3 787	3 290	4 715	0
District 4	261 155	2.56	65.6	51.9	9.0	25.3	19 767	17.9	6 726	3 667	7 976	0
District 5	257 331	2.54	66.8	52.8	10.5	27.8	27 487	8.4	11 375	2 477	1 817	8 321
District 6	274 205	2.70	75.1	64.3	7.6	19.7	4 920	45.4	1 260	1 357	39	0
District 7	259 377	2.50	64.6	45.8	12.5	29.4	9 856	30.8	3 147	2 868	932	191
CONNECTICUT	1 325 443	2.56	67.5	51.4	12.1	27.1	113 079	25.2	20 023	32 223	38 051	2 097
District 1	272 451	2.48	64.3	46.9	13.4	30.0	20 885	32.5	1 055	9 159	5 310	0
District 2	267 234	2.51	68.7	55.1	9.5	25.6	35 369	11.8	11 896	4 781	14 476	2 081
District 3	268 169	2.56	66.8	48.7	14.4	28.3	23 929	22.8	1 365	6 254	10 882	16
District 4	251 808	2.70	70.1	54.0	11.7	24.8	13 898	34.5	880	4 982	4 524	0
District 5	265 781	2.55	67.7	52.4	11.5	26.6	18 998	38.1	4 827	7 047	2 859	0
DELAWARE	320 110	2.59	66.7	49.1	12.9	27.2	24 915	18.2	5 965	4 852	9 394	381
At Large	320 110	2.59	66.7	49.1	12.9	27.2	24 915	18.2	5 965	4 852	9 394	381
DISTRICT OF COLUMBIA	250 456	2.18	43.4	22.3	17.4	47.2	35 225	11.5	2 838	3 759	19 322	927
Delegate District (At Large)	250 456	2.18	43.4	22.3	17.4	47.2	35 225	11.5	2 838	3 759	19 322	927
FLORIDA	7 106 042	2.49	65.2	48.6	12.1	28.0	412 218	24.2	139 148	88 828	54 085	13 457
District 1	267 567	2.41	68.2	50.7	13.6	25.8	35 839	8.9	15 657	4 065	4 412	7 702
District 2	271 750	2.37	63.3	45.2	13.5	28.0	41 208	12.3	19 044	3 904	8 907	527
District 3	257 343	2.55	63.3	34.7	22.3	30.7	23 184	9.6	8 532	2 292	1 572	0
District 4	265 382	2.55	64.5	49.8	10.4	28.8	29 991	12.9	14 104	3 651	1 265	4 036
District 5	343 260	2.44	73.7	61.8	8.2	21.8	15 327	26.6	8 846	3 476	464	0
District 6	298 085	2.44	65.1	50.9	10.2	26.8	24 476	19.1	8 762	3 756	8 349	4
District 7	312 548	2.44	65.3	51.9	10.2	27.1	13 914	27.5	1 636	4 702	5 127	0
District 8	294 024	2.52	64.9	48.2	12.3	26.9	5 216	47.6	879	3 301	1 083	0
District 9	312 495	2.44	65.2	51.9	9.6	28.2	10 296	61.1	81	5 265	452	0
District 10	277 705	2.18	53.9	41.0	8.6	38.4	15 329	45.9	3 269	5 370	1 346	56
District 11	268 097	2.41	59.3	35.9	16.8	33.4	15 012	25.2	3 076	3 095	3 786	412
District 12	303 001	2.49	69.8	51.8	12.8	24.2	16 417	25.8	5 835	3 901	2 392	0
District 13	328 098	2.21	62.6	50.0	8.8	30.1	12 548	52.4	4 010	5 854	756	13
District 14	353 359	2.28	64.8	53.5	7.9	28.0	9 158	32.5	1 709	4 190	238	16
District 15	315 701	2.40	67.4	52.2	10.8	26.2	7 150	39.4	1 621	3 084	1 388	215
District 16	301 592	2.50	68.7	55.1	9.1	25.8	9 277	37.6	4 212	3 995	267	7
District 17	224 044	2.96	65.7	36.1	21.7	28.3	14 437	22.2	4 154	3 635	1 653	262
District 18	259 456	2.41	58.9	40.7	13.3	33.5	12 820	28.9	2 509	2 504	3 594	179
District 19	306 705	2.36	62.4	49.4	10.2	31.6	2 457	65.9	382	2 370	1 356	0
District 20	276 906	2.41	60.1	46.0	10.6	32.9	5 879	56.3	91	2 130	617	0
District 21	221 315	2.94	75.6	52.3	17.7	20.0	15 847	36.6	1 148	2 602	825	11
District 22	293 590	2.33	58.5	47.2	8.0	33.7	8 700	39.7	0	3 667	1 779	11
District 23	225 884	2.94	64.4	36.9	20.9	27.7	28 273	21.2	13 767	3 442	0	0
District 24	287 100	2.51	66.6	52.8	9.6	25.4	19 096	21.3	7 132	2 691	2 457	5
District 25	241 035	3.22	79.3	56.7	16.6	16.5	20 367	10.3	8 692	1 886	0	1
GEORGIA[13]	3 376 763	2.69	68.0	48.5	14.6	26.4	272 931	15.5	81 773	34 812	47 910	25 461
District 1	251 159	2.61	70.6	51.4	14.9	24.5	25 220	14.9	10 727	3 625	167	8 840
District 2	237 465	2.54	69.6	41.6	21.8	26.3	43 118	12.1	7 617	4 275	3 879	9 816
District 3	226 324	2.62	65.5	44.1	16.9	30.1	46 340	14.2	23 414	6 075	3 900	0
District 4	251 746	2.65	57.4	35.7	16.3	34.4	16 946	25.3	3 181	1 881	4 086	0
District 5	262 381	2.43	45.5	26.4	14.7	45.5	36 371	5.0	7 705	1 683	13 612	88

4No spouse present.
13Data are for 109th congressional districts. The boundaries for districts for the 110th Congress have changed.

Table A. 110th Congressional Districts—*Continued*

(Number, percent.)

STATE Congressional district	Education, 2006				Income, 2006			Poverty, 2006		
	School enrollment[5]		Attainment level[6] (percent)		Per capita income (dollars)	Median household income (dollars)	Percent of households with income over $100,000	Persons below poverty level (percent)	Families below poverty level (percent)	Percent of households receiving food stamps in past 12 months
	Total	Private (percent)	High school graduate or more	Bachelor's degree or more						
	37	38	39	40	41	42	43	44	45	46
CALIFORNIA—*Continued*										
District 41	220 469	13.8	81.6	18.4	21 263	47 321	15.6	15.4	11.3	4.8
District 42	212 456	19.0	89.4	36.9	34 396	86 983	42.3	5.5	3.9	0.9
District 43	233 178	7.7	64.5	11.0	16 273	47 002	13.7	15.2	13.2	7.9
District 44	245 755	15.9	80.3	23.9	25 788	63 219	28.4	11.3	7.5	2.7
District 45	214 696	10.6	78.5	19.4	23 547	49 605	18.7	12.3	9.8	3.3
District 46	169 271	16.9	89.8	39.4	37 422	71 257	34.2	7.8	4.9	1.0
District 47	199 435	5.9	55.9	12.6	15 717	50 655	15.5	15.4	13.3	6.0
District 48	193 183	19.0	93.2	52.4	46 181	83 652	42.1	8.0	4.4	0.8
District 49	202 075	12.1	81.1	22.1	24 068	58 571	22.2	10.5	7.5	1.5
District 50	192 743	15.2	88.7	44.5	36 711	74 613	36.4	8.5	5.6	1.1
District 51	215 388	7.8	71.8	16.3	18 451	47 764	16.6	15.0	12.7	5.3
District 52	184 572	15.4	89.9	33.5	31 476	67 366	29.1	7.1	4.9	1.6
District 53	180 092	15.1	84.7	37.5	27 366	47 086	18.0	19.0	13.4	3.7
COLORADO	1 233 278	14.1	88.0	34.3	27 750	52 015	20.3	12.0	8.4	5.0
District 1	141 843	21.0	82.7	36.2	26 931	40 627	15.7	19.7	15.2	6.2
District 2	180 636	16.2	90.0	41.5	30 431	60 410	25.0	10.0	6.2	2.7
District 3	169 029	8.8	86.3	25.0	23 238	42 438	12.0	13.7	10.4	8.6
District 4	197 179	10.0	87.3	31.1	25 277	49 561	17.4	14.0	8.6	6.0
District 5	182 323	12.8	90.5	32.1	25 772	51 727	18.7	10.0	6.7	5.0
District 6	207 616	17.4	95.7	47.2	37 427	80 873	37.4	4.2	3.1	1.3
District 7	154 652	13.5	82.6	26.0	24 072	47 639	15.6	13.5	11.2	5.1
CONNECTICUT	933 817	21.6	88.0	33.7	34 048	63 422	27.8	8.3	5.9	5.6
District 1	181 061	18.9	86.6	29.8	29 644	57 757	22.8	9.9	7.0	7.6
District 2	191 595	17.8	89.7	31.3	31 046	64 708	26.7	5.9	3.6	3.5
District 3	193 090	27.4	88.6	30.9	28 535	57 845	23.3	8.9	6.9	5.8
District 4	192 306	27.2	88.2	43.9	49 052	78 014	39.3	7.8	5.6	4.8
District 5	175 765	16.2	87.1	32.8	32 154	62 510	27.6	8.7	6.3	6.4
DELAWARE	219 609	22.4	85.5	27.0	26 812	52 833	19.7	11.1	7.6	6.9
At Large	219 609	22.4	85.5	27.0	26 812	52 833	19.7	11.1	7.6	6.9
DISTRICT OF COLUMBIA	150 402	36.3	84.3	45.9	37 043	51 847	25.7	19.6	16.3	9.1
Delegate District (At Large)	150 402	36.3	84.3	45.9	37 043	51 847	25.7	19.6	16.3	9.1
FLORIDA	4 269 632	18.1	84.5	25.3	25 297	45 495	15.7	12.6	9.0	7.4
District 1	161 238	13.7	85.6	23.2	23 254	45 824	12.5	14.1	10.6	8.8
District 2	183 339	10.8	82.6	24.7	22 651	41 746	13.0	17.1	11.5	8.6
District 3	177 617	14.0	78.6	15.0	16 460	32 373	6.1	22.8	17.3	12.1
District 4	170 445	20.4	87.0	27.1	26 134	51 585	17.8	10.6	7.3	4.3
District 5	171 874	15.7	84.5	17.9	22 909	44 714	12.0	9.3	6.6	4.0
District 6	191 568	15.5	86.7	22.8	23 050	44 233	13.2	12.8	7.4	4.6
District 7	185 320	20.6	89.2	27.0	28 278	47 595	17.2	10.4	7.4	4.8
District 8	179 467	21.9	87.6	30.2	26 228	48 835	17.0	10.0	7.1	4.6
District 9	187 158	20.3	87.8	28.3	27 718	47 840	18.9	9.7	7.1	4.2
District 10	118 543	18.5	87.6	26.5	27 454	41 624	13.9	11.2	7.3	4.3
District 11	162 820	13.6	82.2	23.7	22 627	37 721	11.4	19.0	15.3	9.3
District 12	176 789	16.4	81.9	19.0	21 257	43 116	11.3	12.7	9.9	6.4
District 13	132 180	18.0	86.5	25.6	28 478	46 176	15.8	11.0	7.2	3.0
District 14	147 779	14.8	86.7	26.9	32 423	50 590	19.5	8.5	5.5	3.2
District 15	168 940	18.9	87.9	24.5	25 609	45 516	14.6	9.9	7.2	4.7
District 16	162 432	13.5	84.5	22.4	25 934	46 572	15.7	9.9	7.5	5.2
District 17	206 207	13.9	74.2	16.1	15 762	35 037	8.1	21.1	16.9	21.1
District 18	135 858	28.6	76.4	31.5	28 560	39 649	17.9	16.8	13.0	16.2
District 19	152 190	19.9	87.9	29.4	29 231	48 370	18.6	8.2	5.2	5.7
District 20	165 507	27.2	88.8	35.2	32 089	52 378	22.8	9.6	6.6	5.3
District 21	180 338	19.5	77.9	27.3	22 031	45 220	17.8	13.8	10.8	18.1
District 22	146 252	29.6	90.8	36.3	38 851	61 093	27.4	7.8	5.2	4.1
District 23	187 164	13.2	75.3	16.1	17 190	38 041	8.6	21.0	17.0	18.5
District 24	189 526	18.9	90.0	28.2	27 092	51 217	18.1	10.7	6.7	3.6
District 25	229 081	18.7	78.2	25.4	20 477	51 474	18.2	11.8	9.6	14.9
GEORGIA[13]	2 543 457	15.5	82.2	26.6	23 716	46 832	16.8	14.7	11.1	8.1
District 1	183 584	11.7	82.4	19.9	21 146	42 840	12.1	15.9	12.4	8.2
District 2	183 913	8.6	76.2	15.3	17 093	31 296	8.1	25.0	20.8	16.8
District 3	170 753	11.7	74.1	14.0	16 189	32 916	7.8	22.8	17.3	14.5
District 4	182 136	23.6	86.0	35.9	25 778	50 285	17.9	14.1	9.7	5.7
District 5	173 843	24.2	84.4	41.1	31 451	45 103	20.9	20.2	16.0	8.7

[5]All persons 3 years old and over enrolled in nursery school through college.
[6]Persons 25 years old and over.
[13]Data are for 109th congressional districts. The boundaries for districts for the 110th Congress have changed.

Table A. 110th Congressional Districts—Continued

(Number, percent.)

STATE Congressional district	Total	Total occupied units	Owner-occupied units						Median cost as percent of income	
			Percent owner-occupied units	Median value (dollars)	Percent valued at $500,000 or more	Median real estate taxes (dollars)	Median monthly costs (dollars)	Percent with second mortgage or home equity loan	With a mortgage	Without a mortgage
	47	48	49	50	51	52	53	54	55	56
CALIFORNIA—Continued										
District 41	313 522	258 892	70.0	330 300	13.4	1 482	1 239	18.0	29.6	13.6
District 42	224 010	217 053	78.1	670 900	78.5	3 496	2 223	32.4	29.1	10.0
District 43	205 773	192 897	61.3	375 400	15.8	1 657	1 493	16.7	34.5	11.1
District 44	259 086	247 888	66.8	528 700	53.8	2 632	1 980	26.6	32.3	11.7
District 45	346 106	278 391	69.6	392 900	27.9	2 194	1 484	20.5	34.6	13.7
District 46	254 894	241 656	62.5	734 600	80.2	2 868	1 901	23.2	29.6	9.8
District 47	158 632	152 064	49.1	563 000	65.2	2 098	1 685	18.4	33.7	9.8
District 48	283 394	263 019	65.1	762 800	77.3	3 784	2 242	28.8	30.0	12.4
District 49	260 762	242 837	68.8	470 300	43.2	2 610	1 830	27.2	33.8	13.2
District 50	272 792	254 837	65.4	652 100	71.6	3 216	2 118	28.0	29.5	10.4
District 51	221 251	200 120	59.4	444 100	38.5	1 711	1 596	23.6	34.9	11.2
District 52	252 764	239 044	66.6	563 200	60.5	2 446	1 894	30.8	29.7	11.3
District 53	281 027	251 953	36.3	549 600	55.8	2 379	1 695	25.1	32.6	11.3
COLORADO	2 095 235	1 846 988	68.7	232 900	10.9	1 347	1 317	26.8	25.8	11.4
District 1	299 233	272 044	54.6	235 400	12.3	1 231	1 291	24.9	28.2	12.1
District 2	319 105	257 853	70.9	271 000	18.0	1 661	1 516	29.4	26.8	12.4
District 3	324 609	265 023	70.4	173 600	10.8	805	886	18.5	25.2	11.5
District 4	292 477	261 155	67.3	213 500	6.9	1 297	1 213	27.5	25.3	11.8
District 5	292 065	257 331	70.2	203 800	6.3	899	1 206	25.1	24.9	9.6
District 6	288 278	274 205	82.8	297 100	15.6	2 071	1 721	34.2	24.6	9.9
District 7	279 468	259 377	64.7	221 300	4.5	1 454	1 307	26.0	27.4	12.3
CONNECTICUT	1 432 250	1 325 443	69.5	298 900	20.1	4 049	1 527	22.7	26.3	16.2
District 1	291 896	272 451	66.2	236 800	5.3	3 770	1 379	20.8	25.7	15.8
District 2	291 327	267 234	74.7	259 600	10.9	3 373	1 412	23.0	25.1	14.2
District 3	288 470	268 169	66.7	284 200	10.0	3 993	1 487	21.3	26.8	18.6
District 4	269 652	251 808	69.7	596 700	58.7	6 022	2 148	25.6	28.0	16.6
District 5	290 905	265 781	70.4	296 000	17.5	4 035	1 490	22.8	26.0	16.9
DELAWARE	382 866	320 110	74.4	227 100	8.0	863	1 003	19.4	23.3	11.6
At Large	382 866	320 110	74.4	227 100	8.0	863	1 003	19.4	23.3	11.6
DISTRICT OF COLUMBIA	282 900	250 456	45.8	437 700	41.6	1 612	1 558	21.9	25.0	10.8
Delegate District (At Large)	282 900	250 456	45.8	437 700	41.6	1 612	1 558	21.9	25.0	10.8
FLORIDA	8 531 860	7 106 042	70.3	230 600	12.8	1 703	1 045	17.1	28.1	14.2
District 1	311 163	267 567	70.8	167 900	5.8	911	814	15.9	23.7	10.8
District 2	357 761	271 750	64.8	165 400	8.1	966	772	13.5	23.9	11.2
District 3	294 637	257 343	51.1	130 700	2.2	873	764	12.1	26.5	11.8
District 4	306 699	265 382	71.2	198 700	8.4	1 440	996	19.5	23.2	11.2
District 5	404 085	343 260	83.9	175 300	4.5	1 228	758	14.0	26.3	12.1
District 6	335 937	298 085	71.7	169 200	4.0	1 296	845	15.2	24.0	11.8
District 7	362 341	312 548	73.0	234 900	12.2	1 623	1 055	17.8	26.2	13.9
District 8	340 159	294 024	66.0	235 100	12.1	1 728	1 136	19.1	26.9	12.6
District 9	357 098	312 495	73.8	221 000	9.5	1 822	1 090	19.1	27.2	14.4
District 10	344 688	277 705	71.0	206 200	13.3	1 492	950	18.9	28.1	15.9
District 11	304 385	268 097	56.2	181 100	7.6	1 434	1 025	16.2	27.6	14.9
District 12	347 527	303 001	70.5	167 000	2.8	1 329	889	14.9	26.7	13.2
District 13	413 115	328 098	77.1	259 400	18.0	1 756	943	16.5	28.4	15.1
District 14	508 471	353 359	76.2	311 800	23.7	2 071	1 129	16.9	29.2	14.5
District 15	387 079	315 701	74.4	229 200	10.3	1 587	1 033	16.8	28.2	14.0
District 16	383 939	301 592	81.5	232 200	13.7	1 699	942	15.7	28.7	14.8
District 17	252 424	224 044	55.0	231 100	4.8	1 715	1 207	13.4	35.0	15.9
District 18	330 971	259 456	51.7	407 700	36.6	3 274	1 496	17.0	34.2	18.1
District 19	370 353	306 705	81.4	264 500	13.2	2 080	1 032	16.5	30.6	18.1
District 20	340 546	276 906	72.5	324 300	23.2	2 756	1 441	21.1	31.7	19.5
District 21	238 932	221 315	64.9	330 000	19.1	2 727	1 449	18.8	32.3	18.4
District 22	379 177	293 590	74.1	400 500	34.2	3 183	1 510	21.2	31.4	16.5
District 23	262 598	225 884	56.2	221 600	5.1	1 595	1 149	17.9	33.3	17.2
District 24	333 745	287 100	76.3	240 000	9.9	1 754	1 106	19.5	26.6	13.5
District 25	264 030	241 035	72.3	329 700	14.6	2 576	1 534	20.1	33.2	16.6
GEORGIA[13]	3 873 405	3 376 763	67.7	156 800	5.9	1 151	1 033	18.8	23.9	11.7
District 1	293 145	251 159	68.4	115 800	5.4	755	693	12.5	21.5	10.9
District 2	276 052	237 465	59.2	87 500	2.0	556	591	10.5	21.7	12.1
District 3	272 264	226 324	65.9	83 900	1.1	542	603	9.7	21.7	12.5
District 4	283 322	251 746	59.4	187 700	7.2	1 822	1 332	22.5	25.9	13.1
District 5	324 059	262 381	48.4	229 900	18.9	2 299	1 462	25.0	26.3	15.4

[13]Data are for 109th congressional districts. The boundaries for districts for the 110th Congress have changed.

Table A. 110th Congressional Districts—*Continued*

(Number, percent.)

STATE Congressional district	Housing units, 2006—*Continued*			Civilian labor force, 2006			Civilian employment and occupation, 2006			
	Renter-occupied units		Sub-standard housing units (percent)[7]	Total	Unemployment		Total civilian employment	Management, professional, and related (percent)	Service, sales, and office (percent)	Construction and production (percent)
	Median gross rent (dollars)	Median gross rent as a percent of income			Total	Rate[8]				
	57	58	59	60	61	62	63	64	65	66
CALIFORNIA—*Continued*										
District 41	905	34.8	6.1	341 384	25 793	7.6	315 591	28.4	44.4	27.0
District 42	1 360	34.2	3.8	355 883	16 640	4.7	339 243	43.0	41.5	15.5
District 43	921	34.4	14.0	332 174	23 327	7.0	308 847	18.1	43.1	38.6
District 44	1 110	32.3	7.7	419 663	31 506	7.5	388 157	31.0	43.5	25.2
District 45	949	35.6	6.7	367 576	26 397	7.2	341 179	25.6	48.4	24.1
District 46	1 318	30.0	4.6	343 183	15 245	4.4	327 938	43.6	42.0	14.3
District 47	1 116	35.1	27.2	312 595	18 810	6.0	293 785	17.3	45.2	36.6
District 48	1 626	29.3	4.1	358 969	13 183	3.7	345 786	52.6	38.4	8.9
District 49	1 176	35.5	7.3	345 910	18 060	5.2	327 850	29.2	43.0	26.9
District 50	1 318	32.6	5.4	358 672	16 124	4.5	342 548	45.8	39.0	14.6
District 51	920	35.4	10.3	288 819	19 013	6.6	269 806	26.4	48.5	23.6
District 52	1 151	31.2	3.2	324 836	14 555	4.5	310 281	42.5	40.6	16.8
District 53	1 053	31.9	7.2	332 578	18 343	5.5	314 235	39.5	42.6	17.8
COLORADO	780	30.2	2.5	2 574 211	141 560	5.5	2 432 651	37.0	41.8	20.6
District 1	722	31.2	3.5	331 669	22 001	6.6	309 668	36.7	42.0	21.2
District 2	943	31.9	2.6	392 240	18 416	4.7	373 824	39.4	41.8	18.6
District 3	699	28.8	2.9	355 786	18 329	5.2	337 457	30.6	43.0	25.3
District 4	718	29.2	2.2	370 450	19 608	5.3	350 842	35.7	39.0	23.3
District 5	736	29.5	2.0	344 600	21 291	6.2	323 309	36.6	44.7	18.6
District 6	973	27.9	0.9	421 572	17 765	4.2	403 807	46.8	40.3	12.7
District 7	766	32.3	3.5	357 894	24 150	6.7	333 744	30.9	42.4	26.5
CONNECTICUT	886	30.0	2.1	1 880 178	115 890	6.2	1 764 288	38.6	42.3	18.9
District 1	817	28.8	2.2	380 052	26 521	7.0	353 531	37.1	43.4	19.4
District 2	860	28.6	1.5	385 545	22 081	5.7	363 464	37.1	43.6	19.0
District 3	917	32.8	2.3	386 461	25 697	6.6	360 764	37.7	42.1	20.1
District 4	1 092	31.7	2.6	353 715	18 827	5.3	334 888	43.2	41.7	15.1
District 5	819	29.1	2.1	374 405	22 764	6.1	351 641	38.3	40.8	20.7
DELAWARE	830	29.5	1.5	432 376	25 512	5.9	406 864	35.2	44.1	20.3
At Large	830	29.5	1.5	432 376	25 512	5.9	406 864	35.2	44.1	20.3
DISTRICT OF COLUMBIA	914	29.1	3.1	315 088	26 728	8.5	288 360	56.1	36.4	7.2
Delegate District (At Large)	914	29.1	3.1	315 088	26 728	8.5	288 360	56.1	36.4	7.2
FLORIDA	872	33.1	2.8	8 825 330	481 222	5.5	8 344 108	31.5	46.5	21.3
District 1	744	31.1	1.7	311 802	17 453	5.6	294 349	30.9	44.4	24.5
District 2	754	32.9	1.8	331 665	20 283	6.1	311 382	33.0	45.0	20.8
District 3	722	32.5	4.2	324 924	26 784	8.2	298 140	22.6	50.6	26.2
District 4	792	28.6	2.0	358 519	17 908	5.0	340 611	33.9	43.7	22.0
District 5	753	28.7	2.7	377 464	24 682	6.5	352 782	28.7	45.9	24.5
District 6	793	30.0	1.7	361 307	22 998	6.4	338 309	32.9	45.0	21.1
District 7	890	32.2	1.4	387 172	15 706	4.1	371 466	34.2	45.2	20.2
District 8	940	32.9	2.0	396 603	21 422	5.4	375 181	34.4	46.6	18.8
District 9	854	33.5	1.4	375 450	19 005	5.1	356 445	37.7	45.4	16.0
District 10	804	32.6	1.5	300 784	13 445	4.5	287 339	33.8	46.0	20.1
District 11	776	32.9	3.7	347 206	23 443	6.8	323 763	28.7	48.7	22.2
District 12	791	29.3	3.9	367 959	20 601	5.6	347 358	27.7	43.9	26.4
District 13	934	34.1	2.3	339 486	14 400	4.2	325 086	32.1	43.2	22.9
District 14	978	31.5	2.8	382 742	14 573	3.8	368 169	30.1	45.8	23.8
District 15	880	34.2	1.8	368 500	19 808	5.4	348 692	31.2	46.6	21.7
District 16	961	32.1	2.1	353 038	17 653	5.0	335 385	28.6	45.9	22.8
District 17	816	36.7	7.3	326 114	28 658	8.8	297 456	21.8	53.9	24.2
District 18	871	37.5	4.2	322 237	12 791	4.0	309 446	33.2	46.0	20.3
District 19	1 139	33.6	2.7	341 739	18 012	5.3	323 727	33.4	48.5	17.9
District 20	1 090	32.6	1.9	348 543	14 836	4.3	333 707	38.3	45.9	15.6
District 21	956	38.2	4.6	331 408	16 474	5.0	314 934	30.2	47.2	22.5
District 22	1 169	31.9	1.4	359 599	14 879	4.1	344 720	39.9	45.1	14.7
District 23	896	35.5	6.5	344 042	27 687	8.0	316 355	21.8	52.0	25.1
District 24	929	33.3	1.8	378 957	16 977	4.5	361 980	35.4	45.7	18.8
District 25	1 039	37.9	4.4	388 070	20 744	5.3	367 326	29.4	47.2	21.4
GEORGIA[13]	738	30.0	2.2	4 692 262	326 019	6.9	4 366 243	33.2	41.1	25.1
District 1	612	25.7	2.0	306 766	17 754	5.8	289 012	29.8	39.6	28.7
District 2	552	32.6	2.9	284 332	25 347	8.9	258 985	27.1	42.2	28.7
District 3	533	30.2	1.9	275 949	22 561	8.2	253 388	25.5	43.0	29.8
District 4	849	29.7	2.4	374 052	33 840	9.0	340 212	38.3	40.7	20.9
District 5	826	31.1	2.5	369 965	31 835	8.6	338 130	41.2	42.9	15.8

[7]Overcrowded or lacking complete plumbing facilities.
[8]Percent of civilian labor force.
[13]Data are for 109th congressional districts. The boundaries for districts for the 110th Congress have changed.

Table A. 110th Congressional Districts—*Continued*

(Number, percent.)

STATE Congressional district	Social Security Beneficiaries (OASDI), December 2006							Supplemental Security Income, December 2006			
	Total	Rate per 1,000 population	Retired workers[9]	Disabled workers	Widow(er)s[10]	Spouses[11]	Children[12]	Total	Aged	Blind	Disabled
	67	68	69	70	71	72	73	74	75	76	77
CALIFORNIA—*Continued*											
District 41	120 274	156.2	76 862	16 277	10 343	6 453	10 339	26 382	4 618	553	21 211
District 42	69 943	101.7	48 369	6 110	6 045	4 594	4 825	10 780	5 543	161	5 076
District 43	61 754	84.7	31 497	10 718	5 998	3 866	9 675	28 097	5 915	545	21 637
District 44	79 512	96.0	49 571	10 108	7 333	4 889	7 611	17 592	4 703	358	12 531
District 45	130 892	158.4	90 503	14 106	10 260	7 151	8 872	21 411	5 391	407	15 613
District 46	97 137	150.7	69 860	7 298	8 501	6 672	4 806	15 695	6 248	255	9 192
District 47	45 675	70.4	27 233	6 325	3 948	3 448	4 721	22 881	9 004	368	13 509
District 48	87 384	126.7	63 348	5 679	8 341	5 991	4 025	8 728	4 195	131	4 402
District 49	103 647	138.4	70 857	10 452	8 771	6 399	7 168	13 885	3 709	273	9 903
District 50	91 089	128.2	63 866	7 623	8 496	6 257	4 847	11 521	4 389	228	6 904
District 51	91 089	133.2	54 191	10 961	9 712	7 962	8 263	35 025	13 537	587	20 901
District 52	94 668	145.5	61 004	11 915	8 598	5 662	7 489	17 366	3 454	322	13 590
District 53	66 834	103.9	42 958	9 420	6 620	4 089	3 747	21 336	5 017	434	15 885
COLORADO	600 316	126.3	392 178	75 836	54 252	34 753	43 297	56 944	8 663	527	47 754
District 1	78 057	125.1	50 837	11 769	7 056	3 649	4 746	13 007	2 554	98	10 355
District 2	65 682	96.4	43 755	8 061	5 366	3 593	4 907	4 659	792	42	3 825
District 3	117 854	174.2	74 647	15 596	11 459	7 277	8 875	12 988	1 585	100	11 303
District 4	93 583	135.9	61 174	11 025	9 120	5 960	6 304	7 426	949	60	6 417
District 5	89 155	131.1	56 457	11 843	8 213	5 645	6 997	7 399	738	93	6 568
District 6	72 772	97.7	50 446	6 647	5 809	4 315	5 555	3 131	674	43	2 414
District 7	83 213	126.4	54 862	10 895	7 229	4 314	5 913	8 334	1 371	91	6 872
CONNECTICUT	587 292	167.6	408 611	67 281	46 686	23 213	41 501	53 318	6 724	467	46 127
District 1	126 109	181.0	87 463	15 136	9 344	4 288	9 878	14 717	2 035	146	12 536
District 2	118 210	167.3	81 735	13 730	9 713	5 066	7 966	6 766	599	66	6 101
District 3	121 604	171.5	83 889	15 016	9 806	4 259	8 634	11 385	1 207	86	10 092
District 4	103 781	149.5	74 358	8 875	8 639	5 383	6 526	8 954	1 611	73	7 270
District 5	117 588	168.5	81 166	14 524	9 184	4 217	8 497	11 496	1 272	96	10 128
DELAWARE	153 544	179.9	100 779	21 685	12 666	6 465	11 949	14 069	1 315	105	12 649
At Large	153 544	179.9	100 779	21 685	12 666	6 465	11 949	14 069	1 315	105	12 649
DISTRICT OF COLUMBIA	71 231	122.5	45 919	10 233	6 211	2 045	6 823	21 672	1 963	152	19 557
Delegate District (At Large)	71 231	122.5	45 919	10 233	6 211	2 045	6 823	21 672	1 963	152	19 557
FLORIDA	3 444 546	190.4	2 349 812	407 268	286 449	170 863	230 154	428 143	100 649	2 773	324 721
District 1	125 449	184.2	75 767	18 988	12 592	7 665	10 437	15 164	1 260	131	13 773
District 2	119 619	174.2	74 055	18 139	11 249	5 693	10 483	17 520	1 732	130	15 658
District 3	104 255	153.4	57 979	21 049	8 914	3 447	12 866	29 007	2 699	212	26 096
District 4	101 294	143.5	64 059	14 235	9 761	5 015	8 224	11 240	1 508	106	9 626
District 5	254 055	298.0	182 404	28 811	17 610	11 918	13 312	14 557	1 556	94	12 907
District 6	154 087	205.0	104 649	19 058	12 231	7 361	10 788	13 386	1 401	119	11 866
District 7	160 935	206.9	109 546	19 441	13 545	7 690	10 713	12 450	1 579	131	10 740
District 8	118 970	159.3	76 824	16 359	10 456	5 896	9 435	14 651	2 368	94	12 189
District 9	151 264	195.9	103 075	18 686	13 250	6 767	9 486	10 355	1 388	55	8 912
District 10	146 328	235.5	101 129	18 343	13 584	6 023	7 249	10 181	1 397	77	8 707
District 11	102 318	154.7	59 657	19 095	9 218	3 888	10 460	27 925	4 036	177	23 712
District 12	150 609	195.2	97 302	21 499	12 487	6 877	12 444	19 136	1 954	91	17 091
District 13	193 852	263.3	144 427	15 468	15 603	10 238	8 116	8 240	1 148	69	7 023
District 14	192 212	236.3	143 216	15 115	14 306	11 180	8 395	8 835	1 379	67	7 389
District 15	167 860	219.5	114 737	19 687	13 799	8 888	10 749	13 085	1 730	69	11 286
District 16	183 515	240.4	133 326	17 352	13 883	9 396	9 558	9 802	1 521	62	8 219
District 17	82 158	121.4	49 420	13 057	6 428	3 382	9 871	29 985	7 955	188	21 842
District 18	112 918	176.8	80 659	10 865	8 546	7 189	5 659	42 843	19 586	177	23 080
District 19	180 530	248.1	139 558	11 176	15 469	8 359	5 968	6 764	2 212	43	4 509
District 20	109 924	163.4	77 169	10 921	10 401	5 239	6 194	11 067	3 795	51	7 221
District 21	96 280	144.7	68 567	8 554	6 698	6 462	5 999	34 160	18 481	183	15 496
District 22	128 286	185.3	94 127	9 601	11 914	7 232	5 412	5 974	1 837	50	4 087
District 23	96 421	139.3	58 231	15 963	7 639	3 280	11 308	23 375	3 923	193	19 259
District 24	130 787	176.5	87 241	16 538	10 976	6 570	9 462	10 191	1 395	82	8 714
District 25	80 620	101.2	52 688	9 268	5 890	5 208	7 566	28 250	12 809	122	15 319
GEORGIA[13]	1 269 987	135.6	764 680	205 249	119 007	53 344	127 707	206 098	26 809	1 972	177 317
District 1	106 850	156.7	60 997	19 127	10 661	5 086	10 979	18 335	1 983	156	16 196
District 2	108 696	168.0	60 360	19 974	11 799	4 475	12 088	27 917	3 434	263	24 220
District 3	116 691	182.2	73 315	17 300	10 327	4 686	11 063	13 597	1 634	152	11 811
District 4	65 058	95.2	38 396	10 503	5 440	2 443	8 276	12 106	1 888	133	10 085
District 5	75 343	111.8	45 330	12 848	7 329	2 657	7 179	19 857	2 554	201	17 102

[9]Includes special age-72 beneficiaries.
[10]Includes nondisabled widow(er)s, disabled widow(er)s, widowed mothers and fathers, and parents receiving payment on the record of a worker who is deceased.
[11]These beneficiaries receive payment on the record of a worker who is retired or disabled.
[12]These beneficiaries receive payment on the record of a worker who is retired, deceased, or disabled.
[13]Data are for 109th congressional districts. The boundaries for districts for the 110th Congress have changed.

Table A. 110th Congressional Districts—*Continued*

(Number, percent.)

STATE Congressional district	Total farms	Farms by size (percent)			Land in farms		Percent of farms where principal operator's primary occupation is farming	Value of all agricultural products sold				Payments from federal farm programs		
		1 to 49 acres	50 to 999 acres	1,000 acres or more	Total acreage	Average size of farms (acres)		Total ($1,000)	Percent of farms with value of:			Total ($1,000)	Number of farms that receive payments	Percent of farms that receive payments
									Less than $50,000	$50,000 to $249,999	$250,000 or more			
	78	79	80	81	82	83	84	85	86	87	88	89	90	91
CALIFORNIA—*Continued*														
District 41	1 061	76.1	21.2	2.7	493 098	465	50.8	296 111	79.8	11.1	9.0	459	31	2.9
District 42	242	84.7	13.2	2.1	16 154	67	51.2	125 169	68.2	11.2	20.7	409	17	7.0
District 43	223	76.2	22.9	0.9	17 463	78	67.7	243 456	46.6	9.4	43.9	753	29	13.0
District 44	962	88.7	10.3	1.0	38 917	40	45.8	188 940	84.3	6.4	9.3	411	19	2.0
District 45	1 379	74.5	20.4	5.0	408 381	296	54.6	601 166	70.3	14.7	15.0	991	52	3.8
District 46	57	77.2	22.8	0.0	1 963	34	57.9	26 226	57.9	17.5	24.6	. . .	2	3.5
District 47	31	80.6	19.4	0.0	855	28	41.9	15 819	71.0	9.7	19.4	21	3	9.7
District 48	106	70.8	26.4	2.8	60 185	568	49.1	190 295	67.0	5.7	27.4	. . .	2	1.9
District 49	3 694	90.0	8.9	1.1	273 023	74	52.5	664 262	79.5	13.7	6.8	452	33	0.9
District 50	912	90.0	9.2	0.8	41 120	45	52.3	212 248	73.2	13.4	13.4	74	5	0.5
District 51	663	33.3	42.7	24.0	548 162	827	74.8	1 066 057	35.4	16.4	48.1	3 301	174	26.2
District 52	1 037	85.8	12.2	1.9	121 241	117	45.9	103 665	83.3	10.7	6.0	76	10	1.0
District 53	61	80.3	19.7	0.0	3 493	57	36.1	6 695	90.2	4.9	4.9	. . .	2	3.3
COLORADO	31 369	32.8	47.7	19.5	31 093 336	991	58.4	4 525 196	80.5	13.5	5.9	125 774	10 163	32.4
District 1	21	61.9	33.3	4.8	3 466	165	57.1	. . .	71.4	14.3	14.3	. . .	4	19.0
District 2	1 158	49.2	41.3	9.5	517 949	447	50.7	58 154	88.8	7.6	3.6	. . .	141	12.2
District 3	12 015	36.8	48.7	14.5	11 532 734	960	57.2	781 245	84.1	11.5	4.4	18 330	2 659	22.1
District 4	12 156	22.2	48.9	28.9	15 135 952	1 245	62.9	3 456 724	70.9	19.6	9.5	97 872	6 317	52.0
District 5	2 418	42.2	45.3	12.5	1 516 812	627	53.8	61 158	92.4	5.6	2.0	998	320	13.2
District 6	2 754	42.1	46.9	10.9	1 676 376	609	51.9	. . .	93.4	5.3	1.3	3 701	463	16.8
District 7	847	47.3	35.7	17.0	710 047	838	57.1	106 077	80.8	12.4	6.8	3 840	259	30.6
CONNECTICUT	4 191	62.3	37.1	0.6	357 154	85	49.6	470 637	85.0	9.1	5.8	3 681	254	6.1
District 1	579	67.9	31.4	0.7	39 192	68	49.4	79 971	82.9	9.8	7.3	305	20	3.5
District 2	2 011	57.9	41.3	0.8	183 720	91	48.8	267 705	85.5	8.7	5.9	2 208	147	7.3
District 3	389	71.5	28.3	0.3	21 617	56	55.3	20 755	85.3	8.7	5.9	324	19	4.9
District 4	201	76.6	23.4	0.0	7 711	38	45.8	24 218	82.1	10.0	8.0	4	3	1.5
District 5	1 011	61.3	38.1	0.6	104 914	104	49.8	77 988	85.9	9.7	4.5	840	65	6.4
DELAWARE	2 391	52.3	41.8	5.9	540 080	226	69.4	618 853	49.6	15.7	34.7	8 643	617	25.8
At Large	2 391	52.3	41.8	5.9	540 080	226	69.4	618 853	49.6	15.7	34.7	8 643	617	25.8
DISTRICT OF COLUMBIA	. . .	. . .	. . .	. . .	. . .	. . .	. . .	. . .	. . .	. . .	. . .	. . .	. . .	. . .
Delegate District (At Large)	. . .	. . .	. . .	. . .	. . .	. . .	. . .	. . .	. . .	. . .	. . .	. . .	. . .	. . .
FLORIDA	44 081	64.9	31.3	3.8	10 414 877	236	52.2	6 242 272	82.8	10.4	6.8	21 818	2 554	5.8
District 1	3 230	47.6	50.9	1.5	417 786	129	50.3	98 006	90.9	6.0	3.1	6 933	809	25.0
District 2	3 857	45.7	50.4	3.9	899 330	233	51.7	376 327	87.2	6.3	6.5	6 744	741	19.2
District 3	1 280	70.5	27.8	1.7	233 062	182	54.1	177 597	79.8	11.0	9.2	156	28	2.2
District 4	2 615	51.0	46.1	2.9	480 130	184	49.1	160 033	89.5	5.5	5.0	1 346	317	12.1
District 5	5 182	68.6	28.7	2.7	807 182	156	51.9	272 377	89.8	7.2	3.0	1 512	138	2.7
District 6	5 073	68.7	29.3	2.0	622 805	123	54.1	247 344	91.9	4.9	3.1	1 326	199	3.9
District 7	1 102	73.2	23.4	3.4	187 718	170	45.2	161 400	81.3	9.2	9.5	102	16	1.5
District 8	1 403	77.4	21.2	1.4	98 812	70	52.0	138 264	85.9	9.4	4.7	134	22	1.6
District 9	1 826	81.8	17.3	1.0	132 013	72	52.8	199 927	85.0	8.9	6.1	115	22	1.2
District 10	78	94.9	5.1	0.0	. . .	. . .	43.6	7 007	88.5	7.7	3.8	18	4	5.1
District 11	290	74.8	24.1	1.0	28 538	98	51.4	72 008	82.4	10.7	6.9	26	3	1.0
District 12	3 690	67.4	29.0	3.6	700 744	190	53.4	422 102	72.4	20.4	7.3	531	42	1.1
District 13	3 502	57.9	35.4	6.7	1 156 599	330	52.4	632 290	75.9	15.6	8.5	409	38	1.1
District 14	730	74.5	20.3	5.2	162 548	223	50.3	201 688	82.5	9.6	7.9	. . .	16	2.2
District 15	1 359	65.2	26.6	8.2	1 015 972	748	55.3	218 552	75.7	14.9	9.4	304	27	2.0
District 16	3 409	58.3	31.7	10.1	2 338 369	686	54.2	1 093 314	74.5	14.7	10.8	884	58	1.7
District 17	5	100.0	0.0	0.0	. . .	. . .	20.0	649	20.0	60.0	20.0	. . .	. . .	. . .
District 18	505	90.7	8.9	0.4	15 368	30	52.1	88 195	76.8	12.7	10.5	. . .	9	1.8
District 19	261	89.3	9.2	1.5	21 560	83	52.1	163 438	67.4	11.5	21.1	. . .	4	1.5
District 20	271	93.7	5.9	0.4	8 047	30	47.2	25 943	83.4	10.3	6.3	163	8	3.0
District 21	46	95.7	4.3	0.0	871	19	78.3	3 950	78.3	15.2	6.5	. . .	. . .	. . .
District 22	324	87.7	12.3	0.0	8 916	28	53.4	31 439	79.9	12.0	8.0	. . .	. . .	. . .
District 23	828	55.7	30.7	13.6	730 595	882	58.9	622 969	62.2	19.3	18.5	838	20	2.4
District 24	1 285	81.9	16.0	2.0	126 714	99	47.9	155 873	81.6	11.2	7.2	44	16	1.2
District 25	1 930	85.5	12.3	2.1	220 096	114	51.1	671 577	72.4	13.2	14.4	84	17	0.9
GEORGIA[13]	49 311	39.2	56.5	4.3	10 744 239	218	50.9	4 911 752	84.1	6.9	9.1	118 535	15 510	31.5
District 1	5 943	34.7	59.9	5.4	1 498 461	252	51.8	585 126	81.8	9.7	8.4	18 045	2 179	36.7
District 2	6 925	29.5	59.3	11.2	2 973 040	429	53.4	944 223	76.3	12.3	11.4	50 009	3 382	48.8
District 3	8 461	27.4	66.8	5.8	2 284 878	270	47.7	671 779	86.7	6.6	6.7	24 369	3 535	41.8
District 4	39	82.1	17.9	0.0	1 108	28	48.7	857	89.7	7.7	2.6	2	4	10.3
District 5	38	71.1	28.9	0.0	2 554	67	65.8	16	100.0	0.0	0.0	29	4	10.5

[13]Data are for 109th congressional districts. The boundaries for districts for the 110th Congress have changed.

. . . = Not available.

Table A. 110th Congressional Districts—*Continued*

(Number, percent.)

STATE Congressional district	Representative	Land area,[1] (sq km)	Total population	Persons per square kilometer	Population and population characteristics, 2006							
					Race alone (percent)				Some other race (percent)	Two or more races (percent)	Hispanic or Latino[2] (percent)	Non-Hispanic White (percent)
					White	Black	American Indian/ Alaska Native	Asian and Pacific Islander				
	1	2	3	4	5	6	7	8	9	10	11	12
GEORGIA[13]—*Continued*												
District 6	Rep. Tom Price (R)	1 764	770 953	437.0	77.6	10.8	0.1	6.3	3.7	1.5	7.1	74.4
District 7	Rep. John Linder (R)	2 518	846 870	336.3	74.3	14.0	0.2	6.1	4.1	1.3	8.9	69.8
District 8	Rep. Jim Marshall (D)	18 573	787 033	42.4	76.5	18.5	0.1	1.7	1.7	1.5	3.8	74.6
District 9	Rep. Nathan Deal (R)	11 224	735 337	65.5	82.2	13.4	0.3	1.7	1.3	1.2	3.2	80.3
District 10	Rep. Paul C. Broun (R)	15 260	794 734	52.1	86.9	5.3	0.3	1.2	5.2	1.1	13.0	79.2
District 11	Rep. Phil Gingrey, (R)	6 974	679 933	97.5	58.3	31.4	0.1	1.4	7.6	1.2	10.8	55.2
District 12	Rep. John Barrow (D)	22 422	663 100	29.6	53.3	42.3	0.2	1.8	1.2	1.3	3.5	51.2
District 13	Rep. David Scott (D)	1 480	759 700	513.3	34.6	50.7	0.2	5.0	8.1	1.3	14.9	28.3
HAWAII		16 635	1 285 498	77.3	26.3	2.2	0.3	48.6	1.1	21.5	7.8	24.6
District 1	Rep. Neil Abercrombie (D)	494	623 230	1 261.6	19.9	2.8	0.2	58.8	0.8	17.6	5.3	19.1
District 2	Rep. Mazie K. Hirono (D)	16 140	662 268	41.0	32.3	1.6	0.4	39.0	1.5	25.2	10.1	29.7
IDAHO		214 314	1 466 465	6.8	92.5	0.5	1.1	1.2	2.6	2.1	9.5	86.3
District 1	Rep. Bill Sali (R)	102 369	779 833	7.6	93.0	0.4	1.1	1.1	2.2	2.3	8.5	87.1
District 2	Rep. Michael K. Simpson (R)	111 946	686 632	6.1	92.1	0.5	1.2	1.3	3.0	2.0	10.6	85.3
ILLINOIS		143 961	12 831 970	89.1	70.7	14.8	0.2	4.2	8.5	1.6	14.7	65.1
District 1	Rep. Bobby L. Rush (D)	253	643 626	2 544.0	27.6	64.4	0.2	1.5	5.3	1.0	8.5	25.0
District 2	Rep. Jesse L. Jackson Jr. (D)	478	640 930	1 340.9	22.5	68.3	0.1	0.6	6.9	1.6	11.5	18.8
District 3	Rep. Daniel Lipinski (D)	322	649 720	2 017.8	67.6	6.7	0.2	3.5	20.3	1.7	29.4	59.4
District 4	Rep. Luis V. Gutierrez (D)	101	603 695	5 977.2	31.0	5.6	0.4	3.0	58.5	1.5	73.1	17.9
District 5	Rep. Rahm Emanuel (D)	148	664 430	4 489.4	67.2	3.1	0.2	6.4	21.1	2.0	29.6	59.6
District 6	Rep. Peter J. Roskam (R)	553	661 838	1 196.8	78.3	3.4	0.4	9.1	7.1	1.6	17.6	68.6
District 7	Rep. Danny K. Davis (D)	146	626 631	4 292.0	32.1	55.8	0.1	5.4	5.2	1.2	8.0	29.4
District 8	Rep. Melissa L. Bean (D)	1 600	738 061	461.3	81.0	3.9	0.1	6.8	6.6	1.7	15.5	72.7
District 9	Rep. Janice D. Schakowsky (D)	195	638 091	3 272.3	67.3	9.7	0.1	14.4	6.7	1.8	12.3	62.3
District 10	Rep. Mark Steven Kirk (R)	646	651 007	1 007.8	81.1	4.8	0.0	7.4	5.5	1.2	14.9	72.0
District 11	Rep. Jerry Weller (R)	10 984	745 974	67.9	85.5	7.7	0.1	0.8	4.1	1.9	10.6	79.8
District 12	Rep. Jerry F. Costello (D)	11 460	651 359	56.8	79.4	17.0	0.2	1.1	1.1	1.2	2.4	78.3
District 13	Rep. Judy Biggert (R)	918	781 037	850.8	78.9	6.7	0.1	8.9	3.7	1.8	9.1	74.1
District 14	Rep. Bill Foster (D)	7 386	795 610	107.7	81.5	4.8	0.2	3.1	8.6	1.8	22.2	69.0
District 15	Rep. Timothy V. Johnson (R)	26 088	662 504	25.4	87.8	6.3	0.1	3.1	1.5	1.1	2.9	86.5
District 16	Rep. Donald A. Manzullo (R)	10 614	722 010	68.0	87.9	5.4	0.3	2.0	3.0	1.3	8.7	82.7
District 17	Rep. Phil Hare (D)	21 031	631 658	30.0	87.6	7.4	0.2	0.7	1.9	2.2	4.5	85.6
District 18	Rep. Ray LaHood (R)	21 202	655 833	30.9	89.3	7.1	0.1	1.3	0.7	1.4	2.1	88.1
District 19	Rep. John Shimkus (R)	29 833	667 956	22.4	94.1	3.3	0.2	0.6	0.4	1.3	1.2	93.5
INDIANA		92 895	6 313 520	68.0	86.0	8.7	0.2	1.3	2.4	1.4	4.7	83.8
District 1	Rep. Peter J. Visclosky (D)	5 722	702 226	122.7	72.5	18.4	0.2	1.1	6.2	1.6	11.5	67.7
District 2	Rep. Joe Donnelly (D)	9 529	678 653	71.2	84.9	8.3	0.3	0.9	3.9	1.6	6.7	82.3
District 3	Rep. Mark E. Souder (R)	8 391	714 551	85.2	87.3	5.8	0.1	1.4	3.4	2.0	6.1	85.0
District 4	Rep. Steve Buyer (R)	10 403	755 830	72.7	93.1	2.7	0.1	2.1	1.1	0.9	3.8	90.4
District 5	Rep. Dan Burton (R)	8 459	777 631	91.9	91.8	3.5	0.2	2.0	1.1	1.4	2.6	90.4
District 6	Rep. Mike Pence (R)	14 375	668 947	46.5	93.4	4.3	0.1	0.6	0.7	0.9	1.8	92.3
District 7	Rep. André Carson (D)	677	641 305	947.3	60.0	32.1	0.2	1.4	4.2	2.1	7.5	56.9
District 8	Rep. Brad Ellsworth (D)	18 238	672 590	36.9	93.8	4.0	0.1	0.7	0.4	1.0	1.1	93.2
District 9	Rep. Baron P. Hill (D)	17 101	701 787	41.0	94.2	2.3	0.2	1.3	0.9	1.2	1.9	93.2
IOWA		144 701	2 982 085	20.6	93.0	2.3	0.3	1.5	1.6	1.4	3.8	91.0
District 1	Rep. Bruce L. Braley (D)	18 691	588 403	31.5	92.5	3.9	0.2	1.2	0.8	1.4	2.4	91.1
District 2	Rep. David Loebsack (D)	19 595	600 154	30.6	92.8	2.7	0.3	1.9	1.3	1.1	3.6	90.7
District 3	Rep. Leonard L. Boswell (D)	18 076	623 821	34.5	90.3	3.3	0.4	2.0	2.0	1.9	4.6	88.2
District 4	Rep. Tom Latham (R)	40 818	591 185	14.5	95.1	0.7	0.2	1.6	1.4	1.0	3.3	93.5
District 5	Rep. Steve King (R)	47 520	578 522	12.2	94.3	0.6	0.3	1.0	2.3	1.5	5.1	91.8
KANSAS		211 900	2 764 075	13.0	85.4	5.6	0.9	2.2	3.4	2.5	8.6	81.0
District 1	Rep. Jerry Moran (R)	148 596	647 996	4.4	90.2	1.5	0.5	1.3	4.2	2.2	12.8	82.5
District 2	Rep. Nancy E. Boyda (D)	36 606	691 312	18.9	87.8	5.0	1.4	1.5	1.8	2.5	4.3	86.0
District 3	Rep. Dennis Moore (D)	2 014	737 283	366.1	81.7	8.5	0.5	3.4	3.7	2.2	9.0	76.9
District 4	Rep. Todd Tiahrt (R)	24 684	687 484	27.9	82.5	6.7	1.0	2.6	3.9	3.2	8.4	78.8
KENTUCKY		102 896	4 206 074	40.9	89.5	7.4	0.2	1.0	0.8	1.2	2.0	88.3
District 1	Rep. Ed Whitfield (R)	30 259	673 899	22.3	90.3	6.6	0.3	0.6	1.1	1.1	1.8	89.5
District 2	Rep. Ron Lewis (R)	19 598	728 259	37.2	91.1	5.8	0.2	0.8	0.7	1.3	2.3	89.6
District 3	Rep. John A. Yarmuth (D)	950	681 111	717.0	75.3	20.1	0.3	2.0	1.0	1.3	2.5	73.9
District 4	Rep. Geoff Davis (R)	14 707	716 879	48.7	94.5	2.8	0.2	0.8	0.7	1.0	1.5	93.9
District 5	Rep. Harold Rogers (R)	27 652	684 339	24.7	97.5	1.2	0.2	0.3	0.2	0.6	. . .	. . .
District 6	Rep. Ben Chandler (D)	9 729	721 587	74.2	87.7	8.0	0.2	1.5	1.0	1.6	3.1	85.7

[1]Dry land or land partially or temporarily covered by water.
[2]May be of any race.
[13]Data are for 109th congressional districts. The boundaries for districts for the 110th Congress have changed.
. . . = Not available.

Table A. 110th Congressional Districts—*Continued*

(Number, percent.)

STATE Congressional district	Percent female	Percent foreign born	Percent born in state of residence	Age (percent)								
				Under 5 years	5 to 18 years	18 to 24 years	25 to 34 years	35 to 44 years	45 to 54 years	55 to 64 years	65 to 74 years	75 years and over
	13	14	15	16	17	18	19	20	21	22	23	24
GEORGIA[13]**—Continued**												
District 6	51.3	14.0	33.2	7.1	21.1	6.8	10.1	18.0	17.2	12.1	4.3	3.4
District 7	49.9	14.3	41.4	7.9	20.8	7.8	14.4	18.5	15.0	9.2	4.1	2.4
District 8	51.3	4.8	58.6	6.7	19.3	9.6	13.8	15.5	14.9	10.4	5.3	4.4
District 9	51.2	3.6	64.4	6.4	18.5	8.7	14.0	14.9	13.9	10.7	7.1	5.8
District 10	50.3	10.3	53.0	7.8	19.3	8.2	14.6	15.9	13.8	10.2	5.9	4.3
District 11	50.6	10.1	60.0	8.3	17.7	10.0	15.5	14.9	13.3	9.3	5.9	5.0
District 12	52.3	4.0	65.7	7.6	17.1	16.8	13.7	12.9	12.3	9.1	5.5	5.0
District 13	50.8	18.4	49.0	8.3	18.8	10.4	17.3	16.5	13.1	8.6	4.3	2.8
HAWAII	50.0	16.3	55.2	6.8	16.3	9.7	13.7	14.1	14.2	11.2	6.6	7.3
District 1	50.4	21.8	53.3	6.5	15.0	9.2	13.7	14.8	13.9	11.0	7.0	8.9
District 2	49.6	11.2	56.9	7.1	17.6	10.3	13.6	13.4	14.5	11.4	6.2	5.9
IDAHO	49.8	5.6	45.1	7.7	19.2	10.4	13.6	13.1	14.0	10.4	6.1	5.5
District 1	49.7	4.6	39.5	7.2	19.4	9.0	13.7	13.9	14.1	11.0	6.3	5.4
District 2	49.9	6.8	51.5	8.2	19.0	12.1	13.5	12.2	13.8	9.8	5.9	5.5
ILLINOIS	50.8	13.8	66.9	6.9	18.1	10.0	13.8	14.6	14.4	10.1	6.0	5.9
District 1	52.7	6.7	74.2	7.4	20.0	10.1	13.3	13.5	13.3	9.7	6.7	5.8
District 2	53.7	6.9	71.9	8.4	21.3	8.4	11.5	13.4	14.0	10.3	6.8	5.9
District 3	50.3	21.7	68.8	7.8	18.3	8.9	12.1	15.1	14.4	10.5	5.8	7.1
District 4	48.2	37.8	49.9	9.5	20.6	11.0	19.8	15.3	10.8	7.2	3.2	2.7
District 5	50.6	30.9	51.2	7.2	14.5	10.4	17.3	17.0	13.6	9.4	5.5	5.1
District 6	49.7	22.2	62.1	7.0	17.2	9.8	13.1	14.5	15.8	11.0	6.1	5.5
District 7	53.0	10.0	64.7	6.7	18.1	10.5	16.0	14.6	13.7	10.0	5.5	4.9
District 8	49.8	17.7	63.6	6.9	19.9	8.9	13.9	16.4	15.7	9.8	4.7	3.8
District 9	51.0	32.6	49.4	5.8	14.1	9.6	13.3	15.2	15.4	11.7	6.9	8.0
District 10	50.7	21.1	58.6	6.6	20.4	8.5	9.3	14.5	16.5	11.0	6.8	6.4
District 11	50.7	6.7	77.9	6.5	18.2	11.7	14.5	14.4	14.2	9.5	5.5	5.4
District 12	51.3	2.2	66.9	6.3	16.9	11.0	14.3	13.4	14.2	9.9	6.6	7.2
District 13	50.9	15.2	66.7	7.0	20.9	8.2	13.2	17.1	15.4	9.6	4.6	4.0
District 14	49.4	15.2	66.7	7.9	19.3	11.2	15.2	15.2	13.3	9.1	4.7	4.1
District 15	50.3	4.3	73.5	5.9	16.0	13.9	13.6	12.5	14.1	10.0	6.8	7.2
District 16	50.7	7.8	68.9	6.7	18.8	8.9	13.1	15.4	14.5	10.2	6.0	6.3
District 17	51.3	2.3	74.6	5.7	16.3	11.0	12.6	12.5	14.6	11.3	7.5	8.6
District 18	50.8	2.2	80.5	6.1	16.3	9.6	13.0	13.3	14.8	11.5	7.5	7.8
District 19	50.3	1.2	77.5	6.4	16.7	9.5	13.2	13.6	14.7	10.7	7.4	7.9
INDIANA	50.8	4.2	68.6	6.9	18.2	9.9	13.2	14.2	14.7	10.6	6.3	6.1
District 1	51.5	5.7	58.9	6.8	18.7	9.6	12.5	13.8	15.3	11.1	6.3	6.0
District 2	50.5	5.6	67.5	6.6	18.2	9.6	12.9	13.7	15.0	11.1	6.3	6.6
District 3	50.5	4.6	70.5	7.8	19.7	8.7	13.5	14.1	14.3	10.3	5.8	5.8
District 4	49.9	4.7	70.4	6.9	18.2	11.3	14.2	14.4	14.0	9.9	5.8	5.4
District 5	51.0	4.3	68.5	6.9	19.1	8.5	13.4	15.4	14.9	10.4	5.9	5.4
District 6	50.9	1.6	74.0	6.2	17.3	9.9	12.3	13.4	14.7	11.7	7.4	7.1
District 7	51.6	6.9	68.3	8.5	17.8	8.9	14.6	15.2	14.6	9.4	5.5	5.4
District 8	50.8	1.6	76.0	6.1	16.9	10.7	12.2	13.5	15.1	11.2	7.1	7.1
District 9	51.0	2.5	63.3	6.1	17.2	11.7	13.2	14.1	14.3	10.8	6.7	6.0
IOWA	50.7	3.8	72.3	6.4	17.6	10.6	11.8	13.5	14.8	10.8	6.9	7.7
District 1	51.1	2.8	73.2	6.3	17.7	10.7	11.2	13.3	15.1	11.2	7.0	7.5
District 2	50.5	4.0	70.2	6.3	17.1	11.6	12.8	13.6	14.5	10.8	6.4	6.9
District 3	50.9	5.1	73.4	7.2	17.8	9.0	13.4	15.0	14.6	10.3	6.1	6.5
District 4	50.2	3.2	75.3	5.7	17.2	12.1	11.0	12.7	14.7	10.7	7.3	8.6
District 5	50.7	3.7	69.4	6.4	17.9	9.7	10.6	12.6	15.3	10.8	7.6	9.1
KANSAS	50.4	6.3	59.1	7.0	18.1	10.8	12.4	13.9	14.5	10.3	6.2	6.7
District 1	50.3	7.2	67.9	7.0	17.7	10.3	10.2	13.2	14.6	10.5	7.4	9.2
District 2	50.0	2.7	62.5	6.4	17.3	12.9	12.3	13.4	14.3	10.6	6.3	6.5
District 3	50.5	9.1	42.9	7.4	18.2	10.5	14.2	15.3	14.4	10.1	4.9	4.9
District 4	50.7	5.8	64.7	7.4	19.1	9.4	12.8	13.7	14.8	10.1	6.2	6.5
KENTUCKY	51.1	2.7	71.8	6.6	17.2	9.3	13.6	14.6	14.7	11.2	6.8	5.9
District 1	51.5	1.7	68.9	6.3	17.1	8.9	13.2	13.6	14.2	11.7	7.9	7.1
District 2	50.4	2.5	74.3	6.5	17.7	9.7	13.9	14.9	14.4	10.9	6.6	5.4
District 3	52.0	4.7	72.0	7.0	17.1	8.2	12.5	14.4	15.7	11.5	6.6	6.9
District 4	50.6	1.9	65.6	6.7	17.9	8.9	13.4	14.8	15.1	11.2	6.5	5.4
District 5	50.5	0.7	80.2	6.3	17.1	8.9	13.9	14.7	15.0	11.6	6.9	5.7
District 6	51.3	4.4	69.9	6.8	16.2	11.3	14.8	14.9	13.9	10.6	6.3	5.3

[13]Data are for 109th congressional districts. The boundaries for districts for the 110th Congress have changed.

Table A. 110th Congressional Districts—*Continued*

(Number, percent.)

STATE Congressional district	Households, 2006						Group quarters, 2006		Group quarters, 2000			
	Number	Average household size	Family households (percent)	Married-couple family (percent)	Female family house-holder[4] (percent)	One-person households (percent)	Total in group quarters	Percent 65 years and over	Persons in correctional institutions	Persons in nursing homes	Persons in college dormitories	Persons in military quarters
	25	26	27	28	29	30	31	32	33	34	35	36
GEORGIA[13]—*Continued*												
District 6	276 095	2.78	73.5	61.0	8.4	21.9	3 498	70.3	34	1 063	0	0
District 7	288 259	2.92	78.4	62.6	11.7	17.0	5 869	19.9	2 167	900	356	0
District 8	279 618	2.77	75.7	59.3	11.9	19.5	12 120	9.7	4 105	1 473	3 727	0
District 9	269 832	2.66	72.4	57.4	10.9	23.4	16 423	28.0	3 361	2 586	2 954	1 084
District 10	277 167	2.84	73.8	58.5	10.8	21.9	8 409	27.7	3 271	2 393	956	0
District 11	246 293	2.69	67.8	44.6	17.2	26.3	16 424	19.2	7 428	3 903	2 026	159
District 12	251 614	2.50	62.6	39.9	18.3	30.6	34 453	9.0	6 328	2 226	11 704	4 657
District 13	258 810	2.91	68.4	42.6	18.2	25.2	7 740	35.4	2 435	2 729	543	817
HAWAII	432 632	2.88	69.6	51.5	12.5	24.5	37 547	19.7	3 233	2 949	4 716	13 992
District 1	219 297	2.77	66.7	49.8	11.6	27.8	16 022	34.5	2 302	1 799	2 984	5 063
District 2	213 335	3.00	72.6	53.2	13.4	21.1	21 525	8.8	931	1 150	1 732	8 929
IDAHO	548 555	2.61	69.8	57.2	8.6	23.9	33 801	28.1	7 401	5 735	8 006	673
District 1	289 460	2.63	71.4	58.9	8.4	22.7	19 934	32.7	4 341	3 233	4 716	0
District 2	259 095	2.60	68.0	55.3	8.8	25.1	13 867	21.4	3 060	2 502	3 290	673
ILLINOIS	4 724 252	2.65	66.6	49.9	12.4	28.1	323 647	26.8	67 820	91 887	90 463	10 865
District 1	228 467	2.76	64.7	32.4	25.7	31.1	12 063	24.5	0	3 128	4 853	0
District 2	225 546	2.81	67.1	36.6	24.8	29.6	6 558	47.7	81	3 092	911	0
District 3	230 160	2.80	69.4	51.1	12.6	26.9	4 302	73.4	0	3 828	327	0
District 4	184 657	3.26	68.1	43.5	16.7	23.2	2 118	21.0	0	831	308	0
District 5	255 921	2.56	56.7	41.8	9.8	34.3	9 015	32.1	0	3 551	2 893	0
District 6	237 134	2.74	71.1	57.7	9.9	25.1	12 186	43.9	718	4 828	3 481	0
District 7	247 212	2.44	53.8	29.4	20.6	40.0	24 332	4.1	11 587	3 450	5 910	0
District 8	258 133	2.83	71.3	58.4	9.2	23.8	6 852	46.5	307	2 385	151	0
District 9	256 755	2.39	55.4	42.6	9.1	37.9	25 653	27.6	35	8 800	7 395	0
District 10	227 614	2.79	72.2	61.2	7.8	25.4	15 105	27.9	846	4 643	2 076	10 432
District 11	263 150	2.74	70.7	55.0	11.7	23.5	25 056	25.9	3 972	5 718	11 025	0
District 12	258 953	2.43	65.2	47.2	14.0	29.9	23 278	22.4	7 433	6 193	5 284	427
District 13	267 334	2.90	74.1	62.8	9.0	22.5	6 937	47.0	2 691	4 007	2 336	0
District 14	265 538	2.93	74.3	60.5	9.2	20.7	18 705	20.7	3 274	4 110	7 676	0
District 15	265 945	2.35	63.3	49.9	9.4	28.6	38 248	23.5	6 999	6 814	16 496	0
District 16	261 414	2.73	70.5	56.0	10.1	25.2	9 129	45.6	1 104	4 659	443	0
District 17	259 571	2.31	64.2	48.2	11.6	30.2	32 831	26.0	5 788	8 296	10 275	0
District 18	265 104	2.37	65.3	52.5	9.7	29.5	27 384	22.3	9 157	6 874	4 950	6
District 19	265 644	2.42	68.3	55.1	9.7	27.1	23 895	27.7	13 828	6 680	3 673	0
INDIANA	2 435 274	2.52	67.6	51.3	11.7	27.2	178 789	28.1	34 676	48 745	69 147	7
District 1	262 096	2.63	69.7	50.6	14.4	25.7	11 896	39.4	1 124	4 161	3 285	0
District 2	257 348	2.53	68.5	52.7	11.5	26.8	27 785	21.4	6 561	4 992	8 879	4
District 3	269 688	2.61	69.7	54.0	10.6	25.2	11 158	53.4	1 952	5 022	1 980	0
District 4	283 672	2.57	69.2	55.8	9.2	24.4	27 889	18.0	3 643	6 127	14 022	0
District 5	293 035	2.60	70.9	57.4	9.7	24.6	15 658	33.3	2 248	4 907	5 001	0
District 6	261 381	2.46	67.5	51.9	10.5	27.4	25 460	27.7	4 086	5 861	6 997	0
District 7	266 402	2.36	57.8	33.9	18.1	35.2	12 777	31.9	4 361	4 955	3 634	0
District 8	270 615	2.39	65.7	50.5	11.0	29.5	25 320	24.3	8 089	7 194	11 492	3
District 9	271 037	2.51	68.5	54.0	10.2	26.1	20 846	29.3	2 612	5 526	13 857	0
IOWA	1 208 765	2.38	65.9	53.1	9.1	27.9	104 071	29.3	11 771	33 428	41 171	4
District 1	238 558	2.39	66.9	53.1	10.2	27.1	17 829	29.5	2 158	5 532	8 724	1
District 2	247 887	2.32	63.1	49.7	10.1	28.9	25 374	18.5	3 579	5 256	9 314	3
District 3	254 129	2.38	66.3	52.8	9.8	27.6	18 864	29.4	2 260	5 534	5 113	0
District 4	237 704	2.39	65.4	54.4	7.1	28.2	23 753	33.9	2 182	9 081	12 969	0
District 5	230 487	2.43	68.1	55.6	8.4	27.7	18 251	37.9	1 592	8 025	5 051	0
KANSAS	1 088 288	2.46	66.6	52.5	10.3	27.9	82 162	30.8	16 703	25 248	24 492	4 580
District 1	260 134	2.38	67.9	55.9	8.6	27.9	27 768	41.4	4 964	9 184	5 934	0
District 2	271 336	2.43	65.6	51.7	10.5	29.1	31 625	16.4	7 674	6 723	8 500	4 067
District 3	283 017	2.56	66.1	51.3	10.7	26.2	11 484	32.8	544	4 101	7 978	0
District 4	273 801	2.47	66.8	51.4	11.2	28.3	11 285	43.2	3 521	5 240	2 080	513
KENTUCKY	1 651 911	2.48	67.0	50.4	12.4	28.2	114 777	24.6	28 388	29 266	31 883	7 277
District 1	267 883	2.44	69.4	53.8	11.6	27.6	19 785	20.4	4 931	6 788	2 980	4 648
District 2	276 937	2.56	70.2	54.0	12.0	24.9	19 217	16.7	4 027	4 667	5 123	2 629
District 3	285 119	2.34	60.2	41.3	15.0	33.9	14 622	43.2	1 169	5 182	2 592	0
District 4	273 264	2.56	69.0	53.1	11.7	25.8	17 172	48.0	6 197	4 284	1 326	0
District 5	257 069	2.60	69.6	52.2	12.4	27.1	17 069	22.6	6 288	4 609	4 446	0
District 6	291 639	2.38	64.0	48.6	11.8	29.6	26 912	9.7	5 776	3 736	15 416	0

[4]No spouse present.
[13]Data are for 109th congressional districts. The boundaries for districts for the 110th Congress have changed.

Table A. 110th Congressional Districts—*Continued*

(Number, percent.)

STATE Congressional district	Education, 2006				Income, 2006			Poverty, 2006		
	School enrollment[5]		Attainment level[6] (percent)		Per capita income (dollars)	Median household income (dollars)	Percent of households with income over $100,000	Persons below poverty level (percent)	Families below poverty level (percent)	Percent of households receiving food stamps in past 12 months
	Total	Private (percent)	High school graduate or more	Bachelor's degree or more						
	37	38	39	40	41	42	43	44	45	46
GEORGIA[13]—*Continued*										
District 6	223 193	20.5	94.7	53.3	38 448	80 175	39.6	5.2	3.5	1.7
District 7	238 031	15.0	88.0	34.7	28 641	68 550	27.4	8.0	6.2	3.6
District 8	218 727	17.5	86.8	25.4	25 738	58 162	20.9	9.8	7.1	6.5
District 9	187 873	13.7	77.8	19.9	21 675	42 284	12.8	13.8	11.0	8.3
District 10	203 007	11.3	77.2	19.2	21 151	46 590	14.7	11.5	8.9	6.4
District 11	173 324	15.7	76.9	18.1	19 642	40 716	10.5	16.2	12.5	8.9
District 12	208 930	12.2	80.1	21.3	18 439	34 136	9.6	20.5	14.5	9.7
District 13	196 143	15.4	80.2	21.1	19 667	44 187	10.3	14.8	11.2	8.6
HAWAII	315 873	23.9	89.0	29.7	27 251	61 160	25.2	9.3	7.1	6.6
District 1	153 984	26.3	88.4	32.8	28 685	61 143	26.2	8.7	6.2	5.8
District 2	161 889	21.7	89.6	26.6	25 901	61 177	24.1	9.8	7.9	7.4
IDAHO	394 245	13.1	87.3	23.3	21 000	42 865	11.3	12.6	9.3	6.1
District 1	201 353	13.5	87.7	22.8	21 693	44 534	12.4	12.0	8.7	5.7
District 2	192 892	12.7	86.8	24.0	20 212	41 494	10.0	13.3	10.0	6.4
ILLINOIS	3 527 824	19.4	85.0	28.9	26 514	52 006	19.9	12.3	9.1	7.9
District 1	194 225	23.1	81.1	21.5	19 493	40 578	12.4	21.8	16.4	16.7
District 2	192 323	17.6	83.4	19.5	19 248	43 830	11.5	18.7	14.4	14.6
District 3	170 875	25.0	80.9	22.9	24 895	53 550	18.8	9.6	7.6	4.5
District 4	170 725	13.5	60.8	18.7	16 641	38 620	10.6	23.3	21.9	15.8
District 5	159 506	32.8	82.0	36.4	30 975	55 561	23.6	11.1	7.7	4.1
District 6	177 117	22.6	88.0	34.6	30 173	65 818	27.0	6.5	4.7	3.0
District 7	175 484	21.0	81.5	36.2	31 520	47 113	23.2	23.2	18.7	15.5
District 8	208 714	18.3	89.1	35.2	31 596	70 694	29.9	6.0	4.3	3.2
District 9	159 052	34.6	86.8	42.0	29 776	51 464	22.1	12.4	8.5	7.3
District 10	187 752	20.0	90.0	50.8	43 773	78 269	38.9	5.4	4.0	2.2
District 11	206 498	17.1	87.4	20.9	24 326	55 759	18.8	9.9	6.8	6.9
District 12	178 002	14.7	85.9	20.8	20 945	40 705	11.4	14.6	10.7	10.8
District 13	238 377	20.6	93.4	45.5	36 394	80 703	37.2	4.1	3.2	2.0
District 14	230 213	14.8	84.9	28.9	26 610	62 067	24.9	8.6	6.3	4.6
District 15	191 420	9.2	87.7	26.0	22 268	42 633	13.0	15.1	9.3	8.2
District 16	192 789	18.2	86.4	23.3	24 623	52 192	18.3	10.2	7.7	6.3
District 17	164 308	15.7	84.5	16.6	20 377	38 792	8.4	15.9	11.9	12.1
District 18	163 296	21.3	88.8	24.3	24 925	47 375	14.0	10.4	7.7	7.4
District 19	167 148	12.2	86.1	20.0	22 263	43 922	12.4	12.4	9.4	8.4
INDIANA	1 655 250	17.0	85.2	21.7	22 781	45 394	12.8	12.7	9.0	8.4
District 1	187 194	17.3	86.5	19.2	22 569	49 029	14.2	14.6	11.5	10.4
District 2	175 827	21.1	82.8	18.3	21 635	43 634	10.8	12.2	8.2	8.8
District 3	183 112	18.6	83.9	20.9	22 556	46 320	12.0	11.1	8.5	7.0
District 4	215 656	12.4	88.0	25.3	24 666	50 676	15.9	10.1	6.4	6.5
District 5	206 548	20.8	90.6	34.7	28 992	58 165	22.4	7.5	5.2	4.3
District 6	167 885	13.7	84.6	16.9	20 599	41 712	9.6	13.2	9.2	9.6
District 7	163 213	20.6	80.6	21.9	20 522	37 265	8.7	19.2	15.6	13.7
District 8	167 861	16.6	84.4	17.4	21 232	40 408	9.6	14.0	9.6	8.7
District 9	187 954	12.2	84.2	18.6	21 047	43 043	10.5	13.8	9.0	7.2
IOWA	791 161	16.9	88.9	24.0	23 115	44 491	12.0	11.0	7.3	7.4
District 1	160 245	19.5	87.9	23.3	22 881	43 352	11.3	12.0	8.7	8.9
District 2	167 411	14.7	89.3	28.4	23 692	44 094	12.5	12.5	7.5	8.1
District 3	160 591	19.8	89.9	26.6	25 387	49 315	15.1	9.8	7.0	7.4
District 4	159 286	12.9	90.7	22.8	22 534	43 489	11.0	10.3	6.1	5.7
District 5	143 628	17.5	86.8	18.7	20 899	42 046	9.6	10.4	7.2	6.8
KANSAS	756 539	13.8	88.5	28.6	23 818	45 478	14.0	12.4	8.6	6.5
District 1	164 357	11.2	84.0	19.4	19 679	39 271	7.4	13.3	9.6	6.8
District 2	198 170	11.7	90.3	26.0	21 755	42 276	12.1	14.3	9.4	7.0
District 3	207 740	16.9	91.8	42.8	30 318	60 104	23.5	9.1	5.7	4.3
District 4	186 272	15.0	87.4	24.6	22 823	43 370	12.5	13.0	9.9	8.1
KENTUCKY	1 042 264	14.9	79.6	20.0	21 112	39 372	11.3	17.0	13.1	12.7
District 1	158 006	9.3	77.0	13.7	18 268	34 442	7.3	17.6	13.4	12.6
District 2	183 535	11.8	79.5	15.6	20 683	40 882	9.9	14.7	11.2	10.4
District 3	172 148	25.5	86.1	28.1	24 961	43 669	14.6	14.8	11.5	10.6
District 4	179 525	17.1	83.0	20.9	23 520	46 629	14.7	13.8	10.7	10.6
District 5	160 406	9.2	68.2	12.6	15 548	26 967	5.8	26.3	21.9	22.8
District 6	188 644	15.6	83.4	28.9	23 452	42 817	14.7	14.9	10.0	10.0

[5]All persons 3 years old and over enrolled in nursery school through college.
[6]Persons 25 years old and over.
[13]Data are for 109th congressional districts. The boundaries for districts for the 110th Congress have changed.

Table A. 110th Congressional Districts—*Continued*

(Number, percent.)

STATE Congressional district	Housing units, 2006									
	Total	Total occupied units	Owner-occupied units							
			Percent owner-occupied units	Median value (dollars)	Percent valued at $500,000 or more	Median real estate taxes (dollars)	Median monthly costs (dollars)	Percent with second mortgage or home equity loan	Median cost as percent of income	
									With a mortgage	Without a mortgage
	47	48	49	50	51	52	53	54	55	56
GEORGIA[13]—*Continued*										
District 6	296 624	276 095	81.7	265 400	15.9	2 238	1 609	31.2	23.4	10.0
District 7	310 313	288 259	82.2	194 000	5.5	1 588	1 400	27.6	24.0	11.6
District 8	308 848	279 618	78.3	167 200	4.0	1 289	1 126	21.2	23.4	10.7
District 9	326 287	269 832	73.6	140 400	4.6	875	815	14.0	23.6	11.4
District 10	315 532	277 167	76.4	156 800	5.6	921	911	16.3	24.1	11.0
District 11	284 169	246 293	64.0	128 300	1.7	788	882	14.7	24.3	11.4
District 12	287 510	251 614	57.1	111 700	2.4	770	806	12.9	23.5	12.2
District 13	295 280	258 810	59.4	143 600	1.1	1 145	1 168	18.4	26.7	11.9
HAWAII	500 021	432 632	59.5	529 700	53.6	1 209	1 465	19.7	28.4	9.1
District 1	244 363	219 297	56.4	530 900	53.8	1 395	1 575	20.5	29.2	8.5
District 2	255 658	213 335	62.8	528 600	53.5	962	1 368	19.0	27.6	9.9
IDAHO	615 703	548 555	71.3	163 900	6.2	1 270	870	20.0	24.1	10.9
District 1	324 467	289 460	74.6	184 500	7.1	1 355	938	21.9	24.6	10.9
District 2	291 236	259 095	67.5	138 900	5.2	1 158	789	17.7	23.3	10.8
ILLINOIS	5 199 743	4 724 252	69.9	200 200	9.5	3 061	1 184	18.0	25.8	14.0
District 1	263 214	228 467	55.5	194 700	3.3	2 154	1 253	16.3	29.9	15.4
District 2	254 358	225 546	65.7	145 600	0.9	2 255	1 148	14.5	28.1	14.9
District 3	249 102	230 160	74.1	249 500	7.1	2 999	1 298	14.9	28.4	15.5
District 4	214 945	184 657	42.7	299 800	12.9	3 018	1 647	14.8	37.9	17.7
District 5	276 965	255 921	57.6	354 500	21.4	3 639	1 702	22.0	31.1	16.2
District 6	249 106	237 134	76.8	295 500	12.9	4 283	1 535	22.7	27.3	15.6
District 7	292 385	247 212	48.4	312 100	23.4	3 515	1 803	20.2	28.3	18.6
District 8	274 309	258 133	80.0	247 900	10.5	4 398	1 605	25.4	26.8	14.6
District 9	284 615	256 755	60.5	352 700	22.8	3 867	1 511	19.9	29.9	15.2
District 10	245 233	227 614	80.1	412 900	37.7	5 814	1 808	22.4	26.8	15.7
District 11	283 741	263 150	76.7	172 100	3.9	3 091	1 178	20.3	25.1	13.9
District 12	291 733	258 953	70.9	91 400	1.0	1 380	700	10.5	21.6	13.0
District 13	283 868	267 334	82.4	319 000	17.0	4 899	1 743	26.6	26.1	14.2
District 14	278 500	265 538	77.0	230 700	8.1	4 355	1 561	21.7	28.3	14.6
District 15	293 039	265 945	69.4	103 500	0.9	1 790	750	11.0	21.1	12.0
District 16	291 167	261 414	78.2	152 600	3.7	3 138	1 072	20.4	24.8	14.8
District 17	287 882	259 571	70.8	83 200	0.7	1 385	647	8.7	20.4	12.6
District 18	290 098	265 104	74.0	107 700	1.2	1 894	791	15.0	21.1	12.2
District 19	295 483	265 644	77.0	97 700	0.9	1 452	675	10.8	21.4	12.2
INDIANA	2 756 583	2 435 274	72.1	120 700	1.9	1 125	874	18.4	21.9	12.2
District 1	291 357	262 096	72.9	134 900	1.5	1 757	1 006	16.9	23.2	14.7
District 2	292 835	257 348	73.7	111 200	2.0	1 042	814	16.7	21.5	12.8
District 3	305 686	269 688	73.9	120 400	2.2	1 039	853	18.2	21.1	11.8
District 4	313 992	283 672	73.6	133 900	2.4	1 288	1 028	22.6	22.4	11.4
District 5	324 120	293 035	76.8	149 900	4.3	1 449	1 081	22.6	21.4	11.1
District 6	294 831	261 381	74.6	100 700	1.0	897	743	14.1	22.0	11.4
District 7	322 133	266 402	55.5	107 400	1.1	1 169	917	18.0	23.7	12.9
District 8	303 569	270 615	73.5	97 600	1.0	779	706	16.0	20.8	12.5
District 9	308 060	271 037	74.1	121 300	1.3	893	782	19.0	21.6	11.7
IOWA	1 319 980	1 208 765	73.3	112 600	1.4	1 416	780	15.4	21.6	12.7
District 1	254 918	238 558	73.1	112 500	1.5	1 402	754	16.0	21.1	12.6
District 2	270 168	247 887	71.2	117 500	1.4	1 500	809	16.6	22.1	13.1
District 3	272 912	254 129	73.3	131 500	1.5	1 804	956	19.2	21.9	12.8
District 4	262 892	237 704	73.8	105 500	1.5	1 266	723	13.9	21.4	12.8
District 5	259 090	230 487	75.3	94 300	1.3	1 194	674	10.7	21.4	12.4
KANSAS	1 207 391	1 088 288	69.9	114 400	1.8	1 402	827	14.3	21.7	12.4
District 1	297 390	260 134	71.8	79 800	0.6	1 073	594	8.2	21.0	12.6
District 2	302 692	271 336	68.8	107 700	1.0	1 306	724	12.8	21.4	12.3
District 3	304 609	283 017	69.6	179 100	4.3	2 191	1 267	22.2	22.8	12.5
District 4	302 700	273 801	69.6	99 400	1.2	1 260	825	13.6	21.3	12.3
KENTUCKY	1 888 336	1 651 911	70.7	111 000	2.1	749	692	15.7	21.5	11.0
District 1	313 247	267 883	72.8	79 200	0.9	457	499	10.3	20.5	10.5
District 2	314 969	276 937	73.1	112 100	1.5	725	704	16.2	21.3	10.7
District 3	317 563	285 119	66.2	142 900	3.4	1 255	952	23.0	22.7	12.6
District 4	307 977	273 264	73.9	128 200	2.8	1 020	878	19.5	21.8	11.0
District 5	311 355	257 069	73.8	65 000	0.4	332	365	5.0	21.3	10.8
District 6	323 225	291 639	64.9	138 900	3.5	1 027	845	20.1	21.1	11.1

[13]Data are for 109th congressional districts. The boundaries for districts for the 110th Congress have changed.

Table A. 110th Congressional Districts—*Continued*

(Number, percent.)

STATE Congressional district	Housing units, 2006—*Continued*			Civilian labor force, 2006			Civilian employment and occupation, 2006			
	Renter-occupied units		Sub-standard housing units (percent)[7]	Total	Unemployment		Total civilian employment	Management, professional, and related (percent)	Service, sales, and office (percent)	Construction and production (percent)
	Median gross rent (dollars)	Median gross rent as a percent of income			Total	Rate[8]				
	57	58	59	60	61	62	63	64	65	66
GEORGIA[13]—*Continued*										
District 6	954	27.8	1.7	406 932	17 585	4.3	389 347	51.1	38.5	10.3
District 7	894	29.0	1.4	461 823	24 448	5.3	437 375	39.3	40.2	20.4
District 8	792	27.9	1.4	409 744	25 467	6.2	384 277	34.5	40.8	24.5
District 9	640	28.1	2.4	352 232	21 073	6.0	331 159	28.5	41.6	29.0
District 10	661	27.7	3.0	393 483	20 244	5.1	373 239	27.6	38.7	32.9
District 11	716	29.8	2.7	333 484	23 071	6.9	310 413	26.1	41.0	32.7
District 12	662	35.8	1.8	312 647	22 474	7.2	290 173	28.3	44.1	26.8
District 13	842	31.5	3.1	410 853	40 320	9.8	370 533	25.2	42.8	31.9
HAWAII	1 116	31.0	9.4	638 345	27 951	4.4	610 394	33.1	48.1	17.8
District 1	1 095	32.2	8.2	303 697	13 463	4.4	290 234	36.4	48.6	14.5
District 2	1 142	29.7	10.7	334 648	14 488	4.3	320 160	30.0	47.6	20.9
IDAHO	623	27.0	3.0	729 018	38 380	5.3	690 638	31.3	40.5	25.4
District 1	661	27.9	3.3	385 829	22 682	5.9	363 147	31.5	40.2	26.2
District 2	598	26.1	2.7	343 189	15 698	4.6	327 491	31.0	40.7	24.5
ILLINOIS	761	29.7	2.7	6 636 049	480 191	7.2	6 155 858	34.5	42.1	23.2
District 1	764	35.0	2.8	291 285	37 769	13.0	253 516	32.1	46.9	21.0
District 2	782	37.7	3.9	293 340	42 998	14.7	250 342	30.7	45.5	23.7
District 3	793	27.8	3.3	319 749	22 471	7.0	297 278	29.0	43.3	27.6
District 4	784	31.7	10.6	298 255	25 164	8.4	273 091	21.5	43.0	35.3
District 5	863	26.8	3.5	383 464	24 517	6.4	358 947	35.8	42.6	21.6
District 6	876	28.5	3.7	365 520	19 631	5.4	345 889	37.3	42.1	20.4
District 7	868	32.9	3.6	307 185	35 358	11.5	271 827	45.1	41.2	13.6
District 8	935	29.4	2.1	416 079	25 978	6.2	390 101	37.7	41.4	20.8
District 9	816	31.8	4.1	338 614	22 416	6.6	316 198	43.0	41.1	15.9
District 10	965	28.2	2.1	324 965	15 678	4.8	309 287	46.1	38.7	15.2
District 11	689	29.0	1.9	401 038	25 283	6.3	375 755	28.6	42.6	28.2
District 12	594	28.2	1.2	321 356	27 986	8.7	293 370	30.0	45.6	23.7
District 13	947	26.7	1.3	424 077	21 977	5.2	402 100	45.1	39.6	15.3
District 14	829	29.6	2.6	428 239	25 121	5.9	403 118	32.3	40.9	26.4
District 15	589	30.5	1.3	341 370	19 940	5.8	321 430	33.6	40.4	25.4
District 16	654	28.6	2.0	384 611	24 242	6.3	360 369	29.5	41.6	28.3
District 17	521	28.0	1.4	316 081	24 635	7.8	291 446	26.6	44.3	28.3
District 18	574	24.0	1.2	339 771	19 147	5.6	320 624	34.7	40.8	23.8
District 19	552	28.4	1.7	341 050	19 880	5.8	321 170	31.8	40.6	26.7
INDIANA	638	29.2	1.8	3 254 182	223 728	6.9	3 030 454	29.9	39.8	29.9
District 1	706	30.8	2.3	353 068	30 117	8.5	322 951	27.2	42.2	30.2
District 2	614	27.2	2.0	343 847	23 698	6.9	320 149	27.0	39.2	33.3
District 3	607	26.6	2.0	372 255	21 736	5.8	350 519	27.9	37.3	34.4
District 4	693	30.9	1.6	396 812	25 426	6.4	371 386	33.5	38.8	27.2
District 5	712	26.7	1.5	419 733	20 795	5.0	398 938	39.9	38.4	21.5
District 6	566	29.8	1.4	334 546	24 524	7.3	310 022	26.5	39.8	33.2
District 7	645	31.0	2.3	332 270	33 355	10.0	298 915	29.1	44.5	26.3
District 8	567	29.6	1.4	341 071	22 345	6.6	318 726	27.1	40.3	32.0
District 9	618	29.8	1.5	360 580	21 732	6.0	338 848	27.9	38.7	32.9
IOWA	584	27.4	1.5	1 624 576	79 517	4.9	1 545 059	32.6	40.8	25.5
District 1	568	27.3	1.7	315 158	16 793	5.3	298 365	30.4	40.4	28.4
District 2	602	28.6	1.2	327 426	17 665	5.4	309 761	36.3	39.5	23.5
District 3	631	28.0	1.7	347 286	16 229	4.7	331 057	34.6	42.5	22.4
District 4	575	27.0	1.5	323 775	13 595	4.2	310 180	32.5	39.6	26.2
District 5	520	25.7	1.3	310 931	15 235	4.9	295 696	29.0	41.7	27.6
KANSAS	609	27.6	1.9	1 471 477	77 880	5.3	1 393 597	34.4	40.5	24.1
District 1	514	24.6	2.1	340 839	13 475	4.0	327 364	29.3	39.2	28.2
District 2	598	28.9	1.4	359 560	19 531	5.4	340 029	33.3	41.5	24.4
District 3	746	27.0	2.0	412 960	22 163	5.4	390 797	41.0	41.5	17.4
District 4	573	29.0	2.1	358 118	22 711	6.3	335 407	32.5	39.4	27.6
KENTUCKY	548	27.9	2.1	2 017 956	139 346	6.9	1 878 610	30.9	40.4	27.9
District 1	498	28.2	1.9	307 117	22 361	7.3	284 756	26.1	39.8	32.8
District 2	545	26.9	2.3	356 133	22 901	6.4	333 232	26.3	40.4	32.7
District 3	613	28.8	1.5	346 492	25 278	7.3	321 214	35.9	42.2	21.7
District 4	583	27.0	1.6	366 176	24 604	6.7	341 572	31.9	40.9	26.6
District 5	417	29.2	3.1	260 997	21 684	8.3	239 313	27.0	39.3	33.1
District 6	578	27.6	2.0	381 041	22 518	5.9	358 523	36.3	39.8	22.8

[7]Overcrowded or lacking complete plumbing facilities.
[8]Percent of civilian labor force.
[13]Data are for 109th congressional districts. The boundaries for districts for the 110th Congress have changed.

Table A. 110th Congressional Districts—*Continued*

(Number, percent.)

STATE Congressional district	Social Security Beneficiaries (OASDI), December 2006							Supplemental Security Income, December 2006			
	Total	Rate per 1,000 population	Retired workers[9]	Disabled workers	Widow(er)s[10]	Spouses[11]	Children[12]	Total	Aged	Blind	Disabled
	67	68	69	70	71	72	73	74	75	76	77
GEORGIA[13]—*Continued*											
District 6	71 620	92.9	50 407	5 840	6 455	4 296	4 622	4 371	1 400	45	2 926
District 7	78 003	92.1	49 742	10 270	6 607	3 302	8 082	8 891	2 100	85	6 706
District 8	117 942	149.9	67 035	22 204	11 177	4 825	12 701	22 248	2 436	224	19 588
District 9	122 650	166.8	78 232	18 449	10 841	5 461	9 667	12 298	1 671	112	10 515
District 10	118 493	149.1	74 395	17 998	10 859	5 116	10 125	15 746	1 987	140	13 619
District 11	103 348	152.0	62 632	17 377	9 356	3 998	9 985	13 057	1 413	131	11 513
District 12	111 631	168.3	62 040	20 502	11 669	4 300	13 120	25 030	2 976	234	21 820
District 13	73 662	97.0	41 799	12 857	6 487	2 699	9 820	12 645	1 333	96	11 216
HAWAII	204 207	158.9	146 599	19 203	15 640	8 960	13 805	22 991	6 471	199	16 321
District 1	106 099	170.2	79 745	7 918	7 870	4 863	5 703	11 969	4 732	87	7 150
District 2	98 108	148.1	66 854	11 285	7 770	4 097	8 102	11 022	1 739	112	9 171
IDAHO	233 766	159.4	150 186	31 318	20 360	13 639	18 263	23 102	1 825	206	21 071
District 1	130 383	167.2	83 619	17 896	11 304	7 474	10 090	12 431	992	108	11 331
District 2	103 383	150.6	66 567	13 422	9 056	6 165	8 173	10 671	833	98	9 740
ILLINOIS	1 906 454	148.6	1 238 100	231 633	187 450	94 649	154 622	260 900	30 423	2 379	228 098
District 1	99 291	154.3	60 075	14 733	10 073	3 106	11 304	31 272	1 654	247	29 371
District 2	100 997	157.6	58 415	15 606	9 923	3 830	13 223	25 183	1 253	227	23 703
District 3	96 844	149.1	66 093	10 038	9 689	4 358	6 666	9 822	1 776	123	7 923
District 4	68 224	113.0	29 476	13 059	8 239	7 051	10 399	18 411	2 542	152	15 717
District 5	75 512	113.6	52 527	8 860	6 455	3 110	4 560	12 129	3 275	126	8 728
District 6	82 662	124.9	59 663	7 361	7 206	3 658	4 774	5 346	1 756	61	3 529
District 7	78 140	124.7	46 174	13 114	7 090	2 254	9 508	31 946	2 579	268	29 099
District 8	82 489	111.8	56 615	9 069	7 081	3 343	6 381	5 578	1 330	61	4 187
District 9	95 651	149.9	68 662	10 097	7 890	3 868	5 134	19 453	5 711	133	13 609
District 10	94 767	145.6	69 870	6 333	8 381	5 494	4 689	6 304	1 786	44	4 474
District 11	113 313	151.9	72 417	14 226	11 381	5 429	9 860	9 113	520	81	8 512
District 12	121 983	187.3	72 221	18 248	14 024	6 541	10 949	18 863	874	153	17 836
District 13	85 217	109.1	60 162	7 490	7 684	3 868	6 013	4 746	1 342	53	3 351
District 14	89 972	113.1	61 062	10 145	7 861	4 063	6 841	5 949	837	68	5 044
District 15	115 356	174.1	74 791	13 386	12 447	6 530	8 202	10 378	562	111	9 705
District 16	116 884	161.9	78 791	14 256	10 058	5 245	8 534	9 150	668	91	8 391
District 17	130 061	205.9	83 675	16 413	13 996	7 299	8 678	14 818	728	152	13 938
District 18	127 265	194.1	84 031	13 377	13 245	7 431	9 181	11 074	549	121	10 404
District 19	131 826	197.4	83 380	15 822	14 727	8 171	9 726	11 365	681	107	10 577
INDIANA	1 080 547	171.1	683 997	148 690	104 580	53 145	90 135	101 202	5 786	937	94 479
District 1	120 617	171.8	72 107	16 305	13 980	7 168	11 057	13 470	775	129	12 566
District 2	121 823	179.5	79 135	16 207	11 333	5 370	9 778	11 470	584	98	10 788
District 3	111 359	155.8	74 112	13 908	9 396	4 773	9 170	8 552	469	72	8 011
District 4	114 180	151.1	75 539	13 756	10 509	5 763	8 613	6 917	391	72	6 454
District 5	116 742	150.1	78 834	12 960	10 508	5 742	8 698	7 089	526	65	6 498
District 6	135 638	202.8	86 475	17 795	13 440	7 406	10 522	11 523	624	92	10 807
District 7	99 243	154.8	58 504	17 924	8 845	3 286	10 684	17 249	1 005	177	16 067
District 8	133 007	197.8	82 099	19 533	13 874	7 041	10 460	13 056	747	122	12 187
District 9	127 938	182.3	77 192	20 302	12 695	6 596	11 153	11 876	665	110	11 101
IOWA	555 803	186.4	369 639	61 782	56 661	32 285	35 436	43 883	3 560	770	39 553
District 1	112 043	190.4	73 520	12 715	11 651	6 938	7 219	10 524	695	166	9 663
District 2	104 771	174.6	70 247	12 633	9 776	5 356	6 759	9 243	588	161	8 494
District 3	101 566	162.8	68 541	12 123	9 299	4 680	6 923	8 529	842	173	7 514
District 4	116 925	197.8	78 909	11 218	12 749	7 362	6 687	6 736	643	129	5 964
District 5	120 498	208.3	78 422	13 093	13 186	7 949	7 848	8 851	792	141	7 918
KANSAS	454 919	164.6	299 083	55 542	43 692	23 194	33 408	39 582	3 225	355	36 002
District 1	127 336	196.5	85 006	12 768	14 017	7 832	7 713	8 635	785	74	7 776
District 2	120 130	173.8	77 004	16 350	11 241	5 781	9 754	11 548	762	98	10 688
District 3	92 048	124.8	62 213	10 979	7 956	4 148	6 752	7 753	797	82	6 874
District 4	115 405	167.9	74 860	15 445	10 478	5 433	9 189	11 646	881	101	10 664
KENTUCKY	812 644	193.2	424 678	167 356	90 047	48 026	82 537	181 700	13 384	1 381	166 935
District 1	150 714	223.6	82 236	29 510	16 663	8 702	13 603	28 455	2 746	199	25 510
District 2	133 550	183.4	73 285	25 733	13 950	7 613	12 969	24 407	2 318	175	21 914
District 3	124 795	183.2	75 203	20 483	13 276	6 072	9 761	20 077	1 515	220	18 342
District 4	121 871	170.0	66 266	22 782	13 518	7 466	11 839	21 501	1 568	196	19 737
District 5	160 527	234.6	58 647	46 628	20 553	12 119	22 580	64 334	3 274	426	60 634
District 6	121 187	167.9	69 041	22 220	12 087	6 054	11 785	22 926	1 963	165	20 798

[9]Includes special age-72 beneficiaries.
[10]Includes nondisabled widow(er)s, disabled widow(er)s, widowed mothers and fathers, and parents receiving payment on the record of a worker who is deceased.
[11]These beneficiaries receive payment on the record of a worker who is retired or disabled.
[12]These beneficiaries receive payment on the record of a worker who is retired, deceased, or disabled.
[13]Data are for 109th congressional districts. The boundaries for districts for the 110th Congress have changed.

Table A. 110th Congressional Districts—*Continued*

(Number, percent.)

STATE Congressional district	Total farms	Farms by size (percent) 1 to 49 acres	Farms by size (percent) 50 to 999 acres	Farms by size (percent) 1,000 acres or more	Land in farms Total acreage	Land in farms Average size of farms (acres)	Percent of farms where principal operator's primary occupation is farming	Value of all agricultural products sold Total ($1,000)	Percent of farms with value of: Less than $50,000	Percent of farms with value of: $50,000 to $249,999	Percent of farms with value of: $250,000 or more	Payments from federal farm programs Total ($1,000)	Number of farms that receive payments	Percent of farms that receive payments
	78	79	80	81	82	83	84	85	86	87	88	89	90	91
GEORGIA[13]—*Continued*														
District 6	443	78.3	21.7	0.0	25 429	57	47.9	16 697	93.5	3.6	2.9	62	67	15.1
District 7	1 211	64.3	35.0	0.7	89 612	74	51.1	87 424	88.3	2.6	9.1	367	213	17.6
District 8	3 700	45.4	52.1	2.5	521 089	141	47.3	145 135	94.4	2.4	3.2	2 253	720	19.5
District 9	10 034	46.3	52.6	1.1	1 197 699	119	54.5	1 330 465	80.5	5.8	13.7	7 362	2 455	24.5
District 10	5 150	53.0	46.4	0.5	478 437	93	50.4	697 426	82.4	5.6	12.0	2 229	837	16.3
District 11	3 537	38.8	59.4	1.8	544 987	154	49.3	208 400	91.3	3.4	5.3	1 678	637	18.0
District 12	3 081	27.5	65.0	7.5	1 043 618	339	48.9	206 660	86.1	8.0	5.8	11 844	1 351	43.8
District 13	749	58.6	40.7	0.7	83 327	111	44.5	17 544	94.5	3.3	2.1	285	126	16.8
HAWAII	5 398	88.0	10.0	2.0	1 300 499	241	57.9	533 423	85.2	10.4	4.4	886	113	2.1
District 1	208	91.3	8.2	0.5	7 200	35	65.9	21 128	80.8	10.1	9.1	. . .	3	1.4
District 2	5 190	87.8	10.1	2.0	1 293 299	249	57.6	512 294	85.4	10.4	4.2	. . .	110	2.1
IDAHO	25 017	49.2	40.2	10.5	11 767 294	470	55.4	3 908 262	79.0	12.2	8.8	93 934	7 098	28.4
District 1	11 260	54.1	37.9	8.0	4 242 845	377	53.6	896 919	84.7	9.3	6.0	22 450	2 435	21.6
District 2	13 757	45.2	42.2	12.6	7 524 449	547	56.9	3 011 342	74.3	14.6	11.2	71 484	4 663	33.9
ILLINOIS	73 027	26.9	62.6	10.5	27 310 833	374	64.1	7 676 239	62.3	26.0	11.7	412 636	47 857	65.5
District 1	. . .	. . .	. . .	. . .	. . .	. . .	. . .	. . .	. . .	. . .	. . .	. . .	. . .	. . .
District 2	211	60.7	37.9	1.4	23 836	113	52.6	21 283	78.2	13.7	8.1	263	60	28.4
District 3	. . .	. . .	. . .	. . .	. . .	. . .	. . .	. . .	. . .	. . .	. . .	. . .	. . .	. . .
District 4	. . .	. . .	. . .	. . .	. . .	. . .	. . .	. . .	. . .	. . .	. . .	. . .	. . .	. . .
District 5	. . .	. . .	. . .	. . .	. . .	. . .	. . .	. . .	. . .	. . .	. . .	. . .	. . .	. . .
District 6	24	70.8	25.0	4.2	2 956	123	50.0	4 991	58.3	16.7	25.0	51	4	16.7
District 7	. . .	. . .	. . .	. . .	. . .	. . .	. . .	. . .	. . .	. . .	. . .	. . .	. . .	. . .
District 8	531	61.0	35.0	4.0	92 926	175	51.8	39 358	73.6	19.0	7.3	1 316	139	26.2
District 9	. . .	. . .	. . .	. . .	. . .	. . .	. . .	. . .	. . .	. . .	. . .	. . .	. . .	. . .
District 10	57	59.6	36.8	3.5	7 390	130	47.4	8 749	75.4	17.5	7.0	132	12	21.1
District 11	5 022	22.6	65.1	12.3	2 158 549	430	71.3	674 408	49.9	35.2	14.9	34 079	3 364	67.0
District 12	5 847	29.9	62.8	7.3	1 707 050	292	55.4	287 086	80.0	14.8	5.2	22 438	3 407	58.3
District 13	148	44.6	52.0	3.4	31 388	212	54.7	16 707	75.7	17.6	6.8	418	52	35.1
District 14	3 518	26.3	62.5	11.2	1 435 883	408	73.7	589 287	47.3	35.4	17.3	24 703	2 232	63.4
District 15	11 576	23.8	61.6	14.6	5 336 908	461	70.1	1 533 084	51.4	32.5	16.1	80 689	8 142	70.3
District 16	6 592	31.5	61.0	7.5	2 069 669	314	65.7	771 054	60.2	27.4	12.5	41 434	4 054	61.5
District 17	10 613	24.0	65.3	10.7	4 059 056	382	65.4	1 133 509	62.1	25.6	12.2	59 894	6 861	64.6
District 18	10 105	23.9	63.8	12.3	4 157 816	411	65.3	1 222 379	58.6	27.0	14.4	58 813	6 749	66.8
District 19	18 783	29.3	62.1	8.6	6 227 406	332	58.1	1 374 345	71.9	20.8	7.3	88 404	12 781	68.0
INDIANA	60 296	39.9	53.8	6.3	15 058 670	250	55.7	4 783 158	74.6	17.6	7.8	224 701	26 841	44.5
District 1	2 336	37.2	48.9	13.9	963 515	412	61.4	392 965	56.5	27.0	16.6	14 393	1 289	55.2
District 2	5 909	40.4	52.0	7.6	1 677 432	284	58.1	562 141	69.4	20.8	9.8	28 134	3 043	51.5
District 3	8 831	43.9	52.8	3.3	1 467 409	166	53.7	567 371	76.7	17.6	5.7	24 283	3 712	42.0
District 4	6 110	44.5	46.8	8.7	1 818 133	298	54.8	597 015	73.0	16.8	10.2	28 439	2 469	40.4
District 5	5 694	42.3	50.3	7.5	1 593 566	280	58.0	547 120	68.8	21.4	9.9	27 365	2 769	48.6
District 6	10 845	38.6	55.0	6.4	2 823 497	260	58.5	859 457	71.5	21.0	7.5	43 180	5 350	49.3
District 7	149	80.5	18.1	1.3	9 716	65	42.3	29 117	69.1	20.8	10.1	93	22	14.8
District 8	8 994	36.8	54.6	8.6	2 686 375	299	54.7	716 990	74.0	16.9	9.1	36 797	3 840	42.7
District 9	11 428	36.4	60.7	2.9	2 019 027	177	52.7	510 981	86.8	9.7	3.6	22 018	4 347	38.0
IOWA	90 655	23.3	68.4	8.3	31 729 490	350	68.3	12 273 634	56.8	29.4	13.8	538 896	63 074	69.6
District 1	14 046	23.6	71.3	5.1	3 983 519	284	68.6	1 642 021	55.3	31.8	12.9	84 588	9 759	69.5
District 2	13 904	24.1	70.2	5.6	3 980 560	286	61.6	1 092 379	69.4	22.6	8.0	77 593	9 388	67.5
District 3	11 642	23.9	68.8	7.3	3 889 325	334	65.8	1 245 663	62.3	26.3	11.4	70 023	8 091	69.5
District 4	24 501	25.7	64.4	10.0	9 100 488	371	69.6	3 813 075	53.4	30.7	16.0	146 304	17 439	71.2
District 5	26 562	20.1	69.5	10.3	10 775 598	406	71.6	4 480 496	51.9	31.8	16.3	160 387	18 397	69.3
KANSAS	64 414	17.4	61.4	21.2	47 227 944	733	63.1	8 746 244	73.1	19.9	7.0	328 244	39 191	60.8
District 1	34 746	12.6	58.3	29.1	33 928 632	976	67.3	7 176 335	66.6	24.1	9.3	251 017	25 088	72.2
District 2	19 459	22.8	67.3	10.0	7 472 712	384	58.1	887 080	82.7	13.6	3.7	48 070	9 274	47.7
District 3	1 041	47.6	47.6	4.7	217 874	209	48.2	39 596	89.0	8.5	2.5	1 462	279	26.8
District 4	9 168	20.7	62.5	16.8	5 608 726	612	59.6	643 234	75.9	18.5	5.6	27 694	4 550	49.6
KENTUCKY	86 541	34.8	63.3	2.0	13 843 706	160	54.2	3 080 080	90.1	7.4	2.5	94 053	22 825	26.4
District 1	24 157	32.2	63.9	3.8	5 020 379	208	54.7	1 289 939	86.6	8.6	4.7	57 210	9 826	40.7
District 2	23 291	36.9	61.7	1.4	3 338 827	143	54.9	600 353	90.8	7.0	2.2	23 064	6 403	27.5
District 3	490	63.9	35.9	0.2	38 251	78	49.4	12 039	90.8	6.3	2.9	79	30	6.1
District 4	15 394	30.7	68.3	1.1	2 243 996	146	53.2	278 945	93.1	6.0	0.8	5 682	2 740	17.8
District 5	10 761	35.5	63.8	0.8	1 383 891	129	52.2	153 909	95.7	3.8	0.5	2 543	1 600	14.9
District 6	12 448	39.1	59.3	1.6	1 818 362	146	55.4	744 895	86.6	10.6	2.9	5 475	2 226	17.9

[13]Data are for 109th congressional districts. The boundaries for districts for the 110th Congress have changed.

. . . = Not available.

Table A. 110th Congressional Districts—Continued

(Number, percent.)

STATE Congressional district	Representative	Land area,[1] (sq km)	Total population	Persons per square kilometer	Race alone (percent) White	Black	American Indian/ Alaska Native	Asian and Pacific Islander	Some other race (percent)	Two or more races (percent)	Hispanic or Latino[2] (percent)	Non-Hispanic White (percent)
	1	2	3	4	5	6	7	8	9	10	11	12
LOUISIANA		112 825	4 287 768	38.0	64.4	31.6	0.6	1.3	1.1	1.0	2.9	62.7
District 1	Vacant	6 221	652 970	105.0	79.8	15.7	0.4	1.5	1.7	1.0	5.2	76.5
District 2	Rep. William J. Jefferson (D)	689	392 934	570.3	37.2	56.4	0.3	3.5	1.9	0.7	5.5	34.2
District 3	Rep. Charlie Melancon (D)	18 157	612 620	33.7	67.2	27.7	1.5	1.2	1.4	0.9	2.5	66.0
District 4	Rep. Jim McCrery (R)	27 881	647 830	23.2	61.4	34.8	0.7	1.0	0.9	1.3	2.5	60.0
District 5	Rep. Rodney Alexander (R)	35 677	637 011	17.9	62.9	34.2	0.5	0.5	1.0	1.0	1.6	62.1
District 6	Rep. Richard H. Baker (R)	7 966	689 923	86.6	60.9	35.5	0.2	1.7	0.7	1.0	2.3	59.4
District 7	Rep. Charles W. Boustany Jr. (R)	16 234	654 480	40.3	70.7	26.9	0.3	0.9	0.5	0.7	1.5	69.9
MAINE		79 931	1 321 574	16.5	95.8	1.0	0.5	0.9	0.3	1.4	1.0	95.3
District 1	Rep. Thomas H. Allen (D)	9 156	668 529	73.0	96.1	1.1	0.2	1.2	0.3	1.0	1.1	95.5
District 2	Rep. Michael H. Michaud (D)	70 775	653 045	9.2	95.4	1.0	0.8	0.6	0.3	1.9	0.9	95.0
MARYLAND		25 314	5 615 727	221.8	61.3	28.9	0.2	5.0	2.7	1.9	6.0	58.3
District 1	Rep. Wayne T. Gilchrest (R)	9 461	712 911	75.4	84.5	11.5	0.2	1.6	0.6	1.6	2.0	83.5
District 2	Rep. C.A. Dutch Ruppersberger (D)	919	690 810	751.7	61.5	31.4	0.2	3.7	1.0	2.2	3.0	59.8
District 3	Rep. John P. Sarbanes (D)	758	691 090	911.7	73.1	18.4	0.2	4.3	1.8	2.2	4.4	70.7
District 4	Rep. Albert Russell Wynn (D)	816	685 190	839.7	28.6	55.7	0.2	7.0	6.5	2.0	11.3	24.2
District 5	Rep. Steny H. Hoyer (D)	3 896	749 580	192.4	54.9	36.1	0.3	3.8	2.4	2.5	5.6	52.0
District 6	Rep. Roscoe G. Bartlett (R)	7 931	722 865	91.1	89.7	5.6	0.2	2.1	1.0	1.3	3.0	87.8
District 7	Rep. Elijah E. Cummings (D)	762	666 605	874.8	34.9	57.8	0.3	4.8	0.9	1.4	2.2	33.7
District 8	Rep. Chris Van Hollen (D)	769	696 676	906.0	60.3	17.4	0.2	12.9	7.4	1.9	16.5	52.2
MASSACHUSETTS		20 306	6 437 193	317.0	82.8	6.1	0.2	4.9	4.3	1.7	7.9	79.3
District 1	Rep. John W. Olver (D)	8 032	644 739	80.3	91.6	2.3	0.2	2.6	1.9	1.4	6.9	86.8
District 2	Rep. Richard E. Neal (D)	2 387	652 262	273.3	83.7	6.1	0.1	1.8	6.3	2.0	11.0	79.7
District 3	Rep. James P. McGovern (D)	1 505	654 597	434.9	87.6	3.2	0.2	4.9	2.5	1.6	8.0	82.7
District 4	Rep. Barney Frank (D)	1 895	662 005	349.3	87.2	3.3	0.2	4.3	3.3	1.7	4.3	85.1
District 5	Rep. Niki Tsongas (D)	1 465	644 889	440.2	79.5	2.3	0.1	6.3	10.3	1.5	13.6	76.3
District 6	Rep. John F. Tierney (D)	1 244	651 354	523.6	90.0	3.3	0.1	3.3	2.0	1.2	5.4	87.7
District 7	Rep. Edward J. Markey (D)	441	647 671	1 468.6	80.5	5.3	0.2	8.6	3.9	1.5	6.9	77.0
District 8	Rep. Michael E. Capuano (D)	105	594 647	5 663.3	56.4	21.8	0.4	9.1	8.6	3.8	17.6	48.7
District 9	Rep. Stephen F. Lynch (D)	811	640 993	790.4	77.4	12.6	0.3	4.9	3.4	1.5	5.1	75.3
District 10	Rep. William D. Delahunt (D)	2 420	644 036	266.1	91.7	2.2	0.6	3.4	0.9	1.1	1.3	90.9
MICHIGAN		147 121	10 095 643	68.6	79.5	14.1	0.5	2.4	1.7	1.8	3.9	77.6
District 1	Rep. Bart Stupak (D)	64 458	662 178	10.3	93.7	1.4	2.2	0.6	0.3	1.8	1.0	93.1
District 2	Rep. Peter Hoekstra (R)	13 895	697 012	50.2	88.5	4.6	0.4	1.1	3.5	2.0	6.1	86.4
District 3	Rep. Vernon J. Ehlers (R)	4 803	694 661	144.6	83.7	8.3	0.3	2.0	3.6	2.1	7.8	80.0
District 4	Rep. Dave Camp (R)	19 299	691 366	35.8	92.9	2.4	0.8	0.9	1.0	1.9	3.0	91.4
District 5	Rep. Dale E. Kildee (D)	4 543	654 879	144.2	77.6	18.4	0.5	0.7	1.3	1.6	3.4	75.8
District 6	Rep. Fred Upton (R)	8 628	674 389	78.2	85.8	8.5	0.5	1.4	1.9	2.0	4.6	83.3
District 7	Rep. Tim Walberg (R)	11 125	684 820	61.6	89.6	5.6	0.4	1.3	1.2	1.9	3.5	87.7
District 8	Rep. Mike Rogers (R)	5 837	696 087	119.3	89.4	4.8	0.3	2.4	0.9	2.1	3.7	87.0
District 9	Rep. Joe Knollenberg (R)	806	672 935	834.9	79.1	10.3	0.2	6.8	2.1	1.4	3.7	77.9
District 10	Rep. Candice S. Miller (R)	9 193	725 901	79.0	93.6	2.0	0.3	1.9	0.7	1.4	2.5	92.0
District 11	Rep. Thaddeus G. McCotter (R)	1 032	712 422	690.3	85.9	6.5	0.3	4.6	1.1	1.7	2.8	84.1
District 12	Rep. Sander M. Levin (D)	415	633 379	1 526.2	76.5	17.3	0.3	3.5	0.4	2.0	1.6	75.7
District 13	Rep. Carolyn C. Kilpatrick (D)	280	607 195	2 168.6	30.8	59.9	0.2	1.4	5.9	1.7	9.7	27.6
District 14	Rep. John Conyers Jr. (D)	318	602 221	1 893.8	34.5	61.7	0.3	1.4	1.1	1.0	1.8	33.8
District 15	Rep. John D. Dingell (D)	2 490	686 198	275.6	78.7	12.6	0.4	5.2	1.2	2.1	3.3	76.6
MINNESOTA		206 189	5 167 101	25.1	87.8	4.4	1.0	3.5	1.6	1.6	3.8	85.9
District 1	Rep. Timothy J. Walz (D)	34 503	631 285	18.3	94.0	1.4	0.4	1.9	1.2	1.0	3.8	91.7
District 2	Rep. John Kline (R)	7 861	709 697	90.3	90.9	2.7	0.4	3.8	1.0	1.2	3.0	88.9
District 3	Rep. Jim Ramstad (R)	1 211	637 106	526.1	83.7	6.7	0.4	5.5	1.8	1.9	3.1	82.4
District 4	Rep. Betty McCollum (D)	523	598 319	1 144.0	77.4	8.8	0.6	7.9	3.0	2.3	6.6	74.4
District 5	Rep. Keith Ellison (D)	321	593 434	1 848.7	73.3	13.8	1.1	5.0	3.9	2.9	8.6	69.0
District 6	Rep. Michele Bachmann (R)	7 979	730 995	91.6	92.5	2.0	0.4	2.7	0.9	1.5	1.9	91.4
District 7	Rep. Collin C. Peterson (D)	82 353	619 053	7.5	93.9	0.5	2.4	0.8	1.1	1.3	3.1	92.2
District 8	Rep. James L. Oberstar (D)	71 439	647 212	9.1	94.5	0.9	2.5	0.7	0.4	1.1	1.0	93.9
MISSISSIPPI		121 488	2 910 540	24.0	60.1	37.4	0.4	0.8	0.6	0.7	1.6	59.3
District 1	Vacant	29 559	762 914	25.8	70.5	27.2	0.3	0.5	0.8	0.7	1.8	69.4
District 2	Rep. Bennie G. Thompson (D)	35 288	687 386	19.5	31.9	66.4	0.1	0.5	0.4	0.6	1.1	31.5
District 3	Rep. Charles W. "Chip" Pickering (R)	34 106	745 531	21.9	63.2	34.1	0.9	0.8	0.5	0.4	1.2	62.6
District 4	Rep. Gene Taylor (D)	22 535	714 709	31.7	72.9	23.6	0.3	1.3	0.8	1.2	. . .	. . .
MISSOURI		178 414	5 842 713	32.7	84.0	11.3	0.4	1.5	1.1	1.8	2.8	82.5
District 1	Rep. Wm. Lacy Clay (D)	562	586 595	1 043.8	41.4	53.8	0.1	2.0	0.7	2.0	1.7	40.4
District 2	Rep. W. Todd Akin (R)	3 232	694 216	214.8	92.4	2.7	0.2	2.9	0.6	1.2	2.2	90.9
District 3	Rep. Russ Carnahan (D)	3 230	646 856	200.3	85.7	10.3	0.3	2.1	0.5	1.1	2.0	84.2
District 4	Rep. Ike Skelton (D)	37 669	657 809	17.5	92.8	3.2	0.4	0.9	1.2	1.6	2.2	91.8
District 5	Rep. Emanuel Cleaver II (D)	1 325	622 642	469.9	67.2	24.9	0.3	1.5	3.5	2.5	7.6	64.0

[1] Dry land or land partially or temporarily covered by water.
[2] May be of any race.
. . . = Not available.

Table A. 110th Congressional Districts—*Continued*

(Number, percent.)

STATE Congressional district	Population and population characteristics, 2006—*Continued*												
	Percent female	Percent foreign born	Percent born in state of residence	Age (percent)									
				Under 5 years	5 to 18 years	18 to 24 years	25 to 34 years	35 to 44 years	45 to 54 years	55 to 64 years	65 to 74 years	75 years and over
	13	14	15	16	17	18	19	20	21	22	23	24
LOUISIANA	51.5	2.9	79.8	7.0	18.4	10.8	12.9	13.6	14.4	10.7	6.5	5.7
District 1	51.9	4.5	75.9	6.6	17.1	9.1	12.3	13.9	15.5	12.0	6.9	6.5
District 2	52.5	6.5	78.2	7.4	18.2	10.5	10.8	13.5	15.7	12.0	6.6	5.4
District 3	51.5	2.1	87.5	7.3	19.3	10.1	13.1	14.4	14.5	9.9	6.3	5.0
District 4	51.1	2.2	72.1	7.2	18.5	10.5	13.5	13.0	13.7	10.5	6.9	6.2
District 5	51.5	1.2	80.0	6.9	18.5	11.8	12.8	13.0	13.3	10.6	7.0	6.2
District 6	51.0	3.3	79.3	6.6	18.1	12.9	14.0	13.9	14.0	10.1	5.5	4.9
District 7	51.5	1.9	85.2	7.3	18.9	10.7	13.1	13.5	14.4	9.9	6.4	5.6
MAINE	51.2	3.2	65.0	5.3	16.0	8.8	11.5	14.7	16.5	12.6	7.4	7.1
District 1	51.2	3.6	58.9	5.2	16.3	8.2	11.3	15.1	16.9	12.7	7.2	7.0
District 2	51.2	2.8	71.3	5.4	15.7	9.4	11.7	14.3	16.0	12.5	7.7	7.2
MARYLAND	51.6	12.2	47.8	6.6	17.7	9.5	12.8	15.7	15.3	10.9	6.1	5.4
District 1	51.1	3.5	60.2	6.0	17.6	8.8	11.5	14.9	15.2	11.7	7.6	6.7
District 2	52.4	7.4	66.2	6.4	17.5	9.9	13.7	15.1	15.1	10.3	6.2	5.9
District 3	51.0	10.1	54.5	6.5	16.1	9.9	14.7	16.2	14.1	10.9	5.8	5.7
District 4	52.0	21.1	22.6	7.2	19.3	9.6	13.5	16.4	15.3	10.4	5.1	3.2
District 5	51.3	10.7	36.1	6.6	18.3	10.7	12.7	16.5	15.5	10.7	5.3	3.7
District 6	50.3	5.1	61.5	6.1	17.8	8.9	12.2	16.3	15.9	10.7	6.2	5.9
District 7	53.4	8.4	62.7	6.7	18.2	10.6	11.8	14.5	15.7	10.6	6.0	6.0
District 8	51.8	31.5	19.2	7.1	16.7	8.0	12.2	15.5	15.8	11.8	6.4	6.5
MASSACHUSETTS	51.6	14.1	64.1	6.0	16.5	10.0	12.7	15.4	15.1	11.0	6.4	6.9
District 1	51.2	6.2	69.7	5.4	16.2	12.5	11.1	14.2	15.5	11.1	6.5	7.6
District 2	52.8	7.2	68.4	6.4	17.4	9.4	12.3	15.1	15.2	11.3	6.2	6.7
District 3	50.7	13.1	62.2	6.1	18.4	9.6	12.7	15.9	15.0	10.3	5.5	6.4
District 4	52.2	13.6	64.4	5.8	17.4	10.3	12.0	14.4	15.3	11.8	5.9	6.9
District 5	51.3	14.4	63.6	7.0	19.4	8.1	11.7	16.3	15.6	10.9	5.7	5.3
District 6	51.2	11.0	71.2	5.7	17.8	8.1	9.5	15.9	16.5	11.9	7.0	7.5
District 7	51.8	22.7	59.5	6.1	14.3	8.9	13.2	16.5	15.3	11.0	7.0	7.8
District 8	51.3	29.0	41.0	5.8	11.5	17.0	22.0	14.1	11.2	8.2	5.2	5.1
District 9	51.1	16.3	69.1	6.6	16.6	8.7	11.9	16.6	15.5	10.5	7.0	6.6
District 10	52.3	8.8	70.0	5.3	15.4	7.8	11.2	15.0	15.8	12.4	8.0	9.1
MICHIGAN	50.8	5.9	75.7	6.3	18.2	9.7	12.5	14.6	15.2	11.0	6.3	6.1
District 1	49.3	1.9	79.8	4.8	15.2	9.5	11.5	13.1	15.8	12.2	9.1	8.8
District 2	50.6	3.5	80.0	6.6	18.3	10.5	13.0	13.9	14.6	10.4	6.5	6.2
District 3	49.9	6.9	74.9	7.3	19.4	9.8	13.8	15.1	14.6	9.5	5.2	5.3
District 4	50.3	2.0	83.4	5.8	16.7	11.7	12.1	13.2	14.7	11.2	7.5	6.9
District 5	52.0	2.0	82.1	6.5	19.0	9.0	12.6	13.9	15.2	10.9	6.7	6.3
District 6	50.9	3.8	68.0	6.4	18.1	10.8	12.2	13.6	15.2	11.1	6.6	6.1
District 7	50.6	2.7	76.6	6.1	18.2	8.9	12.1	14.5	15.6	11.8	6.6	6.3
District 8	50.4	5.3	76.9	6.3	17.8	12.6	12.0	14.7	15.7	11.4	5.2	4.3
District 9	50.9	14.0	67.5	6.1	17.5	8.2	11.0	15.4	16.5	12.6	6.4	6.4
District 10	50.0	6.4	83.6	6.1	18.5	8.3	12.7	15.8	15.4	11.5	6.5	5.2
District 11	50.6	8.4	75.2	6.4	19.1	7.7	10.7	17.5	16.9	10.9	5.4	5.5
District 12	52.1	9.5	75.8	5.8	15.9	8.1	13.7	14.6	15.5	10.9	6.9	8.6
District 13	52.1	6.5	73.3	7.3	23.0	9.0	13.5	13.8	13.7	9.3	4.9	5.5
District 14	52.5	8.0	71.8	7.2	20.4	8.7	12.6	13.8	14.4	10.2	6.2	6.5
District 15	50.2	8.4	64.8	6.4	16.6	12.3	14.2	14.9	14.5	10.8	5.5	4.8
MINNESOTA	50.3	6.6	69.1	6.7	17.6	10.1	13.0	14.7	15.4	10.4	6.0	6.1
District 1	50.3	4.4	69.1	6.4	17.0	11.3	12.0	13.1	15.0	10.3	6.9	8.2
District 2	50.1	6.3	69.2	7.3	19.6	9.5	13.8	16.9	15.3	9.3	4.7	3.6
District 3	51.1	9.7	64.0	6.8	19.3	6.5	10.7	16.6	17.2	11.9	5.9	5.1
District 4	51.8	10.3	65.2	7.2	17.9	10.1	12.3	14.2	15.5	10.4	5.8	6.6
District 5	49.7	14.5	55.6	7.3	14.4	11.3	16.3	15.5	14.6	9.5	5.1	6.1
District 6	49.3	4.5	75.5	7.0	19.2	10.6	14.4	16.1	15.1	9.5	4.6	3.4
District 7	50.4	2.5	73.6	6.3	16.7	11.3	11.3	12.0	15.0	10.8	7.6	9.0
District 8	50.0	1.4	78.4	5.6	16.2	10.3	12.6	12.8	15.5	11.3	7.8	7.9
MISSISSIPPI	51.5	1.8	72.7	7.1	19.0	10.7	12.6	13.7	13.9	10.6	6.6	5.8
District 1	51.4	2.0	63.9	7.2	18.4	10.4	13.4	13.9	13.6	10.9	6.4	5.9
District 2	52.3	1.1	84.4	7.3	20.5	11.9	12.0	12.8	14.0	10.0	6.1	5.5
District 3	51.6	1.5	77.9	6.9	18.3	10.9	12.3	14.2	14.0	10.3	6.7	6.4
District 4	50.7	2.5	65.3	7.0	18.9	9.7	12.8	13.9	14.3	10.9	7.2	5.4
MISSOURI	51.2	3.3	66.3	6.7	17.7	9.8	13.0	13.9	14.8	10.8	6.8	6.6
District 1	54.0	3.8	70.8	6.4	18.9	9.8	11.7	13.1	15.7	11.1	6.6	6.8
District 2	50.7	4.9	67.6	6.2	18.9	8.8	11.6	15.1	16.2	11.4	6.2	5.5
District 3	51.0	5.7	72.6	7.0	17.1	9.5	12.9	15.6	15.1	10.5	6.1	6.3
District 4	50.0	2.1	64.7	6.8	17.4	10.4	13.2	13.3	14.2	10.5	7.4	6.9
District 5	51.7	5.1	58.2	7.4	18.1	8.4	13.6	14.5	14.7	10.7	6.2	6.3

Table A. 110th Congressional Districts—*Continued*

(Number, percent.)

STATE Congressional district	Households, 2006						Group quarters, 2006		Group quarters, 2000			
	Number	Average household size	Family households (percent)	Married-couple family (percent)	Female family house-holder[4] (percent)	One-person households (percent)	Total in group quarters	Percent 65 years and over	Persons in correctional institutions	Persons in nursing homes	Persons in college dormitories	Persons in military quarters
	25	26	27	28	29	30	31	32	33	34	35	36
LOUISIANA	1 564 978	2.66	68.5	47.8	16.1	26.5	122 467	22.9	49 854	31 521	26 959	3 877
District 1	240 749	2.67	69.1	53.2	11.3	26.1	11 079	37.8	3 084	3 563	1 363	0
District 2	126 039	3.00	63.6	39.4	18.5	30.1	14 676	12.6	6 160	3 214	4 726	284
District 3	211 319	2.86	74.0	51.8	16.2	20.7	8 571	41.0	3 168	3 435	744	30
District 4	248 475	2.52	67.3	46.3	17.0	28.1	20 876	25.6	6 708	5 441	2 714	3 563
District 5	235 247	2.57	67.8	45.5	17.7	28.4	32 711	16.4	15 020	7 007	6 863	0
District 6	252 798	2.64	67.6	47.7	16.4	26.2	22 534	12.8	11 998	3 924	7 713	0
District 7	250 351	2.57	68.6	47.3	16.6	27.1	12 020	40.3	3 716	4 937	2 836	0
MAINE	548 247	2.34	65.4	50.5	10.5	27.2	37 484	25.4	2 864	9 339	13 793	688
District 1	277 533	2.36	65.6	51.5	10.2	26.0	13 019	19.6	1 957	3 934	3 880	547
District 2	270 714	2.32	65.1	49.5	10.9	28.4	24 465	28.5	907	5 405	9 913	141
MARYLAND	2 089 031	2.62	67.3	48.7	13.9	26.7	141 501	23.2	35 698	26 716	35 371	7 412
District 1	270 285	2.57	71.5	56.5	10.8	23.4	17 899	12.9	4 635	3 870	3 929	263
District 2	273 686	2.48	63.9	43.4	15.6	29.2	12 568	31.5	1 179	2 908	772	1 570
District 3	266 017	2.48	61.1	45.0	12.1	30.8	31 773	9.4	7 924	3 034	6 918	3 427
District 4	246 334	2.76	67.8	42.9	19.0	27.4	4 516	37.9	1 283	1 196	19	892
District 5	261 667	2.79	72.6	53.7	14.0	21.9	19 075	15.3	846	3 012	10 469	612
District 6	267 658	2.61	70.8	58.3	9.1	23.3	23 475	32.5	11 658	4 591	4 333	254
District 7	241 540	2.67	62.4	36.8	20.3	31.8	22 730	25.6	7 523	3 934	8 590	0
District 8	261 844	2.62	67.9	51.9	11.2	26.2	9 465	57.4	650	4 171	341	394
MASSACHUSETTS	2 446 485	2.54	64.0	48.1	11.9	28.9	215 883	25.0	23 513	55 837	103 583	472
District 1	245 481	2.50	63.6	49.1	10.1	28.4	30 908	17.4	1 441	6 041	18 017	0
District 2	243 391	2.60	67.1	48.5	14.1	27.8	19 230	22.0	2 133	5 649	8 196	0
District 3	245 784	2.60	66.2	50.8	11.8	28.3	15 689	36.6	1 220	5 999	7 870	0
District 4	245 293	2.56	66.8	50.9	11.7	26.5	33 296	16.3	2 824	6 020	12 003	55
District 5	228 388	2.76	70.8	54.1	13.0	24.1	14 422	39.4	5 521	4 844	2 528	0
District 6	240 110	2.66	68.4	53.3	10.8	27.0	13 525	45.6	1 340	6 165	5 175	21
District 7	250 697	2.51	63.5	49.0	10.3	29.4	19 473	39.2	812	5 748	8 695	163
District 8	242 816	2.28	44.9	26.2	14.6	39.7	40 613	6.5	2 088	3 652	35 216	79
District 9	241 475	2.58	64.8	47.0	13.1	28.6	18 058	31.9	4 330	6 207	4 673	97
District 10	263 050	2.41	64.4	51.6	9.3	29.0	10 669	49.3	1 804	5 512	1 210	57
MICHIGAN	3 869 117	2.54	66.7	50.1	12.3	28.0	255 247	22.1	65 330	50 113	69 854	112
District 1	277 473	2.27	66.5	54.7	7.8	27.6	32 948	19.7	11 355	5 196	5 138	63
District 2	258 716	2.62	71.0	57.1	9.9	24.1	18 049	12.6	5 672	3 948	5 207	7
District 3	258 559	2.61	68.7	53.0	11.7	25.8	19 459	21.6	6 740	4 455	3 792	0
District 4	265 843	2.49	67.0	53.9	9.4	26.7	28 383	17.3	7 806	3 769	11 009	0
District 5	261 162	2.46	66.3	45.4	16.4	28.5	11 488	30.5	1 699	2 695	497	0
District 6	259 522	2.54	66.1	51.2	10.4	26.8	15 622	41.3	1 645	3 305	7 998	4
District 7	259 671	2.54	68.4	53.2	11.1	26.7	25 370	18.8	13 350	4 017	4 350	0
District 8	261 707	2.57	69.2	55.6	9.8	24.5	23 932	11.6	1 037	2 127	13 876	0
District 9	265 288	2.50	65.5	52.9	9.3	29.4	10 651	38.5	1 813	2 729	1 554	0
District 10	271 992	2.64	71.5	58.6	8.9	24.4	8 516	48.6	2 717	2 451	0	34
District 11	273 292	2.58	67.6	53.7	10.1	28.0	7 291	23.4	1 953	2 931	77	0
District 12	265 702	2.35	60.0	42.8	12.7	35.4	8 898	38.6	1 316	3 695	283	0
District 13	211 990	2.81	62.6	29.6	26.1	32.8	12 188	15.6	4 151	2 891	193	4
District 14	215 292	2.75	64.0	34.0	24.5	32.5	9 767	41.0	884	3 648	891	0
District 15	262 908	2.52	64.2	48.7	11.3	28.3	22 685	8.0	3 192	2 256	14 989	0
MINNESOTA	2 042 297	2.46	65.1	52.1	9.1	28.1	141 703	31.5	16 999	40 506	44 835	12
District 1	252 393	2.42	65.7	55.0	7.7	28.2	19 707	26.3	2 467	6 343	8 756	0
District 2	260 141	2.68	73.0	60.0	9.1	21.3	12 566	33.4	1 894	2 405	4 690	0
District 3	251 242	2.52	67.4	54.6	9.0	27.2	4 679	43.3	792	2 219	252	0
District 4	240 617	2.41	58.5	41.9	12.5	33.9	18 607	28.7	590	4 701	8 402	0
District 5	253 182	2.25	49.9	34.3	10.6	39.3	23 494	32.9	804	7 481	7 523	0
District 6	263 460	2.69	73.0	61.4	7.5	20.2	22 437	19.2	4 633	2 713	5 261	0
District 7	253 415	2.36	67.3	56.1	7.6	27.5	19 912	51.7	2 092	8 798	6 223	0
District 8	267 847	2.34	65.6	52.7	8.9	27.9	20 301	27.3	3 727	5 846	3 728	12
MISSISSIPPI	1 075 521	2.62	69.0	46.3	17.9	27.4	94 247	22.3	25 778	18 382	29 238	5 722
District 1	285 515	2.58	70.4	50.3	15.3	26.5	26 885	35.2	2 631	4 876	7 377	247
District 2	242 527	2.72	66.9	37.1	25.0	29.5	27 495	13.6	12 515	4 798	11 263	4
District 3	283 559	2.55	68.0	47.6	16.1	28.7	21 109	22.1	5 653	5 092	5 647	628
District 4	263 920	2.64	70.5	48.9	16.2	24.9	18 758	16.6	4 979	3 616	4 951	4 843
MISSOURI	2 305 027	2.46	65.9	50.1	11.9	28.8	167 076	27.7	35 206	48 708	44 587	5 435
District 1	238 738	2.39	60.2	33.8	22.5	35.2	15 338	24.8	1 113	4 782	3 306	0
District 2	258 128	2.66	73.2	61.4	8.6	22.5	8 802	51.2	1 441	4 897	1 950	0
District 3	260 148	2.44	60.8	45.3	11.4	33.1	13 337	33.5	1 386	4 780	3 879	6
District 4	250 601	2.51	69.1	55.1	10.5	26.5	29 773	26.2	7 065	5 827	4 154	5 429
District 5	259 397	2.37	61.5	41.3	15.5	32.7	8 195	44.4	1 602	4 319	1 383	0

[4]No spouse present.

Table A. 110th Congressional Districts—*Continued*

(Number, percent.)

STATE Congressional district	Education, 2006				Income, 2006			Poverty, 2006		
	School enrollment[5]		Attainment level[6] (percent)		Per capita income (dollars)	Median household income (dollars)	Percent of households with income over $100,000	Persons below poverty level (percent)	Families below poverty level (percent)	Percent of households receiving food stamps in past 12 months
	Total	Private (percent)	High school graduate or more	Bachelor's degree or more						
	37	38	39	40	41	42	43	44	45	46
LOUISIANA	1 132 749	18.7	79.4	20.3	20 367	39 337	12.5	19.0	14.4	23.5
District 1	157 145	30.7	85.3	28.2	24 750	48 194	17.9	13.2	9.3	28.2
District 2	110 009	28.3	76.7	20.7	19 059	36 119	12.2	21.8	16.0	35.6
District 3	155 078	17.0	73.2	12.3	18 869	41 786	11.6	18.4	14.1	29.1
District 4	165 681	9.3	81.1	18.5	19 373	35 771	10.1	19.8	15.3	17.2
District 5	171 260	12.2	75.1	16.3	16 958	31 713	7.5	24.1	19.4	16.6
District 6	200 818	20.8	84.8	25.5	22 304	44 339	15.4	18.0	13.1	16.4
District 7	172 758	15.9	77.2	19.3	20 440	36 044	12.2	19.5	14.9	28.0
MAINE	306 812	15.8	88.7	25.8	23 226	43 439	11.8	12.9	8.7	12.3
District 1	156 898	16.7	90.5	31.4	25 924	50 178	15.3	10.0	6.2	9.4
District 2	149 914	14.9	86.9	20.0	20 464	37 107	8.3	16.0	11.3	15.3
MARYLAND	1 521 002	22.3	87.1	35.1	31 888	65 144	28.5	7.8	5.3	4.8
District 1	186 176	22.4	88.1	31.2	31 132	62 617	26.9	6.7	4.4	4.3
District 2	182 180	18.6	84.3	24.7	25 880	53 014	17.6	8.8	6.3	5.5
District 3	184 995	32.3	87.0	41.1	34 637	65 908	29.7	8.4	5.2	4.5
District 4	196 945	20.8	87.0	35.5	30 493	66 963	29.4	6.5	5.1	4.4
District 5	217 221	20.9	90.4	31.9	33 218	79 916	36.4	5.9	3.3	3.2
District 6	183 086	19.7	87.3	27.5	29 245	63 798	25.7	5.8	3.8	4.8
District 7	187 632	16.9	82.0	31.9	26 072	50 778	20.6	15.5	11.5	9.9
District 8	182 767	26.8	90.0	56.3	44 141	82 987	41.4	5.7	3.6	2.5
MASSACHUSETTS	1 703 439	27.6	87.9	37.0	30 686	59 963	25.9	9.9	7.0	6.5
District 1	177 700	15.0	88.1	28.5	24 334	50 610	16.6	12.1	8.2	8.8
District 2	173 265	23.4	85.9	27.9	26 065	52 496	19.8	11.6	8.6	9.7
District 3	177 583	23.4	87.1	35.8	29 876	61 317	27.0	9.2	6.9	6.7
District 4	184 299	32.2	85.9	39.0	34 112	62 923	29.3	9.6	6.9	5.7
District 5	178 136	20.1	86.0	37.3	31 847	66 219	32.5	9.3	6.9	6.7
District 6	171 233	24.1	90.8	39.1	32 125	66 785	31.6	6.4	4.6	3.7
District 7	152 287	31.8	89.6	42.4	33 987	65 537	28.5	7.7	5.6	4.2
District 8	179 133	51.7	82.9	44.9	28 629	45 409	19.8	21.8	17.2	10.6
District 9	166 146	30.6	89.1	37.9	32 486	64 867	28.7	7.6	4.8	5.1
District 10	143 657	22.8	93.0	37.8	33 200	62 386	26.0	5.6	3.7	3.7
MICHIGAN	2 750 796	13.2	87.2	24.5	24 097	47 182	15.9	13.5	9.6	9.8
District 1	150 372	8.3	86.7	18.0	20 376	38 079	7.9	13.8	9.3	10.3
District 2	185 201	15.4	87.9	20.3	21 332	45 731	11.7	11.2	7.6	10.1
District 3	196 271	19.6	87.3	27.3	23 048	47 304	14.1	12.2	9.1	9.0
District 4	188 232	12.6	87.2	21.2	20 834	41 695	10.6	14.9	10.4	10.8
District 5	173 874	9.9	87.0	16.7	20 629	39 246	11.4	18.3	14.6	15.0
District 6	185 211	11.9	86.8	23.7	22 270	43 734	13.2	14.8	9.8	10.2
District 7	177 991	14.8	88.5	21.8	23 119	47 872	13.9	12.4	9.0	8.6
District 8	215 748	11.0	91.7	32.1	26 730	57 105	22.2	10.9	7.0	5.2
District 9	180 524	20.6	92.3	47.3	39 443	69 305	32.2	6.9	4.5	4.5
District 10	191 593	11.5	88.2	20.2	25 975	55 794	19.9	9.3	7.1	7.0
District 11	195 905	13.5	91.7	32.9	30 556	64 630	26.8	6.3	3.6	3.5
District 12	151 577	15.5	85.7	21.8	24 863	47 033	14.1	9.8	7.7	7.9
District 13	179 385	9.3	75.2	14.7	16 843	31 169	8.9	30.3	24.7	23.1
District 14	174 926	12.1	81.2	15.5	17 534	36 070	8.4	23.0	18.5	19.1
District 15	203 986	11.3	87.4	30.2	25 988	52 145	20.1	12.3	7.4	6.8
MINNESOTA	1 349 143	17.3	90.7	30.4	27 591	54 023	19.1	9.8	6.5	5.0
District 1	161 738	16.1	88.6	23.8	24 380	47 531	13.4	9.6	5.4	3.9
District 2	198 345	19.5	93.2	35.4	30 413	70 980	27.5	4.6	3.9	2.5
District 3	165 364	19.1	95.0	42.1	37 740	70 024	31.3	5.6	3.5	3.0
District 4	166 095	26.9	90.6	37.1	27 538	51 832	19.6	13.1	8.4	7.3
District 5	155 228	19.5	88.4	37.8	27 774	47 249	16.8	17.3	12.6	8.4
District 6	206 287	15.8	92.3	28.3	28 212	66 169	23.9	6.8	4.6	2.8
District 7	146 321	9.8	87.5	19.4	21 867	43 053	9.9	11.3	8.0	5.6
District 8	149 765	10.0	89.1	20.0	22 296	44 124	10.5	11.7	7.9	6.3
MISSISSIPPI	787 356	12.3	77.9	18.8	18 165	34 473	9.6	21.1	16.8	17.4
District 1	197 189	9.7	76.3	16.4	18 157	35 831	8.8	19.0	14.6	9.5
District 2	210 912	12.7	74.3	17.7	14 998	27 955	6.9	28.9	23.9	19.8
District 3	192 776	16.0	80.4	22.6	20 302	35 907	11.7	19.6	15.5	13.2
District 4	186 479	10.7	80.3	18.3	18 992	37 970	10.8	17.4	14.3	28.1
MISSOURI	1 494 744	19.9	84.8	24.3	22 916	42 841	12.9	13.6	10.0	10.4
District 1	164 690	21.2	83.0	24.3	21 749	37 439	11.0	20.4	15.8	15.4
District 2	192 891	31.1	92.0	41.6	34 740	69 345	30.5	4.4	2.5	3.1
District 3	166 447	30.9	84.5	27.0	24 374	47 033	14.0	11.3	8.4	8.1
District 4	159 100	14.7	83.4	16.8	19 183	39 203	8.3	14.3	10.8	11.0
District 5	154 683	20.9	86.8	25.2	23 600	42 457	12.1	16.0	12.5	11.6

[5]All persons 3 years old and over enrolled in nursery school through college.
[6]Persons 25 years old and over.

Table A. 110th Congressional Districts—*Continued*

(Number, percent.)

STATE Congressional district	Housing units, 2006									
	Total	Total occupied units	Owner-occupied units							
			Percent owner-occupied units	Median value (dollars)	Percent valued at $500,000 or more	Median real estate taxes (dollars)	Median monthly costs (dollars)	Percent with second mortgage or home equity loan	Median cost as percent of income	
									With a mortgage	Without a mortgage
	47	48	49	50	51	52	53	54	55	56
LOUISIANA	1 829 933	1 564 978	68.5	114 700	2.2	179	648	9.6	21.4	10.6
District 1	283 684	240 749	72.8	177 900	4.5	437	875	12.3	22.9	10.1
District 2	165 669	126 039	58.2	144 500	4.6	212	894	10.2	27.8	12.4
District 3	243 699	211 319	73.6	102 700	0.9	152	571	8.8	20.1	10.2
District 4	295 188	248 475	66.8	86 000	1.5	171	545	7.8	20.3	10.0
District 5	279 497	235 247	67.4	80 700	0.9	142	491	7.0	21.6	11.8
District 6	281 853	252 798	68.1	132 800	2.4	285	818	13.2	20.9	10.2
District 7	280 343	250 351	68.2	93 700	1.8	158	526	7.8	19.5	10.4
MAINE	691 164	548 247	72.8	170 500	5.6	1 768	852	17.5	23.8	14.1
District 1	337 310	277 533	73.5	221 800	8.7	2 258	1 050	21.1	24.9	14.6
District 2	353 854	270 714	72.0	120 900	2.3	1 344	691	13.7	22.3	13.6
MARYLAND	2 300 749	2 089 031	69.4	334 700	23.6	2 334	1 446	23.7	24.5	11.9
District 1	327 865	270 285	79.5	311 500	20.0	1 980	1 251	21.7	23.9	12.0
District 2	294 026	273 686	62.5	219 600	6.9	1 787	1 138	19.3	24.5	12.4
District 3	289 157	266 017	68.8	313 900	19.3	2 213	1 393	24.4	23.4	11.6
District 4	259 564	246 334	65.0	363 400	26.0	2 718	1 757	25.3	27.2	10.7
District 5	278 132	261 667	77.0	369 800	23.4	2 575	1 709	25.7	24.7	10.9
District 6	288 182	267 658	76.0	316 000	19.2	2 125	1 302	26.0	24.1	11.4
District 7	286 902	241 540	58.4	244 600	22.1	1 987	1 211	21.7	24.6	13.5
District 8	276 921	261 844	67.0	527 500	53.2	3 424	1 934	24.8	24.5	11.8
MASSACHUSETTS	2 709 208	2 446 485	64.9	370 400	25.5	3 195	1 546	22.7	27.1	15.8
District 1	274 085	245 481	68.6	226 800	5.1	2 525	1 184	20.6	25.5	14.9
District 2	263 627	243 391	69.0	240 000	6.3	2 662	1 284	22.4	24.8	15.1
District 3	264 204	245 784	66.3	343 000	17.4	3 168	1 607	23.2	26.4	15.7
District 4	264 355	245 293	66.3	390 500	33.5	3 240	1 587	23.1	26.8	15.4
District 5	242 844	228 388	71.5	382 800	26.6	3 693	1 757	24.5	27.3	14.8
District 6	260 961	240 110	71.0	426 000	33.0	3 739	1 719	24.1	27.2	16.1
District 7	267 824	250 697	60.3	443 500	36.4	3 852	1 740	22.1	28.0	17.0
District 8	266 140	242 816	34.3	458 300	41.7	2 792	1 744	19.3	30.2	16.9
District 9	255 843	241 475	66.7	404 300	29.4	3 351	1 765	23.3	27.6	16.1
District 10	349 325	263 050	75.1	416 700	33.6	3 103	1 535	23.0	28.9	16.7
MICHIGAN	4 513 502	3 869 117	75.2	153 300	3.6	1 972	1 010	20.1	24.6	13.9
District 1	413 131	277 473	79.9	112 000	3.0	1 100	673	12.4	23.8	13.0
District 2	318 282	258 716	81.5	141 000	2.9	1 581	887	18.4	24.2	13.5
District 3	279 824	258 559	73.9	148 800	2.9	1 952	1 035	21.1	24.4	13.8
District 4	334 892	265 843	78.0	132 000	2.7	1 360	822	16.0	24.3	12.8
District 5	293 939	261 162	73.4	120 300	0.7	1 525	828	15.3	24.7	13.9
District 6	305 282	259 522	73.7	134 000	3.6	1 561	858	19.0	22.9	12.6
District 7	291 287	259 671	78.2	145 300	3.0	1 760	972	20.6	24.8	13.4
District 8	286 723	261 707	77.3	195 300	4.2	2 507	1 219	26.4	24.3	13.1
District 9	289 913	265 288	75.4	249 500	13.7	3 621	1 473	24.7	23.8	13.4
District 10	302 283	271 992	82.4	189 700	3.0	2 235	1 171	23.9	24.7	14.3
District 11	291 783	273 292	80.5	197 900	5.2	2 868	1 358	25.1	24.1	13.9
District 12	289 244	265 702	74.8	153 600	1.0	2 491	1 070	21.8	25.4	16.2
District 13	271 659	211 990	57.2	102 100	2.9	1 706	949	14.4	29.1	17.0
District 14	258 806	215 292	65.6	121 000	0.8	2 051	1 000	15.5	30.3	17.7
District 15	286 454	262 908	69.8	173 200	3.5	2 603	1 207	23.3	24.8	14.1
MINNESOTA	2 282 837	2 042 297	76.3	208 200	6.8	1 780	1 139	23.0	24.4	12.0
District 1	273 425	252 393	77.8	139 900	2.3	1 193	814	17.0	22.3	11.7
District 2	272 853	260 141	83.7	248 500	8.7	2 237	1 488	30.1	24.9	11.0
District 3	266 707	251 242	77.9	278 400	15.8	2 724	1 529	27.5	24.7	12.0
District 4	257 072	240 617	68.1	225 500	6.4	1 939	1 273	24.2	25.4	11.7
District 5	276 046	253 182	59.1	226 100	6.1	2 224	1 273	25.8	24.9	14.6
District 6	279 206	263 460	84.2	233 500	8.2	1 950	1 387	29.1	25.3	11.3
District 7	303 697	253 415	78.2	126 100	2.3	1 067	707	13.3	22.4	11.9
District 8	353 831	267 847	80.3	160 500	4.0	1 094	832	17.0	25.3	12.0
MISSISSIPPI	1 241 439	1 075 521	70.7	88 600	1.2	437	615	8.2	23.0	12.8
District 1	323 681	285 515	73.8	90 100	0.8	457	650	9.4	23.0	12.4
District 2	282 515	242 527	63.9	72 900	1.0	380	608	6.4	25.4	14.5
District 3	325 009	283 559	72.8	88 500	1.7	396	594	8.2	21.9	12.3
District 4	310 234	263 920	71.3	103 200	1.2	511	610	8.4	22.7	12.5
MISSOURI	2 622 995	2 305 027	70.7	131 900	3.0	1 121	816	14.4	22.4	11.6
District 1	277 996	238 738	62.3	114 100	2.5	1 371	907	14.0	24.9	13.4
District 2	271 820	258 128	82.5	218 900	9.0	2 375	1 278	22.4	22.2	11.8
District 3	288 160	260 148	72.1	153 100	3.0	1 347	960	18.0	23.0	12.3
District 4	308 791	250 601	71.8	112 500	2.0	751	647	9.9	22.4	11.0
District 5	295 531	259 397	63.8	125 600	2.0	1 422	956	17.6	23.3	13.9

Table A. 110th Congressional Districts—*Continued*

(Number, percent.)

STATE Congressional district	Housing units, 2006—*Continued*			Civilian labor force, 2006			Civilian employment and occupation, 2006			
	Renter-occupied units		Sub-standard housing units (percent)[7]	Total	Unemployment		Total civilian employment	Management, professional, and related (percent)	Service, sales, and office (percent)	Construction and production (percent)
	Median gross rent (dollars)	Median gross rent as a percent of income			Total	Rate[8]				
	57	58	59	60	61	62	63	64	65	66
LOUISIANA	618	30.5	3.8	2 011 234	157 338	7.8	1 853 896	29.6	43.7	26.1
District 1	761	29.3	2.9	317 005	19 481	6.1	297 524	37.4	42.6	19.7
District 2	804	40.3	4.5	182 393	21 109	11.6	161 284	26.8	46.3	26.7
District 3	571	25.8	5.6	284 001	17 178	6.0	266 823	22.4	41.8	35.1
District 4	561	28.3	3.3	293 507	23 964	8.2	269 543	28.4	44.0	26.6
District 5	540	33.2	3.6	280 606	26 543	9.5	254 063	27.3	45.1	26.3
District 6	673	32.8	4.5	344 805	27 264	7.9	317 541	32.9	45.1	21.8
District 7	555	29.2	2.9	308 917	21 799	7.1	287 118	29.6	42.1	27.8
MAINE	636	28.7	1.8	701 799	37 066	5.3	664 733	32.7	42.5	22.9
District 1	741	29.1	1.4	371 836	17 304	4.7	354 532	35.7	42.9	19.7
District 2	549	28.2	2.2	329 963	19 762	6.0	310 201	29.2	42.0	26.6
MARYLAND	953	28.6	1.9	3 036 959	160 983	5.3	2 875 976	42.6	40.2	17.0
District 1	824	26.8	1.2	378 282	18 244	4.8	360 038	38.6	41.1	19.7
District 2	889	29.3	1.5	370 522	23 303	6.3	347 219	35.1	43.9	21.0
District 3	995	28.3	1.4	380 627	16 930	4.4	363 697	46.8	38.2	14.8
District 4	1 029	29.2	3.2	382 468	24 803	6.5	357 665	41.6	41.6	16.8
District 5	1 077	26.7	1.7	420 804	21 417	5.1	399 387	43.8	38.5	17.5
District 6	747	27.0	1.3	390 569	14 809	3.8	375 760	36.7	41.4	21.4
District 7	811	29.5	1.9	327 955	25 758	7.9	302 197	42.6	43.0	14.3
District 8	1 225	29.9	2.8	385 732	15 719	4.1	370 013	54.9	34.6	10.5
MASSACHUSETTS	933	30.6	1.9	3 470 663	199 626	5.8	3 271 037	41.2	41.0	17.6
District 1	689	28.8	1.6	345 499	22 689	6.6	322 810	35.5	41.9	22.4
District 2	717	30.7	2.1	344 526	22 914	6.7	321 612	35.8	42.3	21.5
District 3	826	28.4	1.7	352 816	19 773	5.6	333 043	40.9	40.6	18.5
District 4	879	29.3	0.7	347 171	17 635	5.1	329 536	44.0	37.6	18.1
District 5	930	32.0	2.3	334 968	20 154	6.0	314 814	43.5	36.7	19.5
District 6	974	31.6	1.4	347 198	14 603	4.2	332 595	41.8	41.0	17.0
District 7	1 147	29.5	2.3	362 684	20 523	5.7	342 161	45.0	41.2	13.7
District 8	1 097	32.1	3.6	338 604	22 351	6.6	316 253	44.9	44.0	11.1
District 9	1 074	31.0	2.4	347 608	21 064	6.1	326 544	41.0	42.5	16.5
District 10	1 082	31.5	1.4	349 589	17 920	5.1	331 669	39.1	42.7	17.6
MICHIGAN	675	31.1	1.9	5 058 549	481 140	9.5	4 577 409	32.6	42.2	24.7
District 1	501	29.6	2.2	315 675	29 165	9.2	286 510	26.3	45.9	26.7
District 2	596	30.3	2.1	354 918	31 601	8.9	323 317	28.4	40.2	30.3
District 3	651	29.3	1.5	364 033	29 383	8.1	334 650	31.0	42.0	26.5
District 4	592	33.6	2.5	337 285	34 402	10.2	302 883	29.1	43.8	26.1
District 5	590	33.1	1.6	304 697	33 074	10.9	271 623	27.2	44.9	27.7
District 6	592	30.0	1.9	349 720	31 274	8.9	318 446	30.0	40.2	28.7
District 7	644	30.5	1.5	341 614	27 059	7.9	314 555	30.8	39.8	28.8
District 8	698	30.7	1.4	370 246	23 951	6.5	346 295	37.8	41.6	20.2
District 9	835	27.5	1.6	354 454	24 781	7.0	329 673	48.8	36.9	14.2
District 10	701	28.4	2.0	377 852	33 307	8.8	344 545	31.6	40.5	27.4
District 11	759	26.4	0.9	383 160	26 673	7.0	356 487	39.4	40.4	20.1
District 12	725	30.0	2.0	332 357	34 658	10.4	297 699	31.1	43.6	25.3
District 13	695	37.1	2.8	251 857	47 251	18.8	204 606	25.3	50.5	24.0
District 14	719	37.1	3.0	264 086	46 171	17.5	217 915	26.2	49.9	23.9
District 15	773	32.1	1.8	356 595	28 390	8.0	328 205	37.5	40.3	22.1
MINNESOTA	701	29.0	2.0	2 887 040	150 922	5.2	2 736 118	36.5	40.8	22.0
District 1	556	26.4	1.2	352 120	14 644	4.2	337 476	33.3	39.4	25.5
District 2	801	27.2	1.2	413 885	18 069	4.4	395 816	38.0	40.7	20.8
District 3	869	28.0	1.6	361 401	16 099	4.5	345 302	44.0	40.5	15.4
District 4	751	31.4	2.8	322 401	20 996	6.5	301 405	41.0	41.6	17.3
District 5	741	31.0	3.5	344 100	23 423	6.8	320 677	40.0	42.8	17.0
District 6	706	28.8	1.4	418 166	20 695	4.9	397 471	35.5	39.5	24.6
District 7	511	27.9	1.6	336 819	15 419	4.6	321 400	30.8	39.6	27.8
District 8	568	29.2	2.4	338 148	21 577	6.4	316 571	28.8	43.1	27.2
MISSISSIPPI	584	31.8	3.9	1 325 054	118 203	8.9	1 206 851	28.1	40.5	30.1
District 1	536	30.0	3.3	364 159	31 863	8.7	332 296	26.3	37.4	35.2
District 2	562	33.6	4.4	301 331	36 407	12.1	264 924	25.9	45.2	27.4
District 3	602	32.2	3.1	342 337	24 610	7.2	317 727	31.7	39.0	27.6
District 4	645	30.8	4.7	317 227	25 323	8.0	291 904	28.3	41.3	29.6
MISSOURI	607	28.5	2.0	2 989 588	188 143	6.3	2 801 445	31.9	43.1	24.4
District 1	671	32.9	1.7	292 313	29 658	10.1	262 655	32.3	48.2	19.4
District 2	771	27.0	1.2	376 037	14 485	3.9	361 552	42.3	41.3	16.4
District 3	626	29.0	1.8	341 252	22 771	6.7	318 481	33.9	43.9	22.1
District 4	534	25.7	2.9	316 865	17 438	5.5	299 427	26.9	41.6	30.4
District 5	679	29.8	2.4	330 706	26 489	8.0	304 217	33.0	44.2	22.8

[7]Overcrowded or lacking complete plumbing facilities.
[8]Percent of civilian labor force.

Table A. 110th Congressional Districts—*Continued*

(Number, percent.)

STATE Congressional district	Social Security Beneficiaries (OASDI), December 2006							Supplemental Security Income, December 2006			
	Total	Rate per 1,000 population	Retired workers[9]	Disabled workers	Widow(er)s[10]	Spouses[11]	Children[12]	Total	Aged	Blind	Disabled
	67	68	69	70	71	72	73	74	75	76	77
LOUISIANA	722 643	168.5	371 872	114 609	97 808	54 832	83 522	157 977	16 825	1 615	139 537
District 1	114 630	175.6	65 155	16 479	14 602	7 883	10 511	16 813	1 806	157	14 850
District 2	59 164	150.6	30 225	10 719	7 307	3 261	7 652	17 786	1 716	98	15 972
District 3	104 905	171.2	47 254	18 406	15 085	10 279	13 881	22 544	2 025	182	20 337
District 4	114 018	176.0	62 999	17 022	14 729	7 412	11 856	25 332	3 222	310	21 800
District 5	119 378	187.4	60 681	19 004	16 804	8 767	14 122	31 544	3 767	355	27 422
District 6	98 577	142.9	51 234	15 017	12 948	7 151	12 227	20 354	1 761	256	18 337
District 7	111 971	171.1	54 324	17 962	16 333	10 079	13 273	23 604	2 528	257	20 819
MAINE	275 175	208.2	167 240	48 022	23 709	13 479	22 725	32 527	2 354	225	29 948
District 1	136 698	204.5	86 860	21 068	11 539	6 539	10 692	12 623	930	99	11 594
District 2	138 477	212.0	80 380	26 954	12 170	6 940	12 033	19 904	1 424	126	18 354
MARYLAND	778 689	138.7	515 455	94 524	71 121	34 396	63 193	96 375	15 298	649	80 428
District 1	127 856	179.3	89 340	13 388	11 011	5 722	8 395	8 594	1 046	74	7 474
District 2	106 817	154.6	65 517	15 960	11 001	4 533	9 806	14 227	1 178	103	12 946
District 3	100 524	145.5	67 761	11 492	9 832	4 342	7 097	11 885	2 399	77	9 409
District 4	68 732	100.3	44 446	8 864	5 111	2 479	7 832	11 028	2 506	79	8 443
District 5	81 029	108.1	53 536	9 611	6 954	3 593	7 335	7 379	1 287	49	6 043
District 6	113 801	157.4	75 281	13 330	11 221	5 953	8 016	8 378	794	62	7 522
District 7	97 476	146.2	59 113	16 147	8 898	2 861	10 457	26 308	2 190	143	23 975
District 8	82 454	118.4	60 461	5 732	7 093	4 913	4 255	8 576	3 898	62	4 616
MASSACHUSETTS	1 072 305	166.6	695 199	158 781	88 505	44 762	85 058	174 264	44 753	3 726	125 785
District 1	119 241	184.9	73 816	19 866	9 892	4 831	10 836	19 820	3 255	436	16 129
District 2	118 172	181.2	72 842	20 084	9 855	4 401	10 990	23 216	3 922	466	18 828
District 3	103 623	158.3	66 276	16 292	8 447	3 910	8 698	16 998	4 019	357	12 622
District 4	111 265	168.1	72 505	16 428	8 943	4 723	8 666	16 774	4 677	382	11 715
District 5	94 303	146.2	59 676	14 922	7 472	3 893	8 340	18 068	4 434	396	13 238
District 6	113 195	173.8	76 938	13 718	9 805	5 213	7 521	12 496	3 567	255	8 674
District 7	105 562	163.0	72 738	12 818	8 788	4 753	6 465	11 832	3 849	307	7 676
District 8	68 253	114.8	39 584	14 919	4 716	2 280	6 754	30 156	10 499	554	19 103
District 9	104 220	162.6	67 234	15 037	8 873	4 234	8 842	15 179	4 268	330	10 581
District 10	134 471	208.8	93 590	14 697	11 714	6 524	7 946	9 725	2 263	243	7 219
MICHIGAN	1 776 084	175.9	1 103 565	250 351	171 714	97 182	153 272	225 024	16 658	1 695	206 671
District 1	165 932	250.6	106 142	22 084	15 866	11 033	10 807	13 874	972	106	12 796
District 2	127 936	183.5	81 333	18 538	10 793	6 825	10 447	13 191	611	110	12 470
District 3	102 769	147.9	65 116	14 899	8 636	5 006	9 112	13 657	829	97	12 731
District 4	139 048	201.1	89 588	18 102	12 878	8 618	9 862	13 201	651	92	12 458
District 5	127 817	195.2	73 068	21 060	13 217	7 809	12 663	22 063	727	137	21 199
District 6	123 578	183.2	78 916	18 218	10 474	5 647	10 323	15 055	787	146	14 122
District 7	126 263	184.4	80 938	17 710	11 017	6 133	10 465	12 942	592	97	12 253
District 8	99 336	142.7	63 519	12 938	8 663	5 397	8 819	8 946	571	85	8 290
District 9	106 875	158.8	72 725	10 816	10 423	6 291	6 620	8 537	1 668	71	6 798
District 10	120 780	166.4	77 650	14 660	12 065	7 699	8 706	8 773	953	68	7 752
District 11	107 653	151.1	70 740	12 025	11 301	5 775	7 812	7 022	896	52	6 074
District 12	123 720	195.3	77 678	15 884	14 005	6 451	9 702	12 996	2 297	96	10 603
District 13	94 092	155.0	46 723	18 568	10 929	3 994	13 878	35 434	2 055	243	33 136
District 14	108 513	180.2	58 948	18 700	11 450	4 770	14 645	28 098	2 071	205	25 822
District 15	101 772	148.3	60 481	16 149	9 997	5 734	9 411	11 235	978	90	10 167
MINNESOTA	801 237	155.1	537 792	94 885	72 994	42 166	53 400	75 759	10 259	724	64 776
District 1	117 670	186.4	80 107	11 465	12 056	7 472	6 570	7 893	1 153	89	6 651
District 2	78 732	110.9	54 124	8 706	6 356	3 541	6 005	4 827	723	57	4 047
District 3	88 505	138.9	63 592	8 433	7 219	4 130	5 131	6 562	1 252	66	5 244
District 4	87 951	147.0	58 584	11 790	7 326	3 618	6 633	14 690	1 800	130	12 760
District 5	79 282	133.6	52 044	12 713	6 331	2 684	5 510	16 162	2 384	160	13 618
District 6	84 499	115.6	55 789	10 847	6 858	4 106	6 899	5 287	627	54	4 606
District 7	127 604	206.1	84 422	12 774	13 963	8 741	7 704	8 980	1 374	76	7 530
District 8	136 994	211.7	89 130	18 157	12 885	7 874	8 948	11 358	946	92	10 320
MISSISSIPPI	553 844	190.3	296 755	109 531	54 735	23 570	69 253	123 593	14 135	971	108 487
District 1	150 682	197.5	81 937	32 070	13 490	5 518	17 667	27 806	3 525	216	24 065
District 2	125 324	182.3	63 659	25 874	12 781	4 335	18 675	43 517	4 941	374	38 202
District 3	143 308	192.2	78 895	26 289	14 510	6 441	17 173	29 545	3 533	209	25 803
District 4	134 530	188.2	72 264	25 298	13 954	7 276	15 738	22 725	2 136	172	20 417
MISSOURI	1 077 060	184.3	663 590	168 301	101 208	51 092	92 869	119 823	9 231	981	109 611
District 1	109 446	186.6	64 884	18 815	9 549	3 636	12 562	20 880	1 555	164	19 161
District 2	105 635	152.2	73 257	10 152	9 782	5 782	6 662	3 607	440	41	3 126
District 3	102 879	159.0	64 341	16 012	10 049	4 352	8 125	10 553	829	103	9 621
District 4	134 674	204.7	83 439	20 831	12 278	6 635	11 491	12 105	866	112	11 127
District 5	106 691	171.4	67 272	17 223	8 868	3 901	9 427	13 379	1 007	132	12 240

[9]Includes special age-72 beneficiaries.
[10]Includes nondisabled widow(er)s, disabled widow(er)s, widowed mothers and fathers, and parents receiving payment on the record of a worker who is deceased.
[11]These beneficiaries receive payment on the record of a worker who is retired or disabled.
[12]These beneficiaries receive payment on the record of a worker who is retired, deceased, or disabled.

Table A. 110th Congressional Districts—*Continued*

(Number, percent.)

STATE Congressional district	Agriculture, 2002													
	Total farms	Farms by size (percent)			Land in farms		Percent of farms where principal operator's primary occupation is farming	Value of all agricultural products sold				Payments from federal farm programs		
		1 to 49 acres	50 to 999 acres	1,000 acres or more	Total acreage	Average size of farms (acres)		Total ($1,000)	Percent of farms with value of:			Total ($1,000)	Number of farms that receive payments	Percent of farms that receive payments
									Less than $50,000	$50,000 to $249,999	$250,000 or more			
	78	79	80	81	82	83	84	85	86	87	88	89	90	91

LOUISIANA	27 413	41.2	51.5	7.3	7 830 664	286	54.0	1 815 803	82.8	10.3	6.9	123 599	7 562	27.6
District 1	2 509	52.4	47.1	0.5	. . .	. . .	51.3	104 569	83.9	11.4	4.8	3 588	486	19.4
District 2	60	48.3	50.0	1.7	. . .	. . .	51.7	1 722	93.3	3.3	3.3	. . .	4	6.7
District 3	1 917	48.7	40.6	10.7	687 309	359	57.7	255 549	76.6	8.8	14.7	. . .	250	13.0
District 4	5 480	37.1	58.5	4.4	1 260 290	230	51.0	299 063	88.4	6.2	5.4	11 320	1 175	21.4
District 5	8 422	32.0	58.2	9.8	2 956 790	351	57.6	753 248	76.4	13.2	10.4	58 650	3 385	40.2
District 6	2 826	47.5	47.1	5.4	651 500	231	44.6	171 815	87.3	7.9	4.7	5 427	590	20.9
District 7	6 199	47.4	43.6	9.0	1 995 170	322	56.1	229 837	85.9	11.1	3.0	43 633	1 672	27.0
MAINE	7 196	38.6	58.8	2.6	1 369 768	190	47.4	463 603	86.3	9.2	4.6	8 664	1 244	17.3
District 1	2 572	50.0	49.3	0.7	276 575	108	48.5	83 295	88.8	8.7	2.5	1 757	221	8.6
District 2	4 624	32.3	64.1	3.6	1 093 193	236	46.8	380 307	84.8	9.5	5.7	6 907	1 023	22.1
MARYLAND	12 198	47.8	49.0	3.2	2 077 630	170	57.2	1 293 303	77.3	12.2	10.5	33 131	3 372	27.6
District 1	4 051	44.5	48.8	6.7	1 010 337	249	60.1	875 979	63.4	14.6	22.0	18 892	1 748	43.1
District 2	166	61.4	38.0	0.6	12 557	76	54.8	8 882	78.9	15.7	5.4	77	16	9.6
District 3	119	73.9	26.1	0.0	6 107	51	47.9	8 824	85.7	10.9	3.4	7	8	6.7
District 4	261	61.7	36.0	2.3	34 207	131	49.0	31 598	83.9	8.8	7.3	318	32	12.3
District 5	2 033	53.0	45.9	1.1	216 320	106	57.5	39 341	92.5	6.4	1.1	1 583	299	14.7
District 6	4 922	44.8	53.8	1.4	717 861	146	56.2	296 508	80.5	13.2	6.3	10 977	1 151	23.4
District 7	353	63.7	33.4	2.8	38 504	109	51.0	21 903	87.5	7.6	4.8	571	66	18.7
District 8	293	57.7	40.3	2.0	41 737	142	51.2	10 267	88.1	8.2	3.8	706	52	17.7
MASSACHUSETTS	6 075	60.0	39.4	0.5	518 570	85	54.0	384 314	82.3	12.6	5.1	4 268	415	6.8
District 1	2 160	45.2	54.0	0.7	263 787	122	52.5	127 425	83.8	10.6	5.6	2 304	192	8.9
District 2	730	52.2	47.8	0.0	58 060	80	52.5	34 833	83.4	11.5	5.1	527	63	8.6
District 3	371	64.2	35.6	0.3	23 482	63	49.6	35 570	83.6	12.1	4.3	81	16	4.3
District 4	798	67.0	32.5	0.5	54 843	69	58.5	45 590	81.2	14.0	4.8	488	52	6.5
District 5	532	65.4	34.4	0.2	31 987	60	58.3	42 027	81.2	12.4	6.4	366	37	7.0
District 6	366	73.2	26.5	0.3	24 873	68	51.1	27 513	79.8	15.8	4.4	146	12	3.3
District 7	68	79.4	20.6	0.0	2 873	42	58.8	22 884	67.6	16.2	16.2	. . .	1	1.5
District 8	6	66.7	33.3	0.0	281	47	66.7	297	66.7	33.3	0.0	. . .	. . .	. . .
District 9	81	70.4	28.4	1.2	4 913	61	44.4	5 055	81.5	13.6	4.9	. . .	5	6.2
District 10	963	81.4	17.7	0.9	53 471	56	55.9	43 120	81.3	15.2	3.5	335	37	3.8
MICHIGAN	53 315	41.1	55.2	3.7	10 142 958	190	54.5	3 772 435	81.8	12.1	6.1	144 771	18 133	34.0
District 1	6 783	29.4	67.5	3.1	1 356 992	200	53.6	239 550	86.6	9.8	3.5	9 995	1 766	26.0
District 2	5 704	43.4	54.5	2.1	855 633	150	52.4	642 326	80.1	11.5	8.3	12 819	1 330	23.3
District 3	3 167	45.0	51.7	3.4	537 901	170	52.6	277 796	84.1	9.9	6.0	8 931	1 115	35.2
District 4	8 597	34.2	61.9	3.9	1 789 857	208	56.0	521 445	82.0	12.4	5.6	23 631	3 351	39.0
District 5	2 827	44.7	50.3	5.0	599 039	212	59.5	169 889	78.3	14.8	7.0	8 100	1 091	38.6
District 6	5 831	47.1	49.0	3.9	1 084 879	186	56.5	621 052	78.2	13.1	8.7	16 545	1 798	30.8
District 7	8 580	40.4	55.5	4.1	1 655 008	193	50.8	444 832	84.4	11.2	4.4	28 753	3 729	43.5
District 8	3 916	51.5	45.4	3.1	639 493	163	49.7	199 167	85.1	10.0	4.9	9 997	1 084	27.7
District 9	82	67.1	30.5	2.4	7 280	89	43.9	27 125	85.4	6.1	8.5	24	6	7.3
District 10	5 743	40.1	54.9	5.0	1 306 071	227	61.1	482 026	75.2	16.0	8.8	20 900	2 336	40.7
District 11	335	79.4	19.7	0.9	18 835	56	51.9	19 333	87.2	8.4	4.5	139	24	7.2
District 12	10	70.0	30.0	0.0	325	33	60.0	. . .	100.0	0.0	0.0	. . .	. . .	. . .
District 13	17	76.5	23.5	0.0	815	48	11.8	546	76.5	23.5	0.0	. . .	3	17.6
District 14	18	66.7	33.3	0.0	701	39	27.8	. . .	94.4	5.6	0.0	. . .	5	27.8
District 15	1 705	53.5	42.9	3.6	290 129	170	55.1	127 090	79.9	15.4	4.8	4 932	495	29.0
MINNESOTA	80 839	24.9	67.2	7.9	27 512 270	340	62.9	8 575 627	67.1	22.2	10.7	350 709	43 927	54.3
District 1	21 384	25.7	66.5	7.8	7 417 386	347	69.7	3 186 486	53.8	30.3	15.9	108 132	13 291	62.2
District 2	6 784	39.3	56.8	3.9	1 424 134	210	57.5	569 025	70.7	20.6	8.6	21 459	3 360	49.5
District 3	600	60.5	38.2	1.3	64 222	107	51.8	54 034	81.2	13.5	5.3	883	153	25.5
District 4	111	74.8	25.2	0.0	4 653	42	53.2	. . .	73.9	16.2	9.9	19	5	4.5
District 5	21	61.9	38.1	0.0	1 020	49	28.6	. . .	95.2	0.0	4.8	6	4	19.0
District 6	6 691	38.1	59.9	2.0	1 130 137	169	56.9	522 287	77.2	16.5	6.3	14 165	2 525	37.7
District 7	32 629	18.2	69.4	12.4	14 848 949	455	64.8	3 792 754	64.8	23.2	11.9	193 524	21 762	66.7
District 8	12 619	24.0	73.9	2.1	2 621 769	208	53.0	432 003	87.7	9.9	2.4	12 521	2 827	22.4
MISSISSIPPI	42 186	30.0	65.1	5.0	11 097 543	263	48.8	3 116 295	87.1	5.4	7.5	145 508	12 383	29.4
District 1	12 947	28.3	67.5	4.1	3 023 453	234	44.1	370 423	93.1	4.4	2.5	28 559	5 210	40.2
District 2	8 847	21.8	64.8	13.4	4 637 093	524	53.9	1 066 712	80.1	8.2	11.7	102 209	3 626	41.0
District 3	13 241	29.5	68.2	2.2	2 531 167	191	50.8	1 308 446	84.9	4.7	10.4	12 280	2 779	21.0
District 4	7 151	43.9	55.1	1.0	905 830	127	47.2	370 504	89.1	5.0	5.9	2 460	768	10.7
MISSOURI	106 797	23.1	71.5	5.4	29 946 035	280	57.2	4 983 255	84.7	11.4	3.9	264 475	43 379	40.6
District 1	103	52.4	45.6	1.9	13 159	128	57.3	4 488	86.4	6.8	6.8	153	25	24.3
District 2	1 735	34.2	61.4	4.4	391 538	226	51.8	85 698	82.3	14.1	3.6	4 575	749	43.2
District 3	1 491	27.6	69.2	3.2	317 404	213	51.3	31 389	92.2	6.1	1.7	1 402	383	25.7
District 4	26 556	23.7	71.6	4.7	6 986 378	263	58.5	1 169 374	85.0	11.5	3.4	45 830	9 741	36.7
District 5	594	55.6	41.6	2.9	94 515	159	47.5	14 868	92.3	5.2	2.5	533	136	22.9

. . . = Not available.

Table A. 110th Congressional Districts—*Continued*

(Number, percent.)

STATE Congressional district	Representative	Land area,[1] (sq km)	Total population	Persons per square kilometer	White	Black	American Indian/ Alaska Native	Asian and Pacific Islander	Some other race (percent)	Two or more races (percent)	Hispanic or Latino[2] (percent)	Non-Hispanic White (percent)
					Population and population characteristics, 2006 — Race alone (percent)							
	1	2	3	4	5	6	7	8	9	10	11	12
MISSOURI—*Continued*												
District 6	Rep. Sam Graves (R)	33 753	664 783	19.7	92.0	3.1	0.4	1.2	1.2	2.0	2.9	90.4
District 7	Rep. Roy Blunt (R)	14 192	676 969	47.7	92.9	1.2	0.7	1.1	1.3	2.8	3.6	91.0
District 8	Rep. Jo Ann Emerson (R)	48 384	634 998	13.1	92.5	4.6	0.5	0.8	0.2	1.3	1.1	91.8
District 9	Rep. Kenny C. Hulshof (R)	36 067	657 845	18.2	92.7	3.9	0.3	1.2	0.5	1.4	1.4	91.9
MONTANA		376 979	944 632	2.5	89.7	0.5	6.3	0.7	0.9	2.0	2.2	88.6
At Large	Rep. Dennis R. Rehberg (R)	376 979	944 632	2.5	89.7	0.5	6.3	0.7	0.9	2.0	2.2	88.6
NEBRASKA		199 099	1 768 331	8.9	88.6	4.1	0.9	1.7	3.2	1.5	7.4	84.8
District 1	Rep. Jeff Fortenberry (R)	30 952	598 164	19.3	91.4	1.8	1.6	1.9	2.3	1.0	5.6	88.7
District 2	Rep. Lee Terry (R)	1 063	609 320	573.2	80.9	9.9	0.3	2.5	4.0	2.4	8.7	76.6
District 3	Rep. Adrian Smith (R)	167 083	560 847	3.4	94.0	0.2	0.9	0.7	3.1	1.1	7.8	89.7
NEVADA		284 448	2 495 529	8.8	73.6	7.3	1.2	6.4	8.3	3.2	24.4	58.6
District 1	Rep. Shelley Berkley (D)	459	797 562	1 737.6	66.4	12.4	0.6	6.6	10.5	3.5	34.9	43.5
District 2	Rep. Dean Heller (R)	272 153	794 501	2.9	80.3	2.5	2.5	3.6	8.3	2.8	18.7	71.0
District 3	Rep. Jon C. Porter (R)	11 836	903 466	76.3	74.2	7.1	0.6	8.6	6.2	3.3	20.2	61.2
NEW HAMPSHIRE		23 227	1 314 895	56.6	95.1	1.1	0.2	2.0	0.8	0.8	2.3	93.6
District 1	Rep. Carol Shea-Porter (D)	6 342	662 097	104.4	95.6	1.1	0.2	1.8	0.4	0.9	2.2	93.9
District 2	Rep. Paul W. Hodes (D)	16 885	652 798	38.7	94.6	1.0	0.2	2.3	1.1	0.8	2.3	93.3
NEW JERSEY		19 211	8 724 560	454.1	69.6	13.6	0.2	7.5	7.6	1.5	15.6	62.3
District 1	Rep. Robert E. Andrews (D)	867	665 756	767.9	70.6	17.7	0.2	3.7	5.9	1.8	9.8	67.6
District 2	Rep. Frank A. LoBiondo (R)	5 133	683 207	133.1	74.2	14.3	0.3	3.1	6.7	1.3	12.1	69.2
District 3	Rep. Jim Saxton (R)	2 397	698 873	291.6	82.2	9.2	0.1	3.8	2.8	1.8	5.7	79.5
District 4	Rep. Christopher H. Smith (R)	1 862	693 578	372.5	82.5	9.4	0.1	2.8	4.3	0.8	9.7	77.5
District 5	Rep. Scott Garrett (R)	2 846	670 283	235.5	85.2	1.9	0.2	9.3	2.1	1.3	6.2	81.5
District 6	Rep. Frank Pallone Jr. (D)	509	659 998	1 296.7	63.0	15.7	0.3	10.8	8.3	1.9	14.8	57.3
District 7	Rep. Mike Ferguson (R)	1 541	681 380	442.2	79.4	5.6	0.1	10.4	3.4	1.1	9.9	73.0
District 8	Rep. Bill Pascrell Jr. (D)	277	656 603	2 370.4	60.0	13.2	0.1	6.1	18.9	1.6	29.9	49.6
District 9	Rep. Steven R. Rothman (D)	241	654 945	2 717.6	69.8	7.5	0.1	12.9	8.4	1.3	24.1	54.9
District 10	Rep. Donald M. Payne (D)	171	642 024	3 754.5	24.5	58.3	0.4	4.7	10.2	1.9	18.8	17.3
District 11	Rep. Rodney P. Frelinghuysen (R)	1 580	685 030	433.6	84.0	3.0	0.1	8.9	2.9	1.1	9.1	78.4
District 12	Rep. Rush D. Holt (D)	1 640	687 992	419.5	71.7	11.1	0.1	13.5	2.0	1.6	6.0	68.1
District 13	Rep. Albio Sires (D)	147	644 891	4 387.0	53.4	12.4	0.6	8.0	24.0	1.7	50.3	29.6
NEW MEXICO		314 309	1 954 599	6.2	67.8	2.0	9.7	1.4	15.8	3.2	44.0	42.4
District 1	Rep. Heather Wilson (R)	12 216	669 340	54.8	65.7	2.9	4.8	2.3	20.6	3.7	45.2	44.3
District 2	Rep. Stevan Pearce (R)	179 986	632 111	3.5	76.0	1.8	5.4	0.9	12.7	3.3	49.6	41.6
District 3	Rep. Tom Udall (D)	122 108	653 148	5.3	62.1	1.4	18.8	1.0	14.0	2.7	37.4	41.2
NEW YORK		122 283	19 306 183	157.9	66.4	15.5	0.3	6.9	9.2	1.7	16.3	60.2
District 1	Rep. Timothy H. Bishop (D)	1 674	682 472	407.7	87.3	4.3	0.1	3.8	3.0	1.6	9.8	81.2
District 2	Rep. Steve Israel (D)	620	675 077	1 088.8	78.2	11.3	0.2	4.0	5.0	1.3	16.8	67.3
District 3	Rep. Peter T. King (R)	475	660 490	1 390.5	87.7	3.3	0.1	4.4	3.5	1.0	8.0	83.4
District 4	Rep. Carolyn McCarthy (D)	233	641 512	2 753.3	62.7	19.1	0.2	6.5	10.1	1.4	17.1	55.9
District 5	Rep. Gary L. Ackerman (D)	172	654 035	3 802.5	54.1	4.5	0.1	30.3	9.5	1.5	24.9	39.6
District 6	Rep. Gregory W. Meeks (D)	102	671 957	6 587.8	16.7	52.4	0.7	12.8	14.9	2.6	17.3	11.5
District 7	Rep. Joseph Crowley (D)	68	664 805	9 776.5	40.5	16.8	0.2	15.1	25.6	1.9	42.2	25.2
District 8	Rep. Jerrold Nadler (D)	39	692 822	17 764.7	74.0	4.8	0.0	14.8	4.8	1.5	10.8	68.6
District 9	Rep. Anthony D. Weiner (D)	96	674 844	7 029.6	69.4	4.5	0.3	17.4	6.9	1.4	14.8	62.7
District 10	Rep. Edolphus Towns (D)	46	684 607	14 882.8	22.2	61.6	0.2	3.6	10.8	1.5	16.1	18.0
District 11	Rep. Yvette D. Clarke (D)	31	656 345	21 172.4	28.9	57.6	0.3	4.2	6.9	2.1	12.0	25.7
District 12	Rep. Nydia M. Velázquez (D)	49	677 789	13 832.4	45.3	10.6	0.3	18.1	23.9	1.8	47.3	24.2
District 13	Rep. Vito Fossella (R)	168	688 651	4 099.1	74.2	7.4	0.2	11.6	5.1	1.6	13.7	66.6
District 14	Rep. Carolyn B. Maloney (D)	33	642 674	19 475.0	77.4	4.7	0.1	11.7	4.3	1.8	15.0	67.1
District 15	Rep. Charles B. Rangel (D)	27	671 585	24 873.5	28.4	31.2	0.7	3.6	32.8	3.4	46.5	19.9
District 16	Rep. José E. Serrano (D)	31	669 910	21 610.0	11.6	31.7	0.2	2.2	52.2	2.1	65.7	2.2
District 17	Rep. Eliot L. Engel (D)	328	668 624	2 038.5	44.9	32.6	0.2	4.6	15.5	2.2	22.6	38.6
District 18	Rep. Nita M. Lowey (D)	575	671 922	1 168.6	72.2	9.9	0.2	6.5	10.0	1.2	18.4	64.3
District 19	Rep. John J. Hall (D)	3 629	706 420	194.7	82.8	6.1	0.2	3.2	5.8	1.9	10.7	78.4
District 20	Rep. Kirsten E. Gillibrand (D)	18 176	673 470	37.1	93.4	2.6	0.2	1.5	0.8	1.5	2.5	92.1
District 21	Rep. Michael R. McNulty (D)	5 012	664 724	132.6	83.9	8.6	0.3	3.4	2.0	1.7	4.0	82.1
District 22	Rep. Maurice D. Hinchey (D)	8 407	676 625	80.5	80.4	8.3	0.2	3.6	4.9	2.6	10.3	75.9
District 23	Rep. John M. McHugh (R)	34 278	657 220	19.2	93.7	2.5	1.0	0.8	0.7	1.3	2.3	92.5
District 24	Rep. Michael A. Arcuri (D)	15 964	652 981	40.9	92.3	4.0	0.2	1.2	1.0	1.4	2.9	90.7
District 25	Rep. James T. Walsh (R)	4 195	664 395	158.4	86.6	7.9	0.5	2.4	0.7	1.9	2.7	85.1
District 26	Rep. Thomas M. Reynolds (R)	7 073	670 455	94.8	92.2	3.2	0.5	2.3	0.6	1.2	2.2	90.8
District 27	Rep. Brian Higgins (D)	4 740	625 552	132.0	89.4	5.5	0.7	0.5	1.8	2.0	5.2	87.1
District 28	Rep. Louise McIntosh Slaughter (D)	1 383	610 440	441.4	64.5	29.6	0.4	2.1	1.6	1.8	5.9	60.9
District 29	Rep. John R. "Randy" Kuhl Jr. (R)	14 660	653 780	44.6	92.6	2.9	0.6	2.2	0.3	1.3	1.6	91.6

[1]Dry land or land partially or temporarily covered by water.
[2]May be of any race.

Table A. 110th Congressional Districts—*Continued*

(Number, percent.)

STATE Congressional district	Percent female	Percent foreign born	Percent born in state of residence	Population and population characteristics, 2006—*Continued*								
				Age (percent)								
				Under 5 years	5 to 18 years	18 to 24 years	25 to 34 years	35 to 44 years	45 to 54 years	55 to 64 years	65 to 74 years	75 years and over
	13	14	15	16	17	18	19	20	21	22	23	24
MISSOURI—*Continued*												
District 6	50.8	2.7	64.0	6.7	17.6	9.0	13.2	14.6	15.0	11.0	6.5	6.4
District 7	51.1	2.4	57.0	6.7	16.9	11.0	13.9	13.0	13.7	10.8	7.1	6.8
District 8	51.2	1.2	72.0	6.5	17.2	9.3	13.3	12.6	14.0	11.1	8.2	7.8
District 9	50.7	2.0	70.6	6.5	17.0	11.7	13.3	13.7	14.3	10.5	6.6	6.4
MONTANA	50.1	1.9	53.5	6.1	17.0	10.1	11.8	12.7	16.1	12.2	7.2	6.7
At Large	50.1	1.9	53.5	6.1	17.0	10.1	11.8	12.7	16.1	12.2	7.2	6.7
NEBRASKA	50.4	5.6	65.5	7.3	17.9	10.6	13.0	13.2	14.5	10.3	6.4	6.8
District 1	49.6	5.2	68.2	7.0	17.3	11.6	13.7	13.1	14.3	10.1	6.1	6.8
District 2	50.6	7.3	57.2	8.2	18.8	10.3	14.4	14.6	14.2	9.5	5.3	4.8
District 3	51.0	4.2	71.7	6.5	17.6	9.8	10.8	11.9	15.1	11.4	7.8	9.1
NEVADA	49.0	19.1	23.1	7.4	18.1	8.7	14.9	15.3	13.6	11.0	6.3	4.7
District 1	49.1	25.7	22.7	8.5	20.1	8.1	16.1	16.0	12.5	9.5	5.1	4.1
District 2	48.3	13.2	26.8	6.6	17.6	9.7	12.6	14.8	14.5	11.7	7.1	5.5
District 3	49.5	18.4	20.1	7.0	16.8	8.3	16.0	15.2	13.9	11.7	6.6	4.6
NEW HAMPSHIRE	50.8	5.4	41.8	5.6	17.1	9.2	11.7	15.8	16.6	11.8	6.3	6.0
District 1	50.9	5.6	41.3	5.7	17.2	9.4	11.9	16.1	16.5	11.6	6.0	5.5
District 2	50.6	5.2	42.3	5.5	16.9	8.9	11.5	15.5	16.6	12.0	6.7	6.5
NEW JERSEY	51.2	20.1	52.4	6.4	17.5	8.8	12.4	16.0	15.2	10.8	6.4	6.5
District 1	51.4	7.6	54.4	6.1	17.8	10.4	13.5	14.9	15.2	10.5	6.1	5.5
District 2	51.1	9.4	58.6	6.1	17.6	8.5	12.6	16.1	14.6	10.6	6.9	7.0
District 3	51.4	9.1	54.1	5.7	16.9	7.3	12.1	15.7	14.7	11.3	7.5	9.0
District 4	51.3	12.3	60.5	6.9	17.5	8.3	12.1	15.0	14.6	9.9	7.0	8.6
District 5	50.9	14.7	54.6	5.6	19.1	8.2	8.3	16.4	17.1	11.8	6.7	6.8
District 6	50.2	22.2	52.6	6.2	16.3	11.9	14.0	15.1	14.4	10.7	5.7	5.6
District 7	50.7	19.1	57.1	6.5	18.3	7.1	10.1	16.9	17.4	11.0	6.2	6.4
District 8	52.1	27.6	52.0	7.5	18.2	9.0	12.3	15.2	14.4	10.7	6.1	6.6
District 9	51.4	35.5	42.9	6.0	15.1	7.8	13.9	16.4	15.5	11.2	7.3	6.8
District 10	52.8	28.4	49.3	7.5	19.2	10.0	13.8	15.4	13.4	10.4	5.7	4.7
District 11	50.9	17.4	57.3	6.4	18.3	7.6	9.7	16.8	16.5	12.2	6.3	6.0
District 12	51.9	18.7	49.2	6.1	17.7	8.2	11.6	15.9	16.3	11.4	6.4	6.2
District 13	49.0	42.1	37.6	6.8	15.8	9.9	17.9	17.6	13.2	8.8	5.3	4.7
NEW MEXICO	50.7	10.1	50.9	7.3	18.9	10.5	13.1	13.3	13.9	10.8	6.5	5.8
District 1	50.9	11.9	47.8	7.0	17.9	10.2	13.9	14.0	14.4	11.1	5.8	5.6
District 2	50.4	12.2	48.8	7.5	19.5	11.1	12.6	12.6	13.0	10.4	7.3	6.1
District 3	50.8	6.1	56.0	7.2	19.2	10.1	12.9	13.2	14.2	10.8	6.6	5.7
NEW YORK	51.6	21.6	64.5	6.3	17.1	10.1	13.0	15.0	14.6	10.8	6.6	6.5
District 1	51.1	11.0	79.2	6.9	17.8	9.0	10.9	15.8	15.1	11.6	7.1	5.8
District 2	50.2	16.7	74.9	6.3	19.1	9.0	11.0	15.5	16.0	11.1	6.3	5.8
District 3	51.6	12.5	81.2	5.8	17.7	9.1	8.5	15.1	17.1	12.5	6.7	7.5
District 4	51.3	25.2	67.1	6.2	17.6	9.9	10.8	14.6	15.2	11.5	7.1	7.1
District 5	50.8	49.1	45.4	5.6	14.6	8.7	12.9	15.5	15.4	11.5	7.6	8.2
District 6	53.2	43.9	47.3	7.3	19.3	9.4	12.4	15.3	14.9	10.2	6.2	4.9
District 7	52.3	39.2	50.6	6.6	16.4	9.2	14.7	15.8	13.1	11.0	6.6	6.7
District 8	50.4	32.1	45.4	6.6	12.2	8.8	16.9	18.0	13.3	10.4	6.8	6.9
District 9	51.6	41.9	52.7	6.3	15.8	8.1	11.9	15.0	14.8	11.7	7.4	8.9
District 10	54.3	30.9	56.2	8.3	21.8	11.3	13.4	13.7	12.4	9.0	5.6	4.5
District 11	54.5	39.1	47.3	8.2	17.8	10.1	15.4	15.3	13.6	10.1	5.3	4.1
District 12	50.7	41.9	41.8	7.2	15.8	9.7	17.2	16.8	13.6	9.2	5.6	5.0
District 13	51.6	26.6	67.0	6.2	16.8	9.1	12.7	15.8	14.8	11.0	7.2	6.4
District 14	52.8	30.1	45.6	5.2	9.6	7.2	20.9	19.3	13.2	11.3	6.7	6.5
District 15	52.3	33.2	46.9	6.9	15.3	10.9	16.7	15.6	13.3	9.1	6.4	5.9
District 16	52.7	35.5	50.3	9.0	23.9	11.2	14.8	14.5	12.3	7.4	4.4	2.6
District 17	53.1	29.2	57.0	7.8	18.3	10.2	12.5	14.2	13.6	10.6	6.6	6.2
District 18	51.4	22.4	63.1	6.6	18.5	9.0	10.7	15.3	15.0	11.5	6.6	6.9
District 19	50.1	11.8	69.9	6.1	18.8	9.4	10.7	15.9	16.4	11.2	6.2	5.4
District 20	49.9	4.3	76.6	4.9	16.3	9.7	12.1	15.0	15.9	12.0	7.2	6.8
District 21	51.8	6.5	78.9	5.5	16.0	11.7	12.7	13.7	14.5	11.3	6.5	8.1
District 22	50.6	10.6	68.8	5.1	16.0	14.0	13.4	13.4	14.2	10.5	6.6	6.8
District 23	49.6	2.7	80.1	5.4	16.5	12.4	13.6	14.1	14.7	10.5	6.6	6.2
District 24	50.7	4.2	80.5	5.2	16.0	11.6	12.4	13.4	15.2	11.7	7.0	7.5
District 25	51.7	5.5	79.5	5.7	18.3	10.2	11.3	14.3	15.5	10.9	6.7	7.2
District 26	51.1	5.1	83.4	5.6	16.6	10.9	11.3	14.2	15.9	11.1	6.7	7.8
District 27	51.1	3.4	81.9	5.0	17.2	9.8	11.0	14.2	15.6	11.8	7.5	8.0
District 28	52.6	5.8	75.9	5.9	17.4	11.9	12.8	13.1	14.7	10.4	6.4	7.4
District 29	50.8	4.8	77.4	5.7	16.7	11.3	11.6	13.4	15.0	11.9	7.2	7.4

Table A. 110th Congressional Districts—*Continued*

(Number, percent.)

STATE Congressional district	Households, 2006						Group quarters, 2006		Group quarters, 2000			
	Number	Average household size	Family households (percent)	Married-couple family (percent)	Female family house-holder[4] (percent)	One-person households (percent)	Total in group quarters	Percent 65 years and over	Persons in correctional institutions	Persons in nursing homes	Persons in college dormitories	Persons in military quarters
	25	26	27	28	29	30	31	32	33	34	35	36
MISSOURI—*Continued*												
District 6	256 009	2.53	67.7	54.5	9.6	26.8	17 546	27.8	7 902	5 672	4 520	0
District 7	273 464	2.40	65.6	52.3	9.4	28.0	20 451	22.7	1 910	5 090	10 022	0
District 8	251 233	2.45	66.9	52.1	11.1	28.2	19 468	36.0	4 486	7 332	3 641	0
District 9	257 309	2.42	67.8	53.9	9.3	26.2	34 166	16.3	8 301	6 009	11 732	0
MONTANA	372 190	2.47	64.6	53.0	8.1	28.9	25 102	27.9	4 124	6 470	7 035	404
At Large	372 190	2.47	64.6	53.0	8.1	28.9	25 102	27.9	4 124	6 470	7 035	404
NEBRASKA	700 888	2.45	66.0	52.9	9.3	28.3	52 087	33.5	6 060	16 195	18 376	590
District 1	235 548	2.43	65.6	53.9	8.2	28.1	26 694	25.1	3 142	5 242	10 724	0
District 2	237 616	2.51	64.4	48.5	11.8	29.0	11 915	33.2	1 847	3 430	2 836	590
District 3	227 724	2.40	68.0	56.7	7.9	28.0	13 478	50.3	1 071	7 523	4 816	0
NEVADA	936 828	2.63	65.4	47.4	11.6	26.6	33 434	20.1	15 940	4 895	2 498	1 312
District 1	287 476	2.74	65.9	44.7	14.1	26.3	10 074	29.0	4 811	1 918	1 042	0
District 2	298 373	2.60	63.8	47.9	10.4	28.4	17 820	14.8	9 188	2 039	1 456	945
District 3	350 979	2.56	66.2	49.1	10.6	25.2	5 540	20.8	1 941	938	0	367
NEW HAMPSHIRE	504 503	2.53	66.5	53.1	9.1	25.6	37 347	30.7	3 468	9 316	17 574	95
District 1	256 033	2.53	65.6	52.3	9.6	26.6	15 251	36.8	1 422	4 224	7 544	89
District 2	248 470	2.54	67.4	54.0	8.6	24.6	22 096	26.4	2 046	5 092	10 030	6
NEW JERSEY	3 135 490	2.72	69.5	52.0	12.9	25.6	197 712	28.6	47 941	51 493	45 222	3 291
District 1	245 486	2.66	68.4	47.2	16.1	26.8	11 951	18.7	3 610	3 678	2 781	0
District 2	253 919	2.59	67.2	48.2	14.4	27.9	26 431	16.4	10 556	4 555	2 017	355
District 3	263 412	2.60	71.2	56.4	10.7	23.4	12 785	44.9	5 637	4 410	4	1 229
District 4	255 362	2.67	69.3	56.1	9.6	26.2	12 032	30.0	4 396	5 554	796	1 409
District 5	232 603	2.83	76.5	64.6	8.2	19.7	11 751	53.2	267	6 190	1 650	0
District 6	233 261	2.71	66.6	49.7	11.9	27.3	27 519	23.8	19	3 879	10 850	23
District 7	236 104	2.83	75.5	62.4	9.7	21.1	12 214	35.9	5 226	2 852	0	0
District 8	220 340	2.90	70.3	50.5	14.4	25.8	16 663	38.2	1 921	3 653	2 708	0
District 9	251 662	2.58	65.1	48.5	12.0	29.9	5 743	50.6	980	1 609	933	0
District 10	226 087	2.77	65.3	32.2	26.0	30.1	15 008	20.2	4 594	3 038	5 488	0
District 11	239 592	2.81	74.8	62.6	9.0	21.7	12 883	39.6	1 669	4 444	3 187	10
District 12	244 171	2.74	71.5	58.0	10.2	23.3	19 981	19.8	5 240	3 810	12 248	255
District 13	233 491	2.71	62.3	38.5	16.9	29.9	12 751	16.5	3 826	3 821	2 560	10
NEW MEXICO	726 033	2.64	65.8	47.6	12.7	28.4	40 752	24.3	10 940	6 810	7 921	1 827
District 1	268 634	2.46	60.6	43.0	12.2	32.7	9 007	20.8	2 444	1 835	2 377	431
District 2	227 850	2.70	69.5	50.8	13.6	25.0	18 022	9.7	6 324	2 729	3 530	834
District 3	229 549	2.79	68.1	49.8	12.3	26.8	13 723	45.8	2 172	2 246	2 014	562
NEW YORK	7 088 376	2.64	64.5	45.1	14.6	29.4	603 275	24.6	108 088	123 852	174 111	8 598
District 1	232 300	2.88	74.1	59.5	10.4	21.9	14 443	35.8	1 471	4 450	6 959	21
District 2	212 143	3.14	77.9	61.6	11.5	17.2	8 280	61.9	0	3 867	1 406	18
District 3	218 881	2.97	76.2	62.7	9.3	19.8	11 250	33.3	0	3 039	151	4
District 4	206 991	3.04	74.8	57.8	12.6	21.1	11 873	26.5	1 423	3 214	4 142	0
District 5	226 736	2.83	69.5	52.4	11.0	25.2	12 506	49.2	0	4 694	2 566	0
District 6	197 972	3.34	75.5	45.3	23.7	20.6	10 056	45.3	0	4 814	954	0
District 7	241 155	2.71	64.3	37.9	19.2	29.7	10 476	55.0	0	5 561	1 490	0
District 8	309 177	2.17	43.6	34.6	6.4	47.5	22 239	12.5	2 517	2 669	10 558	0
District 9	253 834	2.65	66.2	49.2	12.2	29.9	3 393	72.4	467	2 869	65	0
District 10	225 915	2.96	65.7	30.4	28.9	29.7	15 451	27.6	695	2 710	1 815	0
District 11	235 698	2.75	63.3	30.5	26.0	29.5	7 172	39.6	141	2 198	768	0
District 12	234 804	2.83	61.4	34.1	20.4	29.8	12 576	17.5	1 321	1 306	449	0
District 13	244 837	2.76	71.3	53.5	13.0	24.2	11 829	38.1	944	4 108	1 048	230
District 14	319 236	1.97	39.9	30.2	7.2	50.1	12 783	20.5	620	2 532	5 920	0
District 15	247 609	2.56	51.8	22.1	24.4	41.5	36 780	11.9	13 642	3 176	10 564	0
District 16	222 784	2.92	68.2	22.9	37.4	27.8	18 757	16.2	955	2 669	2 442	0
District 17	229 674	2.82	66.0	40.7	20.7	29.5	19 804	55.1	9	6 659	3 448	0
District 18	232 900	2.79	68.8	54.2	10.7	26.6	22 877	27.1	3 735	5 336	4 292	0
District 19	234 364	2.87	75.3	62.3	7.9	21.0	33 984	19.7	8 686	3 946	6 861	3 695
District 20	258 403	2.48	67.7	53.1	10.7	26.1	31 734	27.0	11 583	4 962	5 126	0
District 21	269 376	2.35	60.3	43.6	12.6	31.9	31 679	25.5	2 318	7 427	14 507	0
District 22	257 572	2.46	61.1	44.8	12.4	30.6	42 381	15.2	5 924	4 959	18 576	1
District 23	248 720	2.45	66.2	51.5	10.1	26.9	46 645	10.8	15 753	4 102	15 623	4 616
District 24	256 252	2.40	65.9	49.3	11.7	27.8	39 246	14.2	11 480	5 614	11 474	13
District 25	261 243	2.48	63.8	48.0	11.9	29.0	16 599	26.6	1 418	4 167	7 028	0
District 26	249 493	2.56	68.0	55.6	8.9	26.1	31 413	23.0	11 383	6 652	10 445	0
District 27	256 556	2.38	62.3	45.6	12.2	31.3	15 627	30.2	6 647	4 623	4 324	0
District 28	251 848	2.34	56.0	33.3	18.3	37.5	20 458	25.9	939	6 330	6 754	0
District 29	251 903	2.47	68.6	52.9	10.9	25.9	30 964	21.6	3 917	5 199	14 356	0

[4]No spouse present.

Table A. 110th Congressional Districts—*Continued*

(Number, percent.)

STATE Congressional district	Education, 2006				Income, 2006			Poverty, 2006		
	School enrollment[5]		Attainment level[6] (percent)		Per capita income (dollars)	Median household income (dollars)	Percent of households with income over $100,000	Persons below poverty level (percent)	Families below poverty level (percent)	Percent of households receiving food stamps in past 12 months
	Total	Private (percent)	High school graduate or more	Bachelor's degree or more						
	37	38	39	40	41	42	43	44	45	46
MISSOURI—*Continued*										
District 6	164 631	16.6	88.9	24.3	23 611	48 358	15.4	9.8	6.9	7.3
District 7	168 003	15.5	83.6	21.7	19 904	36 962	7.4	14.8	10.1	10.8
District 8	148 531	10.0	76.2	13.7	17 399	32 604	6.5	19.5	15.3	18.0
District 9	175 768	15.2	84.0	22.6	20 851	41 448	11.0	13.1	9.2	8.7
MONTANA	231 772	9.8	90.1	27.4	21 067	40 627	10.0	13.6	8.6	7.8
At Large	231 772	9.8	90.1	27.4	21 067	40 627	10.0	13.6	8.6	7.8
NEBRASKA	474 282	17.3	89.5	26.9	23 248	45 474	13.1	11.5	7.8	6.8
District 1	165 376	18.2	90.6	27.1	22 816	47 138	12.6	11.3	7.3	6.6
District 2	172 950	20.4	90.7	34.6	26 245	51 101	17.8	11.1	7.2	6.6
District 3	135 956	12.2	87.2	18.8	20 453	38 709	8.7	12.1	8.9	7.2
NEVADA	594 092	8.8	83.9	20.8	26 340	52 998	18.0	10.3	7.6	3.9
District 1	190 832	8.3	77.2	17.0	23 311	47 991	14.5	13.4	10.6	5.6
District 2	192 008	6.9	86.0	22.0	25 325	51 768	17.5	10.4	7.0	4.0
District 3	211 252	10.9	87.5	22.8	29 906	59 601	21.3	7.6	5.5	2.3
NEW HAMPSHIRE	333 298	20.3	89.9	31.9	28 828	59 683	22.3	8.0	4.9	4.6
District 1	169 187	19.1	90.4	31.5	29 139	61 101	22.3	8.2	5.2	4.9
District 2	164 111	21.4	89.4	32.3	28 513	57 890	22.4	7.8	4.7	4.3
NEW JERSEY	2 276 881	20.9	86.1	33.4	31 877	64 470	29.2	8.7	6.4	4.0
District 1	181 621	19.2	83.7	23.7	26 312	56 305	21.7	10.3	8.0	5.9
District 2	171 759	13.6	83.5	21.3	25 741	53 169	19.1	10.2	7.6	5.6
District 3	169 168	16.6	89.5	30.7	30 696	65 503	27.1	6.1	4.6	2.2
District 4	175 169	28.2	88.0	29.7	29 362	61 418	27.1	7.8	6.5	2.6
District 5	181 507	21.3	92.4	42.1	40 516	84 443	39.9	3.7	2.4	1.6
District 6	180 464	19.6	86.2	34.6	29 550	66 188	29.0	8.6	5.5	3.2
District 7	180 154	21.2	90.9	44.3	41 011	87 020	42.6	3.5	2.2	1.0
District 8	177 004	23.1	82.5	31.6	28 446	57 255	26.8	12.5	9.7	5.0
District 9	155 997	24.8	85.4	33.8	31 567	61 399	28.0	8.2	6.3	4.0
District 10	182 475	17.6	78.9	20.5	21 620	42 717	14.4	17.6	14.4	9.5
District 11	181 195	23.6	92.9	47.7	44 072	92 765	45.5	3.8	2.3	1.6
District 12	190 275	25.2	91.6	47.8	39 715	84 020	41.0	6.0	4.1	2.1
District 13	150 093	17.8	70.9	24.7	24 557	47 048	17.5	15.7	13.3	8.2
NEW MEXICO	540 961	10.6	81.5	25.3	20 913	40 629	12.6	18.5	13.8	8.7
District 1	185 829	13.1	84.1	30.4	23 626	42 762	14.5	15.7	11.9	7.9
District 2	179 720	6.4	77.0	18.9	17 356	36 280	8.2	22.0	17.0	10.9
District 3	175 412	12.3	83.0	26.0	21 576	42 643	14.6	18.0	12.6	7.5
NEW YORK	5 126 012	24.6	84.1	31.2	28 024	51 384	21.5	14.2	10.9	9.6
District 1	184 691	17.4	90.2	31.5	31 995	73 612	33.0	7.2	4.8	2.2
District 2	187 227	18.1	88.4	33.3	33 765	82 196	38.0	5.5	4.0	3.0
District 3	179 236	23.8	91.0	35.0	37 403	86 932	42.3	5.2	2.9	1.5
District 4	174 516	26.5	87.8	36.6	32 141	78 147	36.1	5.8	3.9	3.4
District 5	148 437	25.2	81.5	35.5	31 183	57 811	27.5	10.5	8.0	6.2
District 6	200 118	24.3	78.2	20.8	19 933	53 228	17.9	10.8	9.0	10.3
District 7	164 497	23.7	76.4	21.9	20 198	43 307	11.5	17.2	13.8	12.0
District 8	147 045	53.0	86.7	55.9	53 491	63 613	34.5	17.2	12.7	10.3
District 9	167 640	34.7	86.2	37.2	26 185	54 487	22.0	11.5	9.3	8.0
District 10	224 127	27.7	78.0	22.2	17 784	36 533	11.8	27.5	23.3	18.7
District 11	190 478	26.0	82.2	32.0	23 733	43 737	17.5	19.8	18.6	14.7
District 12	162 251	17.6	66.3	23.5	19 783	36 840	12.8	25.0	22.7	18.5
District 13	173 997	33.0	84.8	27.5	28 106	62 108	27.3	10.2	7.9	7.7
District 14	116 793	50.2	89.8	62.1	63 503	70 628	36.6	10.2	7.3	4.0
District 15	173 726	30.6	72.3	31.9	23 629	32 890	14.1	27.8	24.7	21.7
District 16	219 213	14.2	58.8	10.2	10 931	21 088	3.7	40.8	38.5	35.4
District 17	194 991	34.5	83.4	31.6	26 024	51 992	21.4	14.7	11.3	10.9
District 18	186 404	27.4	88.8	48.3	46 018	81 538	41.8	6.5	4.0	3.9
District 19	198 516	24.6	90.2	34.4	33 675	77 721	36.3	6.8	3.9	2.9
District 20	160 251	18.6	88.8	28.4	26 612	52 704	18.8	8.5	5.7	4.5
District 21	172 677	20.7	88.7	30.5	25 789	49 160	15.7	11.9	7.9	8.2
District 22	196 777	23.5	85.5	26.8	23 351	46 939	15.6	13.9	9.2	7.0
District 23	173 071	13.1	85.9	18.3	19 644	40 602	10.2	15.5	11.3	9.4
District 24	163 683	17.3	85.1	22.4	21 760	43 309	11.3	12.8	9.2	9.7
District 25	184 932	21.7	88.7	30.5	24 464	48 208	16.1	12.2	9.2	7.3
District 26	175 728	15.2	89.9	28.2	24 053	51 281	16.3	9.2	6.4	5.4
District 27	160 582	17.1	86.1	22.1	22 606	41 433	11.7	14.6	11.3	10.5
District 28	169 867	21.8	83.5	23.5	19 723	34 658	8.7	21.6	16.3	16.1
District 29	174 541	26.3	89.3	28.7	24 405	47 319	15.1	10.8	7.9	7.3

[5] All persons 3 years old and over enrolled in nursery school through college.
[6] Persons 25 years old and over.

Table A. 110th Congressional Districts—*Continued*

(Number, percent.)

STATE Congressional district	Housing units, 2006									
	Total	Total occupied units	Owner-occupied units							
			Percent owner-occupied units	Median value (dollars)	Percent valued at $500,000 or more	Median real estate taxes (dollars)	Median monthly costs (dollars)	Percent with second mortgage or home equity loan	Median cost as percent of income	
									With a mortgage	Without a mortgage
	47	48	49	50	51	52	53	54	55	56
MISSOURI—*Continued*										
District 6	287 423	256 009	74.6	132 300	1.6	1 291	870	14.2	21.9	11.1
District 7	305 417	273 464	67.3	109 600	2.1	698	676	12.8	22.5	11.0
District 8	292 278	251 233	70.3	87 900	0.7	520	509	7.9	20.7	10.5
District 9	295 579	257 309	70.9	123 900	3.2	924	691	11.7	21.0	10.8
MONTANA	432 080	372 190	69.9	155 500	6.3	1 371	746	13.5	24.2	12.5
At Large	432 080	372 190	69.9	155 500	6.3	1 371	746	13.5	24.2	12.5
NEBRASKA	774 571	700 888	67.9	119 200	1.9	2 030	862	16.4	22.4	12.9
District 1	257 755	235 548	69.1	126 500	1.8	2 202	892	17.7	22.4	12.2
District 2	256 180	237 616	64.5	139 700	2.5	2 611	1 142	23.6	23.1	12.7
District 3	260 636	227 724	70.2	85 200	1.3	1 392	601	8.1	21.3	13.5
NEVADA	1 065 267	936 828	62.0	315 200	17.3	1 528	1 377	22.4	28.4	11.9
District 1	327 399	287 476	55.8	287 400	10.8	1 537	1 417	22.3	29.5	12.3
District 2	340 638	298 373	64.7	300 000	18.7	1 319	1 197	20.3	26.9	12.1
District 3	397 230	350 979	64.7	347 400	20.7	1 738	1 484	24.3	28.7	11.5
NEW HAMPSHIRE	589 840	504 503	72.1	253 200	9.3	4 136	1 369	21.0	26.2	15.8
District 1	300 543	256 033	71.4	266 500	9.8	4 265	1 457	22.3	26.8	16.4
District 2	289 297	248 470	72.8	242 200	8.9	4 021	1 292	19.6	25.5	15.4
NEW JERSEY	3 472 782	3 135 490	67.3	366 600	26.6	5 773	1 695	21.2	28.0	18.7
District 1	264 867	245 486	71.7	203 200	4.1	4 528	1 361	20.9	26.6	19.0
District 2	339 062	253 919	71.3	236 300	11.1	3 750	1 273	18.2	27.8	18.0
District 3	309 250	263 412	83.6	287 800	13.5	4 418	1 462	21.6	27.9	19.6
District 4	279 459	255 362	77.9	333 200	20.4	4 715	1 461	20.7	27.7	18.6
District 5	246 128	232 603	81.6	465 700	44.2	7 078	1 982	24.2	27.9	18.2
District 6	254 915	233 261	63.5	366 900	20.6	5 495	1 740	22.1	28.7	18.4
District 7	248 173	236 104	79.6	456 400	40.5	7 141	2 032	24.6	26.7	18.2
District 8	234 108	220 340	58.6	422 300	30.5	7 202	1 962	19.2	30.1	21.4
District 9	266 608	251 662	55.3	429 000	31.6	6 393	1 777	18.4	30.4	19.2
District 10	254 625	226 087	39.6	320 000	15.7	5 805	1 788	16.0	33.9	21.8
District 11	251 645	239 592	78.6	496 900	49.4	7 025	2 162	23.7	26.9	16.7
District 12	261 696	244 171	76.8	417 500	33.7	6 418	1 898	23.2	26.3	16.6
District 13	262 246	233 491	31.8	379 800	25.0	5 642	1 830	14.0	32.2	21.5
NEW MEXICO	850 153	726 033	69.7	141 200	4.9	747	736	11.4	22.9	10.1
District 1	291 937	268 634	66.1	166 800	3.8	1 230	971	16.8	24.2	10.0
District 2	277 345	227 850	70.6	94 200	2.7	495	551	5.7	21.5	10.1
District 3	280 871	229 549	73.0	156 400	8.1	652	695	11.3	22.4	10.2
NEW YORK	7 907 514	7 088 376	55.6	303 000	26.8	3 301	1 257	15.8	26.4	15.7
District 1	281 031	232 300	81.8	434 100	34.8	5 879	1 936	20.9	31.4	19.3
District 2	223 147	212 143	81.9	469 900	42.0	6 982	2 120	21.5	31.5	19.5
District 3	230 962	218 881	84.1	483 500	44.8	7 396	2 128	20.1	29.6	21.1
District 4	217 142	206 991	78.7	476 500	42.5	7 218	2 076	17.9	31.4	21.0
District 5	241 390	226 736	56.4	614 400	63.4	3 714	1 516	12.0	29.0	16.4
District 6	214 688	197 972	57.9	434 000	29.7	2 266	1 855	13.9	35.6	16.1
District 7	257 108	241 155	37.1	399 700	33.1	2 213	1 133	9.3	34.3	12.8
District 8	341 412	309 177	29.3	726 100	73.1	3 428	1 852	8.8	23.3	12.6
District 9	274 376	253 834	52.2	500 200	50.0	2 710	1 214	10.5	29.2	14.6
District 10	254 974	225 915	34.4	460 600	41.5	2 259	1 887	11.8	38.2	15.5
District 11	255 411	235 698	26.0	557 500	57.0	2 405	1 618	13.6	27.2	16.8
District 12	253 734	234 804	22.1	545 700	56.7	2 287	1 471	9.5	36.9	16.5
District 13	262 610	244 837	63.5	499 000	49.8	2 659	1 778	16.2	29.5	15.8
District 14	375 290	319 236	29.8	723 300	71.5	3 660	1 825	9.7	21.7	11.3
District 15	273 375	247 609	12.6	590 500	56.8	1 851	1 486	7.4	22.6	8.1
District 16	240 140	222 784	7.1	324 600	9.5	1 270	1 372	10.1	38.8	14.7
District 17	246 830	229 674	45.0	445 800	36.9	4 808	1 735	14.0	29.2	17.9
District 18	247 222	232 900	66.9	607 600	63.7	8 262	2 208	19.5	26.8	16.8
District 19	251 469	234 364	78.4	388 900	29.7	5 747	1 912	24.0	28.0	17.8
District 20	320 235	258 403	73.1	185 600	7.1	2 778	1 068	17.6	24.1	14.6
District 21	299 395	269 376	61.9	150 700	2.2	3 010	1 020	16.4	23.2	13.8
District 22	302 931	257 572	62.0	184 800	4.1	3 059	1 037	15.2	24.8	15.6
District 23	311 831	248 720	71.1	88 800	1.5	1 681	740	11.5	22.3	13.9
District 24	290 616	256 252	69.2	93 200	0.9	2 148	785	11.1	21.7	14.5
District 25	286 116	261 243	70.3	117 800	0.9	3 037	1 005	17.7	22.7	14.8
District 26	268 364	249 493	74.1	119 900	0.5	3 244	1 003	18.2	23.0	15.9
District 27	292 233	256 556	67.4	96 900	0.9	2 500	836	16.8	22.8	15.3
District 28	304 966	251 848	57.6	85 800	0.4	2 260	845	14.7	23.7	15.1
District 29	288 516	251 903	74.3	104 200	1.5	2 529	897	14.9	22.7	14.1

Table A. 110th Congressional Districts—*Continued*

(Number, percent.)

STATE Congressional district	Housing units, 2006—*Continued*			Civilian labor force, 2006			Civilian employment and occupation, 2006			
	Renter-occupied units		Sub-standard housing units (percent)[7]	Total	Unemployment		Total civilian employment	Management, professional, and related (percent)	Service, sales, and office (percent)	Construction and production (percent)
	Median gross rent (dollars)	Median gross rent as a percent of income			Total	Rate[8]				
	57	58	59	60	61	62	63	64	65	66
MISSOURI—*Continued*										
District 6	595	25.5	1.5	353 541	16 076	4.5	337 465	32.5	41.7	25.0
District 7	565	28.4	2.5	344 934	20 482	5.9	324 452	27.2	46.4	25.5
District 8	459	28.6	2.0	293 631	22 144	7.5	271 487	26.6	41.1	30.2
District 9	559	27.8	2.2	340 309	18 600	5.5	321 709	30.6	40.0	28.5
MONTANA	571	28.5	2.0	490 998	23 523	4.8	467 475	33.3	41.3	23.5
At Large	571	28.5	2.0	490 998	23 523	4.8	467 475	33.3	41.3	23.5
NEBRASKA	593	26.8	2.0	974 854	46 891	4.8	927 963	34.2	40.7	23.4
District 1	576	27.4	1.8	336 868	15 047	4.5	321 821	34.7	38.8	25.1
District 2	690	27.8	2.2	331 617	20 019	6.0	311 598	37.7	43.6	18.5
District 3	508	24.5	1.9	306 369	11 825	3.9	294 544	29.9	39.7	26.8
NEVADA	917	30.1	4.0	1 291 287	66 764	5.2	1 224 523	26.5	49.9	23.3
District 1	849	32.3	6.1	398 182	23 552	5.9	374 630	21.8	52.2	25.9
District 2	826	27.7	3.6	406 372	20 613	5.1	385 759	28.0	44.3	27.1
District 3	1 058	30.1	2.6	486 733	22 599	4.6	464 134	29.1	52.8	18.1
NEW HAMPSHIRE	861	29.9	1.4	737 774	33 000	4.5	704 774	35.6	41.8	22.1
District 1	892	29.6	1.3	372 632	18 289	4.9	354 343	34.7	43.3	21.4
District 2	826	30.1	1.5	365 142	14 711	4.0	350 431	36.5	40.3	22.8
NEW JERSEY	974	29.9	2.9	4 546 370	284 815	6.3	4 261 555	38.0	43.3	18.5
District 1	821	29.9	1.9	354 550	23 380	6.6	331 170	34.5	46.1	19.3
District 2	847	31.1	2.2	348 260	27 316	7.8	320 944	28.2	49.2	22.0
District 3	1 072	32.2	1.1	350 933	21 830	6.2	329 103	38.4	43.3	18.1
District 4	1 024	33.6	2.5	345 151	18 958	5.5	326 193	37.0	43.7	18.9
District 5	1 067	29.3	1.2	354 611	15 574	4.4	339 037	44.3	40.1	15.2
District 6	1 052	30.0	4.3	356 074	21 996	6.2	334 078	37.9	43.7	18.4
District 7	1 192	27.8	1.5	357 519	16 793	4.7	340 726	46.2	38.7	15.0
District 8	990	35.6	3.8	326 223	18 039	5.5	308 184	34.5	43.8	21.6
District 9	1 058	28.8	3.9	357 258	21 712	6.1	335 546	36.8	45.9	17.3
District 10	850	29.9	6.2	320 754	35 334	11.0	285 420	25.6	51.9	22.4
District 11	1 132	27.2	1.8	363 923	15 219	4.2	348 704	49.1	38.0	12.8
District 12	1 057	28.5	0.9	361 025	22 074	6.1	338 951	51.3	37.3	11.3
District 13	925	29.1	7.4	350 089	26 590	7.6	323 499	26.7	43.5	29.7
NEW MEXICO	617	29.1	4.2	934 956	59 411	6.4	875 545	34.1	43.0	22.0
District 1	644	29.3	3.2	346 908	19 680	5.7	327 228	37.7	41.6	20.5
District 2	529	28.8	4.4	279 458	20 640	7.4	258 818	28.7	44.2	25.1
District 3	657	29.0	5.4	308 590	19 091	6.2	289 499	34.7	43.5	20.9
NEW YORK	875	30.5	4.7	9 636 401	628 719	6.5	9 007 682	36.7	44.8	18.1
District 1	1 300	35.3	1.9	352 028	15 535	4.4	336 493	35.0	46.3	18.3
District 2	1 404	35.5	2.8	346 451	15 035	4.3	331 416	38.2	41.8	19.9
District 3	1 393	30.1	2.0	338 846	13 993	4.1	324 853	40.2	43.8	15.8
District 4	1 245	35.0	2.8	330 038	16 395	5.0	313 643	39.3	43.7	17.0
District 5	1 143	33.2	8.3	337 897	20 296	6.0	317 601	34.7	48.9	16.3
District 6	976	31.5	9.7	329 604	28 598	8.7	301 006	26.9	52.8	20.2
District 7	953	29.8	9.0	319 094	24 801	7.8	294 293	27.3	52.5	20.2
District 8	1 158	28.2	8.0	379 052	19 699	5.2	359 353	55.4	35.4	9.2
District 9	1 035	30.9	5.6	324 235	18 542	5.7	305 693	35.6	46.1	18.3
District 10	825	31.9	8.0	287 300	26 644	9.3	260 656	31.1	53.1	15.8
District 11	912	30.3	9.3	328 773	28 570	8.7	300 203	38.2	47.5	14.2
District 12	875	30.8	11.6	325 933	20 841	6.4	305 092	28.4	48.1	23.4
District 13	996	31.5	3.9	332 927	18 673	5.6	314 254	35.4	46.9	17.6
District 14	1 325	27.0	5.6	393 282	22 456	5.7	370 826	60.9	32.3	6.7
District 15	760	29.9	9.9	315 191	32 331	10.3	282 860	38.3	48.3	13.3
District 16	773	36.5	15.4	273 903	38 924	14.2	234 979	16.3	60.5	23.1
District 17	972	29.7	5.4	320 018	25 745	8.0	294 273	36.5	47.0	16.4
District 18	1 167	29.8	2.8	332 363	15 994	4.8	316 369	47.2	40.0	12.6
District 19	1 079	31.5	2.3	361 490	18 264	5.1	343 226	39.9	42.6	17.2
District 20	736	28.5	1.5	354 494	20 408	5.8	334 086	37.1	40.2	22.0
District 21	727	28.0	1.5	348 419	19 426	5.6	328 993	37.5	44.5	17.7
District 22	780	31.8	3.1	347 268	20 313	5.8	326 955	35.2	43.7	20.5
District 23	584	29.4	1.7	306 301	23 179	7.6	283 122	28.0	45.0	25.8
District 24	597	27.8	1.7	332 418	21 173	6.4	311 245	32.0	43.1	23.9
District 25	664	29.8	1.0	339 458	19 146	5.6	320 312	36.3	43.5	19.5
District 26	661	27.5	1.1	341 973	18 535	5.4	323 438	36.2	41.5	21.9
District 27	605	29.1	1.4	313 553	19 453	6.2	294 100	30.4	46.2	22.9
District 28	642	34.8	1.2	286 750	23 666	8.3	263 084	33.6	47.5	18.7
District 29	643	29.3	1.2	337 342	22 084	6.5	315 258	37.8	39.2	21.9

[7]Overcrowded or lacking complete plumbing facilities.
[8]Percent of civilian labor force.

Table A. 110th Congressional Districts—*Continued*

(Number, percent.)

STATE Congressional district	Social Security Beneficiaries (OASDI), December 2006							Supplemental Security Income, December 2006			
	Total	Rate per 1,000 population	Retired workers[9]	Disabled workers	Widow(er)s[10]	Spouses[11]	Children[12]	Total	Aged	Blind	Disabled
	67	68	69	70	71	72	73	74	75	76	77
MISSOURI—*Continued*											
District 6	114 158	171.7	73 159	15 183	11 332	5 974	8 510	8 629	745	74	7 810
District 7	133 375	197.0	81 648	21 590	12 403	6 908	10 826	13 727	978	97	12 652
District 8	151 363	238.4	82 426	30 034	15 814	8 152	14 937	26 117	2 086	167	23 864
District 9	118 839	180.6	73 164	18 461	11 133	5 752	10 329	10 826	725	91	10 010
MONTANA	172 920	183.1	111 990	21 611	16 752	10 138	12 429	15 234	1 087	131	14 016
At Large	172 920	183.1	111 990	21 611	16 752	10 138	12 429	15 234	1 087	131	14 016
NEBRASKA	293 935	166.2	194 403	33 915	28 898	16 341	20 378	22 578	2 043	244	20 291
District 1	97 425	162.9	65 321	10 725	9 263	5 193	6 923	6 944	697	110	6 137
District 2	80 908	132.8	52 881	11 279	6 893	3 260	6 595	8 323	601	66	7 656
District 3	115 602	206.1	76 201	11 911	12 742	7 888	6 860	7 311	745	68	6 498
NEVADA	354 321	142.0	240 460	46 966	26 259	14 706	25 930	34 739	8 853	671	25 215
District 1	99 472	124.7	63 708	15 824	7 441	3 694	8 805	15 179	3 687	281	11 211
District 2	127 194	160.1	87 098	16 577	9 538	5 556	8 425	9 891	2 181	208	7 502
District 3	127 655	141.3	89 654	14 565	9 280	5 456	8 700	9 669	2 985	182	6 502
NEW HAMPSHIRE	226 313	172.1	148 322	34 310	16 603	8 575	18 503	14 514	852	157	13 505
District 1	110 664	167.1	72 607	17 072	8 057	4 102	8 826	7 036	452	78	6 506
District 2	115 649	177.2	75 715	17 238	8 546	4 473	9 677	7 478	400	79	6 999
NEW JERSEY	1 381 151	158.3	948 401	158 619	117 395	56 826	99 910	154 347	33 716	959	119 672
District 1	106 504	160.0	65 564	16 294	10 487	4 348	9 811	15 600	1 533	128	13 939
District 2	125 662	183.9	82 726	17 113	10 596	4 728	10 499	13 958	1 630	77	12 251
District 3	143 340	205.1	101 797	14 517	12 057	6 191	8 778	7 130	1 074	40	6 016
District 4	134 760	194.3	96 529	13 626	11 684	5 204	7 717	7 621	1 193	44	6 384
District 5	107 753	160.8	78 041	9 096	9 213	5 108	6 295	5 431	1 642	32	3 757
District 6	91 879	139.2	60 861	12 155	8 312	3 508	7 043	9 712	2 294	64	7 354
District 7	100 316	147.2	72 636	8 245	8 472	4 524	6 439	5 119	1 885	33	3 201
District 8	96 259	146.6	65 805	11 540	7 817	3 842	7 255	15 733	3 867	89	11 777
District 9	102 323	156.2	73 442	10 439	8 487	4 526	5 429	11 186	4 302	56	6 828
District 10	83 733	130.4	51 028	14 165	6 618	2 466	9 456	24 069	3 806	166	20 097
District 11	100 475	146.7	73 969	8 280	8 255	4 468	5 503	4 893	1 817	34	3 042
District 12	111 304	161.8	78 225	10 554	9 094	4 590	8 841	8 509	2 314	41	6 154
District 13	76 843	119.2	47 778	12 595	6 303	3 323	6 844	25 386	6 359	155	18 872
NEW MEXICO	319 935	163.7	192 565	48 044	29 785	20 329	29 212	55 269	8 478	479	46 312
District 1	103 103	154.0	63 311	16 039	9 270	5 970	8 513	15 074	1 798	121	13 155
District 2	115 138	182.1	69 078	16 743	10 883	8 183	10 251	21 072	3 830	199	17 043
District 3	101 694	155.7	60 176	15 262	9 632	6 176	10 448	19 123	2 850	159	16 114
NEW YORK	3 075 081	159.3	2 001 974	416 715	262 721	143 786	249 885	640 570	135 596	2 992	501 982
District 1	121 654	178.3	78 716	16 656	10 638	5 493	10 151	9 465	1 124	60	8 281
District 2	109 441	162.1	71 532	13 847	9 099	5 119	9 844	10 009	1 937	28	8 044
District 3	119 374	180.7	80 379	13 240	11 097	6 197	8 461	6 828	1 378	40	5 410
District 4	109 533	170.7	74 813	11 917	9 943	5 418	7 442	10 014	2 645	50	7 319
District 5	96 393	147.4	71 088	7 332	8 023	5 950	4 000	16 557	8 480	63	8 014
District 6	75 535	112.4	48 817	10 745	5 482	3 081	7 410	24 672	7 176	69	17 427
District 7	90 896	136.7	59 078	12 571	7 427	4 385	7 435	27 813	7 194	113	20 506
District 8	88 675	128.0	61 740	10 434	6 583	3 911	6 007	36 762	12 314	148	24 300
District 9	100 250	148.6	70 031	10 532	9 148	5 383	5 156	27 908	10 655	87	17 166
District 10	75 104	109.7	44 353	12 527	6 031	2 957	9 236	39 841	7 507	142	32 192
District 11	68 706	104.7	44 382	10 318	4 653	2 532	6 821	30 241	8 294	109	21 838
District 12	70 166	103.5	42 353	11 125	6 273	4 045	6 370	39 688	10 892	121	28 675
District 13	105 715	153.5	64 447	16 220	10 041	5 655	9 352	21 068	6 314	78	14 676
District 14	93 741	145.9	70 594	8 128	7 049	4 240	3 730	14 882	4 659	86	10 137
District 15	84 835	126.3	54 117	13 894	6 265	3 236	7 323	50 389	11 438	214	38 737
District 16	63 313	94.5	31 904	13 459	5 203	2 900	9 847	60 645	8 705	173	51 767
District 17	95 137	142.3	65 172	11 464	7 254	3 491	7 756	22 436	4 559	100	17 777
District 18	109 778	163.4	80 301	9 566	8 602	5 197	6 112	10 614	2 859	58	7 697
District 19	106 551	150.8	69 860	13 531	8 760	4 554	9 846	7 786	1 291	48	6 447
District 20	132 193	196.3	86 505	17 713	11 292	6 178	10 505	12 138	1 185	93	10 860
District 21	127 229	191.4	83 169	17 824	10 932	5 116	10 188	17 763	1 854	143	15 766
District 22	123 294	182.2	77 196	19 482	10 351	5 264	11 001	18 774	1 944	124	16 706
District 23	126 723	192.8	74 274	21 087	12 472	7 220	11 670	18 570	1 519	139	16 912
District 24	136 768	209.5	86 580	20 399	11 320	5 954	12 515	18 180	1 689	98	16 393
District 25	126 416	190.3	82 847	17 270	10 193	5 526	10 580	16 014	1 495	144	14 375
District 26	128 350	191.4	85 400	15 704	12 052	6 677	8 517	9 514	1 152	71	8 291
District 27	134 455	214.9	83 228	19 306	14 209	6 786	10 926	18 311	1 657	140	16 514
District 28	121 158	198.5	70 815	22 206	11 049	4 907	12 181	28 630	2 216	161	26 253
District 29	133 698	204.5	88 283	18 218	11 280	6 414	9 503	15 058	1 464	92	13 502

[9]Includes special age-72 beneficiaries.
[10]Includes nondisabled widow(er)s, disabled widow(er)s, widowed mothers and fathers, and parents receiving payment on the record of a worker who is deceased.
[11]These beneficiaries receive payment on the record of a worker who is retired or disabled.
[12]These beneficiaries receive payment on the record of a worker who is retired, deceased, or disabled.

Table A. 110th Congressional Districts—*Continued*

(Number, percent.)

Agriculture, 2002

STATE Congressional district	Total farms	Farms by size (percent): 1 to 49 acres	50 to 999 acres	1,000 acres or more	Land in farms: Total acreage	Average size of farms (acres)	Percent of farms where principal operator's primary occupation is farming	Value of all agricultural products sold: Total ($1,000)	Percent of farms with value of: Less than $50,000	$50,000 to $249,999	$250,000 or more	Payments from federal farm programs: Total ($1,000)	Number of farms that receive payments	Percent of farms that receive payments
	78	79	80	81	82	83	84	85	86	87	88	89	90	91
MISSOURI—*Continued*														
District 6	20 879	20.0	72.8	7.3	6 933 337	332	57.3	1 061 393	82.0	14.1	3.9	87 794	12 467	59.7
District 7	13 028	33.3	64.9	1.8	2 301 046	177	55.8	748 148	87.8	7.9	4.3	9 687	3 139	24.1
District 8	19 816	19.8	73.2	7.0	6 445 021	325	59.0	943 180	84.7	10.5	4.8	51 686	6 226	31.4
District 9	22 595	20.3	74.3	5.4	6 463 637	286	55.6	924 717	84.5	12.0	3.5	62 814	10 513	46.5
MONTANA	27 870	23.3	40.3	36.4	59 612 403	2 139	63.5	1 882 114	71.1	23.1	5.8	210 749	12 389	44.5
At Large	27 870	23.3	40.3	36.4	59 612 403	2 139	63.5	1 882 114	71.1	23.1	5.8	210 749	12 389	44.5
NEBRASKA	49 355	14.8	61.9	23.3	45 903 116	930	73.0	9 703 657	54.6	31.3	14.1	347 517	32 007	64.9
District 1	17 159	21.2	67.2	11.7	7 176 787	418	67.2	2 489 414	62.5	27.9	9.6	104 813	11 727	68.3
District 2	422	45.7	45.0	9.2	112 806	267	54.7	39 718	71.3	20.4	8.3	1 488	181	42.9
District 3	31 774	11.0	59.2	29.8	38 613 523	1 215	76.4	7 174 525	50.1	33.3	16.6	241 217	20 099	63.3
NEVADA	2 989	46.7	36.3	17.0	6 330 622	2 118	58.7	446 989	73.0	16.8	10.2	4 322	439	14.7
District 1	69	81.2	18.8	0.0	2 326	34	49.3	5 204	91.3	2.9	5.8	9	6	8.7
District 2	2 789	44.3	37.6	18.1	6 266 999	2 247	59.8	431 493	71.6	17.7	10.7	4 301	428	15.3
District 3	131	80.2	16.8	3.1	61 297	468	38.9	10 293	91.6	6.1	2.3	13	5	3.8
NEW HAMPSHIRE	3 363	45.9	53.0	1.2	444 879	132	48.6	144 835	88.6	7.7	3.7	3 823	359	10.7
District 1	1 196	51.6	47.9	0.5	119 603	100	49.2	37 468	90.5	5.9	3.6	802	84	7.0
District 2	2 167	42.7	55.7	1.6	325 276	150	48.3	107 367	87.6	8.7	3.7	3 021	275	12.7
NEW JERSEY	9 924	70.5	28.4	1.2	805 682	81	52.3	749 872	85.5	8.5	6.0	4 441	582	5.9
District 1	418	74.6	24.6	0.7	23 707	57	50.7	29 770	85.9	7.4	6.7	195	12	2.9
District 2	2 585	65.7	32.7	1.5	250 568	97	58.8	343 057	78.9	9.7	11.4	1 517	187	7.2
District 3	691	69.6	26.8	3.6	84 923	123	55.7	64 385	79.0	13.9	7.1	427	32	4.6
District 4	1 099	77.1	21.9	1.0	78 343	71	55.8	95 925	84.6	8.6	6.8	326	44	4.0
District 5	1 975	67.5	31.9	0.6	153 759	78	48.5	67 729	89.4	7.9	2.7	...	126	6.4
District 6	97	83.5	16.5	0.0	3 544	37	62.9	11 987	85.6	9.3	5.2	...	1	1.0
District 7	1 352	72.6	26.8	0.6	91 772	68	45.6	29 565	92.5	5.8	1.7	470	82	6.1
District 8	...	...	...	...	...	...	...	...	...	...	...	...	...	...
District 9	...	...	...	...	...	...	...	...	...	...	...	...	...	...
District 10	15	100.0	0.0	0.0	153	10	53.3	737	73.3	20.0	6.7	...	...	...
District 11	466	76.0	23.6	0.4	24 184	52	43.3	42 397	90.1	5.4	4.5	54	13	2.8
District 12	1 208	72.0	26.7	1.3	94 547	78	50.2	57 551	88.2	8.4	3.4	483	85	7.0
District 13	18	100.0	0.0	0.0	182	10	66.7	6 750	72.2	5.6	22.2	...	...	...
NEW MEXICO	15 170	44.7	33.2	22.1	44 810 083	2 954	55.9	1 700 030	84.7	10.0	5.4	50 201	3 246	21.4
District 1	1 400	62.7	24.2	13.1	2 059 643	1 471	50.6	65 761	92.5	4.7	2.8	1 209	153	10.9
District 2	6 724	51.3	27.2	21.5	24 480 558	3 641	54.2	914 991	81.5	12.3	6.2	14 241	1 057	15.7
District 3	7 046	34.8	40.6	24.6	18 269 882	2 593	58.6	719 279	86.1	8.8	5.1	34 751	2 036	28.9
NEW YORK	37 255	30.4	66.9	2.8	7 660 969	206	60.8	3 117 834	74.4	18.7	6.9	110 234	9 896	26.6
District 1	550	74.0	25.8	0.2	28 100	51	62.5	163 986	59.8	21.1	19.1	147	37	6.7
District 2	98	89.8	8.2	2.0	5 956	61	63.3	37 016	70.4	13.3	16.3	...	...	...
District 3	46	87.0	13.0	0.0	832	18	47.8	3 939	73.9	21.7	4.3	...	...	...
District 4	18	83.3	16.7	0.0	353	20	61.1	4 141	61.1	16.7	22.2	...	...	...
District 5	4	100.0	0.0	0.0	...	...	...	350	0.0	100.0	0.0	...	...	...
District 6	...	...	...	...	...	...	...	...	...	...	...	...	...	...
District 7	...	...	...	...	...	...	...	...	...	...	...	...	...	...
District 8	...	...	...	...	...	...	...	...	...	...	...	...	...	...
District 9	3	100.0	0.0	0.0	...	...	...	78	100.0	0.0	0.0	...	...	...
District 10	...	...	...	...	...	...	...	...	...	...	...	...	...	...
District 11	...	...	...	...	...	...	...	...	...	...	...	...	...	...
District 12	4	100.0	0.0	0.0	...	...	...	390	0.0	100.0	0.0	...	...	...
District 13	16	100.0	0.0	0.0	44	3	6.3	1 720	81.3	6.3	12.5	...	...	...
District 14	...	...	...	...	...	...	...	...	...	...	...	...	...	...
District 15	...	...	...	...	...	...	...	...	...	...	...	...	...	...
District 16	...	...	...	...	...	...	...	...	...	...	...	...	...	...
District 17	29	65.5	34.5	0.0	1 076	37	69.0	3 130	65.5	27.6	6.9	...	...	...
District 18	50	70.0	30.0	0.0	3 270	65	64.0	6 700	56.0	34.0	10.0	...	2	4.0
District 19	788	46.2	52.0	1.8	112 781	143	67.3	63 726	75.4	17.0	7.6	...	121	15.4
District 20	4 193	33.0	64.4	2.6	840 858	201	61.1	293 186	77.2	15.8	7.0	11 873	967	23.1
District 21	2 127	30.7	67.7	1.6	386 117	182	59.1	110 513	79.0	15.7	5.4	5 315	561	26.4
District 22	1 784	34.6	64.0	1.3	297 391	167	60.1	113 170	80.6	14.2	5.2	3 139	291	16.3
District 23	6 327	19.0	78.1	2.9	1 624 632	257	64.3	509 814	70.0	23.1	6.9	23 560	1 845	29.2
District 24	6 405	25.0	72.3	2.6	1 398 291	218	60.8	495 145	70.8	22.6	6.6	20 476	1 984	31.0
District 25	1 856	39.0	57.1	4.0	358 638	193	63.5	202 074	70.9	19.2	9.9	7 178	525	28.3
District 26	3 486	37.3	57.5	5.1	870 106	250	60.5	518 978	74.7	15.0	10.3	16 824	1 234	35.4
District 27	2 767	39.5	58.9	1.5	389 152	141	59.7	166 089	77.7	17.4	4.9	5 426	552	19.9
District 28	595	43.4	52.1	4.5	113 437	191	60.0	60 527	81.3	11.1	7.6	1 584	168	28.2
District 29	6 109	24.3	72.9	2.8	1 229 921	201	57.1	363 162	77.9	17.3	4.8	13 288	1 609	26.3

. . . = Not available.

Table A. 110th Congressional Districts—*Continued*

(Number, percent.)

STATE Congressional district	Representative	Land area,[1] (sq km)	Total population	Persons per square kilometer	Race alone (percent) White	Black	American Indian/ Alaska Native	Asian and Pacific Islander	Some other race (percent)	Two or more races (percent)	Hispanic or Latino[2] (percent)	Non-Hispanic White (percent)
	1	2	3	4	5	6	7	8	9	10	11	12
NORTH CAROLINA		126 161	8 856 505	70.2	70.3	21.4	1.1	1.9	3.9	1.4	6.7	67.7
District 1	Rep. G.K. Butterfield (D)	18 645	604 535	32.4	44.2	50.8	0.9	0.7	2.4	1.0	3.6	43.2
District 2	Rep. Bob Etheridge (D)	10 246	695 073	67.8	61.6	28.9	0.5	0.9	6.3	1.8	10.4	57.9
District 3	Rep. Walter B. Jones (R)	16 037	674 334	42.0	76.0	16.7	0.3	1.2	3.8	2.0	5.3	74.8
District 4	Rep. David E. Price (D)	3 246	735 413	226.6	68.0	19.1	0.2	5.6	5.0	2.0	7.2	66.1
District 5	Rep. Virginia Foxx (R)	11 401	656 007	57.5	87.0	7.6	0.1	1.0	3.2	1.0	6.0	84.4
District 6	Rep. Howard Coble (R)	7 624	678 471	89.0	84.4	9.3	0.2	1.5	3.4	1.2	5.7	82.4
District 7	Rep. Mike McIntyre (D)	15 766	692 546	43.9	65.3	20.9	8.0	0.6	3.4	1.8	5.5	63.6
District 8	Rep. Robin Hayes (R)	8 502	657 782	77.4	61.4	29.5	1.6	2.3	3.8	1.4	8.2	57.2
District 9	Rep. Sue Wilkins Myrick (R)	2 566	768 200	299.4	79.1	13.4	0.3	2.6	3.0	1.5	6.1	76.4
District 10	Rep. Patrick T. McHenry (R)	8 552	663 586	77.6	85.0	8.6	0.2	1.8	3.1	1.3	4.8	83.5
District 11	Rep. Heath Shuler (D)	15 605	665 133	42.6	89.9	5.3	1.4	0.6	1.9	0.9	4.1	87.8
District 12	Rep. Melvin L. Watt (D)	2 127	672 120	316.0	45.9	44.0	0.6	2.6	5.6	1.3	11.3	41.0
District 13	Rep. Brad Miller (D)	5 842	693 305	118.7	63.2	27.1	0.3	2.6	5.7	1.1	9.0	59.8
NORTH DAKOTA		178 647	635 867	3.6	91.0	0.9	5.2	0.7	0.8	1.3	1.5	90.4
At Large	Rep. Earl Pomeroy (D)	178 647	635 867	3.6	91.0	0.9	5.2	0.7	0.8	1.3	1.5	90.4
OHIO		106 056	11 478 006	108.2	84.0	11.8	0.2	1.5	0.9	1.5	2.3	82.8
District 1	Rep. Steve Chabot (R)	1 078	607 676	563.7	66.4	28.7	0.2	1.4	1.0	2.4	1.8	65.6
District 2	Rep. Jean Schmidt (R)	6 764	672 493	99.4	92.1	4.5	0.2	2.1	0.2	1.0	0.9	91.4
District 3	Rep. Michael R. Turner (R)	4 132	640 498	155.0	79.1	17.2	0.2	1.5	0.8	1.2	1.8	78.2
District 4	Rep. Jim Jordan (R)	11 966	632 354	52.8	91.8	5.0	0.2	0.6	0.6	1.8	1.4	91.0
District 5	Rep. Robert E. Latta (R)	15 872	636 993	40.1	95.2	1.2	0.2	0.6	1.7	1.2	4.4	93.0
District 6	Rep. Charles A. Wilson (D)	13 461	630 691	46.9	95.2	2.5	0.1	0.7	0.4	1.1	0.8	94.8
District 7	Rep. David L. Hobson (R)	7 377	656 162	88.9	87.4	8.8	0.3	1.4	0.4	1.7	1.6	86.4
District 8	Rep. John A. Boehner (R)	5 216	651 916	125.0	91.2	5.4	0.1	1.6	0.4	1.3	1.7	90.0
District 9	Rep. Marcy Kaptur (D)	2 853	624 654	218.9	80.1	14.7	0.3	1.1	2.1	1.7	4.5	78.4
District 10	Rep. Dennis J. Kucinich (D)	506	605 915	1 197.5	86.6	6.6	0.1	2.2	2.7	1.7	6.0	84.0
District 11	Rep. Stephanie Tubbs Jones (D)	348	565 890	1 626.1	35.9	59.1	0.3	2.2	1.1	1.5	2.1	35.0
District 12	Rep. Patrick J. Tiberi (R)	2 632	696 548	264.6	72.0	22.1	0.2	3.1	1.0	1.7	2.0	71.0
District 13	Rep. Betty Sutton (D)	1 374	647 827	471.5	82.4	12.5	0.2	1.5	1.6	1.8	3.6	80.8
District 14	Rep. Steven C. LaTourette (R)	4 654	653 423	140.4	93.6	3.3	0.1	1.4	0.4	1.2	1.8	92.4
District 15	Rep. Deborah Pryce (R)	3 052	652 582	213.8	84.3	8.9	0.1	4.1	1.1	1.4	3.9	81.7
District 16	Rep. Ralph Regula (R)	4 486	651 351	145.2	92.7	4.9	0.2	0.9	0.3	1.1	1.0	92.0
District 17	Rep. Tim Ryan (D)	2 604	609 894	234.2	84.7	11.7	0.2	1.1	0.6	1.6	1.9	83.5
District 18	Rep. Zachary T. Space (D)	17 680	641 139	36.3	96.1	1.8	0.3	0.2	0.3	1.4	0.7	95.6
OKLAHOMA		177 847	3 579 212	20.1	75.4	7.4	6.8	1.7	2.6	6.1	6.8	72.0
District 1	Rep. John Sullivan (R)	4 498	720 591	160.2	75.3	9.4	5.0	1.5	3.0	5.7	7.8	71.1
District 2	Rep. Dan Boren (D)	53 258	712 531	13.4	70.7	3.8	14.6	0.4	1.1	9.4	3.1	69.1
District 3	Rep. Frank D. Lucas (R)	88 289	699 607	7.9	81.9	3.9	5.7	1.3	3.2	4.0	6.3	79.4
District 4	Rep. Tom Cole (R)	26 449	719 073	27.2	79.0	6.7	5.0	2.3	2.2	4.9	5.6	76.4
District 5	Rep. Mary Fallin (R)	5 353	727 410	135.9	70.2	12.8	3.9	3.1	3.6	6.3	11.3	64.3
OREGON		248 631	3 700 758	14.9	86.1	1.7	1.8	3.9	3.5	3.0	10.2	80.8
District 1	Rep. David Wu (D)	7 618	769 808	101.1	82.3	1.3	1.1	6.7	5.6	3.0	12.2	76.9
District 2	Rep. Greg Walden (R)	179 982	747 548	4.2	90.6	0.4	2.1	1.2	2.6	3.1	10.1	84.2
District 3	Rep. Earl Blumenauer (D)	2 644	717 243	271.3	80.3	5.3	1.6	6.6	3.0	3.2	10.4	74.5
District 4	Rep. Peter A. DeFazio (D)	44 498	716 358	16.1	90.2	0.8	1.8	2.3	2.0	2.9	5.4	87.7
District 5	Rep. Darlene Hooley (D)	13 889	749 801	54.0	87.1	1.0	2.4	2.5	4.1	2.8	12.9	80.6
PENNSYLVANIA		116 074	12 440 621	107.2	83.8	10.4	0.1	2.4	2.1	1.2	4.2	82.0
District 1	Rep. Robert A. Brady (D)	152	638 440	4 200.3	31.8	49.9	0.2	4.9	11.3	1.8	17.3	27.2
District 2	Rep. Chaka Fattah (D)	152	558 248	3 672.7	30.0	60.9	0.2	5.2	2.3	1.4	3.7	29.0
District 3	Rep. Phil English (R)	10 280	647 048	62.9	93.8	3.7	0.1	0.6	0.7	1.2	1.5	93.1
District 4	Rep. Jason Altmire (D)	3 373	647 512	192.0	93.5	3.7	0.1	1.2	0.3	1.1	0.9	92.8
District 5	Rep. John E. Peterson (R)	28 598	636 283	22.2	95.7	1.7	0.1	1.5	0.4	0.6	1.0	95.1
District 6	Rep. Jim Gerlach (R)	2 107	698 397	331.5	84.3	7.8	0.1	3.4	3.0	1.5	5.7	82.0
District 7	Rep. Joe Sestak (D)	751	670 030	892.2	84.7	8.4	0.1	5.0	0.7	1.1	1.7	83.8
District 8	Rep. Patrick J. Murphy (D)	1 603	669 698	417.8	91.0	3.6	0.1	3.4	0.9	1.0	3.1	88.9
District 9	Rep. Bill Shuster (R)	18 543	660 817	35.6	96.6	1.8	0.1	0.5	0.2	0.8	1.3	95.7
District 10	Rep. Christopher P. Carney (D)	16 985	649 330	38.2	95.1	2.4	0.2	0.7	0.7	0.9	2.0	93.9
District 11	Rep. Paul E. Kanjorski (D)	5 744	678 247	118.1	91.5	4.9	0.1	1.3	1.4	0.8	5.1	88.3
District 12	Rep. John P. Murtha (D)	7 127	630 732	88.5	94.7	3.5	0.1	0.4	0.2	1.1	0.7	94.2
District 13	Rep. Allyson Y. Schwartz (D)	660	673 537	1 020.5	81.0	9.2	0.2	5.9	2.1	1.6	4.7	78.7
District 14	Rep. Michael F. Doyle (D)	419	584 384	1 394.7	70.8	23.7	0.1	2.3	0.6	2.3	1.5	70.1
District 15	Rep. Charles W. Dent (R)	2 189	702 359	320.9	85.7	4.1	0.1	2.2	6.2	1.7	10.5	82.1
District 16	Rep. Joseph R. Pitts (R)	3 341	684 119	204.8	87.9	4.6	0.1	1.6	4.6	1.3	10.1	83.0
District 17	Rep. Tim Holden (D)	6 048	662 053	109.5	87.2	7.6	0.2	1.4	2.3	1.3	4.1	85.7
District 18	Rep. Tim Murphy (R)	3 708	649 736	175.2	94.6	2.7	0.1	2.0	0.2	0.6	. . .	. . .
District 19	Rep. Todd Russell Platts (R)	4 294	699 651	162.9	92.0	3.8	0.2	1.6	1.3	1.1	3.6	90.1

[1]Dry land or land partially or temporarily covered by water.
[2]May be of any race.
. . . = Not available.

Table A. 110th Congressional Districts—*Continued*

(Number, percent.)

STATE Congressional district	Percent female	Percent foreign born	Percent born in state of residence	Age (percent)								
				Under 5 years	5 to 18 years	18 to 24 years	25 to 34 years	35 to 44 years	45 to 54 years	55 to 64 years	65 to 74 years	75 years and over
	13	14	15	16	17	18	19	20	21	22	23	24
NORTH CAROLINA	51.0	6.9	59.7	6.8	17.5	9.7	13.5	15.0	14.3	11.0	6.5	5.6
District 1	51.3	3.0	73.3	6.4	17.5	10.5	11.6	13.1	15.1	11.7	7.1	6.9
District 2	49.6	7.8	61.6	7.5	18.4	11.8	14.7	15.2	13.2	9.6	5.3	4.4
District 3	50.0	4.6	55.9	7.5	17.4	12.4	12.8	13.6	13.5	10.6	7.1	5.2
District 4	51.2	12.0	44.7	7.0	18.1	10.0	14.4	17.0	14.9	10.2	4.6	3.9
District 5	51.3	5.4	67.0	5.5	16.7	8.6	12.8	14.4	15.2	12.3	7.9	6.6
District 6	51.3	5.4	65.0	5.9	17.8	8.2	12.5	14.7	15.4	11.5	7.3	6.6
District 7	51.5	4.8	63.9	6.5	17.5	9.5	13.2	13.9	14.3	11.6	7.7	5.8
District 8	51.2	8.0	59.2	7.5	19.0	10.0	14.6	15.2	13.2	9.9	5.7	5.0
District 9	50.8	8.4	48.3	7.5	18.2	7.8	13.6	16.8	15.7	11.0	5.3	4.0
District 10	50.6	4.1	68.9	5.9	17.7	8.1	13.0	15.1	14.5	12.1	7.4	6.2
District 11	51.7	4.7	57.0	5.5	15.2	8.1	12.9	13.5	14.1	12.6	8.9	9.1
District 12	51.4	10.5	58.5	8.4	17.6	10.5	14.7	16.0	13.0	9.7	5.3	4.8
District 13	50.7	10.4	57.1	7.2	16.4	10.3	15.2	16.1	14.1	10.4	5.6	4.9
NORTH DAKOTA	50.1	2.1	71.1	6.1	16.4	13.0	11.7	12.8	14.9	10.5	6.8	7.8
At Large	50.1	2.1	71.1	6.1	16.4	13.0	11.7	12.8	14.9	10.5	6.8	7.8
OHIO	51.3	3.6	75.1	6.4	17.7	9.6	12.6	14.2	15.1	11.0	6.7	6.7
District 1	52.2	3.7	75.7	7.1	18.1	10.5	11.3	14.3	15.3	10.5	6.3	6.7
District 2	51.5	3.1	71.8	6.6	18.9	8.4	13.3	15.0	15.5	10.4	6.1	5.8
District 3	51.1	3.0	70.8	6.7	17.6	9.3	12.5	14.0	14.5	11.4	7.1	7.0
District 4	50.4	1.6	82.6	6.3	17.8	9.6	12.5	13.7	15.0	11.2	7.0	6.9
District 5	50.7	2.0	81.0	6.1	18.0	10.9	12.2	12.9	15.3	11.1	6.8	6.7
District 6	51.3	1.7	68.2	5.3	15.5	11.6	11.8	13.0	15.6	11.8	7.6	7.8
District 7	50.4	2.7	75.6	6.1	17.2	10.0	13.9	14.3	15.1	11.1	6.6	5.7
District 8	50.9	2.9	72.4	6.4	18.2	10.5	13.2	14.5	14.6	10.5	6.4	5.8
District 9	51.2	2.5	78.4	6.4	18.0	9.7	12.6	13.6	15.1	11.3	6.5	6.9
District 10	51.7	8.2	74.9	6.3	16.6	7.9	10.8	15.2	15.9	11.6	7.2	8.4
District 11	54.1	5.5	71.5	6.6	19.1	8.9	12.1	13.3	14.7	10.3	6.9	8.1
District 12	51.4	6.7	66.6	7.4	18.3	9.1	14.5	16.2	14.5	9.8	5.6	4.6
District 13	51.6	3.8	76.2	6.4	18.2	8.7	11.1	14.9	15.7	11.5	6.6	6.8
District 14	50.7	4.5	74.9	5.7	18.3	7.4	10.8	14.6	16.8	12.1	7.1	7.1
District 15	50.3	7.2	70.4	7.6	17.3	11.7	15.5	15.2	13.9	9.2	4.8	4.7
District 16	51.3	2.2	80.6	6.2	17.6	9.2	11.9	13.7	15.6	11.7	6.8	7.3
District 17	51.8	2.7	76.7	5.6	16.3	11.3	12.3	13.1	15.0	11.7	7.4	7.3
District 18	50.8	0.7	84.6	6.5	18.2	8.6	13.6	13.4	14.6	11.1	7.3	6.7
OKLAHOMA	50.7	4.9	61.7	7.0	18.0	10.4	13.1	13.4	14.1	10.8	6.9	6.3
District 1	51.0	6.2	58.2	7.6	18.4	9.1	13.2	14.0	14.7	10.7	6.1	6.0
District 2	50.8	1.9	62.7	6.2	18.0	10.4	11.9	13.2	13.3	11.5	8.3	7.1
District 3	49.9	3.8	65.9	6.6	17.3	11.6	12.1	12.8	14.6	10.9	7.3	6.9
District 4	50.8	3.9	60.5	6.7	18.3	11.0	13.5	13.4	14.2	10.5	6.7	5.6
District 5	51.1	8.6	61.2	8.1	17.9	9.8	14.5	13.3	13.8	10.2	6.4	6.1
OREGON	50.5	9.7	45.0	6.2	17.0	9.2	13.9	13.8	15.1	11.8	6.5	6.4
District 1	49.9	13.9	41.8	6.6	17.8	8.7	15.2	15.5	15.2	10.9	5.3	4.9
District 2	50.7	6.1	42.0	5.7	17.2	8.7	13.0	12.6	15.1	12.3	7.9	7.6
District 3	50.8	13.3	47.3	7.1	16.6	8.3	15.0	15.7	15.5	11.5	5.1	5.1
District 4	50.8	4.8	45.2	5.5	15.6	10.3	12.9	12.1	15.1	12.7	7.9	7.8
District 5	50.1	10.2	49.1	6.2	17.5	10.2	13.2	13.3	14.9	11.9	6.2	6.6
PENNSYLVANIA	51.4	5.1	75.6	5.8	16.7	9.7	11.6	14.3	15.4	11.4	7.1	8.0
District 1	53.4	10.5	70.5	8.5	20.5	10.9	13.3	13.9	13.2	9.0	5.6	5.3
District 2	54.8	8.3	69.8	6.4	16.1	12.0	13.0	13.1	14.2	10.4	6.9	8.0
District 3	50.7	2.3	82.7	5.4	17.2	10.4	11.4	13.7	15.4	11.3	7.0	8.0
District 4	52.2	2.9	81.5	5.4	16.8	7.3	9.3	14.7	16.9	12.5	7.5	9.5
District 5	50.3	2.4	82.2	5.2	14.7	13.4	12.1	13.1	14.5	11.1	7.9	8.0
District 6	50.7	7.0	71.6	6.5	16.7	9.4	12.1	15.1	15.4	11.5	6.7	6.5
District 7	50.9	7.9	73.6	6.0	17.8	9.6	10.4	15.1	15.5	11.3	6.7	7.5
District 8	50.8	8.0	69.2	5.7	17.8	8.5	10.5	15.5	16.7	12.0	6.8	6.6
District 9	50.6	1.3	81.7	5.6	16.1	8.5	12.5	13.9	15.2	11.9	7.9	8.4
District 10	50.5	2.2	71.7	5.0	16.3	9.0	10.9	14.2	15.7	12.4	8.0	8.4
District 11	51.4	4.2	71.0	5.3	15.7	10.6	11.7	14.3	14.8	11.2	7.4	9.0
District 12	51.9	1.0	87.1	4.6	15.3	9.7	11.0	13.3	16.0	12.1	8.1	9.9
District 13	51.8	11.4	73.9	6.3	17.8	8.1	10.2	16.0	16.0	10.9	6.5	8.1
District 14	53.0	4.8	81.5	5.7	14.4	12.6	10.9	13.1	15.9	10.9	7.4	9.2
District 15	50.9	6.9	65.6	5.9	16.8	9.4	11.9	15.1	14.9	11.4	6.7	8.0
District 16	51.2	5.7	71.6	6.9	18.8	9.9	12.4	13.9	14.4	10.1	6.4	7.2
District 17	51.0	3.6	80.4	5.7	16.3	7.9	12.7	14.5	16.1	11.5	7.3	8.0
District 18	51.3	3.2	83.4	5.0	16.1	7.5	10.7	13.7	16.5	12.8	7.8	9.8
District 19	50.8	3.3	69.0	5.6	16.3	9.7	12.6	14.9	15.5	11.5	6.9	7.0

Table A. 110th Congressional Districts—*Continued*

(Number, percent.)

STATE Congressional district	Households, 2006						Group quarters, 2006		Group quarters, 2000			
	Number	Average household size	Family households (percent)	Married-couple family (percent)	Female family house-holder[4] (percent)	One-person households (percent)	Total in group quarters	Percent 65 years and over	Persons in correctional institutions	Persons in nursing homes	Persons in college dormitories	Persons in military quarters
	25	26	27	28	29	30	31	32	33	34	35	36
NORTH CAROLINA	3 454 068	2.49	66.9	49.4	13.2	27.8	270 572	19.1	46 614	50 892	76 018	37 022
District 1	236 882	2.46	66.5	41.9	20.1	29.4	20 673	10.4	6 678	5 476	1 749	4 016
District 2	245 301	2.68	67.0	46.7	14.9	28.3	37 940	9.8	6 490	3 414	11 930	13 857
District 3	262 931	2.42	69.9	54.7	11.5	24.4	37 621	8.9	3 660	2 148	4 877	18 531
District 4	287 725	2.48	63.9	50.0	10.9	28.9	22 336	16.5	958	3 566	14 866	0
District 5	263 187	2.44	67.4	54.8	9.0	28.0	14 367	26.5	731	4 931	4 742	0
District 6	265 714	2.53	70.6	55.9	10.2	25.7	7 493	43.7	1 576	3 267	1 914	0
District 7	275 740	2.47	65.3	47.0	13.6	28.6	12 624	20.8	5 092	2 654	2 627	244
District 8	252 222	2.52	66.6	46.0	15.6	27.9	21 261	18.2	5 094	4 180	5 042	374
District 9	302 198	2.53	69.3	53.8	10.9	25.4	4 315	33.8	556	2 751	796	0
District 10	254 136	2.56	70.5	53.7	12.4	25.2	13 856	27.0	3 898	4 254	2 066	0
District 11	277 529	2.31	66.7	52.5	10.6	28.1	24 316	31.4	2 927	5 871	5 294	0
District 12	261 386	2.47	63.2	38.7	19.2	30.4	27 558	16.0	4 210	4 922	12 876	0
District 13	269 117	2.48	62.8	45.0	13.7	31.0	26 212	30.2	4 744	3 458	7 239	0
NORTH DAKOTA	272 352	2.23	62.1	50.8	7.8	30.6	27 521	24.0	1 518	7 254	10 137	1 244
At Large	272 352	2.23	62.1	50.8	7.8	30.6	27 521	24.0	1 518	7 254	10 137	1 244
OHIO	4 499 506	2.48	65.6	48.9	12.5	29.1	308 323	27.0	68 873	93 157	91 713	369
District 1	243 095	2.43	59.8	39.2	16.9	35.6	16 961	29.7	1 251	5 363	4 916	0
District 2	255 433	2.60	68.7	53.8	11.0	26.5	9 384	39.2	3 152	5 563	221	0
District 3	255 848	2.42	64.1	46.6	13.4	30.9	22 506	31.8	5 432	5 814	7 028	0
District 4	244 234	2.50	68.9	54.8	10.7	26.9	22 426	22.2	12 856	5 856	3 697	0
District 5	245 821	2.52	68.5	55.5	9.1	25.7	17 521	20.8	1 141	5 073	7 398	0
District 6	246 347	2.44	66.7	52.5	10.8	28.2	30 222	25.8	6 504	5 373	9 291	0
District 7	249 556	2.53	69.0	53.9	11.1	24.9	25 814	17.9	12 404	4 694	7 026	341
District 8	245 077	2.59	69.0	53.5	11.3	25.4	17 462	18.3	878	4 323	7 571	0
District 9	249 185	2.44	63.3	45.3	13.6	29.6	17 317	29.8	679	5 772	4 354	17
District 10	251 703	2.38	60.6	42.6	13.2	35.0	7 417	57.1	58	5 422	1 890	0
District 11	233 688	2.35	55.8	29.5	21.7	39.8	17 716	26.3	3 075	6 048	4 755	5
District 12	279 205	2.45	65.9	48.3	12.8	28.7	13 807	23.0	276	4 265	5 748	0
District 13	252 552	2.54	67.7	50.4	13.1	28.7	7 339	40.0	5 007	4 800	554	1
District 14	249 410	2.58	70.3	56.4	9.4	25.8	11 006	54.4	481	4 607	982	5
District 15	261 170	2.40	59.2	44.3	10.8	32.0	25 013	11.9	6 635	3 183	9 531	0
District 16	251 133	2.53	69.7	54.3	11.1	25.7	15 008	35.0	844	6 369	5 438	0
District 17	244 530	2.42	64.7	46.0	14.4	29.4	16 973	19.7	4 629	4 526	7 470	0
District 18	241 519	2.59	69.3	53.3	11.6	26.4	14 431	36.7	3 571	6 106	3 843	0
OKLAHOMA	1 385 300	2.50	66.9	50.5	11.9	28.3	111 393	22.8	33 919	28 021	26 643	7 616
District 1	289 454	2.44	65.5	48.5	12.6	29.1	14 850	31.4	1 303	4 163	3 870	0
District 2	267 067	2.57	70.0	52.8	13.1	26.9	25 813	28.5	9 036	6 779	3 457	4
District 3	262 052	2.56	69.6	54.8	9.7	26.2	29 713	14.2	11 514	6 585	8 180	510
District 4	279 028	2.48	68.5	52.9	11.1	26.5	25 693	22.2	5 969	5 677	6 115	7 102
District 5	287 699	2.48	61.6	44.0	12.8	32.6	15 324	23.0	6 097	4 817	5 021	0
OREGON	1 449 662	2.50	64.0	49.6	10.2	28.0	79 987	24.7	19 523	14 677	18 831	95
District 1	299 239	2.52	63.5	50.9	8.9	29.0	14 360	11.8	3 805	2 305	3 262	45
District 2	295 593	2.47	67.0	52.5	10.1	26.3	17 431	34.7	6 665	3 438	1 748	0
District 3	285 072	2.47	59.2	42.1	12.0	30.4	12 983	36.2	1 953	3 000	3 118	0
District 4	292 493	2.40	63.7	50.0	10.1	27.8	14 004	27.1	1 732	2 524	3 523	33
District 5	277 265	2.63	66.4	52.5	10.0	26.6	21 209	16.7	5 368	3 410	7 180	17
PENNSYLVANIA	4 845 603	2.47	65.5	49.6	11.7	29.3	455 673	27.2	76 553	114 113	147 542	758
District 1	228 966	2.71	58.3	26.5	25.5	37.1	17 636	15.7	1 222	2 710	7 746	531
District 2	231 152	2.31	48.9	23.9	20.3	45.0	24 863	30.5	369	5 347	15 317	0
District 3	251 107	2.45	66.3	51.6	11.3	28.7	30 963	19.9	4 627	7 193	12 362	0
District 4	258 425	2.46	69.6	57.1	9.3	26.6	11 562	52.1	534	6 217	2 540	0
District 5	249 189	2.40	65.6	52.5	8.4	28.5	37 305	18.0	8 054	5 425	16 788	0
District 6	265 823	2.53	67.7	53.3	10.2	25.5	26 581	17.4	4 165	5 855	9 730	0
District 7	250 090	2.57	66.0	51.7	10.5	29.3	26 119	23.3	2 820	5 374	8 161	0
District 8	244 417	2.68	72.1	59.4	8.8	23.2	15 851	36.3	917	4 424	1 203	0
District 9	259 876	2.46	68.5	56.1	8.8	26.5	21 244	26.5	7 081	6 748	3 435	32
District 10	255 651	2.42	69.1	54.5	10.1	26.2	30 569	22.6	9 206	6 216	7 177	0
District 11	267 226	2.45	64.6	48.3	11.4	29.9	24 452	22.3	4 921	6 679	8 669	3
District 12	255 864	2.36	64.9	48.3	12.3	31.0	26 006	23.0	4 379	4 296	8 055	0
District 13	254 021	2.56	65.7	49.0	12.5	29.9	23 196	51.3	6 359	7 933	754	159
District 14	259 999	2.14	50.8	32.0	14.6	42.6	28 340	16.2	4 713	4 657	12 335	0
District 15	266 731	2.54	69.8	53.4	12.1	24.4	25 775	29.3	1 989	6 881	8 732	0
District 16	248 261	2.65	71.9	57.6	10.6	23.0	25 964	31.0	1 029	6 742	10 109	0
District 17	265 010	2.43	66.7	50.8	11.3	28.0	18 202	42.6	7 633	7 733	1 998	0
District 18	261 628	2.41	67.5	55.7	7.8	28.4	18 698	53.1	1 252	6 735	2 811	3
District 19	272 167	2.49	68.6	55.3	9.2	25.7	22 347	19.6	5 283	6 948	9 620	30

[4]No spouse present.

Table A. 110th Congressional Districts—*Continued*

(Number, percent.)

STATE Congressional district	Education, 2006				Income, 2006			Poverty, 2006		
	School enrollment[5]		Attainment level[6] (percent)		Per capita income (dollars)	Median household income (dollars)	Percent of households with income over $100,000	Persons below poverty level (percent)	Families below poverty level (percent)	Percent of households receiving food stamps in past 12 months
	Total	Private (percent)	High school graduate or more	Bachelor's degree or more						
	37	38	39	40	41	42	43	44	45	46
NORTH CAROLINA	2 306 697	14.0	82.0	24.8	22 945	42 625	13.4	14.7	10.7	8.8
District 1	154 482	7.6	75.9	12.5	16 538	30 872	5.8	22.9	18.0	16.6
District 2	195 988	12.4	79.0	17.6	19 035	39 576	9.2	17.0	13.0	11.2
District 3	177 197	10.6	85.6	22.5	21 907	42 349	12.5	13.9	9.5	8.0
District 4	219 357	22.4	90.4	49.8	31 579	60 152	27.3	9.6	6.1	4.4
District 5	157 259	11.6	80.4	21.7	23 048	42 235	12.3	12.5	7.8	6.2
District 6	168 904	16.2	82.7	23.6	24 383	47 868	14.5	11.3	8.0	5.5
District 7	177 337	8.6	78.8	21.0	20 886	38 617	10.3	18.4	13.1	11.3
District 8	183 731	11.4	81.3	19.3	19 872	40 615	9.9	16.1	13.4	9.7
District 9	198 528	21.2	89.7	38.7	32 936	60 531	24.7	7.7	5.0	4.9
District 10	163 433	11.1	77.3	17.3	20 576	38 763	10.5	14.0	10.5	9.4
District 11	151 494	13.2	81.9	23.3	21 735	38 230	10.3	14.8	11.0	8.4
District 12	179 830	16.4	78.2	21.2	19 784	37 436	9.4	19.6	16.0	12.2
District 13	179 157	15.7	82.6	28.6	23 191	44 035	13.9	15.5	10.8	8.8
NORTH DAKOTA	167 120	10.9	88.1	25.6	22 619	41 919	10.1	11.4	7.0	6.2
At Large	167 120	10.9	88.1	25.6	22 619	41 919	10.1	11.4	7.0	6.2
OHIO	2 998 178	18.3	86.2	23.0	23 543	44 532	13.9	13.3	9.8	9.3
District 1	164 221	26.6	84.6	22.7	23 154	40 064	12.4	17.3	13.3	10.1
District 2	173 352	18.5	86.8	31.1	28 314	51 840	20.4	10.7	8.2	7.6
District 3	170 532	19.5	86.3	24.6	23 794	44 089	15.0	13.4	10.3	8.6
District 4	158 621	16.6	85.1	15.4	20 881	42 739	9.9	12.2	9.2	7.9
District 5	171 751	14.2	87.2	15.7	22 084	45 758	11.3	10.3	6.8	6.4
District 6	159 181	12.0	85.6	15.7	19 142	36 374	8.3	17.5	12.9	11.7
District 7	170 404	17.4	86.8	19.8	22 772	48 552	14.2	11.7	8.3	9.3
District 8	173 819	13.2	86.0	20.8	23 365	48 328	15.0	11.4	7.8	7.9
District 9	167 237	18.4	87.0	21.2	23 621	44 807	14.0	15.0	10.8	11.3
District 10	147 445	27.5	85.4	24.3	24 161	43 831	13.4	11.9	9.4	8.6
District 11	160 626	25.1	82.7	25.5	21 458	33 661	10.5	20.8	16.2	15.0
District 12	189 223	22.1	90.1	36.6	29 312	52 216	21.1	12.2	9.1	9.9
District 13	166 229	20.1	87.9	26.5	24 983	48 699	16.3	12.3	9.6	8.7
District 14	159 670	19.8	89.3	28.9	28 620	54 186	20.6	7.4	5.7	5.2
District 15	191 052	14.7	87.6	33.9	25 188	47 341	17.2	15.8	10.7	8.2
District 16	164 604	20.2	86.3	19.9	23 106	46 217	13.2	10.8	8.5	7.4
District 17	158 191	11.0	85.7	16.7	20 203	38 990	8.9	15.2	11.0	10.7
District 18	152 020	13.1	80.9	12.3	18 257	37 084	7.2	15.5	11.8	12.9
OKLAHOMA	938 873	11.1	84.3	22.1	20 935	38 770	10.8	17.0	12.8	10.5
District 1	187 600	17.9	87.5	28.3	23 907	42 196	14.3	15.8	12.5	9.3
District 2	178 364	7.5	80.6	14.4	17 120	32 848	6.4	19.5	15.3	13.0
District 3	184 716	7.6	84.6	19.7	19 818	38 738	9.7	16.9	12.5	9.3
District 4	198 089	7.4	86.1	22.5	20 712	41 880	10.7	15.5	11.0	9.3
District 5	190 104	15.0	82.7	25.8	23 022	38 160	12.3	17.3	12.5	11.6
OREGON	904 926	14.5	87.6	27.5	24 418	46 230	14.8	13.3	9.2	10.7
District 1	193 445	17.6	89.9	35.7	28 735	55 049	21.3	10.9	7.4	8.1
District 2	171 528	10.8	86.6	21.0	21 877	42 875	10.4	13.0	9.7	10.8
District 3	176 652	18.4	87.2	28.8	24 306	45 794	14.4	14.6	10.9	11.3
District 4	172 348	11.5	87.4	23.1	21 851	40 767	10.9	16.0	10.1	13.4
District 5	190 953	13.5	86.8	29.0	25 077	49 832	17.3	12.0	8.2	9.8
PENNSYLVANIA	3 092 591	24.4	86.2	25.4	24 694	46 259	15.8	12.1	8.2	7.4
District 1	189 443	26.0	73.4	15.5	16 131	29 448	7.1	30.7	25.6	19.5
District 2	155 117	37.8	79.8	27.6	21 085	31 730	11.2	26.0	19.5	13.5
District 3	165 196	22.4	87.0	20.0	20 511	40 033	10.3	14.3	9.4	10.0
District 4	154 158	21.1	90.5	31.2	29 031	52 251	19.4	7.6	5.2	5.4
District 5	165 401	9.3	86.2	19.4	19 370	37 213	7.5	14.4	8.9	8.9
District 6	177 840	29.6	89.0	37.7	34 357	64 778	28.3	8.3	5.2	3.9
District 7	185 044	36.8	91.9	39.9	33 047	64 452	30.1	5.6	3.4	3.2
District 8	164 317	29.4	90.1	34.2	33 014	69 660	31.3	4.6	3.1	3.6
District 9	139 970	16.0	83.8	14.9	20 781	41 091	8.7	10.8	7.8	7.1
District 10	148 739	21.6	85.9	19.6	21 453	41 445	10.6	11.7	7.7	6.4
District 11	164 664	21.0	86.4	19.0	20 319	40 233	9.6	13.4	10.0	9.0
District 12	141 964	12.5	85.2	16.3	19 498	35 069	8.1	14.6	10.8	11.4
District 13	171 398	38.2	88.6	34.1	29 165	56 665	23.6	8.3	5.6	4.0
District 14	155 837	27.8	87.6	25.6	20 577	32 466	8.0	19.9	14.3	11.5
District 15	175 544	24.6	85.6	25.1	25 881	52 396	19.7	10.0	7.0	5.2
District 16	174 246	23.0	80.0	25.3	25 385	52 406	18.3	10.5	7.3	5.9
District 17	144 327	16.5	84.7	19.5	23 410	47 318	12.7	9.5	6.7	6.6
District 18	153 006	22.6	92.4	32.4	27 596	52 433	18.9	6.6	4.5	4.1
District 19	166 380	21.5	86.4	24.2	25 889	53 723	16.4	7.2	4.8	3.9

[5]All persons 3 years old and over enrolled in nursery school through college.
[6]Persons 25 years old and over.

Table A. 110th Congressional Districts—*Continued*

(Number, percent.)

STATE Congressional district	Housing units, 2006									
	Total	Total occupied units	Owner-occupied units							
			Percent owner-occupied units	Median value (dollars)	Percent valued at $500,000 or more	Median real estate taxes (dollars)	Median monthly costs (dollars)	Percent with second mortgage or home equity loan	Median cost as percent of income	
									With a mortgage	Without a mortgage
	47	48	49	50	51	52	53	54	55	56
NORTH CAROLINA	4 026 558	3 454 068	68.1	137 200	4.6	1 038	866	19.7	23.1	11.9
District 1	283 257	236 882	60.9	86 300	1.3	719	692	12.5	24.7	15.3
District 2	279 702	245 301	65.9	113 200	1.2	932	844	17.1	23.7	13.2
District 3	334 209	262 931	68.7	136 500	4.9	905	843	18.1	23.3	13.0
District 4	316 592	287 725	65.3	211 200	9.0	1 810	1 331	29.2	21.7	10.7
District 5	307 548	263 187	75.0	133 200	3.7	841	710	19.8	22.1	10.1
District 6	297 988	265 714	75.5	140 000	2.9	940	853	20.6	22.4	11.7
District 7	342 603	275 740	68.2	119 600	5.8	872	730	14.4	24.2	12.8
District 8	288 066	252 222	64.2	116 000	2.4	1 108	853	17.2	23.6	12.9
District 9	328 031	302 198	74.9	182 000	9.7	1 773	1 224	29.8	22.5	11.8
District 10	298 555	254 136	74.9	119 900	3.6	784	722	17.7	23.2	11.2
District 11	344 791	277 529	73.0	151 900	5.2	806	611	14.4	23.3	10.7
District 12	300 537	261 386	54.9	120 500	2.2	1 132	918	19.5	24.5	12.2
District 13	304 679	269 117	61.5	143 600	4.4	1 204	977	22.2	23.1	10.7
NORTH DAKOTA	306 982	272 352	66.7	99 700	1.0	1 436	652	10.0	21.0	11.5
At Large	306 982	272 352	66.7	99 700	1.0	1 436	652	10.0	21.0	11.5
OHIO	5 045 356	4 499 506	70.0	135 200	2.3	1 710	956	20.9	23.6	13.8
District 1	283 302	243 095	61.7	136 100	2.1	1 839	1 041	21.0	24.0	14.6
District 2	288 578	255 433	72.3	161 200	6.0	1 979	1 096	23.0	23.4	13.7
District 3	285 428	255 848	68.1	131 500	2.2	1 908	1 002	20.9	23.8	13.9
District 4	270 634	244 234	74.4	111 800	0.6	1 249	831	18.6	22.5	13.0
District 5	264 801	245 821	77.0	118 900	1.2	1 337	831	21.2	22.4	12.8
District 6	275 996	246 347	73.5	96 400	0.7	928	599	13.2	22.2	12.5
District 7	275 325	249 556	70.7	135 900	1.4	1 647	973	20.6	23.2	12.9
District 8	271 418	245 077	71.3	136 100	1.8	1 650	987	22.2	22.8	13.3
District 9	289 596	249 185	68.4	132 100	1.6	1 748	972	19.8	22.9	14.6
District 10	279 978	251 703	70.1	136 800	1.4	2 437	1 010	21.6	24.8	16.3
District 11	283 914	233 688	55.4	118 900	2.8	1 933	1 022	18.0	28.0	18.7
District 12	314 306	279 205	66.0	181 900	5.4	2 609	1 303	27.7	24.6	13.3
District 13	277 471	252 552	74.1	151 100	2.6	2 030	1 044	22.2	24.1	14.6
District 14	268 385	249 410	78.2	178 400	5.0	2 489	1 154	25.0	24.6	13.9
District 15	297 420	261 170	60.9	158 000	2.9	2 357	1 160	25.3	23.4	13.9
District 16	271 096	251 133	74.3	137 400	2.1	1 538	925	22.2	23.0	13.3
District 17	275 429	244 530	70.2	107 000	0.6	1 368	794	18.5	24.1	15.0
District 18	272 279	241 519	73.8	104 600	1.2	1 070	677	15.1	22.9	12.5
OKLAHOMA	1 607 416	1 385 300	68.6	94 500	1.6	677	673	9.8	21.4	12.0
District 1	320 670	289 454	66.0	115 700	2.1	1 116	873	14.0	21.9	12.3
District 2	327 913	267 067	72.9	78 500	1.3	374	489	5.5	21.1	11.9
District 3	314 095	262 052	72.5	82 400	1.2	493	559	7.0	19.7	11.4
District 4	314 420	279 028	69.2	98 100	0.8	729	726	10.6	21.6	11.9
District 5	330 318	287 699	63.2	101 300	2.6	824	780	12.3	22.4	12.5
OREGON	1 586 600	1 449 662	64.8	236 600	11.1	1 996	1 121	22.0	26.1	12.4
District 1	320 765	299 239	63.4	274 100	12.9	2 481	1 375	27.0	25.2	11.4
District 2	336 412	295 593	67.0	225 400	13.0	1 531	891	16.9	26.3	12.2
District 3	305 619	285 072	61.3	245 900	10.0	2 375	1 314	26.0	27.0	13.8
District 4	316 542	292 493	64.0	200 200	7.0	1 541	887	18.0	26.1	12.1
District 5	307 262	277 265	68.2	234 900	12.5	2 206	1 173	22.3	26.0	12.8
PENNSYLVANIA	5 453 647	4 845 603	71.7	145 200	5.0	2 057	892	17.6	23.7	14.3
District 1	275 626	228 966	58.7	89 100	3.1	943	714	12.0	26.8	16.4
District 2	287 506	231 152	54.0	110 500	4.9	1 121	727	10.9	25.5	17.6
District 3	282 407	251 107	72.7	102 300	1.0	1 665	718	13.2	23.2	13.5
District 4	282 089	258 425	79.2	132 900	3.6	2 420	914	18.1	22.6	14.5
District 5	314 987	249 189	71.2	91 000	1.2	1 348	631	12.3	22.8	13.7
District 6	278 909	265 823	74.5	237 100	14.7	3 390	1 360	24.1	24.1	15.0
District 7	264 169	250 090	76.3	252 800	12.2	3 527	1 366	22.8	24.1	16.2
District 8	257 623	244 417	77.7	319 700	18.6	3 709	1 553	25.9	24.7	15.8
District 9	292 761	259 876	76.7	108 400	1.6	1 266	613	13.8	22.3	12.5
District 10	322 480	255 651	75.3	123 900	2.3	1 592	763	14.4	23.6	14.2
District 11	318 065	267 226	71.3	120 400	1.0	1 828	821	14.6	24.8	15.6
District 12	293 510	255 864	72.2	86 500	0.5	1 253	575	12.2	22.2	13.6
District 13	268 204	254 021	71.8	231 600	9.8	2 577	1 223	20.0	24.9	14.4
District 14	310 276	259 999	57.7	76 900	0.8	1 696	734	14.3	23.8	16.1
District 15	280 726	266 731	73.7	202 100	4.7	2 950	1 109	22.9	24.1	14.8
District 16	261 372	248 261	69.8	184 000	7.1	2 612	1 076	21.3	24.1	12.5
District 17	291 059	265 010	73.5	128 600	1.9	1 945	851	17.4	23.1	13.7
District 18	285 459	261 628	77.8	133 800	2.1	2 497	918	17.9	22.0	13.4
District 19	286 419	272 167	75.3	165 500	3.0	2 146	1 014	21.7	23.5	13.0

Table A. 110th Congressional Districts—*Continued*

(Number, percent.)

STATE Congressional district	Housing units, 2006—*Continued*			Civilian labor force, 2006			Civilian employment and occupation, 2006			
	Renter-occupied units		Sub-standard housing units (percent)[7]	Total	Unemployment		Total civilian employment	Management, professional, and related (percent)	Service, sales, and office (percent)	Construction and production (percent)
	Median gross rent (dollars)	Median gross rent as a percent of income			Total	Rate[8]				
	57	58	59	60	61	62	63	64	65	66
NORTH CAROLINA	656	28.9	2.3	4 445 111	292 883	6.6	4 152 228	32.6	40.1	26.5
District 1	553	31.0	2.9	271 350	24 975	9.2	246 375	23.1	44.2	31.3
District 2	652	28.8	3.6	334 139	26 384	7.9	307 755	27.2	41.1	29.9
District 3	663	27.9	1.5	313 068	18 967	6.1	294 101	32.8	39.8	25.9
District 4	767	29.1	2.2	403 081	20 828	5.2	382 253	52.8	35.1	11.9
District 5	566	28.9	1.6	342 123	17 697	5.2	324 426	28.9	38.8	30.7
District 6	636	27.6	2.1	347 689	18 268	5.3	329 421	31.2	39.6	28.9
District 7	635	29.5	2.6	327 303	21 359	6.5	305 944	28.9	41.0	28.4
District 8	663	28.8	2.4	317 194	22 868	7.2	294 326	28.7	41.0	29.7
District 9	739	26.5	1.2	422 334	21 751	5.2	400 583	40.9	40.8	18.3
District 10	561	27.9	1.8	323 236	25 437	7.9	297 799	27.8	37.6	34.3
District 11	618	28.6	2.4	324 741	15 457	4.8	309 284	28.8	42.3	28.2
District 12	660	29.8	3.1	349 476	33 931	9.7	315 545	27.5	42.9	29.4
District 13	690	29.7	2.9	369 377	24 961	6.8	344 416	35.2	39.6	24.9
NORTH DAKOTA	497	25.8	1.1	346 616	11 606	3.3	335 010	34.0	42.1	22.1
At Large	497	25.8	1.1	346 616	11 606	3.3	335 010	34.0	42.1	22.1
OHIO	627	29.3	1.5	5 891 398	417 031	7.1	5 474 367	32.1	42.1	25.5
District 1	552	31.6	1.7	307 876	24 305	7.9	283 571	30.7	46.5	22.6
District 2	688	26.2	2.0	340 017	21 384	6.3	318 633	38.0	39.5	22.3
District 3	645	31.1	1.3	315 273	23 437	7.4	291 836	34.7	41.8	23.3
District 4	557	27.9	1.5	321 563	19 353	6.0	302 210	26.7	37.2	35.5
District 5	556	25.4	1.4	339 826	21 486	6.3	318 340	25.9	36.1	37.0
District 6	511	31.1	1.4	300 165	22 645	7.5	277 520	27.1	43.4	29.0
District 7	663	28.3	1.6	340 701	21 541	6.3	319 160	32.5	41.8	25.4
District 8	662	28.1	2.1	343 306	20 237	5.9	323 069	31.0	40.8	27.8
District 9	600	29.8	1.0	319 693	26 055	8.2	293 638	29.5	43.3	26.9
District 10	653	29.5	1.4	316 032	24 266	7.7	291 766	31.5	46.7	21.8
District 11	640	32.5	1.3	270 313	33 737	12.5	236 576	34.9	46.4	18.7
District 12	704	28.7	1.8	373 567	24 069	6.4	349 498	42.1	42.2	15.6
District 13	654	29.5	1.0	337 007	22 840	6.8	314 167	33.9	43.8	22.0
District 14	703	29.3	1.3	347 013	16 705	4.8	330 308	35.7	40.7	23.3
District 15	695	30.4	2.5	349 620	22 100	6.3	327 520	38.4	42.8	18.6
District 16	592	28.8	1.4	342 596	22 553	6.6	320 043	30.0	41.7	28.0
District 17	592	30.6	1.2	308 898	25 807	8.4	283 091	26.1	44.4	29.3
District 18	543	28.5	1.8	317 932	24 511	7.7	293 421	26.3	40.4	32.3
OKLAHOMA	580	28.6	2.8	1 734 785	103 313	6.0	1 631 472	30.7	42.8	25.6
District 1	636	29.8	2.4	369 596	20 705	5.6	348 891	33.9	42.9	23.0
District 2	486	27.0	2.8	313 643	22 443	7.2	291 200	26.0	41.7	30.7
District 3	530	28.3	2.9	341 427	19 559	5.7	321 868	29.1	41.6	27.6
District 4	595	27.7	2.8	347 011	19 489	5.6	327 522	32.7	42.5	24.2
District 5	610	29.3	2.9	363 108	21 117	5.8	341 991	31.2	45.2	23.3
OREGON	714	29.9	3.1	1 912 917	120 971	6.3	1 791 946	33.0	42.1	22.8
District 1	751	28.3	3.7	420 397	23 629	5.6	396 768	37.9	40.4	19.6
District 2	677	28.0	3.3	372 749	24 486	6.6	348 263	27.9	43.2	26.4
District 3	741	32.6	3.1	388 402	24 197	6.2	364 205	33.5	42.8	22.9
District 4	662	30.0	2.4	347 908	22 286	6.4	325 622	30.4	42.4	24.8
District 5	725	30.9	3.1	383 461	26 373	6.9	357 088	34.1	41.8	21.1
PENNSYLVANIA	664	28.7	1.4	6 269 806	388 691	6.2	5 881 115	34.0	42.4	23.0
District 1	710	37.3	3.2	271 772	38 628	14.2	233 144	28.0	52.2	19.5
District 2	769	34.4	2.3	253 866	29 884	11.8	223 982	39.0	46.5	14.4
District 3	542	28.8	1.2	320 236	20 875	6.5	299 361	28.4	42.6	28.3
District 4	622	26.6	0.8	329 431	18 502	5.6	310 929	38.7	41.8	19.4
District 5	549	29.0	1.8	312 247	21 178	6.8	291 069	28.7	40.8	29.8
District 6	863	25.1	1.1	376 303	18 258	4.9	358 045	42.1	39.5	18.1
District 7	876	28.5	0.9	349 047	18 706	5.4	330 341	45.9	39.9	14.1
District 8	929	29.6	0.9	364 132	15 878	4.4	348 254	40.1	41.0	18.8
District 9	522	25.2	1.3	325 059	18 047	5.6	307 012	27.4	39.9	31.6
District 10	570	27.6	1.3	322 807	20 617	6.4	302 190	28.7	40.8	29.6
District 11	571	28.6	1.0	336 088	22 366	6.7	313 722	26.9	46.0	26.8
District 12	478	28.3	1.0	292 834	20 410	7.0	272 424	28.6	43.4	27.6
District 13	823	28.7	1.3	340 689	20 544	6.0	320 145	39.1	42.8	17.9
District 14	597	30.0	1.3	286 557	22 125	7.7	264 432	35.9	47.9	16.1
District 15	751	31.1	1.3	365 499	18 763	5.1	346 736	32.3	43.9	23.7
District 16	713	28.0	2.1	353 075	14 007	4.0	339 068	31.8	38.6	27.2
District 17	620	26.3	1.6	351 848	18 373	5.2	333 475	29.7	41.4	28.3
District 18	658	25.9	0.7	332 136	13 941	4.2	318 195	39.6	42.0	18.3
District 19	674	25.0	1.1	386 180	17 589	4.6	368 591	32.6	41.1	25.6

[7]Overcrowded or lacking complete plumbing facilities.
[8]Percent of civilian labor force.

Table A. 110th Congressional Districts—*Continued*

(Number, percent.)

STATE Congressional district	Social Security Beneficiaries (OASDI), December 2006							Supplemental Security Income, December 2006			
	Total	Rate per 1,000 population	Retired workers[9]	Disabled workers	Widow(er)s[10]	Spouses[11]	Children[12]	Total	Aged	Blind	Disabled
	67	68	69	70	71	72	73	74	75	76	77
NORTH CAROLINA	1 550 340	175.1	970 774	261 068	128 785	57 280	132 433	202 478	24 323	1 774	176 381
District 1	135 150	223.6	74 861	27 758	13 258	4 832	14 441	32 838	4 267	243	28 328
District 2	105 267	151.4	60 915	20 853	9 140	3 466	10 893	17 683	2 279	138	15 266
District 3	113 928	168.9	71 205	17 680	10 210	5 298	9 535	13 413	1 740	130	11 543
District 4	83 517	113.6	55 452	11 426	6 413	3 269	6 957	8 477	1 050	96	7 331
District 5	131 462	200.4	86 346	19 785	10 796	5 110	9 425	12 004	1 795	126	10 083
District 6	131 086	193.2	90 266	17 906	9 468	4 759	8 687	8 822	999	71	7 752
District 7	137 307	198.3	80 088	26 799	12 207	5 272	12 941	24 068	2 648	164	21 256
District 8	105 721	160.7	62 466	20 505	8 504	3 279	10 967	16 446	1 621	133	14 692
District 9	103 016	134.1	68 961	13 945	8 257	3 958	7 895	8 223	1 005	71	7 147
District 10	133 663	201.4	86 146	22 938	9 896	3 880	10 803	13 101	1 431	119	11 551
District 11	162 450	244.2	106 227	24 107	14 101	7 929	10 086	15 488	2 198	129	13 161
District 12	100 521	149.6	61 142	18 822	7 942	2 726	9 889	17 245	1 515	192	15 538
District 13	107 252	154.7	66 699	18 544	8 593	3 502	9 914	14 670	1 775	162	12 733
NORTH DAKOTA	115 434	181.5	73 133	11 604	14 578	8 946	7 173	8 040	948	76	7 016
At Large	115 434	181.5	73 133	11 604	14 578	8 946	7 173	8 040	948	76	7 016
OHIO	1 976 174	172.2	1 220 222	251 748	226 863	127 670	149 671	254 034	15 239	1 828	236 967
District 1	100 314	165.1	60 908	15 082	10 671	5 161	8 492	18 265	1 021	117	17 127
District 2	107 994	160.6	65 466	14 298	12 380	7 275	8 575	13 700	844	80	12 776
District 3	114 791	179.2	71 312	15 215	12 536	6 907	8 821	13 682	725	104	12 853
District 4	114 475	181.0	71 409	13 984	13 096	7 662	8 324	11 270	432	89	10 749
District 5	110 367	173.3	69 261	12 774	12 368	7 946	8 018	7 871	362	52	7 457
District 6	129 773	205.8	73 075	17 756	18 138	11 240	9 564	19 980	831	127	19 022
District 7	107 723	164.2	65 146	14 585	12 031	7 336	8 625	12 054	570	105	11 379
District 8	108 332	166.2	65 862	14 788	12 063	7 104	8 515	10 654	467	95	10 092
District 9	109 955	176.0	67 794	14 875	11 926	6 480	8 880	16 699	873	111	15 715
District 10	111 816	184.5	73 180	12 382	12 846	6 441	6 967	14 348	1 214	107	13 027
District 11	103 637	183.1	64 176	14 425	11 398	4 478	9 160	27 187	2 575	204	24 408
District 12	89 954	129.1	56 615	11 868	9 129	4 546	7 796	13 649	1 330	92	12 227
District 13	112 795	174.1	71 379	12 940	13 175	7 456	7 845	13 292	765	95	12 432
District 14	113 178	173.2	76 160	10 747	12 112	7 216	6 943	6 309	492	48	5 769
District 15	81 620	125.1	49 675	11 900	8 916	4 201	6 928	12 177	810	92	11 275
District 16	117 801	180.9	76 036	12 391	13 674	8 459	7 241	9 723	444	91	9 188
District 17	119 328	195.7	72 148	14 724	15 150	8 542	8 764	16 035	722	121	15 192
District 18	122 321	190.8	70 620	17 014	15 254	9 220	10 213	17 139	762	98	16 279
OKLAHOMA	647 067	180.8	394 760	97 042	66 227	34 560	54 478	82 523	7 722	777	74 024
District 1	119 617	166.0	75 707	16 478	11 712	6 195	9 525	13 064	1 113	122	11 829
District 2	156 761	220.0	89 721	27 427	16 430	8 454	14 729	24 572	2 564	232	21 776
District 3	131 484	187.9	80 992	17 700	14 306	7 854	10 632	13 370	1 241	119	12 010
District 4	122 141	169.9	74 785	17 702	12 725	6 786	10 143	13 910	1 283	142	12 485
District 5	117 064	160.9	73 555	17 735	11 054	5 271	9 449	17 607	1 521	162	15 924
OREGON	630 822	170.5	424 170	78 860	55 384	33 286	39 122	28 663	2 517	278	25 867
District 1	100 244	130.2	68 451	11 884	8 632	4 908	6 369	4 183	615	46	3 522
District 2	152 481	204.0	103 609	17 892	13 446	8 528	9 006	5 595	234	47	5 313
District 3	99 772	139.1	64 804	14 967	8 647	4 282	7 072	7 302	1 083	68	6 150
District 4	153 601	214.4	101 236	20 152	13 992	9 184	9 037	6 664	229	67	6 367
District 5	124 724	166.3	86 070	13 965	10 667	6 384	7 638	4 918	355	48	4 514
PENNSYLVANIA	2 438 397	196.0	1 571 817	309 778	250 688	127 231	178 883	326 156	28 822	2 145	295 189
District 1	96 164	150.6	51 249	19 452	9 816	3 369	12 278	50 345	3 952	288	46 105
District 2	101 339	181.5	61 617	16 577	9 984	2 841	10 320	36 744	3 363	262	33 119
District 3	135 677	209.7	83 016	18 938	14 731	8 474	10 518	19 553	1 064	134	18 355
District 4	138 147	213.4	88 633	14 114	17 331	9 996	8 073	11 178	875	68	10 235
District 5	138 188	217.2	87 462	18 815	13 677	8 329	9 905	16 698	1 086	76	15 536
District 6	115 019	164.7	80 045	11 918	10 205	5 137	7 714	7 913	947	55	6 911
District 7	116 833	174.4	80 690	10 844	11 690	5 653	7 956	7 337	1 058	76	6 203
District 8	114 259	170.6	77 976	12 914	10 333	5 155	7 881	6 607	985	67	5 555
District 9	138 038	208.9	86 587	17 958	14 803	9 263	9 427	17 540	1 378	110	16 052
District 10	144 817	223.0	93 966	19 350	13 335	6 998	11 168	14 547	1 296	97	13 154
District 11	150 333	221.6	94 828	22 713	14 070	6 075	12 647	17 005	1 446	112	15 447
District 12	152 735	242.2	87 781	20 723	21 698	11 927	10 606	23 649	1 487	139	22 023
District 13	120 849	179.4	81 946	12 782	12 295	5 511	8 315	15 055	2 898	93	12 064
District 14	125 030	214.0	74 653	18 350	15 980	6 213	9 834	26 140	1 973	164	24 003
District 15	133 900	190.6	90 880	16 024	11 773	5 725	9 498	13 132	1 349	72	11 711
District 16	117 639	172.0	80 314	13 865	9 519	5 703	8 238	12 925	1 166	93	11 666
District 17	132 722	200.5	89 649	16 587	12 065	5 490	8 931	11 978	987	101	10 890
District 18	139 282	214.4	91 972	13 380	16 688	9 676	7 566	8 608	735	61	7 812
District 19	127 426	182.1	88 553	14 474	10 695	5 696	8 008	9 202	777	77	8 348

[9]Includes special age-72 beneficiaries.
[10]Includes nondisabled widow(er)s, disabled widow(er)s, widowed mothers and fathers, and parents receiving payment on the record of a worker who is deceased.
[11]These beneficiaries receive payment on the record of a worker who is retired or disabled.
[12]These beneficiaries receive payment on the record of a worker who is retired, deceased, or disabled.

Table A. 110th Congressional Districts—Continued

(Number, percent.)

STATE Congressional district	Total farms	Farms by size (percent) 1 to 49 acres	50 to 999 acres	1,000 acres or more	Land in farms Total acreage	Average size of farms (acres)	Percent of farms where principal operator's primary occupation is farming	Value of all agricultural products sold Total ($1,000)	Percent of farms with value of: Less than $50,000	$50,000 to $249,999	$250,000 or more	Payments from federal farm programs Total ($1,000)	Number of farms that receive payments	Percent of farms that receive payments
	78	79	80	81	82	83	84	85	86	87	88	89	90	91
NORTH CAROLINA	53 930	45.6	51.1	3.3	9 079 001	168	58.7	6 961 686	79.6	9.0	11.4	97 696	12 312	22.8
District 1	4 356	29.3	58.0	12.7	1 843 684	423	69.0	1 083 751	57.9	18.9	23.2	34 323	1 992	45.7
District 2	4 961	43.9	52.4	3.7	901 841	182	63.4	892 784	73.4	10.3	16.4	8 571	1 328	26.8
District 3	3 206	39.2	50.1	10.7	1 131 915	353	67.9	981 552	58.0	14.2	27.8	17 564	1 131	35.3
District 4	1 447	50.6	48.5	0.9	154 398	107	56.9	62 326	88.1	7.5	4.4	864	255	17.6
District 5	10 156	48.9	50.2	0.8	1 038 572	102	56.0	613 366	84.5	8.6	6.8	5 100	1 493	14.7
District 6	5 227	46.9	52.5	0.6	553 268	106	56.8	339 241	85.1	6.6	8.4	2 923	857	16.4
District 7	4 701	42.1	52.6	5.4	1 100 034	234	64.4	1 641 469	65.8	11.4	22.8	11 603	1 339	28.5
District 8	3 320	41.2	55.4	3.3	583 995	176	56.3	551 749	77.3	5.9	16.8	6 466	921	27.7
District 9	1 246	55.2	42.9	1.9	155 208	125	53.0	196 494	81.4	4.7	14.0	1 283	236	18.9
District 10	5 126	49.4	50.1	0.5	475 329	93	53.0	252 553	91.2	4.9	3.9	2 843	1 051	20.5
District 11	6 305	58.0	41.6	0.4	504 064	80	53.6	184 021	93.4	5.0	1.6	3 740	849	13.5
District 12	1 261	50.4	48.5	1.1	126 959	101	53.9	46 637	92.6	4.5	2.9	807	233	18.5
District 13	2 618	34.3	62.1	3.6	509 734	195	58.6	115 744	83.9	12.0	4.1	1 608	627	23.9
NORTH DAKOTA	30 619	6.7	52.6	40.8	39 294 879	1 283	70.7	3 233 366	58.6	29.6	11.8	293 067	23 892	78.0
At Large	30 619	6.7	52.6	40.8	39 294 879	1 283	70.7	3 233 366	58.6	29.6	11.8	293 067	23 892	78.0
OHIO	77 797	39.5	57.0	3.5	14 583 435	187	55.9	4 263 549	81.8	13.7	4.5	197 425	28 851	37.1
District 1	654	61.9	36.9	1.2	58 769	90	49.2	22 965	88.5	6.9	4.6	563	99	15.1
District 2	5 048	43.2	54.9	1.9	714 003	141	53.2	103 156	91.3	7.4	1.3	5 301	1 416	28.1
District 3	3 518	46.5	49.3	4.2	689 433	196	53.0	144 037	83.1	13.2	3.7	11 635	1 585	45.1
District 4	9 610	35.9	59.0	5.0	2 197 740	229	58.0	598 361	77.0	17.7	5.3	36 471	5 010	52.1
District 5	12 354	33.7	60.0	6.3	3 234 851	262	59.4	859 731	73.5	20.3	6.2	50 501	7 340	59.4
District 6	8 234	30.9	68.3	0.8	1 170 630	142	51.5	174 070	91.7	6.7	1.6	6 333	1 621	19.7
District 7	4 909	45.7	47.8	6.5	1 187 634	242	56.2	304 200	79.1	14.3	6.6	17 338	1 997	40.7
District 8	5 434	44.7	52.1	3.2	968 735	178	58.6	652 468	74.6	16.3	9.1	18 392	2 291	42.2
District 9	1 877	46.0	48.8	5.2	393 275	210	55.9	153 463	76.9	17.2	5.9	5 069	754	40.2
District 10	89	87.6	12.4	0.0	2 128	24	53.9	. . .	76.4	12.4	11.2	. . .	2	2.2
District 11	16	81.3	18.8	0.0	553	35	25.0	. . .	93.8	0.0	6.3	. . .	. . .	. . .
District 12	1 832	54.0	42.8	3.2	325 618	178	54.0	142 861	85.4	10.5	4.1	4 685	519	28.3
District 13	761	68.9	30.7	0.4	59 820	79	49.7	46 111	84.2	12.1	3.7	. . .	103	13.5
District 14	3 267	49.7	49.6	0.7	334 704	102	55.6	160 057	87.6	9.8	2.6	3 234	566	17.3
District 15	2 078	45.0	47.7	7.2	552 482	266	59.8	167 896	75.4	17.4	7.2	9 516	960	46.2
District 16	4 893	47.1	51.3	1.6	621 510	127	57.9	296 288	80.2	14.8	5.0	10 265	1 272	26.0
District 17	1 486	49.3	49.8	0.9	155 079	104	50.4	38 159	88.8	9.1	2.1	1 439	283	19.0
District 18	11 737	30.8	67.4	1.8	1 916 471	163	54.6	386 443	86.5	10.9	2.5	16 270	3 033	25.8
OKLAHOMA	83 300	24.2	67.0	8.8	33 661 826	404	55.3	4 456 404	87.0	9.6	3.4	149 942	24 316	29.2
District 1	3 542	45.1	51.8	3.2	688 644	194	48.3	82 443	92.9	5.5	1.6	1 705	572	16.1
District 2	30 416	26.8	69.0	4.2	8 021 017	264	55.5	1 289 267	90.1	6.5	3.4	14 807	5 127	16.9
District 3	30 462	16.8	67.6	15.6	19 093 990	627	57.4	2 528 847	81.3	14.3	4.3	113 436	14 227	46.7
District 4	14 907	26.8	65.9	7.3	5 083 348	341	54.1	495 593	89.0	8.7	2.4	18 656	3 739	25.1
District 5	3 973	33.1	64.4	2.5	774 827	195	48.4	60 254	95.0	4.3	0.8	1 338	651	16.4
OREGON	40 033	62.5	31.2	6.4	17 080 422	427	53.9	3 195 497	84.9	9.5	5.6	52 085	4 430	11.1
District 1	5 357	72.9	26.1	1.0	411 634	77	48.1	476 529	88.1	7.1	4.8	. . .	453	8.5
District 2	14 768	49.3	36.3	14.4	14 461 305	979	57.7	1 302 248	80.2	13.3	6.5	43 311	2 970	20.1
District 3	2 648	83.8	15.9	0.3	108 249	41	46.8	226 687	88.7	7.1	4.3	. . .	33	1.2
District 4	9 086	62.6	34.5	2.8	1 356 038	149	54.8	393 747	90.2	6.3	3.5	2 710	448	4.9
District 5	8 174	72.3	26.4	1.3	743 196	91	52.2	796 286	83.9	8.6	7.5	3 680	526	6.4
PENNSYLVANIA	58 105	37.8	61.1	1.1	7 745 336	133	56.7	4 256 959	76.9	17.2	5.9	85 794	11 991	20.6
District 1	9	88.9	11.1	0.0	. . .	. . .	66.7	363	66.7	33.3	0.0	. . .	. . .	. . .
District 2	2	100.0	0.0	0.0	. . .	. . .	50.0	. . .	50.0	50.0	0.0	. . .	1	50.0
District 3	5 612	30.3	68.6	1.1	810 906	144	55.4	245 974	82.6	14.4	3.0	6 583	1 162	20.7
District 4	2 037	40.4	59.2	0.5	213 169	105	55.2	52 295	87.6	10.3	2.1	1 660	333	16.3
District 5	6 507	28.0	70.8	1.2	1 010 615	155	52.8	247 496	82.9	14.2	2.9	7 707	1 237	19.0
District 6	1 662	57.8	41.8	0.4	142 425	86	56.9	92 995	74.7	20.4	4.9	2 021	247	14.9
District 7	179	73.2	26.8	0.0	8 822	49	45.8	20 185	85.5	10.6	3.9	. . .	12	6.7
District 8	919	70.2	28.7	1.1	76 851	84	54.8	61 640	82.8	11.1	6.1	773	114	12.4
District 9	8 719	28.0	70.9	1.2	1 435 257	165	61.1	718 203	72.2	19.5	8.3	22 122	2 427	27.8
District 10	7 354	28.5	70.2	1.2	1 191 928	162	56.9	495 114	75.5	19.4	5.2	12 031	1 837	25.0
District 11	1 858	39.8	59.0	1.2	236 805	127	48.7	68 839	86.4	10.7	2.9	2 248	584	31.4
District 12	4 456	31.1	67.8	1.1	612 558	137	48.0	101 852	91.8	6.2	2.0	3 557	720	16.2
District 13	291	71.8	28.2	0.0	16 482	57	51.2	18 588	84.5	9.6	5.8	152	36	12.4
District 14	34	97.1	2.9	0.0	414	12	20.6	. . .	91.2	8.8	0.0	. . .	1	2.9
District 15	1 353	60.8	36.5	2.7	185 234	137	56.8	80 875	82.1	13.2	4.7	2 618	282	20.8
District 16	6 315	46.9	52.7	0.4	512 384	81	72.0	1 121 589	50.6	37.9	11.5	8 168	737	11.7
District 17	4 150	44.2	54.9	0.9	518 343	125	58.9	564 994	69.9	18.5	11.6	8 347	1 065	25.7
District 18	2 309	41.6	58.3	0.2	242 174	105	43.9	32 312	95.2	3.8	1.0	942	335	14.5
District 19	4 339	55.3	43.0	1.7	530 682	122	51.9	332 956	80.4	12.8	6.8	6 830	861	19.8

. . . = Not available.

Table A. 110th Congressional Districts—*Continued*

(Number, percent.)

STATE Congressional district	Representative	Land area,[1] (sq km)	Total population	Persons per square kilometer	Race alone (percent) White	Black	American Indian/ Alaska Native	Asian and Pacific Islander	Some other race (percent)	Two or more races (percent)	Hispanic or Latino[2] (percent)	Non-Hispanic White (percent)
	1	2	3	4	5	6	7	8	9	10	11	12
RHODE ISLAND		2 706	1 067 610	394.5	82.6	5.1	0.4	2.8	6.9	2.2	11.0	78.9
District 1	Rep. Patrick J. Kennedy (D)	841	534 128	635.1	83.8	6.0	0.2	2.5	5.1	2.3	10.1	78.9
District 2	Rep. James R. Langevin (D)	1 865	533 482	286.0	81.5	4.2	0.6	3.0	8.7	2.0	11.9	79.0
SOUTH CAROLINA		77 983	4 321 249	55.4	67.3	28.6	0.3	1.2	1.3	1.3	3.4	65.3
District 1	Rep. Henry E. Brown Jr. (R)	6 849	763 712	111.5	74.8	20.2	0.2	1.6	1.8	1.4	3.5	73.1
District 2	Rep. Joe Wilson (R)	12 347	752 019	60.9	68.1	27.6	0.2	1.1	1.3	1.7	4.7	64.9
District 3	Rep. J. Gresham Barrett (R)	13 966	694 968	49.8	76.5	19.6	0.3	0.9	1.5	1.3	3.0	75.3
District 4	Rep. Bob Inglis (R)	5 570	721 877	129.6	75.5	19.6	0.2	1.9	1.8	1.0	5.3	72.0
District 5	Rep. John M. Spratt Jr. (D)	18 221	711 714	39.1	65.5	31.2	0.5	0.6	1.0	1.3	2.5	64.1
District 6	Rep. James E. Clyburn (D)	21 030	676 959	32.2	41.7	55.6	0.2	0.8	0.6	1.0	1.4	41.1
SOUTH DAKOTA		196 540	781 919	4.0	87.2	0.7	8.6	0.9	1.0	1.6	2.0	86.5
At Large	Rep. Stephanie Herseth Sandlin (D)	196 540	781 919	4.0	87.2	0.7	8.6	0.9	1.0	1.6	2.0	86.5
TENNESSEE		106 752	6 038 803	56.6	79.2	16.8	0.3	1.3	1.3	1.2	3.1	77.5
District 1	Rep. David Davis (R)	10 601	663 745	62.6	95.5	2.2	0.2	0.3	0.5	1.2	2.1	93.8
District 2	Rep. John J. Duncan Jr. (R)	6 285	691 763	110.1	90.1	6.4	0.2	1.2	0.6	1.6	1.8	88.9
District 3	Rep. Zach Wamp (R)	8 834	655 477	74.2	85.3	11.3	0.4	1.1	0.7	1.3	2.2	84.1
District 4	Rep. Lincoln Davis (D)	25 999	666 443	25.6	93.0	4.0	0.2	0.5	0.9	1.4	1.8	92.2
District 5	Rep. Jim Cooper (D)	2 315	653 585	282.3	68.4	25.2	0.4	2.7	2.3	1.0	6.7	64.2
District 6	Rep. Bart Gordon (D)	14 194	728 517	51.3	88.0	7.5	0.2	1.3	2.0	1.0	4.4	85.8
District 7	Rep. Marsha Blackburn (R)	16 296	730 252	44.8	81.9	13.3	0.2	2.2	0.9	1.5	2.5	80.6
District 8	Rep. John S. Tanner (D)	21 398	641 358	30.0	74.2	23.4	0.3	0.5	0.4	1.2	. . .	. . .
District 9	Rep. Steve Cohen (D)	830	607 663	732.1	30.2	63.4	0.2	1.8	3.4	0.9	4.7	28.7
TEXAS[13]		678 051	23 507 783	34.7	69.8	11.6	0.5	3.4	13.0	1.8	35.7	48.1
District 1	Rep. Louie Gohmert (R)	22 036	692 352	31.4	74.5	18.0	0.2	0.8	5.1	1.3	12.1	67.9
District 2	Rep. Ted Poe (R)	5 016	747 541	149.0	65.4	21.6	0.4	3.6	7.7	1.3	17.0	56.7
District 3	Rep. Sam Johnson (R)	686	813 428	1 185.8	67.2	11.4	0.3	11.0	8.6	1.5	20.8	55.5
District 4	Rep. Ralph M. Hall (R)	24 694	780 736	31.6	81.3	10.5	0.8	1.7	4.1	1.7	11.3	74.5
District 5	Rep. Jeb Hensarling (R)	14 061	714 216	50.8	76.3	13.0	0.4	1.9	7.0	1.5	17.9	65.9
District 6	Rep. Joe Barton (R)	16 054	752 355	46.9	68.8	15.6	0.5	3.8	9.5	1.8	21.3	57.7
District 7	Rep. John Abney Culberson (R)	512	763 161	1 490.5	73.3	9.4	0.2	8.1	7.7	1.3	22.5	58.9
District 8	Rep. Kevin Brady (R)	21 108	764 463	36.2	83.8	7.9	0.5	1.3	5.3	1.2	12.0	77.5
District 9	Rep. Al Green (D)	399	697 784	1 748.8	38.8	35.9	0.3	9.7	14.0	1.4	40.9	13.2
District 10	Rep. Michael T. McCaul (R)	9 851	849 012	86.2	72.3	9.6	0.4	5.7	9.9	2.1	25.3	57.8
District 11	Rep. K. Michael Conaway (R)	90 636	677 683	7.5	83.0	4.1	0.5	0.8	9.4	2.2	33.4	60.6
District 12	Rep. Kay Granger (R)	5 616	750 559	133.6	74.5	5.6	0.5	2.7	14.6	2.1	26.3	63.7
District 13	Rep. Mac Thornberry (R)	104 111	654 212	6.3	79.7	6.0	0.7	1.3	10.3	2.0	20.3	70.5
District 14	Rep. Ron Paul (R)	18 376	732 497	39.9	76.6	9.5	0.3	2.6	8.6	2.4	26.8	59.4
District 15	Rep. Rubén Hinojosa (D)	27 758	722 479	26.0	67.3	3.1	0.3	0.6	27.3	1.5	71.8	24.1
District 16	Rep. Silvestre Reyes (D)	1 504	698 733	464.6	75.3	2.9	0.6	1.2	17.9	2.0	81.1	14.2
District 17	Rep. Chet Edwards (D)	19 861	708 405	35.6	80.0	10.1	0.5	1.9	5.5	2.0	18.1	68.4
District 18	Rep. Sheila Jackson-Lee (D)	589	686 965	1 166.3	41.0	38.2	0.4	3.2	15.8	1.4	42.7	15.4
District 19	Rep. Randy Neugebauer (R)	65 445	657 319	10.0	78.7	5.5	0.7	1.0	12.2	2.0	31.7	60.5
District 20	Rep. Charles A. Gonzalez (D)	476	684 044	1 437.1	60.2	6.5	0.6	1.9	28.6	2.3	69.9	20.8
District 21	Rep. Lamar Smith (R)	13 288	785 645	59.1	81.5	3.7	0.3	3.7	8.6	2.2	22.6	68.7
District 22	Rep. Nick Lampson (D)	2 516	808 096	321.2	65.6	13.1	0.6	10.8	8.1	1.9	24.1	50.4
District 23	Rep. Ciro D. Rodriguez (D)	125 501	777 034	6.2	77.8	2.4	0.6	2.0	15.4	1.9	56.6	38.2
District 24	Rep. Kenny Marchant (R)	866	766 447	885.0	69.4	12.1	0.7	8.6	7.4	1.8	25.6	52.2
District 25	Rep. Lloyd Doggett (D)	15 919	746 233	46.9	56.0	6.3	0.6	1.0	34.5	1.6	73.1	18.7
District 26	Rep. Michael C. Burgess (R)	3 346	814 119	243.3	73.9	13.4	0.5	3.2	6.6	2.5	19.3	62.0
District 27	Rep. Solomon P. Ortiz (D)	12 225	708 251	57.9	81.2	2.2	0.5	1.3	13.2	1.7	71.2	24.4
District 28	Rep. Henry Cuellar (D)	35 223	753 251	21.4	68.9	6.3	0.5	0.8	21.9	1.6	64.8	27.5
District 29	Rep. Gene Green (D)	611	689 768	1 128.9	50.5	9.3	0.3	1.7	37.1	1.0	72.9	15.7
District 30	Rep. Eddie Bernice Johnson (D)	822	683 482	831.5	39.9	38.7	0.4	1.3	18.2	1.5	41.5	17.4
District 31	Rep. John R. Carter (R)	18 476	774 224	41.9	74.1	12.5	0.6	3.0	6.9	3.0	19.2	62.9
District 32	Rep. Pete Sessions (R)	413	653 289	1 581.8	70.9	8.8	0.7	3.9	14.4	1.3	42.9	43.1
UTAH		212 751	2 550 063	12.0	89.1	0.9	1.1	2.7	4.5	1.8	11.2	82.8
District 1	Rep. Rob Bishop (R)	53 790	827 128	15.4	89.0	1.4	0.7	2.2	4.7	2.0	13.0	81.4
District 2	Rep. Jim Matheson (D)	118 166	848 581	7.2	89.5	0.7	1.9	2.5	3.7	1.6	7.8	85.8
District 3	Rep. Chris Cannon (R)	40 795	874 354	21.4	88.7	0.6	0.8	3.3	5.0	1.6	12.9	81.3
VERMONT		23 956	623 908	26.0	96.3	0.8	0.4	0.9	0.3	1.3	1.1	95.6
At Large	Rep. Peter Welch (D)	23 956	623 908	26.0	96.3	0.8	0.4	0.9	0.3	1.3	1.1	95.6
VIRGINIA		102 548	7 642 884	74.5	70.8	19.6	0.2	4.9	2.6	1.9	6.2	67.6
District 1	Rep. Robert J. Wittman (R)	9 771	740 228	75.8	73.5	19.3	0.2	2.3	2.2	2.5	5.3	70.9
District 2	Rep. Thelma D. Drake (R)	2 489	648 805	260.7	68.1	22.5	0.3	4.6	1.5	2.9	5.4	64.9
District 3	Rep. Robert C. "Bobby" Scott (D)	2 895	638 296	220.5	38.2	56.1	0.6	1.8	1.6	1.8	3.0	37.2
District 4	Rep. J. Randy Forbes (R)	11 626	724 417	62.3	61.7	33.6	0.4	1.5	1.2	1.6	3.0	60.0
District 5	Rep. Virgil H. Goode Jr. (R)	23 108	664 243	28.7	73.2	23.1	0.1	1.3	1.1	1.3	2.0	72.3

[1]Dry land or land partially or temporarily covered by water.
[2]May be of any race.
[13]Data are for 109th congressional districts. The boundaries for districts for the 110th Congress have changed.

Table A. 110th Congressional Districts—Continued

(Number, percent.)

STATE Congressional district	Percent female	Percent foreign born	Percent born in state of residence	Under 5 years	5 to 18 years	18 to 24 years	25 to 34 years	35 to 44 years	45 to 54 years	55 to 64 years	65 to 74 years	75 years and over
	13	14	15	16	17	18	19	20	21	22	23	24
RHODE ISLAND	51.8	12.6	59.2	5.8	16.5	11.0	12.2	15.0	15.0	10.9	6.3	7.5
District 1	52.8	13.5	54.9	5.9	15.7	10.9	13.0	15.0	14.6	10.4	6.7	7.9
District 2	50.8	11.7	63.5	5.6	17.2	11.0	11.4	14.9	15.4	11.4	5.9	7.1
SOUTH CAROLINA	51.3	4.1	60.8	6.6	17.5	10.1	12.8	14.3	14.3	11.6	7.0	5.8
District 1	51.6	5.1	45.9	6.5	16.6	9.7	13.4	14.5	14.2	12.2	7.3	5.7
District 2	50.9	4.7	54.6	6.6	18.1	10.2	12.5	15.1	14.5	11.2	6.6	5.3
District 3	51.0	3.4	63.1	6.2	16.5	10.1	13.0	13.2	14.4	11.9	7.7	6.9
District 4	51.3	6.2	61.3	6.6	17.5	8.8	13.3	15.2	14.5	11.6	6.7	5.8
District 5	51.3	2.6	65.8	6.6	18.6	9.1	12.9	14.8	14.2	11.6	6.7	5.6
District 6	52.0	2.2	76.3	7.1	17.5	12.8	11.7	13.1	14.0	11.0	6.8	5.9
SOUTH DAKOTA	49.8	2.2	65.2	6.9	17.9	10.6	11.9	13.1	14.7	10.6	6.8	7.5
At Large	49.8	2.2	65.2	6.9	17.9	10.6	11.9	13.1	14.7	10.6	6.8	7.5
TENNESSEE	51.1	3.9	62.6	6.6	17.4	9.2	13.7	14.5	14.5	11.4	6.9	5.8
District 1	51.0	2.4	64.4	5.7	15.7	8.2	13.8	14.1	14.6	12.5	8.4	6.9
District 2	51.4	3.4	63.0	5.9	16.2	9.7	13.3	14.7	14.7	11.9	7.4	6.3
District 3	51.6	2.5	62.6	6.1	16.6	9.1	12.9	13.9	14.5	12.5	7.6	6.8
District 4	50.5	1.9	67.3	6.3	16.6	8.1	13.9	13.7	14.4	12.0	8.3	6.8
District 5	51.5	9.2	55.9	7.5	16.7	9.7	14.8	15.6	14.7	10.1	5.7	5.3
District 6	50.5	4.5	63.2	6.9	17.6	10.0	15.3	15.1	13.9	10.4	6.1	4.9
District 7	50.3	4.1	53.3	6.7	19.5	8.1	12.6	15.8	14.9	11.8	6.1	4.6
District 8	51.7	1.9	71.3	7.0	18.1	9.5	12.8	13.8	14.4	11.1	7.1	6.1
District 9	52.0	5.5	63.7	7.5	19.2	10.4	14.2	13.9	14.7	9.9	5.1	5.1
TEXAS[13]	50.2	15.9	60.9	8.2	19.5	10.4	14.6	14.7	13.5	9.2	5.3	4.6
District 1	51.4	7.0	70.9	7.2	18.2	10.6	12.8	13.0	13.5	10.4	7.2	7.1
District 2	50.5	11.2	61.2	7.2	20.2	8.7	12.6	15.2	15.1	10.8	5.3	5.0
District 3	50.1	22.9	44.5	8.4	19.5	8.7	16.5	17.1	14.4	9.0	3.9	2.5
District 4	50.6	7.0	65.4	7.0	18.8	9.0	14.7	14.7	13.4	10.2	6.5	5.8
District 5	50.2	10.4	68.7	7.0	18.1	9.2	14.0	15.3	14.4	9.8	6.5	5.5
District 6	50.1	13.7	60.6	7.8	19.6	10.0	14.9	15.6	13.4	9.7	5.1	3.9
District 7	50.4	21.9	48.0	7.4	16.6	8.5	15.3	15.9	16.0	10.6	5.1	4.6
District 8	49.7	7.3	65.3	6.5	18.0	10.2	15.0	14.0	14.2	10.4	6.6	5.2
District 9	49.6	35.7	47.3	9.7	18.5	11.4	18.2	14.4	13.4	8.1	3.8	2.5
District 10	49.0	17.5	55.6	8.7	19.6	9.6	16.1	16.1	13.9	8.6	3.9	3.5
District 11	50.9	7.5	73.6	7.0	18.6	10.1	12.2	13.2	13.9	10.6	7.1	7.5
District 12	49.5	13.6	60.0	8.1	18.0	10.2	15.4	15.2	13.8	9.5	5.5	4.2
District 13	49.8	6.7	68.2	7.3	18.0	10.6	13.0	13.0	14.1	10.1	7.1	6.7
District 14	49.9	9.9	67.3	7.5	19.6	9.3	12.9	14.3	15.0	10.2	6.1	5.1
District 15	49.9	15.8	70.1	9.4	21.6	10.7	13.0	13.1	11.8	8.4	5.7	6.2
District 16	52.2	27.1	55.6	9.7	21.6	11.4	12.4	13.4	12.4	8.5	5.6	5.0
District 17	50.0	7.6	72.2	6.6	17.7	16.4	13.2	12.6	12.7	9.2	6.1	5.5
District 18	49.3	22.6	60.1	8.7	20.3	10.6	15.8	15.2	13.3	8.2	4.4	3.4
District 19	50.4	6.5	75.2	7.7	18.7	12.9	12.6	12.6	12.9	9.4	6.8	6.4
District 20	50.7	14.0	66.4	8.6	18.9	12.6	15.8	13.4	12.3	8.7	5.1	4.7
District 21	50.6	8.5	56.9	7.0	17.7	9.7	13.4	16.1	15.3	10.8	5.5	4.6
District 22	51.1	18.5	56.9	7.1	20.0	9.7	14.6	16.1	15.4	9.7	4.5	3.0
District 23	50.6	15.9	61.7	8.6	20.6	10.6	12.1	14.1	13.1	9.6	5.8	5.6
District 24	50.5	19.3	48.0	8.4	21.1	8.4	16.1	16.6	14.8	8.1	3.8	2.8
District 25	50.3	26.6	60.3	10.3	20.6	12.6	16.2	13.9	10.6	7.0	4.4	4.3
District 26	50.6	12.5	55.8	8.3	19.9	10.3	15.3	16.1	13.6	9.2	3.9	3.4
District 27	51.4	16.2	69.4	9.6	21.4	11.1	12.8	12.9	12.7	8.7	5.7	5.1
District 28	50.6	12.7	72.6	8.6	21.3	12.3	13.9	13.6	11.9	8.5	5.1	4.8
District 29	49.0	34.3	56.7	10.4	22.7	10.8	16.1	14.2	11.7	7.6	3.8	2.7
District 30	48.3	22.3	60.7	9.2	19.9	9.9	16.5	16.9	12.0	8.0	4.2	3.4
District 31	50.8	8.5	54.9	8.4	20.6	10.0	15.8	15.3	12.6	8.1	4.8	4.4
District 32	48.1	30.1	46.4	8.6	17.3	9.0	17.9	14.6	13.1	9.5	5.1	4.9
UTAH	49.7	8.3	63.0	9.7	21.4	12.6	15.9	12.2	11.5	7.9	4.6	4.2
District 1	49.7	8.1	62.9	9.7	21.4	12.4	15.8	12.4	11.9	7.9	4.5	4.0
District 2	49.8	7.3	62.0	8.6	20.3	10.6	15.5	12.4	12.7	8.7	5.5	5.7
District 3	49.6	9.3	64.2	10.8	22.4	14.7	16.5	11.9	10.1	7.0	3.9	2.8
VERMONT	50.9	3.9	52.7	5.3	16.2	10.1	11.2	14.5	16.7	12.7	6.9	6.4
At Large	50.9	3.9	52.7	5.3	16.2	10.1	11.2	14.5	16.7	12.7	6.9	6.4
VIRGINIA	50.8	10.1	50.8	6.6	17.0	10.1	13.3	15.6	14.9	10.9	6.2	5.4
District 1	50.9	6.5	48.6	6.5	17.8	10.7	13.8	14.9	14.6	10.2	6.3	5.2
District 2	49.4	7.8	40.8	7.4	18.1	10.8	14.3	15.5	14.5	9.2	5.5	4.7
District 3	52.5	4.6	62.7	7.2	18.2	11.7	12.8	14.8	13.9	9.3	6.0	6.0
District 4	50.7	3.8	64.0	6.4	18.6	10.2	12.6	15.8	15.4	10.6	5.9	4.5
District 5	51.4	3.2	68.8	5.2	16.0	10.5	12.1	14.8	14.3	11.8	8.1	7.1

[13]Data are for 109th congressional districts. The boundaries for districts for the 110th Congress have changed.

Table A. 110th Congressional Districts—*Continued*

(Number, percent.)

STATE Congressional district	Households, 2006						Group quarters, 2006		Group quarters, 2000			
	Number	Average household size	Family households (percent)	Married-couple family (percent)	Female family householder[4] (percent)	One-person households (percent)	Total in group quarters	Percent 65 years and over	Persons in correctional institutions	Persons in nursing homes	Persons in college dormitories	Persons in military quarters
	25	26	27	28	29	30	31	32	33	34	35	36
RHODE ISLAND	405 627	2.53	64.7	47.0	13.4	28.7	43 088	25.7	3 576	9 222	20 551	870
District 1	205 386	2.49	63.6	45.6	14.3	29.4	22 474	28.5	324	5 800	13 308	867
District 2	200 241	2.56	65.8	48.4	12.5	27.8	20 614	22.6	3 252	3 422	7 243	3
SOUTH CAROLINA	1 656 978	2.52	67.8	48.2	15.3	27.3	142 974	18.0	34 909	20 867	39 360	17 102
District 1	312 873	2.40	65.8	48.0	13.7	26.8	11 349	34.9	1 488	2 952	3 678	3 350
District 2	290 780	2.49	68.2	51.3	13.1	26.8	28 827	7.1	8 651	2 923	0	12 829
District 3	263 213	2.54	69.9	52.3	13.1	25.6	25 841	23.1	5 285	4 060	9 450	0
District 4	282 951	2.47	67.7	48.7	14.3	28.1	21 830	19.0	4 309	2 994	7 700	0
District 5	261 775	2.66	68.8	48.1	16.4	27.0	14 180	26.2	5 802	4 501	2 978	830
District 6	245 386	2.59	66.3	39.7	22.1	29.3	40 947	14.4	9 374	3 437	15 554	93
SOUTH DAKOTA	312 477	2.41	65.9	53.2	8.9	28.3	29 816	31.1	4 479	7 791	8 998	566
At Large	312 477	2.41	65.9	53.2	8.9	28.3	29 816	31.1	4 479	7 791	8 998	566
TENNESSEE	2 375 123	2.48	67.2	49.6	13.1	27.8	152 407	25.4	38 481	36 994	45 030	2 593
District 1	267 450	2.43	67.9	52.4	11.0	27.4	15 172	29.6	3 381	4 982	3 142	0
District 2	282 934	2.38	66.2	52.7	9.8	28.3	19 735	21.1	1 241	3 855	8 716	1
District 3	266 645	2.40	67.5	52.2	11.3	27.7	16 804	31.0	1 599	4 293	5 799	10
District 4	258 429	2.53	71.4	55.0	11.5	25.2	13 168	41.8	4 242	5 132	1 494	45
District 5	273 292	2.31	58.3	41.1	14.0	35.1	21 228	8.5	5 947	2 507	11 691	0
District 6	278 024	2.57	69.6	53.1	11.7	24.1	14 907	28.7	1 695	3 978	5 035	0
District 7	265 803	2.70	75.6	60.7	11.2	20.5	13 363	28.6	6 801	3 398	935	2 287
District 8	246 303	2.53	68.6	47.5	16.3	27.0	17 640	33.0	7 198	5 826	4 623	250
District 9	236 243	2.49	59.6	29.5	23.1	35.2	20 390	18.0	6 377	3 023	3 595	0
TEXAS[13]	8 109 388	2.83	70.1	51.5	13.7	24.9	594 214	20.3	244 363	105 052	92 246	34 056
District 1	254 153	2.67	69.9	53.2	13.1	26.4	14 292	25.6	5 488	5 548	6 945	0
District 2	257 910	2.80	71.6	53.5	13.5	23.9	26 101	24.5	19 334	2 498	596	0
District 3	282 836	2.86	70.9	55.4	10.6	23.6	4 636	41.5	162	1 713	245	0
District 4	277 140	2.74	73.0	56.4	12.8	23.9	20 928	29.3	9 930	6 287	2 268	0
District 5	242 392	2.82	73.1	53.8	14.1	23.4	30 718	22.9	17 903	4 522	1 039	0
District 6	263 066	2.83	70.1	54.2	11.4	24.7	8 429	36.2	4 814	3 255	2 283	0
District 7	313 038	2.40	58.3	46.0	9.0	35.6	10 397	47.5	16	2 689	1 310	0
District 8	268 589	2.73	72.9	57.0	11.6	21.6	30 747	10.0	20 710	2 829	2 303	0
District 9	229 829	3.02	66.7	39.0	20.1	27.1	3 969	52.7	0	1 433	220	0
District 10	299 698	2.80	69.1	53.7	10.4	24.7	10 909	33.3	2 017	2 473	3 450	0
District 11	252 619	2.56	70.1	53.6	12.1	26.2	31 070	30.0	10 589	5 952	2 272	1 416
District 12	259 597	2.82	70.0	53.9	11.3	25.5	18 712	17.9	8 635	4 006	3 010	271
District 13	242 015	2.58	68.8	53.0	12.0	27.2	29 164	11.0	20 933	5 237	2 237	4 696
District 14	257 556	2.76	72.8	55.2	12.7	23.0	21 767	25.8	11 781	3 464	903	36
District 15	230 077	3.05	77.5	54.6	18.3	18.8	19 996	17.2	12 575	3 953	902	0
District 16	220 378	3.10	75.8	50.1	19.8	20.5	16 443	11.3	6 220	1 329	179	2 833
District 17	248 041	2.71	67.6	51.0	12.6	25.1	36 048	19.3	10 323	5 249	15 407	0
District 18	227 503	2.94	65.0	36.5	20.8	29.2	19 103	13.9	10 085	1 788	2 599	0
District 19	249 836	2.48	67.1	50.5	12.5	26.2	37 343	16.6	10 077	4 591	9 093	897
District 20	231 718	2.81	66.7	41.6	18.9	27.7	31 798	12.7	4 208	3 176	2 109	7 449
District 21	301 696	2.54	65.7	53.1	9.2	27.4	19 932	16.3	467	3 009	10 030	2 532
District 22	260 598	3.07	76.2	59.8	12.1	20.1	7 867	21.1	4 083	2 161	17	0
District 23	256 064	2.97	74.3	58.9	11.8	21.5	15 286	19.2	6 381	2 425	1 734	271
District 24	280 017	2.72	66.6	50.1	11.6	28.8	3 858	30.7	50	1 817	897	0
District 25	236 504	3.06	72.0	47.7	18.6	21.4	21 810	16.0	9 895	2 891	1 067	0
District 26	270 250	2.94	72.6	55.7	12.7	22.0	20 185	25.8	2 612	2 800	5 435	0
District 27	229 882	3.03	75.4	51.2	18.1	20.3	11 476	7.4	3 472	2 451	1 593	1 307
District 28	227 499	3.22	75.2	51.8	17.7	20.3	21 170	17.9	6 614	3 164	5 238	86
District 29	200 789	3.42	76.3	51.3	17.6	19.8	2 425	12.7	969	1 278	176	0
District 30	230 075	2.88	64.3	38.1	19.3	29.7	20 889	15.8	10 955	2 711	558	0
District 31	264 354	2.85	71.8	56.7	11.0	23.4	20 251	16.8	13 001	4 716	3 105	12 262
District 32	243 669	2.65	61.4	43.7	11.5	32.5	6 495	44.2	64	3 637	3 026	0
UTAH	814 028	3.08	75.5	61.9	9.5	19.1	42 646	14.4	9 921	6 853	9 837	1 760
District 1	270 003	3.02	75.1	61.2	9.6	20.1	12 022	18.6	1 483	2 417	2 157	1 760
District 2	290 613	2.86	72.5	59.1	9.1	21.7	17 323	21.8	6 732	3 113	2 466	0
District 3	253 412	3.40	79.4	65.7	9.8	15.2	13 301	1.1	1 706	1 323	5 214	0
VERMONT	253 808	2.38	64.1	50.1	10.1	27.5	20 760	22.0	1 219	4 037	12 863	22
At Large	253 808	2.38	64.1	50.1	10.1	27.5	20 760	22.0	1 219	4 037	12 863	22
VIRGINIA	2 905 071	2.55	66.8	50.5	12.2	27.8	235 342	18.2	64 036	38 865	65 557	33 752
District 1	274 729	2.62	72.0	55.9	11.6	22.6	21 671	16.7	2 627	3 397	7 075	2 927
District 2	239 181	2.58	68.6	50.9	13.8	25.2	30 786	7.5	9 271	2 664	1 924	20 694
District 3	254 296	2.40	59.7	34.9	20.6	33.8	28 611	17.3	7 809	3 562	6 926	5 185
District 4	257 872	2.70	74.6	56.2	14.0	22.0	27 220	9.7	14 067	3 133	1 846	3 008
District 5	268 221	2.38	65.5	48.1	14.1	29.6	26 401	13.4	10 311	4 415	10 633	0

[4]No spouse present.
[13]Data are for 109th congressional districts. The boundaries for districts for the 110th Congress have changed.

Table A. 110th Congressional Districts—*Continued*

(Number, percent.)

STATE Congressional district	Education, 2006				Income, 2006			Poverty, 2006		
	School enrollment[5]		Attainment level[6] (percent)		Per capita income (dollars)	Median household income (dollars)	Percent of households with income over $100,000	Persons below poverty level (percent)	Families below poverty level (percent)	Percent of households receiving food stamps in past 12 months
	Total	Private (percent)	High school graduate or more	Bachelor's degree or more						
	37	38	39	40	41	42	43	44	45	46
RHODE ISLAND	285 554	26.3	82.4	29.6	25 937	51 814	19.1	11.1	7.8	6.0
District 1	142 123	32.7	80.4	29.2	25 978	50 508	18.1	11.3	8.4	5.9
District 2	143 431	19.9	84.4	30.0	25 896	54 017	20.1	11.0	7.1	6.1
SOUTH CAROLINA	1 095 350	15.2	81.3	22.7	21 875	41 100	11.9	15.7	11.9	10.0
District 1	183 362	16.6	87.5	28.7	26 328	46 466	14.3	13.1	9.4	6.8
District 2	197 262	13.7	87.3	30.8	25 688	48 103	15.7	11.8	9.0	6.4
District 3	174 526	11.9	77.8	19.3	20 118	39 754	10.5	15.0	10.9	9.9
District 4	177 290	19.3	80.3	23.3	22 665	40 824	12.8	13.5	10.9	8.4
District 5	178 905	13.9	77.3	17.4	19 430	37 456	10.3	17.2	13.0	12.5
District 6	184 005	15.8	76.1	15.4	16 149	31 833	6.5	24.6	19.7	17.6
SOUTH DAKOTA	203 460	13.0	88.3	24.8	22 066	42 791	10.5	13.6	8.4	7.2
At Large	203 460	13.0	88.3	24.8	22 066	42 791	10.5	13.6	8.4	7.2
TENNESSEE	1 467 147	16.0	80.9	21.7	22 074	40 315	12.2	16.2	12.4	12.3
District 1	139 958	9.8	77.0	16.9	19 203	34 842	8.2	18.1	14.4	13.4
District 2	164 582	14.5	84.0	26.4	23 781	42 890	13.6	13.9	10.0	10.2
District 3	153 803	21.3	78.9	20.2	21 914	39 112	11.7	14.8	11.4	12.8
District 4	144 893	10.8	76.1	13.3	18 681	35 036	8.0	18.1	14.4	14.2
District 5	166 155	26.4	84.8	30.0	25 440	42 807	14.9	15.2	11.8	10.5
District 6	183 170	10.9	80.9	18.9	21 233	43 755	10.8	14.3	9.9	9.8
District 7	196 074	21.3	87.8	32.1	28 977	58 263	23.7	10.0	7.5	8.0
District 8	155 120	11.5	77.5	14.3	18 255	34 873	8.1	21.0	17.0	16.6
District 9	163 392	15.3	80.4	22.2	20 286	34 357	10.1	22.1	17.6	16.6
TEXAS[13]	6 566 761	11.3	78.6	24.7	22 501	44 922	16.5	16.9	13.3	9.8
District 1	179 847	10.6	81.4	20.0	20 134	38 252	11.3	17.0	13.0	10.6
District 2	200 679	11.8	83.8	24.3	24 908	52 289	21.3	12.6	9.7	9.7
District 3	226 685	15.1	85.8	41.0	31 716	64 954	30.2	9.4	6.8	3.5
District 4	206 721	9.1	82.8	21.4	22 517	46 548	15.6	13.4	9.8	8.6
District 5	172 937	10.2	79.2	19.0	21 577	44 970	15.1	13.1	10.6	9.3
District 6	208 118	11.3	83.1	24.3	23 216	50 909	18.1	12.8	9.9	7.5
District 7	198 470	24.6	90.2	47.3	41 336	61 671	30.3	10.0	7.4	3.1
District 8	189 757	8.7	81.8	20.1	23 381	46 776	17.9	14.9	11.2	10.0
District 9	194 666	10.7	73.0	22.0	17 156	35 467	8.9	23.0	19.1	11.6
District 10	242 337	14.2	86.2	34.3	27 620	58 381	24.1	10.5	7.4	5.3
District 11	170 499	7.6	75.6	18.1	20 882	39 254	11.5	16.9	13.1	10.2
District 12	194 072	18.5	80.1	23.3	24 027	50 084	17.6	12.3	8.8	6.7
District 13	160 668	6.0	79.4	17.7	20 194	38 683	10.3	16.9	12.9	9.6
District 14	202 440	10.2	81.4	22.0	23 613	50 841	19.4	15.2	11.5	7.7
District 15	213 578	5.3	67.2	14.9	14 589	31 502	9.2	30.3	26.2	21.5
District 16	232 338	7.1	69.0	18.3	15 026	32 290	9.0	27.1	24.2	20.9
District 17	228 289	13.4	80.7	21.2	19 392	40 712	11.3	17.5	11.3	9.1
District 18	189 077	7.9	66.6	16.2	16 567	35 414	8.5	24.9	20.8	14.0
District 19	188 417	11.2	76.7	21.0	19 276	37 061	9.9	18.2	13.5	11.5
District 20	193 173	11.7	74.3	15.8	16 109	35 174	7.2	22.2	19.2	14.1
District 21	219 112	17.9	93.3	47.2	34 153	65 036	29.1	8.3	5.2	3.9
District 22	239 256	12.8	86.5	33.2	28 671	64 208	28.7	8.4	6.4	4.8
District 23	234 794	11.9	78.2	28.5	21 979	46 245	17.8	17.7	14.1	11.4
District 24	222 186	14.6	87.0	37.5	29 233	55 687	24.4	9.2	7.8	3.4
District 25	221 844	6.4	63.9	16.2	13 894	32 113	6.8	30.6	25.8	21.0
District 26	240 220	12.1	85.1	29.4	25 703	57 474	23.0	13.2	9.9	6.4
District 27	219 722	6.0	69.9	16.8	15 498	31 990	9.5	28.4	24.2	20.2
District 28	230 622	6.5	69.8	12.1	15 103	36 315	8.5	22.3	17.9	15.9
District 29	198 189	5.1	52.9	7.1	13 309	33 725	6.3	22.0	19.5	12.7
District 30	174 994	11.5	66.3	16.3	17 704	34 683	9.6	25.0	21.6	11.6
District 31	214 210	10.5	88.0	28.3	22 774	51 097	17.1	11.0	8.2	5.7
District 32	158 844	22.4	74.4	35.4	31 689	47 137	21.8	14.7	11.9	5.7
UTAH	819 445	13.5	90.2	28.6	21 016	51 309	15.8	10.6	7.8	5.5
District 1	260 134	8.7	90.1	27.5	21 134	51 154	15.0	10.6	8.2	6.1
District 2	255 039	11.8	91.2	32.6	23 838	51 118	18.5	10.1	7.6	4.5
District 3	304 272	19.0	89.3	25.0	18 166	51 668	13.5	11.0	7.6	5.9
VERMONT	156 039	20.0	89.8	32.4	25 016	47 665	14.9	10.3	6.7	9.0
At Large	156 039	20.0	89.8	32.4	25 016	47 665	14.9	10.3	6.7	9.0
VIRGINIA	1 990 230	17.0	85.4	32.7	29 899	56 277	23.6	9.6	6.8	6.0
District 1	194 439	13.3	88.7	30.0	28 786	60 839	23.8	7.2	5.1	4.2
District 2	171 865	16.9	90.8	29.2	26 959	56 052	18.6	8.0	5.9	4.8
District 3	175 087	13.4	79.5	19.4	20 914	39 984	10.3	17.5	13.5	12.6
District 4	191 393	14.9	82.6	22.0	24 487	54 964	19.1	9.3	6.4	7.1
District 5	171 063	15.1	79.2	21.1	22 100	40 727	10.7	13.5	9.0	9.7

[5]All persons 3 years old and over enrolled in nursery school through college.
[6]Persons 25 years old and over.
[13]Data are for 109th congressional districts. The boundaries for districts for the 110th Congress have changed.

Table A. 110th Congressional Districts—Continued

(Number, percent.)

STATE Congressional district	Total	Total occupied units	Owner-occupied units							
			Percent owner-occupied units	Median value (dollars)	Percent valued at $500,000 or more	Median real estate taxes (dollars)	Median monthly costs (dollars)	Percent with second mortgage or home equity loan	Median cost as percent of income	
									With a mortgage	Without a mortgage
	47	48	49	50	51	52	53	54	55	56
RHODE ISLAND	449 574	405 627	63.0	295 700	13.8	3 186	1 391	21.4	27.6	16.9
District 1	225 727	205 386	58.7	307 100	15.1	3 013	1 395	21.5	27.6	17.2
District 2	223 847	200 241	67.4	286 300	12.6	3 318	1 389	21.3	27.6	16.6
SOUTH CAROLINA	1 975 816	1 656 978	70.3	122 400	4.6	703	772	14.6	22.9	11.6
District 1	403 003	312 873	68.3	181 200	10.3	959	977	18.7	24.7	12.2
District 2	337 484	290 780	72.5	141 200	7.7	940	889	16.0	22.6	11.0
District 3	316 186	263 213	73.8	105 200	2.0	553	651	12.7	21.2	11.3
District 4	315 720	282 951	68.9	122 000	3.1	823	816	17.6	22.8	10.7
District 5	307 013	261 775	74.6	99 600	1.6	526	659	11.8	22.0	11.4
District 6	296 410	245 386	63.8	88 200	1.7	501	639	9.5	23.9	13.0
SOUTH DAKOTA	352 289	312 477	69.2	112 600	2.2	1 470	708	13.4	22.2	11.7
At Large	352 289	312 477	69.2	112 600	2.2	1 470	708	13.4	22.2	11.7
TENNESSEE	2 681 320	2 375 123	69.9	123 100	3.3	860	773	13.3	23.1	11.0
District 1	310 197	267 450	73.6	99 500	1.5	553	499	10.1	21.6	9.8
District 2	311 096	282 934	70.8	136 200	3.7	824	805	14.4	21.8	9.6
District 3	298 087	266 645	69.7	122 400	3.3	836	689	13.5	22.8	11.0
District 4	296 450	258 429	75.5	101 000	2.1	577	558	10.0	23.0	11.8
District 5	301 145	273 292	62.6	155 500	4.8	1 359	1 019	16.6	24.5	11.7
District 6	306 839	278 024	70.7	134 200	2.2	840	823	13.0	22.9	9.8
District 7	292 295	265 803	79.2	170 000	7.5	1 428	1 048	17.9	22.4	10.5
District 8	286 534	246 303	70.1	92 000	0.7	636	661	10.4	22.4	11.7
District 9	278 677	236 243	55.5	95 500	2.9	1 451	982	13.6	28.1	14.3
TEXAS[13]	9 224 920	8 109 388	65.2	114 000	2.8	2 122	956	7.2	23.9	13.6
District 1	294 240	254 153	71.2	86 400	1.2	1 008	614	3.6	20.3	13.3
District 2	287 633	257 910	70.7	115 400	1.1	2 355	1 021	7.3	22.8	12.8
District 3	305 625	282 836	64.4	176 100	4.2	4 006	1 605	13.6	24.0	13.8
District 4	316 490	277 140	74.3	106 800	1.8	1 509	860	6.1	23.4	14.0
District 5	281 371	242 392	71.1	111 400	1.2	1 923	935	6.5	24.1	14.8
District 6	296 910	263 066	67.1	126 200	1.4	2 770	1 152	6.7	24.4	14.1
District 7	343 108	313 038	56.4	183 300	13.3	3 988	1 531	12.4	23.8	12.1
District 8	310 618	268 589	75.8	103 200	2.8	1 328	786	6.8	21.7	12.8
District 9	264 769	229 829	43.2	106 900	0.8	2 303	1 091	7.5	27.5	13.1
District 10	328 182	299 698	69.0	150 000	4.0	3 443	1 341	10.4	24.5	12.2
District 11	301 913	252 619	72.1	73 800	1.8	979	604	2.5	21.6	13.2
District 12	290 990	259 597	68.3	112 300	2.9	2 434	1 064	7.7	24.3	14.2
District 13	289 070	242 015	67.8	76 900	0.9	1 224	628	3.4	21.8	12.9
District 14	311 441	257 556	70.0	118 200	1.4	2 067	958	5.5	22.7	13.0
District 15	273 666	230 077	71.4	69 400	0.9	1 070	550	2.6	24.3	14.4
District 16	239 506	220 378	63.1	89 100	0.5	1 967	723	5.1	24.4	12.9
District 17	286 414	248 041	65.8	101 800	2.2	1 558	803	5.1	23.2	14.4
District 18	268 081	227 503	52.0	103 300	1.5	1 831	938	6.7	27.8	15.0
District 19	289 050	249 836	65.5	74 700	1.0	1 013	623	3.5	20.9	13.3
District 20	256 048	231 718	55.4	81 600	0.4	1 659	740	3.8	23.5	12.7
District 21	331 940	301 696	69.0	182 700	8.7	3 830	1 349	12.9	23.1	11.6
District 22	284 684	260 598	73.9	147 100	1.9	3 407	1 341	10.4	23.5	13.0
District 23	294 929	256 064	71.9	126 100	3.0	2 216	891	6.6	22.8	13.0
District 24	306 538	280 017	59.9	157 200	4.3	3 647	1 465	11.3	24.8	14.7
District 25	279 532	236 504	61.0	79 400	1.0	1 341	645	4.0	27.3	14.0
District 26	296 722	270 250	71.6	145 800	3.2	3 237	1 361	13.8	24.5	14.7
District 27	269 084	229 882	63.8	80 600	1.1	1 347	727	4.0	26.0	15.3
District 28	260 120	227 499	69.6	77 100	0.5	1 322	686	4.2	23.9	12.9
District 29	227 292	200 789	56.6	84 200	0.0	1 454	794	5.3	27.4	14.0
District 30	264 676	230 075	51.0	96 800	1.7	1 694	969	7.1	29.8	14.8
District 31	298 922	264 354	66.3	131 100	1.5	2 539	1 068	8.5	23.3	13.6
District 32	275 356	243 669	50.5	172 300	14.2	3 530	1 335	10.1	25.6	14.5
UTAH	901 322	814 028	72.0	188 500	6.3	1 185	1 093	24.5	24.2	9.7
District 1	305 538	270 003	71.4	166 900	5.1	1 059	1 076	24.9	23.8	9.2
District 2	327 588	290 613	71.6	228 900	9.9	1 312	1 068	23.5	23.8	10.1
District 3	268 196	253 412	73.0	178 800	3.6	1 200	1 128	25.2	25.2	9.6
VERMONT	309 566	253 808	71.9	193 000	5.9	3 036	1 055	17.1	25.4	16.0
At Large	309 566	253 808	71.9	193 000	5.9	3 036	1 055	17.1	25.4	16.0
VIRGINIA	3 230 821	2 905 071	69.9	244 200	20.5	1 565	1 175	23.1	24.1	10.9
District 1	307 113	274 729	72.6	299 900	16.2	1 587	1 253	23.3	24.3	10.3
District 2	265 760	239 181	66.5	237 000	12.6	1 652	1 248	23.9	25.8	12.2
District 3	285 873	254 296	53.5	157 100	3.1	1 316	1 052	20.4	25.1	13.3
District 4	279 539	257 872	73.9	198 800	6.6	1 419	1 136	22.8	24.4	11.9
District 5	312 615	268 221	72.0	129 000	6.7	667	663	15.7	23.0	11.1

[13]Data are for 109th congressional districts. The boundaries for districts for the 110th Congress have changed.

Table A. 110th Congressional Districts—*Continued*

(Number, percent.)

STATE Congressional district	Housing units, 2006—*Continued*			Civilian labor force, 2006			Civilian employment and occupation, 2006			
	Renter-occupied units		Sub-standard housing units (percent)[7]	Total	Unemployment		Total civilian employment	Management, professional, and related (percent)	Service, sales, and office (percent)	Construction and production (percent)
	Median gross rent (dollars)	Median gross rent as a percent of income			Total	Rate[8]				
	57	58	59	60	61	62	63	64	65	66
RHODE ISLAND	840	29.0	1.9	565 481	33 193	5.9	532 288	34.5	44.3	21.1
District 1	835	28.9	1.8	283 323	15 160	5.4	268 163	34.2	43.9	21.9
District 2	845	29.1	2.1	282 158	18 033	6.4	264 125	34.9	44.6	20.3
SOUTH CAROLINA	640	28.7	2.0	2 121 258	156 548	7.4	1 964 710	30.4	41.6	27.5
District 1	778	28.3	2.4	393 959	21 585	5.5	372 374	33.8	44.8	21.3
District 2	706	29.1	1.8	379 259	17 948	4.7	361 311	34.6	42.8	22.3
District 3	565	28.6	2.0	334 017	28 365	8.5	305 652	30.1	37.4	31.8
District 4	607	27.3	1.2	369 657	26 780	7.2	342 877	30.3	40.2	29.3
District 5	569	28.8	2.4	338 793	26 460	7.8	312 333	26.3	40.8	31.9
District 6	575	30.1	2.4	305 573	35 410	11.6	270 163	25.1	43.1	30.8
SOUTH DAKOTA	522	24.7	2.5	423 824	18 362	4.3	405 462	34.9	40.3	22.9
At Large	522	24.7	2.5	423 824	18 362	4.3	405 462	34.9	40.3	22.9
TENNESSEE	613	29.0	2.0	2 987 363	220 468	7.4	2 766 895	30.6	41.5	27.4
District 1	490	26.6	2.1	311 685	20 359	6.5	291 326	27.4	40.7	31.5
District 2	597	28.6	0.7	355 124	21 377	6.0	333 747	34.2	42.4	23.0
District 3	567	27.0	2.4	323 846	23 563	7.3	300 283	30.5	41.3	27.8
District 4	512	27.9	1.6	306 522	25 687	8.4	280 835	27.3	38.0	33.9
District 5	714	29.8	2.1	347 764	20 435	5.9	327 329	36.2	44.0	19.8
District 6	622	28.7	2.3	375 120	25 350	6.8	349 770	28.8	38.4	32.0
District 7	722	27.0	1.7	367 196	21 718	5.9	345 478	35.7	42.8	21.1
District 8	552	30.4	2.3	299 030	28 234	9.4	270 796	25.3	40.2	33.9
District 9	684	33.1	3.0	301 076	33 745	11.2	267 331	27.6	46.1	26.3
TEXAS[13]	711	29.4	5.2	11 536 867	807 572	7.0	10 729 295	32.3	42.6	24.5
District 1	615	30.6	3.3	329 778	25 320	7.7	304 458	31.0	38.1	30.1
District 2	721	27.4	3.9	364 518	26 143	7.2	338 375	32.5	41.7	25.6
District 3	846	26.7	3.7	447 639	21 109	4.7	426 530	42.4	41.0	16.5
District 4	630	28.3	3.0	389 141	25 838	6.6	363 303	31.5	42.9	24.7
District 5	735	30.7	4.3	351 027	24 027	6.8	327 000	30.2	42.5	26.7
District 6	760	29.4	4.1	394 131	29 729	7.5	364 402	31.9	41.8	25.7
District 7	846	27.3	2.9	424 512	20 108	4.7	404 404	48.3	37.5	14.2
District 8	696	29.5	3.5	356 369	25 795	7.2	330 574	30.5	41.9	27.0
District 9	693	32.2	9.1	367 285	33 587	9.1	333 698	25.7	48.5	25.7
District 10	798	28.3	4.0	459 014	24 862	5.4	434 152	39.3	40.4	20.0
District 11	578	27.3	3.2	310 010	14 361	4.6	295 649	28.6	41.9	27.7
District 12	763	28.3	4.1	387 095	26 247	6.8	360 848	31.0	41.2	27.6
District 13	592	29.3	3.0	310 924	18 998	6.1	291 926	28.0	42.0	28.5
District 14	677	28.1	4.0	348 520	24 286	7.0	324 234	32.8	39.7	26.4
District 15	550	30.1	10.0	296 053	23 826	8.0	272 227	28.2	46.0	23.0
District 16	539	30.9	6.2	289 357	23 448	8.1	265 909	29.2	47.4	23.1
District 17	649	32.7	3.3	342 839	27 227	7.9	315 612	30.6	41.2	27.2
District 18	694	32.1	9.0	333 404	31 223	9.4	302 181	23.7	44.8	31.5
District 19	613	31.0	4.5	309 885	17 928	5.8	291 957	30.2	43.9	23.7
District 20	641	29.7	5.0	308 558	23 065	7.5	285 493	26.2	48.2	25.3
District 21	844	26.3	2.1	419 918	20 693	4.9	399 225	48.5	38.4	13.0
District 22	836	25.8	3.0	435 647	28 021	6.4	407 626	39.8	39.8	20.2
District 23	677	28.8	5.4	354 746	24 214	6.8	330 532	36.1	43.9	18.7
District 24	832	27.2	3.6	426 153	24 240	5.7	401 913	38.3	42.3	19.3
District 25	655	31.1	12.1	336 328	29 767	8.9	306 561	26.2	47.6	25.0
District 26	771	31.6	3.4	433 134	31 285	7.2	401 849	34.6	43.9	21.2
District 27	655	33.8	9.3	301 307	25 552	8.5	275 755	27.3	47.5	24.5
District 28	620	31.5	8.5	339 839	28 277	8.3	311 562	22.0	47.9	29.5
District 29	634	31.2	13.1	317 431	32 019	10.1	285 412	12.7	40.0	47.1
District 30	721	32.5	9.1	329 646	33 685	10.2	295 961	22.9	42.5	34.4
District 31	785	27.4	2.8	365 879	23 420	6.4	342 459	36.6	42.4	20.6
District 32	740	29.0	6.7	356 780	19 272	5.4	337 508	32.8	41.0	26.2
UTAH	697	28.0	4.2	1 272 674	56 254	4.4	1 216 420	32.4	43.3	23.9
District 1	654	27.5	3.6	414 670	20 313	4.9	394 357	31.7	43.4	24.6
District 2	734	27.5	3.7	423 044	17 347	4.1	405 697	36.2	42.7	20.8
District 3	705	29.2	5.2	434 960	18 594	4.3	416 366	29.5	43.9	26.2
VERMONT	716	30.5	1.7	350 032	16 953	4.8	333 079	37.4	40.6	20.9
At Large	716	30.5	1.7	350 032	16 953	4.8	333 079	37.4	40.6	20.9
VIRGINIA	846	28.2	1.7	3 977 670	185 464	4.7	3 792 206	39.8	39.1	20.7
District 1	938	28.2	1.4	378 431	16 334	4.3	362 097	37.3	40.9	21.1
District 2	927	28.6	2.1	322 418	14 628	4.5	307 790	36.7	42.2	20.7
District 3	725	30.6	2.1	310 519	25 678	8.3	284 841	29.4	45.5	25.0
District 4	762	27.9	2.3	369 721	17 210	4.7	352 511	32.0	41.7	25.5
District 5	613	27.4	2.0	323 686	19 799	6.1	303 887	31.4	38.5	29.2

[7]Overcrowded or lacking complete plumbing facilities.
[8]Percent of civilian labor force.
[13]Data are for 109th congressional districts. The boundaries for districts for the 110th Congress have changed.

Table A. 110th Congressional Districts—*Continued*

(Number, percent.)

STATE Congressional district	Social Security Beneficiaries (OASDI), December 2006							Supplemental Security Income, December 2006			
	Total	Rate per 1,000 population	Retired workers[9]	Disabled workers	Widow(er)s[10]	Spouses[11]	Children[12]	Total	Aged	Blind	Disabled
	67	68	69	70	71	72	73	74	75	76	77
RHODE ISLAND	193 099	180.9	128 410	29 721	14 414	6 163	14 391	30 710	3 977	194	26 539
District 1	97 720	183.0	66 183	14 421	7 259	3 156	6 701	14 815	2 174	102	12 539
District 2	95 379	178.8	62 227	15 300	7 155	3 007	7 690	15 895	1 803	92	14 000
SOUTH CAROLINA	801 076	185.4	489 743	135 892	70 167	30 760	74 514	105 524	11 771	1 381	92 372
District 1	134 364	175.9	86 185	19 735	11 599	6 001	10 844	12 677	1 297	137	11 243
District 2	124 376	165.4	81 036	16 179	10 996	5 820	10 345	12 996	1 350	195	11 451
District 3	147 094	211.7	91 358	25 954	11 357	5 233	13 192	15 317	1 473	190	13 654
District 4	132 717	183.8	81 034	24 771	10 431	4 624	11 857	14 758	1 394	202	13 162
District 5	135 950	191.0	80 682	24 804	12 466	4 466	13 532	20 422	2 516	244	17 662
District 6	126 575	187.0	69 448	24 449	13 318	4 616	14 744	29 354	3 741	413	25 200
SOUTH DAKOTA	142 953	182.8	94 207	15 038	15 042	9 072	9 594	12 584	1 611	93	10 880
At Large	142 953	182.8	94 207	15 038	15 042	9 072	9 594	12 584	1 611	93	10 880
TENNESSEE	1 115 933	184.8	659 946	190 539	108 804	53 402	103 242	162 660	16 067	1 525	145 068
District 1	155 575	234.4	87 634	29 990	15 985	8 708	13 258	20 881	2 238	173	18 470
District 2	132 319	191.3	81 509	20 884	12 925	6 928	10 073	15 606	1 339	126	14 141
District 3	136 463	208.2	80 751	23 736	13 416	6 910	11 650	18 935	1 678	167	17 090
District 4	152 057	228.2	88 359	27 114	15 422	7 904	13 258	22 288	2 282	178	19 828
District 5	94 766	145.0	59 261	14 523	8 868	3 787	8 327	12 922	1 276	175	11 471
District 6	120 104	164.9	72 043	20 468	10 977	5 106	11 510	14 040	1 687	178	12 175
District 7	107 480	147.2	66 811	15 317	9 774	5 375	10 203	11 784	1 412	119	10 253
District 8	127 325	198.5	73 986	22 533	12 294	5 480	13 032	20 562	2 058	168	18 336
District 9	89 844	147.9	49 592	15 974	9 143	3 204	11 931	25 642	2 097	241	23 304
TEXAS[13]	3 028 901	128.8	1 807 535	410 912	330 751	200 396	279 307	524 347	109 127	6 537	408 683
District 1	129 853	187.6	75 792	19 068	15 258	8 039	11 696	19 487	2 329	263	16 895
District 2	97 990	131.1	56 072	13 535	11 926	6 890	9 567	14 215	1 765	162	12 288
District 3	63 617	78.2	41 238	7 597	5 710	3 453	5 619	8 542	2 664	100	5 778
District 4	131 020	167.8	80 032	19 477	13 478	6 855	11 178	16 677	2 104	187	14 386
District 5	111 798	156.5	70 974	15 470	10 762	5 551	9 041	12 814	1 694	165	10 955
District 6	92 912	123.5	56 591	12 619	9 202	5 189	9 311	11 873	2 002	170	9 701
District 7	75 236	98.6	50 369	6 127	8 062	5 821	4 857	6 761	2 074	94	4 593
District 8	127 765	167.1	76 861	17 037	14 366	9 002	10 499	14 876	1 716	181	12 979
District 9	55 350	79.3	29 860	9 802	5 204	2 810	7 674	20 768	5 194	257	15 317
District 10	79 905	94.1	49 402	9 788	8 224	4 772	7 719	9 396	1 943	165	7 288
District 11	124 739	184.1	76 536	14 905	14 794	9 300	9 204	16 017	3 041	191	12 785
District 12	94 516	125.9	58 589	12 207	10 319	5 725	7 676	10 385	1 651	138	8 596
District 13	112 935	172.6	69 401	13 993	13 788	7 792	7 961	12 787	1 911	149	10 727
District 14	106 475	145.4	63 351	13 560	12 682	7 501	9 381	13 669	2 090	184	11 395
District 15	96 311	133.3	53 166	12 786	11 676	8 492	10 191	32 731	10 020	372	22 339
District 16	92 889	132.9	51 217	12 458	11 044	9 224	8 946	24 596	8 879	278	15 439
District 17	107 968	152.4	67 271	14 362	11 232	6 079	9 024	13 634	1 661	162	11 811
District 18	83 357	121.3	44 912	14 641	9 467	3 860	10 477	26 948	3 896	316	22 736
District 19	109 912	167.2	66 301	13 572	13 269	7 784	8 986	15 282	2 333	227	12 722
District 20	94 904	138.7	51 839	16 678	10 304	6 145	9 938	25 696	4 728	240	20 728
District 21	116 516	148.3	75 737	12 619	11 488	8 008	8 664	9 917	1 333	140	8 444
District 22	80 662	99.8	49 212	9 384	8 592	5 420	8 054	10 278	2 980	119	7 179
District 23	105 093	135.2	58 535	15 070	11 368	8 767	11 353	26 650	7 467	327	18 856
District 24	64 264	83.8	41 128	7 897	5 852	3 349	6 038	7 064	1 611	86	5 367
District 25	93 236	124.9	56 008	13 766	9 689	5 199	8 574	15 455	2 737	252	12 466
District 26	88 210	108.4	54 168	12 056	8 615	4 303	9 068	11 356	1 431	160	9 765
District 27	93 550	132.1	51 572	12 696	11 540	8 000	9 742	27 168	7 514	358	19 296
District 28	95 536	126.8	52 298	12 825	11 147	8 852	10 414	32 165	10 569	417	21 179
District 29	59 918	86.9	31 820	9 145	7 560	4 766	6 627	15 945	3 637	206	12 102
District 30	78 629	115.0	43 166	16 499	7 204	2 791	8 969	22 458	2 856	242	19 360
District 31	94 694	122.3	57 857	12 383	9 770	5 964	8 720	11 191	1 643	139	9 409
District 32	69 141	105.8	46 260	6 890	7 159	4 693	4 139	7 546	1 654	90	5 802
UTAH	282 158	110.6	182 948	32 274	22 884	18 008	26 044	23 521	2 318	257	20 946
District 1	90 696	109.7	58 445	11 222	7 187	5 584	8 258	8 721	887	106	7 728
District 2	113 226	133.4	76 990	10 873	9 235	7 312	8 816	7 207	711	73	6 423
District 3	78 236	89.5	47 513	10 179	6 462	5 112	8 970	7 593	720	78	6 795
VERMONT	114 559	183.6	73 887	16 663	9 867	5 354	8 788	13 404	1 091	89	12 224
At Large	114 559	183.6	73 887	16 663	9 867	5 354	8 788	13 404	1 091	89	12 224
VIRGINIA	1 161 105	151.9	725 945	173 734	107 679	56 034	97 713	139 459	20 529	1 257	117 673
District 1	109 034	147.3	72 915	12 214	10 248	5 652	8 005	7 945	1 111	89	6 745
District 2	84 154	129.7	53 997	10 340	8 452	4 655	6 710	8 790	1 287	99	7 404
District 3	103 579	162.3	59 632	19 277	10 210	3 597	10 863	24 007	1 976	229	21 802
District 4	113 074	156.1	67 872	18 351	10 844	4 765	11 242	15 701	1 517	142	14 042
District 5	144 208	217.1	90 496	23 413	12 417	5 987	11 895	17 610	2 450	116	15 044

[9] Includes special age-72 beneficiaries.
[10] Includes nondisabled widow(er)s, disabled widow(er)s, widowed mothers and fathers, and parents receiving payment on the record of a worker who is deceased.
[11] These beneficiaries receive payment on the record of a worker who is retired or disabled.
[12] These beneficiaries receive payment on the record of a worker who is retired, deceased, or disabled.
[13] Data are for 109th congressional districts. The boundaries for districts for the 110th Congress have changed.

Table A. 110th Congressional Districts—*Continued*

(Number, percent.)

STATE Congressional district	Total farms	Farms by size (percent) 1 to 49 acres	50 to 999 acres	1,000 acres or more	Land in farms Total acreage	Average size of farms (acres)	Percent of farms where principal operator's primary occupation is farming	Value of all agricultural products sold Total ($1,000)	Percent of farms with value of: Less than $50,000	$50,000 to $249,999	$250,000 or more	Payments from federal farm programs Total ($1,000)	Number of farms that receive payments	Percent of farms that receive payments
	78	79	80	81	82	83	84	85	86	87	88	89	90	91
RHODE ISLAND	858	59.8	39.6	0.6	61 223	71	51.5	55 546	80.4	14.1	5.5	528	52	6.1
District 1	308	62.3	37.3	0.3	19 589	64	53.2	22 947	77.6	16.6	5.8	211	17	5.5
District 2	550	58.4	40.9	0.7	41 634	76	50.5	32 599	82.0	12.7	5.3	317	35	6.4
SOUTH CAROLINA	24 541	41.7	54.4	3.8	4 845 923	197	46.4	1 489 750	90.8	4.8	4.4	38 384	6 112	24.9
District 1	1 591	48.7	48.0	3.3	277 012	174	50.6	99 925	87.6	7.4	5.0	1 916	332	20.9
District 2	3 216	42.1	53.9	4.0	731 148	227	44.4	182 062	91.0	4.4	4.6	4 714	820	25.5
District 3	6 543	45.1	53.0	1.9	902 892	138	45.3	266 512	94.0	3.1	2.8	3 345	1 103	16.9
District 4	2 687	53.1	46.1	0.8	273 197	102	45.2	45 459	96.1	2.3	1.6	605	273	10.2
District 5	5 549	35.6	59.7	4.7	1 252 899	226	47.2	568 374	88.9	5.0	6.1	11 874	1 576	28.4
District 6	4 955	35.5	57.4	7.1	1 408 775	284	47.4	327 419	86.7	7.4	5.9	15 931	2 008	40.5
SOUTH DAKOTA	31 736	13.6	54.2	32.2	43 785 079	1 380	72.6	3 834 625	55.2	33.7	11.2	215 084	20 259	63.8
At Large	31 736	13.6	54.2	32.2	43 785 079	1 380	72.6	3 834 625	55.2	33.7	11.2	215 084	20 259	63.8
TENNESSEE	87 595	43.6	54.9	1.5	11 681 533	133	50.3	2 199 814	93.2	4.6	2.2	59 231	16 034	18.3
District 1	13 428	55.1	44.7	0.2	1 029 733	77	52.8	211 833	95.6	3.3	1.1	2 397	1 154	8.6
District 2	6 064	53.2	46.3	0.5	526 333	87	47.7	154 262	95.1	3.1	1.8	2 166	428	7.1
District 3	7 607	47.7	51.9	0.4	730 080	96	51.3	171 995	94.4	3.5	2.1	2 060	857	11.3
District 4	19 059	39.4	59.4	1.2	2 513 707	132	50.0	541 272	91.9	5.6	2.4	9 881	3 678	19.3
District 5	1 974	48.8	50.8	0.4	181 721	92	46.5	24 291	97.2	2.2	0.6	179	138	7.0
District 6	17 959	43.3	55.7	0.9	2 124 154	118	50.5	375 843	93.9	4.4	1.6	6 513	2 502	13.9
District 7	8 728	33.1	64.6	2.3	1 573 162	180	49.0	166 601	94.0	4.2	1.8	8 821	2 700	30.9
District 8	12 620	37.4	57.6	5.1	2 983 641	236	50.5	549 892	88.6	6.8	4.7	27 067	4 538	36.0
District 9	156	48.7	48.7	2.6	19 002	122	37.8	3 824	93.6	4.5	1.9	146	39	25.0
TEXAS[13]	228 926	32.6	57.5	9.9	129 877 666	567	53.6	14 134 744	89.8	7.1	3.1	528 979	42 217	18.4
District 1	21 053	33.4	63.2	3.4	4 468 828	212	54.0	1 136 605	90.5	5.2	4.3	10 511	1 389	6.6
District 2	14 099	43.0	53.9	3.1	2 698 951	191	51.3	365 351	94.9	3.7	1.4	4 518	250	1.8
District 3	925	63.5	33.9	2.6	114 125	123	43.6	22 197	95.5	2.2	2.4	433	52	5.6
District 4	16 085	45.7	51.1	3.2	2 786 930	173	49.5	337 993	94.4	4.2	1.3	5 464	1 096	6.8
District 5	12 764	29.7	65.1	5.2	3 522 032	276	53.7	397 387	92.6	5.7	1.7	3 929	571	4.5
District 6	8 951	43.2	52.8	4.0	1 903 872	213	48.8	181 361	93.7	4.9	1.5	9 107	1 248	13.9
District 7	223	52.5	46.6	0.9	22 740	102	30.5	6 708	97.3	1.3	1.3	43	17	7.6
District 8	1 989	64.4	34.5	1.1	196 716	99	44.2	31 080	97.2	2.1	0.7	135	36	1.8
District 9	2 398	51.5	40.6	7.9	834 325	348	54.3	47 493	90.4	8.3	1.3	6 829	244	10.2
District 10	970	47.3	48.8	3.9	211 359	218	50.9	13 561	93.8	4.9	1.2	628	141	14.5
District 11	13 461	31.0	61.3	7.8	4 835 760	359	52.1	359 118	93.0	5.1	1.8	10 645	2 272	16.9
District 12	3 797	60.0	37.6	2.4	594 681	157	43.4	69 160	96.6	2.4	1.0	377	172	4.5
District 13	17 197	12.6	60.2	27.1	22 993 010	1 337	62.6	5 656 446	72.5	16.7	10.8	158 262	9 679	56.3
District 14	26 242	30.1	63.5	6.4	8 239 677	314	54.4	995 563	91.2	6.5	2.3	44 012	3 833	14.6
District 15	5 690	34.4	54.5	11.1	3 798 707	668	55.2	359 252	87.7	7.6	4.8	14 844	1 199	21.1
District 16	423	75.7	22.2	2.1	57 753	137	49.6	26 747	85.6	9.5	5.0	136	25	5.9
District 17	25 433	22.7	62.5	14.8	18 712 734	736	54.6	1 036 036	88.8	8.7	2.4	76 111	8 264	32.5
District 18	154	50.0	49.4	0.6	17 265	112	39.6	7 212	95.5	2.6	1.9	29	5	3.2
District 19	7 958	18.6	55.4	26.0	9 682 524	1 217	63.1	1 427 265	69.6	19.2	11.1	113 793	5 011	63.0
District 20	519	50.5	47.0	2.5	81 035	156	56.1	47 818	92.5	5.8	1.7	213	57	11.0
District 21	11 022	27.8	60.5	11.7	5 615 781	510	51.8	162 249	95.8	3.7	0.5	4 192	1 368	12.4
District 22	3 177	52.9	41.8	5.3	808 135	254	48.8	82 406	91.1	6.9	2.0	6 847	370	11.6
District 23	7 145	19.8	49.9	30.3	27 065 473	3 788	57.9	522 302	85.2	10.5	4.3	19 466	1 429	20.0
District 24	146	66.4	32.9	0.7	12 279	84	45.2	3 132	92.5	6.2	1.4	. . .	4	2.7
District 25	319	56.4	42.3	1.3	40 680	128	42.9	1 981	98.4	1.6	0.0	293	10	3.1
District 26	2 628	62.2	35.3	2.5	396 781	151	45.3	53 596	95.2	4.0	0.8	1 069	182	6.9
District 27	2 227	47.0	38.8	14.2	1 801 602	809	60.3	171 477	79.4	13.2	7.4	10 755	684	30.7
District 28	7 955	23.7	62.0	14.3	5 624 041	707	54.5	342 195	93.1	5.0	1.9	18 138	1 651	20.8
District 29	145	53.1	44.1	2.8	18 061	125	37.2	940	98.6	1.4	0.0	. . .	2	1.4
District 30	220	62.3	35.0	2.7	30 336	138	57.3	6 073	94.1	3.2	2.7	204	15	6.8
District 31	13 511	38.8	57.7	3.4	2 672 962	198	50.2	258 218	94.2	4.8	1.0	7 975	930	6.9
District 32	100	43.0	54.0	3.0	18 511	185	39.0	5 823	93.0	3.0	4.0	17	11	11.0
UTAH	15 282	54.8	36.8	8.4	11 731 228	768	48.7	1 115 898	84.5	10.3	5.2	26 669	2 987	19.5
District 1	5 334	57.6	34.3	8.1	3 413 726	640	47.8	327 278	83.4	11.1	5.4	11 413	1 176	22.0
District 2	5 394	50.4	40.0	9.5	6 721 729	1 246	49.2	254 272	87.5	9.2	3.3	8 057	939	17.4
District 3	4 554	56.6	35.9	7.5	1 595 773	350	49.3	534 347	82.0	10.7	7.3	7 199	872	19.1
VERMONT	6 571	33.7	64.0	2.3	1 244 909	189	53.1	473 065	76.3	16.9	6.9	24 377	1 296	19.7
At Large	6 571	33.7	64.0	2.3	1 244 909	189	53.1	473 065	76.3	16.9	6.9	24 377	1 296	19.7
VIRGINIA	47 606	35.9	61.1	2.9	8 624 829	181	53.6	2 360 911	87.9	7.5	4.6	54 677	9 206	19.3
District 1	2 827	40.9	53.6	5.6	667 150	236	53.2	137 491	86.2	9.4	4.4	7 710	828	29.3
District 2	675	48.9	44.3	6.8	171 745	254	60.3	162 985	64.4	16.9	18.7	1 863	182	27.0
District 3	577	36.0	57.4	6.6	160 326	278	52.9	36 772	82.7	12.0	5.4	2 732	200	34.7
District 4	3 062	33.7	58.8	7.6	878 218	287	59.5	290 385	80.3	10.9	8.7	12 061	1 090	35.6
District 5	10 059	24.2	72.9	2.9	2 099 927	209	54.8	317 554	90.1	6.9	3.0	8 290	2 587	25.7

[13]Data are for 109th congressional districts. The boundaries for districts for the 110th Congress have changed.
. . . = Not available.

Table A. 110th Congressional Districts—*Continued*

(Number, percent.)

STATE Congressional district	Representative	Land area,[1] (sq km)	Total population	Persons per square kilometer	White	Black	American Indian/ Alaska Native	Asian and Pacific Islander	Some other race (percent)	Two or more races (percent)	Hispanic or Latino[2] (percent)	Non-Hispanic White (percent)
					Race alone (percent)							
	1	2	3	4	5	6	7	8	9	10	11	12
VIRGINIA—*Continued*												
District 6	Rep. Bob Goodlatte (R)	14 625	675 743	46.2	85.7	10.8	0.2	1.1	0.6	1.6	2.7	84.0
District 7	Rep. Eric Cantor (R)	9 102	724 005	79.5	77.5	16.3	0.2	3.1	1.3	1.5	3.2	75.5
District 8	Rep. James P. Moran (D)	319	657 672	2 061.7	67.6	13.3	0.1	9.5	7.1	2.4	16.2	59.1
District 9	Rep. Rick Boucher (D)	22 801	635 771	27.9	93.3	4.1	0.1	1.3	0.4	0.8	1.2	92.5
District 10	Rep. Frank R. Wolf (R)	4 808	786 460	163.6	74.1	7.7	0.1	10.8	5.6	1.7	10.7	69.2
District 11	Rep. Tom Davis (R)	1 004	747 244	744.3	65.6	11.7	0.3	14.6	5.2	2.7	13.6	58.0
WASHINGTON		172 348	6 395 798	37.1	80.5	3.4	1.5	7.1	4.3	3.3	9.1	76.4
District 1	Rep. Jay Inslee (D)	1 138	710 787	624.6	81.4	2.7	0.8	9.8	1.9	3.5	6.1	77.5
District 2	Rep. Rick Larsen (D)	17 002	726 699	42.7	86.9	1.5	1.8	4.3	3.2	2.3	7.0	83.8
District 3	Rep. Brian Baird (D)	19 465	747 336	38.4	88.5	1.4	0.9	3.5	2.5	3.2	5.8	85.9
District 4	Rep. Doc Hastings (R)	49 343	720 159	14.6	76.9	0.9	1.9	1.4	16.5	2.3	29.7	64.7
District 5	Rep. Cathy McMorris Rodgers (R)	59 217	691 800	11.7	89.0	1.3	2.3	2.6	2.0	2.8	4.8	86.7
District 6	Rep. Norman D. Dicks (D)	17 564	687 868	39.2	79.7	5.8	2.3	5.6	2.6	4.1	6.2	76.8
District 7	Rep. Jim McDermott (D)	366	643 402	1 757.9	69.3	8.4	0.9	13.8	3.7	4.0	7.1	66.7
District 8	Rep. David G. Reichert (R)	6 680	771 939	115.6	79.0	2.4	0.8	12.1	2.5	3.2	5.5	76.2
District 9	Rep. Adam Smith (D)	1 574	695 808	442.1	72.5	7.1	1.4	10.9	4.0	4.2	9.2	68.1
WEST VIRGINIA		62 361	1 818 470	29.2	94.6	3.2	0.2	0.6	0.2	1.1	0.8	94.1
District 1	Rep. Alan B. Mollohan (D)	16 281	598 236	36.7	95.8	1.6	0.2	1.0	0.2	1.2	0.8	95.3
District 2	Rep. Shelley Moore Capito (R)	21 909	630 006	28.8	93.8	4.0	0.2	0.7	0.2	1.2	1.1	93.0
District 3	Rep. Nick J. Rahall II (D)	24 170	590 228	24.4	94.4	4.1	0.1	0.3	0.1	1.0	0.4	94.2
WISCONSIN		140 663	5 556 506	39.5	87.5	5.9	0.9	2.0	2.5	1.3	4.6	85.6
District 1	Rep. Paul Ryan (R)	4 351	714 348	164.2	87.8	5.4	0.3	1.0	4.0	1.6	7.8	84.3
District 2	Rep. Tammy Baldwin (D)	9 095	715 067	78.6	89.8	3.7	0.4	2.8	1.6	1.8	4.4	87.2
District 3	Rep. Ron Kind (D)	35 134	708 088	20.2	96.0	0.7	0.6	1.6	0.4	0.8	1.3	95.2
District 4	Rep. Gwen Moore (D)	290	638 284	2 201.0	49.2	35.3	0.7	3.3	9.7	1.8	14.2	45.3
District 5	Rep. F. James Sensenbrenner Jr. (R)	3 298	703 772	213.4	93.2	2.1	0.2	2.5	0.7	1.3	2.9	91.3
District 6	Rep. Thomas E. Petri (R)	14 611	690 565	47.3	93.6	1.5	0.5	1.8	1.7	1.0	3.0	92.5
District 7	Rep. David R. Obey (D)	48 657	686 342	14.1	95.0	0.4	1.6	1.6	0.4	1.1	1.1	94.4
District 8	Rep. Steve Kagen (D)	25 228	700 040	27.7	91.8	0.9	2.7	1.7	1.9	1.0	2.9	91.0
WYOMING		251 489	515 004	2.0	91.8	0.7	2.2	1.0	2.4	1.8	6.9	88.0
At Large	Rep. Barbara Cubin (R)	251 489	515 004	2.0	91.8	0.7	2.2	1.0	2.4	1.8	6.9	88.0
PUERTO RICO		8 870	3 927 776	442.8	75.4	7.7	0.2	0.3	11.9	4.4	98.7	0.9
Delegate District (At Large)	Res. Commissioner Luis G. Fortuño (R)	8 870	3 927 776	442.8	75.4	7.7	0.2	0.3	11.9	4.4	98.7	0.9

[1]Dry land or land partially or temporarily covered by water.
[2]May be of any race.

Table A. 110th Congressional Districts—*Continued*

(Number, percent.)

STATE Congressional district	Percent female	Percent foreign born	Percent born in state of residence	Age (percent)								
				Under 5 years	5 to 18 years	18 to 24 years	25 to 34 years	35 to 44 years	45 to 54 years	55 to 64 years	65 to 74 years	75 years and over
	13	14	15	16	17	18	19	20	21	22	23	24
VIRGINIA—*Continued*												
District 6	51.2	3.8	66.1	5.5	15.9	11.8	11.7	13.9	14.7	11.4	7.4	7.7
District 7	51.7	7.2	59.0	6.6	16.6	8.9	14.0	15.2	15.4	11.3	6.1	5.9
District 8	51.0	26.0	21.1	7.5	13.3	7.1	16.0	18.9	15.3	11.8	5.6	4.5
District 9	50.6	2.0	67.0	5.0	14.1	12.2	12.7	13.2	14.5	12.5	8.6	7.2
District 10	50.3	19.0	36.4	8.0	18.8	8.6	14.3	17.4	14.8	10.2	4.4	3.5
District 11	49.7	24.9	28.1	7.0	19.2	8.6	11.5	16.6	16.4	12.1	5.1	3.5
WASHINGTON	50.2	12.4	47.2	6.4	17.5	9.6	13.9	14.8	15.2	11.1	5.9	5.6
District 1	49.8	14.8	44.6	6.3	17.7	8.2	13.4	16.4	16.5	11.7	5.1	4.7
District 2	50.6	9.2	51.3	6.0	18.0	10.5	13.5	14.2	14.9	10.8	6.1	6.1
District 3	50.6	7.7	41.1	6.3	18.5	9.0	14.2	14.5	14.8	11.0	6.3	5.6
District 4	50.0	15.5	53.7	7.9	20.4	10.6	13.7	12.9	13.3	10.0	6.0	5.3
District 5	50.6	5.4	53.8	6.0	17.2	12.0	13.1	12.9	14.6	11.1	6.5	6.7
District 6	50.3	8.1	50.2	5.8	16.4	9.8	13.8	13.1	14.7	11.6	7.4	7.4
District 7	50.6	19.8	38.8	5.2	11.2	10.3	17.3	16.9	15.8	12.3	5.0	5.9
District 8	49.5	17.0	45.4	6.9	19.7	7.0	12.0	17.6	16.6	10.6	5.6	4.0
District 9	50.1	14.6	45.6	6.8	17.8	9.5	14.4	14.8	15.5	11.0	5.4	4.8
WEST VIRGINIA	51.0	1.2	72.2	5.7	15.7	9.1	12.3	13.7	15.4	12.7	7.9	7.4
District 1	51.1	1.6	70.5	5.5	15.3	10.8	11.6	13.4	14.9	12.8	7.9	7.9
District 2	50.6	1.3	66.4	6.0	16.4	8.1	12.5	14.5	15.6	12.3	7.8	6.8
District 3	51.3	0.7	80.0	5.7	15.4	8.5	12.9	13.2	15.6	13.0	8.0	7.7
WISCONSIN	50.4	4.4	72.1	6.3	17.3	10.1	12.6	14.5	15.4	10.8	6.4	6.6
District 1	50.3	5.4	67.3	6.5	18.3	8.4	12.1	15.1	16.3	10.9	6.3	6.1
District 2	50.4	5.9	68.7	6.1	16.0	12.1	14.1	15.2	15.0	10.4	5.5	5.5
District 3	50.0	2.0	69.0	6.3	16.8	12.3	12.5	13.5	14.8	10.6	6.5	6.8
District 4	52.0	9.0	67.0	8.4	19.4	11.0	14.0	14.5	13.6	9.3	4.8	5.1
District 5	50.4	5.2	75.4	6.2	17.5	8.5	10.4	14.7	16.6	12.0	6.9	7.1
District 6	49.6	3.0	81.1	5.7	16.5	9.5	13.2	14.6	15.4	10.9	6.9	7.3
District 7	50.2	2.0	72.0	5.6	16.8	9.7	11.7	13.7	15.8	11.4	7.4	7.9
District 8	50.1	3.2	76.5	6.1	17.4	9.0	12.4	14.9	15.5	10.7	6.9	6.9
WYOMING	49.7	2.7	42.6	6.6	16.9	10.6	12.7	12.7	16.4	12.0	6.3	5.6
At Large	49.7	2.7	42.6	6.6	16.9	10.6	12.7	12.7	16.4	12.0	6.3	5.6
PUERTO RICO	52.0	2.9	. . .	6.4	19.5	10.4	14.0	13.5	12.5	10.8	7.3	5.6
Delegate District (At Large)	52.0	2.9	. . .	6.4	19.5	10.4	14.0	13.5	12.5	10.8	7.3	5.6

. . . = Not available.

Table A. 110th Congressional Districts—*Continued*

(Number, percent.)

STATE Congressional district	Households, 2006						Group quarters, 2006		Group quarters, 2000			
	Number	Average household size	Family households (percent)	Married-couple family (percent)	Female family house-holder[4] (percent)	One-person households (percent)	Total in group quarters	Percent 65 years and over	Persons in correctional institutions	Persons in nursing homes	Persons in college dormitories	Persons in military quarters
	25	26	27	28	29	30	31	32	33	34	35	36
VIRGINIA—*Continued*												
District 6	267 817	2.38	64.1	48.9	10.5	29.6	37 007	24.2	4 458	6 376	16 797	0
District 7	284 861	2.49	68.7	52.8	11.8	25.7	14 889	24.3	3 854	4 265	3 712	0
District 8	274 875	2.37	51.0	38.9	8.2	41.8	5 580	40.8	926	2 774	641	1 795
District 9	261 921	2.32	65.7	51.1	11.1	28.6	28 916	24.5	5 731	3 874	12 690	2
District 10	266 899	2.92	69.8	56.8	8.3	25.2	7 278	30.7	1 222	2 381	816	77
District 11	254 399	2.91	75.4	60.6	10.7	20.7	6 983	22.0	3 760	2 024	2 497	64
WASHINGTON	2 471 912	2.53	64.5	50.0	10.1	28.3	140 607	20.8	28 871	23 275	30 858	13 868
District 1	281 225	2.49	64.8	52.6	8.6	28.3	9 235	41.2	3 679	1 858	489	879
District 2	280 042	2.54	66.0	51.7	9.9	26.9	15 008	19.9	1 119	2 115	3 339	3 365
District 3	276 800	2.66	69.5	53.1	11.0	24.6	10 515	49.5	2 290	2 405	637	13
District 4	247 897	2.85	70.2	53.6	11.2	24.2	14 515	16.5	2 498	2 657	2 103	9
District 5	273 018	2.42	63.8	49.7	10.4	28.4	31 252	13.0	6 122	3 706	10 644	698
District 6	272 525	2.46	62.4	46.2	11.7	30.3	16 914	15.4	6 116	3 235	2 797	2 049
District 7	289 253	2.14	47.1	35.9	8.2	41.6	25 321	13.9	3 394	3 074	10 642	232
District 8	283 722	2.71	72.2	59.7	7.8	21.4	3 789	55.6	36	1 158	101	0
District 9	267 430	2.55	65.8	47.6	12.8	27.8	14 058	18.5	3 617	3 067	106	6 623
WEST VIRGINIA	743 064	2.39	67.6	52.5	10.9	27.6	45 532	25.9	10 505	11 601	14 300	59
District 1	243 934	2.38	65.6	51.7	10.2	29.0	18 589	24.8	2 416	4 578	8 236	0
District 2	254 757	2.42	68.7	53.5	10.5	26.3	13 257	26.2	2 212	3 380	3 020	59
District 3	244 373	2.36	68.5	52.2	12.0	27.4	13 686	27.1	3 643	3 643	3 044	0
WISCONSIN	2 230 060	2.42	65.3	51.5	9.7	28.2	159 885	30.7	31 068	41 370	51 397	82
District 1	273 813	2.54	69.2	53.5	10.6	26.0	18 575	37.5	5 713	4 116	1 745	5
District 2	286 943	2.41	61.8	50.6	7.9	29.2	23 787	19.1	3 069	3 941	13 483	0
District 3	282 266	2.41	66.6	55.0	7.9	26.9	27 169	23.0	2 696	6 088	13 562	52
District 4	261 560	2.37	55.9	30.7	19.7	36.7	17 847	21.7	2 152	4 151	6 745	13
District 5	276 507	2.50	68.0	56.9	7.9	26.8	11 829	51.9	1 053	5 384	2 063	0
District 6	277 669	2.38	66.0	54.9	7.3	27.9	29 217	20.2	11 286	5 797	5 306	3
District 7	284 209	2.37	67.1	55.2	7.5	25.7	13 204	57.1	1 484	5 985	4 088	2
District 8	287 093	2.37	67.3	53.6	9.4	26.7	18 257	43.2	3 615	5 908	4 405	7
WYOMING	207 302	2.42	66.0	53.2	8.3	27.3	14 146	22.1	4 176	2 869	3 850	545
At Large	207 302	2.42	66.0	53.2	8.3	27.3	14 146	22.1	4 176	2 869	3 850	545
PUERTO RICO	1 240 456	3.13	75.7	47.4	23.2	21.2	46 774	23.7	17 283	7 311	2 174	1 199
Delegate District (At Large)	1 240 456	3.13	75.7	47.4	23.2	21.2	46 774	23.7	17 283	7 311	2 174	1 199

[4]No spouse present.

Table A. 110th Congressional Districts—*Continued*

(Number, percent.)

STATE Congressional district	Education, 2006				Income, 2006			Poverty, 2006		
	School enrollment5		Attainment level6 (percent)		Per capita income (dollars)	Median household income (dollars)	Percent of households with income over $100,000	Persons below poverty level (percent)	Families below poverty level (percent)	Percent of households receiving food stamps in past 12 months
	Total	Private (percent)	High school graduate or more	Bachelor's degree or more						
	37	38	39	40	41	42	43	44	45	46
VIRGINIA—*Continued*										
District 6	177 541	21.7	81.0	23.3	23 019	43 223	13.0	12.7	8.1	6.9
District 7	181 264	18.7	87.2	35.9	30 942	59 929	24.2	6.4	4.1	3.5
District 8	142 392	24.5	91.6	60.4	48 450	84 260	40.8	6.9	5.2	1.9
District 9	155 923	9.1	74.9	14.3	18 414	33 069	6.0	17.4	13.0	11.7
District 10	210 894	21.1	89.5	46.5	40 905	87 512	43.5	5.3	3.5	2.3
District 11	218 369	18.6	91.9	51.7	40 476	97 753	48.8	4.2	2.7	1.6
WASHINGTON	1 631 217	14.5	89.0	30.5	27 346	52 583	19.4	11.8	8.0	8.4
District 1	180 941	17.3	93.5	39.2	33 656	66 048	28.6	6.0	3.9	4.1
District 2	183 623	11.1	88.7	25.0	24 728	51 409	15.7	11.4	7.0	7.2
District 3	192 964	11.2	88.8	24.2	24 798	51 282	16.5	11.5	8.6	9.4
District 4	193 842	7.9	76.9	20.5	19 750	42 214	12.9	18.8	14.1	14.1
District 5	191 020	15.6	90.3	26.1	21 544	41 154	10.9	14.8	9.8	11.2
District 6	161 177	13.9	88.2	21.1	22 870	44 396	12.5	14.7	10.8	11.3
District 7	149 810	24.6	90.8	50.5	37 188	58 137	24.7	12.4	7.6	6.9
District 8	204 245	17.5	93.2	41.3	35 924	76 115	33.9	6.2	3.6	3.8
District 9	173 595	13.2	89.5	24.6	25 808	51 420	17.0	10.9	7.6	8.2
WEST VIRGINIA	412 825	10.0	81.0	16.5	19 417	35 059	8.2	17.3	12.7	12.3
District 1	145 223	8.6	84.6	18.4	19 378	34 198	8.5	17.6	12.2	11.7
District 2	137 451	12.2	82.9	18.2	21 349	39 965	10.3	14.0	10.6	10.5
District 3	130 151	9.2	75.4	12.9	17 394	31 282	5.8	20.6	15.3	14.9
WISCONSIN	1 418 004	17.2	88.4	25.1	24 875	48 772	14.3	11.0	7.3	5.9
District 1	182 970	17.8	88.2	24.0	25 627	54 697	17.6	9.5	6.9	5.3
District 2	201 877	12.5	92.3	36.6	28 510	54 238	19.1	9.9	4.9	4.4
District 3	180 224	11.9	88.8	22.8	22 793	46 638	12.1	11.0	7.0	5.0
District 4	184 994	23.9	79.8	19.2	18 534	34 929	7.2	24.3	19.6	14.1
District 5	177 028	24.6	92.7	37.9	33 314	64 087	25.1	5.1	3.2	2.9
District 6	163 372	17.8	87.3	19.1	23 468	47 276	11.2	8.4	5.4	5.0
District 7	159 391	13.1	87.6	19.1	22 673	44 843	10.4	10.3	6.6	5.8
District 8	168 148	16.3	88.7	21.2	23 348	46 267	11.6	10.4	7.7	5.2
WYOMING	129 477	10.3	90.2	22.7	24 544	47 423	14.1	9.4	6.3	5.0
At Large	129 477	10.3	90.2	22.7	24 544	47 423	14.1	9.4	6.3	5.0
PUERTO RICO	1 119 076	31.6	66.1	20.7	9 474	17 621	3.2	45.4	41.6	29.7
Delegate District (At Large)	1 119 076	31.6	66.1	20.7	9 474	17 621	3.2	45.4	41.6	29.7

5All persons 3 years old and over enrolled in nursery school through college.
6Persons 25 years old and over.

Table A. 110th Congressional Districts—*Continued*

(Number, percent.)

STATE Congressional district	Total	Total occupied units	Housing units, 2006							
			Owner-occupied units							
			Percent owner-occupied units	Median value (dollars)	Percent valued at $500,000 or more	Median real estate taxes (dollars)	Median monthly costs (dollars)	Percent with second mortgage or home equity loan	Median cost as percent of income	
									With a mortgage	Without a mortgage
	47	48	49	50	51	52	53	54	55	56
VIRGINIA—*Continued*										
District 6	297 349	267 817	68.6	156 600	4.2	1 040	779	18.7	22.2	11.0
District 7	306 393	284 861	72.8	239 700	10.7	1 613	1 236	25.5	23.5	10.9
District 8	303 055	274 875	57.9	528 000	53.6	4 039	2 005	28.0	23.9	11.1
District 9	304 022	261 921	72.1	88 800	1.5	499	394	10.0	21.2	9.5
District 10	299 747	266 899	79.0	490 600	48.3	3 610	2 061	31.4	25.5	11.5
District 11	269 355	254 399	79.3	542 500	56.8	4 014	2 101	32.6	25.0	9.9
WASHINGTON	2 699 658	2 471 912	65.5	267 600	15.6	2 356	1 277	23.3	26.5	12.1
District 1	296 842	281 225	67.2	370 900	23.9	3 073	1 684	28.5	26.9	12.9
District 2	312 855	280 042	68.2	275 900	13.1	2 214	1 309	22.6	28.6	13.2
District 3	302 420	276 800	69.9	231 900	8.3	2 067	1 208	26.8	26.3	11.5
District 4	276 974	247 897	66.2	150 300	3.3	1 473	888	13.7	23.6	10.2
District 5	302 525	273 018	65.9	158 000	3.9	1 497	866	16.1	24.7	11.1
District 6	309 443	272 525	62.8	225 000	9.2	1 948	1 055	18.0	26.6	12.8
District 7	316 177	289 253	54.3	422 100	34.9	3 322	1 737	26.3	27.7	12.9
District 8	298 162	283 722	74.9	383 700	32.0	3 279	1 737	30.3	26.3	12.1
District 9	284 260	267 430	60.4	262 600	9.5	2 496	1 373	24.9	26.6	13.0
WEST VIRGINIA	877 587	743 064	74.7	89 700	1.5	422	462	9.3	20.2	9.9
District 1	285 111	243 934	72.8	88 100	1.0	447	489	9.6	20.5	11.2
District 2	300 160	254 757	76.0	112 100	2.9	552	571	11.5	20.1	9.8
District 3	292 316	244 373	75.1	74 800	0.6	284	352	6.6	20.0	9.0
WISCONSIN	2 532 958	2 230 060	70.5	163 500	3.7	2 845	1 052	21.8	24.6	14.2
District 1	303 288	273 813	71.8	185 300	4.0	3 339	1 204	22.5	24.9	14.6
District 2	319 620	286 943	67.2	200 300	4.9	3 506	1 302	26.7	24.9	13.9
District 3	308 382	282 266	74.1	143 700	2.9	2 463	929	18.6	24.4	14.1
District 4	288 536	261 560	49.2	140 100	1.3	3 056	1 061	18.3	26.5	17.8
District 5	291 249	276 507	75.3	234 900	8.8	3 818	1 375	25.9	24.5	14.1
District 6	313 306	277 669	73.6	139 300	2.0	2 550	947	20.6	24.4	14.2
District 7	353 261	284 209	77.4	128 600	2.3	2 020	817	18.1	23.9	13.4
District 8	355 316	287 093	73.7	146 300	2.9	2 412	957	23.1	24.4	14.1
WYOMING	239 088	207 302	69.5	148 900	6.0	792	749	13.5	22.1	9.0
At Large	239 088	207 302	69.5	148 900	6.0	792	749	13.5	22.1	9.0
PUERTO RICO	1 437 597	1 240 456	74.1	98 700	1.8	110	246	2.3	29.1	11.0
Delegate District (At Large)	1 437 597	1 240 456	74.1	98 700	1.8	110	246	2.3	29.1	11.0

Table A. 110th Congressional Districts—*Continued*

(Number, percent.)

STATE Congressional district	Housing units, 2006—*Continued*			Civilian labor force, 2006			Civilian employment and occupation, 2006			
	Renter-occupied units		Sub-standard housing units (percent)[7]	Total	Unemployment		Total civilian employment	Management, professional, and related (percent)	Service, sales, and office (percent)	Construction and production (percent)
	Median gross rent (dollars)	Median gross rent as a percent of income			Total	Rate[8]				
	57	58	59	60	61	62	63	64	65	66
VIRGINIA—*Continued*										
District 6	596	26.4	1.7	341 979	14 274	4.2	327 705	30.9	41.7	26.6
District 7	857	27.5	1.4	392 677	18 161	4.6	374 516	41.3	40.5	17.6
District 8	1 233	27.2	2.1	395 704	11 250	2.8	384 454	57.8	31.9	10.3
District 9	488	28.3	1.1	296 672	19 594	6.6	277 078	27.4	39.8	32.1
District 10	1 173	30.1	1.6	437 041	12 700	2.9	424 341	48.9	35.5	15.4
District 11	1 407	28.8	1.5	408 822	15 836	3.9	392 986	53.0	35.0	11.9
WASHINGTON	779	29.0	2.9	3 296 812	212 160	6.4	3 084 652	36.7	40.7	20.9
District 1	940	28.1	1.7	389 797	18 693	4.8	371 104	44.1	38.8	17.0
District 2	795	30.0	2.8	362 174	18 988	5.2	343 186	29.3	44.1	25.1
District 3	748	30.9	2.3	380 781	25 801	6.8	354 980	32.1	42.3	24.4
District 4	605	29.1	6.5	348 387	32 990	9.5	315 397	28.5	38.6	23.0
District 5	608	29.9	2.1	337 200	23 249	6.9	313 951	34.8	43.6	20.2
District 6	716	29.5	2.5	321 235	27 904	8.7	293 331	30.4	43.7	24.9
District 7	836	27.6	2.9	389 402	20 496	5.3	368 906	49.6	36.0	14.3
District 8	997	27.3	2.5	411 923	21 884	5.3	390 039	44.8	36.6	18.3
District 9	804	28.7	3.3	355 913	22 155	6.2	333 758	32.7	44.3	22.7
WEST VIRGINIA	499	29.0	1.5	820 283	56 115	6.8	764 168	28.3	42.4	28.8
District 1	511	32.1	1.7	282 785	20 793	7.4	261 992	28.6	42.9	28.1
District 2	536	27.2	1.5	296 550	18 225	6.1	278 325	29.2	40.5	29.7
District 3	451	27.8	1.2	240 948	17 097	7.1	223 851	26.7	44.2	28.3
WISCONSIN	658	28.4	1.9	3 056 451	169 015	5.5	2 887 436	31.8	40.8	26.5
District 1	721	28.2	1.6	384 401	22 809	5.9	361 592	32.1	40.0	27.4
District 2	731	28.9	1.7	418 019	17 573	4.2	400 446	39.2	40.3	19.8
District 3	564	27.2	2.1	397 323	18 901	4.8	378 422	29.9	40.6	27.7
District 4	671	32.9	3.8	319 332	31 325	9.8	288 007	27.7	46.6	25.4
District 5	788	27.2	0.9	395 611	14 136	3.6	381 475	39.7	40.1	19.6
District 6	590	26.1	1.4	381 924	18 770	4.9	363 154	26.6	39.6	32.5
District 7	543	26.8	1.9	375 394	21 373	5.7	354 021	27.9	39.9	30.8
District 8	601	26.9	1.6	384 447	24 128	6.3	360 319	28.9	40.7	29.3
WYOMING	601	24.9	2.2	282 679	10 011	3.5	272 668	30.1	39.1	29.7
At Large	601	24.9	2.2	282 679	10 011	3.5	272 668	30.1	39.1	29.7
PUERTO RICO	395	33.5	13.7	1 440 509	226 760	15.7	1 213 749	29.1	47.2	22.8
Delegate District (At Large)	395	33.5	13.7	1 440 509	226 760	15.7	1 213 749	29.1	47.2	22.8

[7]Overcrowded or lacking complete plumbing facilities.
[8]Percent of civilian labor force.

Table A. 110th Congressional Districts—*Continued*

(Number, percent.)

STATE Congressional district	Social Security Beneficiaries (OASDI), December 2006							Supplemental Security Income, December 2006			
	Total	Rate per 1,000 population	Retired workers[9]	Disabled workers	Widow(er)s[10]	Spouses[11]	Children[12]	Total	Aged	Blind	Disabled
	67	68	69	70	71	72	73	74	75	76	77
VIRGINIA—*Continued*											
District 6	135 395	200.4	87 075	20 181	11 908	5 987	10 244	13 100	1 250	136	11 714
District 7	114 176	157.7	76 363	13 730	10 361	5 085	8 637	8 504	1 265	97	7 142
District 8	57 912	88.1	41 866	5 162	4 800	2 898	3 186	7 178	2 952	57	4 169
District 9	162 793	256.1	80 280	39 410	16 960	9 451	16 692	24 574	2 010	151	22 413
District 10	71 640	91.1	49 042	6 863	6 339	3 884	5 512	5 979	2 000	76	3 903
District 11	65 140	87.2	46 407	4 793	5 140	4 073	4 727	6 071	2 711	65	3 295
WASHINGTON	961 739	150.4	631 195	130 146	81 793	52 308	66 297	119 108	15 043	922	103 143
District 1	87 164	122.6	60 687	8 878	7 626	4 780	5 193	7 395	1 680	68	5 647
District 2	116 181	159.9	76 788	15 371	9 779	6 706	7 537	11 725	1 169	102	10 454
District 3	125 425	167.8	79 961	18 190	10 810	6 915	9 549	14 484	1 325	131	13 028
District 4	109 551	152.1	71 940	15 015	8 857	5 702	8 037	14 309	1 414	94	12 801
District 5	123 986	179.2	78 285	18 642	11 006	6 887	9 166	16 373	1 113	107	15 153
District 6	130 368	189.5	83 799	19 166	11 369	7 107	8 927	18 627	1 434	141	17 052
District 7	84 137	130.8	57 113	12 169	6 765	3 602	4 488	15 765	3 318	128	12 319
District 8	87 958	113.9	60 548	8 992	7 089	5 339	5 990	7 360	1 696	46	5 618
District 9	96 969	139.4	62 074	13 723	8 492	5 270	7 410	13 070	1 894	105	11 071
WEST VIRGINIA	419 477	230.7	212 985	83 143	52 459	30 954	39 936	77 999	4 024	576	73 399
District 1	132 860	222.1	74 304	21 174	16 877	10 144	10 361	20 451	1 144	171	19 136
District 2	136 768	217.1	74 424	25 111	15 582	9 250	12 401	21 951	1 500	192	20 259
District 3	149 849	253.9	64 257	36 858	20 000	11 560	17 174	35 597	1 380	213	34 004
WISCONSIN	966 818	174.0	649 341	116 190	87 487	46 138	67 662	93 663	8 191	906	84 566
District 1	120 665	168.9	80 707	15 051	10 652	5 030	9 225	9 767	646	98	9 023
District 2	103 735	145.1	71 347	12 411	8 617	4 229	7 131	9 126	695	91	8 340
District 3	126 434	178.6	84 113	15 021	12 007	6 765	8 528	10 659	1 262	116	9 281
District 4	96 679	151.5	54 835	18 997	8 464	3 110	11 273	31 016	2 008	250	28 758
District 5	119 604	169.9	86 873	10 122	10 747	5 824	6 038	4 748	768	52	3 928
District 6	130 589	189.1	90 109	14 368	11 566	6 196	8 350	8 101	746	93	7 262
District 7	141 213	205.7	94 852	16 350	13 364	7 832	8 815	11 286	1 216	114	9 956
District 8	127 899	182.7	86 505	13 870	12 070	7 152	8 302	8 960	850	92	8 018
WYOMING	82 748	160.7	55 007	9 918	7 576	4 462	5 785	5 951	422	42	5 487
At Large	82 748	160.7	55 007	9 918	7 576	4 462	5 785	5 951	422	42	5 487
PUERTO RICO	723 203	184.1	344 564	139 966	80 944	65 113	65 113	. . .	. . .	. . .	. . .
Delegate District (At Large)	. . .	. . .	. . .	. . .	. . .	. . .	. . .	. . .	. . .	. . .	. . .

[9]Includes special age-72 beneficiaries.
[10]Includes nondisabled widow(er)s, disabled widow(er)s, widowed mothers and fathers, and parents receiving payment on the record of a worker who is deceased.
[11]These beneficiaries receive payment on the record of a worker who is retired or disabled.
[12]These beneficiaries receive payment on the record of a worker who is retired, deceased, or disabled.
. . . = Not available.

Table A. 110th Congressional Districts—*Continued*

(Number, percent.)

STATE Congressional district	Total farms	Farms by size (percent)			Land in farms		Percent of farms where principal operator's primary occupation is farming	Value of all agricultural products sold				Payments from federal farm programs		
		1 to 49 acres	50 to 999 acres	1,000 acres or more	Total acreage	Average size of farms (acres)		Total ($1,000)	Percent of farms with value of:			Total ($1,000)	Number of farms that receive payments	Percent of farms that receive payments
									Less than $50,000	$50,000 to $249,999	$250,000 or more			
	78	79	80	81	82	83	84	85	86	87	88	89	90	91
VIRGINIA—*Continued*														
District 6	7 634	36.0	61.7	2.3	1 278 792	168	55.7	718 577	79.9	9.3	10.8	9 742	1 358	17.8
District 7	4 539	40.6	56.7	2.8	767 654	169	52.5	265 184	87.7	7.0	5.3	4 539	842	18.6
District 8	17	70.6	29.4	0.0	578	34	35.3	950	94.1	0.0	5.9	. . .	. . .	. . .
District 9	14 103	37.0	61.3	1.8	2 050 132	145	51.7	324 654	92.5	5.9	1.6	5 691	1 760	12.5
District 10	3 736	51.0	47.0	2.0	516 614	138	49.4	95 434	92.7	5.4	1.9	1 814	319	8.5
District 11	377	59.2	40.1	0.8	33 690	89	45.9	10 926	93.6	4.0	2.4	234	40	10.6
WASHINGTON	35 939	57.5	34.2	8.3	15 318 008	426	58.5	5 330 740	75.6	14.1	10.3	133 763	7 332	20.4
District 1	727	87.3	12.5	0.1	20 984	29	54.1	86 434	88.7	5.1	6.2	230	24	3.3
District 2	4 258	68.9	30.2	0.9	353 378	83	55.1	609 838	79.9	9.2	10.8	6 947	422	9.9
District 3	4 829	68.0	31.2	0.7	363 097	75	51.8	279 750	90.2	5.5	4.3	1 584	179	3.7
District 4	11 752	55.2	36.8	8.0	5 904 194	502	63.6	2 924 142	63.5	20.5	16.0	54 917	3 026	25.7
District 5	9 367	35.8	43.5	20.7	8 443 095	901	60.8	1 081 288	72.4	18.0	9.6	68 578	3 504	37.4
District 6	1 976	73.5	25.9	0.7	123 993	63	50.3	127 490	91.4	5.0	3.6	504	65	3.3
District 7	116	90.5	9.5	0.0	2 115	18	59.5	9 274	88.8	6.9	4.3	8	12	10.3
District 8	1 782	84.2	15.7	0.1	61 064	34	52.5	96 645	91.1	4.7	4.2	941	73	4.1
District 9	1 132	80.9	18.8	0.3	46 088	41	53.6	115 879	89.1	5.7	5.1	54	27	2.4
WEST VIRGINIA	20 812	27.3	71.0	1.7	3 584 668	172	50.5	482 814	94.8	3.3	1.9	5 180	1 675	8.0
District 1	8 127	25.7	73.3	1.0	1 296 090	159	50.5	100 866	97.0	2.1	0.9	971	426	5.2
District 2	8 207	28.9	68.9	2.2	1 480 527	180	50.7	305 038	92.6	4.0	3.4	3 116	814	9.9
District 3	4 478	27.1	70.9	2.1	808 051	180	50.0	76 910	94.9	4.1	1.0	1 093	435	9.7
WISCONSIN	77 131	27.6	69.9	2.5	15 741 552	204	59.4	5 623 275	72.6	21.4	6.1	247 942	37 234	48.3
District 1	2 966	47.5	48.0	4.6	621 006	209	55.9	269 672	73.2	18.4	8.5	11 025	1 277	43.1
District 2	7 821	36.7	60.3	3.1	1 546 841	198	58.1	678 738	71.9	20.9	7.2	31 962	4 275	54.7
District 3	27 124	22.7	75.0	2.3	5 714 323	211	57.7	1 649 004	74.2	20.7	5.1	87 439	14 812	54.6
District 4	. . .	. . .	. . .	. . .	. . .	. . .	. . .	. . .	. . .	. . .	. . .	. . .	. . .	. . .
District 5	2 335	43.3	54.5	2.2	350 259	150	57.9	165 210	75.8	18.0	6.2	6 520	1 001	42.9
District 6	10 625	31.3	65.9	2.8	2 175 334	205	63.0	981 682	68.4	23.2	8.4	41 084	5 560	52.3
District 7	16 407	21.7	76.2	2.1	3 491 740	213	60.2	1 048 406	73.2	22.3	4.4	37 761	5 685	34.6
District 8	9 853	30.0	67.9	2.1	1 842 049	187	61.0	830 563	70.8	21.8	7.3	32 151	4 624	46.9
WYOMING	9 422	21.4	44.3	34.3	34 402 726	3 651	61.1	863 887	70.2	21.9	7.8	37 913	3 163	33.6
At Large	9 422	21.4	44.3	34.3	34 402 726	3 651	61.1	863 887	70.2	21.9	7.8	37 913	3 163	33.6
PUERTO RICO	. . .	. . .	. . .	. . .	670 743	38	49.3	581 544	91.5	. . .	. . .	56 294	6 051	34.3
Delegate District (At Large)	. . .	. . .	. . .	. . .	670 743	38	49.3	581 544	91.5	. . .	. . .	56 294	6 051	34.3

. . . = Not available.

Table B. 110th Congressional Districts by Counties, 2000

(Number, percent.)

STATE Congressional district County	Land area,[1] (sq km)	Population				Percent with bachelor's degree or more[3]	Median household income, 1999 (dollars)	Percent living in poverty	Percent unem- ployed	Households	
		Total	Percent minority[2]	Percent under 18 years	Percent 65 years and over					Total	Percent owner occupied
	1	2	3	4	5	6	7	8	9	10	11
UNITED STATES	9 161 923	281 421 906	30.9	25.6	12.4	24.4	41 994	12.4	5.8	105 480 101	66.2
ALABAMA	131 426	4 447 100	29.7	25.2	13.0	19.0	34 135	16.1	6.2	1 737 080	72.5
Congressional District 1, Alabama	16 361	635 498	32.2	26.7	13.0	18.5	34 739	16.9	6.8	241 434	73.1
Baldwin County	4 135	140 415	13.9	24.4	15.4	23.1	40 250	10.1	4.3	55 336	79.6
Clarke County (part)	1 123	14 379	30.2	27.0	14.0	14.1	33 537	18.8	6.6	5 534	81.5
Escambia County	2 454	38 440	36.2	24.2	13.4	10.6	28 319	20.9	7.0	14 297	77.1
Mobile County	3 194	399 843	37.5	27.5	12.0	18.6	33 710	18.5	7.6	150 179	68.9
Monroe County	2 657	24 324	42.7	28.2	13.9	11.8	29 093	21.3	8.4	9 383	80.4
Washington County	2 799	18 097	35.4	28.8	12.7	8.6	30 815	18.5	7.7	6 705	88.2
Congressional District 2, Alabama	27 199	635 311	32.9	25.5	13.3	18.0	32 460	17.2	6.4	246 539	71.6
Autauga County	1 544	43 671	20.4	28.6	10.2	18.0	42 013	10.9	4.9	16 003	80.8
Barbour County	2 292	29 038	49.1	25.4	13.5	10.9	25 101	26.8	5.7	10 409	73.2
Bullock County	1 619	11 714	76.1	25.7	12.9	7.7	20 605	33.5	8.6	3 986	74.4
Butler County	2 012	21 399	42.0	26.9	16.4	10.4	24 791	24.6	10.6	8 398	76.2
Coffee County	1 759	43 615	24.1	24.7	14.3	19.3	33 664	14.7	5.7	17 421	71.4
Conecuh County	2 204	14 089	44.8	25.8	15.8	9.2	22 111	26.6	9.8	5 792	81.1
Covington County	2 678	37 631	14.4	23.6	17.9	12.2	26 336	18.4	7.6	15 640	77.7
Crenshaw County	1 579	13 665	26.7	24.7	17.3	11.2	26 054	22.1	5.4	5 577	76.6
Dale County	1 453	49 129	27.2	26.7	11.7	14.0	31 998	15.1	7.7	18 878	64.2
Elmore County	1 609	65 874	23.5	25.6	10.9	16.6	41 243	10.2	5.0	22 737	81.4
Geneva County	1 493	25 764	13.8	24.0	16.3	8.7	26 448	19.6	8.0	10 477	80.6
Henry County	1 455	16 310	34.3	24.2	16.2	14.1	30 353	19.1	6.3	6 525	80.9
Houston County	1 503	88 787	27.1	25.9	13.6	18.4	34 431	15.0	5.2	35 834	69.5
Lowndes County	1 859	13 473	74.2	30.0	12.4	11.0	23 050	31.4	11.9	4 909	83.4
Montgomery County (part)	404	131 547	44.3	24.8	12.3	29.8	36 905	15.9	5.7	52 020	61.0
Pike County	1 738	29 605	39.8	24.2	12.5	18.4	25 551	23.1	9.3	11 933	67.2
Congressional District 3, Alabama	20 290	635 374	35.1	24.6	12.9	16.7	30 806	18.8	6.7	248 689	71.0
Calhoun County	1 576	112 249	21.9	23.6	14.1	15.2	31 768	16.1	6.6	45 307	72.5
Chambers County	1 547	36 583	39.6	24.7	16.1	9.5	29 667	17.0	6.5	14 522	75.7
Cherokee County	1 433	23 988	7.3	22.1	16.0	9.7	30 874	15.6	3.9	9 719	81.7
Clay County	1 567	14 254	18.7	23.8	16.7	7.8	27 885	17.1	5.5	5 765	77.2
Cleburne County	1 451	14 123	6.4	24.2	13.8	9.2	30 820	13.9	5.3	5 590	80.4
Coosa County (part)	976	9 085	47.8	24.4	13.7	8.3	29 900	16.5	7.1	3 373	83.4
Lee County	1 577	115 092	26.8	23.2	8.1	27.9	30 952	21.8	5.8	45 702	62.1
Macon County	1 581	24 105	86.3	25.2	14.0	18.8	21 180	32.8	12.3	8 950	67.3
Montgomery County (part)	1 642	91 963	62.2	27.1	11.1	26.6	34 248	19.4	8.0	34 048	68.7
Randolph County	1 505	22 380	24.3	25.1	15.8	10.0	28 675	17.0	5.3	8 642	79.1
Russell County	1 661	49 756	44.4	26.5	13.1	9.7	27 492	19.9	6.3	19 741	62.4
Talladega County	1 915	80 321	33.6	25.0	13.4	11.2	31 628	17.6	7.7	30 674	76.4
Tallapoosa County	1 859	41 475	26.7	24.1	16.5	14.1	30 745	16.6	6.1	16 656	76.3
Congressional District 4, Alabama	21 684	635 365	9.5	24.2	14.5	11.3	31 344	14.7	5.6	251 545	78.0
Blount County	1 672	51 024	7.6	25.6	12.7	9.6	35 241	11.7	4.8	19 265	83.5
Cullman County	1 913	77 483	4.8	24.2	14.6	11.9	32 256	13.0	4.1	30 706	78.1
DeKalb County	2 015	64 452	9.3	24.7	13.8	8.3	30 137	15.4	5.1	25 113	78.7
Etowah County	1 385	103 459	17.8	23.9	16.0	13.4	31 170	15.7	6.0	41 615	74.4
Fayette County	1 626	18 495	13.5	23.9	16.2	9.2	28 539	17.3	7.7	7 493	77.2
Franklin County	1 646	31 223	12.5	24.2	14.9	9.7	27 177	18.9	5.6	12 259	74.3
Lamar County	1 567	15 904	13.4	23.6	15.9	7.8	28 059	16.1	7.1	6 468	76.9
Marion County	1 920	31 214	5.7	22.5	15.8	8.0	27 475	15.6	8.1	12 697	77.9
Marshall County	1 469	82 231	8.0	24.8	14.3	13.9	32 167	14.7	5.7	32 547	74.7
Morgan County (part)	1 309	49 940	5.4	25.1	12.1	17.5	40 615	9.5	4.8	19 202	83.4
Pickens County (part)	1 215	9 365	18.9	24.1	17.1	9.5	30 841	16.6	4.6	3 759	81.1
St. Clair County (part)	300	5 019	6.4	24.0	12.9	12.6	34 317	11.6	6.0	1 950	82.8
Walker County	2 057	70 713	8.5	23.5	14.7	9.1	29 076	16.5	6.4	28 364	80.0
Winston County	1 591	24 843	3.3	23.7	14.2	8.3	28 435	17.1	6.3	10 107	80.0
Congressional District 5, Alabama	11 618	635 179	22.3	24.9	12.3	23.5	38 054	12.5	5.5	252 745	72.5
Colbert County	1 540	54 984	19.0	23.8	15.4	14.1	31 954	14.0	5.2	22 461	75.7
Jackson County	2 794	53 926	8.7	24.1	13.3	10.4	32 020	13.7	5.1	21 615	77.9
Lauderdale County	1 734	87 966	12.3	23.0	15.1	18.5	33 354	14.4	5.6	36 088	73.2
Lawrence County	1 796	34 803	22.7	25.6	12.1	7.5	31 549	15.3	6.2	13 538	83.1
Limestone County	1 471	65 676	17.5	24.8	11.2	16.9	37 405	12.3	4.3	24 688	77.3
Madison County	2 085	276 700	29.0	25.5	10.8	34.3	44 704	10.5	5.7	109 955	69.9
Morgan County (part)	199	61 124	26.2	25.7	12.4	19.2	35 416	14.6	5.9	24 400	65.1
Congressional District 6, Alabama	11 821	634 742	11.2	24.4	12.3	29.6	46 946	8.1	3.4	249 160	78.0
Bibb County	1 614	20 826	23.8	25.4	11.6	7.1	31 420	20.6	6.2	7 421	80.2
Chilton County	1 797	39 593	14.5	25.7	12.8	9.9	32 588	15.7	4.3	15 287	82.2
Coosa County (part)	713	3 117	2.9	21.7	15.7	7.4	29 776	10.6	7.2	1 309	88.5
Jefferson County (part)	2 205	326 606	10.4	23.3	14.2	33.6	48 878	6.3	3.2	132 030	74.8
St. Clair County (part)	1 341	59 723	10.8	25.5	11.5	11.0	37 642	12.1	4.0	22 193	83.8

[1]Dry land or land partially or temporarily covered by water.
[2]Persons who do not identify themselves as White alone, not of Hispanic origin.
[3]Persons 25 years old and over.

Table B. 110th Congressional Districts by Counties, 2000—Continued

(Number, percent.)

STATE Congressional district County	Land area,[1] (sq km)	Population Total	Population Percent minority[2]	Population Percent under 18 years	Population Percent 65 years and over	Percent with bachelor's degree or more[3]	Median household income, 1999 (dollars)	Percent living in poverty	Percent unemployed	Households Total	Households Percent owner occupied
	1	2	3	4	5	6	7	8	9	10	11
Congressional District 6, Alabama—*Continued*											
Shelby County	2 058	143 293	11.3	26.2	8.4	36.8	55 440	6.3	3.0	54 631	80.9
Tuscaloosa County (part)	2 092	41 584	9.0	24.7	11.3	31.6	47 231	8.4	4.0	16 289	80.5
Congressional District 7, Alabama	22 453	635 631	64.5	26.3	13.0	15.1	26 672	24.7	9.5	246 968	62.8
Choctaw County	2 366	15 922	45.4	25.9	14.4	9.6	24 749	24.5	8.8	6 363	86.3
Clarke County (part)	2 084	13 488	58.9	29.1	12.8	9.8	23 692	26.6	11.6	5 044	80.7
Dallas County	2 540	46 365	64.7	28.5	13.9	13.9	23 370	31.1	11.2	17 841	65.7
Greene County	1 673	9 974	81.4	29.1	15.0	10.5	19 819	34.3	13.1	3 931	75.6
Hale County	1 667	17 185	60.5	29.4	13.6	8.1	25 807	26.9	8.0	6 415	80.2
Jefferson County (part)	677	335 441	73.9	26.3	13.2	15.1	27 298	23.1	9.9	131 235	58.1
Marengo County	2 531	22 539	53.1	28.4	14.8	12.1	27 025	25.9	8.7	8 767	79.2
Perry County	1 863	11 861	69.3	29.8	15.1	10.0	20 200	35.4	14.7	4 333	73.8
Pickens County (part)	1 068	11 584	64.0	29.9	13.6	10.1	23 413	31.7	11.6	4 327	77.5
Sumter County	2 344	14 798	74.3	29.1	13.9	12.4	18 911	38.7	11.5	5 708	72.3
Tuscaloosa County (part)	1 338	123 291	40.5	23.0	11.2	21.1	30 658	20.1	6.9	48 228	57.7
Wilcox County	2 302	13 183	72.7	30.4	13.8	10.1	16 646	39.9	15.2	4 776	83.3
ALASKA	1 481 347	626 932	32.4	30.4	5.6	24.7	51 571	9.4	9.0	221 600	62.5
Congressional District (At Large), Alaska	1 481 347	626 932	32.4	30.4	5.6	24.7	51 571	9.4	9.0	221 600	62.5
Aleutians East Borough	18 099	2 697	80.8	16.1	2.3	4.9	47 875	21.8	41.4	526	58.4
Aleutians West Census Area	11 388	5 465	62.3	17.1	1.7	11.0	61 406	11.9	12.7	1 270	27.8
Anchorage Municipality	4 396	260 283	30.1	29.1	5.3	28.9	55 546	7.3	6.8	94 822	60.0
Bethel Census Area	105 240	16 006	87.9	39.9	5.3	13.1	35 701	20.6	14.6	4 226	60.9
Bristol Bay Borough	1 308	1 258	47.6	31.2	5.0	21.1	52 167	9.5	10.5	490	51.0
Denali Borough	33 021	1 893	15.2	24.0	3.1	22.7	53 654	7.9	11.6	785	64.7
Dillingham Census Area	48 367	4 922	79.0	38.5	5.6	16.4	43 079	21.4	11.5	1 529	60.6
Fairbanks North Star Borough	19 078	82 840	23.9	30.0	4.7	27.0	49 076	7.8	9.1	29 777	54.0
Haines Borough	6 070	2 392	18.5	25.9	10.7	23.8	40 772	10.7	13.7	991	69.7
Juneau City and Borough	7 036	30 711	26.7	27.6	6.2	36.0	62 034	6.0	5.4	11 543	63.8
Kenai Peninsula Borough	41 474	49 691	14.9	30.0	7.3	20.3	46 397	10.0	11.4	18 438	73.7
Ketchikan Gateway Borough	3 194	14 070	27.1	28.2	7.5	20.2	51 344	6.5	7.6	5 399	60.7
Kodiak Island Borough	16 990	13 913	42.9	32.5	4.6	18.7	54 636	6.6	5.2	4 424	54.8
Lake and Peninsula Borough	61 595	1 823	81.0	38.0	5.7	12.4	36 442	18.9	14.3	588	67.5
Matanuska-Susitna Borough	63 925	59 322	13.8	32.2	5.8	18.3	51 221	11.0	10.3	20 556	78.8
Nome Census Area	59 572	9 196	81.1	37.0	6.0	14.7	41 250	17.4	16.4	2 693	58.2
North Slope Borough	230 035	7 385	83.2	38.2	4.2	17.0	63 173	9.1	14.9	2 109	48.8
Northwest Arctic Borough	92 976	7 208	87.9	41.4	5.2	12.7	45 976	17.4	15.6	1 780	56.3
Prince of Wales-Outer Ketchikan Census Area	19 193	6 146	48.0	30.9	5.7	14.2	40 636	12.1	15.0	2 262	70.1
Sitka City and Borough	7 444	8 835	33.5	26.8	7.6	29.5	51 901	7.8	7.8	3 278	58.1
Skagway-Hoonah-Angoon Census Area	20 452	3 436	42.6	26.8	7.1	21.6	40 879	12.8	15.7	1 369	63.6
Southeast Fairbanks Census Area	64 270	6 174	22.0	32.8	6.1	18.2	38 776	18.9	17.7	2 098	69.1
Valdez-Cordova Census Area	88 886	10 195	25.5	29.7	5.7	21.2	48 734	9.8	9.6	3 884	67.8
Wade Hampton Census Area	44 531	7 028	95.1	46.7	5.1	9.1	30 184	26.2	23.9	1 602	66.4
Wrangell-Petersburg Census Area	15 112	6 684	27.5	29.7	9.7	16.3	46 434	7.9	11.0	2 587	70.4
Yakutat City and Borough	19 815	808	50.7	27.5	4.5	17.6	46 786	13.5	7.8	265	59.6
Yukon-Koyukuk Census Area	377 878	6 551	75.7	35.1	7.2	14.2	28 666	23.8	19.9	2 309	67.2
ARIZONA	294 312	5 130 632	36.2	26.6	13.0	23.5	40 558	13.9	5.6	1 901 327	68.0
Congressional District 1, Arizona	151 795	641 710	41.6	28.1	13.7	17.5	32 979	20.3	8.9	223 930	71.5
Apache County	29 021	69 423	82.5	38.4	8.4	11.3	23 344	37.8	21.8	19 971	74.3
Coconino County (part)	41 706	114 993	41.7	28.5	6.8	30.2	38 313	18.1	6.9	40 092	61.4
Gila County	12 348	51 335	31.0	25.1	20.0	13.9	30 917	17.4	9.7	20 140	78.7
Graham County	11 990	33 489	44.8	30.1	11.7	11.8	29 668	23.0	11.6	10 116	73.2
Greenlee County	4 784	8 547	46.7	31.8	9.8	12.2	39 384	9.9	6.3	3 117	51.0
Navajo County (part)	21 487	91 658	55.4	35.5	10.0	12.4	29 115	28.5	11.9	28 381	75.4
Pinal County (part)	9 474	104 748	51.0	26.2	12.7	10.0	34 563	18.2	8.7	31 942	71.7
Yavapai County (part)	20 985	167 517	13.5	21.1	21.9	21.1	34 901	11.9	5.0	70 171	73.4
Congressional District 2, Arizona	52 369	641 435	21.6	23.9	20.5	19.3	42 432	8.9	5.0	249 789	79.3
Coconino County (part)	6 513	1 327	96.6	38.4	9.6	7.4	35 655	27.9	15.6	356	57.3
La Paz County (part)	858	58	0.0	12.1	25.9	9.8	25 972	15.5	0.0	28	67.9
Maricopa County (part)	6 176	479 206	22.3	24.0	20.7	22.5	47 498	6.7	4.3	184 934	81.3
Mohave County	34 477	155 032	16.0	23.0	20.4	9.9	31 521	13.9	7.0	62 809	73.6
Navajo County (part)	4 292	5 812	95.8	36.2	8.8	10.6	20 308	44.6	18.0	1 662	77.3
Yavapai County (part)	54	0	X	X	X	X	X	X	X	0	X
Congressional District 3, Arizona	1 550	640 898	21.4	24.9	10.3	30.3	48 108	8.7	4.0	254 432	66.4
Maricopa County (part)	1 550	640 898	21.4	24.9	10.3	30.3	48 108	8.7	4.0	254 432	66.4
Congressional District 4, Arizona	516	641 430	70.8	32.9	6.8	10.2	30 624	25.6	8.4	196 221	50.8
Maricopa County (part)	516	641 430	70.8	32.9	6.8	10.2	30 624	25.6	8.4	196 221	50.8

[1]Dry land or land partially or temporarily covered by water.
[2]Persons who do not identify themselves as White alone, not of Hispanic origin.
[3]Persons 25 years old and over.
X = Not applicable.

Table B. 110th Congressional Districts by Counties, 2000—*Continued*

(Number, percent.)

STATE Congressional district County	Land area,[1] (sq km)	Population Total	Population Percent minority[2]	Population Percent under 18 years	Population Percent 65 years and over	Percent with bachelor's degree or more[3]	Median household income, 1999 (dollars)	Percent living in poverty	Percent unem- ployed	Households Total	Households Percent owner occupied
	1	2	3	4	5	6	7	8	9	10	11
Congressional District 5, Arizona	3 641	641 348	23.2	22.5	10.3	39.6	51 780	8.4	3.8	261 936	62.9
Maricopa County (part)	3 641	641 348	23.2	22.5	10.3	39.6	51 780	8.4	3.8	261 936	62.9
Congressional District 6, Arizona	1 874	641 360	23.5	27.9	14.4	23.6	47 976	7.7	3.8	233 942	77.5
Maricopa County (part)	810	588 712	24.5	28.5	13.6	24.7	49 375	7.4	3.7	211 750	76.7
Pinal County (part)	1 064	52 648	13.1	20.7	23.6	12.9	37 260	10.6	5.7	22 192	85.0
Congressional District 7, Arizona	59 240	640 996	61.5	29.6	11.4	13.3	30 828	21.8	8.4	216 094	66.1
La Paz County (part)	10 796	19 657	36.4	21.0	26.1	8.7	25 836	19.6	8.0	8 334	78.1
Maricopa County (part)	11 143	80 555	58.7	34.9	5.1	12.0	45 216	15.0	5.6	23 613	77.7
Pima County (part)	18 455	328 825	62.8	28.2	10.0	15.2	28 421	23.8	7.4	115 545	59.9
Pinal County (part)	3 266	17 604	77.0	37.6	6.8	4.0	26 705	33.6	13.9	4 825	71.3
Santa Cruz County (part)	1 297	34 329	89.6	35.5	8.8	11.9	28 658	25.9	8.3	9 929	65.7
Yuma County	14 281	160 026	55.6	28.8	16.6	11.8	32 182	19.2	12.1	53 848	72.2
Congressional District 8, Arizona	23 327	641 455	26.1	22.7	16.7	30.6	40 656	10.5	4.6	264 983	67.1
Cochise County	15 979	117 755	40.0	26.2	14.6	18.8	32 105	17.7	6.7	43 893	67.3
Pima County (part)	5 337	514 921	23.2	22.2	16.8	32.9	42 045	8.9	4.2	216 805	66.6
Pinal County (part)	103	4 727	2.7	1.7	49.9	48.3	62 282	1.5	4.8	2 405	96.5
Santa Cruz County (part)	1 908	4 052	24.8	17.4	25.7	34.7	40 859	12.2	4.1	1 880	80.3
ARKANSAS	134 856	2 673 400	21.4	25.4	14.0	16.7	32 182	15.8	6.1	1 042 696	69.4
Congressional District 1, Arkansas	44 422	668 360	19.8	25.7	15.2	12.3	28 940	18.5	6.4	260 695	69.6
Arkansas County	2 560	20 749	25.1	24.9	15.9	12.2	30 316	17.8	6.2	8 457	67.8
Baxter County	1 436	38 386	2.9	18.9	26.8	12.8	29 106	11.1	4.0	17 052	79.7
Clay County	1 656	17 609	2.0	23.1	19.4	7.4	25 345	17.5	5.6	7 417	74.9
Cleburne County	1 432	24 046	2.6	21.4	21.1	13.9	31 531	13.1	4.9	10 190	80.6
Craighead County	1 841	82 148	11.6	24.2	11.7	20.9	32 425	15.4	5.7	32 301	63.9
Crittenden County	1 580	50 866	49.6	31.1	9.9	12.8	30 109	25.3	6.9	18 471	60.3
Cross County	1 595	19 526	25.7	27.8	13.7	9.9	29 362	19.9	7.6	7 391	70.7
Fulton County	1 601	11 642	2.4	22.8	20.1	10.5	25 529	16.3	5.9	4 810	81.1
Greene County	1 496	37 331	3.3	25.0	14.1	10.9	30 828	13.3	5.6	14 750	71.3
Independence County	1 978	34 233	5.7	24.5	14.5	13.7	31 920	13.0	5.9	13 467	74.4
Izard County	1 504	13 249	4.3	21.0	21.1	11.7	25 670	17.2	4.1	5 440	80.1
Jackson County	1 641	18 418	19.9	22.3	16.2	10.3	25 081	17.4	6.9	6 971	69.6
Lawrence County	1 519	17 774	2.8	23.9	17.5	8.5	27 139	18.4	5.6	7 108	71.2
Lee County	1 558	12 580	59.7	26.2	14.1	7.3	20 510	29.9	13.3	4 182	63.6
Lonoke County	1 984	52 828	9.9	28.8	10.4	14.6	40 314	10.5	3.9	19 262	75.9
Mississippi County	2 326	51 979	36.2	29.6	12.6	11.3	27 479	23.0	8.8	19 349	58.9
Monroe County	1 571	10 254	41.3	28.2	17.7	8.4	22 632	27.5	5.3	4 105	64.9
Phillips County	1 794	26 445	61.3	32.2	13.9	12.4	22 231	32.7	11.3	9 711	56.3
Poinsett County	1 963	25 614	9.9	26.0	14.2	6.3	26 558	21.2	6.3	10 026	66.8
Prairie County	1 673	9 539	15.6	23.9	17.3	9.0	29 990	15.5	4.5	3 894	72.8
Randolph County	1 688	18 195	3.5	24.5	17.1	10.6	27 583	15.3	6.4	7 265	74.5
St. Francis County	1 642	29 329	54.9	27.9	12.1	9.6	26 146	27.5	11.8	10 043	63.2
Searcy County	1 728	8 261	2.9	22.8	19.1	8.4	21 397	23.8	4.7	3 523	77.7
Sharp County	1 565	17 119	3.6	21.7	23.6	10.3	25 152	18.2	6.4	7 211	80.1
Stone County	1 571	11 499	3.0	22.2	18.8	9.8	22 209	18.9	4.4	4 768	77.9
Woodruff County	1 519	8 741	32.1	25.9	16.8	8.0	22 099	27.0	8.0	3 531	65.6
Congressional District 2, Arkansas	15 338	666 058	24.4	25.1	12.1	23.2	37 221	12.7	6.0	263 453	67.1
Conway County	1 440	20 336	17.0	25.5	15.7	11.5	31 209	16.1	6.6	7 967	78.0
Faulkner County	1 677	86 014	12.7	25.6	9.5	25.2	38 204	12.5	6.8	31 882	68.6
Perry County	1 427	10 209	5.6	25.5	14.9	11.1	31 083	14.0	4.7	3 989	82.1
Pulaski County	1 996	361 474	37.1	25.2	11.5	28.1	38 120	13.3	5.3	147 942	60.9
Saline County	1 874	83 529	5.6	25.4	12.4	16.4	42 569	7.2	3.9	31 778	80.7
Van Buren County	1 843	16 192	4.3	21.6	23.4	11.5	27 004	15.4	6.7	6 825	81.1
White County	2 678	67 165	7.5	24.4	13.7	15.5	32 203	14.0	11.3	25 148	73.0
Yell County	2 403	21 139	16.5	25.9	14.9	10.9	28 916	15.4	5.2	7 922	72.9
Congressional District 3, Arkansas	21 989	672 756	12.7	25.7	13.1	17.9	33 915	13.7	5.5	259 465	68.7
Benton County	2 191	153 406	13.3	26.6	14.3	20.3	40 281	10.1	3.4	58 212	72.2
Boone County	1 531	33 948	3.3	23.9	16.6	12.7	29 988	14.8	5.0	13 851	73.3
Carroll County	1 632	25 357	12.4	23.9	15.8	13.8	27 924	15.5	5.5	10 189	73.0
Crawford County	1 542	53 247	9.1	28.2	11.3	9.7	32 871	14.2	6.1	19 702	75.9
Franklin County	1 579	17 771	5.8	25.8	15.7	11.0	30 848	15.2	5.9	6 882	78.0
Johnson County	1 715	22 781	9.8	25.1	14.9	13.1	27 910	16.4	7.8	8 738	73.0
Madison County	2 167	14 243	5.7	26.8	14.3	10.1	27 895	18.6	2.7	5 463	79.0
Marion County	1 548	16 140	3.2	22.2	20.1	10.4	26 737	15.2	5.1	6 776	80.0
Newton County	2 131	8 608	4.1	24.9	14.8	11.8	24 756	20.4	4.5	3 500	81.5
Pope County	2 103	54 469	7.1	25.6	12.7	19.0	32 069	15.2	5.8	20 701	71.2
Sebastian County	1 389	115 071	20.0	25.9	12.9	16.6	33 889	13.6	4.7	45 300	63.5
Washington County	2 460	157 715	15.5	25.0	9.9	24.5	34 691	14.6	7.9	60 151	59.4

[1]Dry land or land partially or temporarily covered by water.
[2]Persons who do not identify themselves as White alone, not of Hispanic origin.
[3]Persons 25 years old and over.

Table B. 110th Congressional Districts by Counties, 2000—*Continued*

(Number, percent.)

| STATE
Congressional district
County | Land
area,[1]
(sq km) | Population | | | | Percent
with
bachelor's
degree
or more[3] | Median
household
income,
1999
(dollars) | Percent
living in
poverty | Percent
unem-
ployed | Households | |
		Total	Percent minority[2]	Percent under 18 years	Percent 65 years and over					Total	Percent owner occupied
	1	2	3	4	5	6	7	8	9	10	11
Congressional District 4, Arkansas	53 107	666 226	28.9	25.2	15.7	13.3	29 675	18.5	6.6	259 083	72.2
Ashley County	2 386	24 209	31.3	26.9	13.8	10.1	31 758	17.5	6.9	9 384	76.2
Bradley County	1 685	12 600	37.6	23.5	17.8	11.9	24 821	26.3	10.8	4 834	72.5
Calhoun County	1 627	5 744	26.3	24.9	15.7	7.3	28 438	16.5	5.3	2 317	82.2
Chicot County	1 668	14 117	57.5	27.3	15.9	11.7	22 024	28.6	10.2	5 205	69.6
Clark County	2 241	23 546	26.4	21.8	14.7	19.8	28 845	19.1	4.7	8 912	65.6
Cleveland County	1 548	8 571	15.6	26.2	13.7	10.0	32 405	15.2	5.5	3 273	82.2
Columbia County	1 984	25 603	38.5	25.1	16.0	16.8	27 640	21.1	7.6	9 981	71.3
Dallas County	1 729	9 210	43.4	26.0	17.0	9.6	26 608	18.9	7.4	3 519	73.9
Desha County	1 981	15 341	50.2	28.9	14.3	11.1	24 121	28.9	8.8	5 922	63.5
Drew County	2 145	18 723	30.1	25.7	13.1	17.3	28 627	18.2	8.9	7 337	68.9
Garland County	1 754	88 068	12.7	21.5	21.4	18.0	31 724	14.6	5.1	37 813	71.2
Grant County	1 636	16 464	4.7	26.0	12.0	11.0	37 182	10.2	4.2	6 241	80.2
Hempstead County	1 888	23 587	40.3	27.3	14.2	11.0	28 622	20.3	6.5	8 959	69.3
Hot Spring County	1 593	30 353	13.3	25.0	15.7	11.2	31 543	14.0	4.9	12 004	78.0
Howard County	1 521	14 300	28.3	26.9	15.3	11.6	28 699	15.5	4.9	5 471	72.0
Jefferson County	2 292	84 278	52.0	26.1	12.8	15.7	31 327	20.5	8.3	30 555	66.1
Lafayette County	1 364	8 559	38.6	25.3	17.6	9.5	24 831	23.2	7.9	3 434	78.4
Lincoln County	1 454	14 492	35.4	22.0	12.0	7.6	29 607	19.5	7.0	4 265	76.2
Little River County	1 377	13 628	26.7	25.2	14.9	9.9	29 417	15.4	6.5	5 465	76.5
Logan County	1 839	22 486	4.5	25.9	16.0	9.4	28 344	15.4	5.3	8 693	77.2
Miller County	1 616	40 443	26.6	26.4	13.3	12.5	30 951	19.3	6.8	15 637	67.9
Montgomery County	2 023	9 245	4.6	23.7	18.9	8.8	28 421	17.0	6.3	3 785	82.8
Nevada County	1 606	9 955	33.3	25.4	15.9	10.7	26 962	22.8	6.3	3 893	74.8
Ouachita County	1 897	28 790	40.5	25.9	17.2	12.7	29 341	19.5	8.5	11 613	71.4
Pike County	1 562	11 303	8.2	24.9	17.1	10.1	27 695	16.8	4.3	4 504	78.6
Polk County	2 226	20 229	6.8	25.5	17.0	10.9	25 180	18.2	5.8	8 047	78.4
Scott County	2 315	10 996	9.3	26.6	14.7	8.4	26 412	18.2	3.9	4 323	74.2
Sevier County	1 461	15 757	27.5	28.2	13.2	9.2	30 144	19.2	4.7	5 708	74.2
Union County	2 691	45 629	34.4	25.9	16.2	14.9	29 809	18.7	6.9	17 989	72.9
CALIFORNIA	403 933	33 871 648	53.4	27.2	10.6	26.6	47 493	14.2	7.0	11 502 870	56.9
Congressional District 1, California	28 505	639 275	28.9	24.4	13.1	25.0	38 918	15.3	6.9	240 381	60.7
Del Norte County	2 610	27 507	29.9	25.1	12.6	11.0	29 642	20.2	10.7	9 170	63.8
Humboldt County	9 253	126 518	18.1	23.1	12.6	23.0	31 226	19.5	8.6	51 238	57.6
Lake County	3 258	58 309	19.4	23.9	19.4	12.1	29 627	17.6	11.0	23 974	70.5
Mendocino County	9 088	86 265	25.3	25.4	13.6	20.2	35 996	15.9	7.3	33 266	61.3
Napa County	1 952	124 279	31.1	24.2	15.3	26.4	51 738	8.3	4.3	45 402	65.1
Sonoma County (part)	1 220	66 933	26.1	25.1	14.2	29.2	55 790	6.4	3.9	24 795	69.9
Yolo County (part)	1 123	149 464	43.0	24.9	8.7	36.1	39 179	19.6	7.3	52 536	50.3
Congressional District 2, California	56 353	638 921	23.9	26.3	14.4	17.4	33 559	17.0	9.5	241 200	63.1
Butte County (part)	3 310	158 701	18.9	22.8	15.2	25.4	32 924	18.1	8.7	62 942	59.0
Colusa County	2 980	18 804	52.5	31.6	11.0	10.6	35 062	16.1	10.7	6 097	63.3
Glenn County	3 405	26 453	38.0	30.6	12.8	10.7	32 107	18.1	9.1	9 172	64.0
Shasta County	9 804	163 256	13.6	26.1	15.2	16.6	34 335	15.4	8.7	63 426	66.1
Siskiyou County	16 283	44 301	16.4	23.9	18.2	17.7	29 530	18.6	9.6	18 556	67.2
Sutter County	1 561	78 930	40.3	28.8	12.1	15.3	38 375	15.5	11.8	27 033	61.5
Tehama County	7 643	56 039	21.5	27.4	15.9	11.3	31 206	17.3	9.7	21 013	67.7
Trinity County	8 233	13 022	13.8	22.9	16.8	15.5	27 711	18.7	13.9	5 587	71.3
Yolo County (part)	1 501	19 196	35.9	27.0	13.4	21.2	51 238	9.2	5.8	6 839	74.6
Yuba County	1 633	60 219	34.5	30.9	10.2	10.3	30 460	20.8	11.3	20 535	54.0
Congressional District 3, California	8 739	639 374	25.7	26.1	12.2	27.0	51 313	8.5	5.3	237 926	68.6
Alpine County	1 913	1 208	28.0	22.8	9.9	28.2	41 875	19.5	8.1	483	67.9
Amador County	1 536	35 100	17.6	20.7	18.1	16.6	42 280	9.2	4.4	12 759	75.4
Calaveras County	2 642	40 554	12.4	22.7	18.0	17.1	41 022	11.8	7.7	16 469	78.7
Sacramento County (part)	1 875	551 128	27.2	26.7	11.4	28.6	52 462	8.1	5.2	204 130	67.3
Solano County (part)	773	11 384	28.3	25.8	12.4	21.3	53 299	9.7	6.9	4 085	71.5
Congressional District 4, California	42 614	639 071	16.3	25.5	13.8	25.2	49 387	8.7	5.5	240 815	73.1
Butte County (part)	936	44 470	24.9	28.0	17.5	9.5	28 635	25.9	12.1	16 624	67.3
El Dorado County	4 431	156 299	15.2	26.0	12.5	26.5	51 484	7.1	5.4	58 939	74.7
Lassen County	11 803	33 828	29.2	21.7	9.0	10.7	36 310	14.0	9.4	9 625	68.1
Modoc County	10 215	9 449	19.5	25.6	17.3	12.4	27 522	21.5	11.9	3 784	70.7
Nevada County	2 480	92 033	9.9	22.9	17.5	26.1	45 864	8.1	4.7	36 894	75.8
Placer County	3 637	248 399	16.6	26.3	13.1	30.3	57 535	5.8	4.0	93 382	73.2
Plumas County	6 614	20 824	11.2	22.7	17.9	17.5	36 351	13.1	9.5	9 000	70.1
Sacramento County (part)	28	30 214	15.7	26.6	11.6	23.5	54 207	6.4	4.7	11 047	72.3
Sierra County	2 469	3 555	10.5	23.4	17.3	17.2	35 827	11.3	9.4	1 520	70.9
Congressional District 5, California	381	638 837	56.6	28.3	10.8	21.4	36 719	19.7	8.2	237 038	49.6
Sacramento County (part)	381	638 837	56.6	28.3	10.8	21.4	36 719	19.7	8.2	237 038	49.6

[1]Dry land or land partially or temporarily covered by water.
[2]Persons who do not identify themselves as White alone, not of Hispanic origin.
[3]Persons 25 years old and over.

Table B. 110th Congressional Districts by Counties, 2000—*Continued*

(Number, percent.)

STATE Congressional district County	Land area,[1] (sq km)	Population				Percent with bachelor's degree or more[3]	Median household income, 1999 (dollars)	Percent living in poverty	Percent unemployed	Households	
		Total	Percent minority[2]	Percent under 18 years	Percent 65 years and over					Total	Percent owner occupied
	1	2	3	4	5	6	7	8	9	10	11
Congressional District 6, California	4 208	638 970	24.0	22.6	12.8	37.9	59 115	7.7	3.8	248 258	63.3
Marin County	1 346	247 289	21.5	20.2	13.5	51.3	71 306	6.6	3.0	100 650	63.6
Sonoma County (part)	2 861	391 681	25.6	24.2	12.3	28.4	52 679	8.3	4.3	147 608	63.1
Congressional District 7, California	904	639 791	56.9	27.3	9.8	22.4	52 778	10.0	6.1	218 711	64.0
Contra Costa County (part)	404	399 619	60.0	27.4	9.7	22.3	51 901	11.2	6.2	138 011	63.1
Solano County (part)	500	240 172	51.7	27.2	9.9	22.5	54 596	8.1	6.0	80 700	65.4
Congressional District 8, California	92	639 362	57.1	14.1	13.2	44.0	52 322	12.2	4.8	276 659	30.2
San Francisco County (part)	92	639 362	57.1	14.1	13.2	44.0	52 322	12.2	4.8	276 659	30.2
Congressional District 9, California	343	639 426	65.0	23.1	10.8	37.4	44 314	16.9	6.8	247 798	45.6
Alameda County (part)	343	639 426	65.0	23.1	10.8	37.4	44 314	16.9	6.8	247 798	45.6
Congressional District 10, California	2 624	638 238	34.7	26.5	11.8	36.2	65 245	6.3	4.5	232 728	69.8
Alameda County (part)	350	75 174	25.2	28.0	7.6	31.7	75 133	5.3	3.4	26 763	72.4
Contra Costa County (part)	1 183	416 758	30.6	25.0	13.7	42.2	67 662	5.7	4.2	158 960	71.0
Sacramento County (part)	217	3 320	42.4	19.3	18.4	12.7	37 383	10.8	10.8	1 387	67.1
Solano County (part)	874	142 986	51.4	30.2	8.5	19.4	53 271	8.5	6.2	45 618	64.1
Congressional District 11, California	5 897	639 625	36.1	28.6	9.7	29.1	61 996	8.8	6.0	219 367	69.0
Alameda County (part)	644	90 433	29.0	25.5	6.7	42.0	84 925	2.7	2.8	31 666	69.9
Contra Costa County (part)	278	132 439	25.5	28.3	8.4	48.3	98 783	3.0	2.7	47 158	81.7
San Joaquin County (part)	3 347	373 958	41.2	29.4	11.2	17.9	47 142	12.8	8.2	127 027	63.6
Santa Clara County (part)	1 628	42 795	39.6	29.9	7.3	32.2	82 647	5.5	5.2	13 516	73.1
Congressional District 12, California	303	638 598	51.9	20.6	13.9	40.7	70 307	5.4	3.1	235 780	62.3
San Francisco County (part)	29	137 371	52.8	15.8	16.6	49.5	68 212	7.3	3.7	53 041	60.1
San Mateo County (part)	274	501 227	51.7	21.9	13.1	38.1	70 744	4.9	2.9	182 739	63.0
Congressional District 13, California	573	638 708	61.7	25.4	10.5	31.8	62 415	7.1	4.8	217 139	60.7
Alameda County (part)	573	638 708	61.7	25.4	10.5	31.8	62 415	7.1	4.8	217 139	60.7
Congressional District 14, California	2 138	639 953	40.4	22.4	11.5	52.2	77 985	6.4	3.6	240 537	58.5
San Mateo County (part)	889	205 934	46.9	25.0	10.9	41.4	71 030	8.0	4.1	71 364	57.7
Santa Clara County (part)	378	361 940	41.1	20.6	12.5	60.5	83 200	5.3	3.1	143 399	56.0
Santa Cruz County (part)	871	72 079	18.3	24.0	8.6	39.0	69 009	7.1	4.9	25 774	74.9
Congressional District 15, California	741	639 090	53.1	24.1	9.4	41.6	74 947	6.6	3.5	222 721	57.9
Santa Clara County (part)	741	639 090	53.1	24.1	9.4	41.6	74 947	6.6	3.5	222 721	57.9
Congressional District 16, California	595	638 760	68.4	27.2	8.0	26.9	67 689	9.8	4.8	186 227	64.1
Santa Clara County (part)	595	638 760	68.4	27.2	8.0	26.9	67 689	9.8	4.8	186 227	64.1
Congressional District 17, California	12 484	638 519	53.9	27.3	9.9	24.9	49 234	13.3	7.8	202 486	55.5
Monterey County	8 604	401 762	59.8	28.4	10.0	22.5	48 305	13.5	8.7	121 236	54.7
San Benito County	3 598	53 234	54.3	32.1	7.9	17.1	57 469	10.0	6.6	15 885	68.1
Santa Cruz County (part)	283	183 523	40.9	23.5	10.4	32.2	49 128	13.8	6.5	65 365	54.1
Congressional District 18, California	7 906	639 004	61.3	33.4	9.5	9.7	34 211	22.7	14.3	193 333	56.8
Fresno County (part)	103	3 109	58.7	25.4	16.1	7.4	37 500	15.7	8.9	935	69.8
Madera County (part)	626	2 843	72.8	33.0	6.8	3.8	30 801	19.4	17.7	765	38.8
Merced County	4 995	210 554	59.7	34.4	9.4	11.0	35 532	21.7	13.1	63 815	58.7
San Joaquin County (part)	277	189 640	75.8	33.9	9.2	7.3	30 201	27.7	15.5	54 602	52.9
Stanislaus County (part)	1 904	232 858	50.7	32.3	9.7	10.5	36 092	19.8	14.5	73 216	58.0
Congressional District 19, California	17 333	638 975	40.2	28.3	11.8	20.3	41 225	14.8	9.0	219 833	64.5
Fresno County (part)	914	232 939	46.5	28.7	10.9	28.0	41 918	14.9	7.3	84 896	60.1
Madera County (part)	4 906	120 266	52.7	29.4	10.8	12.2	36 416	21.4	13.1	35 390	66.8
Mariposa County	3 758	17 130	15.5	22.2	17.0	20.2	34 626	14.8	14.1	6 613	69.9
Stanislaus County (part)	1 965	214 139	34.7	29.7	11.2	17.7	44 710	11.9	8.8	71 930	66.0
Tuolumne County	5 790	54 501	15.2	20.7	18.5	16.1	38 725	11.4	7.7	21 004	71.2
Congressional District 20, California	12 904	639 705	78.7	34.8	7.4	6.3	26 800	32.2	19.3	163 772	50.1
Fresno County (part)	6 133	291 625	83.4	36.1	7.8	6.0	25 297	35.7	19.1	76 986	46.1
Kern County (part)	3 169	218 619	84.5	36.7	6.7	3.8	24 644	34.4	23.1	52 368	52.1
Kings County	3 603	129 461	58.5	28.8	7.5	10.4	35 749	19.5	13.6	34 418	55.9
Congressional District 21, California	20 787	639 755	53.8	32.3	10.3	15.0	36 047	20.7	11.4	200 508	61.6
Fresno County (part)	8 293	271 734	47.7	30.4	11.1	19.4	38 677	16.4	9.7	90 123	61.8
Tulare County	12 494	368 021	58.3	33.7	9.7	11.5	33 983	23.9	12.7	110 385	61.5
Congressional District 22, California	26 980	638 514	33.3	28.5	11.0	18.3	41 801	13.7	7.7	221 335	65.2
Kern County (part)	17 916	443 026	34.0	29.4	10.7	17.5	40 701	14.3	7.7	156 284	65.5
Los Angeles County (part)	1 392	74 177	44.6	30.0	9.4	16.8	41 018	16.8	10.5	24 301	57.1
San Luis Obispo County (part)	7 671	121 311	23.7	23.9	12.9	22.0	47 720	9.4	5.9	40 750	69.0
Congressional District 23, California	2 698	638 854	51.4	25.1	11.7	26.2	44 874	15.7	6.8	213 117	53.7
San Luis Obispo County (part)	887	125 370	24.2	19.2	16.0	31.3	38 897	15.8	6.0	51 989	55.5
Santa Barbara County (part)	1 590	286 840	46.7	23.4	12.4	32.0	46 455	16.2	6.8	97 861	52.3
Ventura County (part)	221	226 644	72.4	30.4	8.5	15.3	47 129	15.0	7.2	63 267	54.4

[1]Dry land or land partially or temporarily covered by water.
[2]Persons who do not identify themselves as White alone, not of Hispanic origin.
[3]Persons 25 years old and over.

Table B. 110th Congressional Districts by Counties, 2000—*Continued*

(Number, percent.)

STATE Congressional district County	Land area,[1] (sq km)	Population				Percent with bachelor's degree or more[3]	Median household income, 1999 (dollars)	Percent living in poverty	Percent unem- ployed	Households	
		Total	Percent minority[2]	Percent under 18 years	Percent 65 years and over					Total	Percent owner occupied
	1	2	3	4	5	6	7	8	9	10	11
Congressional District 24, California	10 057	639 060	31.6	27.6	11.1	30.0	61 453	7.2	4.7	218 728	71.0
Santa Barbara County (part)	5 499	112 507	34.4	28.0	13.4	23.2	47 272	9.5	6.5	38 761	65.4
Ventura County (part)	4 558	526 553	31.0	27.5	10.7	31.5	65 251	6.8	4.4	179 967	72.2
Congressional District 25, California	55 644	638 768	43.0	32.0	8.2	18.8	49 002	12.6	7.8	206 818	70.0
Inyo County	26 426	17 945	25.9	24.5	19.3	17.1	35 006	12.6	5.9	7 703	65.9
Los Angeles County (part)	4 082	454 722	42.2	32.2	7.0	21.2	55 155	11.1	7.3	144 354	73.2
Mono County	7 885	12 853	23.7	22.6	7.3	28.9	44 992	11.5	5.8	5 137	60.1
San Bernardino County (part)	17 251	153 248	49.2	33.1	10.2	10.6	36 589	17.2	10.3	49 624	62.5
Congressional District 26, California	1 947	639 913	47.5	27.0	11.0	32.4	58 968	8.4	5.3	215 830	68.7
Los Angeles County (part)	1 266	388 410	46.5	25.3	13.0	38.5	62 136	7.0	5.0	134 453	70.3
San Bernardino County (part)	682	251 503	49.2	29.6	8.0	22.1	53 386	10.5	5.9	81 377	66.1
Congressional District 27, California	390	638 532	55.4	25.4	10.6	25.8	46 781	13.4	7.3	221 730	54.1
Los Angeles County (part)	390	638 532	55.4	25.4	10.6	25.8	46 781	13.4	7.3	221 730	54.1
Congressional District 28, California	200	639 364	68.9	28.6	8.6	23.7	40 439	19.1	8.7	207 603	43.8
Los Angeles County (part)	200	639 364	68.9	28.6	8.6	23.7	40 439	19.1	8.7	207 603	43.8
Congressional District 29, California	263	638 899	61.0	22.9	13.2	33.4	43 895	14.5	6.6	233 376	44.0
Los Angeles County (part)	263	638 899	61.0	22.9	13.2	33.4	43 895	14.5	6.6	233 376	44.0
Congressional District 30, California	740	639 700	23.9	16.8	14.6	53.5	60 713	9.0	5.6	291 693	47.7
Los Angeles County (part)	740	639 700	23.9	16.8	14.6	53.5	60 713	9.0	5.6	291 693	47.7
Congressional District 31, California	102	639 248	90.3	29.8	7.3	13.7	26 093	30.1	11.2	191 535	23.0
Los Angeles County (part)	102	639 248	90.3	29.8	7.3	13.7	26 093	30.1	11.2	191 535	23.0
Congressional District 32, California	238	638 579	85.2	30.9	9.0	13.6	41 394	18.0	8.2	170 594	55.9
Los Angeles County (part)	238	638 579	85.2	30.9	9.0	13.6	41 394	18.0	8.2	170 594	55.9
Congressional District 33, California	125	638 655	80.2	24.3	10.4	26.9	31 655	23.5	10.4	246 339	30.4
Los Angeles County (part)	125	638 655	80.2	24.3	10.4	26.9	31 655	23.5	10.4	246 339	30.4
Congressional District 34, California	151	638 807	88.6	32.3	7.6	8.7	29 863	26.0	11.4	172 533	30.6
Los Angeles County (part)	151	638 807	88.6	32.3	7.6	8.7	29 863	26.0	11.4	172 533	30.6
Congressional District 35, California	144	638 851	89.6	32.8	7.7	13.3	32 156	26.4	11.2	198 170	39.5
Los Angeles County (part)	144	638 851	89.6	32.8	7.7	13.3	32 156	26.4	11.2	198 170	39.5
Congressional District 36, California	194	639 168	51.7	23.1	10.3	36.9	51 633	12.7	5.6	255 228	44.8
Los Angeles County (part)	194	639 168	51.7	23.1	10.3	36.9	51 633	12.7	5.6	255 228	44.8
Congressional District 37, California	193	638 722	83.4	32.8	8.0	15.2	34 006	25.2	11.2	193 734	44.1
Los Angeles County (part)	193	638 722	83.4	32.8	8.0	15.2	34 006	25.2	11.2	193 734	44.1
Congressional District 38, California	269	639 334	86.6	31.8	9.2	12.5	42 488	16.3	8.6	166 057	62.5
Los Angeles County (part)	269	639 334	86.6	31.8	9.2	12.5	42 488	16.3	8.6	166 057	62.5
Congressional District 39, California	168	639 529	79.2	32.5	8.1	14.7	45 307	15.7	8.3	173 624	59.5
Los Angeles County (part)	168	639 529	79.2	32.5	8.1	14.7	45 307	15.7	8.3	173 624	59.5
Congressional District 40, California	259	638 671	50.9	26.9	10.5	26.4	54 356	10.2	5.4	205 982	60.0
Orange County (part)	259	638 671	50.9	26.9	10.5	26.4	54 356	10.2	5.4	205 982	60.0
Congressional District 41, California	34 484	639 935	36.6	28.4	13.4	18.1	38 721	15.2	8.0	226 258	66.9
Riverside County (part)	1 172	113 441	40.6	27.6	20.1	11.2	31 578	18.7	9.9	41 902	70.3
San Bernardino County (part)	33 311	526 494	35.7	28.6	12.0	19.7	40 525	14.5	7.6	184 356	66.1
Congressional District 42, California	813	640 090	45.8	28.2	8.2	34.8	70 463	6.0	4.3	205 667	76.4
Los Angeles County (part)	123	131 930	67.2	25.9	10.2	38.4	66 096	7.7	4.9	41 250	78.9
Orange County (part)	493	367 735	33.0	28.2	8.7	37.2	72 477	5.1	3.7	125 901	75.4
San Bernardino County (part)	197	140 425	59.2	30.3	4.9	24.5	67 067	6.6	5.6	38 516	77.1
Congressional District 43, California	494	637 764	76.8	36.5	6.2	8.8	37 390	20.7	10.4	174 721	59.9
San Bernardino County (part)	494	637 764	76.8	36.5	6.2	8.8	37 390	20.7	10.4	174 721	59.9
Congressional District 44, California	1 352	639 008	48.8	30.5	8.3	21.1	51 578	12.1	6.6	200 212	65.8
Orange County (part)	398	85 259	21.9	26.2	11.3	41.2	74 766	5.6	3.5	31 346	71.3
Riverside County (part)	954	553 749	53.0	31.2	7.8	17.5	48 484	13.2	7.1	168 866	64.8
Congressional District 45, California	15 488	638 553	50.0	29.0	15.6	17.4	40 468	15.0	7.6	218 350	69.2
Riverside County (part)	15 488	638 553	50.0	29.0	15.6	17.4	40 468	15.0	7.6	218 350	69.2
Congressional District 46, California	683	639 245	37.4	21.9	12.8	36.4	61 567	7.8	4.1	241 898	61.6
Los Angeles County (part)	480	162 711	28.8	19.7	16.8	50.7	73 726	4.1	3.5	67 200	71.3
Orange County (part)	203	476 534	40.3	22.7	11.5	31.2	57 601	9.0	4.3	174 698	57.9
Congressional District 47, California	142	639 242	82.7	33.2	6.4	10.0	41 618	19.1	7.8	150 209	47.4
Orange County (part)	142	639 242	82.7	33.2	6.4	10.0	41 618	19.1	7.8	150 209	47.4

[1]Dry land or land partially or temporarily covered by water.
[2]Persons who do not identify themselves as White alone, not of Hispanic origin.
[3]Persons 25 years old and over.

Table B. 110th Congressional Districts by Counties, 2000—*Continued*

(Number, percent.)

STATE Congressional district County	Land area,[1] (sq km)	Population Total	Population Percent minority[2]	Population Percent under 18 years	Population Percent 65 years and over	Percent with bachelor's degree or more[3]	Median household income, 1999 (dollars)	Percent living in poverty	Percent unemployed	Households Total	Households Percent owner occupied
	1	2	3	4	5	6	7	8	9	10	11
Congressional District 48, California	550	638 848	32.1	23.3	11.7	46.5	69 663	6.3	4.0	247 151	65.1
Orange County (part)	550	638 848	32.1	23.3	11.7	46.5	69 663	6.3	4.0	247 151	65.1
Congressional District 49, California	4 378	639 380	42.1	29.0	12.6	20.7	46 445	11.9	6.4	209 193	66.8
Riverside County (part)	1 053	239 644	41.4	32.6	12.1	15.3	46 293	12.2	7.2	77 100	75.7
San Diego County (part)	3 326	399 736	42.5	26.8	13.0	23.8	46 543	11.7	6.0	132 093	61.6
Congressional District 50, California	778	639 437	34.3	25.2	12.3	40.0	59 813	8.1	4.3	231 948	65.9
San Diego County (part)	778	639 437	34.3	25.2	12.3	40.0	59 813	8.1	4.3	231 948	65.9
Congressional District 51, California	11 868	638 989	78.8	30.7	9.9	15.2	39 243	16.3	8.7	184 647	56.7
Imperial County	10 813	142 361	80.0	31.4	10.2	10.3	31 870	22.6	12.6	39 384	58.3
San Diego County (part)	1 055	496 628	78.4	30.5	9.8	16.6	41 049	14.6	7.8	145 263	56.3
Congressional District 52, California	5 473	639 329	27.6	26.4	11.1	28.6	52 940	8.1	4.9	232 585	63.9
San Diego County (part)	5 473	639 329	27.6	26.4	11.1	28.6	52 940	8.1	4.9	232 585	63.9
Congressional District 53, California	246	638 703	49.2	20.7	9.9	32.2	36 637	20.2	7.4	252 788	34.4
San Diego County (part)	246	638 703	49.2	20.7	9.9	32.2	36 637	20.2	7.4	252 788	34.4
COLORADO	268 627	4 301 261	25.6	25.5	9.7	32.7	47 203	9.3	4.3	1 658 238	67.3
Congressional District 1, Colorado	444	614 139	45.7	21.7	11.3	34.3	39 658	13.7	5.5	266 247	52.2
Adams County (part)	0	0	X	X	X	X	X	X	X	0	X
Arapahoe County (part)	47	59 503	23.5	21.1	11.9	33.2	40 763	8.7	4.0	27 012	49.0
Denver County	397	554 636	48.1	21.8	11.2	34.5	39 500	14.3	5.7	239 235	52.5
Jefferson County (part)	0	0	X	X	X	X	X	X	X	0	X
Congressional District 2, Colorado	14 542	614 289	21.2	24.7	6.6	39.3	55 204	7.4	3.9	233 172	69.2
Adams County (part)	223	239 887	29.7	27.9	7.5	21.1	51 236	6.0	3.9	87 047	72.6
Boulder County (part)	1 731	216 010	14.3	21.2	7.3	59.7	57 413	10.1	4.7	86 439	64.2
Clear Creek County	1 024	9 322	5.7	22.6	7.0	38.8	50 997	5.4	2.0	4 019	75.9
Eagle County	4 372	41 659	25.9	23.4	2.8	42.6	62 682	7.8	3.3	15 148	63.7
Gilpin County	388	4 757	8.0	21.2	6.6	31.2	51 942	4.0	2.1	2 043	78.5
Grand County	4 783	12 442	7.2	21.8	7.9	34.5	47 759	7.3	3.2	5 075	68.3
Jefferson County (part)	237	53 566	16.2	28.6	4.2	36.7	64 017	2.8	2.9	19 643	79.0
Summit County	1 575	23 548	13.9	17.4	3.2	48.3	56 587	9.0	2.8	9 120	59.0
Weld County (part)	210	13 098	26.0	28.5	6.7	19.2	50 590	6.3	4.1	4 638	85.4
Congressional District 3, Colorado	139 765	614 494	25.5	25.0	13.4	23.8	35 970	12.8	5.5	240 911	70.4
Alamosa County	1 872	14 966	45.6	27.4	9.6	27.0	29 447	21.3	8.8	5 467	64.0
Archuleta County	3 497	9 898	20.0	25.3	11.9	29.0	37 901	11.7	4.9	3 980	76.8
Conejos County	3 334	8 400	61.1	32.1	15.1	14.4	24 744	23.0	6.0	2 980	78.6
Costilla County	3 178	3 663	72.0	25.1	16.8	12.8	19 531	26.8	13.2	1 503	78.5
Custer County	1 914	3 503	5.6	22.3	15.0	26.7	34 731	13.3	3.7	1 480	78.9
Delta County	2 958	27 834	14.0	23.9	19.7	17.6	32 785	12.1	5.6	11 058	77.5
Dolores County	2 763	1 844	9.9	21.7	17.5	13.5	32 196	13.1	6.1	785	76.1
Garfield County	7 633	43 791	18.9	27.2	8.7	23.8	47 016	7.5	2.7	16 229	65.1
Gunnison County	8 388	13 956	7.3	18.0	6.7	43.6	36 916	15.0	5.3	5 649	58.4
Hinsdale County	2 895	790	4.3	19.7	11.5	34.9	37 279	7.2	2.2	359	64.9
Huerfano County	4 120	7 862	42.3	20.8	17.1	16.1	25 775	18.0	8.6	3 082	70.6
Jackson County	4 178	1 577	9.1	25.2	12.7	19.9	31 821	14.0	4.3	661	67.9
La Plata County	4 383	43 941	17.6	22.6	9.3	36.4	40 159	11.7	5.7	17 342	68.4
Las Animas County	12 361	15 207	34.9	24.2	18.8	16.2	28 273	17.3	5.7	6 173	70.4
Mesa County	8 619	116 255	13.1	24.9	15.1	22.0	35 864	10.2	5.7	45 823	72.7
Mineral County	2 268	831	5.3	20.0	17.0	31.2	34 844	10.2	2.8	377	73.2
Moffat County	12 282	13 184	11.7	28.2	9.3	12.5	41 528	8.3	5.5	4 983	72.0
Montezuma County	5 275	23 830	22.6	27.6	14.0	21.0	32 083	16.4	6.9	9 201	74.8
Montrose County	5 803	33 432	17.9	26.9	15.3	18.7	35 234	12.6	5.0	13 043	74.9
Otero County (part)	2 581	18 486	43.0	26.8	16.5	15.2	29 508	19.4	8.7	7 230	68.4
Ouray County	1 400	3 742	5.8	22.5	12.3	36.8	42 019	7.2	3.6	1 576	73.0
Pitkin County	2 513	14 872	9.7	16.5	6.7	57.1	59 375	6.2	3.2	6 807	59.1
Pueblo County	6 187	141 472	42.5	25.6	15.3	18.3	32 775	14.9	6.3	54 579	70.4
Rio Blanco County	8 342	5 986	7.4	26.7	11.2	19.5	37 711	9.6	6.0	2 306	70.4
Rio Grande County	2 361	12 413	43.6	28.2	14.9	18.8	31 836	14.5	6.1	4 701	70.8
Routt County	6 116	19 690	4.9	22.5	5.0	42.5	53 612	6.1	3.1	7 953	69.3
Saguache County	8 206	5 917	48.6	28.4	10.6	19.6	25 495	22.6	6.1	2 300	69.4
San Juan County	1 003	558	8.8	19.5	7.5	43.7	30 764	20.9	3.0	269	67.3
San Miguel County	3 332	6 594	9.3	17.7	3.4	48.5	48 514	10.4	2.6	3 015	51.6
Congressional District 4, Colorado	80 025	614 571	20.5	26.0	10.4	28.7	43 389	10.9	4.3	227 695	68.0
Baca County	6 619	4 517	9.3	24.5	22.3	14.0	28 099	16.9	2.4	1 905	76.5
Bent County	3 921	5 998	37.5	23.8	16.0	11.5	28 125	19.5	5.3	2 003	67.7
Boulder County (part)	192	75 278	22.6	27.6	9.2	31.4	51 709	7.7	3.5	28 241	66.5
Cheyenne County	4 614	2 231	8.9	28.6	16.5	14.2	37 054	11.1	1.1	880	75.0
Crowley County	2 043	5 518	33.4	18.8	10.9	11.9	26 803	18.5	5.7	1 358	72.9

[1]Dry land or land partially or temporarily covered by water.
[2]Persons who do not identify themselves as White alone, not of Hispanic origin.
[3]Persons 25 years old and over.
X = Not applicable.

Table B. 110th Congressional Districts by Counties, 2000—*Continued*

(Number, percent.)

STATE Congressional district County	Land area,[1] (sq km)	Population				Percent with bachelor's degree or more[3]	Median household income, 1999 (dollars)	Percent living in poverty	Percent unem- ployed	Households	
		Total	Percent minority[2]	Percent under 18 years	Percent 65 years and over					Total	Percent owner occupied
	1	2	3	4	5	6	7	8	9	10	11
Congressional District 4, Colorado—*Continued*											
Kiowa County	4 587	1 622	6.2	25.9	17.4	16.1	30 494	12.2	3.0	665	71.3
Kit Carson County	5 597	8 011	16.7	26.8	14.9	15.4	33 152	12.1	2.2	2 990	72.1
Larimer County	6 737	251 494	12.4	23.6	9.6	39.5	48 655	9.2	4.2	97 164	67.7
Lincoln County	6 698	6 087	16.4	23.8	14.1	13.2	31 914	11.7	2.3	2 058	68.9
Logan County	4 762	20 504	15.2	24.6	14.5	14.6	32 724	12.2	3.8	7 551	69.8
Morgan County	3 329	27 171	32.4	30.3	12.9	13.5	34 568	12.4	4.2	9 539	68.5
Otero County (part)	689	1 825	19.3	27.2	12.2	17.1	32 452	12.2	4.8	690	78.1
Phillips County	1 781	4 480	13.6	27.1	19.3	19.9	32 177	11.6	2.8	1 781	76.3
Prowers County	4 249	14 483	35.1	29.9	12.8	11.9	29 935	19.5	3.9	5 307	66.2
Sedgwick County	1 420	2 747	12.7	22.5	22.4	13.4	28 278	10.0	1.4	1 165	73.4
Washington County	6 529	4 926	6.6	26.4	18.3	14.3	32 431	11.4	1.6	1 989	73.7
Weld County (part)	10 130	167 838	30.4	28.2	9.2	21.9	41 720	13.0	5.6	58 609	67.3
Yuma County	6 127	9 841	14.0	28.4	16.0	15.5	33 169	12.9	2.4	3 800	71.1
Congressional District 5, Colorado	19 963	614 668	22.6	26.7	9.2	29.8	45 454	8.3	4.6	228 166	66.5
Chaffee County	2 625	16 242	13.0	19.6	16.9	24.3	34 368	11.7	4.7	6 584	73.3
El Paso County	5 507	516 929	23.8	27.5	8.6	31.8	46 844	8.0	4.7	192 409	64.7
Fremont County	3 970	46 145	18.9	20.6	14.5	13.5	34 150	11.7	4.1	15 232	76.0
Lake County	976	7 812	38.4	26.9	6.3	19.5	37 691	12.9	6.0	2 977	68.1
Park County (part)	5 442	6 985	8.2	22.3	8.8	27.5	42 764	8.3	3.8	2 971	83.2
Teller County	1 443	20 555	7.1	25.9	7.3	31.7	50 165	5.4	4.0	7 993	80.9
Congressional District 6, Colorado	10 629	614 491	12.4	29.2	6.5	46.8	73 393	2.7	2.2	221 355	84.9
Arapahoe County (part)	1 934	266 076	16.4	28.4	8.4	44.9	66 694	3.1	2.5	98 244	80.6
Douglas County	2 176	175 766	10.3	31.4	4.1	51.9	82 929	2.1	1.7	60 924	87.9
Elbert County	4 794	19 872	6.7	30.0	6.0	26.6	62 480	4.0	2.4	6 770	89.4
Jefferson County (part)	1 468	145 239	8.8	28.2	6.0	47.7	76 708	2.5	2.3	52 494	88.5
Park County (part)	258	7 538	6.4	24.9	6.2	32.9	60 078	3.1	2.0	2 923	92.4
Congressional District 7, Colorado	3 259	614 609	31.0	25.2	10.2	26.0	46 149	8.9	4.3	240 692	63.2
Adams County (part)	2 864	123 970	50.2	29.6	8.5	9.8	39 548	14.6	6.4	41 109	66.3
Arapahoe County (part)	100	162 388	43.2	25.8	7.7	25.4	43 912	9.1	4.2	65 653	57.1
Jefferson County (part)	295	328 251	17.8	23.4	12.1	31.7	49 966	6.7	3.6	133 930	65.3
CONNECTICUT	12 548	3 405 565	22.6	24.7	13.8	31.4	53 935	7.9	5.3	1 301 670	66.8
Congressional District 1, Connecticut	1 691	680 851	28.5	24.4	14.8	28.2	50 227	9.6	6.4	268 880	63.6
Hartford County (part)	1 145	613 977	30.6	24.5	14.9	28.1	49 310	10.2	6.7	241 956	62.6
Litchfield County (part)	442	36 498	5.4	24.5	13.9	25.1	55 233	4.2	3.6	14 205	77.4
Middlesex County (part)	104	30 376	12.6	22.5	13.6	33.8	58 871	3.9	3.1	12 719	66.8
Congressional District 2, Connecticut	5 253	681 092	11.4	24.2	12.3	28.8	54 498	5.8	4.4	255 470	72.0
Hartford County (part)	339	74 603	10.4	23.9	12.6	29.1	61 006	3.5	3.3	26 628	80.3
Middlesex County (part)	705	84 088	5.2	23.6	13.3	36.2	64 784	3.5	5.6	31 919	81.8
New Haven County (part)	94	17 858	4.6	28.1	14.3	57.2	87 497	1.3	2.1	6 515	88.3
New London County (part)	1 725	259 088	15.4	24.3	13.0	26.2	50 646	6.4	4.1	99 835	66.7
Tolland County	1 062	136 364	9.0	23.1	10.2	32.8	59 044	5.6	3.7	49 431	73.5
Windham County	1 328	109 091	11.5	25.1	12.3	19.0	45 115	8.5	5.8	41 142	67.4
Congressional District 3, Connecticut	1 189	681 085	24.0	23.7	14.7	28.0	49 752	8.8	5.8	267 105	63.6
Fairfield County (part)	60	59 822	17.7	23.1	19.0	24.9	54 125	4.8	4.3	23 688	79.3
Middlesex County (part)	147	40 607	19.6	23.0	14.2	29.0	48 509	7.5	4.5	16 703	57.5
New Haven County (part)	983	580 656	25.0	23.8	14.3	28.3	49 163	9.3	6.1	226 714	62.4
Congressional District 4, Connecticut	1 183	681 176	29.1	25.9	13.3	42.2	66 598	7.4	5.2	250 230	67.8
Fairfield County (part)	1 098	671 355	29.5	25.9	13.4	42.3	66 416	7.5	5.2	246 887	67.5
New Haven County (part)	85	9 821	3.7	27.3	8.8	32.2	77 126	2.1	3.1	3 343	91.1
Congressional District 5, Connecticut	3 231	681 361	19.8	25.1	13.8	29.9	53 118	7.7	4.7	259 985	67.5
Fairfield County (part)	463	151 390	19.5	25.0	10.4	35.3	66 004	5.2	3.2	53 657	72.8
Hartford County (part)	421	168 603	21.1	25.0	14.5	35.3	51 649	8.7	5.4	66 514	63.9
Litchfield County (part)	1 941	145 695	5.5	24.5	14.3	28.1	56 553	4.5	3.9	57 346	74.7
New Haven County (part)	407	215 673	28.6	25.7	15.3	23.1	44 840	11.0	5.8	82 468	62.0
DELAWARE	5 060	783 600	27.5	24.8	13.0	25.0	47 381	9.2	5.2	298 736	72.3
Congressional District (At Large), Delaware	5 060	783 600	27.5	24.8	13.0	25.0	47 381	9.2	5.2	298 736	72.3
Kent County	1 527	126 697	27.8	27.2	11.6	18.6	40 950	10.7	5.6	47 224	70.0
New Castle County	1 104	500 265	29.3	24.8	11.6	29.5	52 419	8.4	5.2	188 935	70.1
Sussex County	2 428	156 638	21.5	22.5	18.5	16.6	39 208	10.5	4.9	62 577	80.7
DISTRICT OF COLUMBIA	159	572 059	72.3	20.0	12.3	39.1	40 127	20.2	10.8	248 338	40.8
Delegate District (At Large), District of Columbia	159	572 059	72.3	20.0	12.3	39.1	40 127	20.2	10.8	248 338	40.8

[1]Dry land or land partially or temporarily covered by water.
[2]Persons who do not identify themselves as White alone, not of Hispanic origin.
[3]Persons 25 years old and over.

Table B. 110th Congressional Districts by Counties, 2000—*Continued*

(Number, percent.)

STATE Congressional district County	Land area,[1] (sq km)	Population				Percent with bachelor's degree or more[3]	Median household income, 1999 (dollars)	Percent living in poverty	Percent unem- ployed	Households	
		Total	Percent minority[2]	Percent under 18 years	Percent 65 years and over					Total	Percent owner occupied
	1	2	3	4	5	6	7	8	9	10	11
FLORIDA	139 670	15 982 378	34.6	22.7	17.6	22.3	38 819	12.5	5.6	6 337 929	70.1
Congressional District 1, Florida	12 022	639 335	22.0	24.3	12.7	20.2	36 738	13.1	5.8	242 696	70.6
Escambia County	1 715	294 410	29.2	23.5	13.3	21.0	35 234	15.4	6.6	111 049	67.3
Holmes County	1 250	18 564	10.5	23.1	14.8	8.8	27 923	19.1	6.2	6 921	81.6
Okaloosa County (part)	2 390	156 781	20.0	24.5	11.8	21.9	40 108	9.3	4.9	60 973	65.2
Santa Rosa County	2 634	117 743	10.8	26.4	11.0	22.9	41 881	9.8	5.3	43 793	80.4
Walton County (part)	2 531	30 864	15.3	23.5	14.8	9.3	29 626	16.8	5.2	12 029	79.7
Washington County	1 502	20 973	19.7	23.5	15.2	9.2	27 922	19.2	5.5	7 931	81.9
Congressional District 2, Florida	24 410	639 190	28.5	22.8	12.0	24.1	34 718	16.5	6.7	248 547	68.4
Bay County	1 978	148 217	17.2	24.0	13.3	17.7	36 092	13.0	4.9	59 597	68.6
Calhoun County	1 469	13 017	23.1	23.0	13.8	7.7	26 575	20.0	6.5	4 468	80.2
Dixie County	1 823	13 827	11.7	22.0	17.0	6.8	26 082	19.1	7.4	5 205	86.5
Franklin County	1 410	11 057	20.3	18.1	16.0	12.4	26 756	17.7	3.6	4 096	79.2
Gadsden County	1 337	45 087	64.1	26.5	12.3	12.9	31 248	19.9	7.6	15 867	78.0
Gulf County	1 436	13 332	21.3	21.5	16.3	10.1	30 276	16.7	6.0	4 931	81.0
Jackson County	2 372	46 755	31.3	22.3	14.6	12.8	29 744	17.2	5.7	16 620	77.9
Jefferson County (part)	1 102	6 371	35.0	25.1	14.9	18.6	34 909	14.0	5.3	2 463	84.6
Lafayette County	1 406	7 022	24.6	21.5	12.1	7.2	30 651	17.5	4.5	2 142	80.4
Leon County (part)	1 620	227 067	35.7	21.2	8.4	42.5	36 946	18.9	8.6	92 035	55.8
Liberty County	2 165	7 021	25.6	21.9	10.4	7.4	28 840	19.9	5.0	2 222	81.7
Okaloosa County (part)	33	13 717	7.4	25.3	15.2	49.0	63 852	3.5	2.6	5 296	79.3
Suwannee County	1 781	34 844	19.1	24.0	16.9	10.5	29 963	18.5	7.3	13 460	81.0
Taylor County	2 699	19 256	22.6	24.7	13.8	8.9	30 032	18.0	5.5	7 176	79.8
Wakulla County	1 571	22 863	15.1	25.7	10.2	15.7	37 149	11.3	3.9	8 450	84.2
Walton County (part)	208	9 737	7.1	16.1	19.0	35.5	44 553	7.0	2.3	4 519	77.2
Congressional District 3, Florida	4 652	640 123	61.6	28.4	10.8	12.9	29 785	21.5	7.8	236 276	55.6
Alachua County (part)	473	47 695	52.2	24.2	9.5	22.3	23 443	30.4	10.6	18 732	48.6
Clay County (part)	253	14 486	19.2	23.6	16.2	21.2	43 711	9.7	7.3	5 396	67.0
Duval County (part)	230	252 271	67.4	29.2	11.4	11.6	29 373	21.4	7.8	96 547	53.8
Lake County (part)	776	19 591	16.8	26.8	13.3	9.9	33 942	14.5	4.3	7 410	82.9
Marion County (part)	883	8 774	6.0	21.5	21.8	6.3	27 095	18.5	8.0	3 809	88.1
Orange County (part)	251	218 791	73.3	29.7	7.8	13.7	31 445	20.7	7.4	74 557	49.4
Putnam County (part)	1 401	39 037	26.7	25.5	16.5	8.9	28 079	22.4	6.8	15 055	78.9
Seminole County (part)	25	25 033	60.8	28.2	12.5	10.5	26 503	23.7	7.7	9 488	50.6
Volusia County (part)	361	14 445	48.1	27.2	17.5	10.5	28 843	24.1	10.6	5 282	70.1
Congressional District 4, Florida	10 665	638 922	22.1	24.3	10.9	24.4	43 947	9.1	4.1	246 246	69.4
Baker County	1 516	22 259	17.7	27.5	9.0	8.2	40 035	14.7	4.5	7 043	81.3
Columbia County	2 064	56 513	22.0	25.3	14.0	10.9	30 881	15.0	6.0	20 925	77.1
Duval County (part)	1 098	438 069	21.1	24.0	10.4	29.3	47 091	6.9	3.7	175 423	65.5
Hamilton County	1 333	13 327	45.1	23.5	11.0	7.3	25 638	26.0	7.1	4 161	77.3
Jefferson County (part)	446	6 531	48.8	20.4	14.1	15.3	30 077	20.7	4.2	2 232	76.8
Leon County (part)	107	12 385	37.6	22.7	6.8	30.4	46 851	4.8	3.0	4 486	81.6
Madison County	1 792	18 733	44.3	25.4	14.6	10.2	26 533	23.1	5.4	6 629	78.4
Nassau County	1 688	57 663	11.1	25.0	12.6	18.9	46 022	9.1	4.8	21 980	80.7
Union County	622	13 442	28.3	21.9	7.3	7.5	34 563	14.0	4.0	3 367	74.5
Congressional District 5, Florida	10 474	639 719	12.4	20.2	25.7	14.3	34 815	10.6	4.9	263 218	85.2
Citrus County	1 512	118 085	7.1	17.1	32.3	13.2	31 001	11.7	6.7	52 634	85.6
Hernando County	1 239	130 802	10.9	18.8	30.9	12.7	32 572	10.3	5.2	55 425	86.5
Lake County (part)	1 020	78 316	16.1	20.3	23.9	18.9	41 313	7.2	3.2	31 977	83.6
Levy County (part)	2 677	26 669	11.9	22.9	18.8	10.4	26 860	17.9	5.8	10 935	84.7
Marion County (part)	345	14 138	10.9	18.3	30.3	14.1	32 725	12.2	6.8	6 209	88.0
Pasco County (part)	1 685	164 457	13.2	22.9	20.8	15.6	37 460	10.1	4.6	64 958	85.1
Polk County (part)	583	53 907	11.3	24.8	16.3	14.5	41 812	9.0	4.0	20 301	81.5
Sumter County	1 413	53 345	21.7	16.2	27.6	12.2	32 073	13.7	4.8	20 779	86.4
Congressional District 6, Florida	7 541	638 952	21.2	22.9	15.4	21.4	36 846	13.4	5.3	247 789	72.9
Alachua County (part)	1 792	170 260	24.2	18.9	9.5	43.4	34 620	20.6	6.1	68 777	56.7
Bradford County	759	26 088	24.9	21.8	12.9	8.4	33 140	14.6	4.8	8 497	79.0
Clay County (part)	1 304	126 328	14.8	28.4	9.0	19.9	49 578	6.5	4.4	44 847	79.2
Duval County (part)	676	88 539	23.9	29.2	7.7	11.6	42 658	9.6	4.2	31 777	78.2
Gilchrist County	904	14 437	11.1	24.3	13.6	9.4	30 328	14.1	4.4	5 021	86.2
Lake County (part)	149	44 429	17.7	17.9	35.8	13.4	32 133	11.8	4.8	19 983	80.6
Levy County (part)	220	7 781	33.9	26.0	15.0	11.5	27 276	20.9	7.3	2 932	79.3
Marion County (part)	1 738	161 090	22.2	20.6	25.7	14.8	32 225	13.3	6.1	65 955	78.8
Congressional District 7, Florida	4 654	639 140	18.5	22.0	18.2	24.5	40 525	10.1	5.0	259 281	74.1
Flagler County	1 256	49 832	16.5	17.9	28.6	21.2	40 214	8.7	4.3	21 294	84.1
Orange County (part)	8	9 641	6.2	27.1	15.0	61.7	75 016	1.5	2.5	3 625	90.9
Putnam County (part)	469	31 386	21.9	23.5	20.9	10.0	28 291	19.1	4.4	12 784	81.3
St. Johns County	1 577	123 135	11.0	23.0	15.9	33.1	50 099	8.0	3.3	49 614	76.4
Seminole County (part)	314	161 950	20.9	24.6	11.3	30.8	50 588	6.6	3.4	62 354	71.1
Volusia County (part)	1 029	263 196	21.0	20.3	21.4	17.8	33 328	12.8	7.3	109 610	71.5

[1]Dry land or land partially or temporarily covered by water.
[2]Persons who do not identify themselves as White alone, not of Hispanic origin.
[3]Persons 25 years old and over.

Table B. 110th Congressional Districts by Counties, 2000—*Continued*

(Number, percent.)

| STATE Congressional district County | Land area,[1] (sq km) | Population | | | | Percent with bachelor's degree or more[3] | Median household income, 1999 (dollars) | Percent living in poverty | Percent unemployed | Households | |
		Total	Percent minority[2]	Percent under 18 years	Percent 65 years and over					Total	Percent owner occupied
	1	2	3	4	5	6	7	8	9	10	11
Congressional District 8, Florida	2 556	639 026	30.0	23.2	13.9	25.9	41 568	9.4	4.3	254 858	66.4
Lake County (part)	524	68 192	14.0	19.9	26.9	17.8	36 428	9.6	4.1	29 043	79.5
Marion County (part)	1 123	74 914	17.2	23.6	21.3	12.0	31 793	12.1	4.9	30 782	79.3
Orange County (part)	884	492 684	34.3	23.6	11.0	29.2	43 958	9.0	4.3	193 759	62.4
Osceola County (part)	24	3 236	12.6	28.4	5.3	54.7	63 036	7.4	2.0	1 274	52.0
Congressional District 9, Florida	1 642	638 563	15.0	21.9	20.5	24.6	40 742	8.6	3.9	266 733	76.3
Hillsborough County (part)	1 165	245 935	20.8	26.8	9.6	34.7	55 352	6.4	3.4	91 295	76.6
Pasco County (part)	244	180 308	7.3	17.5	32.3	11.1	30 248	11.2	4.7	82 608	80.2
Pinellas County (part)	233	212 320	14.6	19.9	23.1	26.3	40 780	8.9	3.8	92 830	72.6
Congressional District 10, Florida	452	639 428	12.0	17.9	23.5	22.6	37 168	8.9	4.0	294 533	71.7
Pinellas County (part)	452	639 428	12.0	17.9	23.5	22.6	37 168	8.9	4.0	294 533	71.7
Congressional District 11, Florida	632	639 059	51.6	25.0	12.0	21.2	33 559	17.5	7.3	257 770	55.4
Hillsborough County (part)	544	541 862	47.7	24.2	11.9	22.6	35 009	16.3	7.2	221 799	55.4
Manatee County (part)	48	27 463	73.5	30.8	13.0	7.3	26 888	26.1	6.9	8 366	54.0
Pinellas County (part)	40	69 734	73.1	29.1	13.1	14.4	26 908	23.3	8.8	27 605	55.4
Congressional District 12, Florida	5 066	640 096	27.9	25.1	17.1	16.6	37 769	12.4	5.5	243 267	72.7
Hillsborough County (part)	1 014	211 151	27.0	26.0	15.0	20.2	43 831	9.9	4.4	78 263	74.3
Osceola County (part)	91	13 583	60.5	34.2	8.0	9.8	37 172	12.8	6.6	4 147	78.6
Polk County (part)	3 961	415 362	27.4	24.4	18.5	14.9	35 136	13.7	6.1	160 857	71.7
Congressional District 13, Florida	6 732	639 216	14.1	18.0	28.6	23.7	40 187	9.4	3.8	281 788	77.5
Charlotte County (part)	79	17 573	3.4	10.2	45.6	19.2	33 945	7.0	3.3	8 845	84.9
DeSoto County	1 651	32 209	38.9	22.5	19.4	8.4	30 714	23.6	5.3	10 746	74.7
Hardee County	1 651	26 938	44.9	27.6	13.6	8.4	30 183	24.6	9.7	8 166	73.4
Manatee County (part)	1 871	236 539	13.2	19.4	26.3	22.0	39 771	8.3	3.2	104 094	75.3
Sarasota County	1 480	325 957	10.4	16.2	31.4	27.4	41 957	7.8	3.7	149 937	79.1
Congressional District 14, Florida	2 736	639 298	16.2	18.2	27.3	24.4	42 541	8.8	3.4	279 398	77.3
Charlotte County (part)	236	26 680	7.7	18.3	26.4	14.5	38 312	8.1	3.2	11 378	86.2
Collier County (part)	420	171 730	12.9	14.8	32.3	33.8	51 155	6.4	2.7	79 421	77.9
Lee County	2 081	440 888	18.1	19.6	25.4	21.1	40 319	9.7	3.7	188 599	76.5
Congressional District 15, Florida	6 591	639 133	22.1	22.1	20.2	22.3	39 397	9.8	4.8	261 939	73.2
Brevard County (part)	1 669	355 857	16.6	21.3	21.0	24.9	39 781	9.3	4.9	151 171	73.3
Indian River County	1 303	112 947	16.5	19.2	29.2	23.1	39 635	9.3	4.5	49 137	77.6
Osceola County (part)	3 308	155 674	39.0	26.1	11.7	15.4	37 906	11.5	4.9	55 556	67.3
Polk County (part)	310	14 655	21.1	19.5	20.5	16.1	41 061	7.1	2.8	6 075	89.7
Congressional District 16, Florida	11 755	638 817	18.2	21.0	25.5	20.0	39 408	10.0	4.1	262 341	81.7
Charlotte County (part)	1 481	97 374	11.2	15.9	35.0	18.1	36 272	8.5	3.6	43 641	82.8
Glades County	2 004	10 576	31.5	22.1	19.2	9.8	30 774	15.2	8.8	3 852	81.6
Hendry County (part)	1 430	28 831	51.0	30.0	10.6	8.9	34 839	23.2	6.7	8 949	74.8
Highlands County	2 663	87 366	23.5	19.3	33.1	13.6	30 160	15.2	4.4	37 471	79.7
Martin County (part)	930	121 950	12.3	18.2	29.1	27.0	43 557	8.0	4.0	54 268	80.4
Okeechobee County	2 005	35 910	28.6	25.2	16.5	8.9	30 456	16.0	4.7	12 593	74.9
Palm Beach County (part)	467	102 406	18.1	27.1	13.8	32.6	61 841	4.6	3.2	37 484	84.9
St. Lucie County (part)	774	154 404	14.8	20.6	25.6	16.4	38 417	8.9	4.1	64 083	83.6
Congressional District 17, Florida	250	639 593	81.5	29.3	10.8	13.5	30 426	23.3	11.1	213 285	57.4
Broward County (part)	67	166 109	62.5	26.4	12.5	16.7	35 394	14.2	6.5	62 512	60.0
Miami-Dade County (part)	183	473 484	88.2	30.3	10.2	12.3	28 209	26.5	13.0	150 773	56.4
Congressional District 18, Florida	919	639 753	70.2	19.2	17.8	25.6	32 298	19.3	7.8	255 055	47.9
Miami-Dade County (part)	539	560 206	77.0	19.5	18.3	25.6	30 834	20.7	8.6	219 997	45.6
Monroe County (part)	381	79 547	22.7	16.9	14.6	25.4	42 319	10.2	3.2	35 058	62.5
Congressional District 19, Florida	598	638 503	22.5	18.9	29.7	25.7	42 237	7.7	4.8	283 625	79.1
Broward County (part)	123	209 314	25.2	19.5	25.6	23.5	40 010	8.2	4.6	93 096	73.6
Palm Beach County (part)	476	429 189	21.2	18.6	31.7	26.8	43 718	7.5	4.9	190 529	81.8
Congressional District 20, Florida	416	639 795	33.3	21.2	17.3	29.6	44 034	9.6	4.8	275 276	69.9
Broward County (part)	378	543 879	32.1	22.2	16.3	27.9	44 477	9.2	4.7	227 698	71.6
Miami-Dade County (part)	38	95 916	39.9	15.2	22.9	38.3	41 924	12.0	5.5	47 578	62.0
Congressional District 21, Florida	349	639 005	79.0	24.3	12.8	22.9	41 426	13.0	7.2	211 014	61.9
Broward County (part)	95	73 875	60.1	31.9	4.7	37.0	74 448	3.9	3.3	23 183	91.7
Miami-Dade County (part)	255	565 130	81.5	23.4	13.9	21.2	38 235	14.2	7.8	187 831	58.2
Congressional District 22, Florida	694	640 100	17.7	18.6	20.8	34.1	51 200	7.1	3.7	285 359	74.3
Broward County (part)	212	277 945	18.8	19.9	17.1	33.6	50 799	7.8	3.9	122 484	72.3
Palm Beach County (part)	481	362 155	16.8	17.7	23.6	34.5	51 517	6.5	3.6	162 875	75.7
Congressional District 23, Florida	8 708	639 781	70.7	28.1	12.2	12.8	31 309	21.9	8.3	224 530	56.5
Broward County (part)	2 247	351 896	72.3	27.5	13.1	12.2	31 597	20.4	8.2	125 472	60.4
Hendry County (part)	1 555	7 379	73.9	30.3	6.5	5.1	28 523	28.4	12.7	1 901	61.3
Martin County (part)	509	4 781	65.2	26.2	6.7	7.2	24 583	36.3	11.6	1 020	48.3
Palm Beach County (part)	3 688	237 434	68.4	28.5	11.3	14.6	31 817	22.2	8.2	83 287	51.6
St. Lucie County (part)	709	38 291	70.1	30.1	11.0	8.4	24 685	31.9	9.5	12 850	50.2

[1]Dry land or land partially or temporarily covered by water.
[2]Persons who do not identify themselves as White alone, not of Hispanic origin.
[3]Persons 25 years old and over.

Table B. 110th Congressional Districts by Counties, 2000—*Continued*

(Number, percent.)

STATE Congressional district County	Land area,[1] (sq km)	Population				Percent with bachelor's degree or more[3]	Median household income, 1999 (dollars)	Percent living in poverty	Percent unem-ployed	Households	
		Total	Percent minority[2]	Percent under 18 years	Percent 65 years and over					Total	Percent owner occupied
	1	2	3	4	5	6	7	8	9	10	11
Congressional District 24, Florida	4 101	639 516	20.1	23.1	14.6	25.5	43 954	8.7	4.2	248 930	74.3
Brevard County (part)	968	120 373	15.7	23.7	16.6	19.3	40 980	10.0	5.0	47 024	78.8
Orange County (part)	1 207	175 228	28.7	23.9	9.8	29.6	45 075	10.7	4.7	64 345	67.1
Seminole County (part)	459	178 213	23.2	25.4	9.6	33.9	51 426	5.9	3.4	67 730	70.6
Volusia County (part)	1 467	165 702	10.7	19.3	23.7	18.0	38 467	8.6	4.1	69 831	81.6
Congressional District 25, Florida	11 054	638 315	75.8	28.6	8.6	20.3	44 489	13.7	7.0	194 175	72.7
Collier County (part)	4 826	79 647	55.5	30.6	7.4	10.4	41 234	18.7	5.5	23 552	67.8
Miami-Dade County (part)	4 027	558 626	78.7	28.3	8.7	21.6	45 147	12.9	7.2	170 595	73.4
Monroe County (part)	2 201	42	0.0	0.0	0.0	0.0	36 250	0.0	0.0	28	0.0
GEORGIA	149 976	8 186 453	37.3	26.5	9.6	24.3	42 433	13.0	5.4	3 006 369	67.5
Congressional District 1, Georgia	29 542	630 068	31.2	27.2	10.6	17.4	34 912	15.9	4.9	229 864	69.3
Appling County	1 317	17 419	24.9	27.3	12.0	8.4	30 266	18.6	4.8	6 606	79.0
Atkinson County	876	7 609	37.6	30.2	9.3	6.9	26 470	23.0	5.2	2 717	74.2
Bacon County	738	10 103	20.4	25.7	13.0	6.6	26 910	23.7	4.5	3 833	74.9
Berrien County	1 172	16 235	15.4	27.2	12.4	9.4	30 044	17.7	4.4	6 261	75.6
Brantley County	1 151	14 629	6.4	28.3	10.1	6.2	30 361	15.6	4.9	5 436	86.9
Bryan County	1 144	23 417	18.3	31.1	7.2	19.3	48 345	11.7	2.9	8 089	78.0
Camden County	1 631	43 664	27.0	31.7	4.9	16.0	41 056	10.1	4.5	14 705	63.2
Charlton County	2 022	10 282	31.6	27.5	9.9	6.4	27 869	20.9	5.2	3 342	80.7
Chatham County (part)	558	74 285	20.6	23.3	13.7	38.1	53 908	5.3	3.0	29 472	73.3
Clinch County	2 096	6 878	31.9	28.0	12.2	10.4	26 755	23.4	4.2	2 512	72.4
Coffee County	1 551	37 413	33.9	28.1	9.7	10.0	30 710	19.1	6.4	13 354	74.4
Cook County	593	15 771	33.5	28.8	13.1	8.1	27 582	20.7	5.3	5 882	74.9
Echols County	1 047	3 754	28.9	29.7	9.0	8.4	25 851	28.7	3.7	1 264	75.7
Glynn County	1 094	67 568	31.0	25.3	14.6	23.8	38 765	15.1	5.5	27 208	65.5
Jeff Davis County	863	12 684	21.0	27.0	11.9	9.4	27 310	19.4	5.2	4 828	77.4
Lanier County	484	7 241	29.6	27.3	10.5	8.8	29 171	18.5	6.0	2 593	76.3
Liberty County	1 344	61 610	55.7	31.9	4.0	14.5	33 477	15.0	5.2	19 383	50.7
Long County	1 038	10 304	35.5	32.8	5.6	5.8	30 640	19.5	7.6	3 574	66.2
Lowndes County (part)	890	82 698	39.9	26.1	9.2	20.8	31 874	18.9	5.4	29 695	58.2
McIntosh County	1 123	10 847	38.9	28.2	11.4	11.1	30 102	18.7	5.6	4 202	83.5
Pierce County	889	15 636	13.9	26.3	12.3	10.1	29 895	18.4	4.0	5 958	80.7
Telfair County	1 142	11 794	40.6	22.5	15.1	8.3	26 097	21.2	6.4	4 140	78.3
Ware County	2 337	35 483	31.1	24.7	15.5	11.4	28 360	20.5	6.3	13 475	70.3
Wayne County	1 670	26 565	25.3	25.6	11.3	11.6	32 766	16.7	5.0	9 324	76.5
Wheeler County	771	6 179	37.7	22.3	12.6	7.1	24 053	25.3	5.0	2 011	77.4
Congressional District 2, Georgia	28 079	629 617	52.2	27.6	12.0	13.6	29 843	21.9	7.4	226 742	64.5
Baker County	889	4 074	53.8	27.4	13.5	10.7	30 338	23.4	8.3	1 514	77.6
Brooks County	1 278	16 450	43.0	27.2	15.1	11.3	26 911	23.4	5.2	6 155	76.9
Calhoun County	726	6 320	62.1	22.0	12.8	11.7	24 588	26.5	5.6	1 962	71.6
Chattahoochee County	644	14 882	45.0	28.5	1.8	25.0	31 148	10.6	2.0	2 932	27.9
Clay County	506	3 357	61.7	25.7	19.5	10.1	21 448	31.3	6.8	1 347	74.2
Crawford County	842	12 495	27.5	27.5	9.1	6.8	37 848	15.4	4.6	4 461	84.8
Crisp County	709	21 996	46.4	29.1	12.8	12.8	26 547	29.3	7.0	8 337	60.5
Decatur County	1 546	28 240	44.1	28.6	13.3	12.1	28 820	22.7	6.5	10 380	72.5
Dooly County	1 018	11 525	55.1	25.5	11.5	9.6	27 980	22.1	6.4	3 909	71.4
Dougherty County	854	96 065	62.8	27.6	11.8	17.8	30 934	24.8	9.8	35 552	53.5
Early County	1 324	12 354	49.9	28.6	16.2	12.6	25 629	25.7	8.1	4 695	72.4
Grady County	1 187	23 659	36.8	27.3	13.2	10.6	28 656	21.3	7.4	8 797	73.3
Lee County	921	24 757	18.4	30.6	6.3	17.0	48 600	8.2	3.4	8 229	78.3
Lowndes County (part)	416	9 417	34.0	26.2	7.9	10.3	36 673	12.8	5.2	2 959	86.9
Macon County	1 045	14 074	62.6	27.6	13.0	10.0	24 224	25.8	9.1	4 834	73.2
Marion County	951	7 144	41.7	28.5	10.8	8.9	29 145	22.4	3.6	2 668	78.1
Miller County	733	6 383	30.4	26.3	17.2	11.3	27 335	21.2	4.0	2 487	76.9
Mitchell County	1 326	23 932	51.0	27.5	11.9	9.1	26 581	26.4	6.2	8 063	72.0
Muscogee County (part)	132	119 318	68.5	27.9	11.3	12.9	28 440	21.8	8.3	43 011	49.4
Peach County	391	23 668	51.0	25.9	9.8	16.8	34 453	20.2	12.9	8 436	68.4
Quitman County	392	2 598	47.6	24.0	19.8	6.1	25 875	21.9	5.8	1 047	80.4
Randolph County	1 112	7 791	61.0	27.3	15.4	9.5	22 004	27.7	7.9	2 909	68.8
Schley County	434	3 766	34.4	29.1	11.2	13.7	32 035	19.9	5.7	1 435	76.3
Seminole County	617	9 369	39.0	26.0	15.7	8.6	27 094	23.2	6.8	3 573	80.8
Stewart County	1 188	5 252	63.5	25.0	18.4	9.3	24 789	22.2	10.1	2 007	72.5
Sumter County	1 257	33 200	52.8	28.0	12.5	19.3	30 904	21.4	6.8	12 025	63.9
Talbot County	1 018	6 498	63.9	24.1	14.4	7.9	26 611	24.2	8.7	2 538	82.7
Taylor County	978	8 815	45.2	26.9	13.1	8.5	25 148	26.0	8.0	3 281	76.8
Terrell County	869	10 970	62.5	28.7	13.3	10.7	26 969	28.6	8.5	4 002	66.3
Thomas County	1 420	42 737	41.8	27.1	14.0	16.8	31 115	17.4	6.5	16 309	70.0
Webster County	543	2 390	50.6	24.8	14.7	9.1	27 992	19.3	7.5	911	81.4
Worth County (part)	816	16 121	36.6	28.7	13.0	8.6	31 234	19.9	7.2	5 977	74.7

[1]Dry land or land partially or temporarily covered by water.
[2]Persons who do not identify themselves as White alone, not of Hispanic origin.
[3]Persons 25 years old and over.

Table B. 110th Congressional Districts by Counties, 2000—*Continued*

(Number, percent.)

STATE Congressional district County	Land area,[1] (sq km)	Population				Percent with bachelor's degree or more[3]	Median household income, 1999 (dollars)	Percent living in poverty	Percent unem- ployed	Households	
		Total	Percent minority[2]	Percent under 18 years	Percent 65 years and over					Total	Percent owner occupied
	1	2	3	4	5	6	7	8	9	10	11
Congressional District 3, Georgia	10 650	630 052	23.6	27.4	10.5	21.5	47 553	9.0	4.1	227 878	75.9
Carroll County (part)	778	46 523	19.9	25.2	10.0	20.5	39 928	13.4	5.1	16 514	71.4
Coweta County	1 146	89 215	22.8	28.7	8.5	20.6	52 706	7.8	3.9	31 442	78.0
Douglas County (part)	257	16 092	11.1	27.4	8.2	13.6	53 998	4.8	2.5	5 532	89.3
Fayette County	510	91 263	18.0	29.0	9.0	36.2	71 227	2.6	2.6	31 524	86.6
Harris County	1 201	23 695	22.5	25.4	12.0	21.1	47 763	8.2	3.4	8 822	86.1
Heard County	767	11 012	13.2	28.7	11.6	7.3	33 038	13.6	5.7	4 043	77.3
Henry County (part)	708	79 667	16.0	29.3	7.7	19.0	57 890	5.2	2.8	27 514	86.3
Lamar County	479	15 912	32.4	24.5	12.9	11.3	37 087	11.2	5.5	5 712	72.4
Meriwether County	1 303	22 534	44.4	26.9	13.8	10.8	31 870	17.8	7.0	8 248	74.1
Muscogee County (part)	428	66 973	20.9	24.7	12.4	32.0	47 532	5.3	3.1	26 808	67.7
Pike County	566	13 688	17.2	27.6	11.0	14.0	44 370	9.6	3.4	4 755	81.5
Rockdale County (part)	79	8 685	13.8	30.4	8.2	25.0	66 549	6.5	3.2	2 803	92.1
Spalding County	513	58 417	34.5	27.2	11.6	12.5	36 221	15.5	6.2	21 519	62.8
Troup County	1 072	58 779	34.9	27.8	12.6	18.0	35 469	14.8	5.2	21 920	64.5
Upson County	843	27 597	30.1	25.5	14.9	11.5	31 201	14.7	7.0	10 722	69.9
Congressional District 4, Georgia	854	629 724	70.2	26.6	6.7	29.3	47 943	10.3	5.5	222 861	60.1
DeKalb County (part)	514	470 688	76.5	26.6	6.9	31.0	47 893	10.3	5.7	168 732	60.7
Gwinnett County (part)	81	97 610	65.9	26.1	3.8	25.4	46 062	11.6	4.9	32 880	49.5
Rockdale County (part)	259	61 426	29.4	27.2	9.5	23.1	51 958	8.4	4.3	21 249	72.2
Congressional District 5, Georgia	636	629 438	65.6	22.4	9.8	36.5	37 802	21.2	11.0	253 957	44.9
Clayton County (part)	38	12 415	74.2	30.6	6.4	6.4	32 029	15.9	6.4	4 223	40.3
DeKalb County (part)	91	120 835	48.1	18.5	11.7	47.1	45 856	15.3	5.6	51 388	50.2
Fulton County (part)	507	496 188	69.6	23.1	9.5	34.4	35 957	22.7	12.5	198 346	43.6
Congressional District 6, Georgia	1 764	630 613	19.1	25.9	7.0	50.6	71 699	4.5	2.9	237 679	71.8
Cherokee County	1 097	141 903	10.2	28.1	6.6	27.0	60 896	5.3	2.7	49 495	83.9
Cobb County (part)	188	162 129	15.4	26.2	6.6	56.6	80 602	2.9	2.6	60 335	79.2
DeKalb County (part)	55	62 182	34.0	19.7	10.9	54.0	66 598	7.2	3.5	25 281	55.7
Fulton County (part)	423	264 399	22.6	26.0	6.6	58.1	76 299	4.4	3.0	102 568	65.7
Congressional District 7, Georgia	2 518	630 511	24.5	28.6	6.3	31.8	60 450	5.4	3.2	218 221	77.1
Barrow County	420	46 144	16.3	28.1	9.3	10.9	45 019	8.3	4.2	16 354	75.5
Forsyth County (part)	45	15 317	7.1	32.3	3.4	58.9	102 829	2.2	1.5	5 043	96.7
Gwinnett County (part)	1 040	490 838	26.3	28.6	5.6	35.7	63 831	4.5	2.9	169 437	76.9
Newton County (part)	161	17 525	31.4	27.2	10.3	17.8	45 007	12.4	8.3	6 080	71.0
Walton County	853	60 687	17.8	28.4	9.6	13.0	46 479	9.7	3.4	21 307	76.5
Congressional District 8, Georgia	18 573	629 231	37.0	27.0	11.7	15.9	36 294	15.8	5.7	233 321	69.5
Baldwin County (part)	136	5 848	42.5	27.4	11.1	11.4	34 107	13.1	7.1	2 155	78.3
Ben Hill County	652	17 484	37.9	27.6	13.1	9.5	27 100	22.3	6.3	6 673	66.7
Bibb County	647	153 887	50.4	26.6	12.7	21.3	34 532	19.1	7.5	59 667	58.8
Bleckley County	563	11 666	27.5	26.7	13.6	12.5	33 448	15.9	6.0	4 372	76.1
Butts County	483	19 522	31.6	24.0	10.0	8.6	39 879	11.5	3.8	6 455	76.6
Colquitt County	1 430	42 053	35.0	27.3	13.0	11.4	28 539	19.8	6.1	15 495	66.7
Dodge County	1 296	19 171	31.5	26.0	13.3	11.6	27 607	17.4	5.4	7 062	73.8
Houston County	976	110 765	31.1	28.1	9.4	19.8	43 638	10.2	4.4	40 911	68.5
Irwin County	924	9 931	28.2	29.0	14.4	9.9	30 257	17.8	6.0	3 644	76.8
Jasper County	959	11 426	30.2	27.3	11.8	11.5	39 890	14.2	4.7	4 175	79.1
Jones County	1 020	23 639	25.6	27.1	10.3	15.0	43 301	10.2	4.5	8 659	85.8
Laurens County	2 104	44 874	37.1	26.8	13.2	14.4	32 010	18.4	5.1	17 083	71.3
Monroe County	1 025	21 757	30.3	26.2	10.0	17.1	44 195	9.8	3.4	7 719	79.4
Newton County (part)	555	44 476	23.6	27.8	9.8	13.3	44 826	9.1	4.0	15 917	80.3
Pulaski County	641	9 588	38.4	23.1	13.2	12.9	31 895	16.4	5.5	3 407	73.7
Tift County	686	38 407	37.1	27.4	11.6	15.6	32 616	19.9	6.7	13 919	67.2
Turner County	741	9 504	44.3	29.6	12.8	10.5	25 676	26.7	8.0	3 435	71.4
Twiggs County	933	10 590	46.2	27.0	11.7	5.4	31 608	19.7	8.3	3 832	82.7
Wilcox County	985	8 577	38.5	22.9	13.6	7.0	27 483	21.0	4.9	2 785	79.9
Wilkinson County	1 157	10 220	42.8	27.1	13.3	9.6	32 723	17.9	6.7	3 827	82.3
Worth County (part)	660	5 846	17.3	28.3	10.1	8.6	36 599	14.7	7.3	2 129	80.4
Congressional District 9, Georgia	11 224	629 678	13.9	25.8	11.0	16.2	41 116	10.8	3.5	230 256	76.5
Catoosa County	420	53 282	4.5	25.8	11.8	13.8	39 998	9.4	3.3	20 425	77.0
Dade County	451	15 154	3.0	23.8	12.0	10.9	35 259	9.7	5.4	5 633	80.2
Dawson County	547	15 999	3.0	25.2	9.3	18.1	47 486	7.6	3.4	6 069	81.4
Fannin County	999	19 798	3.1	21.0	19.0	10.4	30 612	12.4	3.9	8 369	82.6
Forsyth County (part)	540	83 090	7.8	27.1	7.8	30.2	63 728	6.1	2.2	29 522	86.6
Gilmer County	1 105	23 456	8.8	24.2	13.2	12.9	35 140	12.5	4.2	9 071	78.1
Gordon County (part)	544	17 306	5.3	28.2	8.2	9.7	40 532	8.5	3.3	6 123	83.6
Hall County	1 020	139 277	28.9	26.9	9.4	18.7	44 908	12.4	3.8	47 381	71.1
Lumpkin County	737	21 016	7.6	24.2	9.8	17.6	39 167	13.2	3.9	7 537	72.3
Murray County	892	36 506	7.2	27.8	8.0	7.2	36 996	12.7	4.0	13 286	73.7

[1]Dry land or land partially or temporarily covered by water.
[2]Persons who do not identify themselves as White alone, not of Hispanic origin.
[3]Persons 25 years old and over.

Table B. 110th Congressional Districts by Counties, 2000—*Continued*

(Number, percent.)

STATE Congressional district County	Land area,[1] (sq km)	Population				Percent with bachelor's degree or more[3]	Median household income, 1999 (dollars)	Percent living in poverty	Percent unemployed	Households	
		Total	Percent minority[2]	Percent under 18 years	Percent 65 years and over					Total	Percent owner occupied
	1	2	3	4	5	6	7	8	9	10	11
Congressional District 9, Georgia—*Continued*											
Pickens County	601	22 983	4.6	23.5	13.2	15.6	41 387	9.2	2.3	8 960	82.1
Union County	835	17 289	2.5	19.7	21.6	12.5	31 893	12.5	3.2	7 159	82.3
Walker County	1 157	61 053	6.2	24.6	13.8	10.2	32 406	12.5	4.3	23 605	77.0
White County	626	19 944	5.8	23.1	14.5	15.4	36 084	10.5	2.8	7 731	79.3
Whitfield County	751	83 525	27.5	27.1	10.4	12.8	39 377	11.5	3.6	29 385	67.6
Congressional District 10, Georgia	15 260	629 818	26.1	24.1	11.8	22.7	36 615	14.8	5.5	239 239	68.6
Banks County	605	14 422	8.5	26.1	10.4	8.6	38 523	12.5	3.0	5 364	81.0
Clarke County	313	101 489	38.0	17.9	8.0	39.8	28 403	28.3	10.1	39 706	42.1
Columbia County	751	89 288	18.7	29.5	8.0	32.0	55 682	5.1	3.6	31 120	82.1
Elbert County	955	20 511	34.2	26.0	15.1	9.8	28 724	17.3	5.8	8 004	75.9
Franklin County	682	20 285	11.5	23.9	15.4	10.3	32 134	13.9	4.2	7 888	79.3
Greene County	1 006	14 406	47.9	25.0	14.4	17.6	33 479	22.3	6.7	5 477	76.2
Habersham County	720	35 902	15.2	23.3	13.8	15.8	36 321	12.2	4.2	13 259	76.2
Hart County	601	22 997	21.5	23.6	16.4	13.5	32 833	14.8	5.3	9 106	80.8
Jackson County	887	41 589	12.3	26.8	10.4	11.7	40 349	12.0	3.4	15 057	74.9
Lincoln County	547	8 348	36.1	24.4	14.9	10.1	31 952	15.3	5.9	3 251	81.8
McDuffie County	673	21 231	40.1	27.9	12.4	11.7	31 920	18.4	7.6	7 970	71.4
Madison County	735	25 730	12.1	26.3	10.9	10.9	36 347	11.6	2.7	9 800	80.2
Morgan County	906	15 457	31.7	26.6	12.5	18.7	40 249	10.9	5.1	5 558	77.6
Oconee County	481	26 225	12.1	30.3	8.5	39.8	55 211	6.5	3.7	9 051	80.2
Oglethorpe County	1 142	12 635	21.7	25.5	12.2	15.6	35 578	13.2	3.0	4 849	82.5
Putnam County	892	18 812	33.5	23.2	14.4	14.4	36 956	14.6	3.8	7 402	79.5
Rabun County	961	15 050	7.0	22.0	18.1	17.6	33 899	11.1	4.9	6 279	79.4
Richmond County (part)	286	80 000	42.7	21.6	12.6	30.3	35 459	15.4	6.2	31 835	49.1
Stephens County	464	25 435	15.0	23.3	15.7	14.1	29 466	15.1	4.2	9 951	72.7
Towns County	432	9 319	2.8	16.2	25.9	17.4	31 950	11.8	3.8	3 998	85.2
Wilkes County	1 221	10 687	45.9	24.0	17.5	12.0	27 644	17.5	4.4	4 314	75.5
Congressional District 11, Georgia	6 974	628 748	19.7	26.8	9.3	21.7	45 710	9.8	4.2	229 653	72.6
Bartow County	1 190	76 019	13.6	27.8	9.4	14.1	43 660	8.6	4.0	27 176	75.2
Carroll County (part)	514	40 745	21.7	26.8	9.9	12.1	37 878	14.0	4.5	15 054	69.5
Chattooga County	812	25 470	14.3	23.0	14.2	7.7	30 664	14.3	5.6	9 577	75.4
Cobb County (part)	405	223 656	26.2	27.0	6.5	37.6	59 614	6.9	3.6	81 841	70.3
Floyd County	1 329	90 565	21.0	24.5	13.9	15.8	35 615	14.4	6.7	34 028	66.8
Gordon County (part)	377	26 798	17.1	24.8	11.8	11.2	37 726	10.7	3.6	10 050	64.5
Haralson County	731	25 690	7.4	26.1	13.2	9.0	31 656	15.5	4.1	9 826	75.2
Paulding County	812	81 678	10.5	30.7	6.0	15.2	52 161	5.5	2.5	28 089	86.8
Polk County	806	38 127	22.0	25.9	13.2	8.0	32 328	15.5	6.0	14 012	71.3
Congressional District 12, Georgia	22 422	629 552	49.2	26.9	11.5	13.9	30 383	21.9	8.1	227 952	65.2
Baldwin County (part)	534	38 852	46.9	20.8	10.5	16.9	35 394	17.4	6.0	12 603	64.4
Bulloch County	1 767	55 983	32.1	22.3	9.4	25.4	29 499	24.5	10.2	20 743	58.1
Burke County	2 151	22 243	53.2	31.3	11.0	9.5	27 877	28.7	9.2	7 934	76.0
Candler County	639	9 577	37.3	26.8	15.1	10.2	25 022	26.1	7.1	3 375	73.2
Chatham County (part)	576	157 763	57.7	25.8	12.6	18.1	30 437	20.7	7.3	60 393	54.1
Effingham County	1 242	37 535	16.2	29.9	8.0	13.6	46 505	9.3	4.2	13 151	82.7
Emanuel County	1 776	21 837	37.3	27.9	13.2	10.1	24 383	27.4	4.4	8 045	71.2
Evans County	479	10 495	39.8	27.8	12.3	9.0	25 447	27.0	8.1	3 778	71.4
Glascock County	373	2 556	9.9	23.6	18.4	6.5	29 743	17.2	12.3	1 004	80.2
Hancock County	1 226	10 076	78.8	24.3	12.2	9.8	22 003	29.4	13.7	3 237	76.5
Jefferson County	1 367	17 266	58.0	28.5	13.7	9.1	26 120	23.0	11.8	6 339	72.2
Jenkins County	906	8 575	44.1	28.6	13.9	10.8	24 025	28.4	10.7	3 214	73.4
Johnson County	788	8 560	37.9	30.2	15.6	7.8	23 848	22.6	5.4	3 130	79.8
Montgomery County	635	8 270	30.5	24.9	10.5	13.5	30 240	19.9	3.9	2 919	78.2
Richmond County (part)	553	119 775	64.3	30.3	9.8	10.4	31 667	22.1	10.2	42 085	64.6
Screven County	1 679	15 374	46.9	27.8	14.1	10.2	29 312	20.1	9.4	5 797	77.7
Taliaferro County	506	2 077	61.8	24.3	18.6	8.4	23 750	23.4	9.8	870	77.1
Tattnall County	1 253	22 305	40.6	23.1	11.3	7.9	28 664	23.9	6.8	7 057	70.5
Toombs County	950	26 067	33.9	28.5	12.2	12.7	26 811	23.9	5.7	9 877	65.5
Treutlen County	520	6 854	35.2	25.7	13.6	8.5	24 644	26.3	9.4	2 531	74.9
Warren County	739	6 336	60.6	26.5	16.1	8.0	27 366	27.0	9.4	2 435	76.8
Washington County	1 762	21 176	54.4	26.9	12.7	10.5	29 910	22.9	9.5	7 435	74.1
Congressional District 13, Georgia	1 480	629 403	53.1	27.5	7.0	22.5	46 477	8.8	5.0	228 746	63.8
Clayton County (part)	331	224 102	64.5	29.8	5.8	17.2	43 452	9.8	5.4	78 020	61.7
Cobb County (part)	287	221 966	47.9	24.7	7.6	29.2	47 262	8.7	4.9	85 311	58.3
DeKalb County (part)	35	12 160	93.2	30.8	3.7	24.3	53 581	6.6	6.5	3 938	90.7
Douglas County (part)	259	76 082	26.9	27.6	7.5	20.4	49 301	8.4	4.1	27 290	71.9
Fulton County (part)	439	55 419	73.5	27.8	9.5	19.2	42 797	10.0	6.6	20 328	65.5
Henry County (part)	128	39 674	27.8	29.0	6.7	20.7	56 423	4.3	2.6	13 859	83.2

[1]Dry land or land partially or temporarily covered by water.
[2]Persons who do not identify themselves as White alone, not of Hispanic origin.
[3]Persons 25 years old and over.

Table B. 110th Congressional Districts by Counties, 2000—*Continued*

(Number, percent.)

STATE Congressional district County	Land area,[1] (sq km)	Population Total	Population Percent minority[2]	Population Percent under 18 years	Population Percent 65 years and over	Percent with bachelor's degree or more[3]	Median household income, 1999 (dollars)	Percent living in poverty	Percent unem- ployed	Households Total	Households Percent owner occupied
	1	2	3	4	5	6	7	8	9	10	11
HAWAII	16 635	1 211 537	77.2	24.3	13.3	26.2	49 820	10.7	6.3	403 240	56.5
Congressional District 1, Hawaii	494	606 610	82.3	21.6	15.2	28.9	50 798	9.7	5.8	209 847	53.1
Honolulu County (part)	494	606 610	82.3	21.6	15.2	28.9	50 798	9.7	5.8	209 847	53.1
Congressional District 2, Hawaii	16 140	604 927	72.1	27.0	11.4	23.1	48 686	11.7	6.8	193 393	60.2
Hawaii County	10 433	148 677	70.5	26.1	13.4	22.1	39 805	15.7	8.0	52 985	64.5
Honolulu County (part)	1 059	269 546	74.7	28.4	9.7	25.1	55 736	10.2	7.4	76 603	58.6
Kalawao County	34	147	90.5	0.0	49.7	10.2	9 333	40.1	0.0	115	0.0
Kauai County	1 612	58 463	72.3	26.4	13.9	19.4	45 020	10.5	5.3	20 183	61.3
Maui County	3 002	128 094	68.1	25.5	11.5	22.4	49 489	10.5	5.0	43 507	57.5
IDAHO	214 314	1 293 953	12.0	28.5	11.3	21.7	37 572	11.8	5.8	469 645	72.4
Congressional District 1, Idaho	102 369	648 922	11.1	28.1	11.6	20.3	38 364	11.0	6.2	237 288	75.7
Ada County (part)	2 261	164 438	8.4	30.7	7.8	28.5	52 281	5.5	3.6	56 010	83.2
Adams County	3 534	3 476	5.2	23.7	16.3	14.9	28 423	15.1	7.7	1 421	79.0
Benewah County	2 010	9 171	12.2	26.8	14.3	11.4	31 517	14.1	13.9	3 580	78.4
Boise County	4 927	6 670	6.2	27.0	11.1	19.9	38 651	12.9	7.2	2 616	83.3
Bonner County	4 501	36 835	4.6	25.4	13.2	16.9	32 803	15.5	7.3	14 693	77.8
Boundary County	3 286	9 871	6.6	29.2	13.4	14.7	31 250	15.7	10.0	3 707	78.4
Canyon County	1 527	131 441	22.4	31.0	10.9	14.9	35 884	12.0	5.9	45 018	73.3
Clearwater County	6 375	8 930	6.6	22.9	15.6	13.4	32 071	13.5	11.5	3 456	77.9
Gem County	1 457	15 181	9.9	28.0	15.7	11.4	34 460	13.1	5.1	5 539	79.9
Idaho County	21 976	15 511	6.6	25.0	16.7	14.4	29 515	15.6	10.2	6 084	77.0
Kootenai County	3 225	108 685	6.0	27.1	12.3	19.1	37 754	10.5	7.8	41 308	74.5
Latah County	2 789	34 935	7.5	20.3	9.4	41.0	32 524	16.7	7.6	13 059	58.7
Lewis County	1 241	3 747	8.9	25.1	18.4	14.8	31 413	12.0	8.6	1 554	74.5
Nez Perce County	2 199	37 410	9.0	23.7	16.8	18.9	36 282	12.2	4.6	15 286	68.7
Owyhee County	19 886	10 644	28.7	31.3	12.3	10.2	28 339	16.9	6.8	3 710	69.7
Payette County	1 055	20 578	15.4	30.3	13.3	10.6	33 046	13.2	6.2	7 371	74.2
Shoshone County	6 822	13 771	4.6	23.0	17.4	10.2	28 535	16.4	11.8	5 906	72.6
Valley County	9 526	7 651	4.0	23.7	14.7	26.3	36 927	9.3	6.1	3 208	79.1
Washington County	3 772	9 977	17.5	27.1	17.2	12.7	30 625	13.3	7.8	3 762	73.8
Congressional District 2, Idaho	111 946	645 031	12.9	28.8	11.0	23.1	36 934	12.6	5.4	232 357	69.0
Ada County (part)	471	136 466	10.7	22.9	10.7	34.2	40 077	10.3	4.3	57 398	58.4
Bannock County	2 883	75 565	10.4	28.0	10.3	24.9	36 683	13.9	6.9	27 192	70.6
Bear Lake County	2 516	6 411	3.6	32.8	15.8	11.7	32 162	9.6	7.2	2 259	83.2
Bingham County	5 425	41 735	21.1	35.0	10.4	14.4	36 423	12.4	5.8	13 317	79.4
Blaine County	6 850	18 991	13.2	23.9	7.7	43.1	50 496	7.8	4.2	7 780	68.7
Bonneville County	4 839	82 522	9.6	32.0	10.2	26.1	41 805	10.1	5.0	28 753	74.7
Butte County	5 783	2 899	9.6	28.9	14.9	13.0	30 473	18.2	5.8	1 089	77.1
Camas County	2 784	991	3.4	24.7	13.1	22.2	34 167	8.3	4.0	396	77.8
Caribou County	4 574	7 304	4.8	31.7	13.6	15.9	37 609	9.6	4.8	2 560	79.5
Cassia County	6 647	21 416	20.5	34.0	12.7	13.9	33 322	13.6	5.2	7 060	72.6
Clark County	4 570	1 022	37.4	34.8	9.2	12.6	31 576	19.9	6.1	340	68.2
Custer County	12 757	4 342	5.7	25.7	14.4	17.4	32 174	14.3	6.2	1 770	74.7
Elmore County	7 971	29 130	20.1	27.8	7.1	17.3	35 256	11.2	6.6	9 092	57.4
Franklin County	1 723	11 329	6.6	37.2	11.7	13.6	36 061	7.4	5.3	3 476	80.8
Fremont County	4 835	11 819	13.1	33.1	12.5	12.0	33 424	14.2	5.3	3 885	84.3
Gooding County	1 893	14 155	19.5	29.7	15.5	12.0	31 888	13.8	3.4	5 046	72.4
Jefferson County	2 836	19 155	11.6	36.2	9.3	15.2	37 737	10.4	4.4	5 901	84.7
Jerome County	1 554	18 342	19.9	31.6	12.3	14.0	34 696	13.9	5.9	6 298	70.0
Lemhi County	11 821	7 806	4.2	25.5	16.7	17.9	30 185	15.3	8.6	3 275	76.1
Lincoln County	3 122	4 044	17.0	30.5	13.2	13.0	32 484	13.1	3.9	1 447	74.4
Madison County	1 221	27 467	5.6	26.2	6.0	24.4	32 607	30.5	7.3	7 129	59.2
Minidoka County	1 967	20 174	27.8	31.6	13.1	10.1	32 021	14.8	6.5	6 973	76.9
Oneida County	3 109	4 125	3.9	32.0	16.0	15.0	34 309	10.8	4.3	1 430	82.3
Power County	3 640	7 538	25.5	33.8	10.2	14.3	32 226	16.1	4.7	2 560	74.5
Teton County	1 166	5 999	13.0	31.8	7.4	28.1	41 898	12.9	3.3	2 078	73.7
Twin Falls County	4 986	64 284	12.3	27.8	14.1	16.0	34 506	12.7	5.9	23 853	68.3
ILLINOIS	143 961	12 419 293	32.2	26.1	12.1	26.1	46 590	10.7	6.0	4 591 779	67.3
Congressional District 1, Illinois	253	654 203	72.6	28.3	12.6	18.7	37 222	19.7	12.9	233 426	54.4
Cook County (part)	253	654 203	72.6	28.3	12.6	18.7	37 222	19.7	12.9	233 426	54.4
Congressional District 2, Illinois	478	654 078	74.5	29.5	11.6	18.1	41 330	15.2	10.4	228 365	66.2
Cook County (part)	457	643 430	74.5	29.4	11.7	18.0	41 199	15.4	10.5	224 654	66.3
Will County (part)	21	10 648	72.8	33.0	6.5	25.5	51 516	7.0	5.9	3 711	60.3
Congressional District 3, Illinois	322	653 292	31.9	25.7	14.5	20.5	48 048	8.3	5.7	236 791	72.6
Cook County (part)	322	653 292	31.9	25.7	14.5	20.5	48 048	8.3	5.7	236 791	72.6
Congressional District 4, Illinois	101	653 654	81.4	31.7	6.2	13.6	35 935	20.2	9.3	193 008	39.2
Gooding County	101	653 654	81.4	31.7	6.2	13.6	35 935	20.2	9.3	193 008	39.2

[1]Dry land or land partially or temporarily covered by water.
[2]Persons who do not identify themselves as White alone, not of Hispanic origin.
[3]Persons 25 years old and over.

Table B. 110th Congressional Districts by Counties, 2000—*Continued*

(Number, percent.)

STATE Congressional district County	Land area,[1] (sq km)	Population				Percent with bachelor's degree or more[3]	Median household income, 1999 (dollars)	Percent living in poverty	Percent unem- ployed	Households	
		Total	Percent minority[2]	Percent under 18 years	Percent 65 years and over					Total	Percent owner occupied
	1	2	3	4	5	6	7	8	9	10	11
Congressional District 5, Illinois	148	654 116	34.2	19.8	11.7	33.9	48 531	8.5	4.8	266 664	49.8
Cook County (part)	148	654 116	34.2	19.8	11.7	33.9	48 531	8.5	4.8	266 664	49.8
Congressional District 6, Illinois	553	654 549	24.8	26.0	10.3	34.6	62 640	4.3	3.6	232 718	75.8
Cook County (part)	158	165 297	32.7	24.9	9.9	28.8	57 218	5.0	4.0	60 049	71.6
DuPage County (part)	395	489 252	22.1	26.4	10.4	36.6	65 217	4.1	3.5	172 669	77.3
Congressional District 7, Illinois	146	653 521	72.7	26.6	9.6	32.1	40 361	24.0	12.2	250 442	41.9
Cook County (part)	146	653 521	72.7	26.6	9.6	32.1	40 361	24.0	12.2	250 442	41.9
Congressional District 8, Illinois	1 600	652 805	21.1	28.2	8.1	32.1	62 762	4.4	3.4	234 592	77.6
Cook County (part)	234	221 890	28.8	25.0	8.4	35.7	61 395	4.2	3.3	85 163	71.3
Lake County (part)	784	329 213	19.4	30.1	7.7	33.1	66 100	4.5	3.5	113 624	81.5
McHenry County (part)	582	101 702	9.8	28.9	8.9	20.9	58 300	4.5	3.4	35 805	80.5
Congressional District 9, Illinois	195	653 117	37.6	20.4	15.6	39.6	46 531	11.0	5.3	268 430	54.7
Cook County (part)	195	653 117	37.6	20.4	15.6	39.6	46 531	11.0	5.3	268 430	54.7
Congressional District 10, Illinois	646	654 062	24.9	27.0	12.3	47.5	71 663	4.8	3.8	229 591	78.7
Cook County (part)	271	338 919	16.3	25.5	15.0	49.9	74 472	2.7	2.5	126 918	82.6
Lake County (part)	375	315 143	34.1	28.5	9.4	44.6	68 514	7.0	5.2	102 673	73.7
Congressional District 11, Illinois	10 984	653 861	16.4	26.7	11.9	18.5	47 800	8.4	5.7	236 533	74.6
Bureau County (part)	1 794	28 108	6.5	24.9	17.7	15.6	40 353	7.3	4.3	11 280	76.5
Grundy County	1 088	37 535	6.1	26.8	12.2	15.2	51 719	4.8	4.6	14 293	72.3
Kankakee County	1 753	103 833	22.1	27.0	13.1	15.0	41 532	11.4	6.4	38 182	69.4
La Salle County	2 939	111 509	8.2	25.1	16.5	13.3	40 308	9.1	5.4	43 417	75.1
Livingston County (part)	94	399	2.3	24.6	10.0	10.6	48 304	1.8	1.8	145	82.1
McLean County (part)	1 351	81 911	13.1	21.3	9.1	27.6	39 534	14.1	9.3	29 316	61.8
Will County (part)	1 730	287 466	21.0	29.0	9.9	20.7	57 621	6.3	4.7	98 713	80.3
Woodford County (part)	236	3 100	1.3	27.9	19.0	15.5	45 564	7.5	3.7	1 187	80.1
Congressional District 12, Illinois	11 460	653 456	20.3	25.1	14.5	16.8	35 198	15.0	7.0	255 599	69.4
Alexander County	612	9 590	37.8	25.9	16.8	6.9	26 042	26.1	10.6	3 808	72.0
Franklin County	1 067	39 018	2.1	23.1	18.6	11.3	28 411	16.2	6.8	16 408	77.7
Jackson County	1 523	59 612	20.3	19.2	11.1	32.0	24 946	25.2	7.9	24 215	53.3
Madison County (part)	304	120 972	14.7	25.5	15.4	11.4	35 080	14.0	7.6	49 106	70.0
Monroe County	1 006	27 619	1.4	26.5	13.3	20.4	55 320	3.4	2.5	10 275	80.2
Perry County	1 142	23 094	10.7	21.9	16.1	10.1	33 281	13.2	8.0	8 504	78.6
Pulaski County	520	7 348	34.1	27.4	17.4	7.1	25 361	24.7	9.6	2 893	75.7
Randolph County	1 498	33 893	11.8	22.2	15.5	8.6	37 013	10.0	5.7	12 084	79.4
St. Clair County	1 719	256 082	33.1	27.7	13.1	19.3	39 148	14.5	6.8	96 810	67.0
Union County	1 078	18 293	5.1	23.2	17.5	15.8	30 994	16.5	10.7	7 290	75.4
Williamson County (part)	991	57 935	5.1	23.2	16.7	17.1	31 586	14.9	6.7	24 206	73.0
Congressional District 13, Illinois	918	652 879	18.5	28.2	8.8	42.4	71 686	2.9	3.2	230 918	80.7
Cook County (part)	164	85 302	7.8	28.0	12.4	33.3	74 639	2.9	2.9	28 636	91.5
DuPage County (part)	338	363 425	18.7	26.5	9.5	49.7	71 701	2.8	2.9	137 164	74.5
Will County (part)	416	204 152	22.5	31.2	6.0	32.5	70 750	2.9	3.8	65 118	88.9
Congressional District 14, Illinois	7 386	654 031	26.1	28.7	9.0	26.3	56 314	7.0	4.7	220 953	74.8
Bureau County (part)	282	923	2.4	29.6	14.4	8.7	32 241	13.8	3.4	331	68.0
DeKalb County (part)	1 011	73 039	16.5	22.0	9.7	28.8	43 323	13.1	6.6	25 958	55.3
DuPage County (part)	131	51 484	31.4	30.8	5.3	31.3	71 911	4.9	3.4	15 768	83.0
Henry County (part)	1 321	22 762	2.0	26.0	15.8	19.7	46 230	5.8	3.1	8 745	80.0
Kane County	1 348	404 119	32.4	30.3	8.3	27.7	59 351	6.7	4.7	133 901	76.0
Kendall County	830	54 544	11.5	29.5	8.4	25.3	64 625	3.0	2.9	18 798	84.1
Lee County	1 879	36 062	9.7	24.2	14.7	13.2	40 967	7.7	5.3	13 253	73.9
Whiteside County (part)	584	11 098	8.6	24.8	15.6	8.9	41 096	10.7	4.7	4 199	78.6
Congressional District 15, Illinois	26 088	653 618	11.5	23.5	14.0	23.2	38 583	11.7	5.0	257 248	68.8
Champaign County	2 582	179 669	22.3	21.0	9.8	38.0	37 780	16.1	5.5	70 597	55.7
Clark County	1 299	17 008	1.4	24.8	17.9	13.6	35 967	9.2	4.8	6 971	77.5
Coles County	1 316	53 196	5.4	19.7	13.3	20.8	32 286	17.5	5.5	21 043	61.9
Crawford County	1 149	20 452	8.0	22.8	16.7	10.3	32 531	11.2	5.4	7 842	80.2
Cumberland County	896	11 253	1.5	26.6	15.9	10.1	36 149	9.5	5.4	4 368	82.0
De Witt County	1 030	16 798	2.7	24.6	15.9	13.4	41 256	8.2	5.3	6 770	74.9
Douglas County	1 080	19 922	5.0	27.1	16.0	13.8	39 439	6.4	2.8	7 574	76.9
Edgar County	1 615	19 704	2.8	23.8	17.8	13.3	35 203	10.5	4.8	7 874	74.6
Edwards County (part)	68	1 115	1.6	24.3	15.8	6.7	30 185	6.5	4.9	474	75.7
Ford County	1 258	14 241	2.7	25.9	19.4	13.9	38 073	7.0	3.3	5 639	76.0
Gallatin County (part)	208	1 180	1.4	24.6	16.8	5.0	24 808	21.4	7.9	491	83.1
Iroquois County	2 892	31 334	5.6	25.5	18.1	11.8	38 071	8.7	3.8	12 220	76.4
Lawrence County (part)	516	8 709	2.5	21.9	22.9	11.9	28 838	14.3	6.3	3 614	74.8
Livingston County (part)	2 610	39 279	9.2	25.0	15.3	12.7	41 281	8.9	5.3	14 229	74.1
McLean County (part)	1 714	68 522	10.5	25.9	10.6	44.7	56 432	5.1	2.2	27 430	71.5

[1]Dry land or land partially or temporarily covered by water.
[2]Persons who do not identify themselves as White alone, not of Hispanic origin.
[3]Persons 25 years old and over.

Table B. 110th Congressional Districts by Counties, 2000—*Continued*

(Number, percent.)

STATE Congressional district County	Land area,[1] (sq km)	Population Total	Population Percent minority[2]	Population Percent under 18 years	Population Percent 65 years and over	Percent with bachelor's degree or more[3]	Median household income, 1999 (dollars)	Percent living in poverty	Percent unemployed	Households Total	Households Percent owner occupied
	1	2	3	4	5	6	7	8	9	10	11
Congressional District 15, Illinois—*Continued*											
Macon County (part)	394	15 396	4.6	23.1	16.1	23.1	51 969	4.6	3.9	6 087	87.7
Moultrie County	869	14 287	1.8	25.5	17.7	14.7	40 084	7.8	3.3	5 405	78.4
Piatt County	1 140	16 365	2.3	25.2	15.4	21.0	45 752	5.0	2.9	6 475	80.3
Saline County (part)	142	6 468	1.6	24.4	21.8	9.6	26 118	18.7	9.6	2 722	75.2
Vermilion County	2 329	83 919	15.5	25.0	16.0	12.5	34 071	13.3	7.6	33 406	71.8
Wabash County (part)	303	10 773	2.8	24.1	17.8	12.6	34 525	14.1	6.7	4 344	73.1
White County (part)	680	4 028	2.6	22.2	18.9	7.3	34 222	12.6	4.1	1 673	79.1
Congressional District 16, Illinois	10 614	653 467	14.3	27.6	12.0	21.1	48 960	7.3	4.9	244 751	75.5
Boone County	728	41 786	14.9	29.8	10.7	14.5	52 397	7.0	4.4	14 597	78.6
Carroll County	1 151	16 674	3.8	24.4	19.2	13.1	37 148	9.6	6.9	6 794	76.7
DeKalb County (part)	631	15 930	6.5	28.8	10.0	19.1	55 225	4.0	3.5	5 716	79.4
Jo Daviess County	1 557	22 289	2.0	23.1	17.9	15.2	40 411	6.7	4.0	9 218	77.3
McHenry County (part)	981	158 375	10.6	31.1	7.4	32.2	69 221	3.1	3.5	53 598	84.9
Ogle County	1 965	51 032	7.7	27.4	13.4	17.0	45 448	7.1	4.6	19 278	74.5
Stephenson County	1 461	48 979	11.4	25.2	16.3	15.6	40 366	9.0	6.2	19 785	74.8
Whiteside County (part)	810	19 984	4.7	24.5	17.0	14.4	42 154	5.6	3.8	7 785	77.7
Winnebago County	1 331	278 418	20.7	26.4	12.7	19.4	43 886	9.6	5.8	107 980	70.1
Congressional District 17, Illinois	21 031	653 531	12.7	24.0	16.2	14.7	35 066	12.5	6.8	260 924	71.0
Adams County (part)	775	55 875	5.9	24.5	18.1	19.3	33 936	10.5	5.3	22 272	71.8
Calhoun County	657	5 084	1.6	23.0	19.1	9.4	34 375	9.0	4.9	2 046	80.8
Christian County (part)	127	6 892	1.3	24.6	20.7	7.3	30 553	15.5	4.9	2 800	73.2
Fayette County (part)	281	2 495	0.6	26.4	16.3	7.9	29 973	12.2	5.8	982	79.4
Fulton County	2 242	38 250	5.5	22.0	18.3	11.4	33 952	9.9	6.7	14 877	76.3
Greene County (part)	951	8 443	2.4	25.6	16.7	8.8	30 866	14.6	7.3	3 270	76.5
Hancock County	2 058	20 121	1.3	24.6	18.2	15.6	36 654	8.3	4.8	8 069	80.3
Henderson County	981	8 213	2.3	23.3	16.7	10.0	36 405	9.5	5.2	3 365	78.9
Henry County (part)	811	28 258	7.7	24.8	16.8	12.4	35 813	9.8	5.5	11 311	77.8
Jersey County (part)	419	3 736	3.1	26.8	11.7	11.6	42 354	7.1	8.0	1 369	80.6
Knox County (part)	1 029	49 414	13.0	21.7	17.5	14.7	34 940	11.8	7.0	19 462	70.2
McDonough County	1 526	32 913	7.5	17.7	14.1	26.9	32 141	19.8	11.1	12 360	63.1
Macon County (part)	374	69 874	23.2	24.9	15.3	13.5	31 915	18.1	9.6	28 742	64.7
Macoupin County	2 237	49 019	2.4	24.7	17.5	11.8	36 190	9.4	5.2	19 253	79.0
Madison County (part)	81	1 760	1.6	25.0	16.4	10.0	40 000	7.9	6.0	722	84.5
Mercer County	1 453	16 957	1.9	24.7	16.0	12.6	40 893	7.8	5.9	6 624	79.7
Montgomery County (part)	752	15 259	1.9	25.1	17.5	10.8	31 722	16.0	6.3	6 144	76.5
Pike County (part)	809	4 808	1.1	25.4	17.0	9.0	29 572	13.4	6.6	1 957	81.3
Rock Island County	1 105	149 374	18.5	23.8	15.0	17.1	38 608	10.7	6.3	60 712	69.7
Sangamon County (part)	298	36 546	36.7	28.3	13.7	12.7	27 308	24.0	9.5	14 993	52.2
Shelby County (part)	278	1 934	0.9	27.3	17.8	3.5	33 594	11.8	5.8	728	85.6
Warren County	1 405	18 735	5.6	23.1	16.4	15.8	36 224	9.2	6.5	7 166	74.4
Whiteside County (part)	380	29 571	17.0	25.7	15.8	10.1	38 760	9.5	5.7	11 700	70.8
Congressional District 18, Illinois	21 202	653 426	10.0	24.3	15.1	20.7	41 934	8.9	4.6	257 236	73.6
Adams County (part)	1 444	12 402	2.9	27.0	14.9	10.2	37 912	7.8	3.7	4 588	83.1
Brown County	792	6 950	22.1	17.7	12.7	9.2	35 445	8.5	3.5	2 108	74.1
Bureau County (part)	173	6 472	7.3	23.8	18.2	17.0	40 721	6.2	4.9	2 571	74.8
Cass County	974	13 695	10.0	25.3	15.6	12.6	35 243	12.0	5.8	5 347	75.2
Knox County (part)	826	6 422	1.9	23.4	17.4	13.9	38 376	6.3	2.8	2 594	81.5
Logan County	1 601	31 183	9.0	21.9	14.9	14.2	39 389	8.1	6.3	11 113	71.3
Macon County (part)	736	29 436	8.8	24.5	15.0	21.2	46 234	5.3	3.5	11 732	80.6
Marshall County	1 000	13 180	2.3	23.4	18.8	14.5	41 576	5.6	3.7	5 225	80.2
Mason County	1 396	16 038	1.9	24.3	17.2	11.2	35 985	9.7	6.1	6 389	76.7
Menard County	814	12 486	2.3	26.6	13.3	20.5	46 596	8.2	3.9	4 873	78.9
Morgan County	1 473	36 616	8.1	22.7	15.7	19.9	36 933	9.7	6.1	14 039	70.3
Peoria County	1 605	183 433	21.5	25.1	14.1	23.3	39 978	13.7	5.8	72 733	67.8
Pike County (part)	1 341	12 576	3.5	23.6	20.1	10.3	31 755	12.0	6.1	4 919	75.6
Putnam County	414	6 086	4.8	25.1	16.0	12.1	45 492	5.5	4.9	2 415	82.3
Sangamon County (part)	1 274	86 539	7.7	23.1	14.8	31.8	46 424	5.8	2.9	36 931	72.3
Schuyler County	1 133	7 189	1.5	23.2	19.3	11.7	35 233	10.1	5.7	2 975	79.0
Scott County	650	5 537	0.8	24.9	16.5	12.1	36 566	9.7	4.6	2 222	77.6
Stark County	746	6 332	2.4	25.1	19.1	13.4	35 826	8.6	6.9	2 525	77.4
Tazewell County	1 681	128 485	3.2	24.3	14.9	18.1	45 250	6.3	4.0	50 327	76.1
Woodford County (part)	1 132	32 369	2.2	26.6	14.5	21.7	52 071	4.0	2.6	11 610	83.0

[1]Dry land or land partially or temporarily covered by water.
[2]Persons who do not identify themselves as White alone, not of Hispanic origin.
[3]Persons 25 years old and over.

Table B. 110th Congressional Districts by Counties, 2000—*Continued*

(Number, percent.)

STATE Congressional district County	Land area,[1] (sq km)	Population				Percent with bachelor's degree or more[3]	Median household income, 1999 (dollars)	Percent living in poverty	Percent unem- ployed	Households	
		Total	Percent minority[2]	Percent under 18 years	Percent 65 years and over					Total	Percent owner occupied
	1	2	3	4	5	6	7	8	9	10	11
Congressional District 19, Illinois	29 833	653 627	6.0	24.3	15.3	17.1	38 955	9.1	4.7	253 590	78.1
Bond County	985	17 633	10.2	21.9	14.6	15.0	37 680	9.3	5.3	6 155	79.6
Christian County (part)	1 709	28 480	4.9	23.9	16.5	11.3	38 342	8.1	4.9	11 121	77.0
Clay County	1 215	14 560	1.3	23.9	19.2	9.7	30 599	11.8	5.6	5 839	79.8
Clinton County	1 228	35 535	6.4	24.9	14.5	13.0	44 618	6.4	3.3	12 754	80.3
Edwards County (part)	508	5 856	1.8	22.8	19.0	10.4	32 102	10.4	3.7	2 431	82.3
Effingham County	1 240	34 264	2.0	28.6	13.9	15.1	39 379	8.1	4.5	13 001	76.0
Fayette County (part)	1 574	19 307	7.2	23.3	15.9	9.2	32 025	12.2	5.8	7 164	79.8
Gallatin County (part)	631	5 265	2.9	21.7	18.3	8.3	26 269	20.5	6.7	2 235	80.6
Greene County (part)	455	6 318	1.7	25.1	18.6	11.8	32 702	9.5	3.5	2 487	76.3
Hamilton County	1 127	8 621	2.5	24.0	19.2	10.5	30 496	12.9	4.6	3 462	81.5
Hardin County	462	4 800	5.6	20.5	18.6	9.6	27 693	18.6	5.9	1 987	80.5
Jasper County	1 280	10 117	0.8	25.9	16.5	11.2	34 721	9.9	3.5	3 930	83.2
Jefferson County	1 479	40 045	11.2	24.3	15.3	13.7	33 555	12.3	5.6	15 374	74.4
Jersey County (part)	537	17 932	2.4	25.2	14.9	12.8	42 003	7.1	5.5	6 727	77.1
Johnson County	893	12 878	17.1	18.6	13.5	11.7	33 326	11.3	7.5	4 183	84.9
Lawrence County (part)	448	6 743	1.9	23.7	16.7	6.8	31 836	12.8	6.2	2 695	79.9
Madison County (part)	1 493	136 209	7.5	24.4	13.2	26.3	50 207	6.0	3.5	52 125	77.3
Marion County	1 482	41 691	6.2	25.5	16.6	12.1	35 227	11.3	7.0	16 619	76.6
Massac County	619	15 161	7.9	22.9	17.8	10.7	31 498	13.5	5.9	6 261	78.6
Montgomery County (part)	1 071	15 393	9.0	22.1	16.4	11.6	34 783	10.5	4.8	5 363	80.4
Pope County	961	4 413	7.0	21.5	17.7	10.5	30 048	18.2	11.2	1 769	82.1
Richland County	933	16 149	1.9	24.5	17.6	15.2	31 185	12.9	7.4	6 660	76.4
Saline County (part)	851	20 265	7.5	23.9	17.9	12.9	29 869	12.8	7.3	8 270	76.9
Sangamon County (part)	676	65 866	6.6	25.4	12.1	32.2	49 174	5.8	3.0	26 798	76.8
Shelby County (part)	1 686	20 959	1.2	24.7	17.7	12.2	37 762	8.9	3.5	8 328	80.6
Wabash County (part)	276	2 164	1.4	24.7	13.0	12.0	34 325	14.3	5.9	848	85.8
Washington County	1 457	15 148	1.7	25.3	16.7	13.4	40 932	6.0	3.2	5 848	81.0
Wayne County	1 849	17 151	2.2	23.8	18.8	10.0	30 481	12.4	6.6	7 143	79.6
White County (part)	602	11 343	1.7	21.2	21.6	11.6	28 301	12.5	6.3	4 861	77.6
Williamson County (part)	106	3 361	13.1	18.5	14.0	17.9	46 033	9.0	7.2	1 152	87.8
INDIANA	92 895	6 080 485	14.1	25.9	12.4	19.4	41 567	9.5	4.9	2 336 306	71.4
Congressional District 1, Indiana	5 722	675 541	30.3	26.6	12.6	17.1	44 087	10.5	6.5	252 348	71.0
Benton County	1 052	9 421	4.7	27.5	15.8	13.0	39 813	5.5	3.3	3 558	75.8
Jasper County	1 450	30 043	4.2	27.5	12.4	13.0	43 369	6.7	6.0	10 686	77.5
Lake County	1 287	484 564	39.5	26.8	13.0	16.2	41 829	12.2	7.5	181 633	69.0
Newton County	1 041	14 566	4.5	26.5	13.0	9.6	40 944	6.9	4.4	5 340	80.0
Porter County (part)	892	136 947	8.2	25.6	10.9	22.2	52 345	6.1	4.0	51 131	75.6
Congressional District 2, Indiana	9 529	675 685	15.5	26.1	13.3	17.2	40 381	9.5	5.0	256 650	72.8
Carroll County	964	20 165	3.8	26.3	14.0	12.9	42 677	6.8	3.9	7 718	79.7
Cass County	1 069	40 930	9.5	25.8	14.4	12.0	39 193	7.4	4.0	15 715	73.6
Elkhart County (part)	189	85 958	23.8	28.4	10.8	13.5	40 139	10.1	4.6	32 282	66.2
Fulton County	954	20 511	5.0	25.8	15.3	10.3	38 290	7.6	4.7	8 082	78.3
Howard County (part)	76	35 837	16.2	25.3	14.4	12.7	34 063	14.2	6.7	15 454	64.1
LaPorte County	1 549	110 106	15.1	24.5	13.6	14.0	41 430	8.7	4.3	41 050	75.2
Marshall County	1 151	45 128	7.7	28.0	13.2	14.9	42 581	6.8	4.2	16 519	76.8
Porter County (part)	191	9 851	3.2	26.3	9.8	27.3	64 091	4.1	3.4	3 518	90.9
Pulaski County	1 123	13 755	3.9	26.9	15.3	10.3	35 422	8.3	4.3	5 170	80.7
St. Joseph County	1 185	265 559	19.2	25.7	13.6	23.6	40 420	10.4	5.6	100 743	71.7
Starke County	801	23 556	3.5	26.7	13.8	8.4	37 243	11.1	6.2	8 740	80.8
White County (part)	276	4 329	3.3	26.0	14.2	7.2	41 684	5.0	3.2	1 659	82.2
Congressional District 3, Indiana	8 391	675 533	12.3	28.2	11.4	18.4	44 013	7.8	3.9	252 847	75.0
Allen County (part)	1 330	319 253	18.6	27.6	11.4	23.1	42 472	9.3	4.7	124 188	70.4
DeKalb County	940	40 285	2.9	28.2	11.4	12.4	44 909	5.9	4.2	15 134	81.5
Elkhart County (part)	1 013	96 833	10.3	29.2	11.0	17.3	49 089	5.8	2.6	33 872	78.0
Kosciusko County	1 392	74 057	7.1	27.7	12.0	14.9	43 939	6.4	3.4	27 283	78.9
LaGrange County	983	34 909	4.3	33.7	10.0	8.9	42 848	7.7	2.5	11 225	81.4
Noble County	1 065	46 275	8.6	28.9	11.0	11.1	42 700	7.9	3.3	16 696	78.0
Steuben County	800	33 214	3.8	25.6	11.9	15.5	44 089	6.7	4.5	12 738	78.3
Whitley County	869	30 707	1.9	26.8	13.1	13.3	45 503	4.9	2.5	11 711	83.3
Congressional District 4, Indiana	10 403	675 272	6.5	25.7	11.0	22.1	45 947	8.0	4.2	252 284	73.5
Boone County	1 095	46 107	2.6	28.3	11.7	27.6	49 632	5.2	3.0	17 081	78.7
Clinton County	1 049	33 866	8.0	27.3	14.6	10.1	40 759	8.6	5.4	12 545	72.9
Fountain County (part)	442	5 974	1.9	27.6	13.7	8.9	39 539	7.4	4.4	2 322	81.5
Hendricks County	1 058	104 093	4.3	28.0	9.7	23.1	55 208	3.6	2.1	37 275	82.9
Johnson County (part)	442	96 991	3.4	27.6	11.1	24.6	53 705	5.2	3.3	36 112	76.1

[1]Dry land or land partially or temporarily covered by water.
[2]Persons who do not identify themselves as White alone, not of Hispanic origin.
[3]Persons 25 years old and over.

Table B. 110th Congressional Districts by Counties, 2000—*Continued*

(Number, percent.)

STATE Congressional district County	Land area,[1] (sq km)	Population Total	Percent minority[2]	Percent under 18 years	Percent 65 years and over	Percent with bachelor's degree or more[3]	Median household income, 1999 (dollars)	Percent living in poverty	Percent unemployed	Households Total	Percent owner occupied
	1	2	3	4	5	6	7	8	9	10	11
Congressional District 4, Indiana—*Continued*											
Lawrence County	1 162	45 922	2.9	24.5	14.8	10.7	36 280	9.8	5.7	18 535	78.9
Marion County (part)	101	40 056	12.0	26.7	9.7	28.7	56 744	4.5	3.3	15 130	83.7
Monroe County (part)	367	28 052	5.0	27.1	10.2	19.7	41 720	7.0	4.0	10 958	75.4
Starke County	1 307	37 629	3.6	25.9	13.9	14.7	41 297	8.3	3.9	14 595	73.3
Morgan County	1 053	66 689	2.1	27.2	10.7	12.6	47 739	6.6	3.0	24 437	79.7
Tippecanoe County	1 294	148 955	13.5	20.9	9.0	33.2	38 652	15.4	6.9	55 226	55.9
White County (part)	1 032	20 938	7.9	25.6	15.0	11.1	40 403	7.4	3.5	8 068	75.4
Congressional District 5, Indiana	8 459	675 753	6.7	26.8	11.3	30.6	52 800	5.2	3.3	258 319	76.0
Grant County	1 072	73 403	11.9	23.7	14.9	14.1	36 162	11.8	7.3	28 319	73.2
Hamilton County	1 031	182 740	6.6	30.7	7.5	48.9	71 026	2.9	2.3	65 933	80.9
Hancock County	793	55 391	2.0	26.4	11.3	22.2	56 416	3.0	3.0	20 718	81.4
Howard County (part)	683	49 127	7.3	25.8	12.7	21.9	51 630	6.1	3.6	19 346	77.8
Huntington County	991	38 075	2.8	26.2	14.0	14.2	41 620	5.5	3.8	14 242	77.0
Johnson County (part)	137	5 985	2.3	23.2	9.9	23.0	57 470	3.2	2.8	1 957	76.9
Marion County (part)	248	144 594	9.3	25.1	11.2	43.0	58 597	3.7	2.2	59 532	69.6
Miami County	973	36 082	7.0	26.0	12.9	10.4	39 184	8.0	3.7	13 716	76.0
Shelby County (part)	787	38 819	3.5	26.5	12.0	12.5	43 191	7.8	3.6	14 872	72.1
Tipton County	674	16 577	2.3	25.0	14.6	12.4	48 546	5.1	2.6	6 469	79.9
Wabash County	1 070	34 960	3.5	24.5	15.6	13.7	40 413	6.9	4.5	13 215	75.9
Congressional District 6, Indiana	14 375	675 819	6.6	25.1	14.1	14.7	39 002	9.7	5.2	262 371	74.3
Adams County	879	33 625	4.0	31.2	13.5	10.7	40 625	9.1	2.9	11 818	77.0
Allen County (part)	372	12 596	17.3	27.6	11.3	11.7	48 620	5.9	3.4	4 557	86.6
Bartholomew County (part)	631	37 641	5.1	27.4	11.5	27.7	50 570	5.7	3.4	14 261	80.1
Blackford County	428	14 048	2.4	24.7	15.4	10.3	34 760	8.7	4.4	5 690	78.6
Dearborn County (part)	159	14 607	1.5	30.0	7.3	21.7	61 711	3.4	2.5	4 937	89.4
Decatur County	965	24 555	2.7	26.3	13.3	11.5	40 401	9.3	3.8	9 389	73.2
Delaware County	1 019	118 769	9.8	22.1	13.5	20.4	34 659	15.1	7.1	47 131	67.2
Fayette County	557	25 588	2.8	24.4	15.6	7.8	38 840	7.9	6.4	10 199	71.6
Franklin County	1 000	22 151	1.5	28.1	12.7	12.5	43 530	7.1	4.0	7 868	81.4
Henry County	1 018	48 508	2.2	24.1	15.7	11.7	38 150	7.8	4.9	19 486	77.1
Jay County	994	21 806	3.3	26.9	14.7	9.9	35 700	9.1	4.2	8 405	77.8
Johnson County (part)	251	12 233	5.5	26.1	10.2	11.3	44 550	9.8	4.5	4 365	79.9
Madison County	1 171	133 358	10.8	23.8	14.9	14.4	38 925	9.3	5.7	53 052	74.2
Randolph County	1 173	27 401	2.2	25.3	15.8	9.9	34 544	11.1	5.5	10 937	75.9
Rush County	1 057	18 261	3.3	26.7	14.8	10.3	38 152	7.3	3.7	6 923	74.1
Shelby County (part)	282	4 626	0.9	27.3	13.6	14.3	49 549	5.6	4.0	1 689	85.0
Union County	418	7 349	1.5	27.2	12.9	11.1	36 672	9.7	5.2	2 793	75.0
Wayne County	1 045	71 097	8.5	24.2	15.9	13.7	34 885	11.4	6.5	28 469	68.7
Wells County	958	27 600	2.9	27.4	14.1	14.3	43 934	5.9	3.0	10 402	80.8
Congressional District 7, Indiana	677	675 804	36.9	25.8	11.2	21.2	36 522	13.5	6.3	277 502	55.8
Marion County (part)	677	675 804	36.9	25.8	11.2	21.2	36 522	13.5	6.3	277 502	55.8
Congressional District 8, Indiana	18 238	675 693	6.4	24.4	14.4	15.9	36 732	10.7	5.6	263 037	73.9
Clay County	926	26 556	2.0	26.2	15.1	12.8	36 865	8.7	5.2	10 216	79.1
Daviess County	1 115	29 820	3.4	29.0	14.6	9.7	34 064	13.8	4.3	10 894	78.6
Fountain County (part)	583	11 980	1.5	25.6	16.5	10.6	37 149	9.1	5.1	4 719	76.2
Gibson County	1 266	32 500	4.0	24.8	15.6	12.4	37 515	8.2	5.0	12 847	77.9
Greene County	1 403	33 157	2.0	24.7	15.3	10.5	33 998	11.0	5.4	13 372	80.0
Knox County	1 336	39 256	4.3	23.0	15.3	14.4	31 362	16.0	8.7	15 552	68.9
Martin County	871	10 369	1.1	25.2	14.3	8.8	36 411	11.2	5.8	4 183	81.3
Owen County	998	21 786	2.6	26.7	12.8	9.2	36 529	9.4	4.5	8 282	81.6
Parke County	1 152	17 241	3.6	24.0	14.7	11.6	35 724	11.5	4.1	6 415	80.3
Pike County	871	12 837	2.0	24.0	15.3	8.4	34 759	8.0	5.4	5 119	82.7
Posey County	1 058	27 061	2.4	27.3	12.4	14.8	44 209	7.4	4.1	10 205	81.9
Putnam County	1 244	36 019	6.1	23.7	12.4	13.1	38 882	8.0	4.8	12 374	78.6
Sullivan County	1 158	21 751	6.6	22.6	14.1	9.4	32 976	10.9	6.9	7 819	79.8
Vanderburgh County	608	171 922	11.3	23.1	15.3	19.3	36 823	11.2	5.6	70 623	66.8
Vermillion County	665	16 788	2.5	23.8	15.9	11.2	34 837	9.5	5.4	6 762	79.2
Vigo County	1 045	105 848	10.1	22.8	14.3	21.4	33 184	14.1	7.1	40 998	67.4
Warren County	945	8 419	1.4	26.3	14.0	14.0	41 825	6.5	2.9	3 219	80.9
Warrick County	995	52 383	2.3	26.8	10.8	21.8	48 814	5.3	3.8	19 438	83.3

[1]Dry land or land partially or temporarily covered by water.
[2]Persons who do not identify themselves as White alone, not of Hispanic origin.
[3]Persons 25 years old and over.

Table B. 110th Congressional Districts by Counties, 2000—*Continued*

(Number, percent.)

STATE Congressional district County	Land area,[1] (sq km)	Population Total	Percent minority[2]	Percent under 18 years	Percent 65 years and over	Percent with bachelor's degree or more[3]	Median household income, 1999 (dollars)	Percent living in poverty	Percent unemployed	Households Total	Percent owner occupied
	1	2	3	4	5	6	7	8	9	10	11
Congressional District 9, Indiana	17 101	675 385	5.9	24.2	12.1	17.3	39 011	10.5	4.3	260 948	71.7
Bartholomew County (part)	423	33 794	9.3	25.3	13.0	15.8	38 426	9.2	4.0	13 675	68.1
Brown County	809	14 957	3.0	23.3	12.9	18.5	43 708	8.9	3.6	5 897	85.0
Clark County	971	96 472	10.5	24.2	12.4	14.3	40 111	8.1	4.5	38 751	70.0
Crawford County	792	10 743	1.3	25.6	12.8	8.4	32 646	16.8	5.3	4 181	82.9
Dearborn County (part)	632	31 502	2.6	26.5	12.9	12.6	42 795	8.1	3.7	11 895	74.1
Dubois County	1 114	39 674	3.2	27.4	12.9	14.5	44 169	5.3	2.5	14 813	78.0
Floyd County	383	70 823	7.3	25.8	12.2	20.4	44 022	8.7	3.9	27 511	72.5
Harrison County	1 257	34 325	2.4	26.0	11.4	13.1	43 423	6.4	4.0	12 917	84.1
Jackson County	1 319	41 335	4.7	25.6	13.3	11.5	39 401	8.5	3.3	16 052	74.2
Jefferson County	936	31 705	4.6	24.4	13.1	16.4	38 189	9.6	5.6	12 148	74.6
Jennings County	977	27 554	3.5	27.7	10.7	8.4	39 402	9.2	7.3	10 134	79.1
Monroe County (part)	654	92 511	11.6	15.1	8.8	47.3	30 632	23.2	4.2	35 940	47.4
Ohio County	225	5 623	1.6	24.8	13.8	11.6	41 348	7.1	4.8	2 201	77.6
Orange County	1 035	19 306	2.4	25.7	14.8	10.2	31 564	12.4	5.1	7 621	79.2
Perry County	988	18 899	2.6	23.0	14.9	9.6	36 246	9.4	4.9	7 270	79.2
Ripley County	1 156	26 523	1.7	28.1	13.4	11.5	41 426	7.5	3.3	9 842	76.9
Scott County	493	22 960	2.3	26.2	11.1	8.8	34 656	13.1	4.5	8 832	75.8
Spencer County	1 033	20 391	2.5	26.5	12.9	13.0	42 451	6.9	4.6	7 569	83.4
Switzerland County	573	9 065	1.5	26.2	12.7	7.6	37 092	13.9	7.7	3 435	77.8
Washington County	1 332	27 223	1.6	26.5	12.1	10.2	36 630	10.6	4.4	10 264	81.1
IOWA	144 701	2 926 324	7.3	25.0	14.9	21.2	39 469	9.1	4.2	1 149 276	72.3
Congressional District 1, Iowa	18 691	585 302	7.8	25.3	14.5	20.0	38 727	10.1	4.7	227 405	72.6
Black Hawk County	1 469	128 012	12.3	23.1	14.0	23.0	37 266	13.1	4.8	49 683	68.9
Bremer County	1 134	23 325	2.3	24.1	15.9	21.5	40 826	5.1	5.8	8 860	78.1
Buchanan County	1 480	21 093	2.5	28.5	14.5	12.7	38 036	9.4	4.3	7 933	78.1
Butler County	1 503	15 305	1.1	24.6	20.2	12.4	35 883	8.0	3.1	6 175	80.4
Clayton County	2 017	18 678	1.8	25.3	18.6	12.8	34 068	8.6	3.7	7 375	76.6
Clinton County	1 800	50 149	4.6	25.6	15.8	14.4	37 423	10.2	5.0	20 105	72.9
Delaware County	1 497	18 404	1.4	29.0	15.0	13.0	37 168	7.9	3.4	6 834	78.0
Dubuque County	1 575	89 143	3.3	25.5	14.8	21.3	39 582	7.8	4.5	33 690	73.5
Fayette County	1 893	22 008	3.1	25.0	19.0	13.8	32 453	10.8	4.6	8 778	75.6
Jackson County	1 647	20 296	1.1	26.0	17.3	12.1	34 529	10.3	3.7	8 078	75.8
Jones County	1 490	20 221	4.3	24.2	15.8	12.7	37 449	8.6	3.9	7 560	75.8
Scott County	1 186	158 668	13.2	26.3	11.9	24.9	42 701	10.5	5.2	62 334	70.5
Congressional District 2, Iowa	19 595	585 241	7.5	24.1	13.3	25.0	40 121	9.9	4.1	232 880	70.8
Appanoose County	1 285	13 721	3.0	23.8	20.0	12.2	28 612	14.5	5.9	5 779	74.1
Cedar County	1 501	18 187	2.0	25.3	16.2	16.3	42 198	5.5	2.3	7 147	76.9
Davis County	1 303	8 541	1.7	27.2	17.4	11.4	32 864	11.9	3.6	3 207	79.8
Des Moines County	1 078	42 351	6.8	24.3	16.7	16.0	36 790	10.7	5.5	17 270	74.2
Henry County	1 125	20 336	6.5	24.6	14.8	16.2	39 087	8.8	4.4	7 626	73.1
Jefferson County	1 128	16 181	4.5	24.5	13.7	31.2	33 851	10.9	4.1	6 649	67.4
Johnson County	1 591	111 006	11.0	20.0	7.5	47.6	40 060	15.0	3.9	44 080	56.7
Lee County	1 340	38 052	7.0	24.3	16.5	12.5	36 193	9.7	5.8	15 161	75.5
Linn County	1 858	191 701	6.8	25.2	12.2	27.7	46 206	6.5	3.5	76 753	72.7
Louisa County	1 041	12 183	13.6	27.7	13.9	12.7	39 086	9.3	4.3	4 519	77.3
Muscatine County	1 136	41 722	14.4	26.9	12.9	17.2	41 803	8.9	3.9	15 847	75.4
Van Buren County	1 256	7 809	1.0	24.7	18.9	11.8	31 094	12.7	3.7	3 181	79.3
Wapello County	1 118	36 051	4.8	23.2	17.8	14.6	32 188	13.2	6.7	14 784	75.6
Washington County	1 473	20 670	3.7	26.1	17.8	16.4	39 103	7.6	2.6	8 056	75.3
Wayne County	1 361	6 730	1.9	23.8	23.6	12.1	29 380	14.0	4.0	2 821	79.5
Congressional District 3, Iowa	18 076	585 305	9.8	25.5	13.3	24.6	43 176	8.0	4.4	231 632	71.5
Benton County	1 855	25 308	1.3	27.3	15.4	13.9	42 427	6.1	2.9	9 746	79.4
Grundy County	1 302	12 369	1.4	25.2	19.3	17.2	39 396	4.6	3.6	4 984	79.7
Iowa County	1 519	15 671	1.4	26.3	17.1	15.8	41 222	5.0	2.3	6 163	77.9
Jasper County	1 891	37 213	3.2	24.6	16.0	15.9	41 683	6.5	3.1	14 689	75.7
Keokuk County	1 500	11 400	1.4	25.8	20.2	11.6	34 025	10.1	3.9	4 586	78.8
Lucas County	1 115	9 422	1.8	25.4	19.3	11.1	30 876	13.7	4.9	3 811	78.4
Mahaska County	1 479	22 335	3.7	25.7	16.3	16.5	37 314	9.8	4.5	8 880	71.1
Marion County	1 435	32 052	2.9	25.4	16.0	18.9	42 401	7.6	3.4	12 017	75.5
Monroe County	1 123	8 016	2.0	25.4	19.6	12.6	34 877	9.0	3.7	3 228	78.5
Polk County	1 475	374 601	13.5	25.6	11.1	29.7	46 116	7.9	4.7	149 112	68.8
Poweshiek County	1 515	18 815	3.6	22.6	17.6	18.5	37 836	9.8	5.0	7 398	71.9
Tama County	1 868	18 103	10.1	26.6	18.7	12.9	37 419	10.5	4.0	7 018	77.6

[1]Dry land or land partially or temporarily covered by water.
[2]Persons who do not identify themselves as White alone, not of Hispanic origin.
[3]Persons 25 years old and over.

Table B. 110th Congressional Districts by Counties, 2000—*Continued*

(Number, percent.)

STATE Congressional district County	Land area,[1] (sq km)	Population				Percent with bachelor's degree or more[3]	Median household income, 1999 (dollars)	Percent living in poverty	Percent unem-ployed	Households	
		Total	Percent minority[2]	Percent under 18 years	Percent 65 years and over					Total	Percent owner occupied
	1	2	3	4	5	6	7	8	9	10	11
Congressional District 4, Iowa	40 818	585 305	5.2	24.4	16.4	20.4	38 242	8.9	3.9	229 320	73.3
Allamakee County	1 656	14 675	5.1	25.5	18.4	14.4	33 967	9.6	3.9	5 722	76.5
Boone County	1 480	26 224	2.0	24.8	16.4	18.8	40 763	7.6	2.6	10 374	75.6
Calhoun County	1 477	11 115	2.3	22.9	22.1	15.4	33 286	10.1	3.3	4 513	77.4
Cerro Gordo County	1 472	46 447	5.1	24.0	17.7	20.3	35 867	8.5	4.7	19 374	71.5
Chickasaw County	1 307	13 095	1.5	26.0	17.9	12.2	37 649	8.3	6.4	5 192	80.4
Dallas County	1 519	40 750	7.5	28.2	11.1	26.8	48 528	5.6	2.6	15 584	76.4
Emmet County	1 025	11 027	5.1	23.8	19.2	13.0	33 305	8.2	4.7	4 450	75.2
Floyd County	1 296	16 900	2.0	25.2	19.1	14.8	35 237	9.3	4.5	6 828	74.1
Franklin County	1 508	10 704	6.9	24.2	20.5	14.5	36 042	8.0	4.1	4 356	74.8
Greene County	1 472	10 366	2.5	25.6	21.7	14.6	33 883	8.1	4.8	4 205	75.6
Hamilton County	1 494	16 438	3.4	25.5	18.0	17.5	38 658	6.3	2.5	6 692	72.8
Hancock County	1 479	12 100	3.7	26.7	17.8	15.4	37 703	6.0	2.7	4 795	78.2
Hardin County	1 474	18 812	3.5	24.5	20.7	17.1	35 429	8.0	4.4	7 628	74.6
Howard County	1 226	9 932	0.7	26.2	20.0	12.6	34 641	9.3	3.4	3 974	79.2
Humboldt County	1 125	10 381	2.9	24.8	21.0	15.4	38 201	8.3	3.5	4 295	75.9
Kossuth County	2 520	17 163	1.8	25.7	20.1	13.6	34 562	10.2	3.8	6 974	77.6
Madison County	1 453	14 019	2.0	27.0	15.2	14.4	41 845	6.7	4.2	5 326	78.0
Marshall County	1 482	39 311	11.8	25.3	16.6	17.0	38 268	10.2	4.4	15 338	73.8
Mitchell County	1 215	10 874	0.2	26.4	21.5	12.8	34 843	10.7	3.1	4 294	81.5
Palo Alto County	1 460	10 147	2.0	24.2	21.4	13.9	32 409	10.6	2.1	4 119	74.0
Pocahontas County	1 496	8 662	1.0	25.5	21.7	15.0	33 362	9.1	3.3	3 617	79.2
Story County	1 484	79 981	9.6	19.0	9.7	44.5	40 442	14.1	4.4	29 383	58.3
Warren County	1 481	40 671	2.8	27.0	11.8	21.2	50 349	5.1	3.5	14 708	79.9
Webster County	1 852	40 235	7.5	24.5	17.4	16.9	35 334	10.0	4.3	15 878	71.2
Winnebago County	1 037	11 723	3.3	23.9	18.9	16.5	38 381	8.4	3.0	4 749	76.1
Winneshiek County	1 786	21 310	2.9	22.7	15.8	20.5	38 908	8.0	4.5	7 734	73.6
Worth County	1 036	7 909	3.0	24.1	19.4	12.7	36 444	8.3	3.8	3 278	79.0
Wright County	1 504	14 334	5.5	24.5	21.1	13.5	36 197	7.0	3.7	5 940	74.1
Congressional District 5, Iowa	47 520	585 171	6.1	25.7	17.1	16.1	36 773	8.9	3.8	228 039	73.6
Adair County	1 474	8 243	1.3	24.0	22.1	11.2	35 179	7.6	3.4	3 398	75.3
Adams County	1 097	4 482	1.0	23.8	21.3	12.0	30 453	9.3	4.9	1 867	74.8
Audubon County	1 148	6 830	1.2	25.8	23.6	12.3	32 215	7.7	4.1	2 773	79.0
Buena Vista County	1 489	20 411	18.4	25.3	16.8	18.7	35 300	10.5	3.8	7 499	70.5
Carroll County	1 475	21 421	1.4	27.0	18.7	16.0	37 275	6.5	2.4	8 486	74.3
Cass County	1 462	14 684	1.8	23.7	20.8	16.6	32 922	11.1	5.0	6 120	74.6
Cherokee County	1 495	13 035	1.9	24.5	20.3	15.2	35 142	7.3	3.6	5 378	73.5
Clarke County	1 117	9 133	5.0	26.2	17.0	12.1	34 474	8.5	5.9	3 584	72.3
Clay County	1 473	17 372	2.9	24.7	18.0	16.3	35 799	8.2	3.8	7 259	69.2
Crawford County	1 850	16 942	10.8	26.6	17.3	12.4	33 922	11.1	3.6	6 441	73.1
Decatur County	1 377	8 689	3.5	23.1	17.6	15.1	27 343	15.5	7.5	3 337	71.1
Dickinson County	987	16 424	1.6	21.9	20.6	21.3	39 020	6.0	2.8	7 103	78.0
Fremont County	1 324	8 010	3.1	24.9	19.8	14.0	38 345	9.5	2.8	3 199	74.5
Guthrie County	1 530	11 353	2.4	23.5	20.6	14.9	36 495	8.0	3.8	4 641	79.6
Harrison County	1 805	15 666	1.6	26.2	17.7	12.7	38 141	7.1	4.3	6 115	76.6
Ida County	1 118	7 837	1.4	25.5	21.6	13.6	34 805	8.8	3.9	3 213	73.2
Lyon County	1 522	11 763	0.8	28.1	18.7	14.2	36 878	7.0	2.4	4 428	81.7
Mills County	1 131	14 547	2.8	26.7	12.6	16.3	42 428	8.3	4.9	5 324	79.5
Monona County	1 795	10 020	1.7	23.3	23.9	13.4	33 235	9.4	3.8	4 211	76.2
Montgomery County	1 098	11 771	2.3	24.7	20.2	12.9	33 214	9.1	5.0	4 886	73.2
O'Brien County	1 484	15 102	3.0	24.9	21.2	14.7	35 758	7.3	3.0	6 001	76.8
Osceola County	1 033	7 003	3.0	26.0	19.1	13.4	34 274	7.0	3.3	2 778	77.8
Page County	1 385	16 976	4.1	23.3	19.7	16.6	35 466	12.5	6.0	6 708	71.7
Plymouth County	2 237	24 849	2.0	28.3	15.9	19.3	41 638	6.0	1.9	9 372	77.4
Pottawattamie County	2 472	87 704	5.7	25.8	13.8	15.0	40 089	8.4	4.1	33 844	71.1
Ringgold County	1 393	5 469	1.4	24.0	24.1	13.4	29 110	14.3	4.1	2 245	75.5
Sac County	1 491	11 529	2.6	24.1	22.7	13.6	32 874	9.9	3.1	4 746	76.8
Shelby County	1 530	13 173	1.6	26.3	20.5	15.3	37 442	6.0	2.6	5 173	77.1
Sioux County	1 989	31 589	3.6	27.2	15.0	19.8	40 536	6.4	1.8	10 693	80.4
Taylor County	1 383	6 958	4.6	24.0	22.1	12.0	31 297	12.1	3.9	2 824	76.6
Union County	1 099	12 309	2.4	23.4	18.7	14.7	31 905	11.4	3.9	5 242	72.0
Woodbury County	2 260	103 877	16.2	27.3	13.4	18.9	38 509	10.3	4.2	39 151	68.6

[1]Dry land or land partially or temporarily covered by water.
[2]Persons who do not identify themselves as White alone, not of Hispanic origin.
[3]Persons 25 years old and over.

Table B. 110th Congressional Districts by Counties, 2000—*Continued*

(Number, percent.)

STATE Congressional district County	Land area,[1] (sq km)	Population Total	Percent minority[2]	Percent under 18 years	Percent 65 years and over	Percent with bachelor's degree or more[3]	Median household income, 1999 (dollars)	Percent living in poverty	Percent unem-ployed	Households Total	Percent owner occupied
	1	2	3	4	5	6	7	8	9	10	11
KANSAS	211 900	2 688 418	16.9	26.5	13.2	25.8	40 624	9.9	4.2	1 037 891	69.3
Congressional District 1, Kansas	148 596	672 051	15.4	26.4	16.3	18.0	34 869	11.0	4.1	260 475	71.4
Barber County	2 937	5 307	3.4	24.9	21.5	21.0	33 407	10.1	2.0	2 235	75.3
Barton County	2 315	28 205	11.2	26.0	17.9	16.6	32 176	12.9	5.3	11 393	72.0
Chase County	2 010	3 030	3.7	24.1	18.7	19.6	32 656	8.6	2.7	1 246	73.5
Cheyenne County	2 641	3 165	3.2	23.6	26.6	16.0	30 599	9.4	2.8	1 360	77.4
Clark County	2 524	2 390	6.0	26.3	21.6	22.1	33 857	12.7	2.6	979	76.5
Clay County	1 668	8 822	3.2	24.9	20.8	16.5	33 965	10.1	3.5	3 617	77.0
Cloud County	1 853	10 268	2.5	22.3	23.2	18.0	31 758	10.8	4.3	4 163	74.4
Comanche County	2 042	1 967	2.8	22.3	25.7	15.1	29 415	10.2	0.2	872	73.5
Decatur County	2 314	3 472	3.1	23.6	26.3	15.4	30 257	11.6	1.1	1 494	76.0
Dickinson County	2 196	19 344	5.2	25.8	18.6	15.2	35 975	7.5	3.2	7 903	74.8
Edwards County	1 611	3 449	12.2	24.6	21.3	16.3	30 530	10.4	2.7	1 455	77.5
Ellis County	2 331	27 507	3.9	22.2	14.3	29.2	32 339	12.9	4.1	11 193	63.3
Ellsworth County	1 854	6 525	9.2	20.8	20.2	16.4	35 772	7.2	3.5	2 481	79.6
Finney County	3 372	40 523	48.3	34.3	6.7	14.3	38 474	14.2	4.9	12 948	64.8
Ford County	2 845	32 458	42.8	30.9	11.0	16.4	37 860	12.4	4.9	10 852	64.8
Geary County (part)	927	23 682	38.1	27.7	11.1	15.8	31 837	12.3	5.5	9 377	56.1
Gove County	2 775	3 068	2.9	25.7	22.8	18.4	33 510	10.3	1.9	1 245	79.7
Graham County	2 327	2 946	5.4	22.4	23.5	17.4	31 286	11.5	2.7	1 263	79.3
Grant County	1 489	7 909	36.7	32.7	9.4	15.2	39 854	10.1	4.7	2 742	74.7
Gray County	2 250	5 904	11.1	31.6	12.4	16.3	40 000	9.1	3.2	2 045	72.7
Greeley County	2 015	1 534	12.1	28.7	18.1	17.4	34 605	11.6	2.5	602	75.1
Greenwood County (part)	1 250	2 127	4.7	26.2	20.9	16.3	30 734	14.6	3.6	862	75.4
Hamilton County	2 581	2 670	22.5	28.0	18.2	17.4	32 033	15.7	2.0	1 054	69.7
Haskell County	1 495	4 307	26.7	32.9	10.6	17.5	38 634	11.6	2.9	1 481	72.2
Hodgeman County	2 227	2 085	4.8	29.1	19.0	19.7	35 994	11.5	1.4	796	78.4
Jewell County	2 355	3 791	2.4	21.8	26.0	13.8	30 538	11.6	2.3	1 695	79.9
Kearny County	2 256	4 531	28.7	34.4	11.4	15.0	40 149	11.7	2.9	1 542	73.5
Kiowa County	1 871	3 278	3.7	23.8	21.3	18.9	31 576	10.8	3.4	1 365	71.8
Lane County	1 858	2 155	4.0	25.3	20.6	18.5	36 047	8.2	1.9	910	77.0
Lincoln County	1 862	3 578	2.3	23.1	23.4	17.4	30 893	9.7	2.4	1 529	78.7
Logan County	2 779	3 046	3.0	25.3	20.8	17.5	32 131	7.3	3.8	1 243	76.3
Lyon County	2 204	35 935	22.7	25.8	11.5	23.0	32 819	14.5	6.0	13 691	60.9
McPherson County	2 330	29 554	4.3	25.3	17.3	22.2	41 138	6.6	4.1	11 205	73.9
Marion County	2 443	13 361	3.5	24.9	21.1	17.9	34 500	8.3	2.9	5 114	79.9
Marshall County	2 338	10 965	2.6	25.0	22.1	13.2	32 089	9.2	3.5	4 458	79.7
Meade County	2 534	4 631	13.7	29.7	17.8	19.6	36 761	9.3	2.9	1 728	73.9
Mitchell County	1 813	6 932	2.7	24.6	21.3	16.9	33 385	9.5	4.2	2 850	74.7
Morris County	1 806	6 104	5.0	25.1	21.0	16.0	32 163	9.0	2.9	2 539	78.2
Morton County	1 890	3 496	18.0	29.6	13.8	17.6	37 232	10.5	3.8	1 306	71.6
Nemaha County (part)	655	7 028	2.5	27.4	23.7	16.6	35 794	7.3	1.7	2 625	78.2
Ness County	2 784	3 454	2.6	22.8	24.2	17.9	32 340	8.7	1.8	1 516	76.1
Norton County	2 274	5 953	8.0	21.9	19.5	15.4	31 050	10.5	4.0	2 266	77.9
Osborne County	2 311	4 452	2.4	23.9	25.8	15.5	29 145	10.4	3.7	1 940	78.6
Ottawa County	1 868	6 163	2.4	25.6	17.6	16.3	38 009	8.6	4.4	2 430	82.2
Pawnee County	1 953	7 233	10.8	24.1	18.7	21.8	35 175	11.8	12.0	2 739	74.4
Phillips County	2 295	6 001	2.0	24.7	21.9	16.1	35 013	10.0	2.1	2 496	77.9
Pratt County	1 904	9 647	5.4	24.8	19.3	21.0	35 529	9.4	4.6	3 963	73.4
Rawlins County	2 770	2 966	4.0	23.9	26.0	15.9	32 105	12.5	2.0	1 269	76.8
Reno County	3 249	64 790	10.9	24.4	16.3	17.3	35 510	10.9	4.6	25 498	70.7
Republic County	1 855	5 835	2.4	22.3	26.2	14.9	30 494	9.1	2.4	2 557	78.9
Rice County	1 882	10 761	8.2	24.6	18.1	17.5	35 671	10.7	5.8	4 050	76.6
Rooks County	2 301	5 685	3.6	25.2	21.5	15.4	30 457	9.8	4.1	2 362	77.1
Rush County	1 860	3 551	1.5	22.2	25.5	16.4	31 268	9.7	2.7	1 548	82.4
Russell County	2 291	7 370	2.7	22.0	24.3	16.7	29 284	12.0	4.2	3 207	75.2
Saline County	1 864	53 597	12.9	26.2	13.8	20.4	37 308	8.8	3.4	21 436	69.0
Scott County	1 858	5 120	7.5	26.9	16.4	23.0	40 534	5.1	2.2	2 045	74.4
Seward County	1 656	22 510	50.5	32.0	8.4	13.6	36 752	16.9	4.9	7 419	64.1
Sheridan County	2 322	2 813	1.1	26.4	20.2	15.9	33 547	15.7	0.6	1 124	82.3
Sherman County	2 735	6 760	10.0	24.5	17.0	15.0	32 684	12.9	3.1	2 758	68.9
Smith County	2 319	4 536	2.2	21.8	27.6	16.7	28 486	10.7	2.3	1 953	79.7
Stafford County	2 051	4 789	7.5	26.5	21.0	18.4	31 107	11.8	3.5	2 010	77.7
Stanton County	1 761	2 406	25.5	30.8	13.3	16.9	40 172	14.9	2.8	858	67.8
Stevens County	1 884	5 463	25.1	31.1	13.4	17.5	41 830	10.3	3.8	1 988	75.4
Thomas County	2 784	8 180	3.2	26.1	14.7	25.0	37 034	9.7	5.8	3 226	69.0
Trego County	2 301	3 319	0.8	24.0	24.3	14.0	29 677	12.3	1.8	1 412	81.4

[1]Dry land or land partially or temporarily covered by water.
[2]Persons who do not identify themselves as White alone, not of Hispanic origin.
[3]Persons 25 years old and over.

Table B. 110th Congressional Districts by Counties, 2000—*Continued*

(Number, percent.)

STATE Congressional district County	Land area,[1] (sq km)	Population Total	Population Percent minority[2]	Population Percent under 18 years	Population Percent 65 years and over	Percent with bachelor's degree or more[3]	Median household income, 1999 (dollars)	Percent living in poverty	Percent unemployed	Households Total	Households Percent owner occupied
	1	2	3	4	5	6	7	8	9	10	11
Congressional District 1, Kansas—*Continued*											
Wabaunsee County	2 065	6 885	2.6	26.6	15.6	17.3	41 710	7.3	2.7	2 633	82.9
Wallace County	2 367	1 749	7.8	28.9	18.1	17.2	33 000	16.1	1.5	674	76.6
Washington County	2 327	6 483	1.5	23.7	25.0	15.2	29 363	10.1	2.2	2 673	79.5
Wichita County	1 861	2 531	20.5	28.5	16.2	15.5	33 462	14.8	3.0	967	74.3
Congressional District 2, Kansas	36 606	672 302	12.7	25.3	13.5	23.2	37 855	11.2	4.3	257 846	69.0
Allen County	1 303	14 385	6.2	25.4	18.0	15.2	31 481	14.9	4.3	5 775	74.9
Anderson County	1 510	8 110	2.8	25.6	20.2	11.7	33 244	12.8	3.7	3 221	80.0
Atchison County	1 120	16 774	10.3	26.7	16.3	18.0	34 355	13.3	6.2	6 275	73.5
Bourbon County	1 650	15 379	6.2	25.8	18.2	17.8	31 199	13.5	3.9	6 161	74.1
Brown County	1 478	10 724	14.1	26.4	19.8	19.0	31 971	12.9	5.8	4 318	71.3
Cherokee County	1 521	22 605	8.6	26.5	15.2	11.3	30 505	14.3	5.5	8 875	76.2
Coffey County	1 631	8 865	4.5	26.8	16.3	20.1	37 839	6.6	4.4	3 489	78.3
Crawford County	1 536	38 242	7.8	22.8	15.5	23.9	29 409	16.0	4.9	15 504	64.3
Doniphan County	1 016	8 249	5.1	25.2	16.1	14.8	32 537	11.9	7.0	3 173	74.6
Douglas County (part)	796	36 949	11.7	24.0	9.7	45.7	48 804	11.6	3.1	14 292	61.3
Franklin County	1 486	24 784	6.0	27.5	13.9	16.5	39 052	7.7	3.5	9 452	73.5
Geary County (part)	69	4 265	40.0	40.3	0.2	29.0	32 480	10.8	18.5	1 081	0.8
Jackson County	1 698	12 657	10.4	28.3	14.9	15.4	40 451	8.8	3.4	4 727	80.6
Jefferson County	1 389	18 426	3.6	27.3	12.8	17.9	45 535	6.7	3.4	6 830	85.1
Labette County	1 680	22 835	12.3	25.5	17.5	15.9	30 875	12.7	3.6	9 194	73.3
Leavenworth County	1 200	68 691	18.1	26.6	9.9	23.1	48 114	6.7	3.4	23 071	67.0
Linn County	1 551	9 570	3.5	24.9	18.3	12.7	35 906	11.0	5.5	3 807	82.5
Miami County	1 494	28 351	5.1	27.9	11.9	19.4	46 665	5.5	2.5	10 365	78.5
Nemaha County (part)	1 205	3 689	1.4	30.3	18.7	10.6	31 632	12.3	2.2	1 334	84.9
Neosho County	1 481	16 997	6.8	25.6	17.3	15.0	32 167	13.0	4.9	6 739	74.5
Osage County	1 822	16 712	3.1	27.0	15.8	14.3	37 928	8.4	3.5	6 490	79.8
Pottawatomie County	2 187	18 209	4.7	29.2	13.4	22.7	40 176	9.7	3.1	6 771	78.5
Riley County	1 579	62 843	17.0	18.7	7.5	40.5	32 042	20.6	7.0	22 137	47.3
Shawnee County	1 424	169 871	20.0	25.2	13.7	26.0	40 988	9.6	4.0	68 920	67.5
Wilson County	1 486	10 332	3.7	25.4	19.9	10.9	29 747	11.3	4.2	4 203	78.1
Woodson County	1 297	3 788	3.6	21.8	24.8	11.4	25 335	13.2	3.6	1 642	81.4
Congressional District 3, Kansas	2 014	671 981	20.4	26.5	10.1	39.1	51 118	7.8	3.8	258 464	67.7
Douglas County (part)	387	63 013	17.5	18.2	6.9	40.6	33 224	18.7	5.5	24 194	46.4
Johnson County	1 235	451 086	11.0	27.0	10.0	47.7	61 455	3.4	2.3	174 570	72.3
Wyandotte County	392	157 882	48.4	28.4	11.7	12.0	33 784	16.5	8.2	59 700	62.9
Congressional District 4, Kansas	24 684	672 084	19.0	27.6	13.0	23.0	40 917	9.6	4.8	261 106	68.9
Butler County	3 698	59 482	6.4	28.6	12.5	20.4	45 474	7.3	3.6	21 527	77.7
Chautauqua County	1 662	4 359	7.1	23.4	24.4	12.3	28 717	12.2	4.8	1 796	81.8
Cowley County	2 917	36 291	11.9	25.9	15.9	18.3	34 406	12.9	7.8	14 039	70.9
Elk County	1 676	3 261	5.4	22.5	25.6	10.6	27 267	13.8	4.7	1 412	80.8
Greenwood County (part)	1 702	5 546	4.5	22.9	23.4	13.8	29 948	11.7	4.6	2 372	75.2
Harper County	2 076	6 536	3.3	24.6	23.1	14.0	29 776	11.6	3.8	2 773	74.6
Harvey County	1 397	32 869	11.8	26.0	17.0	23.0	40 907	6.4	3.7	12 581	71.9
Kingman County	2 236	8 673	3.3	27.4	19.6	17.8	37 790	10.6	1.4	3 371	78.1
Montgomery County	1 671	36 252	15.9	25.0	18.3	16.0	30 997	12.6	4.7	14 903	71.7
Sedgwick County	2 588	452 869	23.6	28.1	11.4	25.4	42 485	9.5	4.8	176 444	66.2
Sumner County	3 061	25 946	7.5	28.5	15.4	15.7	39 415	9.5	5.0	9 888	76.7
KENTUCKY	102 896	4 041 769	10.7	24.6	12.5	17.1	33 672	15.8	5.7	1 590 647	70.7
Congressional District 1, Kentucky	30 259	673 723	10.3	24.1	14.6	11.8	30 360	16.5	6.3	267 297	74.0
Adair County	1 054	17 244	4.3	23.5	14.6	10.9	24 055	24.0	10.8	6 747	80.1
Allen County	896	17 800	2.4	25.9	13.7	9.1	31 238	17.3	4.9	6 910	79.0
Ballard County	651	8 286	6.4	23.0	16.1	10.6	32 130	13.6	4.2	3 395	81.9
Butler County	1 109	13 010	2.7	25.3	12.9	6.4	29 405	16.0	4.8	5 059	79.5
Caldwell County	899	13 060	6.5	22.4	18.0	10.0	28 686	15.9	5.5	5 431	77.4
Calloway County	1 000	34 177	7.2	18.8	14.9	24.0	30 134	16.6	9.6	13 862	68.3
Carlisle County	499	5 351	2.3	23.3	18.3	10.6	30 087	13.1	6.2	2 208	84.0
Casey County	1 154	15 447	3.1	24.4	15.2	7.4	21 580	25.5	5.9	6 260	81.1
Christian County	1 868	72 265	31.6	28.2	9.7	12.5	31 177	15.0	6.8	24 857	55.3
Clinton County	511	9 634	2.8	22.8	15.0	8.0	19 563	25.8	6.1	4 086	77.2
Crittenden County	938	9 384	1.7	23.2	16.3	7.3	29 060	19.1	6.7	3 829	80.3
Cumberland County	792	7 147	4.9	23.6	17.8	7.1	21 572	23.8	6.5	2 976	77.6
Fulton County	541	7 752	25.3	24.9	17.4	11.5	24 382	23.1	8.6	3 237	64.2
Graves County	1 439	37 028	7.9	24.4	16.2	12.6	30 874	16.4	5.5	14 841	77.9
Henderson County	1 140	44 829	9.7	24.7	13.2	13.8	35 892	12.3	5.4	18 095	67.3

[1]Dry land or land partially or temporarily covered by water.
[2]Persons who do not identify themselves as White alone, not of Hispanic origin.
[3]Persons 25 years old and over.

Table B. 110th Congressional Districts by Counties, 2000—*Continued*

(Number, percent.)

STATE Congressional district County	Land area,[1] (sq km)	Population				Percent with bachelor's degree or more[3]	Median household income, 1999 (dollars)	Percent living in poverty	Percent unem- ployed	Households	
		Total	Percent minority[2]	Percent under 18 years	Percent 65 years and over					Total	Percent owner occupied
	1	2	3	4	5	6	7	8	9	10	11
Congressional District 1, Kentucky—*Continued*											
Hickman County	633	5 262	12.0	22.0	18.7	8.8	31 615	17.4	6.5	2 188	81.4
Hopkins County	1 426	46 519	8.6	24.1	14.7	10.6	30 868	16.5	7.0	18 820	74.7
Lincoln County (part)	222	5 942	1.2	24.8	13.6	5.9	28 088	16.2	5.0	2 341	80.4
Livingston County	819	9 804	1.7	22.5	15.0	8.4	31 776	10.3	4.7	3 996	85.2
Logan County	1 439	26 573	10.1	25.7	13.9	9.6	32 474	15.5	4.2	10 506	75.2
Lyon County	559	8 080	8.3	15.6	16.9	10.1	31 694	12.7	5.5	2 898	82.2
McCracken County	650	65 514	13.6	23.3	15.9	18.1	33 865	15.1	6.0	27 736	68.7
McLean County	659	9 938	2.8	24.3	14.4	8.7	29 675	16.0	6.1	3 984	80.3
Marshall County	790	30 125	2.4	21.7	17.5	13.7	35 573	9.5	4.2	12 412	82.6
Metcalfe County	753	10 037	3.6	24.7	15.0	6.6	23 540	23.6	6.5	4 016	79.3
Monroe County	857	11 756	5.1	24.0	15.2	8.4	22 356	23.4	10.1	4 741	75.1
Muhlenberg County	1 230	31 839	6.1	22.6	15.3	8.1	28 566	19.7	7.6	12 357	82.9
Ohio County (part)	581	12 875	3.6	24.5	15.7	8.2	28 994	17.4	5.6	5 099	74.1
Russell County	657	16 315	2.1	22.4	16.5	9.6	22 042	24.3	6.5	6 941	79.4
Simpson County	612	16 405	12.3	26.2	13.3	11.9	36 432	11.6	3.2	6 415	71.8
Todd County	975	11 971	11.2	26.6	14.0	9.2	29 718	17.2	4.4	4 569	76.5
Trigg County	1 148	12 597	12.3	22.7	16.8	12.0	33 002	12.3	4.9	5 215	81.3
Union County	894	15 637	15.7	25.2	12.8	10.9	35 018	17.7	12.8	5 710	77.9
Webster County	867	14 120	8.1	24.2	14.9	7.1	31 529	15.4	4.7	5 560	78.0
Congressional District 2, Kentucky	19 598	673 201	9.2	25.7	11.5	13.9	35 724	13.3	5.3	255 468	73.5
Barren County	1 272	38 033	6.0	24.1	14.9	11.1	31 240	15.6	5.4	15 346	72.3
Breckinridge County	1 483	18 648	4.4	24.9	14.2	7.4	30 554	15.8	6.0	7 324	81.9
Bullitt County	775	61 236	2.4	27.2	7.8	9.2	45 106	7.9	3.2	22 171	83.9
Daviess County	1 198	91 545	6.5	25.7	13.9	17.0	36 813	12.3	5.8	36 033	70.3
Edmonson County	784	11 644	1.9	23.5	14.4	4.9	25 413	18.4	6.9	4 648	85.6
Grayson County	1 305	24 053	2.2	24.6	14.0	7.7	27 639	18.1	5.7	9 596	77.3
Green County	748	11 518	3.3	22.7	16.9	9.1	25 463	18.4	5.1	4 706	78.4
Hancock County	489	8 392	3.2	26.8	10.9	8.1	36 914	13.6	5.1	3 215	82.5
Hardin County	1 626	94 174	19.2	27.5	9.7	15.4	37 744	10.0	5.7	34 497	66.9
Hart County	1 077	17 445	7.5	25.7	13.8	7.0	25 378	22.4	6.6	6 769	77.3
Jefferson County (part)	48	19 593	9.5	28.3	7.1	7.3	39 060	12.1	4.4	6 978	72.3
Larue County	682	13 373	6.4	25.0	15.1	10.9	32 056	15.4	4.8	5 275	80.3
Marion County	897	18 212	11.3	25.2	12.9	9.1	30 387	18.6	5.9	6 613	78.2
Meade County	799	26 349	8.4	29.7	8.2	11.3	36 966	11.3	7.2	9 470	73.9
Nelson County	1 095	37 477	7.4	27.6	10.6	13.4	39 010	12.2	3.7	13 953	78.0
Ohio County (part)	957	10 041	1.0	25.2	12.8	6.5	30 494	17.1	5.0	3 800	88.5
Shelby County	995	33 337	15.0	25.4	10.6	18.7	45 534	9.9	3.9	12 104	72.7
Spencer County	481	11 766	3.2	27.1	9.1	11.1	47 042	8.8	4.1	4 251	82.6
Taylor County	699	22 927	7.3	23.4	15.3	12.2	28 089	17.5	7.3	9 233	72.3
Warren County	1 412	92 522	13.9	23.1	10.4	24.7	36 151	15.4	5.8	35 365	64.0
Washington County	779	10 916	10.1	25.5	14.8	13.3	33 136	13.5	4.6	4 121	79.9
Congressional District 3, Kentucky	950	674 011	23.9	24.1	13.7	25.3	39 468	12.4	5.1	280 034	64.7
Jefferson County (part)	950	674 011	23.9	24.1	13.7	25.3	39 468	12.4	5.1	280 034	64.7
Congressional District 4, Kentucky	14 707	673 619	4.9	25.9	11.6	17.5	40 150	11.4	4.7	257 417	73.4
Bath County (part)	544	8 276	3.9	24.6	15.1	10.5	25 856	22.5	6.4	3 316	78.3
Boone County	638	85 991	6.0	28.4	8.1	22.8	53 593	5.6	3.1	31 258	74.2
Boyd County	415	49 752	5.0	21.8	15.6	14.1	32 749	15.5	8.5	20 010	72.9
Bracken County	526	8 279	1.4	25.5	13.5	9.5	34 823	10.8	4.9	3 228	76.9
Campbell County	393	88 616	4.1	25.6	12.6	20.5	41 903	9.3	3.9	34 742	69.0
Carroll County	337	10 155	6.8	25.0	12.8	8.3	35 925	14.9	6.7	3 940	66.8
Carter County	1 063	26 889	1.3	24.6	12.5	8.9	26 427	22.3	8.2	10 342	81.0
Elliott County	606	6 748	0.6	25.2	13.4	7.8	21 014	25.9	10.5	2 638	82.3
Fleming County	909	13 792	3.0	25.3	13.4	8.8	27 990	18.6	6.7	5 367	78.8
Gallatin County	256	7 870	2.5	28.6	10.3	6.9	36 422	13.4	3.5	2 902	77.0
Grant County	673	22 384	2.0	28.6	9.5	9.4	38 438	11.1	5.4	8 175	74.1
Greenup County	896	36 891	2.8	23.6	14.6	11.5	32 142	14.1	7.3	14 536	81.8
Harrison County	802	17 983	5.0	25.1	13.4	10.6	36 210	12.0	3.6	7 012	70.5
Henry County	749	15 060	6.9	25.5	12.2	9.8	37 263	13.7	3.7	5 844	77.4
Kenton County	419	151 464	6.6	26.3	11.0	22.9	43 906	9.0	3.5	59 444	66.4
Lewis County	1 255	14 092	1.4	25.2	12.5	6.4	22 208	28.5	11.7	5 422	81.2
Mason County	624	16 800	9.9	24.2	15.4	14.4	30 195	16.8	5.4	6 847	67.4
Nicholas County	509	6 813	2.5	23.5	15.5	7.5	29 886	13.2	9.6	2 710	74.8
Oldham County	490	46 178	7.0	27.4	7.0	30.6	63 229	4.1	2.5	14 856	86.8
Owen County	912	10 547	3.5	25.4	14.0	9.1	33 310	15.5	5.3	4 086	78.2
Pendleton County	727	14 390	1.7	28.3	10.4	9.7	38 125	11.4	5.0	5 170	77.9
Robertson County	259	2 266	1.8	24.1	16.9	8.7	30 581	22.2	5.7	866	77.9
Scott County (part)	319	4 258	2.1	26.2	8.7	13.7	51 705	9.4	2.6	1 569	84.8
Trimble County	386	8 125	2.7	26.5	11.4	7.6	36 192	13.6	5.2	3 137	80.6

[1]Dry land or land partially or temporarily covered by water.
[2]Persons who do not identify themselves as White alone, not of Hispanic origin.
[3]Persons 25 years old and over.

Table B. 110th Congressional Districts by Counties, 2000—*Continued*

(Number, percent.)

STATE Congressional district County	Land area,[1] (sq km)	Population				Percent with bachelor's degree or more[3]	Median household income, 1999 (dollars)	Percent living in poverty	Percent unemployed	Households	
		Total	Percent minority[2]	Percent under 18 years	Percent 65 years and over					Total	Percent owner occupied
	1	2	3	4	5	6	7	8	9	10	11
Congressional District 5, Kentucky	27 652	673 654	2.9	24.6	12.4	9.6	21 915	28.1	8.9	262 110	76.3
Bath County (part)	180	2 809	1.4	23.9	12.9	8.6	26 563	20.1	7.2	1 129	84.2
Bell County	934	30 060	4.2	24.4	13.4	9.0	19 057	31.1	11.1	12 004	67.5
Breathitt County	1 283	16 100	1.9	25.5	11.6	10.0	19 155	33.2	10.1	6 170	76.5
Clay County	1 220	24 556	7.2	25.4	10.3	8.0	16 271	39.7	10.7	8 556	74.8
Floyd County	1 021	42 441	2.9	23.6	12.2	9.7	21 168	30.3	10.0	16 881	76.2
Harlan County	1 210	33 202	4.7	25.0	13.9	8.9	18 665	32.5	13.2	13 291	73.5
Jackson County	897	13 495	1.3	26.0	11.9	6.8	20 177	30.2	8.8	5 307	80.2
Johnson County	677	23 445	1.5	23.9	12.7	9.3	24 911	26.6	8.4	9 103	76.4
Knott County	912	17 649	2.7	24.6	11.4	10.2	20 373	31.1	15.6	6 717	79.6
Knox County	1 004	31 795	2.5	26.1	12.7	8.8	18 294	34.8	8.9	12 416	71.4
Laurel County	1 128	52 715	2.8	25.4	11.4	10.6	27 015	21.3	5.4	20 353	77.0
Lawrence County	1 085	15 569	0.7	25.2	12.3	6.6	21 610	30.7	11.5	5 954	78.0
Lee County	544	7 916	4.3	22.6	14.4	6.3	18 544	30.4	9.4	2 985	76.8
Leslie County	1 046	12 401	1.4	24.6	11.5	6.3	18 546	32.7	10.2	4 885	82.1
Letcher County	878	25 277	1.7	23.8	12.5	7.7	21 110	27.1	11.0	10 085	80.8
McCreary County	1 108	17 080	2.6	27.4	10.5	6.7	19 348	32.2	11.3	6 520	75.6
Magoffin County	801	13 332	0.6	26.7	10.5	6.3	19 421	36.6	12.8	5 024	81.9
Martin County	598	12 578	1.1	28.1	9.7	9.0	18 279	37.0	12.8	4 776	79.3
Menifee County	528	6 556	2.7	24.9	11.7	8.4	22 064	29.6	8.3	2 537	81.2
Morgan County	987	13 948	6.0	22.4	11.8	7.7	21 869	27.2	8.4	4 752	79.9
Owsley County	513	4 858	1.2	24.3	15.3	7.7	15 805	45.4	8.8	1 894	78.4
Perry County	886	29 390	3.0	24.3	11.3	8.9	22 089	29.1	11.6	11 460	77.4
Pike County	2 040	68 736	1.9	23.7	12.4	9.9	23 930	23.4	9.0	27 612	78.7
Pulaski County	1 714	56 217	3.2	23.5	15.0	10.5	27 370	19.1	5.1	22 719	76.0
Rockcastle County	822	16 582	1.5	24.3	13.3	8.3	23 475	23.1	6.7	6 544	79.6
Rowan County	727	22 094	4.9	20.3	10.4	21.9	28 055	21.3	8.1	7 927	69.7
Wayne County	1 190	19 923	4.4	25.4	13.4	7.2	20 863	29.4	7.9	7 913	76.4
Whitley County	1 140	35 865	2.4	25.7	12.9	13.4	22 075	26.4	6.7	13 780	72.7
Wolfe County	577	7 065	0.7	26.0	12.7	10.6	19 310	35.9	9.1	2 816	73.8
Congressional District 6, Kentucky	9 729	673 561	12.9	23.1	10.9	24.6	37 544	13.2	5.0	268 321	63.2
Anderson County	525	19 111	4.1	26.6	10.6	12.0	45 433	7.5	4.0	7 320	79.8
Bourbon County	755	19 360	10.4	25.0	13.4	13.5	35 038	14.0	3.8	7 681	65.5
Boyle County	471	27 697	13.0	22.7	14.2	19.3	35 241	11.9	4.3	10 574	69.3
Clark County	659	33 144	7.2	24.7	12.4	15.6	39 946	10.6	4.6	13 015	68.6
Estill County	658	15 307	1.0	24.3	13.5	6.9	23 318	26.4	7.4	6 108	73.9
Fayette County	737	260 512	20.8	21.3	10.0	35.6	39 813	12.9	5.4	108 288	55.3
Franklin County	545	47 687	12.5	22.8	12.3	23.8	40 011	10.7	6.2	19 907	64.8
Garrard County	599	14 792	6.0	24.4	13.1	10.5	34 284	14.7	5.1	5 741	76.4
Jessamine County	448	39 041	6.4	26.3	9.5	21.5	40 096	10.5	4.3	13 867	67.1
Lincoln County (part)	648	17 419	5.2	26.1	13.0	9.3	26 099	22.8	5.0	6 865	78.4
Madison County	1 141	70 872	7.6	21.8	9.8	21.8	32 861	16.8	5.0	27 152	59.7
Mercer County	650	20 817	7.1	24.4	14.6	13.5	35 555	12.9	3.6	8 423	74.5
Montgomery County	514	22 554	5.8	24.8	12.8	13.4	31 746	15.2	5.9	8 902	71.5
Powell County	467	13 237	1.8	26.6	10.6	6.5	25 515	23.5	5.6	5 044	74.0
Scott County (part)	419	28 803	9.5	26.3	9.0	21.4	46 740	8.7	3.9	10 541	67.5
Woodford County	494	23 208	9.1	25.3	10.4	25.9	49 491	7.3	2.6	8 893	72.4
LOUISIANA	112 825	4 468 976	37.5	27.3	11.6	18.7	32 566	19.6	7.3	1 656 053	67.9
Congressional District 1, Louisiana	6 221	637 543	20.4	24.8	12.7	27.4	40 948	12.1	4.8	250 838	70.3
Jefferson Parish (part)	120	252 900	19.6	21.2	14.8	28.4	42 274	8.6	4.1	106 874	62.2
Orleans Parish (part)	25	37 501	10.4	18.5	18.5	54.7	49 898	7.7	2.9	17 927	63.0
St. Charles Parish (part)	83	11 360	18.8	32.8	5.4	34.6	61 142	5.6	2.5	3 759	87.2
St. Tammany Parish	2 212	191 268	15.0	28.4	10.0	28.3	47 883	9.7	3.8	69 253	80.5
Tangipahoa Parish	2 047	100 588	31.3	27.7	10.6	16.3	29 412	22.7	8.6	36 558	73.3
Washington Parish	1 734	43 926	33.2	26.8	14.8	10.9	24 264	24.7	8.2	16 467	76.5
Congressional District 2, Louisiana	689	639 048	71.6	28.3	10.3	19.4	27 514	26.8	9.6	236 008	50.4
Jefferson Parish (part)	246	191 875	55.4	30.4	8.3	11.4	32 628	20.4	8.1	65 684	65.1
Orleans Parish (part)	442	447 173	78.6	27.3	11.1	22.8	25 782	29.7	10.2	170 324	44.8
Congressional District 3, Louisiana	18 157	638 674	30.3	28.8	10.7	10.8	34 463	18.6	7.1	223 921	77.5
Ascension Parish (part)	551	39 811	35.6	29.3	9.7	10.3	36 045	18.3	7.0	14 008	76.1
Assumption Parish	877	23 388	33.8	28.4	11.0	7.4	31 168	21.8	9.3	8 239	84.1
Iberia Parish	1 490	73 266	35.7	30.0	11.4	11.2	31 204	23.6	9.2	25 381	73.4
Jefferson Parish (part)	427	10 691	13.1	27.2	9.0	9.2	40 083	12.9	4.2	3 676	87.6
Lafourche Parish	2 809	89 974	17.8	27.3	11.2	12.4	34 910	16.5	5.9	32 057	77.9

[1]Dry land or land partially or temporarily covered by water.
[2]Persons who do not identify themselves as White alone, not of Hispanic origin.
[3]Persons 25 years old and over.

Table B. 110th Congressional Districts by Counties, 2000—*Continued*

(Number, percent.)

STATE Congressional district County	Land area,[1] (sq km)	Population Total	Population Percent minority[2]	Population Percent under 18 years	Population Percent 65 years and over	Percent with bachelor's degree or more[3]	Median household income, 1999 (dollars)	Percent living in poverty	Percent unemployed	Households Total	Households Percent owner occupied
	1	2	3	4	5	6	7	8	9	10	11
Congressional District 3, Louisiana—*Continued*											
Plaquemines Parish	2 187	26 757	31.2	29.3	9.9	10.8	38 173	18.0	6.7	9 021	78.9
St. Bernard Parish	1 204	67 229	15.4	25.2	13.7	8.9	35 939	13.1	5.8	25 123	74.7
St. Charles Parish (part)	652	36 712	32.6	29.6	10.2	12.2	40 727	13.2	6.2	12 663	79.7
St. James Parish	637	21 216	50.3	29.5	11.3	10.1	35 277	20.7	10.2	6 992	85.6
St. John the Baptist Parish	567	43 044	49.1	31.1	8.1	12.9	39 456	16.7	6.9	14 283	81.0
St. Martin Parish	1 916	48 583	34.6	29.5	10.1	8.5	30 701	21.5	8.6	17 164	81.7
St. Mary Parish	1 587	53 500	38.2	29.6	11.1	9.4	28 072	23.6	8.6	19 317	73.9
Terrebonne Parish	3 250	104 503	26.9	29.1	9.6	12.3	35 235	19.1	5.9	35 997	75.5
Congressional District 4, Louisiana	27 881	638 366	38.0	27.1	13.0	16.7	31 085	20.0	8.3	241 288	68.5
Allen Parish (part)	938	11 591	28.4	24.6	11.6	8.3	31 453	17.8	5.8	3 781	77.8
Beauregard Parish	3 005	32 986	16.5	27.4	11.8	13.8	32 582	15.6	7.2	12 104	79.8
Bienville Parish	2 100	15 752	45.5	27.2	17.7	11.5	23 663	26.1	10.0	6 108	77.8
Bossier Parish	2 174	98 310	27.0	28.0	10.5	18.1	39 203	13.7	5.6	36 628	69.5
Caddo Parish	2 284	252 161	47.8	26.8	13.7	20.6	31 467	21.1	9.3	97 974	63.8
Claiborne Parish	1 955	16 851	48.5	25.5	17.4	12.4	25 344	26.5	9.4	6 270	75.8
De Soto Parish	2 272	25 494	44.9	28.4	14.5	10.2	28 252	25.1	8.1	9 691	76.6
Grant Parish	1 671	18 698	14.8	28.2	12.8	9.8	29 622	21.5	7.0	7 073	81.7
Natchitoches Parish	3 252	39 080	42.8	25.9	12.2	18.4	25 722	26.5	9.9	14 263	64.5
Red River Parish	1 008	9 622	42.7	30.1	14.5	8.7	23 153	29.9	11.9	3 414	76.2
Sabine Parish	2 241	23 459	28.9	26.2	16.5	11.1	26 655	21.5	8.2	9 221	81.0
Vernon Parish	3 441	52 531	28.5	29.1	8.0	13.5	31 216	15.3	8.5	18 260	56.7
Webster Parish	1 542	41 831	34.8	25.7	16.3	12.6	28 408	20.2	8.1	16 501	74.5
Congressional District 5, Louisiana	35 677	638 726	36.6	27.0	13.2	15.5	27 453	23.6	8.6	233 533	70.3
Allen Parish (part)	1 042	13 849	34.9	24.7	11.7	10.0	24 897	21.7	8.8	4 321	74.5
Avoyelles Parish	2 156	41 481	32.2	26.8	13.8	8.3	23 851	25.9	8.1	14 736	74.4
Caldwell Parish	1 371	10 560	20.5	24.9	13.8	8.8	26 972	21.2	7.4	3 941	79.2
Catahoula Parish	1 822	10 920	28.6	25.8	14.2	9.4	22 528	28.1	8.6	4 082	83.0
Concordia Parish	1 802	20 247	40.1	27.7	14.8	9.6	22 742	29.1	9.9	7 521	76.1
East Carroll Parish	1 092	9 421	69.0	30.4	13.0	12.3	20 723	40.5	15.0	2 969	62.1
Evangeline Parish (part)	1 192	12 898	12.0	29.3	10.8	10.3	27 547	21.2	3.9	4 532	83.1
Franklin Parish	1 615	21 263	33.4	28.0	15.7	9.8	22 964	28.4	8.3	7 754	76.2
Iberville Parish (part)	761	15 204	58.0	30.0	11.2	10.3	26 040	26.7	9.1	5 212	73.9
Jackson Parish	1 476	15 397	29.3	25.3	16.4	12.9	28 352	19.8	5.4	6 086	77.3
La Salle Parish	1 616	14 282	14.6	26.1	14.6	11.2	28 189	18.7	5.5	5 291	83.5
Lincoln Parish	1 221	42 509	43.0	22.2	11.4	31.8	26 977	26.5	13.3	15 235	59.9
Madison Parish	1 616	13 728	63.4	33.0	11.4	11.0	20 509	36.7	12.5	4 469	61.9
Morehouse Parish	2 057	31 021	44.6	27.5	15.4	9.7	25 124	26.8	11.1	11 382	71.6
Ouachita Parish	1 581	147 250	36.2	27.8	11.8	22.7	32 047	20.7	8.2	55 216	64.1
Pointe Coupee Parish (part)	1 158	12 749	56.0	29.5	12.3	8.1	25 048	29.4	10.5	4 515	76.6
Rapides Parish	3 425	126 337	34.3	27.3	13.0	16.5	29 856	20.5	7.1	47 120	68.0
Richland Parish	1 446	20 981	39.5	27.2	15.2	12.8	23 668	27.9	6.9	7 490	72.3
Tensas Parish	1 560	6 618	57.0	26.4	15.5	14.8	19 799	36.3	11.6	2 416	69.4
Union Parish	2 273	22 803	30.6	25.7	14.8	11.8	29 061	18.6	7.0	8 857	81.2
West Carroll Parish	931	12 314	20.8	25.6	15.5	9.5	24 637	23.4	12.2	4 458	79.0
Winn Parish	2 462	16 894	34.0	24.8	14.4	9.4	25 462	21.5	7.7	5 930	74.7
Congressional District 6, Louisiana	7 966	638 209	37.2	26.7	9.6	24.1	37 931	16.6	6.0	232 902	68.7
Ascension Parish (part)	204	36 816	10.8	30.9	5.4	19.1	53 728	7.3	3.9	12 683	89.1
East Baton Rouge Parish	1 180	412 852	44.9	26.1	9.9	30.8	37 224	17.9	6.3	156 365	61.6
East Feliciana Parish	1 174	21 360	48.6	25.7	11.1	11.3	31 631	23.0	11.2	6 699	82.4
Iberville Parish (part)	841	18 116	45.6	23.0	10.8	9.0	31 764	19.6	5.7	5 462	80.5
Livingston Parish	1 678	91 814	6.6	29.4	8.7	11.4	38 887	11.4	4.8	32 630	83.8
Pointe Coupee Parish (part)	285	10 014	18.7	24.2	15.5	18.1	37 561	15.0	3.7	3 882	79.0
St. Helena Parish	1 058	10 525	53.8	29.0	12.5	11.2	24 970	26.8	9.5	3 873	85.0
West Baton Rouge Parish	495	21 601	37.9	28.0	9.8	11.1	37 117	17.0	5.6	7 663	78.8
West Feliciana Parish	1 052	15 111	52.0	20.4	7.0	10.6	39 667	19.9	5.6	3 645	74.5
Congressional District 7, Louisiana	16 234	638 410	28.0	28.1	11.7	16.6	31 453	19.9	7.4	237 563	70.3
Acadia Parish	1 697	58 861	20.0	29.8	12.3	9.4	26 684	24.5	7.1	21 142	72.2
Calcasieu Parish	2 774	183 577	27.2	27.4	11.9	16.9	35 372	15.4	6.9	68 613	71.5
Cameron Parish	3 401	9 991	7.3	28.3	10.5	7.9	34 232	12.3	4.6	3 592	85.2
Evangeline Parish (part)	528	22 536	40.5	29.6	13.9	9.0	17 101	38.7	9.6	8 204	61.8
Jefferson Davis Parish	1 689	31 435	20.1	29.4	13.2	9.9	27 736	20.9	7.9	11 480	74.9
Lafayette Parish	699	190 503	27.6	27.3	9.5	25.5	36 518	15.7	6.9	72 372	66.1
St. Landry Parish	2 405	87 700	44.0	29.4	13.5	10.7	22 855	29.3	10.4	32 328	70.7
Vermilion Parish	3 040	53 807	18.2	28.2	13.6	10.7	29 500	22.1	7.0	19 832	77.0

[1]Dry land or land partially or temporarily covered by water.
[2]Persons who do not identify themselves as White alone, not of Hispanic origin.
[3]Persons 25 years old and over.

Table B. 110th Congressional Districts by Counties, 2000—*Continued*

(Number, percent.)

STATE Congressional district County	Land area,[1] (sq km)	Population				Percent with bachelor's degree or more[3]	Median household income, 1999 (dollars)	Percent living in poverty	Percent unem-ployed	Households	
		Total	Percent minority[2]	Percent under 18 years	Percent 65 years and over					Total	Percent owner occupied
	1	2	3	4	5	6	7	8	9	10	11
MAINE	79 931	1 274 923	3.5	23.6	14.4	22.9	37 240	10.9	4.8	518 200	71.6
Congressional District 1, Maine	9 156	637 450	3.6	23.9	13.9	27.9	42 044	8.6	3.7	258 917	70.8
Cumberland County	2 164	265 612	4.7	23.3	13.3	34.2	44 048	7.9	3.7	107 989	66.7
Kennebec County (part)	1 640	76 648	2.9	24.2	13.7	21.3	37 577	10.4	4.3	31 482	72.6
Knox County	947	39 618	2.0	22.4	17.3	26.2	36 774	10.1	3.4	16 608	74.0
Lincoln County	1 181	33 616	1.9	22.6	18.1	26.6	38 686	10.1	4.3	14 158	83.1
Sagadahoc County	658	35 214	3.9	25.7	12.3	25.0	41 908	8.6	3.3	14 117	72.0
York County	2 566	186 742	2.9	24.7	13.6	22.9	43 630	8.2	3.5	74 563	72.6
Congressional District 2, Maine	70 775	637 473	3.3	23.3	14.9	17.7	32 600	13.3	5.9	259 283	72.4
Androscoggin County	1 218	103 793	3.7	23.8	14.4	14.4	35 794	11.1	5.1	42 028	63.4
Aroostook County	17 279	73 938	3.4	22.6	17.0	14.6	28 837	14.3	6.5	30 356	73.1
Franklin County	4 397	29 467	2.3	23.7	14.2	20.9	31 459	14.6	7.3	11 806	76.0
Hancock County	4 112	51 791	2.9	22.3	15.9	27.1	35 811	10.2	5.4	21 864	75.6
Kennebec County (part)	607	40 466	3.2	23.1	15.2	19.3	33 929	12.6	5.4	16 201	68.5
Oxford County	5 382	54 755	2.5	24.1	16.1	15.7	33 435	11.8	5.3	22 314	77.0
Penobscot County	8 795	144 919	3.7	22.8	13.1	20.3	34 274	13.7	5.6	58 096	69.8
Piscataquis County	10 272	17 235	2.4	23.3	17.3	13.3	28 250	14.8	8.0	7 278	79.4
Somerset County	10 170	50 888	2.1	24.7	14.3	11.8	30 731	14.9	6.3	20 496	77.9
Waldo County	1 890	36 280	2.7	24.2	13.5	22.3	33 986	13.9	5.7	14 726	79.8
Washington County	6 652	33 941	6.9	22.9	17.3	14.7	25 869	19.0	8.5	14 118	77.6
MARYLAND	25 314	5 296 486	37.9	25.6	11.3	31.4	52 868	8.5	4.7	1 980 859	67.7
Congressional District 1, Maryland	9 461	663 097	15.2	25.0	13.4	27.3	51 918	7.3	3.9	248 619	78.5
Anne Arundel County (part)	205	101 788	8.2	26.6	10.2	41.0	76 571	3.1	2.5	35 677	88.7
Baltimore County (part)	258	59 152	7.8	23.4	15.8	43.3	70 984	2.4	2.3	22 304	89.5
Caroline County	829	29 772	19.3	26.8	13.6	12.1	38 832	11.7	4.8	11 097	74.0
Cecil County (part)	902	85 951	7.2	27.7	10.4	16.4	50 510	7.2	4.1	31 223	74.9
Dorchester County (part)	1 444	30 674	31.2	23.3	17.9	12.0	34 077	13.8	5.8	12 706	70.1
Harford County (part)	389	106 254	6.9	27.7	10.6	34.1	65 178	2.5	2.3	38 051	85.9
Kent County (part)	724	19 197	21.5	20.9	19.2	21.7	39 869	13.0	4.4	7 666	70.3
Queen Anne's County (part)	964	40 563	11.7	25.3	12.8	25.4	57 037	6.3	2.8	15 315	83.2
Somerset County (part)	847	24 747	44.3	18.5	14.3	11.6	29 903	20.1	9.7	8 361	69.7
Talbot County (part)	697	33 812	18.7	21.6	20.5	27.8	43 532	8.3	3.4	14 307	71.6
Wicomico County (part)	977	84 644	28.3	24.7	12.8	21.9	39 035	12.8	5.5	32 218	66.5
Worcester County (part)	1 226	46 543	19.5	20.5	20.2	21.6	40 650	9.6	6.8	19 694	75.0
Congressional District 2, Maryland	919	661 945	33.8	25.6	12.3	20.3	44 309	9.8	5.0	260 455	62.4
Anne Arundel County (part)	134	106 857	27.6	28.4	8.2	18.1	52 488	6.6	3.6	38 041	68.1
Baltimore County (part)	430	359 278	26.1	23.5	14.7	23.0	45 810	7.6	4.5	145 768	63.2
Harford County (part)	305	83 190	27.0	28.1	9.5	19.3	48 129	8.5	4.2	31 509	65.0
Baltimore city (part)	50	112 620	69.2	28.1	10.6	13.9	31 554	20.6	8.7	45 137	53.0
Congressional District 3, Maryland	758	661 068	24.2	23.0	12.6	36.5	52 906	7.7	4.0	262 186	67.5
Anne Arundel County (part)	392	232 055	24.3	23.1	10.5	32.2	59 889	5.6	3.4	86 886	70.4
Baltimore County (part)	193	185 149	17.9	23.1	15.0	39.9	53 473	6.1	3.8	74 370	68.1
Howard County (part)	99	76 164	31.4	27.6	6.8	52.1	69 750	4.5	2.8	28 403	72.6
Baltimore city (part)	74	167 700	27.7	20.8	16.1	31.8	38 091	13.6	5.9	72 527	61.4
Congressional District 4, Maryland	816	661 651	72.5	28.4	7.3	32.7	57 727	7.3	5.3	236 464	62.8
Montgomery County (part)	438	251 141	45.5	27.4	7.6	49.9	70 345	5.3	3.1	88 955	69.0
Prince George's County (part)	379	410 510	89.0	28.9	7.0	21.7	51 500	8.6	6.7	147 509	59.1
Congressional District 5, Maryland	3 896	662 203	39.5	26.2	8.7	28.7	62 661	5.6	4.1	234 188	74.8
Anne Arundel County (part)	346	48 956	9.9	25.0	10.7	26.8	68 938	4.1	2.4	18 066	89.3
Calvert County (part)	557	74 563	16.9	29.6	8.9	22.5	65 945	4.4	3.0	25 447	85.2
Charles County (part)	1 194	120 546	32.7	28.8	7.8	20.0	62 199	5.5	3.4	41 668	78.2
Prince George's County (part)	863	331 927	56.5	24.3	8.5	35.2	63 983	5.6	4.7	118 365	70.0
St. Mary's County (part)	936	86 211	19.6	27.9	9.0	22.6	54 706	7.2	4.5	30 642	71.8
Congressional District 6, Maryland	7 931	661 559	8.4	25.9	12.0	23.7	50 957	6.7	3.6	240 769	75.7
Allegany County	1 102	74 930	7.6	20.5	17.9	14.1	30 821	14.8	8.9	29 322	70.1
Baltimore County (part)	546	30 610	4.3	26.0	11.5	41.8	70 962	2.7	2.2	11 426	83.6
Carroll County	1 163	150 897	5.0	27.7	10.8	24.8	60 021	3.8	2.7	52 503	82.0
Frederick County	1 717	195 277	11.9	27.5	9.6	30.0	60 276	4.5	3.1	70 060	75.8
Garrett County	1 678	29 846	1.0	25.1	14.9	13.8	32 238	13.3	5.6	11 476	77.9
Harford County (part)	447	29 146	4.1	27.1	10.4	24.6	59 570	3.6	2.5	10 107	88.6
Montgomery County (part)	92	18 930	10.9	32.6	6.0	41.8	72 440	4.0	1.9	6 149	88.3
Washington County	1 187	131 923	10.7	23.4	14.2	14.6	40 617	9.5	3.3	49 726	65.6
Congressional District 7, Maryland	762	662 615	65.8	26.0	11.7	27.5	38 885	17.6	8.6	247 981	55.5
Baltimore County (part)	123	120 103	55.8	24.5	14.0	29.3	50 114	6.6	5.2	46 009	65.9
Howard County (part)	554	171 678	25.8	28.1	8.2	53.3	77 245	3.6	2.2	61 640	74.3
Baltimore city (part)	85	370 834	87.6	25.5	12.7	14.4	25 564	28.0	14.0	140 332	43.7
Congressional District 8, Maryland	769	662 348	44.1	24.3	12.4	53.7	68 306	6.2	3.6	250 197	65.3
Montgomery County (part)	753	603 270	39.6	24.1	12.8	56.8	72 040	5.6	3.2	229 461	68.1
Prince George's County (part)	16	59 078	90.1	25.8	7.7	18.3	38 924	12.9	7.7	20 736	34.9

[1]Dry land or land partially or temporarily covered by water.
[2]Persons who do not identify themselves as White alone, not of Hispanic origin.
[3]Persons 25 years old and over.

Table B. 110th Congressional Districts by Counties, 2000—*Continued*

(Number, percent.)

STATE Congressional district County	Land area,[1] (sq km)	Population				Percent with bachelor's degree or more[3]	Median household income, 1999 (dollars)	Percent living in poverty	Percent unem-ployed	Households	
		Total	Percent minority[2]	Percent under 18 years	Percent 65 years and over					Total	Percent owner occupied
	1	2	3	4	5	6	7	8	9	10	11
MASSACHUSETTS	20 306	6 349 097	18.1	23.6	13.5	33.2	50 502	9.3	4.6	2 443 580	61.7
Congressional District 1, Massachusetts	8 032	634 484	11.1	24.2	13.9	25.4	42 570	10.5	5.0	245 029	65.5
Berkshire County	2 412	134 953	5.9	22.5	18.0	26.0	39 047	9.5	5.1	56 006	66.9
Franklin County	1 818	71 535	5.2	23.4	14.3	29.1	40 768	9.4	4.5	29 466	67.0
Hampden County (part)	804	123 424	20.3	25.8	14.4	21.1	40 253	15.6	5.2	47 450	59.1
Hampshire County (part)	1 175	101 284	10.7	20.2	10.2	36.0	46 988	10.0	5.5	35 630	66.6
Middlesex County (part)	205	23 190	3.0	30.2	7.3	30.1	62 885	4.4	3.3	7 931	82.8
Worcester County (part)	1 617	180 098	12.3	26.1	13.4	20.3	44 201	9.2	4.9	68 546	65.7
Congressional District 2, Massachusetts	2 387	634 444	17.6	25.5	13.7	23.1	44 386	10.8	4.7	242 706	65.8
Hampden County (part)	797	332 804	27.6	26.0	14.5	20.2	39 456	14.4	5.8	127 838	63.0
Hampshire County (part)	195	50 967	10.2	18.1	15.6	41.2	44 325	8.2	4.4	20 361	62.1
Norfolk County (part)	48	15 314	3.6	26.9	9.5	22.0	64 496	2.5	3.6	5 557	83.9
Worcester County (part)	1 346	235 359	6.0	26.2	12.3	23.3	51 230	6.8	3.3	88 950	69.7
Congressional District 3, Massachusetts	1 505	634 466	13.9	25.5	12.9	30.8	50 223	9.0	4.4	240 491	62.9
Bristol County (part)	386	180 528	8.1	24.8	14.2	20.1	44 649	8.7	4.8	70 009	61.4
Middlesex County (part)	204	78 076	10.3	26.4	9.9	43.6	67 302	4.4	3.2	29 460	73.3
Norfolk County (part)	185	60 245	4.2	29.6	9.6	40.3	70 723	3.1	3.1	20 745	81.2
Worcester County (part)	730	315 617	20.1	24.8	13.6	32.1	46 433	11.5	4.7	120 277	58.1
Congressional District 4, Massachusetts	1 895	634 697	12.2	23.9	13.7	36.9	53 169	8.4	4.9	241 784	65.1
Bristol County (part)	981	331 851	12.3	24.4	14.5	18.5	41 561	11.3	6.5	127 913	60.5
Middlesex County (part)	88	88 029	13.0	21.7	14.9	68.4	87 167	4.2	3.0	32 624	70.6
Norfolk County (part)	266	141 248	14.4	22.9	11.6	65.5	77 103	5.6	3.1	53 913	65.1
Plymouth County (part)	561	73 569	6.7	25.9	13.2	25.3	52 322	6.0	3.9	27 334	80.0
Congressional District 5, Massachusetts	1 465	635 223	20.4	27.2	11.0	33.6	56 217	8.9	3.9	227 344	67.2
Essex County (part)	243	206 048	31.4	28.0	12.1	25.3	44 992	13.3	5.0	75 276	56.4
Middlesex County (part)	998	409 286	15.2	26.9	10.5	36.8	62 230	6.9	3.5	145 914	71.9
Worcester County (part)	225	19 889	12.1	25.3	8.8	49.5	83 498	2.9	2.6	6 154	86.0
Congressional District 6, Massachusetts	1 244	636 554	10.2	24.2	14.4	35.1	57 826	6.3	4.0	243 310	68.9
Essex County (part)	1 054	517 371	11.1	24.0	14.5	33.4	54 513	7.2	4.5	200 143	66.2
Middlesex County (part)	190	119 183	6.5	25.1	13.7	42.5	74 105	2.3	2.2	43 167	81.5
Congressional District 7, Massachusetts	441	634 385	16.5	20.4	15.5	39.5	56 110	6.7	3.5	255 260	57.1
Middlesex County (part)	421	568 799	16.4	20.5	15.4	42.0	58 143	6.1	3.3	227 954	57.9
Suffolk County (part)	20	65 586	17.3	20.1	16.6	17.9	41 650	12.1	5.3	27 306	50.9
Congressional District 8, Massachusetts	105	635 185	51.2	18.3	9.4	39.8	39 300	19.9	7.1	254 471	28.4
Middlesex County (part)	27	178 833	32.0	13.8	9.7	54.1	47 159	12.7	5.0	74 170	31.5
Suffolk County (part)	78	456 352	58.7	20.1	9.2	33.6	35 880	22.6	8.1	180 301	27.0
Congressional District 9, Massachusetts	811	633 846	20.5	23.8	14.1	33.8	55 407	7.5	4.2	238 738	64.4
Bristol County (part)	74	22 299	5.8	24.4	9.5	39.6	69 144	2.0	3.1	7 489	81.7
Norfolk County (part)	423	284 227	11.6	24.2	16.3	40.2	65 899	3.6	3.0	105 028	76.7
Plymouth County (part)	261	159 451	27.2	26.8	11.0	18.4	46 976	10.2	5.7	55 106	63.6
Suffolk County (part)	53	167 869	31.0	20.1	14.0	35.5	47 152	12.4	4.9	71 115	44.9
Congressional District 10, Massachusetts	2 420	635 813	7.8	22.7	16.7	33.5	51 928	5.9	3.9	254 447	73.6
Barnstable County	1 024	222 230	6.6	20.4	23.1	33.6	45 933	6.9	5.2	94 822	77.8
Bristol County (part)	0	0	X	X	X	X	X	X	X	0	X
Dukes County	269	14 987	10.6	22.7	14.2	38.4	45 559	7.3	2.7	6 421	71.3
Nantucket County	124	9 520	14.0	19.3	10.4	38.4	55 522	7.5	4.3	3 699	63.1
Norfolk County (part)	113	149 274	14.9	19.6	15.9	31.1	49 891	6.5	3.5	63 584	56.9
Plymouth County (part)	890	239 802	4.1	26.9	11.8	34.4	62 857	4.5	3.2	85 921	81.8
MICHIGAN	147 121	9 938 444	21.5	26.1	12.3	21.8	44 667	10.5	5.8	3 785 661	73.8
Congressional District 1, Michigan	64 458	662 583	6.2	23.1	17.0	15.6	34 076	11.2	8.0	266 115	80.1
Alcona County (part)	1 747	11 719	3.0	19.2	24.5	10.9	31 362	12.6	10.0	5 132	89.5
Alger County (part)	2 377	9 862	12.7	20.4	17.1	14.7	35 892	10.3	8.6	3 785	82.4
Alpena County (part)	1 487	31 314	2.6	23.7	17.1	13.2	34 177	10.5	7.3	12 818	79.3
Antrim County (part)	1 235	23 110	3.5	24.4	17.6	19.4	38 107	9.0	6.4	9 222	85.0
Arenac County (part)	950	17 269	5.6	23.2	16.5	9.1	32 805	13.9	8.4	6 710	84.3
Baraga County (part)	2 341	8 746	21.7	22.8	16.3	10.9	33 673	11.1	7.9	3 353	77.7
Bay County (part)	803	30 855	4.0	25.3	12.7	12.2	45 034	7.4	5.8	11 436	90.0
Charlevoix County (part)	1 080	26 090	4.1	26.0	14.8	19.8	39 788	8.0	6.0	10 400	81.2
Cheboygan County (part)	1 853	26 448	5.7	23.6	17.9	13.9	33 417	12.2	14.3	10 835	82.8
Chippewa County (part)	4 043	38 543	25.0	21.3	12.7	15.0	34 464	12.8	10.0	13 474	74.0
Crawford County	1 446	14 273	4.6	24.4	16.6	12.9	33 364	12.7	7.5	5 625	82.8
Delta County (part)	3 030	38 520	4.7	23.8	17.1	17.1	35 511	9.5	7.5	15 836	79.6
Dickinson County	1 985	27 472	2.5	25.1	18.1	16.7	34 825	9.1	5.6	11 386	80.1
Emmet County (part)	1 212	31 437	5.8	25.3	14.3	26.2	40 222	7.4	7.3	12 577	75.5
Gladwin County	1 313	26 023	2.9	23.2	18.3	9.2	32 019	13.8	8.4	10 561	85.6

[1]Dry land or land partially or temporarily covered by water.
[2]Persons who do not identify themselves as White alone, not of Hispanic origin.
[3]Persons 25 years old and over.
X = Not applicable.

Table B. 110th Congressional Districts by Counties, 2000—*Continued*

(Number, percent.)

STATE Congressional district County	Land area,[1] (sq km)	Population Total	Percent minority[2]	Percent under 18 years	Percent 65 years and over	Percent with bachelor's degree or more[3]	Median household income, 1999 (dollars)	Percent living in poverty	Percent unem- ployed	Households Total	Households Percent owner occupied
	1	2	3	4	5	6	7	8	9	10	11
Congressional District 1, Michigan—*Continued*											
Gogebic County (part)	2 854	17 370	6.0	20.5	22.6	15.8	27 405	14.4	9.4	7 425	78.7
Houghton County (part)	2 620	36 016	4.9	21.9	15.5	23.0	28 817	16.8	7.9	13 793	71.5
Iosco County (part)	1 422	27 339	3.7	22.3	21.5	11.3	31 321	12.7	9.0	11 727	82.0
Iron County	3 021	13 138	4.0	20.6	25.1	13.7	28 560	11.3	9.4	5 748	82.5
Keweenaw County (part)	1 401	2 301	5.0	22.5	20.2	19.1	28 140	12.7	11.1	998	89.3
Luce County (part)	2 339	7 024	18.0	21.4	15.4	11.8	32 031	14.9	8.7	2 481	79.6
Mackinac County (part)	2 646	11 943	20.7	22.3	18.3	14.9	33 356	10.5	14.8	5 067	79.1
Marquette County (part)	4 717	64 634	5.1	21.4	13.5	23.7	35 548	10.9	6.2	25 767	69.8
Menominee County (part)	2 703	25 326	4.1	24.1	17.3	11.0	32 888	11.5	5.1	10 529	79.5
Montmorency County	1 418	10 315	2.3	20.4	23.8	8.2	30 005	12.8	12.4	4 455	86.1
Ogemaw County	1 462	21 645	3.4	23.5	18.7	9.6	30 474	14.0	8.5	8 842	85.0
Ontonagon County (part)	3 397	7 818	3.5	20.2	21.6	13.0	29 552	10.4	9.6	3 456	84.9
Oscoda County	1 463	9 418	2.7	23.3	20.3	8.0	28 228	14.6	8.8	3 921	85.3
Otsego County	1 333	23 301	3.2	26.7	13.8	17.4	40 876	6.8	5.6	8 995	81.9
Presque Isle County (part)	1 710	14 411	1.9	20.9	22.5	11.5	31 656	10.3	10.9	6 155	85.5
Schoolcraft County (part)	3 051	8 903	11.5	22.9	18.6	11.3	31 140	12.2	12.4	3 606	81.8
Congressional District 2, Michigan	13 895	663 003	12.6	27.6	12.3	18.3	42 589	8.9	5.0	242 071	80.0
Allegan County (part)	733	38 872	10.8	28.9	11.5	19.0	49 223	5.9	2.2	14 061	83.6
Benzie County (part)	832	15 998	4.9	23.3	17.5	20.0	37 350	7.0	6.2	6 500	85.8
Kent County (part)	340	30 254	8.9	27.5	9.8	14.6	43 603	7.6	4.4	11 347	70.3
Lake County	1 470	11 333	16.0	22.0	19.6	7.8	26 622	19.4	8.4	4 704	82.9
Manistee County (part)	1 408	24 527	7.3	22.8	18.1	14.2	34 208	10.3	6.5	9 860	81.0
Mason County (part)	1 282	28 274	6.5	24.2	16.9	15.9	34 704	11.0	7.3	11 406	78.3
Muskegon County (part)	1 319	170 200	20.4	27.4	12.9	13.9	38 008	11.4	5.4	63 330	77.7
Newaygo County	2 182	47 874	7.0	29.1	12.8	11.4	37 130	11.6	5.8	17 599	84.5
Oceana County (part)	1 400	26 873	14.3	28.1	13.9	12.6	35 307	14.7	7.9	9 778	82.7
Ottawa County (part)	1 465	238 314	11.5	28.7	10.1	26.0	52 347	5.5	4.0	81 662	80.8
Wexford County	1 465	30 484	3.4	26.8	14.0	15.3	35 363	10.3	6.9	11 824	79.2
Congressional District 3, Michigan	4 803	662 354	17.8	28.1	10.5	23.9	45 936	8.6	4.4	243 184	72.5
Barry County	1 440	56 755	3.4	27.2	11.7	14.7	46 820	5.5	4.7	21 035	85.9
Ionia County	1 485	61 518	9.0	26.9	10.0	10.8	43 074	8.7	4.6	20 606	80.1
Kent County (part)	1 878	544 081	20.3	28.3	10.4	26.4	46 128	8.9	4.4	201 543	70.3
Congressional District 4, Michigan	19 299	662 497	7.1	24.6	13.6	18.6	39 020	10.5	6.2	252 141	77.8
Clare County	1 468	31 252	3.4	24.5	17.3	8.8	28 845	16.0	8.6	12 686	82.2
Grand Traverse County (part)	1 205	77 654	4.5	25.4	13.1	26.1	43 169	5.9	4.6	30 396	77.3
Gratiot County	1 477	42 285	10.0	23.8	13.5	12.9	37 262	10.3	5.7	14 501	77.5
Isabella County	1 487	63 351	9.5	20.4	9.0	23.9	34 262	20.4	7.2	22 425	63.3
Kalkaska County	1 453	16 571	3.0	25.6	13.8	9.7	36 072	10.5	6.4	6 428	85.4
Leelanau County (part)	903	21 119	7.7	24.4	17.4	31.4	47 062	5.4	5.0	8 436	84.7
Mecosta County	1 439	40 553	7.9	22.5	13.1	19.1	33 849	16.1	11.6	14 915	73.6
Midland County	1 350	82 874	5.6	26.9	12.0	29.3	45 674	8.4	5.1	31 769	78.4
Missaukee County	1 468	14 478	2.5	27.1	14.9	10.2	35 224	10.7	6.5	5 450	83.5
Montcalm County	1 834	61 266	6.6	27.2	12.1	10.8	37 218	10.9	5.5	22 079	81.6
Osceola County	1 466	23 197	3.3	27.1	14.1	11.3	34 102	12.7	6.6	8 861	81.3
Roscommon County	1 350	25 469	2.7	19.9	23.7	10.9	30 029	12.4	8.8	11 250	85.8
Saginaw County (part)	1 661	121 164	12.5	24.0	14.1	18.2	45 084	7.1	5.4	46 830	77.9
Shiawassee County (part)	739	41 264	4.0	25.9	13.6	11.6	38 650	9.1	6.2	16 115	76.1
Congressional District 5, Michigan	4 543	662 584	25.0	27.3	12.3	15.1	39 675	13.7	7.5	257 373	73.8
Bay County (part)	348	79 302	8.5	24.0	15.4	14.9	36 570	10.6	6.5	32 494	75.6
Genesee County	1 657	436 141	25.8	27.4	11.6	16.2	41 951	13.1	7.1	169 825	73.2
Saginaw County (part)	434	88 875	48.4	30.1	12.5	12.4	30 523	23.1	11.1	33 600	68.2
Tuscola County (part)	2 104	58 266	5.3	26.9	12.8	10.6	40 174	8.2	6.2	21 454	84.1
Congressional District 6, Michigan	8 628	662 305	15.7	25.9	12.5	21.1	40 943	11.4	5.8	253 892	72.9
Allegan County (part)	1 410	66 793	8.6	28.7	10.8	14.0	44 040	8.2	5.4	24 104	82.4
Berrien County (part)	1 479	162 453	21.8	25.9	14.5	19.6	38 567	12.7	5.5	63 569	72.2
Calhoun County (part)	123	4 667	3.9	28.0	13.0	15.5	48 939	7.8	4.9	1 701	90.1
Cass County	1 275	51 104	11.3	25.6	13.6	12.1	41 264	9.9	5.0	19 676	81.9
Kalamazoo County	1 455	238 603	16.6	24.0	11.3	31.2	42 022	12.0	6.6	93 479	65.8
St. Joseph County	1 305	62 422	8.8	27.4	13.0	12.7	40 355	11.3	4.6	23 381	76.9
Van Buren County (part)	1 582	76 263	15.6	28.1	12.3	14.3	39 365	11.1	5.8	27 982	79.5
Congressional District 7, Michigan	11 125	662 535	11.5	26.0	12.5	19.1	45 181	7.9	4.9	248 411	76.7
Branch County	1 314	45 787	7.8	25.6	13.0	10.6	38 760	9.3	4.8	16 349	78.9
Calhoun County (part)	1 713	133 318	18.0	25.9	13.8	16.0	38 579	11.4	5.8	52 399	72.4
Eaton County	1 493	103 655	11.4	26.1	11.3	21.7	49 588	5.8	4.3	40 167	74.1
Hillsdale County	1 551	46 527	3.2	26.3	13.3	12.0	40 396	8.2	5.3	17 335	79.9
Jackson County	1 830	158 422	12.5	25.6	12.9	16.3	43 171	9.0	5.5	58 168	76.5
Lenawee County	1 944	98 890	10.7	25.9	12.7	16.3	45 739	6.7	4.7	35 930	78.2
Washtenaw County (part)	1 280	75 936	6.5	27.0	9.8	39.8	68 241	3.0	2.9	28 063	83.9

[1]Dry land or land partially or temporarily covered by water.
[2]Persons who do not identify themselves as White alone, not of Hispanic origin.
[3]Persons 25 years old and over.

Table B. 110th Congressional Districts by Counties, 2000—*Continued*

(Number, percent.)

STATE Congressional district County	Land area,[1] (sq km)	Population Total	Population Percent minority[2]	Population Percent under 18 years	Population Percent 65 years and over	Percent with bachelor's degree or more[3]	Median household income, 1999 (dollars)	Percent living in poverty	Percent unem- ployed	Households Total	Households Percent owner occupied
	1	2	3	4	5	6	7	8	9	10	11
Congressional District 8, Michigan	5 837	662 349	12.4	26.3	8.8	29.0	52 510	8.4	4.4	245 099	75.2
Clinton County	1 480	64 753	5.4	28.1	10.8	21.2	52 806	4.6	3.0	23 653	85.2
Ingham County	1 448	279 320	23.1	23.4	9.4	33.0	40 774	14.6	5.7	108 593	60.7
Livingston County	1 472	156 951	3.9	28.7	8.2	28.2	67 400	3.4	3.3	55 384	88.1
Oakland County (part)	780	130 902	5.1	28.5	7.1	28.9	68 788	4.3	3.5	46 688	86.1
Shiawassee County (part)	656	30 423	3.5	28.2	9.8	16.8	49 047	6.2	4.3	10 781	86.2
Congressional District 9, Michigan	806	662 892	18.6	24.4	12.4	43.5	65 358	5.4	3.6	264 060	74.3
Oakland County (part)	806	662 892	18.6	24.4	12.4	43.5	65 358	5.4	3.6	264 060	74.3
Congressional District 10, Michigan	9 193	662 510	6.4	26.6	11.1	16.9	52 690	6.0	4.5	244 523	82.1
Huron County (part)	2 167	36 079	3.2	24.3	19.5	10.9	35 315	10.2	5.9	14 597	83.5
St. Joseph County	1 694	87 904	5.2	28.2	9.5	12.7	51 717	5.4	5.5	30 729	85.0
Macomb County (part)	960	329 745	7.3	26.4	9.4	21.8	63 412	4.1	3.5	120 254	82.5
St. Clair County (part)	1 876	164 235	6.4	26.6	12.3	12.6	46 313	7.8	5.2	62 072	79.6
Sanilac County (part)	2 496	44 547	4.3	26.9	15.4	10.0	36 870	10.4	6.0	16 871	81.9
Congressional District 11, Michigan	1 032	662 505	10.4	25.4	11.6	28.5	59 177	4.3	3.4	257 783	78.5
Oakland County (part)	543	196 207	6.9	27.5	8.2	34.0	65 085	3.7	3.0	74 584	80.6
Wayne County (part)	489	466 298	11.9	24.5	13.0	26.3	56 594	4.6	3.5	183 199	77.7
Congressional District 12, Michigan	415	662 559	18.4	22.6	15.7	19.5	46 784	7.3	4.7	274 732	73.0
Lenawee County	285	458 404	9.5	22.4	16.7	14.7	46 258	6.7	4.6	188 949	76.6
Oakland County (part)	131	204 155	38.4	23.2	13.3	30.6	48 099	8.5	4.7	85 783	64.9
Congressional District 13, Michigan	280	662 844	71.1	30.0	11.5	14.1	31 165	24.4	12.9	239 745	55.7
Wayne County (part)	280	662 844	71.1	30.0	11.5	14.1	31 165	24.4	12.9	239 745	55.7
Congressional District 14, Michigan	318	662 468	67.8	28.9	12.4	14.2	36 099	19.7	9.8	243 452	64.9
Wayne County (part)	318	662 468	67.8	28.9	12.4	14.2	36 099	19.7	9.8	243 452	64.9
Congressional District 15, Michigan	2 490	662 456	20.8	24.5	10.0	27.5	48 963	10.3	4.5	253 080	68.4
Monroe County (part)	1 427	145 945	5.8	27.3	11.1	14.3	51 743	7.0	3.5	53 772	80.9
Washtenaw County (part)	559	246 959	29.4	20.4	7.5	51.0	47 703	13.7	4.1	97 264	52.7
Wayne County (part)	503	269 552	21.0	26.7	11.6	15.0	48 313	9.1	5.6	102 044	76.7
MINNESOTA	206 189	4 919 479	11.8	26.2	12.1	27.4	47 111	7.9	4.1	1 895 127	74.5
Congressional District 1, Minnesota	34 503	614 952	6.7	25.5	15.1	21.6	40 941	8.5	4.0	237 886	76.9
Blue Earth County	1 949	55 941	5.7	21.3	12.1	26.6	38 940	12.9	4.6	21 062	66.4
Brown County	1 582	26 911	3.5	25.3	17.5	16.5	39 800	6.4	5.4	10 598	80.1
Cottonwood County	1 658	12 167	5.0	25.0	22.0	14.2	31 943	11.7	3.8	4 917	80.4
Dodge County	1 138	17 731	4.3	30.3	12.1	17.1	47 437	5.8	3.5	6 420	84.4
Faribault County	1 848	16 181	5.0	24.4	22.3	13.8	34 440	8.6	4.6	6 652	80.6
Fillmore County	2 231	21 122	1.4	26.1	19.3	15.1	36 651	10.1	3.5	8 228	80.7
Freeborn County	1 833	32 584	7.9	23.9	18.9	12.8	36 964	8.4	4.3	13 356	78.7
Houston County	1 446	19 718	1.9	27.2	16.0	20.5	40 680	6.5	3.9	7 633	81.1
Jackson County	1 817	11 268	3.4	24.6	20.5	14.2	36 746	8.6	3.5	4 556	79.1
Le Sueur County (part)	9	586	0.0	27.3	12.3	14.8	38 500	7.4	5.2	240	84.2
Martin County	1 837	21 802	3.0	25.0	19.8	16.1	34 810	10.5	4.1	9 067	77.4
Mower County	1 843	38 603	6.6	25.0	19.5	14.7	36 654	9.2	3.9	15 582	78.3
Murray County	1 824	9 165	2.8	24.9	21.3	11.9	34 966	8.3	3.7	3 722	84.5
Nicollet County	1 171	29 771	4.5	24.7	10.9	29.3	46 170	7.5	4.5	10 642	75.6
Nobles County	1 853	20 832	16.9	26.6	17.3	13.5	35 684	11.7	3.9	7 939	75.1
Olmsted County	1 691	124 277	10.8	27.0	10.8	34.7	51 316	6.4	3.7	47 807	76.0
Pipestone County	1 207	9 895	3.7	25.7	21.4	13.9	31 909	9.5	2.5	4 069	77.5
Rock County	1 250	9 721	3.1	26.3	20.5	15.4	38 102	8.0	1.7	3 843	78.0
Steele County	1 113	33 680	6.5	27.8	13.1	20.1	46 106	6.2	3.4	12 846	80.2
Wabasha County	1 360	21 610	2.9	27.1	14.9	16.9	42 117	6.0	2.9	8 277	82.5
Waseca County	1 096	19 526	7.2	25.8	14.2	16.2	42 440	6.5	2.5	7 059	80.0
Watonwan County	1 125	11 876	17.1	27.7	18.6	13.7	35 441	9.8	3.5	4 627	77.0
Winona County	1 622	49 985	4.9	22.8	13.1	23.2	38 700	12.0	5.3	18 744	71.0
Congressional District 2, Minnesota	7 861	615 117	8.1	29.8	7.5	31.2	61 344	3.9	3.0	217 641	82.2
Carver County	925	70 205	5.6	31.6	7.3	34.3	65 540	3.5	3.2	24 356	83.5
Dakota County (part)	1 411	295 704	9.5	30.2	5.9	36.4	64 973	3.3	2.4	106 239	80.9
Goodhue County	1 964	44 127	4.1	26.4	15.0	19.1	46 972	5.7	3.1	16 983	78.9
Hennepin County (part)	1	0	X	X	X	X	X	X	X	0	X
Le Sueur County (part)	1 153	24 840	5.4	27.4	14.1	16.9	46 089	6.9	3.8	9 390	82.9
Rice County	1 289	56 665	9.6	25.2	11.3	22.4	48 651	6.9	6.3	18 888	77.9
Scott County	924	89 498	7.4	31.2	6.1	29.4	66 612	3.4	2.6	30 692	86.6
Washington County (part)	195	34 078	7.2	32.3	5.1	25.7	66 839	2.6	2.6	11 093	92.2

[1] Dry land or land partially or temporarily covered by water.
[2] Persons who do not identify themselves as White alone, not of Hispanic origin.
[3] Persons 25 years old and over.
X = Not applicable.

Table B. 110th Congressional Districts by Counties, 2000—*Continued*

(Number, percent.)

STATE Congressional district County	Land area,[1] (sq km)	Population				Percent with bachelor's degree or more[3]	Median household income, 1999 (dollars)	Percent living in poverty	Percent unemployed	Households	
		Total	Percent minority[2]	Percent under 18 years	Percent 65 years and over					Total	Percent owner occupied
	1	2	3	4	5	6	7	8	9	10	11
Congressional District 3, Minnesota	1 211	614 979	11.3	26.6	10.2	40.1	63 816	3.5	2.8	237 651	77.4
Anoka County (part)	55	58 414	7.7	28.5	7.3	21.1	54 656	5.0	3.9	21 485	79.4
Hennepin County (part)	1 156	556 565	11.7	26.4	10.5	41.9	65 160	3.4	2.6	216 166	77.2
Congressional District 4, Minnesota	523	614 911	22.2	25.8	11.7	33.0	46 811	9.6	4.2	242 046	65.3
Dakota County (part)	64	60 200	11.9	24.0	15.1	27.9	49 052	5.1	3.6	24 912	66.8
Ramsey County (part)	401	508 730	24.7	25.6	11.6	34.3	45 791	10.6	4.4	199 981	63.7
Washington County (part)	57	45 981	8.1	29.7	8.5	25.8	56 072	3.8	2.8	17 153	81.8
Congressional District 5, Minnesota	321	614 874	28.7	21.5	11.7	34.9	41 569	12.7	4.8	263 486	57.2
Anoka County (part)	41	53 402	13.1	21.8	14.3	20.8	44 838	6.9	3.4	22 437	69.8
Hennepin County (part)	279	559 167	30.2	21.5	11.4	36.3	41 328	13.3	5.0	239 794	56.2
Ramsey County (part)	2	2 305	19.5	12.5	21.1	33.1	37 458	7.1	3.9	1 255	33.1
Congressional District 6, Minnesota	7 979	614 793	5.1	29.2	7.6	24.5	56 862	4.7	3.0	214 072	82.8
Anoka County (part)	1 001	186 268	5.6	31.1	4.8	21.5	62 871	3.1	3.1	62 506	89.7
Benton County	1 057	34 226	4.7	27.0	11.1	17.2	41 968	7.1	3.4	13 065	67.1
Hennepin County (part)	6	468	5.6	23.9	6.0	12.3	70 417	1.9	0.7	169	97.6
Ramsey County (part)	0	0	X	X	X	X	X	X	X	0	X
Sherburne County	1 130	64 417	3.8	30.9	7.1	19.4	57 014	4.4	2.6	21 581	84.0
Stearns County (part)	2 310	118 357	4.6	25.4	10.1	23.3	43 407	8.8	3.7	42 070	72.8
Washington County (part)	762	121 071	7.4	28.6	7.8	39.0	70 419	2.6	2.5	43 216	85.8
Wright County	1 711	89 986	2.7	31.2	8.8	17.9	53 945	4.7	3.0	31 465	84.3
Congressional District 7, Minnesota	82 353	615 129	6.8	26.1	16.9	16.4	36 453	10.3	5.0	238 530	77.8
Becker County	3 394	30 000	10.9	26.6	16.3	16.7	34 797	12.2	6.3	11 844	80.4
Beltrami County (part)	5 459	29 293	27.3	28.5	12.0	22.5	31 069	20.2	8.3	10 520	69.4
Big Stone County	1 287	5 820	1.5	24.9	24.2	11.4	30 721	12.0	5.3	2 377	85.1
Chippewa County	1 509	13 088	3.7	25.3	20.0	13.7	35 582	8.6	5.6	5 361	76.5
Clay County	2 707	51 229	7.7	25.0	13.0	24.7	37 889	13.2	5.3	18 670	71.6
Clearwater County	2 576	8 423	9.8	26.1	17.3	14.7	30 517	15.1	10.3	3 330	81.6
Douglas County	1 643	32 821	1.8	24.0	17.9	17.3	37 703	8.5	3.9	13 276	77.2
Grant County	1 415	6 289	1.5	23.7	23.0	15.7	33 775	8.4	4.8	2 534	82.2
Kandiyohi County	2 062	41 203	9.5	26.6	15.0	18.3	39 772	9.2	3.6	15 936	75.5
Kittson County	2 841	5 285	3.4	25.1	21.6	14.8	32 515	10.2	5.0	2 167	82.7
Lac qui Parle County	1 981	8 067	1.3	24.5	23.3	13.0	32 626	8.5	3.3	3 316	80.7
Lake of the Woods County	3 358	4 522	3.2	24.5	17.3	17.2	32 861	9.8	4.8	1 903	85.4
Lincoln County	1 391	6 429	0.9	23.7	24.3	14.1	31 607	9.7	3.5	2 653	80.4
Lyon County	1 850	25 425	8.1	26.1	14.6	21.4	38 996	10.1	5.1	9 715	68.4
McLeod County	1 274	34 898	4.6	27.8	13.9	15.4	45 953	4.8	3.8	13 449	78.5
Mahnomen County	1 440	5 190	37.3	29.4	16.9	12.4	30 053	16.7	6.7	1 969	77.3
Marshall County	4 590	10 155	4.4	25.3	18.6	12.0	34 804	9.8	8.7	4 101	83.8
Meeker County	1 576	22 644	2.8	27.1	16.3	13.9	40 908	7.1	4.8	8 590	81.5
Norman County	2 270	7 442	6.0	25.6	21.0	13.1	32 535	10.3	6.1	3 010	81.1
Otter Tail County	5 127	57 159	3.5	25.0	18.9	17.2	35 395	10.1	5.2	22 671	80.0
Pennington County	1 597	13 584	2.9	24.3	15.9	14.9	34 216	11.1	7.6	5 525	74.6
Polk County	5 103	31 369	7.6	25.9	17.3	17.6	35 105	10.9	5.9	12 070	74.0
Pope County	1 736	11 236	1.1	24.8	21.6	14.7	35 633	8.8	3.6	4 513	80.8
Red Lake County	1 120	4 299	3.5	25.4	19.0	10.7	32 052	10.8	9.1	1 727	79.4
Redwood County	2 278	16 815	5.3	26.5	19.3	13.4	37 352	7.7	3.1	6 674	80.0
Renville County	2 546	17 154	6.3	26.6	19.8	12.6	37 652	8.8	3.8	6 779	81.0
Roseau County	4 306	16 338	4.7	29.8	12.6	14.9	39 852	6.6	3.3	6 190	84.1
Sibley County	1 525	15 356	6.5	27.6	16.5	11.6	41 458	8.1	2.7	5 772	80.9
Stearns County (part)	1 172	14 809	3.6	28.4	18.2	12.6	36 845	8.4	3.6	5 534	81.0
Stevens County	1 456	10 053	4.3	21.6	16.9	20.6	37 267	13.6	5.3	3 751	70.2
Swift County	1 926	11 956	9.5	23.0	18.7	14.0	34 820	8.4	4.3	4 353	77.1
Todd County	2 440	24 426	3.8	27.4	16.1	10.0	32 281	12.9	5.2	9 342	82.9
Traverse County	1 487	4 134	4.2	25.5	26.5	10.7	30 617	12.0	5.2	1 717	80.5
Wilkin County	1 946	7 138	3.1	27.9	16.1	14.0	38 093	8.1	3.7	2 752	80.6
Yellow Medicine County	1 963	11 080	5.4	25.8	20.4	14.4	34 393	10.4	5.5	4 439	79.3
Congressional District 8, Minnesota	71 439	614 724	5.4	24.8	15.8	17.7	37 911	10.4	6.0	243 815	80.1
Aitkin County	4 712	15 301	4.2	20.9	23.0	11.3	31 139	11.6	7.7	6 644	85.3
Beltrami County (part)	1 029	10 357	13.8	29.5	10.4	26.1	39 544	10.5	5.2	3 817	88.3
Carlton County	2 228	31 671	8.7	25.4	15.1	14.9	40 021	7.9	5.8	12 064	82.0
Cass County	5 226	27 150	13.5	25.1	18.0	16.6	34 332	13.6	6.8	10 893	86.0
Chisago County	1 082	41 101	3.7	30.1	9.8	15.3	52 012	5.1	3.4	14 454	87.0

[1] Dry land or land partially or temporarily covered by water.
[2] Persons who do not identify themselves as White alone, not of Hispanic origin.
[3] Persons 25 years old and over.
X = Not applicable.

Table B. 110th Congressional Districts by Counties, 2000—*Continued*

(Number, percent.)

STATE Congressional district County	Land area,[1] (sq km)	Population Total	Population Percent minority[2]	Population Percent under 18 years	Population Percent 65 years and over	Percent with bachelor's degree or more[3]	Median household income, 1999 (dollars)	Percent living in poverty	Percent unem- ployed	Households Total	Households Percent owner occupied
	1	2	3	4	5	6	7	8	9	10	11
Congressional District 8, Michigan—*Continued*											
Cook County	3 757	5 168	10.6	20.1	17.3	28.8	36 640	10.1	6.2	2 350	78.2
Crow Wing County	2 581	55 099	2.7	24.8	17.1	18.4	37 589	9.8	5.5	22 250	79.6
Hubbard County	2 389	18 376	3.7	24.6	17.9	20.2	35 321	9.7	6.6	7 435	83.4
Isanti County	1 137	31 287	2.9	28.6	10.9	14.5	50 127	5.7	4.3	11 236	85.2
Itasca County	6 902	43 992	5.6	24.3	16.8	17.6	36 234	10.6	6.7	17 789	82.9
Kanabec County	1 360	14 996	2.8	27.5	14.1	10.5	38 520	9.5	6.2	5 759	84.0
Koochiching County	8 035	14 355	4.4	23.9	17.9	15.1	36 262	12.1	5.5	6 040	80.4
Lake County	5 437	11 058	2.5	22.3	20.1	19.5	40 402	7.4	5.3	4 646	84.0
Mille Lacs County	1 488	22 330	6.8	27.0	16.1	12.2	36 977	9.6	5.4	8 638	79.8
Morrison County	2 912	31 712	1.8	28.0	15.6	12.6	37 047	11.1	5.7	11 816	82.0
Pine County	3 655	26 530	7.2	25.5	15.1	10.3	37 379	11.3	6.8	9 939	83.7
St. Louis County	16 123	200 528	5.6	22.4	16.1	21.9	36 306	12.1	6.8	82 619	74.7
Wadena County	1 386	13 713	3.2	25.8	19.7	13.4	30 651	14.1	5.6	5 426	77.4
MISSISSIPPI	121 488	2 844 658	39.2	27.2	12.1	16.9	31 330	19.9	7.4	1 046 434	72.4
Congressional District 1, Mississippi	29 559	711 113	28.7	26.6	12.4	13.9	32 535	16.4	6.1	267 649	75.1
Alcorn County	1 036	34 558	13.1	23.8	14.8	11.7	29 041	16.6	4.7	14 224	73.5
Benton County	1 054	8 026	38.0	26.9	15.4	7.8	24 149	23.2	7.1	2 999	84.3
Calhoun County	1 519	15 069	31.5	25.3	16.6	10.2	27 113	18.1	6.5	6 019	76.2
Chickasaw County	1 299	19 440	44.1	28.6	13.1	9.5	26 364	20.0	5.2	7 253	77.8
Choctaw County	1 085	9 758	32.3	27.8	14.8	11.2	27 020	24.7	11.7	3 686	81.3
Clay County	1 058	21 979	57.5	28.8	13.4	14.6	27 372	23.5	8.1	8 152	73.4
DeSoto County	1 238	107 199	15.2	28.1	8.9	14.3	48 206	7.1	3.6	38 792	79.2
Grenada County	1 092	23 263	42.3	27.2	14.5	13.5	27 385	20.9	6.0	8 820	69.1
Itawamba County	1 379	22 770	8.2	24.3	14.1	8.8	31 156	14.0	7.2	8 773	82.5
Lafayette County	1 635	38 744	28.8	19.6	9.9	31.1	28 517	21.3	6.6	14 373	60.6
Lee County	1 164	75 755	27.0	27.6	11.5	18.1	36 165	13.4	4.9	29 200	69.2
Lowndes County	1 301	61 586	44.0	28.5	11.3	20.5	32 123	21.3	7.9	22 849	66.6
Marshall County	1 829	34 993	52.1	26.5	11.4	9.0	28 756	21.9	8.9	12 163	80.5
Monroe County	1 979	38 014	32.4	27.2	13.8	10.9	30 307	17.2	6.7	14 603	79.0
Panola County	1 772	34 274	50.2	29.5	12.4	10.8	26 785	25.3	7.8	12 232	77.9
Pontotoc County	1 288	26 726	16.4	27.5	12.7	11.4	32 055	13.8	5.5	10 097	78.1
Prentiss County	1 075	25 556	14.1	25.1	13.6	9.9	28 446	16.5	5.6	9 821	78.0
Tate County	1 048	25 370	32.5	27.2	11.3	12.3	35 836	13.5	10.3	8 850	78.3
Tippah County	1 186	20 826	18.9	25.0	14.5	9.0	29 300	16.9	5.3	8 108	78.1
Tishomingo County	1 098	19 163	5.2	22.9	17.0	8.7	28 315	14.1	5.7	7 917	78.7
Union County	1 076	25 362	17.3	26.0	14.4	13.2	32 682	12.6	4.8	9 786	77.6
Webster County (part)	1 052	9 485	21.9	25.8	16.9	13.3	28 639	17.9	6.1	3 609	77.8
Winston County (part)	86	146	15.8	19.9	21.2	42.7	27 083	30.1	0.0	63	100.0
Yalobusha County	1 210	13 051	39.9	25.6	16.1	9.6	26 315	21.8	7.0	5 260	79.0
Congressional District 2, Mississippi	35 288	710 996	65.5	29.4	11.5	16.8	26 894	27.3	10.4	245 770	65.7
Attala County	1 904	19 661	42.0	26.0	17.3	11.6	24 794	21.8	7.0	7 567	77.7
Bolivar County	2 270	40 633	66.9	29.5	11.0	18.8	23 428	33.3	15.1	13 776	61.1
Carroll County	1 626	10 769	38.3	24.3	14.1	10.9	28 878	16.0	7.4	4 071	84.8
Claiborne County	1 261	11 831	84.8	26.3	10.5	18.9	22 615	32.4	18.0	3 685	80.3
Coahoma County	1 435	30 622	70.8	33.0	12.3	16.2	22 338	35.9	10.1	10 553	57.3
Copiah County	2 011	28 757	52.6	26.9	13.2	11.6	26 358	25.1	11.0	10 142	79.8
Hinds County (part)	2 207	219 002	69.2	29.1	9.9	21.4	31 423	21.9	8.7	76 996	62.9
Holmes County	1 958	21 609	79.8	32.1	12.5	11.2	17 235	41.1	17.3	7 314	73.2
Humphreys County	1 083	11 206	73.0	32.8	12.2	11.6	20 566	38.2	11.4	3 765	61.4
Issaquena County	1 070	2 274	63.9	27.6	10.7	7.1	19 936	33.2	13.5	726	67.4
Jefferson County	1 345	9 740	86.8	28.6	11.1	10.6	18 447	36.0	14.2	3 308	80.4
Leake County (part)	734	11 397	53.5	27.4	14.7	13.7	24 922	25.9	7.4	3 972	76.5
Leflore County	1 533	37 947	70.4	29.8	12.1	16.1	21 518	34.8	15.9	12 956	53.3
Madison County (part)	1 223	27 393	75.0	31.5	11.4	18.2	31 162	28.6	10.9	8 271	70.9
Montgomery County	1 054	12 189	46.1	26.8	16.7	11.0	25 270	24.3	6.9	4 690	76.9
Quitman County	1 049	10 117	69.7	31.9	13.3	10.6	20 636	33.1	8.4	3 565	68.8
Sharkey County	1 108	6 580	71.2	33.1	11.1	12.6	22 285	38.3	14.5	2 163	65.7
Sunflower County	1 797	34 369	71.6	27.9	9.7	12.0	24 970	30.0	12.9	9 637	61.9
Tallahatchie County	1 668	14 903	60.7	30.1	13.3	10.9	22 229	32.2	9.6	5 263	76.1
Tunica County	1 178	9 227	73.1	31.5	9.8	9.1	23 270	33.1	9.3	3 258	51.8
Warren County	1 519	49 644	45.4	28.5	11.8	20.8	35 056	18.7	6.7	18 756	68.3
Washington County	1 875	62 977	66.3	31.4	11.7	16.4	25 757	29.2	11.9	22 158	59.5
Yazoo County	2 381	28 149	59.0	28.4	12.6	11.8	24 795	31.9	10.7	9 178	68.9

[1]Dry land or land partially or temporarily covered by water.
[2]Persons who do not identify themselves as White alone, not of Hispanic origin.
[3]Persons 25 years old and over.

Table B. 110th Congressional Districts by Counties, 2000—*Continued*

(Number, percent.)

STATE Congressional district County	Land area,[1] (sq km)	Population				Percent with bachelor's degree or more[3]	Median household income, 1999 (dollars)	Percent living in poverty	Percent unem- ployed	Households	
		Total	Percent minority[2]	Percent under 18 years	Percent 65 years and over					Total	Percent owner occupied
	1	2	3	4	5	6	7	8	9	10	11
Congressional District 3, Mississippi	34 106	711 409	36.3	26.4	12.8	20.2	31 907	19.2	6.7	269 154	75.7
Adams County	1 192	34 340	54.4	26.7	15.6	17.5	25 234	25.9	9.1	13 677	70.2
Amite County	1 890	13 599	44.0	25.8	15.6	9.4	26 033	22.6	8.9	5 271	85.9
Covington County	1 072	19 407	36.9	28.6	12.9	11.4	26 669	23.5	7.7	7 126	84.9
Franklin County	1 462	8 448	37.5	27.5	15.2	10.5	24 885	24.1	8.7	3 211	86.1
Hinds County (part)	45	31 798	19.2	19.5	18.3	59.5	52 885	6.9	3.1	14 034	69.3
Jasper County (part)	628	7 293	54.6	27.9	15.3	10.3	22 260	25.4	7.6	2 713	83.9
Jefferson Davis County	1 058	13 962	58.8	28.2	13.8	10.4	21 834	28.2	12.9	5 177	84.5
Jones County (part)	136	2 126	37.5	27.0	13.5	10.9	29 612	17.1	5.2	797	84.7
Kemper County	1 984	10 453	60.6	25.3	15.1	10.3	23 998	26.0	12.6	3 909	83.9
Lauderdale County	1 822	78 161	40.3	26.6	14.2	16.2	30 768	20.8	7.5	29 990	67.8
Lawrence County	1 115	13 258	33.7	27.5	13.1	12.0	28 495	19.6	6.3	5 040	84.3
Leake County (part)	775	9 543	33.2	26.8	14.3	9.2	28 541	20.4	6.7	3 639	88.0
Lincoln County	1 517	33 166	30.8	26.8	13.9	12.4	27 279	19.2	7.1	12 538	78.1
Madison County (part)	634	47 281	20.4	26.9	8.8	47.7	54 559	6.0	2.6	18 948	70.8
Marion County (part)	676	9 800	24.7	28.3	11.8	7.8	25 995	23.4	6.3	3 608	87.4
Neshoba County	1 476	28 684	34.3	28.4	14.2	11.4	28 300	21.0	7.4	10 694	79.5
Newton County	1 497	21 838	34.9	26.2	14.8	12.1	28 735	19.9	5.2	8 221	81.8
Noxubee County	1 799	12 548	70.8	30.7	12.9	10.9	22 330	32.8	9.4	4 470	79.7
Oktibbeha County	1 185	42 902	41.4	21.1	8.8	34.8	24 899	28.2	11.7	15 945	55.6
Pike County	1 059	38 940	49.0	27.7	14.3	12.5	24 562	25.3	9.4	14 792	74.3
Rankin County	2 006	115 327	19.8	25.8	9.1	23.8	44 946	9.5	3.8	42 089	77.2
Scott County	1 578	28 423	45.2	28.6	12.3	8.6	26 686	20.7	6.0	10 183	78.4
Simpson County	1 525	27 639	36.2	27.9	13.0	10.9	28 343	21.6	6.3	10 076	81.2
Smith County	1 647	16 182	24.2	27.5	14.2	9.1	30 840	16.9	5.9	6 046	87.0
Walthall County	1 046	15 156	45.8	28.5	14.0	10.4	22 945	27.8	9.8	5 571	83.2
Webster County (part)	42	809	36.1	28.2	13.0	9.3	30 962	27.6	12.1	296	85.5
Wilkinson County	1 753	10 312	68.9	25.9	13.9	10.0	18 929	37.7	10.4	3 578	83.1
Winston County (part)	1 486	20 014	45.4	26.8	15.1	13.6	28 261	23.7	7.4	7 515	79.4
Congressional District 4, Mississippi	22 535	711 140	26.5	26.5	11.7	16.7	33 023	16.9	6.7	263 861	72.4
Clarke County	1 790	17 955	36.3	26.8	15.4	9.6	26 610	23.0	8.5	6 978	84.2
Forrest County	1 208	72 604	36.5	24.4	11.2	22.8	27 420	22.5	7.9	27 183	60.4
George County	1 239	19 144	11.3	28.9	11.2	9.1	34 730	16.7	9.1	6 742	86.2
Greene County	1 846	13 299	27.6	24.0	10.3	8.0	28 336	19.6	10.4	4 148	86.9
Hancock County	1 235	42 967	10.7	25.2	14.0	17.3	35 202	14.4	6.9	16 897	79.6
Harrison County	1 505	189 601	28.2	26.0	11.1	18.4	35 624	14.6	6.1	71 538	62.7
Jackson County	1 883	131 420	25.8	27.6	10.3	16.5	39 118	12.7	6.7	47 676	74.6
Jasper County (part)	1 123	10 856	53.4	27.9	13.4	9.4	25 737	20.9	8.7	3 995	88.8
Jones County (part)	1 661	62 832	29.3	25.7	14.2	14.1	28 760	19.9	5.7	23 478	76.6
Lamar County	1 287	39 070	15.0	28.1	9.8	26.8	37 628	13.3	4.3	14 396	75.8
Marion County (part)	728	15 795	38.8	27.5	15.4	13.8	23 577	25.6	7.5	5 728	76.0
Pearl River County	2 101	48 621	15.5	27.0	12.5	13.9	30 912	18.4	7.3	18 078	79.8
Perry County	1 676	12 138	24.0	28.6	11.1	7.7	27 189	22.0	7.1	4 420	84.6
Stone County	1 153	13 622	21.0	27.0	11.2	12.4	30 495	17.5	6.8	4 747	81.3
Wayne County	2 099	21 216	38.9	29.2	11.9	9.5	25 918	25.4	7.8	7 857	84.9
MISSOURI	178 414	5 595 211	16.2	25.5	13.5	21.6	37 934	11.7	5.3	2 194 594	70.3
Congressional District 1, Missouri	562	621 497	54.0	26.4	13.9	22.4	36 314	15.8	8.3	249 256	62.1
St. Louis County (part)	469	458 398	43.0	26.4	13.6	24.1	41 598	10.1	5.8	182 789	70.0
St. Louis city (part)	93	163 099	85.1	26.7	14.5	17.4	21 802	32.2	16.8	66 467	40.2
Congressional District 2, Missouri	3 232	621 422	6.8	27.3	11.3	38.3	61 416	3.6	3.1	230 452	81.6
Lincoln County	1 633	38 944	4.6	30.0	10.8	9.7	42 592	8.3	4.8	13 851	80.8
St. Charles County (part)	913	245 678	6.5	28.9	8.6	25.4	55 881	4.1	3.8	88 279	80.8
St. Louis County (part)	686	336 800	7.2	25.8	13.4	50.0	69 833	2.8	2.4	128 322	82.1
Congressional District 3, Missouri	3 230	622 148	14.3	24.8	13.0	23.2	41 091	10.1	5.6	251 895	68.9
Jefferson County	1 701	198 099	3.1	27.9	9.2	12.1	46 338	6.8	4.6	71 499	83.4
Ste. Genevieve County	1 301	17 842	2.4	26.5	14.6	8.1	39 200	8.2	3.2	6 586	82.3
St. Louis County (part)	160	221 117	10.1	21.8	16.3	35.7	47 476	6.5	5.4	93 201	71.2
St. Louis city (part)	67	185 090	32.3	24.8	13.0	20.5	31 100	18.0	7.3	80 609	52.4
Congressional District 4, Missouri	37 669	621 882	7.6	25.5	14.4	15.6	34 541	12.1	4.6	238 497	73.5
Barton County	1 539	12 541	3.7	27.4	16.5	10.6	29 275	13.0	3.0	4 895	73.4
Bates County	2 198	16 653	3.0	26.6	17.4	10.1	30 731	14.5	5.0	6 511	75.0
Benton County	1 827	17 180	2.9	20.5	22.4	8.8	26 646	15.7	6.1	7 420	82.2
Camden County (part)	1 487	35 020	2.8	20.4	18.9	17.8	35 808	11.5	4.8	14 911	82.1
Cass County (part)	1 559	39 076	3.7	27.6	12.2	16.5	49 199	5.2	2.7	14 424	80.4
Cedar County	1 233	13 733	3.6	24.6	20.8	10.0	26 694	17.4	4.3	5 685	78.3
Cole County	1 014	71 397	13.5	24.1	11.3	27.4	42 924	8.7	3.7	27 040	67.8
Dade County	1 270	7 923	3.2	24.3	20.3	9.9	29 097	13.4	5.2	3 202	78.8
Dallas County	1 403	15 661	3.2	27.2	15.2	9.5	27 346	17.9	4.9	6 030	79.2
Henry County	1 819	21 997	3.8	23.7	18.3	11.7	30 949	14.3	5.0	9 133	73.0

[1] Dry land or land partially or temporarily covered by water.
[2] Persons who do not identify themselves White, not of Hispanic origin.
[3] Persons 25 years old and over.

Table B. 110th Congressional Districts by Counties, 2000—*Continued*

(Number, percent.)

STATE Congressional district County	Land area,[1] (sq km)	Population Total	Population Percent minority[2]	Population Percent under 18 years	Population Percent 65 years and over	Percent with bachelor's degree or more[3]	Median household income, 1999 (dollars)	Percent living in poverty	Percent unemployed	Households Total	Households Percent owner occupied
	1	2	3	4	5	6	7	8	9	10	11
Congressional District 4, Missouri—*Continued*											
Hickory County	1 032	8 940	4.2	19.9	26.0	7.7	25 346	19.7	8.1	3 911	84.5
Jackson County (part)	74	18 952	6.7	28.2	10.3	17.5	46 265	7.0	3.3	7 231	66.2
Johnson County	2 151	48 258	11.4	25.2	9.4	23.2	35 391	14.9	6.1	17 410	61.5
Laclede County	1 984	32 513	3.8	26.7	14.2	11.3	29 562	14.3	4.8	12 760	72.8
Lafayette County	1 630	32 960	5.1	26.0	15.4	13.8	38 235	8.8	3.7	12 569	75.4
Moniteau County	1 079	14 827	7.6	25.8	14.0	13.0	37 168	9.9	3.0	5 259	77.7
Morgan County	1 547	19 309	3.5	23.8	19.6	10.7	30 659	16.2	4.8	7 850	82.9
Pettis County	1 774	39 403	8.8	26.3	15.5	15.0	31 822	12.8	5.1	15 568	72.5
Polk County (part)	753	6 113	3.3	24.4	19.2	8.4	27 688	15.9	4.3	2 418	83.4
Pulaski County	1 417	41 165	24.3	27.5	7.9	18.8	34 247	10.3	6.8	13 433	58.0
Ray County	1 475	23 354	3.9	27.6	12.7	10.8	41 886	6.8	5.5	8 743	79.5
St. Clair County	1 753	9 652	4.0	23.1	21.2	9.0	25 321	19.6	6.3	4 040	79.5
Saline County	1 957	23 756	11.6	24.4	16.2	15.8	32 743	13.2	4.6	9 015	69.1
Vernon County	2 160	20 454	3.4	26.6	16.3	14.2	30 021	14.9	4.4	7 966	72.3
Webster County	1 537	31 045	4.6	28.9	11.5	11.0	31 929	14.8	4.0	11 073	78.0
Congressional District 5, Missouri	1 325	621 496	33.7	25.5	13.0	22.9	38 311	12.4	5.9	254 560	62.3
Cass County (part)	251	43 016	7.9	28.9	11.3	18.8	49 903	6.3	3.4	15 744	78.8
Jackson County (part)	1 073	578 480	35.6	25.3	13.1	23.2	37 462	12.9	6.0	238 816	61.3
Congressional District 6, Missouri	33 753	621 790	7.6	25.3	13.3	21.2	41 225	8.7	3.8	241 504	72.0
Andrew County	1 127	16 492	2.6	26.2	14.4	18.8	40 688	8.2	3.1	6 273	80.0
Atchison County	1 411	6 430	3.5	24.1	21.1	16.6	30 959	11.6	3.7	2 722	69.2
Buchanan County	1 061	85 998	8.8	24.3	15.0	16.9	34 704	12.2	5.9	33 557	67.5
Caldwell County	1 112	8 969	2.2	27.1	16.9	11.7	31 240	11.9	3.1	3 523	77.4
Carroll County	1 799	10 285	3.9	25.1	20.1	14.0	30 643	13.7	4.1	4 169	74.0
Chariton County	1 958	8 438	3.7	23.8	22.4	11.4	32 285	11.6	4.0	3 469	80.5
Clay County	1 027	184 006	9.5	25.8	10.8	24.9	48 347	5.5	3.3	72 558	70.7
Clinton County	1 085	18 979	4.2	26.8	14.1	14.5	41 629	9.3	4.4	7 152	79.0
Cooper County	1 463	16 670	11.7	22.8	15.4	13.7	35 313	10.7	3.4	5 932	74.2
Daviess County	1 468	8 016	1.2	27.1	17.6	12.0	30 855	15.2	4.3	3 178	76.8
DeKalb County	1 099	11 597	11.5	20.6	14.0	10.7	31 654	10.8	3.8	3 528	73.4
Gentry County	1 273	6 861	1.3	26.0	21.7	14.5	28 750	12.0	5.3	2 747	74.5
Grundy County	1 129	10 432	4.0	23.2	20.5	12.5	27 333	15.8	4.8	4 382	71.8
Harrison County	1 878	8 850	2.0	23.9	22.1	9.3	28 707	13.5	3.8	3 658	74.7
Holt County	1 196	5 351	1.6	23.7	21.5	11.7	29 461	13.0	2.2	2 237	74.4
Howard County	1 206	10 212	9.3	23.9	16.2	17.9	31 614	11.6	5.2	3 836	75.2
Jackson County (part)	419	57 448	7.4	29.5	7.2	28.2	57 265	4.3	2.8	20 247	80.7
Linn County	1 607	13 754	2.7	25.2	20.5	10.8	28 242	14.9	3.4	5 697	77.0
Livingston County	1 384	14 558	4.3	24.0	19.0	13.1	32 290	12.4	3.2	5 736	70.8
Mercer County	1 176	3 757	0.7	22.8	21.9	12.2	29 640	13.3	3.8	1 600	76.8
Nodaway County	2 270	21 912	3.6	19.3	13.8	23.6	31 781	16.5	5.6	8 138	63.8
Platte County	1 089	73 781	10.2	25.7	8.8	33.3	55 849	4.8	2.6	29 278	67.4
Putnam County	1 341	5 223	1.5	24.0	20.6	11.2	26 282	16.0	4.6	2 228	77.2
Schuyler County	797	4 170	1.4	24.6	19.8	11.6	27 385	17.0	4.8	1 725	75.2
Sullivan County	1 686	7 219	9.4	25.2	18.3	8.4	26 107	16.5	5.2	2 925	71.7
Worth County	690	2 382	1.4	24.2	22.5	11.3	27 471	14.3	5.9	1 009	76.8
Congressional District 7, Missouri	14 192	621 746	7.1	24.5	13.9	18.8	32 929	13.0	5.6	246 008	68.9
Barry County	2 018	34 010	7.6	26.2	16.1	10.7	28 906	16.6	4.8	13 398	75.7
Christian County	1 459	54 285	3.5	27.8	10.6	20.9	38 085	9.1	3.2	20 425	75.9
Greene County	1 748	240 391	7.5	22.2	13.7	24.2	34 157	12.1	5.5	97 859	63.6
Jasper County	1 657	104 686	8.9	25.7	13.8	16.5	31 323	14.5	6.6	41 412	67.0
Lawrence County	1 588	35 204	5.8	27.2	15.6	12.1	31 239	14.1	4.4	13 568	74.3
McDonald County	1 397	21 681	15.9	28.8	11.2	7.0	27 010	20.7	4.2	8 113	71.5
Newton County	1 622	52 636	7.4	26.2	14.1	16.1	35 041	11.6	4.6	20 140	76.6
Polk County (part)	898	20 879	3.3	26.0	14.1	16.8	30 165	16.4	4.7	7 499	69.6
Stone County	1 200	28 658	2.8	21.4	18.9	14.2	32 637	12.8	9.6	11 822	81.2
Taney County (part)	606	29 316	5.7	22.4	14.4	16.5	31 598	12.1	10.1	11 772	64.6
Congressional District 8, Missouri	48 384	621 746	7.6	25.1	15.8	11.9	27 865	18.2	6.5	245 519	72.0
Bollinger County	1 608	12 029	2.8	26.2	14.7	6.9	30 462	13.8	6.2	4 576	81.6
Butler County	1 807	40 867	8.2	24.1	16.7	11.6	27 228	18.6	6.6	16 718	68.9
Cape Girardeau County	1 499	68 693	8.3	23.4	13.7	24.2	36 458	11.1	5.0	26 980	68.4
Carter County	1 315	5 941	5.3	25.2	15.9	10.8	22 863	25.2	8.1	2 378	76.7
Dent County	1 952	14 927	3.1	24.7	17.8	10.1	27 193	17.2	7.1	5 982	74.1
Douglas County	2 110	13 084	3.6	25.8	17.0	9.9	25 918	17.5	4.7	5 201	79.0
Dunklin County	1 413	33 155	12.5	26.0	16.6	9.1	24 878	24.5	6.2	13 411	65.9
Howell County	2 403	37 238	4.4	25.9	16.8	10.9	25 628	18.7	6.4	14 762	73.5
Iron County	1 428	10 697	3.9	24.9	17.1	8.4	26 080	19.0	6.7	4 197	75.9
Madison County	1 287	11 800	2.4	24.5	18.0	7.8	25 601	17.2	6.8	4 711	76.0

[1]Dry land or land partially or temporarily covered by water.
[2]Persons who do not identify themselves White, not of Hispanic origin.
[3]Persons 25 years old and over.

Table B. 110th Congressional Districts by Counties, 2000—*Continued*

(Number, percent.)

STATE Congressional district County	Land area,[1] (sq km)	Population Total	Percent minority[2]	Percent under 18 years	Percent 65 years and over	Percent with bachelor's degree or more[3]	Median household income, 1999 (dollars)	Percent living in poverty	Percent unemployed	Households Total	Percent owner occupied
	1	2	3	4	5	6	7	8	9	10	11
Congressional District 8, Missouri—*Continued*											
Mississippi County	1 070	13 427	22.7	26.4	15.9	9.6	23 012	23.7	8.8	5 383	63.5
New Madrid County	1 756	19 760	17.2	26.4	15.4	9.6	26 826	22.1	6.0	7 824	66.1
Oregon County	2 050	10 344	6.3	24.2	17.9	9.1	22 359	22.0	7.3	4 263	78.3
Ozark County	1 922	9 542	3.5	21.9	19.5	8.3	25 861	21.6	5.9	3 950	81.6
Pemiscot County	1 277	20 047	29.4	29.9	15.1	8.4	21 911	30.4	8.6	7 855	58.4
Perry County	1 229	18 132	3.0	26.0	15.7	9.9	36 632	9.0	3.0	6 904	79.9
Phelps County	1 743	39 825	7.5	23.9	13.9	21.1	29 378	16.4	6.5	15 683	65.6
Reynolds County	2 101	6 689	5.8	23.9	16.3	7.5	25 867	20.1	10.2	2 721	77.1
Ripley County	1 630	13 509	3.2	24.8	17.3	7.8	22 761	22.0	8.4	5 416	78.0
St. Francois County	1 164	55 641	4.4	23.9	15.0	10.2	31 199	14.9	7.5	20 793	73.2
Scott County	1 090	40 422	12.6	27.4	13.8	10.6	31 352	16.1	6.3	15 626	69.3
Shannon County	2 600	8 324	4.1	26.2	14.9	7.6	20 878	26.9	6.7	3 319	79.7
Stoddard County	2 142	29 705	3.4	23.8	17.2	10.1	26 987	16.5	6.0	12 064	72.3
Taney County (part)	1 032	10 387	4.2	22.4	21.1	10.7	28 940	13.2	10.1	4 386	80.3
Texas County	3 052	23 003	4.9	24.9	17.9	10.8	24 545	21.4	6.5	9 378	76.6
Washington County	1 967	23 344	5.2	26.6	11.7	7.5	27 112	20.8	7.8	8 406	79.9
Wayne County	1 971	13 259	2.6	23.3	19.9	6.8	24 007	21.9	9.3	5 551	78.2
Wright County	1 767	17 955	3.6	27.0	16.5	9.8	24 691	21.7	5.9	7 081	73.1
Congressional District 9, Missouri	36 067	621 484	7.3	25.1	13.0	19.9	36 693	11.8	4.6	236 903	72.6
Adair County	1 469	24 977	5.0	19.2	12.2	28.5	26 677	23.3	4.8	9 669	60.4
Audrain County	1 795	25 853	9.3	24.6	17.2	12.7	32 057	14.8	4.0	9 844	74.1
Boone County	1 775	135 454	15.3	22.8	8.6	41.7	37 485	14.5	5.3	53 094	57.5
Callaway County	2 173	40 766	8.7	25.4	10.9	16.5	39 110	8.5	3.9	14 416	76.8
Camden County (part)	210	2 031	3.4	16.7	19.5	17.2	36 313	8.7	2.2	868	85.7
Clark County	1 314	7 416	1.6	25.0	16.7	10.7	29 457	14.1	5.3	2 966	78.5
Crawford County	1 923	22 804	2.7	26.1	15.8	8.4	30 860	16.3	6.0	8 858	76.7
Franklin County	2 390	93 807	3.2	27.4	12.1	12.8	43 474	7.0	3.5	34 945	78.0
Gasconade County	1 349	15 342	1.6	24.7	18.9	10.4	35 047	9.5	4.1	6 171	80.3
Knox County	1 310	4 361	1.7	24.8	21.3	12.8	27 124	18.0	4.7	1 791	77.1
Lewis County	1 308	10 494	4.4	25.1	16.1	13.0	30 651	16.1	4.8	3 956	76.5
Macon County	2 082	15 762	3.8	24.1	19.1	13.0	30 195	12.5	3.9	6 501	75.9
Maries County	1 367	8 903	3.2	26.0	15.9	11.0	31 925	13.1	3.6	3 519	81.5
Marion County	1 135	28 289	6.9	25.8	16.7	15.6	31 774	12.1	6.7	11 066	70.4
Miller County	1 534	23 564	3.3	26.3	15.3	11.4	30 977	14.2	5.4	9 284	75.0
Monroe County	1 673	9 311	5.5	25.9	17.7	9.5	30 871	11.9	4.5	3 656	78.5
Montgomery County	1 392	12 136	4.6	25.3	17.4	9.9	32 772	11.8	6.1	4 775	78.7
Osage County	1 570	13 062	1.5	26.4	14.7	10.4	39 565	8.3	2.7	4 922	83.0
Pike County	1 743	18 351	12.2	23.5	14.6	10.2	32 373	15.5	4.8	6 451	74.1
Ralls County	1 220	9 626	2.3	25.2	14.3	12.3	37 094	8.7	4.9	3 736	82.3
Randolph County	1 249	24 663	10.3	23.8	14.9	11.7	31 464	12.5	4.6	9 199	72.0
St. Charles County (part)	538	38 205	4.2	29.2	9.4	32.2	68 525	3.5	3.7	13 384	89.5
Scotland County	1 136	4 983	2.1	28.7	18.9	11.2	27 409	16.8	4.6	1 902	76.7
Shelby County	1 297	6 799	2.0	25.3	19.9	12.5	29 448	16.3	4.8	2 745	75.1
Warren County	1 117	24 525	5.4	26.8	13.0	11.1	41 016	8.6	4.3	9 185	83.1
MONTANA	376 979	902 195	10.5	25.5	13.4	24.4	33 024	14.6	6.3	358 667	69.1
Congressional District (At Large), Montana	376 979	902 195	10.5	25.5	13.4	24.4	33 024	14.6	6.3	358 667	69.1
Beaverhead County	14 355	9 202	5.9	24.5	13.4	26.4	28 962	17.1	3.8	3 684	63.7
Big Horn County	12 936	12 671	64.7	35.9	8.2	14.3	27 684	29.2	14.0	3 924	64.9
Blaine County	10 946	7 009	47.3	32.5	12.9	17.4	25 247	28.1	10.9	2 501	61.0
Broadwater County	3 086	4 385	4.1	25.3	16.4	15.0	32 689	10.8	4.6	1 752	79.3
Carbon County	5 304	9 552	3.0	24.0	16.9	23.3	32 139	11.6	4.7	4 065	74.2
Carter County	8 649	1 360	1.4	26.4	17.8	13.6	26 313	18.1	0.5	543	74.6
Cascade County	6 998	80 357	10.5	26.0	14.1	21.5	32 971	13.5	6.3	32 547	64.9
Chouteau County	10 291	5 970	15.7	28.8	17.4	20.5	29 150	20.5	5.7	2 226	68.6
Custer County	9 798	11 696	4.6	24.9	17.1	18.8	30 000	15.1	5.4	4 768	70.1
Daniels County	3 694	2 017	3.8	22.3	23.6	14.1	27 306	16.9	3.1	892	77.9
Dawson County	6 146	9 059	2.7	23.3	17.6	15.1	31 393	14.9	4.4	3 625	74.0
Deer Lodge County	1 909	9 417	5.6	22.2	18.8	14.7	26 305	15.8	10.3	3 995	73.9
Fallon County	4 197	2 837	1.5	25.7	17.9	14.4	29 944	12.5	3.1	1 140	77.3
Fergus County	11 238	11 893	3.6	24.5	19.9	19.1	30 409	15.4	5.3	4 860	73.7
Flathead County	13 205	74 471	4.7	25.8	12.9	22.4	34 466	13.0	6.4	29 588	73.3
Gallatin County	6 749	67 831	5.0	21.8	8.5	41.0	38 120	12.8	6.1	26 323	62.4
Garfield County	12 090	1 279	0.7	24.9	19.3	16.8	25 917	21.5	3.1	532	73.3
Glacier County	7 756	13 247	64.1	35.2	9.5	16.5	27 921	27.3	15.4	4 304	62.0
Golden Valley County	3 044	1 042	1.3	27.8	16.4	16.2	27 308	25.8	1.9	365	77.5
Granite County	4 474	2 830	6.1	24.5	15.7	22.1	27 813	16.8	5.4	1 200	74.0

[1]Dry land or land partially or temporarily covered by water.
[2]Persons who do not identify themselves White, not of Hispanic origin.
[3]Persons 25 years old and over.

Table B. 110th Congressional Districts by Counties, 2000—Continued

(Number, percent.)

STATE Congressional district County	Land area,[1] (sq km)	Population				Percent with bachelor's degree or more[3]	Median household income, 1999 (dollars)	Percent living in poverty	Percent unemployed	Households	
		Total	Percent minority[2]	Percent under 18 years	Percent 65 years and over					Total	Percent owner occupied
	1	2	3	4	5	6	7	8	9	10	11
Congressional District (At Large), Montana—*Continued*											
Hill County	7 502	16 673	21.0	28.1	12.8	20.0	30 781	18.4	10.0	6 457	64.4
Jefferson County	4 291	10 049	4.8	27.8	10.2	27.7	41 506	9.0	5.1	3 747	83.2
Judith Basin County	4 843	2 329	2.1	27.0	17.2	23.6	29 241	21.1	2.5	951	77.2
Lake County	3 869	26 507	29.0	28.0	14.5	22.2	28 740	18.7	8.0	10 192	71.5
Lewis and Clark County	8 964	55 716	5.8	25.6	11.7	31.6	37 360	10.9	5.1	22 850	70.0
Liberty County	3 703	2 158	0.8	26.0	19.5	17.6	30 284	20.3	3.5	833	71.9
Lincoln County	9 357	18 837	4.7	25.2	15.1	13.7	26 754	19.2	13.8	7 764	76.5
McCone County	6 844	1 977	4.2	24.7	18.9	16.4	29 718	16.8	2.2	810	77.7
Madison County	9 289	6 851	4.3	22.9	17.2	25.5	30 233	12.1	5.2	2 956	70.4
Meagher County	6 195	1 932	2.8	25.2	18.3	18.7	29 375	18.9	5.4	803	73.2
Mineral County	3 159	3 884	5.7	24.1	14.1	12.3	27 143	15.8	7.4	1 584	73.0
Missoula County	6 729	95 802	7.1	22.8	10.1	32.8	34 454	14.8	6.2	38 439	61.9
Musselshell County	4 836	4 497	4.2	23.6	17.5	16.7	25 527	19.9	7.6	1 878	76.9
Park County	7 258	15 694	4.2	23.4	14.8	23.1	31 739	11.4	5.0	6 828	66.4
Petroleum County	4 284	493	2.0	25.8	16.4	17.4	24 107	23.2	2.1	211	74.4
Phillips County	13 311	4 601	11.6	27.1	17.4	17.1	28 702	18.3	4.2	1 848	70.5
Pondera County	4 208	6 424	16.7	29.5	16.1	19.8	30 464	18.8	6.9	2 410	70.2
Powder River County	8 540	1 858	3.4	26.8	18.3	16.0	28 398	12.9	3.6	737	72.9
Powell County	6 024	7 180	8.4	21.3	14.3	13.1	30 625	12.6	5.6	2 422	71.3
Prairie County	4 498	1 199	1.8	19.2	24.2	14.8	25 451	17.2	3.8	537	77.7
Ravalli County	6 201	36 070	4.2	25.7	15.4	22.5	31 992	13.8	5.9	14 289	75.7
Richland County	5 398	9 667	4.8	27.3	15.7	17.2	32 110	12.2	6.1	3 878	72.3
Roosevelt County	6 101	10 620	58.5	34.6	11.6	15.6	24 834	32.4	15.7	3 581	65.3
Rosebud County	12 982	9 383	36.4	33.5	8.7	17.6	35 898	22.4	8.4	3 307	67.2
Sanders County	7 154	10 227	9.0	23.7	16.9	15.5	26 852	17.2	9.8	4 273	76.5
Sheridan County	4 342	4 105	5.5	22.4	23.5	18.4	29 518	14.7	3.5	1 741	80.1
Silver Bow County	1 860	34 606	6.4	23.7	15.9	21.7	30 402	14.9	6.8	14 432	70.4
Stillwater County	4 649	8 195	4.6	25.2	14.5	17.8	39 205	9.8	6.8	3 234	76.0
Sweet Grass County	4 805	3 609	3.4	25.8	17.6	23.6	32 422	11.4	2.3	1 476	74.1
Teton County	5 886	6 445	4.5	27.3	16.9	20.8	30 197	16.6	3.7	2 538	75.7
Toole County	4 949	5 267	6.6	25.6	15.7	16.8	30 169	12.9	4.3	1 962	71.5
Treasure County	2 535	861	4.9	27.4	16.7	18.2	29 830	14.7	4.2	357	71.4
Valley County	12 745	7 675	11.9	25.2	19.0	15.7	30 979	13.5	5.4	3 150	75.9
Wheatland County	3 686	2 259	3.5	26.6	19.1	13.5	24 492	20.4	5.9	853	72.2
Wibaux County	2 303	1 068	2.7	25.9	21.3	16.0	28 224	15.3	4.9	421	73.2
Yellowstone County	6 825	129 352	9.0	25.6	13.3	26.4	36 727	11.1	4.5	52 084	69.2
NEBRASKA	199 099	1 711 263	12.6	26.3	13.6	23.7	39 250	9.7	3.5	666 184	67.4
Congressional District 1, Nebraska	30 952	570 423	9.5	25.4	13.4	23.9	40 021	9.2	3.6	220 835	67.4
Burt County	1 276	7 791	3.0	25.7	21.7	14.2	33 954	8.9	2.8	3 155	75.9
Butler County	1 511	8 767	1.8	27.9	17.7	13.6	36 331	8.2	4.0	3 426	75.5
Cass County	1 448	24 334	3.3	27.9	12.3	18.7	46 515	5.2	2.6	9 161	79.7
Cedar County (part)	662	3 092	1.1	27.4	21.8	16.0	33 138	7.5	3.0	1 199	75.5
Colfax County	1 070	10 441	27.3	29.0	16.0	11.5	35 849	10.8	3.5	3 682	75.4
Cuming County	1 481	10 203	6.1	27.1	20.3	12.3	33 186	9.0	2.0	3 945	71.5
Dakota County	683	20 253	28.4	30.6	9.9	12.4	38 834	11.4	3.9	7 095	67.5
Dixon County	1 234	6 339	7.0	27.4	18.2	14.1	34 201	10.0	3.1	2 413	76.3
Dodge County	1 384	36 160	5.6	24.7	17.6	15.0	37 188	8.6	3.3	14 433	67.9
Gage County	2 215	22 993	2.7	24.2	19.1	15.4	34 908	8.7	2.8	9 316	71.4
Johnson County	974	4 488	8.1	24.1	22.1	14.7	32 460	8.9	4.6	1 887	75.0
Lancaster County	2 173	250 291	11.3	23.5	10.4	32.6	41 850	9.5	3.6	99 187	60.5
Madison County	1 483	35 226	11.5	26.8	14.4	17.0	35 807	11.2	4.7	13 436	65.8
Nemaha County	1 060	7 576	2.0	23.1	18.4	22.9	32 588	12.6	6.2	3 047	72.5
Otoe County	1 595	15 396	4.2	26.3	18.4	18.1	37 302	8.1	4.0	6 060	74.0
Pawnee County	1 118	3 087	0.9	22.5	27.1	14.4	29 000	11.0	3.4	1 339	81.0
Richardson County	1 433	9 531	4.4	25.5	21.5	13.6	29 884	10.1	4.9	3 993	74.7
Sarpy County (part)	417	15 872	4.2	29.3	7.8	31.5	60 609	2.4	1.8	5 621	87.6
Saunders County	1 953	19 830	2.4	27.9	15.2	16.9	42 173	6.6	2.4	7 498	79.6
Seward County	1 489	16 496	2.5	24.9	15.2	22.6	42 700	7.0	3.0	6 013	72.0
Stanton County	1 113	6 455	3.3	29.7	13.5	13.7	36 676	6.8	2.7	2 297	80.1
Thurston County	1 020	7 171	54.2	37.0	13.2	12.0	28 170	25.6	12.6	2 255	60.8
Washington County	1 011	18 780	2.7	27.1	13.1	22.7	48 500	6.0	3.3	6 940	77.3
Wayne County	1 148	9 851	3.6	21.7	13.6	28.0	32 366	14.5	2.9	3 437	64.8
Congressional District 2, Nebraska	1 063	570 308	20.3	27.3	10.1	30.5	45 235	8.8	3.8	219 999	63.8
Douglas County	857	463 585	21.8	26.5	11.0	30.6	43 209	9.8	3.9	182 194	63.2
Sarpy County (part)	206	106 723	14.0	30.7	6.4	30.1	52 682	4.5	3.1	37 805	66.5

[1] Dry land or land partially or temporarily covered by water.
[2] Persons who do not identify themselves White, not of Hispanic origin.
[3] Persons 25 years old and over.

Table B. 110th Congressional Districts by Counties, 2000—*Continued*

(Number, percent.)

STATE Congressional district County	Land area,[1] (sq km)	Population				Percent with bachelor's degree or more[3]	Median household income, 1999 (dollars)	Percent living in poverty	Percent unemployed	Households	
		Total	Percent minority[2]	Percent under 18 years	Percent 65 years and over					Total	Percent owner occupied
	1	2	3	4	5	6	7	8	9	10	11
Congressional District 3, Nebraska	167 083	570 532	8.0	26.2	17.3	17.1	33 866	11.1	3.3	225 350	71.0
Adams County	1 459	31 151	7.8	24.3	15.9	19.9	37 160	9.3	3.5	12 141	66.8
Antelope County	2 220	7 452	1.3	27.5	19.9	14.3	30 114	13.6	2.2	2 953	76.4
Arthur County	1 853	444	2.7	24.3	17.3	15.7	27 375	13.8	1.2	185	63.8
Banner County	1 933	819	3.5	28.0	16.5	19.6	31 339	13.6	1.7	311	64.6
Blaine County	1 841	583	0.3	26.9	16.5	12.3	25 278	19.4	1.4	238	65.1
Boone County	1 779	6 259	1.5	29.1	20.6	13.1	31 444	10.4	1.5	2 454	75.2
Box Butte County	2 785	12 158	12.1	28.2	14.4	15.3	39 366	10.7	5.1	4 780	70.1
Boyd County	1 399	2 438	1.0	24.8	24.2	12.8	26 075	15.2	2.0	1 014	80.4
Brown County	3 163	3 525	1.5	24.5	22.5	17.2	28 356	11.1	1.6	1 530	74.4
Buffalo County	2 507	42 259	6.5	24.8	11.6	30.2	36 782	11.2	2.7	15 930	63.6
Cedar County (part)	1 255	6 523	1.3	30.5	19.2	11.4	33 573	9.9	2.5	2 424	82.6
Chase County	2 317	4 068	3.6	25.4	21.0	16.6	32 351	9.6	1.4	1 662	77.1
Cherry County	15 438	6 148	6.2	26.7	17.2	19.4	29 268	12.3	1.8	2 508	62.2
Cheyenne County	3 099	9 830	5.8	26.4	17.2	16.8	33 438	10.0	2.1	4 071	72.8
Clay County	1 484	7 039	4.5	27.4	18.2	16.2	34 259	10.4	2.8	2 756	77.8
Custer County	6 671	11 793	2.3	26.2	21.0	16.1	30 677	12.4	2.5	4 826	73.2
Dawes County	3 616	9 060	7.4	21.2	14.9	28.4	29 476	18.9	4.1	3 512	62.6
Dawson County	2 623	24 365	27.1	29.3	14.3	14.4	36 132	10.8	3.8	8 824	69.1
Deuel County	1 139	2 098	3.9	23.3	23.0	17.4	32 981	9.1	2.2	908	78.0
Dundy County	2 382	2 292	3.9	23.2	22.3	16.7	27 010	13.6	1.5	961	72.4
Fillmore County	1 493	6 634	2.5	26.2	21.4	15.7	35 162	7.8	2.2	2 689	74.7
Franklin County	1 492	3 574	1.3	24.5	23.7	15.8	29 304	13.2	2.5	1 485	81.3
Frontier County	2 524	3 099	2.6	26.0	16.6	17.9	33 038	12.2	2.0	1 192	73.0
Furnas County	1 860	5 324	2.0	24.2	23.8	16.1	30 498	10.6	3.6	2 278	76.6
Garden County	4 414	2 292	3.8	21.8	24.1	14.2	26 458	14.8	1.9	1 020	70.8
Garfield County	1 476	1 902	1.5	23.3	24.9	13.4	27 407	12.6	1.8	813	72.6
Gosper County	1 187	2 143	2.1	23.6	20.7	17.6	36 827	7.9	0.8	863	75.6
Grant County	2 010	747	1.9	29.2	13.9	24.7	34 821	9.7	1.0	292	67.8
Greeley County	1 476	2 714	1.1	26.9	23.4	13.5	28 375	14.6	2.1	1 077	78.4
Hall County	1 415	53 534	16.3	27.1	14.1	15.9	36 972	12.0	4.5	20 356	65.9
Hamilton County	1 408	9 403	1.2	29.0	15.3	18.6	40 277	7.5	2.5	3 503	75.2
Harlan County	1 432	3 786	1.8	24.3	22.7	15.3	30 679	10.1	2.6	1 597	80.2
Hayes County	1 847	1 068	3.3	26.5	20.3	11.6	26 667	18.4	2.1	430	71.9
Hitchcock County	1 839	3 111	3.8	24.1	22.1	13.8	28 287	14.9	2.6	1 287	78.0
Holt County	6 249	11 551	1.2	27.0	19.8	14.5	30 738	13.0	2.2	4 608	73.5
Hooker County	1 868	783	2.8	23.9	26.7	15.7	27 868	6.9	1.3	335	74.0
Howard County	1 475	6 567	1.8	28.1	17.2	14.2	33 305	11.7	2.9	2 546	77.2
Jefferson County	1 484	8 333	2.2	23.3	22.7	14.4	32 629	8.9	3.6	3 527	75.7
Kearney County	1 337	6 882	4.0	26.8	16.6	21.3	39 247	8.5	4.1	2 643	74.0
Keith County	2 749	8 875	6.1	25.3	18.4	16.8	32 325	9.3	3.3	3 707	73.1
Keya Paha County	2 003	983	2.4	24.0	20.5	15.7	24 911	26.9	1.7	409	71.4
Kimball County	2 465	4 089	6.0	24.7	21.2	13.5	30 586	11.1	2.0	1 727	76.5
Knox County	2 870	9 374	8.5	25.6	23.1	14.4	27 564	15.6	3.7	3 811	74.9
Lincoln County	6 641	34 632	6.9	26.1	15.3	16.2	36 568	9.7	4.0	14 076	69.2
Logan County	1 478	774	5.2	27.6	17.6	10.5	33 125	10.5	1.8	316	71.5
Loup County	1 476	712	2.0	27.2	19.4	13.3	26 250	17.7	0.9	289	77.5
McPherson County	2 225	533	2.3	27.4	18.4	22.2	25 750	16.2	0.0	202	67.3
Merrick County	1 256	8 204	2.4	27.6	17.4	14.9	34 961	8.9	3.0	3 209	74.3
Morrill County	3 687	5 440	12.2	27.3	16.8	14.3	30 235	14.7	5.1	2 138	71.4
Nance County	1 143	4 038	2.1	27.6	19.6	11.4	31 267	13.1	2.8	1 577	74.8
Nuckolls County	1 490	5 057	1.4	23.7	24.5	13.1	28 958	11.2	2.4	2 218	80.0
Perkins County	2 287	3 200	3.0	26.6	19.4	17.6	34 205	13.6	2.5	1 275	75.6
Phelps County	1 399	9 747	4.1	26.4	18.2	20.4	37 319	8.9	3.0	3 844	73.2
Pierce County	1 486	7 857	2.4	29.1	17.1	13.3	32 239	11.8	2.3	2 979	77.8
Platte County	1 756	31 662	7.7	29.0	13.8	17.2	39 359	7.7	2.5	12 076	73.3
Polk County	1 137	5 639	1.2	25.1	21.3	13.5	37 819	5.8	1.8	2 259	76.9
Red Willow County	1 856	11 448	3.4	24.9	19.0	15.2	32 293	9.6	2.8	4 710	70.6
Rock County	2 612	1 756	2.6	22.7	22.1	12.2	25 795	21.8	2.3	763	73.1
Saline County	1 490	13 843	9.2	24.7	17.2	14.0	35 914	9.4	2.5	5 188	70.8
Scotts Bluff County	1 915	36 951	20.2	25.9	17.4	17.3	32 016	14.5	5.8	14 887	66.2
Sheridan County	6 322	6 198	12.0	25.4	21.6	17.2	29 484	13.2	2.7	2 549	69.9
Sherman County	1 466	3 318	2.1	24.5	22.9	10.8	28 646	12.9	2.9	1 394	80.6
Sioux County	5 352	1 475	3.4	24.5	16.3	21.5	29 851	15.4	4.1	605	66.8
Thayer County	1 488	6 055	1.7	24.0	24.6	15.0	30 740	10.7	2.2	2 541	80.0
Thomas County	1 846	729	2.9	23.9	20.6	17.2	27 292	14.3	2.0	325	73.5
Valley County	1 471	4 647	2.1	24.7	24.1	16.4	27 926	12.8	3.2	1 965	75.8
Webster County	1 489	4 061	2.5	23.6	24.3	13.7	30 026	11.2	5.9	1 708	78.3
Wheeler County	1 490	886	1.8	28.9	16.9	14.9	26 771	20.9	3.2	352	70.2
York County	1 491	14 598	3.6	25.3	17.4	17.0	37 093	8.5	3.5	5 722	69.6

[1] Dry land or land partially or temporarily covered by water.
[2] Persons who do not identify themselves White, not of Hispanic origin.
[3] Persons 25 years old and over.

Table B. 110th Congressional Districts by Counties, 2000—*Continued*

(Number, percent.)

STATE Congressional district County	Land area,[1] (sq km)	Population Total	Population Percent minority[2]	Population Percent under 18 years	Population Percent 65 years and over	Percent with bachelor's degree or more[3]	Median household income, 1999 (dollars)	Percent living in poverty	Percent unemployed	Households Total	Households Percent owner occupied
	1	2	3	4	5	6	7	8	9	10	11
NEVADA	284 448	1 998 257	34.9	25.5	10.9	18.2	44 581	10.5	6.2	751 165	60.9
Congressional District 1, Nevada	459	666 442	48.5	26.5	9.9	14.6	39 480	13.9	7.8	244 538	51.8
Clark County (part)	459	666 442	48.5	26.5	9.9	14.6	39 480	13.9	7.8	244 538	51.8
Congressional District 2, Nevada	272 153	666 470	25.1	25.8	11.3	19.3	43 879	10.1	5.6	253 503	63.6
Churchill County	12 766	23 982	20.1	28.9	11.8	16.7	40 808	8.7	5.9	8 912	65.8
Clark County (part)	8 193	43 978	44.1	28.8	7.1	9.3	36 455	14.4	7.0	14 591	47.6
Douglas County	1 839	41 259	12.0	23.9	15.2	23.2	51 849	7.3	5.9	16 401	74.2
Elko County	44 493	45 291	27.4	32.4	6.2	14.8	48 383	8.9	5.7	15 638	69.8
Esmeralda County	9 294	971	18.6	20.2	17.2	9.6	33 203	15.3	3.3	455	66.4
Eureka County	10 815	1 651	14.7	27.9	12.5	13.6	41 417	12.6	4.0	666	74.0
Humboldt County	24 988	16 106	25.9	31.4	7.4	14.2	47 147	9.7	8.3	5 733	73.0
Lander County	14 228	5 794	24.9	32.1	6.9	10.8	46 067	12.5	7.8	2 093	77.1
Lincoln County	27 541	4 165	9.9	30.2	15.9	15.1	31 979	16.5	5.2	1 540	74.7
Lyon County	5 164	34 501	16.6	27.0	13.8	11.3	40 699	10.4	6.9	13 007	75.9
Mineral County	9 729	5 071	29.6	24.2	20.4	10.1	32 891	15.2	12.9	2 197	72.7
Nye County	47 000	32 485	14.8	23.4	18.3	10.1	36 024	10.7	7.1	13 309	76.4
Pershing County	15 635	6 693	30.3	25.4	7.8	8.7	40 670	11.4	7.6	1 962	69.4
Storey County	682	3 399	10.2	19.2	13.4	18.0	45 490	5.8	5.2	1 462	79.7
Washoe County	16 426	339 486	27.0	24.8	10.5	23.7	45 815	10.0	5.0	132 084	59.3
White Pine County	22 989	9 181	20.6	24.1	13.5	11.2	36 688	11.0	7.6	3 282	76.5
Carson City	371	52 457	21.6	23.3	14.9	18.5	41 809	10.0	4.6	20 171	63.1
Congressional District 3, Nevada	11 836	665 345	30.9	24.2	11.6	20.4	50 749	7.5	5.4	253 124	66.9
Clark County (part)	11 836	665 345	30.9	24.2	11.6	20.4	50 749	7.5	5.4	253 124	66.9
NEW HAMPSHIRE	23 227	1 235 786	4.9	25.0	12.0	28.7	49 467	6.5	3.8	474 606	69.7
Congressional District 1, New Hampshire	6 342	617 575	5.0	25.0	11.7	28.5	50 135	6.7	3.4	238 422	68.6
Belknap County (part)	887	50 267	3.4	23.6	15.2	23.7	43 421	6.2	3.3	20 130	74.2
Carroll County (part)	2 418	43 666	2.1	22.6	17.8	26.5	39 990	7.9	3.8	18 351	77.7
Hillsborough County (part)	351	167 328	8.0	24.9	11.7	27.4	49 447	7.8	3.4	64 971	58.6
Merrimack County (part)	94	11 721	4.6	24.4	9.0	29.4	61 491	4.0	8.8	4 147	79.7
Rockingham County (part)	1 638	232 360	3.9	26.4	10.1	31.5	56 894	4.7	2.7	88 242	74.2
Strafford County	955	112 233	4.4	23.6	11.2	26.4	44 803	9.2	4.1	42 581	64.4
Congressional District 2, New Hampshire	16 885	618 211	4.9	25.0	12.3	28.9	48 762	6.4	4.2	236 184	70.9
Belknap County (part)	153	6 058	2.6	23.9	14.2	19.7	44 985	5.1	4.1	2 329	73.3
Carroll County (part)	0	0	X	X	X	X	X	X	X	0	X
Cheshire County	1 832	73 825	2.6	23.1	13.7	26.6	42 382	8.0	7.0	28 299	70.9
Coos County	4 663	33 111	2.1	22.8	18.5	11.9	33 593	10.0	5.4	13 961	71.1
Grafton County	4 438	81 743	5.1	21.9	13.5	32.7	41 962	8.6	4.8	31 598	68.6
Hillsborough County (part)	1 919	213 513	7.5	27.4	9.8	32.2	57 504	5.1	3.4	79 484	70.2
Merrimack County (part)	2 326	124 504	3.5	24.9	12.7	29.1	47 391	6.1	3.9	47 696	68.6
Rockingham County (part)	162	44 999	4.7	26.0	10.3	32.5	66 458	3.4	2.8	16 287	83.1
Sullivan County	1 392	40 458	2.2	23.8	15.8	19.7	40 938	8.5	3.3	16 530	72.1
NEW JERSEY	19 211	8 414 350	34.0	24.7	13.2	29.8	55 146	8.5	5.8	3 064 645	65.6
Congressional District 1, New Jersey	867	647 392	28.7	26.5	12.0	20.7	47 473	9.9	6.2	236 875	70.0
Burlington County (part)	17	28 929	17.7	20.5	15.2	23.0	47 002	4.9	3.7	12 532	56.9
Camden County (part)	419	428 482	35.3	27.2	11.7	20.3	45 151	11.6	6.4	155 992	67.4
Gloucester County (part)	431	189 981	15.7	25.6	12.1	21.3	52 864	6.6	6.2	68 351	78.1
Congressional District 2, New Jersey	5 133	647 080	28.3	25.2	14.1	17.9	44 173	10.3	7.7	238 517	71.1
Atlantic County	1 453	252 552	36.3	25.3	13.5	18.7	43 933	10.5	7.5	95 024	66.3
Burlington County (part)	373	6 302	5.2	30.2	7.6	33.9	72 659	3.3	2.6	2 016	93.5
Camden County (part)	94	10 485	9.0	25.5	8.8	12.8	59 075	5.6	7.5	3 525	87.8
Cape May County	661	102 326	9.8	22.3	20.3	22.0	41 591	8.6	8.2	42 148	74.3
Cumberland County	1 267	146 438	41.5	25.4	12.9	11.7	39 150	15.0	9.9	49 143	67.9
Gloucester County (part)	410	64 692	10.1	28.4	10.1	24.0	58 440	4.8	5.3	22 366	85.3
Salem County	875	64 285	20.5	25.6	14.4	15.2	45 573	9.5	6.6	24 295	73.0
Congressional District 3, New Jersey	2 397	647 300	16.6	24.0	17.0	27.2	55 282	5.1	4.4	243 939	82.4
Burlington County (part)	1 414	320 738	24.1	25.7	12.2	30.0	60 577	4.6	3.9	115 608	79.5
Camden County (part)	63	69 965	16.7	23.5	18.0	46.2	69 421	4.0	3.7	26 227	82.9
Ocean County (part)	921	256 597	7.1	21.8	22.8	18.9	46 769	5.9	5.3	102 104	85.6
Congressional District 4, New Jersey	1 862	647 357	18.8	25.0	16.3	25.4	54 073	6.6	4.5	241 042	77.7
Burlington County (part)	281	67 425	25.7	23.6	13.8	22.6	56 132	5.2	4.3	24 215	76.6
Mercer County (part)	205	165 333	29.6	24.1	13.4	24.7	54 124	7.1	4.3	62 444	68.7
Monmouth County (part)	649	160 280	13.5	27.0	12.1	35.7	69 801	4.4	4.0	56 085	83.0
Ocean County (part)	727	254 319	13.2	24.7	21.5	20.1	46 108	8.0	5.0	98 298	80.7

[1]Dry land or land partially or temporarily covered by water.
[2]Persons who do not identify themselves White, not of Hispanic origin.
[3]Persons 25 years old and over.
X = Not applicable.

Table B. 110th Congressional Districts by Counties, 2000—*Continued*

(Number, percent.)

STATE Congressional district County	Land area,[1] (sq km)	Population Total	Population Percent minority[2]	Population Percent under 18 years	Population Percent 65 years and over	Percent with bachelor's degree or more[3]	Median household income, 1999 (dollars)	Percent living in poverty	Percent unemployed	Households Total	Households Percent owner occupied
	1	2	3	4	5	6	7	8	9	10	11
Congressional District 5, New Jersey	2 846	647 338	13.7	26.1	13.3	38.6	72 781	3.6	3.3	229 150	81.6
Bergen County (part)	417	390 710	18.0	25.6	14.9	47.1	82 753	2.8	3.0	136 653	83.7
Passaic County (part)	298	52 974	8.5	26.4	9.0	29.1	73 561	3.4	3.8	18 246	87.1
Sussex County (part)	1 205	101 217	6.0	27.7	9.8	24.4	61 469	4.8	3.7	35 591	80.1
Warren County	927	102 437	7.7	26.0	12.9	24.4	56 100	5.4	3.8	38 660	72.8
Congressional District 6, New Jersey	509	647 121	38.3	23.7	11.7	29.7	55 681	9.1	5.8	234 071	61.3
Middlesex County (part)	236	286 000	42.0	22.5	10.4	33.5	59 293	8.2	5.7	99 394	59.0
Monmouth County (part)	245	295 032	25.0	24.3	13.4	27.7	53 418	9.0	5.7	113 027	64.8
Somerset County (part)	12	18 260	66.0	24.5	11.7	31.1	58 693	8.3	3.7	6 513	59.6
Union County (part)	16	47 829	88.1	27.5	9.3	18.5	46 683	15.9	7.9	15 137	50.1
Congressional District 7, New Jersey	1 541	647 269	20.9	24.7	13.1	41.5	74 823	3.4	3.2	233 383	78.7
Hunterdon County (part)	730	97 985	8.4	26.3	9.5	43.1	82 017	2.5	2.5	34 355	84.8
Middlesex County (part)	96	144 317	36.6	23.1	13.1	31.9	66 436	4.6	4.4	50 046	74.6
Somerset County (part)	558	182 890	21.5	26.2	10.4	45.2	78 062	3.6	2.9	65 941	78.4
Union County (part)	158	222 077	15.8	23.8	16.9	44.1	75 532	3.0	3.1	83 041	78.8
Congressional District 8, New Jersey	277	647 130	46.4	25.0	13.4	28.0	51 954	10.7	6.5	225 542	56.7
Essex County (part)	110	232 981	29.9	22.8	15.3	41.1	64 691	5.2	4.2	88 535	66.1
Passaic County (part)	167	414 149	55.7	26.2	12.3	19.9	45 390	13.9	8.1	137 007	50.7
Congressional District 9, New Jersey	241	647 477	38.9	21.2	14.8	29.5	52 437	7.6	5.4	251 055	52.8
Bergen County (part)	189	493 408	35.7	20.7	15.5	31.5	55 180	6.7	4.8	194 164	55.5
Hudson County (part)	43	135 851	54.4	22.8	12.3	22.7	44 208	11.6	7.8	49 631	40.3
Passaic County (part)	9	18 218	10.8	21.7	15.7	25.6	55 340	3.4	2.9	7 260	65.2
Congressional District 10, New Jersey	171	647 109	78.6	27.0	10.9	18.3	38 177	17.5	10.9	228 419	38.6
Essex County (part)	92	375 695	88.2	28.4	10.0	18.5	34 094	21.9	13.5	132 369	31.7
Hudson County (part)	8	69 234	78.9	26.8	11.3	22.1	39 391	17.0	10.6	24 007	39.4
Union County (part)	70	202 180	60.8	24.5	12.5	16.9	45 468	9.6	6.8	72 043	50.9
Congressional District 11, New Jersey	1 580	647 127	17.1	25.0	11.9	45.2	79 009	3.5	3.4	233 258	77.9
Essex County (part)	104	66 561	13.8	24.6	15.8	53.8	94 184	2.3	2.4	23 276	83.9
Morris County	1 215	470 212	18.0	24.7	11.6	44.1	77 340	3.9	3.5	169 711	76.0
Passaic County (part)	6	3 708	9.2	18.6	15.2	23.1	68 929	5.9	5.2	1 343	81.5
Somerset County (part)	110	63 697	20.9	25.7	13.3	52.8	84 106	3.2	3.3	23 688	78.1
Sussex County (part)	145	42 949	7.8	28.2	7.2	33.8	74 721	2.2	3.3	15 240	88.6
Congressional District 12, New Jersey	1 640	647 253	27.7	24.8	12.6	42.3	69 668	5.2	5.5	233 010	75.1
Hunterdon County (part)	384	24 004	4.0	22.9	12.2	36.9	72 451	3.0	2.5	9 323	79.5
Mercer County (part)	380	185 428	41.4	23.7	11.7	42.8	60 716	10.2	10.5	63 363	65.4
Middlesex County (part)	438	245 189	26.5	24.1	14.3	39.0	66 973	3.5	3.8	92 358	74.4
Monmouth County (part)	329	159 989	15.2	28.2	11.5	46.3	84 481	3.4	3.2	55 124	86.0
Somerset County (part)	109	32 643	38.5	21.7	11.2	49.5	72 305	3.2	3.4	12 842	78.3
Congressional District 13, New Jersey	147	647 397	67.7	23.4	10.9	20.5	37 129	18.0	9.5	236 384	28.9
Essex County (part)	21	118 396	71.7	25.0	9.5	8.6	30 563	23.6	12.4	39 556	24.0
Hudson County (part)	70	403 890	65.8	21.6	11.2	26.7	38 907	16.6	8.6	156 908	26.3
Middlesex County (part)	32	74 656	64.8	27.2	11.9	11.2	42 046	14.5	9.7	24 017	52.9
Union County (part)	24	50 455	77.5	27.7	9.9	8.4	32 549	21.0	10.6	15 903	31.5
NEW MEXICO	314 309	1 819 046	55.3	27.9	11.7	23.5	34 133	18.4	7.3	677 971	70.0
Congressional District 1, New Mexico	12 216	606 729	51.5	25.7	11.3	29.5	38 413	14.0	5.8	238 379	65.4
Bernalillo County (part)	1 889	543 181	51.6	25.1	11.6	30.6	38 589	13.7	5.8	216 172	63.3
Sandoval County (part)	565	16 784	54.5	27.2	9.1	29.1	46 691	11.6	4.8	6 170	86.3
Santa Fe County (part)	137	4 876	18.6	31.0	6.1	32.8	55 875	6.5	2.7	1 721	93.3
Torrance County	8 663	16 911	42.6	30.3	10.1	14.4	30 446	19.0	6.0	6 024	83.9
Valencia County (part)	962	24 977	59.8	32.7	9.2	13.2	32 468	19.5	7.5	8 292	87.4
Congressional District 2, New Mexico	179 986	606 110	55.8	28.8	13.1	16.9	29 269	22.4	8.7	218 546	72.0
Bernalillo County (part)	1 106	3 742	98.0	36.3	6.9	4.2	23 083	29.4	13.8	1 133	92.1
Catron County	17 943	3 543	23.8	20.9	18.8	18.4	23 892	24.5	8.9	1 584	80.4
Chaves County	15 723	61 382	48.1	29.0	14.8	16.2	28 513	21.3	9.0	22 561	70.9
Cibola County	11 757	25 595	75.3	30.7	11.1	12.0	27 774	24.8	11.5	8 327	77.1
De Baca County	6 021	2 240	35.5	23.9	26.3	16.2	25 441	17.7	5.4	922	77.8
Dona Ana County	9 861	174 682	67.5	29.7	10.7	22.3	29 808	25.4	9.2	59 556	67.5
Eddy County	10 831	51 658	42.6	28.7	14.7	13.5	31 998	17.2	6.8	19 379	74.3
Grant County	10 272	31 002	51.4	26.2	16.4	20.5	29 134	18.7	8.0	12 146	74.5
Guadalupe County	7 849	4 680	83.7	24.4	13.1	10.3	24 783	21.6	7.7	1 655	74.1
Hidalgo County	8 924	5 932	57.3	31.8	13.5	9.9	24 819	27.3	9.7	2 152	67.8
Lea County	11 378	55 511	45.9	30.1	12.5	11.6	29 799	21.1	9.1	19 699	72.6
Lincoln County	12 512	19 411	29.1	22.7	18.0	22.8	33 886	14.9	3.9	8 202	77.2
Luna County	7 680	25 016	60.1	29.9	18.2	10.4	20 784	32.9	17.1	9 397	75.0
McKinley County (part)	1 123	6 895	94.0	34.5	7.2	6.5	23 145	41.7	17.9	1 672	88.6
Otero County	17 163	62 298	44.8	29.5	11.5	15.4	30 861	19.3	8.1	22 984	66.9
Sierra County	10 827	13 270	29.4	20.0	27.9	13.1	24 152	20.9	6.6	6 113	74.8
Socorro County	17 214	18 078	62.3	28.2	11.1	19.4	23 439	31.7	9.1	6 675	71.0
Valencia County (part)	1 803	41 175	60.8	28.3	11.0	15.7	35 027	15.0	5.6	14 389	81.9

[1]Dry land or land partially or temporarily covered by water.
[2]Persons who do not identify themselves White, not of Hispanic origin.
[3]Persons 25 years old and over.

Table B. 110th Congressional Districts by Counties, 2000—*Continued*

(Number, percent.)

STATE Congressional district County	Land area,[1] (sq km)	Population Total	Population Percent minority[2]	Population Percent under 18 years	Population Percent 65 years and over	Percent with bachelor's degree or more[3]	Median household income, 1999 (dollars)	Percent living in poverty	Percent unemployed	Households Total	Households Percent owner occupied
	1	2	3	4	5	6	7	8	9	10	11
Congressional District 3, New Mexico	122 108	606 207	58.6	29.2	10.7	23.7	35 058	19.0	7.7	221 046	72.9
Bernalillo County (part)	25	9 755	40.8	28.1	9.0	33.9	56 728	6.3	3.2	3 631	78.0
Colfax County	9 730	14 189	49.8	25.1	17.4	18.5	30 744	14.8	6.4	5 821	72.7
Curry County	3 641	45 044	41.3	30.1	11.4	15.3	28 917	19.0	6.9	16 766	59.4
Harding County	5 505	810	49.1	20.1	29.4	18.1	26 111	16.3	3.2	371	75.2
Los Alamos County	283	18 343	17.8	25.9	12.4	60.5	78 993	2.9	2.0	7 497	78.6
McKinley County (part)	12 989	67 903	87.3	38.3	6.8	12.6	25 184	35.5	17.1	19 804	71.0
Mora County	5 002	5 180	82.5	26.9	17.1	15.5	24 518	25.4	13.2	2 017	82.5
Quay County	7 446	10 155	41.1	24.9	19.4	13.7	24 894	20.9	5.2	4 201	70.5
Rio Arriba County	15 171	41 190	86.3	28.5	10.8	15.4	29 429	20.3	8.2	15 044	81.7
Roosevelt County	6 342	18 018	37.2	27.9	12.1	22.6	26 586	22.7	8.0	6 639	62.7
Sandoval County (part)	9 043	73 124	48.6	30.1	10.8	23.8	44 526	12.3	6.5	25 241	83.0
San Juan County	14 281	113 801	53.8	32.6	9.0	13.5	33 762	21.5	9.1	37 711	75.3
San Miguel County	12 217	30 126	81.0	27.6	11.8	21.2	26 524	24.4	8.7	11 134	73.2
Santa Fe County (part)	4 808	124 416	56.0	23.7	10.9	37.1	41 735	12.2	4.8	50 761	67.7
Taos County	5 706	29 979	65.8	24.5	12.2	25.9	26 762	20.9	8.9	12 675	75.5
Union County	9 920	4 174	37.1	27.4	17.8	13.0	28 080	18.1	1.9	1 733	72.9
NEW YORK	122 283	18 976 457	38.0	24.6	12.9	27.4	43 393	14.6	7.1	7 056 860	53.0
Congressional District 1, New York	1 674	654 458	15.6	25.6	12.1	27.2	61 884	6.0	4.1	223 885	79.4
Suffolk County (part)	1 674	654 458	15.6	25.6	12.1	27.2	61 884	6.0	4.1	223 885	79.4
Congressional District 2, New York	620	654 346	28.6	26.6	11.6	30.6	71 147	5.9	3.8	206 854	81.7
Nassau County (part)	36	48 498	10.6	25.2	17.0	53.5	97 897	3.2	2.7	16 079	93.1
Suffolk County (part)	584	605 848	30.1	26.8	11.1	28.7	69 556	6.1	3.8	190 775	80.8
Congressional District 3, New York	475	653 934	13.1	24.3	14.6	31.3	70 561	4.3	3.4	225 221	81.7
Nassau County (part)	370	494 871	13.8	24.1	15.1	33.6	72 514	4.1	3.4	170 582	82.9
Suffolk County (part)	105	159 063	11.0	25.2	13.1	23.9	64 665	5.1	3.4	54 639	78.0
Congressional District 4, New York	233	654 691	37.7	25.1	14.3	31.0	66 799	6.4	4.0	212 562	77.3
Nassau County (part)	233	654 691	37.7	25.1	14.3	31.0	66 799	6.4	4.0	212 562	77.3
Congressional District 5, New York	172	654 253	55.8	21.8	14.8	33.6	51 156	12.1	6.0	228 362	53.3
Nassau County (part)	103	136 484	20.5	23.9	17.2	55.6	93 381	4.4	3.6	48 164	80.0
Queens County (part)	68	517 769	65.1	21.2	14.2	27.8	44 954	14.0	6.6	180 198	46.1
Congressional District 6, New York	102	654 946	87.2	26.8	10.6	18.0	43 546	14.5	9.5	204 235	52.7
Queens County (part)	102	654 946	87.2	26.8	10.6	18.0	43 546	14.5	9.5	204 235	52.7
Congressional District 7, New York	68	652 943	72.4	23.5	13.0	19.8	36 990	17.7	8.8	238 573	32.3
Bronx County (part)	48	372 882	71.5	25.2	14.0	17.6	35 164	18.9	9.3	141 322	31.4
Queens County (part)	20	280 061	73.5	21.1	11.6	22.5	40 003	16.1	8.1	97 251	33.5
Congressional District 8, New York	39	654 429	31.2	17.7	13.8	47.8	47 061	18.7	6.7	303 343	26.1
Kings County (part)	22	318 887	35.0	26.7	16.4	20.4	27 604	27.1	8.3	112 290	26.1
New York County (part)	16	335 542	27.5	9.3	11.2	68.2	63 630	10.4	5.9	191 053	26.1
Congressional District 9, New York	96	654 916	36.0	21.0	16.7	31.0	45 426	12.2	5.9	255 970	46.2
Kings County (part)	35	203 549	22.8	22.1	17.9	30.3	39 554	15.5	5.8	77 830	43.4
Queens County (part)	60	451 367	42.0	20.5	16.2	31.2	47 400	10.7	6.0	178 140	47.4
Congressional District 10, New York	46	655 668	83.7	30.0	9.6	17.5	30 212	29.0	13.5	226 363	28.6
Kings County (part)	46	655 668	83.7	30.0	9.6	17.5	30 212	29.0	13.5	226 363	28.6
Congressional District 11, New York	31	654 134	78.5	27.0	9.2	25.0	34 082	23.2	11.6	238 213	21.6
Kings County (part)	31	654 134	78.5	27.0	9.2	25.0	34 082	23.2	11.6	238 213	21.6
Congressional District 12, New York	49	653 346	76.9	25.6	9.5	17.1	29 195	28.3	11.0	224 653	18.8
Kings County (part)	31	422 197	77.2	27.0	8.3	17.8	29 288	29.7	11.3	141 983	20.4
New York County (part)	3	110 526	88.2	20.6	14.2	15.3	21 476	33.6	11.5	41 048	6.2
Queens County (part)	14	120 623	65.8	25.1	9.2	16.2	35 904	18.8	9.1	41 622	25.9
Congressional District 13, New York	168	654 619	29.2	23.5	13.4	24.0	50 092	11.9	6.1	240 389	54.0
Kings County (part)	16	210 891	30.4	19.5	17.1	25.6	40 425	15.8	6.6	84 048	35.7
Richmond County	151	443 728	28.6	25.4	11.6	23.2	55 039	10.0	5.9	156 341	63.8
Congressional District 14, New York	33	654 165	33.9	13.2	13.2	56.9	57 152	12.4	5.2	340 543	25.8
New York County (part)	17	449 552	24.0	10.2	14.0	69.3	66 908	8.8	4.3	259 325	27.5
Queens County (part)	16	204 613	55.7	19.7	11.5	25.0	35 658	20.2	7.8	81 218	20.1
Congressional District 15, New York	27	654 355	83.7	23.9	10.8	25.0	27 934	30.5	14.5	247 218	10.0
Bronx County (part)	2	12 780	91.5	3.9	0.0	0.0	X	X	X	0	X
New York County (part)	24	641 575	83.5	24.3	11.0	25.6	27 934	30.5	14.5	247 218	10.0
Queens County (part)	1	0	X	X	X	X	X	X	X	0	X
Congressional District 16, New York	31	654 400	97.1	34.5	6.7	7.8	19 311	42.2	20.3	211 904	7.1
Bronx County (part)	31	654 400	97.1	34.5	6.7	7.8	19 311	42.2	20.3	211 904	7.1

[1] Dry land or land partially or temporarily covered by water.
[2] Persons who do not identify themselves White, not of Hispanic origin.
[3] Persons 25 years old and over.
X = Not applicable.

Table B. 110th Congressional Districts by Counties, 2000—*Continued*

(Number, percent.)

STATE Congressional district County	Land area,[1] (sq km)	Population				Percent with bachelor's degree or more[3]	Median household income, 1999 (dollars)	Percent living in poverty	Percent unem-ployed	Households	
		Total	Percent minority[2]	Percent under 18 years	Percent 65 years and over					Total	Percent owner occupied
	1	2	3	4	5	6	7	8	9	10	11
Congressional District 17, New York	328	654 283	58.9	26.6	12.8	28.5	44 868	16.0	7.6	235 347	41.2
Bronx County (part)	29	292 588	76.8	25.8	13.3	24.2	37 370	19.9	10.3	109 986	28.1
Rockland County (part)	267	197 862	28.9	28.9	11.9	38.4	65 836	11.1	3.8	63 450	68.5
Westchester County (part)	33	163 833	63.2	25.1	13.0	24.4	41 769	15.0	7.6	61 911	36.3
Congressional District 18, New York	575	654 696	32.9	24.7	14.4	43.8	68 887	7.8	3.9	235 623	63.7
Rockland County (part)	65	60 981	31.7	26.6	11.7	38.2	75 412	6.5	3.7	19 368	77.6
Westchester County (part)	510	593 715	33.1	24.5	14.6	44.4	68 099	8.0	3.9	216 255	62.5
Congressional District 19, New York	3 629	653 397	16.5	26.8	10.9	32.3	64 337	6.4	4.2	223 647	75.2
Dutchess County (part)	699	151 102	19.6	25.1	11.2	28.2	58 590	5.3	5.5	52 633	71.7
Orange County (part)	1 634	212 729	14.8	29.1	10.0	25.0	56 957	9.2	4.8	69 478	72.6
Putnam County	599	95 745	10.4	26.3	9.6	33.9	72 279	4.4	3.5	32 703	82.2
Rockland County (part)	119	27 910	18.1	24.7	10.5	30.0	68 190	4.9	3.1	9 857	80.5
Westchester County (part)	578	165 911	19.3	26.1	12.8	43.9	78 200	5.2	3.1	58 976	76.6
Congressional District 20, New York	18 176	655 277	6.6	24.4	13.7	24.7	44 239	7.9	4.7	250 312	73.8
Columbia County	1 647	63 094	8.8	23.9	16.5	22.6	41 915	9.0	4.3	24 796	70.5
Delaware County (part)	2 968	41 851	4.8	22.8	18.7	17.5	32 724	12.7	5.9	16 749	75.7
Dutchess County (part)	1 364	99 177	10.7	24.4	12.7	29.0	54 387	6.1	5.3	34 889	75.8
Essex County (part)	1 740	14 279	12.4	19.9	15.7	20.7	34 907	10.1	3.8	5 241	67.4
Greene County	1 678	48 195	11.4	22.8	15.6	16.4	36 493	12.2	6.1	18 256	72.2
Otsego County (part)	823	12 037	2.8	24.1	16.4	20.4	35 924	10.6	7.2	4 743	81.5
Rensselaer County (part)	1 456	60 179	3.0	25.9	12.5	23.9	50 251	5.4	3.6	22 786	81.2
Saratoga County (part)	2 086	192 120	5.2	25.1	11.3	31.4	49 584	5.7	3.9	74 668	72.7
Warren County	2 251	63 303	3.1	24.0	15.1	23.2	39 198	9.7	5.3	25 726	69.9
Washington County	2 164	61 042	6.1	24.6	14.0	14.3	37 668	9.4	4.9	22 458	74.3
Congressional District 21, New York	5 012	654 374	14.5	23.3	15.5	27.0	40 254	11.2	6.5	265 380	60.8
Albany County	1 356	294 565	18.2	22.4	14.6	33.3	42 935	10.6	6.8	120 512	57.7
Fulton County (part)	208	31 090	6.0	23.9	17.9	13.8	30 808	15.4	6.7	12 550	62.6
Montgomery County	1 048	49 708	9.2	24.5	19.1	13.6	32 128	12.0	5.8	20 038	67.1
Rensselaer County (part)	238	92 359	13.8	23.1	14.3	23.6	38 025	12.3	7.7	37 108	54.9
Saratoga County (part)	17	8 515	3.3	23.6	14.2	18.9	46 362	5.7	4.0	3 497	59.0
Schenectady County	534	146 555	13.7	24.3	16.6	26.3	41 739	10.9	5.1	59 684	65.4
Schoharie County	1 611	31 582	4.8	24.0	14.9	17.3	36 585	11.4	7.2	11 991	75.3
Congressional District 22, New York	8 407	654 522	20.0	23.8	13.6	23.9	38 586	14.3	6.5	248 893	61.2
Broome County (part)	933	155 671	11.2	22.1	17.1	24.0	33 772	14.2	5.6	63 783	60.3
Delaware County (part)	779	6 204	4.1	24.4	18.1	10.9	30 958	13.8	8.0	2 521	75.8
Dutchess County (part)	13	29 871	50.2	25.8	13.7	19.5	29 389	22.7	8.2	12 014	36.8
Orange County (part)	481	128 638	35.0	28.8	10.9	18.4	46 138	12.6	5.7	45 310	58.4
Sullivan County	2 512	73 966	20.1	24.8	14.3	16.7	36 998	16.3	9.2	27 661	68.1
Tioga County (part)	544	31 890	3.5	26.9	13.8	21.6	40 561	8.6	5.1	12 224	75.4
Tompkins County (part)	228	50 533	23.0	12.5	9.0	61.9	31 376	27.4	7.5	17 881	39.0
Ulster County	2 918	177 749	14.4	23.4	13.3	25.0	42 551	11.4	6.3	67 499	68.0
Congressional District 23, New York	34 278	654 216	7.1	25.1	12.5	16.0	35 434	13.5	8.2	240 431	71.0
Clinton County	2 691	79 894	7.7	23.0	11.9	17.8	37 028	13.9	6.2	29 423	68.5
Essex County (part)	2 913	24 572	3.3	24.4	16.3	16.8	34 773	12.3	8.5	9 787	77.3
Franklin County	4 226	51 134	16.5	22.6	12.8	13.0	31 517	14.6	10.6	17 931	70.3
Fulton County (part)	1 077	23 983	3.4	25.9	14.2	13.1	37 436	8.9	5.8	9 334	85.0
Hamilton County	4 456	5 379	2.2	19.8	20.1	18.4	32 287	10.4	9.7	2 362	79.3
Jefferson County	3 295	111 738	12.8	26.4	11.4	16.0	34 006	13.3	9.1	40 068	59.8
Lewis County	3 303	26 944	1.9	27.7	13.8	11.7	34 361	13.2	7.8	10 040	77.0
Madison County	1 699	69 441	4.5	25.0	12.5	21.6	40 184	9.8	7.1	25 368	74.9
Oneida County (part)	1 193	26 823	2.5	27.2	12.9	12.3	37 069	10.6	5.7	10 090	80.0
Oswego County	2 469	122 377	3.6	26.8	11.3	14.4	36 598	14.0	9.3	45 522	72.8
St. Lawrence County	6 956	111 931	6.3	23.4	13.0	16.4	32 356	16.9	8.5	40 506	70.6
Congressional District 24, New York	15 964	654 390	7.9	24.3	15.2	19.3	36 082	12.6	6.5	251 360	69.8
Broome County (part)	898	44 865	3.6	26.0	14.1	18.2	40 290	8.3	4.5	16 966	83.1
Cayuga County (part)	1 374	70 664	8.5	24.4	15.1	16.2	37 213	11.3	5.1	26 475	70.1
Chenango County	2 316	51 401	3.2	26.2	14.9	14.4	33 679	14.4	5.6	19 926	75.3
Cortland County	1 294	48 599	3.7	23.6	12.5	18.8	34 364	15.5	8.5	18 210	64.3
Herkimer County	3 655	64 427	2.5	24.3	16.9	15.7	32 924	12.5	6.7	25 734	71.2
Oneida County (part)	1 948	208 646	12.7	23.5	17.0	19.1	35 765	13.4	5.9	80 406	65.6
Ontario County (part)	60	16 945	18.6	23.4	16.5	22.3	34 078	14.4	7.3	6 425	57.5
Otsego County (part)	1 774	49 639	5.5	22.3	14.8	22.5	32 728	16.0	14.1	18 548	70.9
Seneca County	842	33 342	6.4	24.9	15.1	17.5	37 140	11.5	6.0	12 630	73.7
Tioga County (part)	799	19 894	3.3	27.0	12.0	16.5	39 780	8.0	5.0	7 501	81.6
Tompkins County (part)	1 005	45 968	8.3	26.3	10.2	36.5	42 433	9.0	4.0	18 539	68.0
Congressional District 25, New York	4 195	654 484	13.4	25.9	13.8	27.8	43 188	10.4	5.0	255 813	69.1
Cayuga County (part)	422	11 299	3.1	28.9	10.5	11.5	40 015	9.5	5.6	4 083	84.2
Monroe County (part)	188	91 084	6.2	24.8	16.1	36.6	56 497	3.6	3.3	35 669	82.5
Onondaga County	2 021	458 336	16.3	25.8	13.8	28.5	40 847	12.2	5.4	181 153	64.5
Wayne County	1 565	93 765	7.2	27.4	12.1	17.0	44 157	8.6	5.1	34 908	77.6

[1]Dry land or land partially or temporarily covered by water.
[2]Persons who do not identify themselves White, not of Hispanic origin.
[3]Persons 25 years old and over.

Table B. 110th Congressional Districts by Counties, 2000—*Continued*

(Number, percent.)

STATE Congressional district County	Land area,[1] (sq km)	Population Total	Percent minority[2]	Percent under 18 years	Percent 65 years and over	Percent with bachelor's degree or more[3]	Median household income, 1999 (dollars)	Percent living in poverty	Percent unem- ployed	Households Total	Percent owner occupied
	1	2	3	4	5	6	7	8	9	10	11
Congressional District 26, New York	7 073	654 343	7.6	24.6	14.1	25.5	46 653	6.9	5.7	243 482	75.0
Erie County (part)	544	193 269	8.6	23.4	16.7	39.2	54 225	5.2	7.1	73 202	76.6
Genesee County	1 280	60 370	5.5	25.9	14.3	16.3	40 542	7.6	4.3	22 770	72.9
Livingston County	1 637	64 328	7.0	23.3	11.4	19.2	42 066	10.4	6.1	22 150	74.5
Monroe County (part)	630	144 491	7.0	25.8	12.8	26.2	51 370	5.3	4.6	53 671	76.2
Niagara County (part)	728	112 598	5.4	24.9	14.1	18.8	42 252	7.9	4.9	44 419	72.0
Orleans County (part)	718	35 863	14.5	25.8	12.6	12.3	36 788	11.5	6.9	12 364	73.3
Wyoming County	1 536	43 424	9.4	24.0	12.1	11.5	39 895	8.4	6.1	14 906	76.9
Congressional District 27, New York	4 740	654 200	11.1	23.9	15.8	19.9	36 884	12.0	6.3	261 614	66.2
Chautauqua County	2 751	139 750	8.0	24.4	16.0	16.9	33 458	13.8	6.3	54 515	69.3
Erie County (part)	1 990	514 450	11.9	23.8	15.7	20.7	37 904	11.5	6.3	207 099	65.4
Congressional District 28, New York	1 383	654 464	38.1	26.1	14.3	21.2	31 751	18.7	8.7	268 193	55.4
Erie County (part)	171	242 546	42.9	25.9	15.9	20.9	30 531	19.1	9.6	100 572	57.0
Monroe County (part)	290	296 362	43.3	26.8	12.1	23.6	31 827	20.5	8.4	121 195	48.9
Niagara County (part)	626	107 248	15.2	24.4	16.9	15.9	33 653	13.4	7.4	43 427	67.7
Orleans County (part)	295	8 308	3.8	28.1	11.5	15.8	42 452	7.9	6.8	2 999	84.9
Congressional District 29, New York	14 660	654 208	7.4	25.0	14.1	26.1	41 875	9.9	6.2	248 477	74.0
Allegany County	2 668	49 927	3.5	24.3	14.0	17.2	32 106	15.5	9.0	18 009	73.9
Cattaraugus County	3 393	83 955	5.9	26.1	14.7	14.9	33 404	13.7	7.4	32 023	74.4
Chemung County	1 057	91 070	10.1	24.3	15.6	18.6	36 415	13.0	7.8	35 049	68.9
Monroe County (part)	599	203 406	12.1	23.9	13.2	42.6	58 588	5.1	5.1	75 977	74.9
Ontario County (part)	1 609	83 279	3.3	25.8	12.6	25.1	46 411	6.0	4.0	31 945	76.8
Schuyler County	851	19 224	4.3	25.3	14.7	15.5	36 010	11.8	7.4	7 374	77.2
Steuben County	3 607	98 726	3.7	25.9	15.2	17.9	35 479	13.2	7.0	39 071	73.2
Yates County	876	24 621	3.2	26.7	15.6	18.2	34 640	13.1	6.4	9 029	77.0
NORTH CAROLINA	126 161	8 049 313	29.8	24.4	12.0	22.5	39 184	12.3	5.3	3 132 013	69.4
Congressional District 1, North Carolina	18 645	619 249	55.6	26.0	14.1	12.0	28 410	21.1	8.5	236 646	63.4
Beaufort County (part)	806	16 351	46.4	25.8	15.5	10.5	24 848	25.3	7.9	6 767	66.0
Bertie County	1 811	19 773	64.0	26.1	16.0	8.8	25 177	23.5	7.1	7 743	74.9
Chowan County	447	14 526	39.8	24.1	18.1	16.4	30 928	17.6	6.7	5 580	72.3
Craven County (part)	764	38 975	42.5	25.8	10.4	16.2	29 273	16.8	7.0	13 587	54.4
Edgecombe County	1 308	55 606	60.8	27.1	12.6	8.5	30 983	19.6	9.6	20 392	64.0
Gates County	882	10 516	41.4	26.6	14.3	10.5	35 647	17.0	4.4	3 901	82.0
Granville County (part)	182	11 753	54.0	25.1	17.8	17.6	35 260	17.9	5.9	4 512	64.1
Greene County	687	18 974	49.8	25.1	11.9	8.2	32 074	20.2	7.3	6 696	74.7
Halifax County	1 879	57 370	57.7	26.2	14.9	11.1	26 459	23.9	8.1	22 122	67.0
Hertford County	915	22 601	63.0	25.4	16.1	11.1	26 422	18.3	8.7	8 953	70.0
Jones County (part)	721	6 835	49.0	26.7	15.2	10.2	30 211	18.1	5.1	2 627	78.1
Lenoir County (part)	410	30 801	64.6	26.0	16.1	9.4	26 069	22.4	10.7	12 596	58.6
Martin County	1 194	25 593	48.4	25.5	15.4	11.6	28 793	20.2	8.0	10 020	71.8
Nash County (part)	22	14 920	66.6	27.7	15.7	12.1	24 314	27.7	10.4	5 929	43.0
Northampton County	1 389	22 086	61.0	24.4	17.6	10.8	26 652	21.3	8.6	8 691	76.8
Pasquotank County	588	34 897	43.5	24.8	14.1	16.4	30 444	18.4	9.8	12 907	65.7
Perquimans County	640	11 368	29.2	22.9	19.8	12.3	29 538	17.9	5.9	4 645	78.6
Pitt County (part)	918	54 809	59.8	27.1	11.0	14.3	28 242	25.0	8.7	20 998	53.5
Vance County (part)	415	28 373	57.7	26.4	14.7	12.9	30 366	20.8	7.6	10 872	61.9
Warren County	1 110	19 972	61.4	23.5	17.4	11.6	28 351	19.4	8.3	7 708	77.2
Washington County	903	13 723	52.2	25.8	15.5	11.6	28 865	21.8	7.1	5 367	73.5
Wayne County (part)	237	52 666	54.4	27.0	12.1	15.4	31 017	16.4	8.2	20 343	52.2
Wilson County (part)	416	36 761	70.8	27.4	12.2	6.9	23 745	27.8	11.5	13 690	48.7
Congressional District 2, North Carolina	10 246	618 753	40.9	25.5	10.0	15.9	36 510	14.3	7.4	223 122	66.5
Chatham County (part)	1 338	33 094	34.6	23.2	14.8	14.6	37 697	11.5	3.8	12 588	77.9
Cumberland County (part)	264	108 028	59.9	27.2	6.1	18.5	33 101	16.2	14.5	33 612	44.2
Franklin County	1 274	47 260	35.8	25.3	11.1	13.2	38 968	12.6	4.7	17 843	77.8
Harnett County	1 541	91 025	31.3	26.8	10.4	12.8	35 105	14.9	8.3	33 800	70.3
Johnston County	2 051	121 965	24.7	26.2	9.9	15.9	40 872	12.8	4.0	46 595	73.4
Lee County	666	49 040	34.0	25.6	13.0	17.2	38 900	12.8	4.6	18 466	71.7
Nash County (part)	1 088	45 667	41.4	24.6	11.6	14.2	36 824	11.7	5.8	17 262	70.0
Sampson County	1 580	32 741	57.2	26.2	13.7	10.2	28 237	20.5	8.5	12 027	70.6
Vance County (part)	241	14 581	45.7	28.4	9.1	6.2	33 492	19.9	9.5	5 327	75.1
Wake County (part)	201	75 352	54.0	20.6	7.8	24.0	37 554	15.2	10.8	25 602	54.7
Congressional District 3, North Carolina	16 037	618 810	23.6	23.8	11.6	20.1	37 510	12.4	5.2	234 158	70.9
Beaufort County (part)	1 338	28 607	25.3	22.3	16.2	18.9	34 567	16.1	5.5	11 552	80.4
Camden County	623	6 885	19.2	24.7	13.4	16.2	39 493	10.1	3.7	2 662	83.5
Carteret County	1 346	59 383	10.9	20.6	17.1	19.8	38 344	10.7	5.0	25 204	76.6
Craven County (part)	1 071	52 461	23.3	23.4	15.4	21.1	41 199	10.5	4.3	20 995	74.7
Currituck County	678	18 190	10.4	25.2	11.9	13.3	40 822	10.7	3.7	6 902	81.5

[1]Dry land or land partially or temporarily covered by water.
[2]Persons who do not identify themselves White, not of Hispanic origin.
[3]Persons 25 years old and over.

Table B. 110th Congressional Districts by Counties, 2000—*Continued*

(Number, percent.)

STATE Congressional district County	Land area,[1] (sq km)	Population				Percent with bachelor's degree or more[3]	Median household income, 1999 (dollars)	Percent living in poverty	Percent unem- ployed	Households	
		Total	Percent minority[2]	Percent under 18 years	Percent 65 years and over					Total	Percent owner occupied
	1	2	3	4	5	6	7	8	9	10	11
Congressional District 3, North Carolina—*Continued*											
Dare County	993	29 967	6.5	21.3	13.8	27.7	42 411	8.0	4.9	12 690	74.5
Duplin County (part)	606	14 122	28.7	25.4	11.5	9.9	32 020	16.1	5.5	5 245	76.2
Hyde County	1 587	5 826	38.0	20.4	17.2	10.6	28 444	15.4	5.3	2 185	78.4
Jones County (part)	502	3 546	21.5	23.8	15.5	8.2	32 154	14.7	4.9	1 434	82.2
Lenoir County (part)	625	28 847	23.3	24.6	13.2	17.4	37 872	10.3	5.5	11 266	76.4
Nash County (part)	289	26 833	19.8	25.5	12.5	24.9	47 581	8.4	2.9	10 453	77.8
Onslow County	1 986	150 355	30.5	26.2	6.4	14.8	33 756	12.9	6.9	48 122	58.1
Pamlico County	873	12 934	27.4	21.0	18.7	14.7	34 084	15.3	5.7	5 178	82.1
Pitt County (part)	770	78 989	24.7	21.0	8.7	35.3	37 651	16.9	5.6	31 541	61.2
Tyrrell County	1 010	4 149	44.4	22.5	16.8	10.6	25 684	23.3	6.1	1 537	74.8
Wayne County (part)	1 194	60 663	27.8	25.5	10.9	14.6	37 097	11.6	4.9	22 269	77.3
Wilson County (part)	546	37 053	22.4	23.5	13.4	22.2	43 045	9.5	3.6	14 923	72.7
Congressional District 4, North Carolina	3 246	619 432	31.2	24.6	8.0	48.0	53 847	9.2	3.7	240 099	64.1
Chatham County (part)	430	16 235	15.6	20.7	17.2	52.1	55 371	6.1	1.1	7 153	76.0
Durham County	752	223 314	51.8	22.8	9.6	40.1	43 337	13.4	5.1	89 015	54.2
Orange County	1 036	118 227	24.2	20.3	8.3	51.5	42 372	14.1	3.7	45 863	57.6
Wake County (part)	1 028	261 656	17.7	28.3	5.9	52.8	70 448	3.8	2.6	98 068	75.2
Congressional District 5, North Carolina	11 401	619 433	12.0	23.1	13.5	20.1	39 710	9.5	3.9	249 357	76.8
Alexander County	674	33 603	8.8	24.3	11.8	9.3	38 684	8.5	2.5	13 137	80.5
Alleghany County	608	10 677	7.5	19.3	19.3	11.7	29 244	17.2	4.6	4 593	79.0
Ashe County	1 104	24 384	3.7	19.9	17.9	12.1	28 824	13.5	4.6	10 411	81.0
Davie County	687	34 835	11.3	24.4	13.9	17.6	40 174	8.6	3.7	13 750	83.3
Forsyth County (part)	806	175 683	14.0	23.6	12.9	35.9	51 616	4.7	2.6	73 106	76.0
Iredell County (part)	1 060	68 486	24.8	24.9	13.5	13.6	37 942	10.0	4.9	26 441	72.9
Rockingham County (part)	263	11 160	8.7	25.3	11.1	10.6	42 846	8.3	4.1	4 237	83.9
Stokes County	1 170	44 711	7.5	24.5	11.7	9.3	38 808	9.1	5.9	17 579	82.0
Surry County	1 390	71 219	11.7	23.6	15.4	12.0	33 046	12.4	3.4	28 408	76.3
Watauga County	809	42 695	4.8	16.2	11.1	33.2	32 611	17.9	8.2	16 540	62.9
Wilkes County	1 961	65 632	8.8	22.6	14.2	11.3	34 258	11.9	3.8	26 650	77.9
Yadkin County	869	36 348	10.3	23.9	14.2	10.3	36 660	10.0	3.1	14 505	80.3
Congressional District 6, North Carolina	7 624	619 228	14.6	23.8	13.7	22.7	43 503	8.2	3.6	246 278	76.7
Alamance County (part)	921	90 976	16.3	22.9	13.9	23.7	43 084	8.6	4.4	36 180	75.4
Davidson County (part)	890	73 877	8.4	23.7	13.0	11.6	39 514	8.9	4.0	29 248	77.9
Guilford County (part)	1 248	178 594	14.7	23.7	12.2	37.6	53 919	5.5	2.9	72 626	75.3
Moore County	1 807	74 769	21.1	22.1	22.0	26.8	41 240	11.4	5.5	30 713	78.6
Randolph County	2 039	130 454	13.9	25.1	12.1	11.1	38 348	9.1	3.1	50 659	76.6
Rowan County (part)	719	70 558	13.4	25.1	12.4	11.0	38 382	8.9	3.6	26 852	79.3
Congressional District 7, North Carolina	15 766	619 603	37.0	24.5	12.7	17.8	33 998	16.7	6.7	243 322	73.1
Bladen County	2 266	32 278	44.0	24.7	14.6	11.3	26 877	21.0	5.6	12 897	77.8
Brunswick County	2 214	73 143	19.0	21.2	16.9	16.1	35 888	12.6	4.6	30 438	82.2
Columbus County	2 426	54 749	37.2	25.8	13.9	10.1	26 805	22.7	7.7	21 308	76.4
Cumberland County (part)	1 251	72 063	34.5	26.7	10.4	16.6	38 194	13.3	6.8	27 399	72.5
Duplin County (part)	1 511	34 941	51.2	26.5	13.0	10.7	28 388	20.8	8.2	13 022	74.4
New Hanover County	515	160 307	21.1	20.9	12.8	31.0	40 172	13.1	5.7	68 183	64.7
Pender County	2 255	41 082	28.4	23.2	14.0	13.6	35 902	13.6	5.7	16 054	82.6
Robeson County	2 457	123 339	69.2	29.0	9.9	11.4	28 202	22.8	9.6	43 677	72.8
Sampson County (part)	869	27 420	26.2	25.3	11.8	12.1	35 894	14.0	5.2	10 246	76.9
Scotland County (part)	1	281	10.3	23.8	4.3	53.5	67 188	3.6	4.9	98	100.0
Congressional District 8, North Carolina	8 502	618 465	38.1	26.1	10.6	18.2	38 390	12.4	6.0	233 377	66.2
Anson County	1 377	25 275	50.7	25.2	14.4	9.2	29 849	17.8	6.0	9 204	76.0
Cabarrus County (part)	843	125 451	19.5	25.9	11.8	19.0	45 747	7.2	4.3	47 474	74.0
Cumberland County (part)	175	122 872	44.2	29.2	7.6	21.2	40 462	10.0	5.9	46 347	62.6
Hoke County	1 013	33 646	58.2	29.8	7.8	10.9	33 230	17.7	7.0	11 373	75.0
Mecklenburg County (part)	110	107 178	51.9	21.9	7.9	29.9	39 979	11.4	6.7	43 151	47.1
Montgomery County	1 273	26 822	34.4	24.9	14.0	10.0	32 903	15.4	5.1	9 848	76.5
Richmond County	1 228	46 564	36.4	25.8	13.6	10.1	28 830	19.6	6.9	17 873	72.0
Scotland County (part)	826	35 717	48.9	28.2	11.1	15.6	30 848	20.7	10.0	13 301	68.9
Stanly County	1 023	58 100	16.4	24.9	14.3	12.7	36 898	10.7	4.5	22 223	76.2
Union County (part)	634	36 840	43.4	27.1	11.2	12.8	38 782	16.5	8.4	12 583	62.8
Congressional District 9, North Carolina	2 566	619 705	17.0	25.3	10.0	35.9	55 059	6.2	3.7	243 854	72.8
Gaston County (part)	700	164 160	19.0	24.6	12.6	15.1	39 568	10.9	5.7	63 941	67.6
Mecklenburg County (part)	849	368 708	17.7	24.8	9.2	47.5	62 753	4.4	3.2	149 106	72.0
Union County (part)	1 017	86 837	10.3	28.3	8.2	24.7	55 675	4.7	2.7	30 807	87.8
Congressional District 10, North Carolina	8 552	618 943	15.0	24.3	13.1	14.1	37 649	10.6	4.1	241 060	75.1
Avery County	640	17 167	7.5	19.5	15.7	14.5	30 627	15.3	7.0	6 532	80.5
Burke County	1 312	89 148	15.0	24.0	13.4	12.8	35 629	10.7	4.2	34 528	74.1
Caldwell County	1 221	77 415	9.0	23.3	13.4	10.4	35 739	10.7	3.4	30 768	74.9
Catawba County	1 036	141 685	17.7	24.3	12.2	17.0	40 536	9.1	3.3	55 533	72.6
Cleveland County	1 203	96 287	23.7	25.2	13.7	13.3	35 283	13.3	5.4	37 046	72.9

[1]Dry land or land partially or temporarily covered by water.
[2]Persons who do not identify themselves White, not of Hispanic origin.
[3]Persons 25 years old and over.

Table B. 110th Congressional Districts by Counties, 2000—*Continued*

(Number, percent.)

STATE Congressional district County	Land area,[1] (sq km)	Population Total	Population Percent minority[2]	Population Percent under 18 years	Population Percent 65 years and over	Percent with bachelor's degree or more[3]	Median household income, 1999 (dollars)	Percent living in poverty	Percent unem- ployed	Households Total	Households Percent owner occupied
	1	2	3	4	5	6	7	8	9	10	11
Congressional District 10, North Carolina—*Continued*											
Gaston County (part)	223	26 205	15.0	24.5	13.4	8.4	38 938	10.8	5.1	9 995	77.1
Iredell County (part)	430	54 174	12.2	26.3	10.8	22.2	47 757	5.8	2.8	20 919	78.4
Lincoln County	774	63 780	13.2	24.8	11.6	13.0	41 421	9.2	3.9	24 041	78.5
Mitchell County	573	15 687	3.0	21.0	18.6	12.2	30 508	13.8	4.1	6 551	80.9
Rutherford County (part)	1 139	37 395	10.8	24.3	15.3	10.8	30 615	14.5	6.3	15 147	76.9
Congressional District 11, North Carolina	15 605	619 224	10.3	21.3	17.8	20.5	34 720	12.0	5.2	257 331	75.4
Buncombe County	1 699	206 330	12.3	21.8	15.4	25.3	36 666	11.4	4.8	85 776	70.3
Cherokee County	1 179	24 298	6.1	20.6	19.8	11.0	27 992	15.3	5.5	10 336	82.1
Clay County	556	8 775	2.2	18.5	22.6	15.4	31 397	11.4	4.0	3 847	84.6
Graham County	756	7 993	9.2	21.9	18.1	11.2	26 645	19.5	5.9	3 354	82.7
Haywood County	1 434	54 033	4.1	20.8	19.1	16.0	33 922	11.5	4.6	23 100	77.3
Henderson County	969	89 173	10.3	20.8	21.7	24.1	38 109	9.7	4.6	37 414	78.8
Jackson County	1 271	33 121	14.8	19.0	14.0	25.5	32 552	15.1	10.2	13 191	72.5
McDowell County	1 144	42 151	9.2	22.9	14.2	9.0	32 396	11.6	4.5	16 604	77.2
Macon County	1 338	29 811	4.4	20.3	22.4	16.2	32 139	12.6	4.9	12 828	81.3
Madison County	1 164	19 635	3.6	21.3	15.9	16.1	30 985	15.4	5.2	8 000	76.5
Polk County	616	18 324	9.9	20.1	23.7	25.7	36 259	10.1	4.1	7 908	78.6
Rutherford County (part)	322	25 504	18.5	23.4	17.1	14.9	32 145	13.0	5.6	10 044	70.8
Swain County	1 368	12 968	32.9	24.3	15.1	13.9	28 608	18.3	10.1	5 137	76.9
Transylvania County	980	29 334	7.4	20.4	21.4	23.7	38 587	9.5	4.9	12 320	79.4
Yancey County	809	17 774	4.0	21.3	18.1	13.1	29 674	15.8	4.5	7 472	80.2
Congressional District 12, North Carolina	2 127	619 269	55.4	25.5	10.8	19.2	35 775	15.9	7.7	235 533	56.8
Cabarrus County (part)	100	5 612	8.6	27.3	8.2	21.8	57 430	4.0	2.5	2 045	89.0
Davidson County (part)	540	73 369	20.7	24.6	12.4	14.0	37 781	11.2	4.2	28 908	70.5
Forsyth County (part)	255	130 384	60.7	24.2	12.6	17.6	30 751	20.0	7.6	50 745	50.6
Guilford County (part)	223	130 551	61.2	25.8	11.2	20.7	35 193	15.9	8.7	49 588	55.8
Mecklenburg County (part)	404	219 568	68.0	26.6	7.7	21.3	37 907	16.3	8.0	81 159	52.6
Rowan County (part)	606	59 782	31.9	24.0	15.9	18.0	36 461	12.7	9.6	23 088	66.9
Congressional District 13, North Carolina	5 842	619 199	36.8	23.1	10.8	27.3	41 060	11.6	4.6	247 876	62.4
Alamance County (part)	193	39 824	53.4	26.0	14.4	8.7	30 193	16.9	6.9	15 404	57.6
Caswell County	1 100	23 501	39.2	23.3	13.1	8.3	35 018	14.4	6.5	8 670	79.4
Granville County (part)	1 193	36 745	36.6	23.5	9.4	11.5	41 384	9.5	4.0	12 142	79.2
Guilford County (part)	210	111 900	44.5	20.9	11.5	28.4	36 370	13.0	6.2	46 453	50.2
Person County	1 016	35 623	31.9	24.1	13.9	10.3	37 159	12.0	4.7	14 085	74.6
Rockingham County (part)	1 204	80 768	26.0	23.0	15.3	10.8	32 609	13.4	6.0	32 752	72.4
Wake County (part)	926	290 838	35.1	23.3	8.5	40.3	48 772	9.8	3.4	118 370	60.6
NORTH DAKOTA	178 647	642 200	8.2	25.1	14.7	22.0	34 604	11.9	4.6	257 152	66.6
Congressional District (At Large), North Dakota	178 647	642 200	8.2	25.1	14.7	22.0	34 604	11.9	4.6	257 152	66.6
Adams County	2 559	2 593	2.6	23.4	24.2	16.6	29 079	10.4	1.9	1 121	70.9
Barnes County	3 863	11 775	2.1	22.2	19.7	22.1	31 166	10.8	4.7	4 884	71.1
Benson County	3 576	6 964	48.9	36.3	13.8	10.9	26 688	29.1	13.0	2 328	68.3
Billings County	2 982	888	0.3	24.5	15.9	18.8	32 667	12.8	2.8	366	76.2
Bottineau County	4 322	7 149	2.9	22.1	21.2	14.9	29 853	10.7	4.7	2 962	80.0
Bowman County	3 010	3 242	1.0	24.0	21.9	17.9	31 906	8.2	2.1	1 358	79.5
Burke County	2 858	2 242	1.7	20.9	24.8	12.0	25 330	15.4	2.6	1 013	84.6
Burleigh County	4 230	69 416	5.1	24.8	12.5	28.7	41 309	7.8	3.5	27 670	68.0
Cass County	4 572	123 138	5.7	23.5	9.6	31.3	38 147	10.1	3.9	51 315	54.4
Cavalier County	3 855	4 831	1.2	24.4	22.9	13.1	31 868	11.5	3.8	2 017	81.5
Dickey County	2 929	5 757	2.8	23.7	21.3	16.6	29 231	14.8	3.8	2 283	71.4
Divide County	3 262	2 283	1.6	20.1	29.4	13.3	30 089	14.6	4.4	1 005	81.9
Dunn County	5 205	3 600	13.3	27.7	17.3	16.3	30 015	17.5	6.4	1 378	79.9
Eddy County	1 632	2 757	2.6	23.6	24.7	15.9	28 642	9.7	4.7	1 164	75.3
Emmons County	3 911	4 331	1.0	24.7	25.6	12.3	26 119	20.1	3.3	1 786	84.2
Foster County	1 645	3 759	1.4	26.2	21.3	19.8	32 019	9.3	3.3	1 540	74.3
Golden Valley County	2 595	1 924	2.2	28.5	21.0	19.8	29 967	15.3	3.9	761	77.8
Grand Forks County	3 724	66 109	8.2	23.8	9.7	27.8	35 785	12.3	4.4	25 435	53.7
Grant County	4 298	2 841	3.1	23.6	24.5	11.2	23 165	20.3	2.3	1 195	79.6
Griggs County	1 835	2 754	0.6	22.7	25.6	15.7	29 572	10.1	3.2	1 178	78.4
Hettinger County	2 933	2 715	1.1	23.3	25.3	14.4	29 209	14.8	4.9	1 152	84.3
Kidder County	3 499	2 753	1.5	23.3	24.1	11.0	25 389	19.8	4.9	1 158	81.9
LaMoure County	2 971	4 701	1.1	24.2	23.3	13.9	29 707	14.7	2.8	1 942	81.0
Logan County	2 571	2 308	1.4	22.9	27.1	12.9	27 986	15.1	2.9	963	85.4
McHenry County	4 854	5 987	1.4	24.0	21.7	13.2	27 274	15.8	5.1	2 526	81.5
McIntosh County	2 526	3 390	1.3	19.3	34.2	9.9	26 389	15.4	2.5	1 467	82.8
McKenzie County	7 102	5 737	22.7	30.7	15.9	15.7	29 342	17.2	6.6	2 151	73.9
McLean County	5 465	9 311	7.9	23.6	20.3	15.1	32 337	13.5	5.6	3 815	82.3
Mercer County	2 708	8 644	4.2	29.0	14.2	14.4	42 269	7.5	5.4	3 346	84.4
Morton County	4 989	25 303	4.4	27.0	14.7	17.0	37 028	9.6	3.8	9 889	75.6

[1]Dry land or land partially or temporarily covered by water.
[2]Persons who do not identify themselves White, not of Hispanic origin.
[3]Persons 25 years old and over.

Table B. 110th Congressional Districts by Counties, 2000—*Continued*

(Number, percent.)

STATE Congressional district County	Land area,[1] (sq km)	Population Total	Population Percent minority[2]	Population Percent under 18 years	Population Percent 65 years and over	Percent with bachelor's degree or more[3]	Median household income, 1999 (dollars)	Percent living in poverty	Percent unem- ployed	Households Total	Households Percent owner occupied
	1	2	3	4	5	6	7	8	9	10	11
Congressional District (At Large), North Dakota—*Continued*											
Mountrail County	4 724	6 631	34.5	28.2	17.6	15.6	27 098	19.3	5.9	2 560	72.6
Nelson County	2 542	3 715	1.5	22.3	27.5	17.5	28 892	10.3	3.3	1 628	80.3
Oliver County	1 874	2 065	2.8	27.6	14.6	12.0	36 650	14.9	5.0	791	85.6
Pembina County	2 898	8 585	5.6	24.8	19.5	16.4	36 430	9.2	4.8	3 535	78.3
Pierce County	2 636	4 675	1.5	23.8	24.0	14.7	26 524	12.5	4.1	1 964	73.1
Ramsey County	3 069	12 066	8.2	25.0	18.9	18.8	35 600	12.6	7.0	4 957	64.9
Ransom County	2 235	5 890	2.5	25.1	21.1	15.8	37 672	8.8	3.2	2 350	75.5
Renville County	2 266	2 610	3.2	23.2	21.9	16.1	30 746	11.0	1.8	1 085	77.7
Richland County	3 721	17 998	3.8	24.5	15.4	15.2	36 098	10.4	6.1	6 885	69.5
Rolette County	2 337	13 674	74.4	36.6	9.8	14.7	26 232	31.0	14.3	4 556	67.4
Sargent County	2 224	4 366	1.5	26.3	17.1	12.7	37 213	8.2	1.9	1 786	79.6
Sheridan County	2 517	1 710	1.1	21.2	26.8	9.7	24 450	21.0	7.5	731	84.8
Sioux County	2 834	4 044	83.4	40.7	5.8	11.2	22 483	39.2	23.3	1 095	46.1
Slope County	3 154	767	0.0	25.8	17.9	16.0	24 667	16.9	2.9	313	87.2
Stark County	3 466	22 636	3.1	25.5	15.5	22.3	32 526	12.3	4.9	8 932	70.3
Steele County	1 845	2 258	1.4	27.6	19.6	19.8	35 757	7.1	2.9	923	76.9
Stutsman County	5 753	21 908	2.3	22.9	17.6	19.7	33 848	10.4	3.4	8 954	67.2
Towner County	2 654	2 876	2.9	24.8	23.4	16.1	32 740	8.9	2.3	1 218	74.9
Traill County	2 232	8 477	3.1	24.9	19.2	21.8	37 445	9.2	3.2	3 341	72.4
Walsh County	3 320	12 389	7.0	24.8	19.5	13.3	33 845	10.9	6.2	5 029	76.8
Ward County	5 213	58 795	8.6	26.2	12.5	22.1	33 670	10.8	4.5	23 041	62.7
Wells County	3 293	5 102	1.5	22.5	26.0	13.7	31 894	13.5	6.0	2 215	76.5
Williams County	5 362	19 761	7.4	26.1	16.5	16.5	31 491	11.9	5.7	8 095	71.6
OHIO	106 056	11 353 140	16.0	25.4	13.3	21.1	40 956	10.6	5.0	4 445 773	69.1
Congressional District 1, Ohio	1 078	630 545	31.3	26.4	13.0	22.3	37 414	13.9	5.7	254 914	57.6
Butler County (part)	349	21 619	2.2	26.1	10.5	15.5	55 579	2.7	2.5	7 662	90.6
Hamilton County (part)	729	608 926	32.4	26.4	13.1	22.5	36 927	14.3	5.8	247 252	56.6
Congressional District 2, Ohio	6 764	630 893	8.3	26.1	12.3	29.0	46 813	8.4	4.1	247 290	71.5
Adams County	1 512	27 330	2.4	26.3	13.4	7.2	29 315	17.4	7.6	10 501	73.9
Brown County	1 274	42 285	2.3	27.6	11.6	8.8	38 303	11.6	5.3	15 555	79.5
Clermont County	1 171	177 977	3.4	27.9	9.4	20.8	49 386	7.1	3.5	66 013	74.8
Hamilton County (part)	326	236 377	15.3	24.3	14.5	44.8	52 293	5.5	3.1	99 538	67.9
Pike County	1 143	27 695	4.0	27.1	13.5	9.7	31 649	18.6	9.5	10 444	70.1
Scioto County (part)	860	44 942	5.4	23.5	17.0	10.1	25 638	21.4	9.9	18 589	64.2
Warren County (part)	478	74 287	6.5	28.4	8.9	33.5	60 218	3.9	3.1	26 650	77.2
Congressional District 3, Ohio	4 132	630 804	20.6	24.9	13.6	22.7	41 591	10.2	4.9	252 297	67.4
Clinton County	1 064	40 543	4.7	26.4	12.1	14.1	40 467	8.6	4.4	15 416	68.9
Highland County	1 433	40 875	3.4	27.0	13.7	9.7	35 313	11.8	6.1	15 587	75.3
Montgomery County (part)	1 078	465 290	26.1	24.3	14.4	24.4	40 571	11.1	5.2	191 978	64.7
Warren County (part)	557	84 096	5.9	27.1	9.9	23.9	56 080	4.5	2.9	29 316	79.8
Congressional District 4, Ohio	11 966	630 549	8.3	25.9	13.6	13.1	40 100	9.4	4.2	238 920	73.9
Allen County	1 047	108 473	15.9	25.9	14.1	13.4	37 048	12.1	5.7	40 646	72.1
Auglaize County	1 039	46 611	2.4	27.6	14.4	13.4	43 367	6.2	3.2	17 376	77.9
Champaign County	1 110	38 890	4.3	26.2	12.6	10.6	43 139	7.6	4.3	14 952	76.0
Hancock County	1 376	71 295	6.2	25.7	13.2	21.7	43 856	7.5	3.0	27 898	73.1
Hardin County	1 218	31 945	3.2	24.3	13.0	11.4	34 440	13.2	4.1	11 963	73.0
Logan County	1 187	46 005	4.7	26.6	13.9	11.5	41 479	9.3	3.7	17 956	75.6
Marion County	1 046	66 217	8.2	24.4	13.4	11.1	38 709	9.7	4.5	24 578	72.9
Morrow County	1 052	31 628	1.7	27.3	11.4	9.5	40 882	9.0	4.3	11 499	82.2
Richland County	1 287	128 852	12.2	24.8	14.1	12.6	37 397	10.6	4.8	49 534	71.6
Shelby County	1 060	47 910	4.7	28.6	12.2	12.8	44 507	6.7	3.2	17 636	74.4
Wyandot County (part)	542	12 723	3.2	25.9	15.8	8.0	38 360	6.2	2.8	4 882	74.6
Congressional District 5, Ohio	15 872	630 826	6.3	26.3	13.1	14.6	41 701	7.6	4.6	237 945	76.5
Ashland County (part)	422	11 922	1.2	29.9	10.5	8.0	43 142	9.2	3.4	4 000	88.4
Crawford County	1 041	46 966	2.9	25.0	15.2	9.7	36 227	10.4	5.2	18 957	72.5
Defiance County	1 065	39 500	10.2	26.5	12.8	14.3	44 938	5.6	3.7	15 138	79.6
Fulton County	1 054	42 084	7.3	28.2	12.8	13.2	44 074	5.4	3.3	15 480	80.1
Henry County	1 079	29 210	7.1	27.6	14.0	11.1	42 657	7.0	4.3	10 935	80.5
Huron County	1 276	59 487	6.1	28.2	12.4	10.9	40 558	8.5	5.1	22 307	72.2
Lucas County (part)	186	16 463	3.3	28.1	10.9	26.6	55 792	3.4	3.3	5 868	86.9
Mercer County (part)	671	9 603	1.6	27.1	14.1	9.2	44 138	4.7	2.7	3 414	86.5
Paulding County	1 078	20 293	4.9	26.6	12.5	7.8	40 327	7.7	3.3	7 773	83.9
Putnam County	1 253	34 726	5.2	29.6	13.3	12.9	46 426	5.6	2.9	12 200	84.1

[1] Dry land or land partially or temporarily covered by water.
[2] Persons who do not identify themselves White, not of Hispanic origin.
[3] Persons 25 years old and over.

Table B. 110th Congressional Districts by Counties, 2000—*Continued*

(Number, percent.)

STATE Congressional district County	Land area,[1] (sq km)	Population Total	Population Percent minority[2]	Population Percent under 18 years	Population Percent 65 years and over	Percent with bachelor's degree or more[3]	Median household income, 1999 (dollars)	Percent living in poverty	Percent unemployed	Households Total	Households Percent owner occupied
	1	2	3	4	5	6	7	8	9	10	11
Congressional District 5, Ohio—*Continued*											
Sandusky County (part)	1 060	61 792	10.9	26.1	14.5	11.9	40 584	7.5	4.3	23 717	75.3
Seneca County	1 426	58 683	6.4	25.9	14.1	12.5	38 037	9.0	5.1	22 292	75.1
Van Wert County	1 062	29 659	3.6	26.0	15.4	12.0	39 497	5.5	4.9	11 587	81.7
Williams County	1 092	39 188	4.8	26.2	13.9	10.7	40 735	6.0	3.4	15 105	76.8
Wood County	1 599	121 065	6.7	23.6	10.9	26.2	44 442	9.6	6.2	45 172	70.6
Wyandot County (part)	508	10 185	2.4	25.7	15.1	12.2	39 419	4.7	2.9	4 000	74.9
Congressional District 6, Ohio	13 461	630 529	4.9	23.0	15.4	14.2	32 888	14.0	6.9	246 659	75.1
Athens County (part)	939	43 279	8.7	15.7	8.5	35.1	28 157	28.8	11.2	15 059	57.0
Belmont County (part)	1 169	55 178	3.7	22.7	18.6	9.3	28 068	15.9	7.5	22 996	74.5
Columbiana County	1 379	112 075	4.6	24.4	15.0	10.8	34 226	11.5	4.9	42 973	76.0
Gallia County	1 214	31 069	5.3	25.0	13.4	11.6	30 191	18.1	9.5	12 060	74.8
Jefferson County	1 061	73 894	7.9	21.4	18.6	11.8	30 853	15.1	7.6	30 417	74.3
Lawrence County	1 178	62 319	4.2	24.4	14.4	10.3	29 127	18.9	8.5	24 732	74.8
Mahoning County (part)	825	102 901	4.0	22.7	17.7	23.4	43 504	5.5	3.9	41 202	77.8
Meigs County	1 112	23 072	3.0	23.9	14.8	7.4	27 287	19.8	10.0	9 234	79.4
Monroe County	1 180	15 180	1.7	23.5	16.2	8.4	30 467	13.9	6.8	6 021	80.7
Noble County	1 033	14 058	7.9	22.7	13.1	8.1	32 940	11.4	6.0	4 546	79.8
Scioto County (part)	726	34 253	5.7	25.5	12.2	10.1	32 463	16.4	8.1	12 282	79.1
Washington County	1 645	63 251	3.2	23.5	14.9	15.0	34 275	11.4	7.4	25 137	76.2
Congressional District 7, Ohio	7 377	630 805	11.3	25.4	11.9	18.7	43 248	8.8	4.6	236 171	71.1
Clark County	1 036	144 742	12.4	25.1	14.7	14.9	40 340	10.7	5.9	56 648	71.5
Fairfield County	1 308	122 759	5.5	26.8	11.2	20.8	47 962	5.9	3.3	45 425	76.2
Fayette County	1 053	28 433	4.8	25.3	14.3	10.7	36 735	10.1	4.9	11 054	66.6
Franklin County (part)	201	86 161	24.2	27.4	9.5	14.7	41 729	8.5	3.4	34 182	61.5
Greene County	1 075	147 886	11.6	23.8	11.7	31.1	48 656	8.5	5.2	55 312	69.6
Perry County	1 061	34 078	1.8	28.2	12.0	6.9	34 383	11.8	5.9	12 500	79.4
Pickaway County	1 300	52 727	8.3	24.1	10.8	11.4	42 832	9.5	4.1	17 599	74.6
Ross County (part)	343	14 019	17.2	19.4	6.2	9.5	46 162	9.7	3.4	3 451	83.9
Congressional District 8, Ohio	5 216	630 795	8.3	26.2	11.8	18.7	43 753	8.8	4.2	238 870	71.2
Butler County (part)	861	311 188	10.2	25.9	10.7	24.1	47 340	9.1	4.2	115 420	70.3
Darke County	1 553	53 309	2.3	26.2	15.2	10.1	39 307	8.0	4.2	20 419	76.6
Mercer County (part)	529	31 321	2.3	30.5	14.5	13.8	42 365	6.9	3.4	11 342	78.3
Miami County	1 054	98 868	4.6	25.9	13.3	16.3	44 109	6.7	3.1	38 437	72.3
Montgomery County (part)	118	93 772	14.3	26.5	10.5	14.9	37 906	12.1	6.1	37 251	64.5
Preble County	1 100	42 337	1.8	26.0	13.1	10.1	42 093	6.1	4.3	16 001	78.9
Congressional District 9, Ohio	2 853	630 711	20.4	25.6	13.7	19.8	40 265	12.0	5.7	250 985	68.4
Erie County (part)	660	79 551	12.5	24.6	15.6	16.6	42 746	8.3	4.4	31 727	72.0
Lorain County (part)	837	71 584	7.3	25.0	12.7	18.1	52 137	5.5	3.3	25 805	81.7
Lucas County (part)	695	438 591	25.4	26.1	13.2	21.1	37 376	14.3	6.4	176 979	64.6
Ottawa County (part)	660	40 985	5.5	23.2	16.4	16.0	44 224	5.9	4.1	16 474	80.7
Congressional District 10, Ohio	506	631 003	12.8	23.4	16.2	23.3	41 841	9.1	4.6	262 940	68.0
Cuyahoga County (part)	506	631 003	12.8	23.4	16.2	23.3	41 841	9.1	4.6	262 940	68.0
Congressional District 11, Ohio	348	630 668	60.9	26.2	15.4	23.4	31 998	19.5	8.8	258 965	54.2
Cuyahoga County (part)	348	630 668	60.9	26.2	15.4	23.4	31 998	19.5	8.8	258 965	54.2
Congressional District 12, Ohio	2 632	630 744	27.8	27.3	9.7	32.1	47 289	10.0	4.4	248 615	62.5
Delaware County	1 146	109 989	6.4	28.2	8.1	41.0	67 258	3.8	3.8	39 674	80.4
Franklin County (part)	482	433 332	37.9	27.4	9.5	31.4	42 432	12.5	4.9	175 836	55.7
Knox County (part)	0	0	X	X	X	X	X	X	X	0	X
Licking County (part)	1 004	87 423	5.0	25.4	12.3	24.4	50 660	5.2	3.1	33 105	77.5
Congressional District 13, Ohio	1 374	630 928	18.4	25.8	13.6	22.3	44 524	9.4	4.9	244 563	72.7
Cuyahoga County (part)	182	87 499	6.0	25.2	12.8	36.8	65 554	2.3	3.4	33 176	82.2
Lorain County (part)	438	213 080	21.0	26.6	12.5	16.1	42 702	10.2	4.7	80 031	71.7
Medina County (part)	214	50 648	3.6	27.1	8.8	20.7	59 332	4.1	3.4	17 814	84.7
Summit County (part)	540	279 701	23.1	25.2	15.5	22.5	38 582	12.0	5.9	113 542	68.6
Congressional District 14, Ohio	4 654	630 655	6.0	26.0	13.4	27.1	51 304	5.7	3.5	238 653	79.6
Ashtabula County (part)	1 819	102 728	7.1	26.1	14.6	11.1	35 607	12.1	5.1	39 397	74.1
Cuyahoga County (part)	151	44 808	9.3	27.5	14.7	52.6	79 389	2.8	2.3	16 376	88.3
Geauga County	1 045	90 895	3.0	28.3	11.9	31.7	60 200	4.6	2.8	31 630	87.3
Lake County (part)	591	227 511	5.5	24.2	14.1	21.5	48 763	5.1	3.5	89 700	77.5
Portage County (part)	265	28 047	3.5	25.3	12.9	29.3	57 946	3.9	3.3	10 208	81.8
Summit County (part)	325	124 836	7.9	26.4	11.9	38.7	61 009	3.3	3.1	47 504	79.2
Trumbull County (part)	457	11 830	2.1	32.0	10.7	10.2	40 069	12.0	4.4	3 838	83.5
Congressional District 15, Ohio	3 052	630 607	14.9	23.3	10.0	32.1	43 885	10.8	3.7	256 778	59.1
Franklin County (part)	715	549 485	16.1	22.9	10.0	34.8	43 209	11.5	3.8	228 760	57.1
Madison County	1 205	40 213	8.7	24.7	10.9	13.0	44 212	7.8	3.1	13 672	72.3
Union County	1 131	40 909	4.8	27.5	9.7	15.9	51 743	4.6	2.3	14 346	77.5

[1]Dry land or land partially or temporarily covered by water.
[2]Persons who do not identify themselves White, not of Hispanic origin.
[3]Persons 25 years old and over.
X = Not applicable.

Table B. 110th Congressional Districts by Counties, 2000—*Continued*

(Number, percent.)

STATE Congressional district County	Land area,[1] (sq km)	Population Total	Population Percent minority[2]	Population Percent under 18 years	Population Percent 65 years and over	Percent with bachelor's degree or more[3]	Median household income, 1999 (dollars)	Percent living in poverty	Percent unem- ployed	Households Total	Households Percent owner occupied
	1	2	3	4	5	6	7	8	9	10	11
Congressional District 16, Ohio	4 486	630 710	7.6	25.7	14.0	19.2	41 801	8.3	4.1	241 013	73.6
Ashland County (part)	677	40 601	3.1	24.6	15.0	18.1	38 049	9.5	4.5	15 524	72.3
Medina County (part)	878	100 447	3.8	27.7	11.4	26.8	54 097	4.8	3.3	36 728	79.5
Stark County	1 492	378 098	10.2	24.8	15.1	17.9	39 824	9.2	4.5	148 316	72.4
Wayne County	1 438	111 564	3.7	27.5	12.2	17.2	41 538	8.0	3.2	40 445	73.3
Congressional District 17, Ohio	2 604	630 316	15.5	23.8	14.8	15.8	36 705	12.3	6.0	249 550	70.1
Mahoning County (part)	250	154 654	31.3	24.3	17.8	13.3	30 177	17.3	8.2	61 385	69.5
Portage County (part)	1 010	124 014	6.3	23.3	10.5	19.0	41 602	10.5	4.8	46 241	68.9
Summit County (part)	204	138 362	13.1	23.6	13.5	18.0	37 553	11.7	5.2	56 742	65.9
Trumbull County (part)	1 140	213 286	10.8	23.9	16.0	14.7	38 214	10.2	5.8	85 182	73.8
Congressional District 18, Ohio	17 680	631 052	4.2	26.1	13.7	11.3	34 462	12.6	5.6	240 645	74.3
Athens County (part)	373	18 944	4.0	24.2	11.1	9.2	25 852	24.6	10.9	7 442	67.4
Belmont County (part)	223	15 048	12.2	18.2	17.1	17.6	36 181	9.0	5.5	5 313	77.5
Carroll County	1 022	28 836	1.9	25.2	14.1	9.1	35 509	11.4	4.3	11 126	80.0
Coshocton County	1 461	36 655	3.0	26.2	14.7	9.8	34 701	9.1	5.7	14 356	76.0
Guernsey County	1 352	40 792	4.3	26.2	14.4	10.0	30 110	16.0	6.9	16 094	73.4
Harrison County	1 045	15 856	3.5	23.0	17.7	9.0	30 318	13.3	4.7	6 398	77.5
Hocking County	1 095	28 241	2.5	25.4	13.1	9.8	34 261	13.5	5.7	10 843	75.6
Holmes County	1 096	38 943	1.7	35.6	10.5	8.3	36 944	12.9	2.3	11 337	76.9
Jackson County	1 089	32 641	3.6	26.0	13.6	11.0	30 661	16.5	7.7	12 619	73.8
Knox County (part)	1 365	54 500	2.8	24.8	13.8	16.7	38 877	10.1	6.1	19 975	75.7
Licking County (part)	775	58 068	4.8	26.9	11.2	9.3	36 764	10.8	4.8	22 504	69.9
Morgan County	1 082	14 897	6.2	25.3	15.3	9.1	28 868	18.4	8.4	5 890	78.2
Muskingum County	1 721	84 585	6.5	26.0	14.3	12.6	35 185	12.9	5.8	32 518	73.5
Ross County	1 440	59 326	6.5	25.1	13.5	11.8	35 822	12.3	5.7	23 685	72.0
Tuscarawas County	1 470	90 914	2.7	25.5	15.0	12.2	35 489	9.4	4.1	35 653	75.0
Vinton County	1 072	12 806	2.5	27.1	12.2	6.0	29 465	20.0	9.0	4 892	77.8
OKLAHOMA	177 847	3 450 654	25.9	25.8	13.2	20.3	33 400	14.7	5.3	1 342 293	68.4
Congressional District 1, Oklahoma	4 498	690 419	26.2	26.3	12.0	25.6	38 610	11.3	4.7	275 329	64.8
Creek County (part)	139	5 802	19.0	30.2	9.6	9.7	37 623	10.7	4.3	2 079	80.9
Rogers County (part)	345	14 831	17.5	29.6	9.0	19.9	53 750	6.7	3.4	5 169	87.8
Tulsa County	1 477	563 299	27.5	26.2	11.8	26.9	38 213	11.6	4.8	226 892	61.8
Wagoner County	1 458	57 491	20.9	28.1	10.1	15.4	41 744	8.9	3.7	21 010	81.0
Washington County	1 080	48 996	20.3	25.1	17.7	25.8	35 816	11.9	4.9	20 179	74.0
Congressional District 2, Oklahoma	53 258	689 974	29.8	26.0	15.2	13.2	27 885	18.5	6.5	264 390	74.3
Adair County	1 491	21 038	52.3	30.5	12.1	9.8	24 881	23.2	7.2	7 471	73.3
Atoka County	2 534	13 879	24.7	23.8	14.9	10.1	24 752	19.8	6.6	4 964	76.4
Bryan County	2 354	36 534	21.0	24.7	15.4	17.9	27 888	18.4	6.5	14 422	69.3
Cherokee County	1 945	42 521	44.6	26.2	12.1	22.1	26 536	22.9	8.2	16 175	66.8
Choctaw County	2 004	15 342	32.3	25.9	17.4	9.9	22 743	24.3	7.1	6 220	70.9
Coal County	1 342	6 031	25.5	26.6	17.8	12.4	23 705	23.1	6.9	2 373	75.3
Craig County	1 971	14 950	31.8	24.0	16.5	10.5	30 997	13.7	3.9	5 620	74.9
Delaware County	1 918	37 077	30.6	24.5	17.6	13.3	27 996	18.3	6.6	14 838	79.2
Haskell County	1 495	11 792	22.0	26.0	17.0	10.3	24 553	20.5	4.7	4 624	77.3
Hughes County	2 089	14 154	28.2	22.9	18.5	9.7	22 621	21.9	7.6	5 319	75.8
Johnston County	1 669	10 513	24.4	25.6	15.5	13.3	24 592	22.0	6.1	4 057	73.7
Latimer County	1 870	10 692	27.7	25.6	16.0	12.0	23 962	22.7	7.8	3 951	74.5
Le Flore County	4 107	48 109	21.7	26.1	13.6	11.3	27 278	19.1	6.3	17 861	75.1
McCurtain County	4 797	34 402	30.5	27.9	13.9	10.8	24 162	24.7	7.4	13 216	73.3
McIntosh County	1 606	19 456	27.8	22.6	21.6	13.1	25 964	18.2	6.6	8 085	78.9
Mayes County	1 699	38 369	28.5	26.6	14.7	12.1	31 125	14.3	5.4	14 823	77.0
Muskogee County	2 108	69 451	37.3	25.8	15.5	15.4	28 438	17.9	7.3	26 458	69.6
Nowata County	1 463	10 569	28.5	26.2	17.2	9.5	29 470	14.1	3.9	4 147	77.7
Okfuskee County	1 618	11 814	35.0	24.7	16.3	9.2	24 324	23.0	12.5	4 270	76.0
Okmulgee County	1 805	39 685	31.0	26.9	15.4	11.4	27 652	18.9	7.8	15 300	72.6
Ottawa County	1 221	33 194	26.9	25.7	16.8	12.2	27 507	16.6	6.0	12 984	73.9
Pittsburg County	3 382	43 953	23.7	23.5	17.2	12.9	28 679	17.2	7.2	17 157	76.0
Pushmataha County	3 619	11 667	23.0	26.1	18.3	12.4	22 127	23.2	6.7	4 739	77.8
Rogers County (part)	1 403	55 810	22.2	28.4	11.9	16.1	41 899	9.1	3.8	20 555	79.4
Sequoyah County	1 745	38 972	32.4	27.4	13.6	10.9	27 615	19.8	6.2	14 761	75.2
Congressional District 3, Oklahoma	88 289	689 994	19.0	25.5	14.2	18.1	32 098	15.0	5.1	263 332	72.5
Alfalfa County	2 245	6 105	10.9	19.4	20.7	14.9	30 259	13.7	2.8	2 199	81.7
Beaver County	4 699	5 857	14.8	26.7	17.0	17.6	36 715	11.7	2.6	2 245	79.1
Beckham County	2 336	19 799	15.0	24.3	15.4	15.5	27 402	18.2	6.3	7 356	71.1
Blaine County	2 405	11 976	26.5	24.0	16.6	14.0	28 356	16.9	5.3	4 159	76.9
Caddo County	3 311	30 150	36.1	28.5	14.9	14.2	27 347	21.7	8.0	10 957	73.5

[1] Dry land or land partially or temporarily covered by water.
[2] Persons who do not identify themselves White, not of Hispanic origin.
[3] Persons 25 years old and over.

Table B. 110th Congressional Districts by Counties, 2000—*Continued*

(Number, percent.)

STATE Congressional district County	Land area,[1] (sq km)	Population				Percent with bachelor's degree or more[3]	Median household income, 1999 (dollars)	Percent living in poverty	Percent unem- ployed	Households	
		Total	Percent minority[2]	Percent under 18 years	Percent 65 years and over					Total	Percent owner occupied
	1	2	3	4	5	6	7	8	9	10	11
Congressional District 3, Oklahoma—*Continued*											
Canadian County (part)	2 133	63 074	15.5	27.2	10.2	20.4	42 061	9.0	3.8	22 895	76.9
Cimarron County	4 753	3 148	17.5	27.4	18.8	17.7	30 625	17.6	2.0	1 257	72.6
Creek County (part)	2 336	61 565	18.7	27.2	13.2	11.9	32 792	13.7	4.8	23 210	77.8
Custer County	2 555	26 142	20.5	24.3	13.7	22.8	28 524	18.5	4.7	10 136	63.7
Dewey County	2 590	4 743	9.1	23.1	21.3	16.6	28 172	15.0	3.3	1 962	79.0
Ellis County	3 183	4 075	5.1	22.0	21.9	19.2	27 951	12.5	2.3	1 769	80.7
Garfield County	2 741	57 813	13.1	25.0	15.9	19.6	33 006	13.9	5.1	23 175	70.2
Grant County	2 591	5 144	4.8	25.4	21.5	16.2	28 977	13.7	2.7	2 089	78.8
Greer County	1 656	6 061	21.1	19.8	20.2	12.6	25 793	19.6	6.9	2 237	74.8
Harmon County	1 393	3 283	34.1	25.7	20.4	12.1	22 365	29.7	6.9	1 266	77.2
Harper County	2 691	3 562	7.0	23.4	21.5	19.2	33 705	10.2	1.4	1 509	78.7
Jackson County	2 079	28 439	28.2	29.2	11.9	18.5	30 737	16.2	5.2	10 590	60.3
Kay County	2 379	48 080	17.3	26.4	16.9	18.3	30 762	16.0	7.7	19 157	71.7
Kingfisher County	2 339	13 926	13.8	27.3	15.4	16.1	36 676	10.8	3.5	5 247	78.2
Kiowa County	2 628	10 227	20.0	24.0	20.3	14.8	26 053	19.3	6.0	4 208	75.2
Lincoln County	2 481	32 080	14.1	27.4	14.0	11.1	31 187	14.5	4.9	12 178	80.1
Logan County	1 928	33 924	19.8	25.4	12.0	19.1	36 784	12.9	5.7	12 389	78.4
Major County	2 478	7 545	6.5	24.6	19.3	14.4	30 949	12.0	3.3	3 046	81.0
Noble County	1 896	11 411	14.1	25.3	15.2	15.8	33 968	12.8	3.7	4 504	75.2
Osage County	5 830	44 437	34.1	26.3	13.1	14.6	34 477	13.2	5.6	16 617	80.5
Pawnee County	1 475	16 612	18.2	26.6	14.7	12.1	31 661	13.0	5.1	6 383	80.0
Payne County	1 778	68 190	16.8	19.5	10.8	34.2	28 733	20.3	4.8	26 680	55.9
Roger Mills County	2 957	3 436	10.1	23.6	18.8	15.8	30 078	16.3	2.4	1 428	78.8
Texas County	5 276	20 107	33.3	28.9	10.3	17.7	35 872	14.1	4.9	7 153	67.1
Washita County	2 599	11 508	9.5	26.1	18.6	15.1	29 563	15.5	4.0	4 506	74.7
Woods County	3 332	9 089	8.6	18.8	19.9	23.7	28 927	15.0	4.1	3 684	69.6
Woodward County	3 218	18 486	9.5	26.0	14.2	15.2	33 581	12.0	6.1	7 141	72.0
Congressional District 4, Oklahoma	26 449	690 400	22.4	25.7	12.1	20.2	35 510	13.1	5.1	262 143	69.7
Canadian County (part)	197	24 623	13.8	29.6	7.5	22.2	52 635	5.2	2.6	8 589	84.4
Carter County	2 134	45 621	23.1	26.2	16.3	15.1	29 405	16.6	5.6	17 992	71.1
Cleveland County	1 389	208 016	18.5	24.4	8.4	28.0	41 846	10.6	4.2	79 186	67.0
Comanche County	2 770	114 996	38.1	27.5	9.7	19.1	33 867	15.6	7.6	39 808	60.3
Cotton County	1 649	6 614	17.1	25.5	18.0	14.0	27 210	18.2	4.8	2 614	76.4
Garvin County	2 091	27 210	16.7	24.7	17.8	12.0	28 070	15.9	5.6	10 865	73.9
Grady County	2 851	45 516	13.9	26.6	13.0	14.4	32 625	13.9	4.8	17 341	75.7
Jefferson County	1 965	6 818	16.4	24.0	20.1	10.6	23 674	19.2	5.5	2 716	74.1
Love County	1 335	8 831	18.6	25.7	16.2	10.8	32 558	11.8	5.2	3 442	81.8
McClain County	1 475	27 740	14.6	26.6	11.9	15.7	37 275	10.5	3.7	10 331	81.3
Marshall County	961	13 184	23.7	23.5	19.4	11.4	26 437	17.9	4.2	5 371	79.2
Murray County	1 083	12 623	20.6	23.7	18.4	14.9	30 294	14.1	5.7	5 003	74.2
Oklahoma County (part)	162	60 996	26.4	26.2	12.6	19.4	39 161	10.5	4.4	23 850	67.3
Pontotoc County	1 864	35 143	25.1	24.7	14.9	21.8	26 955	16.5	6.8	13 978	67.0
Stephens County	2 264	43 182	13.7	24.5	18.4	16.6	30 709	14.6	6.5	17 463	75.6
Tillman County	2 258	9 287	30.3	27.0	19.3	12.5	24 828	21.9	4.3	3 594	77.2
Congressional District 5, Oklahoma	5 353	689 867	32.3	25.5	12.5	24.5	33 893	15.8	5.4	277 099	61.3
Oklahoma County (part)	1 674	599 452	33.6	25.4	12.2	26.0	34 621	15.7	5.3	242 984	59.7
Pottawatomie County	2 040	65 521	21.3	25.8	13.9	15.5	31 573	14.6	5.7	24 540	72.2
Seminole County	1 638	24 894	30.1	26.3	16.8	12.1	25 568	20.8	8.6	9 575	72.3
OREGON	248 631	3 421 399	16.5	24.7	12.8	25.1	40 916	11.6	6.5	1 333 723	64.2
Congressional District 1, Oregon	7 618	684 351	18.9	25.2	10.1	33.3	48 464	8.7	5.2	268 505	59.6
Clatsop County	2 143	35 630	9.4	23.6	15.5	19.1	36 301	13.2	6.6	14 703	64.2
Columbia County	1 701	43 560	6.9	27.3	11.7	14.0	45 797	9.1	6.3	16 375	76.1
Multnomah County (part)	47	74 827	14.3	13.5	12.1	55.2	38 909	14.1	6.8	39 533	40.0
Washington County	1 874	445 342	22.2	26.8	8.8	34.5	52 122	7.4	4.6	169 162	60.5
Yamhill County	1 853	84 992	15.5	26.6	11.7	20.6	44 111	9.2	6.4	28 732	69.6
Congressional District 2, Oregon	179 982	684 184	14.0	25.5	15.1	19.0	35 600	13.0	7.8	264 616	68.2
Baker County	7 946	16 741	4.9	24.3	19.2	16.4	30 367	14.7	8.3	6 883	70.0
Crook County	7 717	19 182	9.0	26.5	14.5	12.6	35 186	11.3	7.7	7 354	74.2
Deschutes County	7 817	115 367	7.1	24.7	13.0	25.0	41 847	9.3	5.2	45 595	72.3
Gilliam County	3 119	1 915	3.6	23.1	19.0	13.4	33 611	9.1	6.8	819	69.6
Grant County	11 729	7 935	5.3	25.9	16.7	15.7	32 560	13.7	11.9	3 246	73.3
Harney County	26 248	7 609	11.2	25.9	14.8	11.9	30 957	11.8	9.4	3 036	72.6
Hood River County	1 353	20 411	29.6	28.0	12.8	23.1	38 326	14.2	6.6	7 248	64.9
Jackson County	7 214	181 269	11.4	24.3	16.0	22.3	36 461	12.5	7.3	71 532	66.5
Jefferson County	4 612	19 009	35.4	29.7	12.4	13.7	35 853	14.6	8.6	6 727	71.3
Josephine County (part)	401	51 363	8.8	23.4	21.0	14.2	31 918	13.7	9.8	21 075	66.9

[1]Dry land or land partially or temporarily covered by water.
[2]Persons who do not identify themselves White, not of Hispanic origin.
[3]Persons 25 years old and over.

Table B. 110th Congressional Districts by Counties, 2000—Continued

(Number, percent.)

| STATE Congressional district County | Land area,[1] (sq km) | Population | | | | Percent with bachelor's degree or more[3] | Median household income, 1999 (dollars) | Percent living in poverty | Percent unemployed | Households | |
		Total	Percent minority[2]	Percent under 18 years	Percent 65 years and over					Total	Percent owner occupied
	1	2	3	4	5	6	7	8	9	10	11
Congressional District 2, Oregon—*Continued*											
Klamath County	15 395	63 775	16.1	25.9	14.9	15.9	31 537	16.8	10.0	25 205	68.0
Lake County	21 072	7 422	10.6	24.7	17.7	15.5	29 506	16.1	8.5	3 084	68.8
Malheur County	25 607	31 615	31.3	27.4	13.6	11.1	30 241	18.6	11.1	10 221	63.8
Morrow County	5 264	10 995	28.9	30.7	10.5	11.0	37 521	14.8	10.7	3 776	73.1
Sherman County	2 132	1 934	9.5	26.3	18.1	19.0	35 142	14.6	7.3	797	70.4
Umatilla County	8 327	70 548	22.5	27.8	12.2	16.0	36 249	12.7	7.5	25 195	64.9
Union County	5 275	24 530	6.5	24.6	14.8	21.8	33 738	13.8	7.9	9 740	66.6
Wallowa County	8 146	7 226	2.6	24.1	19.0	20.3	32 129	14.0	11.8	3 029	71.8
Wasco County	6 167	23 791	16.1	25.2	16.7	15.7	35 959	12.9	7.9	9 401	68.4
Wheeler County	4 442	1 547	5.6	22.8	23.0	14.3	28 750	15.6	7.3	653	72.1
Congressional District 3, Oregon	2 644	684 502	22.8	23.9	11.0	24.8	42 063	11.7	6.4	268 551	61.3
Clackamas County (part)	1 588	125 218	12.1	25.3	10.5	21.4	48 638	7.2	5.7	47 332	70.7
Multnomah County (part)	1 056	559 284	25.2	23.6	11.1	25.6	40 925	12.7	6.5	221 219	59.3
Congressional District 4, Oregon	44 498	684 512	10.3	23.3	15.1	21.4	35 796	13.7	6.9	275 607	65.7
Benton County (part)	1 516	49 806	13.2	24.2	11.0	45.2	41 781	12.9	4.6	20 111	59.1
Coos County	4 145	62 779	9.8	21.8	19.1	15.0	31 542	15.0	8.5	26 213	68.2
Curry County	4 215	21 137	9.0	19.0	26.9	16.4	30 117	12.2	7.3	9 543	72.9
Douglas County	13 045	100 399	8.0	23.9	17.8	13.3	33 223	13.1	7.6	39 821	71.7
Josephine County (part)	3 846	24 363	8.2	22.2	18.2	13.8	29 864	17.7	9.8	9 925	76.8
Lane County	11 795	322 959	11.4	22.8	13.3	25.5	36 942	14.4	6.4	130 453	62.3
Linn County	5 937	103 069	8.8	26.0	14.4	13.4	37 518	11.4	7.9	39 541	67.9
Congressional District 5, Oregon	13 889	683 850	16.4	25.6	12.7	27.0	44 409	10.9	6.2	256 444	66.5
Benton County (part)	236	28 347	13.5	16.4	8.7	51.9	42 088	18.0	5.3	10 034	53.6
Clackamas County (part)	3 251	213 173	10.1	26.5	11.4	32.5	54 417	6.2	4.6	80 869	71.3
Lincoln County	2 537	44 479	11.8	21.4	19.4	20.8	32 769	13.9	8.4	19 296	65.7
Marion County	3 066	284 834	23.5	27.3	12.4	19.8	40 314	13.5	7.7	101 641	62.9
Multnomah County (part)	24	26 375	13.4	19.2	9.5	58.2	62 792	6.9	3.6	11 346	69.3
Polk County	1 919	62 380	14.4	25.4	14.7	25.3	42 311	11.5	6.2	23 058	68.4
Tillamook County	2 855	24 262	8.5	22.2	19.6	17.6	34 269	11.4	4.4	10 200	71.9
PENNSYLVANIA	116 074	12 281 054	15.9	23.8	15.6	22.4	40 106	11.0	5.7	4 777 003	71.3
Congressional District 1, Pennsylvania	152	645 422	66.7	28.3	12.1	13.9	28 261	26.9	12.8	238 648	60.3
Delaware County (part)	41	75 324	73.6	29.4	12.8	11.7	31 387	19.8	12.1	26 986	56.0
Philadelphia County (part)	111	570 098	65.8	28.2	12.0	14.2	27 752	27.8	12.9	211 662	60.9
Congressional District 2, Pennsylvania	152	647 350	70.1	24.2	13.9	24.2	30 646	23.8	11.7	259 903	53.4
Montgomery County (part)	23	36 875	34.6	22.7	18.6	49.2	61 713	5.1	7.4	14 346	64.5
Philadelphia County (part)	129	610 475	72.2	24.3	13.6	22.5	29 446	24.9	12.0	245 557	52.8
Congressional District 3, Pennsylvania	10 280	646 332	6.3	24.3	15.4	18.0	35 884	11.6	5.7	247 374	73.5
Armstrong County (part)	1 131	32 386	1.2	23.7	17.0	10.2	32 311	11.4	6.8	12 487	82.5
Butler County (part)	1 613	112 716	2.5	23.1	15.5	16.8	37 056	11.5	5.2	43 189	75.5
Crawford County (part)	2 419	80 015	3.8	24.4	15.3	15.0	34 225	12.4	5.9	30 633	76.6
Erie County	2 077	280 843	10.2	25.0	14.3	20.9	36 627	12.0	5.8	106 507	69.2
Mercer County (part)	1 639	105 658	5.0	23.4	17.4	17.9	35 488	10.6	5.7	40 581	76.7
Venango County (part)	419	6 495	1.9	23.7	16.5	10.5	32 602	12.4	7.4	2 564	81.5
Warren County (part)	981	28 219	1.3	24.8	16.4	15.8	35 449	10.4	4.9	11 413	74.8
Congressional District 4, Pennsylvania	3 373	646 555	5.8	23.9	17.3	27.1	43 547	7.5	4.4	254 233	78.4
Allegheny County (part)	745	274 460	4.4	24.1	16.7	36.2	50 852	5.1	3.5	107 952	80.2
Beaver County (part)	1 065	179 197	8.0	22.6	18.6	15.8	36 880	9.4	5.4	71 783	74.7
Butler County (part)	429	61 367	2.6	27.4	12.1	35.7	54 578	4.8	3.0	22 673	82.1
Lawrence County	934	94 643	5.5	23.1	19.3	15.1	33 152	12.1	6.1	37 091	77.3
Mercer County (part)	101	14 635	24.0	23.3	22.7	13.0	30 193	17.9	8.5	6 131	73.2
Westmoreland County (part)	99	22 253	4.8	24.8	15.5	42.5	58 101	3.5	2.3	8 603	86.4
Congressional District 5, Pennsylvania	28 598	646 326	3.9	22.2	15.4	16.9	33 254	13.5	5.8	250 231	72.9
Cameron County	1 029	5 974	1.0	24.6	19.9	12.1	32 212	9.4	6.3	2 465	75.0
Centre County (part)	2 868	135 758	9.2	17.9	10.3	36.3	36 165	18.8	5.5	49 323	60.2
Clarion County	1 560	41 765	2.1	21.7	15.2	15.3	30 770	15.4	6.6	16 052	72.2
Clearfield County (part)	2 506	75 339	3.2	22.6	17.0	11.6	31 737	12.3	6.8	29 659	78.5
Clinton County	2 307	37 914	2.0	21.5	16.7	13.4	31 064	14.2	5.8	14 773	73.0
Crawford County (part)	204	10 351	1.5	26.7	17.3	12.5	28 427	15.3	6.7	4 045	66.7
Elk County	2 146	35 112	1.4	24.0	17.3	12.3	37 550	7.0	4.5	14 124	79.4
Forest County	1 109	4 946	5.0	22.8	19.5	8.9	27 581	16.4	7.1	2 000	82.6
Jefferson County	1 698	45 932	1.6	23.6	17.9	11.7	31 722	11.8	6.7	18 375	77.2
Juniata County (part)	103	3 253	0.2	25.5	14.2	9.6	30 653	9.5	2.5	1 218	76.4
Lycoming County (part)	1 692	47 222	3.5	23.5	15.8	12.9	36 673	8.1	3.9	18 112	77.4
McKean County	2 542	45 936	4.5	23.8	16.7	14.0	33 040	13.1	6.0	18 024	74.8
Mifflin County (part)	550	30 804	2.0	23.3	16.9	10.5	31 773	12.6	4.7	12 728	70.4
Potter County	2 800	18 080	2.5	25.9	16.6	12.3	32 253	12.7	6.2	7 005	77.4
Tioga County (part)	2 848	41 226	2.3	23.7	16.0	14.2	32 033	13.5	6.0	15 862	76.1
Venango County (part)	1 330	51 070	2.6	24.3	16.8	13.4	32 221	13.5	7.2	20 183	75.8
Warren County (part)	1 307	15 644	1.4	22.8	17.1	11.3	37 435	8.9	5.4	6 283	84.5

[1]Dry land or land partially or temporarily covered by water.
[2]Persons who do not identify themselves White, not of Hispanic origin.
[3]Persons 25 years old and over.

Table B. 110th Congressional Districts by Counties, 2000—*Continued*

(Number, percent.)

STATE Congressional district County	Land area,[1] (sq km)	Population				Percent with bachelor's degree or more[3]	Median household income, 1999 (dollars)	Percent living in poverty	Percent unem- ployed	Households	
		Total	Percent minority[2]	Percent under 18 years	Percent 65 years and over					Total	Percent owner occupied
	1	2	3	4	5	6	7	8	9	10	11
Congressional District 6, Pennsylvania	2 107	645 741	13.6	24.5	14.0	34.2	55 611	6.1	5.0	245 016	73.7
Berks County (part)	804	207 176	10.6	23.3	16.3	21.2	46 446	7.0	4.8	80 230	74.3
Chester County (part)	1 004	243 416	11.9	26.7	11.6	40.6	64 453	4.8	3.3	90 293	77.0
Lehigh County (part)	19	2 187	5.9	24.5	10.6	36.2	59 479	1.4	3.8	819	83.4
Montgomery County (part)	280	192 962	19.1	23.1	14.6	39.9	58 274	6.7	7.2	73 674	68.8
Congressional District 7, Pennsylvania	751	646 355	11.6	23.8	15.4	36.1	56 126	5.4	3.6	246 445	74.3
Chester County (part)	163	74 697	7.7	24.6	14.2	54.7	73 989	3.3	2.9	28 832	78.1
Delaware County (part)	436	475 540	12.0	24.0	16.0	32.7	52 554	6.1	3.9	179 334	74.3
Montgomery County (part)	153	96 118	12.3	22.2	13.2	37.9	60 392	3.5	2.9	38 279	71.3
Congressional District 8, Pennsylvania	1 603	644 798	9.1	25.5	12.6	30.7	59 207	4.5	3.5	236 264	77.5
Bucks County	1 573	597 635	8.8	25.7	12.4	31.2	59 727	4.5	3.5	218 725	77.3
Lehigh County (part)	0	0	X	X	X	X	X	X	X	0	X
Montgomery County (part)	13	16 348	19.9	24.2	15.7	37.9	57 652	5.3	3.3	6 354	74.3
Philadelphia County (part)	17	30 815	9.8	22.9	13.7	16.8	52 280	4.4	4.1	11 185	82.4
Congressional District 9, Pennsylvania	18 543	647 032	3.6	23.6	15.9	13.0	34 910	11.1	5.3	250 103	76.6
Bedford County	2 628	49 984	1.6	23.6	16.4	10.2	32 731	10.3	5.7	19 768	80.2
Blair County	1 362	129 144	2.7	22.7	17.3	13.9	32 861	12.6	6.2	51 518	72.9
Cambria County (part)	549	21 696	4.5	21.4	16.7	9.6	28 678	12.8	11.3	7 751	81.0
Clearfield County (part)	466	8 043	0.9	23.9	16.3	6.7	28 272	14.7	8.1	3 126	85.4
Cumberland County (part)	820	40 574	3.9	26.4	11.7	18.7	46 523	5.5	2.4	14 904	82.4
Fayette County (part)	1 028	33 777	1.7	23.7	15.4	9.9	29 408	17.1	7.7	13 040	77.2
Franklin County (part)	1 999	129 313	5.6	24.0	16.0	14.8	40 476	7.6	3.7	50 633	74.0
Fulton County	1 133	14 261	1.8	24.5	14.5	9.3	34 882	10.8	3.9	5 660	79.0
Huntingdon County	2 264	45 586	7.1	21.6	14.9	11.9	33 313	11.3	5.6	16 759	77.6
Indiana County (part)	1 885	66 964	2.6	23.2	15.9	15.1	30 929	14.5	7.1	26 391	75.4
Juniata County (part)	911	19 568	3.0	24.9	15.3	8.7	35 362	9.4	3.7	7 366	77.9
Mifflin County (part)	517	15 682	1.0	27.5	17.2	11.7	33 565	12.4	2.8	5 685	82.3
Perry County (part)	901	21 824	1.9	25.7	12.4	11.4	41 866	7.8	3.3	8 385	81.3
Somerset County (part)	2 055	50 055	4.3	22.5	17.1	10.8	31 089	12.8	5.5	19 027	77.1
Westmoreland County (part)	26	561	28.7	23.0	4.6	23.0	29 107	2.1	0.0	90	92.2
Congressional District 10, Pennsylvania	16 985	646 627	4.4	23.5	16.6	17.1	35 996	10.3	5.2	250 693	75.7
Bradford County	2 980	62 761	2.2	25.5	15.7	14.8	35 038	11.8	5.5	24 453	75.5
Centre County (part)	0	0	X	X	X	X	X	X	X	0	X
Lackawanna County (part)	1 018	85 019	2.1	23.5	17.1	24.1	40 077	7.3	4.3	33 155	79.0
Luzerne County (part)	553	63 018	1.6	21.6	18.9	24.3	39 615	8.0	4.3	25 645	75.1
Lycoming County (part)	1 507	72 822	8.3	23.0	16.1	16.5	32 140	13.8	7.8	28 891	64.5
Montour County	339	18 236	3.4	24.4	17.1	22.1	38 075	8.7	7.2	7 085	72.8
Northumberland County	1 191	94 556	3.5	21.8	19.1	11.1	31 314	11.9	5.2	38 835	73.6
Pike County	1 416	46 302	10.1	26.5	15.1	19.0	44 608	6.9	5.4	17 433	84.8
Snyder County	858	37 546	2.4	24.0	14.0	12.5	35 981	9.9	3.8	13 654	76.5
Sullivan County	1 165	6 556	4.9	20.8	21.8	12.8	30 279	14.5	8.9	2 660	80.4
Susquehanna County	2 131	42 238	1.9	25.5	15.6	13.2	33 622	12.3	4.3	16 529	79.5
Tioga County (part)	89	147	2.7	21.1	16.3	15.5	27 500	15.6	13.6	63	93.7
Union County	820	41 624	12.4	20.0	13.4	18.0	40 336	8.8	3.9	13 178	73.4
Wayne County	1 889	47 722	4.1	24.1	17.5	14.6	34 082	11.3	5.7	18 350	80.5
Wyoming County	1 029	28 080	2.0	25.3	13.3	15.4	36 365	10.2	4.9	10 762	79.0
Congressional District 11, Pennsylvania	5 744	646 148	6.6	22.2	17.9	15.9	34 979	11.3	6.1	256 175	70.2
Carbon County	987	58 802	3.0	22.1	18.5	11.0	35 113	9.5	5.5	23 701	78.2
Columbia County	1 258	64 151	2.7	20.8	15.9	15.8	34 094	13.1	7.3	24 915	72.2
Lackawanna County (part)	170	128 276	5.1	20.6	21.1	16.6	30 867	12.7	6.0	53 063	60.5
Luzerne County (part)	1 754	256 232	4.8	20.9	19.8	14.4	32 348	11.9	5.7	105 042	69.1
Lycoming County (part)	0	0	X	X	X	X	X	X	X	0	X
Monroe County	1 576	138 687	15.0	26.6	12.2	20.5	46 257	9.0	6.6	49 454	78.3
Congressional District 12, Pennsylvania	7 127	646 419	5.0	21.3	19.1	13.7	30 612	13.6	7.4	262 370	73.4
Allegheny County (part)	17	6 586	5.5	22.4	16.4	11.8	27 634	15.7	6.6	2 847	62.1
Armstrong County (part)	563	40 006	2.8	22.2	18.8	10.6	31 020	11.9	5.7	16 518	73.4
Cambria County (part)	1 233	130 902	4.7	20.9	20.2	14.4	30 377	12.4	8.4	52 780	73.8
Fayette County (part)	1 019	114 867	6.0	22.4	19.0	11.9	26 911	18.3	8.4	46 929	72.0
Greene County	1 491	40 672	5.8	22.0	15.2	12.2	30 352	15.9	9.2	15 060	74.1
Indiana County (part)	263	22 641	6.1	14.6	11.9	24.6	27 096	27.0	11.1	7 732	59.4
Somerset County (part)	729	29 968	1.0	22.2	19.7	10.8	30 607	10.2	6.1	12 195	79.5
Washington County (part)	644	103 114	6.9	20.4	19.8	14.5	31 624	12.7	6.8	42 924	71.1
Westmoreland County (part)	1 169	157 663	4.4	21.7	20.0	14.6	33 271	10.4	5.9	65 385	76.3
Congressional District 13, Pennsylvania	660	647 976	14.3	23.3	17.2	28.6	49 319	7.1	4.6	251 044	72.3
Montgomery County (part)	567	341 814	11.9	24.7	15.5	40.4	63 467	3.3	3.3	129 377	76.9
Philadelphia County (part)	93	306 162	17.1	21.8	19.2	15.6	37 196	11.5	6.2	121 667	67.4
Congressional District 14, Pennsylvania	419	645 809	27.0	20.9	18.0	21.4	30 139	17.1	8.4	280 228	57.9
Allegheny County (part)	419	645 809	27.0	20.9	18.0	21.4	30 139	17.1	8.4	280 228	57.9

[1]Dry land or land partially or temporarily covered by water.
[2]Persons who do not identify themselves White, not of Hispanic origin.
[3]Persons 25 years old and over.
X = Not applicable.

Table B. 110th Congressional Districts by Counties, 2000—*Continued*

(Number, percent.)

STATE Congressional district County	Land area,[1] (sq km)	Population Total	Population Percent minority[2]	Population Percent under 18 years	Population Percent 65 years and over	Percent with bachelor's degree or more[3]	Median household income, 1999 (dollars)	Percent living in poverty	Percent unemployed	Households Total	Households Percent owner occupied
	1	2	3	4	5	6	7	8	9	10	11
Congressional District 15, Pennsylvania	2 189	646 544	13.6	24.0	15.5	22.2	45 330	8.2	4.4	248 049	71.6
Berks County (part)	126	3 595	1.3	25.9	11.9	20.1	46 650	6.3	2.4	1 353	85.1
Lehigh County (part)	879	309 903	16.8	23.8	15.9	23.2	43 312	9.3	4.4	121 087	68.7
Montgomery County (part)	215	65 980	6.4	27.0	13.1	21.9	54 796	4.6	3.5	24 068	77.9
Northampton County	968	267 066	11.9	23.3	15.7	21.2	45 234	7.9	4.6	101 541	73.3
Congressional District 16, Pennsylvania	3 341	646 602	15.4	26.9	13.2	22.8	45 934	9.4	3.7	233 454	69.9
Berks County (part)	92	60 556	49.0	30.5	12.3	12.6	28 918	24.9	8.6	22 114	56.5
Chester County (part)	791	115 388	17.7	26.1	10.5	37.7	61 123	7.5	4.6	38 780	73.3
Lancaster County	2 458	470 658	10.6	26.6	14.0	20.5	45 507	7.8	3.0	172 560	70.9
Congressional District 17, Pennsylvania	6 048	646 550	12.5	23.3	16.0	17.4	40 473	8.4	4.6	255 934	72.7
Berks County (part)	1 202	102 311	4.2	23.9	15.0	16.2	49 989	5.0	4.0	37 873	83.0
Dauphin County	1 360	251 798	24.3	24.3	14.2	23.5	41 507	9.7	4.5	102 670	65.4
Lebanon County	937	120 327	7.6	23.7	16.4	15.4	40 838	7.5	4.0	46 551	72.7
Perry County (part)	532	21 778	1.8	25.4	12.1	11.3	41 945	7.5	4.2	8 310	77.9
Schuylkill County	2 016	150 336	3.9	20.8	19.9	10.7	32 699	9.5	5.9	60 530	77.9
Congressional District 18, Pennsylvania	3 708	646 325	4.6	22.3	17.6	29.3	44 938	6.3	4.3	260 857	77.3
Allegheny County (part)	711	354 811	5.9	22.0	18.3	34.7	48 174	5.3	4.2	146 123	74.9
Beaver County (part)	60	2 215	3.3	24.9	9.5	14.0	47 500	3.4	5.2	793	92.3
Washington County (part)	1 576	99 783	3.2	24.0	16.0	23.3	45 604	6.9	3.8	38 206	83.9
Westmoreland County (part)	1 362	189 516	2.9	21.8	17.3	22.3	38 934	7.7	4.9	75 735	78.5
Congressional District 19, Pennsylvania	4 294	646 143	7.8	23.7	14.1	21.3	45 345	6.8	3.6	249 982	74.8
Adams County	1 347	91 292	6.3	24.8	13.9	16.7	42 704	7.1	4.2	33 652	76.8
Cumberland County (part)	605	173 100	7.2	20.9	15.7	30.0	46 754	6.8	3.4	68 111	71.0
Franklin County (part)	0	0	X	X	X	X	X	X	X	0	X
York County	2 343	381 751	8.4	24.6	13.5	18.4	45 268	6.7	3.6	148 219	76.1
RHODE ISLAND	2 706	1 048 319	18.1	23.6	14.6	25.6	42 090	11.9	5.6	408 424	60.0
Congressional District 1, Rhode Island	841	524 189	17.4	22.7	15.4	26.0	40 616	11.9	5.5	208 498	55.7
Bristol County	64	50 648	3.9	22.9	16.8	34.3	50 737	6.3	4.8	19 033	71.2
Newport County	269	85 433	9.8	22.5	14.4	38.3	50 448	7.1	5.3	35 228	61.6
Providence County (part)	508	388 108	20.8	22.7	15.5	22.1	37 605	13.8	5.7	154 237	52.4
Congressional District 2, Rhode Island	1 865	524 130	18.8	24.5	13.7	25.2	44 129	11.9	5.7	199 926	64.6
Kent County	441	167 090	5.3	23.1	15.2	24.8	47 617	6.6	4.3	67 320	71.6
Providence County (part)	563	233 494	35.1	26.3	13.3	19.8	35 761	18.3	7.2	85 699	54.5
Washington County	862	123 546	6.1	23.2	12.7	35.5	53 103	7.3	5.1	46 907	72.9
SOUTH CAROLINA	77 983	4 012 012	33.8	25.2	12.1	20.4	37 082	14.1	5.9	1 533 854	72.2
Congressional District 1, South Carolina	6 849	668 462	26.2	24.0	11.8	25.4	40 713	11.5	4.6	263 896	69.4
Berkeley County (part)	809	111 447	27.5	28.0	7.0	15.7	41 826	9.7	4.3	38 978	70.3
Charleston County (part)	1 719	246 044	30.1	22.8	11.7	35.3	42 057	12.5	4.8	100 123	63.8
Dorchester County (part)	309	76 935	24.2	29.7	8.1	24.6	46 901	8.0	4.4	27 849	72.4
Georgetown County (part)	1 076	37 407	32.8	22.6	17.6	25.3	40 056	13.9	5.5	15 146	79.5
Horry County	2 936	196 629	20.1	21.3	15.0	18.7	36 470	12.0	4.6	81 800	73.0
Congressional District 2, South Carolina	12 347	668 374	31.8	25.2	11.2	28.5	42 915	11.0	4.3	254 578	73.4
Aiken County (part)	1 238	26 928	27.7	27.5	10.9	15.7	36 023	13.7	5.7	10 272	81.7
Allendale County	1 057	11 211	73.1	26.4	12.8	9.3	20 898	34.5	10.2	3 915	72.5
Barnwell County	1 420	23 478	45.1	28.2	12.6	11.6	28 591	20.9	7.7	9 021	75.5
Beaufort County	1 520	120 937	32.4	23.1	15.6	33.2	46 992	10.7	4.3	45 532	73.3
Calhoun County (part)	419	6 827	42.0	26.0	9.6	11.1	35 013	13.6	5.6	2 657	88.4
Hampton County	1 450	21 386	58.8	27.7	12.0	10.1	28 771	21.8	6.1	7 444	78.1
Jasper County	1 699	20 678	59.0	26.8	10.9	8.7	30 727	20.7	3.9	7 042	77.8
Lexington County	1 811	216 014	16.9	26.0	10.2	24.6	44 659	9.0	3.7	83 240	77.2
Orangeburg County (part)	766	22 370	44.2	27.1	12.0	20.9	36 616	13.4	5.6	8 520	85.4
Richland County (part)	967	198 545	36.9	24.3	9.4	40.2	46 780	8.2	3.8	76 935	65.4
Congressional District 3, South Carolina	13 966	668 657	24.0	24.3	13.4	17.1	36 092	13.3	5.4	258 800	75.5
Abbeville County	1 316	26 167	31.8	25.2	14.9	12.8	32 635	13.7	5.1	10 131	80.4
Aiken County (part)	1 541	115 624	30.0	25.8	13.3	20.9	38 396	13.9	5.9	45 315	74.3
Anderson County	1 860	165 740	19.1	24.6	13.7	15.9	36 807	12.0	4.3	65 649	76.3
Edgefield County	1 300	24 595	44.4	24.0	10.8	12.5	35 146	15.5	6.4	8 270	80.4
Greenwood County	1 180	66 271	35.9	25.4	13.8	18.9	34 702	14.2	6.3	25 729	69.3
Laurens County (part)	1 760	64 149	29.4	24.7	13.6	12.1	33 333	14.7	7.2	24 432	76.7
McCormick County	931	9 958	55.3	19.4	16.4	16.0	31 577	17.9	5.8	3 558	81.1
Oconee County	1 620	66 215	11.9	22.8	15.5	18.2	36 666	10.8	4.3	27 283	78.4
Pickens County	1 287	110 757	10.6	22.3	11.3	19.1	36 214	13.7	5.4	41 306	73.4
Saluda County	1 172	19 181	37.6	24.9	14.6	11.9	35 774	15.6	5.0	7 127	80.6
Congressional District 4, South Carolina	5 570	668 706	25.3	24.7	12.2	22.3	39 417	11.4	5.1	261 236	70.1
Greenville County	2 046	379 616	24.4	24.6	11.8	26.2	41 149	10.5	4.6	149 556	68.2
Laurens County (part)	92	5 418	24.4	33.0	6.8	6.1	39 245	10.3	6.0	1 858	86.8
Spartanburg County	2 100	253 791	26.0	24.8	12.5	18.2	37 579	12.3	5.5	97 735	72.0
Union County	1 332	29 881	32.5	23.8	15.6	9.8	31 441	14.3	7.3	12 087	76.7

[1]Dry land or land partially or temporarily covered by water.
[2]Persons who do not identify themselves White, not of Hispanic origin.
[3]Persons 25 years old and over.
X = Not applicable.

Table B. 110th Congressional Districts by Counties, 2000—*Continued*

(Number, percent.)

STATE Congressional district County	Land area,[1] (sq km)	Population				Percent with bachelor's degree or more[3]	Median household income, 1999 (dollars)	Percent living in poverty	Percent unemployed	Households	
		Total	Percent minority[2]	Percent under 18 years	Percent 65 years and over					Total	Percent owner occupied
	1	2	3	4	5	6	7	8	9	10	11
Congressional District 5, South Carolina	18 221	668 451	35.9	26.3	11.9	14.8	35 416	15.2	6.9	251 219	74.7
Cherokee County	1 017	52 537	23.8	25.9	12.4	11.8	33 787	13.9	6.2	20 495	73.9
Chester County	1 504	34 068	40.4	26.9	12.7	9.6	32 425	15.3	6.8	12 880	78.3
Chesterfield County	2 068	42 768	36.4	26.7	12.2	9.7	29 483	20.3	8.9	16 557	76.2
Darlington County	1 453	67 394	43.4	26.2	12.1	13.5	31 087	20.3	8.0	25 793	77.0
Dillon County	1 049	30 722	50.2	29.1	11.7	9.2	26 630	24.2	8.7	11 199	72.0
Fairfield County	1 778	23 454	60.9	26.2	13.2	11.7	30 376	19.6	6.9	8 774	77.5
Florence County (part)	178	12 487	55.9	25.3	13.8	21.9	35 721	16.7	7.9	4 571	70.3
Kershaw County	1 881	52 647	29.2	26.1	12.8	16.3	38 804	12.8	5.3	20 188	82.0
Lancaster County	1 422	61 351	29.4	25.4	12.3	10.2	34 688	12.8	6.4	23 178	75.2
Lee County (part)	817	17 559	62.6	25.4	12.6	9.2	26 804	20.5	8.9	5 972	79.2
Marlboro County	1 242	28 818	55.6	26.2	12.3	8.3	26 598	21.7	8.2	10 478	70.8
Newberry County	1 634	36 108	38.2	24.1	14.9	14.8	32 867	17.0	7.8	14 026	76.7
Sumter County (part)	409	43 924	43.2	28.5	10.8	22.3	37 691	12.7	6.0	16 057	64.0
York County	1 768	164 614	23.6	26.3	10.3	20.9	44 539	10.0	6.1	61 051	73.1
Congressional District 6, South Carolina	21 030	669 362	59.8	26.3	12.1	14.1	28 967	22.4	9.3	244 125	70.2
Bamberg County	1 019	16 658	63.5	25.4	14.2	15.4	24 007	27.8	11.7	6 123	74.8
Berkeley County (part)	2 034	31 204	53.6	27.7	11.3	10.2	31 662	19.2	7.9	10 944	88.0
Calhoun County (part)	566	8 358	57.6	24.2	17.3	16.6	31 188	18.4	6.1	3 260	80.9
Charleston County (part)	660	63 925	73.3	27.2	12.6	11.6	22 281	32.3	11.9	23 203	49.1
Clarendon County	1 573	32 502	55.6	25.9	14.2	11.4	27 131	23.1	6.7	11 812	79.1
Colleton County	2 736	38 264	45.1	27.3	13.0	11.5	29 733	21.1	6.4	14 470	80.2
Dorchester County (part)	1 179	19 478	52.1	25.3	12.9	9.5	31 095	16.4	6.8	6 860	85.6
Florence County (part)	1 893	113 274	40.2	26.0	11.6	18.3	35 059	16.4	7.9	42 576	73.3
Georgetown County (part)	1 034	18 390	57.5	30.4	10.3	7.4	27 743	23.4	7.9	6 513	85.4
Lee County (part)	245	2 560	85.1	27.6	11.1	9.0	27 944	29.8	16.0	914	80.1
Marion County	1 267	35 466	58.8	27.6	12.4	10.2	26 526	23.2	9.8	13 301	73.4
Orangeburg County (part)	2 099	69 212	69.3	25.6	13.6	14.7	27 355	24.1	9.6	25 598	72.4
Richland County (part)	992	122 132	73.3	24.1	10.1	18.9	29 460	23.1	11.7	43 166	54.3
Sumter County (part)	1 314	60 722	55.8	27.8	11.7	11.3	30 817	18.8	8.7	21 671	73.5
Williamsburg County	2 419	37 217	67.5	28.7	13.1	11.5	24 214	27.9	9.1	13 714	80.7
SOUTH DAKOTA	196 540	754 844	11.9	26.9	14.3	21.5	35 282	13.2	4.4	290 245	68.2
Congressional District (At Large), South Dakota	196 540	754 844	11.9	26.9	14.3	21.5	35 282	13.2	4.4	290 245	68.2
Aurora County	1 834	3 058	5.5	27.5	21.8	12.7	29 783	11.4	1.8	1 165	76.1
Beadle County	3 260	17 023	3.5	24.8	19.4	18.3	30 510	11.9	3.2	7 210	67.7
Bennett County	3 070	3 574	59.1	36.3	11.0	12.7	25 313	39.2	10.5	1 123	59.5
Bon Homme County	1 459	7 260	5.0	23.2	20.8	15.3	30 644	12.9	2.1	2 635	76.1
Brookings County	2 058	28 220	3.9	20.8	11.0	32.2	35 438	14.0	4.9	10 665	58.2
Brown County	4 437	35 460	4.6	23.6	16.1	23.6	35 017	9.9	3.5	14 638	66.3
Brule County	2 121	5 364	10.8	30.6	16.9	20.6	32 370	14.3	6.9	1 998	71.2
Buffalo County	1 219	2 032	83.3	41.7	6.3	5.4	12 692	56.9	21.7	526	43.2
Butte County	5 824	9 094	5.8	28.2	15.0	12.2	29 040	12.8	5.7	3 516	73.4
Campbell County	1 906	1 782	0.9	26.2	21.9	14.8	28 793	14.1	1.5	725	82.1
Charles Mix County	2 843	9 350	31.3	32.2	17.3	14.1	26 060	26.9	8.5	3 343	68.3
Clark County	2 481	4 143	1.4	26.9	22.2	11.4	30 208	14.8	3.0	1 598	80.7
Clay County	1 066	13 537	7.4	18.9	10.2	38.7	27 535	21.2	8.0	4 878	54.4
Codington County	1 781	25 897	3.4	26.8	14.1	18.8	36 257	9.0	3.9	10 357	70.1
Corson County	6 405	4 181	62.6	36.7	10.7	11.3	20 654	41.0	13.2	1 271	59.2
Custer County	4 034	7 275	7.1	24.1	16.4	24.4	36 303	9.4	3.3	2 970	77.0
Davison County	1 128	18 741	3.4	25.4	16.3	20.2	33 476	11.5	2.9	7 585	61.8
Day County	2 664	6 267	9.6	25.3	23.4	15.4	30 227	14.3	4.6	2 586	76.1
Deuel County	1 615	4 498	2.6	25.4	20.6	13.3	31 788	10.3	1.3	1 843	80.0
Dewey County	5 964	5 972	75.8	39.0	8.6	12.2	23 272	33.6	14.3	1 863	55.3
Douglas County	1 123	3 458	1.8	27.6	22.8	14.5	28 478	14.6	1.4	1 321	81.0
Edmunds County	2 967	4 367	0.8	26.7	22.2	15.5	32 205	13.8	2.4	1 681	82.0
Fall River County	4 506	7 453	10.8	22.8	22.3	19.2	29 631	13.6	6.9	3 127	69.5
Faulk County	2 590	2 640	1.4	26.6	22.8	13.1	30 237	18.1	1.8	1 014	81.5
Grant County	1 768	7 847	1.7	26.9	19.1	14.8	33 088	9.9	3.3	3 116	77.4
Gregory County	2 631	4 792	7.4	24.4	24.8	12.0	22 732	20.1	3.8	2 022	74.7
Haakon County	4 696	2 196	3.7	25.3	17.9	15.4	29 894	13.9	3.5	870	76.9
Hamlin County	1 313	5 540	2.3	29.7	19.2	12.8	33 851	12.1	2.6	2 048	81.8
Hand County	3 721	3 741	1.0	24.8	24.4	15.6	32 377	9.2	1.2	1 543	74.1
Hanson County	1 126	3 139	0.7	29.7	15.0	14.0	33 049	16.6	2.1	1 115	79.2
Harding County	6 917	1 353	2.5	32.7	13.5	17.8	25 000	21.1	1.6	525	73.7
Hughes County	1 919	16 481	11.1	27.7	13.6	32.0	42 970	8.0	2.7	6 512	66.2
Hutchinson County	2 105	8 075	1.5	24.8	26.2	14.1	30 026	13.0	1.9	3 190	78.8
Hyde County	2 230	1 671	6.2	25.8	22.3	16.0	31 103	12.3	1.5	679	71.6
Jackson County	4 841	2 930	50.5	36.2	12.0	16.2	23 945	36.5	15.7	945	63.6

[1]Dry land or land partially or temporarily covered by water.
[2]Persons who do not identify themselves White, not of Hispanic origin.
[3]Persons 25 years old and over.

Table B. 110th Congressional Districts by Counties, 2000—*Continued*

(Number, percent.)

STATE Congressional district County	Land area,[1] (sq km)	Population				Percent with bachelor's degree or more[3]	Median household income, 1999 (dollars)	Percent living in poverty	Percent unem- ployed	Households	
		Total	Percent minority[2]	Percent under 18 years	Percent 65 years and over					Total	Percent owner occupied
	1	2	3	4	5	6	7	8	9	10	11
Congressional District (At Large), South Dakota—*Continued*											
Jerauld County	1 372	2 295	0.5	21.4	25.5	12.3	30 690	20.6	2.5	987	72.1
Jones County	2 514	1 193	4.4	25.7	17.6	17.8	30 288	15.8	3.0	509	72.5
Kingsbury County	2 171	5 815	1.9	24.7	24.3	16.2	31 262	10.0	3.0	2 406	76.1
Lake County	1 459	11 276	3.3	23.7	16.3	21.1	34 087	9.7	3.4	4 372	70.5
Lawrence County	2 072	21 802	5.6	23.2	14.5	24.0	31 755	14.8	9.1	8 881	64.8
Lincoln County	1 497	24 131	2.6	29.7	10.3	25.5	48 338	4.4	1.8	8 782	79.7
Lyman County	4 247	3 895	34.5	32.3	13.6	15.9	28 509	24.3	9.5	1 400	68.8
McCook County	1 488	5 832	1.8	28.4	19.5	16.3	35 396	8.1	1.8	2 204	78.9
McPherson County	2 945	2 904	0.6	22.1	29.3	10.7	22 380	22.6	2.2	1 227	83.2
Marshall County	2 170	4 576	8.1	27.2	21.1	16.2	30 567	13.9	4.4	1 844	77.9
Meade County	8 989	24 253	8.2	28.3	10.5	16.8	36 992	9.4	3.9	8 805	68.2
Mellette County	3 384	2 083	55.4	35.3	12.9	16.6	23 219	35.8	11.5	694	65.0
Miner County	1 477	2 884	1.4	25.6	23.8	13.5	29 519	11.8	1.3	1 212	76.4
Minnehaha County	2 097	148 281	8.0	26.2	11.0	26.0	42 566	7.5	3.0	57 996	64.7
Moody County	1 346	6 595	15.6	29.1	15.2	17.4	35 467	9.6	3.0	2 526	72.5
Pennington County	7 190	88 565	14.5	26.6	11.7	25.0	37 485	11.5	4.5	34 641	66.2
Perkins County	7 437	3 363	3.8	23.9	23.8	14.6	27 750	16.9	3.9	1 429	76.6
Potter County	2 244	2 693	1.2	23.3	25.3	16.2	30 086	12.6	1.4	1 145	79.1
Roberts County	2 852	10 016	31.6	30.0	16.9	13.4	28 322	22.1	7.2	3 683	68.9
Sanborn County	1 474	2 675	3.4	25.6	19.2	14.8	33 375	14.9	2.3	1 043	77.7
Shannon County	5 423	12 466	95.1	45.0	4.7	12.1	20 916	52.3	33.0	2 785	49.6
Spink County	3 895	7 454	2.9	25.9	19.0	14.4	31 717	12.8	3.3	2 847	73.8
Stanley County	3 738	2 772	7.2	27.1	11.0	22.1	41 170	8.7	1.4	1 111	76.6
Sully County	2 608	1 556	2.3	25.4	17.5	16.4	32 500	12.1	2.0	630	75.9
Todd County	3 595	9 050	86.3	43.9	6.2	12.1	20 035	48.3	18.4	2 462	45.0
Tripp County	4 179	6 430	12.3	27.9	19.6	13.5	28 333	19.9	4.2	2 550	75.0
Turner County	1 598	8 849	1.1	25.7	20.6	17.0	36 059	7.2	1.7	3 510	77.4
Union County	1 192	12 584	4.6	27.0	13.5	26.3	44 790	5.5	1.9	4 927	74.5
Walworth County	1 833	5 974	13.6	24.4	21.9	15.8	27 834	18.2	6.1	2 506	71.2
Yankton County	1 351	21 652	6.0	25.7	14.6	23.0	35 374	9.6	2.4	8 187	69.1
Ziebach County	5 082	2 519	73.5	40.5	7.6	12.0	18 063	49.9	17.4	741	59.6
TENNESSEE	106 752	5 689 283	20.8	24.6	12.4	19.6	36 360	13.5	5.5	2 232 905	69.9
Congressional District 1, Tennessee	10 601	632 216	5.0	22.0	14.5	15.0	31 228	14.8	5.5	259 389	74.2
Carter County	883	56 742	2.9	21.3	15.0	12.8	27 371	16.9	5.9	23 486	74.9
Cocke County	1 125	33 565	4.7	22.9	13.6	6.2	25 553	22.5	8.8	13 762	75.5
Greene County	1 610	62 909	4.5	22.3	14.8	12.8	30 382	14.5	5.6	25 756	76.7
Hamblen County	417	58 128	11.2	23.1	13.3	13.3	32 350	14.4	4.2	23 211	72.5
Hancock County	576	6 786	3.1	23.2	15.7	10.2	19 760	29.4	5.7	2 769	78.7
Hawkins County	1 260	53 563	3.1	23.2	13.2	10.0	31 300	15.8	5.1	21 936	78.7
Jefferson County (part)	196	11 136	2.8	23.4	12.7	9.2	32 093	13.1	4.2	4 424	81.5
Johnson County	773	17 499	3.7	19.7	15.0	6.9	23 067	22.6	7.0	6 827	79.7
Sevier County (part)	1 364	53 975	3.9	22.3	13.1	13.4	33 564	11.4	6.6	21 951	70.2
Sullivan County	1 070	153 048	3.9	21.8	15.9	18.1	33 529	12.9	4.6	63 556	75.8
Unicoi County	482	17 667	3.2	20.5	18.1	10.6	29 863	13.1	6.8	7 516	76.6
Washington County	845	107 198	7.1	21.2	13.9	22.9	33 116	13.9	5.4	44 195	68.2
Congressional District 2, Tennessee	6 285	632 112	10.0	22.7	13.2	23.3	36 796	12.2	4.9	258 049	70.9
Blount County	1 447	105 823	5.8	22.8	14.1	17.9	37 862	9.7	4.5	42 667	75.9
Knox County	1 317	382 032	12.6	22.3	12.6	29.0	37 454	12.6	4.8	157 872	66.9
Loudon County	593	39 086	4.8	21.8	16.0	17.0	40 401	10.0	3.6	15 944	79.1
McMinn County	1 114	49 015	7.9	24.0	14.4	10.8	31 919	14.5	5.3	19 721	75.7
Monroe County	1 644	38 961	5.8	24.7	13.2	10.1	30 337	15.5	7.5	15 329	78.3
Sevier County (part)	170	17 195	3.3	25.1	11.0	13.9	38 924	8.4	6.2	6 516	83.9
Congressional District 3, Tennessee	8 834	632 100	14.7	23.4	13.6	18.9	35 434	13.4	5.4	253 042	70.5
Anderson County	874	71 330	7.2	23.1	16.6	20.8	35 483	13.1	5.3	29 780	72.5
Bradley County	851	87 965	7.9	23.7	11.6	15.9	35 034	12.2	5.0	34 281	68.6
Claiborne County	1 125	29 862	2.7	23.6	13.5	8.9	25 782	22.6	7.3	11 799	78.5
Grainger County	726	20 659	2.0	22.9	12.6	7.8	27 997	18.7	4.9	8 270	83.6
Hamilton County	1 405	307 896	24.4	23.2	13.8	23.9	38 930	12.1	5.5	124 444	65.9
Jefferson County (part)	513	33 158	5.7	22.7	12.9	14.1	33 140	13.5	5.8	12 731	76.7
Meigs County	505	11 086	2.3	25.0	11.7	7.0	29 354	18.3	6.3	4 304	81.9
Polk County	1 127	16 050	2.1	22.5	14.4	7.5	29 643	13.0	4.9	6 448	80.8
Rhea County	818	28 400	5.1	23.7	13.7	9.1	30 418	14.7	6.4	11 184	75.4
Roane County (part)	311	7 886	5.9	24.8	12.7	30.2	49 719	6.6	2.8	3 059	85.0
Union County	579	17 808	1.6	25.9	10.9	5.8	27 335	19.6	5.2	6 742	80.9

[1]Dry land or land partially or temporarily covered by water.
[2]Persons who do not identify themselves White, not of Hispanic origin.
[3]Persons 25 years old and over.

Table B. 110th Congressional Districts by Counties, 2000—*Continued*

(Number, percent.)

STATE Congressional district County	Land area,[1] (sq km)	Population Total	Population Percent minority[2]	Population Percent under 18 years	Population Percent 65 years and over	Percent with bachelor's degree or more[3]	Median household income, 1999 (dollars)	Percent living in poverty	Percent unemployed	Households Total	Households Percent owner occupied
	1	2	3	4	5	6	7	8	9	10	11
Congressional District 4, Tennessee	25 999	631 842	7.3	24.1	14.5	11.3	31 645	15.2	5.6	248 234	76.7
Bledsoe County	1 052	12 367	5.5	23.1	11.6	7.1	28 982	18.1	6.6	4 430	81.7
Campbell County	1 243	39 854	2.8	22.8	15.2	7.0	25 285	22.8	6.7	16 125	73.4
Coffee County	1 111	48 014	7.5	24.8	14.7	17.5	34 898	14.3	6.0	18 885	71.5
Cumberland County	1 765	46 802	2.6	21.3	20.6	13.7	30 901	14.7	5.2	19 508	80.6
Fentress County	1 291	16 625	1.1	24.2	13.6	8.3	23 238	23.1	7.3	6 693	79.1
Franklin County	1 436	39 270	8.5	23.0	15.3	15.3	36 044	13.2	5.0	15 003	78.5
Giles County	1 582	29 447	13.7	24.5	14.5	10.6	34 824	11.7	4.3	11 713	75.4
Grundy County	934	14 332	1.8	25.1	13.9	7.1	22 959	25.8	6.4	5 562	82.1
Hickman County (part)	903	12 938	4.6	25.6	14.1	6.7	29 182	15.2	5.1	5 012	77.4
Lawrence County	1 598	39 926	3.7	26.1	14.7	8.7	30 498	14.6	7.6	15 480	77.1
Lewis County	731	11 367	4.4	25.9	13.6	8.5	30 444	13.4	7.9	4 381	79.5
Lincoln County	1 477	31 340	10.1	23.8	15.5	11.9	33 434	13.6	5.6	12 503	76.2
Marion County	1 291	27 776	5.7	23.7	12.8	9.5	31 419	14.1	5.4	11 037	80.5
Maury County	1 587	69 498	18.8	26.3	12.0	13.6	41 591	10.9	4.2	26 444	72.8
Moore County	335	5 740	5.0	23.3	15.1	11.8	36 591	9.6	4.9	2 211	83.7
Morgan County	1 352	19 757	4.0	23.2	11.6	6.0	27 712	16.0	7.0	6 990	82.8
Pickett County	422	4 945	1.4	21.5	17.8	9.1	24 673	15.6	4.0	2 091	84.3
Roane County (part)	624	44 024	4.9	21.9	16.7	12.0	31 457	15.2	6.2	18 141	76.3
Scott County	1 378	21 127	1.9	26.0	11.4	7.5	24 093	20.2	7.3	8 203	76.5
Sequatchie County	689	11 370	2.2	24.5	12.2	10.2	30 959	16.5	5.1	4 463	76.2
Van Buren County	708	5 508	1.4	23.0	14.0	7.8	28 165	15.2	6.7	2 180	85.6
Warren County	1 121	38 276	9.4	24.0	14.0	9.1	30 920	16.6	4.7	15 181	72.9
White County	975	23 102	4.2	23.6	15.3	7.9	29 383	14.3	6.2	9 229	79.7
Williamson County (part)	392	18 437	15.4	25.8	12.0	22.4	44 787	10.3	3.7	6 769	75.3
Congressional District 5, Tennessee	2 315	632 173	31.7	22.9	10.8	27.9	40 419	12.2	5.0	258 235	58.1
Cheatham County (part)	430	24 333	3.9	27.9	8.2	13.5	45 281	6.9	2.8	8 695	82.2
Davidson County (part)	1 239	542 892	35.8	22.2	11.1	29.1	38 706	13.4	5.4	225 839	54.4
Wilson County (part)	646	64 948	7.9	26.8	8.5	23.1	55 135	4.7	3.0	23 701	84.8
Congressional District 6, Tennessee	14 194	632 118	10.9	25.4	10.9	16.3	39 721	11.1	4.6	238 975	73.3
Bedford County	1 227	37 586	17.2	25.7	12.7	11.1	36 729	13.1	4.4	13 905	73.5
Cannon County	688	12 826	3.5	25.5	13.6	8.4	32 809	12.8	4.6	4 998	78.5
Clay County	612	7 976	3.4	21.3	15.8	6.8	23 958	19.1	7.6	3 379	80.0
DeKalb County	789	17 423	6.3	23.3	14.1	11.3	30 359	17.0	5.2	6 984	75.0
Jackson County	800	10 984	3.2	22.2	15.0	8.4	26 502	18.1	6.3	4 466	80.8
Macon County	795	20 386	3.2	26.1	12.7	5.6	29 867	15.1	5.0	7 916	78.6
Marshall County	972	26 767	11.3	25.6	12.5	10.6	38 457	10.0	4.3	10 307	73.0
Overton County	1 122	20 118	1.9	23.1	15.0	8.3	26 915	16.0	5.5	8 110	80.8
Putnam County	1 039	62 315	6.8	22.2	13.2	20.2	30 914	16.4	5.0	24 865	65.6
Robertson County	1 234	54 433	12.6	26.8	10.8	11.9	43 174	9.0	3.4	19 906	76.5
Rutherford County	1 603	182 023	15.4	26.4	7.5	22.9	46 312	9.0	5.0	66 443	69.8
Smith County	814	17 712	5.0	25.5	13.4	9.3	35 625	12.2	4.4	6 878	78.8
Sumner County	1 371	130 449	9.4	26.2	10.6	18.6	46 030	8.1	3.7	48 941	75.5
Trousdale County	296	7 259	14.0	24.0	14.4	8.9	32 212	13.4	3.4	2 780	76.3
Wilson County (part)	832	23 861	12.8	24.8	12.8	10.1	39 461	12.0	6.5	9 097	72.7
Congressional District 7, Tennessee	16 296	632 793	16.6	27.2	9.7	29.2	50 090	8.0	3.8	229 831	79.3
Cheatham County (part)	354	11 579	4.4	27.2	9.3	18.4	47 273	8.6	2.7	4 183	86.5
Chester County	747	15 540	12.5	24.4	13.8	11.2	34 349	14.4	6.8	5 660	77.3
Davidson County (part)	62	26 999	13.4	22.3	11.2	56.1	64 508	4.7	2.1	11 566	73.4
Decatur County	865	11 731	7.0	21.6	18.1	7.3	28 741	16.0	5.2	4 908	80.1
Dickson County (part)	0	0	X	X	X	X	X	X	X	0	X
Fayette County	1 825	28 806	38.2	25.7	13.1	12.8	40 279	14.3	5.4	10 467	80.3
Hardeman County	1 729	28 105	43.3	24.0	12.7	7.8	29 111	19.7	6.6	9 412	74.1
Hardin County	1 497	25 578	5.5	23.2	16.1	9.8	27 819	18.8	5.3	10 426	77.3
Henderson County	1 347	25 522	10.0	24.3	14.2	9.3	32 057	12.4	4.5	10 306	79.2
Hickman County (part)	683	9 357	9.2	23.2	9.4	6.6	33 548	12.9	3.8	3 069	84.8
McNairy County	1 451	24 653	8.8	23.7	15.8	8.8	30 154	15.9	5.2	9 980	80.0
Montgomery County (part)	885	102 704	30.4	29.4	6.4	20.3	41 022	8.3	5.9	35 762	64.5
Perry County	1 075	7 631	3.7	24.4	16.3	7.1	28 061	15.4	5.4	3 023	85.8
Shelby County (part)	759	189 545	13.1	28.6	8.3	40.2	70 653	3.2	2.4	67 177	86.0
Wayne County	1 901	16 842	8.6	21.4	13.8	8.0	26 576	16.3	7.4	5 936	82.9
Williamson County (part)	1 117	108 201	9.2	30.1	7.0	48.2	74 256	3.8	2.4	37 956	82.6
Congressional District 8, Tennessee	21 398	632 189	25.5	25.9	13.2	12.5	33 001	15.0	6.5	242 466	70.3
Benton County	1 023	16 537	4.4	21.9	17.8	6.3	28 679	15.6	7.3	6 863	80.6
Carroll County	1 551	29 475	12.5	23.2	17.2	11.1	30 463	13.9	8.3	11 779	79.0
Crockett County	687	14 532	20.6	25.2	16.0	9.1	30 015	16.9	5.1	5 632	74.9
Dickson County (part)	1 268	43 156	6.8	26.7	11.6	11.3	39 056	10.2	4.4	16 473	76.1
Dyer County	1 322	37 279	14.9	25.7	13.4	12.0	32 788	15.9	7.6	14 751	65.6

[1] Dry land or land partially or temporarily covered by water.
[2] Persons who do not identify themselves White, not of Hispanic origin.
[3] Persons 25 years old and over.
X = Not applicable.

Table B. 110th Congressional Districts by Counties, 2000—*Continued*

(Number, percent.)

STATE Congressional district County	Land area,[1] (sq km)	Population Total	Percent minority[2]	Percent under 18 years	Percent 65 years and over	Percent with bachelor's degree or more[3]	Median household income, 1999 (dollars)	Percent living in poverty	Percent unem- ployed	Households Total	Percent owner occupied
	1	2	3	4	5	6	7	8	9	10	11
Congressional District 8, Tennessee—*Continued*											
Gibson County	1 561	48 152	21.6	24.0	17.6	10.1	31 105	12.8	5.8	19 518	72.1
Haywood County	1 381	19 797	54.1	27.0	13.8	11.1	27 671	19.5	6.8	7 558	65.9
Henry County	1 455	31 115	11.4	22.2	18.1	12.1	30 169	14.3	6.1	13 019	77.4
Houston County	519	8 088	5.3	24.3	16.7	10.3	29 968	18.1	3.7	3 216	77.0
Humphreys County	1 378	17 929	5.5	23.8	14.8	9.3	35 786	10.8	4.6	7 238	77.9
Lake County	423	7 954	33.9	18.1	13.3	5.4	21 995	23.6	8.6	2 410	60.0
Lauderdale County	1 218	27 101	36.6	24.9	11.9	7.7	29 751	19.2	6.9	9 567	65.0
Madison County	1 443	91 837	35.6	25.8	12.3	21.5	36 982	14.0	6.9	35 552	67.0
Montgomery County (part)	512	32 064	24.3	25.0	11.9	16.2	31 276	15.4	7.4	12 568	60.7
Obion County	1 411	32 450	12.7	23.4	15.2	10.3	32 764	13.3	5.3	13 182	71.5
Shelby County (part)	365	76 187	60.6	33.7	8.1	10.8	32 555	20.3	8.5	26 505	62.0
Stewart County	1 187	12 370	4.7	23.8	14.9	10.2	32 316	12.4	7.6	4 930	79.3
Tipton County	1 190	51 271	22.7	29.2	9.9	10.8	41 856	12.1	4.9	18 106	76.2
Weakley County	1 503	34 895	10.4	21.6	14.2	15.3	30 008	16.0	6.1	13 599	68.8
Congressional District 9, Tennessee	830	631 740	65.1	27.4	10.7	22.1	33 806	19.4	8.1	244 684	56.9
Shelby County (part)	830	631 740	65.1	27.4	10.7	22.1	33 806	19.4	8.1	244 684	56.9
TEXAS	678 051	20 851 820	47.6	28.2	9.9	23.2	39 927	15.4	6.1	7 393 354	63.8
Congressional District 1, Texas	22 036	651 562	29.4	26.2	14.1	17.6	33 461	16.0	6.9	245 088	71.9
Angelina County	2 076	80 130	30.6	27.5	12.5	14.7	33 806	15.8	6.0	28 685	72.4
Cass County (part)	397	3 035	14.0	27.9	16.8	11.0	31 146	14.8	4.7	1 191	88.3
Gregg County	710	111 379	31.0	26.8	13.5	19.5	35 006	15.1	6.9	42 687	64.1
Harrison County	2 328	62 110	30.8	26.9	13.1	15.4	33 520	16.7	7.4	23 087	77.2
Marion County	987	10 941	28.2	22.4	19.3	8.5	25 347	22.4	8.2	4 610	82.1
Nacogdoches County	2 452	59 203	29.8	23.9	12.0	22.8	28 301	23.3	10.7	22 006	61.5
Panola County	2 074	22 756	22.5	25.4	16.1	13.4	31 909	14.1	6.4	8 821	80.8
Rusk County	2 392	47 372	28.9	24.9	15.6	12.8	32 898	14.6	5.5	17 364	79.9
Sabine County	1 270	10 469	13.0	21.1	24.9	10.6	27 198	15.9	9.2	4 485	86.2
San Augustine County	1 367	8 946	32.4	23.7	21.3	11.8	27 025	21.2	7.0	3 575	81.6
Shelby County	2 057	25 224	30.4	26.5	16.5	12.2	29 112	19.4	5.2	9 595	78.2
Smith County	2 405	174 706	32.0	26.6	14.0	22.5	37 148	13.8	6.5	65 692	69.7
Upshur County	1 522	35 291	15.4	26.9	14.3	11.1	33 347	14.9	5.2	13 290	81.7
Congressional District 2, Texas	5 016	651 605	35.8	27.4	9.9	23.2	47 029	11.4	5.8	233 043	70.1
Harris County (part)	982	349 152	27.3	28.7	7.1	30.3	59 565	6.7	4.2	123 949	72.6
Jefferson County	2 340	252 051	48.2	25.9	13.6	16.3	34 706	17.4	8.1	92 880	65.9
Liberty County (part)	1 693	50 402	32.5	26.9	10.0	8.5	37 288	15.4	7.1	16 214	74.7
Congressional District 3, Texas	686	651 782	36.7	28.5	5.3	41.4	60 878	7.0	3.7	239 947	61.3
Collin County (part)	484	389 809	26.1	28.0	4.8	52.5	73 371	4.7	3.0	147 517	65.0
Dallas County (part)	201	261 973	52.5	29.3	6.1	23.8	45 155	10.5	4.9	92 430	55.5
Congressional District 4, Texas	24 694	651 500	20.7	26.7	13.2	18.0	38 276	12.8	4.9	241 494	74.5
Bowie County	2 300	89 306	29.7	24.9	14.0	16.1	33 001	17.7	6.9	33 058	70.9
Camp County	512	11 549	35.1	26.7	15.6	12.2	31 164	20.9	6.0	4 336	74.8
Cass County (part)	2 031	27 403	23.6	24.5	17.8	12.1	28 073	18.0	5.8	10 999	77.6
Collin County (part)	1 711	101 866	15.5	31.1	6.6	26.7	61 578	5.4	2.9	34 453	84.3
Delta County	718	5 327	13.5	25.5	17.9	13.9	29 094	17.6	5.6	2 094	77.1
Fannin County	2 309	31 242	15.6	23.3	16.0	12.6	34 501	13.9	5.2	11 105	74.7
Franklin County	740	9 458	14.0	24.5	18.3	16.2	31 955	15.6	4.5	3 754	79.0
Grayson County	2 418	110 595	15.7	25.2	15.1	17.2	37 178	11.3	4.7	42 849	70.5
Hopkins County	2 026	31 960	18.7	26.2	15.1	15.1	32 136	14.6	4.8	12 286	71.4
Hunt County	2 179	76 596	20.1	26.5	12.7	16.8	36 752	12.8	5.8	28 742	71.4
Lamar County	2 375	48 499	19.2	26.1	15.8	14.5	31 609	16.4	5.6	19 077	67.2
Morris County	659	13 048	29.6	25.0	18.6	11.2	29 011	18.3	6.5	5 215	77.8
Rains County	601	9 139	10.1	23.9	16.3	11.5	33 712	14.9	6.1	3 617	82.7
Red River County	2 720	14 314	24.2	23.9	19.5	9.0	27 558	17.3	5.9	5 827	75.0
Rockwall County	334	43 080	17.2	30.1	8.4	32.7	65 164	4.7	1.8	14 530	82.7
Titus County	1 063	28 118	40.0	30.4	12.5	13.2	32 452	18.5	5.9	9 552	72.4
Congressional District 5, Texas	14 061	651 919	28.5	26.5	12.0	18.6	41 007	11.0	5.1	237 891	70.7
Anderson County	2 773	55 109	36.8	20.6	11.5	11.1	31 957	16.5	7.5	15 678	73.9
Cherokee County	2 725	46 659	30.6	26.3	15.1	11.4	29 313	17.9	5.6	16 651	73.8
Dallas County (part)	381	320 669	35.1	28.2	8.7	25.7	48 493	7.8	4.2	119 613	63.0
Henderson County	2 264	73 277	15.2	24.4	18.2	12.1	32 533	15.1	6.5	28 804	80.0
Kaufman County	2 036	71 313	23.7	29.0	10.7	12.3	44 783	10.5	4.5	24 367	79.2
Van Zandt County	2 198	48 140	11.6	25.5	17.1	11.6	35 029	13.3	5.9	18 195	80.9
Wood County	1 684	36 752	13.3	21.9	20.9	14.5	32 885	14.3	8.4	14 583	81.4

[1]Dry land or land partially or temporarily covered by water.
[2]Persons who do not identify themselves White, not of Hispanic origin.
[3]Persons 25 years old and over.

Table B. 110th Congressional Districts by Counties, 2000—*Continued*

(Number, percent.)

STATE Congressional district County	Land area,[1] (sq km)	Population Total	Population Percent minority[2]	Population Percent under 18 years	Population Percent 65 years and over	Percent with bachelor's degree or more[3]	Median household income, 1999 (dollars)	Percent living in poverty	Percent unem- ployed	Households Total	Households Percent owner occupied
	1	2	3	4	5	6	7	8	9	10	11
Congressional District 6, Texas	16 053	651 691	34.0	28.2	8.9	24.4	45 857	10.4	4.6	237 167	64.9
Ellis County	2 434	111 360	28.5	30.1	9.2	17.1	50 350	8.6	5.2	37 020	76.2
Freestone County	2 273	17 867	28.2	23.3	16.4	10.9	31 283	14.2	4.2	6 588	78.6
Houston County	3 188	23 185	36.3	23.2	17.7	12.2	28 119	21.0	6.1	8 259	76.1
Leon County	2 777	15 335	18.8	24.2	20.2	12.1	30 981	15.6	5.4	6 189	82.8
Limestone County (part)	735	11 879	36.3	25.9	16.4	12.4	29 288	18.1	6.6	4 364	73.9
Navarro County	2 610	45 124	34.2	27.6	14.5	12.2	31 268	18.2	7.8	16 491	70.7
Tarrant County (part)	608	421 674	36.2	28.4	6.7	30.1	49 346	8.9	4.1	156 085	59.1
Trinity County (part)	1 430	5 267	15.3	24.5	19.8	8.1	24 220	19.6	5.5	2 171	83.6
Congressional District 7, Texas	512	651 682	32.6	23.5	9.2	50.0	57 846	7.4	3.8	277 148	55.1
Harris County (part)	512	651 682	32.6	23.5	9.2	50.0	57 846	7.4	3.8	277 148	55.1
Congressional District 8, Texas	21 108	651 755	20.1	26.8	11.4	17.7	40 459	12.6	6.0	232 204	78.4
Hardin County	2 316	48 073	11.1	27.7	12.2	13.0	37 612	11.2	5.7	17 805	82.5
Jasper County	2 428	35 604	23.5	26.5	15.7	10.5	30 902	18.1	7.2	13 450	80.6
Liberty County (part)	1 310	19 752	7.0	29.2	11.0	7.0	40 712	11.8	6.4	7 028	89.0
Montgomery County	2 704	293 768	18.8	29.3	8.7	25.3	50 864	9.4	4.5	103 296	78.2
Newton County	2 416	15 072	25.8	26.2	14.1	5.5	28 500	19.1	10.5	5 583	84.5
Orange County	923	84 966	14.2	27.2	12.6	11.0	37 586	13.8	7.9	31 642	77.2
Polk County	2 738	41 133	25.4	22.7	18.0	10.4	30 495	17.4	6.7	15 119	81.6
San Jacinto County	1 478	22 246	19.1	25.4	16.0	9.6	32 220	18.8	7.5	8 651	87.9
Trinity County (part)	364	8 512	19.5	21.9	23.4	10.2	28 438	16.4	7.5	3 552	79.0
Tyler County	2 390	20 871	16.8	23.1	18.0	9.7	29 808	15.8	6.4	7 775	84.0
Walker County	2 039	61 758	39.9	17.7	9.0	18.3	31 468	18.4	8.8	18 303	59.9
Congressional District 9, Texas	399	651 086	82.6	29.5	5.7	24.2	34 870	18.4	7.5	229 350	42.0
Fort Bend County (part)	70	81 175	83.9	33.7	3.6	25.6	52 198	8.0	6.2	24 121	83.1
Harris County (part)	328	569 911	82.4	28.9	6.0	24.0	32 804	19.9	7.7	205 229	37.1
Congressional District 10, Texas	9 851	651 523	33.7	27.4	7.5	35.2	52 465	8.2	4.1	241 672	66.1
Austin County	1 690	23 590	28.2	27.0	14.8	17.3	38 615	12.1	4.4	8 747	77.2
Bastrop County (part)	671	20 605	38.5	27.4	9.4	15.9	43 393	12.5	4.2	6 675	81.1
Burleson County (part)	1 147	12 897	29.4	26.0	16.6	13.2	32 683	17.1	4.9	5 022	79.6
Harris County (part)	1 056	235 146	25.5	33.2	4.7	37.0	69 083	4.5	3.7	76 069	84.3
Lee County	1 628	15 657	31.5	28.8	14.3	13.1	36 280	11.9	2.6	5 663	79.4
Travis County (part)	750	280 592	39.6	23.1	7.1	42.5	50 495	8.7	3.5	117 617	50.2
Waller County	1 330	32 663	49.9	25.6	9.4	16.8	38 136	16.0	13.8	10 557	72.5
Washington County	1 578	30 373	29.3	24.7	16.7	19.0	36 760	12.9	4.3	11 322	73.5
Congressional District 11, Texas	90 636	651 590	35.5	27.3	14.8	17.0	32 711	15.8	6.1	243 501	71.6
Andrews County	3 887	13 004	43.7	31.4	12.1	12.4	34 036	16.4	8.1	4 601	79.7
Brown County	2 445	37 674	20.9	25.7	16.3	15.0	30 974	17.2	7.0	14 306	72.2
Burnet County	2 580	34 147	17.8	24.6	17.7	17.4	37 921	13.0	2.9	13 133	78.4
Coke County	2 328	3 864	19.5	24.2	23.9	14.7	29 085	13.0	4.4	1 544	78.8
Coleman County	3 264	9 235	17.5	23.5	23.0	11.7	25 658	19.9	6.4	3 889	74.6
Comanche County	2 429	14 026	23.1	25.3	20.1	13.0	28 422	17.3	4.4	5 522	76.2
Concho County	2 568	3 966	43.3	16.1	14.0	14.1	31 313	11.9	3.6	1 058	75.0
Crane County	2 035	3 996	47.8	31.6	10.8	12.8	32 194	13.4	8.3	1 360	85.3
Dawson County	2 336	14 985	57.5	25.5	14.4	10.5	28 211	19.7	8.2	4 726	73.4
Ector County	2 334	121 123	48.9	30.4	10.7	12.0	31 152	18.7	7.7	43 846	68.6
Gillespie County	2 748	20 814	17.4	21.4	25.3	22.9	38 109	10.2	3.7	8 521	77.5
Glasscock County	2 333	1 406	31.4	34.1	8.7	18.7	35 655	14.7	3.5	483	67.3
Irion County	2 723	1 771	26.0	26.7	15.8	21.5	37 500	8.4	2.6	694	77.7
Kimble County	3 239	4 468	22.5	23.9	21.2	17.3	29 396	18.8	3.0	1 866	73.6
Lampasas County	1 844	17 762	20.3	27.6	14.6	16.2	36 176	14.1	4.7	6 554	74.0
Llano County	2 421	17 044	6.3	15.9	30.6	21.0	34 830	10.3	2.9	7 879	80.9
Loving County	1 743	67	17.9	20.9	14.9	5.9	40 000	0.0	0.0	31	80.6
McCulloch County	2 769	8 205	28.9	26.5	20.0	14.0	25 705	22.5	6.9	3 277	72.7
Martin County	2 369	4 746	43.8	34.1	13.2	11.8	31 836	18.7	4.9	1 624	74.3
Mason County	2 414	3 738	22.6	22.4	23.5	18.7	30 921	13.2	1.6	1 607	80.5
Menard County	2 336	2 360	34.2	24.4	22.1	17.2	24 762	25.8	3.5	990	75.4
Midland County	2 332	116 009	38.1	30.2	11.7	24.8	39 082	12.9	5.4	42 745	69.5
Mills County	1 938	5 151	13.8	25.6	23.0	20.2	30 579	18.4	2.6	2 001	80.9
Mitchell County	2 357	9 698	45.0	20.1	14.4	10.4	25 399	17.7	3.8	2 837	76.0
Nolan County (part)	339	13 933	36.9	27.3	16.3	12.4	25 336	22.9	6.8	5 417	65.6
Reagan County	3 044	3 326	54.0	34.2	10.8	9.2	33 231	11.8	3.3	1 107	78.4
Runnels County	2 721	11 495	32.6	26.8	20.0	13.1	27 806	19.2	5.7	4 428	77.4
San Saba County	2 938	6 186	26.4	27.9	20.7	15.8	30 104	16.6	3.7	2 289	75.6
Schleicher County	3 394	2 935	46.0	27.7	16.2	17.6	29 746	21.5	1.8	1 115	75.7
Scurry County	2 337	16 361	34.6	25.1	15.3	11.8	31 646	16.0	6.0	5 756	73.9

[1] Dry land or land partially or temporarily covered by water.
[2] Persons who do not identify themselves White, not of Hispanic origin.
[3] Persons 25 years old and over.

Table B. 110th Congressional Districts by Counties, 2000—*Continued*

(Number, percent.)

STATE Congressional district County	Land area,[1] (sq km)	Population Total	Population Percent minority[2]	Population Percent under 18 years	Population Percent 65 years and over	Percent with bachelor's degree or more[3]	Median household income, 1999 (dollars)	Percent living in poverty	Percent unemployed	Households Total	Households Percent owner occupied
	1	2	3	4	5	6	7	8	9	10	11
Congressional District 11, Texas—*Continued*											
Sterling County	2 391	1 393	31.6	28.4	14.4	17.1	35 129	16.8	2.0	513	76.2
Sutton County (part)	2 198	1 206	28.4	24.5	19.3	22.9	42 250	12.6	0.7	475	64.8
Tom Green County	3 942	104 010	37.0	26.1	13.5	19.5	33 148	15.2	7.4	39 503	64.1
Upton County	3 216	3 404	45.6	29.1	13.7	11.8	28 977	19.9	5.5	1 256	75.6
Ward County	2 164	10 909	48.2	30.5	14.0	12.4	29 386	17.9	8.4	3 964	78.2
Winkler County	2 178	7 173	46.8	29.9	14.4	10.5	30 591	18.7	8.2	2 584	83.2
Congressional District 12, Texas	5 615	651 770	33.5	27.5	10.0	21.1	41 735	11.3	4.7	236 645	65.1
Parker County	2 340	88 495	10.7	27.6	10.5	18.6	45 497	8.3	4.2	31 131	80.6
Tarrant County (part)	932	514 482	39.3	27.4	9.8	22.3	41 201	12.0	4.8	188 336	61.1
Wise County	2 343	48 793	13.7	28.2	10.6	13.0	41 933	9.9	4.2	17 178	81.3
Congressional District 13, Texas	104 110	651 665	26.3	26.3	14.1	17.2	33 501	14.0	5.3	243 086	69.4
Archer County (part)	461	4 932	5.7	29.4	11.1	18.2	44 145	6.7	3.0	1 790	85.3
Armstrong County	2 366	2 148	5.5	26.0	19.1	20.5	38 194	10.6	3.4	802	79.1
Baylor County	2 255	4 093	13.5	22.9	24.9	12.1	24 627	16.1	4.8	1 791	72.6
Briscoe County	2 332	1 790	26.5	27.3	18.8	17.5	29 917	16.0	3.4	724	77.1
Carson County	2 391	6 516	9.8	27.9	15.4	15.5	40 285	7.3	2.9	2 470	83.6
Childress County	1 840	7 688	36.3	22.2	15.0	8.6	27 457	17.6	5.7	2 474	70.7
Clay County	2 843	11 006	6.0	24.8	16.0	13.9	35 738	10.3	3.5	4 323	83.0
Collingsworth County	2 380	3 206	28.7	26.4	22.0	15.3	25 438	18.7	4.3	1 294	78.9
Cooke County (part)	1 509	9 848	6.7	29.0	12.7	16.9	44 761	8.7	2.3	3 573	79.3
Cottle County	2 334	1 904	28.6	24.2	25.6	15.3	25 446	18.4	5.8	820	71.6
Crosby County	2 330	7 072	53.2	30.7	15.4	10.5	25 769	28.1	8.2	2 512	69.3
Dallam County	3 897	6 222	31.8	32.0	10.4	9.6	27 946	14.1	4.7	2 317	63.0
Dickens County	2 342	2 762	32.2	18.4	18.8	8.4	25 898	17.4	5.1	980	77.7
Donley County	2 408	3 828	11.5	22.6	21.7	15.8	29 006	15.9	9.5	1 578	74.4
Foard County	1 830	1 622	20.2	26.0	23.2	10.5	25 813	14.3	2.2	664	75.0
Gray County	2 404	22 744	22.3	23.8	18.2	11.9	31 368	13.8	5.4	8 793	77.4
Hall County	2 339	3 782	36.4	27.2	21.0	10.3	23 016	26.3	9.0	1 548	74.3
Hansford County	2 382	5 369	33.5	29.1	15.3	18.6	35 438	16.4	4.0	2 005	74.4
Hardeman County	1 801	4 724	22.4	25.1	20.2	12.8	28 312	17.8	4.2	1 943	73.2
Hartley County	3 787	5 537	22.6	20.8	11.8	17.6	46 327	6.6	1.2	1 604	76.4
Haskell County	2 339	6 093	24.8	23.6	25.5	14.4	23 690	22.8	5.2	2 569	78.9
Hemphill County	2 356	3 351	17.9	27.6	14.9	17.9	35 456	12.6	3.1	1 280	77.3
Hutchinson County	2 298	23 857	19.9	27.4	15.4	14.3	36 588	11.1	5.6	9 283	78.9
Jack County	2 374	8 763	15.3	23.5	15.1	12.8	32 500	12.9	4.0	3 047	76.8
Jones County	2 411	20 785	33.8	22.4	13.9	8.2	29 572	16.8	6.1	6 140	79.2
King County	2 363	356	7.0	33.4	10.7	24.6	35 625	20.7	0.0	108	38.9
Knox County	2 199	4 253	34.0	27.9	22.5	11.8	25 453	22.9	6.4	1 690	75.4
Lipscomb County	2 414	3 057	22.0	27.4	18.6	18.9	31 964	16.7	4.2	1 205	77.9
Montague County	2 410	19 117	7.4	24.1	19.8	11.3	31 048	14.0	5.6	7 770	78.7
Moore County	2 330	20 121	50.1	33.6	10.5	11.0	34 852	13.5	4.3	6 774	70.5
Motley County	2 562	1 426	18.0	23.8	24.3	14.7	28 348	19.4	2.2	606	77.4
Ochiltree County	2 376	9 006	33.4	30.7	11.5	16.1	38 013	13.0	4.6	3 261	72.5
Oldham County	3 887	2 185	16.6	35.1	11.0	19.4	33 713	19.8	6.9	735	66.3
Palo Pinto County	2 468	27 026	17.6	25.7	16.4	12.1	31 203	15.9	5.1	10 594	71.9
Potter County	2 355	113 546	42.3	28.0	11.7	13.5	29 492	19.2	7.1	40 760	60.1
Randall County	2 368	104 312	14.3	25.9	11.9	28.9	42 712	8.1	4.2	41 240	70.3
Roberts County	2 393	887	2.6	24.9	14.4	25.4	44 792	7.2	1.3	362	79.6
Sherman County	2 391	3 186	29.2	31.0	13.6	20.4	33 179	16.1	4.5	1 124	74.2
Stonewall County	2 379	1 693	17.6	22.3	24.0	12.6	27 935	19.3	3.0	713	78.5
Swisher County	2 332	8 378	42.2	28.3	15.9	16.2	29 846	17.4	5.8	2 925	70.4
Throckmorton County	2 363	1 850	9.0	25.6	20.6	18.2	28 277	13.5	4.4	765	77.3
Wheeler County	2 368	5 284	16.6	24.9	20.9	13.0	31 029	13.0	1.8	2 152	78.0
Wichita County	1 626	131 664	26.8	25.0	12.7	20.0	33 780	13.2	5.9	48 441	62.3
Wilbarger County	2 515	14 676	31.3	28.0	16.8	17.1	29 500	13.1	3.8	5 537	66.3
Congressional District 14, Texas	18 376	651 837	37.8	28.1	10.9	19.3	41 335	13.3	6.1	234 340	69.3
Aransas County	652	22 497	26.7	23.8	19.9	16.7	30 702	19.9	7.4	9 132	75.1
Brazoria County (part)	3 417	181 250	35.3	28.4	9.0	15.1	43 993	11.8	6.2	60 765	71.1
Calhoun County	1 327	20 647	47.7	28.6	13.4	12.1	35 849	16.4	7.4	7 442	72.8
Chambers County	1 552	26 031	22.0	28.9	8.9	12.1	47 964	11.0	5.0	9 139	83.6
Fort Bend County (part)	627	26 776	25.8	33.6	6.1	47.9	85 820	5.1	3.1	8 760	90.0
Galveston County (part)	657	197 012	36.7	26.5	10.6	25.2	42 976	13.2	6.8	74 995	63.8
Jackson County	2 148	14 391	33.8	27.5	15.7	12.8	35 254	14.7	5.0	5 336	73.7
Matagorda County	2 886	37 957	47.5	29.8	12.9	12.5	32 174	18.5	8.4	13 901	66.8
Victoria County	2 286	84 088	47.1	29.2	11.8	16.2	38 732	12.9	4.7	30 071	67.4
Wharton County	2 823	41 188	46.8	28.7	13.8	14.3	32 208	16.5	6.0	14 799	68.8

[1]Dry land or land partially or temporarily covered by water.
[2]Persons who do not identify themselves White, not of Hispanic origin.
[3]Persons 25 years old and over.

Table B. 110th Congressional Districts by Counties, 2000—*Continued*

(Number, percent.)

STATE Congressional district County	Land area,[1] (sq km)	Population Total	Percent minority[2]	Percent under 18 years	Percent 65 years and over	Percent with bachelor's degree or more[3]	Median household income, 1999 (dollars)	Percent living in poverty	Percent unemployed	Households Total	Percent owner occupied
	1	2	3	4	5	6	7	8	9	10	11
Congressional District 15, Texas	27 758	651 580	80.4	32.3	11.6	13.2	26 840	30.5	10.1	193 921	72.5
Bee County	2 280	32 359	65.1	23.3	10.4	12.2	28 392	24.0	8.0	9 061	65.5
Brooks County	2 443	7 976	92.2	31.5	15.2	6.8	18 622	40.2	8.5	2 711	73.1
Cameron County (part)	355	87 160	76.5	31.5	14.7	15.1	29 746	26.1	8.9	28 002	67.7
DeWitt County	2 355	20 013	39.3	23.7	19.3	11.8	28 714	19.6	5.8	7 207	76.6
Duval County	4 643	13 120	88.9	29.4	14.0	8.9	22 416	27.2	9.5	4 350	80.8
Goliad County	2 211	6 928	40.6	26.0	17.6	12.3	34 201	16.4	3.2	2 644	80.3
Hidalgo County (part)	3 315	380 063	88.6	34.9	9.8	14.2	25 706	34.5	11.9	105 986	72.6
Jim Wells County	2 239	39 326	77.1	31.3	12.3	10.9	28 843	24.1	6.6	12 961	76.5
Karnes County	1 943	15 446	59.3	21.7	14.1	9.4	26 526	21.9	6.5	4 454	74.0
Live Oak County	2 684	12 309	41.9	22.3	16.4	12.0	32 057	16.5	5.8	4 230	81.4
Refugio County	1 995	7 828	52.9	26.1	16.9	11.6	29 986	17.8	4.9	2 985	74.7
San Patricio County (part)	1 296	29 052	72.7	31.1	12.5	8.3	27 712	26.3	8.6	9 330	72.9
Congressional District 16, Texas	1 504	652 363	82.7	31.6	10.0	17.0	31 245	23.6	9.4	203 161	62.8
El Paso County (part)	1 504	652 363	82.7	31.6	10.0	17.0	31 245	23.6	9.4	203 161	62.8
Congressional District 17, Texas	19 921	651 509	28.6	25.4	11.9	20.0	35 253	17.0	6.7	236 230	64.5
Bosque County	2 562	17 204	15.5	24.4	20.7	15.4	34 181	12.7	5.2	6 726	77.5
Brazos County	1 517	152 415	33.9	21.5	6.7	37.0	29 104	26.9	8.5	55 202	45.6
Burleson County (part)	576	3 573	37.0	29.8	13.6	13.2	34 390	17.6	3.3	1 341	79.3
Grimes County	2 055	23 552	37.3	24.7	13.8	10.3	32 280	16.6	6.2	7 753	77.8
Hill County	2 493	32 321	22.4	25.7	17.1	12.5	31 600	15.7	4.9	12 204	75.0
Hood County	1 092	41 100	9.5	23.8	17.8	20.5	43 668	8.5	4.8	16 176	81.2
Johnson County	1 889	126 811	16.7	28.7	10.1	13.8	44 621	8.8	4.6	43 636	78.9
Limestone County (part)	1 619	10 172	30.2	24.5	16.3	9.7	29 464	17.3	4.2	3 542	76.1
McLennan County	2 698	213 517	35.3	26.6	13.0	19.1	33 560	17.6	7.6	78 859	60.2
Madison County	1 216	12 940	40.3	21.3	14.2	11.5	29 418	15.8	5.8	3 914	77.0
Robertson County (part)	1 717	11 095	42.1	27.2	18.7	11.4	27 151	21.7	7.4	4 439	69.8
Somervell County	485	6 809	14.7	28.2	13.2	17.2	39 404	8.6	4.7	2 438	74.7
Congressional District 18, Texas	589	651 789	80.2	28.9	8.3	14.4	31 291	23.3	9.5	222 454	48.8
Harris County (part)	589	651 789	80.2	28.9	8.3	14.4	31 291	23.3	9.5	222 454	48.8
Congressional District 19, Texas	65 445	651 610	36.6	27.1	12.9	18.7	31 575	17.5	6.5	239 851	65.3
Archer County (part)	1 895	3 922	7.3	26.4	17.7	13.2	32 146	11.9	3.7	1 555	76.5
Bailey County	2 141	6 594	50.8	30.3	14.8	9.3	27 901	16.7	8.7	2 348	71.3
Borden County	2 328	729	20.3	25.0	15.4	21.4	29 205	14.0	3.7	292	73.3
Callahan County	2 327	12 905	8.1	26.1	17.2	12.3	32 463	12.2	5.0	5 061	80.8
Castro County	2 327	8 285	56.2	33.1	12.2	14.7	30 619	19.0	5.8	2 761	71.0
Cochran County	2 008	3 730	51.0	31.5	14.4	10.2	27 525	27.0	11.1	1 309	74.1
Deaf Smith County	3 878	18 561	60.6	33.4	11.8	11.8	29 601	20.6	8.6	6 180	67.4
Eastland County	2 398	18 297	14.1	23.4	20.7	12.7	26 832	16.8	7.9	7 321	76.7
Fisher County	2 334	4 344	25.3	24.0	22.9	12.4	27 659	17.5	4.4	1 785	76.8
Floyd County	2 570	7 771	50.0	31.3	16.0	12.3	26 851	21.5	6.7	2 730	74.0
Gaines County	3 891	14 467	39.5	34.8	10.2	10.5	30 432	21.7	5.5	4 681	78.6
Garza County	2 319	4 872	44.1	28.0	14.1	10.0	27 206	22.3	5.7	1 663	70.9
Hale County	2 602	36 602	55.3	30.2	12.8	14.4	31 280	18.0	6.7	11 975	64.8
Hockley County	2 352	22 716	42.2	29.1	12.3	13.6	31 085	18.9	6.9	7 994	74.4
Howard County	2 338	33 627	42.9	24.2	14.7	11.1	30 805	18.6	6.7	11 389	69.5
Kent County	2 337	859	11.4	20.5	25.3	15.1	30 433	10.4	3.8	353	78.5
Lamb County	2 632	14 709	49.1	29.6	17.2	11.1	27 898	20.9	5.8	5 360	75.6
Lubbock County	2 330	242 628	37.5	25.6	11.0	24.4	32 198	17.8	5.8	92 516	59.2
Lynn County	2 310	6 550	48.0	31.1	14.2	13.4	26 694	22.6	6.1	2 354	74.6
Nolan County (part)	2 023	1 869	7.8	25.3	19.8	18.6	32 059	13.1	3.5	753	80.5
Parmer County	2 283	10 016	51.5	33.0	12.7	13.4	30 813	17.0	5.3	3 322	72.3
Shackelford County	2 367	3 302	9.1	27.1	18.0	20.8	30 479	13.6	1.8	1 300	78.7
Stephens County	2 317	9 674	19.7	24.4	17.6	13.4	29 583	15.6	3.7	3 661	72.4
Taylor County	2 371	126 555	27.3	26.6	12.3	22.5	34 035	14.5	8.2	47 274	61.5
Terry County	2 305	12 761	50.5	28.3	14.5	9.5	28 090	23.3	5.7	4 278	71.1
Yoakum County	2 071	7 322	47.1	32.2	11.0	10.2	32 672	19.6	9.2	2 469	78.2
Young County	2 389	17 943	13.6	24.9	19.7	14.4	30 499	15.7	5.2	7 167	73.8
Congressional District 20, Texas	476	651 603	76.7	28.7	10.4	15.4	31 937	19.9	7.1	223 059	54.3
Bexar County (part)	476	651 603	76.7	28.7	10.4	15.4	31 937	19.9	7.1	223 059	54.3
Congressional District 21, Texas	13 287	651 930	32.0	24.4	12.3	37.5	49 036	9.2	4.1	254 810	66.7
Bandera County	2 051	17 645	15.5	24.7	16.1	19.4	39 013	10.8	4.8	7 010	82.9
Bexar County (part)	623	350 249	41.6	25.2	11.9	35.8	48 968	7.9	4.1	138 605	62.6
Blanco County	1 842	8 418	17.9	24.3	16.6	22.2	39 369	11.2	2.9	3 303	78.6
Comal County	1 454	78 021	25.4	25.6	14.7	26.2	46 147	8.6	3.8	29 066	77.2
Kendall County	1 716	23 743	18.9	27.3	13.9	31.4	49 521	10.5	3.3	8 613	79.6

[1] Dry land or land partially or temporarily covered by water.
[2] Persons who do not identify themselves White, not of Hispanic origin.
[3] Persons 25 years old and over.

Table B. 110th Congressional Districts by Counties, 2000—*Continued*

(Number, percent.)

STATE Congressional district County	Land area,[1] (sq km)	Population				Percent with bachelor's degree or more[3]	Median household income, 1999 (dollars)	Percent living in poverty	Percent unem- ployed	Households	
		Total	Percent minority[2]	Percent under 18 years	Percent 65 years and over					Total	Percent owner occupied
	1	2	3	4	5	6	7	8	9	10	11
Congressional District 21, Texas—*Continued*											
Kerr County	2 865	43 653	22.3	22.7	24.6	23.3	34 283	14.5	4.6	17 813	73.3
Real County	1 813	3 047	23.7	23.7	20.5	17.3	25 118	21.2	3.6	1 245	77.0
Travis County (part)	925	127 154	19.0	21.4	6.6	61.9	67 871	10.4	4.1	49 155	64.3
Congressional District 22, Texas	2 516	651 657	39.4	29.1	7.2	32.4	57 932	7.3	4.8	226 585	72.0
Brazoria County (part)	174	60 517	32.7	28.7	8.1	32.6	62 810	5.5	3.6	21 189	82.6
Fort Bend County (part)	1 569	246 501	46.9	31.3	6.3	39.2	66 563	7.1	4.6	78 034	79.1
Galveston County (part)	375	53 146	38.1	27.2	12.4	13.5	41 134	13.3	6.6	19 787	75.5
Harris County (part)	399	291 493	34.7	27.6	6.9	30.2	54 865	6.9	4.9	107 575	64.1
Congressional District 23, Texas	125 500	651 149	70.0	31.4	10.0	17.9	33 574	20.9	7.5	208 355	72.4
Bexar County (part)	1 841	376 425	66.0	30.7	9.0	22.1	40 418	16.6	5.7	122 474	71.8
Brewster County	16 039	8 866	46.3	22.2	14.6	27.7	27 386	18.2	10.7	3 669	59.4
Crockett County	7 271	4 099	55.7	29.1	12.7	10.4	29 355	19.4	6.6	1 524	71.5
Culberson County	9 874	2 975	74.9	32.0	10.6	13.9	25 882	25.1	6.1	1 052	70.4
Dimmit County	3 447	10 248	87.1	33.0	12.9	10.1	21 917	33.2	14.2	3 308	73.9
Edwards County	5 490	2 162	45.9	28.3	16.2	17.3	25 298	31.6	4.9	801	79.7
El Paso County (part)	1 120	27 259	91.2	40.2	4.8	4.8	26 677	28.4	11.1	6 861	86.7
Hudspeth County	11 839	3 344	76.9	34.2	10.0	9.7	21 045	35.8	8.2	1 092	81.0
Jeff Davis County	5 865	2 207	37.9	24.5	16.4	35.1	32 212	15.0	5.8	896	70.2
Kinney County	3 531	3 379	52.9	25.7	24.7	17.7	28 320	24.0	9.4	1 314	77.9
Maverick County	3 315	47 297	96.8	37.0	9.6	9.1	21 232	34.8	17.6	13 089	69.5
Medina County	3 439	39 304	49.5	29.0	12.3	13.3	36 063	15.4	5.2	12 880	79.7
Pecos County	12 338	16 809	66.7	27.6	11.6	12.9	28 033	20.4	5.7	5 153	74.2
Presidio County	9 986	7 304	85.7	32.9	14.2	11.7	19 860	36.4	13.0	2 530	70.1
Reeves County	6 827	13 137	77.6	29.8	12.7	8.0	23 306	28.9	12.4	4 091	77.6
Sutton County (part)	1 567	2 871	62.7	30.5	12.2	8.4	32 147	20.2	4.7	1 040	75.3
Terrell County	6 106	1 081	52.6	26.5	18.1	19.0	24 219	25.2	5.3	443	77.7
Uvalde County	4 031	25 926	67.4	31.4	13.9	13.8	27 164	24.3	6.7	8 559	72.0
Val Verde County	8 211	44 856	78.3	32.0	10.8	14.1	28 376	26.1	11.3	14 151	66.0
Zavala County	3 363	11 600	92.6	33.8	11.5	7.6	16 844	41.8	16.7	3 428	73.0
Congressional District 24, Texas	866	651 137	36.1	27.3	5.7	36.2	56 098	6.3	3.3	248 764	57.1
Dallas County (part)	445	333 393	45.5	28.0	6.5	32.1	52 681	7.7	3.9	122 543	59.1
Denton County (part)	118	104 502	32.0	25.0	3.3	42.2	56 183	5.0	2.9	43 564	46.5
Tarrant County (part)	303	213 242	23.5	27.2	5.7	39.5	61 755	4.8	2.7	82 657	59.7
Congressional District 25, Texas	15 919	651 477	47.1	25.2	8.8	27.7	39 794	15.1	4.8	242 456	56.8
Bastrop County (part)	1 630	37 128	32.4	28.1	10.8	17.7	43 665	11.2	3.8	13 422	79.9
Caldwell County	1 413	32 194	51.0	28.4	12.7	13.3	36 573	13.1	5.5	10 816	69.6
Colorado County	2 494	20 390	35.5	25.5	18.6	14.4	32 425	16.2	5.1	7 641	76.7
Fayette County	2 461	21 804	20.2	23.1	22.1	14.6	34 526	11.4	3.4	8 722	78.2
Gonzales County	2 765	18 628	49.2	27.9	16.9	10.7	28 368	18.6	4.8	6 782	69.2
Hays County	1 756	97 589	35.5	24.4	7.7	31.3	45 006	14.3	6.3	33 410	64.9
Lavaca County	2 512	19 210	19.3	24.1	21.6	11.4	29 132	13.2	2.5	7 669	78.4
Travis County (part)	888	404 534	54.2	24.8	6.4	32.4	40 458	15.8	4.6	153 994	48.4
Congressional District 26, Texas	3 346	651 858	33.9	28.7	7.8	26.9	48 714	11.0	5.1	232 209	67.7
Cooke County (part)	754	26 515	18.5	26.8	15.6	15.3	35 539	16.2	5.6	10 070	69.5
Dallas County (part)	16	48	0.0	56.3	0.0	19.0	25 938	0.0	50.0	14	100.0
Denton County (part)	2 183	328 474	21.5	28.4	5.6	34.8	59 106	7.2	4.1	115 339	71.3
Tarrant County (part)	393	296 821	49.1	29.2	9.6	19.5	40 350	14.8	6.3	106 786	63.6
Congressional District 27, Texas	12 225	651 843	72.3	30.9	10.6	16.2	31 327	25.3	9.4	209 011	63.9
Cameron County (part)	1 991	248 067	88.7	34.5	10.0	12.7	24 994	35.5	12.3	69 265	67.7
Kenedy County	3 773	414	86.0	30.2	11.6	20.3	25 000	15.3	6.5	138	40.6
Kleberg County	2 256	31 549	71.6	27.3	10.9	20.4	29 313	26.7	10.6	10 896	58.6
Nueces County	2 165	313 645	62.3	28.3	11.2	18.8	35 959	18.2	7.6	110 365	61.3
San Patricio County (part)	496	38 086	40.0	30.9	8.8	16.7	40 079	11.6	6.3	12 763	64.8
Willacy County	1 545	20 082	88.8	31.6	11.8	7.5	22 114	33.2	13.8	5 584	77.3
Congressional District 28, Texas	35 223	651 259	79.8	34.0	9.5	12.6	28 866	29.9	9.6	188 199	73.6
Atascosa County	3 191	38 628	60.7	31.7	11.0	10.5	33 081	20.2	6.0	12 816	78.5
Bexar County (part)	290	14 654	28.5	30.9	8.0	16.4	43 042	8.3	5.0	4 804	68.3
Frio County	2 935	16 252	79.2	28.7	11.1	8.4	24 504	29.0	7.3	4 743	69.0
Guadalupe County	1 842	89 023	40.6	28.3	11.1	19.1	43 949	9.8	5.4	30 900	77.0
Hidalgo County (part)	751	189 400	91.7	35.8	9.9	10.3	23 196	38.6	12.4	50 838	74.0
Jim Hogg County	2 943	5 281	91.1	31.6	14.1	9.5	25 833	25.9	8.1	1 815	77.6
La Salle County	3 856	5 866	81.7	29.1	12.2	6.4	21 857	29.8	7.9	1 819	74.7
McMullen County	2 883	851	35.7	23.0	19.0	16.2	32 500	20.7	1.7	355	80.8
Starr County	3 168	53 597	98.4	37.4	8.1	6.9	16 504	50.9	20.9	14 410	79.4
Webb County	8 694	193 117	95.2	36.2	7.7	13.9	28 100	31.2	9.3	50 740	65.7
Wilson County	2 090	32 408	39.2	29.2	11.4	12.8	40 006	11.3	4.9	11 038	85.0
Zapata County	2 582	12 182	85.2	33.0	14.6	8.7	24 635	35.8	11.1	3 921	81.9
Congressional District 29, Texas	611	651 405	78.2	33.4	7.0	6.5	31 751	21.9	9.3	193 092	55.3
Harris County (part)	611	651 405	78.2	33.4	7.0	6.5	31 751	21.9	9.3	193 092	55.3

[1]Dry land or land partially or temporarily covered by water.
[2]Persons who do not identify themselves White, not of Hispanic origin.
[3]Persons 25 years old and over.

Table B. 110th Congressional Districts by Counties, 2000—*Continued*

(Number, percent.)

STATE Congressional district County	Land area,[1] (sq km)	Population Total	Percent minority[2]	Percent under 18 years	Percent 65 years and over	Percent with bachelor's degree or more[3]	Median household income, 1999 (dollars)	Percent living in poverty	Percent unem-ployed	Households Total	Households Percent owner occupied
	1	2	3	4	5	6	7	8	9	10	11
Congressional District 30, Texas	822	652 261	78.1	29.5	7.9	16.0	33 505	21.4	8.8	220 701	49.1
Dallas County (part)	822	652 261	78.1	29.5	7.9	16.0	33 505	21.4	8.8	220 701	49.1
Congressional District 31, Texas	18 476	651 868	34.0	28.6	8.8	24.1	43 381	9.6	5.1	225 600	64.8
Bell County	2 745	237 974	42.8	28.9	8.7	19.8	36 872	12.1	6.8	85 507	55.7
Coryell County	2 724	74 978	39.6	26.2	5.6	12.4	35 999	9.5	6.7	19 950	54.8
Erath County	2 814	33 001	17.6	24.6	13.4	25.0	30 708	16.0	10.7	12 568	63.1
Falls County	1 992	18 576	44.3	27.7	16.8	9.6	26 589	22.6	7.4	6 496	71.7
Hamilton County	2 164	8 229	8.4	23.8	23.2	16.8	31 150	14.2	2.6	3 374	77.8
Milam County	2 633	24 238	31.1	27.3	17.0	11.6	33 186	15.9	4.7	9 199	73.0
Robertson County (part)	496	4 905	35.0	30.7	12.2	15.8	31 918	18.2	3.5	1 740	76.1
Williamson County	2 908	249 967	26.5	29.8	7.2	33.6	60 642	4.8	2.8	86 766	74.2
Congressional District 32, Texas	413	650 555	49.8	25.3	9.3	36.4	45 725	12.5	4.5	252 320	46.5
Dallas County (part)	413	650 555	49.8	25.3	9.3	36.4	45 725	12.5	4.5	252 320	46.5
UTAH	212 751	2 233 169	14.7	32.1	8.5	26.1	45 726	9.4	5.0	701 281	71.5
Congressional District 1, Utah	53 790	744 337	16.7	32.3	8.6	24.7	45 058	9.5	5.4	238 384	70.8
Box Elder County	14 823	42 745	9.0	36.1	10.4	19.5	44 630	7.1	5.2	13 144	80.0
Cache County	3 016	91 391	10.1	31.2	7.1	31.9	39 730	13.5	5.1	27 543	64.6
Davis County	789	238 994	10.3	35.2	7.3	28.8	53 726	5.1	4.4	71 201	77.6
Juab County (part)	6 365	1 062	11.4	33.9	10.1	7.9	30 769	15.5	6.8	368	71.5
Morgan County	1 578	7 129	3.0	36.9	8.8	23.3	50 273	5.2	3.8	2 046	88.3
Rich County	2 664	1 961	2.3	34.8	14.1	22.0	39 766	10.2	4.2	645	83.7
Salt Lake County (part)	270	94 051	45.8	26.1	10.1	18.4	30 277	21.0	8.2	34 730	44.9
Summit County	4 846	29 736	10.5	29.8	4.9	45.5	64 962	5.4	2.8	10 332	75.5
Tooele County	17 950	40 735	14.9	35.1	7.5	15.9	45 773	6.7	5.6	12 677	78.3
Weber County	1 491	196 533	17.3	30.9	10.4	19.9	44 014	9.3	6.0	65 698	74.9
Congressional District 2, Utah	118 166	744 287	12.0	29.6	10.8	30.9	45 583	9.0	4.6	252 500	70.6
Carbon County	3 829	20 422	13.8	28.3	13.2	12.3	34 036	13.4	8.9	7 413	77.4
Daggett County	1 809	921	8.7	23.1	13.9	11.9	30 833	5.5	7.7	340	70.6
Duchesne County	8 387	14 371	10.5	36.8	9.3	12.7	31 298	16.8	7.8	4 559	80.8
Emery County	11 530	10 860	7.3	35.4	10.2	11.6	39 850	11.5	6.4	3 468	82.0
Garfield County	13 401	4 735	4.7	32.4	14.1	20.3	35 180	8.1	8.1	1 576	79.0
Grand County	9 535	8 485	11.1	26.8	12.7	22.9	32 387	14.8	8.8	3 434	70.9
Iron County	8 542	33 779	8.4	31.2	8.5	23.8	33 114	19.2	5.3	10 627	66.3
Kane County	10 339	6 046	5.5	29.1	17.0	21.1	34 247	7.9	5.3	2 237	78.1
Piute County	1 963	1 435	4.6	31.1	17.0	14.4	29 625	16.2	6.4	509	87.2
Salt Lake County (part)	924	437 788	12.6	26.6	10.3	37.2	50 962	6.8	3.7	155 607	67.1
San Juan County	20 254	14 413	60.5	39.3	8.4	13.9	28 137	31.4	15.1	4 089	79.3
Uintah County	11 596	25 224	14.5	34.6	9.9	13.2	34 518	14.5	7.7	8 187	77.0
Utah County (part)	351	57 730	5.0	41.0	6.3	32.0	56 861	4.4	3.9	14 882	82.5
Wasatch County	3 049	15 215	7.2	34.2	8.4	26.3	49 612	5.2	4.3	4 743	80.6
Washington County	6 285	90 354	8.6	31.1	17.0	21.0	37 212	11.2	5.5	29 939	74.0
Wayne County	6 372	2 509	3.2	32.4	14.3	20.9	32 000	15.4	3.3	890	77.6
Congressional District 3, Utah	40 795	744 545	15.4	34.4	6.2	22.1	46 568	9.7	4.9	210 397	73.5
Beaver County	6 708	6 005	9.4	33.4	13.9	12.1	34 544	8.3	2.2	1 982	78.9
Juab County (part)	2 420	7 176	3.8	39.2	9.8	12.9	39 063	9.7	3.0	2 088	81.1
Millard County	17 066	12 405	9.5	37.3	12.5	16.8	36 178	13.1	5.9	3 840	79.6
Salt Lake County (part)	716	366 548	20.0	35.8	4.9	16.5	50 718	6.1	4.7	104 804	79.9
Sanpete County	4 113	22 763	9.5	33.2	11.0	17.3	33 042	15.9	6.8	6 547	78.8
Sevier County	4 948	18 842	5.2	34.5	13.0	15.2	35 822	10.8	6.3	6 081	82.0
Utah County (part)	4 824	310 806	11.7	32.7	6.5	31.3	43 890	13.4	4.9	85 055	64.1
VERMONT	23 956	608 827	3.9	24.2	12.7	29.4	40 856	9.4	4.2	240 634	70.6
Congressional District (At Large), Vermont	23 956	608 827	3.9	24.2	12.7	29.4	40 856	9.4	4.2	240 634	70.6
Addison County	1 995	35 974	4.0	24.8	11.3	29.8	43 142	8.6	4.5	13 068	75.0
Bennington County	1 752	36 994	2.9	23.8	16.6	27.1	39 926	10.0	4.6	14 846	71.4
Caledonia County	1 685	29 702	3.1	25.4	14.3	22.5	34 800	12.3	6.2	11 663	72.9
Chittenden County	1 396	146 571	5.6	23.5	9.4	41.2	47 673	8.8	4.0	56 452	66.1
Essex County	1 723	6 459	3.7	25.5	15.0	10.8	30 490	13.7	6.2	2 602	79.7
Franklin County	1 650	45 417	4.2	28.1	10.9	16.6	41 659	9.0	3.7	16 765	75.0
Grand Isle County	214	6 901	2.8	24.9	12.3	25.0	43 033	7.6	3.4	2 761	81.3
Lamoille County	1 194	23 233	3.7	24.3	11.3	31.2	39 356	9.6	4.6	9 221	70.8
Orange County	1 783	28 226	2.6	25.6	12.8	23.9	39 855	9.1	4.4	10 936	78.1
Orleans County	1 807	26 277	3.4	25.1	15.1	16.1	31 084	14.1	6.7	10 446	74.1
Rutland County	2 415	63 400	2.4	23.2	14.9	23.2	36 743	10.9	4.7	25 678	69.8
Washington County	1 785	58 039	3.9	23.5	12.8	32.2	40 972	8.0	3.2	23 659	68.5
Windham County	2 043	44 216	3.9	23.6	14.0	30.5	38 204	9.4	4.0	18 375	67.9
Windsor County	2 515	57 418	2.8	23.4	15.8	30.2	40 688	7.7	3.2	24 162	71.5

[1]Dry land or land partially or temporarily covered by water.
[2]Persons who do not identify themselves White, not of Hispanic origin.
[3]Persons 25 years old and over.

Table B. 110th Congressional Districts by Counties, 2000—*Continued*

(Number, percent.)

STATE Congressional district County	Land area,[1] (sq km)	Population Total	Population Percent minority[2]	Population Percent under 18 years	Population Percent 65 years and over	Percent with bachelor's degree or more[3]	Median household income, 1999 (dollars)	Percent living in poverty	Percent unem- ployed	Households Total	Households Percent owner occupied
	1	2	3	4	5	6	7	8	9	10	11
VIRGINIA	102 548	7 078 515	29.9	24.5	11.2	29.5	46 677	9.6	4.2	2 699 173	68.1
Congressional District 1, Virginia	9 771	642 404	25.4	26.4	11.3	26.8	50 257	6.7	4.6	237 490	72.7
Caroline County (part)	1 033	12 074	37.8	24.5	14.7	11.6	38 394	9.6	4.5	4 403	79.1
Essex County	668	9 989	42.6	23.0	17.3	17.4	37 395	11.2	3.2	3 995	77.2
Fauquier County (part)	858	28 479	12.7	28.3	8.6	22.1	60 981	5.4	2.8	9 933	78.6
Gloucester County	561	34 780	14.6	26.2	12.0	17.6	45 421	7.7	4.0	13 127	81.4
James City County (part)	370	48 102	19.1	23.3	16.7	41.5	55 594	6.4	3.6	19 003	77.0
King and Queen County	819	6 630	38.6	22.8	16.9	10.3	35 941	10.9	4.1	2 673	82.3
King George County	466	16 803	23.6	27.7	9.6	23.6	49 882	5.6	4.2	6 091	71.8
King William County	713	13 146	26.7	26.0	11.7	14.8	49 876	5.5	3.1	4 846	85.1
Lancaster County	345	11 567	30.5	19.1	28.6	24.5	33 239	12.5	6.4	5 004	83.0
Mathews County	222	9 207	13.8	19.9	21.3	19.2	43 222	6.0	3.2	3 932	84.7
Middlesex County	337	9 932	22.2	19.3	22.4	18.9	36 875	13.0	3.9	4 253	83.0
Northumberland County	498	12 259	27.9	18.6	26.3	21.7	38 129	12.3	3.9	5 470	87.4
Prince William County (part)	207	37 827	45.8	32.2	3.3	27.5	51 653	6.0	4.2	12 682	53.2
Richmond County	496	8 809	36.7	18.4	17.4	9.9	33 026	15.4	5.0	2 937	77.2
Spotsylvania County (part)	421	71 275	19.5	30.1	8.0	25.9	59 781	3.7	3.2	24 682	81.0
Stafford County	700	92 446	19.9	31.5	5.8	29.6	66 809	3.5	3.0	30 187	80.6
Westmoreland County	594	16 718	35.8	23.0	19.2	13.3	35 797	14.7	4.1	6 846	79.2
York County	274	56 297	21.4	29.1	9.2	37.4	57 956	3.5	2.8	20 000	75.8
Fredericksburg city	27	19 279	28.9	17.7	13.1	30.5	34 585	15.5	9.6	8 102	35.5
Hampton city (part)	38	31 662	47.1	26.9	8.3	23.7	45 774	6.3	4.4	12 034	64.3
Newport News city (part)	62	71 559	29.9	24.4	12.6	27.6	41 533	7.7	3.4	29 505	57.2
Poquoson city	40	11 566	4.9	26.9	11.3	31.6	60 920	4.5	3.2	4 166	84.1
Williamsburg city	22	11 998	22.0	9.9	11.9	45.0	37 093	18.3	41.7	3 619	44.3
Congressional District 2, Virginia	2 489	643 367	32.7	25.5	9.4	25.5	44 193	8.7	5.0	231 653	63.5
Accomack County	1 179	38 305	38.0	24.3	16.9	13.5	30 250	18.0	7.6	15 299	75.0
Northampton County	537	13 093	47.6	23.5	21.6	15.7	28 276	20.5	7.0	5 321	68.7
Hampton city (part)	53	54 637	31.5	21.6	9.9	27.4	45 398	8.6	4.7	18 512	65.6
Norfolk city (part)	77	112 075	37.5	21.0	9.2	19.2	35 022	13.1	8.3	38 066	48.5
Virginia Beach city	643	425 257	30.6	27.4	8.4	28.1	48 705	6.5	4.1	154 455	65.6
Congressional District 3, Virginia	2 895	643 917	62.2	25.9	11.7	17.2	32 238	18.9	7.9	250 417	52.1
Charles City County	473	6 926	64.5	21.9	13.3	10.5	42 745	10.6	3.7	2 670	84.9
Henrico County (part)	351	65 440	54.1	26.3	11.2	13.2	42 016	8.3	3.7	25 755	69.7
Isle of Wight County (part)	0	0	X	X	X	X	X	X	X	0	X
James City County (part)	0	0	X	X	X	X	X	X	X	0	X
New Kent County	543	13 462	20.2	24.9	9.7	16.3	53 595	4.9	3.8	4 925	88.8
Prince George County (part)	395	15 059	37.1	23.2	8.3	17.0	52 079	9.9	3.8	4 810	82.1
Surry County	723	6 829	53.6	25.2	14.1	12.8	37 558	10.8	5.3	2 619	77.0
Hampton city (part)	44	60 138	72.4	25.1	11.9	15.1	31 836	16.2	9.4	23 341	50.1
Newport News city (part)	115	108 591	59.8	29.4	8.4	14.3	32 587	17.9	7.2	40 181	48.9
Norfolk city (part)	62	122 328	67.4	26.8	12.5	19.9	29 365	24.3	9.6	48 144	43.2
Portsmouth city	86	100 565	54.7	25.7	13.8	13.8	33 742	16.2	7.7	38 170	58.5
Richmond city (part)	103	144 579	71.3	23.2	12.4	22.8	27 133	26.1	9.9	59 802	42.5
Congressional District 4, Virginia	11 626	643 670	38.0	26.6	10.6	19.6	45 249	9.5	4.4	231 889	73.5
Amelia County	924	11 400	29.6	25.4	13.2	9.8	40 252	8.4	2.9	4 240	82.0
Brunswick County (part)	412	3 319	53.2	23.5	15.8	7.1	28 167	18.8	7.4	1 304	77.4
Chesterfield County (part)	731	127 191	28.5	27.7	7.4	24.3	55 394	5.5	3.8	45 194	80.5
Dinwiddie County	1 305	24 533	35.5	24.0	12.2	11.0	41 582	9.3	3.8	9 107	79.2
Greensville County	765	11 560	61.5	18.1	11.5	11.0	32 002	14.7	4.4	3 375	78.3
Isle of Wight County (part)	818	29 728	29.2	25.4	12.0	17.5	45 387	8.3	4.1	11 319	80.9
Nottoway County	815	15 725	43.3	23.0	17.0	11.1	30 866	20.1	5.9	5 664	70.9
Powhatan County	677	22 377	18.8	23.9	8.4	19.1	53 992	5.7	1.8	7 258	88.9
Prince George County (part)	292	17 988	44.5	26.9	6.2	21.9	47 846	6.3	4.5	5 349	64.9
Southampton County	1 553	17 482	44.2	22.8	14.4	11.7	33 995	14.6	4.7	6 279	74.3
Sussex County	1 271	12 504	63.5	19.7	13.4	10.0	31 007	16.1	5.3	4 126	69.5
Chesapeake city	882	199 184	34.2	28.8	8.8	24.7	50 743	7.3	4.1	69 900	74.9
Colonial Heights city	19	16 897	10.9	22.5	18.7	19.0	43 224	5.5	2.3	7 027	69.4
Emporia city	18	5 665	59.7	25.3	20.0	14.2	30 333	16.0	6.8	2 226	52.1
Franklin city	22	8 346	54.3	24.9	18.5	16.4	31 687	19.8	7.0	3 384	53.6
Hopewell city	27	22 354	38.8	26.8	14.5	10.2	33 196	14.9	6.7	9 055	55.9
Petersburg city	59	33 740	81.9	24.9	15.6	14.8	28 851	19.6	8.9	13 799	51.5
Suffolk city	1 036	63 677	46.9	27.8	11.6	17.3	41 115	13.2	4.9	23 283	72.2

[1]Dry land or land partially or temporarily covered by water.
[2]Persons who do not identify themselves White, not of Hispanic origin.
[3]Persons 25 years old and over.
X = Not applicable.

Table B. 110th Congressional Districts by Counties, 2000—*Continued*

(Number, percent.)

STATE Congressional district County	Land area,[1] (sq km)	Population				Percent with bachelor's degree or more[3]	Median household income, 1999 (dollars)	Percent living in poverty	Percent unem-ployed	Households	
		Total	Percent minority[2]	Percent under 18 years	Percent 65 years and over					Total	Percent owner occupied
	1	2	3	4	5	6	7	8	9	10	11
Congressional District 5, Virginia	23 108	643 323	27.5	22.5	14.8	19.0	35 739	13.2	5.1	253 996	72.4
Albemarle County	1 872	79 236	16.4	24.8	12.5	47.7	50 749	6.7	3.1	31 876	65.8
Appomattox County	864	13 705	24.3	24.7	15.0	10.5	36 507	11.4	2.9	5 322	81.0
Bedford County (part)	1 234	35 681	8.0	22.2	14.7	13.9	39 114	7.7	3.3	14 356	87.3
Brunswick County (part)	1 055	15 100	59.6	19.7	14.3	11.6	31 771	15.9	7.2	4 973	77.7
Buckingham County	1 504	15 623	41.0	22.4	13.6	8.5	29 882	20.0	5.5	5 324	77.9
Campbell County	1 307	51 078	17.1	24.0	13.7	14.6	37 280	10.6	3.1	20 639	77.3
Charlotte County	1 230	12 472	35.1	24.4	17.8	10.3	28 929	18.1	5.6	4 951	77.4
Cumberland County	773	9 017	40.2	24.7	15.0	11.8	31 816	15.1	3.5	3 528	77.2
Fluvanna County	744	20 047	21.1	23.7	13.9	24.5	46 372	5.9	2.9	7 387	85.3
Franklin County	1 792	47 286	11.8	22.0	14.3	14.8	38 056	9.7	3.8	18 963	81.2
Greene County	406	15 244	9.8	27.1	9.8	19.8	45 931	6.6	2.7	5 574	81.5
Halifax County	2 122	37 355	40.1	23.3	17.4	9.5	29 929	15.7	7.4	15 018	76.0
Henry County (part)	635	34 868	26.3	22.2	14.4	11.3	34 065	9.9	5.1	14 529	75.7
Lunenburg County	1 118	13 146	41.7	21.4	16.9	9.2	27 899	20.0	5.2	4 998	77.8
Mecklenburg County	1 616	32 380	41.3	21.5	17.8	12.1	31 380	15.5	6.6	12 951	74.3
Nelson County	1 223	14 445	18.5	21.4	16.7	20.8	36 769	12.1	4.8	5 887	80.8
Pittsylvania County	2 514	61 745	25.7	23.0	14.3	9.3	35 153	11.8	4.3	24 684	80.1
Prince Edward County	914	19 720	38.1	20.3	14.1	19.2	31 301	18.9	13.3	6 561	68.5
Bedford city	18	6 299	25.3	21.6	21.8	15.2	28 792	19.7	13.3	2 519	60.3
Charlottesville city	27	45 049	31.4	15.2	10.0	40.8	31 007	25.9	4.3	16 851	40.9
Danville city	112	48 411	46.7	23.3	19.7	13.9	26 900	20.0	10.1	20 607	58.0
Martinsville city	28	15 416	46.0	22.6	20.9	16.6	27 441	19.2	8.7	6 498	60.2
Congressional District 6, Virginia	14 625	643 630	15.1	22.4	15.0	20.8	37 773	11.0	4.4	254 321	69.2
Alleghany County (part)	448	5 085	4.5	24.7	15.7	16.7	41 275	7.0	7.8	2 022	81.2
Amherst County	1 231	31 894	22.8	23.4	13.7	13.1	37 393	10.7	5.0	11 941	78.1
Augusta County	2 513	65 615	5.4	23.6	12.8	15.4	43 045	5.8	2.5	24 818	83.2
Bath County	1 378	5 048	7.8	20.7	17.1	11.1	35 013	7.8	4.2	2 053	79.8
Bedford County (part)	720	24 690	9.2	26.7	10.2	31.8	51 290	6.3	2.4	9 482	85.5
Botetourt County	1 405	30 496	5.4	23.3	13.2	19.6	48 731	5.2	2.7	11 700	87.7
Highland County	1 077	2 536	0.7	19.9	20.2	13.2	29 732	12.6	6.8	1 131	83.7
Roanoke County (part)	330	71 310	6.1	22.6	16.4	29.0	47 380	4.7	2.1	29 112	74.6
Rockbridge County	1 553	20 808	5.0	22.1	15.6	18.7	36 035	9.6	3.6	8 486	77.6
Rockingham County	2 204	67 725	5.3	24.7	13.9	17.6	40 748	8.2	3.4	25 355	78.0
Shenandoah County	1 327	35 075	6.0	22.4	17.2	14.7	39 173	8.2	2.7	14 296	73.1
Buena Vista city	18	6 349	7.0	22.3	16.2	10.5	32 410	10.4	3.9	2 547	70.6
Covington city (part)	2	1 364	13.9	25.1	17.9	5.8	27 798	13.1	5.3	571	55.7
Harrisonburg city	45	40 468	19.6	15.2	9.3	31.2	29 949	30.1	9.3	13 133	39.1
Lexington city	6	6 867	14.3	10.5	16.4	42.6	28 982	21.6	9.9	2 232	55.2
Lynchburg city	128	65 269	34.0	22.2	16.4	25.2	32 234	15.9	6.7	25 477	58.5
Roanoke city	111	94 911	31.4	22.6	16.4	18.7	30 719	15.9	5.8	42 003	56.3
Salem city	38	24 747	8.7	20.8	16.9	19.8	38 997	6.7	3.8	9 954	67.6
Staunton city	51	23 853	16.7	19.9	18.1	20.4	32 941	11.7	3.9	9 676	61.4
Waynesboro city	40	19 520	15.2	23.8	17.5	20.6	32 686	12.8	6.5	8 332	61.2
Congressional District 7, Virginia	9 102	643 583	21.9	25.0	12.1	33.2	50 990	6.1	2.8	252 282	72.9
Caroline County (part)	346	10 047	38.5	25.0	11.1	12.7	42 840	9.0	4.2	3 618	85.6
Chesterfield County (part)	372	132 712	21.0	28.6	8.7	40.4	61 779	3.6	2.6	48 578	81.4
Culpeper County	987	34 262	22.9	25.6	12.0	15.7	45 290	9.2	3.2	12 141	70.5
Goochland County	737	16 863	27.5	21.2	12.3	29.4	56 307	6.9	1.7	6 158	86.7
Hanover County	1 224	86 320	12.3	27.1	10.7	28.7	59 223	3.6	2.2	31 121	84.3
Henrico County (part)	265	196 860	25.0	24.1	12.9	41.9	51 379	5.4	2.7	82 366	64.5
Louisa County	1 288	25 627	23.9	24.4	12.9	14.0	39 402	10.2	3.4	9 945	81.4
Madison County	832	12 520	13.5	23.8	15.2	19.4	39 856	9.6	3.2	4 739	76.9
Orange County	885	25 881	16.6	23.0	17.3	18.5	42 889	9.2	2.9	10 150	77.1
Page County	806	23 177	4.4	22.9	15.8	9.8	33 359	12.5	3.9	9 305	73.9
Rappahannock County	690	6 983	8.3	22.6	13.8	22.9	45 943	7.6	2.2	2 788	75.4
Spotsylvania County (part)	617	19 120	16.2	29.3	8.5	11.8	48 880	8.8	3.1	6 626	86.6
Richmond city (part)	52	53 211	37.5	18.3	16.1	46.0	43 376	8.3	3.5	24 747	55.0
Congressional District 8, Virginia	319	643 764	42.9	19.6	8.8	53.8	63 430	7.5	3.0	277 916	50.1
Arlington County	67	189 453	39.5	16.3	9.1	60.2	63 001	7.8	2.8	86 352	43.3
Fairfax County (part)	207	315 651	44.3	22.6	8.4	49.1	66 992	6.8	3.1	125 204	59.5
Alexandria city	39	128 283	46.3	16.8	8.9	54.3	56 054	8.9	3.2	61 889	40.0
Falls Church city	5	10 377	20.3	23.6	12.3	63.7	74 924	4.2	2.9	4 471	60.5
Congressional District 9, Virginia	22 801	643 561	6.7	20.7	14.6	14.0	29 783	16.2	5.7	259 829	74.2
Alleghany County (part)	704	7 841	3.0	21.7	15.7	11.6	37 228	7.2	3.7	3 127	87.2
Bland County	929	6 871	5.4	19.2	14.8	9.2	30 397	12.4	4.5	2 568	86.1
Buchanan County	1 305	26 978	3.4	21.7	11.4	8.0	22 213	23.2	8.3	10 464	82.9
Carroll County	1 234	29 245	3.1	20.9	17.2	9.5	30 597	12.5	6.1	12 186	81.7
Craig County	856	5 091	1.3	23.6	13.7	10.8	37 314	10.3	2.8	2 060	81.4

[1]Dry land or land partially or temporarily covered by water.
[2]Persons who do not identify themselves White, not of Hispanic origin.
[3]Persons 25 years old and over.

Table B. 110th Congressional Districts by Counties, 2000—*Continued*

(Number, percent.)

STATE Congressional district County	Land area,[1] (sq km)	Population Total	Percent minority[2]	Percent under 18 years	Percent 65 years and over	Percent with bachelor's degree or more[3]	Median household income, 1999 (dollars)	Percent living in poverty	Percent unemployed	Households Total	Percent owner occupied
	1	2	3	4	5	6	7	8	9	10	11
Congressional District 9, Virginia—*Continued*											
Dickenson County	859	16 395	1.4	22.0	14.5	6.7	23 431	21.3	7.2	6 732	82.1
Floyd County	987	13 874	4.2	22.3	15.8	12.5	31 585	11.7	3.6	5 791	81.8
Giles County	925	16 657	3.4	21.9	16.6	12.4	34 927	9.5	5.4	6 994	79.0
Grayson County	1 146	17 917	9.6	19.5	17.0	8.0	28 676	13.6	3.6	7 259	81.3
Henry County (part)	355	23 062	28.8	22.4	15.7	6.6	29 394	14.3	5.9	9 381	78.7
Lee County	1 132	23 589	2.2	22.6	15.5	9.5	22 972	23.9	8.0	9 706	74.4
Montgomery County	1 005	83 629	10.7	17.3	8.6	35.9	32 330	23.2	5.4	30 997	55.1
Patrick County	1 251	19 407	9.2	21.8	16.5	8.6	28 705	13.4	4.0	8 141	80.2
Pulaski County	830	35 127	7.7	20.5	15.4	12.5	33 873	13.1	5.5	14 643	73.6
Roanoke County (part)	320	14 468	9.7	23.3	12.8	24.3	48 962	3.2	2.2	5 574	90.5
Russell County	1 229	30 308	4.5	21.2	13.3	9.4	26 834	16.3	6.9	11 789	81.1
Scott County	1 390	23 403	2.0	20.7	17.7	8.3	27 339	16.8	5.9	9 795	78.3
Smyth County	1 171	33 081	3.6	21.6	16.3	10.6	30 083	13.3	4.7	13 493	74.1
Tazewell County	1 346	44 598	3.9	21.5	15.4	11.0	27 304	15.3	9.1	18 277	77.3
Washington County	1 458	51 103	3.0	20.7	15.3	16.1	32 742	10.9	4.2	21 056	77.3
Wise County	1 046	40 123	3.4	23.0	14.0	10.8	26 149	20.0	7.2	16 013	75.2
Wythe County	1 200	27 599	4.8	21.7	15.8	12.1	32 235	11.0	4.3	11 511	77.4
Bristol city	33	17 367	8.0	20.2	20.4	17.0	27 389	16.2	6.5	7 678	65.0
Clifton Forge city	8	4 289	17.7	21.0	23.8	9.6	26 090	19.4	7.3	1 841	62.7
Covington city (part)	13	4 939	16.9	20.2	21.2	6.5	30 941	12.8	4.6	2 264	73.4
Galax city	21	6 837	18.8	23.2	18.6	11.1	28 236	18.6	2.7	2 950	66.1
Norton city	20	3 904	9.8	22.0	15.7	14.0	22 788	22.8	7.3	1 730	56.0
Radford city	25	15 859	12.0	12.9	9.8	34.1	24 654	31.4	6.4	5 809	44.5
Congressional District 10, Virginia	4 808	643 714	23.0	28.2	7.3	43.1	71 560	4.4	2.4	228 202	75.4
Clarke County	457	12 652	9.5	23.3	14.7	23.9	51 601	6.6	2.1	4 942	75.5
Fairfax County (part)	306	222 465	29.6	28.8	6.0	61.9	96 039	2.7	2.0	75 734	78.5
Fauquier County (part)	825	26 660	13.1	25.3	12.7	32.1	63 871	5.5	2.3	9 909	73.7
Frederick County	1 074	59 209	6.2	26.4	10.7	18.6	46 941	6.4	2.5	22 097	80.3
Loudoun County	1 346	169 599	20.6	29.7	5.5	47.2	80 648	2.8	2.0	59 900	79.4
Prince William County (part)	190	52 535	30.8	27.8	5.5	29.6	61 819	5.9	2.4	18 521	65.0
Warren County	553	31 584	8.7	25.6	12.4	15.0	42 422	8.5	3.4	12 087	74.1
Manassas city	26	35 135	33.7	29.7	5.3	28.1	60 409	6.3	3.7	11 757	69.8
Manassas Park city	6	10 290	33.0	30.9	4.6	20.3	60 794	5.2	2.2	3 254	78.7
Winchester city	24	23 585	20.8	21.8	14.3	23.7	34 335	13.2	4.6	10 001	45.7
Congressional District 11, Virginia	1 004	643 582	33.2	26.9	7.4	48.9	80 397	3.8	2.7	221 178	76.6
Fairfax County (part)	510	431 633	32.6	25.6	8.3	55.6	86 282	3.8	2.5	149 776	76.7
Prince William County (part)	478	190 451	34.6	30.8	4.6	32.7	70 120	3.7	3.0	63 367	77.4
Fairfax city	16	21 498	32.7	20.1	12.6	45.7	67 642	5.7	2.4	8 035	69.1
WASHINGTON	172 348	5 894 121	21.1	25.6	11.2	27.7	45 776	10.6	6.2	2 271 398	64.6
Congressional District 1, Washington	1 138	654 799	18.4	25.4	9.5	36.4	58 565	5.6	3.8	250 775	67.9
King County (part)	217	238 540	18.8	23.3	9.9	45.1	62 694	5.4	3.3	96 035	65.8
Kitsap County (part)	573	109 143	16.1	27.1	10.2	33.8	54 092	5.6	4.6	39 607	72.6
Snohomish County (part)	347	307 116	19.0	26.4	8.9	30.3	56 592	5.7	4.0	115 133	68.1
Congressional District 2, Washington	17 002	654 984	14.4	26.4	11.5	22.4	45 441	10.0	6.4	247 566	67.2
Island County	540	71 558	14.8	25.4	14.3	27.0	45 513	7.0	5.7	27 784	70.1
King County (part)	961	648	6.9	19.4	15.0	14.5	43 661	13.2	10.7	299	78.9
San Juan County	453	14 077	6.1	19.4	19.1	40.2	43 491	9.2	3.2	6 466	73.6
Skagit County	4 494	102 979	17.1	26.2	14.6	20.8	42 381	11.1	6.9	38 852	69.7
Snohomish County (part)	5 064	298 908	14.2	28.3	9.4	18.2	50 224	8.0	6.0	109 719	67.4
Whatcom County	5 490	166 814	13.6	24.1	11.6	27.2	40 005	14.2	7.4	64 446	63.4
Congressional District 3, Washington	19 465	654 992	12.4	27.1	11.4	21.4	44 426	10.5	6.5	249 432	67.9
Clark County	1 627	345 238	13.5	28.7	9.6	22.1	48 376	9.1	5.9	127 208	67.3
Cowlitz County	2 949	92 948	10.2	26.8	13.3	13.3	39 797	14.0	7.7	35 850	67.6
Lewis County	6 236	68 600	9.3	26.5	15.6	12.9	35 511	14.0	9.0	26 306	71.4
Pacific County	2 416	20 984	12.0	21.4	22.4	15.2	31 209	14.4	7.8	9 096	74.7
Skamania County (part)	4 067	7 034	8.3	26.4	10.9	16.7	38 912	13.1	10.3	2 676	72.5
Thurston County (part)	1 485	116 364	13.2	24.5	10.9	32.8	46 868	9.2	5.6	46 743	66.1
Wahkiakum County	684	3 824	6.7	23.4	18.6	14.8	39 444	8.1	8.1	1 553	79.7
Congressional District 4, Washington	49 343	654 851	32.3	30.4	11.2	18.7	37 764	16.2	9.7	228 819	66.0
Thurston County (part)	339	11 170	67.2	36.9	8.3	9.9	31 406	20.8	9.7	3 235	67.7
Benton County	4 411	142 475	18.3	29.7	10.3	26.3	47 044	10.3	6.1	52 866	68.8
Chelan County	7 566	66 616	22.6	28.0	14.0	21.9	37 316	12.4	10.4	25 021	64.6
Douglas County	4 715	32 603	22.7	29.4	12.7	16.2	38 464	14.4	9.0	11 726	71.0
Franklin County	3 218	49 347	52.7	34.5	8.4	13.6	38 991	19.2	10.8	14 840	65.7
Grant County	6 944	74 698	34.4	32.1	11.6	13.7	35 276	17.4	11.7	25 204	66.7
Kittitas County	5 950	33 362	10.5	20.6	11.6	26.2	32 546	19.8	9.1	13 382	58.3
Klickitat County	4 849	19 161	15.1	26.8	13.9	16.4	34 267	17.0	10.4	7 473	68.8
Skamania County (part)	223	2 838	8.5	27.6	11.2	17.0	40 610	13.1	13.3	1 079	77.4
Yakima County	11 127	222 581	43.5	31.7	11.2	15.3	34 828	19.7	11.1	73 993	64.4

[1]Dry land or land partially or temporarily covered by water.
[2]Persons who do not identify themselves White, not of Hispanic origin.
[3]Persons 25 years old and over.

Table B. 110th Congressional Districts by Counties, 2000—*Continued*

(Number, percent.)

STATE Congressional district County	Land area,[1] (sq km)	Population Total	Percent minority[2]	Percent under 18 years	Percent 65 years and over	Percent with bachelor's degree or more[3]	Median household income, 1999 (dollars)	Percent living in poverty	Percent unem-ployed	Households Total	Percent owner occupied
	1	2	3	4	5	6	7	8	9	10	11
Congressional District 5, Washington	59 217	654 935	12.4	25.4	13.0	23.8	35 720	14.4	8.5	253 204	66.0
Adams County (part)	4 646	5 258	12.0	28.6	16.1	15.9	39 271	12.5	6.6	1 994	69.7
Asotin County	1 646	20 551	5.4	25.4	16.2	18.0	33 524	15.4	6.4	8 364	67.1
Columbia County	2 250	4 064	9.8	24.0	18.8	17.5	33 500	12.6	9.0	1 687	69.6
Ferry County	5 708	7 260	24.2	26.9	12.7	13.5	30 388	19.0	18.8	2 823	73.0
Garfield County	1 840	2 397	2.7	26.0	20.7	17.0	33 398	14.2	4.9	987	73.8
Lincoln County	5 986	10 184	5.6	25.2	18.9	18.8	35 255	12.6	6.2	4 151	76.6
Okanogan County	13 644	39 564	28.6	27.7	14.1	15.9	29 726	21.3	12.0	15 027	68.6
Pend Oreille County	3 627	11 732	8.3	26.3	15.1	12.3	31 677	18.1	10.4	4 639	77.4
Spokane County	4 568	417 939	10.3	25.6	12.5	25.0	37 308	12.3	8.0	163 611	65.5
Stevens County	6 419	40 066	10.5	28.7	12.8	15.3	34 673	15.9	9.9	15 017	78.1
Walla Walla County	3 291	55 180	21.2	24.4	14.7	23.3	35 900	15.1	8.2	19 647	65.2
Whitman County	5 593	40 740	13.1	18.1	9.3	44.0	28 584	25.6	9.7	15 257	47.8
Congressional District 6, Washington	17 564	655 068	22.3	25.0	13.9	20.1	39 205	13.2	7.5	259 518	63.5
Clallam County	4 505	64 525	12.7	21.8	21.3	20.8	36 449	12.5	7.7	27 164	72.8
Grays Harbor County	4 965	67 194	13.3	25.7	15.4	12.7	34 160	16.1	8.3	26 808	69.1
Jefferson County	4 699	25 953	8.8	19.7	21.0	28.4	37 869	11.3	6.7	11 645	76.1
Kitsap County (part)	452	122 826	19.8	26.4	10.9	17.6	41 398	11.5	7.3	46 809	63.0
Mason County	2 489	49 405	13.7	23.4	16.4	15.6	39 586	12.2	8.3	18 912	79.0
Pierce County (part)	454	325 165	29.5	25.6	12.3	22.5	40 216	13.7	7.3	128 180	57.0
Congressional District 7, Washington	366	655 016	33.1	16.9	11.9	44.1	45 864	11.5	5.2	292 385	50.5
King County (part)	366	655 016	33.1	16.9	11.9	44.1	45 864	11.5	5.2	292 385	50.5
Congressional District 8, Washington	6 680	655 029	18.1	27.7	8.8	37.4	63 854	5.1	4.0	240 810	75.6
King County (part)	3 670	524 456	19.8	26.9	9.3	42.0	66 039	5.1	3.7	196 233	73.6
Pierce County (part)	3 010	130 573	11.0	30.9	6.6	17.4	57 263	5.3	5.4	44 577	84.1
Congressional District 9, Washington	1 574	654 447	26.8	26.3	9.9	22.3	46 495	9.2	5.6	248 889	59.6
King County (part)	292	318 374	30.8	25.6	9.9	23.0	46 422	9.7	5.1	125 964	55.4
Pierce County (part)	885	245 082	23.7	27.2	9.3	19.7	46 322	9.0	6.0	88 043	62.5
Thurston County (part)	398	90 991	21.1	26.2	11.8	26.0	47 085	8.4	6.5	34 882	67.3
WEST VIRGINIA	62 361	1 808 344	5.5	22.2	15.3	14.8	29 696	17.9	7.3	736 481	75.2
Congressional District 1, West Virginia	16 281	602 545	4.3	21.8	15.8	16.3	30 303	17.0	7.3	245 352	74.0
Barbour County	883	15 557	2.6	23.0	15.6	11.8	24 729	22.6	8.8	6 123	78.5
Brooke County	230	25 447	2.3	20.4	18.3	13.4	32 981	11.7	5.1	10 396	76.6
Doddridge County	830	7 403	2.9	25.4	14.9	10.2	26 744	19.8	8.9	2 845	81.3
Gilmer County	881	7 160	2.9	20.2	15.4	17.1	22 857	25.9	14.9	2 768	72.3
Grant County	1 236	11 299	1.1	22.7	15.3	11.4	28 916	16.3	5.7	4 591	80.8
Hancock County	215	32 667	4.3	20.9	18.4	11.5	33 759	11.1	5.6	13 678	77.0
Harrison County	1 078	68 652	4.3	23.1	16.5	16.3	30 562	17.2	7.6	27 867	74.8
Marion County	802	56 598	5.7	20.5	17.8	16.0	28 626	16.3	7.9	23 652	74.7
Marshall County	795	35 519	2.4	22.9	16.3	10.7	30 989	16.6	7.5	14 207	77.5
Mineral County	849	27 078	4.4	23.4	15.1	11.7	31 149	14.7	5.8	10 784	77.8
Monongalia County	935	81 866	8.3	18.1	10.7	32.4	28 625	22.8	7.3	33 446	61.0
Ohio County	275	47 427	6.1	21.3	18.7	23.1	30 836	15.8	8.7	19 733	68.6
Pleasants County	339	7 514	2.3	24.0	14.9	9.7	32 736	13.7	6.6	2 887	80.5
Preston County	1 679	29 334	1.9	23.7	14.9	10.8	27 927	18.3	6.8	11 544	83.1
Ritchie County	1 175	10 343	2.0	22.9	15.2	7.1	27 332	19.1	7.5	4 184	81.7
Taylor County	448	16 089	3.4	23.0	15.7	11.3	27 124	20.3	7.4	6 320	79.6
Tucker County	1 085	7 321	1.7	21.2	18.1	10.6	26 250	18.1	7.7	3 052	82.5
Tyler County	667	9 592	1.3	23.2	16.6	8.5	29 290	16.6	10.1	3 836	83.7
Wetzel County	930	17 693	1.3	23.7	16.2	10.4	30 935	19.8	10.1	7 164	78.5
Wood County	951	87 986	3.3	23.0	15.5	15.2	33 285	13.9	6.5	36 275	73.4
Congressional District 2, West Virginia	21 909	602 243	6.1	23.0	14.6	16.2	33 198	14.8	5.9	244 587	75.5
Berkeley County	832	75 905	8.1	25.7	11.1	15.1	38 763	11.5	4.3	29 569	74.1
Braxton County	1 330	14 702	1.6	22.6	15.9	9.2	24 412	22.0	8.7	5 771	78.1
Calhoun County	727	7 582	2.5	22.3	16.7	9.3	21 578	25.1	12.1	3 071	79.0
Clay County	887	10 330	2.2	25.5	13.7	7.3	22 120	27.5	11.5	4 020	79.1
Hampshire County	1 662	20 203	2.3	25.0	14.5	11.3	31 666	16.3	5.0	7 955	81.1
Hardy County	1 511	12 669	3.9	23.4	14.8	9.4	31 846	13.1	3.5	5 204	80.5
Jackson County	1 206	28 000	1.2	24.0	15.3	12.4	32 434	15.2	5.9	11 061	79.5
Jefferson County	543	42 190	9.9	23.6	11.2	21.6	44 374	10.3	4.6	16 165	75.9
Kanawha County	2 339	200 073	10.0	21.3	16.5	20.6	33 766	14.4	5.7	86 226	70.3
Lewis County	990	16 919	1.2	22.2	16.4	11.2	27 066	19.9	7.6	6 946	73.0
Mason County	1 118	25 957	2.0	22.6	15.3	8.8	27 134	19.9	10.1	10 587	80.9
Morgan County	593	14 943	2.6	22.4	16.5	11.2	35 016	10.9	4.1	6 145	83.3
Pendleton County	1 807	8 196	3.7	21.8	17.9	10.8	30 429	11.4	7.0	3 350	79.2
Putnam County	897	51 589	2.6	24.9	11.6	19.7	41 892	9.3	4.5	20 028	84.0
Randolph County	2 693	28 262	2.4	22.3	15.1	13.6	27 299	18.0	6.9	11 072	75.8

[1]Dry land or land partially or temporarily covered by water.
[2]Persons who do not identify themselves White, not of Hispanic origin.
[3]Persons 25 years old and over.

Table B. 110th Congressional Districts by Counties, 2000—*Continued*

(Number, percent.)

STATE Congressional district County	Land area,[1] (sq km)	Population				Percent with bachelor's degree or more[3]	Median household income, 1999 (dollars)	Percent living in poverty	Percent unemployed	Households	
		Total	Percent minority[2]	Percent under 18 years	Percent 65 years and over					Total	Percent owner occupied
	1	2	3	4	5	6	7	8	9	10	11
Congressional District 2, West Virginia—*Continued*											
Roane County	1 252	15 446	2.4	23.3	14.8	9.0	24 511	22.6	12.6	6 161	79.6
Upshur County	919	23 404	2.5	22.6	14.8	13.8	26 973	20.0	7.0	8 972	76.7
Wirt County	603	5 873	1.2	25.2	12.9	9.9	30 748	19.6	6.2	2 284	83.1
Congressional District 3, West Virginia	24 170	603 556	6.0	21.8	15.6	12.0	25 630	21.9	9.0	246 542	76.0
Boone County	1 303	25 535	1.8	23.3	13.6	7.2	25 669	22.0	8.5	10 291	78.9
Cabell County	729	96 784	7.0	19.9	16.1	20.9	28 479	19.2	7.9	41 180	64.6
Fayette County	1 720	47 579	8.0	21.7	16.2	10.7	24 788	21.7	11.9	18 945	77.2
Greenbrier County	2 645	34 453	5.6	21.6	17.6	13.6	26 927	18.2	8.5	14 571	76.5
Lincoln County	1 133	22 108	1.1	23.4	13.1	5.9	22 662	27.9	10.1	8 664	79.0
Logan County	1 176	37 710	4.4	22.1	14.4	8.8	24 603	24.1	10.5	14 880	76.8
McDowell County	1 385	27 329	12.7	23.3	16.1	5.6	16 931	37.7	14.4	11 169	79.8
Mercer County	1 089	62 980	8.1	21.1	17.5	13.8	26 628	19.7	9.8	26 509	76.9
Mingo County	1 095	28 253	3.9	24.3	12.5	7.3	21 347	29.7	10.8	11 303	77.8
Monroe County	1 226	14 583	7.5	20.1	15.3	8.2	27 575	16.2	5.2	5 447	84.4
Nicholas County	1 680	26 562	1.4	23.3	15.0	9.8	26 974	19.2	7.7	10 722	82.9
Pocahontas County	2 435	9 131	2.2	21.0	17.2	11.8	26 401	17.1	6.3	3 835	80.3
Raleigh County	1 572	79 220	11.0	21.5	15.5	12.7	28 181	18.5	7.7	31 793	76.5
Summers County	935	12 999	3.5	20.4	19.9	10.1	21 147	24.4	12.5	5 530	79.1
Wayne County	1 310	42 903	1.4	23.3	14.9	11.9	27 352	19.6	6.6	17 239	78.1
Webster County	1 440	9 719	0.7	23.0	15.2	8.7	21 055	31.8	14.6	4 010	79.1
Wyoming County	1 297	25 708	1.4	22.4	14.0	7.1	23 932	25.1	9.5	10 454	83.3
WISCONSIN	140 663	5 363 675	12.6	25.5	13.1	22.4	43 791	8.7	4.7	2 084 544	68.4
Congressional District 1, Wisconsin	4 351	670 359	12.4	26.0	12.4	21.5	50 372	6.3	4.6	254 793	70.8
Kenosha County (part)	707	149 577	14.6	27.0	11.5	19.2	46 970	7.5	5.8	56 057	69.1
Milwaukee County (part)	217	115 659	8.7	22.1	14.7	26.4	53 042	3.5	2.7	46 806	65.7
Racine County (part)	863	188 831	20.1	27.0	12.4	20.3	48 059	8.4	6.0	70 819	70.6
Rock County (part)	752	79 212	5.8	26.2	12.6	18.6	47 470	6.1	4.5	30 956	70.2
Walworth County (part)	1 425	81 179	8.4	26.0	13.3	20.9	48 159	6.3	3.8	30 743	73.3
Waukesha County (part)	388	55 901	3.2	28.0	8.6	25.9	66 243	1.8	2.8	19 412	85.5
Congressional District 2, Wisconsin	9 095	670 670	10.9	23.4	10.9	32.1	46 979	8.7	4.3	267 211	62.3
Columbia County	2 004	52 468	4.0	25.1	14.4	16.7	45 064	5.2	3.5	20 439	74.9
Dane County	3 113	426 526	12.5	22.4	9.3	40.6	49 223	9.4	3.8	173 484	57.6
Green County	1 513	33 647	2.2	26.5	14.7	16.7	43 228	5.1	3.2	13 212	73.7
Jefferson County (part)	804	43 886	5.7	25.0	13.5	19.4	47 132	5.9	4.2	17 059	72.0
Rock County (part)	1 114	73 095	16.1	26.7	13.1	14.6	43 175	8.6	6.9	27 661	72.2
Sauk County (part)	534	28 468	4.6	24.8	14.8	20.0	40 585	7.2	4.5	11 577	69.0
Walworth County (part)	13	12 580	9.3	11.6	9.6	33.4	31 824	27.2	13.4	3 779	34.8
Congressional District 3, Wisconsin	35 134	670 473	3.8	25.3	13.5	19.5	40 006	9.8	4.5	254 520	72.1
Sauk County (part)	1 773	13 804	1.6	25.2	16.7	14.0	37 200	7.5	3.8	5 511	76.5
Clark County (part)	2 303	19 558	2.3	30.1	14.8	10.3	34 679	13.7	4.2	7 028	82.5
Crawford County	1 483	17 243	3.2	26.2	15.9	13.2	34 135	10.2	4.8	6 677	76.9
Dunn County	2 207	39 858	4.3	23.3	11.2	21.1	38 753	12.9	7.2	14 337	69.0
Eau Claire County	1 651	93 142	5.5	23.4	12.2	27.0	39 219	10.9	4.7	35 822	65.0
Grant County	2 973	49 597	2.3	23.6	15.3	17.2	36 268	11.2	4.7	18 465	72.4
Iowa County	1 975	22 780	1.5	27.1	13.4	18.5	42 518	7.3	3.9	8 764	75.8
Jackson County	2 557	19 100	11.1	24.1	15.0	11.3	37 015	9.6	8.3	7 070	75.0
Juneau County	1 988	24 316	4.0	25.5	16.8	10.0	35 335	10.1	6.1	9 696	76.9
La Crosse County	1 173	107 120	6.1	23.6	12.6	25.4	39 472	10.7	4.1	41 599	65.1
Lafayette County	1 641	16 137	1.0	27.2	15.8	13.3	37 220	9.1	2.6	6 211	77.4
Monroe County	2 333	40 899	4.4	28.0	13.9	13.2	37 170	12.0	4.8	15 399	73.7
Pepin County	602	7 213	1.4	26.4	16.9	13.3	37 609	9.1	4.4	2 759	79.6
Pierce County	1 493	36 804	2.6	24.4	9.6	24.6	49 551	7.7	4.7	13 015	73.1
Richland County	1 518	17 924	2.4	25.1	17.2	14.1	33 998	10.1	4.8	7 118	74.5
St. Croix County	1 870	63 155	2.7	27.9	9.8	26.3	54 930	4.0	2.6	23 410	76.4
Sauk County (part)	1 635	26 757	2.2	27.5	14.2	14.9	43 990	7.3	3.8	10 067	78.3
Trempealeau County	1 901	27 010	1.7	25.3	16.4	13.3	37 889	8.3	3.5	10 747	74.3
Vernon County	2 059	28 056	1.3	27.4	17.1	14.0	33 178	14.2	4.2	10 825	79.1
Congressional District 4, Wisconsin	290	670 373	49.3	28.0	11.4	17.8	33 121	19.8	8.8	264 190	46.6
Milwaukee County (part)	290	670 373	49.3	28.0	11.4	17.8	33 121	19.8	8.8	264 190	46.6
Congressional District 5, Wisconsin	3 298	670 392	6.0	25.3	13.7	35.0	58 594	3.4	2.7	261 626	73.4
Jefferson County (part)	411	11 584	4.3	24.7	11.3	13.4	49 004	4.2	3.4	4 377	78.8
Milwaukee County (part)	119	154 132	9.2	22.3	18.2	43.0	51 596	4.5	2.6	66 733	67.2
Ozaukee County (part)	601	82 317	3.9	26.6	12.6	38.6	62 745	2.6	2.2	30 857	76.3
Washington County	1 116	117 493	3.2	26.6	11.2	21.9	57 033	3.6	2.7	43 842	76.0
Waukesha County (part)	1 051	304 866	6.2	25.9	12.6	35.6	62 161	2.9	2.8	115 817	75.0

[1] Dry land or land partially or temporarily covered by water.
[2] Persons who do not identify themselves White, not of Hispanic origin.
[3] Persons 25 years old and over.

Table B. 110th Congressional Districts by Counties, 2000—*Continued*

(Number, percent.)

STATE Congressional district County	Land area,[1] (sq km)	Population Total	Percent minority[2]	Percent under 18 years	Percent 65 years and over	Percent with bachelor's degree or more[3]	Median household income, 1999 (dollars)	Percent living in poverty	Percent unem- ployed	Households Total	Percent owner occupied
	1	2	3	4	5	6	7	8	9	10	11
Congressional District 6, Wisconsin	14 611	670 609	5.8	24.8	14.3	17.1	44 242	6.1	3.7	258 274	73.4
Adams County	1 678	18 643	3.4	20.7	21.0	10.0	33 408	10.4	7.8	7 900	85.4
Calumet County (part)	819	29 723	1.9	27.5	12.4	17.4	51 387	3.4	2.2	11 043	82.4
Dodge County	2 285	85 897	6.1	24.8	14.0	13.2	45 190	5.3	3.3	31 417	73.5
Fond du Lac County (part)	1 872	97 296	4.9	25.2	14.3	16.9	45 578	5.8	4.3	36 931	73.0
Green Lake County	918	19 105	3.1	24.0	18.8	14.5	39 462	7.0	5.1	7 703	77.2
Jefferson County (part)	228	18 551	6.3	26.1	11.3	15.0	45 542	6.1	4.4	6 769	66.4
Manitowoc County (part)	1 532	82 887	4.9	25.4	15.6	15.5	43 286	6.1	3.6	32 721	76.0
Marquette County	1 180	15 832	7.6	21.1	18.1	10.1	35 746	7.7	5.4	5 986	82.3
Outagamie County (part)	11	10 112	2.1	29.2	11.5	21.9	53 095	2.6	1.6	3 766	76.8
Sheboygan County (part)	1 330	112 646	8.9	25.5	14.0	17.9	46 237	5.2	2.6	43 545	71.4
Waushara County	1 621	23 154	4.8	23.6	19.1	11.7	37 000	9.1	6.6	9 336	83.4
Winnebago County (part)	1 136	156 763	6.1	23.8	12.5	22.8	44 445	6.7	3.7	61 157	68.0
Congressional District 7, Wisconsin	48 657	670 432	4.8	25.3	15.2	16.6	39 026	8.6	5.3	263 682	76.1
Ashland County	2 703	16 866	13.0	25.5	16.0	16.5	31 628	11.9	8.1	6 718	70.6
Barron County	2 235	44 963	2.8	25.3	16.4	14.9	37 275	8.8	4.7	17 851	75.9
Bayfield County (part)	3 823	15 013	11.4	24.7	16.4	21.6	33 390	12.5	8.5	6 207	82.6
Burnett County	2 128	15 674	6.9	22.1	20.3	14.0	34 218	8.8	5.8	6 613	84.5
Chippewa County	2 617	55 195	2.4	26.5	14.6	14.7	39 596	8.2	4.7	21 356	75.6
Clark County (part)	846	13 999	2.9	29.7	17.8	10.4	34 440	11.2	4.1	5 019	79.5
Douglas County (part)	3 391	43 287	4.9	23.6	14.5	18.3	35 226	11.0	7.1	17 808	71.5
Iron County (part)	1 961	6 861	1.7	19.4	23.2	13.2	29 580	11.1	8.9	3 083	80.7
Langlade County (part)	1 216	15 852	3.0	23.9	19.6	12.3	32 699	10.5	5.7	6 515	76.2
Lincoln County	2 288	29 641	3.0	25.5	16.3	13.6	39 120	6.9	5.3	11 721	78.3
Marathon County	4 001	125 834	6.2	26.7	13.0	18.3	45 165	6.6	3.8	47 702	75.7
Oneida County (part)	1 445	20 110	2.4	23.5	16.6	18.5	36 067	8.3	7.0	8 228	75.5
Polk County	2 376	41 319	2.9	26.2	15.2	15.6	41 183	7.1	3.9	16 254	80.1
Portage County	2 088	67 182	5.0	24.0	10.9	23.4	43 487	9.5	5.9	25 040	70.9
Price County	3 244	15 822	1.7	23.9	19.0	13.0	35 249	8.9	5.7	6 564	80.8
Rusk County	2 365	15 347	1.9	24.7	18.5	11.2	31 344	11.8	6.3	6 095	78.6
Sawyer County	3 254	16 196	18.6	24.1	18.0	16.5	32 287	12.7	6.6	6 640	76.9
Taylor County	2 525	19 680	2.0	27.1	15.2	11.0	38 502	9.8	5.2	7 529	80.4
Washburn County	2 097	16 036	3.4	23.8	18.6	15.2	33 716	9.9	6.1	6 604	80.9
Wood County	2 053	75 555	4.2	25.7	15.4	16.9	41 595	6.5	5.0	30 135	74.3
Congressional District 8, Wisconsin	25 228	670 367	7.7	25.8	13.5	19.1	43 274	6.8	4.0	260 248	73.4
Brown County (part)	1 369	226 778	10.3	26.0	10.6	22.5	46 447	6.9	3.8	87 295	65.4
Calumet County (part)	9	10 908	8.8	31.7	6.4	30.7	55 879	3.8	2.2	3 867	74.5
Door County (part)	1 250	27 961	2.7	22.0	18.7	21.4	38 813	6.4	5.4	11 828	79.3
Florence County	1 264	5 088	0.8	23.0	17.6	12.4	34 750	9.1	5.7	2 133	85.6
Forest County	2 626	10 024	14.5	25.4	19.3	10.0	32 023	13.1	7.7	4 043	78.9
Kewaunee County (part)	887	20 187	1.9	25.7	15.3	11.4	43 824	5.8	2.6	7 623	81.9
Langlade County (part)	1 044	4 888	2.2	25.4	16.8	9.8	34 455	8.7	6.0	1 937	87.0
Marinette County (part)	3 631	43 384	2.0	23.6	17.6	12.9	35 256	8.3	5.4	17 585	79.5
Menominee County	927	4 562	87.9	39.0	9.2	12.9	29 440	28.8	16.5	1 345	74.5
Oconto County (part)	2 585	35 634	2.5	25.8	15.1	10.6	41 201	7.1	3.9	13 979	82.9
Oneida County (part)	1 468	16 666	2.9	21.1	21.3	21.7	38 721	6.3	4.9	7 105	84.6
Outagamie County (part)	1 647	150 859	7.4	27.5	10.9	22.6	49 349	4.8	3.3	56 764	72.1
Shawano County	2 312	40 664	8.9	25.7	16.8	12.6	38 069	7.9	3.8	15 815	78.2
Vilas County	2 263	21 033	10.6	20.7	23.0	17.6	33 759	8.0	6.1	9 066	82.0
Waupaca County	1 945	51 731	2.6	25.7	16.6	14.8	40 910	6.8	3.6	19 863	76.9
WYOMING	251 489	493 782	11.2	25.9	11.6	21.9	37 892	11.4	5.3	193 608	70.0
Congressional District (At Large), Wyoming	251 489	493 782	11.2	25.9	11.6	21.9	37 892	11.4	5.3	193 608	70.0
Albany County	11 066	32 014	12.3	18.3	8.2	44.1	28 790	21.0	5.4	13 269	51.3
Big Horn County	8 125	11 461	8.5	28.7	16.8	15.9	32 682	14.1	6.3	4 312	74.4
Campbell County	12 424	33 698	6.5	31.1	5.0	15.7	49 536	7.6	4.4	12 207	73.6
Carbon County	20 451	15 639	18.0	24.0	12.0	17.2	36 060	12.9	5.3	6 129	70.9
Converse County	11 020	12 052	7.9	28.3	11.3	14.7	39 603	11.6	4.6	4 694	74.1
Crook County	7 404	5 887	1.8	27.0	14.7	17.5	35 601	9.1	3.3	2 308	80.1
Fremont County	23 782	35 804	25.4	27.4	13.1	19.7	32 503	17.6	8.9	13 545	72.8
Goshen County	5 764	12 538	10.4	23.8	17.3	18.6	32 228	13.9	6.4	5 061	70.7
Hot Springs County	5 190	4 882	5.7	22.1	20.0	17.9	29 888	10.6	1.8	2 108	68.6
Johnson County	10 791	7 075	3.7	24.3	18.1	22.2	34 012	10.1	6.1	2 959	73.7
Laramie County	6 957	81 607	16.9	25.3	11.4	23.4	39 607	9.1	4.9	31 927	69.1
Lincoln County	10 539	14 573	4.2	30.9	12.3	17.2	40 794	9.0	3.8	5 266	81.4
Natrona County	13 830	66 533	8.3	25.9	12.6	20.0	36 619	11.8	5.2	26 819	69.9
Niobrara County	6 801	2 407	2.6	22.4	18.9	15.3	29 701	13.4	3.4	1 011	72.9
Park County	17 981	25 786	5.5	24.4	14.5	23.7	35 829	12.7	5.0	10 312	71.3

[1]Dry land or land partially or temporarily covered by water.
[2]Persons who do not identify themselves White, not of Hispanic origin.
[3]Persons 25 years old and over.

Table B. 110th Congressional Districts by Counties, 2000—*Continued*

(Number, percent.)

STATE Congressional district County	Land area,[1] (sq km)	Population				Percent with bachelor's degree or more[3]	Median household income, 1999 (dollars)	Percent living in poverty	Percent unem-ployed	Households	
		Total	Percent minority[2]	Percent under 18 years	Percent 65 years and over					Total	Percent owner occupied
	1	2	3	4	5	6	7	8	9	10	11
Congressional District (At Large), Wyoming—*Continued*											
Platte County	5 400	8 807	7.2	25.2	16.6	15.2	33 866	11.7	4.3	3 625	75.8
Sheridan County	6 535	26 560	5.4	24.2	15.5	22.4	34 538	10.7	4.5	11 167	68.9
Sublette County	12 646	5 920	3.9	25.9	12.0	21.6	39 044	9.7	4.8	2 371	73.5
Sweetwater County	27 001	37 613	13.4	28.6	8.0	17.0	46 537	7.8	5.7	14 105	75.1
Teton County	10 380	18 251	8.6	19.3	6.9	45.8	54 614	6.0	2.9	7 688	54.8
Uinta County	5 391	19 742	8.2	33.2	7.0	15.0	44 544	9.9	6.4	6 823	75.2
Washakie County	5 802	8 289	12.8	27.2	15.7	18.7	34 943	14.1	8.3	3 278	73.1
Weston County	6 210	6 644	5.2	24.0	15.6	14.5	32 348	9.9	5.6	2 624	78.0
NONVOTING DELEGATES											
AMERICAN SAMOA	200	57 291	98.8	44.6	3.3	7.4	18 219	61.0	21.4	9 349	77.2
Delegate District (At Large), American Samoa	200	57 291	98.8	44.6	3.3	7.4	18 219	61.0	21.4	9 349	77.2
Eastern District	67	23 441	99.2	43.9	3.5	6.4	18 271	58.6	21.1	3 845	77.6
Manu'a District	57	1 378	99.1	46.5	8.6	3.9	14 338	65.2	19.5	273	94.1
Rose Island	0	0	X	X	X	X	X	X	X	0	X
Swains Island	2	37	100.0	43.2	2.7	6.3	18 125	52.8	31.8	7	85.7
Western District	75	32 435	98.5	45.0	3.0	8.3	18 445	62.6	21.7	5 224	76.0
GUAM	544	154 805	93.1	35.4	5.2	20.0	39 317	23.0	7.0	38 769	48.4
Delegate District (At Large), Guam	544	154 805	93.1	35.4	5.2	20.0	39 317	23.0	7.0	38 769	48.4
COMMONWEALTH OF THE NORTHERN MARIANA ISLANDS	464	69 221	98.2	25.6	1.5	15.5	22 898	46.0	3.2	14 055	32.4
Delegate District (At Large)	464	69 221	98.2	25.6	1.5	15.5	22 898	46.0	3.2	14 055	32.4
Northern Islands Municipality	155	6	100.0	16.7	0.0	0.0	26 250	83.3	0.0	1	0.0
Rota Municipality	85	3 283	98.4	35.6	2.7	15.7	28 708	34.2	6.6	757	51.8
Saipan Municipality	115	62 392	98.2	24.8	1.4	15.2	22 555	46.9	2.9	12 507	31.0
Tinian Municipality	108	3 540	97.9	30.8	1.8	20.8	23 542	41.2	6.3	790	35.3
PUERTO RICO	8 870	3 808 610	99.0	28.6	11.1	18.3	14 412	48.2	19.2	1 261 325	72.9
Delegate District (At Large), Puerto Rico	8 870	3 808 610	99.0	28.6	11.1	18.3	14 412	48.2	19.2	1 261 325	72.9
Adjuntas Municipio	173	19 143	99.6	32.1	10.4	10.9	9 888	65.4	30.9	5 895	71.8
Aguada Municipio	80	42 042	99.3	29.7	8.7	12.8	11 384	59.3	22.1	13 520	80.6
Aguadilla Municipio	95	64 685	98.5	27.4	11.7	15.7	11 476	55.0	25.3	22 087	66.5
Aguas Buenas Municipio	79	29 032	99.5	29.4	10.0	12.4	12 957	51.7	15.5	9 240	73.5
Aibonito Municipio	81	26 493	99.5	30.5	10.8	14.7	12 725	51.8	23.2	8 408	75.1
Añasco Municipio	102	28 348	99.2	28.3	10.0	12.3	12 620	51.6	23.7	9 398	80.5
Arecibo Municipio	326	100 131	99.3	26.4	12.6	15.7	12 496	50.9	20.7	34 245	75.1
Arroyo Municipio	39	19 117	98.8	31.5	10.0	13.4	11 484	55.1	33.4	6 166	75.1
Barceloneta Municipio	48	22 322	99.4	29.5	11.1	9.1	11 706	56.0	23.8	7 508	79.4
Barranquitas Municipio	89	28 909	99.6	35.3	8.3	14.4	11 322	61.3	25.1	8 663	71.2
Bayamón Municipio	115	224 044	99.0	26.7	12.3	21.7	19 861	34.9	13.1	73 693	73.3
Cabo Rojo Municipio	182	46 911	99.1	25.4	13.8	17.3	13 580	47.1	18.5	17 114	79.3
Caguas Municipio	152	140 502	99.2	27.7	11.4	21.1	16 522	41.7	16.2	46 937	73.4
Camuy Municipio	120	35 244	99.1	29.4	10.4	14.0	13 168	51.9	20.1	11 457	78.9
Canóvanas Municipio	85	43 335	99.1	31.4	8.5	10.9	13 034	54.2	21.1	13 446	82.8
Carolina Municipio	117	186 076	98.7	26.3	11.3	21.5	21 236	33.7	12.6	63 546	73.0
Cataño Municipio	12	30 071	99.4	31.9	10.0	18.2	12 852	50.0	20.9	9 638	64.9
Cayey Municipio	134	47 370	99.3	28.2	11.4	15.0	13 452	50.3	17.9	15 634	69.7
Ceiba Municipio	75	18 004	87.5	28.8	8.7	16.3	16 440	38.6	18.4	5 750	63.8
Ciales Municipio	173	19 811	99.3	33.3	10.0	9.5	10 981	63.1	23.7	6 047	75.3
Cidra Municipio	93	42 753	99.3	30.5	8.6	15.9	15 557	46.9	18.6	13 204	76.0
Coamo Municipio	202	37 597	99.1	32.1	10.5	14.9	12 064	56.1	26.4	11 749	76.9
Comerío Municipio	74	20 002	99.5	31.4	9.2	11.0	10 892	61.6	22.2	6 311	76.0
Corozal Municipio	110	36 867	99.4	31.7	9.2	11.8	11 786	58.2	16.3	11 264	77.7
Culebra Municipio	30	1 868	92.0	25.5	10.9	11.7	17 008	37.0	16.8	699	75.7
Dorado Municipio	60	34 017	98.4	28.9	9.0	19.1	16 460	41.4	14.8	10 887	81.9
Fajardo Municipio	77	40 712	98.2	28.7	12.5	16.2	15 410	42.1	18.6	14 176	76.3
Florida Municipio	39	12 367	99.5	30.8	9.1	10.0	11 123	57.0	26.6	3 962	78.0
Guánica Municipio	96	21 888	99.7	29.8	11.5	9.2	9 721	63.7	35.7	7 291	75.6
Guayama Municipio	169	44 301	99.5	30.4	9.7	14.9	12 112	52.8	27.5	14 225	72.8

[1]Dry land or land partially or temporarily covered by water.
[2]Persons who do not identify themselves White, not of Hispanic origin.
[3]Persons 25 years old and over.
X = Not applicable.

Table B. 110th Congressional Districts by Counties, 2000—*Continued*

(Number, percent.)

STATE Congressional district County	Land area,[1] (sq km)	Population				Percent with bachelor's degree or more[3]	Median household income, 1999 (dollars)	Percent living in poverty	Percent unem- ployed	Households	
		Total	Percent minority[2]	Percent under 18 years	Percent 65 years and over					Total	Percent owner occupied
1		2	3	4	5	6	7	8	9	10	11
Delegate District (At Large), Puerto Rico—*Continued*											
Guayanilla Municipio	110	23 072	99.3	29.9	10.9	13.2	11 361	57.0	27.3	7 209	80.8
Guaynabo Municipio	70	100 053	97.9	26.2	12.5	35.9	26 211	31.1	9.4	34 068	77.0
Gurabo Municipio	72	36 743	99.1	29.5	8.5	21.2	16 451	43.1	14.5	11 741	81.4
Hatillo Municipio	108	38 925	98.9	29.2	10.4	14.9	12 378	55.8	22.5	12 685	77.9
Hormigueros Municipio	29	16 614	98.8	23.5	14.6	18.1	16 745	38.4	19.4	5 820	80.3
Humacao Municipio	116	59 035	98.8	28.4	10.7	15.0	14 345	47.2	18.6	19 293	76.0
Isabela Municipio	143	44 444	99.0	27.6	12.0	13.3	11 685	55.5	24.3	14 970	76.3
Jayuya Municipio	115	17 318	99.7	34.2	8.7	10.9	11 220	62.8	31.1	5 083	70.5
Juana Díaz Municipio	156	50 531	99.5	32.6	8.9	15.3	12 892	56.7	27.4	14 954	80.4
Juncos Municipio	69	36 452	99.3	29.5	9.8	13.2	13 072	54.1	22.5	11 933	76.7
Lajas Municipio	156	26 261	99.5	27.3	12.6	13.1	11 384	56.5	26.4	9 007	78.8
Lares Municipio	159	34 415	99.5	30.5	11.4	12.7	9 685	65.5	20.2	10 974	73.3
Las Marías Municipio	120	11 061	99.3	30.0	10.0	9.6	9 472	65.5	30.2	3 564	71.4
Patillas Municipio	88	34 485	99.1	29.1	9.2	13.1	14 622	47.3	22.5	11 145	78.1
Loíza Municipio	50	32 537	99.8	35.2	7.0	9.1	11 200	59.7	26.8	9 597	84.2
Luquillo Municipio	67	19 817	98.6	29.2	10.9	17.6	13 631	51.7	23.1	6 573	78.2
Manatí Municipio	117	45 409	99.4	29.7	10.8	14.9	12 796	51.7	24.0	15 266	73.6
Maricao Municipio	95	6 449	99.5	32.3	9.4	6.1	9 243	68.0	28.9	2 013	72.7
Maunabo Municipio	54	12 741	99.8	29.8	11.0	11.5	11 638	59.1	26.1	3 994	77.7
Mayagüez Municipio	201	98 434	99.3	24.0	13.5	18.6	11 775	52.2	23.0	34 742	60.2
Moca Municipio	130	39 697	99.2	30.3	8.8	12.6	11 271	58.7	23.9	12 712	78.0
Morovis Municipio	101	29 965	99.3	34.7	8.1	11.8	12 090	59.5	23.5	8 801	79.2
Naguabo Municipio	134	23 753	98.8	29.0	11.1	12.3	11 461	56.0	21.5	7 872	75.7
Naranjito Municipio	70	29 709	99.2	31.6	9.1	12.0	12 484	55.5	17.4	8 932	80.6
Orocovis Municipio	164	23 844	99.1	34.3	9.3	11.1	9 945	68.0	26.0	7 083	78.0
Patillas Municipio	121	20 152	99.0	30.2	11.3	12.3	12 021	54.6	28.5	6 576	78.5
Peñuelas Municipio	115	26 719	99.3	34.4	8.2	12.8	12 194	59.7	26.3	7 698	81.2
Ponce Municipio	297	186 475	99.1	29.3	11.6	19.8	12 998	52.3	25.1	59 607	69.7
Quebradillas Municipio	59	25 450	99.1	29.9	9.9	11.2	12 210	55.4	22.8	8 280	74.1
Rincón Municipio	37	14 767	98.3	26.1	12.3	11.8	11 460	56.3	22.0	5 147	78.6
Río Grande Municipio	157	52 362	99.2	29.8	9.2	13.6	15 006	46.6	20.4	16 430	82.3
Sabana Grande Municipio	93	25 935	99.4	28.6	11.5	13.3	12 485	52.0	22.3	8 865	79.0
Salinas Municipio	179	31 113	99.4	31.8	10.0	12.8	11 391	57.2	27.8	10 184	78.1
San Germán Municipio	141	37 105	99.3	26.1	13.0	18.3	13 089	49.6	23.5	12 809	74.6
San Juan Municipio	124	434 374	98.6	24.7	14.8	28.9	17 367	40.8	13.7	163 462	55.6
San Lorenzo Municipio	138	40 997	99.4	29.8	10.0	11.7	12 226	54.1	22.0	13 138	78.8
San Sebastián Municipio	183	44 204	99.6	27.9	12.6	12.7	10 962	57.5	25.1	14 970	75.4
Santa Isabel Municipio	88	21 665	99.6	33.3	9.3	13.0	11 895	57.4	23.9	6 781	76.7
Toa Alta Municipio	71	63 929	99.4	32.6	6.7	20.0	20 134	39.0	12.3	19 420	84.4
Toa Baja Municipio	60	94 085	98.9	29.1	9.2	16.6	18 331	39.6	15.1	30 453	79.0
Trujillo Alto Municipio	54	75 728	99.0	29.2	9.0	27.1	21 980	34.0	11.5	24 160	77.5
Utuado Municipio	294	35 336	99.4	30.7	11.8	11.9	9 948	63.6	30.0	11 207	71.5
Vega Alta Municipio	72	37 910	99.4	30.4	9.5	11.9	13 495	51.3	18.5	11 894	80.2
Vega Baja Municipio	119	61 929	99.1	30.4	10.1	14.4	13 933	50.6	20.8	19 758	80.1
Vieques Municipio	132	9 106	98.2	29.8	14.1	10.1	9 331	64.6	28.2	3 319	80.1
Villalba Municipio	92	27 913	99.5	34.5	8.3	12.8	11 728	62.5	28.9	7 722	80.9
Yabucoa Municipio	143	39 246	99.3	29.9	9.4	12.1	12 292	54.5	23.8	12 242	82.1
Yauco Municipio	176	46 384	99.3	29.8	10.8	15.8	11 924	56.6	25.2	15 012	76.9
VIRGIN ISLANDS	346	108 612	88.7	31.6	8.1	16.8	24 704	32.5	5.6	40 648	46.0
Delegate District (At Large), Virgin Islands	346	108 612	88.7	31.6	8.1	16.8	24 704	32.5	5.6	40 648	46.0
St. Croix Island	215	53 234	91.2	34.1	8.2	15.1	21 401	38.7	6.9	19 455	50.4
St. John Island	51	4 197	62.9	24.9	7.0	26.8	32 482	18.5	2.1	1 735	47.7
St. Thomas Island	81	51 181	88.3	29.5	8.2	17.5	26 893	27.2	4.6	19 458	41.4

[1]Dry land or land partially or temporarily covered by water.
[2]Persons who do not identify themselves White, not of Hispanic origin.
[3]Persons 25 years old and over.

SOURCE NOTES AND DEFINITIONS

PART I: MAPS

The U.S. Census Bureau produced maps that reflected the boundaries and geographic relationships for the 109th congressional districts. For the most part, these maps also reflect the boundaries of the 110th congressional districts. In this volume, the state-level Census Bureau maps of the 109th/110th congressional districts have been reprinted for each state, except for the six states with at-large representatives. For these states, the maps are from the *National Atlas of the United States* series from the Department of the Interior's U.S. Geological Survey. The *National Atlas* maps are also used for the individual congressional district maps, as well as the county maps for Georgia and Texas. The U.S. map of all of the 109th congressional districts, which can be found in the introduction, is a product of the Census Bureau, as is the map of the Northern Mariana Islands.

The "Congressional Districts by Counties" relationship tables are from the Census Bureau. The counties are listed alphabetically and show the congressional district(s) in which they fall. As congressional district boundaries often cross county lines, a county may be split into more than one district, as in the case of Los Angeles County (which includes 18 different congressional districts). The Census Bureau also has tables that show the relationships between the congressional districts and counties or county equivalents, incorporated places and Census designated places (including consolidated cities), county subdivisions (for 18 states), American Indian areas, census tracts, ZIP Code Tabulation Areas (ZCTAs), urban/rural population and land area, and school districts.

There are no Census Bureau relationship tables for states with at-large representatives, the District of Columbia, or the territories. However, lists of counties, where applicable, for these areas have been included.

For more information on the Census Bureau maps:
Click on *Maps,* under Geography.
Click on *Map Products*
Click on *109th Congressional District Maps and Related Information*
Listed are the individual, state-based, and national 109th congressional districts maps

For more information on the *National Atlas* maps:
Click on *Printable Maps*
Click on *Learn More,* under the heading *Congressional Districts for the 110th Congress–Printable Maps*

For more information on the congressional districts by counties relationship tables:
<http://www.census.gov/geo/www/cd110th/tables110.html>

Click on a state name to find the table included in this volume, as well as seven other relationship tables listed below:
Congressional districts and counties
Congressional districts by counties
Congressional districts by American Indian areas
Congressional districts by places
Congressional districts by census tracts
Congressional districts by ZIP Code Tabulation Areas (ZCTAs)
Congressional districts by school districts
Congressional districts by urban/rural population and land area

PART II: TABLES

The data in this volume are from the 2006 American Community Survey (ACS), the U.S. Social Security Administration (SSA), the 2002 Census of Agriculture, and the 2000 Census of Population and Housing. Most of this information can be found on the Internet. The 2006 ACS data have been tabulated for the congressional districts of the 109th Congress, including redistricting changes made in Maine, Pennsylvania, and Texas. The 2002 Census of Agriculture data were tabulated for the congressional districts of the 108th Congress, and do not reflect the current congressional district boundaries in Georgia, Maine, Pennsylvania, and Texas. The 2000 decennial census data have been retabulated for the 110th congressional districts.

The definitions in this section refer to the United States and the District of Columbia. Some slight variations may apply to data from Puerto Rico.

Table A presents 92 items for the United States as a whole, each state, the District of Columbia, Puerto Rico, each congressional district, and the delegate districts for the District of Columbia and Puerto Rico.

2000 Census of Population and Housing and the 2006 American Community Survey (ACS)

As established by Article 1, Section 2 of the Constitution, the purpose of the decennial census is to enumerate the population for the establishment of 435 congressional districts of approximately equal populations. Each state is assigned at least 1 congressional seat, and the remaining 385 seats are divided proportionally among the states based on population counts from the decennial census. The American Community Survey (ACS) is a new nationwide survey designed to provide communities a fresh look at how they are changing. It is a critical element in the Census Bureau's reengineered 2010 census plan. The ACS collects information such as age, race, income, commute time to work, home value, veteran status, and other important data from U.S. households. Data users can access this detailed demographic and housing data annually instead of waiting 10 years for decennial census data, which helps these users make more accurate, timely, and informed decisions. 2006 ACS data are available for geographic areas with populations of 65,000 or more. In 2008, data will be available for all areas with 20,000 inhabitants or more, as a 3-year period estimate (2005–2007).

To access the data through American FactFinder: <www.census.gov/> Click on *American FactFinder* Click on *Data Set.* Under *American Community Survey* tab, select *2006 American Community Survey*

REPRESENTATIVE
Table A, Item 1
Source: Office of the Clerk, U.S. House of Representatives
<http://clerk.house.gov/member_info/olm110.html>

Congressional representatives for the 110th Congress are listed.

LAND AREA
Table A, Item 2
Source: U.S. Census Bureau—2006 American Community Survey
Table B, Item 1
Source: U.S. Census Bureau—2000 Census of Population and Housing

Land area measurements are shown to the nearest square kilometer. Land area includes dry land and land temporarily or partially covered by water, such as marshland, swamps, and river floodplains. In Table B, there are some county parts within congressional districts that have no land area and no population. These unpopulated areas are so small that they round to zero square kilometers, or they are water areas where the congressional district boundary is on a river or inlet.

POPULATION AND POPULATION DENSITY
Table A, Items 3 and 4
Source: U.S. Census Bureau—2006 American Community Survey
Table B, Item 2
Source: U.S. Census Bureau—2000 Census of Population and Housing

In Table A, the population data are estimates from the 2006 American Community Survey. Data were tabulated for the 109th Congress and some boundary changes have occurred in Georgia and Texas.

In Table B, the total population is the estimate from the sample of the 2000 census, for consistency with other items. Data were tabulated for the 109th Congress and some boundary changes have occurred in Georgia and Texas. Because the 100-percent population number was

used for apportionment, all congressional districts within each state usually have exactly the same official population, which can be found in the 100-percent file. The estimate from the sample includes slight variations among congressional districts as a result of the weighting process.

POPULATION BY RACE AND HISPANIC ORIGIN AND SEX
Table A, Items 5–13
Source: U.S. Census Bureau—2006 American Community Survey
Table B, Item 3
Source: U.S. Census Bureau—2000 Census of Population and Housing

Data on race were derived from answers to the question on race that was asked of all respondents. The concept of race, as used by the Census Bureau, reflects self-identification by respondents according to the race or races with which they most closely identify. These categories are sociopolitical constructs and should not be interpreted as being scientific or anthropological in nature. Furthermore, the race categories include both racial and national origin groups.

In Table A, items 5 through 8 refer to individuals who identified with each racial category alone.

The **White** population is defined as persons who indicated their race as White, as well as persons who did not classify themselves in one of the specific race categories listed on the questionnaire but entered a nationality such as Irish, German, Italian, Lebanese, Near Easterner, Arab, or Polish.

The **Black** population includes persons who indicated their race as "Black, African Am., or Negro," as well as persons who did not classify themselves in one of the specific race categories but reported entries such as African American, Afro American, Kenyan, Nigerian, or Haitian.

The **American Indian or Alaska Native** population includes persons who indicated their race as American Indian or Alaska Native, as well as persons who did not classify themselves in one of the specific race categories but reported entries such as Canadian Indian, French-American Indian, Spanish-American Indian, Eskimo, Aleut, Alaska Indian, or any of the American Indian or Alaska Native tribes.

The **Asian and Pacific Islander** population combines two census groupings: **Asian** and **Native Hawaiian or Other Pacific Islander**. The **Asian** population includes persons who indicated their race as Asian Indian, Chinese, Filipino, Japanese, Korean, Vietnamese, or "Other Asian," as well as persons who provided write-in entries of such groups as Cambodian, Laotian, Hmong, Pakistani, or Taiwanese. The **Native Hawaiian or Other Pacific Islander** population includes persons who indicated their race as "Native Hawaiian," "Guamanian or Chamorro,"

"Samoan," or "Other Pacific Islander," as well as persons who reported entries such as Part Hawaiian, American Samoan, Fijian, Melanesian, or Tahitian.

The **Some other race** category includes all other responses not included in the "White," "Black or African American," "American Indian or Alaska Native," "Asian," and "Native Hawaiian or Other Pacific Islander" race categories described above. Respondents providing write-in entries such as multiracial, mixed, interracial, or a Hispanic/Latino group (for example, Mexican, Puerto Rican, or Cuban) in the "Some other race" write-in space are included in this category.

Two or more races. Respondents may have chosen to provide two or more races either by checking two or more race response check boxes, by providing multiple write-in responses, or by some combination of check boxes and write-in responses. The race response categories shown on the questionnaire are collapsed into the five minimum races identified by the OMB and the Census Bureau "Some other race" category. For data product purposes, "Two or more races" refers to combinations of two or more of the following race categories:

The **Hispanic population** is based on a complete-count question that asked respondents "Is this person Spanish/ Hispanic/Latino?" Persons marking any one of the four Hispanic categories (i.e., Mexican, Puerto Rican, Cuban, or other Spanish) are collectively referred to as Hispanic.

The **Non-Hispanic White** alone number in Column 12 includes only those persons who were not Hispanic and whose race was "White only."

The **female** population is shown as a percentage of total population.

FOREIGN-BORN POPULATION
Table A, Item 14
Source: U.S. Census Bureau—2006 American Community Survey

The foreign-born population includes all people who were not U.S. citizens at birth. Foreign-born people are those who indicated they were either U.S. citizens by naturalization or they were not citizens of the United States. The foreign-born population includes immigrants (legal permanent residents), temporary migrants (e.g., students), humanitarian migrants (e.g., refugees), and unauthorized migrants (people illegally residing in the United States).

BORN IN STATE OF RESIDENCE
Table A, Item 15
Source: U.S. Census Bureau—2006 American Community Survey

This category includes persons who indicated that they currently reside in the state in which they were born.

POPULATION BY AGE
Table A, Items 16–24
Source: U.S. Census Bureau—2006 American Community Survey
Table B, Items 4 and 5
Source: U.S. Census Bureau—2000 Census of Population and Housing

Age is defined as age at last birthday (number of completed years since birth).

HOUSEHOLD CHARACTERISTICS
Table A, Items 25–30
Source: U.S. Census Bureau—2006 American Community Survey
Table B, Item 10
Source: U.S. Census Bureau—2000 Census of Population and Housing

Households. A household includes all of the people who occupy a housing unit. (People not living in households are classified as living in group quarters.) A housing unit is a house, an apartment, a mobile home, a group of rooms, or a single room occupied (or if vacant, intended for occupancy) as separate living quarters. Separate living quarters are those in which the occupants live separately from any other people in the building and have direct access from the outside of the building or through a common hall. The occupants may be a single family, one person living alone, two or more families living together, or any other group of related or unrelated people who share living quarters. The number of households is the same as the number of year-round occupied housing units.

Average household size is a measure obtained by dividing the number of people in households by the total number of households (or householders).

A **family** includes a householder and one or more other people living in the same household who are related to the householder by birth, marriage, or adoption. All people in a household who are related to the householder are regarded as members of his/her family. A family household may contain people not related to the householder, but those people are not included as part of the householder's family in census tabulations. Thus, the number of family households is equal to the number of families, but family households may include more members than do families. A household can contain only one family for purposes of census tabulations. Not all households contain families, since a household may comprise a group of unrelated people or one person living alone.

Families are classified by type as either a "married-couple family" or "other family" according to the presence of a spouse. "Other family" is further broken down according to the sex of the householder.

The category **female family householder** includes only female-headed family households with no spouse present.

A **one-person household** consists of a householder living alone.

GROUP QUARTERS
Table A, Items 31 and 32
Source: U.S. Census Bureau—2006 American Community Survey

The group quarters population includes all people not living in households.

GROUP QUARTERS
Table A, Items 28 through 31
Source: U.S. Census Bureau—2000 Census of Population and Housing

For Georgia, Maine, Pennsylvania, and Texas, data apply to the 108th congressional districts. The group quarters population includes all people not living in households. Two general categories of people in group quarters are used: (1) the institutionalized population and (2) the non-institutionalized population.

Institutionalized population. The institutionalized population includes people under formally authorized, supervised care or custody in institutions at the time of enumeration, such as **correctional institutions, nursing homes**, and juvenile institutions.

Correctional institutions. Includes prisons, federal detention centers, military disciplinary barracks and jails, police lockups, halfway houses used for correctional purposes, local jails, and other confinement facilities, including work farms.

Nursing homes. Comprises a heterogeneous group of places providing continuous nursing and other services to patients. The majority of patients are elderly, although people who require nursing care because of chronic physical conditions may be found in these homes regardless of their age. Included in this category are skilled-nursing facilities, intermediate-care facilities, long-term care rooms in wards or buildings on the grounds of hospitals, or long-term care rooms/nursing wings in congregate housing facilities. Also included are nursing, convalescent, and rest homes such as soldiers', sailors', veterans', and fraternal or religious homes for the aged, with nursing care.

Noninstitutionalized population. The noninstitutionalized population includes all people who live in group quarters other than institutions, such as **college dormitories, military quarters**, and group homes. Also included are staff residing at institutional group quarters.

College dormitories. Includes college students in dormitories (provided the dormitory is restricted to students who do not have their families living with them), fraternity and sorority houses, and on-campus residential quarters used exclusively for those in religious orders who are attending college. College dormitory housing includes university-owned on-campus and off-campus housing for unmarried residents.

Military quarters. Includes military personnel living in barracks and dormitories on base, transient quarters on base for temporary residents (both civilian and military), and military ships. However, patients in military hospitals receiving treatment for chronic diseases or who had no usual home elsewhere, and people being held in military disciplinary barracks, were included as part of the institutionalized population.

SCHOOL ENROLLMENT AND TYPE OF SCHOOL
Table A, Items 37 and 38
Source: U.S. Census Bureau—2006 American Community Survey

Data on school enrollment were derived from a sample of the population. Persons were classified as enrolled in school if they reported attending a "regular" public or private school (or college) during the year. The instructions were to "include only nursery school, kindergarten, elementary school, and schooling which would lead to a high school diploma or a college degree" as regular school. The Census Bureau defines a public school as "any school or college controlled and supported by a local, county, state, or federal government." Schools primarily supported and controlled by religious organizations or other private groups are defined as private schools.

EDUCATIONAL ATTAINMENT
Table A, Items 39 and 40
Source: U.S. Census Bureau—2006 American Community Survey
Table B, Item 6
Source: U.S. Census Bureau—2000 Census of Population and Housing

Data on educational attainment are tabulated for the population 25 years old and over. The data were derived from a question that asked respondents for the highest level of school completed or the highest degree received. Persons who had passed a high school equivalency examination were considered high school graduates. Schooling received in foreign schools was to be reported as the equivalent grade or years in the regular American school system.

Vocational and technical training, such as barber school training; business, trade, technical, and vocational schools; or other training for a specific trade are specifically excluded.

High school graduate or more. This category includes those who have received a high school diploma or its equivalent, and those who reported any level of educational attainment above a high school diploma.

Bachelor's degree or more. This category includes those who have received bachelor's degrees, master's degrees, professional school degrees (such as law school or medical school degrees), and doctoral degrees.

INCOME
Table A, Items 41–43
Source: U.S. Census Bureau—2006 American Community Survey
Table B, Item 7
Source: U.S. Census Bureau—2000 Census of Population and Housing

The data on income were derived from responses of a sample of persons 15 years old and over. Total money income is the sum of the amounts reported separately for wage or salary income; net self-employment income; interest, dividends, or net rental or royalty income or income from estates and trusts; Social Security or railroad retirement income; Supplemental Security Income (SSI); public assistance or welfare payments; retirement, survivor, or disability pensions; and all other income. Receipts from the following sources are not included as income: capital gains; money received from the sale of property (unless the recipient was engaged in the business of selling such property); the value of income "in kind" from food stamps, public housing subsidies, medical care, employer contributions for individuals, etc.; withdrawal of bank deposits; money borrowed; tax refunds; exchange of money between relatives living in the same household; and gifts, lump-sum inheritances, insurance payments, and other types of lump-sum receipts.

Per capita income is the mean income computed for every man, woman, and child in a particular group. It is derived by dividing the aggregate income of a particular group by the resident population in that. Per capita income is rounded to the nearest whole dollar.

Household income includes the income of the householder and all other individuals 15 years old and over in the household (whether or not they are related to the householder). Since many households consist of only one person, median household income is usually less than median family income.

POVERTY
Table A, Items 44–46
Source: U.S. Census Bureau—2006 American Community Survey
Table B, Item 8
Source: U.S. Census Bureau—2000 Census of Population and Housing

The **poverty status** data were derived from data collected on the number of persons in a household from questionnaire item 3, which provided data on each person's relationship to the householder, and questionnaire items 41 and 42, which were also used to derive the income data. The Social Security Administration (SSA) developed the original poverty definition in 1964, which federal interagency committees subsequently revised in 1969 and 1980. The Office of Management and Budget's (OMB) *Directive 14* prescribes the SSA's definition as the official poverty measure for federal agencies to use in their statistical work. Poverty statistics presented in American Community Survey products adhere to the standards defined by OMB in *Directive 14*.

Poverty thresholds vary depending on three criteria: size of family, number of children, and, for one- and two-person families, age of householder. In determining the poverty status of families and unrelated individuals, the Census Bureau uses thresholds (income cutoffs) arranged in a two-dimensional matrix. The matrix consists of family size (from one person to nine or more persons), cross-classified by presence and number of family members under 18 years old (from no children present to eight or more children present). Unrelated individuals and two-person families are further differentiated by age of reference person (under 65 years old and 65 years old and over). To determine a person's poverty status, the person's total family income over the previous 12 months is compared to with the poverty threshold appropriate for that person's family size and composition. If the total income of that person's family is less than the threshold appropriate for that family, then the person is considered poor or "below the poverty level," together with every member of his or her family. If a person is not living with anyone related by birth, marriage, or adoption, then the person's own income is compared with his or her poverty threshold. The total number of persons below the poverty level is the sum of persons in families and the number of unrelated individuals with incomes below the poverty level over the previous 12 months. The average poverty threshold for a four-person family was $17,603 in 2000 and $20,614 in 2006.

The data on **poverty status of family households** were derived from answers to the income questions. The income items were asked on a sample basis. Since poverty is defined at the family level and not at the household level, the poverty status of the household is determined by the poverty status of the householder. Households are classified as poor when the total income of the householder's family in calendar year is below the appropriate poverty threshold. (For nonfamily householders, the person's income is compared with the appropriate threshold.) The income of persons living in the household who are unrelated to the householder is not considered when determining the poverty status of a household, nor does their presence affect the family size in determining the appropriate threshold. The poverty thresholds vary depending upon three criteria: size of family, number of children, and, for one- and two-person families, age of the householder.

Food stamp receipt. The data on participation in the Food Stamp Program are designed to identify households in which one or more of the current members received food stamps during the past 12 months. Once a food stamp household was identified, a question was asked about the total value of all food stamps received by the household during that 12 month period. The Food Stamp Act of 1977 defines this federally funded program as one intended to "permit low-income households to obtain a more nutritious diet" (from title XIII of P.L. 95-113, The Food Stamp Act of 1977, declaration of policy). Providing eligible households with coupons that can be used to purchase food increases food purchasing power. The Food and Nutrition Service (FNS) of the U.S. Department of Agriculture (USDA) administers the Food Stamp program through state and local welfare offices. The Food Stamp program is the major national income support program for which all low-income and low-resource households, regardless of household characteristics, are eligible.

HOUSING UNITS, TENURE, COSTS, AND CONDITION
Table A, Items 47–59
Source: U.S. Census Bureau—2006 American Community Survey
Table B, Item 11
Source: U.S. Census Bureau—2000 Census of Population and Housing

A **housing unit** is a house, apartment, mobile home or trailer, group of rooms, or single room occupied or, if vacant, intended for occupancy as separate living quarters. Separate living quarters are those in which the occupants do not live and eat with any other person in the structure and which have direct access from the outside of the building through a common hall. For vacant units, the criteria of separateness and direct access are applied to the intended occupants whenever possible. If that information cannot be obtained, these criteria are applied to the previous occupants.

The occupants of a housing unit may be a single family, one person living alone, two or more families living together, or any other group of related or unrelated persons who share living arrangements. Both occupied and vacant housing units are included in the housing inventory, although recreational vehicles, tents, caves, boats, railroad cars, and the like are included only if they are occupied as a person's usual place of residence.

A housing unit is classified as occupied if it is the usual place of residence of the person or group of persons living in it at the time of enumeration, or if the occupants are only temporarily absent (away on vacation). A household consists of all persons who occupy a housing unit as their usual place of residence.

Owner occupied. A housing unit is owner occupied if the owner or co-owner lives in the unit, even if it is mortgaged or not fully paid for. The owner or co-owner must live in the unit and usually is Person 1 on the questionnaire. The unit is "Owned by you or someone in this household with a mortgage or loan" if it is being purchased with a mort-

gage or some other debt arrangement, such as a deed of trust, contract to purchase, land contract, or purchase agreement. The unit is also considered owned with a mortgage if it is built on leased land and there is a mortgage on the unit. Mobile homes occupied by owners with installment loans balances are also included in this category. A housing unit is "Owned by you or someone in this household free and clear (without a mortgage or loan)" if there is no mortgage or other similar debt on the house, apartment, or mobile home, including units built on leased land if the unit is owned outright without a mortgage.

Median value is the dollar amount that divides the distribution of specified owner-occupied housing units into two equal parts, with half of all units below the median value and half above the median value. Value is defined as the respondent's estimate of what the house would sell for if it were for sale. Data are presented for single-family units on fewer than 10 acres of land that have no business or medical office on the property.

Real estate taxes data were obtained from Housing Question 20 on the 2006 American Community Survey. The question was asked at owner-occupied units. The statistics from this question refer to the total amount of all real estate taxes on the entire property (land and buildings) payable to all taxing jurisdictions, including special assessments, school taxes, county taxes, and so forth.

Real estate taxes include state, local, and all other real estate taxes even if delinquent, unpaid, or paid by someone who is not a member of the household. However, taxes due from prior years are not included. If taxes are paid on other than a yearly basis, the payments are converted to a yearly basis.

The payment for real estate taxes is added to payments for fire, hazard, and flood insurance; utilities and fuels; and mortgages (both first and second mortgages, home equity loans, and other junior mortgages) to derive "Selected Monthly Owner Costs" and "Selected Monthly Owner Costs as a Percentage of Household Income." A separate question (Question 22c on the 2006 American Community Survey) determines whether real estate taxes are included in the mortgage payment to the lender(s). This makes it possible to avoid counting taxes twice in the computations.

Median monthly costs is derived from dividing the monthly housing costs distribution into two equal parts: one-half of the cases falling below the median monthly housing costs and one-half above the median. Medians are shown separately for units "with a mortgage" and for units "not mortgaged." Median monthly housing costs are computed on the basis of a standard distribution. Median monthly housing costs are rounded to the nearest whole dollar.

Second mortgage or home equity loan. The data on second mortgages or home equity loan payments were obtained from Housing Questions 23a and 23b on the 2006 American Community Survey. The questions were asked at owner-occupied units. Question 23a asks whether a second mortgage or a home equity loan exists on the property. Question 23b provides the regular monthly amount required to be paid to the lender on all second and junior mortgages and home equity loans. Amounts are included even if the payments are delinquent or paid by someone else. The amounts reported are included in the computation of "Selected Monthly Owner Costs" and "Selected Monthly Owner Costs as a Percentage of Household Income" for units with a mortgage.

All mortgages other than first mortgages (for example, second, third, etc.) are classified as "junior" mortgages. A second mortgage is a junior mortgage that gives the lender a claim against the property that is second to the claim of the holder of the first mortgage. Any other junior mortgage(s) would be subordinate to the second mortgage. A home equity loan is a line of credit available to the borrower that is secured by real estate. It may be placed on a property that already has a first or second mortgage, or it may be placed on a property that is owned free and clear.

If the respondents answered that no first mortgage existed, but a second mortgage or a home equity loan did, a computer edit assigned the unit a first mortgage and made the first mortgage monthly payment the amount reported in the second mortgage. The second mortgage/home equity loan data were then made "No" in Question 23a and left blank in Question 23b.

Housing cost, as a percentage of income, is shown separately for owners with mortgages, owners without mortgages, and renters. Rent as a percentage of income is a computed ratio of gross rent and monthly household income (total household income divided by 12). Selected owner costs include utilities and fuels, mortgage payments, insurance, taxes, etc. In each case, the ratio of housing cost to income is computed separately for each housing unit. The housing cost ratios for half of all units are above the median shown in this book, and half are below the median shown in the book.

Renter occupied. All occupied housing units that are not owner occupied, whether they are rented for cash rent or occupied without payment of cash rent, are classified as renter occupied. "No cash rent" units are separately identified in the rent tabulations. Such units are generally provided free by friends or relatives or in exchange for services, such as resident manager, caretaker, minister, or tenant farmer. Housing units on military bases also are classified in the "No cash rent" category. "Rented for cash rent" includes units in continuing care, sometimes called "life care arrangements." These arrangements usually involve a contract between one or more individuals and a service provider guaranteeing

the individual shelter—usually a house or apartment—and services, such as meals or transportation to shopping or recreation.

Median gross rent divides the distribution of renter-occupied housing units into two equal parts. The rent concept used in this volume is gross rent, which includes the amount of cash rent a renter pays (contract rent) plus the estimated average cost of utilities and fuels, if these are paid by the renter. The rent is the amount of rent only for living quarters and excludes any business or other space occupied. Single-family houses on lots of 10 or more acres of land are excluded.

Median gross rent as a percentage of household income. This measure divides the gross rent as a percentage of household income distribution into two equal parts, with one-half of the cases below the median gross rent as a percentage of household income and one-half above the median. Median gross rent as a percentage of household income is computed on the basis of a standard distribution. Median gross rent as a percentage of household income is rounded to the nearest tenth.

Substandard units are occupied units that are overcrowded or lack complete plumbing facilities. For the purposes of this item, "overcrowded" is defined as having 1.01 persons or more per room. Complete plumbing facilities include hot and cold piped water, a flush toilet, and a bathtub or shower. These facilities must be located inside the housing unit but do not have to be in the same room.

CIVILIAN LABOR FORCE
Table A, Items 60–62
Source: U.S. Census Bureau—2006 American Community Survey
Table B, Item 9
Source: U.S. Census Bureau—2000 Census of Population and Housing

The civilian labor force consists of all civilians 16 years old and over who are either employed or unemployed.

Unemployment includes all persons who did not work during the survey week, made specific efforts to find a job during the previous four weeks, and were available for work during the survey week (except for temporary illness). Persons waiting to be called back to a job from which they had been laid off and those waiting to report to a new job within the next 30 days are included in unemployment figures.

Unemployment rate. The unemployment rate is the number of unemployed persons as a percentage of the civilian labor force.

NOTE: The Census Bureau is aware that there may be a problem or problems in the employment-status data of

Census 2000. The labor force data for some places where colleges are located appear to overstate the number in the labor force, the number unemployed, and the percent unemployed. Research into this "college-town" issue indicates that the problem extended beyond places with colleges to the country in general. It stems from the tendency of many working-age people living in civilian noninstitutional group quarters (GQ), such as college dormitories, worker dormitories, and group homes (for the mentally ill or physically handicapped), to exhibit a particular pattern of entries to the employment questions in Census 2000. They now estimate that the pattern affected the employment data for about 15 percent of the civilian noninstitutional GQ population 16 years old and over in the United States, or around 500,000 people. It had an impact on the Census 2000 labor force statistics for the entire country, but its effects were most visible and substantial for places such as college towns, which have high concentrations of people living in civilian noninstitutional group quarters.

The data on employment status (referred to as labor force status in previous censuses) were derived from answers to long-form questionnaire Items 21and 25, which were asked of a sample of the population 15 years old and over. The series of questions on employment status was designed to identify, in this sequence: (1) people who worked at any time during the reference week; (2) people who did not work during the reference week, but who had jobs or businesses from which they were temporarily absent (excluding people on layoff); (3) people on temporary layoff who expected to be recalled to work within the next 6 months or who had been given a date to return to work, and who were available for work during the reference week; and (4) people who did not work during the reference week, who had looked for work during the reference week or the three previous weeks, and who were available for work during the reference week.

The employment status data shown in the 2000 census tabulations relate to people 16 years old and over.

CIVILIAN EMPLOYMENT AND OCCUPATIONS
Table A, Items 63–66
Source: U.S. Census Bureau—2006 American Community Survey

Total civilian employment includes all civilians 16 years old and over who were either (1) "at work"—those who did any work at all during the reference week as paid employees, worked in either their own business or profession, worked on their own farm, or worked 15 hours or more as unpaid workers in a family farm or business; or were (2) "with a job, but not at work"—those who had a job but were not at work that week due to illness, weather, industrial dispute, vacation, or other personal reasons.

Occupation. The data on occupation were derived from answers to Questions 39 and 40. Written responses to the occupation questions are coded using the occupational classification system developed for the 2000 census and modified in 2002. This system consists of 509 specific occupational categories, including military, for employed people, arranged into 23 major occupational groups. This classification was developed based on the *Standard Occupational Classification (SOC) Manual: 2000*, published by the Executive Office of the President, Office of Management and Budget. Some occupation groups are related closely to certain industries. Operators of transportation equipment, farm operators and workers, and healthcare providers account for major portions of their respective industries of transportation, agriculture, and health care. However, the industry categories include people in other occupations. For example, people employed in agriculture include truck drivers and book-keepers; people employed in the transportation industry include mechanics, freight handlers, and payroll clerks; and people employed in health care include janitors, security guards, and secretaries.

This volume includes three combined groupings of the major categories. **Management, Professional, and Related** occupations include managers, business and financial specialists, computer specialists, doctors, lawyers, teachers, and similar occupations. **Service, Sales, and Office** occupations include health care support workers, firefighting and law enforcement workers, food preparation workers, building workers, maintenance workers, sales workers, and administrative support workers. **Construction and Production** occupations include construction trades supervisors and workers; extraction workers; installation, maintenance, and repair workers; production workers; and transportation and material moving workers, such as traffic controllers and motor vehicle operators.

Social Security Data, 2006

To access the data on the Internet:

The main page for Social Security data is: <http://www.ssa.gov/policy/data_subject.html> Old-Age (retirement), Survivors, and Disability Insurance (OASDI) Congressional district data (Table 1) and Supplemental Security Income data (Table 2) can be found at: <http://www.ssa.gov/policy/docs/factsheets/ cong_stats/2006/index.html>

Social Security Beneficiaries (OASDI)
Table A, Items 67– 73
Source: Social Security Administration—Congressional Statistics, December 2006

Old-Age (retirement), Survivors, and Disability Insurance (OASDI)—popularly referred to as Social Security—provides monthly benefits to workers and their families when earnings stop or are reduced because the worker retires, dies, or becomes disabled. The amount of benefits received is based on the worker's level of earnings in employment or self-employment covered by the Social Security program.

Supplemental Security Income (SSI)
Table A, Items 74–77
Source: Social Security Administration—Congressional Statistics, December 2006

Supplemental Security Income (SSI) is a federal cash assistance program that provides monthly payments to low-income aged, blind, or disabled persons in the 50 states, the District of Columbia, and the Northern Mariana Islands. (U.S. totals do not include territories.)

2002 Census of Agriculture

The census of agriculture is the leading source of facts and statistics about the nation's agricultural production. It provides a detailed picture of U.S. farms and ranches every 5 years and is the only source of uniform, comprehensive agricultural data for every state and county or county equivalent in the United States.

The first agriculture census was taken in 1840 as part of the sixth decennial census of population. The agriculture census continued to be taken as part of the decennial census through 1950. A separate mid-decade census of agriculture was conducted in 1925, 1935, and 1945. From 1954 to 1974, the census was taken for the years ending in 4 and 9. In 1976, Congress authorized the census of agriculture to be taken for 1978 and 1982 to adjust the data reference year to coincide with other economic censuses. This adjustment in timing established the agriculture census on a 5-year cycle, with data being collected for years ending in 2 and 7.

For 156 years (1840 to 1996), the U.S. Department of Commerce, Bureau of the Census was responsible for collecting census of agriculture data. The 1997 Appropriations Act contained a provision that transferred the responsibility for the census of agriculture from the Census Bureau to the U.S. Department of Agriculture (USDA)'s National Agricultural Statistics Service (NASS). The 2002 Census of Agriculture is the 26th federal census of agriculture and the second conducted by NASS. For Georgia, Maine, Pennsylvania, and Texas, data apply to the 108th congressional districts.

To access the data on the Internet:

The main page for the 2002 Census of Agriculture is:
Under *2002 Census*,
Under *2002 Congressional Districts*,
Select *Rankings* or *Profiles*
Additional items can by found by returning to the main page, under *congressional districts* click on *profiles* or *rankings*.

FARMS
Table A, Item 78
Source: U.S. Department of Agriculture, National Agricultural Statistics Service—2002 Census of Agriculture

The census definition of a farm is any place from which $1,000 or more of agricultural products were produced and sold, or normally would have been sold, during the census year.

FARMS BY SIZE
Table A, Items 79–83
Source: U.S. Department of Agriculture, National Agricultural Statistics Service—2002 Census of Agriculture

All **farms** were classified into size groups according to the total land area in the farm. The land area of a farm is an operating unit concept and includes land owned and operated, as well as land rented from others. Land rented to or assigned to a tenant was considered part of the tenant's farm and not part of the owner's.

The approximate land area represents the total land area as determined by records and calculations as of January 1, 2000. The proportion of land area in farms may exceed 100 percent because some operations have land in two or more counties, but all acres are tabulated in the principal county of operation.

The **acreage** designated as "land in farms" consists primarily of agricultural land used for crops, pasture, or grazing. It also includes woodland and wasteland not actually under cultivation or used for pasture or grazing, provided it was part of the farm operator's total operation. Large acreages of woodland or wasteland held for nonagricultural purposes were deleted from individual reports during the edit process. Land in farms includes acres in the Conservation Reserve and Wetlands Reserve Programs.

Land in farms is an operating unit concept and includes land owned and operated as well as land rented from others. Land used rent free was reported as land rented from others. All grazing land, except land used under government permits on a per-head basis, was included as "land in farms" (provided it was part of a farm or ranch). Land under the exclusive use of a grazing association was reported by the grazing association and included as land in farms. All land on American Indian reservations used for growing crops or grazing livestock was included as land in farms. Land on reservations not reported by individual American Indians or non-Native Americans was reported in the name of the cooperative group that used the land. In many instances, an entire American Indian reservation was reported as one farm.

PRINCIPAL OPERATOR
Table A, Item 84
Source: U.S. Department of Agriculture, National Agricultural Statistics Service—2002 Census of Agriculture

The **principal operator** is the person primarily responsible for the on-site, day-to-day operation of the farm or ranch business. This person may be a hired manager or business manager.

The term "operator" designates a person who operates a farm, either doing the work or making day-to-day decisions about such things as planting, harvesting, feeding, and marketing. The operator may be the owner, a member of the owner's household, a hired manager, a tenant, a renter, or a sharecropper. If a person rents land to others or has land worked on shares by others, he/she is considered the operator only of the land that is retained for his/her own operation.

The primary occupation classifications used were:

* *Farming.* The operator spent 50 percent or more of his/her work time during 2002 at farming or ranching.
* *Other.* The operator spent more than 50 percent of his/her work time during 2002 in occupations other than farming or ranching. Also, operators who spent the majority of their work time working for another agricultural operation for wages were included in this classification.

All farms were classified by tenure of operators in the 2002 census.
The classifications used were:

* Full owners operated only land they owned.
* Part owners operated land they owned and land they rented from others.
* Tenants only operated land they rented from others or worked on shares for others.

Farms with hired managers are classified according to the land ownership characteristics reported. For example, a corporation owns all the land used on the farm and hires a manager to run the farm. The hired manager is considered the farm operator, and the farm is classified with a tenure type of "full owner" even though the hired manager owns none of the land he/she operates.

VALUE OF AGRICULTURAL PRODUCTS SOLD
Table A, Items 85–88

Source: U.S. Department of Agriculture, National Agricultural Statistics Service—2002 Census of Agriculture

This category represents the gross market value before taxes and production expenses of all agricultural products sold or removed from the farm in 2002 regardless of who received the payment. It is equivalent to total sales. It includes sales by the operators and the value of any shares received by partners, landlords, contractors, or others associated with the operation. The value of commodities placed in the Commodity Credit Corporation (CCC) loan program is included in this figure. Market value of agricultural products sold does not include payments received for participation in other federal farm programs. It also excludes income from farm-related sources such as "customwork" and other agricultural services, as well as income from non-farm sources. The value of crops sold in 2002 does not necessarily represent the sales from crops harvested in 2002. Data may include sales from crops produced in earlier years and may exclude some crops produced in 2002 but held in storage and not sold. For commodities such as sugarbeets and wool sold through a co-op that made payments in several installments, respondents were requested to report the total value received in 2002.

The value of agricultural products sold was requested of all operators. If the operators failed to report this information, estimates were made based on the amount of crops harvested, livestock or poultry inventory, or number sold.

PAYMENTS RECEIVED FROM FEDERAL FARM PROGRAMS
Table A, Items 89–91
Source: U.S. Department of Agriculture, National Agricultural Statistics Service—2002 Census of Agriculture

This category consists of direct cash payments received by the farm operators in 2002. It includes disaster payments, loan deficiency payments from prior participation, payments from the Conservation Reserve Program (CRP), the Wetlands Reserve Program (WRP), other conservation programs, and all other federal farm programs under which payments were made directly to farm operators. Commodity Credit Corporation (CCC) proceeds and federal crop insurance payments were not tabulated in this category.